Major Problems
in American Foreign Policy
Volume II: Since 1914

DOCUMENTS AND ESSAYS

THIRD EDITION

EDITED BY
THOMAS G. PATERSON
UNIVERSITY OF CONNECTICUT

1989

D. C. HEATH AND COMPANY
Lexington, Massachusetts   Toronto

For Aaron M. Paterson

Cover painting: *Flags, Beacon Street, Boston* by Dodge Macknight. Watercolor on paper, 16½ × 23⅛″. (Museum of Fine Arts, Boston. Bequest of Mrs. Edward Jackson Holmes)

Published simultaneously in Canada.

Printed in the United States of America.

International Standard Book Number: 0-669-15857-7

Library of Congress Catalog Card Number: 88-80720

Major Problems
in American Foreign Policy

MAJOR PROBLEMS IN AMERICAN HISTORY SERIES

GENERAL EDITOR
THOMAS G. PATERSON

Preface

The writing of diplomatic history changes, and so, happily, must this volume. In this third edition, new documents and essays have been included and chapters revised to reflect recent research and interpretations. The original goal remains: to provide students and instructors with the most distinguished, readable, stimulating, and up-to-date scholarship in the field.

The first chapter presents the diversity of scholarly opinion on the chief characteristics of American foreign policy. After this general opening, each chapter addresses a major issue in the history of American diplomacy. The primary documents introduce the problem, identify key issues, reveal the flavor of the times, and convey the intense spirit and conviction that usually marked debate. The essays in each chapter, by outstanding historians, political scientists, diplomats, and others, reveal how different interpretations can emerge from readings of the same documents or from observations of the same phenomena. The chapter introductions and section headnotes set the readings in historical and interpretive perspective. The aim is to encourage readers to reach their own interpretations. A list of books and articles for further reading, with emphasis on recent works, appears at the end of each chapter.

In the late 1970s the People's Republic of China adopted a new system for rendering Chinese phonetic characters into the Roman alphabet. This method, the Pinyin, replaced the Wade-Giles technique. The Pinyin system is now commonly used, but we remain in a transitional stage in which the old spellings still appear. Because some of the documents and essays in this volume were written in the old manner, I have retained Wade-Giles spellings. In the titles, introductions and headnotes, however, the Pinyin spellings are followed by the old spellings in parentheses.

Many friends, colleagues, and students contributed, through their generous suggestions, to the shaping of this edition. J. Garry Clifford and Kenneth J. Hagan made excellent recommendations, as did Randall B. Woods. I also received helpful advice and research assistance from Michael Barnhart, John Coogan, Bruce Cumings, Bruce dePyssler, Richard Finnegan, Laura Grant, Melvyn Leffler, James Matray, Barney J. Rickman, Rodney Scudder, and Duane Tananbaum. My thanks to them.

I am also pleased to recognize again the help I received during the preparation of the first and second editions from Harold Barto, Richard Dean Burns, Bruce Cumings, Joe Decker, John Dobson, Michael Ebner, Gerald Gordon, Gregg Herken, James Hindman, Michael Hunt, Donald Johnson, Lawrence Kaplan, Ellen Kerley, Warren Kimball, Karen Kupperman, Melvyn Leffler, Douglas Little, Jean Manter, James Matray, John

Merrill, Jean-Donald Miller, Charles Neu, Holly Izard Paterson, Stephen Pelz, Carol Petillo, Sister Eileen Rice, Harlow Sheidley, Kenneth Shewmaker, Mark Stoler, Harry Stout, William Stueck, John Sylvester, Paul Varg, and Thomas Zoumaras. As always, the staff of D. C. Heath, including Linda Halvorson, Sylvia Mallory, James Miller, Margaret Roll, and Bryan Woodhouse, has improved this book, and I thank them for their care and encouragement.

Finally, I gratefully acknowledge the comments and support of the many students and instructors who have enthusiastically received *Major Problems in American Foreign Policy* over the years. This classroom success has prompted D. C. Heath to launch a new series—Major Problems in American History—modeled upon this book's format of primary-source documents and analytical essays. The several volumes in this series, edited by distinguished scholars, will explore a variety of topics in American history. As these volumes appear during the next few years, we invite comments and suggestions on their content.

T.G.P.

Contents

C H A P T E R 4
Diplomacy in the 1920s
Page 109

C H A P T E R 5
Franklin D. Roosevelt, Isolationism, and World War II
Page 165

C H A P T E R 6
The Grand Alliance of the Second World War
Page 231

C H A P T E R 7
The Origins of the Cold War
Page 272

C H A P T E R 10

The Eisenhower-Dulles Foreign Policy of the 1950s

Page 447

C H A P T E R 11

Cuba and the Missile Crisis

Page 498

E S S A Y S

C H A P T E R 12
The Vietnam War
Page 568

D O C U M E N T S

E S S A Y S

C H A P T E R 13
Nixon, Kissinger, and Détente
Page 618

D O C U M E N T S

E S S A Y S

CHAPTER 14
Carter, Reagan, Cold War, and Global Crisis
Page 674

Explaining Modern American Foreign Policy

In the twentieth century, the United States became a global power. Building on decades of domestic and foreign expansion, American leaders utilized the nation's power to enlarge and protect it's worldwide economic, strategic, and political interests. The United States, however hesitantly, entered two world wars, and its military forces frequently intervened abroad—in Cuba in the 1900s, in Nicaragua in the 1920s, in Vietnam in the 1960s, and in Lebanon in the 1980s, to cite a few examples. As foreign aid, American dollars flowed overseas to help develop and influence other countries. The American economy became deeply intertwined with an international economy that presented both opportunities and challenges. Covert and subversive operations provided American presidents with a variety of new instruments to exert influence abroad. The presidency gained tremendous leverage at the expense of Congress in the making of foreign policy, a huge foreign affairs bureaucracy emerged to administer America's far-flung programs and to project American authority, and interest groups learned to cooperate with Washington to satisfy their respective private and national objectives.

By the 1960s, the United States had become the world's giant—conducting a major share of international trade and investment; managing a host of naval, military, and intelligence bases; sending teachers, social workers, investors, technicians, soldiers, and spies to distant lands; lecturing other peoples about the virtues of democracy and private enterprise; dominating international communications; spreading its culture to others; and maintaining an arsenal of frightening nuclear weapons. Most scholars agree that the United States in the twentieth century has grown into a global, even hegemonic, power and that it has spawned foreign affairs-related institutions at home and abroad that have transformed American life. But they differ in their explanations of why Americans became active and often successful interventionists, why they stumbled and failed at times—that is, why they did not always use their power effectively—and why, finally, they found themselves in the 1970s and 1980s in danger of losing their preeminent position. How do we explain the rise and decline of American power? What have been the fundamental characteristics of modern American foreign policy, the root sources of American activism, the mainsprings of American foreign policy: economic needs? economic dreams or ambitions? physical security? hegemony? arrogance? racism? emotionalism? domestic politics? corporatist organization? a reformist zeal? ideology—but which ideas in particular? The following essays, by accomplished historians, suggest ways to explain American behavior in this century's international relations.

✳ E S S A Y S

The first essay, by diplomat and historian George F. Kennan, finds "moralism-legalism" at the core of American diplomacy. This approach, he posits, has inhibited an understanding of power realities and has left American foreign policy susceptible to abrupt shifts whenever fickle public opinion changes. In the second essay, William Appleman Williams, for many years a professor at the University of Wisconsin and Oregon State University, argues that American diplomacy has been driven by "open door" economic expansionism. This drive has produced "tragedy," because in coercing foreign peoples in order to exploit their markets and remake their societies, Americans have violated their own noble ideals. Building upon Williams, among others, Emily S. Rosenberg of Macalester College agrees in the third essay that Americans have sought open access to trade and investment, but she enlarges the concept of expansionism to include cultural factors. She defines "liberal-developmentalism" as a multifaceted ideology and notes how Americans looked to their national government to satisfy their ideals and their needs.

In the fourth essay, Michael J. Hogan of Ohio State University introduces another term: "corporatism." Some scholars use this concept not only to describe an ideology similar to liberal-developmentalism but also to identify an American economic-political system whose goals both at home and abroad are political order, social harmony, and economic progress. The fifth essay, by Thomas McCormick of the University of Wisconsin, explains the history of modern American diplomacy by stressing American capitalist expansion and the development after World War II of United States "hegemony," or dominance, in the "world system." By the early 1970s, according to McCormick, this hegemonic power had seriously eroded, confronting American leaders with a crisis of contraction quite different from their traditional expansion. Americans then set out to restore their diminished power, in large part by improving their military stature. In the contrasting final essay, Robert Dallek of the University of California, Los Angeles, explores what he believes is the "non-rational" character of twentieth-century American foreign policy. Dallek concludes that Americans have attempted to relieve their domestic fears, unrest, or yearnings by taking action abroad. Seeming to share Kennan's views, although not dismissing ideological, strategic, political, or economic elements, Dallek finds a "persistent irrationality" in American foreign policy.

Moralism-Legalism

GEORGE F. KENNAN

After many years of official duty in the Foreign Service of the United States, it fell to me to bear a share of the responsibility for forming the foreign policy of the United States in the difficult years following World War II. The Policy Planning Staff—it was my duty to set up this office and direct it through the first years of its existence—was the first regular office of the Department of State to be charged in our time with looking at problems from the standpoint of the totality of American national interest, as distinct from a single portion of it. People working in this institutional framework soon became conscious of the lack of any general agreement, both within and without our government, on the basic concepts underlying the conduct of the external relations of the United States.

It was this realization of the lack of an adequately stated and widely accepted theoretical foundation to underpin the conduct of our external relations which aroused my curiosity about the concepts by which our statesmen had been guided in recent decades. After all, the novel and grave problems with which we were forced to deal seemed in large measure to be the products of the outcome of these past two world wars. The rhythm of international events is such that the turn of the century seemed a suitable starting point for an examination of American diplomacy and its relation to these two great cycles of violence. One and a half decades elapsed between the conclusion of the war with Spain and the dispatch of the first "Open Door" notes, on the one hand, and the outbreak of World War I, on the other. Measured against what we know of the relationships between cause and effect in the great matters of international life, this is a respectable period of time and one in which the influence of a country as powerful as the United States of that day could, if exerted consistently and with determination, have affected perceptibly the course of world affairs. The same was plainly true of the interval between the two world wars. By 1900 we were generally aware that our power had world-wide significance and that we could be affected by events far afield; from that time on our interests were constantly involved in important ways with such events.

By what concepts were our statesmen animated in their efforts to meet these new problems? What assumptions had they made concerning the basic purposes of this country in the field of foreign policy? What was it they felt they were trying to achieve? And were these concepts, in the light of retrospect, appropriate and effective ones? Did they reflect some deeper understanding of the relationship of American democracy to its world environment—something which we, perhaps, had forgotten but ought to resurrect and place again at the foundation of our conduct? Or had they been inadequate and superficial all along?. . .

George F. Kennan, *American Diplomacy, 1900–1950* (Chicago: University of Chicago Press, 1951), v–vi, 65–66, 95–101. Copyright © 1951 by The University of Chicago Press.

It is surely a curious characteristic of democracy: this amazing ability to shift gears overnight in one's ideological attitudes, depending on whether one considers one's self at war or at peace. Day before yesterday, let us say, the issues at stake between ourselves and another power were not worth the life of a single American boy. Today, nothing else counts at all; our cause is holy; the cost is no consideration; violence must know no limitations short of unconditional surrender.

Now I know the answer to this one. A democracy is peace-loving. It does not like to go to war. It is slow to rise to provocation. When it has once been provoked to the point where it must grasp the sword, it does not easily forgive its adversary for having produced this situation. The fact of the provocation then becomes itself the issue. Democracy fights in anger— it fights for the very reason that it was forced to go to war. It fights to punish the power that was rash enough and hostile enough to provoke it— to teach that power a lesson it will not forget, to prevent the thing from happening again. Such a war must be carried to the bitter end.

This is true enough, and, if nations could afford to operate in the moral climate of individual ethics, it would be understandable and acceptable. But I sometimes wonder whether in this respect a democracy is not uncomfortably similar to one of those prehistoric monsters with a body as long as this room and a brain the size of a pin: he lies there in his comfortable primeval mud and pays little attention to his environment; he is slow to wrath—in fact, you practically have to whack his tail off to make him aware that his interests are being disturbed; but, once he grasps this, he lays about him with such blind determination that he not only destroys his adversary but largely wrecks his native habitat. You wonder whether it would not have been wiser for him to have taken a little more interest in what was going on at an earlier date and to have seen whether he could not have prevented some of these situations from arising instead of proceeding from an undiscriminating indifference to a holy wrath equally undiscriminating. . . .

As you have no doubt surmised, I see the most serious fault of our past policy formulation to lie in something that I might call the legalistic-moralistic approach to international problems. This approach runs like a red skein through our foreign policy of the last fifty years. It has in it something of the old emphasis on arbitration treaties, something of the Hague Conferences and schemes for universal disarmament, something of the more ambitious American concepts of the role of international law, something of the League of Nations and the United Nations, something of the Kellogg Pact, something of the idea of a universal "Article 51" pact, something of the belief in World Law and World Government. But it is none of these, entirely. Let me try to describe it.

It is the belief that it should be possible to suppress the chaotic and dangerous aspirations of governments in the international field by the acceptance of some system of legal rules and restraints. This belief undoubtedly represents in part an attempt to transpose the Anglo-Saxon concept of individual law into the international field and to make it applicable to governments as it is applicable here at home to individuals. It must also stem in part from the memory of the origin of our own political system—from the recollection that we were able, through acceptance of a common institutional and juridical framework, to reduce to harmless dimensions the conflicts of interest and aspiration among the original thirteen colonies and to bring them all into an ordered and peaceful relationship with one another. Remembering this, people are unable to understand that what might have been possible for the thirteen colonies in a given set of circumstances might not be possible in the wider international field.

It is the essence of this belief that, instead of taking the awkward conflicts of national interest and dealing with them on their merits with a view to finding the solutions least unsettling to the stability of international life, it would be better to find some formal criteria of a juridical nature by which the permissible behavior of states could be defined. There would then be judicial entities competent to measure the actions of governments against these criteria and to decide when their behavior was acceptable and when unacceptable. Behind all this, of course, lies the American assumption that the things for which other peoples in this world are apt to contend are for the most part neither creditable nor important and might justly be expected to take second place behind the desirability of an orderly world, untroubled by international violence. To the American mind, it is implausible that people should have positive aspirations, and ones that they regard as legitimate, more important to them than the peacefulness and orderliness of international life. From this standpoint, it is not apparent why other peoples should not join us in accepting the rules of the game in international politics, just as we accept such rules in the competition of sport in order that the game may not become too cruel and too destructive and may not assume an importance we did not mean it to have.

If they were to do this, the reasoning runs, then the troublesome and chaotic manifestations of the national ego could be contained and rendered either unsubstantial or subject to easy disposal by some method familiar and comprehensible to our American usage. Departing from this background, the mind of American statesmanship, stemming as it does in so large a part from the legal profession in our country, gropes with unfailing persistence for some institutional framework which would be capable of fulfilling this function.

I cannot undertake in this short lecture to deal exhaustively with this thesis or to point out all the elements of unsoundness which I feel it contains. But some of its more outstanding weaknesses are worthy of mention.

In the first place, the idea of the subordination of a large number of states to an international juridical regime, limiting their possibilities for aggression and injury to other states, implies that these are all states like our own, reasonably content with their international borders and status, at least to the extent that they would be willing to refrain from pressing for change without international agreement. Actually, this has generally been true only of a portion of international society. We tend to underestimate the violence of national maladjustments and discontents elsewhere in the world if we think that they would always appear to other people as less important than the preservation of the juridical tidiness of international life.

Second, while this concept is often associated with a revolt against nationalism, it is a curious thing that it actually tends to confer upon the concept of nationality and national sovereignty an absolute value it did not have before. The very principle of "one government, one vote," regardless of physical or political differences between states, glorifies the concept of national sovereignty and makes it the exclusive form of participation in international life. It envisages a world composed exclusively of sovereign national states with a full equality of status. In doing this, it ignores the tremendous variations in the firmness and soundness of national divisions: the fact that the origins of state borders and national personalities were in many instances fortuitous or at least poorly related to realities. It also ignores the law of change. The national state pattern is not, should not be, and cannot be a fixed and static thing. By nature, it is an unstable phenomenon in a constant state of change and flux. History has shown that the will and the capacity of individual peoples to contribute to their world environment is constantly changing. It is only logical that the organizational forms (and what else are such things as borders and governments?) should change with them. The function of a system of international relationships is not to inhibit this process of change by imposing a legal straitjacket upon it but rather to facilitate it: to ease its transitions, to temper the asperities to which it often leads and moderate the conflicts to which it gives rise, and to see that these conflicts do not assume forms too unsettling for international life in general. But this is a task for diplomacy, in the most old fashioned sense of the term. For this, law is too abstract, too inflexible, too hard to adjust to the demands of the unpredictable and the unexpected.

By the same token, the American concept of world law ignores those means of international offense—those means of the projection of power and coercion over other peoples—which bypass institutional forms entirely or even exploit them against themselves: such things as ideological attack, intimidation, penetration, and disguised seizure of the institutional paraphernalia of national sovereignty. It ignores, in other words, the device of the puppet state and the set of techniques by which states can be converted into puppets with no formal violation of, or challenge to, the outward attributes of their sovereignty and their independence.

This is one of the things that has caused the peoples of the satellite countries of eastern Europe to look with a certain tinge of bitterness on the United Nations. The organization failed so completely to save them from domination by a great neighboring country, a domination no less invidious by virtue of the fact that it came into being by processes we could not call "aggression." And there is indeed some justification for their feeling, because the legalistic approach to international affairs ignores in general the international significance of political problems and the deeper sources of international instability. It assumes that civil wars will remain civil and not grow into international wars. It assumes the ability of each people to solve its own internal political problems in a manner not provocative of its international environment. It assumes that each nation will always be able to construct a government qualified to speak for it and cast its vote in the international arena and that this government will be acceptable to the rest of the international community in this capacity. It assumes, in other words, that domestic issues will not become international issues and that the world community will not be put in the position of having to make choices between rival claimants for power within the confines of the individual state.

Finally, this legalistic approach to international relations is faulty in its assumptions concerning the possibility of sanctions against offenses and violations. In general, it looks to collective action to provide such sanction against the bad behavior of states. In doing so, it forgets the limitations on the effectiveness of military coalition. It forgets that, as a circle of military associates widens in any conceivable political-military venture, the theoretical total of available military strength may increase, but only at the cost of compactness and ease of control. And the wider a coalition becomes, the more difficult it becomes to retain political unity and general agreement on the purposes and effects of what is being done. As we are seeing in the case of Korea, joint military operations against an aggressor have a different meaning for each participant and raise specific political issues for each one which are extraneous to the action in question and affect many other facets of international life. The wider the circle of military associates, the more cumbersome the problem of political control over their actions, and the more circumscribed the least common denominator of agreement. This law of diminishing returns lies so heavily on the possibilities for multilateral military action that it makes it doubtful whether the participation of smaller states can really add very much to the ability of the great powers to assure stability of international life. And this is tremendously important, for it brings us back to the realization that even under a system of world law the sanction against destructive international behavior might continue to rest basically, as it has in the past, on the alliances and relationships among the great powers themselves. There might be a state, or perhaps more than one state, which all the rest of the world community together could not successfully coerce into following a line of action to which it was violently averse. And if this is true, where are we? It seems to me that we are right back in the realm of the forgotten art of diplomacy from which we have spent fifty years trying to escape.

These, then, are some of the theoretical deficiencies that appear to me to be inherent in the legalistic approach to international affairs. But there is a greater deficiency still that I should like to mention before I close. That is the inevitable association of legalistic ideas with moralistic ones: the carrying-over into the affairs of states of the concepts of right and wrong, the assumption that state behavior is a fit subject for moral judgment. Whoever says there is a law must of course be indignant against the lawbreaker and feel a moral superiority to him. And when such indignation spills over into military contest, it knows no bounds short of the reduction of the law-breaker to the point of complete submissiveness—namely, unconditional surrender. It is a curious thing, but it is true, that the legalistic approach to world affairs, rooted as it unquestionably is in a desire to do away with war and violence, makes violence more enduring, more terrible, and more destructive to political stability than did the older motives of national interest. A war fought in the name of high moral principle finds no early end short of some form of total domination.

The Open Door Policy

WILLIAM APPLEMAN WILLIAMS

A re-examination of the history of twentieth-century American foreign relations (and the relationship between foreign policy and the domestic economy) offers the most promising approach to . . . a reconsideration of our assumptions. First, we thereby confront directly what happened. We learn the ideas and the actions of the men who made or influenced policy, and the consequences of those events at home and abroad. Second, at the end of such a review of the past, we return to the present better informed. Finally, that increased knowledge and understanding may help us to muster the nerve to act in ways that can transform the tragedy into a new beginning.

For history is a way of learning, of getting closer to the truth. It is only by abandoning the clichés that we can even define the tragedy. When we have done that, we will no longer be merely acquiescing in the deadly inertia of the past. We will have taken the first and vital step in making history. Such a reexamination of history must be based upon a searching review of the way America has defined its own problems and objectives, and its relationship with the rest of the world. The reason for this is simple: realism goes nowhere unless it starts at home. Combined with a fresh look at Soviet behavior, such an understanding of American policy should help in the effort to outline new programs and policies designed to bring America's ideals and practical objectives closer to realization.

In the realm of ideas and ideals, American policy is guided by three conceptions. One is the warm, generous, humanitarian impulse to help other people solve their problems. A second is the principle of self-determination applied at the international level, which asserts the right of every society to establish its own goals or objectives, and to realize them internally through the means it decides are appropriate. These two ideas can be reconciled; indeed, they complement each other to an extensive degree. But the third idea entertained by many Americans is one which insists that

From *The Tragedy of American Diplomacy,* 9–11, 49–50, 53–58, 303–308, by William Appleman Williams. Copyright © 1959 by William Appleman Williams. Reprinted by permission of Harper & Row, Publishers, Inc.

other people cannot *really* solve their problems and improve their lives unless they go about it in the same way as the United States.

This feeling is not peculiar to Americans, for all other peoples reveal some degree of the same attitude toward the rest of the world. But the full scope and intensity of the American version is clearly revealed in the blunt remark of former Secretary of State Dean G. Acheson. He phrased it this way in explaining and defending the American program of foreign aid as it was being evolved shortly after the end of World War II: "We are willing to help people who believe the way we do, to continue to live the way they want to live."

This insistence that other people ought to copy America contradicts the humanitarian urge to help them and the idea that they have the right to make such key decisions for themselves. In some cases, the American way of doing things simply does not work for the other people. In another instance it may be satisfactory, but the other society may prefer to do it in a different way that produces equally good results—perhaps even better ones. But even if the American way were the *only* effective approach, the act of forcing it upon the other society—and economic and political pressure are forms of force—violates the idea of self-determination. It also angers the other society and makes it even less apt to accept the American suggestion on its own merits. Hence it is neither very effective nor very idealistic to try to help other people by insisting from the outset that they follow closely the lead and the example of the United States on all central and vital matters.

The same kind of difficulty arises in connection with the economic side of American foreign policy. The United States needs raw materials and other goods and services from foreign countries, just as it needs to sell some of its own goods and services to them. It might be able literally to isolate itself and survive, but that is not the issue. Not even the isolationists of the late 1920's and early 1930's advocated that kind of foreign policy. The vital question concerns instead the way in which America gets what it needs and exports what it wants to sell.

Most Americans consider that trade supplies the answer to this problem. But trade is defined as the exchange of goods and services between producers dealing with each other in as open a market as it is possible to create, and doing this without one of them being so beholden to the other that he cannot bargain in a meaningful and effective way. Trade is not defined by the transfer of goods and services under conditions established and controlled largely by one of the parties.

Here is a primary source of America's troubles in its economic relations with the rest of the world. For in expanding its own economic system throughout much of the world, America has made it very difficult for other nations to retain any economic independence. This is particularly true in connection with raw materials. Saudi Arabia, for example, is not an independent oil producer. Its oil fields are an integrated and controlled part of the American oil industry. But a very similar, if often less dramatic, kind of relationship also develops in manufacturing industries. This is the case in countries where established economic systems are outmoded or lethargic, as well as in the new, poor nations that are just beginning to industrialize. American corporations exercise very extensive authority, and even commanding power, in the political economy of such nations.

Unfortunately, there is an even more troublesome factor in the economic aspect of American foreign policy. That is the firm conviction, even dogmatic belief, that America's *domestic* well-being depends upon such sustained, everincreasing overseas economic expansion. Here is a convergence of economic practice with intellectual analysis and emotional involvement that creates a very powerful and dangerous propensity to define the essentials of American welfare in terms of activities outside the United States.

It is dangerous for two reasons. First, it leads to an indifference toward or a neglect of, internal developments which are nevertheless of primary importance. And second, this strong tendency to externalize the sources or causes of good things leads naturally enough to an even greater inclination to explain the lack of the good life by blaming it on foreign individuals, groups, and nations. This kind of externalizing evil serves not only to antagonize the outsiders, but further intensifies the American determination to make them over in the proper manner or simply push them out of the way.

The over-all result of these considerations is that America's humanitarian urge to assist other peoples is undercut—even subverted—by the way it goes about helping them. Other societies come to feel that American policy causes them to lose their economic, political, and even psychological independence. . . .

In summation, the true nature and full significance of the Open Door Policy can only be grasped when its four essential features are fully understood.

First: it was neither a military strategy nor a traditional balance-of-power policy. *It was conceived and designed to win the victories without the wars.* In a truly perceptive and even noble sense, the makers of the Open Door Policy understood that war represented the failure of policy. Hence it is irrelevant to criticize the Open Door Policy for not emphasizing, or not producing, extensive military readiness.

Second: it was derived from the proposition that America's overwhelming economic power would cast the economy and the politics of the poorer, weaker, underdeveloped countries in a pro-American mold. American leaders assumed the opposition of one or many industrialized rivals. Over a period of two generations the policy failed because some of those competitors, among them Japan and Germany, chose to resort to force when they concluded (on solid grounds) that the Open Door Policy was working only too well; and because various groups inside the weaker countries such as China and Cuba decided that America's extensive influence in and upon their societies was harmful to their specific and general welfare.

Third (and clearly related to the second point): the policy was neither legalistic nor moralistic in the sense that those criticisms are usually offered. It was extremely hard-headed and practical. In some respects, at any rate, it was the most impressive intellectual achievement in the area of public policy since the generation of the Founding Fathers.

Fourth: unless and until it, and its underlying *Weltanschauung,* were modified to deal with its own consequences, the policy was certain to produce foreign policy crises that would become increasingly severe.

Once these factors are understood, it becomes useful to explore the way that ideological and moralistic elements became integrated with the fundamentally secular and economic nature of the Open Door Policy. The addition of those ingredients served to create a kind of expansionism that aimed at the marketplace of the mind and the polls as well as of the pocketbook.

Taken up by President Theodore Roosevelt and his successors, the philosophy and practice of secular empire that was embodied in the Open Door Notes became the central feature of American foreign policy in the twentieth century. American economic power gushed into some underdeveloped areas within a decade and into many others within a generation. It also seeped, then trickled, and finally flooded into the more developed nations and their colonies until, by 1939, America's economic expansion encompassed the globe. And by that time the regions where America's position was not extensively developed were precisely the areas in which the United States manifested a determination to retain and expand its exploratory operations—or to enter in force for the first time.

Throughout these same years,the rise of a new crusading spirit in American diplomacy contributed an outward thrust of its own and reinforced the secular expansion. This righteous enthusiasm was both secular, emphasizing political and social ideology, and religious, stressing the virtues (and necessities) of Protestant Christianity. In essence, this twentieth-century Manifest Destiny was identical with the earlier phenomenon of the same name.

Americans assumed a posture of moral and ideological superiority at an early date. Despite the persistence of the Puritan tradition, however, this assertiveness took predominantly secular forms. Supernatural authority was invoked to explain and account for the steady enlargement of the United States, but the justifications for expansion were generally based on standards derived from this world. The phrase "Manifest Destiny," for example, symbolized the assertion that God was on America's side rather than the more modest claim that the country had joined the legions of the Lord. As that logic implied, the argument was that America was the "most progressive" society whose citizens made "proper use of the soil." For these and similar reasons, it was added, the laws of "political gravitation" would bring many minor peoples into the American system.

Though it had appeared as early as the eve of the American Revolution, the assertion that the expansion of the United States "extended the area of freedom" gained general currency after the War of 1812. President Andrew Jackson seems to have coined the phrase, with his wildcatting intellectual supporters making many variations. One of the more persuasive and popular, which won many converts during and after the war with Mexico, stressed America's responsibility to extend its authority over "semi-barbarous people." By thus taking up the duty of "regeneration and civilization," America could perform the noble work of teaching inferiors to appreciate the blessings they already enjoyed but were inclined to overlook. In turn, this would prepare them for the better days to follow under America's benevolent leadership.

Near the end of the century, American missionaries and domestic religious leaders began to impart a more theological tone to this crusading fervor. This resulted in part from the effort by the clergy to marry traditional Christianity with the new doctrine of evolution and in that way adjust their theology to the latest revelations, and also to sustain their influence in the age of science. Josiah Strong was an innovator of that kind. As a Congregationalist minister in whom the frontier experience and outlook exercised an important influence, Strong concluded that the theory of evolution only substantiated the doctrine of predestination. America had been hand-picked by the Lord to lead the Anglo-Saxons in transforming the world. "It would seem," he explained with reference to the American Indians and other benighted peoples, "as if these inferior tribes were only precursors of a superior race, voices in the wilderness crying: Prepare ye the way of the Lord."

Ever since New England ministers had accepted the challenge of saving the heathens of Hawaii, a crusade that began in the eighteenth century, American missionaries had been noticeably concerned about Asia—and in particular China. As the Reverend Hudson Taylor explained in 1894, there was "a great Niagara of souls passing into the dark in China." Though they never lost faith, a growing number of missionaries did get discouraged enough to question whether hell-fire sermons on the dangers of damnation were an approach sufficient unto the need. Some thought fondly of the sword of righteousness, and toyed with the idea of a "Society for the Diffusion of Cannon Balls." That kind of crusade was never organized, but the missionaries did begin in the 1890's to demand formal support and protection from the American government.

This request, while never acted upon with the same vigor as those from business groups, did receive sympathetic and favorable consideration. For one thing, the religious stake in China was significant: America had over 500 missionaries in that country, and their schools claimed a total student body of nearly 17,000 Chinese. Many churches had also supported intervention in Cuba. But the most important factor was the way that the missionary movement began to evolve an approach that offered direct support to secular expansion.

Missionaries had always tended to operate on an assumption quite similar to the frontier thesis. "Missionaries are an absolute necessity," explained the Reverend Henry Van Dyke of Princeton in 1896, "not only for the conversion of the heathen, but also, and much more, for the preservation of the Church. Christianity is a religion that will not keep." Religious leaders began to link the missionary movement with economic expansion in what the Reverend Francis E. Clark of the Christian Endeavor organization called "the widening of our empire." The Board of Foreign Missions also welcomed such expansion as "an ally."

Then, beginning in the mid-1890's, the missionaries began to change their basic strategy in a way that greatly encouraged such liaison with secular expansionists. Shifting from an emphasis on the horrors of hell to a concern with practical reform as the lever of conversion, they increasingly stressed the need to remake the underdeveloped societies. Naturally enough, they were to be reformed in the image of the United States. Such changes would lead to regeneration identified with Christianity and witnesses for the Lord would accordingly increase.

Not only did this program mesh with the idea of American secular influence (how else were the reforms to be initiated?), but it was very similar to the argument that American expansion was justified because it created more progressive societies. Missionaries came to sound more and more like political leaders, who were themselves submerging their domestic ideological differences at the water's edge in a general agreement on expansion as a reform movement.

The domestic reformer La Follette offers an excellent example of this convergence of economic and ideological expansion that took place across political lines. He approved taking the Philippines because it would enable America "to conquer [its] rightful share of that great market now opening [in China] for the world's commerce." Expansion was also justified because the United States had a "bounden duty to establish and maintain stable government" in the islands. Pointing out that from the beginning "the policy of this government has been to expand," La Follette justified it on the grounds that "it has *made men free.*" Thus, he concluded, "we can legally and morally reserve unto ourselves perpetual commercial advantages of priceless value to our foreign trade for all time to come" by taking the Philippines.

Theodore Roosevelt's outlook reveals an even more significant aspect of this progressive integration of secular and ideological expansionism. His concern for economic expansion was complemented by an urge to extend Anglo-Saxon ideas, practices, and virtues throughout the world. Just as his Square Deal program centered on the idea of responsible leaders using the national government to regulate and moderate industrial society at home, so did his international outlook revolve around the idea of American supremacy being used to define and promote the interests of "collective civilization."

Thus it was necessary, he warned in his Presidential Message of December 1901, to exercise restraint in dealing with the large corporations. "Business concerns which have the largest means at their disposal . . . take the lead in the strife for commercial supremacy among the nations of the world. America has only just begun to assume the commanding position in the international business world which we believe will more and more be hers. It is of the utmost importance that this position be not jeopardized, especially at a time when the overflowing abundance of our own natural resources and the skill, business energy, and mechanical aptitude of our people make foreign markets essential."

Roosevelt integrated that kind of expansion with ideological considerations and imperatives to create an all-inclusive logic and set of responsibilities which made peace itself the consequence of empire. In his mind, at any rate, it was America's "duty toward the people living in barbarism to see that they are freed from their chains, and we can free them only by destroying barbarism itself." Thus, he concluded "peace cannot be had until the civilized nations have expanded in some shape over the barbarous nations."

The inherent requirements of economic expansion coincided with such religious, racist, and reformist drives to remake the world. The reason for this is not difficult to perceive. As they existed, the underdeveloped countries were poor, particularistic, and bound by traditions which handicapped business enterprise. They were not organized to link up with the modern industrial system in a practical and efficient manner. It was economically necessary to change them *in certain ways and to a limited degree* if the fruits of expansion were to be harvested. As with the missionaries, therefore, the economic and political leaders of the country decided that what was good for Americans was also good for foreigners. Humanitarian concern was thus reinforced by hard-headed economic requirements.

The administrations of Theodore Roosevelt understood this relationship between economic expansion and overseas reform, and explicitly integrated it into the strategy of the Open Door Policy. It was often commented upon in dispatches and policy statements concerning China and Latin America. In his famous Corollary to the Monroe Doctrine, for example, Roosevelt (who thought of the Open Door Policy as the Monroe Doctrine for Asia) stressed the need for reforms and asserted the right and the obligation of the United States to see that they were made—and honored. . . .

The integration of these elements was carried forward, and given classic expression in rhetoric, style, and substance, in the diplomacy of President Woodrow Wilson and Secretary of State William Jennings Bryan. Both men were leaders of the secular American reform movement, and both brought to their conduct of foreign affairs a religious intensity and righteousness that was not apparent in earlier administrations and that has not been matched since their time. As Protestants imbued with a strong sense of Anglo-Saxon self-consciousness, they personified the assertive idealism that complemented and reinforced the economic drive for markets. . . .

By the time of World War I, therefore, the basic dilemma of American foreign policy was clearly defined. Its generous humanitarianism prompted it to improve the lot of less fortunate peoples, but that side of its diplomacy was undercut by two other aspects of its policy. On the other hand, it defined helping people in terms of making them more like Americans. This subverted its ideal of self-determination. On the other hand, it asserted and acted upon the necessity of overseas economic expansion for its own material prosperity. But by defining such expansion in terms of markets for American exports, and control of raw materials for American industry, the ability of other peoples to develop and act upon their own patterns of development was further undercut. . . .

America can neither take its place in nor make its contribution to the world community until it believes and demonstrates that it can sustain prosperity and democracy without recourse to open-door imperial expansion.

Liberal-Developmentalism

EMILY S. ROSENBERG

Liberal-developmentalism merged nineteenth-century liberal tenets with the historical experience of America's own development, elevating the beliefs and experiences of America's unique historical time and circumstance into developmental laws thought to be applicable everywhere.

The ideology of liberal-developmentalism can be broken into five major features: (1) belief that other nations could and should replicate America's own developmental experience; (2) faith in private free enterprise; (3) support for free or open access for trade and investment; (4) promotion of free flow of information and culture; and (5) growing acceptance of governmental activity to protect private enterprise and to simulate and regulate American participation in international economic and cultural exchange.

To many Americans, their country's economic and social history became a universal model. In order to become a modern society, a nation needed extensive capital investment generated by foreign borrowing and by exports; development of educational, transportation, communication, and banking institutions; a steady supply of cheap labor; maximization of individual initiative for people deemed most efficient; wide-open land use and free-wheeling environmental practices; and a robust private business sector solidly linked to capital-intensive, labor-saving technology. This blueprint, drawn from America's experience, became the creed of most Americans who dealt with foreign nations. . . .

Belief in America's mission helped drive its internationalist impulse. As long as internationalists believed the world was destined to follow American patterns, they could remain confident that there was no fundamental conflict between national advancement and global progress. A strong internationalist spirit and an accompanying faith in American-led progress . . . would recur again and again.

Central to the developmental process were tenets drawn from nineteenth-century liberalism. . . .

Encouraging individual initiative through private enterprise was an important canon of nineteenth-century liberalism. Liberalism, of course, grew up in opposition to artificial, statist monopoly or government-conferred privilege. Freedom, in the American tradition, meant absence of the autocratic state and the full play of competing individual initiatives through private ownership. Private enterprise was free because it was not shackled by an overbearing governmental structure. And celebrants of the American system generally credited private business, above all, with producing rapid industrial development and increasing abundance. To be sure, nineteenth-century

Selections from *Spreading the American Dream: American Economic and Cultural Expansion, 1890–1945*, 7, 9–12, 230–234, by Emily Rosenberg. Copyright © 1982 by Emily S. Rosenberg. Reprinted by permission of Hill and Wang, a division of Farrar, Straus and Giroux, Inc.

government, particularly states and localities, did not remain aloof from the process of economic growth. But government intervened in the economy primarily in order to release the energies of the private sector. Government kept the pump of American business in working order, but it did not raise and lower the handle.

Throughout the twentieth century, the national government adopted ever more elaborate ways of oiling and repairing the pump and of insuring a ready supply of water and pumpers. And while government became increasingly involved with the operation of the private sector, many businesses became so internationalized and so huge that they bore little resemblance to the enterprises America had known. Still, the mystique of the transforming qualities of private ownership remained intact and profoundly shaped American attitudes and policies toward others. Why should private entrepreneurs, unrestrained and encouraged by government—liberal-developmentalists asked—not duplicate their American success story in other parts of the world? Minimal interference by foreign governments in the supposedly free play of private initiatives became a fairly consistent American goal abroad.

Belief in free trade and investment accompanied the faith in private enterprise. The classical economists David Ricardo and Adam Smith and their popularizers bequeathed to American liberalism the law of comparative advantage: a division of labor in which specialization by each economic unit would result in increased efficiency within the worldwide system. The avid pursuit of *individual* gain, regulated by an "invisible hand," would promote the *general* welfare by enriching all those nations and people who participated in the free marketplace. To American entrepreneurs, comparative advantage translated into a practical article of faith: the gains of unregulated private business were synonymous with the advance of society as a whole. In an international setting, as at home, the invisible hand would convert the narrow self-interest of corporations (and nations) into general well-being and raise standards of living.

In practice, the faith in liberal rules of economic exchange had an important qualification. Throughout most of its history, the United States was a strongly protectionist nation. Those who favored protective tariffs on foreign goods expressed their liberalism in terms of equal access, or the open door. Nations, liberal protectionists argued, had a right to use tariffs to develop their own special endowments, as long as the duties did not discriminate in favor of certain trading partners and create privileged spheres of influence. For much of the twentieth century, both low-tariff and protectionist interests agreed that equal access for trade and investment, rather than the absolute doctrine of free trade, provided the fundamental ingredient of a liberal order.

In the twentieth century, Americans increasingly questioned the supposedly self-regulating nature of a liberal order. Especially during the 1930s, international cartels and nationalistic restrictions distorted the free play of economic forces. The national government increasingly became a regulator, its visible hand replacing Adam Smith's mythical invisible one. But despite intervention in the economic system on both the national and the international levels, Americans retained the core of their liberal beliefs. The beneficence and fairness of the international division of labor, organized by private enterprise and maintained through policies promoting equal access for trade and investments, remained a fundamental faith for most policymakers.

The free flow of ideas related closely to free trade. In fact, liberal-developmentalists assumed that one free marketplace was a necessary condition for the other. Free flow was also largely defined as the absence of governmental control. Communications media were free if they were not servants of government; if private enterprise controlled communications, the cause of free expression was—almost by definition—advanced. Americans supported private ownership of broadcasting and news services abroad, and they championed the spread of the same advertiser-shaped mass culture developed at home.

Because the American government itself did not usually generate or severely censor information, liberal-developmentalists could not perceive American culture as either value-laden or ideological, because it was based on mass appeal and appeared inherently democratic. Was not America's own success story proof that the best ideas come to the fore in a liberal society? The notion that "the best idea wins" was the counterpart, in the realm of ideas, to the economic law of comparative advantage. Liberal-developmentalists thus saw America's free-flow doctrines as helping to spread truth and knowledge in an essentially democratic marketplace. Free flow, they argued, was nonideological and anti-authoritarian.

The marketplace metaphor permeated liberal-developmentalism. The ideal world was a great open market: each buyer and thinker had access to a separate stall and freedom to peddle his or her wares. But the buyer was sovereign, and because the buyer's decisions were critical in determining what goods or thoughts would be accepted, the marketplace was inherently democratic and anti-authoritarian. Because all met as equals, the marketplace eroded barriers that separated people; differences of class and nationality broke down, and all producers were judged solely by the merit of their products. Governments might arrange the marketing booths, keep the lanes of commerce open, and enforce minimal standards of fairness and safety, but the interaction of private buyers and sellers provided the dynamics of the system, bringing the best-quality products to the greatest number of people. The liberal marketplace (both economic and intellectual), then, was supposed to generate efficiency, abundance, democracy, wisdom, and social integration. It could be noisy and turbulent, but it was always, in the end, uplifting and fair. The ideology of the American Dream—both its domestic and its global versions—was a full rendition of this liberal marketplace utopia.

As the marketplace ideal implied, the role of private citizens was crucial. It is not surprising that in the late nineteenth and early twentieth centuries private Americans, more than government policymakers, tended to shape America's role in the world. As traders, investors, missionaries, philanthropists, international societies, and purveyors of mass communications pushed beyond America's continental frontiers, the private sector spearheaded

American expansion. Even though private impulses have often had only peripheral status in traditional diplomatic histories, a study of America's foreign affairs must, to a large degree, focus upon these nongovernmental forces.

But during the course of the twentieth century, the federal government increasingly intervened to rationalize or extend contacts originated by private interests. Liberal-developmentalists gradually devised governmental structures to promote or guide American participation within the international system. The relationships between private initiatives and governmental structures thus became more complex. For each historical period, it is important to view American expansion within the context of both private and governmental activities and to try to understand the changing relationship between the two. . . .

This relationship progressed through three general stages: the promotional state, the cooperative state, and the regulatory state. Throughout, economic and cultural expansion were closely related.

From the Administration of Benjamin Harrison to Woodrow Wilson, most of the framework for the promotional state was hammered into place: a big navy; bargaining tariffs; the open-door policy; attempts to spread the gold standard; legislation allowing monopolistic combinations in the export trade, in foreign investment and in overseas branch banking; many new or improved executive-branch bureaucracies such as the Tariff Commission, the Federal Trade Commission, the Bureau of Foreign and Domestic Commerce, and the consular corps of the State Department; and some coordination of private philanthropy through the Red Cross and the American Relief Administration. All of this new governmental activity in support of cultural and economic expansion remained compatible with America's liberal tradition of limited government. Promotional activities encouraged the growth of the private sector; they presumably liberated, rather than restricted, the free-enterprise system that lay at the heart of a liberal order.

Following World War I, the world experienced an even greater surge of American expansion. Promotional activities continued, especially the effort to make the tariff a tool for expanding the most-favored-nation principle, but government undertook more vigorous steps to shape the international impact of private citizens and groups. Herbert Hoover symbolized the cooperative strategy by which public goals were to be carried out through private means. The hallmarks of the cooperative state were "voluntary" guidelines set for investors by government and the chosen instrument, in which policymakers informally awarded a private group or corporation official blessing or monopolistic privileges in return for carrying out some element of American foreign policy. The chosen-instrument approach developed in every sector the American government considered essential to American expansion—international communications, international investment banking, strategic raw materials. By cooperating with businesses and various kinds of private associations, the government hoped to improve America's competitive position in the world. Through the private approach of the cooperative state, policymakers believed the United States could expand its global influence and yet preserve the liberal tradition of limited government.

With the collapse of the international system after 1929 and the onset of worldwide depression and then war, the cooperative, private emphasis of the 1920s gave way to more direct governmental involvement in the international economic and cultural order. Government officials believed that the difficulties of the 1930s stemmed from inadequate international economic mechanisms (because of the limitations of working through the private sector) and from a lack of military preparedness to halt countries that desired to carve out restricted spheres of influence. According to this view, the road to stability, prosperity, and peace required new governmental mechanisms to guide the world economy, new agencies to disperse American information and relief, and a powerful military presence (enhanced by military-assistance programs and possession of the new atomic weaponry) to prevent the growth of closed spheres of influence. Though government still promoted private expansion and still used cooperative, chosen-instrument relationships (as in resource policy), expansion became an elaborate process directed by a variety of official cultural and economic agencies. Governmental or intergovernmental agencies such as IMF, IBRD, GATT, AID, USIA,* and other technical-assistance agencies assumed functions previously conducted by private citizens.

In each of these stages, the realities of American expansion increasingly diverged from the liberal-developmental theories invoked by policymakers. More precisely, policymakers tended to apply their liberal canons selectively— upholding those that would favor American expansion and modifying or ignoring those that might not.

The Americans who guided foreign relations from 1890 to 1945 tried to create an international order based on certain liberal tenets. For commerce, American policymakers sought stable exchange rates based on gold, equal access to markets, and (after 1934) freer trade. All these were to promote wider markets for American exports, greater production and employment at home, and rising levels of world trade. For investment, Americans desired stability, open access, and nonsocialist forms of economic organization that would not threaten American investors' property rights abroad. For various cultural and philanthropic exchanges, policymakers also sought to promote unrestricted access—that is, the doctrine of free flow. In all areas, Americans stressed private ownership and denounced the restrictions or monopolies that foreign governments imposed. This brand of liberalism—emphasizing equal trading opportunity, open access, free flow, and free enterprise— was advanced as a formula for global development, a formula that the Americans liked to think had succeeded in the United States.

---

*International Monetary Fund, International Bank for Reconstruction and Development, General Agreement on Tariffs and Trade, Agency for International Development, United States Information Agency

There were many problems with liberal-developmentalist goals. First, America's own development did not arise from following these liberal principles but from an expedient mix of individual initiatives and government policies promoting growth. American policymakers did many of the things they cautioned foreigners against. They restrained trade through protective tariffs and, after they began to lower their tariff barriers, used import quotas. They indirectly subsidized the export sector through taxpayer-financed promotional bureaus and lending agencies. During two wars, they effectively nationalized key sectors of the economy and vigorously pursued foreign expansion, taking advantage of the temporary merger of public and private spheres to outmaneuver foreign competitors. They supported American producers' monopolies and price setting cartels (though, of course, America's cartels were privately owned). They carefully nurtured domestically owned communications and transportation, making sure that foreign companies never dominated the technology of dissemination of information. After World War II, they created many governmental agencies that directly dispersed American loans, relief, and information, thus manipulating to political advantage what might have been an unguided flow of information and capital. By all these means, America's governing elites retained control; they shaped domestic growth and diversification and then guided its expansion into the world.

By pressing free flow, free enterprise, and open access on others, the American government, in effect, was prescribing a developmental process for foreigners quite unlike their own—a "development" dominated by strong American-based structures and organized by American capital and expertise. For weaker states, the influx of foreign ownership and foreign-dominated communications that accompanied policies of open access could ultimately mean a surrender of national control over basic decisions regarding the organization of economic and social life. For twentieth-century American policymakers, international liberalism, a Pax Americana, and global development were synonymous goals. Nationalists, especially in Latin America, Asia, or Africa, increasingly believed that policies promoting free flow, free enterprise, and open access integrated them into a global system dominated by others and were thus incompatible with well-balanced, or nationally controlled, development in their own countries.

Second, America's liberal approach of maximizing the power of private capital and minimizing governmental restrictions did not rid the world of obstacles within the mythical free marketplace but merely made it easier for such obstacles to grow within the private sector. American-dominated private cartels and huge international businesses could practice monopolistic arrangements behind a shield of rhetoric extolling American individualism and free enterprise. And the American government supported them by denouncing restraints by foreign governments as autocratic interference with the freedom of the private sector. Americans, in short, did not really seek a free marketplace but a *privately owned* marketplace which they mistakenly labeled "free."

Third was another problem relating to the power of private capital. In order to become more competitive with European enterprises in a global rivalry, American companies—Firestone Rubber, Standard Oil, or Pan American Airways, for example—might carve out a dominant position in an economically weak nation. The United States government, invoking the principle of advancing international competition, might assist that effort as part of an antimonopoly campaign against Europeans. But the private corporation and, behind it, the cooperating hand of government might then exert a monopolistic, or illiberal, control on the smaller nation. Similarly, a joint government-industry effort to increase American information abroad might be justified by the liberal doctrine of free flow. Yet a strong American communications sector could, in weak states, exert a dominance that was positively stifling. Liberalism in the international order, then, could run directly counter to both liberalism and balanced, nationally controlled development in weaker nations. That the advance of international liberalism could generate its polar opposite—entrenched conservatism and a narrow range of options—in many areas of the world was a contradiction that exporters of the American dream persistently refused to acknowledge. In powerless states, archconservative regimes catering to domineering American private interests or agencies often directly resulted from America's expansion within a liberal international order; they were not unfortunate accidents brought about by America's insufficient attention to "human rights" abroad.

Fourth, although American liberal-developmentalists posited an open, global contest between alternative visions of human possibilities, they clearly believed that America's own formula for advancement would inevitably triumph in the global marketplace. The dilemma constantly presented itself: how could foreign countries who resisted American-prescribed "development" (often called "civilization" or later "modernization") be handled without violating their "liberty" to try out competing ideas and techniques? Each generation of liberal-developmentalists found ways around this difficulty by developing theories of America's special mission to uplift the world. Doctrines of racial superiority and evangelical mission prevailed early in the century; a faith in granting prerogatives to new middle-class professionals emerged with turn-of-the-century progressivism and grew stronger between the wars; and a fervent anti-Communism justified much illiberal conduct after World War II. There could, American liberal-expansionists believed, be no truly enlightened dissent against the ultimate acceptance of American ways, and this faith bred an intolerance, a narrowness, that was the very opposite of liberality.

The American dream as represented in the ideal of liberal-developmentalism differed from the reality of America's expanding cultural and economic influence. Americans involved in international affairs could preach and even believe in the basic tenets of free enterprise, open access, and free flow, while they themselves applied them selectively and ignored their contradictions.

Corporatism

MICHAEL J. HOGAN

Historians of the New School use the terms corporatism, corporate liberalism, neo-capitalism, and associationalism more or less interchangeably to describe a political-economic system that is characterized by certain organizational forms, by a certain ideology, and by a certain trend in the development of public policy. Organizationally, corporatism refers to a system that is founded on officially recognized economic or functional groups, including organized labor, business, and agriculture. In such a system, institutional regulating, coordinating, and planning mechanisms integrate these groups into an organic whole; elites in the private and public sectors collaborate to guarantee order, progress, and stability; and this collaboration creates a pattern of interpenetration and power sharing that makes it difficult to determine where one sector leaves off and the other begins. Ellis W. Hawley defines corporatism primarily in these terms. His definition parallels Philippe Schmitter's "ideal-type" corporatism, and his work on the 1920s, which traces what Robert Wiebe called "the search for order" in modern history, sheds new light on the process by which American leaders have sought to adapt the liberal institutions of an earlier day to the imperatives of an organized capitalism. Influenced by the work of neo-institutional and neo-organizational historians, Hawley has called our attention to the emergence of an administrative state with limited but important responsibilities, the concurrent appearance of organized units of private economic power, the collaborative systems that fused these units into concerts of group action and self-government, and the administrative networks that link private governments and public authorities.

Other New School historians have focused on the ideology that corporate liberals used to explain and rationalize the institutional and organizational adaptations described by Hawley. They have identified a body of liberal thought that envisioned a "middle way" between the older laissez-faire system of classical theory and the paternalistic statism of an Orwellian nightmare. According to the most recent of these accounts, the spokesmen of corporate liberalism favored positive programs, including those administered by government, to tame the business cycle, nurture growth, and protect elements of the population that did not yet share in the material benefits of modern capitalism. But they also sought to contain the state by entrusting much of the responsibility for public policy to semiautonomous agencies of economic coordination and control, to supposedly nonpartisan experts from the private sector, and to corporative systems of economic planning, voluntary regulation, and social welfare. Aside from depoliticizing divisive issues and "privatizing" public power in the name of private enterprise and democracy, these strategies would help to discipline the selfish pursuit

Michael J. Hogan, "Corporatism: A Positive Appraisal," *Diplomatic History,* X (Fall 1986), 363–367. Reprinted by permission of Scholarly Resources Inc.

of individual and group interests. They would weld ostensibly competing private groups into an organic unit and thus maximize the chances for political stability and for an economic growth in which all could share. The idea of growth, what Charles S. Maier calls "productionism," formed another component of the ideology of corporatism. Corporate liberals perceived growth as both a goal in its own right and as the key to social harmony, the survival of private enterprise, and the preservation of political democracy. By focusing on growth, it was possible to define a common political and economic agenda for different private groups, thus widening the area of collaboration between them while shrinking the area of competition. And by generating growth it was possible to avoid the dangerous social divisions, the battles over redistribution, and the excessive expansion of state power that might otherwise result from economic stagnation and retrenchment.

Generating growth, however, required more than a common commitment to productionism and particular organizational adaptations. It also required appropriate public programs, especially in such areas as fiscal, monetary, and budgetary policy, international economic policy, and labor policy broadly defined to include measures of social welfare. Corporate liberals have differed among themselves over the nature of these policies, and their recommendations have changed over time. Nevertheless, the general direction of corporatist thinking remained consistent with what American historians would identify as "progressive," and then "liberal," opinion in the public and private sectors. Works that might be fitted into the New School thus talk of an *evolving* corporate liberalism. They tend to view the modern American experience as a single process, but they do not deny the reality of historical change. Indeed, they are particularly interested in the liberal policy innovations growing out of the New Deal, and at least some have linked these changes to interrelated transformations in the structure of American industry and politics.

This is the case with Thomas Ferguson and other historians who have sought to explain the rise and fall of the "System of '96," by which they mean the political alignment that took shape in the United States at the end of the nineteenth century. The Republican party presided over this system, organizing a dominant political coalition centered on a nearly homogeneous community of business and banking leaders. By the 1920s, however, the business community had split into capital-intensive and labor-intensive blocs. Ferguson notes how each bloc adopted different positions on labor and trade policy, a list that later would include fiscal, monetary, and budgetary policy as well.

On the labor question, capital-intensive firms adopted a conciliatory approach similar to the one urged by Republican progressives like Herbert Hoover, out of which came support for employee representation schemes, corporate programs of welfare capitalism, and the eight-hour day in the steel industry. Labor-intensive firms remained wedded to the antilabor policies of an earlier age. Unable to afford the higher wages, better benefits, and improved working conditions that it would take to buy a more malleable and cooperative work force, they resorted to the "big stick" in dealing with labor strikes, launched a crusade for the "Open Shop," and applauded the use of antilabor court injunctions by the Justice Department. The same firms also belonged to the nationalist wing of the business community and the Republican party. Fearful of more efficient producers abroad, they sought to shelter the home market behind a wall of restrictions and generally complained about reducing war debts and raising taxes in order to underwrite the recovery of foreign competitors. Their position set them at odds with the capital-intensive firms for whom the world was an oyster to be enjoyed without penalty in the home market. These latter firms had emerged as world leaders in their industries. And, together with their partners among the great international investment houses, they led the campaign to reduce war debts, eliminate trade restrictions, and organize an Open Door world economy.

These divisions help to account for many of the inconsistencies that typified domestic and foreign policy during the Republican Ascendancy. They arose from underlying changes in the industrial structure and resulted in a political stalemate that persisted into the 1930's, when the gradual convergence of progressive opinion in the public and private sectors finally led to a major realignment. But out of this realignment came the dominant coalition, the so-called New Deal coalition, that would set the political agenda under Democratic and Republican administrations alike over the next forty years. The New Deal coalition included at its core the capital-intensive bloc of firms and their allies in the investment community, the leading trade unions, and the major farm associations. Each of these groups stood to gain from policies that buttressed the private sector, promoted overseas expansion, fostered social welfare, or facilitated labor's collaboration in a tripartite partnership with government and business. Their alliance enabled the New Deal to overcome domestic opposition, eliminate some of the earlier contradictions in public policy, and take the nation farther down the road to a corporative political economy than Republican progressives had been able to go in the 1920s. Hoover's concept of countercyclical stabilization now gave way to Keynesian strategies of demand management, welfare capitalism and company unionism to the welfare state and the Wagner Act, and "independent internationalism" to multilateralism.

As the last transformation suggests, the search for order in the United States had an international counterpart. Corporate liberals saw parallels between national policies of economic autarky and the unbridled pursuit of self-interest at home, between state trading and paternalistic government, and between international rivalries and domestic social divisions. From their point of view, moreover, these international dangers could be eliminated by restructuring the world system along lines similar to the corporative order that was emerging in the United States. To the open and competitive system envisioned in classical theory—one founded on the principles of specialization, comparative advantage, stable currencies, and fixed exchanges—corporate liberals would append new mechanisms of economic planning, new institutions of coordination and control, and new partnerships between public and private elites in the collective administration of world trade and development. These were to be the bricks and mortar in an international edifice that Hoover and progressive Republicans started to build in the 1920s, and that Cold War liberals later would seek to protect by adding military alliances and other collective security arrangements. In the final design as drawn after World War II, multinational frameworks would limit competitive nationalisms; market forces and institutional co-ordinators would integrate economies; and economic, as well as military integration, would help to deter aggressors, clear a path to stable growth, and forge a prosperous community of free nations.

The corporatist synthesis, then, can be used to analyze modern American efforts to organize a neo-capitalist system at home and to reorganize the international system along similar lines; to link both efforts to underlying transformations in the structure of American industry and politics; to explain the innovations in public policy that resulted; and to describe the ideology articulated to legitimize both policy innovations and organizational adaptations.

Hegemony and World System

THOMAS McCORMICK

Capitalism has *always* been *international* in nature. The key to capital accumulation and profit maximization has always been the mobility of capitalists—especially large capitalists with political connections and economic reserves—to shift their activity from one place to another in order to secure greater returns, even if that other place be both distant and foreign. That was true of a Hanseatic grain merchant in the sixteenth century who rerouted his ships from the Baltic to the Adriatic to take advantage of local famine and exorbitant prices; it is true today of a multinational automobile corporation that relocates its engine production from Detroit to São Paulo to take advantage of lower factors of production. Moreover, that same fluidity of capital across international borders was not only key to initiating success but key to renewing capitalism's success after long slumps like those of 1650–1730 and 1870–1900. Such periodic slumps flowed from two antithetical tendencies: the tendency of individual capitalists both to maximize production to protect and enlarge market shares; and to minimize wage bills to reduce competitive costs of production. The social consequence of such cumulative individual decisions was a real or potential overproduction/underconsumption and a decline in the rate of profit. And historically, the major countervailing force to falling profits was international fluidity of capital and goods that optimized opportunities and options to enhance profits and capital accumulation.

In the last decade, a number of academic observers have suggested

Thomas McCormick, " 'Every System Needs a Center Sometimes': An Essay on Hegemony and Modern American Foreign Policy," in Lloyd C. Gardner, ed., *Redefining the Past: Essays in Diplomatic History in Honor of William Appleman Williams,* 196–201, 204–5, 211–12, 213–16, 218–20. Reprinted with permission of Oregon State University Press.

that this international fluidity had produced, by 1650, a configuration that could properly be described as a world system or a world economy. Rooted in the dense empiricism of Fernand Braudel and the sociological imagination of Immanuel Wallerstein, this analysis posits three central characteristics for that world system—as true in 1950 as in 1650.

1. At any given point in time, the system occupies a "given geographic space"—"one portion of our planet, to the degree that it forms an economic whole." Moreover, that "geographic space" has tended to expand historically to integrate more and more of the earth and its inhabitants into a world market economy; that is, to enlarge the arena of capital mobility and profit maximization.

2. At any given point in time, the system requires a pole or center—a dominant city to act as the coordinator and clearing house of international capital: Venice in 1450, Antwerp in 1550, Amsterdam in 1650, London in 1850, and New York City in 1950.

3. At any given point in time, the system consists of successive zones, each performing a specialized function in a complex international division of labor. The center, or core countries, monopolize high-tech, high-value added, high-profit enterprises and their auxiliaries of finance and insurance; the hinterlands, or peripheral areas, are the "hewers of wood and the carriers of water," specializing in production of primary commodities both agricultural and extractive; and in between, the semiperiphery performs intermediate functions of semifinishing products, mobilizing local capital, and sharing in transport.

What is striking about this world system is that it is *always* changing and *never* changing. The geographic boundary of the world system is always expanding or (on occasion) contracting; but a discernible boundary is always there between the capitalist world economy and its external world—the minisystem of subsistence or the maxi-empires of the Ottomans, the Russians, the Chinese. The center is forever shifting, from the Mediterranean to Northern Europe to North America; but there is always some center. There is always mobility between zones, both upward as in the United States' case or downward as in Spain's; but the zones and their division of labor are always there. What constitutes high technology and low technology is forever changing; wheat, shipbuilding, textiles, or steel may have been high value in earlier epochs but are intermediate or low value in this age of electrical equipment. What remains constant is the monopolization of high tech (and high profits), at any given moment, by core countries. Hence, in 1685, a world system where northwestern Europe constituted the core (with Amsterdam its center) and specialized in diversified agriculture, textiles, shipbuilding, and metal wares; Eastern Europe, Scandinavia, Scotland, Ireland, and the Americas, as its periphery, produced grain, bullion, wool, sugar, and cotton; and the Mediterranean, as its semiperiphery, specialized in silk and in credit and specie transactions. Hence, in 1985, a world system where North America, Japan, and Europe constitute the core (with New York City as its center) and specialize in electronics, capital goods, durable consumer goods, diversified agriculture, and finance; the Less Developed

Countries (LDCs) of Africa, Southeast Asia, and the Caribbean basin, as the periphery, specialize in nonpetroleum raw materials; and the Newly Industrializing Countries (NICs) of Mexico, Brazil, South Africa, Israel, Iran, India, China, Eastern Europe, and the Asian rimlands, as the semi-periphery, specialize in consumer goods, shipping, petroleum, and credit transactions.

In its *real* life, the system's norm has been a state of tension between "haves" and "have-nots"; between tendencies toward concentration and toward redistribution; between cooperation and competition; between the general utility of peace and prosperity and the cyclical necessity for war and depression to weed out the inefficient, revive profits, and restore vitality. In its *ideal* life, the circumstances are rather different; and, on rare occasions, the real has come close to approximating the ideal—principally in the three golden ages of capitalism that followed the end of the Thirty Years War in 1648, the Napoleonic Wars in 1815, and the two World Wars in 1945. And the key to each of those epochs of peace and prosperity has been the same: the ability and will of a single power to arrogate to itself the role of hegemonic power in the world system.

Hegemony rests upon the indispensable underpinning of economic supremacy. Any hegemonic power must simultaneously contain the dominant financial urban center; possess clear comparative advantage in a wide range of product lines, usually based on technological and managerial superiority (e.g., Fordism and Taylorism in 1920s America); and dominate world trade both quantitatively and qualitatively. But beyond mere economic power, a hegemonic nation must possess clear military superiority; it must be able to exert its political will over allies and enemies alike; and it must obtain ideological hegemony over the rest of the system—that is, have its basic ideas and principles command deference. In other words, it must be both feared and respected.

Why the utility of single power hegemony to the capitalist system? What makes it preferable to general competition or a balance of power? Simply put, hegemony historically has been the surest way to overcome the essential contradiction of a system that is economically internationalist but politically nationalist. On the one hand, as has been noted, the ability to accumulate capital and maximize profits depends on the fluidity and mobility of factors of production; there is an economic imperative that drives the system toward internationalization, integration, and interdependence. On the other hand, the system is compartmentalized into political units called nation states; and those units are wedded to specific territory and preoccupied with specific functions of sustenance and military defense. Those concerns for territory, sustenance, and defense create a bias on the part of state apparatus to interfere with the fluidity and mobility of factors of production through farm subsidies, military spending, protective tariffs, capital controls, currency convertibility regulation, and the like. That bias is immensely intensified in nation states using various forms of mercantilism as catch-up strategies to overtake more advanced, perhaps even hegemonic core countries—like the effort of British mercantilism to overtake the Dutch in the seventeenth century; or of Napoleon's Continental System to pass the British in the early nineteenth century; or of Germany's New Plan to supplant the British and withstand the Americans in the early twentieth century; or of Russia's "we will bury capitalism" program in the 1960s. Given such biases, the overwhelming inclination of nation states, in periods of competition or balance of power, is to pursue policies of economic autarky—of capitalism in one country or in one self-contained trading bloc. But such approaches are transparently inefficient; they tend to create a series of fragmented national economies that are redundant, not optimally sized, and uneconomical. And, in the long run, such inefficiency compounds the tendency of the rate of profit to fall.

Single power hegemony acts to counter the tendency to national capital and self-sufficiency. It gives to one power an unequivocal interest to opt for an international capital approach rather than a national. As the dominant industrial, commercial, and financial center, it has the most to gain from a world of free trade, free capital movements, and free convertibility—a *free world;* and the most to lose from a world of mercantilist state interventions that seriously limit those freedoms. So it possesses built-in incentives to use its position as *workshop* and *banker* of the world system to create institutions and ground rules that foster the internationalization of capital; and to use its position as *theologian* of the system to preach the universality of freedom of the seas (the Dutch), and free trade (the British), and the open door (the Americans), and comparative advantage and specialized division of labor (all of the above); and to use its position as *umpire* and *cop* of the system to protect it against external antagonists, internal rebellions, and internecine differences; and to generally see that the ground rules are not impeded by friend or foe.

There are two consequences. First, hegemonic periods have tended to be the most prosperous, since the hegemonic country uses its power to sustain an economic order that both expands and integrates simultaneously; economic internationalism is more efficient and more profitable for the system as a whole than competitive economic nationalism. Second, hegemonic periods tend to be the most peaceful (at least within the core). The economic expansiveness of the system (the antithesis of a zero-sum game) often means that the material rewards (how the economic pie is sliced) are satisfactory enough to dampen the temptation of nonhegemonic core powers to use force (war) as a strategy of income/power redistribution. And even if the temptation persists, the military capacity of the hegemonic country to chastise, or to withhold protection against external enemies, tends to act as a deterrent to independent, autarkic action.

Hegemony is always impermanent. There are ultimately tendencies at work to transform hegemonic countries into *rentier* nations and into warfare states; and the transformations, in turn, undermine hegemony itself. On the one hand, there is a cumulative tendency to neglect investment in the hegemonic country's own industrial plant in favor of investment and lending abroad. Higher wage bills at home for both production and managerial workers combined with greater accessibility to the world system (the major price and the major perk of hegemony) make the export of capital more profitable than the export of goods. The resulting deterioration in domestic capital spending is then compounded by the hegemonic state's overspending on military power. Essential to the system as its military shield and its penetrating sword, that military spending always is a mixed blessing for the hegemonic country. On the one hand, it counteracts the tendency to a falling rate of profit by state subsidization of high profits. On the other hand, this forced consumption (by taxpayers) at artificially high prices (and profits) tends to divert capital from civilian production into military production—which again leads to the neglect of modernizing needs of the domestic industrial plant. Over time, both these *rentier* and military tendencies diminish the very comparative advantage, the very industrial supremacy, upon which hegemony originally rested. And, further, that decline in industrial supremacy may tempt the hegemonic power to overstress other major components of its dominance—chiefly its monopolization of the military protection racket and its continued financial might—to exact concessions from other powers to halt its decline. But such "imperial preference" (if you will) is itself uneconomical and inefficient for the system as a whole; and, to the degree that it rests on yet greater military spending, only further contributes to the deterioration in comparative advantage possessed by the declining hegemonic power.

This impermanent character of hegemony helped produce the crisis of capitalism between 1870 and 1950, encompassing a thirty year slump (1870–1900) and a thirty-year war (World Wars I and II, sandwiched around an even more serious depression). The key to this crisis in the capitalist world system was the decline in British hegemony, manifested by lower productivity and the loss of advantage in more and more product lines; by the increasing use of military force to create, perpetuate, and protect a formal, colonial empire in the periphery; and by its partial emasculation of free trade and multilateralism in favor of trading privileges for its own sterling bloc.

That decline in both British power and the deference accorded it made it possible for four other countries to pursue catch-up strategies of their own: the United States, Germany, Japan, and (more belatedly) Russia. Each built upon domestic catharsis and renewal—the American Civil War, German reunification, the Meiji restoration, and the Russian Revolution. Each initially used state intervention in the economy (national capital) to counteract British dominance in the world system (international capital): American import substitution and tariff protectionism, German central banking and trading quotas, Japanese oversight of investment strategies and capital flows, and Russian state ownership. Each participated in the new imperialism movement in Asia, Africa, or Latin America at the turn of the century, but with mixed results: a greater strategic presence astride world trading routes but little tangible and direct economic rewards. Each initially opted for a strategy of regional autarky—that is, partially removing a geographic area from the British-dominated international economy and integrating it into their own national economies: the Pan-Americanism of the United States; the *Mittel-Europe* of Germany; the Pan-Asianism of Japan; and socialism in one country (i.e., state capitalism in the Eurasian continent) by Russia. . . .

World War II . . . was the means by which the United States asserted and assumed hegemony in the world system. Became the system's workshop and banker; its umpire and its cop; its preacher and its teacher. The potential for such arrogation of power had existed since 1919, but now war provided the last ingredients: the will to power by elite leaders and the popular acceptance of the legitimacy and propriety of that will. Now the process begun in the first phase of this new Thirty Years War ended in the second. British hegemony was dead and so too any German pretense to hegemony. The twentieth century would yet be the American Century. Novelist Gore Vidal caught the full sense of it well in his *Washington, D. C.* when he described the last days of a fictionalized Franklin Roosevelt and the first days of his successor.

> The elegant, ravaged old President . . . continued to pursue, even as he was dying, the high business of reassembling the fragments of broken empires into a new pattern with himself at center, proud creator of the new imperium. Now, though he was gone, the work remained. The United States was master of the earth. No England, no France, no Germany, no Japan . . . left to dispute the Republic's will. Only the mysterious Soviet would survive to act as other balance in the scale of power.

By 1945, it had become axiomatic to American leaders that two prerequisites were necessary for the world system to function in an economically efficient and politically stable way. First, there had to be a constantly expanding world economic pie. Second, there had to be a hegemonic power capable of enforcing rules of behavior necessary to ensure that expansion, and punishing or isolating those who refused to accede to those rules. Neither prerequisite had obtained during the 1930s, and the lack of each had produced World War II. The economic pie had contracted and kicked off a scramble for scarce resources and profits; and the lack of a clearly dominant capitalist power removed any restraints on the more aggressive scramblers. Those American leaders emerged from World War II determined to rectify those glaring deficiencies, and to put the global "humpty dumpty" back together again after ten years of history's worst depression and six years of one of history's worst wars, to assume the burden of power themselves (as well as the profits and prestige), and to wield it in ways that would breathe life back into a nearly moribund system.

In the five years that followed World War II (what some have called the First Cold War), American efforts concerned themselves primarily with reconstruction of the European and Japanese industrial cores—especially the revival of industrial productivity. For the first two years, the effort was *ad hoc* and piecemeal, parceled out on a country-by-country basis through UN agencies, the American Export-Import Bank, German and Japanese occupation funding, and the $3.75 billion loan to Great Britain. Those interim efforts failed. The goals of multilateral trade and free currency convertibility were as remote as ever; and the institutions designed to promote them—the World Bank, the International Monetary Fund, the International Trade Organization—were either nonfunctional or nonexistent. The shorthand symbol of that failure was the Dollar Gap that reached critical proportions by 1947. Europe and Japan had an almost insatiable need for American capital goods, raw materials, and food to effect their recovery, but they lacked the dollars to pay for them. The consequent trade deficit forced them to cut back on purchases from the United States—both hurting their recovery and threatening American prosperity—and led them to experiment with autarkic measures to protect their currencies and minimize the deficit. In effect, it led Europe to consider nationalist rather than internationalist roads to reconstruction. This was especially true in governments where organized labor wielded some clout and pushed for economic policies geared to full employment and income redistribution (redividing the pie) rather than increased productivity for world markets (expanding the pie). . . .

American efforts between 1947 and 1950 were bold, imaginative, sophisticated endeavors to end those autarkic experiments and commit Europe and Japan irrevocably to the course of multilateralism and interdependence. Of these, the Marshall Plan (European Economic Recovery program) was clearly the most stunning; indeed, the most revolutionary. Not only was its scale, duration, and governmental involvement unprecedented. More important (more important than the dollars themselves) was the use of leverage to force Europe to take the American road. Marshall Plan aid was used to move Europe in the direction of a common market and an industrial economy organized around the principles of comparative advantage and the economies of scale; and its veto over counterpart funds was used to force Europe to soft-pedal welfare programs, limit wages, control inflation, and create an environment conducive for capital investment—part of it financed out of labor's pocket. This was hegemony with a vengeance: American control over Europe's internal social and economic policies, in return for aid in making Europe more competitive with American capital. At the same time, in Japan, the infusion of capital through military subcontracting and the reduction of costs through austerity wages (the Dodge Plan) sought to make Japan independent of American occupation support and capable of competing again in world markets. In effect, the United States made some shortrun sacrifices to restore European and Japanese competition, on the assumption that, in the long run, the new economic equilibrium would revive world trade to pre-1929 levels (at least) and make America's own prosperity both better and more enduring.

There were two potential enemies to this exercise in American hegemony—one within, one without. The external adversary was the Soviet Union, which re-entered the world system in World War II after twenty years of semi-isolation. . . .

If Russia was the external devil, there was also an "enemy within" that threatened America's hegemonic internationalism. The major component of that internal opposition was the residue of the 1930s antiwar, anti-intervention movement, augmented by a much smaller component of radical labor leaders and popular front politicians. The former was clearly the greater enemy that forever bedeviled New Dealers and business internationalists with the penultimate fear: a revival of isolation. Made politically potent by the Republican election victory in 1946, apparent representatives of such sentiments made abundantly clear their wariness about foreign aid, downward revision of the tariff, or participation in international banking and monetary agencies. They simply did not buy the logic or accept the imperatives of economic internationalism—either for the interests of their constituents or for the nation as a whole. Ultimately, the threat of such nationalists was blunted in several ways: symbolic politics were invoked, such as the notion of bipartisanship: that peace like war had its perils, and required that politics stop at the water's edge. Home market businessmen were persuaded that subcontracts from foreign market multinationals were crucial to their own prosperity. Center-right labor leaders were persuaded that popular front politics and redistributive strategies were dead in the postwar Republican revival, and that only global economic expansion offered any real hope for full employment.

But the major method was to invoke the communist menace. Not the very real Russian menace that elites themselves feared, but a simpler, more stark, more militarized, more (secularly) evangelical menace. A button that, once pushed, would evoke the deepest fears about threats to the bedrock values of American life and to the very physical security of the American nation. And that button was pushed: first in the overblown Greek crisis of 1947; and finally even in the Marshall Plan debates when economic and humanitarian arguments seemed insufficient to carry the day. The same button, pushed to disarm nationalist critics of American hegemonic policies, could be used to disgrace and discredit more radical critics. Indeed it was: in 1947, to denounce leftist opposition to the Truman Doctrine; in 1948, to condemn Henry Wallace and the Progressive Party as tools or dupes of international communism; and in 1949, to purge the American labor movement of radical influences. (A liberal version of McCarthyism before the real thing ironically turned to devour liberals themselves.)

The contours of the Cold War have paralleled those of the international business cycle. What some have called the Second Cold War coincided with the Long Boom that made the period between 1950 and 1973 the most sustained and profitable period of economic growth in the history of world capitalism. Over that quarter of a century, the Gross *World* Product grew to be 2.25 times larger, and global industrial output averaged an increase of 5.5 percent per year. That compared favorably with the world economy's best previous record: the 4.5 percent annual average during the 1899–1914 period. Capital became more fluid and free to maneuver in the world system than ever before, and the extent of world economic integration and interdependence was unprecedented, perhaps even sufficient to realize the American goal of rendering autarkic options simply unfeasible. And, of course, hegemonic America reaped its share of this growth and integration. By 1967 22 percent of American profits were being earned in overseas economic activity, and the annual gross product of American multinational corporations, estimated at $120 billion, was larger than the GNP of any other capitalist country, including Germany or Japan.

Both the Long Boom and the Second Cold War grew out of American responses to a network of crises. . . .

For five years [1945–1950], American elites had attempted to use their hegemonic power and position to effect the recovery of the European and Japanese industrial machines and to restore world trade to predepression levels and, at the same time, to isolate ("contain") the Soviet bloc that declined to defer to American hegemony and accept its rules of the game. Now all that seemed terribly jeopardized. Japan's economic recovery was in shambles and Europe's was disappointing. Most of Eurasia, from the Elbe to the Amur, had partially withdrawn from the world economy. The Asian rimlands seemed destined soon to follow and, who knew, could much of the Third World be far behind? In addition, America's atomic diplomacy and the credibility of its military shield appeared much in doubt. In short, 1950 seemed frighteningly like 1930, with strong centrifugal tendencies pushing nation states to revert to their inherent nationalist tendencies; to protect their own economies through state regulation of trade and investment; and to play their Russian cards and China cards to ease their own deficit/debtor dilemmas. In other words, American hegemony was facing its first and severest postwar test and, if the hegemony could not be maintained, there were serious questions in the minds of American elites as to whether the capitalist world economy and the American free enterprise system could survive and prosper.

The American response to this midcentury crisis established the central tendencies of American paramountcy for more than two decades thereafter. First, American leaders chose to militarize the Cold War. They built the H-bomb, quadrupled the military budget, replaced foreign aid with military aid, transformed NATO from a political alliance to a military pact, rearmed Germany, and held open the option of rearming Japan. All this would maintain the credibility of the American military shield for its allies and would be easier to sell than tariff revision and foreign aid at home. Second, they attempted to speed the integration of European economies and the creation of a common market, hoping to create a larger internal market for European trade. This European integrationism and the Cold War's militarization were intimately connected, for German rearmament was a powerful incentive to European economic cooperation, the major means of subsuming German freedom of action—including the freedom to do military mischief—within a matrix of economic interdependence. Third, they determined upon a concerted effort to develop Third World extractive economies and integrate them into the industrial cores of Europe and Japan; to provide the markets and raw materials essential for full recovery. This object too was tied to militarization, for parts of the periphery—especially the Asian rimlands—were so immersed in revolution and civil war that military pacification seemed necessary as a prelude to stable economic growth. Militarization, European integration, and Third World orientation—these were the dominant characteristics of American foreign policy from 1950 to 1973.

All of these facets contributed to the Long Boom. . . .

The militarism and economic intergrationism of the Second Cold War helped create an interdependent and fluid world economy, but they also laid the groundwork for a crisis in American hegemony. Militarization ultimately distorted the American economy grotesquely, creating a kind of "war capitalism" as mirror image to Russia's "war socialism." Cost-overrun contracts and skewed bidding made military spending a state subsidy for guaranteed exorbitant profits; and, as such, magnetically lured capital and credit that otherwise would have gone into civilian research, modernization, and production. As a consequence, American industry sharply declined in its productivity and lost its comparative advantage to Japan and Germany in a whole range of product lines long dominated by the United States. By 1973, America's only significant comparative advantage was in "guns and butter": military hardware, commercial aircraft, and agriculture.

Relatedly, the success in integrating Germany into the common market, Japan into the Asian rimlands, and both into the mainstream of world triangular patterns only reinforced their competitiveness relative to the United States. Once more, the measure and the metaphor was the dollar—only a dollar drain rather than a dollar gap; an American trade deficit. . . . Clearly, by 1973, the economic base of hegemony—its veritable underpinning—was seriously stressed.

So too, ironically, was its credibility base. The American pretense of hegemony rested on its claim that its leadership could give maximum economic efficiency and peace to the world system. And the Long Boom and the nonappearance of World War III endowed that claim with some legitimacy. But efficiency is not necessarily equity (indeed, it may come at the expense of equity); and the absence of global wars between core powers did not mean the end of neocolonial wars waged on alienated parts of the periphery. So it came to pass that America presided over an international division of labor that was predicated upon core exploitation of the periphery—in which prices of periphery commodities declined and the terms of trade worsened; in which the profits of fledgling industrialization in the semiperiphery were repatriated to corporate headquarters in New York, Frankfurt, Antwerp, London, and Tokyo; in which dependency became a palpable reality and not simply an economic theory. "Rich lands and poor," as Gunnar Myrdal described it—and the rich indeed got richer, and the poor got poorer. And so too it came to pass that America, as hegemonic power, had to confront the revolt of parts of the periphery, spurred on by mixtures of economic radicalism, political nationalism, cultural pride, and racial backlash—Vietnam and Cuba, Indonesia and Chile, Egypt and India, Algeria and Guatemala, the Congo and Bolivia. Hegemony required the confrontation, but the manner of its resolution often weakened the very credibility upon which hegemony rested.

Vietnam was the quintessential example during the Long Boom. The American commitment began in 1950 as part of a concerted policy of preventing the Asian rimlands (Korea, Taiwan, Southeast Asia) from drifting into the Sino-Soviet Asian trading bloc, and tempting a depressed Japan to follow suit; or, more positively, to integrate Japan and the rimlands into the world system and ultimately tempt China to junk its Russian connection and follow the path marked international capital. From its inception in 1950 to its fateful conclusion in 1973 (the same temporal frame as the Boom),the American policy was a conscious act of hegemony. America itself had little direct interest of its own in Southeast Asia, either materially or strategically. But Japan did—with its pressing need for markets, food, and raw materials, and its dependence on Persian Gulf oil that had to traverse the narrow straits of the Southeast Asian archipelagos. In effect, the United States acted as surrogate for Japan, acted in its police role to militarily stabilize Southeast Asia in order to effect political stability and to render economic development and integration into Japan's "workshop" economy finally possible. . . . Not only was American economic supremacy in question by 1973, but so was the efficacy of its military shield and its political preachments.

Cold War and business cycle have continued to follow their symbiotic course since 1973. Just as Russo-American détente gave way first to ambivalence and then to a Third Cold War, so too did stage one of an extended economic contraction (the Long Slump) give way first to uneven recovery and then to a second, harsher stage of tough times. Moreover, the changes in both the Cold War and the international economy facilitated the emergence of new power centers in American society, and the unfolding of an ongoing debate over the status of American hegemony and the best means, if any, of revitalizing it. . . .

This economic contraction [1979–1983] coincided with the failure of America's regional surrogate policy, witnessed by the revolutionary overthrow of the Shah in Iran and Somoza in Nicaragua. The interaction of both forced a great debate in policy-making circles, one that would partly end the confusion and ambivalence of the short recovery period. In some ways, it was a replay of the 1950 debate over NSC-68 [National Security Council Paper 68] and the recommendation to militarize the Cold War.

There were still those, like Cyrus Vance [secretary of state under Carter], who argued against remilitarization. More representative of old wealth and old power, they were more inclined to be sanguine and accept the loss of hegemony and make do in a more multipolar world; to consign limits to America's police role; to stress moral leadership and human rights instead; to put their faith in reindustrialization to restore America's capacity to compete and prosper in the world system; to explore the possibilities of renewed détente and arms agreements; and to coexist with and profit from Third World revolutions—knowing that whatever they were and whatever they called themselves (Marxist-Leninists, African socialists, Sandinistas) they could not deliver on their material promises to their subjects without coming to the West, hat in hand, for trade, capital, and technology.

Two factors damned this group and gave victory to their opponents. First, changes within American society produced new challengers to old wealth. Partly, this was the product of demographic changes that shifted the regional locus of power south and west. Partly, it grew out of the Long Slump itself, which produced an economic shakedown that, in purging the inefficient and rewarding vitality, tended to diminish the ranks of the old and enhance the power of the new. And finally, it reflected the regional distortions created by military spending and its disproportionate outlays in the west and the south. This new power group, dubbed by some the "Prussians," was not disposed to be sanguine about the loss of hegemony; as newcomers, recently arrived at the economic trough, they were not inclined to accept limits at the very moment of their greatest opportunity. Nor were they inclined to relinquish America's military function, integrated as they were into the war capitalism sector.

At the same time, events in the world system shifted the framework of the debate in their favor. The collapse of the world economy and the decline of American hegemony sparked a rash of revolutionary crises throughout the Third World: from Poland to Portugal, from Afghanistan to El Salvador, from Iran to Nicaragua, from Lebanon to Grenada, from Angola to Argentina, from South Africa to the Philippines. Almost all spilled over into the Third Cold War and exacerbated Russo-American conflict. Sometimes the initiative was American; sometimes Russian; and often as not, it was the tail wagging the dog—Third World client states soliciting aid that their patrons could not refuse without risking (in America's case) hegemonic credentials or (in Russia's case) revolutionary legitimacy.

The "Prussians" won the debate in 1979 during the late Carter administration, and ratified it with Reagan's victories in 1980 and 1984. Like Dean Acheson [secretary of state under Truman] and Paul Nitze [chief author of NSC-68] in 1950, they determined to rebuild and solidify American hegemony on the basis of an enlarged and modernized military shield. Their assumptions were that American dominance of the world "protection racket" would merit special rewards and preferences not due other core powers; that human rights diplomacy was ineffectual—that deference based on fear was more real than deference based on sentimentality; that an open door for Third World revolutions may be profitable, but negated the major *raison d'être* for remilitarization, and was not so profitable as a wholly capitalist road; and that restoring American economic supremacy—the basis of hegemony—could not be done by reindustrializing weak and archaic industries, but only by a massive state sponsorship of a technological revolution that would make America the first truly postindustrial society. Star Wars: the defense system that probably won't; the economic system that might.

There is compelling logic to the "stand-tall-in-the-saddle" position. The system does seem to need a center in order to survive. Certainly it has not done well in past periods of competing power centers and autarkic policies. So the revival of world protectionist sentiment and the drift toward competition and new coalitions (the EEC, Russia, Japan-China, and North America) are not reassuring. The New Imperialism was tried a century ago and found wanting as a guarantor of global peace and a provider of profits. On the other hand, hegemony too has been tried and likewise found wanting; found to rest on an hierarchical and often cruel division of labor, and upon harsh repression, when need be, to sustain that hierarchy. Such a choice: where efficiency exploits and peace kills. Somehow an old political catchphrase comes to mind: "The system isn't the solution. The system is the problem."

The Non-Rational

ROBERT DALLEK

Immediately after World War II, when the United States took unprecedented responsibility for international peace and security, curiosity about the American style of foreign policy was intense. Partly generated by a desire to avoid future blunders, interest understandably centered on past misdeeds—on why we had fought a seemingly pointless war with Spain, committed ourselves to unrealized goals in World War I, retreated into political isolationism in the twenties, ignored transparent threats in the thirties, and emerged from World War II imperfectly prepared to act constructively in foreign affairs. The answers to these questions produced a rich and varied literature on American diplomatic history. Where some scholars saw selfish economic interest or an imperial drive to make the world safe for capitalism as the principal influence on national actions abroad, others stressed the importance of domestic politics, the use of external events to promote internal political control. Still others found the central ingredient of America's foreign misadventures in legalism or a reverence for the rule of law, evangelism or a Protestant sense of responsibility for the disadvantaged, moralism or a tradition of free security ignoring the importance of power. . . .

[My] book aims to rekindle discussion about U.S. foreign affairs. More than that, it is an attempt to probe nonrational influences on foreign policy. After almost two decades of reading, thinking, and writing about American diplomatic history, I remain unsatisfied with existing explanations for past crusading fervor, visions of eternal peace, denials of basic realities, and overblown fears in response to events abroad. Were such distortions merely quaint relics of the past, one might see them as aberrations worthy of only casual attention. But their enduring hold on the American imagination in dealing with the outside world heightens my interest in explaining them. I share with the diplomat and historian George Kennan the belief that our current "preoccupation with nuclear war is a form of illness [which] can be understood only as some form of subconscious despair on the part of its devotees—some sort of death wish, a readiness to commit suicide for fear of death—a state of mind explicable only by some inability to face the normal hazards and vicissitudes of the human predicament—a lack of faith, or better a lack of strength that it takes to have faith, as countless of our generations have had it before us."

[My] book, then, is an exploration of what I would describe as the hidden side of American foreign policy. I do not mean conspiratorial schemes consciously pursued by unscrupulous men. I mean those subjective influences that makers and backers of foreign policy barely glimpse themselves. It is a study of undercurrents, of mood, tone, or milieu, of a climate of feeling that almost imperceptibly insinuates itself into concrete ideas and actions.

Like the atmosphere, these matters are not easily described. Yet they are there. More precisely, I am interested in the ways Americans have given foreign affairs symbolic meanings or made them into something other than what they actually were. I am concerned with foreign policy as a product of emotional displacement, of the impulse to make overseas affairs a vehicle for expressing unresolved internal tensions. For most Americans, the external world has been a remote, ill-defined sphere which can be molded into almost anything they wish. More often than we might care to think, this attitude has translated into foreign policies which have relieved and encouraged a nation struggling with tormenting domestic concerns. . . .

None of this is to suggest that political, strategic, and economic interests played no part in what the United States did abroad. These substantive matters, especially after World War II, loomed large in the country's overseas actions. But material and psychological or symbolic aims are not mutually exclusive. In our approach to foreign affairs, style and substance have always gone hand in hand. The fact that I have so much less to say about traditional influences on foreign policy than about the psychological ones is not meant to suggest that I wish to replace one explanation with the other. My objective is to expand our understanding of American foreign affairs by looking at them in a somewhat different way. As the historian Richard Hofstadter concluded, "people not only seek their interests but also express and even in a measure define themselves in politics; that political life acts as a sounding board for identities, values, fears, and aspirations."

What I have found particularly striking in pursuing this idea is how consistently domestic mood or climate of feeling registered in all its complexity on foreign policy. It is well known that before 1945 the country's shift from an agricultural, rural, largely homogeneous society to an industrial, urban one with a heterogeneous population spawned economic, political, and social unrest. It has been less clearly recognized that this development also found release in actions overseas. Indeed, I would go so far as to say that during these years foreign policy was less a reaction to events abroad than to conditions at home, where economic, political, and social change substantially blotted out overseas affairs and largely made them an irrational extension of internal hopes and fears.

The way America fought and ended the Spanish-American war, for instance, expressed yearnings across the whole society for a way out of the tensions between the modern industrialized world and the earlier rural culture. At one level the struggle with Spain became a celebration of old-style individualism and localism, while the peace arrangements reflected the contrary belief that new, worldwide responsibilities might compel the country to accommodate itself to modern trends. When it did not, the progressives used foreign policy in every part of the globe to encourage hopes for greater harmony, democracy, individual, opportunity, and social justice in the United States. The Caribbean, with small island countries that barely registered on American thought, became a perfect focus for these domestic absorptions. [Theodore] Roosevelt's Corollary to Monroe's

Doctrine and [Woodrow] Wilson's Missionary Diplomacy said less about American intentions in the Caribbean than about the quest for progressive advance in the United States. To be sure, the Roosevelt and Wilson policies also served selfish national interests, but the emotional or symbolic satisfaction which their actions provided seems to have been foremost in American minds.

Remote areas like East Asia were particularly susceptible to this sort of symbolic politics: When Americans invested China with visions of self-determination or freedom from alien control, they were more intent on combatting corporate influences destroying autonomy at home than on assuring independence for the Chinese. Even Europe, the most familiar foreign area of the world for Americans, could not escape the national preoccupation with internal affairs. Although the Great European War of 1914–18 was the most compelling event of the progressive era, it also became enmeshed in domestic concerns: American participation in the war was as much a device for relieving frustrations at home as a means of advancing national interests abroad.

The triumph of political reaction in the twenties and the subsequent revival of liberalism in the thirties and forties did not alter this pattern. Tied to enduring tensions over national self-image, the impulse to attach domestic goals to foreign relations survived the shifts between progressive and conservative political control. After World War I, when social cleavages between city and town, foreign- and native-born, agitated the country and heightened longings for a homogeneous America, foreign affairs reflected both these trends: Economic nationalism and political isolationism expressed the reality of special interest struggles in the United States, while treaties limiting naval arms and outlawing war were more symbolic wishes for lost domestic unity than sensible advances toward world peace. Moreover, World War II, the most serious international crisis of the century, repeated the national habit of viewing foreign relations in domestic terms: Universalism in the forties was more a statement about felt American harmony than a realistic assessment of the possibilities for "one world."

This impulse to invest overseas affairs with domestic meanings made American foreign policy before 1945 highly erratic. False assumptions about the outside world abounded. But as long as national survival did not seem particularly threatened by external conditions, Americans were loath to give up this psychologically satisfying way of seeing foreign affairs. After World War II, however, when national security could no longer be taken for granted and democratic and anticommunist nations everywhere depended on American power for their safety, U.S. foreign policy became more realistic than it had been. Interest in the United States mounted not only in past failures overseas but also in understanding how other people thought and international relations worked. "Realism" became a kind of national obsession in everything to do with foreign affairs.

But this self-conscious effort to be rational and toughminded about foreign relations could not entirely overturn traditional habits, especially because tensions over the character of American life continued to trouble the domestic scene. Though the New Deal persuaded Americans of the necessity of accommodating themselves to a more centralized society of large-scale organizations and less individual autonomy, nagging doubts remained. However considerable the success of the New Deal, however popular many of its ideas and its spirit of humane responsibility for the disadvantaged, it did not advance a new national self-image or fresh systematic conception of social relations to replace the old ideology of self-help and free enterprise. Consequently, the postwar period witnessed enduring tensions over national character and the proper role of federal authority in American life. Periodic bursts of organized demand for less government and greater freedom, culminating in the Reagan presidency, testify to continuing dreams of restoring an earlier, simpler style of life. Yet the country has been willing to follow this traditional ideology only up to a point, suggesting that it remains stuck somewhere between the new and the old, the modern technology world of huge bureaucracies and the nineteenth-century small-town culture of greater autonomy and personal control.

This ongoing conflict over national character partly explains the persistent irrationality in postwar foreign policy. A central element of the American response to the outside world in this period has been an unthinking anti-communism, an impulse to see a significant Communist threat to American security where it was either small or nonexistent. Policy toward Iran in the 1950s, Vietnam in the 1960s, and Chile in the 1970s reflected this distortion. The Eisenhower, Kennedy, Johnson, and Nixon administrations successively turned nationalistic movements in each of these countries into international Communist advances threatening dire harm to the United States. American ideas of what went on in these countries and what it meant to the United States were greatly at variance with the facts. As demonstrated by post-1975 events in Southeast Asia, for example, a Communist government in all Vietnam produced not Communist control throughout the area, but rather a clash of the two most powerful Communist countries in Asia—China and Vietnam. My point here is not to make a virtue out of the triumph of Communist arms in Vietnam but to consider why so many Americans reached false conclusions about the meaning of events in three widely separated countries over a long period of time.

As with the pre-1945 period, I see part of the answer in the response to changes in the United States. Shortly after World War II, the sociologist David Riesman suggested that Americans were uncomfortable with recent alterations in American life. ". . . Why is war so likely, when few people want it?" he asked. ". . . One reason—certainly not the only one!—is simply that great numbers of people do not in fact enjoy life enough. They are not passionately attached to their lives, but rather cling to them. . . . The person who is not autonomous," he explained, "loses much of the joy that comes through strength—through the effort to live one's life, not necessarily heroically, but come what may, in full commitment to it." Though feeling alienated and powerless, this "other-directed" person, as Riesman calls him, refuses to confront the sources of his distress. Instead, he lays the blame for his discontent on conditions beyond his reach: It is not the industrial culture of organized conformity which provides so much material comfort and against which he refuses to turn, but a distant external threat—Russian communism, for example—to which he ascribes his sense of dread. In short, the "Communist threat" has become a convenient excuse for not facing up to troubling domestic concerns.

The Communist danger served yet another function. It justified the need for "togetherness," conformity, or organizational loyalty as a substitute for the traditional individualism to which so many Americans are still drawn. Tied to the material benefits provided by the impersonal machine culture, Americans rationalize its necessity by pointing to Communist threats. Though other influences contribute to this exaggerated fear, its usefulness as a device for encouraging "Americanism" or "belongingness" has been a consistent reason for its centrality in U.S. foreign policy since the Second World War.

The other side of the struggle over national character—the attraction to old-style individualism—has also made itself felt in the post war debate on foreign affairs. Advocates of the idea that there is no substitute for victory in the contest with communism and that we may have to fight a nuclear war which we could survive see such policies as ultimately restoring a nineteenth-century world of greater personal freedom. The destruction of Communist power would end the Cold War, partly eliminate the need for a powerful centralized government, reduce the pressure for conformity, and allow the individual more leeway to follow his own star. Viewing the Cold War as a major contributor to conformity in American life, many proponents of traditional individualism favor all-out steps to bring it to an end. They have also expressed their commitment to individualism more benignly in repeated calls for national self-determination all over the globe. Vietnamization during Nixon's presidency, for example, had less to do with the unrealistic goal of turning a client state into an independent South Vietnam than with finding a way out of the war and symbolically reasserting personal liberty in the United States. Despite the considerable movement toward a more rational view of international relations in recent years, then, the country has continued to use foreign policy in nonrational ways to express current hopes and fears.

✳ *F U R T H E R   R E A D I N G*

Richard J. Barnet, *Roots of War* (1972)

William H. Becker and Samuel F. Wells, eds., *Economics and World Power* (1984)

Jules R. Benjamin, "The Framework of U.S. Relations with Latin America in the Twentieth Century," *Diplomatic History*, 11 (1987), 91–112

Barton J. Bernstein, ed., *Towards a New Past* (1968)

Edward M. Burns, *The American Idea of Mission* (1957)

Jerald A. Combs, *American Diplomatic History: Two Centuries of Changing Interpretations* (1982)

Charles DeBenedetti, *The Peace Reform in American History* (1980)

Alexander DeConde, ed., *Encyclopedia of American Foreign Policy* (1978)

Arthur A. Ekirch, Jr., *Ideas, Ideals, and American Diplomacy* (1966)
Frances FitzGerald, *America Revised* (1979)
John L. Gaddis, "The Corporatist Synthesis: A Skeptical View," *Diplomatic History*, 10 (1986), 357–62
Lloyd C. Gardner, ed., *Redefining the Past* (1986)
Norman A. Graebner, *Ideas and Diplomacy* (1964)
Gerald K. Haines and J. Samuel Walker, eds., *American Foreign Relations: A Historiographical Review* (1981)
Ellis W. Hawley, "The Discovery and Study of a 'Corporate Liberalism,' " *Business History Review*, 52 (1978), 309–20
John Higham, "The Cult of the 'American Consensus,' " *Commentary*, 27 (1959), 93–100
——, *History* (1965)
Stanley Hoffmann, *Gulliver's Troubles, or the Setting of American Foreign Policy* (1968)
Michael Hogan, *The Marshall Plan* (1987)
——, "Revival and Reform: America's Twentieth-Century Search for a New Economic Order Abroad," *Diplomatic History*, 8 (1984), 287–310
Michael H. Hunt, *Ideology and U.S. Foreign Policy* (1987)
Akira Iriye, "Culture and Power: International Relations as Intercultural Relations," *Diplomatic History*, 3 (1979), 115–28
Gabriel Kolko, *The Roots of American Foreign Policy* (1969)
Walter LaFeber, " 'Ah, If We Had Studied It More Carefully': The Fortunes of American Diplomatic History," *Prologue*, 11 (1979), 121–31
Walter Lippmann, *U.S. Foreign Policy: Shield of the Republic* (1943)
Thomas J. McCormick, "Drift or Mastery?" *Reviews in American History*, 10 (1982), 318–30
Charles S. Maier, "Marking Time: The Historiography of International Relations," in Michael Kamman, ed., *The Past before Us* (1980)
Frank Merli and Theodore A. Wilson, eds., *Makers of American Diplomacy* (1974)
Hans J. Morgenthau, *In Defense of the National Interest* (1951)
Charles E. Neu, "The Rise of the National Security Bureaucracy," in Louis Galambos, ed., *The New American State* (1987)
Robert E. Osgood, *Ideals and Self-Interest in America's Foreign Relations* (1953)
Robert A. Packenham, *Liberal America and the Third World* (1973)
Dexter Perkins, *The Evolution of American Foreign Policy* (1948)
David Potter, *People of Plenty* (1954)
Arthur M. Schlesinger, Jr., *The Cycles of American History* (1986)
——, *The Imperial Presidency* (1973)
Franz Schurmann, *Logic of World Power* (1974)
"Symposium: Responses to Charles S. Maier, 'Marking Time,' " *Diplomatic History*, 5 (1981), 353–71
Robert Tucker, *The Radical Left and American Foreign Policy* (1971)
E. L. Tuveson, *Redeemer Nation* (1968)
Immanuel Wallerstein, *The Capitalist World-Economy* (1979)
Albert K. Weinberg, *Manifest Destiny* (1935)
Rubin F. Weston, *Racism in U.S. Imperialism* (1972)
Robert H. Wiebe, *The Search for Order* (1967)
William A. Williams, *The Contours of American History* (1966)
——, *Empire as a Way of Life* (1980)
——, *History as a Way of Learning* (1973)

CHAPTER

2

United States Entry

into World War I

In August 1914 Europe descended into war. Because the United States was a
major power and a substantial trader on the high seas, it became ensnared in
the conflict. Until early 1917, the Wilson administration struggled to define a
policy toward World War I that would protect America's interests and principles,
keep the country out of the conflagration, end the bloodshed, and permit the
United States to shape the peace settlement and hence the postwar world. In
April of that year, President Woodrow Wilson finally decided for war. Why?

Most historians point to the German U-boat as the catalyst but disagree on
why Wilson reacted to submarine warfare as he did. Some historians have
claimed that Germany posed a dangerous threat to American political and stra-
tegic interests and that the President grasped that reality. Others have empha-
sized the negative impact of German actions on the American economy. Still
other scholars have stressed Wilson's defense of honor and ideals. Another set of
questions surrounds the issue of neutrality. Did the United States follow a neu-
tral policy? What personal, domestic, and foreign factors made neutrality diffi-
cult? Does "unneutrality" better describe American policy, as some historians
have suggested? Finally, what other options did Wilson have? Would they have
worked to end the war without United States entry?

※ DOCUMENTS

The German submarine, the U-boat, loomed as a major obstacle in German-
American relations when U-20 sank the British liner *Lusitania* on May 7, 1915,
killing 1,198 people, 128 of them Americans. The first document is a firm note
that Woodrow Wilson sent to Berlin on May 13 warning it to disavow submarine
warfare and to respect the right of Americans to sail on the high seas. The second document, a failed resolution by Senator Thomas P. Gore and Representative Jeff: McLemore, sought in February 1916 to prevent Americans from traveling on armed belligerent vessels, thereby reducing the chances for a clash with

43

the Germans. The third document is the memorandum of a conversation between Secretary of State Robert Lansing and Count Johann-Heinrich Bernstorff, the German Ambassador to the United States. The meeting took place on April 20, 1916, less than a month after the torpedoing of the *Sussex*. The conversation helped produce a German pledge not to attack merchant vessels and liners without warning.

The Zimmermann Telegram of January 1917, the fourth document, caused a serious deterioration of relations between Berlin and Washington. Intended for Mexico, the message was intercepted by the British and turned over to American authorities. Germany now seemed a threat in America's own backyard. When the Germans initiated unrestricted submarine warfare in February, Wilson broke diplomatic relations. On April 2, after the sinking of several vessels, the President asked Congress for a declaration of war, reprinted here as the fifth document. One of the few dissenters in the Senate (the vote for war was 82 to 6) was Robert LaFollette of Wisconsin; in a speech of April 4, the last document, he feared the consequences of American entry into the First World War.

The First *Lusitania* Note, 1915

In view of the recent acts of the German authorities in violation of American rights on the high seas which culminated in the torpedoing and sinking of the British steamship *Lusitania* on May 7th, 1915, by which over 100 American citizens lost their lives, it is clearly wise and desirable that the Government of the United States and the Imperial German Government should come to a clear and full understanding as to the grave situation which has resulted.

The sinking of the British passenger steamer *Falaba* by a German submarine on March 28, through which Leon C. Thrasher, an American citizen, was drowned; the attack on April 28 on the American vessel *Cushing* by a German aeroplane; the torpedoing on May 1 of the American vessel *Gulflight* by a German submarine, as a result of which two or more American citizens met their death; and, finally, the torpedoing and sinking of the steamship *Lusitania,* constitute a series of events which the Government of the United States has observed with growing concern, distress, and amazement. . . .

The Government of the United States has been apprised that the Imperial German Government considered themselves to be obliged by the extraordinary circumstances of the present war and the measures adopted by their adversaries in seeking to cut Germany off from all commerce, to adopt methods of retaliation which go much beyond the ordinary methods of warfare at sea, in the proclamation of a war zone from which they have warned neutral ships to keep away. This Government has already taken occasion to inform the Imperial German Government that it cannot admit the adoption of such measures or such a warning of danger to operate as in any degree an abbreviation of the rights of American shipmasters or of American citizens bound on lawful errands as passengers on merchant ships of belligerent nationality; and that it must hold the Imperial German Government to a strict accountability for any infringement of those rights, intentional or incidental. It does not understand the Imperial German Government to question those rights. It assumes, on the contrary, that the Imperial Government accept, as of course, the rule that the lives of noncombatants, whether they be of neutral citizenship or citizens of one of the nations at war, can not lawfully or rightfully be put in jeopardy by the capture or destruction of an unarmed merchantman, and recognize also, as all other nations do, the obligation to take the usual precaution of visit and search to ascertain whether a suspected merchantman is in fact of belligerent nationality or is in fact carrying contraband of war under a neutral flag.

The Government of the United States, therefore, desires to call the attention of the Imperial German Government with the utmost earnestness to the fact that the objection to their present method of attack against the trade of their enemies lies in the practical impossibility of employing submarines in the destruction of commerce without disregarding those rules of fairness, reason, justice, and humanity, which all modern opinion regards as imperative. It is practically impossible for the officers of a submarine to visit a merchantman at sea and examine her papers and cargo. It is practically impossible for them to make a prize of her; and, if they can not put a prize crew on board of her, they can not sink her without leaving her crew and all on board of her to the mercy of the sea in her small boats. These facts it is understood the Imperial German Government frankly admit. We are informed that, in the instances of which we have spoken, time enough for even that poor measure of safety was not given, and in at least two of the cases cited, not so much as a warning was received. Manifestly submarines can not be used against merchantmen, as the last few weeks have shown, without an inevitable violation of many sacred principles of justice and humanity.

American citizens act within their indisputable rights in taking their ships and in traveling wherever their legitimate business calls them upon the high seas, and exercise those rights in what should be the well-justified confidence that their lives will not be endangered by acts done in clear violation of universally acknowledged international obligations, and certainly in the confidence that their own Government will sustain them in the exercise of their rights. . . .

Long acquainted as this Government has been with the character of the Imperial German Government and with the high principles of equity by which they have in the past been actuated and guided, the Government of the United States can not believe that the commanders of the vessels which committed these acts of lawlessness did so except under a misapprehension of the orders issued by the Imperial German naval authorities. It takes it for granted that, at least within the practical possibilities of every such case, the commanders even of submarines were expected to do nothing that would involve the lives of non-combatants or the safety of neutral ships, even at the cost of failing of their object of capture or destruction. It confidently expects, therefore, that the Imperial German Government will disavow the acts of which the Government of the United States complains, that they will make reparation so far as reparation is possible for injuries which are without measure, and that they will take immediate steps to prevent the recurrence of anything so obviously subversive of the principles of warfare for which the Imperial German Government have in the past so wisely and so firmly contended.

The Government and people of the United States look to the Imperial German Government for just, prompt, and enlightened action in this vital matter with the greater confidence because the United States and Germany are bound together not only by special ties of friendship but also by the explicit stipulations of the treaty of 1828 between the United States and the Kingdom of Prussia.

Expressions of regret and offers of reparation in case of the destruction of neutral ships sunk by mistake, while they may satisfy international obligations, if no loss of life results, can not justify or excuse a practice, the natural and necessary effect of which is to subject neutral nations and neutral persons to new and immeasurable risks.

The Imperial German Government will not expect the Government of the United States to omit any word or any act necessary to the performance of its sacred duty of maintaining the rights of the United States and its citizens and of safeguarding their free exercise and enjoyment.

The Gore-McLemore Resolution, 1916

Whereas a number of leading powers of the world are now engaged in a war of unexampled proportions: and

Whereas the United States is happily at peace with all of the belligerent nations; and

Whereas it is equally the desire and interest of the American people to remain at peace with all nations; and

Whereas the President has recently afforded fresh and signal proofs of the superiority of diplomacy to butchery as a method of settling international disputes; and

Whereas the right of American citizens to travel on unarmed belligerent vessels has recently received renewed guaranties of respect and inviolability; and

Whereas the right of American citizens to travel on armed belligerent vessels rather than upon unarmed vessels is essential neither to their life, liberty, or safety, nor to the independence, dignity, or security of the United States; and

Whereas Congress alone has been vested with the power to declare war, which involves the obligations to prevent war by all proper means consistent with the honor and vital interest of the Nation:

Now, therefore, be it

Resolved by the Senate (the House of Representatives concurring), That it is the sense of the Congress, vested as it is with the sole power to declare war, that all persons owing allegiance to the United States should, in behalf of their own safety and the vital interest of the United States, forbear to exercise the right to travel as passengers upon any armed vessel of any belligerent power, whether such vessel be armed for offensive or defensive purposes: and it is the further sense of the Congress that no passport should be issued or renewed by the Secretary of State or by anyone acting under him to be used by any person owing allegiance to the United States for purpose of travel upon any such armed vessel of a belligerent power.

Lansing and Bernstorff Discuss Submarine Warfare, 1916

L: Good morning.

B: Good morning, Sir. You handed me a copy of the note yesterday, and in the present state of affairs of course my chief object is to find a way how this break can be avoided, because I hope it can be avoided. My idea is to find a way out of it, but of course I had to telegraph my Government that this Government seemed to offer little opportunity for settlement. If it means the entire stopping of the use of submarines, I am afraid that it cannot be arranged.

L: You will recall that we said in the first *Lusitania* note that we thought it was impossible to use submarines in a really humane way and that later, in our note of July 21, we said that the way submarine warfare had been conducted for the past two months showed that is was possible and therefore we hoped that course would be pursued. Then we had the sinking of the *Arabic* right on top of that, which was another great disaster. Our position is that, if submarine warfare had been conducted in that way, that possibly there would have been no further question raised. But it has not. It has been conducted in the most indiscriminate way and we cannot help but believe that it is ruthless. In those conditions submarine warfare should stop against commercial vessels, unless visit and search is observed.

B: That, of course, is impossible. Germany cannot abandon submarine warfare. No government could come out and say—"We give up the use of submarines." They would have to resign.

L: What possible methods in the use of submarines, that are effective from a belligerent standpoint, can be suggested which will comply with the law?

B: I had always supposed that warning was to be given.

L: We do not consider that the people on board—the non-combatants on board the vessels—are in a place of safety when put into an open boat a hundred miles from land. It might be calm there, but in the two days it would take them to reach land there might be a severe storm. That is one of the grounds of complaint.

B: That, of course, speaking of neutral vessels—

L: The fact that we do not have Americans on these vessels does not remove the menace to American lives. The sinking of neutral vessels shows that Americans cannot travel with safety on neutral vessels even. That is the serious part of it and I do not know how your government can modify submarine warfare and make it effective and at the same time obey the law and the dictates of humanity.

B: Humanity. Of course war is never humane.

L:. "Humanity" is a relative expression when used with "war" but the whole tendency in the growth of international law in regard to warfare in the past 125 years has been to relieve non-combatants of needless suffering.

B: Of course I think it would be an ideal state of affairs, but our enemies violate all the rules and you insist on their being applied to Germany.

L: One deals with life; the other with property.

B: Yes.

L: The German method seems reckless to me. It is as if a man who has a very dim vision should go out on the street with a revolver in search of an enemy and should see the outline of a figure and should immediately fire on him and injure him seriously and then go up and apologize and say he made a mistake. I do not think that would excuse him. That seems to be the course pursued by your submarine commanders—they fire first and inquire afterwards.

B: I myself cannot at all explain how it comes that so many neutral vessels have been attacked. I have not the slightest evidence. I do not know anything about it from our communications.

L: Of course we are gradually collecting the evidence. We have not in all the cases but we have in certain ones. The *Tubantia,* for example, seems to have been torpedoed by a German torpedo—a Schwartz kopf.

B: She was at anchor.

L: No. I do not think she had let her anchor down but she was preparing to anchor. She was at rest.

B: Yes, I know. And then there was a Spanish vessel which—

L: Of course there is this, Mr. Ambassador, that any discussion of the submarine and its present method of attack cannot go on indefinitely.

B: What was your idea to prevent the break—that we should for the time being stop?

L: I think the only way is to declare an abandonment and then if the German Government desires to discuss a method of renewal—

B: An absolute abandonment, to my mind, is impossible. It might be possible to announce stopping for a time for discussion and giving the reason plainly for the purpose of quieting our public opinion, that might be possible.

L: I understand you are speaking entirely without instructions.

B: I am not at all instructed. I am speaking to you purely from my desire to prevent a break.

L: In view of our note I would not want to say that that would be satisfactory, but if it was made—

B: I am only trying to see what can be done because a declaration to my Government to absolutely abandon submarine warfare would make a break absolutely necessary. To abandon it would mean the overthrow of the Chancellor.

L: Probably you would get a more radical man. I realize that.

B: So the question is what we can do.

L: There would have to be a complete abandonment first and then if the German Government desires to discuss the matter—

B: I want to do what I can, because I am perfectly convinced they do not want to break; quite apart from the sentimental side I think they do not want a break. A break would prolong the war. It would last for years.

L: We do not any of us want to prolong the war.

B: That is exactly why I want to get out of this present difficulty. From the present state of affairs it looks as if the end is coming and if now there was a break and the United States was brought into the war it would prolong it. It would cause new complications.

L: New complications?

B: New economic difficulties.

L: I think that would be Germany's problem. The only possible course is an abandonment of submarine warfare, whether limited or not would depend on the terms. I would want to see an abandonment first and then possibly a discussion could follow as to how submarine warfare can be conducted within the rules of international law and entire safety of non-combatants, because, of course, in my viewpoint that is the chief question of international law in regard to attacks by belligerents on enemy's commerce.

B: Then I am to understand that you do not recognize the law of retaliation?

L: We do not recognize retaliation when it affects the rights of neutrals.

B: The British retaliate by stopping all commerce to Germany.

L: It is a very different thing. The right to life is an inherent right, which man has from birth; the right of property is a purely legal right.

B: Only in this case, England's methods affect the lives of non-combatants of Germany.

L: Not neutrals.

B: No, but it affects non-combatants.

L: Does it affect their lives? I thought from the statements which have been made that Germany was not suffering from want of food.

B: But they are trying to starve them. You do not stop England but insist we must stop our retaliation.

L: But you must appreciate that we care more for the lives of our people than we do for the property.

B: We have the same difficulty—our people are getting to care more for lives. That is the whole difficulty—we are dealing with a warlike population.

L: I realize that. I appreciate that you have great difficulty with your public.

B: If you and I were to have the say in settling the case it would be an easy matter, because one can discuss the matter without heat.

L: I realize that. It makes it very difficult, but I do not think there is any other course. That certainly may be an impossible course for your Government to pursue, yet I see no other way, and I think I am as anxious to preserve peace as anyone.

B: I wanted to find out what I could do, because I do not see how they can do it though they might do it temporarily. I am sure that in the first place they would say they believed in the submarine entirely and that secondly the rules of international law must be modified by conditions. Your idea is that the submarine cannot be used if it does comply with the rules.

L: That is true. My view is that certain instruments of war are not proper to use under certain conditions, and that is the viewpoint that has largely been held in regard to the submarine as a commerce destroyer. You can not and do not know the nationality of the boat attacking. It attacks without being seen and so avoids responsibility. It gives every opportunity to kill indiscriminately and recklessly.

B: I perfectly agree with you that sinking without warning would have to stop entirely, sinking without warning is an international offense, and that is why I thought possibly my Government might give up the retaliation, but I do not think it would be possible to say we would give up submarine warfare. I do not think we would do it.

L: And if they should now sink another vessel it would be very serious— that is the way I look at the situation.

B: And if they continue the submarine warfare and an instance should happen directly after the break of diplomatic relations, if that should come, it would be still more serious.

L: That is logical.

B: That is why I look at it so seriously.

L: I do not feel that breaking off of diplomatic relations necessarily means war.

B: I do not say it myself but I do not see how it can be avoided. If we refuse it will be because we are to continue submarine warfare and then something might happen which would mean war. I came to see if something could not be done.

L: I am very much obligated to you for coming in, sir.

B: Good bye, Mr. Secretary.

L: Good bye.

The Zimmermann Telegram, 1917

It is our purpose on the 1st of February to commence the unrestricted U-boat war. The attempt will be made to keep America neutral in spite of it all.

In case we should not be successful in this, we propose Mexico an alliance upon the following terms: Joint conduct of the war. Joint conclusion of peace. Ample financial support and an agreement on our part that Mexico shall gain back by conquest the territory lost by her at a prior period in

Texas, New Mexico, and Arizona. Arrangement as to details is entrusted to your Excellency.

Your Excellency will make the above known to the President [Carranza] in strict confidence at the moment that war breaks out with the United States, and you will add the suggestion that Japan be requested to take part at once and that he simultaneously mediate between ourselves and Japan.

Please inform the President that the unrestricted use of our U-boats now offers the prospect of forcing England to sue for peace in the course of a few months.

Confirm receipt.

Woodrow Wilson's War Message, 1917

I have called the Congress into extraordinary session because there are serious, very serious, choices of policy to be made, and made immediately, which it was neither right nor constitutionally permissible that I should assume the responsibility of making.

On the third of February last I officially laid before you the extraordinary announcement of the Imperial German Government that on and after the first day of February it was its purpose to put aside all restraints of law of humanity and use its submarines to sink every vessel that sought to approach either the ports of Great Britain and Ireland or the western coasts of Europe or any of the ports controlled by the enemies of Germany within the Mediterranean. That had seemed to be the object of the German submarine warfare earlier in the war, but since April of last year the Imperial Government had somewhat restrained the commanders of its undersea craft in conformity with its promise then given to us that passenger boats should not be sunk and that due warning would be given to all other vessels which its submarines might seek to destroy, when no resistance was offered or escape attempted, and care taken that their crews were given at least a fair chance to save their lives in their open boats. The precautions taken were meagre and haphazard enough, as was proved in distressing instance after instance in the progress of the cruel and unmanly business, but a certain degree of restraint was observed. The new policy has swept every restriction aside. Vessels of every kind, whatever their flag, their character, their cargo, their destination, their errand, have been ruthlessly sent to the bottom without warning and without thought of help or mercy for those on board, the vessels of friendly neutrals along with those of belligerents. Even hospital ships and ships carrying relief to the sorely bereaved and stricken people of Belgium, though the latter were provided with safe conduct through the proscribed areas by the German Government itself and were distinguished by unmistakable marks of identity, have been sunk with the same reckless lack of compassion or of principle.

I was for a little while unable to believe that such things would in fact be done by any government that had hitherto subscribed to the humane practices of civilized nations. International law had its origin in the attempt to set up some law which would be respected and observed upon the seas, where no nation had right of dominion where lay the free highways of the world. By painful stage after stage has that law been built up, with meagre enough results, indeed, after all was accomplished that could be accomplished, but always with a clear view, at least of what the heart and conscience of mankind demanded. This minimum of right the German Government has swept aside under the plea of retaliation and necessity and because it had no weapons which it could use at sea except these which it is impossible to employ as it is employing them without throwing to the winds all scruples of humanity or of respect for the understandings that were supposed to underlie the intercourse of the world. I am not now thinking of the loss of property involved, immense and serious as that is, but only of the wanton and wholesale destruction of the lives of noncombatants, men, women, and children, engaged in pursuits which have always, even in the darkest periods of modern history, been deemed innocent and legitimate. Property can be paid for; the lives of peaceful and innocent people cannot be. The present German submarine warfare against commerce is a warfare against mankind.

It is a war against all nations. American ships have been sunk, American lives taken, in ways which it has stirred us very deeply to learn of, but the ships and people of other neutral and friendly nations have been sunk and overwhelmed in the waters in the same way. There has been no discrimination. The challenge is to all mankind. Each nation must decide for itself how it will meet it. The choice we make for ourselves must be made with a moderation of counsel and a temperateness of judgment benefiting our character and our motives as a nation. We must put excited feeling away. Our motive will not be revenge or the victorious assertion of the physical might of the nation, but only the vindication of right, of human right, of which we are only a single champion.

When I addressed the Congress on the twenty-sixth of February last I thought that it would suffice to assert our neutral rights with arms, our right to use the seas against unlawful interference, our right to keep our people safe against unlawful violence. But armed neutrality, it now appears, is impracticable. Because submarines are in effect outlaws when used as the German submarines have been used against merchant shipping, it is impossible to defend ships against their attacks as the law of nations has assumed that merchantmen would defend themselves against privateers or cruisers, visible craft giving chase upon the open sea. It is common prudence in such circumstances, grim necessity indeed, to endeavour to destroy them before they have shown their own intention. They must be dealt with upon sight, if dealt with at all. The German Government denies the right of neutrals to use arms at all within the areas of the sea which it has proscribed, even in the defense of rights which no modern publicist has ever before questioned their right to defend. The intimation is conveyed that the armed guards which we have placed on our merchant ships will be treated as beyond the pale of law and subject to be dealt with as pirates would be. Armed neutrality is ineffectual enough at best; in such circumstances and in the face of such pretensions it is worse than ineffectual: it is likely only to produce what it was meant to prevent; it is practically certain to draw us into the war without either the rights or the effectiveness of belligerents. There is one choice we cannot make, we are incapable of making: we will not choose the path of submission and suffer the most sacred rights of our nation and our people to be ignored or violated. The wrongs against which we now array ourselves are no common wrongs; they cut to the very roots of human life.

With a profound sense of the solemn and even tragical character of the step I am taking and of the grave responsibilities which it involves, but in unhesitating obedience to what I deem my constitutional duty, I advise that the Congress declare the recent course of the Imperial German Government to be in fact nothing less than war against the government and people of the United States; that it formally accept the status of belligerent which has thus been thrust upon it; and that it take immediate steps not only to put the country in a more thorough state of defense but also to exert all its power and employ all its resources to bring the Government of the German Empire to terms and end the war. . . .

While we do these things, these deeply momentous things, let us be very clear, and make very clear to all the world what our motives and our objects are. My own thought has not been driven from its habitual and normal course by the unhappy events of the last two months, and I do not believe that the thought of the nation has been altered or clouded by them. . . . Our object now, as then, is to vindicate the principles of peace and justice in the life of the world as against selfish and autocratic power and to set up amongst the really free and self-governed peoples of the world such a concert of purpose and of action as will henceforth ensure the observance of those principles. Neutrality is no longer feasible or desirable where the peace of the world is involved and the freedom of its peoples, and the menace to that peace and freedom lies in the existence of autocratic governments backed by organized force which is controlled wholly by their will, not by the will of their people. We have seen the last of neutrality in such circumstances. We are at the beginning of an age in which it will be insisted that the same standards of conduct and of responsibility for wrong done shall be observed among nations and their governments that are observed among the individual citizens of civilized states.

We have no quarrel with the German people. We have no feeling toward them but one of sympathy and friendship. It was not upon their impulse that their government acted in entering this war. It was not with their previous knowledge or approval. It was a war determined upon as wars used to be determined upon in the old, unhappy days when peoples were nowhere consulted by their rulers and wars were provoked and waged in the interest of dynasties or of little groups of ambitious men who were accustomed to use their fellow men as pawns and tools. Self-governed nations do not fill their neighbour states with spies or set the course of intrigue to bring about some critical posture of affairs which will give them an opportunity to strike and make conquest. Such designs can be successfully worked out only under cover and where no one has the right to ask questions. Cunningly contrived plans of deception or aggression, carried, it may be, from generation to generation, can be worked out and kept from the light only within the privacy of courts or behind the carefully guarded confidences of a narrow and privileged class. They are happily impossible where public opinion commands and insists upon full information concerning all the nation's affairs.

A steadfast concert for peace can never be maintained except by a partnership of democratic nations. No autocratic government could be trusted to keep faith within it or observe its covenants. It must be a league of honour, a partnership of opinion. . . .

Does not every American feel that assurance has been added to our hope for the future peace of the world by the wonderful and heartening things that have been happening within the last few weeks in Russia? Russia was known by those who knew it best to have been always in fact democratic at heart, in all the vital habits of her thought, in all the intimate relationships of her people that spoke their natural instinct, their habitual attitude towards life. The autocracy that crowned the summit of her political structure, long as it had stood and terrible as was the reality of its power, was not in fact Russian in origin, character, or purpose; and now it has been shaken off and the great, generous Russian people have been added in all their naive majesty and might to the forces that are fighting for freedom in the world, for justice, and for peace. Here is a fit partner for a League of Honour.

One of the things that has served to convince us that the Prussian autocracy was not and could never be our friends is that from the very outset of the present war it has filled our unsuspecting communities and even our offices of government with spies and set criminal intrigues everywhere afoot against our national unity of counsel, our peace within and without, our industries and our commerce. . . . That it means to stir up enemies against us at our very doors the intercepted note to the German Minister at Mexico City is eloquent evidence.

We are accepting this challenge of hostile purpose because we know that in such a government, following such methods, we can never have a friend; and that in the presence of its organized power, always lying in wait to accomplish we know not what purpose, there can be no assured security for the democratic governments of the world. We are now about to accept gauge of battle with this natural foe to liberty and shall, if necessary, spend the whole force of the nation to check and nullify its pretensions and its power. We are glad, now that we see the facts with no veil of false pretence about them, to fight thus for the ultimate peace of the world and for the liberation of its peoples, the German peoples included: for the rights of nations great and small and the privilege of men everywhere to choose their way of life and of obedience. The world must be made safe for democracy. . . .

It is a distressing and oppressive duty, Gentlemen of the Congress, which I have performed in thus addressing you. There are, it may be, many months of fiery trial and sacrifice ahead of us. It is a fearful thing to lead this great peaceful people into war, into the most terrible and disastrous of all wars, civilization itself seeming to be in the balance. But the right is more precious than peace, and we shall fight for the things which we have always carried nearest our hearts,—for democracy, for the right of those who submit to authority to have a voice in their own governments, for the rights and liberties of small nations, for a universal dominion of right by such a concert of free peoples as shall bring peace and safety to all nations and make the world itself at last free. To such a task we can dedicate our lives and our fortunes, everything that we are and everything that we have, with the pride of those who know that the day has come when America is privileged to spend her blood and her might for the principles that gave her birth and happiness and the peace which she has treasured. God helping her, she can do no other.

Robert M. LaFollette's Dissent, 1917

The poor, sir, who are the ones called upon to rot in the trenches, have no organized power, have no press to voice their will upon this question of peace or war; but, oh, Mr. President, at some time they will be heard. I hope and I believe they will be heard in an orderly and a peaceful way. I think they may be heard from before long. I think, sir, if we take this step, when the people to-day who are staggering under the burden of supporting families at the present prices of the necessaries of the life find those prices multiplied, when they are raised a hundred percent, or 200 percent, as they will be quickly, aye, sir, when beyond that those who pay taxes come to have their taxes doubled and again doubled to pay the interest on the nontaxable bonds held by Morgan and his combinations, which have been issued to meet this war, there will come an awakening; they will have their day and they will be heard. It will be as certain and as inevitable as the return of the tides, and as resistless, too. . . .

Just a word of comment more upon one of the points in the President's address. He says that this is a war "for the things which we have always carried nearest to our hearts—for democracy, for the right of those who submit to authority to have a voice in their own government." In many places throughout the address is this exalted sentiment given expression.

It is a sentiment peculiarly calculated to appeal to American hearts and, when accompanied by acts consistent with it, is certain to receive our support; but in this same connection, and strangely enough, the President says that we have become convinced that the German Government as it now exists—"Prussian autocracy" he calls it—can never again maintain friendly relations with us. His expression is that "Prussian autocracy was not and could never be our friend," and repeatedly throughout the address the suggestion is made that if the German people would overturn their Government it would probably be the way to peace. So true is this that the dispatches from London all hailed the message of the President as sounding the death knell of Germany's Government.

But the President proposes alliance with Great Britain, which, however liberty-loving its people, is a hereditary monarchy, with a hereditary ruler, with a hereditary House of Lords, with a hereditary landed system, with a limited and restricted suffrage for one class and a multiplied suffrage power for another, and with grinding industrial conditions for all the wageworkers. The President has not suggested that we make our support of Great Britain conditional to her granting home rule to Ireland, or Egypt, or India. We rejoice in the establishment of a democracy in Russia, but it will hardly be contended that if Russia was still an autocratic Government, we would not be asked to enter this alliance with her just the same. Italy and the lesser powers of Europe, Japan in the Orient; in fact all of the countries with whom we are to enter into alliance, except France and newly revolutionized Russia, are still of the old order—and it will be generally conceded that no one of them has done as much for its people in the solution of municipal problems and in securing social and industrial reforms as Germany.

Is it not a remarkable democracy which leagues itself with allies already far overmatching in strength the German nation and holds out to such beleaguered nation the hope of peace only at the price of giving up their Government? I am not talking now of the merits or demerits of any government, but I am speaking of a profession of democracy that is linked in action with the most brutal and domineering use of autocratic power. Are the people of this country being so well represented in this war movement that we need to go abroad to give other people control of their governments? Will the President and the supporters of this war bill submit it to a vote of the people before the declaration of war goes into effect? Until we are willing to do that, it illy becomes us to offer as an excuse for our entry into the war the unsupported claim that this war was forced upon the German people by their Government "without their previous knowledge or approval."

Who has registered the knowledge or approval of the American people of the course this Congress is called upon in declaring war upon Germany? Submit the question to the people, you who support it. You who support it dare not do it, for you know that by a vote of more than ten to one the American people as a body would register their declaration against it.

In the sense that this war is being forced upon our people without their knowing why and without their approval, and that wars are usually forced upon all peoples in the same way, there is some truth in the statement; but I venture to say that the response which the German people have made to the demands of this war shows that it has a degree of popular support which the war upon which we are entering has not and never will have among our people. The espionage bills, the conscription bills, and other forcible military measures which we understand are being ground out of the war machine in this country is the complete proof that those responsible for this war fear that it has no popular support and that armies sufficient to satisfy the demand of the entente allies can not be recruited by voluntary enlistments.

❋ *E S S A Y S*

In the first essay, Ross Gregory of Central Michigan University explores the several influences that moved Woodrow Wilson to a decision for intervention in the war. In suggesting that American entry into the war was inevitable, Gregory gives special weight to rights and interests and the necessity of a major nation like the United States to defend them. John G. Coogan of Michigan State University is less sympathetic toward Wilson's diplomacy. In emphasizing American "unneutrality" in the second essay, Coogan writes that the president could have pursued policy alternatives to prevent both United States entry into the war and a German victory. Coogan also concludes that Wilson's failure to follow a truly neutral course ultimately undermined the President's own goal of a "peace without victory."

Rights, Honor, and Interests

ROSS GREGORY

In light of the controversy which later surrounded America's entry into the First World War, and the momentous effect that war had on the future of the world, it seems appropriate here to offer some final observations about Wilsonian diplomacy and the factors responsible for intervention. Wilson asked Congress to declare war in 1917 because he felt Germany had driven him to it. He could find no way, short of an unthinkable abandonment of rights and interests, to avoid intervention. He briefly had tried armed neutrality, and, as he said in the war message, that tactic had not done the job. Germany was making war on the United States, and Wilson had no reasonable alternative to a declaration of hostilities. Hence submarine warfare must bear the immediate responsibility for provoking the decision for war. It nonetheless is not enough to say that the United States went to war simply because of the submarines, or that the events of January-March 1917 alone determined the fate of the United States, for a number of factors helped bring the nation to that point where it seemed impossible to do anything else. During the period of neutrality the American government made certain decisions, avoided others, found itself pulled one way or another by national sentiment and need and by the behavior of the belligerent nations.

Any account of American intervention would go amiss without some reference to the pro-Ally nature of American neutrality. American money and supplies allowed the Allies to sustain the war effort. While Wilson did not act openly partial to the Allies, he did promote American economic enterprise and declined to interfere—indeed showed no signs of dismay—when the enterprise developed in ways that were beneficial to Britain and France. Although Wilson did experience a considerable hardening of attitude

---

toward the Allies in 1916 (his major advisers did not), he could not bring himself to limit the provisioning of Britain and France; and it was this traffic that brought on submarine warfare. Without American assistance to the Allies, Germany would have had no reason to adopt policy injurious to the interests of the United States.

There were several reasons why American policy functioned in a manner which favored the Allies. The first was a matter of circumstances: Britain controlled the sea, and the Allies were in desperate need of American products—conditions which assured that most American trade would go to Britain and France. The second factor was an assumption by much of the American population, most members of the administration, and the president that the political and material well-being of the United States was associated with preservation of Britain and France as strong, independent states. Germany unintentionally confirmed the assumption with the invasion of Belgium, use of submarines, and war tactics in general. While pro-Ally feeling was tempered by a popular desire to stay out of the conflict and by the president's wish to remain fair and formally neutral, it was sufficiently strong to discourage any policy that would weaken the Allied war effort. [Wilson adviser "Colonel" Edward] House, [Secretary of State Robert] Lansing, and [Ambassador to England Walter Hines] Page were so partial to the Allies that they acted disloyally to the president. Wilson frequently complained about Britain's intolerable course; he sent notes of protest and threatened to do more. He grumbled about Page's bias for the British and questioned the usefulness of his ambassador in Britain. Yet he did nothing to halt Britain's restrictions on trade with continental Europe, and Page stayed on in London until the end of the war. Wilson declined to press the British because he feared that such action would increase Germany's chances of winning and lead to drastic economic repercussions in the United States. Favoritism for the Allies did not cause the United States to go to war with Germany. It did help create those conditions of 1917 in which war seemed the only choice.

The United States (or much of the population) preferred that Britain and France not collapse, and the nation was equally anxious that Germany not succeed, at least not to the extent of dominating Europe. A prewar suspicion of German militarism and autocratic government, and accounts, during the war, of "uncivilized" German warfare influenced Wilson and a majority of the American people to believe that the United States faced an evil world force, that in going to war with Germany the nation would be striking a blow for liberty and democracy. This general American attitude toward the war of 1914–18 probably influenced Wilson's decision to resist submarine warfare, and thus affected his neutrality policies. More important, it made the decision to intervene seem all the more noble and did much to determine the way the United States, once it became belligerent, prosecuted the war. It was not, however, the major reason for accepting intervention. For all the popular indignation over the invasion of Belgium and other allegedly atrocious German warfare, there still did not develop in the United

States a large movement for intervention. Even in 1917 Wilson showed the utmost reluctance to bring the nation into the war. Americans evidently were willing to endure German brutality, although they did not like it, as long as it did not affect their interests; and one must wonder what the American response—and the response of the president—would have been had no Americans been aboard the *Lusitania*. Wilson's vilification on April 2 of the German political system was more a means of sanctifying the cause than a reason for undertaking it. He was a curious crusader. Before April 1917 he would not admit that there was a need for America to take up the sword of righteousness. Against his will he was driven to the barricades, but once he was in the streets he became the most thorough and enthusiastic of street fighters.

The most important influence on the fate of the United States 1914–17 was the nation's world position. National need and interests were such that it was nearly impossible to avoid the problems which led the nation into war. Even if the administration had maintained a rigidly neutral position and forced Britain to respect all maritime rights of the United States, it is doubtful that the result would have been different. Grey testified that Britain would have yielded rather than have serious trouble with the United States, which means that, faced with American pressure, Britain would have allowed a larger amount of American trade through to Germany. This was the most the Germans could have expected from the United States, and it would not have affected the contraband trade with the Allies. Germany used submarines not because of the need to obtain American supplies, but from a desire to prevent the Allies from getting them.

The course that would have guaranteed peace for the United States was unacceptable to the American people and the Wilson administration. Only by severing all its European ties could the nation obtain such a guarantee. In 1914 that act would have placed serious strain on an economy that already showed signs of instability; by 1916 it would have been economically disastrous. At any time it would have been of doubtful political feasibility, even if one were to premise American popular disinterest in who won the war. The British understood this fact and reacted accordingly. If such thoughts suggest that the United States was influenced by the needs of an expanding capitalist economy, so let it be. It is by no means certain that another economic structure would have made much difference.

One might argue that measures short of a total embargo, a different arrangement of neutral practices—for instance, stoppage of the munitions traffic, and/or a ban on American travel on belligerent ships—would have allowed a profitable, humane, yet nonprovocative trade with Europe. Though a reply to that contention can offer no stronger claim to truth than the contention itself, one can offer these points: Wilson argued that yielding one concession on the seas ultimately would lead to pressure to abandon all rights. The pragmatic behavior of belligerents, especially the Germans, makes that assessment seem fair. Lest the German chancellor appear a hero to opponents of American intervention, it is well to remember that

Bethmann's views on submarine warfare were not fashioned by love of the United States, or by the agony of knowing his submarines were sending innocent victims to their death. He was guided by simple national interest and the desire to use submarines as fully as circumstances allowed. It also is worth noting that Germany, when it reopened submarine warfare in 1917, was interested not merely in sinking munitions ships, but wanted to prevent all products going to Britain and was especially anxious to halt shipments of food. Had the United States wished to consider Bryan's proposals, keeping people and property out of the danger zone, it would have been easier early in the war, perhaps in February 1915, than after the sinkings began, and above all after the *Lusitania* went down. Yielding in the midst of the *Lusitania* crisis involved nothing short of national humiliation. If Bryan's proposals would have eliminated the sort of incident that provoked intervention, they also would have required a huge sacrifice—too great, as it turned out, for Wilson to accept. The United States would have faced economic loss, loss of national prestige, and probably the eventual prospect of a Europe dominated by Hindenburg, Ludendorff, and Wilhelm II.

No less than the nation as a whole, Wilson found himself accountable for the world standing of the United States. He felt a need and an obligation to promote economic interests abroad. When dealing with Germany he usually spoke in terms of principle; in relations with the Allies he showed awareness of practical considerations. In the hectic days of August 1914, he took steps to get American merchant ships back to sea. In the summer of 1915, advisers alerted him to the financial strain Britain had come to experience, the weakening of the pound sterling and the need to borrow funds in the United States. The secretary of the treasury recommended approval of foreign loans. "To maintain our prosperity we must finance it," he said. Lansing, who believed similarly, wrote the president: "If the European countries cannot find the means to pay for the excess of goods sold them over those purchased from them, they will have to stop buying and our present export trade will shrink proportionately. The result will be restriction of output, industrial depression, idle capital, idle labor, numerous failures, financial demoralization, and general unrest and suffering among the laboring masses." Shortly afterward the administration acquiesced as the House of Morgan floated loans of $500 million for the British and French governments. War traffic with the Allies prompted the German attempt to stop it with submarines. Submarine warfare led to destruction of property and loss of American lives. What had started as efforts to promote prosperity and neutral rights developed into questions of national honor and prestige. Wilson faced not merely the possibility of abandoning economic rights but the humiliating prospect of allowing the Germans to force him to it. The more hazardous it became to exercise American rights, the more difficult it was to yield them.

Wilson's definition of right and honor was itself conditioned by the fact that he was president of the United States and not some less powerful nation. His estimate of what rights belonged to the United States, what was for belligerents fair and humane warfare, rested not simply on a statement of principle, but on the power of the United States to compel observance of these principles. He could not send demands to the German government without some reason for believing the Germans would obey. Interpretation of national honor varies with national economic and military strength. The more powerful the nation, the more the world expects of it and the more the nation expects of itself. Such small seafaring states as Denmark and the Netherlands suffered extensive losses from submarine warfare, and yet these governments did not feel themselves honor bound to declare war. Wilson credited his right to act as a mediator to his position as leader of the most powerful neutral state. Indeed, he sometimes felt obligated to express moral principle. He could not, and would not, have acted these ways had he been, let us say, president of the Dominican Republic. It is thus possible to say that despite Wilson's commanding personality, his heavy-handedness in foreign policy and flair for self-righteousness, American diplomacy in final analysis was less a case of the man guiding affairs of the nation than the nation, and belligerent nations, guiding the affairs of the man.

It is tempting to conclude that inasmuch as the United States was destined to enter the conflict, it might as well have accepted that fact and reacted accordingly. Presumably this response would have involved an earlier declaration of war, certainly a large and rapid rearmament program. In recent years some "realist" scholars, notably George F. Kennan, have considered that this course would have been practical. However wise that policy might have been, it did not fit conditions of the period of neutrality. Wilson opposed entering the war earlier, and had he thought differently, popular and congressional support were highly questionable. People did not know in 1914 that commercial relations would lead them into the World War; most of them believed during the entire period that they could have trade and peace at the same time. The body of the United States was going one way during the period of neutrality, its heart and mind another. For a declaration of war there needed to be a merging of courses.

Then, too, it was not absolutely certain that the United States had to enter the conflict, for the nation after all did avoid intervention for over two and one-half years, two-thirds of the war's fighting time. That same strength which eventually brought the nation into the war for a while helped it avoid intervention. From this perspective the campaign for mediation might have represented some of Wilson's soundest thinking. German officials never were certain about American strength, and the longer they had to endure a costly, indecisive conflict, the more they were willing to consider the type of gamble taken in 1917. American intervention was all but certain unless the United States made a drastic change in policy—which, as we have seen, it was unwilling to do—or unless someone beforehand brought the war to an end. It incidentally also seems fair to say that an indecisive settlement, a "peace without victory," would have better served the interests of the United States, not to mention the interests of the world, than the vindictive treaty drawn up in 1919. These thoughts, of course, are hindsight, but it is ironic that Wilson made the same observations weeks before the United States entered the war. . . .

One of the most provocative features of Wilsonian diplomacy was the president's apparent obsession with moral principle and international law. To critics this tendency suggested blindness to realistic goals, ignorance of the way nations deal with one another, if not a profession of personal superiority. In some ways the critics were right. Wilson was dedicated to principle. He thought the old system of interstate relations was unsatisfactory and looked to a time when nations would find rules to govern relations among themselves no less effective than laws within individual states. He wished to have a large part in making those rules. His propensity to quibble about shipments of cargo and techniques of approaching ships at sea seemed a ridiculous and remote abstraction at a time when the fate of nations hung in balance. It was naive to expect nations to respect legal principles when they had so much at stake. If they obeyed Wilson's command, their obedience was due less to principle than to his nation's ability to retaliate. At the same time international law was to Wilson more than an ideal; it was a manifestation of neutral intent and a device for defining American neutrality. Unless the United States decided to declare war or to stay out of the mess entirely, it would have to deal with complicated questions of neutral rights. International law was not merely convenient, it was the only device available. There fortunately was no conflict between Wilsonian principle and American rights and needs—the principle could be used to uphold the need. That the United States found an attraction for international law is not surprising: the restraints the law placed on belligerents would benefit any nation wishing to engage in neutral wartime commerce. International law looked to an orderly international society, and the United States, a satisfied nation, would profit from order. The chaos of 1914–17 strengthened feeling in the United States that American interests coincided with world interests, or, put another way, that what was good for the United States was good for the world.

Even so, it is not adequate to say that Wilson was a realist who clothed practical considerations with moral rhetoric. He was both practical and idealistic, at least during the period of American neutrality. If he believed that upholding principle would advance American interests, he also hoped that promoting American interests would serve the cause of international morality. By demonstrating that the United States would not condone brutality, disorder, and lawlessness, he hoped to set a standard for other nations to follow. Wilson wanted to help reform the world, but he would have settled for protecting the interests of the United States and keeping the nation at peace.

Evidence from various quarters supports these final conclusions: there is no indication that Wilson went to war to protect American loans to the Allies and large business interests, although these interests, and economic factors in general, helped bring the United States to a point where war seemed unavoidable. There is no evidence that Wilson asked for war to prevent the defeat of Britain and France. It could well have been, as several scholars have written, that preservation of Britain and France was vital to the interests of the United States. American neutrality, incidentally or by design, functioned to sustain that thesis. Even so, Wilson did not intervene to prevent these nations' collapse; the Allies, while not winning, were not on the verge of losing in the spring of 1917. Nor did Wilson go to war to preserve American security. This is not to say that he was not concerned with security; he simply did not see it in jeopardy. The president did ask his countrymen for war as a means of protecting American honor, rights, and general interest—for both moral and practical reasons. He saw no contradiction between the two. But Wilson's idea of right and interest grew out of what the nation was at the time, and the First World War made clear what had been true for some years: the United States was in all respects a part of the world, destined to profit from its riches and suffer from its woes.

Wilson's Unneutrality and Its Costs

JOHN G. COOGAN

Any evaluation of American neutrality during the first six months of World War I must begin with the recognition that the Wilson administration permitted, and in some cases encouraged, systematic British violation of American neutral rights on a scale unprecedented at the height of the Napoleonic Wars. Wilson, who possessed every advantage in his dealings with the British government, had given away the very neutral rights which Washington, Adams, Jefferson, and Madison had refused to yield at gunpoint. The American response to the blockade was not neutrality, as Arthur Link argues, or "benevolent neutrality," as Ernest May argues. It was simple unneutrality. . . .

This failure to hold the British maritime system within some recognized legal system paralleled a failure to maintain specific doctrines of maritime law traditionally upheld by the United States. In five broad areas, British measures constituted substantial departures from existing Anglo-American prize law. In none of these areas had the Wilson administration taken effective action by the end of January 1915 to assert American rights or interests.

During the first six months of war, British authorities had systematically eroded the distinction between absolute and conditional contraband. In most cases the contraband control officials made no effort to prove that a particular cargo was destined for enemy military use, and indeed they sometimes disregarded conclusive evidence that a cargo was destined for use by neutral civilians. . . .

Reprinted from John W. Coogan: *The End of Neutrality: The United States, Britain, and Maritime Rights, 1899–1915,* 209–214, 221–222, 235–236, 249–256. Copyright © 1981 by Cornell University Press. Used by permission of the publisher.

The British government had added raw materials such as iron ore and copper to the absolute contraband list, contrary to both the Declaration of London and customary Anglo-American law. Ores and metals were on the free list of the declaration and thus could not be declared contraband of either sort under that agreement. They might be declared conditional contraband under existing law, but capture could be justified only when the captor could prove destination to the enemy armed forces. The British, by their own admission, were never able to provide this proof during World War I. They seized the metals anyway, with only pro forma objections from Washington.

The British government had declared food to be conditional contraband. It had then, on the basis of unfounded rumors that the German government had assumed control of food stocks, seized both direct and indirect food shipments to Germany on grounds that they would become the property of the German government and thus were good prize under the Declaration of London. The British continued to seize food shipments after they had formally repudiated the declaration and after they had received incontrovertible evidence that German food imports did not come under government control. Again, Washington did nothing. . . .

The administration's record in the second broad area of conflict between British policies and neutral rights, the nature of the evidence that would justify seizure of a neutral ship by a belligerent, was as unneutral as its record in regard to contraband. The British government claimed and enforced the right to seize neutral ships on mere suspicion. It then required the owners of the ship and cargo to prove their innocence, at their own expense, to the satisfaction of British contraband control authorities. The penalty for failure to establish innocence ranged from continued detention at enormous expense to outright confiscation. This rule of "presumed guilty until you prove yourself innocent" was contrary to every principle of Anglo-Saxon jurisprudence, to the Declaration of London, to customary international law, and to the sovereign rights of neutral citizens and states. Britain had been ready to go to war rather than submit to enforcement of a more limited version of this rule by Russia in 1904. When Britain applied the principle to American trade by *force majeure* on a far more extensive scale a decade later, Wilson made only the mildest protest.

The administration was only slightly more active in a third area of concern, that of visit and search. The British government claimed and enforced a belligerent right to divert neutral ships found on the high seas into British ports where they would be searched at the convenience of British officials and often held for prolonged periods without prize court proceedings. This practice violated both the Declaration of London and customary international law. It violated most grievously the rule of law defined by Britain's own Law Officers in 1899 and 1904. The British government had threatened war when Russia attempted to enforce a version of this rule less offensive to neutral rights in 1904. Wilson's response in 1914 was to have Ambassador Page ask the Foreign Office for relief in individual cases. This action won the release of few American ships or cargoes and certainly did nothing to challenge a flagrantly illegal practice.

In a fourth area, the doctrine of continuous voyage, British practice also went far beyond either the Declaration of London or established international law. The system of controls Britain established over Dutch, Danish, Swedish, and Norwegian imports was deliberately designed to keep those neutrals so short of food, raw materials, and other products that they would have no surplus for export to Germany. This application of continuous voyage was illegal under both the Declaration of London and customary law. It violated the sovereignty of the affected European neutrals, as well as that of the United States. Wilson accepted this illegal system with hardly a whimper.

The American government also accepted the British proclamation of November 3, 1914, which declared the North Sea a war zone. Neutral ships that failed to call at a British port for sailing instructions—and not incidentally a thorough and likely prolonged inspection by contraband control officials—risked destruction by British mines. By sowing mines in international waters, Britain deliberately replaced the belligerent right of visit and search in the North Sea with a new rule: explode and sink. This action, which threatened to send American ships, seamen, and cargoes to the bottom simply for exercising their basic right to sail the high seas, was a direct contradiction of the principle of freedom of the seas. Wilson ignored it.

By the end of January 1915, the British government was systematically violating every rule of international law which it believed might hinder its campaign against German imports. Only the Declaration of Paris remained in theory, although British seizure of conditional contraband under the neutral flag without evidence of enemy military destination constituted de facto violation of that agreement. Yet the United States, traditionally a strong advocate of neutral rights, had offered no meaningful resistance and only the most apologetic, pro forma protest. . . .

Did Wilson then deliberately mislead an isolationist public with promises of neutrality, all the while pursuing a "realistic" policy of nonbelligerent aid to the Allies under the justification of national security and in hope of creating a better world? The evidence indicates that such was his effect but not his intent. The president saw no contradiction between his public promises of neutrality and his unneutral actions on maritime rights because he never admitted, in public, in private, or to himself, that those actions were in any way unneutral. He continued to believe that the blockade was substantially within the rules of international law, although admitting that there might be occasional technical variations from traditional American principles. He continued to believe that the blockade did little real harm to legitimate American commerce with Europe and that any problems which did arise were best dealt with privately on a case-by-case basis. He continued to believe that the British government in general and Sir Edward Grey in particular were honest and conciliatory, and that Grey was doing his best to lead Britain and its Allies to adopt liberal war aims. These beliefs were ludicrously wrong, but Wilson held to them tenaciously, despite overwhelming contrary evidence, because they fit so comfortably his perceptions of the war and his vision of the peace. . . .

On February 4, 1915, the Imperial German Government announced that "beginning on February 18, 1915 it will endeavour to destroy every enemy merchant ship that is found" within a war zone including "all the waters surrounding Great Britain." This campaign was to be conducted primarily by submarines and admittedly would not be in accordance with the rules of cruiser warfare in existing international law. In addition, because Allied shipping often flew neutral flags as a *ruse de guerre,* the German proclamation acknowledged the possibility that a submarine might sink a neutral merchantman in the mistaken belief that it was an enemy hiding under the neutral flag. Germany regretted, but could not promise to avoid, such flagrant violations of neutral rights. Nevertheless, Britain had pleaded its "vital interests" to justify violation of established maritime law, and "the neutral powers seem to satisfy themselves with theoretical protest." The German government expected all true neutrals to accept the submarine with the same attitude.

Six days later, on February 10, William Jennings Bryan instructed the American ambassador in Berlin to lodge an immediate protest. The note was signed by the secretary of state, but the words were those of President Wilson:

> If the commanders of German vessels of war should act upon the presumption that the flag of the United States was not being used in good faith and should destroy on the high seas an American vessel or the lives of American citizens, it would be difficult for the Government of the United States to view the act in any other light than as an indefensible violation of neutral rights which it would be very hard indeed to reconcile with the friendly relations now so happily subsisting between the two governments.
>
> If such a deplorable situation should arise, the Imperial German Government can readily appreciate that the Government of the United States would be constrained to hold the Imperial German Government to a strict accountability for such acts of their naval authorities and to take any steps it might be necessary to take to safeguard American lives and property and to secure to American citizens the full enjoyment of their acknowledged rights on the high seas.

In marked contrast to the apologetic tone of American notes to London during previous months, the "Strict Accountability" note had the unmistakable ring of an ultimatum. . . .

The ultimate measure of American neutrality during World War I is a comparison between the February 10 protest to Berlin and the March 30 protest to London. When Germany had warned that it would regret but might not be able to avoid violation of certain American maritime rights in the course of military operations directed against the Allies, Wilson took six days to send an ultimatum. When Britain committed what Grey privately admitted were more serious and more extensive violations, Wilson took a month to send a note that even [British Assistant Undersecretary] Eyre

Crowe, who was coming to dislike Americans almost as much as Germans, had to admit was "altogether friendly" in tone. The differences in substance and in tone between the two notes demonstrate the gulf between the president's public calls for neutrality and his actions. As [State Department officer James B.] Scott, Lansing, and [Secretary of War Lindley] Garrison had warned, the American failure to enforce neutral rights equally against the two belligerents constituted under international law a hostile act against the German Empire. By the end of March 1915, the United States was no longer entitled to the legal status of "neutral."

Wilson and Lansing later claimed that they protested more vigorously against the submarine than against the blockade because the latter took property, which was replaceable, whereas the former took lives, which were not. This position must be regarded as an ex post facto rationalization for unneutral behavior and an inconsistent one at that. No such distinction appears in the "Strict Accountability" note, which stated explicitly that the United States would hold Germany accountable for destruction of "American lives and property," and would secure "to American citizens the full enjoyment of their acknowledged rights on the high seas." Nor had Wilson made any effort in November 1914 to defend the right of American ships to free passage through Britain's North Sea war zone. The German war zone was to be enforced by submarines, whose captains were ordered to make every effort to spare neutral ships. The British war zone was enforced by automatic contact mines, which could not distinguish a German battleship from an American tanker carrying oil between two neutral ports. Yet the administration was willing and even eager to assert the right of Americans to sail unmolested through the German zone, while citizens who entered the British zone did so at their own risk. The real difference between blockade and submarine in Wilson's view was not that the former took property and the latter took lives, but that the former was British and the latter was German.

Two years to the day after Page presented the American note of April 2, 1915, to Grey, Woodrow Wilson asked the Congress of the United States to declare war on Germany. He emphasized in his request that, although other concerns had influenced his decision, the primary motivation had been defense of American maritime rights against the German submarine: "We enter this war only where we are clearly forced into it because there are no other means of defending our rights." At best this statement indicates Wilson's capacity for self-delusion; at worst it demonstrates his capacity for hypocrisy. The system for international law Wilson claimed to be defending in 1917 had been undermined two years earlier by his own failure to maintain American neutrality. The United States went to war not in defense of neutral rights, but to enforce the principle that a nation purporting to be neutral could violate the rules of neutrality while avoiding the consequences of belligerency. . . .

Woodrow Wilson publicly pledged in August 1914 to maintain American neutrality. He did not keep this pledge, as Arthur Link maintains he did. Nor was his policy "benevolent neutrality," as Ernest May argues. American policy toward Britain during the Boer War had been benevolent neutrality. American policy during World War I was precisely what James Brown Scott had warned it would be if the United States failed to defend its rights against flagrant British violation: "non-neutrality toward Germany" and "a manifest failure to safeguard the interests of United States citizens engaged in perfectly legitimate business." American maritime neutrality during the first eight months of World War I was incompatible with the traditional American principles contained in John Bassett Moore's magisterial 1907 *Digest of International Law,* incompatible with John Hay's statements during the Boer and Russo-Japanese Wars, incompatible with the Naval War Code of 1900 and the teachings of the Naval War College, incompatible with the positions taken by the United States at the Hague and London Conferences, and incompatible with the recommendations of the president's own Anglophilic advisers such as Lansing, Scott, [Admiral of the Navy George] Dewey, and [Chandler Parsons] Anderson. Only by Wilson's personal definition, which had no reference to either international law or American history, was the United States entitled to the status of "neutral" by March 1915.

Several historians have concluded from this evidence that Wilson deliberately compromised Americans neutrality in order to aid the Allies and eventually bring the United States into the war at their side. For the first eight months of war, at least, this interpretation overestimates Wilson's deviousness and underestimates his capacity for self-delusion. The president did shape American neutrality so it aided the Allies, but there is no evidence that he recognized his actions were in any way unneutral. On the contrary, surrounded by advisers eager to present Allied actions in the best possible light and convinced of his own moral superiority, Wilson continued to believe that he could define true neutrality better than could lawyers and textbooks. Lansing and Garrison saw the flaw in this reasoning—that other nations were more likely to accept the rule of law than to accept the rule of Wilson—but they were never able to make the president see it. The best summation of Wilson's attitude on maritime rights was written by Shakespeare in regard to Cardinal Wolsey: "His own opinion was his law."

If Wilson's personality explains how he could continue to believe in all sincerity that his administration was neutral despite overwhelming evidence to the contrary, another explanation is needed for the failure of the American people to insist on strict adherence to traditional policies. The president's greatest fear was a public outcry against the blockade which would compromise his leadership and thus recreate the "tragical" circumstances of 1812. Lansing and others warned consistently that British actions were on the verge of provoking such a reaction. Yet the outcry never developed, despite obvious British violations of neutral rights and the evident failure of the administration to prevent them. The fact that public opinion ultimately turned against Germany, and not against Britain, the initial offender, is one of the most puzzling aspects of American maritime rights policy.

The first, and most important, factor working against a popular demand that Wilson follow traditional neutrality policies was that a majority of the American people sympathized with the Allies. Two decades of Anglo-American rapprochement, historical friendship with France, both real and imagined German brutality in Belgium, and other influences had predisposed most Americans to accept administration claims that Anglo-American differences over the blockade were technical and relatively minor. The complexity of maritime law prevented all but a handful from understanding the real issues involved, and both London and Washington deliberately sought to maintain this confusion. The most vocal Republicans, led by Theodore Roosevelt, openly supported the Allies and thus allowed Wilson to picture himself as the man of peace dedicated to true neutrality. Grey and [British Ambassador Cecil] Spring Rice were careful to justify British actions in terms least likely to offend American sensibilities, as when the ambassador cited supposed Civil War precedents and the foreign secretary used the word "blockade" inaccurately but effectively to describe the reprisals Order in Council of March 1915. The Allies eased the pain their economic campaign inflicted on such key American industries as copper, cotton, and meat with huge purchases of their own. All these factors joined to create the extraordinary passivity of American public opinion in response to the blockade and the administration's failure to challenge it effectively.

To say that Wilson was unneutral and that he led the United States into an unneutral policy on maritime rights is not to say that he was necessarily wrong in what he did. Link, though wrong in asserting that the president did maintain neutrality, makes a convincing case for the position that the failure to challenge the blockade was a wise strategic decision:

> The results of destroying the British blockade would have been the wrecking of American friendship with the two great European democracies and the probable victory of the Central Powers, without a single compensatory gain for the interests and security of the United States. Only the sure achievement of some great political objective like a secure peace settlement, certainly not the winning of a commercial advantage or the defense of doubtful neutral rights, would have justified Wilson in undertaking a determined challenge to British sea power.

This argument is particularly impressive in light of what is now known of German war aims. There no longer is room for doubt that the Kaiser's government, from shortly after the war began to shortly before it ended, was committed to a massive program of territorial aggrandizement. The details of this program remained vague, but two essential elements were Continental domination and destruction of British maritime supremacy. Had Germany achieved this position, a challenge to the Monroe Doctrine almost certainly would have followed.

The failure to challenge the illegal aspects of the Allied blockade thus gained one clear advantage for the United States. The economic campaign proved a decisive factor in preventing a German victory that would have threatened American security. Britain and France remained Great Powers for two more decades, during which American power grew enormously. When the United States did have to face a victorious Germany in 1941, it was far more ready for the challenge than it would have been in 1914.

Wilson's fears of German agents building heavy artillery emplacements in the United States and disguising them as tennis courts were paranoid fantasies, but his belief that German victory in Europe would pose an unacceptable threat to American national security seems entirely realistic.

Evaluation of American maritime rights policy thus rests on weighing this advantage against the costs of unneutrality. For there were costs, despite the president's failure to acknowledge or even to recognize them. By aiding the Allies in order to block German aggrandizement, Wilson's policies ultimately identified the United States with the postwar aggrandizement of Britain, France, Japan, and Italy. He compromised not only the American tradition of neutrality in colonial and European conflicts, but the entire system of international relations based on the concepts of neutrality and limited war. He sacrificed on the altar of Anglo-American friendship any possibility that the United States could use its immense power to preserve the existing international system, to mitigate the horrors of war for neutrals and perhaps for belligerent civilians, and to mediate a compromise peace. Wilson ignored these costs, but the historian must weigh them in his balance.

A sincerely neutral United States could have reduced wartime suffering among the weaker neutrals and among the civilian populations of the belligerents. The best indication of what might have been done in this regard is Wilson's success in using American power to delay the German decision for unrestricted submarine warfare by two full years. A similar stand against British interference with food shipments to the European neutrals, to Germany, and to Austria-Hungary would have saved innocent lives and prevented enormous suffering. Such a stand also would have done much to establish American good faith in German eyes and perhaps would have opened the way to other limitations on war's barbarism.

Another cost of Wilson's failure to challenge the blockade, destruction of the existing legal order on the seas, is more difficult to evaluate. The general historical view, that the system of maritime rights existing in 1914 was "ambiguous," "obsolete," or "very nearly unworkable," would have found few supporters in either the British or the American government. Britain violated what its leaders privately acknowledged to be established international law for reasons of military expediency; the United States permitted these violations for reasons of presidential policy. Wilson had the power to command respect for neutral rights from all belligerents. He chose to use that power only against Germany. By doing so he forfeited America's claim to neutrality. The established system of international maritime law broke down in 1914 not because of its own flaws, but because one man refused to uphold it. Wilson tried to replace the system he destroyed with a new order, "freedom of the seas," but failed. The result has been an enduring anarchy.

The American failure to challenge the blockade destroyed more than traditional maritime law. Wilson perverted the very concept of neutrality and thereby undermined the entire system of international relations which had dominated Western civilization since the rise of the nation-state. The old system had drawn a clear distinction between belligerents and neutrals, and had defined certain rights and duties for each. The American failure to fulfill the obligations of neutrality was a primary factor in the disintegration of this distinction. Wilson instead drew a moral distinction between the Allies and the Central Powers and shaped American "neutrality" to favor the "good" belligerent. For the rest of his Presidency he sought to build a new world order in which his own moral universalism would replace nationalism as the foundation of international relations. The heart of this order was to be the League of Nations, which was to replace national self-interest with international justice. The League's failure was also the failure of Wilson's vision.

The national system of international relations had its flaws, as World War I demonstrates. But it did deal with the twentieth century's dominant historical force, nationalism, more effectively than Wilson's system of moral universalism. The old system sought to limit and localize conflicts by providing guidelines for belligerent and neutral conduct which discouraged outside intervention. The new system invited nations not directly involved in a conflict to intervene in accordance with their moral judgments. The history of neither the League of Nations nor the United Nations supports Wilson's assurance that a world organization would evaluate such local conflicts fairly and ensure that any outside intervention would be on the side of justice. Like many before him, Woodrow Wilson learned that to destroy an existing system is easier than to replace it with a better system. His role in undermining the traditional national system of international relations might ultimately prove to have been the greatest cost of American unneutrality in 1914.

Evaluation of American maritime rights policy during World War I rests essentially on the answer to one question: could the United States have blocked a German victory while preserving its own neutrality within the existing system of international relations, avoiding identification with Allied aggrandizement, and preventing the innocent deaths and suffering caused by the blockade? This question can never be answered with certainty because the Wilson administration refused to explore any alternatives to its own policy. Nevertheless, it is possible to sketch a scenario in which both belligerent camps, denied by firm American resistance the sustaining hope of victory through illegal surface or submarine blockade, sicken of the carnage in the trenches. In such circumstances, with each side recognizing that supplies from America could sustain its foe indefinitely and with neither able to afford antagonizing the United States, the promise of American mediation and a compromise peace does not seem totally unrealistic. Ironically, it was the genius of Woodrow Wilson which recognized that a lasting peace must be "a peace without victory." It was the tragedy of Woodrow Wilson that his own unneutrality would be a major factor in bringing about the decisive Allied victory that made a healing peace impossible.

✖ F U R T H E R   R E A D I N G

Thomas A. Bailey and Paul B. Ryan, *The Lusitania Disaster* (1975)

Paul Birdsall, "Neutrality and Economic Pressure, 1914–1917," *Science and Society,* 3 (1939), 217–28

John M. Blum, *Woodrow Wilson and the Politics of Morality* (1956)

Henry Blumenthal, *Illusion and Reality in Franco-American Diplomacy, 1914–1945* (1986)

Edward H. Buehrig, ed., *Wilson's Foreign Policy in Perspective* (1957)

Kathleen Burk, *Britain, America, and the Sinews of War, 1914–1918* (1985)

Kendrick A. Clements, *Woodrow Wilson: World Statesman* (1988)

John Garry Clifford, *The Citizen Soldiers* (1972)

John M. Cooper, Jr., " 'An Irony of Fate': Woodrow Wilson's Pre-World War I Diplomacy," *Diplomatic History,* 3 (1979), 425–37

———, *The Vanity of Power* (1969)

———, *The Warrior and the Priest: Woodrow Wilson and Theodore Roosevelt* (1983)

Patrick Devlin, *Too Proud to Fight* (1975)

Robert H. Ferrell, *Woodrow Wilson and World War I* (1985)

Lloyd C. Gardner, *Safe for Democracy* (1984)

Alexander L. George and Juliette George, *Woodrow Wilson and Colonel House: A Personality Study* (1956)

———, "*Woodrow Wilson and Colonel House:* A Reply to Weinstein, Anderson, and Link," *Political Science Quarterly,* 96 (1981–82), 641–65

Ross Gregory, "To Do Good in the World: Woodrow Wilson and America's Mission," in Frank J. Merli and Theodore A. Wilson, eds., *Makers of American Diplomacy* (1974)

———, *Walter Hines Page* (1970)

N. Gordon Levin, *Woodrow Wilson and World Politics* (1968)

Arthur S. Link, *Wilson,* 5 vols. (1947–1965)

———, *Woodrow Wilson: Revolution, War and Peace* (1979)

Ernest R. May, *The World War and American Isolation 1914–1917* (1959)

Walter Millis, *Road to War* (1935)

Charles E. Neu, "The Search for Woodrow Wilson," *Reviews in American History,* 10 (1982), 223–28

Daniel M. Smith, *The Great Departure* (1965)

———, *Robert Lansing and American Neutrality, 1914–1917* (1958)

Charles C. Tansill, *America Goes to War* (1938)

Barbara Tuchman, *The Zimmermann Telegram* (1958)

Edwin A. Weinstein, *Woodrow Wilson: A Medical and Psychological Biography* (1981)

———, James W. Anderson, and Arthur S. Link, "Woodrow Wilson's Political Personality," *Political Science Quarterly,* 93 (1978–79), 585–98

Woodrow Wilson, Henry Cabot Lodge, and the League Fight

During the First World War, President Woodrow Wilson called for a lenient "peace without victory," and some historians have concluded that he had decided for war in April 1917 to ensure himself a place at the peace table. Less than a year later, the President issued his peace program of Fourteen Points. For Wilson, the fourteenth point proposing a League of Nations ranked first in importance. The war ended on November 11, 1918, and in January of the following year, Wilson became an active participant in the Paris Peace Conference at Versailles. For several months, he worked to write a peace treaty and a covenant for his cherished League.

At home, however, many Americans began to question Wilson's diplomacy, especially because they knew that he had made several compromises with his own "points" in order to win approval for his League plan. Critics also feared that an international organization would undermine American sovereignty. They grew particularly alarmed over Article 10 of the League Covenant, which prescribed collective security. The President battled back in a vigorous national debate, on the whole refused to compromise, and ultimately witnessed the Senate's rejection of both the peace treaty and American membership in the League.

Historians disagree in their explanations for the rejection. Some have concentrated on the personal feud between Wilson and Republican Senator Henry Cabot Lodge, the influential chairman of the Foreign Relations Committee. Others have emphasized the President's arrogance and stubbornness in the face of overwhelming political odds. And some have related Wilson's poor health, especially after a serious stroke, to his unwillingness or inability to compromise with his Senate foes. Finally, some scholars have concluded that the League fight represented a fundamental debate over the essence of American foreign policy— whether it would adhere to the tradition of unilateralism or shift to collective security. As Lodge once put it, "Are you ready to put your soldiers and your *sailors at the deposition of other nations?'' One question looks to the future: Did it matter that the United States did not join the League of Nations?*

✖ *D O C U M E N T S*

Wilson issued his Fourteen Points in a speech on January 8, 1918, reprinted here as the first document. The League of Nations was created at Versailles and its Article 10, the second document, aroused heated controversy in the United States; Wilson considered the article the heart of the Covenant and the key to collective security. The third document is the speech Wilson gave in San Francisco on September 17, 1919, defending the League against mounting criticism. Led by Senator Henry Cabot Lodge of Massachusetts, critics offered a number of reservations to the Covenant and incorporated them in a Lodge resolution dated November 19, 1919, reprinted as the last document.

The Fourteen Points, 1918

We entered this war because violations of right had occurred which touched us to the quick and made the life of our own people impossible unless they were corrected and the world secured once for all against their recurrence. What we demand in this war, therefore, is nothing peculiar to ourselves. It is that the world be made fit and safe to live in; and particularly that it be made safe for every peace-loving nation which, like our own, wishes to live its own life, determine its own institutions, be assured of justice and fair dealing by the other peoples of the world as against force and selfish aggression. All the peoples of the world are in effect partners in this interest, and for our own part we see very clearly that unless justice be done to others it will not be done to us. The programme of the world's peace, therefore, is our programme; and that programme, the only possible programme, as we see it, is this:

I. Open covenants of peace, openly arrived at, after which there shall be no private international understandings of any kind but diplomacy shall proceed always frankly and in the public view.

II. Absolute freedom of navigation upon the seas, outside territorial waters, alike in peace and in war, except as the seas maybe closed in whole or in part by international action for the enforcement of international covenants.

III. The removal, so far as possible, of all economic barriers and the establishment of an equality of trade conditions among all the nations consenting to the peace and associating themselves for its maintenance.

IV. Adequate guarantees given and taken that national armaments will be reduced to the lowest point consistent with domestic safety.

V. A free, open-minded, and absolutely impartial adjustment of all colonial claims, based upon a strict observance of the principle that in determining all such questions of sovereignty the interests of the populations concerned must have equal weight with the equitable claims of the government whose title is to be determined.

VI. The evacuation of all Russian territory and such a settlement of all questions affecting Russia as will secure the best and freest cooperation of the other nations of the world in obtaining for her an unhampered and unembarrassed opportunity for the independent determination of her own political development and national policy and assure her of a sincere welcome into the society of free nations under institutions of her own choosing; and, more than a welcome, assistance also of every kind that she may need and may herself desire. The treatment accorded Russia by her sister nations in the months to come will be the acid test of their good will, of their comprehension of her needs as distinguished from their own interests, and of their intelligent and unselfish sympathy.

VII. Belgium, the whole world will agree, must be evacuated and restored, without any attempt to limit the sovereignty which she enjoys in common with all other free nations. No other single act will serve as this will serve to restore confidence among the nations in the laws which they have themselves set and determined for the government of their relations with one another. Without this healing act the whole structure and validity of international law is forever impaired.

VIII. All French territory should be freed and the invaded portions restored, and the wrong done to France by Prussia in 1871 in the matter of Alsace-Lorraine, which has unsettled the peace of the world for nearly fifty years, should be righted, in order that peace may once more be made secure in the interest of all.

IX. A readjustment of the frontiers of Italy should be effected along clearly recognizable lines of nationality.

X. The peoples of Austria-Hungary, whose place among the nations we wish to see safeguarded and assured, should be accorded the freest opportunity of autonomous development.

XI. Rumania, Serbia, and Montenegro should be evacuated; occupied territories restored; Serbia accorded free and secure access to the sea; and the relations of the several Balkan states to one another determined by friendly counsel along historically established lines of allegiance and nationality; and international guarantees of the political and economic independence and territorial integrity of the several Balkan states should be entered into.

XII. The Turkish portions of the present Ottoman Empire should be assured a secure sovereignty, but the other nationalities which are now under Turkish rule should be assured an undoubted security of life and an absolutely unmolested opportunity of autonomous development, and the Dardanelles should be permanently opened as a free passage to the ships and commerce of all nations under international guarantees.

XIII. An independent Polish state should be erected which should include the territories inhabited by indisputably Polish populations, which should be assured a free and secure access to the sea, and whose political and economic independence and territorial integrity should be guaranteed by international covenant.

XIV. A general association of nations must be formed under specific covenants for the purpose of affording mutual guarantees of political independence and territorial integrity to great and small states alike. . . .

We have spoken now, surely, in terms too concrete to admit of any further doubt or question. An evident principle runs through the whole programme I have outlined. It is the principle of justice to all peoples and nationalities, and their right to live on equal terms of liberty and safety with one another, whether they be strong or weak. Unless this principle be made its foundation no part of the structure of international justice can stand. The people of the United States could act upon no other principle; and to the vindication of this principle they are ready to devote their lives, their honor, and everything that they possess. The moral climax of this the culminating and final war for human liberty has come, and they are ready to put their own strength, their own highest purpose, their own integrity and devotion to the test.

Article 10 of the League Covenant, 1919

Article 10. The Members of the League undertake to respect and preserve as against external aggression the territorial integrity and existing political independence of all Members of the League. In case of any such aggression or in case of any threat or danger of such aggression the Council shall advise upon the means by which this obligation shall be fulfilled.

Wilson Defends the League, 1919

It is my purpose, fellow citizens, to analyze the objections which are made to this great League, and I shall be very brief. In the first place, you know that one of the difficulties which have been experienced by those who are objecting to this League is that they do not think that there is a wide enough door open for us to get out. For my own part, I am not one of those who, when they go into a generous enterprise, think first of all how they are going to turn away from those with whom they are associated. I am not one of those who, when they go into a concert for the peace of the world, want to sit close to the door with their hand on the knob and constantly trying the door to be sure that it is not locked. If we want to go into this thing—and we do want to go into it—we will go in it with our whole hearts and settled purpose to stand by the great enterprise to the end. Nevertheless, you will remember—some of you, I dare say—that when I came home in March for an all too brief visit to this country, which seems to me the fairest and dearest in the world, I brought back with me the first draft of the Covenant of the League of Nations. I called into consultation the Committees on Foreign Affairs and on Foreign Relations of the House and

Senate of the United States, and laid the draft of the Covenant before them. One of the things that they proposed was that it should be explicitly stated that any member of the League should have the right to withdraw. I carried that suggestion back to Paris, and without the slightest hesitation it was accepted and acted upon; and every suggestion which was made in that conference at the White House was accepted by the conference of peace in Paris. There is not a feature of the Covenant, except one, now under debate upon which suggestions were not made at that time, and there is not one of those suggestions that was not adopted by the conference of peace.

The gentlemen say,"You have laid a limitation upon the right to withdraw. You have said that we can withdraw upon two years' notice, if at that time we shall have fulfilled all our international obligations and all our obligations under the Covenant." "Yes," I reply; "is it characteristic of the United States not to fulfill her international obligations? Is there any fear that we shall wish to withdraw dishonorably? Are gentlemen willing to stand up and say that they want to get out whether they have the moral right to get out or not?" I for one am too proud as an American to debate that subject on that basis. The United States has always fulfilled its international obligations, and, God helping her, she always will. There is nothing in the Covenant to prevent her acting upon her own judgment with regard to that matter. The only thing she has to fear, the only thing she has to regard, is the public opinion of mankind, and inasmuch as we have always scrupulously satisfied the public opinion of mankind with regard to justice and right, I for my part am not afraid at anytime to go before that jury. It is a jury that might condemn us if we did wrong, but it is not a jury that could oblige us to stay in the League, so that there is absolutely no limitation upon our right to withdraw.

One of the other suggestions I carried to Paris was that the committees of the two Houses did not find the Monroe Doctrine safeguarded in the Covenant of the League of Nations. I suggested that to the conference in Paris, and they at once inserted the provision which is now there that nothing in the Covenant shall be construed as affecting the Monroe Doctrine. What is the validity of the Monroe Doctrine? The Monroe Doctrine means that if any outside power, any power outside this hemisphere, tries to impose its will upon any portion of the Western Hemisphere the United States is at liberty to act independently and alone in repelling the aggression; that it does not have to wait for the action of the League of Nations; that it does not have to wait for anything but the action of its own administration and its own Congress. This is the first time in the history of international diplomacy that any great government has acknowledged the validity of the Monroe Doctrine. Now for the first time all the great fighting powers of the world except Germany, which for the time being has ceased to be a great fighting power, acknowledge the validity of the Monroe Doctrine and acknowledge it as part of the international practice of the world.

They are nervous about domestic questions. They say, "It is intolerable to think that the League of Nations should interfere with domestic questions," and whenever they begin to specify they speak of the question of immigration, of the question of naturalization, of the question of the tariff. My fellow citizens, no competent or authoritative student of international law would dream of maintaining that these were anything but exclusively domestic questions, and the Covenant of the League expressly provides that the League can take no action whatever about matters which are in the practice of international law regarded as domestic questions. We did not undertake to enumerate samples of domestic questions for the very good reason, which will occur to any lawyer, that if you made a list it would be inferred that what you left out was not included. Nobody with a thoughtful knowledge of international practice has the least doubt as to what are domestic questions, and there is no obscurity whatever in this Covenant with regard to the safeguarding of the United States, along with other sovereign countries, in the control of domestic questions. I beg that you will not fancy, my fellow citizens, that the United States is the only country that is jealous of its sovereignty. Throughout these conferences it was necessary at every turn to safeguard the sovereign independence of the several governments who were taking part in the conference, and they were just as keen to protect themselves against outside intervention in domestic matters as we were. Therefore the whole heartiness of their concurrent opinion runs with this safeguarding of domestic questions.

It is objected that the British Empire has six votes and we have one. The answer to that is that it is most carefully arranged that our one vote equals the six votes of the British Empire. Anybody who will take the pains to read the Covenant of the League of Nations will find out that the assembly—and it is only in the assembly that the British Empire has six votes—is not a voting body. . . .

Not a single affirmative act or negative decision upon a matter of action taken by the League of Nations can be validated without the vote of the United States of America. We can dismiss from our dreams the six votes of the British Empire, for the real underlying conception of the assembly of the League of Nations is that it is the forum of opinion, not of action. It is the debating body; it is the body where the thought of the little nation along with the thought of the big nation is brought to bear upon those matters which affect the peace of the world, is brought to bear upon those matters which affect the good understanding between nations upon which the peace of the world depends; where this stifled voice of humanity is at last to be heard, where nations that have borne the unspeakable sufferings of the ages that must have seemed to them like aeons will find voice and expression, where the moral judgment of mankind can sway the opinion of the world. That is the function of the assembly. The assembly is the voice of mankind. The council, where unanimous action is necessary, is the only means through which that voice can accomplish action.

You say, "We have heard a great deal about Article X." I just now said that the only substitute for the League of Nations which is offered by the opponents is a return to the old system. What was the old system? That the strong had all the rights and need pay no attention to the rights of the weak; that if a great powerful nation saw what it wanted, it had the right to go and take it; that the weak nations could cry out and cry out as they pleased and there would be no hearkening ear anywhere to their rights.

The Lodge Reservations, 1919

Resolved . . . That the Senate advise and consent to the ratification of the treaty of peace with Germany . . . subject to the following reservations and understandings . . . which ratification is not to take effect or bind the United States until the said reservations and understandings . . . have been accepted by . . . at least three of the four principal allied and associated powers. . . .

1. . . . in case of notice of withdrawal from the league of nations, as provided in said article [Article 1], the United States shall be the sole judge as to whether all its international obligations . . . have been fulfilled, and notice of withdrawal . . . may be given by a concurrent resolution of the Congress of the United States.

2. The United States assumes no obligation to preserve the territorial integrity or political independence of any other country . . . under the provisions of article 10, or to employ the military or naval forces of the United States under any article of the treaty for any purpose, unless in any particular case the Congress, which . . . has the sole power to declare war . . . shall . . . so provide.

3. No mandate shall be accepted by the United States under article 22 . . . except by action of the Congress of the United States.

4. The United States reserves to itself exclusively the right to decide what questions are within its domestic jurisdiction. . . .

5. The United States will not submit to arbitration or to inquiry by the assembly or by the council of the league of nations . . . any questions which in the judgment of the United States depend upon or relate to . . . the Monroe doctrine; said doctrine is to be interpreted by the United States alone and is . . . wholly outside the jurisdiction of said league of nations. . . .

6. The United States withholds its assent to articles 156, 157, and 158 [Shantung clauses]. . . .

7. The Congress of the United States will provide by law for the appointment of the representatives of the United States in the assembly and the council of the league of nations, and may in its discretion provide for the participation of the United States in any commission. . . . no person shall represent the United States under either said league of nations or the treaty of peace . . . except with the approval of the Senate of the United States. . . .

9. The United States shall not be obligated to contribute to any expenses of the league of nations . . . unless and until an appropriation of funds . . . shall have been made by the Congress of the United States.

10. If the United States shall at any time adopt any plan for the limitation of armaments proposed by the council of the league . . . it reserves the

right to increase such armaments without the consent of the council whenever the United States is threatened with invasion or engaged in war. . . .

14. The United States assumes no obligation to be bound by any election, decision, report, or finding of the council or assembly in which any member of the league and its self-governing dominions, colonies, or parts of empire, in the aggregate have cast more than one vote.

E S S A Y S

Woodrow Wilson's perspective on the League of Nations and the American debate over it is developed by Arthur S. Link of Princeton University in the first essay. A major Wilson biographer, Link explains the politics of the question and lauds Wilson as a prophet. William C. Widenor of the University of Illinois, in the second essay, a selection from his *Henry Cabot Lodge and the Search for an American Foreign Policy* (1980), studies the Massachusetts senator's opposition to Wilson's League and his recommended changes. Widenor disputes the view of a demonic Lodge locked in a personal feud with the President; he stresses instead the importance of ideas in the debate.

Woodrow Wilson's Perspective

ARTHUR S. LINK

Wilson returned to the United States in June 1919 to face the crucial task of winning the support of the American people and the approval of the Senate for the Versailles Treaty, the underpinning of the Paris settlements. During the months following Wilson's homecoming, indeed until the election of 1920, there ensued in the United States a debate no less important than the great debate of 1787–1789 over ratification of the Constitution. At stake was the issue of American participation in a new world order capped by the League of Nations, an instrumentality designed to promote world cooperation and peace and armed with sanctions (including military force) to prevent aggression.

Some details of the well-known parliamentary struggle and of the bitter personal controversy between Wilson and his chief antagonist, Senator Henry Cabot Lodge of Massachusetts, cannot be ignored. However, the emphasis of this chapter will be upon what has often been obscured by too much focus on the dramatic details—how the great debate of 1919–1920 revealed differences in opinion concerning the role that the United States should play in world affairs. These differences were fundamental and authentic because they transcended partisanship and personality. They also are as relevant to Americans in the latter part of this century as they were in Wilson's day.

Arthur S. Link, *Woodrow Wilson: Revolution, War, Peace,* 104–113, 119–128, Copyright © 1979. Reprinted by permission of Harlan Davidson, Inc.

The general lines of battle over ratification of the Treaty of Versailles were drawn before Wilson went to Paris, and largely by Wilson himself. Wilson's appeal during the congressional campaign had given a partisan coloration to the whole process of peacemaking. Many Republicans had regarded Wilson's appointment to the American Peace Commission of only one nominal Republican—Henry White, a career diplomat—as a slap in the face. By ignoring the Senate in his appointment of the commission, moreover, Wilson made it inevitably certain that the fight over the Treaty would renew in virulent form the old conflict between the President and the upper house for control of foreign policy.

It would be a great mistake to assume, as some historians have done, that the fate of the Treaty was foreordained by the injection of partisanship into the question of peacemaking or by Wilson's failure to appoint senators to the commission. In the subsequent controversy, Wilson had the warm support of the League to Enforce Peace, composed mainly of prominent Republicans, including former President William Howard Taft. The debate in the country over the Treaty was not a partisan one; and, in the final analysis, the votes in the Senate were partisan only to the degree that a large number of Democratic senators followed Wilson's demands. The important point is that the country at large and the Senate, to a large degree, divided over profoundly important issues, not along party lines. Finally, the fact that Wilson took no senators with him to Paris was of no consequence for the final result.

While Wilson was in Paris, there were unmistakable signs at home that he would encounter significant opposition in the Senate. The most ominous of these was the so-called Round Robin resolution that Lodge read to the Senate on March 4, 1919. It was signed by thirty-seven senators, more than enough to defeat the Treaty, and declared that the Covenant of the League of Nations, "in the form now proposed to the peace conference, was unacceptable. At the same time, isolationists in the Senate were already beginning a furious rhetorical attack against the Covenant.

Although Wilson was defiant in a speech in New York just before he sailed for Paris, he did accept the advice of his friends who urged him to conciliate his critics. He first tried, through Henry White, to ascertain precisely why the Covenant was not acceptable to Lodge and the signers of the Round Robin. Then, when Lodge refused to give any specifics, Wilson consulted Taft and other Republican supporters of the League and, in response to their suggestions, obtained changes in the Covenant. They provided for the right of member nations of the League to withdraw after giving due notice, exempted domestic questions from the League's jurisdiction, permitted member nations to refuse to accept a colonial mandate, and, most important, accorded formal recognition to the Monroe Doctrine.

Wilson was exhausted by the end of the peace conference and showed numerous indications of an unwillingness to compromise further with his senatorial critics. Colonel House, on the day that Wilson left Paris, urged him to meet the Senate in a conciliatory spirit. "I have found," Wilson is alleged to have replied, "that one can never get anything in this life that is worthwhile without fighting for it.'' This self-referential statement suggests that Wilson felt a great burden of guilt because of the compromises that he had made. If this was true, then the guilt feelings were reinforcing his determination to make no further compromises.

Refreshed by the return voyage, Wilson returned to Washington on July 8 in a confident mood. And with good reason. Much of the senatorial criticism of the Treaty was captious. Most important, by this time thirty-two state legislatures had endorsed the Covenant in concurrent resolutions; thirty-three governors had expressed their approval; and a *Literary Digest* poll indicated overwhelming support for the Covenant among editors of newspapers and magazines. Indeed, the whole country seemed to be in a fever of excitement about the League.

Wilson was, therefore, in the mood of a triumphant leader presenting his adversaries with a *fait accompli* when he laid the Treaty formally before the Senate on July 10. He did not refer to the senators, as he had often done, as his ''colleagues,'' and he did not use his favorite phrase ''common counsel,'' that is, the necessity of reasonable give and take before arriving at a final decision. On the contrary, he ''informed'' the senators that a world settlement had been made and then took the highest possible ground to urge prompt and unqualified approval. The League of Nations, he exclaimed, was the best hope of mankind. ''Dare we reject it and break the heart of the world?'' He gave the answer in an impromptu peroration at the end:

> The stage is set, the destiny disclosed. It has come about by no plan of our conceiving, but by the hand of God who led us into this way. We cannot turn back. We can only go forward, with lifted eyes and freshened spirit, to follow the vision. It was of this that we dreamed at our birth. America shall in truth show the way. The light streams upon the path ahead, and nowhere else.

Wilson met reporters in an informal press conference after delivering this address. He was relaxed and confident. There had been much talk of reservations to the Treaty. What did the President think of that idea? Wilson replied that he was determined to oppose all reservations, for they would require a two-thirds vote of the Senate and necessitate renegotiation of the Treaty. It is significant that a constitutional scholar should have made such a mistake. He had no doubt that the Treaty would be ratified just as it stood.

Actually, the situation was far less simple and reassuring than Wilson imagined at the beginning of the great debate. For one thing, powerful voices were already raised in outright and violent condemnation of the Treaty on various grounds. Idealists, who had thrilled at Wilson's vision of a new world, condemned the Treaty because it failed to establish a millennial order. The German-Americans believed that the Treaty was a base betrayal of the Fatherland; the Italian-Americans were angry over Wilson's opposition to Italy's demands. Most important, the several million Irish-Americans, inflamed by the civil war then raging in Ireland, were up in arms because Wilson had refused to win Irish independence at Paris and because the Treaty allegedly benefited the hated English. The powerful chain of Hearst newspapers was marshaling and inciting all the hyphenate protests. Out-and-out isolationists believed that American membership in the League of Nations would mean entanglement in all of Europe's rivalries and wars. They had powerful advocates in a small group of so-called ir-reconcilables or bitter-enders in the Senate, led by Hiram W. Johnson of California, William E. Borah of Idaho, and James A. Reed of Missouri, who opposed the Treaty for various deeply rooted reasons—nationalism, chauvinism, and idealism.

These were the major groups who opposed ratification of the Treaty. In the ensuing debate, they were the loudest and busiest participants of all. They were, however, a minority among the leaders of thought and political opinion, and they spoke for a minority of the people, at least before 1920, if not afterward. This is a simple point but a vital one, because, in its important aspects, the debate over the Treaty was not a struggle between advocates of complete withdrawal on the one side and proponents of total international commitment on the other. It was, rather, a contest between the champions of a potentially strong system of collective security and a group who favored a more limited commitment. It was a choice between these alternatives, and not between complete isolation or complete inter-nationalism, that Wilson, the Senate, and the American people eventually had to make. We will, therefore, let the arguments of the isolationists pass without analysis and concentrate our attention upon the two main and decisive courses of the debate.

Differences of opinion in the United States over the territorial and other provisions of the Treaty were insignificant as compared to the differences evoked by the Covenant of the League and its provisions to prevent aggression and war. Those provisions were clear and for the most part unequivocal. Article 10 guaranteed the political independence and territorial integrity of every member nation throughout the world. Articles 11, 12, 13, 15, 16, and 17 established the machinery of arbitration for all international disputes susceptible to that procedure and decreed that an act of war against one member nation should "ipso facto be deemed to . . . [be] an act of war against all the other Members" and should be followed automatically by an economic blockade against the aggressor and by Council action to determine what military measures should be used to repel the aggression. These were almost ironclad guarantees of mutual security, meant to be effective and unencumbered by the right of any nation involved in a dispute to veto action by the League's Council. Whether such a worldwide system could work, and whether the American people were prepared at this stage of their development to support such a system even if it did work—these were the two main issues of the great debate of 1919–1920.

The decisive opposition to the Versailles Treaty came from a group of men who, to a varying degree, would have answered no to both these questions. This group included some of the most distinguished leaders in and out of the Senate, like Senator Frank B. Kellogg of Minnesota, President

Nicholas Murray Butler of Columbia University, former Secretary of State Elihu Root, and Charles Evans Hughes, Republican presidential candidate in 1916. Most of them were Republicans, because few Democrats active in politics dared to incur the President's wrath by opposing him. They were not isolationists but limited internationalists who believed that the United States should play, in a varying degree, an active role in preserving the peace of the world. Most of them favored, for example, arbitration, the establishment of something like a World Court to interpret and codify international law, and international agreements for disarmament, economic cooperation, and the like. Some of them even supported the idea of alliances with certain powers for specific purposes.

On the other hand, all the limited internationalists opposed any such approval of the Treaty as would commit the United States unreservedly to the kind of collective security the Covenant of the League had created. Their arguments might be summarized as follows:

First, a system of collective security that is worldwide in operation is not likely either to work or to endure the strains that will inevitably be put upon it, because in practice the great powers will not accept the limitations that the Covenant places upon their sovereignty, and no nation will go to war to vindicate Article 10 unless its vital interests compel it to do so. Such sweeping guarantees as the Covenant affords are, therefore, worse than no guarantees at all because they offer only an illusory hope of security.

Second, the Covenant's fundamental guarantee, embodied in Article 10, is impossible to maintain because its promise to perpetuate the *status quo* defies the very law of life. As Elihu Root put it:

> If perpetual, it would be an attempt to preserve for all time unchanged the distribution of power and territory made in accordance with the views and exigencies of the Allies in this present juncture of affairs. It would necessarily be futile. . . . It would not only be futile; it would be mischievious. Change and growth are the law of life, and no generation can impose its will in regard to the growth of nations and the distribution of power upon succeeding generations.

Third, the American people are not ready to support the Covenant's sweeping commitments and in fact should not do so unless their vital interests are involved in a dispute. They would and should be ready to act to prevent the outbreak or any conflict that threatened to lead to a general war, but it is inconceivable that they would or should assume the risk of war to prevent a border dispute in the Balkans, or to help maintain Japanese control of Shantung Province or British supremacy in Ireland and India. Unconditional ratification of the Treaty by the United States would, therefore, be worse than outright rejection, for it would mean the making of promises that the American people could not possibly honor in the future.

Fourth, unqualified membership in the League will raise grave dangers to American interests and the American constitutional system. It will menace American control over immigration and tariff policies, imperil the Monroe

Doctrine, increase the power of the President at the expense of Congress, and necessitate the maintenance of a large standing army for the fulfillment of obligations under the Covenant.

Fifth, and most important, full-fledged participation in such a system of collective security as the Covenant establishes will spell the end of American security in foreign affairs, because it will mean transferring the power of decision over questions of peace and war from the President and Congress to an international agency which the United States could not control.

The limited internationalists, voicing these objections day in and day out as the great debate reached its crescendo in the autumn of 1919, made their purposes and program indelibly clear. They would accept most of the provisions of the Treaty unrelated to the League and acquiesce in the ones that they did not like. They would also sanction American membership in the League of Nations. But they would also insist upon reserving to the United States, and specifically to Congress, the power of decision concerning the degree of American participation in the League; and they would make no binding promise to enforce collective security anywhere in the future. This strategy was devised by Elihu Root in July 1919.

This was also the final, public position of Senator Lodge, the man who devised and executed the Republican strategy in the upper house during the parliamentary phase of the Treaty struggle. Personally, Lodge had little hope for the success of the League, a profound contempt for Wilson, and almost a sardonic scorn for Wilson's international ideals. The Massachusetts Senator was an ardent nationalist, almost a jingoist. He was no isolationist, but a believer in a strong balance of power. His solution would have been harsh terms, including dismemberment of Germany, and the formation of an Anglo-Franco-American alliance as the best insurance for future peace. But, as chairman of the Foreign Relations Committee and leader of his party in the Senate, it was his duty to subordinate his own strong feelings and to find a common ground upon which most Republicans could stand. That common ground, that program acceptable to an overwhelming majority of Republicans inside the Senate and out, was, in brief, to approve the Treaty and to accept membership in the League. This would be subject to certain amendments and reservations that would achieve the objectives of the limited internationalists.

Amendments and reservations designed to satisfy the moderate internationalists were embodied in the report that the Republican majority of the Foreign Relations Committee presented to the Senate on September 10, 1919. During the following weeks, that body rejected the amendments (on the ground that they would require renegotiation of the Treaty) and adopted most of them in the form of reservations, fourteen in all. Most of them were unimportant, but there was one that constituted a virtual rejection of the kind of collective security that Wilson had envisaged. It was Reservation 2, which declared that the United States assumed no obligations to preserve the territorial integrity or political independence of any other country, unless

Congress should by act or joint resolution specifically assume such an obligation. In addition, the preamble to the reservations provided that American ratification of the Treaty should not take effect until at least three of the four principal Allied powers had accepted the reservations in a formal exchange of notes.

This, then, was the program to which most of Wilson's opponents stood committed by the time that the Senate moved toward a formal vote on the Versailles Treaty. Whether Lodge himself was an irreconcilable who desired the defeat of the Treaty, or whether he was merely a strong reservationist, is an important question but an irrelevant one at this point. The significant fact is that he had succeeded in uniting most Republicans and in committing them to a program that affirmed limited internationalism at the same time that it repudiated American support of a tentative collective security system.

Meanwhile, despite his earlier show of intransigence, Wilson had been hard at work in preparation for the impending struggle. In an effort to split the Republican ranks, he held a series of conferences in late July with eleven Republican senators who he thought would favor approval of the Treaty after the adoption of a few interpretive reservations. On August 19, the President met the Foreign Relations Committee at the White House for a three-hour grilling on all phases of the settlement. The interchange produced no new support for the Treaty. What Wilson did not know, and never did seem to know, was that virtually all of the so-called mild reservationists had already coalesced into the central hard-core Republican pro-League group in the Senate. They were the men who voted with Democrats to convert Lodge's amendments into reservations. They were the ones who forced Lodge, for the sake of party unity, to support the treaty with reservations. Finally, they were the real authors of the reservations. Thus, confer as much as he could, Wilson made no headway in winning the support that would be vital when the Senate voted on the Treaty.

In response Wilson made one of the most fateful decisions of his career. It was, as he put it, to go to the people and purify the wells of public opinion that had been poisoned by the isolationists and opponents of unreserved ratification. He was physically weakened by his labors at Paris, and his physician warned that a long speaking tour might endanger his life. Even so, he insisted upon making the effort to rally the people, the sources of authority, who had always sustained him in the past.

Wilson left Washington on September 3, 1919, and headed for the heartland of America, into Ohio, Indiana, Missouri, Iowa, Nebraska, Minnesota, and the Dakotas—into the region where isolationist sentiment was strongest. From there he campaigned through the Northwest and the major cities of the Pacific Coast. The final leg of his journey took him through Nevada, Utah, Wyoming, and Colorado, where the tour ended after Wilson's partial breakdown on September 25 and 26. In all he traveled 8,000 miles in twenty-two days and delivered thirty-two major addresses and eight minor ones. It was not only the greatest single speaking effort of Wilson's career, but also one of the most notable forensic accomplishments in American history.

Everywhere that he went, Wilson pleaded in good temper, not as a partisan, but as a leader who stood above party strife and advantage. He was making his tour, he explained, first of all so that the people might know the truth about the Treaty of Versailles and no longer be confused by the misrepresentations of its enemies. . . .

There remained the greatest threat of all to the integrity of the Covenant, the challenge of the reservation to Article 10. This reservation, Wilson warned, would destroy the foundation of any collective security, because it was a notice to the world that the American people would fulfill their obligations only when it suited their purposes to do so. "That," the President exclaimed at Salt Lake City, "is a rejection of the Covenant. That is an absolute refusal to carry any part of the same responsibility that the other members of the League carry." "In other words, my fellow citizens," he added at Cheyenne,

> what this proposes is this: That we should make no general promise, but leave the nations associated with us to guess in each instance what we were going to consider ourselves bound to do and what we were not going to consider ourselves bound to do. It is as if you said, "We will not join the League definitely, but we will join it occasionally. We will not promise anything, but from time to time we may cooperate. We will not assume any obligations. . . ." This reservation proposes that we should not acknowledge any moral obligation in the matter; that we should stand off and say, "We will see, from time to time; consult us when you get into trouble, and then we will have a debate, after two or three months we will tell you what we are going to do." The thing is unworthy and ridiculous, and I want to say distinctly that, as I read this, it would change the entire meaning of the Treaty and exempt the United States from all responsibility for the preservation of peace. It means the rejection of the Treaty, my fellow countrymen, nothing less. It means that the United States would take from under the structures its very foundations and support.

The irony of it all was, Wilson added, the reservation was actually unnecessary, *if the objective of its framers was merely to reserve the final decision for war to the American government.* In the case of all disputes to which it was not a party, the United States would have an actual veto over the Council's decision for war, because that body could not advise member nations to go to war except by unanimous vote, exclusive of the parties to the dispute. Thus, Wilson explained, there was absolutely no chance that the United States could be forced into war against its will, unless it was itself guilty of aggression, in which case it would be at war anyway.

These were, Wilson admitted, legal technicalities, and, he added, he would not base his case for American participation in the League of Nations upon them. The issue was not who had the power to make decisions for war, but whether the American people were prepared to go wholeheartedly into the League, were determined to support a collective security system unreservedly, and were willing to make the sacrifices that were necessary to preserve peace. Wilson summarized all his pleading with unrivaled feeling at the Mormon capital:

> Instead of wishing to ask to stand aside, get the benefits of the League, but share none of its burdens or responsibilities, I for my part want to go in and accept what is offered to us, the leadership of the world. A leadership of what sort, my fellow citizens? Not a leadership that leads men along the lines by which great nations can profit out of weak nations. Not an exploiting power, but a liberating power—a power to show the world that when America was born it was indeed a finger pointed toward those lands into which men could deploy some of these days and live in happy freedom, look each other in the eyes as equals, see that no man was put upon, that no people were forced to accept authority which was not of their own choice, and that, out of the general generous impulse of the human genius and the human spirit, we were lifted along the levels of civilization to days when there should be wars no more, but men should govern themselves in peace and amity and quiet. That is the leadership we said we wanted, and now the world offers it to us. It is inconceivable that we should reject it.

We come now to the well-known tragic sequel. Following his address at Pueblo, Colorado, on September 25, 1919, Wilson showed such obvious signs of exhaustion that his physician canceled his remaining engagements and sped the presidential train to Washington. On October 2, Wilson suffered a severe stroke and paralysis of the left side of his face and body. For several days his life hung in the balance; then he gradually revived, and by the end of October he was clearly out of danger. But his recovery was only partial at best. His mind remained relatively clear; but he was physically enfeebled, and the disease had wrecked his emotional constitution and aggravated all his more unfortunate personal traits.

Meanwhile, the Senate was nearing the end of its long debate over the Treaty of Versailles. Senator Lodge presented his revised fourteen reservations on behalf of the Foreign Relations Committee to the upper house on November 6, 1919. Senator Gilbert M. Hitchcock of Nebraska, the Democratic minority leader, countered with five reservations, four of which Wilson had approved in substance before he embarked upon his western tour. They simply sought to make clear the American understanding of Article 10 and other provisions of the Treaty. The issue before the Senate, therefore, now seemed clear— whether to approve the Treaty with reservations that did not impair the American obligation to uphold the Covenant, or whether to approve the Treaty with reservations that permitted repudiation of all compelling obligations and promised American support for only a limited international system.

Lodge beat down the Hitchcock reservations with the help of the irreconcilables and then won adoption of his own. Now Wilson had to choose between acceptance of the Lodge reservations or run the risk of the outright defeat of the Treaty. He gave his decision to Hitchcock in a brief conference at the White House on November 17 and in a letter on the following day: Under no circumstances could he accept the Lodge reservation to Article

10, for it meant nullification of the Treaty. When the Senate voted on November 19, therefore, most of the Democrats joined the irreconcilables to defeat approval with the Lodge reservations by a count of thirty-nine ayes to fifty-five nays. The Democratic leaders, hoping to split the Republican ranks and win the support of the mythical mild reservationists then moved unconditional approval of the Treaty. This strategy, upon which Wilson had placed all his hopes, failed, as a firm Republican majority defeated the resolution with the help of the irreconcilables by a vote of thirty-eight ayes to fifty-three nays.

The great mystery is why Wilson rejected the Lodge reservation to Article 10. Before he left on his western tour, Wilson handed Hitchcock four "interpretive" reservations to the articles relating to the right of member nations to withdraw, Article 10, the nonjurisdiction of the League over domestic matters like immigration, and the Monroe Doctrine. Wilson's reservation to Article 10 said that the Senate understood that the advice of the League Council with regard to the use of armed force was to be "regarded only as advice and leaves each member free to exercise its own judgment as to whether it [were] wise or practicable to act upon that advice or not." Hitchcock's own reservation, which presumably Wilson had approved, went even further and said that Congress would have to approve the use of armed force if so requested by the Council.

Why, when the two sides were so close together, did Wilson reject the Lodge reservation to Article 10? Having built so grandly at Paris, having fought so magnificently at home for his creation, why did he remove by his own hand the cornerstone of his edifice of peace? Were there inner demons of pride and arrogance driving him to what Thomas A. Bailey has called "the supreme infanticide"?

Dr. Weinstein has described the effects of the devastating stroke on Wilson's personality and perceptions at this time. He is convinced that, had Wilson been in full health, he would have found the formula to reconcile the differences between the Lodge and Hitchcock reservations. There is a great deal of evidence to support this hypothesis. When Wilson made his decision, on November 17, to reject the Lodge reservation, he was still a very sick man. His mind could function well in certain circumstances, but his whole emotional balance had been shattered. He was sick, petulant, and rigid. He saw very few people between his stroke and November 17, and those who talked to him were careful not to upset him. From his lonely isolation in a sickroom, he saw the outside world from a limited and distorted view. A healthy Wilson certainly would have spent most of his time from his return to Washington from the West to mid-November conferring, cajoling, and doing everything possible to find an acceptable compromise on the reservation to Article 10. This was part of the genius of his leadership. He had displayed it many times before, most notably in negotiating the writing of the Federal Reserve Act and the Versailles Treaty.

Wilson's isolation and the unfortunate pathological effects of his stroke might well have caused him to give the most literal reading possible to the Lodge reservation to Article 10. Taken literally, this reservation could be read as an emphatic repudiation of American responsibilities under the Covenant. It read:

> The United States assumes no obligation to preserve the territorial integrity or political independence of any other country or to interfere in controversies between nations—whether members of the league or not—under the provisions of Article 10, or to employ the military or naval forces of the United States under any article of the treaty for any purpose, unless in any particular case the Congress, which, under the Constitution, has the sole power to declare war or authorize the employment of the military or naval forces of the United States shall by act or joint resolution so provide.

Even a healthy Wilson might have concluded that this reservation amounted, as he put it, to nullification of the Treaty. And any strong President would have bridled at the closing phrases of the reservation, for they constituted the first important congressional constraints against the President as commander in chief to this point in American history and were probably unconstitutional.

Wilson, whether because of his illness or not, did read the reservation literally. He believed, very deeply, that the one issue now at stake was whether the United States would join the League of Nations and give leadership to it wholeheartedly and without reservations, or whether it would join the League grudgingly, with no promises to help maintain the peace of the world. To Wilson, the difference between what he stood for and what the Republicans would agree to was the difference between the success or failure and the life or death of mankind's best hope for peace.

The vote on November 19 was not the end of the struggle, for during the following months an overwhelming majority of the leaders of opinion in the United States refused to accept the vote as the final verdict. In the absence of any reliable indices, it is impossible to measure the division of public opinion as a whole; but there can be little doubt that an overwhelming majority of thoughtful people favored ratification with some kind of reservations, even with the Lodge reservations, if that was necessary to obtain the Senate's consent.

Consequently, there was enormous pressure upon the leaders in both parties for compromise during the last weeks of 1919 and the early months of 1920. Prominent Republicans who had taken leadership in a nonpartisan campaign for the League (including former President Taft), scores of editors, the spokesmen of various academic, religious, and labor organizations, and Democratic leaders who dared oppose the President (like William J. Bryan and Colonel House) begged Lodge and Wilson to find a common ground. Alarmed by the possibility of American rejection of the Treaty, spokesmen for the British government declared publicly that limited American participation in the League would be better than no participation at all.

Under this pressure, the moderate leaders in both camps set to work in late December and early January to find a basis for agreement. Even Lodge began to weaken and joined the bipartisan conferees who were attempting to work out an acceptable reservation to Article 10. But the

Massachusetts Senator and his friends would not yield the essence of their reservation, and it was Wilson who had to make the final choice.

By January, Wilson had recovered sufficient strength to take personal leadership of the Democrats in the Senate. One effect of his stroke was a strong if not complete tendency to deny that he was ill. For example, he would refer to his paralyzed left arm as "it" and not as a part of his body. He was absolutely convinced that he had the great mass of the people behind him and that they would crush any senator or party who opposed him. Living as he did in a world of unreality, Wilson concocted two stratagems.

The first stratagem was to challenge the fifty-seven senators from thirty-eight states who opposed the Treaty altogether or supported the Lodge reservations to resign and then run for reelection in special elections. Should they be reelected, Wilson would appoint a leader of the opposition as Secretary of State and he, Wilson, and his Vice President would resign and the Republican leader would become President. This plan proved to be unfeasible because of variations in state election laws.

Then Wilson, ever innovative, turned to his second stratagem—to make the treaty the leading issue of the coming presidential campaign. Moreover, he would be the Democratic nominee; he would go once again to the people and win an overwhelming mandate for the League. He even drafted a Democratic platform and his speech of acceptance. He set this plan in motion in a letter to the Jackson Day Dinner in Washington, then the chief meeting of Democrats preliminary to a presidential campaign, on January 8, 1920. He repeated his principal arguments for ungrudging approval, declared that "the overwhelming majority" of the people desired ratification of the Treaty, and concluded:

> If there is any doubt as to what the people of the country think on this vital matter, the clear and single way out is to submit it for determination at the next election to the voters of the nation, to give the next election the form of a great and solemn referendum, a referendum as to the part the United States is to play in completing the settlements of the war and in the prevention in the future of such outrages as Germany attempted to perpetrate.

The Jackson Day letter spelled disaster for ratification of the Treaty in any form. Wilson committed the supreme error of converting what had really not been a partisan issue, except in the parliamentary sense, into a hostage of party loyalty and politics. Henceforth most Republican senators would have to vote as Republicans, most Democrats as Democrats, even though they might want to put the interests of the country above those of party and vote for ratification with reservations.

Secondly, in spite of his unshakable faith in the wisdom of the people, Wilson, an expert in the American constitutional and political systems, should have known that there is no way to convert a presidential election into a referendum upon a single issue. Bryan had tried to make the election of 1900 a referendum upon the question of imperialism and had failed utterly to do so. As it turned out in 1920, Warren G. Harding, the Republican nominee and a strong reservationist, had no trouble in muting and sidestepping the League issue. Indeed, a group of thirty-one prominent pro-League Republicans issued a statement during the campaign assuring their fellow Republicans that Harding's election would be the best assurance of ratification and American membership in the League of Nations!

Thirdly, and ironically, Wilson's Jackson Day letter destroyed Wilson's leadership among the various segments of elite opinion makers who had heretofore been his strongest supporters—religious leaders, educational leaders, publicists, editors, and politically active professionals. A reading of their correspondence, journals, editorials, and resolutions reveals a sharp and sudden turn in their opinion. In their view, Wilson was a petulant and sick man and now the principal obstacle to ratification. These leaders of opinion were in utter despair and confusion. Most of them simply gave up the fight. The effect would be devastating for Democratic fortunes during the presidential campaign.

However, Wilson continued to hope that he would lead the Democrats to victory as their presidential candidate. He made plans to have his name put in nomination at the Democratic national convention and to have himself nominated by acclamation. A group of his closest friends had to tell him that it was impossible.

Meanwhile, the parliamentary phase of the struggle moved to its inexorable conclusion when the Senate took its second and final vote on the Treaty on March 19, 1920. The only hope for approval lay in the chance that enough Democrats would defy Wilson, as many friends of the League were urging them to do, to obtain a two-thirds majority for the Lodge reservations. Twenty-one Democrats did follow their consciences rather than the command from the White House, but not enough of them defected to put the Treaty across. The Treaty with the Lodge reservations failed by seven votes.

In this, the last and greatest effort of his life, did Wilson spurn the role of statesman for that of prophet? It is easy enough from our vantage point to say that, in rejecting ratification on the only possible terms and in throwing the issue into the party arena, he did not act as a statesman. It is also clear that his illness gravely impaired his perceptions of political reality and was probably the principal cause of his strategic errors.

However, when we view the situation through Wilson's eyes, his behavior seems neither irrational nor quixotic. As has been said many times, he believed that he had the overwhelming support of the people. He had gone to them many times before, and, except in 1918, with resounding success. He was confident that he, or another pro-League Democrat, could do so again in 1920.

His friends feared that he would be devastated by Harding's victory. On the contrary, he was serene and confident on the morning after the election. He told his private secretary, "The Republicans have committed suicide." To the end of his life he was confident of the ultimate outcome and of the rectitude of his own position. As he put it: "I would rather fail in a cause that will ultimately triumph than triumph in a cause that will ultimately fail."

Wilson was fundamentally right in the one great principle at stake in the Treaty fight. The most immoral thing that a nation (or individual) can do is to refuse to exercise power responsibly when it possesses it. The United States exercised the greatest economic and potentially the greatest military power in the world in 1920. At least for a time it spurned the responsibility that accompanied its power.

Moreover, Wilson was fundamentally right in the long run. As he put it in a speech on Armistice Day in 1923: "We shall inevitably be forced by the moral obligations of freedom and honor to retrieve that fatal error and assume once more the role of courage, self-respect, and helpfulness which every true American must wish to regard as our natural part in the affairs of the world."

The postwar version of collective security failed in the crucial tests of the 1930s, not because the Treaty of Versailles was responsible or the peace-keeping machinery of the League of Nations was defective, but because the people of Great Britain, France, and the United States were unwilling to confront aggressors with the threat of war. Consequently, a second and more terrible world conflict came in 1939, as Wilson had prophesied it would.

The American people, and other peoples, learned the lesson that Wilson taught in 1919 and 1920, but at a fearful cost. And it is Wilson the prophet and pivot of the twentieth century who survives in history, in the hopes and aspirations of mankind for a peaceful world, and in whatever ideals of international service that the American people still cherish. One thing is certain, now that nations have the power to sear virtually the entire face of the earth: The prophet of 1919–1920 was right in his vision; the challenge that he raised then is today no less real and no less urgent than it was in his own time.

Henry Cabot Lodge's Perspective

WILLIAM C. WIDENOR

Just as Wilson was heralding the formation of his "league for peace" Charles Evans Hughes warned that "it is not the part of wisdom to create expectations on the part of the people of the world which the Covenant cannot satisfy." On that point Wilson would have differed, for Hughes's advice ran counter to the president's conception of political leadership. Believing that in international relations idealism could be a self-fulfilling proposition, Wilson saw his duty in inspiring the people to believe that they need no longer be content with human imperfection, that the war could be a war to end all wars and the league a means of ensuring perpetual

From *Henry Cabot Lodge and the Search for an American Foreign Policy.* © 1980 The Regents of the University of California, reprinted by permission of the University of California Press.

peace. He first engaged and then ultimately commanded and personified the hopes and aspirations of millions both at home and abroad. Many Americans came to believe (no other word is as descriptive) in the League of Nations. Their acceptance of the League bore many of the marks of an act of faith rather than of careful analysis of the factors (other than faith) requisite for the successful operation of a collective security system. When their hopes did not materialize, when the Senate developed reservations with respect to American entry into the League and international relations returned to their normal desultory pattern, it was easier to believe that this state of affairs was the result of the machinations of "evil" men than to entertain the proposition that their own faith might have been misplaced. The corollary of the "self-righteous martyred saint attitude" adopted toward Wilson by his many disciples was the idea that the will of the American people had been frustrated by "a little group of powerful men" or, more specifically, by the "craft and acumen," "the consummate cunning" of Lodge, who almost single-handedly "beat back this enormous movement" and kept the United States out of the League. Hence, the prominent place in American demonology which Lodge has long occupied.

Such interpretations vary in their sophistication, but share a common quality: their defense of Wilson and of his conception of a league rests primarily on impugning the motives and character of those who opposed him. That alone should be sufficient to arouse suspicion. Moreover, such criticism has inhibited rational consideration of the problems involved in the enforcement of peace, and it is precisely on that point that American thinking has tended to imprecision. Apparently, as Lodge once suggested, we will always have with us "those who wish to have the world's peace assured by force, without using force to do it." The conclusions of those who have made the most thorough study of the issues involved (John Chalmers Vinson's work on Article X and Warren Kuehl's careful comparison of Wilson's conception of a league with that of other prominent American internationalists) indicate that ideas did play an important, even determinant, role in the struggle over the league. It served the interests of many of those involved to believe that the struggle was essentially one of partisan politics and personal hatred, but the real problem was that Americans could not agree upon the nature of the League they wanted or upon the arrangements necessary to make it work.

Both Wilson and Taft occupied an uncomfortable position. As Walter Lippmann later recognized, "in them the idealism which prompts Americans to make large and resounding commitments was combined with the pacifism which causes Americans to shrink from the measures of force that are needed to support the commitments." Wishing to minimize the exertions so important to the Europeans (the commitment to come to their aid with troops), hoping and often convincing himself that the United States would never in practice be called upon to fulfill its commitment to use force on behalf of the territorial integrity of other states, Wilson came to depict the League in a manner reflecting the isolationism to which it was the supposed antithesis. Trapped by the contradictions inherent in their own desires (a contradiction laid bare by Borah when he pointedly asked "What will your league amount to if it does not contain powers that no one dreams of giving it"), it is perhaps understandable that when it came their turn to write the nation's history Wilsonians found it profitable to argue personalities and motives rather than issues.

It also behooves us to be suspicious of those interpretations which depict Lodge as the villain of the fight over the League because that was the manner in which it pleased Wilson to view the struggle. Lodge was singled out by name in the 1920 Democratic platform for his alleged inconsistency on the League and peace issue, and "the Republican Senate" was condemned for "its refusal to ratify the treaty merely because it was the product of Democratic statesmanship, thus interposing partisan envy and personal hatred in the way of peace and renewed prosperity of the world." The objections to such an interpretation are manifold. Apart from the fact that it denigrates the role of ideas in the determination of human behavior, it remains a little too convenient. The Democrats found it politic to run against Lodge in 1918 and again in 1920, and Wilsonians have been doing so ever since. Lodge was never a popular figure on the American political scene. Indeed, he presented an inviting target and outside New England his very virtues were readily converted into liabilities. As even the admiring Barrett Wendell noted, Lodge was "not sympathetic in either temper or in address"; even when "really large and constructive in his purposes, he . . . managed to impress people as a rather cynical opportunist at best." It was Lodge's misfortune that his demeanor presented a standing invitation to opponents to disregard the issues he wanted to stress, but it would not seem unreasonable to expect historians to endeavor to surmount that obstacle.

Implicit in all "Wilsonian" interpretations is the assumption that Lodge would have supported a league such as Wilson advocated if a Republican had proposed it. Certainly Lodge hated Wilson and was intent on effecting his political demise, but that does not mean that his animosity was solely a function of personal or partisan feelings. He also hated what Wilson stood for and the way he did things, not least the manner in which he conducted the nation's foreign policy. It is one thing to claim that Lodge had a political and even personal interest in the defeat of the League, which is obvious, and yet quite another to say that interest so dominated his thinking that he would have supported a league such as Wilson fashioned if only its sponsorship had been different. That goes in the face of Lodge's course with respect to the Taft arbitration treaties and of everything which I have been able to discover about his foreign policy views. Lodge's views on Wilson's league were not only compatible with, but flowed directly out of his perception of the type of foreign policy most appropriate under American conditions. . . .

Wilson preferred as in May of 1916 and January of 1917 to let the league be all things to all men. He made no attempt to educate public opinion on what Lodge considered the all important details of prospective world organization. Both personally and politically he found it convenient to ignore the problems inherent in the relationship between force and peace. The league as depicted in his Fourteen Points Address seemed to rest on an implied threat to use force against would-be violators of the new international order, and yet the pacifist impulse in his thinking and in that of many of his followers was so strong that it was tempting to picture a league so morally ascendant that force would never have to be employed. It was this particularly Wilsonian straddle that caused Roosevelt to focus on the problem of credibility, and to fear that Wilson would inevitably make the league a thing of words and do his best to substitute "some fake policy of permanent pacifism" for one based on permanent preparation.

While the war was in progress Lodge also had little to say on the subject of a league. To him all talk of a league still carried the connotation of a desire for a negotiated settlement, and he saw no reason to change the position detailed in his February 1, 1917 speech on "The President's Plan For World Peace." When the subject of the league again came to the fore he had only to reach back to that speech for his arguments. It continued to serve his purposes. He had emphasized the practical and political difficulties involved in the construction of a system to actually enforce peace, had warned against entangling the question of how to make peace permanent with the peace to end the present war, and had insisted that "a treaty which cannot or will not be scrupulously fulfilled is infinitely worse than no treaty at all." He recurred to the latter point during the war, characterizing the maintenance of the sanctity of treaties as "one of the war's great features and objects." But like most Congressmen he focused his attention on more immediate issues and left it to Roosevelt, the publicist in the partnership of parliamentarian and publicist, to carry on discussion of the league proposal.

To Roosevelt the spirit behind a league remained of more significance than its institutional arrangements. He thought it might be possible to limit future wars, but only "by wise action, based equally on observed good faith and on thoroughly prepared strength" and those, he insisted, were the precise characteristics in which his countrymen were wanting. Hence, he accorded a higher priority to the cultivation of those characteristics than to the formation of a league. "Sound nationalism" was still a necessary antecedent to "sound internationalism." Roosevelt was ready to see the United States join a league to enforce peace, but only on condition that "we do not promise what will not or ought not to be performed" and "do not surrender our right and duty to prepare our own strength for our own defense." Above all he wanted the country to be wary of those who thought it possible "to secure peace without effort and safety without service and sacrifice. . . ." His greatest problem with Wilson's version of a league was that the President seemed to be telling the American people that a league and preparedness need not go hand in hand, that if they accepted the league they could safely reject preparedness. Roosevelt, on the contrary, felt that only on the basis of the adoption of a policy of permanent national preparedness could the U.S. afford to try the league experiment. He and Taft were eventually able to get together on the league issue because Taft came out for universal military training, and this allowed Roosevelt to say that he backed the League to Enforce Peace as an addition to, and not as a substitute for, national preparation.

The battle lines, drawn since the winter of 1916–17, became ever more taut as the war neared its conclusion. "Unanimity in approving a world organization," as Lansing later so aptly put it, "did not mean that opinion might not differ radically in working out its forms and functions." Just under the surface of support for the principle lay a plethora of qualifications. Roosevelt in conditioning his support for league membership on a prior commitment to national preparedness was engaged in something of a personal crusade, but there was also a widespread feeling (at least in Republican ranks) that the league was already a reality, that the Allies constituted a de facto league. Lodge thought the Allies a "good enough league for the present at least," and even Taft and Lowell felt the league might initially consist of only the major Allied powers—England, France, Italy, Japan, and the U.S. Other and predictable Republican concerns were the preservation of the Monroe Doctrine (with Roosevelt taking up Cosmos's idea and suggesting the reservation of specific spheres of influence under any league arrangement) and the revitalization of the Hague Tribunal, a way of expressing their continued interest in a juridically based internationalism. Most people were still talking about a league in general terms, but the magic phrase "league for peace" already masked many different and even contradictory ideas about how it ought to be constituted. Many people had already formulated distinct reservations with respect to a league. . . .

It was "easy to talk about a league of nations and the beauty and necessity of peace," he [Lodge] said, "but the hard practical demand is, are you ready to put your soldiers and your sailors at the disposition of other nations?" In public he left the answer open, but, aware of the strength of the pacifist and isolationist blocs in Congress, he never for a moment thought a plan for an international army could get through the Senate. There was an insuperable obstacle to the formation of an effective league. That obstacle lay deep in the American character and in the nature of the American political system. Hence Lodge could confidently state that "the strength of our position is to show up the impossibility of any of the methods proposed and invite them, when they desire our support, to produce their terms; they cannot do it." What was required for the construction of an effective collective security organization was never politically feasible at home. It was a dilemma from which Lodge determined that Wilson should not be permitted to escape.

Though he was already in close contact with people like Beveridge who were reassuming the traditional "isolationist" posture, Lodge's concerns were never theirs. True, their arguments were often the same and Lodge was as opposed as anyone to any derogation of national sovereignty. But Lodge cared about the peace settlement in Europe in a way that the "isolationists" never did (was concerned not only about its morality but about its viability), and many of the considerations which impelled him to oppose a league of Wilsonian design were "internationalist" reasons. During the war he often made the "internationalist" point that, the Monroe Doctrine notwithstanding, we *were* interfering in Europe and there was no longer any place for talk about the war being three thousand miles away and of no concern. Naturally, he still believed in Washington's injunction against permanent alliances, but, as he expressed it, "we must make up our minds that as we have shared in the war we must share in the settlement of peace." He also had a concern for the preservation of close relations with the Allies unknown among those who became isolationists. Though technically the U.S. had no treaty of alliance with those on whose side it fought, technicalities, he maintained, were of no consequence in the presence of facts. "To encourage or even to permit any serious differences to arise between the United States and Great Britain, or with France, or Italy, or Belgium, would be a world calamity of the worst kind." Carrying out the peace with Germany would be the work of a generation and would necessitate the closest cooperation among the Allies.

Another measure of Lodge's internationalism can be derived from the fact that on the eve of the Peace Conference he seemed willing to go considerably further than Wilson in making the United States a guarantor of the European settlement. He considered it imperative that the Slavic nationalities be helped in establishing themselves as independent states, and privately he even suggested the possibility of the United States becoming a mandatory for such trouble spots as Constantinople. At a time when Wilson was trying to distance himself from the Allied governments, Lodge wanted to tie the United States more closely to them.

> We cannot halt or turn back now. We must do our share to carry out the peace as we have done our share to win the war, of which the peace is an integral part. We must do our share in the occupation of German territory. . . . We can not escape doing our part in aiding the peoples to whom we have helped to give freedom and independence in establishing themselves with ordered governments, for in no other way can we erect the barriers which are essential to prevent another outbreak by Germany upon the world. . . .

Lodge's outlook, in short, was no more isolationist than Wilson's and, in its emphasis on sacrifice and on the responsibilities of the United States, perhaps less so. Even Taft was prompted to remark in response to Lodge's Senate speech on the 21st of December that it "was the best yet made on the aims of the Allies and the elements of a satisfactory treaty of peace. . . . Its great merit is in its broad vision of the real purposes of the United States and her present obligation. . . . He [Lodge] is not a little American."

Both Lodge and Wilson were internationalists interested in making the peace secure, but there the similarity ended. Their respective priorities were quite different. The President's mind, as Lodge suggested, was "fixed on general questions lying outside the making of a peace with Germany." Lodge could not have been too surprised that immediately upon reaching Paris, Wilson announced that the foundation of a League of Nations would be the first and foremost task of the conference. The Senator believed, on the other hand, that "the first and controlling purpose of the peace must be to put Germany in such a position that it will be physically impossible for her to break out again upon other nations with a war for world conquest." Lodge saw no alternative. Only by building on present conditions, only by the "existing and most efficient league" [the Allies], could the peace be effectively implemented. "The attempt to form now a league of nations— and I mean an effective league, with power to enforce its decrees—no other is worth discussing—can tend at this moment only to embarrass the peace that we ought to make at once with Germany." Both privately in a memorandum prepared to be shown to Balfour, Clemenceau, and Nitti, and publicly in the Senate he warned that the consequences of Wilson's persistence could be dire:

> . . . under no circumstances must provisions for such a league be made a part of the peace treaty which concludes the war with Germany. Any attempt to do this would not only long delay the signature of the treaty peace, which should not be unduly postponed, but it would make the adoption of the treaty, unamended, by the Senate of the United States and other ratifying bodies, extremely doubtful.

There developed out of this what Arno Mayer has described as a "transnational political confrontation." The patterns of allegiance and mistrust formed in the years of America's neutrality were too strong to be overcome. Lodge so distrusted the President that he was quite willing to undermine his position at the Peace Conference. In his affinity for the British, Lodge was prepared to undercut Wilson as Hamilton had once undercut John Jay. His views had long been more in accord with those of the leaders of the Allies, and now he sought to encourage them to stand up to Wilson, particularly on the league issue and the exaction of physical guarantees. The memorandum he gave to Henry White might "in certain contingencies be very important to them [Balfour, Clemenceau, and Nitti] in strengthening their position." His December 21 Senate speech was "intended chiefly for the benefit of the Allies."

Wilson for his part distrusted not only Lodge but also the Allied leaders and told his advisers that the men with whom they were about to deal did not really represent their respective nations. Tragically, events had long since precluded even the possibility of Lodge and Wilson listening to one another. Lodge's warnings probably only increased Wilson's determination to put his own stamp on the Peace Conference. Perhaps even more unfortunate, their disdain for each other also precluded an appreciation of their respective abilities and strengths. As a result Wilson began to think in terms of arranging things so that the Senate would be forced to accept a league and Lodge, having confidence only in the sense of the Allies, determined to "force Wilson, as we forced him before, to do what ought to be done but which he is not planning to do." Thus did they underestimate one another and thus did a historic and (if there be any logic in history) well-nigh inevitable struggle begin. . . .

The initiative was entirely Wilson's. It was his League that was before the Peace Conference and his League that would eventually come before the Senate. Only if Lodge, Root, or Roosevelt had been in actual control of American foreign policy could they have constructed an alternative to the Wilsonian settlement. As it was, their ideas were little more than hypotheses. The time was opportune; the United States was ripe for an abandonment of the isolation against which Lodge had long, and Wilson more recently, contended. But there remained the question of what kind of internationalism would take its place. Root was convinced that Wilson was on the wrong track and told Lodge that if his proposal is not materially amended "the world will before very long wake up to realize that a great opportunity has been wasted in the doing of a futile thing." Lodge also felt that a great opportunity was being wasted and urged Root to "show the public what ought to be done to accomplish as much as can practically be accomplished by a union of the nations to promote general peace and disarmament." This Root soon did in a March 29 letter to Republican National Chairman Will Hays, a letter which culminated in six far-reaching amendments to Wilson's draft. But their position was defensive by definition; they could try to amend Wilson's proposal but they had no power to put anything in its place. The President was in a position to force them to adopt a narrow, insular nationalism in order to prevent the construction of what they regarded as a dangerous, unstable form of internationalism. "In trying to do too much," Lodge feared (prophetically as it turned out) that "we might lose all." It might have been otherwise. As Root recounted, when the proposal had been laid before the Paris Conference, the French representative, Leon Bourgeois, emphasized that "we do not present it as something that is final, but only as the result of an honest effort to be discussed and to be examined not only by this conference but the public opinion of the world."

But this was not the manner in which Wilson presented the League to the American people. He offered a finished product, a *fait accompli*. On his return to Paris, Wilson did try to meet some of Taft's suggestions for amendments, did try, for example, to secure some recognition of the Monroe Doctrine and establish a category of domestic issues over which the League would have no jurisdiction, but one would be hard pressed to argue that the Covenant underwent any substantial revision between February 15 and April 28, 1919, when the final draft was published. Lodge called Root that night to say that he found the amendments unsatisfactory and thought the League in its new form "but slight improvement over the first draft." His complaints were essentially the same as in February. Still he was probably not too surprised. At the time of the Round Robin he still hoped to jolt the Peace Conference into a full reconsideration of the Covenant, but only two weeks later (after Wilson's uncompromising New York Opera speech) he had despaired of this happening and had suggested that it would have to be done elsewhere—plainly in the Senate. . . .

Never a universalist, Lodge early sought to differentiate between a "general, indefinite, unlimited scheme of always being called upon to meddle in European, Asian and African questions" and a policy designed to ensure that the strong barrier-states necessary to fetter Germany were erected. As he saw it, the future peace of the world depended, not on the universal prevalence of American ideals, but rather on the strength of France, a fact which Wilson seemed not to appreciate.

Lodge's conception of America's world role was as idealistic as Wilson's, but there was a crucial difference. Lodge believed that America had evolved a special, historical individuality and a unique system of values which were as much the product of propitious circumstance as anything else. Though he was prepared to go to great lengths to defend and preserve that individuality, he did not, like Wilson, seek its preservation in an attempt to secure its universal acceptance. The United States, at least toward Europe, served best as an example; it would remain mankind's best hope only so long as it did not destroy itself by becoming involved in every broil that desolated the earth. Conservative in his assessment of the human condition and too particularist to believe it possible to universalize American values, he readily conceded that Europe had different interests and priorities and understood its own needs better than could any American. The United States, in his view, did have an interest in the European settlement, but he was quick to emphasize that "there is a wide difference between taking a suitable part and bearing due responsibility in world affairs and plunging the United States into every controversy and conflict on the face of the globe."

Lodge and Root would have done it differently:

> It seemed to me at the time and has seemed to me ever since so clear what the President ought to have done; that he should have said to the Powers associated with us in the war: "We want the world made safe against Germany and as long as that is done we are content. So far as European matters are concerned, you are the people to settle them. Settle them all among yourselves and we will back you up. When it comes to Asia and Africa, of course we expect to have a voice; and we ask to be let alone in our own hemisphere." If that had been done the situation today would have been wholly different. But Mr. Wilson has undertaken to be the final umpire in every European question, incurring hostility both for himself and for his country, and meddling with things in which the United States has no interest whatsoever.

But Wilson, having less appreciation of the factors that circumscribed the nation's ability to act wisely in foreign affairs, so influenced the Peace Conference that they "made omnipotence their province and occupied the entire sphere on national and international relations the world over." Policy divorced from the reality of interest produced such aberrations as the Conference's decisions respecting Fiume, Danzig, and Shantung. It probably would have turned out better, Lodge felt, had it all been in Clemenceau's hands. At any rate, the sooner a country that so mismanaged things got out of the business of meddling in other nation's affairs the better.

Shantung, like Fiume, had an importance which transcended the significance of the territory involved or the alleged "immorality" of the Conference's disposition of it. Lodge seems actually to have believed that "the taking of Shantung . . . from an ally and handing it over to another ally as the price of a signature to the League is one of the blackest things in the history of diplomacy," equalling even the partition of Poland. This was probably not so much because he was a staunch defender of China as because he was suspicious of "the Prussia of the East." It was the Shantung question that triggered massive attrition on the left flank of Wilson's support, and Lodge used the issue to the hilt in the struggle for domestic political advantage. But perhaps of even more significance to Lodge and Root was the fact that Article X of the Covenant appeared to bind the United States to defend the Shantung settlement, to sustain Japan against China should the latter rise up and attack Japan in an effort to undo "the great wrong" of the cession of control over Shantung. Public reaction to the Shantung arrangement convinced them that this was something the United States would never do, and this in turn made them regard Article X with even greater suspicion. What had a telling effect on public opinion in the short run, and put Wilson at a political disadvantage, was also predictive of the form American public opinion would take were the United States ever asked to support its pledge under Article X. Therein lay a justification for exploiting the Shantung issue and also proof that one can not readily draw a line between "political" and "principled" opposition to the League. . . .

Another measure of the nature and extent of Lodge's internationalism would follow if we could give a definite answer to Arthur Link's question whether Lodge was himself "an irreconcilable who desired the defeat of the treaty, or . . . merely a strong reservationist. . . ." Another way of putting it would be to ask whether he sincerely advocated ratification with reservations and made a sincere effort to effect the compromises that would have made ratification possible. While some evidence supports the claim that Lodge was just going through the motions and had no intention of compromising with the Democrats, those who have emphasized Lodge's "willingness to accept the treaty with reservations" and the fact that "he actually tried to get the treaty through with his reservations" have slightly the better of the argument. Among the evidence they adduce is the negotiation Lodge undertook with Colonel House through Stephen Bonsal in an effort to work out compromise language, Lodge's allowing the treaty to come to a second vote, his willingness to enter into a bipartisan conference in January of 1920 which sought to devise reservations language acceptable to most Senators, and finally his support of changes in his own reservations that were designed to meet Wilson's objections (as when he vainly tried to secure a provision making American withdrawal dependent on a joint, rather than on a concurrent resolution of Congress).

Of more than passing interest are Lodge's relationships with other principals in the struggle over the League and their opinion of him and his position. Revealing, both in its praise of Lodge and in its foreclosure of any other route to ratification, is a letter from Root to Lodge dated December 1, 1919, well after the vote in November. In Root's view Lodge's leadership in the Senate had been "extraordinarily able"; he termed it "one of the greatest examples of parliamentary leadership" he had ever known and expressed the wish that all the friends of the Treaty could understand that it was Lodge who had given the Treaty "its only chance for ratification. . . ." Another important figure, Viscount Grey, sent by the British Government as its Ambassador to the United States with the special mission of composing American differences of opinion on the League, apparently came to the same conclusion as Root. He is said to have commented sympathetically on Lodge's handling of the treaty, and in a letter to the London *Times* he advocated British acceptance of the Lodge reservations as the best means of securing American participation.

The relationship between Lodge and the irreconcilables also deserves attention. Senator Knox thought that only pressure from the irreconcilables had kept Lodge in line, that "on one occasion he was on the point of surrendering to the mild reservationists. . . . ." It is not an unreasonable construction of Borah's January 24, 1920, letter to Lodge (threatening to bolt the party unless Lodge dropped his backstage compromise negotiation with the Democrats) to say it demonstrated that Borah believed Lodge was doing his best to get the treaty ratified. The irreconcilables forced him to break off those negotiations, but in the following weeks he reasserted his independence and continued to modify his reservations, their views notwithstanding. He taunted the irreconcilables with the claim that his reservations had "acquired a sanctity with some of my friends which they did not have, I think, until after the 19th of November," announced his intention to support improvements in both substance and phraseology which might lead to securing a two-thirds vote for the treaty, and finally even suggested a substitute for that most sacrosanct of reservations, that to Article X. In addition he wrote a letter to Beveridge on February 16, 1920, which seemed to anticipate a favorable vote on ratification and which had the evident purpose of consoling Beveridge by telling him, first, that the reservations made the League safe for the United States and, second, that no one would be able to say it was a victory for Wilson since the reservations were "too clearly ours to allow such a charge to have any effect." Admittedly, the evidence cited here is selective. But it seems sufficient to make a fairly good case for the argument that Lodge was willing to acquiesce in ratification on the basis of strong and effective reservations. Nevertheless, that leaves much unsaid, for some of those reservations embodied principles which Lodge was not ready to compromise.

Many, however, have not been convinced of Lodge's willingness to accept ratification on the basis of his own reservations. A frequent charge has been that the reservations were a device to secure the treaty's defeat, and that if Wilson had shown any signs of accepting them Lodge would have come up with more drastic ones. These charges apparently had their origin in a 1928 Council on Foreign Relations publication alleging that Lodge had "declared privately" that he "had proposed reservations which he was confident the President would reject, and that he was prepared to add to them if it were necessary, his purpose being to have the League rejected." However, there is no hard evidence to support such an accusation. It has the markings of a rationalization employed by those seeking to defend Wilson's intransigence and is devoid of political logic. The Lodge who knew within what tight limits he had to operate would never have risked such an affront to the mild reservationists.

A better case has been made in support of the view that Lodge was really an irreconcilable and opposed to any league whatsoever. Some historians have argued against Lodge's sincerity by citing remarks and publications from a later date. However, all their damaging evidence postdates the final vote on the treaty. Lodge did gradually become more irreconcilable. Will Hays remarked on that and so did Root who, though he continued to believe that Lodge initially wanted to join the League with reservations, recognized that he had gradually fallen under the influence of Brandegee and the other irreconcilables. Lodge came eventually to feel that the Senate's rejection of the League had been "a fortunate result." He may even have thought so shortly after the vote. There is considerable psychological resonance in Alice Longworth's observation that though he "at one time persuaded himself to believe that he was in favor of the League of Nations if amply safeguarded by reservations, my opinion is that in his heart he was really as opposed to it in any shape as an irreconcilable. . . ." His views changed in response to the country's mood; as the country became more irreconcilable (not an unreasonable interpretation of the 1920 election results) he moved in the same direction, the more easily as the country's mood confirmed his view that America was not ready for such undertakings. But does that necessarily reflect on his sincerity in advocating ratification of the League before March 19, 1920, or on his willingness to compromise toward that end? It doesn't directly, but it seems to suggest that we may have been asking the wrong questions. Since Lodge appears to have abandoned his support for ratification rather readily after March 19, we might better ask whether he ever believed in the League and whether he thought the differences between his conception of a league and Wilson's—between his conception of the proper scope of American internationalism and the President's— could be compromised. . . .

Lodge was skeptical about the League from the outset and never entertained high hopes for it. In confidence he predicted its failure and to Lord Bryce he expressed the opinion that the League was "a mere ornament" since "the real force under the treaty with Germany is placed in the hands of the five great Powers." While sure that reservations would "do more for the chances of life to the League than anything else," he felt bound "to confess that this League is altogether too much like a political alliance to make me feel that it is likely to be either enduring or successful." Even worse from his point of view, the League arrangements sought to deny the power realities that underlay its existence and to that end made extravagant promises incapable of fulfillment. Lodge saw through to the heart of the dilemma confronting those trying to construct a workable universal collective security organization: "Really to fulfill the advertised intention of its framers, it would have been necessary to put force behind the League, . . ." and to have provided for an international army with an international command.

That being politically unacceptable, the result was the murky compromise known as Article X under which Member States pledged to defend one another's territorial integrity and political independence, it being left to the League Council to "advise upon the means by which this obligation shall be fulfilled." This uneasy compromise caused Wilson considerable difficulty at home; it permitted his opponents to attack the League from both sides in the manner of Borah's famous question: "What will your league amount to if it does not contain powers that no one dreams of giving it." This same uneasy compromise haunted the League throughout its history. Canada tried to have Article X suppressed in 1920, and the League Council could not in 1923 even decide whether its advice was binding.

Wilson, as John Chalmers Vinson has observed, never gave a compelling interpretation of American responsibilities under Article Ten. He was damned if he did and damned if he didn't. He could only equivocate. Though claiming that Article X was "the very backbone of the whole Covenant," he dared not claim that the Council's advice derogated from Congress's right "to exercise its independent judgment in all matters of peace and war." Consequently, he was left to resolve the contradictions inherent in American participation in the Covenant in the following unsatisfactory manner. The engagement under Article X, he claimed:

> . . . constitutes a very grave and solemn moral obligation. But it is a moral, not a legal obligation, and leaves our Congress absolutely free to put its own interpretation upon it in all cases that call for action. It is binding in conscience only, not in law.

At first glance it would appear that Wilson and Lodge were not far apart; Lodge wanted only a reservation saying that the United States "assumes no obligation" under Article X "unless in any particular case the Congress . . . shall by act or joint resolution so provide." But appearances were in this case particularly deceiving. To Wilson and his supporters the moral obligation was real (if only as a matter of faith), and their objection to Lodge's reservation to Article X was that it specifically removed that moral obligation. This was not a minor point, but rather *the* obstacle to ratification; the nature of the obligation assumed by Member States would determine what kind of organization the League would be. To Lodge and Root it appeared as if Wilson and the Democrats wanted to accept an obligation which the United States might thereafter refuse, while their position has been characterized as one of wanting to refuse an obligation which might thereafter be accepted. Believing that under American conditions it was important to make all commitments as definite as possible, they could never accept Wilson's attempt to distinguish between a moral and a legal obligation. It begged the question of whether the obligation was binding. Root denounced Wilson's "curious and childlike casuistry" and thought the attempted distinction "false, demoralizing and dishonest." Lodge, believing that such an obligation could only be moral, wanted to prevent there arising a situation where Congress could not exert its Constitutional rights without breaking that moral obligation. That was the purpose of his reservation to Article X; it "made us the judges of whether we should carry out the guarantees of Article 10 or not, and in case of our refusal this reservation prevented its being a breach of the treaty. . . ."

Since the success of a collective security organization would seem to rest on the absence of doubt as to the intentions of its members, that is, on the credibility of their commitments, Lodge's reservation stating that the United States assumed no obligation was a denial of the theory on which collective security was based. His reservations, though leaving the League a useful instrument of collaboration (which was the way he had conceived it in the first place), "would have transformed the League into a non-coercive or an intermediate type of international organization," That, of course, is essentially what it became.

But there remains the question of Lodge's intent and his understanding of what he was doing. Many of the irreconcilables were convinced that the reservations never amounted to anything, that once the League was set up they would influence its operation very little. Some historians in their eagerness to criticize Wilson's handling of the matter have also come to regard the Lodge reservations as innocuous. They claim that Lodge hardly hoped for more than party unity and face-saving reservations, and that therefore a "reasonably sagacious political approach" by Wilson would have assured ratification. Such arguments can, of course, be used to bolster either the case for Lodge's partisanship or the case for the "sincerity" of his internationalism, but they also carry the implication that Lodge was unfamiliar and unconcerned with the problems inherent in the application of force to ensure peace and neither appreciated Wilson's ploy nor understood how to meet it. Given what we now know about his thinking since the winter of 1916–17, that is difficult to accept. Despite the fact that he eventually became an irreconcilable, Lodge never wavered in the view that the reservations would have made the League safe for the United States. And making it safe for the United States could not help but change its structure. Lodge took his reservations seriously and so did Wilson; they both knew they had profound implications. They were so far apart in their views on Article X that it is reasonable to assume there was virtually no prospect for compromise. However, Americans have an abiding faith in their ability to compromise and that made Lodge's task more difficult. But Wilson at least would probably have understood and agreed with James Beck's observation that "the reservations would have driven a 'coach and four' through the League of Nations and made the obligations of the United States thereunder almost nominal. . . ."

Lodge was unyielding on two crucial points. In October of 1919 he told the Senate that "this treaty will never be ratified unless the Monroe Doctrine is finally and absolutely reserved from the jurisdiction of the League." In February of 1920 he declared that he could "never assent to any change in principle in the two reservations relating to the Monroe Doctrine and Article 10." This could lead one to conclude that his efforts to reach a compromise in the context of the bipartisan committee were "an elaborate charade," but perhaps a fairer interpretation would be that, though he was convinced that compromise was impossible, he found it necessary to demonstrate that fact to others. Nothing short of an actual demonstration that nothing could be done by way of compromise would satisfy public opinion, he told Beveridge. Lodge attributed this to the press, which seemed "to overlook the fact that with the mass of the Senators this is not a question of personal fortune or party advantage but a great question of principle on which they cannot yield any essential point.'' To the end he complained that ''the differences between what Hitchcock offers and what we are willing to accept are much deeper and broader than people generally understand.'' It was to counteract that situation that he agreed to the bipartisan conferences. ''It was,'' he wrote to a confidant, ''something we had to go through.'' It might also be described as the culmination of the educative process in which he had long been engaged. Viewed in that light the fact that he made up his mind ''that if the conference was to break up without an agreement it should be on Article 10'' appears less Machiavellian. Article 10 was ''the crucial point throughout the contest over the covenant. . . .'' What Lodge did was to arrange to break off the negotiations ''on a question not only where I knew we could stand before the country but where, also, I could have my votes of more than one-third.''

This suggests not necessarily the sincere advocate of ratification with reservations, nor yet the reasonable compromiser, but a man strongly opposed to the Wilsonian conception of a League and determined to reveal its faults and prevent the United States from getting deeply involved in it. As Lodge saw it, the League was grievously flawed and would not work. Thomas Bailey once observed that Lodge was a failure if he really wanted the Treaty, but he could scarcely have ''really wanted'' something in which he did not believe. Whether the United States joined the League was never of as much concern to him as were the conditions under which it joined. Those, as Wilson also understood, would determine the nature of the organization and involved ''great principles.'' Lodge's detached view on the matter of American entry gave him a considerable tactical advantage and permitted him to maintain close working relations both with those who wanted and with those who did not want the United States in the League. He thereby maximized his control of the situation and ensured that no matter which way the final vote went his views would prevail. . . .

Wilson claimed not only that the United States had gone to war to establish a League of Nations, but that ''the opinion of the whole world swung to our support and the support of the nations associated with us in the great struggle'' because of that advocacy. Moreover, he insisted that any reservation to Article X would plunge the world back into imperialism and reaction, a clear invitation to the American people to attribute anything short of perfection in international relations to Lodge's reservations. Never willing to admit that there were serious problems involved in the formation of a league to enforce peace, Wilson sought to limit such discussion by the introduction of yet another myth, namely that the Republican Senate ''interposing partisan envy and personal hatred in the way of the peace and prosperity of the world'' had refused to ratify the treaty ''merely because it was the product of Democratic statesmanship.'' Wilson knew something about lost causes and the manner in which they were romanticized. As a result, under the influence of another and even more horrible war, a new generation of Americans found it easy to believe that had the United States joined the League that war might not have occurred. In their devotion to atoning for the "mistake" of 1919–20 by constructing a new international organization for securing the world's peace, they were as blind to some of the other requisites of a lasting peace settlement as Wilson had been twenty-five years earlier. Instead of learning from their elders' mistakes, they only compounded their tragedy.

✻ *F U R T H E R   R E A D I N G*

Lloyd Ambrosius, *Woodrow Wilson and the American Diplomatic Tradition: The League Fight in Perspective* (1987)
Thomas A. Bailey, *Woodrow Wilson and the Great Betrayal* (1945)
——, *Woodrow Wilson and the Lost Peace* (1944)
Paul Birdsall, *Versailles Twenty Years After* (1941)
Robert H. Ferrell, *Woodrow Wilson and World War I* (1985)
Denna F. Fleming, *The United States and the League of Nations 1918–1920* (1942)
Inga Floto, *Colonel House in Paris* (1973)
John A. Garraty, *Henry Cabot Lodge* (1953)
Lawrence E. Gelfand, *The Inquiry: American Preparations for Peace* (1963)
W. Stull Holt, *Treaties Defeated by the Senate* (1933)
Herbert Hoover, *The Ordeal of Woodrow Wilson* (1958)
Warren F. Kuehl, *Seeking World Order* (1969)
A. Lentin, *Lloyd George, Woodrow Wilson, and the Guilt of Germany* (1985)
N. Gordon Levin, *Woodrow Wilson and World Politics* (1968)
Arno Mayer, *Politics and Diplomacy of Peacemaking* (1967)
Keith Nelson, *Victors Divided* (1973)
Robert E. Osgood, *Ideals and Self-Interest in American Foreign Relations* (1953)
Stuart I. Rochester, *American Liberal Disillusionment in the Wake of World War I* (1977)
Klaus Schwabe, *Woodrow Wilson, Revolutionary Germany, and Peacemaking, 1918–1919* (1985)
Ralph A. Stone, *The Irreconcilables* (1970)
John Thompson, *Russia, Bolshevism, and the Versailles Peace* (1966)
Seth P. Tillman, *Anglo-American Relations at the Paris Peace Conference, 1919* (1961)
Marc Trachtenburg, *Reparations in World Politics* (1986)
Arthur Walworth, *Wilson and the Peacemakers* (1986)

CHAPTER

4

Diplomacy in the 1920s

Historians used to treat the 1920s as a backwater between the fast-moving streams of the First and Second World War eras. It was supposedly a time of "isolationism," when the American people, disillusioned over the souring experience of World War I and the League fight at home, pressed their government to reduce its international obligations, to return to unilateralism. New scholarship has revised that view. Historians now find a mix of unilateralism and internationalism, with the United States significantly involved in world affairs—helping Europe resolve its debts-reparations problem, for example. The United States remained a major trader; indeed, it had become an economic giant. Business-government cooperation helped advance the American economic frontier abroad. With adequate military power to meet threats to national security, the United States participated in disarmament conferences and continued to count Latin America as its sphere of influence. In a world beset by economic dislocations, the challenging ideology of Bolshevism, and revolutionary nationalism like that in Mexico, the United States did not shrink from trying to influence international relations. American confusion there seemed to be, but not weakness, except perhaps in Asia, and certainly not withdrawal. The characteristics of 1920s diplomacy are the subject of this chapter.

❀ D O C U M E N T S

At the Washington Conference of 1921-1922, Secretary of State Charles Evans Hughes insisted on substantial naval disarmament in a major opening address on November 12, 1921, reprinted here as the first document. The three conference treaties are reprinted as the second document. The third document, dated July 19, 1923, is a Hughes letter explaining why the United States still refused to recognize the government of Soviet Russia. Secretary of Commerce Herbert Hoover was an economic expansionist who mobilized his department to aid American business abroad. In a March 16, 1926, speech (the fourth document) he explained foreign trade's place in the American economic system. In late 1926 the Coolidge administration ordered troops into Nicaragua when that Latin American country erupted in civil war, threatening the power of the American-backed Conservative party. In the fifth document, a leading anti-imperialist, Senator Burton

K. Wheeler of Montana, in a speech of January 26, 1927, condemned this new United States intervention. At the Pan American Conference in Havana, Cuba, the United States faced Latin American criticism. When, on February 18, 1928, one delegate introduced a resolution reading, "That no state has the right to intervene in the internal affairs of another," Charles Evans Hughes, the head of the United States delegation, rose to speak against it. The resolution was withdrawn after his speech, part of which is reprinted here as the sixth document. The seventh document is the antiwar Kellogg-Briand Pact, signed by the United States and most of the world's nations in August 1928. Finally, on January 7, 1932, after the Japanese overran Manchuria, Secretary of State Henry L. Stimson issued what has become known as the Stimson Doctrine, a policy of nonrecognition that guided the United States for the rest of the decade.

Charles Evans Hughes on Naval Disarmament, 1921

But if we are warned by the inadequacy of earlier endeavors for limitation of armament, we can not fail to recognize the extraordinary opportunity now presented. We not only have the lessons of the past to guide us, not only do we have the reaction from the disillusioning experiences of war, but we must meet the challenge of imperative economic demands. What was convenient or highly desirable before is now a matter of vital necessity. If there is to be economic rehabilitation, if the longings for reasonable progress are not to be denied, if we are to be spared the uprisings of peoples made desperate in the desire to shake off burdens no longer endurable, competition in armament must stop. The present opportunity not only derives its advantage from a general appreciation of this fact, but the power to deal with the exigency now rests with a small group of nations, represented here, who have every reason to desire peace and to promote amity. The astounding ambition which lay athwart the promise of the Second Hague Conference no longer menaces the world, and the great opportunity of liberty-loving and peace-preserving democracies has come. Is it not plain that the time has passed for mere resolutions that the responsible Powers should examine the question of limitation of armament? We can no longer content ourselves with investigations, with statistics, with reports, with the circumlocution of inquiry. The essential facts are sufficiently known. The time has come, and this Conference has been called, not for general resolutions or mutual advice, but for action. . . .

It is apparent that this can not be accomplished without serious sacrifices. Enormous sums have been expended upon ships under construction and building programs which are now under way can not be given up without heavy loss. Yet if the present construction of capital ships goes forward other ships will inevitably be built to rival them and this will lead to still others. Thus the race will continue so long as ability to continue lasts. The effort to escape sacrifices is futile. We must face them or yield our purpose. . . .

In making the present proposal the United States is most solicitous to deal with the question upon an entirely reasonable and practicable basis, to the end that the just interests of all shall be adequately guarded and that national security and defense shall be maintained. Four general principles have been applied:

1. That all capital-ship building programs, either actual or projected, should be abandoned;
2. That further reduction should be made through the scrapping of certain of the older ships;
3. That in general regard should be had to the existing naval strength of the Powers concerned;
4. That the capital ship tonnage should be used as the measurement of strength for navies and a proportionate allowance of auxiliary combatant craft prescribed.

The principle features of the proposed agreement are as follows:

Capital Ships

United States.   The United States is now completing its program of 1916 calling for 10 new battleships and 6 battle cruisers. One battleship has been completed. The others are in various stages of construction; in some cases from 60 to over 80 per cent of the construction has been done. On these 15 capital ships now being built over $330,000,000 have been spent. Still, the United States is willing in the interest of an immediate limitation of naval armament to scrap all these ships.
The United States proposes, if this plan is accepted—

1. To scrap all capital ships now under construction. This includes 6 battle cruisers and 7 battleships on the ways and in course of building, and 2 battleships launched.

The total number of new capital ships thus to be scrapped is 15. The total tonnage of the new capital ships when completed would be 618,000 tons.

2. To scrap all of the older battleships up to, but not including, the *Delaware* and *North Dakota*. The number of these old battleships to be scrapped is 15. Their total tonnage is 227,740 tons.

Thus the number of capital ships to be scrapped by the United States, if this plan is accepted, is 30, with an aggregate tonnage (including that of ships in construction, if completed) of 845,740 tons.

Great Britain.   The plan contemplates that Great Britain and Japan shall take action which is fairly commensurate with this action on the part of the United States.
It is proposed that Great Britain—

1. Shall stop further construction of the 4 new Hoods, the new capital

ships not laid down but upon which money has been spent. These 4 ships, if completed, would have tonnage displacement of 172,000 tons.

2. Shall, in addition, scrap her pre-dreadnaughts, second line battleships, and first line battleships up to, but not including, the *King George V* class.

These, with certain pre-dreadnaughts which it is understood have already been scrapped, would amount to 19 capital ships and a tonnage reduction of 411,375 tons.

The total tonnage of ships thus to be scrapped by Great Britain (including the tonnage of the 4 Hoods, if completed) would be 583,375 tons.

Japan.   It is proposed that Japan

1. Shall abandon her program of ships not yet laid down, viz., the *Kii*, *Owari*, *No. 7* and *No. 8* battleships, and *Nos. 5, 6, 7,* and *8,* battle cruisers.

It should be observed that this does not involve the stopping of construction, as the construction of none of these ships has been begun.

2. Shall scrap 3 capital ships (the *Mutsu* launched, the *Tosa*, and *Kago* in course of building) and 4 battle cruisers (the *Amagi* and *Akagi* in course of building, and the *Atoga* and *Takao* not yet laid down, but for which certain material has been assembled).

The total number of new capital ships to be scrapped under this paragraph is seven. The total tonnage of these new capital ships when completed would be 289,100 tons.

3. Shall scrap all pre-dreadnaughts and battleships of the second line. This would include the scrapping of all ships up to, but not including, the *Settsu*; that is, the scrapping of 10 older ships, with a total tonnage of 159,828 tons.

The total reduction of tonnage on vessels existing, laid down, or for which material has been assembled (taking the tonnage of the new ships when completed), would be 448,928 tons.

Thus, under this plan there would be immediately destroyed, of the navies of the three Powers, 66 capital fighting ships, built and building, with a total tonnage of 1,878,043.

It is proposed that it should be agreed by the United States, Great Britain, and Japan that their navies, with respect to capital ships, within three months after the making of the agreement shall consist of certain ships designated in the proposal and numbering for the United States 18, for Great Britain 22, for Japan 10.

The tonnage of these ships would be as follows: Of the United States, 500,650; of Great Britain, 604,450; of Japan, 299,700. In reaching this result, the age factor in the case of the respective navies has received appropriate consideration. . . .

With the acceptance of this plan the burden of meeting the demands of competition in naval armament will be lifted. Enormous sums will be released to aid the progress of civilization. At the same time the proper demands of national defense will be adequately met and the nations will have ample opportunity during the naval holiday of 10 years to consider their future course. Preparation for offensive naval war will stop now. . . .

The Washington Conference Treaties, 1922

The Five-Power Treaty

Article III.   Subject to the provisions of Article II, the Contracting Powers shall abandon their respective capital ship building programs, and no new capital ships shall be constructed or acquired by any of the Contracting Powers except replacement tonnage which may be constructed or acquired as specified in Chapter II, Part 3. . . .

Article IV.   The total capital ship replacement tonnage of each of the Contracting Powers shall not exceed in standard displacement, for the United States, 525,000 tons (533,400 metric tons); for the British Empire 525,000 tons (533,400 metric tons); for France 175,000 tons (177,800 metric tons); for Italy 175,000 tons (177,800 metric tons): for Japan 315,000 tons (320,040 metric tons).

Article V.   No capital ship exceeding 35,000 tons (35,560 metric tons) standard displacement shall be acquired by, or constructed by, for, or within the jurisdiction of, any of the Contracting Powers.

Article VI.   No capital ship of any of the Contracting Powers shall carry a gun with a calibre in excess of 16 inches (406 millimetres).

Article VII.   The total tonnage for aircraft carriers of each of the Contracting Powers shall not exceed in standard displacement, for the United States 135,000 tons (137,160 metric tons); for the British Empire 135,000 tons (137,160 metric tons); for France 60,000 tons (60,960 metric tons); for Italy 60,000 tons (60,960 metric tons); for Japan 81,000 tons (82,296 metric tons). . . .

Article XI.   No vessel of war exceeding 10,000 tons (10,160 metric tons) standard displacement, other than a capital ship or aircraft carrier, shall be acquired by, or constructed by, for, or within the jurisdiction of, any of the Contracting Powers. Vessels not specifically built as fighting ships nor taken in time of peace under government control for fighting purposes, which are employed on fleet duties or as troop transports or in some other way for the purpose of assisting in the prosecution of hostilities otherwise than as fighting ships, shall not be within the limitations of this Article. . . .

Article XIX. The United States, the British Empire and Japan agree that the status quo at the time of the signing of the present Treaty, with regard to fortifications and naval bases, shall be maintained in their respective territories and possessions specified hereunder:

1. The insular possessions which the United States now holds or may hereafter acquire in the Pacific Ocean, except (a) those adjacent to the coast of the United States, Alaska and the Panama Canal Zone, not including the Aleutian Islands, and (b) the Hawaiian Islands;
2. Hongkong and the insular possessions which the British Empire now holds or may hereafter acquire in the Pacific Ocean, east of the meridian of 110° east longitude, except (a) those adjacent to the coast of Canada, (b) the Commonwealth of Australia and its Territories, and (c), New Zealand;
3. The following insular territories and possessions of Japan in the Pacific Ocean, to wit: the Kurile Islands, the Bonin Islands, Anami-Oshima, the Loochoo Islands, Formosa and the Pescadores, and any insular territories or possessions in the Pacific Ocean which Japan may hereafter acquire.

The maintenance of the status quo under the foregoing provisions implies that no new fortifications or naval bases shall be established in the territories and possessions specified, that no measures shall be taken to increase the existing naval facilities for the repair and maintenance of naval forces, and that no increase shall be made in the coast defenses of the territories and possessions above specified. This restriction, however, does not preclude such repair and replacement of worn-out weapons and equipment as is customary in naval and military establishments in time of peace. . . .

The Nine-Power Treaty

Article I. The Contracting Powers, other than China, agree:

1. To respect the sovereignty, the independence, and the territorial and administrative integrity of China;
2. To provide the fullest and most unembarrassed opportunity to China to develop and maintain for herself an effective and stable government;
3. To use their influence for the purpose of effectually establishing and maintaining the principle of equal opportunity for the commerce and industry of all nations throughout the territory of China;
4. To refrain from taking advantage of conditions in China in order to seek special rights or privileges which would abridge the rights of subjects or citizens of friendly States, and from countenancing action inimical to the security of such States.

Article II. The Contracting Powers agree not to enter into any treaty, agreement, arrangement or understanding, either with one another, or, individually or collectively, with any Power or Powers, which would infringe or impair the principles stated in Article I.

Article III.   With a view to applying more effectually the principles of the Open Door or equality of opportunity in China for the trade and industry of all nations, the Contracting Powers, other than China, agree that they will not seek, nor support their respective nationals in seeking—

a. any arrangement which might purport to establish in favor of their interests any general superiority of rights with respect to commercial or economic development in any designated region of China;

b. any such monopoly or preference as would deprive the nationals of any other Power of the right of undertaking any legitimate trade or industry in China, or of participating with the Chinese Government, or with any local authority, in any category of public enterprise, or which by reason of its scope, duration or geographical extent is calculated to frustrate the practical application of the principle of equal opportunity.

It is understood that the foregoing stipulations of this Article are not to be so construed as to prohibit the acquisition of such properties or rights as may be necessary to the conduct of a particular commercial, industrial or financial undertaking or to the encouragement of invention and research.

China undertakes to be guided by the principles stated in the foregoing stipulations of this Article in dealing with applications for economic rights and privileges from Governments and nationals of all foreign countries, whether parties to the present Treaty or not.

Article IV.   The Contracting Powers agree not to support any agreements by their respective nationals with each other designed to create Spheres of Influence or to provide for the enjoyment of mutually exclusive opportunities in designated parts of Chinese territory.

Article V.   China agrees that, throughout the whole of the railways in China, she will not exercise or permit unfair discrimination of any kind. In particular there shall be no discrimination whatever, direct or indirect, in respect of charges or of facilities on the ground of the nationality of passengers or the countries from which or to which they are proceeding, or the origin or ownership of goods or the country from which or to which they are consigned, or the nationality or ownership of the ship or other means of conveying such passengers or goods before or after their transport on the Chinese Railways.

The Contracting Powers, other than China, assume a corresponding obligation in respect of any of the aforesaid railways over which they or their nationals are in a position to exercise any control in virtue of any concession, special agreement or otherwise.

Article VI.   The Contracting Powers, other than China, agree fully to respect China's rights as a neutral in time of war to which China is not a party; and China declares that when she is a neutral she will observe the obligations of neutrality.

Article VII.   The Contracting Powers agree that, whenever a situation arises which in the opinion of any one of them involves the application of the stipulations of the present Treaty, and renders desirable discussion of such application, there shall be full and frank communication between the Contracting Powers concerned. . . .

The Four-Power Treaty

I. The High Contracting Parties agree as between themselves to respect their rights in relation to their insular possessions and insular dominions in the region of the Pacific Ocean.

If there should develop between any of the High Contracting Parties a controversy arising out of any Pacific question and involving their said rights which is not satisfactorily settled by diplomacy and is likely to affect the harmonious accord now happily subsisting between them, they shall invite the other High Contracting Parties to a joint conference to which the whole subject will be referred for consideration and adjustment.

II. If the said rights are threatened by the aggressive action of any other Power, the High Contracting Parties shall communicate with one another fully and frankly in order to arrive at an understanding as to the most efficient measures to be taken, jointly or separately, to meet the exigencies of the particular situation.

Hughes Opposes Recognition of Soviet Russia, 1923

You refer with just emphasis to the tyrannical exercise of power by this regime. The seizure of control by a minority in Russia came as a grievous disappointment to American democratic thought which had enthusiastically acclaimed the end of the despotism of the Czars and the entrance of free Russia into the family of democratic nations. Subsequent events were even more disturbing. The right of free speech and other civil liberties were denied. Even the advocacy of those rights which are usually considered to constitute the foundation of freedom was declared to be counter-revolutionary and punishable by death. Every form of political opposition was ruthlessly exterminated. There followed the deliberate destruction of the economic life of the country. Attacks were made not only upon property in its so-called capitalistic form, but recourse was had also to the requisitioning of labor. All voluntary organizations of workers were brought to an end. To unionize or strike was followed by the severest penalties. When labor retaliated by passive resistance, workmen were impressed into a huge labor army. The practical effect of this program was to plunge Russia once more into medievalism. Politically there was a ruthless despotism and economically the situation was equally disastrous.

It is true that, under the pressure of the calamitous consequences, the governing group in Russia has yielded certain concessions. The so-called new economic policy permitted a partial return to economic freedom. The termination of forcible requisitions of grain has induced the peasantry to endeavor to build up production once more and favorable weather conditions have combined to increase the agricultural output. How far the reported exports of Russian grain are justified by the general economy of the country is at least an open question. Manufacturing industry has to a great extent disappeared. The suffrage, so far as it may be exercised, continues to be limited to certain classes and even among them the votes of some categories count more than the votes of others. A new constitution has just now been promulgated providing in effect for the continuance of the regime of the 1917 *coup d'etat* under a new title. The Constitution, it is understood, contains no bill of rights, and the civil liberties of the people remain insecure. There is no press except the press controlled by the regime, and the censorship is far-reaching and stringent. Labor is understood to be still at the mercy of the State. While membership in official unions is no longer obligatory, workmen may not organize or participate in voluntary unions. . . .

But while a foreign regime may have securely established itself through the exercise of control and the submission of the people to, or their acquiescence in, its exercise of authority, there still remain other questions to be considered. Recognition is an invitation to intercourse. It is accompanied on the part of the new government by the clearly implied or express promise to fulfill the obligations of intercourse. These obligations include, among other things, the protection of the persons and property of the citizens of one country lawfully pursuing their business in the territory of the other and abstention from hostile propaganda by one country in the territory of the other. In the case of the existing regime in Russia, there has not only been the tyrannical procedure to which you refer, and which has caused the question of the submission or acquiescence of the Russian people to remain an open one, but also a repudiation of the obligations inherent in international intercourse and a defiance of the principles upon which alone it can be conducted.

The persons of our citizens in Russia are for the moment free from harm. No assurance exists, however, against a repetition of the arbitrary detentions which some of them have suffered in the past. The situation with respect to property is even more palpable. The obligations of Russia to the taxpayers of the United States remain repudiated. The many American citizens who have suffered directly or indirectly by the confiscation of American property in Russia remain without the prospect of indemnification. We have had recent evidence, moreover, that the policy of confiscation is by no means at an end. The effective jurisdiction of Moscow was recently extended to Vladivostok and soon thereafter Moscow directed the carrying out in that city of confiscatory measures such as we saw in Western Russia during 1917 and 1918.

What is most serious is that there is conclusive evidence that those in control at Moscow have not given up their original purpose of destroying existing governments wherever they can do so throughout the world. Their efforts in this direction have recently been lessened in intensity only by the reduction of the cash resources at their disposal. You are well aware from the experiences of the American Federation of Labor of this aspect of the situation which must be kept constantly in view. I had occasion to refer to it last March in addressing the Women's Committee for the Recognition of Russia. It is worth while to repeat the quotations which I then gave from utterances of the leaders of the Bolshevik Government on the subject of world revolution, as the authenticity of these has not been denied by their authors. Last November Zinoviev said, "The eternal in the Russian revolution is the fact that it is the beginning of the world revolution." Lenin, before the last Congress of the Third Internationale, last fall, said that "the revolutionists of all countries must learn the organization, the planning, the method and the substance of revolutionary work." "Then, I am convinced," he said, "the outlook of the world revolution will not be good but excellent." And Trotsky, addressing the Fifth Congress of the Russian Communist Youths at Moscow last October,—not two years ago but last October,—said this: "That means, comrades, that revolution is coming in Europe as well as in America, systematically, step by step, stubbornly and with gnashing of teeth in both camps. It will be long protracted, cruel and sanguinary."

The only suggestion that I have seen in answer to this portrayal of a fixed policy is that these statements express the views of the individuals in control of the Moscow regime rather than of the regime itself. We are unable, however, to find any reason for separating the regime, and its purpose from those who animate it, and control it, and direct it so as to further their aims.

While this spirit of destruction at home and abroad remains unaltered, the question of recognition by our Government of the authorities at Moscow cannot be determined by mere economic considerations or by the establishment in some degree of a more prosperous condition, which of course we should be glad to note, or simply by a consideration of the probable stability of the regime in question. There cannot be intercourse among nations any more than among individuals except upon a general assumption of good faith. We would welcome convincing evidence of a desire of the Russian authorities to observe the fundamental conditions of international intercourse and the abandonment by them of the persistent attempts to subvert the institutions of democracy as maintained in this country and in others. It may confidently be added that respect by the Moscow regime for the liberties of other peoples will most likely be accompanied by appropriate respect for the essential rights and liberties of the Russian people themselves. The sentiment of our people is not deemed to be favorable to the acceptance into political fellowship of this regime so long as it denies the essential bases of intercourse and cherishes, as an ultimate and definite aim, the destruction of the free institutions which we have laboriously built up, containing as they do the necessary assurances of the freedom of labor upon which our prosperity must depend.

Herbert Hoover on Foreign Trade, 1926

Foreign trade has become a vital part of the whole modern economic system. The war brought into high relief the utter dependence of the life of nations upon it. The major strategy of war is to crush the enemy by depriving him of it. In peace time our exports and imports are the margins upon which our well-being depends. The export of our surplus enables us to use in full our resources and energy. The creation of a wider range of customers to each production unit gives to that unit greater stability in production and greater security to the workers.

And we may quite well view our exports from the other side of the trade balance sheet. They enable us to purchase and import those goods and raw materials which we can not produce ourselves. We could probably get along as a nation if we had to suppress the 7 to 10 per cent of our production which goes to export, but our standard of living and much of the joy of living is absolutely dependent upon certain import commodities. We could not carry on our material civilization without some of the fibers, rubber, and some metals. Without diamonds we would not be able to get satisfactorily engaged to marry. The prosperity of our people in many ways can be measured by the volume of imports. . . .

The Government can chart the channels of foreign trade and keep them open. It can assist American firms in advancing their goods. In the improvement of all the foreign services the Department of Commerce has made great progress in the past five years, and it has been developed into organizing in internal cooperation and consultation with our industries and our merchants. I can refer to the success of that service without egotism, for it has been the work of Doctor Klein and his assistants. Some indication of the degree of their success is shown by the increased demand upon the services of the bureau they direct. The requests of merchants, manufacturers, and farm cooperatives for information and assistance have grown from some 15,000 inquiries per month four years ago to a total of 170,000 inquiries per month during the past year, a total of over 2,040,000 during the year.

I believe the effect of the efforts of the department in establishment of standards, elimination of waste, and the provision of wider information has been to expand the possibilities of foreign trade to many concerns not hitherto able to extend into this field. One of the interesting and encouraging facts is the rapid increase in the number of small concerns participating in export business. The surprisingly large number of inquiries now being received by the department from such firms amply proves that the virtues of high quality, specialized production, good service, precise export technique, and farsighted policy are by no means monopolized by big corporations. Literally thousands of small dealers and manufacturers, whose commodities have a strong specialty appeal and meet a definite need, are now successfully cultivating overseas markets. Foreign trade is thus becoming a national asset in the fullest sense of the word. . . .

We have the question propounded daily as to whether, with a stabilized Europe, we can continue successfully to hold our own share in the growth of the world's trade in competitive goods. It permits argument both ways, and we may recede on some particular commodities. I have the firm view, however, that the recovery of Europe will, by and large, help our foreign trade. Trade grows on prosperity, not on poverty. I believe that in most trades it has been more difficult to compete with Europe in neutral markets during the past few years against the underpaid labor and lower overhead costs of depreciating currencies than it will be when Europe is more stable and they have recovered their pre-war standards of living. Moreover, as Europe gains in stability and their living standards increase, they will become better customers for our goods in direct trade.

In a large sense the major proportion of foreign trade is a cooperative effort among nations to secure the greatest total output and total consumption. Foreign trade is too often visualized as a sort of battle. It is a misfortune that the terminology of trade has been so much infected by military terms. We speak of export trade as a matter of conquest, we talk of trade wars, trade strategy, of economic power—all carrying many implications of extermination. In larger vision our export trade does not grow by supplanting the other fellow but from the increased consuming power of the world.

I do not wish to be understood as saying that we are going to obtain our share of these increases without effort and without competition. What I wish to get clear is that, in the large view, our exports are not based on the destruction of our competitors but on insistence that we shall participate with them in the growth of world demand. . . .

Without entering upon any partisan discussion of the protective tariff, which I, of course, support, there is one phase of the tariff which I believe experience shows has less effect upon the volume of international movement of commodities than had at one time been assumed.

As a result of the hardships suffered by many people of both combatant and neutral nations during the war, there came to all nations a deep resolution, in so far as the resources of their countries permitted, to produce as far as possible their essential commodities. The struggle to overcome post-war unemployment has added to this impulse. The result is that 52 of the 70 nations of the world, including almost every important trading nation, increased their tariffs after the war. It might seem that these widespread protective policies would tend to localize industry and thus decrease the total volume of international trade. But it certainly appears that internal economic and social currents which make for prosperity or depression in a nation have a much larger effect upon the total volume of imports than the tariffs and thus more largely affect world trade as a whole. In our case, far from our present tariff diminishing our total imports, they have increased about 35 per cent since the higher tariff came into effect. This has also been the case with other nations which have progressed in internal economy. In any event our experience surely indicates that in considering the broad future of our trade we can dismiss the fear that our increased tariff would so diminish our total imports as to destroy the ability of other nations to buy from us.

The most commonly remarked revolution in our foreign economic relations is our shift from a debtor to a creditor nation upon a gigantic scale. It is the father of much speculative discussion as to its future effect upon our merchandise trade. Alarm has been repeatedly raised that repayment of the war debts must necessitate the increase of imports of competitive goods in order to provide for these payments—to the damage of our industry and workmen. These ideas are out of perspective. Our war debt when settled upon our own views of the capacity to pay will yield about $300,000,000 per annum, although as yet the actual payments are much less than this. The private foreign loans and investments to-day require repayments in principal and interest of about $600,000,000 annually, or nearly twice the war debt. I have heard of no suggestion that interest and repayment of these private debts will bring the disaster attributed to the war debt. The question is of importance, however, as to how this $800,000,000 or $900,000,000 of annual payments may affect our merchandise movement. There is a compensating factor in American trade relations unique to our country which has a large bearing upon this question—that is, the vast dimension of our invisible exports in the form of tourist expenditure, emigrants' remittances, and other forms of American expenditure abroad. These items in 1925 amounted to about $900,000,000, or about $100,000,000 more than our incoming payments on debts of all kinds. In other words, at this stage of calculation the balance of trade should be in our favor by about $100,000,000. But beyond this we are making, and shall long continue to make, loans abroad. For the last four years these loans have averaged nearly $700,000,000 a year, and in fact the merchandise balance in our favor has been running just about this amount.

Now the summation and purpose of all these words is the conclusion that there is no disastrous shift in our imports and exports of merchandise in prospect from debt causes.

The making of loans to foreign countries for reproductive purposes not only increases our direct exports but builds up the prosperity of foreign countries and is an economic blessing to both sides of the transaction. And I do not put this business of loans upon any sentimental footing, although the economic advantage to foreign countries of our great financial strength in these times can not be denied. Nor did we get this financial strength out of war profits. We lost enormously by the war. We created this reserve of capital, as any study of our economy will show, from our growth of efficiency, by hard work, and savings since the war. . . .

In conclusion, if we can keep in motion the social and economic forces which we have developed so greatly in the last decade, if we can multiply and improve education and skill, if we still further stimulate scientific research, if we continue to eliminate industrial waste, if we still continue to improve our business organization and maintain private initiative, we shall hold our own in our share in the world's trade.

By contributing to peace and economic stability, by the loan of our surplus savings abroad for productive purposes, by the spread of inventions over the world, we can contribute to the elevation of standards of living in foreign countries and the demand for all goods.

Burton K. Wheeler
Condemns Intervention in Nicaragua, 1927

Mr. President, for days I have had in mind discussing the administration policy in Latin America. I confess I have found it a difficult task, owing to the fact that its policy has changed with every pressure that has been brought to bear upon it.

First we learned that the marines were sent to the little Republic to protect American lives and property; then they were sent there to protect the paper canal which we wrung from the people of Nicaragua by questionable means; at the end of the week we were there to protect the Americans from Bolshevism.

While men are tramping our streets with arms off, legs off, blind, deaf, and insane as a result of the last war, this administration begins preaching the hymn of hate, spreading false propaganda against a sister republic of Central America, all in the interest of those who seek to exploit and enslave other peoples. The American people are not fooled. They knew that this cry of Bolshevism and the protection of lives and property in Nicaragua is but an effort of this administration to justify war with Mexico. . . .

Why did not the President [Coolidge] frankly tell us why Vice President Sacasa left Nicaragua? Why did he not tell us that he was driven out by a usurper exercising dictatorial power at the head of the military forces of the country? Why did he not tell us that this usurper was aided and abetted by Diaz, whom we have recognized as President? Why did he not tell us why Doctor Sacasa did not return to the Corinto conference instead of suggesting that his absence meant that he had abandoned his claim to the Presidency? Why did not the President confide to Congress and through Congress to the country that Chamorro and Diaz, the two chief personages through whom our State Department has operated in Nicaragua, are professional revolutionists who have looted their country of millions of dollars, and are known and detested throughout Latin-speaking America as traitors of the meanest kind? Why did he not state fairly the character of the Congress that elected Diaz? Why, in a word, did he not candidly confess that Diaz was just as much a violator of the five-power treaty that was held to exclude Chamorro from the presidency as Chamorro himself, and that Diaz was thrust into power because he was known by experience to be the most perfect instrument available to enable the New York bankers to have their will of the defenseless people of Nicaragua? Why, oh why, did not President Coolidge frankly admit, what every person of average intelligence who looks into the matter can not fail to realize, that Dr. Juan B. Sacasa is the constitutional President of Nicaragua? . . .

It is impossible, in a speech of reasonable length, to follow in detail the rough-shod, antirepublican rule of our State Department in Nicaragua. To do so would be an arousing revelation to any American whose heart still beats in sympathy with the founders of our Republic.

The followers of Doctor Sacasa are to-day fighting for just those same principles of liberty and free government for which our forefathers fought in 1776. Indeed it is not too much to say that one would seek in vain in the history of our struggle for independence for a parallel to the brazen tyranny of our State Department in its dealings with the overwhelming majority of the people of Nicaragua. George III never dared to perpetrate upon the American Colonies such fiscal and political iniquities as our State Department has not hesitated to perpetrate upon the defenseless people of Nicaragua.

When it is generally known how our State Department, undeterred by the manifest disapproval of the United States Senate, has robbed the little State of Nicaragua of its every vestige of sovereignty, men and women of honor throughout our land will hang their heads in shame. The wretched instrument made use of by the State Department for the accomplishment of this great wrong was Adolfo Diaz. . . .

From the beginning of our active intervention in Nicaragua in the interest of profitable investments for bankers, to this moment—and never more than this very moment—Brown Bros. and J. & W. Seligman, New York, were and are the niggers in the Nicaraguan woodpile. Other American concession seekers and holders—notably the Knox group, La Luz & Los Angeles Mining Co.—have played a big bad part. But the State Department policy is built around the exploitation of Nicaragua by Brown Bros. and J. & W. Seligman. The big stake being played for at this moment and on which the future of Nicaragua absolutely depends is the control of 51 per cent of the stock of the National Bank of Nicaragua with the concessions.

Permit me to digress one moment to say that the concessions which go with that bank and which were in the possession of these people at one time, and which they are now seeking to get back, were the most unconscionable concessions that have ever been granted in the history of any country, I think, with the possible exception of the case of Haiti, when they turned over the rule of their country to one of the banks of the city of New York. . . .

Think of it; the railroads down there are incorporated in this country, and those people down there are paying income taxes to the United States upon their own railroads. The railroad and the bank have been absolutely the things that have dominated and controlled that country. They have had men in there collecting the taxes of that country, they have run the elections of the country, and they have absolutely taken away, as nearly as possibly could be taken away, the freedom of the people of that little country.

Wholesale graft has characterized the banker–State Department control of Nicaragua for the past 17 years. Patriotic Liberals and Conservatives agree on this. Behind the paper statements of prosperity the real conditions stick out plain to one who looks. Declared by the native business men and the populace to be intolerably bad. The operating expenses of the railroad increased from $30,000 to approximately $300,000, and no improvements were made. The railroads constantly deteriorated during the time they were under the charge of American business men, notwithstanding the fact that they promised to make certain improvements and extend the railroads. None were ever made. They violated not only their moral obligations, but their legal obligations as well. The customs duties were increased 100 per cent. . . .

Some people have been particularly severe in their criticism of Mr. Kellogg because of the fact that he gave out a statement charging that everybody and everything was caused in these countries by Bolshevism. But the people of this country should not be too harsh in their criticism of Mr. Kellogg. They should be reminded of the fact that a coup d'état took place out in Minnesota some years ago, when the Scandinavians took part in it, and ever since that coup d'état, which elevated Mr. Kellogg to the position of Secretary of State, he has been seeing Bolsheviks under every sagebrush throughout the entire length and breadth of this continent. . . .

Ever since the World War we have been manufacturing more goods than we can sell. We are looking for new markets. Latin America and South America afford these markets. And yet in order to allow a few bankers to exploit Nicaragua, our oil interests to exploit Mexico, we are willing to ruin the legitimate commercial business of this country. We are willing to let thousands of men remain out of employment who could be working in the manufacturing plants of this country if we by peaceful means sought the friendship and the trade of Central and South America.

It seems to me that the Senate's duty is clear. In view of these facts I think the time has come to assert ourselves, and I for one am no longer going to sit silent while the interests of this country are being compromised and the country's legitimate, material interests jeopardized by certain ruthless international bankers and their bureaucratic puppets in the State Department.

Hughes on Intervention at the Pan American Conference, 1928

We desire to respect the rights of every country and to have the rights of our own country equally respected. We do not wish the territory of any American Republic. We do not wish to govern any American Republic. We do not wish to intervene in the affairs of any American Republic. We simply wish peace and order and stability and recognition of honest rights properly acquired so that this hemisphere may not only be the hemisphere of peace but the hemisphere of international justice. Much has been said of late with regard to Nicaragua. . . . We are there simply to aid them in obtaining free elections, in order that they may have a sovereign and independent government. I mention that merely because I speak in a spirit of entire frankness.

Now what is the real difficulty? Let us face the facts. The difficulty, if there is any, in any one of the American Republics, is not of any external aggression. It is an internal difficulty, if it exists at all. From time to time there arises a situation most deplorable and regrettable in which sovereignty is not at work, in which for a time in certain areas there is no government at all, in which for a time and within a limited sphere there is no possibility of performing the functions of sovereignty and independence. Those are the conditions that create the difficulty with which at times we find ourselves confronted. What are we to do when government breaks down and American citizens are in danger of their lives? Are we to stand by and see them killed because a government in circumstances which it cannot control and for which it may not be responsible can no longer afford reasonable protection? I am not speaking of sporadic acts of violence, or of the rising of mobs, or of those distressing incidents which may occur in any country however well administered. I am speaking of the occasions where government itself is unable to function for a time because of difficulties which confront it and which it is impossible for it to surmount.

Now it is a principle of international law that in such a case a government is fully justified in taking action—I would call it interposition of a temporary character—for the purpose of protecting the lives and property of its nationals. I could say that that is not intervention.

The Kellogg-Briand Pact, 1928

Article 1. The high contracting parties solemnly declare in the names of their respective peoples that they condemn recourse to war for the solution of international controversies, and renounce it as an instrument of national policy in their relations with one another.

Article 2. The high contracting parties agree that the settlement or solution of all disputes or conflicts of whatever nature or of whatever origin they may be, which may arise among them, shall never be sought except by pacific means. . . .

The Stimson Doctrine, 1932

With the recent military operations about Chinchow, the last remaining administrative authority of the Government of the Chinese Republic in South Manchuria, as it existed prior to September 18th, 1931, has been destroyed. The American Government continues confident that the work of the neutral commission recently authorized by the Council of the League of Nations will facilitate an ultimate solution of the difficulties now existing between China and Japan. But in view of the present situation and of its own rights and obligations therein, the American Government deems it to be its duty to notify both the Imperial Japanese Government and the Government of the Chinese Republic that it cannot admit the legality of any situation *de facto* nor does it intend to recognize any treaty or agreement entered into between those Governments, or agents thereof which may impair the treaty rights of the United States or its citizens in China, including those which relate to the sovereignty, the independence, or the territorial administrative integrity of the Republic of China, or to the international policy relative to China, commonly known as the open door policy; and that it does not intend to recognize any situation, treaty or agreement which may be brought about by means contrary to the covenants and obligations of the Pact of Paris of August 27, 1928, to which Treaty both China and Japan, as well as the United States, are parties.

✷ E S S A Y S

Both essays in this chapter reflect the recent scholarship that depicts the United States as a major power and international participant in the interwar years. In the first, Melvyn P. Leffler of the University of Virginia studies the goals of American foreign policy for the period. He discovers an American consensus on open door expansionism but also a debate over the tactics to implement the American objective of a stable, capitalist international order. Especially when the Great Depression hit in the early 1930s, Leffler argues, domestic priorities conflicted with foreign policy goals. The second essay, by John Braeman of the University of Nebraska, studies the issue of American security. Braeman questions the once-popular view that the United States was militarily weak during the interwar era, suffering a gap between goals and capabilities. After surveying American military preparedness, Braeman concludes that United States power was adequate for its interests at the time.

Open Door Expansionism, World Order, and Domestic Constraints

MELVYN P. LEFFLER

After World War I, economic considerations assumed a position of primacy in the shaping of American foreign policy. Economic factors played a decisive role because they were closely linked to ideological values, moral constructs, and legal concepts. Indeed the full impact of economic considerations cannot be assessed in quantitative terms. Studies of exports, imports, loans, and investments, however revealing they may be, do not elucidate the complex web of legal, institutional, ideological, and economic interrelationships that came to fruition in the aftermath of the Great War. American officials could extol the virtues of peace, support arbitration treaties, defend the rights of property, champion the sanctity of contracts, cultivate multinational efforts of cooperation in the private sector, and oppose revolutionary movements abroad because they realized that efforts to avert war, disseminate American ideals, and encourage world economic progress were compatible with the interests of a net creditor, exporting nation, increasingly concerned with foreign supplies of raw materials.

Excerpted from "1921–1932: Expansionist Impulses and Domestic Constraints" by Melvyn P. Leffler in *Economics and World Power: An Assessment of American Diplomacy Since 1789*, 225–35, 237–59, 261–62, 264–67, William H. Becker and Samuel F. Wells, Jr., eds. Copyright © 1984 Columbia University Press. Used by permission.

The primacy of economic considerations resulted at least in part from the absence of strategic apprehensions. With Germany defeated and Britain weakened, the vital security interests of the United States appeared safe. Japan was a potential menace to American interests in the western Pacific and in East Asia. But the Japanese did not seem to jeopardize the nation's security. No great power threatened the continental coastlines, challenged the Monroe Doctrine, or endangered the Panama Canal. Not having to worry about the nation's safety, even military thinking became increasingly linked to the vortex of economic factors. In part, this reflected the navy's effort to capitalize upon the nation's overseas commercial and financial interests in order to enhance its own organizational goals; in part, it reflected the ascendancy of economic factors in the shaping of diplomatic and military thinking.

American foreign policy goals were aimed at creating a stable and peaceful international order conducive to the expansion of American exports, the protection of American overseas investments, the control of foreign supplies of raw materials, and the dissemination of American ideals and values. The policy known as the open door, first applied to the Far East and subsequently universalized by Woodrow Wilson, increasingly influenced the conceptualization of policy objectives. American officials sought the right to trade and invest on equal terms with any other nation. They also wanted American access to raw materials and championed the cause of national self-determination. Such goals were expected to enhance American material interests. But these goals were also tied to ideological and legal principles that were considered prerequisite to world order, international prosperity, and universal justice.

Within the United States controversy did not center on the fundamental open-door objectives of American foreign policy. Instead debate focused on the tactics to implement foreign policy goals. Partisan politics, ethnocultural divisions, bureaucratic rivalries, and rifts within the business community very much influenced the debates over tactics. And these disputes were significant because they implicitly revealed the degree of importance attached to foreign policy goals by interest groups, legislative representatives, and executive officials. The rejection of the League of Nations, imposition of higher tariff duties, insistence on war debt repayments, and antipathy to military commitments in Europe and East Asia revealed that as important as was the search for an open-door, liberal capitalist order, it did not take precedence over domestic priorities, many of them economic, nor supersede traditional non-entanglement inclinations.

In short, the matrix of economic-ideological concerns encompassed in the open-door approach to a stable, liberal capitalist world order determined the conceptualization of foreign policy goals. Yet the pursuit of these goals was not seen as *vital* to the national security or the economic well-being of the United States. Hence, when the depression came, and when there was not yet a threat from a totalitarian power, almost everyone concurred on the primacy (although not exclusiveness) or domestic tactics to solve the depression and on the need to refrain from military embroilments and political alliances that might divert energy and dissipate resources from these domestic approaches.

World War I significantly influenced the position of the United States in the world economy. The nation entered the war as a net debtor on private account and emerged as a net creditor with a balance of over $3.5 billion. In addition, foreign governments owed the American government over $10 billion as a result of Allied war debt obligations. Not so dramatic, but also important, was the tremendous expansion of American trade during the war and immediate postwar years. The proportion of total world exports belonging to the United States climbed from 12.4 percent in 1913 to 16.9 percent in 1922. The percentage of total world imports going to the United States rose from 8.3 percent to 12.9 percent during the same period. If the effect of the 1921–22 recession is disregarded for a moment, the impact of world conflict on American exports and imports is even more startling. Between 1913 and 1920, American merchandise exports increased from $2.5 billion to $8 billion while American imports grew from $1.75 billion to over $5 billion. One of the most impressive developments between 1914 and 1920 was the 500 percent increase in the overseas sales of finished man-ufactured goods. In 1919, 14 percent of all manufactured goods produced in the country were exported compared to less than 10 percent in 1914. . . .

Farm commodities and raw materials were especially dependent on foreign markets. Using 1920 figures, the President's Committee on Un-employment reported that 61.5 percent of the cotton produced in the country was exported, 51.5 percent of the copper, 53.2 percent of the rice, 46.5 percent of the rye, 44.5 percent of the tobacco, 23.5 percent of the wheat, 19 percent of the zinc, and 17.8 percent of the tin plate. Statistics of this sort and pressures from farm groups and their congressional spokesmen impelled Republican officials to reactivate the War Finance Corporation in 1921 as a temporary expedient to help relieve the agricultural overproduction problem. Subsequently, when agricultural distress persisted, the Treasury Department and the Federal Reserve Bank of New York (FRBNY) sought to expedite Europe's financial stabilization and to augment her purchasing power in order to boost domestic farm prices and relieve agrarian discontent.

Hoover and his colleagues in the Commerce Department did not think that farm problems could be solved permanently through overseas sales, but they were equally concerned with the nation's foreign trade. They maintained that crop diversification, more efficient marketing procedures, and an increasing home market would gradually eliminate agricultural distress. Accordingly, they focused their primary attention on the expansion of in-dustrial exports. Foreign sales of manufactured goods, Commerce officials claimed, made "it possible to use our resources and energy to greater advantage; by widening the range of markets it gives to industry greater stability in output and thereby makes employment more secure." By the middle 1920s, the Bureau of Foreign and Domestic Commerce (BFDC) was answering 9,000 business requests daily for trade information. Export associations claimed that because prices were set in international markets, "our interest in foreign trade is far greater than the mere proportion which it bears to our total commerce."

In order to maintain and expand American exports, policymakers recognized that private American capital would have to assume a more important role in the international economy. As early as April 1919 State and Commerce Department officials concurred that foreign investment "on a substantial scale is almost essential to the maintenance and extension of foreign trade on a sound financial basis." With the support of the Treasury Department, Congress passed the Edge Act in 1919. This legislation permitted new forms of business to engage in foreign lending. During the following year, hundreds of the nation's most prominent bankers and businessmen met in Chicago to support the formation of a new corporation under the Edge Act. As economic conditions worsened during 1921, businessmen continually reminded one another that, as a creditor nation, the United States had an obligation to make foreign loans in order to support foreign currencies and promote American exports. When the Harding administration took office in 1921, Secretary of State Charles Evans Hughes, Secretary of the Treasury Andrew W. Mellon, and Hoover focused immediate attention on how to promote the outflow of American capital for the well-being of the international community and for the advancement of the American economy.

The evidence is now overwhelming that at the end of the Great War, executive officials and business leaders were cognizant of the creditor status of the United States and of its significance for American foreign policy. In the autumn of 1919, the State Department Economic Liaison Committee, including representatives from every important executive agency, discussed the commercial ramifications of the nation's creditor status. A new subcommittee was established "to prepare an exposition of the problems arising from the permanently adverse balance of trade which the United States, as a creditor nation, seems destined to have in the future." Although imports did increase faster than exports in the postwar decade, the unfavorable merchandise balance did not materialize. Throughout the 1920s, officials in the Commerce Department paid close attention to the relationship of imports to exports. They maintained that capital outflows, immigrant remittances, tourist expenditures, and other so-called "invisible" items enabled the United States to reconcile a favorable trade balance with its creditor status. Yet they sensed that this was a temporary phenomenon.

Indeed, one of the most striking aspects of the official American attitude toward the international economy after World War I was the growing belief in the nation's dependence on foreign supplies of raw materials. Hoover and Julius Klein, chief of the BFDC, repeatedly emphasized that "our standard of living is absolutely dependent upon certain import commodities." As the United States became increasingly industrialized, it seemed destined to import larger amounts of raw materials. The Commerce Department's systematic effort to expand exports was geared to the assumption that exports would eventually prove essential to pay for indispensable imports.

"Foreign trade," the Commerce Department declared, "is of greater importance to our manufacturing industry in furnishing its raw materials than in providing markets for its finished products." Imports of raw materials and semi-manufactured goods constituted a growing proportion of all such materials used by American industry. The Commerce Department emphasized American dependence on foreign supplies of rubber, silk, and wood pulp, while the Navy noted the importance of nitrates, tin, nickel, rubber, wool, and coffee imports. In the mid-1920s, awareness of the growing dependence of an industrial nation on raw material imports impelled Hoover to combat the efforts of foreign government-sponsored cartels to control the marketing of important products, like rubber.

At the conclusion of the Great War nothing worried American civilian and military officials more than the prospect of America's dependence on foreign petroleum sources. Oil seemed absolutely vital to American industry and the United States Navy. The assumption that America was quickly exhausting its oil reserves caused widespread alarm. State, Commerce, and Navy Department officials prodded private corporations to accelerate their search for foreign oil supplies. In negotiations with foreign governments, American policymakers insisted upon equal opportunity for American corporations and threatened to retaliate if such rights were not recognized. Even in 1926, when new domestic discoveries were alleviating the worst apprehensions, the State Department's Economic Advisor's office maintained that "our whole industrial being as well as our security as a nation depends in a great measure on an assured supply of petroleum and in order to assure ourselves of supplies from foreign fields, we want the control of those supplies to be in the hands of American companies." By this time American oil corporations were working out cooperative arrangements with their British counterparts to control much of the world's known oil reserves.

After World War I, the search for export markets, the dependence on foreign supplies of raw materials, and the recognition of America's role as a creditor nation convinced policymakers and businessmen of the essential unity of the international economy. Technological advancement and industrial progress bred worldwide interdependence. If it were not for the exchange of commodities, Hoover acknowledged, "Not a single automobile would run; not a dynamo would turn; not a telephone, telegraph, or radio would operate . . . Therefore, let no one think that international trade is but the noisy dickering of merchants and bankers,—it is the lifeblood of modern civilization." This viewpoint impelled American officials to try to create a stable world order along open-door liberal capitalist lines. Such an order, they believed, would redound to the benefit of the American economy, promote international economic progress, and contribute to world peace. Peace, stability, prosperity, and capitalism were interlocking phenomena, each dependent upon the other. Such an all-encompassing Weltanschauung enabled American policymakers to reconcile their ideals with their self-interest, to blend their search for peace with their quest for markets, and to harmonize their ethnocentrism with their generosity.

During the 1920s, in speech after speech, Harding, Hoover, Hughes,

Mellon, Kellogg, and other influential officials dedicated American foreign policy to the construction of a peaceful and stable world order. Peace and stability, they never tired of saying, were prerequisite to the growth of world trade and the free flow of private capital. In turn, commercial exchange and private investment contributed to economic growth, fostered social stability, and destroyed the causes of mass discontent. Backwardness and poverty were the sources of social upheaval and revolutionary disorder; private investment and economic growth their cure. For Americans, self-interest and selflessness went hand in hand. "Were it not for commerce," Harding declared, "there would be no civilization." With genuine sincerity, the National Foreign Trade Council also emphasized the mutuality of interests between American businessmen and the "other peoples of the world. We wish them all peace, stability, and prosperity, so will their trade grow and thrive. So will ours advance." And as economic growth took place, the seeds of conflict would be removed and the prospects for peace would be enhanced.

This outlook meant that the defeat of the League of Nations did not terminate American efforts to create a stable, liberal capitalist order. In fact, the League of Nations was not an end in itself, but a means toward an end. . . .

When Harding, Hughes, and Hoover supported the creation of a Central American tribunal and advocated American membership in the Permanent Court for International Justice, they were resuming the prewar American internationalist tradition. This orientation linked international law to a peaceful world order conducive to the flow of private capital, the advance of backward economies, and the growth of world trade. Republican officials did not expect legal institutions to insure world peace. Indeed, they believed it was naive to expect any international organization, however much force it might theoretically have as its disposal, to eliminate conflict. Their aim was to proceed gradually to establish legal processes that constituted alternatives to military force. Hughes and Hoover spoke frequently of codifying international law and enlarging the area of administered justice. They had no illusions but that this would be a slow, painful process. Yet respect for legal processes was indispensable to national and international stability. According to Hoover, "the whole great fabric of international commerce upon which the world is today dependent for its very existence rests . . . upon the sanctity of contract honestly entered upon under the laws of each country. But for confidence in the courts of different nations, the whole of our international economic relations would become hazardous and weakened. And the just decisions of the courts remove the friction of our respective citizens out of the field of diplomatic relations into the field of abstract justice."

Viable judicial institutions and respect for legal processes were considered necessary for the maintenance of international stability, the cultivation of world commerce, and the protection of contractual obligations. Bolshevism constituted a challenge to the economic and legal world order sought by American officials. Bolshevik confiscation of private property, abrogation of contracts, and fomenting of revolutionary activity posed a long-term threat to the interests of a capitalist, creditor nation intent on expanding world trade and promoting economic growth in a stable international environment. Consequently, from 1919 to 1933, American officials refused to recognize the Soviet regime. This posture was not an ideological stand divorced from economic self-interest. Although a nonrecognition policy prevented the extension of long-term credits that might have aided exports to the Soviet Union, the loss of some direct trade with Soviet Russia was not considered as harmful to American interests as would be the adoption of Soviet precedents in other parts of the world. In a speech President Harding intended to deliver just before his death, he emphasized that "international good faith forbids any sort of sanction of the Bolshevist policy. . . . If there are no property rights there is little, if any, foundation for national rights, which we are ever being called upon to safeguard. The whole fabric of international commerce and righteous international relationship will fail if any great nation like ours shall abandon the underlying principles relating to sanctity of contract and the honor involved in respected rights." Such rhetoric did not compartmentalize ideology and economics; it blended them. . . .

The defense of property rights and aversion to revolution were integral parts of the American effort to disseminate open-door, liberal capitalist principles in the 1920s. American military officials accepted this as the major goal of American foreign policy. . . .

Without question the military's emphasis on economic considerations was prompted, at least in part, by organizational and bureaucratic imperatives. Nevertheless, it is significant that military leaders assumed that the best means of pursuing organizational interests was by underscoring the imperatives of open-door expansion. Such arguments, the army and navy believed, were most likely to win favor with other executive officials and congressional leaders. Yet once they admitted that the international environment was quiescent and that no strategic threats were on the horizon, military spokesmen found themselves in a very difficult position.

The absence of a threat to vital national security interests encouraged civilian leaders, especially Hoover, to press forward with arms limitation proposals. These officials assumed that their quest for an open-door, liberal capitalist world order would have a better chance of survival if it were built upon solid economic foundations than if it were imposed through military force. Moreover, there was a widespread consensus among Republican officials in the early 1920s that expenditures on armaments were one of the major causes of financial chaos, fluctuating exchange rates, commercial stagnation, and economic dislocation. By limiting armaments, Harding, Hughes, and Hoover hoped to curtail government expenditures, balance budgets, stabilize currencies, and establish an environment conducive to world economic growth.

This was the great achievement of the Washington Naval Conference of 1921–22. The agreements limited armaments, reaffirmed the principles of equal opportunity and self-determination in China, and provided for consultation among the great powers in the Pacific. With Germany no longer a military threat and Japanese power limited to the western Pacific, civilian officials believed that the best chance of stabilizing the international arena was by demonstrating the economic benefits to be derived from arms limitation and cooperative competition according to the principles of the open door. The policymakers believed this orientation would redound to their domestic political advantage does not mean they were unconcerned with foreign policy considerations. Indeed, the political appeal of the Washington Conference illustrates the American people's readiness to accept a foreign policy based on the economic and ideological foundations of the open door and arms limitation.

Throughout the 1920s, Republican officials promoted arms limitation as an integral part of their foreign economic policy. This was not an unrealistic pursuit when implemented cautiously in an unthreatening international environment. Their aim was to establish the economic basis of a permanent peace. They also sought to end the dissipation of capital resources on military weaponry, find peaceful ways of settling contentious issues, and outlaw war as an acceptable means of pursuing national objectives. No great miracles were expected from any one of these developments. After the signing of the Kellogg-Briand Pact in 1928, Myron Herrick, the American ambassador to France, sarcastically remarked that "treaties are somewhat like children's games. When some child does not want to play any longer, he breaks up the game and that's the end of it." Yet American officials hoped that the slow evolution of arms limitation treaties, judicial processes, arbitration agreements, and antiwar pacts would gradually turn men's energy and attention from military preparations to economic undertakings. . . .

Yet in the early 1920s both Republican officials and American businessmen agreed that the most important task of American foreign policy was to help rehabilitate European economies and stabilize European finances. Prior to the war Europe had consumed over 60 percent of American exports, including 83 percent of all crude material exports, and 71 percent of all foodstuff exports. Because the agricultural and raw material sectors of the American economy were so badly hit by the economic slump of 1920–22, it was natural for policymakers and businessmen to dwell upon the significance of Europe's pacification and reconstruction. Moreover, they felt certain that the recovery of the Old World was necessary for the growth of backward economies, including those of Latin American nations. Europe constituted a critical market for the tropical goods and natural resources of underdeveloped areas. In turn, the latter purchased the manufactured goods and finished products of western Europe. Furthermore, with American capital still expected to find many lucrative opportunities at home, European capital was assumed to have a vital role to play in generating future international economic growth.

The perception of an interdependent world economy, with the Old World occupying a major place in it, impelled American officials to grapple with European economic and financial problems. Even before the Washington Conference had been concluded, officials in the State, Commerce, Treasury, and Agriculture Departments as well as those in the FRBNY had begun to prepare for the reassessment of Germany's reparations burden, the reduction of Allied war debt obligations, the mobilization of private American capital for European reconstruction, and the readjustment of American tariff duties. These tasks were not easily undertaken because they clashed with protectionist demands, fiscal priorities, inflationary fears, and isolationist sentiment. Yet Harding, Hughes, Hoover, Mellon, Culbertson, and Benjamin Strong, governor of the FRBNY, moved cautiously and steadily to establish the World War Foreign Debt Commission, to strengthen the Tariff Commission, to oversee the outflow of private capital, to prepare for cooperation between European central banks and the FRBNY, and to depoliticize, so far as was possible, the European reparations imbroglio.

By the latter part of 1923, Republican officials were ready to play a significant role in the financial rehabilitation of Germany and the stabilization of European currencies. With the mark worthless, the Weimar Republic on the verge of collapse, and revolutionary ardor on the upswing, American policymakers repeatedly emphasized that an American contribution to European stabilization efforts was prerequisite to sustained prosperity at home and to the prevention of revolution abroad. In the middle 1920s, American financial leverage, through capital outflows and war debt reductions, was applied to help arrange the Dawes Plan, consummate the Locarno treaties, stabilize European currencies, and establish the gold exchange standard. As European tensions abated, Franco-German relations improved, and economic growth resumed, Republican officials took great pride in their contribution to the restoration of stability in the Old World. Maintaining that a prosperous Germany would be a peaceful Germany, they reaffirmed their view that nations acted out of economic self-interest. They assumed that while they were laying the basis for Europe's recuperation and America's prosperity, they were also establishing the framework for a stable and peaceful world order along liberal capitalist lines. . . .

With regard to Latin America . . . , the Monroe Doctrine still served as the cornerstone of American policy, but it no longer constituted a viable guide to action because European colonialism in the western hemisphere was almost over and European encroachments on the independence of Latin American nations were unlikely. American officials repeatedly proclaimed their desire to respect the territorial integrity of their Latin American neighbors, to refrain from direct military interventions, and to withdraw American troops from occupied countries. Nevertheless, the quest for stability remained the fundamental objective of American policy. Hughes and Hoover insisted that political instability "was the greatest menace to progress and prosperity." Indeed, American officials often promoted free elections because they considered them prerequisite to a stable order; yet the curtailment of democratic liberties also could be condoned when such liberties threatened to engender chaos. Hughes and other policymakers believed that disorder and revolution disrupted the flow of private capital, retarded economic growth, set back educational, agricultural, and industrial advancements upon which democracy depended. They assumed that if stability could be preserved, American economic opportunities would multiply, Latin American economies would grow, and democratic institutions would flourish. The search for stability, then, was not simply a product of dollar diplomacy or economic imperialism. Nor was it a policy designed to protect the interests of any single firm or interest group. Instead, it was a policy that accepted the economic interdependence of the modern world; contemplated the parallel advancement of developed and undeveloped economies; postulated the mutual benefits of open-door commerce and overseas investments; linked democratic institutions to economic foundations.

With the exception of America's military intervention in Nicaragua in 1926, Republican officials steadily reduced America's military presence in Caribbean and Central American countries. They also began to withdraw from formal control over many of those nations' customs houses. Even in Mexico where pressure to intervene in the mid-1920s was substantial, President Calvin Coolidge and Secretary of State Kellogg resorted to more sophisticated and conciliatory tactics. Outright military intervention no longer maximized the interests of the United States. In fact, strong-arm tactics appeared to alienate Latin American peoples, stiffen resistance to American economic penetration, establish precedents for military solutions to other inter-American disputes, and encourage the growth of statist policies and confiscatory measures.

Therefore, American policymakers increasingly sought alternative means to achieve stability. State Department officials declared their respect for the sovereignty of other nations in the hemisphere, sought to limit armament expenditures, devised arbitration procedures for the peaceful resolution of inter-American disputes, endeavored to sign commercial treaties incorporating the equality of treatment principle, and tried to protect property rights. They also encouraged private corporate efforts to work out international agreements for American control of critical radio and cable facilities as well as petroleum resources. At the same time, Commerce Department officials encouraged the flow of private capital into Latin America's natural resource industries, advocated the construction of an inter-American transportation network, especially the Pan-American highway, and supported the efforts of unofficial American advisory missions to stabilize Latin American currencies and improve the management of Latin American finance ministries and central banks.

In East Asia, as elsewhere, the quest for a stable, liberal capitalist order dominated American policymaking. But in this area of the world, American policy was beset by the complications emanating from the disorder in China, the proximity of Japanese power, the vulnerability of the Philippines, and the uncertainty of whether to take a unilateral or cooperative approach toward Far Eastern affairs. The Washington Conference treaties aimed at establishing a cooperative orientation based on the acceptance of open-door principles, a subordination of military imperatives, and a concern for orderly economic growth in China. . . .

Throughout the 1920s, American policymakers never ceased stating that stability in China was the essential precondition for the growth of American exports and the extension of American loans. Whether they were institutionalizing multinational cooperation along open-door lines, condemning the proliferation of internal strife in China, or acting unilaterally to recognize the Nationalists, American policymakers were seeking to establish a stable order conducive to the safety of American lives and property and hospitable to the expansion of American commerce, investments, and values. The fundamental problem in the middle and late 1920s, however, was that the United States was unable to establish a policy that reconciled its ambitions in China with its existing interests in Japan.

Throughout the postwar decade there remained much potential for friction with Japan, America's number one economic partner in East Asia. Influential State and Commerce Department officials like William R. Castle and Julius Klein were well aware of this. In fact, as late as 1929 and 1930, the persistence of chaos in China and the brief revival of Japanese civilian efforts to cooperate with the West encouraged American policymakers to reaffirm the importance of Japanese-American relations. At this time Japanese-American trade still was more than twice the value of Chinese-American commerce. At the London Naval Conference of 1930, Secretary of State Henry L. Stimson and the rest of the American delegation worked hard to reconcile Japanese-American differences. Japan's concurrent return to the gold standard seemed to bode well for the future development of economic relations in East Asia. Still not foreseeing the long-term ramifications of the stock market crash and the economic downturn, the Hoover administration desired to underscore naval arms limitation as a key component of America's economic diplomacy in East Asia and the rest of the world. Although plagued by the difficulty of coordinating their quest for stability in China with their cultivation of a harmonious partnership with Japan, economic considerations remained critical to the conduct of diplomacy in East Asia.

Despite the problems encountered by policymakers in some regions of the world, American exports, imports, loans, and investments grew steadily in the 1920s. Once the war-inspired cycle of boom and bust was over, the value of merchandise exports grew from $3,832,000,000 in 1922 to over $5,100,000,000 in 1929. Particularly significant was the growth of finished manufactured products, which by 1929 totaled almost 50 percent of all American exports. Most striking of all was the enormous surge in automobile exports. By the end of the decade automobiles constituted almost 10 percent of all exports and the value of automobile exports had increased almost 2,000 percent since the prewar era. In 1929, approximately 10 percent of all motor vehicles produced in the United States were exported abroad compared to 5.5 percent in 1913. Indeed the growth of the automobile industry in the 1920s was very much related to the increase in overseas sales. And since the automobile industry consumed 14 percent of the steel, 82 percent of the rubber, 63 percent of the plate glass, 60 percent of the upholstery leather, and 26 percent of the aluminum produced in the United States, overseas car sales had a bearing on the well-being of the entire economy. But in addition to automobile exports, foreign sales of other mass-produced goods also mounted. All through the 1920s overseas sales of cash registers, typewriters, sewing machines, and agricultural machinery were especially noteworthy, and in 1930 machinery replaced unmanufactured cotton as America's number one export item.

At the same time that exports were increasing, imports also were growing from $3,113,000,000 in 1922 to $4,399,000,000 in 1929. Prior to the war, the value of imports was approximately 78 percent of exports; during the latter 1920s imports amounted to 84.4 percent of exports. Compared to the prewar years, the growth in the value of wood pulp, newsprint, silk, and petroleum imports was especially impressive. The quantitative leap in rubber imports was also dramatic (over 800 percent), but price declines minimized its significance. Commerce Department officials were captivated by the rapid industrialization of the nation and worried about American dependence upon foreign supplies of raw materials. "Upon these highly essential imports," Hoover wrote, "is dependent not only much of our comfort but even the very existence of the major part of our industrial life."

Preoccupied with maintaining access to raw materials, American officials were pleased by the overseas investments of American corporations in natural resource industries. During the 1920s, private long-term American investments abroad grew dramatically, amounting to a little over $15 billion at the end of the decade. Approximately $7.5 billion were in direct investments. Of this amount slightly over 50 percent was in supply-oriented fields, including mining, smelting, and oil production. In Latin America, Asia, and even Africa, Americans began challenging Europe's control of raw materials and developing access to their own supplies. Investments in foreign nitrates, oil, tin, copper, and rubber grew dramatically. At the same time, market-oriented investments also increased, especially in Europe. New manufacturing investments in Europe in 1928 and 1929 equalled the entire number of such investments up to World War I. Yet the fastest growth of American overseas foreign investments was in public utilities. In sum, between 1922 and 1930, direct investments increased by nearly $2.5 billion; portfolio investments by almost $7 billion. The result of these increments was that by 1930, United States direct foreign investments alone exceeded the direct *and* portfolio investments of France, Holland, and Germany *combined*. At the time of the stock market crash, American investments in Latin America for the first time equalled those of Great Britain. Between 1912 and 1928, United States investments in Colombia had increased by 15,150 percent; in Venezuela, by 4,566 percent; in Chile, by 4,200 percent; in Argentina, by 1,412 percent. . . .

The expansion of American trade and investments, however, was more a function of postwar international economic and financial developments than of any official American policies or actions. The great growth in manufacturing exports came in those very industries that had introduced mass production techniques and that benefitted from economies of scale. Official Commerce Department reports emphasized the relationship between efficient American mass production techniques and the growth of overseas sales of automobiles, agricultural machinery, and cash registers. In fact, there does not seem to have been any cause-and-effect relationship between the promotion of the unconditional most-favored-nation clause and the growth of these exports. Likewise, an incisive study of American business firms in China suggests that government advocacy of the open door had little to do with the success or failure of American corporate marketing practices in that nation. As the increment in manufactured exports can be best explained in terms of technological and industrial developments, the relative decline in overseas agricultural sales was related to the drive of many nations for national self-sufficiency in foodstuffs after the Great War as well as to the growth of foreign competition. Even the value of American imports may well have been affected more by the general level of prosperity in the United States and by fluctuations in prices set in international markets than by the setting of American customs duties. The value of imports increased markedly in the mid-1920s despite the rate hikes in the Fordney-McCumber tariff schedule. At the end of the decade the quantity of imports reached an all-time high; but the unit value of these imports already was declining because of market forces somewhat beyond American control. Seen in this perspective, even the Hawley-Smoot tariff may well have had a smaller impact on world trade and American imports than is usually attributed to it.

As with trade, the policies of the American government were not the key influence affecting the magnitude of overseas investments. Market-oriented direct investments in branch factories, for example, were most frequently the consequence of corporate attempts to leap over foreign tariff walls. Indeed Republican officials tended to be very circumspect about investments in branch factories because there was considerable apprehension that branch factories sacrificed American jobs. On the other hand, American policymakers certainly supported overseas investments in raw materials like oil, rubber, and nitrates. Repeatedly, they called upon foreign governments to adhere to the open door for investment and to allow equal American access to undeveloped raw materials. Yet even in respect to these supply-oriented investments, official policy had only a marginal influence. Private American corporations, influenced by the dynamics of the marketplace benefitting from superior technology and plentiful capital, and often encouraged by the governments of undeveloped nations, acted in accord with their own self-interest. As a result, the United States government often acquiesced in private corporate practices. In the cable, radio, and petroleum industries, for example, the open-door policy was compromised as Republican officials accepted private efforts to limit competition and establish multinational cooperation.

In a similar manner, official efforts to encourage foreign loans and guide their use had little influence on events. The corporations established under the Edge legislation did not significantly augment the outflow of long-term capital. In the early 1920s, domestic economic recession and European financial and political instability undermined the efficacy of the Edge Act. As soon as recovery began at home and stability returned to Europe, there was an unprecedented outflow of American capital. As is well-known, State, Commerce, and Treasury officials tried informally to channel this capital into so-called productive pursuits. Yet their efforts were unsuccessful. Bankers ignored implicit warnings about the dangers of loans to German municipalities and found ingenious ways to circumvent an explicit ban on loans to France. New York did become the world's financial center, but this had more to do with the impact of the war on London than with any concrete measures taken by Washington. With the important exceptions of the State Department's informal support of the Dawes and Young Plans and the Treasury Department's strong encouragement of cooperation between the FRBNY and European central banks, financial developments were more closely related to the impact of the war, the evolution of political developments abroad, and the workings of the marketplace than to any official acts in Washington.

This is not to say that Washington did not *try* to influence postwar economic, commercial, and financial developments. As outlined earlier in this essay, American officials very much sought to create a stable and prosperous world order conducive to the spread of liberal capitalist values and open-door principles. Yet there often was a gap between official aspirations and subsequent developments. Part of this related to the deep divisions within the business community and among economic interest groups. Disparate business organizations could agree on the need for a stable world order hospitable to the expansion of American trade, investments, and values. Recent studies demonstrate, however, that there was no consensus on tactics. Tariff debates pitted small manufacturers against international bankers, export-import interests against the Home Market Club, refiners against planters, meatpackers against ranchers, etc. Similarly, oil producers and international bankers disagreed on how the government should react to Mexican legislation implementing Article 27 of the 1917 constitution. J. P. Morgan and Company and Standard Oil could concur on the merits of a stable, liberal capitalist order, but their interests clashed when tax revenues on oil property might be used to liquidate outstanding debts. In China, members of the banking consortium and American exporters agreed on the wisdom of the open-door policy. Yet this did not stop businessmen from complaining bitterly about the reluctance of the consortium to finance major development projects.

Rifts within the business community over tactics resulted not only from clashing interests but from honest differences of opinion over the importance to be attributed to foreign policy goals. Everyone, for example, wanted to restore financial stability in Europe. But one's willingness to reduce or cancel the Allied war debts and thereby accept a heavier tax burden depended on just how much importance one attached to the goal of European reconstruction. And this assessment would depend on whether one was an international banker in New York holding European securities, a cotton farmer in Mississippi seeking to recover European markets, an auto manufacturer in Detroit aspiring to expand overseas sales, or a haberdasher in Shenandoah, Iowa, hoping to increase business as a result of higher hog prices and enlarged farm income. Of course, the position one took was not exclusively based on a rational assessment of economic self-interest. The cotton farmer in Mississippi might be a Klansman who hated Catholics and therefore opposed any reduction of the Italian war debt. The essential point is that individuals and interest groups who shared a common goal might disagree sharply on tactics. And these tactical differences were significant because they reflected contrasting assessments of just how important foreign policy goals were vis-à-vis domestic priorities, like reducing taxes, protecting the local market, winning elections, or preventing speculation and inflation.

American policymakers had to pursue foreign policy goals and reconcile clashing business interests without resorting to tactics that jeopardized domestic priorities or that engendered international complications out of proportion to the value attributed to the diplomatic objectives themselves. This was no easy task because competing interest groups often raised legitimate, albeit self-interested, concerns about difficult matters that were easy prey for politicians looking for demagogic issues. That complicated foreign policy questions might become the subject of political controversy always worried Hughes and Hoover. They were sensitive to ethnocultural divisions among the American people as well as to interest group pressures. Hence they sought to remove foreign policy issues from the political arena. They endeavored to establish general principles of policy that were designed to subordinate the narrow interests of particular firms, balance conflicting domestic pressures, and reconcile divergent national ambitions.

With regard to trade and investment American officials championed the unconditional most-favored-nation clause and the open-door policy. If all foreigners were treated equally in each nation's market, Hughes, Culbertson, and Hoover believed that world commerce would grow, international stability would be enhanced, and American exports would multiply. Accordingly, they were willing to sacrifice preferential treatment in the Brazilian market in order to disseminate the equality-of-treatment principle around the globe. At the same time, Republican officials were able to persuade Congress to strengthen the Tariff Commission, adopt a flexible tariff policy, and grant the President authority to adjust duties according to the difference in the costs-of-production at home and abroad. Hoover and Culbertson hoped that "scientific" protectionism would end congressional logrolling over customs duties and would permit experts on the Tariff Commission to adjust rates according to the needs of the national and international economy. Likewise, an open door for investments was advocated because this was considered the best means of promoting the unrestricted flow of private capital into productive pursuits. State and Commerce Department officials also believed that the open door would promote fair competition, stabilize international relations, and obviate the need to support any particular American firm. When necessary, however, Republican policymakers accepted business arrangements that established multinational monopolies so long as these could be justified in terms of maximizing efficiency, cultivating international cooperation, and enhancing overall American economic and strategic interests.

In other ways as well Republican officials sought to depoliticize foreign policy issues, reconcile domestic pressures bearing on these issues, and harmonize competing national interests. The World War Foreign Debt Commission was established in 1922. Dominated by Mellon and Hoover, the commission negotiated war debt agreements with the Allied debtors in a way that balanced a desire to lower taxes with an eagerness to expand commerce and promote European financial stability. During the mid-1920s, the Treasury Department also encouraged the FRBNY to support European efforts to stabilize their currencies. The FRBNY extended credits, adjusted discount rates, and conducted operations in the open market in an effort to restore the gold standard and promote American exports without encouraging speculation, generating inflation, or injuring domestic business.

Perhaps most importantly Republican officials made a calculated decision to rely upon the private sector and unofficial experts to implement foreign policy goals. The bankers' consortium in China was intended to preserve the open door, enhance Japanese-American amity, and foster Chinese economic growth. Private financiers and businessmen, like Owen D. Young, J. P. Morgan, Thomas W. Lamont, Charles G. Dawes, and S. Parker Gilbert, were selected as unofficial experts to help settle the European reparations enigma and to arrange the financing of German indemnity payments. Hughes and Hoover looked to the major petroleum, electrical, mining, and rubber corporations to gain American control of critical overseas natural resources and communication facilities. The State Department relied upon private banking firms and professional economists, like Edwin Kemmerer, to mobilize capital and improve financial conditions in Central America, the Caribbean, and South America.

Republican officials' reliance on the private sector reflected their views of how to structure and govern an industrial society in an interdependent world economy of competitive nation-states. The private sector was presumed to have the expertise to handle these complex matters. Moreover, by assigning responsibility to the private sector, government officials were trying both to minimize overt state intervention in the marketplace and reduce the chances that controversial foreign policy questions would become embroiled in partisan politics at home. They were also hoping to depoliticize the international economic environment. If economic and financial rivalries could be removed from the realm of government action, the prospects for peace would be greatly enhanced. Hoover, for example, deplored government-subsidized foreign cartels not only because they raised the price of critical raw materials but also because they further injected political considerations into international economic affairs and thereby increased the likelihood that economic competition could lead to war.

The dependence upon private businessmen, professional experts, and supposedly apolitical agencies eventually contributed to serious problems. Businessmen could not be counted upon to pursue the interests of the national polity when their self-interest was at stake. Relying upon the bankers' consortium in China proved an ineffective way to implement the open door. Financiers would not make loans when persistent instability meant probable default. Nor would private bankers forgo the lure of high profits on German loans despite official warnings of their dangers. Hoover and Mellon still depended upon central bankers and private experts to maintain European currency stability and to lighten Germany's reparations burden. Yet these methods were unlikely to succeed so long as American officials sought to avoid a clash with Congress over additional war debt reductions and so long as the Tariff Commission refused to use the flexible provisions of the Fordney-McCumber Act to reduce duties. Even while the balance of payments problems of many nations mounted, Hoover and other officials continued to place great faith in the salutary effect of direct private foreign investments in backward economies. They disregarded or underestimated the significance of many things, including the decline in raw material and agricultural prices, the growth in the absolute value of America's export surplus, the weaknesses inherent in the gold exchange standard, and the discrepancy between supply and demand as well as between world-wide productive capacity and international purchasing power.

In short, in the late 1920s American diplomacy became complacent and overly decentralized. Too much faith was placed in the efficacy of private market forces and too much responsibility was assigned to the private sector. Disconcerting developments were downplayed and tough decisions were postponed. The prevailing prosperity created great self-satisfaction and engendered a feeling that there was plenty of time to grapple with potential problems. Inertia set in. Policymaking mechanisms became routinized; old formulas institutionalized. The risks of changing policies seemed greater than the hazards of perpetuating them. Moreover, in the late 1920s, there was no widespread pressure for tariff or debt reductions or for recognition of Russia. Kellogg's recognition of the Chinese nationalists, Hoover's goodwill tour to Latin America, the State Department's rejection of military interventionism, and the FRBNY's experiments in central bank cooperation were about as innovative and progressive as anyone was proposing at the time. Hence no major initiatives were launched in the late 1920s to reduce tariffs, scale down the war debts, tackle European payments problems, bolster sagging raw material prices, stabilize conditions in China, or reintegrate Russia into the world economy. The stultification of the policymaking process was not so much a byproduct of bureaucratic imperatives as a reflection of officials' belief that they had already developed the best means of reconciling conflicting business pressures, of balancing internal and external economic imperatives, of harmonizing immediate market and investment demands with long-term ideological and economic aspirations.

During 1930 and 1931, of course, worldwide economic, financial, and political developments transformed the policymaking environment. The stock market crash in the autumn of 1929, the gradual erosion of values and growing political ferment in 1930, the dramatic financial crisis in the spring and summer of 1931, the eruption of warfare in Manchuria in September 1931, the precipitous decline in international trade, and the proliferation of revolutions throughout Latin America presented the Hoover administration with unprecedented foreign policy problems. Indeed, the very growth of American exports, imports, loans, and investments all through the 1920s had underscored the interdependence of the American and international economies and now highlighted the significance of unfolding events.

Under the circumstances, Hoover, Stimson, Mellon, and Treasury Undersecretary Ogden Mills reaffirmed the viability of the open-door economic orientation of the 1920s and tried to resuscitate outworn economic, commercial, and financial policies. Hoover emphasized the importance of arms limitation as a method of reducing expenditures, balancing budgets, stabilizing currencies, and revitalizing commerce. He sought to strengthen the flexible provisions of the tariff act, but still committed his administration to a policy of protectionism—scientifically applied. Stimson supported the open-door policy, chastised Japanese violations of the Washington treaties and Kellogg-Briand Pact, and proved unable to reconcile American rhetoric in China with American interests in Japan. Neither the lure of Russian markets nor the fear of Japanese ambitions persuaded Hoover or Stimson of the wisdom of recognizing the Soviet government. The potential for revolutionary ferment around the globe made Bolshevik precedents all the more threatening to the creditor and commercial interests of the United States. In Europe, Hoover proposed a one-year moratorium on debt payments. Yet he still depended on private financiers to maintain their credits in Germany, hoped that central bankers could preserve the gold standard, and proposed the recreation of the debt commission as a means of resolving the long-term problem of Allied war debt payments.

Throughout the crisis of 1931–32, Hoover and Stimson refused to cancel the war debts, scale down tariffs, extend government loans to financially pressed nations in Latin America, assume strategic commitments in Europe, or intervene militarily in East Asia. Such actions might have contributed to the stable, open-door, liberal capitalist order that policymakers sought to establish. But these efforts also would have diverted attention from and interfered with domestic priorities that were considered of even greater importance. Likewise, such efforts would have conflicted with prevailing Republican views on the proper role of the government in economic affairs and on the appropriate responsibilities of the United States in the international arena. In other words, open-door, economic expansion remained critical to the conceptualization and implementation of American foreign policy during this era, but foreign policy goals remained of distinctly secondary importance to domestic concerns and to prevailing practices of privatism and independent internationalism. This had been true all through the 1920s. During the first postwar decade, however, prosperity had eased the difficulty of making tactical choices. Once the depression set in, the subordination of "internationalist" options illustrated not the irrelevance of economic concerns to foreign policy goals but the subordination of foreign policy to domestic pursuits.

To understand this development, it is necessary to emphasize that during the 1920s foreign economic interests did not become proportionately more important to the functioning of the American economy. Notwithstanding the impressive gains in exports, imports, and investments, their relationship to domestic economic developments, albeit important, was not critical. Looking at broad trends, the proportion of exports to the total production of movable goods actually declined from 12.8 percent in 1899 to 9.8 percent in 1929. The percentage of farm income derived from overseas sales diminished from 16.5 percent in 1914 to 15.0 percent in 1929. Likewise, the book value of United States foreign direct investments as a percentage of gross national product did not change between 1914 and 1929. Manufactured exports, to be sure, constituted a larger percentage of overseas sales. But the proportion of manufactured goods exported in relation to their total production decreased from a little less than 10 percent in 1914 to a little under 8 percent in 1929. The importance of exports to the automobile industry, the fastest growing industry of the 1920s, cannot be denied. But petroleum refining was the fastest growing component of the nation's second most rapidly growing industrial grouping and the proportion of exports to total production dropped from 61 percent in 1899 to 36 percent in 1914 to 22 percent in 1927. Chemicals constituted the third fastest growing industry and the proportion of exports to production remained less than 5 percent. The textile industry was the largest manufacturing industry in the 1920s and exports constituted less than 4 percent of production. Machinery was the second largest industry and machinery exports became the nation's number one export item in 1930. Yet the proportion of machinery exports to total machinery production decreased from 10.6 percent in 1914 to 8.6 percent in 1929. Radios constituted one of the fastest growing sectors of the machinery industry. But once again exports remained a fairly constant 5 percent of production. Cast iron pipe was the fastest growing component of the iron and steel industry, the nation's third largest. Exports in 1927, however, constituted only 3.6 percent of production. Notwithstanding the growing interest in export markets, Commerce Department officials estimated in 1927 that only 4-5 percent of all manufacturers in the United States were engaged in foreign trade. . . .

This orientation helps to explain why the Hoover administration focused its primary, although not exclusive, attention on domestic palliatives once the depression worsened. . . .

This is not to suggest that the business community or Republican policymakers were repudiating the economic basis of American foreign policy. Support for the limitation of armaments, the stabilization of currencies, the maintenance of the open door, the sanctity of contracts, and the peaceful resolution of disputes remained the focal points of American diplomacy. But tactical attempts to implement such policies were too costly when they interfered with or diverted energy from domestic priorities as well as too dangerous when they demanded an enhanced role for government. In January 1931, the Department of Commerce rejected proposals to make a long-term silver loan to China. "The burden would largely fall on the American people" and this could not be accepted. Similar fears about the budgetary and fiscal consequence of war debt readjustments prompted Congress to reject Hoover's proposal to recreate the debt commission. The President himself would not contemplate tariff reductions for fear that foreign goods might saturate the home market. Nor would he consider strong measures to enforce the open door in China. Most State, Commerce, and Naval officials concurred that Japanese actions in Manchuria did not threaten important American economic interests. Hence they rejected measures that might risk war and distract attention from domestic reconstruction efforts. Foreign economic concerns, although critical to the conceptualization of diplomatic policy, remained subordinate to domestic economic approaches to American prosperity. "While reestablishment of stability abroad is helpful to us and to the world," Hoover insisted, "we can make a very large measure of recovery irrespective of foreign influence."

The subordination of foreign to domestic policy was sustained, at least in part by the belief that international developments, ominous as they were, did not jeopardize the nation's security. During 1932 military officials sneered at Stimson's efforts to bluff the Japanese into respect for the Kellogg-Briand Pact and the Nine-Power Treaty. Although naval officers worried about the growing strength of the Japanese navy relative to the American navy, they did not think Japanese actions in Manchuria threatened vital American interests. . . .

Without a clear-cut threat to the nation's security, and there was none in 1931–32, foreign economic interests did not impel the Hoover administration to incur overseas strategic commitments. This did not mean that the United States was indifferent to European developments. Indeed Hoover was making real attempts at this time to alleviate financial distress in the Old World in order to promote prosperity at home. But foreign economic objectives, while continuing to demand certain types of economic and financial initiatives, did not lead to strategic obligations so long as policymakers did not think that national security interests were jeopardized.

Throughout the years 1921 to 1933, economic considerations were critical to the conceptualization of diplomatic goals, but foreign policy remained subordinate to domestic concerns and priorities. In the absence of any imminent threats to the nation's security, economic factors assumed a position of primacy because they were inextricably linked to a legalist-moralist framework that postulated the superiority of American values and institutions. But "realist" historians and political scientists are misleading students when they highlight the legal and moral aspects of American foreign policy in this era and treat them in isolation from the economic interests of a capitalist creditor nation. American officials sought to join the World Court, sign arbitration treaties, outlaw war, and protect property because they wanted to construct a stable world order conducive to the expansion of American interests and values. They did not expect these efforts to bring about any great and immediate changes in the nature of international relations. They did not assume any natural harmony among democratic nations. Modern industrialism and technology, they perceived, bred interdependence. But it did not eliminate the potentiality of conflict. Republican policymakers recognized the need for continuous efforts to cultivate worldwide stability and international economic growth. That they failed to achieve their task was not because they were naive but because they grew complacent in the late 1920s, bowed to domestic political expedients, mismanaged domestic economic affairs, exaggerated the benefits of the private marketplace, and shared in the pervasive economic ignorance of the time.

As important as the open door was to the molding of foreign policy, it was not considered *vital* to the nation's economic well-being or its national security. Revisionists err when they intimate that American officials during the Republican ascendancy believed that survival of the capitalist system at home depended upon the expansion of the open door abroad. This mistake is unfortunate because the Wisconsin School of diplomatic historians [led by William Appleman Williams] and their adherents have performed an important service in underscoring the domestic roots of foreign policy. Yet if further progress is to be made in our understanding, we must grapple not only with domestic expansionist imperatives but also with domestic economic constraints. Foreign policy, at least in this era, grew out of *and was limited by* internal economic imperatives and by prevailing ideas about the legitimate role of government in international economic affairs. Contemporaries viewed open door expansion as only one of several ways of coping with cyclical fluctuations, overproduction, and unemployment. Open-door expansion did not take precedence over domestic tactics; indeed it was subordinate to them. Encouraging foreign trade, as Hoover emphasized, was very valuable but not nearly so important as cultivating and protecting the domestic market. Business periodicals, trade association literature, and annual corporate reports indicate that once the depression intensified, efforts to balance production to meet consumption and proposals to cut government expenditures assumed greater importance than export expansion.

By the late 1920s, moreover, the perceived dependence on foreign raw materials may not have seemed as ominous as it had in the immediate postwar years. The discovery of new domestic sources of petroleum diminished the pervasive fears of oil shortages that had characterized the early 1920s. In fact, in its annual assessments of the international situation in the early 1930s, the navy stopped voicing concern over the inadequacy of petroleum supplies. In the plans drawn up in 1928 and 1930 for possible wars with Japan and Great Britain, the Joint Board of the Army and Navy noted that in an emergency the nation could fulfill most of its requirements for raw materials within the western hemisphere. This may help to explain why in the early 1930s there was so much reluctance to intervene militarily in East Asia or to assume commitments in Europe. If most essential raw materials could be found in Latin America and Canada, and if European and Chinese markets were not vital to the nation's economic well-being, there were fewer reasons to take risks that were disproportionate to the nation's interests.

Prior to 1933, it was not unreasonable or unrealistic for American officials to pursue foreign policy objectives without incurring strategic obligations. It was a time when the Nazis still had not achieved power in Germany and when the Japanese still had limited ambitions. Moreover, since economic dislocation contributed to both German and Japanese bellicosity, and since American security interests were not immediately endangered, it was natural for the United States to play down geopolitical considerations and to concentrate on economic problems. Herein rested an area where the United States potentially could make a contribution to international stability. But Republican officials failed to devise a comprehensive approach that reconciled internal and external economic priorities. Ensnared by conflicting pressures and entrapped by an overzealous faith in the wisdom of the private sector and the beneficence of the open marketplace, policymakers failed to develop tactical approaches not only capable of achieving, but also commensurate with, their economic goals.

American Military Power and Security

JOHN BRAEMAN

Since Pearl Harbor, American foreign policy during the Harding-Coolidge-Hoover years has received a largely negative appraisal from historians. In the aftermath of World War II, the adherents of Wilsonian internationalism dominated the writing of American diplomatic history. The crux of their indictment of the Republican administrations of the twenties was that this country's refusal to participate in collective-security arrangements for upholding the peace was responsible for the breakdown of international order in the years that followed. If the United States had joined the League of Nations, or at the minimum cooperated with the peace-loving nations, Britain, France, and, until the illusions of the wartime alliance collapsed, the Soviet Union, against would-be or actual aggressors, the Second World War could have been avoided. Although this view has continued to have its champions, the hardening of Cold War tensions—and the accompanying disillusionment with the efficacy of the United Nations—spurred a major counterattack upon what George F. Kennan has termed the "legalistic-moralistic approach to international problems." With the emergence of the so-called realist school came a different—though no more positive—evaluation of the role played by the United States during the age of normalcy.

The dominant intellectual figure in the post–World War II realist movement was University of Chicago political scientist Hans J. Morgenthau. Morgenthau's starting point was a complex of assumptions about the behavior of nations and, more fundamentally, about human nature, which were in striking contrast to the nineteenth-century liberal faith in the existence of an inherent harmony of interests that underlay the Wilsonian vision of collective security.

"The primordial social fact," he postulated in *Scientific Man vs. Power*

From "Power and Diplomacy: The 1920s Reappraised," *The Review of Politics*, 44 (July 1982). Reprinted with the permission of the editor of *The Review of Politics*, Notre Dame, Indiana 46556.

Politics, "is conflict, actual or potential. . . ." Or as he put the matter more bluntly still in his now-classic *Politics Among Nations*, "the struggle for power is universal in time and space and is an undeniable fact of experience." Within most nations, he acknowledged, there existed a community of interests and values that tended to reduce the intensity of conflict. But the international arena was different. "The history of the nations active in international politics shows them continuously preparing for, actively involved in, or recovering from organized violence in the form of war." In such an anarchical world, force remained the ultimate arbiter. Thus, whatever the long-term goals of a nation, "Power is always the immediate aim." And given this country's geopolitical situation, he defined as the American national interest "to preserve the unique position of the United States as a predominant power without rival" in the Western Hemisphere and "the maintenance of the balance of power" in Europe and Asia.

The trouble was, runs the realist indictment, few Americans in the age of normalcy grasped those truths. Robert E. Osgood lamented that the post–World War I revulsion against Wilsonian utopianism had fostered a no less dangerous set of illusions: a millennialist hope for "peace by incantation," "a blind aversion to war and the instruments of war as absolute evils abstracted from the conflicts of power and national self-interest which lead to war," and, thus, a refusal to accept "the uses of force and the threat of force as indispensable instruments of national policy." Robert H. Ferrell placed much of the responsibility for this situation upon the organized peace movement, which was in the 1920's at the zenith of its influence; more still upon an "immature" and "appallingly naive" public. But the elite was as much at fault as the man in the street. Betty Glad penned a damning portrait of Secretary of State Charles Evans Hughes, the chief architect of American foreign policies in the 1920's, belaboring his "evasion of the role of power in international politics." Herbert Feis blamed the ineffectiveness of American "dollar diplomacy" during the Harding-Coolidge-Hoover administrations upon "the hazy, lazy faith"—shared by the public, business leaders, and government policymakers—that trade, loans, and investments would automatically promote world peace without backing "the dollar with our diplomacy and, if essential, by arms." "Far from coordinating force and diplomacy," J. Chalmers Vinson summed up, "the American statesmen and people set the two up as incompatible." The dominant ethos was rather that peace could, and would, be maintained, "by persuasion and example rather than force."

Military historians deplored the lack of machinery for civilian-military consultation in formulating foreign policies, the resulting widening gap between goals and capabilities, and the flight from "reality" in the services' own strategic planning. The United States's refusal to assume a share of the burdens of economic reconstruction, its aloofness from foreign political involvements, and what Edward W. Bennett has stigmatized as its "indifference to, or even revulsion from, the principle of the balance of power" were blamed for undercutting the Versailles settlement in Europe. Even heavier fire was directed against this country's Far Eastern policies. A minority of the postwar realists questioned the wisdom of American hostility to Japanese ambitions; and the revulsion against the Vietnam war has given this line new popularity. But the preponderant view among the post–Pearl Harbor generation of historians was that the fault lay in this country's failure to maintain sufficient military strength to meet the Japanese challenge. Popular hostility to naval spending, congressional economizing, and the naval limitations agreements undercut the deterrent power of the navy. And when Japan in Manchuria launched the first major direct attack upon the world order, the United States responded with no more than words.

There is no question that the political and intellectual atmosphere in the United States during the twenties opposed large-scale military and naval expenditures. But a nation's military capability cannot be measured by any absolute standard. Even in the narrow sense of armed forces-in-being, what matters is their relative size and efficiency vis-à-vis those of potential enemies. And in the larger sense, a nation's "military potential" depends upon a number of factors: its geographical vulnerability; the kind of war to be fought; and most importantly, as World War I had demonstrated, its technological and economic capacity. Perhaps the most salient feature of the Republican era was this country's overwhelming superiority in the economic sphere. In the late 1920's, the United States produced an output of manufactures larger than that of the other six major powers—Great Britain, Germany, France, the Soviet Union, Italy, and Japan—combined. The extent to which a nation translates its available resources into mobilized strength is a political decision. That decision, as Klaus Knorr has pointed out, reflects a "cost-gain calculation" of the advantages and disadvantages anticipated from the maintenance of military strength at different levels. "The desirability of ready combat strength depends, first, on the importance of the prevailing goals for the achievement of which military power is a means and, secondly, on the prevailing assumptions about the amount of military resources necessary to achieve these goals." If such variables are taken into account, substantial evidence exists for a reappraisal of the conventional wisdom about American policies during the Harding-Coolidge-Hoover years.

In the first place, the extent of pacifist influence upon American policy during the 1920's should not be exaggerated. Although the organized peace groups mobilized impressive shows of public support on such issues as naval disarmament and outlawing war, the military services could, and did, rally the backing of veterans' organizations, patriotic societies, and special interest groups. Viewing the world as a competitive arena in which each nation pursued its self-interest, the increasingly influential professional careermen in the State Department had no illusions that moral force did, or could, regulate international relations. And their thinly veiled hostility toward those peace enthusiasts who hoped for a radical transformation of the international order was shared by their politically responsible superiors. Nor was there any lack of consultation with the services on matters involving national security; even Hoover, the most pacifist-minded of the chief executives of the era, took pains to do so. The crux of the services' grievance was that their advice was not always followed when purely military considerations conflicted with larger policy goals. Most important, the Republican administrations remained committed to the basic principles of military and naval policy that had been formulated during the preceding two decades: "a strong Navy and battle fleet, second to none, as a first line of defense capable of dominating the western Atlantic and the eastern Pacific"; "a small Regular Army devoted primarily to the preservation and increase of military knowledge, the training of civilian components, and the preparation of plans for future wars"; and "a strong civilian industrial economy capable of conversion to war production in an emergency."

Post–World War I army planning was based upon an "insurance" concept of preparedness resting upon a small professional force capable of emergency defense, while providing the nucleus for the mobilization and training of a mass "citizen" army. Funding limitations did keep the army's enlisted strength in the latter twenties and early thirties to 118,750 men— a far cry from the 280,000 maximum envisaged by the National Defense Act of 1920 and below the 165,000 figure estimated by the General Staff as required for carrying out the army's responsibilities. But even in the midst of the depression, appropriations were more than double the pre– World War I level. And while during the years of prosperity recruiters found difficulty in attracting and retaining high-caliber enlistees, the impact of hard times allowed the army to upgrade its standards. The officer corps remained at approximately twice the prewar level, thus providing the cadre that was able to lead the vastly expanded army of World War II. This pool of potential leaders was reinforced by the continuation of Citizens' Military Training Camps and the expansion of the Reserve Officers' Training Corps in the colleges. Reflecting the World War I experience, Section 5A of the 1920 National Defense Act provided for a new assistant secretary of war responsible for procurement and industrial mobilization planning. At first, this office concentrated upon improving procurement procedures, but in the latter 1920's—drawing upon studies by the newly established Industrial War College and in cooperation with business leaders—formulated the landmark "Industrial Mobilization Plan" of 1930.

Far from a time of stagnation, the Republican years witnessed significant improvements in the army's effectiveness: the introduction of a more rational promotion system; expanded theoretical education for officers; and the establishment of a War Plans Division within the General Staff responsible for strategic planning. The General Staff's intelligence branch (G-2) displayed an impressive breadth of interest in foreign events, making a continuing effort to view military questions in their larger political, social, and economic context. Despite the handicaps of higher-echelon conservatism, financial stringency and the fact that the theories of mechanized warfare advocates outran the existing technology, a group of younger officers pushed forward with the beginnings of a modern tank force. Under the stimulus of depression-inspired demand for economy, the pace of innovation to make the most efficient use of limited resources accelerated during the Hoover years. Up until 1929 the army had relied largely upon equipment left over from World War I. Although funds were not available for any large-scale reequipment, the War Department in late 1929 inaugurated a systematic program of research and development aimed at developing pilot models of new equipment that could be mass-produced when more monies became available, with the General Staff setting as its top priority work on what became the Garand semiautomatic rifle. In 1932, Chief of Staff General Douglas A. MacArthur put through a sweeping revamping of the army's organizational structure—the so-called four-army plan—for the more rapid deployment of combat units in the event of war.

Nor was there any threat on the European side warranting a larger American buildup. The military establishments of all the major European powers—except for the Soviet Union—suffered during the twenties from popular suspicion, stringent budgetary limitations, and a loss of self-confidence that bordered upon defeatism. From 1919 until its abrogation in 1932, British military policy was shaped by the "Ten Year Rule" that the Empire would not become involved in a major war during the next decade. Given this assumption, the strength of pacifist sentiment, and the country's near-desperate need for financial retrenchment, the British army was cut back to a level barely capable of handling its routine peacetime responsibilities. Although France as of 1933 had 450,000 officers and men under arms—with plans to mobilize within two weeks sufficient reserves to raise the total to a million—Paris' anxiety over Germany's superior population and industry, and its potential military superiority, bred a state-of-siege mentality. The Treaty of Versailles had bound the German army by a network of restrictions down to the equipping and arming of units. Despite the growing evasion of these limitations after mid-decade, the *Reichswehr* in the years before Hitler did not envisage the possibility of mobilizing more than a maximum 300,000-man force in the event of war and doubted their ability to equip even that many. The Soviet Union was probably the most formidable military power on the continent. In the late twenties, its regular army numbered 562,000 men, and starting in 1931 a large-scale program of expansion and reequipment was launched under a leadership committed to an offensive strategy based on mobility, maneuver, and mechanization. But the USSR's technological and industrial backwardness, its continuing internal problems, and its leaders' obsession with the threat of "capitalist encirclement" made the avoidance of war the keystone of Soviet policy.

Similarly exaggerated are the charges, made then and since, that American policymakers were blind to the revolutionary potentialities of air power. The Army Reorganization Act of 4 June 1920 provided formal recognition of the Air Service as a combatant arm, while the Air Force Act of 1926 provided for a new assistant secretary of war to deal with aviation matters, added an air section to each of the General Staff divisions, and authorized a five-year program of expansion in personnel and equipment. Insufficient money prevented achievement of the authorized 1800-plane force. But appropriations did rise sharply, with the result that by 1933 the Air Corps boasted 1619 planes, of which over 1100 were regarded as first-line craft. While balking at granting the air arm full autonomy as an independent service, the General Staff in its contingency war planning from 1923 on envisaged establishment of a consolidated air strike force under a single commander directly responsible to Army General Headquarters. By the early 1930's, army officialdom was gradually moving toward acceptance of this organizational setup for peacetime. Although the most vocal champion of the supremacy of air power, Brigadier General "Billy" Mitchell, was forced out of the service, his ideas about the airplane as primarily an offensive weapon whose function was to destroy the enemy's industrial base had come to permeate Air Corps' thinking. If the air power enthusiasts failed to achieve all their goals, the reasons were not simply old-guard obstruction and congressional parsimony. The major obstacles were the limits of the existing technology, substantive differences over strategy and tactics, and the absence of any immediate threat. "Despite popular legend," World War II Air Corps chief H. H. "Hap" Arnold acknowledged, "we could not have had any real air power much sooner than we got it."

The same factors retarded air power development abroad. In structure and theory, Britain was in advance of the United States. An independent Royal Air Force and Air Ministry had been established in World War I, and the air staff's doctrine of the deterrent role of strategic bombing directed against an enemy's industrial base was accepted as official government policy. Yet financial stringency prevented full implementation of the 52-squadron Home Defense Force program authorized in 1923. Thus, in 1930, the RAF had 770 front-line aircraft compared to France's 1300, Italy's 1100, and the United States's 900. By the spring of 1932, Britain's first-line air strength had slipped to fifth place, behind France, the Soviet Union, the United States, and Italy. Although the world leader in number of aircraft, the French air force remained until 1933 a branch of the army, which envisaged for air power no more than a limited auxiliary role in support of ground forces. Notwithstanding an impressive short-run showing in the 1920's, Italy lacked the resource base to remain a major air power. Despite the increasing momentum of German secret air rearmament after 1926, the *Reichswehr* had by the spring of 1932 only 228 aircraft—with a goal of 274 for the following year—of which 192 were converted civilian planes. Probably no government of the time was more air conscious than the Soviet, which rapidly expanded the size of the Red Air Force to roughly 2200 planes by the end of 1932. But the Soviets continued to lag behind the Western powers in technology and training. And given the domination of the air force by the Red Army, major emphasis was placed upon providing tactical support for ground campaigns.

Most important, aviation technology still left the oceans as safe defenses. Even the head of the Air Service acknowledged in the fall of 1925 that the United States was not in any immediate danger of air attack. Eight years later, a board headed by Major General Hugh A. Drum, the army's deputy chief of staff—pointing to the difficulties attending the flight of the highly rated Italian bombers to the Chicago World Fair—reaffirmed that this country need not fear attack by land-based planes. As late as 1935, Britain's top heavy bomber, the Hawker "Hendon," could carry 1,500 pounds of bombs for no more than a thousand miles round trip. Despite the enthusiasm of *Reichswehr* air planners from the early twenties for a long-range strategic bomber, the first steps toward implementing its development were not undertaken until late 1933, and Germany would remain without an operational heavy bomber at the beginning of World War II. Rather than lagging behind, the United States was in the forefront of long-range bomber development. The landmark breakthrough came in 1931 with the appearance of the Martin B-10, an all-metal monoplane that was the first of the modern bombers. In July 1933 the Air Corps Materiel Division began work on the plans for what would become the B-17 Flying Fortress. And what would prove decisive in the long run, the growth of civilian aviation and the aircraft industry— stimulated by the Air Mail Act of 1925, the Air Commerce Act of 1926, Charles Lindbergh's 1927 transatlantic flight, and the Air Corps's policy of encouraging private manufacturers to build up their design and engineering staffs through placing orders for experimental prototypes—gave the United States an industrial and technological infrastructure in the aeronautics field that no rival could match.

The most controversial issue involved the state of the navy. Whereas the army command acquiesced without major protest in civilian decisions about funding and manpower levels, most naval officers made no secret of their unhappiness. Their anger was first roused by the restrictions placed upon capital ships by the Five Power Treaty of the Washington Conference of 1921-1922: a ten-year ban upon new construction; maximum tonnage quotas; and a 5:5:3 ratio for the United States, Britain, and Japan. Their anxieties about the navy's deterrent capability was heightened by the agreement reached at the London Conference of 1930. That pact continued the holiday in capital ship construction until 1936 and reduced further the tonnage allowances; fixed tonnage quotas for heavy cruisers, light cruisers, destroyers, and submarines; and provided for a 10:10:7 ratio in the first three categories with parity in submarines. Domestic political realities were an important factor in the American government's championship of naval limitation. The struggle over the naval appropriations bill of 1921 demonstrated the resistance to implementing the Wilson administration's planned building program. But the key point, and what made the agreements possible, was that similar forces were at work in this country's two major sea rivals. In Britain, the mood of pacifism and the demand for financial retrenchment joined to exert tremendous pressure for major cutbacks in naval expenditures. Similarly, the balance of political forces in Japan up until the Great Depression worked in favor of a policy of accommodation with the United States: the backlash against military interventionism spurred by the unsuccessful Siberian invasion; the growing influence of the political parties; the acceptance by the civilian decision-making elite that Japan's interests in China were primarily economic; the financial burdens of a naval arms race; Japan's dependence on this country for vital raw materials; and the sense of security given the existing favorable power balance in the western Pacific.

Qualitatively, the agreements were, as William R. Braisted has suggested, "a service to the Navy" by requiring the service to make the most efficient use of its available resources. The reduced capital ship tonnage required by the Five Power Treaty allowed the navy to eliminate overaged and obsoletely equipped vessels. With new construction halted, the navy concentrated upon an extensive program of modernization of its remaining battleships. The installation of new engines and the conversion from coal to oil increased speed and range; new electrical power systems were developed; improvements in the elevating mechanism of turreted guns resulted in increased firing power; and the substitution of plastics and aluminum for heavier materials allowed improved armor while keeping within the tonnage limitations. Naval researchers made important advances in radio communications, in radar, and in radio-controlled torpedoes. And despite their reputed obsession with the battleship, naval planners in the 1920's were committed to the construction and maintenance of a balanced fleet. Most of the eighteen of the 8-inch-gunned cruisers the navy had in 1941 were authorized between 1922 and 1933. As for light cruisers, the ten *Omaha* class commissioned between 1923 and 1925 were regarded by foreign sources as the finest of their type in the world. The large number of destroyers—349—built or building at the end of World War I precluded the construction of additional vessels until the existing ships reached overage classification twelve years after their commissioning. But starting in 1931–1932, Congress authorized the beginning of an extensive replacement program that would be continued by the Roosevelt administration. When the test came after Pearl Harbor, the American treaty-era ships proved "effective if not optimal military units, capable of performing their fundamentally defensive strategic function."

Similarly impressive were the innovations in strategy. In line with its assigned mission of capturing Japanese bases in Micronesia in support of the fleet in the western Pacific, the Marine Corps during the twenties worked out the basic principles of amphibious assault doctrine, gave increased emphasis in its training, course work, and maneuvers to landing operations, and worked out techniques of air support for such landings. The navy's most glaring weakness was in submarines. But the Naval Research Laboratory worked to improve submarine technology; submarine officers engaged in an ongoing study of design and tactics; and the London Conference's restrictions on tonnage forced a rethinking of submarine design to maximize cruising distance and torpedo power. Probably most significant for the future was the progress achieved in naval aviation. Despite its ponderousness and slowness, the airplane carrier *Langley*—a converted old fleet collier commissioned in 1922—proved invaluable for training and experimental purposes. When commissioned in 1927, the *Saratoga* and *Lexington* were the finest carriers afloat. Although the undersized *Ranger* proved a misstep, the navy in 1933 gained congressional authorization for the *Yorktown* and *Enterprise*. At the same time, a group of younger aviation-oriented officers pioneered in formulating the concept of the carrier as an independent striking force. By contrast, British carrier development lagged because of the Royal Air Force's preoccupation with long-range, land-based strategic bombers. And though more active than the British in this area, the Japanese continued to view the carrier as an auxiliary in support of the main battle fleet. This country's fleet aircraft, Rear Admiral Ernest J. King, chief of the Bureau of Aeronautics, reported in 1934, "have reached a degree of efficiency not equaled by any other power."

Even quantitatively, American negotiators struck a hard bargain. Memories of World War I disputes over neutral rights, the existence of a wide range of continuing frictions, and sensitivity to the possible threat to the Western Hemisphere from British bases in the West Indies made Washington adamant in its demand for naval parity with Britain. Despite angry protests from the Admiralty about the disparity in defensive responsibilities borne by the two fleets, Whitehall, hobbled by British financial weakness and anxious to conciliate the United States, yielded to the American position. What remained in dispute was the mix of different type vessels and the tonnage levels that would constitute parity. The differences about cruisers were sufficiently formidable to block agreement at Geneva in 1927. When a compromise was reached at London in 1930, the British made the larger concessions, accepting a future cruiser total far below what the Admiralty had deemed the minimum required. Whereas American naval planners were convinced in the aftermath of the Washington Conference that Britain's navy remained actually superior in fighting strength, they regarded the London treaty as leaving the British battle fleet inferior to this country's. After 1929, Britain ceased to appear as a possible enemy in the annual estimates drawn up by the navy's War Plans Division, and in 1932, the division's director reported optimistically that "as Britain's power wanes, the power of the United States should be increasingly effective, particularly in matters relating to the Western Pacific." In 1933, the British government formalized its longstanding assumption in practice when the Defense Requirements Subcommittee was instructed to exclude any consideration of preparations for war against the United States when drawing up its rearmament program.

In view of congressional and public attitudes toward large naval expenditures, the Five Power Treaty's 10:6 ratio for this country vis-à-vis Japan in capital ships was, as Ernest R. Andrade, Jr., has pointed out, "not a great sacrifice for the United States but instead a diplomatic achievement of major importance" since the Navy General Board's own figures showed "that without the treaty the ratio might have been even more unfavorable." Given this country's failure in the years that followed to keep pace with Japanese building in the unrestricted categories, the limitations adopted at London similarly gave the United States a more favorable balance than existed in practice. Japan would have to halt all new cruiser construction for five years to allow the United States to build up, while the tonnage allowed for submarines was below what the Japanese navy strategists viewed as a safe minimum. While American admirals fumed at the abandonment of the 10:6 ratio, Tokyo's Naval General Staff bitterly protested that the agreement jeopardized Japanese national security. The explanation for the outcry by naval officialdom on the two sides of the Pacific lies in the mirror-image complex of strategic principles that each side held. There was no question that the United States retained sufficient naval strength—except in what even American planners acknowledged was the highly unlikely circumstance of a joint Anglo-Japanese assault—to defend the Western Hemisphere and the eastern Pacific. The crux of the issue was the ability of the United States to undertake offensive operations in the western Pacific.

In their planning for possible war with Japan, so-called War Plan Orange, American naval planners assumed—as did their Japanese counterparts— that the outcome of a United States–Japanese war would be decided by a showdown battle between the two main battle fleets in the western Pacific. Given this country's lack of advanced bases in the area, the distance to be sailed from Hawaii, and the attrition the fleet would suffer en route from Japanese cruiser, destroyer, submarine, and air assaults, they estimated that the attacking fleet would require to start out with a 2:1 superiority to assure victory. Hence the grievance at the 10:6 ratio for capital ships; the much deeper alarm over the London Conference's 10:7 ratio; and, worse still, the failure by the administration and Congress even to build up to the allowed totals. Reversing these assumptions, the Japanese Naval General Staff postulated a 10:7 ratio as the minimum to guarantee Japanese victory. Its dissatisfaction with the Washington Conference's 10:6 ratio for capital ships was mitigated by the absence of any restrictions on building in the other categories. But that advantage was lost at London. The net result was a balance of strategic power that left neither side confident of winning. That men convinced of the likelihood of war would be unhappy over this situation is understandable. But why should the two countries come to blows? Although American big-navy advocates talked much about the threat of a possible attack on the Philippines, their underlying assumption—again shared by Japanese strategists—was that hostilities would result from a clash over Japanese expansionism in China. Thus, the question of the adequacy of the American navy—and of American military capability generally—rests in the final analysis upon what were this country's foreign policy objectives.

Generally, the more ambitious a nation's foreign policy objectives, the larger its armed forces will be. Or to put the matter in different terms, a nation's mobilized strength is a function of what its decision-makers—and to the extent that their policies require popular support, what its public opinion—regards as the "national interest." Given the multiplicity of definitions that have been advanced, many political scientists deny that there is, in any objective sense, such a thing as "the national interest." But what counts is how men at any given time view the situation of their nation vis-à-vis other nations. To take over Donald E. Nuechterlein's definition, *"the national interest is the perceived needs and desires of one sovereign state in relation to other sovereign states comprising the external environment."* In this broad sense, national interests may be strategic, economic, or ideological. All interests do not weigh in the balance the same. The stakes involved are felt, on an ascending scale of "intensity," as "peripheral," "major," "vital," and "survival." The most crucial question is what makes an interest "vital." As a rule of thumb, a "vital" interest exists when "serious harm will very likely result to the state unless strong measures"—

including military force—are taken to deter or counter "an adverse action by another state."

The most important single factor shaping, and delimiting, United States foreign policymaking in the Republican era was this country's overwhelming sense of security. While favoring the expansion of overseas trade and investment, American officials were not willing to incur excessive costs and risk in their pursuit. Washington was most activist in backing American business abroad when such action coincided with its larger strategic and political goals: the World War I–inspired desire for American control over petroleum reserves, cables, and banking facilities in Latin America; defense of the traditional Open Door policy in China; and access to the oil of the Middle East and Dutch East Indies because of the feared depletion of American reserves. Where such political and strategic objectives were not at stake, State Department support for private interests was limited to routine calls for equal opportunities for American firms. Exports and overseas investments represented no more than a minor factor in the total national economy. The country remained self-sufficient in most mineral resources; by the latter 1920's even the anxieties over oil supplies had largely faded. The third world, as we now call it, remained under colonial rule; most of the underdeveloped countries that were independent, far from resisting, welcomed American investment from a wish to play this country off against more immediately threatening powers, to tap new sources of revenue, or to promote economic growth.

American strategic planning for Latin America up to the late thirties envisaged United States interests almost exclusively in terms of the Caribbean region as this country's "soft underbelly." Although plans were drawn up for intervention in each of the South American countries, these were more conceptual and intellectual exercises than operational realities. Even with regard to the Caribbean area, the absence of any meaningful danger from Europe after World War I led American policymakers to inaugurate a shift away from military intervention in favor of other methods of promoting order and stability. When temporary intervention was required to safeguard American lives and property, the forces at the disposal of the navy's Special Squadron were sufficient for the purpose. Only in Nicaragua was there significant resistance—and the *Sandinistas* were more a political embarrassment than a military threat. Nor was there—except for Mexico—any effective challenge to American primacy south of the border from the larger Latin American countries. Developments during and after World War I had strengthened the bonds of Latin American economic dependency upon this country. Notwithstanding the strain of anti-Americanism among Latin American intellectuals, most local elites welcomed the Yankee dollar. Apart from Argentina, the South American republics deferred to American leadership in political matters. The 1920's did witness major frictions with Mexico, partly because of the threat to American property rights from Mexican revolutionary nationalism, partly because of the Mexican government's anti-clerical campaign. But, despite rumors to the contrary, American officials never seriously contemplated using force. And a judicious mixture of pragmatic official and unofficial diplomacy with economic pressure brought a resolution of the differences on terms satisfactory to Washington.

Despite the popular distrust of Old World entanglements, the Republican administrations of the age of normalcy were not indifferent to, nor aloof from, European problems. On the contrary, the establishment of a peaceful and prosperous Europe ranked high upon their list of priorities. American negotiators disregarded congressional guidelines to scale down substantially the Allied war debts. Convinced of the adverse political and economic effects of excessive reparations, Washington simultaneously labored to work out a "realistic" solution based upon Germany's capacity to pay. After the failure of his efforts to forestall the French occupation of the Ruhr, Secretary of State Charles Evans Hughes took the lead in arranging for the Dawes Plan settlement of the deadlock. The Federal Reserve—encouraged and supported by the Treasury—cooperated with the European central banks to achieve currency stabilization. Although the United States took no formal part in the security arrangements reached at Locarno, American officials exerted behind-the-scenes pressure in favor of the accord by warning that continued American loans depended upon the return of political stability. In contrast with the later ridicule of the naiveté of outlawing war, the Kellogg-Briand treaty was hailed by contemporaries as the harbinger of a larger role by the United States in world affairs, while influential elements in this country saw in the pact an opening wedge for American cooperation with collective action against aggressors.

The question is not the fact of United States involvement in European affairs, but its extent. The promotion of European recovery did take a secondary place in the calculations of American officialdom to what was regarded as more important priorities, such as tariff protection for the home market and reducing the burden on American taxpayers. Nor did support for European political stability extend to a willingness to make binding diplomatic or military commitments. Yet, even leaving aside the domestic political constraints upon American decision-makers, what more *should* the United States have done? American political and business leaders remained confident—and here Herbert Hoover was simply the most articulate spokesman of a widely shared optimism—that the United States could prosper economically, regardless of what happened in Europe. Diplomatic and military commitments meant in the context of the time support for France against Germany. Although regarding a strong France as indispensable for a European balance of power, Washington did not accept Paris' definition of what constituted French security. American officials were convinced that the French hard line on reparations, their refusal to meet Germany's legitimate grievances, and their efforts to keep Germany down were self-defeating by undermining the possibility of a prosperous, satisfied, republican Germany. Thus, they worried that any commitments on this country's part would strengthen French intransigence. Nor were they alone in this view. Their British counterparts were no more willing to underwrite the *status quo.*

If from the vantage point of the Second World War, the failure to back up France appears misguided, was that the wisest course in the 1920's? Despite the Treaty of Versailles, Germany remained potentially the most powerful nation in Europe. Nothing short of the massing of overwhelming military force could have kept Germany in a permanently inferior status. The disastrous results of Hitler's rise to power showed the validity of the American view that future European peace depended upon the success of the Weimar Republic. More immediately relevant, American policies appeared to have been successful. The influx of American loans that followed adoption of the Dawes Plan, and the achievement of currency stabilization, led to a spurt of economic growth and a new mood of optimism in Europe. The resulting prosperity contributed to muting the social conflicts that had wracked the domestic politics of the European nations in the first half of the decade. American leaders shared the contemporary optimism about the Locarno settlement as the dawn of a new era of cooperation and peace. With the benefit of hindsight, historians have emphasized the fragility of the "spirit of Locarno." While the historian can only speculate about what might have been, there is no difficulty in imagining a better Europe in the 1930's were it not for the devastating impact of the Great Depression. In the context of the time, the pact did establish, as William J. Newman has persuasively argued, "a viable and stable balance . . . which held considerable promise of diplomatic and international stability in Europe."

When this structure began to crumble under the impact of the Great Depression, the Hoover administration was not blind to the dangers. In the face of the German financial crisis in the spring of 1931, the President moved boldly to forestall the threatened collapse of the Central European banking and financial structure with his moratorium, while simultaneously working behind the scenes to promote a new debt-reparations settlement. By 1932, he had become sufficiently alarmed at the deadlock at the Geneva Disarmament Conference to take new initiatives that went far toward meeting the French demand for security guarantees. Reversing its long-standing position, Washington endorsed a system of international supervision and control as part of any new arms limitation agreement. Although Hoover continued to balk at making commitments in advance—even if no more than a formal consultative pact—American officials repeatedly assured the Western Europeans that this country would not interfere with collective action against aggressors. That Hoover's efforts to unravel the debt-reparations tangle proved a failure was due as much to the intransigence of the European powers as to domestic political impediments. The administration's decision not to go further in meeting French security anxieties reflected in part popular and congressional hostility to involvement in European power rivalries, partly the chief executive's own fear that such involvement might entangle the United States in responsibilities and dangers, such as in Eastern Europe, not commensurate with its interests.

Limited interest similarly shaped United States policy in the Far East. Although firms with a large economic stake in China, such as Standard Oil, were not without political muscle, this country's trade with and investment in China were relatively minor—and substantially below trade with and investment in Japan. Nor did American bankers, despite State Department urgings, show any enthusiasm for loans to China. American interests in China were primarily ideological, or, to put the matter more bluntly, sentimental. Captivated by the image of this country as the protector and friend of China, a vocal body of American opinion spearheaded by the missionary lobby indulged in fanciful visions of the United States as the mentor to China's evolution into a modern liberal democracy. Responsible government officials had a more realistic grasp of the rampant confusion and chaos in China, and were painfully aware of this country's limited ability to shape events in the Celestial Empire to its liking. Taking as axiomatic their duty to protect the lives, property, and rights of American citizens abroad, American diplomats kept up a drumfire of protests when those were threatened. Wishing to maintain a show of the flag, the State Department overruled the army's wish to withdraw the tiny force stationed in China. But the major thrust of American policy toward China during the twenties was toward accommodation with Chinese nationalism. The Hoover administration even accepted in principle, and entered into negotiations for, the gradual relinquishment of the keystone of the so-called unequal treaty system, the right of extraterritoriality.

Those historians who fault American policymakers for failing to take a firmer stand against Japan fail to ask what was the alternative to the attempt at a *modus vivendi* inaugurated by Secretary of State Charles Evans Hughes. China was a weak reed; Russia in the aftermath of the war was in temporary eclipse as a Far Eastern power; and Britain, painfully aware of its vulnerability in Asia, was anxious to avoid provoking the Japanese. American efforts first under Taft and then under Wilson to resist Japanese ambitions in China had antagonized the Japanese without any substantive gain for the United States. Most importantly, Hughes did not think the Open Door a sufficiently vital interest for the United States to be worth fighting for. Even if he had, the public and their representatives in Congress were not willing to make the military and naval expenditures required to deter Japan if she determined to close the door. Given this situation, Hughes achieved at the Washington Conference a diplomatic triumph that gained for the United States the abrogation of the long-suspect Anglo-Japanese Alliance, Japan's formal withdrawal of Group V of the Twenty-One Demands, and its pledge to respect the Open Door and China's independence and territorial integrity. And until 1931, Tokyo remained committed to the "Washington system" of peaceful economic expansion in China and cooperation with the Anglo-American powers.

The United States was not without blame for the breakdown of Japanese adherence to the "Washington system." The Japanese exclusion provision of the 1924 immigration act contributed to undercutting the pro-Western moderates, as did this country's unilateral support for Chinese nationalism. But more important were forces beyond Washington's control: the continued strength of traditional attitudes and values antagonistic to the new "cooperative diplomacy"; the shifting balance of power on the Asiatic mainland with the rise of Chinese nationalism and the reemergence of Russia as a Far Eastern power; and Japan's worsening economic difficulties. Would a stronger United States navy have deterred the invasion of Manchuria? The militants who precipitated the crisis were not moved by a feeling of strength but rather by a sense of weakness: by anxieties about Japan's isolation in the world; by fear that the London naval agreement of 1930 jeopardized Japanese supremacy in the western Pacific; and by alarm over Chiang Kai-shek's growing pressure on the Japanese position in Manchuria. When a broad cross section of Japanese opinion forced the government in Tokyo to sanction the actions taken by the soldiers in the field, what could the United States do? As Christopher Thorne has brilliantly shown, given the Japanese domestic political situation and Japan's preponderant military power in the area, "there was little that the United States, Britain and France, singly or even together, could do to make the Japanese surrender over Manchuria . . . without accepting a high risk of extensive costs."

Was the risk worth taking? The answer to that question depends upon an estimate of if, and how much, Japanese ambitions menaced American national interests. Throughout the interwar period, naval planners predicated their strategic thinking upon the probability, if not inevitability, of war with Japan. In part, naval officers exploited the supposed Japanese menace as a stratagem to win larger appropriations; in part, they continued to hew to the Mahan thesis that United States prosperity depended upon access to the China market. But there were dissenting voices even within the naval establishment. Admiral William V. Pratt, chief of Naval Operations from 1930 to 1933, never shared his colleagues' belief in the inevitability of a United States-Japanese war. Admiral Montgomery Taylor, commander of the Asiatic fleet during the Manchurian crisis, dismissed the possibility of saving China as a hopeless proposition; his successor, Admiral F. B. Upham, questioned the importance of trade with China given the costs of maintaining an American position there. Although paying lip service to War Plan Orange, army planners had grown increasingly dubious about the possibility of its successful execution, doubts that would culminate in 1935 in their calling for writing off the Philippines as a military liability and adopting the Alaska-Hawaii-Panama triangle as this country's strategic perimeter. Army officials down graded—at least until the late thirties—the likelihood of war with Japan in the foreseeable future. In contrast to their naval counterparts, they did not regard Japanese expansionism on the Asiatic continent as a threat to any vital American interests.

That view was shared by the public at large, Congress, and administration leaders. Although popular and congressional sentiment was strongly anti-Japanese and there was a widespread feeling that the United States should do something, the near-universal opinion was against any action that carried the danger of war. The support that existed for economic sanctions rested upon the assumption that such pressure would suffice to force Tokyo to retreat without further escalation of the crisis. But Hoover was convinced that the result would be war. And while he believed that the United States could not allow Japan's treaty violation to pass without protest, he regarded this country's vital interests as limited to the defense of the Western Hemisphere. His secretary of state, Henry L. Stimson, was more enamored of the importance of the China market, more disposed by temperament to trying to bluff Japan into backing down, and more optimistic about the success of economic sanctions. At the same time, he was no more willing than his chief to risk a showdown with Japan. Nor were his top advisers. No one was more committed to the importance of maintaining the Open Door or more imbued with the sense of America's special responsibility to China than was Stanley K. Hornbeck, chief of the State Department's Division of Far Eastern Affairs. Yet when faced with the Japanese challenge in Manchuria, Hornbeck was torn between militancy and caution—with caution gaining the upper hand. Even when the Japanese in the spring of 1933 advanced into Northern China, he acknowledged that the "United States has not much to lose . . . there is nothing there that is vital to us."

The post-Pearl Harbor argument to the contrary rests, in the final analysis, upon the assumption—at times made explicit, but more generally implicitly accepted—that there was a direct line of planned aggression from Manchuria culminating in Pearl Harbor. But perhaps the most striking feature of Japanese policymaking after 1931 was its ambivalence, confusion, and *ad hoc* quality. Recent Japanese scholarship indicates that the general staff blundered into, rather than plotted, the war with China that began in 1937 and thereafter was unable to find a way out of that deepening morass. And the Japanese decision to move southward—which, rather than the war in China, would be the major precipitating factor bringing on conflict with the United States— was not the result of any long-hatched master plan, but was rather a response to what appeared to be the opportunities made possible by the European war. Japanese army planners did not seriously envisage the possibility of war with the United States until mid-1940. Up to then, the army had looked first upon the Soviet Union, then upon Britain as Japan's most likely antagonist. Even the navy, which had long viewed the United States as Japan's most probable foe, drifted into the "determination" to go to war without much thought about what that involved. Not until mid-1941 did Japanese decision-makers come to accept—more fatalistically than optimistically—that the decision to advance south would inevitably bring war with the United States.

The basic flaw in the realist indictment of American foreign and military policies during the so-called age of normalcy is a case of confusing the 1920's with the 1930's. The years after 1933 did witness an extraordinary rapid shift in the world balance of power. That shift was due partly to the accelerating pace of technological innovation, but more to the differing willingness by the major powers to allocate resources to arms. If the United States was ill-prepared to meet the resulting challenges, the fault lay with the men in charge when those changes took place. In the context of 1921–1933, however, American policies were neither naive nor unwise. Perhaps at no time in its history—before or since—has the United States been more secure. Nor did his Republican successors have Wilson's messianic zeal to create a new global order. "The foreign policy of small nations is often determined for them," the British scholar A. E. Campbell has pointed out, "but in a nation complex, powerful, and unusually secure the assessment of the national interest can only rest on a general conception of the world situation. . . . Politically conscious men will have such a conception at the back of their minds, if not always at the forefront, and against that conception they will test the importance or unimportance for their nation of specific world events, and so the need for government action." Thus, what must be kept in mind about the years after World War I is that "the United States possessed a unique combination of great power and an isolated position."

✳ *F U R T H E R   R E A D I N G*

Derek H. Aldcroft, *From Versailles to Wall Street, 1919–1929* (1977)

Jules R. Benjamin, *The United States and Cuba* (1978)

John Braeman, "American Foreign Policy in the Age of Normalcy: Three Histo-riographical Traditions," *Amerikastudian/American Studies*, 26 (1981), 125–58

Thomas Buckley, *The United States and the Washington Conference, 1921–1922* (1970)

————, and Edwin B. Strong, *American Foreign and National Security Policies, 1914–1945* (1987)

Bruce J. Calder, *The Impact of Intervention* (1984)

Warren I. Cohen, *Empire Without Tears* (1987)

Frank Costigliola, *Awkward Dominion: American Political, Economic, and Cultural Relations with Europe, 1919–1933* (1984)

Charles DeBenedetti, *Origins of the Modern American Peace Movement, 1915–1929* (1978)

Roger Dingman, *Power in the Pacific: The Origins of Naval Arms Limitations, 1914–1922* (1976)

L. Ethan Ellis, *Republican Foreign Policy, 1921–1933* (1968)

Robert H. Ferrell, *American Diplomacy in the Great Depression* (1957)

————, *Frank B. Kellogg and Henry L. Stimson* (1963)

————, *Peace in Their Time* (1952)

Peter Filene, *Americans and the Soviet Experiment, 1917–1933* (1967)

Betty Glad, *Charles Evans Hughes and the Illusions of Innocence* (1966)

Kenneth J. Grieb, *The Latin American Policy of Warren G. Harding* (1976)

Ellis W. Hawley, ed., *Herbert Hoover, Secretary of Commerce, 1921–1928* (1981)

Michael J. Hogan, *Informal Entente: The Private Structure of Cooperation in Anglo-American Economic Diplomacy* (1977)

Jon Jacobson, "Is There a New International History of the 1920s?" *American Historical Review*, 88 (1983), 617–45

Harold Josephson, *James T. Shotwell and the Rise of Internationalism in America* (1976)

William Kamman, *A Search for Stability: United States Diplomacy Toward Nicaragua, 1925–1933* (1968)

Walter LaFeber, *Inevitable Revolutions* (1983)

Melvyn P. Leffler, *The Elusive Quest: America's Pursuit of European Stability and French Security, 1919–1933* (1979)

————, "Political Isolationism, Economic Expansionism, or Diplomatic Realism? American Policy toward Western Europe, 1921–1933," *Perspectives in American History*, 8 (1974), 413–61

Richard Lowitt, *George W. Norris: The Persistence of a Progressive, 1913–1933* (1971)

Sally Marks, *The Illusion of Peace: International Relations, 1918–1933* (1976)

Elting E. Morison, *Turmoil and Tradition* (1960)

Robert K. Murray, *The Harding Era* (1969)

Carl Parrini, *Heir to Empire* (1969)

Stephen J. Randall, *United States Foreign Oil Policy, 1919–1948* (1986)

Robert D. Schulzinger, *The Making of the Diplomatic Mind: The Training, Outlook, and Style of United States Foreign Service Officers, 1908–1931* (1975)

Michael S. Sherry, *The Rise of American Air Power* (1987)

Robert F. Smith, "Republican Policy and Pax Americana, 1921–1932," in William Appleman Williams, ed., *From Colony to Empire* (1972), 253–92.

George Soule, *Prosperity Decade* (1947)

Joan Hoff Wilson, *Herbert Hoover* (1975)

———, *Ideology and Economics: U. S. Relations with the Soviet Union, 1918–1933* (1974)

———, "A Reevaluation of Herbert Hoover's Foreign Policy," in Martin L. Fausold and George T. Mazuzan, eds., *The Hoover Presidency: A Reappraisal* (1974), 164–86

William Appleman Williams, "The Legend of Isolationism in the 1920s," *Science and Society*, 18 (1954), 1–20

Franklin D. Roosevelt,

Isolationism,

and World War II

The rise of German and Japanese aggression in the 1930s presented Americans once again with questions of war or peace, neutrality or alliance. Americans protested this aggression—witness the Stimson Doctrine after Japan seized Manchuria—but they sought to avoid entanglement in the cascading crises that engulfed both Europe and Asia. Congress passed Neutrality Acts, and President Franklin D. Roosevelt publicly endorsed America's neutral position. Recalling the horrors of World War I and beset by a terrible depression at home, many Americans embraced what was popularly known as isolationism. After the outbreak of full-scale war in Europe in September 1939, Roosevelt and the nation gradually moved toward an interventionist posture, repealing the arms embargo and sending Britain and the Soviet Union Lend-Lease supplies.

When war came to the United States, it struck not in Europe but in Asia. For more than a decade, the United States had opposed Japanese expansion into China. In the late 1930s, as the Sino-Japanese war intensified, the United States began to expand its navy and grant loans to China. And Washington did not invoke the Neutrality Acts, thereby permitting China to buy armaments from the United States. In September 1940, after Japan gained bases in French Indochina and signed a Tripartite Pact with Germany and Italy, the United States embargoed shipments of scrap iron and steel to the island nation. The economic war accelerated in July 1941 after Japanese troops occupied French Indochina. The Roosevelt administration froze Japanese assets in the United States, thereby crippling Japanese-U.S. trade and denying Japan vital petroleum imports. Tokyo and Washington exchanged proposals and counterproposals for the rest of the year, but to no avail. On December 7, in a surprise attack, Japanese pilots bombed the American naval base at Pearl Harbor, the Hawaiian Islands. The United States declared war on Japan, and Germany declared war on the United States. Americans once again braced themselves for world war.

Historians have grappled with controversial questions in explaining America's road to war. Almost all study Franklin D. Roosevelt as decision maker, probing his ideas, leadership, and choices, and the results of his policies. Was he an isolationist, like most other Americans? Or was he an internationalist who found it difficult to act on his views because of restraining domestic politics and public opinion? Was he a leader or a follower? Was he in command of the making of foreign policy, or did he leave crucial decisions to subordinates, who complicated his diplomacy? Did he have command of the foreign affairs bureaucracy? Did he permit Secretary of State Cordell Hull too much authority in handling Asian affairs while he concentrated on Europe, thus failing to coordinate policy?

Another set of questions focuses on events and decisions leading to Pearl Harbor. Was Japanese-American conflict inevitable? Was war between Japan and the United States inevitable? Or could different American policies toward unacceptable Japanese expansion have produced a different outcome? How important was timing? Did the United States push Japan into war? Was the issue of China solvable? Were American proposals realistic? Finally, although most historians reject any notion of a Rooseveltian conspiracy, questions of this nature persist: Did Roosevelt, eager to enter the European war, devise policies toward Japan that guaranteed entry into war through the Asian "back door"? Did the President deliberately set up Pearl Harbor for disaster, or did American leaders simply err in not alerting the base to possible attack?

D O C U M E N T S

In the first selection, Senator Gerald P. Nye explains the results of his investigation into alleged business pressure on the Wilson administration for American entry into the First World War. His speech on May 28, 1935, reflected ideas that helped to pass the Neutrality Acts, reprinted here as the second document. In the third document, a speech on August 14, 1936, at Chautauqua, New York, President Franklin D. Roosevelt passionately condemned war. On October 5, 1937, he told a Chicago audience that aggressors should be "quarantined" (the fourth selection). He obviously directed his words at Japan, but he offered no concrete plans.

The next document is the President's address to the nation in a "fireside chat" on December 29, 1940; he announced that he would make the United States the "arsenal of democracy." Congress passed the Lend-Lease Act the following March. The sixth selection is distinguished historian Charles A. Beard's 1941 testimony before a Senate committee protesting Lend-Lease as a step toward war. In July 1941, Secretary of State Cordell Hull submitted an American proposal for a Sino-Japanese settlement and lectured Ambassador Kichisaburo Nomura that some Japanese government officials had obstructed opportunities for peace by applauding the Tripartite Alliance. A high-level meeting in Tokyo conducted by Foreign Minister Yosuke Matsuoka heard his adviser, Yoshie Saito, analyze the divisive issues in Japanese-American relations. Saito's comments are reprinted here as the seventh document. The eighth selection is the Atlantic Charter penned by Roosevelt and British Prime Minister Winston Churchill on August 14, 1941, after their summit meeting off the coast of Newfoundland. These principles were popularly considered the war objectives of the

Allies. The ninth document, the American proposals to Japan dated November 29, 1941, sought to roll back Japanese expansion and revive the Open Door principles. The Japanese position paper of December 7, 1941 (the tenth selection), handed to Hull as the rising sun's warriors descended upon Pearl Harbor, outlined Japan's case against the United States and for mastery of China. The final document is Roosevelt's war message to Congress, delivered on December 8, 1941.

Gerald P. Nye on the
Causes of War, 1935

This past year has witnessed the most intensive inquiry into the questions of arms traffic, munitions, war profits, and profits from preparedness for war that the world ever saw undertaken. It has been my privilege to work with six other Members of the United States Senate in this study. I am happy tonight to say that it grows increasingly evident that our labors have not been in vain and that truly worth-while legislation will be forthcoming to meet the frightful challenge which the inquiry disclosures have been. Largely because the people have shown tremendous interest in the subject, I am sure that substantial legislation is on the way to restrain those racketeers who find large profit in breeding hate, fear, and suspicion as a base for large preparedness programs, and who have learned that while there is large profit in preparing for war, there is larger profit for them in war itself.

But out of this year of study has come tremendous conviction that our American welfare requires that great importance be given the subject of our neutrality when others are at war.

Tonight I think we will do well to give some thought to causes behind our entry into the Great War. Those causes as well as the results which have since followed are an experience we should not soon forget.

Nineteen hundred and fourteen found America just as determined, just as anxious for peace as it is now. But less than 3 years later we were in the greatest of all wars, creating obligations and burdens which even to this day bend our backs. What was it that took us into that war in spite of our high contrary resolve? . . .

Let us be as frank before the next war comes as Wilson was frank after the last war was over. Let us know that it is sales and shipments of munitions and contraband, and the lure of the profits in them, that will get us into another war, and that when the proper time comes and we talk about national honor, let us know that simply means the right to go on making money out of a war.

Let us have done with all the fraud, and we will have done with all the postwar friction.

There are many who have tried to keep us from being involved in entangling foreign political alliances. But since wars are for economic causes basically, it is as important to avoid becoming involved in entangling foreign economic alliances. That is the crux of the matter. It is useless to pretend that our isolation from foreign political entanglements means anything if we open wide the gates to foreign loans and credits for munitions and spread out a network of munition ships that will be ignition points of another war.

What are the facts behind these conclusions of men familiar with the real causes of our entering the war?

From the year ending June 30, 1914, to the year ending June 30, 1916, our exports to the Allies increased almost 300 percent, or from $825,000,000 to $3,214,000,000. During the same period our exports to the Central Powers fell from $169,000,000 to $1,000,000. Long before we declared war on Germany we had ceased to have any economic interests in her fate in the war, because she was buying nothing from us.

The bulk of our sales during this pre-war period were in munitions and war materials. It must be remembered that the World War inaugurated war on the scale of whole nations pitted against nations—not simply of armies, however large, against armies. Consequently, foodstuffs and raw materials for the manufacture of items essential to modern war were declared contraband by one belligerent or another. In the year 1914 more than half of our total exports to all countries were munitions and war materials of this kind. In 1915 our sales of such materials were 179 percent greater than they had been in the preceding year and constituted 86 percent of our total exports to all countries. In 1916 our sales of these articles were 287 percent greater than in 1914 and totaled $3,700,000,000, which was 88 percent of our total exports. The growth of our sales of explosives may be taken as a single example. In the year ending June 30, 1914, we exported only $10,000,000 worth of explosives. In the year ending June 30, 1915, this figure had grown to $189,000,000, and in the next year it reached $715,000,000. . . .

Now, we must not forget that this enormous trade required financing also on an enormous scale. Our State Department at the outset of the war announced that "in the judgment of this Government loans by American bankers to any foreign nation which is at war are inconsistent with the true spirit of neutrality." But once we had recognized and encouraged the trade in war materials as a neutral right, it proved impossible to deny the demands for normal financing of that trade.

While the State Department was officially opposed to loans, our bankers were not. Mr. Lamont has written that J. P. Morgan & Co. was whole-heartedly in back of the Allies from the start. Mr. Davison was sent to England to place the firm's services at England's disposal. As early as February 1915 Morgan signed his first contract with the Du Pont Co. as agent for an allied power. Of the total sales by Du Pont to France and England, totalling practically half a billion dollars, over 70 percent were made through Morgan & Co., although Morgan & Co. acted as agents for the Allies only from the spring of 1915 until shortly after we entered the war—a little over 2 years.

From the early days of the war the State Department did not object to bank credits being extended to belligerents as distinguished from loans. In November 1914 France received $10,000,000 on 1-year treasury notes from the National City Bank, and in May 1915 Russia received $10,200,000 for a year from the same source. In April 1915 France received short-term credit of about $30,000,000 arranged by J. P. Morgan. Brown Bros. opened a commercial line of credit of $25,000,000 for French merchants in the summer of 1915.

In October 1915 America's bankers ceased distinguishing between credits and loans and the Government was helpless to prevent this. American investors began to finance the Allies in earnest with the flotation of the great Anglo-French loan of $500,000,000 through a huge banking syndicate headed by J. P. Morgan & Co. Similar loans followed fast, and by 1917 total loans and credits to the Allies of well over $2,000,000,000 were outstanding. Morgan & Co. had a demand loan or overdraft due from Great Britain of approximately $400,000,000, which obviously could not be paid at that time. Instead Great Britain deliberately needed enormous new credits.

By this time the history of the bank credits up to October 1915 had been repeated—on a far larger scale. In the early part of 1917 it was clear that our private financial and banking resources were exhausted. Unless the great credit of the American Nation could itself be pledged, the flow of goods to Europe would end and the claims of our banks, who had made possible this flow of goods in the past, would not be paid. No one stopped to inquire whether new funds would not similarly be burned up in the holocaust of European war and would be used in the natural course of events to bail out the American banks. The facts are that by November 11, 1918, $7,000,000,000 were lent to Europe by our Government and, though most of this is still unpaid, the private loans were redeemed and the securities behind them have disappeared.

We are now discussing things that have heretofore been whispered only—things that most of us felt couldn't be true because they shouldn't be true. But if a recognition of ugly facts will help us prevent another disaster we must discuss them openly. . . .

The experience of the last war includes the lesson that neutral rights are not a matter for national protection unless we are prepared to protect them by force. Senator Clark and I, and, I believe, Representative Maverick and other colleagues in Congress, believe that the only hope of our staying out of war is through our people recognizing and declaring as a matter of considered and fervently held national policy, that we will not ship munitions to aid combatants and that those of our citizens who ship other materials to belligerent nations must do so at their own risk and without any hope of protection from our Government. If our financiers and industrialists wish to speculate for war profits, let them be warned in advance that they are to be limited to speculation with their own capital and not with the lives of their countrymen and the fabric of their whole nation.

The Neutrality Acts, 1935–1939

The 1935 Act

Resolved by the Senate and House of Representatives of the United States of America in Congress assembled, That upon outbreak or during the progress of war between, or among, two or more foreign states, the President shall proclaim such fact, and it shall thereafter be unlawful to export arms, ammunition, or implements of war from any place in the United States, or possessions of the United States, to any port of such belligerent states, or to any neutral port for transshipment to, or for the use of a belligerent country.

The President, by proclamation, shall definitely enumerate the arms, ammunition, or implements of war, the export of which is prohibited by this Act.

The President may, from time to time, by proclamation, extend such embargo upon the export of arms, ammunition, or implements of war to other states as and when they may become involved in such war. . . .

The 1936 Act

Resolved by the Senate and House of Representatives of the United States of America in Congress assembled, That section 1 of the joint resolution . . . approved August 31, 1935, be, and the same hereby is, amended by striking out in the first section, on the second line, after the word "assembled" the following words: "That upon the outbreak or during the progress of war between", and inserting therefor the words: "Whenever the President shall find that there exists a state of war between"; and by striking out the word "may" after the word "President" and before the word "from" in the twelfth line, and inserting in lieu thereof the word "shall". . . .

Section 2.   There are hereby added to said joint resolution two new sections, to be known as sections 1a and 1b, reading as follows:

"Section 1a.   Whenever the President shall have issued his proclamation as provided for in section 1 of this Act, it shall thereafter during the period of the war be unlawful for any person within the United States to purchase, sell, or exchange bonds, securities, or other obligations of the government of any belligerent country, or of any political subdivision thereof, or of any person acting for or on behalf of such government, issued after the date of such proclamation, or to make any loan or extend any credit to any such government or person. . . ."

The 1937 Act

Whenever the President shall have issued a proclamation under the authority of section 1 of this Act it shall thereafter be unlawful for any citizen of the United States to travel on any vessel of the state or states named in such proclamation, except in accordance with such rules and regulations as the President shall prescribe. . . .

The 1939 Act

Section 1.   (a) That whenever the President, or the Congress by concurrent resolution, shall find that there exists a state of war between foreign states, and that it is necessary to promote the security or preserve the peace of the United States or to protect the lives of citizens of the United States, the President shall issue a Proclamation naming the states involved; and he shall, from time to time, by proclamation, name other states as and when they may become involved in the war. . . .

Section 2.   (a) Whenever the President shall have issued a proclamation under the authority of section 1 (a) it shall thereafter be unlawful for any American vessel to carry any passengers or any articles or materials to any state named in such proclamation. . . .

(c) Whenever the President shall have issued a proclamation under the authority of section 1 (a) it shall thereafter be unlawful to export or transport or attempt to export or transport, or cause to be exported or transported, from the United States to any state named in such proclamation, any articles or materials (except copyrighted articles or materials) until all right, title, and interest therein shall have been transferred to some foreign government, agency, institution, association, partnership, corporation, or national. . . .

Franklin D. Roosevelt on War, at Chautauqua, 1936

We are not isolationists except insofar as we seek to isolate ourselves completely from war. Yet we must remember that so long as war exists on earth there will be some danger that even the nation which most ardently desires peace may be drawn into war.

I have seen war. I have seen war on land and sea. I have seen blood running from the wounded. I have seen men coughing out their gassed lungs. I have seen the dead in the mud. I have seen cities destroyed. I have seen 200 limping, exhausted men come out of line—the survivors of a regiment of 1,000 that went forward 48 hours before. I have seen children starving. I have seen the agony of mothers and wives. I hate war.

I have passed unnumbered hours, I shall pass unnumbered hours thinking and planning how war may be kept from this nation.

I wish I could keep war from all nations, but that is beyond my power. I can at least make certain that no act of the United States helps to produce or to promote war. I can at least make clear that the conscience of America revolts against war and that any nation which provokes war forfeits the sympathy of the people of the United States. . . .

The Congress of the United States has given me certain authority to provide safeguards of American neutrality in case of war.

The President of the United States, who, under our Constitution, is vested with primary authority to conduct our international relations, thus has been given new weapons with which to maintain our neutrality.

Nevertheless—and I speak from a long experience—the effective maintenance of American neutrality depends today, as in the past, on the wisdom and determination of whoever at the moment occupy the offices of President and Secretary of State.

It is clear that our present policy and the measures passed by the Congress would, in the event of a war on some other continent, reduce war profits which would otherwise accrue to American citizens. Industrial and agricultural production for a war market may give immense fortunes to a few men; for the nation as a whole it produces disaster. It was the prospect of war profits that made our farmers in the west plow up prairie land that should never have been plowed but should have been left for grazing cattle. Today we are reaping the harvest of those war profits in the dust storms which have devastated those war-plowed areas.

It was the prospect of war profits that caused the extension of monopoly and unjustified expansion of industry and a price level so high that the normal relationship between debtor and creditor was destroyed.

Nevertheless, if war should break out again in another continent, let us not blink [at] the fact that we would find in this country thousands of Americans who, seeking immediate riches—fool's gold—would attempt to break down or evade our neutrality.

They would tell you—and, unfortunately, their views would get wide publicity—that if they could produce and ship this and that and the other article to belligerent nations the unemployed of America would all find work. They would tell you that if they could extend credit to warring nations that credit would be used in the United States to build homes and factories and pay our debts. They would tell you that America once more would capture the trade of the world.

It would be hard to resist that clamor. It would be hard for many Americans, I fear, to look beyond, to realize the inevitable penalties, the inevitable day of reckoning that comes from a false prosperity. To resist the clamor of that greed, if war should come, would require the unswerving support of all Americans who love peace.

If we face the choice of profits or peace, the Nation will answer—must answer—"we choose peace." It is the duty of all of us to encourage such a body of public opinion in this country that the answer will be clear and for all practical purposes unanimous. . . .

We can keep out of war if those who watch and decide have a sufficiently detailed understanding of international affairs to make certain that the small decisions of each day do not lead toward war, and if, at the same time, they possess the courage to say "no" to those who selfishly or unwisely would let us go to war.

Of all the nations of the world today we are in many ways most singularly blessed. Our closest neighbors are good neighbors. If there are remoter nations that wish us not good but ill, they know that we are strong; they know that we can and will defend ourselves and defend our neighborhood.

We seek to dominate no other nation. We ask no territorial expansion. We oppose imperialism. We desire reduction in world armaments.

We believe in democracy; we believe in freedom; we believe in peace. We offer to every nation of the world the handclasp of the good neighbor. Let those who wish our friendship look us in the eye and take our hand.

Roosevelt's "Quarantine" Speech, 1937

Some fifteen years ago the hopes of mankind for a continuing era of international peace were raised to great heights when more than sixty nations solemnly pledged themselves not to resort to arms in furtherance of their national aims and policies. The high aspirations expressed in the Briand-Kellogg Peace Pact and the hopes for peace thus raised have of late given way to a haunting fear of calamity. The present reign of terror and international lawlessness began a few years ago.

It began through unjustified interference in the internal affairs of other nations or the invasion of alien territory in violation of treaties; and has now reached a stage where the very foundations of civilization are seriously threatened. The landmarks and traditions which have marked the progress of civilization toward a condition of law, order and justice are being wiped away.

Without a declaration of war and without warning or justification of any kind, civilians, including vast numbers of women and children, are being ruthlessly murdered with bombs from the air. In times of so-called peace, ships are being attacked and sunk by submarines without cause or notice. Nations are fomenting and taking sides in civil warfare in nations that have never done them any harm. Nations claiming freedom for themselves deny it to others.

Innocent peoples, innocent nations, are being cruelly sacrificed to a greed for power and supremacy which is devoid of all sense of justice and humane considerations. . . .

The peace-loving nations must make a concerted effort in opposition to those violations of treaties and those ignorings of humane instincts which today are creating a state of international anarchy and instability from which there is no escape through mere isolation or neutrality.

Those who cherish their freedom and recognize and respect the equal right of their neighbors to be free and live in peace must work together for the triumph of law and moral principles in order that peace, justice and confidence may prevail in the world. There must be a return to a belief in the pledged word, in the value of a signed treaty. There must be recognition of the fact that national morality is as vital as private morality.

A bishop wrote me the other day: "It seems to me that something greatly needs to be said in behalf of ordinary humanity against the present practice of carrying the horrors of war to helpless civilians, especially women and children. It may be that such a protest might be regarded by many, who claim to be realists, as futile, but may it not be that the heart of mankind is so filled with horror at the present needless suffering that

that force could be mobilized in sufficient volume to lessen such cruelty in the days ahead. Even though it may take twenty years, which God forbid, for civilization to make effective its corporate protest against this barbarism, surely strong voices may hasten the day."

There is a solidarity and interdependence about the modern world, both technically and morally, which makes it impossible for any nation completely to isolate itself from economic and political upheavals in the rest of the world, especially when such upheavals appear to be spreading and not declining. There can be no stability or peace either within nations or between nations except under laws and moral standards adhered to by all. International anarchy destroys every foundation for peace. It jeopardizes either the immediate or the future security of every nation, large or small. It is, therefore, a matter of vital interest and concern to the people of the United States that the sanctity of international treaties and the maintenance of international morality be restored.

The overwhelming majority of the peoples and nations of the world today want to live in peace. They seek the removal of barriers against trade. They want to exert themselves in industry, in agriculture and in business, that they may increase their wealth through the production of wealth-producing goods rather than striving to produce military planes and bombs and machine guns and cannon for the destruction of human lives and useful property.

In those nations of the world which seem to be piling armament on armament for purposes of aggression, and those other nations which fear acts of aggression against them and their security, a very high proportion of their national income is being spent directly for armaments. It runs from thirty to as high as fifty percent. We are fortunate. The proportion that we in the United States spend is far less—eleven or twelve percent.

How happy we are that the circumstances of the moment permit us to put our money into bridges and boulevards, dams and reforestation, the conservation of our soil and many other kinds of useful works rather than into huge standing armies and vast supplies of implements of war.

I am compelled and you are compelled, nevertheless, to look ahead. The peace, the freedom and the security of ninety percent of the population of the world is being jeopardized by the remaining ten percent who are threatening a breakdown of all international order and law. Surely the ninety percent who want to live in peace under law and in accordance with moral standards that have received almost universal acceptance through the centuries, can and must find some way to make their will prevail.

The situation is definitely of universal concern. The questions involved relate not merely to violations of specific provisions of particular treaties; they are questions of war and of peace, of international law and especially of principles of humanity. It is true that they involve definite violations of agreements, and especially of the Covenant of the League of Nations, the Briand-Kellogg Pact and the Nine Power Treaty. But they also involve problems of world economy, world security and world humanity.

It is true that the moral consciousness of the world must recognize the importance of removing injustices and well-founded grievances; but at the same time it must be aroused to the cardinal necessity of honoring sanctity of treaties, of respecting the rights and liberties of others and of putting an end to acts of international aggression.

It seems to be unfortunately true that the epidemic of world lawlessness is spreading.

When an epidemic of physical disease starts to spread, the community approves and joins in a quarantine of the patients in order to protect the health of the community against the spread of the disease.

It is my determination to pursue a policy of peace. It is my determination to adopt every practicable measure to avoid involvement in war. It ought to be inconceivable that in this modern era, and in the face of experience, any nation could be so foolish and ruthless as to run the risk of plunging the whole world into war by invading and violating, in contravention of solemn treaties, the territory of other nations that have done them no real harm and are too weak to protect themselves adequately. Yet the peace of the world and the welfare and security of every nation, including our own, is today being threatened by that very thing.

Roosevelt on the "Arsenal of Democracy," 1940

Never before since Jamestown and Plymouth Rock has our American civilization been in such danger as now.

For, on September 27, 1940, by an agreement signed in Berlin, three powerful nations, two in Europe and one in Asia, joined themselves together in the threat that if the United States of America interfered with or blocked the expansion program of these three nations—a program aimed at world control—they would unite in ultimate action against the United States.

The Nazi masters of Germany have made it clear that they intend not only to dominate all life and thought in their own country, but also to enslave the whole of Europe, and then to use the resources of Europe to dominate the rest of the world. . . .

Does anyone seriously believe that we need to fear attack anywhere in the Americas while a free Britain remains our most powerful naval neighbor in the Atlantic? Does anyone seriously believe, on the other hand, that we could rest easy if the Axis powers were our neighbors there?

If Great Britain goes down, the Axis powers will control the continents of Europe, Asia, Africa, Australia, and the high seas—and they will be in a position to bring enormous military and naval resources against this hemisphere. It is no exaggeration to say that all of us, in all the Americas, would be living at the point of a gun—a gun loaded with explosive bullets, economic as well as military.

We should enter upon a new and terrible era in which the whole world, our hemisphere included, would be run by threats of brute force. To survive in such a world, we would have to convert ourselves permanently into a militaristic power on the basis of war economy.

Some of us like to believe that even if Great Britain falls, we are still safe, because of the broad expanse of the Atlantic and of the Pacific.

But the width of those oceans is not what it was in the days of clipper ships. At one point between Africa and Brazil the distance is less than from Washington to Denver, Colorado—five hours for the latest type of bomber. And at the North end of the Pacific Ocean America and Asia almost touch each other. . . .

There are those who say that the Axis powers would never have any desire to attack the Western Hemisphere. That is the same dangerous form of wishful thinking which has destroyed the powers of resistance of so many conquered peoples. The plain facts are that the Nazis have proclaimed, time and again, that all other races are their inferiors and therefore subject to their orders. And most important of all, the vast resources and wealth of this American Hemisphere constitute the most tempting loot in all the round world. . . .

The experience of the past two years has proven beyond doubt that no nation can appease the Nazis. No man can tame a tiger into a kitten by stroking it. There can be no appeasement with ruthlessness. There can be no reasoning with an incendiary bomb. We know now that a nation can have peace with the Nazis only at the price of total surrender. . . .

The history of recent years proves that shootings and chains and concentration camps are not simply the transient tools but the very altars of modern dictatorships. They may talk of a "new order" in the world, but what they have in mind is only a revival of the oldest and the worst tyranny. In that there is no liberty, no religion, no hope.

The proposed "new order" is the very opposite of a United States of Europe or a United States of Asia. It is not a Government based upon the consent of the governed. It is not a union of ordinary, self-respecting men and women to protect themselves and their freedom and their dignity from oppression. It is an unholy alliance of power and pelf to dominate and enslave the human race.

The British people and their allies today are conducting an active war against this unholy alliance. Our own future security is greatly dependent on the outcome of that fight. Our ability to "keep out of war" is going to be affected by that outcome.

Thinking in terms of today and tomorrow, I make the direct statement to the American people that there is far less chance of the United States getting into war, if we do all we can now to support the nations defending themselves against attack by the Axis than if we acquiesce in their defeat, submit tamely to an Axis victory, and wait our turn to be the object of attack in another war later on.

If we are to be completely honest with ourselves, we must admit that there is risk in any course we may take. But I deeply believe that the great majority of our people agree that the course that I advocate involves the least risk now and the greatest hope for world peace in the future.

The people of Europe who are defending themselves do not ask us to do their fighting. They ask us for the implements of war, the planes, the tanks, the guns, the freighters which will enable them to fight for their liberty and for our security. Emphatically we must get these weapons to them in sufficient volume and quickly enough, so that we and our children will be saved the agony and suffering of war which others have had to endure. . . .

We must be the great arsenal of democracy. For us this is an emergency as serious as war itself. We must apply ourselves to our task with the same resolution, the same sense of urgency, the same spirit of patriotism and sacrifice as we would show were we at war.

We have furnished the British great material support and we will furnish far more in the future.

There will be no "bottlenecks" in our determination to aid Great Britain. No dictator, no combination of dictators, will weaken that determination by threats of how they will construe that determination.

The British have received invaluable military support from the heroic Greek army, and from the forces of all the governments in exile. Their strength is growing. It is the strength of men and women who value their freedom more highly than they value their lives.

Charles A. Beard Criticizes
Lend-Lease, 1941

There is no question here of sympathy for Britain; this nation is almost unanimous in its sympathy. There is no question here of aid to Britain; the Nation is agreed on that. Our immediate task is to analyze the meaning of the language employed in this bill, and to calculate as far as may be humanly possible the consequences for our country that are likely to flow from its enactment into law—to rend, if we can, some corner of the dark veil that hides the future from our vision.

Unless this bill is to be regarded as a mere rhetorical flourish—and respect for its authors precludes the thought of such frivolity—then, I submit, it is a bill for waging an undeclared war. We should entertain no delusions on this point. We should now face frankly and with such knowledge and intelligence as we may have the nature and probable consequences of that war. Without indulging in recriminations, we are bound to consider that fateful prospect.

The contention that this is a war measure has been, I know, hotly denied. The bill has been called a bill to keep the United States out of war. It has been said that we are "buying peace" for ourselves, while others are fighting our war for democracy and defense. I invite your special attention to this line of argument. I confess, gentlemen of the committee, an utter inability to understand the reasoning and morals of those who use this formula. My code of honor may be antiquated, but under it I am bound to say that if this is our war for democracy and if foreign soldiers are now fighting and dying for the defense of the United States, then it is shameful for us to be buying peace with gold, when we should be offering our bodies as living sacrifices. As I am given to see things, buying peace for ourselves, if this is our war, buying it with money renders us contemptible in the eyes of the world and, if I understand the spirit of America, contemptible in our own eyes. However, that may be, there is no guaranty that this bill will buy peace and keep us out of war, despite professions to that effect.

If the bill is enacted into law and efficiently carried into execution, it will engage our government in war activities, involve us officially in the conflicts of Europe and Asia, and place in jeopardy everything we cherish in the United States. . . .

The history of Europe and Asia is long and violent. Tenacious emotions and habits are associated with it. Can the American people, great and ingenious though they be, transform those traditions, institutions, systems, emotions, and habits by employing treasure, arms, propaganda, and diplomatic lectures? Can they, by any means at their disposal, make over Europe and Asia, provide democracy, a bill of rights, and economic security for everybody, everywhere, in the world? With all due respect for those Americans who clamor that this is the mission of the United States, I am compelled to say that, in my opinion, their exuberance is on a par with the childish exuberance of the Bolshevik internationalists who preach the gospel of one model for the whole world. And I am bound to say, furthermore, that it is an exuberance more likely to bring disasters upon our own country than to carry happiness and security to the earth's weary multitudes.

Against embarking on such a crusade, surely we are put on our guard by the history of the last World War. For public consumption and partly with a view to influencing American public opinion, several European belligerents put forth numerous formulations of war origins and war aims. Later, unexpected revolutions in Russia, Germany, and Austria ripped open the diplomatic archives of those countries. Then were revealed to us the maneuvers, negotiations, and secret treaties spread over many years, which preceded and accompanied that World War. I have spent many weary months studying these documents, and I will say, gentlemen of the committee, that these documents do not show that the European conflict was, in the aims of the great powers, a war for democracy, or for the defense of he United States, or had anything to do with protecting the interests of the United States. . . .

This is not to say that the present war is identical with the last war or to recite that false phrase, "History repeats itself"—for it never does. Yet we do know that the present war did not spring out of a vacuum, nor merely out of the Versailles Treaty. Its origins, nature, and course are rooted in the long history of the Old World and the long conflicts of the great powers. . . .

Does Congress intend to guarantee the present extent, economic resources, and economic methods of the British Empire forever to the government of Great Britain by placing the unlimited resources of the United States forever at the disposal of the British government, however, constituted?

Does Congress intend to supply money, ships, and commodities of war until the French Republic is restored? Until the integrity of its empire is assured? Until all the lands run over by Hitler are once more vested with full sovereignty? Until Russia has returned to Finland and Poland the territories wrested from them? Until democracy is reestablished in Greece? Until the King of Albania has recovered his throne?

Is Congress prepared to pour out American wealth until the Chungking government in China has conquered the Nanking government? Until Japan is expelled from the continent? Until Japanese Communists are finally suppressed? And until Soviet Russia is pushed back within the old Russian borders?

And if European or Asiatic powers should propose to make settlements without providing democracy, a bill of rights, and economic security for everybody, everywhere, will Congress insist that they keep on fighting until the President of the United States is satisfied with the results? If none of the countries deemed under the terms of this bill to be defending the United States succeeds in defeating its enemy with the material aid rendered by the United States, will Congress throw millions of boys after the billions of dollars?

Two more crucial questions are before our Nation in council. After Europe has been turned into flaming shambles, with resolutions exploding right and left, will this Congress be able to supply the men, money, and talents necessary to reestablish and maintain order and security there? Are the members of Congress absolutely sure, as they think about this bill, that the flames of war and civil commotion will not spread to our country? That when the war boom of fools' gold has burst with terrific force, Congress will be able to cope at home with the problems of unemployment and debts with which it had wrestled for years prior to this present false prosperity by borrowing money to meet the needs of distressed farmers, distressed industries, the distressed third of the nation?

As a nation in council, we should not mislead ourselves by phrases and phantoms. The present business of our Congress, it seems to me, is not to split hairs over the mere language of this bill to restrict its consequences to one or two years of presidential experimentation. The present business of Congress is to decide now, in voting on this bill, whether it is prepared on a showdown to carry our country into war in Europe and Asia, and thus set the whole world on fire, or whether it is resolved, on a showdown, to stay out to the last ditch and preserve one stronghold of order and sanity even against the gates of hell. Here, on this continent, I believe we may be secure and should make ourselves secure from the kind of conflict and terrorism in which the old worlds have indulged for such long ages of time.

Japanese Officials on China
and American Pressure, July 1941

SAITO: I have studied the present proposal, and find many reasons, to be explained shortly, why it is unacceptable.

The present world, divided into those who are for the maintenance of

---

Reprinted from *Japan's Decision for War: Records of the 1941 Policy Conferences*, 94–97, edited and translated by Nobutaka Ike, with the permission of the publishers, Stanford University Press. © 1967 by the Board of Trustees of the Leland Stanford Junior University.

the status quo and those who are for its destruction, the democracies and the totalitarian states, is in the midst of a war. Hull's reply is for the status quo and for democracy. It is obvious that America sent it after consultation with Britain and China. Thus I think the countries that are for the status quo are getting together to put pressure on Japan. On the matter of Sino-Japanese negotiations, the United States hopes to make us negotiate on the basis of conditions existing prior to the China Incident. In this proposal the phrase "Chinese Government" is used. I think this tricky wording is tantamount to saying that we should renounce the basic treaty between Japan and China. Cancelling our recognition of the Nanking Government would mean reviving the moribund Chungking Government. We must consider and study this phrase "Chinese Government."

The Americans think that Manchuria should revert to China. This proposal says, in effect, that Japan and China should negotiate after Japan has renounced the joint declaration made by Japan, Manchukuo, and China. If we begin negotiations by doing this at a time when Chungking is trying to regain lost territory, it is certain that from the very beginning things would go against us.

This proposal does not recognize the stationing of troops [in China] to maintain peace and order; it seeks the unconditional withdrawal of all troops. The stationing of troops to maintain peace and order is a most important element in our national policy. If we withdrew our troops unconditionally, the Chinese Communists, the Nationalists, the Nanking Government, and Chungking would fight, causing great disorder. If this happened, Britain and the United States would intervene. Accordingly, the unconditional withdrawal of troops will deadlock our negotiations with the United States.

The proposal does not recognize the stationing of troops as a defense against Communism. Whereas the Japanese draft tries to recognize the treaties that have been concluded to date, the United States proposal tries to invalidate them. That the United States does not recognize the stationing of troops as a defense against Communism is indicated in Hull's Statement.

Japan aims at complete cooperation between Japan and China. By contrast, the United States is advocating nondiscriminatory treatment. This makes it impossible to establish a New Order in East Asia. Britain and the United States have continued to aid Chiang until the present time; and they are planning to obtain an advantageous position in China in the future. When an overall peace comes to China, the influence of American "dollars," which are backed by 80 per cent of the world's gold supply, will spread all over China, working from today's special position. America's intention is to bring about peace between Japan and China by means of an agreement between Japan and the United States, and then to let Japan and China negotiate directly within the limits thus set. This procedure will transfer leadership in East Asia to the United States. It will interfere with the implementation of an independent policy by our Empire. It will give the United States the right to have a say in the China Problem.

The attitudes of Japan and the United States toward European war differ greatly. Stated another way, we can only suppose that they mean to enter the war but are telling us to keep quiet. The United States has interpreted her right of self-defense very broadly. She has also practically said that Japan should renounce the Tripartite Pact. We must naturally reject such ideas.

As for trade between Japan and America, America plans to limit it to the pre-Incident level. In short, a maintain-the-status-quo mentality is evident. Moreover, the proposal talks about ordinary commercial transactions, but in the future we must increase trade in vital materials, such as steel and scrap iron; and by keeping trade at the pre-Incident level the United States will be legally preventing the development of Japan's foreign trade. That is, this action will interfere with Japan's future economic development, and the United States will freely control the markets of the Far East. The fact that the Americans have eliminated the word "Southwest" from "Southwest Pacific" is evidence that they are also greatly concerned with the North Pacific. They say "normal trade relations"; but Japan has in mind not only trade, but also mining and industry. The United States, by talking about "trade relations," is clearly limiting Japan's demands.

On the question of Japanese emigration to the United States, the previous draft stated that Japan would be treated the same as other countries; but this statement has been eliminated in the present draft.

We made a proposal regarding the independence of the Philippines; but the American proposal simply states that the Philippines has not yet developed to the point of independence.

Hull's "Oral Statement" contains especially outrageous language. For instance, it says, "We have no intention of considering the stationing of troops a defense against Communism." Or again: "There are differences of opinion within the Japanese Government. I understand that there are Cabinet members who say Japan should ally herself with the Axis and fight side-by-side with Hitler. We cannot make an agreement with a Japanese Government of that kind. If you want to facilitate an improvement in Japanese-American relations, you had better change your Cabinet." His attitude is one of contempt for Japan. I have been in the foreign service for a long time. This language is not the kind one would use toward a country of equal standing: it expresses an attitude one would take toward a protectorate or a possession. These words are inexcusable.

MATSUOKA: In general, I am in agreement with Adviser Saito's report; but I would like to state one or two thoughts.

First of all, Hull's "Statement" is outrageous. Never has such a thing occurred since Japan opened diplomatic relations with other countries. Nomura and I are good friends, but it is inexcusable for him to transmit such an outrageous statement. I was truly amazed that he would listen without protest to a demand that Japan, a great world power, change her Cabinet. I sent a message to him right away, saying: "You should not have transmitted such a statement. Was there not some misunderstanding? Inform me of the circumstances at the time." But I have not yet received an answer from him.

Second, we cannot dissolve the Tripartite Pact.

Third, acceptance of the American proposal would threaten the establishment of a Greater East Asia Co-prosperity Sphere, and this would be a very grave matter.

Fourth, I think that Britain and the United States are trying to meddle in the settlement of the Sino-Japanese problem in one way or another. I am unhappy that among our people there are those who believe it would be better to achieve peace through the mediation of a third party, even though we have fought for four years trying to secure the leadership of East Asia. Such people use as a precedent the times when we sought the aid of third parties, including the United States, in the peace negotiations during the Sino-Japanese and Russo-Japanese wars; but they forget the position that the Empire occupies thirty years later.

The Atlantic Charter, August 1941

Joint declaration of the President of the United States of America and the Prime Minister, Mr. Churchill, representing His Majesty's Government in the United Kingdom, being met together, deem it right to make known certain common principles in the national policies of their respective countries on which they base their hopes for a better future for the world.

First, their countries seek no aggrandizement, territorial or other;

Second, they desire to see no territorial changes that do not accord with the freely expressed wishes of the peoples concerned;

Third, they respect the right of all peoples to choose the form of government under which they will live; and they wish to see sovereign rights and self-government restored to those who have been forcibly deprived of them;

Fourth, they will endeavor, with due respect for their existing obligations, to further the enjoyment by all states, great or small, victor or vanquished, of access, on equal terms, to the trade and to the raw materials of the world which are needed for their economic prosperity;

Fifth, they desire to bring about the fullest collaboration between all nations in the economic field with the object of securing, for all improved labor standards, economic advancement, and social security;

Sixth, after the final destruction of the Nazi tyranny, they hope to see established a peace which will afford to all nations the means of dwelling in safety within their own boundaries, and which will afford assurance that all the men in all the land may live out their lives in freedom from fear and want;

Seventh, such a peace should enable all men to traverse the high seas and oceans without hindrance;

Eighth, they believe that all of the nations of the world, for realistic as well as spiritual reasons, must come to the abandonment of the use of force. Since no future peace can be maintained if land, sea, or air armaments continue to be employed by nations which threaten, or may threaten, aggression outside of their frontiers, they believe pending the establishment of a wider and permanent system of general security, that the disarmament of such nations is essential. They will likewise aid and encourage all other practicable measures which will lighten for peace-loving peoples the crushing burden of armaments.

American Proposals to Japan, November 1941

Section I   Draft Mutual Declaration of Policy

The Government of the United States and the Government of Japan both being solicitous for the peace of the Pacific affirm that their national policies are directed toward lasting and extensive peace throughout the Pacific area, that they have no territorial designs in that area, that they have no intention of threatening other countries or of using military force aggressively against any neighboring nation, and that, accordingly, in their national policies they will actively support and give practical application to the following fundamental principles upon which their relations with each other and with all other governments are based:

1. The principle of inviolability of territorial integrity and sovereignty of each and all nations.
2. The principle of non-interference in the internal affairs of other countries.
3. The principle of equality, including equality of commercial opportunity and treatment.
4. The principle of reliance upon international cooperation and conciliation for the prevention and pacific settlement of controversies and for improvement of international conditions by peaceful methods and processes.

The Government of Japan and the Government of the United States have agreed that toward eliminating chronic political instability, preventing recurrent economic collapse, and providing a basis for peace, they will actively support and practically apply the following principles in their economic relations with each other and with other nations and peoples:

1. The principle of non-discrimination in international commercial relations.
2. The principle of international economic cooperation and abolition of extreme nationalism as expressed in excessive trade restrictions.
3. The principle of non-discriminatory access by all nations to raw material supplies.
4. The principle of full protection of the interests of consuming countries and populations as regards the operation of international commodity agreements.
5. The principle of establishment of such institutions and arrangements of international finance as may lend aid to the essential enterprises and

the continuous development of all countries and may permit payments through processes of trade consonant with the welfare of all countries.

Section II   Steps To Be Taken by the Government of the United States and by the Government of Japan

The Government of the United States and the Government of Japan propose to take steps as follows:

1. The Government of the United States and the Government of Japan will endeavor to conclude a multilateral non-aggression pact among the British Empire, China, Japan, the Netherlands, the Soviet Union, Thailand and the United States.

2. Both Governments will endeavor to conclude among the American, British, Chinese, Japanese, the Netherland and Thai Governments an agreement whereunder each of the Governments would pledge itself to respect the territorial integrity of French Indochina and, in the event that there should develop a threat to the territorial integrity of Indochina, to enter into immediate consultation with a view to taking such measures as may be deemed necessary and advisable to meet the threat in question. Such agreement would provide also that each of the Governments party to the agreement would not seek or accept preferential treatment in its trade or economic relations with Indochina and would use its influence to obtain for each of the signatories equality of treatment in trade and commerce with French Indochina.

3. The Government of Japan will withdraw all military, naval, air and police forces from China and from Indochina.

4. The Government of the United States and the Government of Japan will not support—militarily, politically, economically—any government or regime in China other than the National Government of the Republic of China with capital temporarily at Chungking.

5. Both Governments will give up all extraterritorial rights in China, including rights and interests in and with regard to international settlements and concessions, and rights under the Boxer Protocol of 1901.

Both Governments will endeavor to obtain the agreement of the British and other governments to give up extraterritorial rights in China, including rights in international settlements and in concessions and under the Boxer Protocol of 1901.

6. The Government of the United States and the Government of Japan will enter into negotiations for the conclusion between the United States and Japan of a trade agreement, based upon reciprocal most-favored-nation treatment and reduction of trade barriers by both countries, including an undertaking by the United States to bind raw silk on the free list.

7. The Government of the United States and the Government of Japan will, respectively, remove the freezing restrictions on Japanese funds in the United States and on American funds in Japan.

8. Both Governments will agree upon a plan for the stabilization of the

dollar-yen rate, with the allocation of funds adequate for this purpose, half to be supplied by Japan and half by the United States.

9. Both Governments will agree that no agreement which either has concluded with any third power or powers shall be interpreted by it in such a way as to conflict with the fundamental purpose of this agreement, the establishment and preservation of peace throughout the Pacific area.

10. Both Governments will use their influence to cause other governments to adhere to and to give practical application to the basic political and economic principles set forth in this agreement.

The Japanese Position, December 1941

Ever since the China Affair broke out owing to the failure on the part of China to comprehend Japan's true intentions, the Japanese Government has striven for the restoration of peace and it has consistently exerted its best efforts to prevent the extension of war-like disturbances. It was also to that end that in September last year Japan concluded the Tripartite Pact with Germany and Italy.

However, both the United States and Great Britain have resorted to every possible measure to assist the Chungking regime so as to obstruct the establishment of a general peace between Japan and China, interfering with Japan's constructive endeavors toward the stabilization of East Asia. Exerting pressure on the Netherlands East Indies, or menacing French Indo-China, they have attempted to frustrate Japan's aspiration to the ideal of common prosperity in cooperation with these regions. Furthermore, when Japan in accordance with its protocol with France took measures of joint defence of French Indo-China, both American and British Governments, willfully misinterpreting it as a threat to their own possessions, and inducing the Netherlands Government to follow suit, they enforced the assets freezing order, thus severing economic relations with Japan. While manifesting thus an obviously hostile attitude, these countries have strengthened their military preparations perfecting an encirclement of Japan, and have brought about a situation which endangers the very existence of the Empire. . . .

From the beginning of the present negotiation the Japanese Government has always maintained an attitude of fairness and moderation, and did its best to reach a settlement, for which it made all possible concessions often in spite of great difficulties. As for the China question which constituted an important subject of the negotiation, the Japanese Government showed a most conciliatory attitude. As for the principle of non-discrimination in international commerce, advocated by the American Government, the Japanese Government expressed its desire to see the said principle applied throughout the world, and declared that along with the actual practice of this principle in the world, the Japanese Government would endeavor to apply the same in the Pacific Area including China, and made it clear that Japan had no intention of excluding from China economic activities of third powers pursued on an equitable basis. Furthermore, as regards the question of withdrawing troops from French Indo-China, the Japanese Government even volunteered, as mentioned above, to carry out an immediate evacuation of troops from Southern French Indo-China as a measure of easing the situation.

It is presumed that the spirit of conciliation exhibited to the utmost degree by the Japanese Government in all these matters is fully appreciated by the American Government.

On the other hand, the American Government, always holding fast to theories in disregard of realities, and refusing to yield an inch on its impractical principles, caused undue delay in the negotiation. It is difficult to understand this attitude of the American Government and the Japanese Government desires to call the attention of the American Government especially to the following points:

1. The American Government advocates in the name of world peace those principles favorable to it and urges upon the Japanese Government the acceptance thereof. The peace of the world may be brought about only by discovering a mutually acceptable formula through recognition of the reality of the situation and mutual appreciation of one another's position. An attitude such as ignores realities and imposes one's selfish views upon others will scarcely serve the purpose of facilitating the consummation of negotiations.

Of the various principles put forward by the American Government as a basis of the Japanese-American Agreement, there are some which the Japanese Government is ready to accept in principle, but in view of the world's actual conditions, it seems only a utopian ideal on the part of the American Government to attempt to force their immediate adoption.

Again, the proposal to conclude a multilateral non-aggression pact between Japan, United States, Great Britain, China, the Soviet Union, the Netherlands and Thailand, which is patterned after the old concept of collective security, is far removed from the realities of East Asia.

2. The American proposal contained a stipulation which states—"Both Governments will agree that no agreement, which either has concluded with any third power or powers, shall be interpreted by it in such a way as to conflict with the fundamental purpose of this agreement, the establishment and preservation of peace throughout the Pacific area." It is presumed that the above provision has been proposed with a view to restrain Japan from fulfilling its obligations under the Tripartite Pact when the United States participates in the War in Europe, and, as such, it cannot be accepted by the Japanese Government.

The American Government, obsessed with its own views and opinions, may be said to be scheming for the extension of the war. While it seeks, on the one hand, to secure its rear by stabilizing the Pacific Area, it is engaged, on the other hand, in aiding Great Britain and preparing to attack, in the name of self-defense, Germany and Italy, two Powers that are striving to establish a new order in Europe. Such a policy is totally at variance with the many principles upon which the American Government proposes to found the stability of the Pacific Area through peaceful means.

3. Whereas the American Government, under the principles it rigidly upholds, objects to settle international issues through military pressure, it is exercising in conjunction with Great Britain and other nations pressure by economic power. Recourse to such pressure as a means of dealing with international relations should be condemned as it is at times more inhumane than military pressure.

4. It is impossible not to reach the conclusion that the American Government desires to maintain and strengthen, in coalition with Great Britain and other Powers, its dominant position it has hitherto occupied not only in China but in other areas of East Asia. It is a fact of history that the countries of East Asia for the past hundred years or more have been compelled to observe the *status quo* under the Anglo-American policy of imperialistic exploitation and to sacrifice themselves to the prosperity of the two nations. The Japanese Government cannot tolerate the perpetuation of such a situation since it directly runs counter to Japan's fundamental policy to enable all nations to enjoy each its proper place in the world.

The stipulation proposed by the American Government relative to French Indo-China is a good exemplification of the above-mentioned American policy. Thus six countries,—Japan, the United States, Great Britain, the Netherlands, China and Thailand,—excepting France, should undertake among themselves to respect the territorial integrity and sovereignty of French Indo-China and equality of treatment in trade and commerce would be tantamount to placing the territory under the joint guarantee of the Governments of those six countries. Apart from the fact that such a proposal totally ignores the position of France, it is unacceptable to the Japanese Government in that such an arrangement cannot but be considered as an extension to French Indo-China of a system similar to the Nine Power Treaty structure which is the chief factor responsible for the present predicament of East Asia.

5. All the items demanded of Japan by the American Government regarding China such as wholesale evacuation of troops or unconditional application of the principle of non-discrimination in international commerce ignored the actual conditions of China, and are calculated to destroy Japan's position as the stabilizing factor of East Asia. The attitude of the American Government in demanding Japan not to support militarily, politically or economically any regime other than the regime at Chungking, disregarding thereby the existence of the Nanking Government, shatters the very basis of the present negotiation. This demand of the American Government falling, as it does, in line with its above-mentioned refusal to cease from aiding the Chungking regime, demonstrates clearly the intention of the American Government to obstruct the restoration of normal relations between Japan and China and the return of peace to East Asia.

In brief, the American proposal contains certain acceptable items such as those concerning commerce, including the conclusion of a trade agreement, mutual removal of the freezing restrictions and stabilization of yen and dollar exchange, or the abolition of extra-territorial rights in China. On the other hand, however, the proposal in question ignores Japan's sacrifices in the four years of the China Affair, menaces the Empire's existence itself and disparages its honour and prestige. Therefore, viewed in its entirety, the Japanese Government regrets that it cannot accept the proposal as a basis of negotiations.

Roosevelt's War Message, 1941

Yesterday, December 7, 1941—a date which will live in infamy—the United States of America was suddenly and deliberately attacked by naval and air forces of the Empire of Japan.

The United States was at peace with that Nation and, at the solicitation of Japan, was still in conversation with its Government and its Emperor looking toward the maintenance of peace in the Pacific. Indeed, one hour after Japanese air squadrons had commenced bombing in Oahu, the Japanese Ambassador to the United States and his colleague delivered to the Secretary of State a formal reply to a recent American message. While this reply stated that it seemed useless to continue the existing diplomatic negotiations, it contained no threat or hint of war or armed attack.

It will be recorded that the distance of Hawaii from Japan makes it obvious that the attack was deliberately planned many days or even weeks ago. During the intervening time the Japanese Government has deliberately sought to deceive the United States by false statements and expressions of hope for continued peace.

The attack yesterday on the Hawaiian Islands has caused severe damage to American naval and military forces. Very many American lives have been lost. In addition American ships have been reported torpedoed on the high seas between San Francisco and Honolulu.

Yesterday the Japanese Government also launched an attack against Malaya.

Last night Japanese forces attacked Hong Kong.

Last night Japanese forces attacked Guam.

Last night Japanese forces attacked the Philippine Islands.

Last night the Japanese attacked Wake Island.

This morning the Japanese attacked Midway Island.

Japan has, therefore, undertaken a surprise offensive extending throughout the Pacific area. The facts of yesterday speak for themselves. The people of the United States have already formed their opinions and well understand the implications to the very life and safety of our Nation.

As Commander-in-Chief of the Army and Navy I have directed that all measures be taken for our defense.

Always will we remember the character of the onslaught against us.

No matter how long it may take us to overcome this premeditated invasion, the American people in their righteous might will win through to absolute victory.

I believe I interpret the will of the Congress and of the people when I assert that we will not only defend ourselves to the uttermost but will make very certain that this form of treachery shall never endanger us again.

Hostilities exist. There is no blinking at the fact that our people, our territory, and our interests are in grave danger.

With confidence in our armed forces—with the unbounded determination of our people—we will gain the inevitable triumph—so help us God.

I ask that the Congress declare that since the unprovoked and dastardly attack by Japan on Sunday, December seventh, a state of war has existed between the United States and the Japanese Empire.

⚹ *E S S A Y S*

Robert A. Divine of the University of Texas, in discussing Franklin D. Roosevelt's reactions to the crises of the 1930s, argues in the first essay that the President was a sincere isolationist who shared the views of a majority of Americans against involvement in another war. In the second essay, Robert Dallek of the University of California, Los Angeles, depicts Roosevelt more as a frustrated internationalist swayed by isolationist public opinion. According to Dallek, Roosevelt was determined to throw America's weight first against the Germans in the European war; thus he tried to play for time in Asia while he strove to persuade the American people to back the Allies. Dallek also sees Roosevelt as the chief policymaker. In the last essay, Jonathan G. Utley of the University of Tennessee disputes interpretations that credit Roosevelt with sound leadership. Utley concludes that Japanese-American conflict was inevitable because of a fundamental clash between the American Open Door and the Japanese New Order. But because neither side wanted to fight the other, effective diplomacy might have worked to prevent war or at least to create coexistence. Finding that Cordell Hull, more than Roosevelt, guided Asian policy, Utley faults American diplomats on a number of counts, including seeking a comprehensive peace that had no chance of success.

Roosevelt the Isolationist

ROBERT A. DIVINE

Roosevelt's foreign policy in the 1930's toward the totalitarian threat of Germany, Italy, and Japan would seem to offer little room for historical controversy. The record is clear—Roosevelt pursued an isolationist policy, refusing to commit the United States to the defense of the existing international order. He accepted a series of isolationist neutrality laws passed by Congress, objecting only to those provisions which infringed on his freedom of action as President; he acquiesced in Italy's seizure of Ethiopia, Japan's invasion of China, and Germany's takeover of Austria and the Sudetenland in Czechoslovakia. The sole exception that can be cited is the Quarantine speech

Robert A. Divine, *Roosevelt and World War II* (Baltimore: The Johns Hopkins University Press, 1969), 5–11, 20–30, 30–37, 38–40, 43–48. Copyright © 1969 by The Johns Hopkins University Press. Reprinted by permission of The Johns Hopkins University Press.

in 1937, and even this apparently bold statement was so ambiguous that historians have never been able to agree on the President's precise intention.

Yet this isolationist policy does not square with the usual image of Franklin Roosevelt as a perceptive world leader who recognized the danger to the United States from Axis aggression and who eventually led his nation into war to preserve American security. Troubled by this contradiction, historians have argued that Roosevelt subordinated his own internationalist preferences and gave in to the isolationist mood of the American people. As a shrewd politician, he knew that the electorate would not tolerate an active foreign policy in the midst of the depression, and so he wisely surrendered to the public will. His major desires in the mid-thirties were to achieve recovery and carry out sweeping domestic reforms; he could not jeopardize these vital goals with an unpopular foreign policy. Implicit in this interpretation is the belief that Roosevelt was an internationalist at heart. Thus Basil Rauch argues that the President acted wisely in drifting with the current in the 1930's; later in the decade, when the totalitarian threat became more intense, he was finally able to win the people over to an active policy. James MacGregor Burns is less charitable. He accuses Roosevelt of floating helplessly on a flood tide of isolationism and thus failing to fulfill his obligation of leadership. "As a foreign policy maker," Burns concludes, "Roosevelt during his first term was more pussyfooting politician than political leader."

Charles A. Beard, in his book *American Foreign Policy in the Making, 1932–1940*, offers a simpler and more convincing explanation of Roosevelt's behavior. In the 1930's, Beard contends, Roosevelt *was* an isolationist. Though Beard in a later book accuses the President of lying the nation into war, his earlier study provides a sound interpretation of Roosevelt's foreign policy. If we accept Roosevelt's own public statements at their face value, then we can dismiss the concept of two Roosevelts, one the public figure saying what the people wanted to hear, the other the private man with an entirely different set of beliefs. Equally important, we no longer have to explain Roosevelt's conduct on the basis of a devious political expediency. Instead, we can state simply that Roosevelt pursued an isolationist policy out of genuine conviction.

It is not surprising that F.D.R. shared in the isolationist temper of his times. The mood was deep and pervasive in the 1930's. The First World War had led to a profound sense of disillusion that found expression in an overwhelming national desire to abstain from future world conflicts. The generation of the thirties embraced pacifism as a noble and workable ideal— students demonstrated on college campuses every spring in massive antiwar strikes; religious and pacifist societies waged a campaign to remove ROTC units from colleges and universities; millions of Americans applauded the limited naval disarmament of the 1920's and followed with intense interest the futile disarmament conference that went on at Geneva through the early years of the decade. Feeding this pacifism was the belief that the same wicked businessmen who had destroyed the economic health of the nation were responsible for fomenting war. The Nye investigation struck a responsive chord with the airing of charges that it was merchants of death like Pierre Du Pont and J. P. Morgan who had brought the United States into the First World War. And many Americans accepted the argument that the depression was the final legacy of that war.

Roosevelt, in his speeches and letters, constantly reiterated his belief that the United States should avoid all future conflicts. In his first two years in office, he tended to ignore foreign policy as he concentrated on the problems of economic recovery at home. But in 1935, as the world crisis unfolded with Hitler's rearmament of Germany and Mussolini's attack on Ethiopia, the President began to speak out on international issues. In an Armistice Day address in 1935, after commenting on the rising danger in Europe, he said, "the primary purpose of the United States of America is to avoid being drawn into war." The nation's youth, he continued, "know that the elation and prosperity which may come from a new war must lead—for those who survive it—to economic and social collapse more sweeping than any we have experienced in the past." He concluded by stating that the proper American role was to provide an example to all mankind of the virtues of peace and democracy. In a letter to William Dodd, the American ambassador to Germany, a few weeks later, he repeated this advice, writing, "I do not know that the United States can save civilization but at least by our example we can make people think and give them the opportunity of saving themselves."

Roosevelt's initial response to the rising totalitarian threat was thus in the classic tradition of American isolationism. The United States was to play a passive role as the beacon of liberty to mankind, providing a model for the world to follow, but avoiding any active participation in a foreign conflict. In his annual message in January, 1936, for the first time he dwelt at some length on foreign policy, warning the congressmen and senators of the dangers to peace that were developing in Europe. If war came, he declared, the only course the United States could follow was neutrality, "and through example and all legitimate encouragement and assistance to persuade other Nations to return to the ways of peace and good-will." In a Dallas speech in mid-1936, he spoke again of the troubles plaguing the European nations and expressed his sympathy for their plight. "We want to help them all that we can," he stated, "but they have understood very well in these latter years that help is going to be confined to moral help, and that we are not going to get tangled up with their troubles in the days to come."

Roosevelt voiced his isolationist convictions most forthrightly in his famous Chautauqua address in August, 1936. This speech came after he had been renominated for the presidency by the Democratic Party, and it was the only speech he made in the 1936 campaign that dealt with foreign policy. Once again he concentrated on the perilous world situation, and again he reaffirmed his determination to keep the nation out of any conflict that might arise. He played on the merchants of death theme, warning that the lure of "fool's gold" in the form of trade with belligerents would lead many greedy Americans to attempt to evade the neutrality laws. "If we face the choice of profit or peace," Roosevelt demanded, "the nation will answer—must answer—'we choose peace.'" He went on to point our how hard it would be to keep out of a major war and said that only careful day-by-day conduct of foreign policy by the Secretary of State and the President would keep the nation at peace.

The most striking passage came when Roosevelt revealed his own emotional distaste for war:

> I have seen war. I have seen war on land and sea. I have seen blood running from the wounded. I have seen men coughing out their gassed lungs. I have seen the dead in the mud. I have seen cities destroyed. I have seen two hundred limping, exhausted men come out of line—the survivors of a regiment of one thousand that went forward forty-eight hours before. I have seen children starving. I have seen the agony of mothers and wives. I hate war.
>
> I have passed unnumbered hours, I shall pass unnumbered hours, thinking and planning how war may be kept from this nation.

Here Roosevelt laid bare the source of his isolationism. Some commentators dismissed his words as campaign rhetoric, empty phrases designed simply to win votes in the coming election. But the words carry a sense of conviction and honesty that belies such hypocrisy. Samuel Rosenman testifies to Roosevelt's sincerity, stating that the President considered the Chautauqua address one of his most important speeches. The following Christmas, after he had been safely re-elected, Roosevelt sent close friends a specially printed and inscribed copy of the speech as a holiday gift. For Roosevelt, the Chautauqua address was more than a campaign speech; it was a clear and precise statement of his innermost beliefs. He shared fully in the hatred of war that was at the root of American isolationism in the depression decade, and he was determined to insure that the United States would remain a beacon of peace and sanity in a world going mad.

Roosevelt's fundamental aversion to war determined his responses to the hostile acts committed by Italy, Japan, and Germany in the 1930's. As these totalitarian powers expanded into Ethiopia, China, and Central Europe, Roosevelt was torn between his strong distaste for their aggression and his conviction that the United States should stay out of war at any cost. In subtle ways, he tried to throw the weight of American influence against the totalitarian states, but never at the risk of American involvement.

The Italian invasion of Ethiopia in early October of 1935 touched off the first major foreign crisis that Roosevelt faced as President. The Ethiopian war had been developing for over a year, and the imminence of this conflict had goaded Congress into passing the first Neutrality Act in late August. This legislation instructed the President to apply an embargo on the export of arms to nations at war and permitted him, at his discretion, to warn American citizens against traveling on belligerent ships. The idea of preventing munitions-makers from selling weapons to countries at war appealed to Roosevelt, but he was distressed at the mandatory nature of the arms embargo, preferring discretionary power that would enable him to decide when and against whom such embargoes should be levied. Nevertheless, he decided not to veto the Neutrality Act when Congress limited it to a six-month trial period. Roosevelt realized that this legislation would not hamper him if war broke out in Africa. Italy, which had the money and ships to import arms from the United States, would be adversely affected, while Ethiopia would be no worse off.

Thus, when reporters asked him his opinion of the Neutrality Act on August 28, he could reply candidly that he found it "entirely satisfactory." "The question of embargoes as against two belligerents meets the need of the existing situation," he explained. "What more can one ask?" . . .

When Hitler announced plans for German rearmament in 1935 and then marched into the Rhineland the next year, the Roosevelt administration remained silent. In both cases, Germany was violating the Treaty of Versailles, but the fact that the United States was not a party to this agreement meant that there were no grounds for an American protest. Privately, Roosevelt did speak out, commenting to his associates that Hitler was an international gangster, a bandit who someday would have to be halted. After the German seizure of Austria in March, 1938, Cordell Hull issued a cautious statement expressing American concern over the effect of this German act on world peace. Roosevelt was also disturbed, but he was not ready to alter his policy. In a letter to the American ambassador in Ireland in April, 1938, he commented that the only hopeful sign about the world situation was "that we in the United States are still better off than the people or the governments of any other great country."

The real test of Roosevelt's policy came with the Czech crisis in September of 1938 which culminated in the Munich Conference. Moving inexorably toward his goal of uniting all German people in Europe into a Greater Third Reich, Hitler began demanding the cession of the Sudeten provinces of Czechoslovakia. The Czechs refused and turned to England and France for help. Neville Chamberlain, the British Prime Minister, flew to Germany on September 15 to confer with Hitler. A week later, England and France announced that Czechoslovakia would turn over to Hitler the districts in which Germans were in the majority. But the German dictator refused to be content with these concessions. Instead he stepped up his demands to include areas in which the Germans were in the minority and insisted that the transfer be accomplished by October 1. British and French public opinion stiffened, and by September 25 it seemed likely that Chamberlain and Edouard Daladier, the French Premier, would fight rather than surrender completely to Hitler.

As the deadline approached, William Bullitt, the American ambassador in Paris, sent a series of urgent cables asking Roosevelt to call for an international conference to head off a major war. At one point, Bullitt even suggested that Roosevelt offer his services as a neutral arbitrator. The idea of personal diplomatic intervention appealed to the President, but Hull and other State Department advisers cautioned him against any dramatic step. Finally, on September 26, Roosevelt issued a public appeal to Hitler, Chamberlain, Daladier, and Eduard Beneš, the Czech leader, calling for a resumption of the negotiations. When Hitler sent back a negative reply, Roosevelt dispatched a personal appeal to Mussolini, asking him to do everything possible to continue the diplomatic negotiations. Then, late on September 27, the President sent a telegram to Hitler appealing once again for a peaceful solution and suggesting an international conference at some neutral spot in Europe. The next afternoon, the British and French leaders announced that they would meet with Hitler and Mussolini at Munich on September 29 to continue the quest for peace. When Roosevelt heard the news, he immediately cabled Chamberlain the brief but enthusiastic message, "Good man."

Historians still debate Roosevelt's responsibility for the Munich Conference. Basil Rauch, in a tortuous reading of the sequence of events, interprets Roosevelt's actions as an effort to bolster the willingness of Chamberlain and Daladier to stand up to Hitler! In a more carefully reasoned article, John McVickar Haight argues that Roosevelt was indeed trying to stand behind England and France, but that the French in particular misinterpreted his actions. "The president's messages," Haight concluded, "were couched in such cautious terms they were misread." William L. Langer and S. Everett Gleason deal with the Munich Conference briefly at the outset of *The Challenge to Isolation*, where they flatly state that "there is no reason to suppose that the President's appeal influenced Hitler in his decision to call the Munich Conference." James MacGregor Burns is even harsher, charging that Roosevelt pursued "a policy of pinpricks and righteous protest." "No risks, no commitments," writes Burns, "was the motto of the White House."

A careful reading of the texts of the messages Roosevelt sent on September 26 and 27 indicates that the President was genuinely perplexed by the Czech crisis. He realized that war impended; he hoped desperately to use American influence to prevent it; but he was still paralyzed by his fear of war. "Should hostilities break out, the lives of millions of men, women, and children in every country involved will most certainly be lost under circumstances of unspeakable horror," he wrote. He recognized that the United States would inevitably be affected by such a conflict, stating that "no nation can escape some measure of the consequences of such a world catastrophe." But while he urged the European leaders to come together again and seek a peaceful solution, he refrained from making any specific American commitments. Thus, in his appeal to Hitler on September 27 in which he proposed a major international conference, he made it clear that the United States would not attend. "The Government of the United States has no political involvements in Europe," Roosevelt informed Hitler, "and will assume no obligations in the conduct of the present negotiations." Nothing he might have said could have been more damaging. In effect, he gave Hitler a green light, saying that the United States would not concern itself in any meaningful way with the settlement of the gravest international crisis since the end of World War I. In that limited and indirect way, he must bear some of the responsibility for the Munich debacle.

But what is most significant is Roosevelt's inner turmoil. In a letter on

September 15 to William Phillips, the American ambassador to Italy, he confessed his fear that negotiations with Hitler might only postpone "what looks to me like an inevitable conflict within the next five years." "Perhaps when it comes," he commented, "the United States will be in a position to pick up the pieces of European civilization and help them to save what remains of the wreck—not a cheerful prospect." Yet in the same letter he goes on to say, "if we get the idea that the future of our form of government is threatened by a coalition of European dictators, we might wade in with everything we have to give." A month later, after Munich, he revealed the same contradiction in his thought in a note to Canadian Prime Minister Mackenzie King. He began by saying that he rejoiced in the peaceful solution of the Czech crisis, claiming that it proved that the people of the world had a clear perception of how terrible a general European war would be. Yet, he continued, "I am still concerned, as I know you are, when we consider prospects for the future." He concluded with the fatalistic estimate that world peace depended on Hitler's continued willingness to co-operate.

It does seem clear that by the end of 1938, Roosevelt was no longer the confirmed isolationist he had been earlier in the decade. The brutal conquests by Italy, Japan, and Germany had aroused him to their ultimate threat to the United States. But he was still haunted by the fear of war that he voiced so often and so eloquently. His political opponents and subsequent historians have too readily dismissed his constant reiteration of the horrors of war as a politician's gesture toward public opinion. I contend that he was acting out of a deep and sincere belief when he declared that he hated war, and it was precisely this intense conviction that prevented him from embracing an interventionist foreign policy in the late 1930's. In the Munich crisis, he reveals himself in painful transition from the isolationist of the mid-1930's who wanted peace at almost any price to the reluctant internationalist of the early 1940's who leads his country into war in order to preserve its security.

No aspect of Roosevelt's foreign policy has been more controversial than his role in American entry into World War II. Although much of the discussion centers on the events leading to Pearl Harbor, I do not intend to enter into that labyrinth. The careful and well-researched studies by Herbert Feis, Roberta Wohlstetter, and Paul Schroeder demonstrate that while the administration made many errors in judgment, Roosevelt did not deliberately expose the fleet to a Japanese attack at Pearl Harbor in order to enter the war in Europe by a back door in the Pacific. This revisionist charge has already received far more attention than it deserves and has distracted historians from more significant issues.

What is more intriguing is the nature of Roosevelt's policy toward the war in Europe. There are a number of tantalizing questions that historians have not answered satisfactorily. Why was Roosevelt so devious and indirect in his policy toward the European conflict? When, if ever, did F.D.R. decide that the United States would have to enter the war in Europe to protect its own security? And finally, would Roosevelt have asked Congress for a declaration of war against Germany if Japan had not attacked Pearl Harbor?

In the months that followed the Munich Conference, President Roosevelt gradually realized that appeasement had served only to postpone, not to prevent, a major European war. In January, 1939, he sought to impart this fact in his annual message to Congress. He warned the representatives and senators that "philosophies of force" were loose in the world that threatened "the tenets of faith and humanity" on which the American way of life was founded. "The world has grown so small and weapons of attack so swift," the President declared, "that no nation can be safe" when aggression occurs anywhere on earth. He went on to say that the United States had "rightly" decided not to intervene militarily to prevent acts of aggression abroad and then added, somewhat cryptically, "There are many methods short of war, but stronger and more effective than mere words, of bringing home to aggressor governments the aggregate sentiments of our own people." Roosevelt did not spell out these "methods short of war," but he did criticize the existing neutrality legislation, which he suggested had the effect of encouraging aggressor nations. "We have learned, he continued, "that when we deliberately try to legislate neutrality, our neutrality laws may operate unevenly and unfairly—may actually give aid to an aggressor and deny it to the victim. The instinct of self-perservation should warn us that we ought not to let that happen anymore."

Most commentators interpreted the President's speech as a call to Congress to revise the existing neutrality legislation, and in particular the arms embargo. Yet for the next two months, Roosevelt procrastinated. Finally, after Hitler's armies overran the remainder of Czechoslovakia in mid-March, Senator Key Pittman came forward with an administration proposal to repeal the arms embargo and permit American citizens to trade with nations at war on a cash-and-carry basis. The Pittman bill obviously favored England and France, since if these nations were at war with Nazi Germany, they alone would possess the sea power and financial resources to secure arms and supplies from a neutral United States. At the same time, the cash-and-carry restrictions would guard against the loss of American lives and property on the high seas and thus minimize the risk of American involvement.

Although the Pittman bill seemed to be a perfect expression of Roosevelt's desire to bolster the European democracies yet not commit the United States, the President scrupulously avoided any public endorsement in the spring of 1939. His own political stock was at an all-time low as a result of the courtpacking dispute, a sharp economic recession, and an unsuccessful effort to purge dissident Democrats in the 1938 primaries. By May, Roosevelt's silence and Pittman's inept handling had led to a deadlock in the Senate. The President then turned to the House of Representatives, meeting with the leaders of the lower chamber on May 19 and telling them that passage of the cash-and-carry measure was necessary to prevent the outbreak of war in Europe. Yet despite this display of concern, Roosevelt refused to take the issue to the people, asking instead that Cordell Hull champion neutrality revision. The presidential silence proved fatal. In late June, a rebellious House of Representatives voted to retain the arms embargo and thus sabotage the administration's effort to align the United States with Britain and France.

Belatedly, Roosevelt decided to intervene. He asked the Senate Foreign Relations Committee to reconsider the Pittman bill, but in early July the Committee rebuffed the President by voting 12 to 11 to postpone action until the next session of Congress. Roosevelt was furious. He prepared a draft of a public statement in which he denounced congressional isolationists "who scream from the housetops that this nation is being led into a world war" as individuals who "deserve only the utmost contempt and pity of the American People." Hull finally persuaded him not to release this inflammatory statement. Instead, Roosevelt invited a small bipartisan group of senators to meet with him and Cordell Hull at the White House. The senators listened politely while the President and Secretary of State warned of the imminence of war in Europe and the urgent need of the United States to do something to prevent it. Senator William Borah, a leading Republican isolationist, then stunned Roosevelt and Hull by announcing categorically that there would be no war in Europe in the near future, that he had access to information from abroad that was far more reliable than the cables arriving daily at the State Department. When the other senators expressed their belief that Congress was not in the mood to revise the Neutrality Act, the meeting broke up. In a press release the next day, Roosevelt stated that the administration would accept the verdict of Congress, but he made it clear that he and Hull still believed that its failure to revise the neutrality legislation "would weaken the leadership of the United States . . . in the event of a new crisis in Europe." In a press conference three days later, Roosevelt was even blunter, accusing the Republicans of depriving him of the only chance he had to prevent the outbreak of war in Europe.

When the German invasion of Poland on September 1, 1939, touched off World War II, Roosevelt immediately proclaimed American neutrality and put the arms embargo and other restrictions into effect. In a radio talk to the American people on the evening of September 3, he voiced his determination to keep the country out of the conflict. "We seek to keep war from our firesides," he declared, "by keeping war from coming to the Americas." Though he deliberately refrained from asking the people to remain neutral in thought as Wilson had done in 1914, he closed by reiterating his personal hatred of war and pledging that, "as long as it remains within my power to prevent, there will be no blackout of peace in the United States."

President Roosevelt did not give up his quest for revision of the Neutrality Act, however. After a careful telephone canvass indicated that a majority of the Senate would now support repeal of the arms embargo, the President called Congress into special session. On September 21, Roosevelt urged the senators and representatives to repeal the arms embargo and thereby return to the traditional American adherence to international law. Calling Jefferson's embargo and the neutrality legislation of the 1930's the sole exceptions to this historic policy, he argued that the removal of the arms embargo was a way to insure that the United States would not be involved in the European conflict, and he promised that the government would also insist that American citizens and American ships be barred from entering the war zones. Denying that repeal was a step toward war, Roosevelt asserted that his proposal "offers far greater safeguards than we now possess or have ever possessed to protect American lives and property from danger. . . . There lies the road to peace." He then closed by declaring that America must stand aloof from the conflict so that it could preserve the culture of Western Europe. "Fate seems now to compel us to assume the task of helping to maintain in the western world a citadel wherein that civilization may be kept alive," he concluded.

It was an amazing speech. No less than four times the President declared that his policy was aimed at keeping the United States out of the war. Yet the whole intent of arms embargo repeal was to permit England and France to purchase arms and munitions from the United States. By basing his appeal on a return to international law and a desire to keep out of the war, Roosevelt was deliberately misleading the American people. The result was a long and essentially irrelevant debate in Congress over the administration bill to repeal the arms embargo and to place all trade with belligerents on a cash-and-carry basis. Advocates of the bill followed the President's cue, repeatedly denying that the legislation was aimed at helping Britain and France and insisting that the sole motive was to preserve American neutrality. Isolationist opponents quite logically asked, if the purpose was to insure neutrality, why did not the administration simply retain the arms embargo and add cash-and-carry for all other trade with countries at war. With heavy majorities already lined up in both houses, administration spokesmen refused to answer this query. They infuriated the isolationists by repeating with parrot-like precision the party line that the substitution of cash-and-carry for the arms embargo would keep the nation out of war.

The result was an overwhelming victory for Roosevelt. In late October the Senate, thought to be the center of isolationist strength, voted for the administration bill by more than two to one; in early November the House concurred after a closer ballot. Now Britain and France could purchase from the United States anything they needed for their war effort, including guns, tanks, and airplanes, provided only that they paid cash and carried away these supplies in their own ships.

Roosevelt expressed his thoughts most clearly in a letter to William Allen White a month later. "Things move with such terrific speed, these days," he wrote, "that it really is essential to us to think in broader terms and, in effect, to warn the American people that they, too, should think of possible ultimate results in Europe. . . . Therefore, my sage old friend, my problem is to get the American people to think of conceivable consequences without scaring the American people into thinking that they are going to be dragged into this war." In 1939, Roosevelt evidently decided that candor was still too risky, and thus he chose to pursue devious tactics in aligning the United States indirectly on the side of England and France.

The blitzkrieg that Adolf Hitler launched in Europe in the spring of 1940 aroused Americans to their danger in a way that Roosevelt never could. Norway and Denmark fell in April, and then on May 10 Germany launched an offensive thrust through the low countries into northern France that drove Holland and Belgium out of the war in less than a week and forced the British into a humiliating retreat from the continent at Dunkirk before the month was over. The sense of physical security from foreign danger that the United States had enjoyed for over a century was shattered in a matter of days. The debate over policy would continue, but from May 1940 on, virtually all Americans recognized that the German victories in Europe imperiled the United States. . . .

In early June, the news from Europe became even worse. As he sat in his White House study one evening reading the latest dispatches, Roosevelt remarked to his wife, "All bad, all bad." He realized that a vigorous defense program was not enough—that American security depended on the successful resistance of England and France to German aggression. As Hitler's armies swept toward Paris and Mussolini moved his troops toward the exposed French frontier on the Mediterranean, Roosevelt sought to throw American influence into the balance. On June 10, he was scheduled to deliver a commencement speech at the University of Virginia in Charlottesville. Going over the State Department draft, he stiffened the language, telling a diplomat who called at the White House that morning that his speech would be a " 'tough' one—one in which the issue between the democracies and the Fascist powers would be drawn as never before." News that Italy had attacked France reached the President just before he boarded the train to Charlottesville and reinforced his determination to speak out boldly.

Addressing the graduates that evening, President Roosevelt condemned the concept of isolationism that he himself had held so strongly only a few years before. He termed the idea that the United States could exist as a lone island of peace in a world of brute force "a delusion." "Such an island," he declared, "represents to me and to the overwhelming majority of Americans today a helpless nightmare of a people without freedom— the nightmare of a people lodged in prison, handcuffed, hungry, and fed through the bars from day to day by the contemptuous, unpitying masters of other continents." In clear and unambiguous words, he declared that his sympathies lay wholly on the side of "those nations that are giving their life blood in combat" against Fascist aggression. Then, in his most significant policy statement, he announced that his administration would follow a twofold course of increasing the American defense effort and extending to England and France "the material resources of this nation."

The Charlottesville speech marks a decisive turn in Roosevelt's policy. At the time, most commentators focused on one dramatic sentence, written in at the last moment, in which he condemned the Italian attack on France by saying, "the hand that held the dagger has struck it into the back of its neighbor." But far more important was the President's pledge to defend American security by giving all-out aid to England and France. By promising to share American supplies with these two belligerents, Roosevelt was gambling that they could successfully contain Germany on the European continent and thus end the threat to American security. Given the German military advantages, the risks were enormous. If Roosevelt diverted a large portion of the nation's limited supply of weapons to England and France and then they surrendered to Hitler, the President would be responsible for leaving this country unprepared to meet a future German onslaught.

At the same time, the President's admirers have read too much into the Charlottesville speech. Basil Rauch argues that the speech ended America's status as a neutral. Robert Sherwood goes even further, claiming that at Charlottesville Roosevelt committed the United States "to the assumption of responsibility for nothing less than the leadership of the world." Samuel Rosenman is more moderate, labeling this address as "the beginning of all-out aid to the democracies," but noting that it stopped short of war. But is it even accurate to say that the speech signified all-out aid short of war? An examination of Roosevelt's subsequent steps to help France and England reveals that the President was still extremely reluctant to do anything that would directly involve the United States in the European conflict.

The French quickly discovered the limitations of the President's new policy. Heartened by Roosevelt's words at Charlottesville, Paul Reynaud, the French Premier, immediately tried to secure American military intervention to save his country. In a personal appeal to Roosevelt on June 14, Reynaud asked him to send American troops as well as American supplies in France's hour of greatest need. The next day, the President replied. The United States admired the stubborn and heroic French resistance to German aggression, Roosevelt wrote, and he promised to do all he could to increase the flow of arms and munitions to France. But there he drew the line. "I know that you will understand that these statements carry with them no implication of military commitments," the President concluded. "Only the Congress can make such commitments." On June 17, the French, now fully aware that American military involvement was out of the question, surrendered to Germany.

The British, left waging the fight alone against Germany, also discovered that Roosevelt's actions failed to live up to the promise of his words. On May 15, five days after he replaced Neville Chamberlain as Prime Minister, Winston Churchill sent an urgent message to President Roosevelt. Churchill eloquently expressed his determination to fight Hitler to the bitter end, but he warned that Britain had to have extensive aid from the United States. Above all else, England needed forty or fifty American destroyers to protect the Atlantic supply line from German submarine attacks. Churchill pointed out that England had lost thirty-two destroyers since the war began, and she needed most of her remaining sixty-eight in home waters to guard against a German invasion. "We must ask, therefore," Churchill concluded, "as a matter of life or death, to be reinforced with these destroyers."

Despite the urgency of the British request, Roosevelt procrastinated. On June 5, the President told Secretary of the Interior Harold Ickes that it would require an act of Congress to transfer the destroyers to Great Britain. Even pressure from several other cabinet members, including Henry Morgenthau and the two new Republicans Roosevelt appointed in June, Secretary of War Henry Stimson and Secretary of the Navy Frank Knox, failed to move Roosevelt. His reluctance was increased when Congress decreed on June 28 that the President could not transfer any warships to a belligerent until the Chief of Naval Operations certified that they were "not essential to the defense of the United States."

Roosevelt's inaction caused deep concern among members of the Committee to Defend America by Aiding the Allies, the pro-British pressure group headed by William Allen White. A few of the more interventionist members of White's committee developed the idea in mid-July of arranging a trade whereby the United States would give Britain the needed destroyers in return for the right to build naval and air bases on British islands in the Western Hemisphere. On August 1, a three-man delegation called at the White House to present this idea to the President, who received it noncommittally. Lord Lothian, the British ambassador, had suggested as far back as May 24 that England grant the United States the rights for bases on Newfoundland, Bermuda, and Trinidad, and in July, in talks with Secretary of the Navy Frank Knox, Lothian linked the possibility of these bases with the transfer of destroyers. Knox liked the idea, but he could not act without the President's consent. And Roosevelt remained deaf to all pleas, including one by Churchill on July 21 in which the British Prime Minister said, "Mr. President, with great respect I must tell you that in the long history of the world this is a thing to do NOW."

Churchill's appeal and the possibility of justifying the transfer of the destroyers as a trade for bases evidently persuaded Roosevelt to act. On August 2, when Frank Knox raised the issue in a cabinet meeting, Roosevelt approved the idea of giving Britain the destroyers in return for the right to build bases on British islands in the Atlantic and Caribbean, and, in addition, in return for a British pledge to send its fleet to the New World if Germany defeated England. Roosevelt still believed that the destroyer transfer would require an act of Congress, and the cabinet advised him to secure the support of Wendell Willkie, the Republican candidate for the presidency in the forthcoming campaign, to insure favorable Congressional action. Through William Allen White, who acted as an intermediary, Roosevelt received word that while Willkie refused to work actively to line up Republican support in Congress, he did agree not to make the destroyer deal a campaign issue.

Roosevelt called his advisers together on August 13 to make a final decision. With the help of Morgenthau, Knox, Stimson, and Undersecretary of State Sumner Welles, Roosevelt drafted a cable to Churchill proposing the transfer of fifty destroyers in return for eight bases and a private pledge in regard to the British fleet. The next day a joyous Churchill cabled back his acceptance of these terms, saying that "each destroyer you can spare to us is measured in rubies." But Churchill realized that the deal meant more than just help at sea. "The moral value of this fresh aid from your Government and your people at this critical time," he cabled the President, "will be very great and widely felt."

It took two more weeks to work out the details of the transaction, and during that period a group of distinguished international lawyers convinced the Attorney General that the administration could transfer the destroyers without the approval of Congress. One final hitch developed when Churchill insisted that the bases be considered free gifts from the British; Roosevelt finally agreed that two of the sites would be gifts, but that the remaining six would have to be considered a *quid pro quo* for the destroyers. On September 3, the President made the transaction public in a message to Congress in which he bore down heavily on the advantages to be gained by the United States. Barely mentioning the transfer of the destroyers, the President called the acquisition of eight naval and air bases stretching in an arc from Newfoundland to British Guiana "an epochal and far-reaching act of preparation for continental defense in the face of grave danger." Searching desperately for a historical precedent, Roosevelt described the trade as "the most important action in the reinforcement of our national defense that has been taken since the Louisiana Purchase."

What is most striking about the destroyer-for-bases deal is the caution and reluctance with which the President acted. In June he announced a policy of all-out aid to Britain, yet he delayed for nearly four months after receiving Churchill's desperate plea for destroyers. He acted only after interventionists had created strong public support, only after the transfer could be disguised as an act in support of the American defense program, only after the leader of the opposition Party had agreed not to challenge him politically on this issue, and only after his legal advisers found a way to bypass Congress. What may have appeared on the surface to be a bold and courageous act by the President was in reality a carefully calculated and virtually fool proof maneuver.

It would be easy to dismiss the destroyer-for-bases deal as just another example of Roosevelt's tendency to permit political expediency to dictate his foreign policy. Certainly Roosevelt acted in this case with a careful eye on the political realities. This was an election year, and he was not going to hand Wendell Willkie and the Republicans a ready-made issue. But I believe that Roosevelt's hesitation and caution stem as much from his own uncertainty as from political calculation. He realized that the gift of vessels of war to a belligerent was a serious departure from traditional neutrality, and one that might well give Germany the grounds on which to declare war against the United States. He wanted to give England all-out aid short of war, but he was not at all sure that this step would not be an act of war. Only when he convinced himself that the destroyer-for-bases deal could be construed as a step to defend the nation's security did he give his consent. Thus his rather extravagant public defense of his action was not just a political move to quiet isolationist critics; rather it was his own deeply felt rationalization for a policy step of great importance that undoubtedly moved the United States closer to participation in the European conflict.

Perhaps even more significant is the pattern that emerges from this review of Roosevelt's policy in the spring and summer of 1940, for it is one that recurs again and again in his conduct of foreign policy. Confronted by a major crisis, he makes a bold and forthright call at Charlottesville for a policy of all-out aid short of war. But then, having pleased the interventionists with his rhetoric, he immediately retreats, turning down the French appeal for intervention and delaying on the British plea for destroyers, thus reassuring his isolationist critics. Then, as a consensus begins to form, he finally enters into the destroyer-for-bases deal and thus redeems the pledge he had made months before at Charlottesville. Like a child playing a game of giant steps, Roosevelt moved two steps forward and one back before he took the giant step ahead. Movement in a straight and unbroken line seems to have been alien to his nature—he could not go forward until he had tested the ground, studied all the reactions, and weighed all the risks. . . .

After his triumphant election to a third term, Roosevelt relaxed on a Caribbean cruise. But after only a week, a navy seaplane arrived with an urgent dispatch from Winston Churchill. The Prime Minister gave a lengthy and bleak description of the situation in Europe and then informed the President that England was rapidly running out of money for continued purchases of American goods. "The moment approaches when we shall no longer be able to pay cash for shipping and other supplies," Churchill wrote, concluding with the confident assertion that Roosevelt would find "ways and means" to continue the flow of munitions and goods across the Atlantic.

When the President returned to Washington in mid-December, he called in the press, and in his breeziest and most informal manner began to outline the British dilemma and his solution to it. His advisers were working on several plans, he said, but the one that interested him most was simply to lend or lease to England the supplies she needed, in the belief that "the best defense of Great Britain is the best defense of the United States." Saying that he wanted to get rid of the dollar sign, Roosevelt compared his scheme to the idea of lending a garden hose to a neighbor whose house was on fire. When the fire is out, the neighbor either returns the hose or, if it is damaged, replaces it with a new one. So it would be, Roosevelt concluded, with the munitions the United States would provide Britain in the war against Nazi Germany.

In a fireside chat to the American people a few days later, Roosevelt justified this lend-lease concept on grounds of national security. Asserting that Hitler aimed not just at victory in Europe but at world domination, Roosevelt repeated his belief that the United States was in grave peril. If England fell, he declared, "all of us in the Americas would be living at the point of a gun." He admitted that the transfer of arms and munitions to Britain risked American involvement in the conflict, but he argued that "there is far less chance of the United States getting into war if we do all we can now to support the nations defending themselves against attack by the Axis than if we acquiesce in their defeat, submit tamely to an Axis victory, and wait our turn to be the object of attack in another war later on." He declared that he had no intention of sending American troops to Europe; his sole purpose was to "keep war away from our country and our people." Then, in a famous phrase, he called upon the United States to become "the great arsenal of democracy."

Congress deliberated over the lend-lease bill for the next two months, and a strong consensus soon emerged in favor of the measure. Leading Republicans, including Wendell Willkie, endorsed the bill, and most opponents objected only to the leasing provision, suggesting instead an outright loan to Britain. The House acted quickly, approving lend-lease by nearly 100 votes in February; the Senate took longer but finally gave its approval by a margin of almost two to one in early March. After the President signed the legislation into law, Congress granted an initial appropriation of seven billion dollars to guarantee the continued flow of vital war supplies to Great Britain.

Roosevelt had thus taken another giant step forward, and this time without any hesitation. His election victory made him bolder than usual, and Churchill's candid plea had convinced him that speed was essential. The granting of lend-lease aid was very nearly an act of war, for it gave Britain unrestricted access to America's enormous industrial resources. But the President felt with great sincerity that this policy would lead not to American involvement but to a British victory that alone could keep the nation out of war. . . .

In the six months preceding Pearl Harbor, Franklin Roosevelt moved slowly but steadily toward war with Germany. On July 7, he announced that he had sent 4,000 American marines to Iceland to prevent that strategic island from falling into German hands. Secretary of War Stimson, though pleased with this action, expressed disappointment over the President's insistence on describing it solely as a measure of hemispheric self-defense. Iceland was the key to defending the supply route across the Atlantic, and Stimson believed that the President should have frankly told Congress that the United States was occupying the island to insure the delivery of goods to Britain.

Once American forces landed in Iceland, Roosevelt authorized the Navy to convoy American ships supplying the marines on the island. In addition, he at first approved a naval operations plan which permitted British ships to join these convoys and thus receive an American escort halfway across the Atlantic, but in late July he reversed himself ordering the Navy to restrict its convoys to American and Icelandic vessels. In August, at the famous Atlantic Conference with Churchill, Roosevelt once again committed himself to the principle of convoying British ships halfway across the Atlantic, but he failed to give the necessary order to the Navy after his return to Washington.

Roosevelt's hesitancy and indecision finally ended in early September when a German submarine fired a torpedo at the American destroyer *Greer*. Though subsequent reports revealed that the *Greer* had been following the U-boat for more than three hours and had been broadcasting its position to nearby British naval units, Roosevelt interpreted this incident as a clear-cut case of German aggression. In a press release on September 5, he called the attack on the *Greer* deliberate, and on the same day he told Samuel Rosenman to begin drafting a statement that would express his determination "to use any means necessary to get the goods to England." Rosenman and Harry Hopkins prepared a strongly worded speech, and after a few revisions the President delivered it over a worldwide radio network on the evening of September 11.

In biting phrases, Roosevelt lashed out against Hitler and Nazi Germany. He described the attack on the *Greer* as part of a concerted German effort to "acquire absolute control and domination of the seas for themselves." Such control, he warned, would lead inevitably to a Nazi effort to dominate the Western Hemisphere and "create a permanent world system based on force, terror, and murder." The attack on the *Greer* was an act of piracy, Roosevelt declared; German submarines had become the "rattlesnakes of the Atlantic." Then, implying but never openly saying that American ships would shoot German submarines on sight, Roosevelt declared that henceforth the United States Navy would escort "all merchant ships—not only American ships but ships of any flag—engaged in commerce in our defensive waters."

Contemporary observers and many historians labeled this the "shoot-on-sight" speech, seeing its significance primarily in the orders to American naval officers to fire at German submarines in the western Atlantic. "The undeclared war" speech would be a better label, for its real importance was that Roosevelt had finally made a firm decision on the convoy issue on which he had been hedging ever since the passage of lend-lease by Congress. Branding the Germans as "pirates" and their U-boats as "rattlesnakes" distracted the American people from the fact that the President was now putting into practice the policy of convoying British ships halfway across the ocean, and thereby assuming a significant share of the responsibility for the Battle of the Atlantic. The immediate effect was to permit the British to transfer forty destroyers from the western Atlantic to the submarine-infested waters surrounding the British Isles. In the long run, the President's decision meant war with Germany, since from this time forward there would inevitably be more and more U-boat attacks on American destroyers, increasingly heavy loss of life, and a direct challenge to the nation's honor and prestige. Only Hitler's reluctance to engage in war with the United States while he was still absorbed in the assault on Russia prevented an immediate outbreak of hostilities.

With the convoy issue now resolved, Roosevelt moved to revise the Neutrality Act. In mid-October he asked the House to permit the arming of American merchant ships with deck guns, and then later in the month he urged the Senate to remove the "carry" provision of the law so that American merchantmen could take supplies all the way across the Atlantic to British ports. When a German submarine torpedoed the destroyer *Kearney* near Iceland, Roosevelt seized on the incident to speed up action in Congress.

"America has been attacked," the President declared in a speech on October 27. "The U.S.S. *Kearney* is not just a Navy ship. She belongs to every man, women, and child in this Nation." Describing Nazi efforts at infiltration in South America, the President bluntly charged that Germany was bent on the conquest of "the United States itself." Then, coming very close to a call for war, he asserted, "The forward march of Hitlerism can be stopped—and it will be stopped. Very simply and very bluntly—we are pledged to pull our own oar in the destruction of Hitlerism." Although he called only for the revision of the Neutrality Act, the tone of the entire address was one of unrelieved belligerency, culminating in the following peroration: "Today in the face of this newest and greatest challenge, we Americans have cleared our decks and taken our battle stations. We stand ready in the defense of our Nation and the faith of our fathers to do what God has given us the power to see as our full duty."

Two weeks later, by quite slim majorities, Congress removed nearly all restrictions on American commerce from the Neutrality Act. For the first time since the war began in 1939, American merchant vessels could carry supplies all the way across the Atlantic to British ports. The significance of this action was obscured by the Japanese attack on Pearl Harbor which triggered American entry into the war in December and gave rise to the subsequent charge that Roosevelt led the nation into the conflict via the back door. Revision of the Neutrality Act was bound to lead to war with Germany within a matter of months. Hitler could be forbearing when it was only a question of American escort vessels operating in the western Atlantic. He could not have permitted American ships to carry a major portion of lend-lease supplies to Britain without giving up the Battle of the Atlantic. With the German offensive halting before Leningrad and Moscow in December, Hitler would have been compelled to order his submarine commanders to torpedo American ships as the only effective way to hold Britain in check. And once Germany began sinking American ships regularly, Roosevelt would have had to ask Congress for a declaration of war.

The crucial question, of course, is why Roosevelt chose such an oblique policy which left the decision for peace or war in the hands of Hitler. His apologists, notably Robert Sherwood and Basil Rauch, insist that he had no choice. The isolationists were so powerful that the President could not lay the issue squarely before Congress and ask for a declaration of war. If he had, writes Basil Rauch, he would have "invited a prolonged, bitter, and divisive debate" and thereby have risked a defeat which would have discredited the administration and turned the nation back to isolationism. Sherwood sadly agrees, saying, "He had no more tricks left. The hat from which he had pulled so many rabbits was empty. The President of the United States was now the creature of circumstance which must be shaped not by his own will or his own ingenuity but by the unpredictable determination of his enemies."

In part this was true, but these sympathetic historians fail to point out that Roosevelt was the prisoner of his own policies. He had told the nation time and time again that it was not necessary for the United States to enter the war. He had propounded the doctrine that America could achieve Hitler's downfall simply by giving all-out aid to England. He had repeatedly denied that his measures would lead the nation to war. In essence, he had foreclosed to himself the possibility of going directly to the people and bluntly stating that the United States must enter the war as the only way to guarantee the nation's security. All he could do was edge the country closer and closer, leaving the ultimate decision to Germany and Japan.

We will never know at what point Roosevelt decided in his own mind that it was essential that the United States enter the war. His own personal hatred of war was deep and genuine, and it was this conviction that set him apart from men like Stimson and Morgenthau, who decided that American participation was necessary as early as the spring of 1941. William Langer and Everett Gleason believe that Roosevelt realized by the fall of 1941 that there was no other way to defeat Hitler, but they conclude that, even so, he thought the American military contribution could be limited to naval and air support and not include the dispatch of an American army to the European battlefields.

It is quite possible that Roosevelt never fully committed himself to American involvement prior to Pearl Harbor. His hesitancy was not just a catering to isolationist strength but a reflection of his own inner uncertainty. Recognizing that Hitler threatened the security of the United States, he took a series of steps which brought the nation to the brink of war, but his own revulsion at the thought of plunging his country into the most devastating conflict in history held him back until the Japanese attack left him no choice.

Roosevelt's Leadership, Public Opinion, and Playing for Time in Asia

ROBERT DALLEK

At the same time that Roosevelt had been working on Hemisphere defense, he had tried to restrain Japan and prevent the outbreak of a Pacific war. Reflecting the mood of the country, the Congress, and the administration in the summer and fall of 1939, he had told Joseph Grew, the American Ambassador to Tokyo, that the United States would not be forced out of China and would support its position in the Far East by reinforcing Manila and Pearl Harbor and holding maneuvers in Hawaiian waters. More specifically, in September 1939, when Japan renewed its pressure on Britain and France to withdraw from China, Hull had warned Tokyo against actions that would further undermine Japanese-American relations and encourage the introduction of financial and trade policies injurious to Japan. In October, with Roosevelt's explicit approval, Grew had bluntly told an America-Japan Society luncheon in Tokyo that opinion in the United States highly resented Japanese actions in China and favored economic retaliation against further violations of American rights.

In the three months before the Commercial Treaty with Japan expired in January 1940, international and domestic pressure mounted for stronger action against Japan. Steps toward the creation of a puppet regime in

Excerpted from *Franklin D. Roosevelt and American Foreign Policy, 1932–1945*, 236–43, 269, 270–75, 299, 303, 306, 308–13, 529–31, by Robert Dallek. Copyright © 1979 by Oxford University Press, Inc. Reprinted by permission.

Nanking and continuing efforts to drive Anglo-French forces from China suggested that words alone would not alter Tokyo's course. Only economic sanctions, Chiang Kai-shek told FDR, would force Japan into a negotiated settlement "based on reason and justice." [Henry] Morgenthau, [Harold] Ickes, Stanley K. Hornbeck, the State Department's senior Far Eastern adviser, congressional leaders, and, according to an opinion poll, 75 per cent of the American public agreed.

Others were not so sure. Fearful that continued resistance to Japanese control in China, especially by the use of sanctions, would lead Tokyo into an attack on their Asian colonies, Britain and France urged Washington to help negotiate a settlement of the China Incident and to renew its trade treaty with Japan. Ambassador Grew also counselled restraint. Seeing "a marked trend" in Japan toward better relations with the United States, he recommended against talk of an embargo and urged negotiations for a new trade treaty. While Hull opposed immediate trade talks, he also opposed the introduction of economic sanctions as likely to "arouse" the Japanese. Instead, he urged the President simply to continue with existing trade practices when the treaty expired.

Roosevelt's own impulse was to deal harshly with Japan. In the summer of 1939 he had spoken of intercepting the Japanese fleet if it moved south against Indochina or the Dutch East Indies; in September he had answered a Chinese plea for additional credits by telling Morgenthau "to do everything . . . that we can get away with"; in October he had complimented Grew on his blunt speech, saying that "you did it in the right way and at the right time"; and in November he had predicted that Americans would question continued relations with Tokyo "if the Japanese government were to fail to speak as civilized twentieth-century human beings."

In December, however, when he had to make up his mind about economic pressure on Japan, he had adopted a middle ground between advocates of sanctions and conciliation. While accepting Hull's recommendation not to impose sanctions at the expiration of the treaty, he also asked him to tell the Japanese that the withholding of sanctions was "a temporary measure" which would stand as long as there was a reasonable possibility of reaching some accord. Should this possibility disappear, Hull was also to say, the President would restrict trade with Japan. He hoped that such a policy would strengthen Japanese proponents of better relations with the United States and weaken impulses to recoup potential trade losses by seizing Allied colonies to the south.

Though hopes for improved relations rose when a moderate Japanese Cabinet under Admiral Mitsumasa Yonai took power in mid-January, unbridgeable tensions over China kept the two countries apart. Opinion in Japan was practically unanimous on achieving the "new order" in East Asia, which was a euphemism for control of China. During the first three months of 1940 attacks on China's supply line through Indochina and the creation of a collaborationist regime in Nanking made this clear. In response, the administration lent Chiang another $20 million and denounced the Puppet government in Nanking as "a further step in a program of one country by armed force to impose its will upon a neighboring country." The United States, Hull declared, would continue to recognize Chiang's regime as the legitimate government of China.

German victories in Scandinavia in April 1940 further sharpened Japanese-American tensions. Hitler's defeat of Denmark followed by Britain's occupation of Iceland aroused concern in Tokyo and Washington about the Dutch East Indies. Anticipating a German attack on Holland and a Dutch request for American occupation of their overseas territory, Japan's Foreign Minister publicly warned against any change in their control. Believing this foretold a Japanese move into the territory, Roosevelt and Hull responded with a statement of American dependence on the islands for rubber and tin and declared against any change in their status quo as inimical to peace throughout the Pacific. Tokyo, in turn, objected to Washington's interpretation of its statement and to the movement of the American Fleet to Hawaii as an unneeded deterrent against Japanese expansion to the south.

In May, Germany's conquest of Holland followed by Britain's occupation of the Dutch West Indies accentuated these concerns. Hull publicly reiterated American support for the status quo in the Dutch East Indies, while he and Roosevelt privately persuaded London to disavow any intention of intervention there. Despite these actions, Tokyo pressed the Dutch to guarantee minimum annual exports from the islands of thirteen raw materials, including principally oil. German victories persuaded the administration to concede these demands and to renew the search for a settlement with Japan. In late May, Roosevelt told Morgenthau that he "would like to do something with Japan, [a] sort of joint treaty to keep peace in the Pacific." Simultaneously, Hull asked his Far Eastern experts "to take a fine-tooth comb and a microscope and go back over our relations with Japan and see if it is humanly possible to find something with which to approach them and prevail upon them not to gallop off on a wild horse." Conversations initiated in Tokyo by the administration on June 10 only highlighted the gulf between the two sides.

In June 1940 Allied losses in Europe touched off a new round of Japanese aggressiveness. Taking advantage of French defeat and British weakness, the Yonai government revived demands for Allied withdrawal from China, pressed France to shut the Indochina border and Britain to close Chinese supply routes through Hong Kong and Burma, and declared "the regions of the South Seas" part of Japan's Greater East Asia Co-Prosperity Sphere. In response, the French asked Washington to oppose their expulsion from China and to send arms to Indochina; the Chinese urged a declaration of American backing for the status quo in Indochina; and the British suggested either halting all exports to Japan or sending a part of the American fleet to Singapore. The only alternative to these steps, London advised, was to attempt to negotiate a full-scale settlement with Japan which would end the war in China and guarantee the safety of Western possessions in the Pacific.

Roosevelt and Hull refused to alter course. Believing that strong measures would provoke an unwanted Pacific crisis and that appeasement would encourage further Japanese demands, they continued to urge a middle ground. If, Hull told the British, the Western Powers acquiesced in, but did not assent to, Japanese impairment of some of their rights and interests, and if Britain continued to resist Berlin and the United States kept its Fleet in Hawaii, Japan would refrain from any major move. But London thought otherwise. Since it believed that Britain could not hold out against Japanese demands without direct American support, London agreed to close the principal supply route to Nationalist China, the Burma Road, in July and to work for a settlement in China.

Britain's action forced Washington into a hot debate on Far Eastern policy. On July 18, when Morgenthau, Stimson, and Knox questioned the Burma Road decision in a conversation at the British Embassy, Lord Lothian, the Ambassador, protested that Washington's refusal to back strong measures against Japan had forced London's hand. "After all," Lothian said, "you are continuing to ship aviation gasoline to Japan." If, he contended, the United States would stop such shipments and Britain would blow up the oil wells in the Dutch East Indies, Japan would be without fuel for its war machine. Morgenthau, who had been battling to halt the export of strategic materials, put this plan before the President on the following day. Proposing a total embargo on all American oil exports, British acquisition of sufficient supplies from Venezuela and Colombia, Anglo-Dutch destruction of the Dutch East Indies wells, and British air attacks on German synthetic-oil plants, Morgenthau predicted "that this thing might give us peace in three to six months."

Roosevelt was of two minds. On the one hand, he wished to take a stronger stand against Japan. Unhappy over the closing of the Burma Road and aware that Tokyo was about to exert "the utmost efforts" to block inter-American economic cooperation at the Havana Conference and to step up strategic imports from the United States, Roosevelt was "tremendously interested" in Morgenthau's proposal and discussed it with Stimson, Knox, and Welles. At the same time, though, he remained determined to avoid a war in the Pacific. A conflict with Japan would not only reduce Anglo-American power to defeat Berlin, it would also jeopardize the President's political future. Having just been nominated for a third term on a platform of no participation in foreign wars unless attacked, Roosevelt felt constrained to avoid provacative steps. Hence, when Welles argued that this plan would cause Japan to attack Britain, the President ordered more discussion with the British and left the proposal in the air.

But Morgenthau and Stimson would not leave it there. Angered by Welles's "beautiful Chamberlain talk," which suggested that "everything is going to be lovely" and that Japan will come over and "kiss our big toe," Morgenthau asked the President on July 22 to use the Defense Act of July 2, 1940, to forbid the export of petroleum, petroleum products, and scrap metals. In receipt of reports that Japan had significantly increased its orders in the United States for high-grade aviation fuel, Roosevelt directed Welles to limit the export of this gasoline. On the 25th, after hearing from Stimson that Japan was trying to corner the American market on aviation fuel and that delivery of these orders might leave United States forces without adequate supplies for six to nine months, Roosevelt signed a Treasury Department proclamation limiting the export of all oil and scrap metal. . . .

Though Tokyo objected at once, these restrictions had little to do with the fact that Japan now intensified its drive for an East Asian sphere of control. In the second half of July, in the belief that the Yonai government was not taking enough advantage of German victories, Japanese militants established Prince Fumimaro Konoye at the head of a Cabinet that included avowed expansionists like Yosuke Matsuoka and General Hideki Tojo, the new Foreign Affairs and War ministers. Outlining its policies in formal documents of July 26 and 27, the Konoye government pledged itself to settle the China Incident and solve "the problem of the south" by using stronger measures against the foreign concessions in China, the Netherlands East Indies, and French Indochina. These plans took specific form in August and September when the Japanese intimidated the British into withdrawing troops from Shanghai, the Dutch into discussing Japan's economic demands on the Dutch East Indies, and the French into recognizing Japan's preponderant interest in Indochina.

Roosevelt and Hull felt as constrained as ever in answering these challenges. With the outcome of an air battle over Britain and control of the Atlantic in doubt, they remained firmly opposed to a Pacific war. To ease Japan's need for oil and to control its impulse to seize it in the Dutch East Indies, the State Department interpreted the President's Order of July 26 to include only high-octane aviation fuels. This allowed Japan to buy middle-octane gasolines which were entirely satisfactory for their planes. Though this loophole in the President's proclamation was an open secret in the administration, Roosevelt had no desire to close it. In a conversation with Morgenthau about oil and scrap on August 16, he spoke "in [the] same vein as S. Welles," saying that "we must not push Japan too much at this time as we might push her to take [the] Dutch East Indies." In September and October, moreover, when Japanese negotiators in the islands were pressing Dutch authorities for a sixfold increase in annual oil shipments for five years, the State Department, with Roosevelt's approval, endorsed a settlement satisfying 60 per cent of this demand.

Other developments made Roosevelt less accommodating about scrap metal. In August and September, despite repeated verbal protests by Washington, the Japanese had pressed French Indochina into conceding transit rights for troops, permission to construct airfields, and close economic ties. On September 12, in a telegram that impressed FDR, Grew advised further efforts to conciliate Japan or attempts to protect American interests merely by expressions of disapproval. Describing Japan as a predatory power temporarily without ethical or moral sense, Grew urged a policy of striving by every means to preserve the status quo in the Pacific. At the same time, increased Japanese purchases of American scrap metal threatened to create shortages in the United States. Roosevelt responded to all this on September 13 by asking Morgenthau to find ways of halting scrap shipments to Japan without denying them to Britain. On the 26th, after Britain had shown itself likely to withstand the German air assault and Japanese forces had marched into Indochina, the administration announced a full embargo on all iron and steel scrap.

These steps were insufficient to deter Japan from the completion of a Tripartite Pact with Berlin and Rome on September 27, 1940. Marked chiefly by an agreement to help each other if attacked by a Power not currently involved in the European or Sino-Japanese fighting, the treaty aimed to prevent the United States from either joining Britain against Berlin or directly opposing Japan's creation of an East Asian sphere. For Tokyo, it was also a way of securing German approval for its drive to the south and help in settling differences with Russia to the north. . . .

Roosevelt's preference was for active opposition to Japan. . . . Yet at the same time, he continued to hold the conviction that meeting problems in the Atlantic and winning reelection required peace in the Pacific. Consequently, he would not risk an oil embargo, telling Morgenthau, who pressed him on this point, to get out of the oil business and leave foreign affairs to him and Hull. Shortly after, he told Hull and Welles that "we were not to shut off oil from Japan . . . and thereby force her into a military expedition against the Dutch East Indies." He also decided against any move into Singapore and abandoned his talk of Pacific patrols. The fact that Tokyo showed no determination to fight over the reopening of the Burma Road also seemed to reduce the need for such steps. Further, the fact that American declarations on the Tripartite Pact led Tokyo to use softer words suggested that the administration's measured response was all it now need do in opposing Japan. . . .

From the fall of 1940 to the summer of 1941, while Roosevelt struggled to aid Britain against Berlin, the Far East continued to force itself on his attention. Though he remained eager to keep things as quiet as possible in the Pacific and to divert the fewest possible resources from the Atlantic and the Middle East, continuing Japanese pressure on China and Southeast Asia denied him that option.

On October 18, 1940, Chiang Kai-shek sent word that continued resistance to Japan depended on prompt additional help from the United States. He contended that the loss of American and Russian supplies after the closing of the Burma Road in July, rampant inflation, and Communist exploitation of current difficulties in order to weaken Nationalist rule were sapping China's ability and resolve to fight. To meet these difficulties, Chiang asked for 500 planes in the next three months, American volunteers to fly them, and "a single big loan rather than small piecemeal credits" as given in the past. The planes and crews would allow Chiang's Chungking government to oppose Japan's uncontested control of the skies and to defend the recently reopened Burma Road; they would permit raids on naval bases in Japan and Formosa and thus impair Tokyo's ability to fight the United States. . . .

Though Roosevelt rejected Chiang's proposal for an alliance, he shared his apprehension that Japanese recognition of the Nanking government would further undermine "free China," and he tried to "do something fast." Asking Welles and Morgenthau to arrange a hundred-million-dollar loan at once, he pressed Morgenthau to go ahead with the credit even if it meant defying Congress. "It is a matter of life and death . . .," he told the Secretary. "If I don't do it . . . it may mean war in the Far East." On November 30, the same day Tokyo recognized the Nanking regime, Roosevelt announced a contemplated credit to the Chinese government of $100 million, and Hull expressed American determination to continue to recognize "the legally constituted Government at Chungking."

At the same time, Roosevelt encouraged a plan to give the Chinese a limited number of long-range bombers to attack Japan. Since, as Morgenthau told T. V. Soong, Chiang's Personal Representative in Washington, "asking for 500 planes is like asking for 500 stars," Roosevelt saw the idea of giving bombers as a relatively cheap way to bolster Chungking. Originating with the Chinese, who proposed to use foreign pilots and mechanics operating from airfields within 650 miles of Tokyo, the scheme received enthusiastic support from the President, Morgenthau, and Hull. "Wonderful," FDR replied when Morgenthau put the plan before him. "If we could only find some way to have them [the Chinese] drop some bombs on Tokyo," Hull remarked to Morgenthau. When the two of them tried to work out the details of such an operation, however, it drew fire from Stimson and Marshall as "rather half baked" and too costly to the British war effort. Instead, with London's reluctant acquiescence, Stimson and Marshall agreed to divert 100 pursuit planes from British orders to help defend the Burma Road. This help, while less than Chiang had asked or Washington wished to give, promised to keep China fighting and, most importantly, help deter Japan from attacking French, Dutch, or British possessions to the South. . . .

When a fresh crisis arose in the Far East in February 1941 over reports of a Japanese offensive against Southeast Asia, circumstances dictated that Roosevelt not challenge Japan. Though he considered giving a strong response, the battle of the Atlantic and the Lend-Lease debate constrained him. More specifically, the need to answer Hitler's offensive with additional Atlantic patrols and concerns that a war scare would provoke opposition to Lend-Lease decided Roosevelt against moving more ships to the Pacific or sending a naval force to cruise the Philippines as a warning to Japan.

Instead of strong measures, Roosevelt relied on "moral steps" of doubtful consequence. On February 11 he advised Americans in China, the Philippines, and Malaya to leave the Far East, and on the 14th he had "a very serious talk" with Admiral Kichisaburo Nomura, Japan's new Ambassador. Declaring that Japanese movements southward were giving "this country very *serious* concern," he warned that an incident like the destruction of the [American gunboat] *Panay* could "cause an overnight uprising . . . of American sentiment against the authors." Though the Ambassador assented to everything the President said, Roosevelt thought the conversation of little importance and made light of it in a discussion with [Assistant Secretary of State Adolf

A.] Berle. Describing himself as "really emotional," he recounted his "speech" to the Ambassador, "interspersing it with [mock] sobs. . . . He hoped Admiral Nomura would make it plain to his Government that . . . everybody here was doing their best to keep things quiet . . . should the dikes ever break (three sobs), civilization would be ended."

The British, who took a strong verbal stand against Tokyo, pressed Roosevelt to go beyond these "moral steps." Describing "the awful enfeeblement of our war effort" that would result from a conflict with Japan, Churchill implored the President to inspire the Japanese "with the fear of a double war." From Churchill's perspective, if this helped check Japan, all to the good, and if not, it would link the United States in a military alliance with Britain in the Far East and almost certainly assure her involvement in the European war. Roosevelt, however, remained convinced that a war scare would jeopardize the "pending" Lend-Lease bill and that the public would oppose initiatives that risked war in the Far East. An opinion survey sent to him on February 15, the same day as Churchill's message, showed 59 per cent favoring American action to keep Japan out of the Dutch East Indies and Singapore, but only 39 per cent willing to risk war to achieve this end. It was with considerable relief, then, that London and Washington saw Tokyo back away from any warlike act in Southeast Asia during the next nine days.

For four months after this crisis subsided in February 1941, Roosevelt continued to aim for peace in the Pacific through diplomatic talks, limited displays of strength, and additional aid to China. Since negotiations with the Japanese held out some possibility of a settlement and since discussions even if unproductive would at least delay the onset of a war. Roosevelt encouraged further talks. In a conversation with Nomura in March, he endorsed the idea that "matters between our two countries could undoubtedly be worked out without a military clash." Though the ensuing discussions between Nomura and Hull principally confirmed American suspicions of Japanese intentions, Roosevelt was content to let them run on through the spring. They continued to seem not only the best immediate bar to war, but also the best means to help Japan's moderates resist, and possibly overcome, advocates of strong action and firm ties to Berlin. . . .

In June and July, despite his undiminished desire to avoid greater involvement in the Pacific, pressures beyond his control pushed Roosevelt toward a confrontation with Japan. Hitler's attack on Russia forced Tokyo into a grand debate on whether to join Germany by invading Soviet Siberia, take advantage of Russian preoccupation in the north to step up expansion and control of raw materials to the south, or redouble its efforts to avoid war and gain its principal ends in China and Southeast Asia through negotiations with the United States. As long as such a debate was in progress, Roosevelt, who was under heavy domestic pressure to relieve American petroleum shortages by embargoing oil to Japan, refused to do anything which might "tip the delicate scales and cause Japan to decide to attack Russia or . . . the Dutch East Indies." "The Japs," he told Ickes on July 1, "are having a real drag-down and knock-out fight among themselves . . . trying to decide which way they are going to jump—attack Russia, attack the South Seas (thus throwing in their lot definitely with Germany), or whether they will sit on the fence and be more friendly with us. No one knows what the decision will be but . . . it is terribly important for the control of the Atlantic for us to help to keep peace in the Pacific. I simply have not got enough Navy to go round—and every little episode in the Pacific means fewer ships in the Atlantic."

Roosevelt did not know that American diplomatic action was discouraging Japan from an accommodation with the United States. On June 21, in response to developments in the talks going on since April, Hull had sent Tokyo a comprehensive statement of America's position on the issues between them. Since Nomura had initially misled his government into thinking that the United States would negotiate on far more generous terms than those outlined in the June 21 proposal, the Japanese interpreted this document as a deliberate stiffening of position in response to Berlin's imminent attack on the Soviet Union. This apparent change in attitude contributed to a high-level Japanese decision of July 2 to proceed with the advance to the south, even if it meant war with Britain and the United States. More specifically, the Japanese now decided to consolidate their hold on Indochina and Siam as a prelude to closing the Burma Road and dominating the Dutch East Indies.

Evidence of this decision provoked a strong response. Believing that negotiation and appeasement had done little to check Japan and would be a highly unpopular answer to its current action, Roosevelt laid plans to answer new Japanese demands for control in Southeast Asia with "various embargoes, both economic and financial." On July 18, after Tokyo had demanded Vichy's acquiescence in the occupation of eight air and two naval bases in southern Indochina, the President worked out a program of sanctions with his Cabinet. Though giving them "quite a lecture" against a total oil embargo, which would be a goad to war in the Pacific, he agreed to answer Japan's action with a freeze on assets, a reduction in oil exports to amounts received in past years, and a limit on gasoline sales to 67 octane or lower. On the 24th, therefore, when Vichy acceded to Tokyo's demands, Welles issued a public condemnation of the action as a prelude to "further and more obvious movements of conquest," and Roosevelt confirmed his decision to freeze Japanese funds and further restrict her trade.

Yet Roosevelt still had no intention of closing off all oil to Japan. While he wanted a comprehensive order that would allow him to do so at any time, he had no inclination to do it at once. The President, Ickes complained, "was still unwilling to draw the noose tight. He thought that it might be better to slip the noose around Japan's neck and give it a jerk now and then. . . . The effect of the freezing order is to require an export license before any goods can be shipped to Japan but the President indicated that we would still continue to ship oil and gasoline." As Roosevelt explained it to a group of civilian defense volunteers on July 24, oil exports to Japan served American and British self-interest by keeping the Japanese out of the Dutch East Indies and thereby preventing a war in the South Pacific which would disrupt essential lines of supply. Roosevelt also tried to forestall a crisis with Japan by proposing that if Tokyo withdrew from Indochina, the Powers would neutralize the area and guarantee equal access to all its resources. Though Roosevelt had little hope of a favorable response to his plan, he saw it as "one more effort to avoid Japanese expansion to [the] South Pacific."

Neither of these efforts at appeasement, however, made an impression on the Japanese. They refused to take the President's neutralization scheme seriously, and they saw no evidence of his intention to permit further oil exports. So as to leave petroleum policy open, the White House announcement of the President's freezing order said nothing about oil. This left the impression both in the United States and Japan that all trade between them, including petroleum exports, had been suspended. Though an announcement of August 1 indicated that applications for petroleum export licenses could be resubmitted if they did not exceed prewar quantities or involve fuels and oils suitable for use in aircraft, the administration's failure to state its policy clearly allowed government agencies to reject these applications and establish a de facto embargo on oil to Japan. Roosevelt, who left on August 3 for a conference with Churchill on board a ship in the Atlantic did not realize that a full embargo had been introduced until early September, and by then he saw a shift in policy as a show of weakness which Japan would exploit and London and American leaders would deplore.

Roosevelt's acceptance of the full embargo was one expression of his growing belief that only a firm policy would have an impact on Japan. An initial report on the results of the freezing action indicated that it had thrown the Japanese off balance and put them in a quandary about future policy. On the one hand, they asked for further conversations with the United States, even proposing a meeting between Prince Konoye and the President. On the other hand, they made plans for further expansion to the south. Since Roosevelt was aware of these plans because Japanese diplomatic cables could be read through a code-breaking device called "Magic," he viewed their suggestions for talks as insincere. "You will . . . find the President quite ready to talk freely about Japan and about the question of joint action with ourselves if the Japs go for ourselves or the Dutch," Lord Halifax, the British Ambassador to Washington since January, had cabled Churchill in early August. "Opinion has moved so fast during the last few weeks that I don't think you need have any inhibitions about speaking quite freely." Yet, as his actions would shortly demonstrate, Roosevelt remained eager to extend the discussions with Tokyo as a means of deferring a war in the Pacific for as long as he could. . . .

The Pearl Harbor attack on December 7, 1941, ended the long struggle to check Japan without going to war. In August at Argentia, after the British had also answered Japan's move into southern Indochina with sanctions, Churchill had pressed Roosevelt to confront Tokyo with an ultimatum. Under pressure from the Dutch and the Australians to win a commitment from the President to follow a Japanese attack on the Netherlands East Indies or Malaya with a request to Congress for a declaration of war, Churchill proposed parallel warnings to Tokyo by America, Britain, and Holland. These were to say that further encroachment in the Southwest

Pacific would compel countermeasures that might lead to war. The American note was also to indicate that Japanese aggression against British or Dutch possessions would move the President to ask Congress for authority to aid them. Churchill asserted that only some such declaration could restrain Japan and that without it there would almost certainly be a war which would destroy all of Britain's merchant shipping in the Indian Ocean and the Pacific and cut the lifelines between the Dominions and the British Isles. "The blow to the British Government," Churchill declared, "might be almost decisive."

Since Churchill wished to assure that America would not leave Britain to fight Japan alone, he also saw such a warning as a way to bring the United States into the war. As he shortly indicated to one American representative in London, his preference was for the United States to enter the conflict in the Atlantic without Japanese involvement. But as a second choice, he favored American and Japanese belligerency over noninvolvement by both. The "unthinkable" possibility was Japanese involvement without America. An ultimatum to Japan such as he proposed to Roosevelt at Argentia, therefore, would rule out the last possibility and enhance the likelihood that the United States would join the fighting.

Roosevelt would not make the commitments Churchill asked. He refused to give "an assurance that [he] would go to Congress for authority to give armed support" if Japan attacked British or Dutch possessions, and only after considerable pressure from Churchill did he agree to send Tokyo a warning. Though he promised to maintain the economic measures against Japan "in full force . . . he seemed to think that this was the most that he could do. He did not offer to give any further warning to Japan," Churchill reported to his War Cabinet. But after further discussion, "he finally agreed" to warn the Japanese Ambassador that in response to further military expansion "various steps would have to be taken by the United States notwithstanding the President's realization that the taking of such further measures might result in war between the United States and Japan." Since the British were subsequently to associate themselves with the President's statement, Churchill took FDR's agreement to issue this "severe warning" as "a very great advance towards the gripping of Japanese aggression by united forces."

While Roosevelt shared Churchill's concern that Britain not fight Japan alone, he saw the warning to Tokyo as chiefly another means to deter Japan from going to war. The President's "chief objective in the Pacific for the time being," Welles had told [British Permanent Undersecretary Sir Alexander] Cadogan on the first day of the Atlantic Conference, was "the avoidance of war with Japan." Two days later Roosevelt himself told Churchill "that he felt very strongly that every effort should be made to prevent the outbreak of war with Japan." His idea, as he also told Churchill, was to seize on possibilities, slim as they were, for continued negotiations which could give them at least thirty more days to strengthen Pacific defenses. . . .

Yet Roosevelt actually had little hope that a meaningful rapprochement was possible. While he talked with Nomura, a large Japanese force on the Siberian border seemed poised to attack the Soviet Union, and Japanese newspapers discussed the possibility of an attack on American oil tankers headed for Vladivostok. The progress of the Nazi-Soviet conflict rather than "regard for the United States," FDR told Halifax on August 18, was the principal influence on current Japanese policy. For FDR, the realistic objective in these talks was not a fundamental shift in Japanese-American relations, which seemed almost certainly beyond reach, but time—the extension of peace in the Pacific while America, Britain, and Russia increased their military strength. If matters could be strung out long enough, or until Hitler could be destroyed, the change in international circumstance might even force Japan to shift policy without a war.

Consequently, on August 28, when Prime Minister Konoye responded with an "urgent" plea for a meeting as soon as possible, Roosevelt "complimented the tone and spirit" of the reply and declared himself "keenly interested in having three or four days" with him. According to Hull, Roosevelt "relished a meeting with Konoye, and . . . was excited at the prospect." Vice President Henry Wallace left a Cabinet meeting on the following day with the impression that Roosevelt was ready to adopt an "appeasing or partially appeasing stand" toward Japan.

Yet Roosevelt would take only limited risks in these negotiations. While describing himself as looking forward to his meeting with the Prince, he also "cynically" asked Nomura "whether [an] invasion of Thailand can be expected during these conversations just as an invasion of French Indochina occurred during Secretary Hull's conversations with your Excellency." Fearful that a meeting with Konoye would produce only vague commitments which could be bent in almost any direction later, Roosevelt now followed the State Department's advice that he and Nomura resolve fundamental differences before a meeting. In another conversation with Nomura on September 3, therefore, the President asked for assurances of Japan's detachment from the Tripartite Pact, its readiness to withdraw troops from China, and its adherence to principles of nondiscrimination in economic relations.

High-level Japanese conferences between September 3 and 6 demonstrated that Japanese-American differences were irreconcilable. Convinced that they must act before American economic sanctions and weather conditions hindered their ability to fight, Japan's military leaders now insisted that Konoye be given only until mid-October to settle matters with the United States. If there were no agreement by that date, Japan was to prepare itself for war against America, England, and Holland. The conditions for a settlement agreed to by an Imperial Conference on September 6 set Japan firmly on the road to war. At a minimum, America and Britain were not to interfere with Japan's efforts to conclude the China Incident, were to do nothing that threatened Japan in the Far East, including the establishment of additional military bases or the strengthening of existing forces, and were to cooperate with Japan's efforts to secure adequate supplies of raw materials and assure her economic well-being. In return, Japan would promise not to use Indochina as a military base against other countries, except China, would agree to follow a Far Eastern settlement by withdrawal from Indochina, and would guarantee the neutrality of the Philippines. As for China, it was shortly decided that troops would remain for "a necessary period" in Inner Mongolia and north China to defend against Communism, while other army units would be withdrawn at the close of the China Incident. Manchukuo was not to be returned to China.

The statement to the American government of these conditions in documents of September 22 and 25 simply confirmed Roosevelt's determination not to hold a summit meeting without prior guarantees. Even if FDR believed that he could extend these discussions by a personal meeting with Konoye, he appreciated that sentiment in the United States and China made it nearly impossible without preliminary assurances against trading Chinese interests for peace. Newspaper, public, and official opinion was uniformly opposed to any appeasement of Japan. In September, for example, Roosevelt had learned that 67 per cent of the public was ready to risk war with Japan to keep her from becoming more powerful. Moreover, because Japanese aggression and German aggression were firmly linked in American minds, Roosevelt feared that any appeasement of Japan would produce a cynical outcry in the United States which weaken public resolve to oppose Berlin. At the same time, his principal advisers counseled against anything that further weakened Chinese resistance, pointing out that the combination of ineffective aid and the current negotiations left the Chinese feeling neglected and resentful. They "feel the same way the Czechs did when Chamberlain and Hitler were deciding upon their fate," [White House aide] Lauchlin Currie advised FDR.

In these circumstances, Roosevelt simply tried to string out the negotiations for as long as he could. At the end of September, in response to Hull's outline of what they should say next to Japan, Roosevelt "wholly" agreed that Hull should "recite the more liberal original attitude of the Japanese when they first sought the meeting, point out their much narrowed position now, earnestly ask if they cannot go back to their original attitude, start discussions again on agreement in principle, and reemphasize my hope for a meeting." "Very little was going on as regards these talks," Roosevelt told the British Charge d'Affaires on October 1, adding that nevertheless he was "gaining useful time." . . .

Japan's final proposals offered little hope of forestalling the threatened war. Divided into parts "A" and "B," with the "B" section to be presented only if negotiations stalled on "A," Nomura put the first set of proposals before FDR on November 10. Though addressing their central differences on relations with the Axis, trade, and China, Tokyo's review of these issues offered no way around the impasse. Japan would not withdraw from the Tripartite Pact. If we went into an agreement with Japan while she maintained an obligation to Germany to go to war with us, Hull told Nomura, "it would cause so much turmoil in the country that I might well be lynched." On China, a "Magic" intercept indicated that Tokyo would only try to dispel suspicions by shifting regions of occupation. "We will call it evacuation; but . . . in the last analysis this would be out of the question."

By November 14, Tokyo had given up on these initial proposals and ordered Nomura and Saburo Kurusu, a professional diplomat flown to the United States to help in the negotiations, to present plan "B." But reluctant to take an "irretrievable" step, Kurusu proposed a temporary arrangement that would buy more time for the discussion of fundamental differences. On November 18, he suggested a modus vivendi to Hull in which the United States would ease its economic pressure on Japan in return for a Japanese withdrawal from Indochina. Tokyo at once rejected this suggestion, however, and ordered its diplomats to seek a temporary agreement conforming to proposal "B." Consequently, on November 20 the envoys presented a five-point program to Hull which they described as "an amplification" of their previous suggestions. Under its terms, Japan and the United States were to make no armed advances in Southeast Asia and the southern Pacific, with the exception of French Indochina, where Japan could still move against China; Japan was to withdraw troops from southern Indochina and transfer them to northern Indochina at once and pull out completely after the establishment of an equitable Pacific peace; both governments were to cooperate in the acquisition of goods from the Dutch East Indies; both sides were to restore trade to pre-freeze conditions; and the United States was not to interfere with efforts to restore Sino-Japanese peace. . . .

Though they [Hull and Roosevelt] now agreed to give Japan a ten-point outline of a "proposed basis for agreement," which had been drafted simultaneously with the modus vivendi, neither had serious hopes that it would lead anywhere. Both agreed that negotiations with Japan were for "all practical purposes" at an end, and that hostile action by Japan was "possible at any moment." At a War Cabinet meeting on November 28, it was everyone's opinion that the Japanese troopships moving south posed a "terrific" threat to "Britain at Singapore, the Netherlands, and ourselves in the Philippines," and that the next move was for the President to address a secret warning to the Japanese Emperor and a public message to the Congress alerting it to the danger. With intercepted messages from Tokyo indicating that nothing would happen for at least a few days, the President left it to his advisers to draft these messages while he took a belated Thanksgiving holiday in Warm Springs. . . .

The President needed no reply from the Emperor to know that his appeal would fail. The same evening his message went to Tokyo he received thirteen parts of a fourteen-part Japanese reply to the ten-point American proposal of November 26. "This means war," he told Hopkins. "Since war was undoubtedly going to come at the convenience of the Japanese." Hopkins answered, "it was too bad that we could not strike the first blow and prevent any sort of surprise." "No, we can't do that," the President said. "We are a democracy and a peaceful people." Raising his voice, he added: "But we have a good record." As the military courier who delivered the intercept to the President understood him, the United States would stand on that record and not make the first overt move. "We would have to wait until it came." As Stimson explained it later to a congressional investigating committee, despite the risk involved "in letting the Japanese fire the first shot, we realized that in order to have the full support of the

American people it was desirable to make sure that the Japanese be the ones to do this so that there should remain no doubt in anyone's mind as to who were the aggressors."

Even at this late date, Roosevelt had strong reason to fear that American opinion would be divided and unenthusiastic about full-scale involvement in the war. To be sure, a public opinion survey that reached him on December 5 had shown 69 per cent of the country willing to risk war with Japan to prevent her from becoming more powerful; but only 51 per cent of this group believed the United States would go to war with Japan in the near future. At the same time, a summary of editorial opinion indicated that most of the press saw "American involvement in a Pacific war as an imminent probability." But these papers had "by no means relinquished hope that war may be avoided." Indeed, a majority of the press held "to the hope that the Axis can be defeated without full-scale American participation at the actual fighting fronts."

An oppressive fear as to the economic consequences of fuller American involvement fueled this wish. A detailed report to the President in November on the current public mood had concluded that, unlike the people of many warring countries, Americans believed "that the sun will never shine as brightly after the storm as it did before." Despite expectations of military victory, between 60 and 70 per cent of the public foresaw themselves working harder for less money, paying higher prices, and suffering higher unemployment after a war.

There was also disturbing evidence of resistance to full-scale involvement in a report from Professor Paul Douglas of the University of Chicago on public sentiment in downstate Illinois. In a one-month speaking tour of twenty-two cities and towns, Douglas had found "*no* evidence" that public opinion was ahead of the President "or that any large section demands more violent action. . . . There is a tremendous fear of another A. E. F. [American Expeditionary Force] with its heavy losses," Douglas wrote. "I think the people are in favor of (a) economic aid (b) material aid and probably even (c) use of an airforce but they are opposed at present to an A. E. F." This more or less echoed a national survey of mid-November in which 47 per cent favored and 44 per cent opposed sending a large American Army to Europe, even if it were required for German defeat. Though there was stronger sentiment in the country for directly confronting Japan, the cumulative evidence suggested that the nation would be less than united in a war sparked by Japanese aggression against Thailand, or British or Dutch possessions.

The Japanese solved the President's dilemma on December 7, 1941. At approximately 7:55 A.M., Hawaii time, 190 carrier-based Japanese dive bombers, torpedo planes, and fighters struck at the American fleet and military installations in and around Pearl Harbor, Honolulu, Hawaii. Followed by a second wave of 170 planes, the attack lasted almost two hours. Catching the American defenders by surprise, the Japanese planes killed 2403 Americans and wounded an additional 1178 men. Though no American aircraft carriers were in the Harbor, the bulk of the American battle fleet, seven battleships, along with most of the Navy and Army aircraft on the Island of Oahu were destroyed or put out of commission. However successful in immediate military terms, the Pearl Harbor attack principally served to unite the American people for a war against Japan as nothing else could have.

Though the surprise attack profoundly distressed FDR, it also relieved him. As told by Hopkins, the President said it took the question of peace and war "entirely out of his hands, because the Japanese had made the decision for him." He had always believed that the Japanese would try to avoid fighting the United States while they moved against the other Powers in the Pacific. This would have left him "with the very difficult problem of protecting our interests. . . . Hence his great relief at the method that Japan used. In spite of the disaster at Pearl Harbor . . . it completely solidified the American people and made the war upon Japan inevitable." "In spite of his anxiety," Eleanor Roosevelt later said of her husband, that day "Franklin was in a way more serene than he had appeared in a long time." . . .

Even after Japan's attack, Roosevelt remained intensely concerned with assuring public unity. When Cabinet members led by Hull pressed him to present a long war message to Congress reviewing the whole history of "Japan's lawless conduct," he resisted. Because he believed it essential to have the message read by as many people as possible, he insisted on making it brief and confining it to "the treachery of the present attack." Further, when Churchill inquired whether he wanted him to wait to ask Parliament for a war declaration until the President had acted, Roosevelt answered: "I think it best on account of psychology here that Britain's declaration of war be withheld until after my speech." On December 8 Roosevelt put his war message before the Congress. "Yesterday, December 7, 1941—a day which will live in infamy—the United States of America was suddenly and deliberately attacked by naval and air forces of the Empire of Japan." Describing in some 500 words the diplomatic background to and the consequences of Japan's surprise offensive throughout the Pacific, the President asked for a Declaration of War, which the Congress promptly gave with only one dissenting vote.

Despite strong pressure from Stimson, Roosevelt refused to include Germany and Italy in his request. The President, Halifax advised Churchill on December 9, still felt that he had to persuade part of the American public to fight Germany as well as Japan. "I seem to be conscious of a still lingering distinction in some quarters of the public between war with Japan and war with Germany," FDR told Halifax. Hopeful, because of intercepts of Japanese messages, that Hitler would take the initiative and relieve him of a step that seemed likely to generate debate in the United States, Roosevelt waited to see what Germany would do. On December 11, Hitler and Mussolini obliged him by declaring war on the United States, an act, in their view, of anticipating the inevitable.

In the years after Pearl Harbor, critics of Roosevelt's leadership argued that the President had provoked the Japanese attack as a "backdoor" to the European war. They even suggested that FDR expected the Pearl Harbor assault but allowed American forces to be surprised in order to assure unity at home. This argument, as Roberta Wohlstetter has shown, is without merit. The surprise at Pearl Harbor, she effectively demonstrates, resulted from a national failure to anticipate. The country's political and military leaders simply discounted or underestimated the likelihood of a Japanese attack on Hawaii. Yet the authors of the assertion that FDR allowed American forces to be surprised did not enunciate it simply to discredit FDR. Voiced by a group of writers who believed the United States would have done better to stay out of the war, the refusal to see the Pearl Harbor attack as a surprise was essential to a vindication of old isolationist beliefs. Having consistently argued that American security was not at stake in the war, or that the United States was invulnerable to attack, diehard isolationists tried to answer a devastating refutation of this theme by placing the blame for Pearl Harbor on FDR. Only by explaining away America's vulnerability to attack as the product of something Roosevelt and others around him contrived could isolationists keep their faith alive.

The isolationist tenet that described involvement in the war as certain to damage the nation's democratic institutions was a more realistic concern. By setting precedents for arbitrary use of Executive power, Roosevelt and subsequent Presidents gave meaning to isolationist warnings that the defense of democracy abroad would compromise it at home. It is an irony of history that in his determination to save democracy from Nazism, Roosevelt contributed to the rise of some undemocratic practices in the United States. But it is an even greater irony that the isolationist failure to appreciate the threat posed by Nazi might helped force Roosevelt into the machinations which later Presidents used to rationalize abuses of power on more questionable grounds. . . .

In the years since 1945, Roosevelt has come under sharp attack for his handling of foreign affairs. To be sure, historians generally agree that he was an architect of victory in World War II, but they find little to compliment beyond that: his response to the London Economic Conference of 1933, his neutrality and peace plans of the thirties, his pre–Pearl Harbor dealings with Japan, and his wartime approach to China, France, and Russia have evoked complaints of superficiality and naivete; his cautious reactions to the Italian conquest of Ethiopia, the demise of the Spanish Republic, Japanese expansion in China, Nazi victories from 1938 to 1941, the destruction of Europe's Jews, and apparent wartime opportunities for cementing ties with Russia, transforming China, ending colonialism, and establishing a truly effective world body have saddled him with a reputation for excessive timidity about world affairs; his indirection and guarded dealings with the public before Pearl Harbor and his secret wartime agreements have provoked charges of arbitrary leadership destructive to American democracy.

These complaints certainly have some merit. Roosevelt made his share of errors in response to foreign affairs. His acceptance of Britain's lead in dealing with the Spanish Civil War, his sanction of wiretaps and mail openings, his wartime internment of the Japanese, and his cautious response to appeals for help to Jewish victims of Nazi persecution were unnecessary and destructive compromises of legal and moral principles. Beyond these matters, however, I believe that too much has been made of Roosevelt's shortcomings and too little of the constraints under which he had to work in foreign affairs.

During the thirties, when public and congressional opinion fixed its attention on national affairs and opposed any risk of involvement in "foreign wars," Roosevelt felt compelled to rely on symbols to answer challenges and threats from abroad. His handling of the London Economic Conference, for example, was less the expression of confusion or overblown visions of curing the Depression from outside the United States than of an abortive effort to restore a measure of faith in international cooperation. Likewise, his suggestions for preserving peace during the thirties were less the product of an idealized view of world affairs than of a continuing desire to encourage leaders and peoples everywhere to work against war and, specifically, to signal aggressor nations that the United States was not indifferent to their plans.

Similarly, his acceptance of the Neutrality laws of the thirties was less an act of conviction than of realistic calculation about what he could achieve at home and abroad. Since winning congressional approval for domestic programs essential to national economic and political stability ruled out bold initiatives in foreign affairs, Roosevelt acquiesced in the widespread preference for a passive foreign policy. Instead, he aimed to meet worldwide attacks on democracy by preserving it in the United States. "You have made yourself the trustee for those in every country who seek to mend the evils of our condition by reasoned experiment within the framework of the existing social system," John Maynard Keynes, the noted economist, publicly told him in December 1933. "If you fail, rational change will be gravely prejudiced throughout the world, leaving orthodoxy and revolution to fight it out." Between 1935 and 1938, his reluctance openly to oppose aggression in Ethiopia, Spain, China, Austria, or Czechoslovakia rested not on an isolationist impulse or a desire to appease aggressors but chiefly on a determination to retain his ability to influence crucial developments at home. Roosevelt turned this influence to good account abroad. Under his leadership, a Montevideo newspaper commented, the United States had again become "the victorious emblem around which may rally the multitudes thirsting for social justice and human fraternity." "His moral authority, the degree of confidence which he inspired outside his own country," the historian Isaiah Berlin later said, ". . . has no parallel. . . . Mr. Roosevelt's example strengthened democracy everywhere."

Yet Roosevelt's contribution to the survival of international democracy came not through symbolic gestures in the thirties but through substantive actions during World War II. His appreciation that effective action abroad required a reliable consensus at home and his use of dramatic events overseas to win national backing from a divided country for a series of pro-Allied steps were among the great presidential achievements of this century. In the years 1939–41 Roosevelt had to balance the country's desire to stay out of war against its contradictory impulse to assure the defeat of Nazi power. Roosevelt's solution was not to intensify the conflict by choosing one goal over the other but rather to weave the two together: the surest road to peace, he repeatedly urged the nation to believe throughout this difficult period, was material aid to the Allies. And even when he concluded that the country would eventually have to join the fighting, as I believe he did in the spring of 1941, he refused to force an unpalatable choice upon the nation by announcing for war.

Roosevelt's dissembling created an unfortunate precedent for arbitrary action in foreign affairs which subsequent Presidents have been quick to use. This consequence, however, needs to be evaluated alongside two other considerations: first that Roosevelt's indirection forestalled a head-on clash with the Congress and majority opinion which would have weakened his ability to lead before and after Pearl Harbor; and, second, that for all his willingness to deceive the public in the interest of persuading it to go to war, he never lost sight of the fact that a national commitment to fight required events beyond his control to arrange. Indeed, what seems most striking in this period was not Roosevelt's arbitrariness in pushing the country toward war but rather his caution and restraint. For all his talk at Argentia of needing an "incident," and for all his efforts even to manufacture one in the case of the *Greer* [an American destroyer fired upon by a German submarine in September 1941], he refused to ask for a declaration of war until a genuine provocation from abroad made the nation ready to fight.

Did Roosevelt, then, maneuver or, at the very least, permit the country to become involved in a war with Japan as a backdoor to the European fighting? "Had FDR been determined to avoid war with the Japanese if at all possible," George Kennan has argued, "he would have conducted American policy quite differently . . . than he actually did. He would not, for example, have made an issue over Japanese policy in China, where the Japanese were preparing, anyway, to undertake a partial withdrawal . . . and where this sort of American pressure was not really essential. He would not have tried to starve the Japanese navy of oil. And he would have settled down to some hard and realistic dealings with the Japanese." This picture of Roosevelt's options leaves out the domestic context in which he had to operate. The struggle against fascism in American minds was indelibly linked with China's fight against Japan. Though mindful of the advantage of concentrating American power against Berlin, Roosevelt also appreciated that opposition to Japan was an essential part of the moral imperative Americans saw for fighting. To have acquiesced in Japan's domination of China and allowed oil and other vital supplies to fuel Japan's war machine would have provoked an outcry in the United States against cynical power politics and weakened the national resolve to confront power outside of the Western Hemisphere. In short, to gain a consensus for fighting fascism overseas, Roosevelt could not discriminate between Germany and Japan; both had to be opposed at the same time.

Roosevelt's Failure of Leadership, Bureaucracy, and War with Japan

JOHNATHAN G. UTLEY

The Japanese-American conflict grew out of two mutually exclusive views of world order. Japan, seeing itself as a poor nation surrounded by richer and more powerful nations, sought to gain security through the establishment of a New Order. By dominating the political and economic life of East Asia, then Greater East Asia, and ultimately Greater East Asia and the South Seas, Japanese leaders hoped to assure safe access to the markets and raw materials vital to Japan's role as a great nation. American leaders could agree that a secure source of raw materials and markets was essential for all nations but they flatly rejected Japan's autarchic approach. Americans favored the liberal commercial world order, characterized by free trade and free investment. If Germany succeeded in establishing its autarchic order over Europe and Japan over Asia, the world would be set back 750 years, or so Roosevelt and Hull believed. The United States would never accept Japan's New Order in Greater East Asia and the South Seas. It was learning to live with Japan in China, but expansion farther south was intolerable.

Since each nation equated its own system with national survival, it is tempting to conclude that this was a conflict not susceptible to peaceful resolution and that it could be resolved only on the field of battle. Yet neither side wanted to fight the other. Japanese leaders looked upon the massive economic and military resources of the United States and concluded that almost anything would be better than a war with such a great power. American leaders, while not respecting the Japanese, saw America's real interests in Europe and wished to avoid war in Asia. This mutual desire for peace meant an opportunity for diplomacy.

The purpose of diplomacy is to find a way for nations with conflicting interests to resolve their differences other than on the battlefield, and if not to resolve those differences at least to learn to coexist with them. By this criterion, American foreign policy managers failed. During a period of more than four years they were unable to guide either American or Japanese policy in a direction that would avoid war.

Where did American leaders go wrong? Or phrased more discreetly, how might they have acted differently?

To begin with, Cordell Hull and his staff approached Japan with strongly held preconceptions. They could not see Japan, they could not understand what Japan was saying, they could not believe that any Japanese leader was both sincere and capable of delivering on promises. This negative view of Japan and the Japanese led Hull and company to make many tactical errors. When, as early as 1938, [Ambassador Joseph] Grew warned that the Japanese people would never turn on the military and that sanctions would only unite the nation, Washington ignored his advice. When Grew and Foreign Minister Nomura negotiated the first tentative steps toward understanding in December 1939, Hull turned a cold shoulder. When [American diplomat Joseph W.] Ballantine noted in the summer of 1941 that Japan had legitimate complaints about its treatment at the hands of the Western powers, his advice caused not even a ripple within State. It fell to someone from the Treasury Department, Harry Dexter White, to draft a plan that recognized Japan's legitimate economic needs and proposed to meet them. And when the State Department was finished with that proposal it offered Japan nothing and demanded much.

Though Hull turned a deaf ear to the voices of conciliation in the administration, he also refused to heed those who called for confrontation. As Ickes, Maxwell, Stimson, Knox, Morgenthau, Leahy, Davis, and even the president discovered, when Hull set his mind to something he was a formidable opponent. Though he won the vast majority of his battles with the hawks of the Roosevelt administration, neither Hull nor the president managed to maintain control over the constantly growing and increasingly complex foreign policy bureaucracy. By losing control over the execution of policy, they lost control over the direction the nation moved.

None of the bureaucratic sleights of hand that proliferated during 1940 and 1941 was critical. But the cumulative effect of these little actions moved the United States further toward economic sanctions than Hull or Roosevelt intended. As a result, Japan felt increasingly encircled, and responded by expanding into the resource-rich areas of Southeast Asia. When it moved into southern Indochina in July 1941, and Dean Acheson transformed Roosevelt's financial freeze into sweeping economic sanctions, the damage to American foreign policy was irreparable. This is not to say that without Acheson's machinations there would have been no war. But in the summer of 1941 time was the critical factor. If a confrontation with Japan could have been put off to the spring of 1942 it might have been avoided indefinitely, because by then American military power would have been much greater and German victory in Europe less certain. Acheson and the others who moved the nation toward economic warfare denied the United States that time.

As the two nations inched their way along the road to Pearl Harbor, Hull committed his most serious tactical error. He tried to establish a lasting peace with Japan through negotiation of a comprehensive agreement. To the secretary, peace was not merely the absence of war but the maintenance of fair, decent, and equal relations between nations. But to achieve a diplomatic agreement that would bring about a change of that magnitude was beyond Hull's grasp. In 1938 and 1939 that did not seem to make much difference because the United States could afford to wait for Japan to see the futility of its chosen path of conquest. Hull and Roosevelt saw a war coming in Europe, but they did not foresee the collapse of France with the resulting disruption of the world balance of power. That event, more than any other, outmoded the policy of waiting for Japan to undergo a regeneration of spirit before reaching an agreement. That was the time when Hull should have set aside his search for a comprehensive peace and begun working on a limited understanding, something to avoid war. If he could not bring himself to do this in June 1940, then he should have done so in October, after Japan moved closer to the Axis and into Indochina. An even better opportunity to shift the focus came with the Hull-Nomura talks in the spring of 1941. Or if Hull was waiting for a position of strength to seek a compromise, he had it in August when the freeze was imposed and the talks reopened. In September 1941, when Hull learned that the freeze had cut off Japan's access to oil, the secretary had all the incentive he needed to change his diplomatic objective.

Through all these events Hull tenaciously held to his goal of a sweeping agreement with Japan on fundamentals. This policy was not inspired by a slavish devotion to the sanctity of treaties or a sentimental attachment to China—it was the result of Hull's belief that anything less would be a futile appeasement of Japan. The fact that it was pragmatic, however, did not make it wise.

If the secretary had so little faith in temporary agreements as to shun becoming involved in them, then Roosevelt should have intervened to change the focus of Japanese-American talks. But the president never did so, and permitted his secretary of state to lead the nation along a diplomatic path that could only end in tragedy.

Roosevelt's failure of leadership might be explained by any of a number of factors. He too was deeply suspicious of Japanese intentions. He was also preoccupied with the pressing matters of Europe and did not have the time to devote to Asian affairs. Moreover, to take charge of the negotiations with Japan meant taking them away from Hull, who jealously guarded his territory. Beyond all these reasons, the problem of Japanese-American relations was clearly a diplomatic question, and Roosevelt was not comfortable with the intricacies of diplomacy. He enjoyed meeting with Churchill and would have enjoyed meeting with Konoye. He liked to think in terms of a quarantine, naval blockades, and simple economic sanctions. The stuff of which the negotiations with Japan were made did not suit him.

A variety of factors brought Cordell Hull to that point on the morning of November 26, 1941 when he gave up on diplomacy and accepted war. The American faith in the liberal commercial world order and Japan's attempt to establish a New Order in Asia at the point of a gun assured Japanese-American tension. In responding to this tension, the Roosevelt administration failed to employ diplomatic efforts that were consistent with American national interest. The rigidly anti-Japanese Washington mind-set and Cordell Hull's fixation with a comprehensive settlement made diplomacy ineffectual. Even had Hull and Roosevelt been more sensitive to Japan's concerns and more flexible in their diplomatic negotiations, they still faced the problem of a bureaucracy that was out of control. The president and the secretary of state had a policy, but so did Morgenthau, Ickes, Stimson, Knox, Acheson, Grew, Welles, Hornbeck, Maxwell, Yost, Green, Leahy, Stark, and the rest. As a result, the course Roosevelt and Hull charted was not the one that the nation followed. Perhaps stronger control over the bureaucracy would have made no difference, but the chaos that characterized the execution of American policy left no chance for success.

✳ *F U R T H E R   R E A D I N G*

Patrick Abbazia, *Mr. Roosevelt's Navy* (1975)
Frederick Adams, *Economic Diplomacy* (1976)
Selig Adler, *The Isolationist Impulse* (1957)
Irvine H. Anderson, *The Standard-Vacuum Oil Company and United States East Asia Policy* (1975)
Michael Barnhart, *Japan Prepares for Total War* (1987)
Charles A. Beard, *President Roosevelt and the Coming of the War, 1941* (1948)
Michael Beschloss, *Kennedy and Roosevelt* (1980)
Dorothy Borg, *The United States and the Far Eastern Crisis of 1933–1938* (1964)
———— and Shumpei Okamoto, eds., *Pearl Harbor as History* (1973)
Russell D. Buhite, *Nelson T. Johnson and American Policy Toward China, 1925–1941* (1968)
James M. Burns, *The Lion and the Fox* (1956)
Richard D. Burns and Edward M. Bennett, eds., *Diplomats in Crisis* (1974)
Robert J. C. Butow, *The John Doe Associates: Backdoor Diplomacy for Peace, 1941* (1974)
————, *Tojo and the Coming of the War* (1961)
Mark Chadwin, *The Hawks of World War II* (1968)
J. Garry Clifford and Samuel R. Spencer, Jr., *The First Peacetime Draft* (1986)
Warren I. Cohen, *America's Response to China* (1980)
Wayne S. Cole, *America First: The Battle Against Intervention, 1940–1941* (1953)
————, *Charles A. Lindbergh and the Battle Against Intervention in World War II* (1974)
————, *Roosevelt and the Isolationists, 1932–1945* (1983)
————, *Senator Gerald P. Nye and American Foreign Relations* (1962)
James V. Compton, *The Swastica and the Eagle* (1967)
James Crowley, *Japan's Quest for Autonomy* (1966)
David H. Culbert, *News for Everyman: Radio and Foreign Affairs in Thirties America* (1976)
Roger Dingman, *Power in the Pacific* (1976)
Robert A. Divine, *The Illusion of Neutrality* (1962)
————, *The Reluctant Belligerent* (1979)
Jean-Baptiste Duroselle, *From Wilson to Roosevelt* (1963)
Herbert Feis, *The Road to Pearl Harbor* (1950)
Lloyd Gardner, *Economic Aspects of New Deal Diplomacy* (1964)
Martin Gilbert, *Winston S. Churchill: Finest Hour, 1939–1941* (1983)
John M. Haight, Jr., *American Aid to France, 1938–1940* (1970)
Patrick Hearden, *Roosevelt Confronts Hitler* (1987)
Waldo H. Heinrichs, Jr., *American Ambassador* (1966) (on Joseph Grew)
————, *Threshold of War* (1988)
Saburo Ienaga, *The Pacific War* (1978)
Akira Iriye, *Across the Pacific* (1967)
————, *After Imperialism* (1969)
————, *The Origins of the Second World War in Asia and the Pacific* (1987)
Manfred Jonas, *Isolationism in America* (1966)
Kenneth P. Jones, *U. S. Diplomats in Europe, 1919–1941* (1981)
Thomas C. Kennedy, *Charles A. Beard and American Foreign Policy* (1975)

Warren F. Kimball, *The Most Unsordid Act: Lend-Lease, 1939–1941* (1969)

Charles P. Kindleberger, *The World in Depression, 1929–1939* (1973)

William E. Kinsella, Jr., *Leadership in Isolation* (1978)

William L. Langer and S. E. Gleason, *The Challenge to Isolation, 1937–1940* (1952)

———, *The Undeclared War, 1940–1941* (1953)

William E. Leuchtenburg, *Franklin D. Roosevelt and the New Deal* (1963)

Mark M. Lowenthal, "Roosevelt and the Coming of the War," *Journal of Contemporary History*, 16 (1981), 413–40

Thomas R. Maddux, *Years of Estrangement: American Relations with the Soviet Union, 1933–1941* (1980)

Frederick W. Marks III, *Wind over Sand: The Diplomacy of Franklin Roosevelt* (1988)

Martin V. Melosi, *The Shadow of Pearl Harbor* (1977)

James W. Morley, ed., *Deterrent Diplomacy* (1976)

———, ed., *The Fateful Choice: Japan's Advance into Southeast Asia, 1939–1941* (1979)

Charles Neu, *The Troubled Encounter* (1975)

William L. Neumann, *America Encounters Japan* (1963)

Arnold Offner, *American Appeasement* (1969)

———, *The Origins of the Second World War* (1975)

Stephen Pelz, *Race to Pearl Harbor* (1974)

Gordon W. Prange, *At Dawn We Slept: The Untold Story of Pearl Harbor* (1981)

Julius Pratt, *Cordell Hull* (1964)

Willard Range, *Franklin D. Roosevelt's World Order* (1959)

David Reynolds, *The Creation of the Anglo-American Alliance, 1937–41* (1982)

Bruce Russett, *No Clear and Present Danger* (1972)

Michael Schaller, *The U. S. Crusade in China, 1938–1945* (1978)

David F. Schmitz, *The United States and Fascist Italy, 1922–1940* (1988)

Paul W. Schroeder, *Axis Alliance and Japanese-American Relations, 1941* (1958)

Raymond Sontag, *A Broken World, 1919–1939* (1971)

Richard Steele, "Franklin D. Roosevelt and His Foreign Policy Critics," *Political Science Review*, 94 (1979), 15–32.

———, *Propaganda in an Open Society: The Roosevelt Administration and the Media, 1933–1941* (1985)

Charles C. Tansill, *Back Door to War* (1952)

James C. Thomson, Jr., Peter W. Stanley, and John C. Perry, *Sentimental Imperialists* (1981)

John Toland, *Infamy: Pearl Harbor and Its Aftermath* (1982)

Paul A. Varg, *The Closing of the Door* (1973)

Gerald E. Wheeler, *Prelude to Pearl Harbor: The United States Navy and the Far East, 1921–1931* (1963)

John Wiltz, *From Isolation to War, 1919–1939* (1971)

———, *In Search of Peace: The Senate Munitions Inquiry* (1963)

Lawrence Wittner, *Rebels Against War* (1984)

Roberta Wohlstetter, *Pearl Harbor: Warning and Decision* (1962)

CHAPTER
6

The Grand Alliance
of the Second World War

The Grand Alliance of Great Britain, the United States, and the Soviet Union won the Second World War. In the process of hurling defeat at Germany and Japan, and in the final triumph itself, the structure of international relations was transformed. World War II was a true watershed in world history, a time when power shifted from some states to others, when decolonization ate into traditional empires, when war-ravaged economic and political institutions took new shapes. The major objective of Allied leaders Winston S. Churchill, Franklin D. Roosevelt, and Josef Stalin was, of course, to win the war. But they did not always agree on military strategy, and because military decisions carried postwar political consequences, they debated the principles that might guide them in the transition to peace. As they gradually ground down the Axis powers, the Allies negotiated among themselves. They exchanged strong views on the opening of a second, or western, front; they differed over the location for new military campaigns; they suspected each other of flirting with separate peaces; they jockeyed for political position in the countries liberated from Nazi control, such as Poland; they struggled to define the configuration of world power in the postwar era. After Germany and Japan were crushed, the Grand Alliance came apart.

The politics of the Grand Alliance and the linkage between World War II and the Cold War have sparked considerable historical debate. Some critics have faulted President Roosevelt for making military choices without adequately considering their long-term diplomatic impact. Some have held him responsible for the Russian domination of Eastern Europe, a divided Germany, and the onset of the Cold War. The wartime conferences, such as the Yalta Conference, have stirred controversy because they produced plans for winning the war and fashioning the peace that generated Allied tensions and failed to supply postwar stability. The most common charge against Roosevelt after the war was that, naive and unrealistic, he gave in to the Russians, encouraging their expansionist ambitions. Other commentators treat Roosevelt's wartime diplomacy more favorably, emphasizing the unique complexities of conducting a global war, American dependency upon Soviet military forces in Europe, and Roosevelt's grasp of power realities. After all, the Allies did achieve the impressive feat of smashing power-

ful enemies, and if the peace plans did not hold, Roosevelt's successors must share some responsibility. Some scholars have argued, moreover, that the United States used the opportunity of war to weaken the British Empire, expand American interests, including new overseas bases, and thwart a rising political left. The United States under Roosevelt's leadership, then, self-consciously developed and protected a larger American sphere of influence while offering to honor the spheres of the other great powers. Whichever interpretation they express, historians agree that Roosevelt was the central figure in defining policy and that the Second World War elevated the United States to global leadership.

✖ D O C U M E N T S

When to open a second or western front was a major Allied issue until June 6, 1944, when British and American troops crossed the channel into France. Until that time, the Russians pressed hard for action. In a Washington meeting between Franklin D. Roosevelt and Soviet Commissar for Foreign Affairs V. M. Molotov on May 30, 1942 (the first document), the President promised such an operation before year's end. But delays set in, and Soviet Premier Josef Stalin grew impatient. His letter of June 24, 1943, to Churchill, the second document, demonstrates his concern. At an Allied conference held in Teheran, Iran, during late November and early December 1943, Roosevelt and Stalin exchanged ideas about having "Four Policemen" govern the postwar world; the American record of the conference is reprinted as the third selection.

The interest in spheres of influence is illustrated by the fourth document: a Churchill-Stalin agreement of October 1944, delineating the British and Russian roles in the liberated countries. This account is drawn from Churchill's memoirs. The next two documents emerged from the important Yalta Conference of February 4–11, 1945, when the Allied leaders were near victory over Germany. In the seventh selection, a letter dated April 5, 1945, Roosevelt chided Stalin for suggesting that the United States was negotiating with the Germans in Switzerland behind Russian backs. Just before his death, in response to Churchill's growing irritation over Soviet manipulation of Poland, Roosevelt wrote the British Prime Minister. His letter of April 11, 1945, is reprinted here as the last document.

Roosevelt's Promise of a Second Front, 1942

Opening the general discussion, the President remarked to Admiral King and General Marshall that he first wished to place them *au courant* with the questions Mr. Molotov had raised, and he hoped that Mr. Molotov himself would then put the situation before them in detail. Mr. Molotov, the President continued, had just come from London, where he had been discussing with the British authorities the problem of a second (invasion) front in Western Europe. He had, the President added, been politely received, but had as yet obtained no positive commitment from the British. There was no doubt that on the Russian front the Germans had enough superiority in aircraft and mechanized equipment to make the situation precarious. The Soviets wished the Anglo-American combination to land sufficient combat troops on the continent to draw off 40 German divisions from the Soviet front. We appreciated, he continued, the difficulties of the situation and viewed the outlook as serious. We regarded it as our obligation to help the Soviets to the best of our ability, even if the extent of this aid was for the moment doubtful. That brought up the question, what we can do even if the prospects for permanent success might not be especially rosy. Most of our difficulties lay in the realm of ocean transport, and he would in this connection merely remark that getting any one convoy through to Murmansk was already a major naval operation. The President then suggested that Mr. Molotov should treat the subject in such detail as suited his convenience.

Mr. Molotov thereupon remarked that, though the problem of the second front was both military and political, it was predominantly political. There was an essential difference between the situation in 1942 and what it might be in 1943. In 1942 Hitler was the master of all Europe save a few minor countries. He was the chief enemy of everyone. To be sure, as was devoutly to be hoped, the Russians might hold and fight on all through 1942. But it was only right to look at the darker side of the picture. On the basis of his continental dominance, Hitler might throw in such reinforcements in manpower and material that the Red Army might *not* be able to hold out against the Nazis. Such a development would produce a serious situation which we must face. The Soviet front would become secondary, the Red Army would be weakened, and Hitler's strength would be correspondingly greater, since he would have at his disposal not only more troops, but also the foodstuffs and raw materials of the Ukraine and the oil-wells of the Caucasus. In such circumstances the outlook would be much less favorable for all hands, and he would not pretend that such developments were all outside the range of possibility. The war would thus become tougher and longer. The merit of a new front in 1942 depended on the prospects of Hitler's further advantage, hence the establishment of such a front should not be postponed. The decisive element in the whole problem lay in the question, when are the prospects better for the United Nations: in 1942 or in 1943.

Amplifying his remarks, Mr. Molotov observed that the forces on the Soviet front were large, and, objectively speaking, the balance in quantity of men, aviation, and mechanized equipment was slightly in Hitler's favor. Nevertheless, the Russians were reasonably certain they could hold out. This was the most optimistic prospect, and the Soviet morale was as yet unimpaired. But the main danger lay in the probability that Hitler would try to deal the Soviet Union a mighty crushing blow. If, then, Great Britain and the United States, as allies, were to create a new front and to draw off 40 German divisions from the Soviet front, the ratio of strength would be so altered that the Soviets could either beat Hitler this year or insure beyond question his ultimate defeat.

Mr. Molotov therefore put this question frankly: could we undertake such offensive action as would draw off 40 German divisions which would be, to tell the truth, distinctly second-rate outfits? If the answer should be in the affirmative, the war would be decided in 1942. If negative, the Soviets would fight on alone, doing their best, and no man would expect more from them than that. He had not, Mr. Molotov added, received any positive answer in London. Mr. Churchill had proposed that he should return through London on his homeward journey from Washington, and had promised Mr. Molotov a more concrete answer on his second visit. Mr. Molotov admitted he realized that the British would have to bear the brunt of the action if a second front were created, but he also was cognizant of the role the United States plays and what influence this country exerts in questions of major strategy. Without in any way minimizing the risks entailed by a second front action this summer. Mr. Molotov declared his government wanted to know in frank terms what position we take on the question of a second front, and whether we were prepared to establish one. He requested a straight answer.

The difficulties, Mr. Molotov urged, would not be any less in 1943. The chances of success were actually better at present while the Russians still have a solid front. "If you postpone your decision," he said, "you will have eventually to bear the brunt of the war, and if Hitler becomes the undisputed master of the continent, next year will unquestionably be tougher than this one."

The President then put to General Marshall the query whether developments were clear enough so that we could say to Mr. Stalin that we are preparing a second front. "Yes," replied the General. The President then authorized Mr. Molotov to inform Mr. Stalin that we expect the formation of a second front this year.

Josef Stalin's Impatience over a Second Front, 1943

I fully realise the difficulty of organising an Anglo-American invasion of Western Europe, in particular, of transferring troops across the Channel. The difficulty could also be discerned in your communications.

From your messages of last year and this I gained the conviction that you and the President were fully aware of the difficulties of organising such an operation and were preparing the invasion accordingly, with due regard to the difficulties and the necessary exertion of forces and means. Even last year you told me that a large-scale invasion of Europe by Anglo-American troops would be effected in 1943. In the Aide-Memoire handed to V. M. Molotov on June 10, 1942, you wrote:

> Finally, and most important of all, we are concentrating our maximum effort on the organization and preparation of a large-scale invasion of the Continent of Europe by British and American forces in 1943. We are setting no limit to the scope and objectives of this campaign, which will be carried out in the first instance by over a million men, British and American, with air forces of appropriate strength.

Early this year you twice informed me, on your own behalf and on behalf of the President, of decisions concerning an Anglo-American invasion of Western Europe intended to "divert strong German land and air forces from the Russian front." You had set yourself the task of bringing Germany to her knees as early as 1943, and named September as the latest date for the invasion.

In your message of January 26 you wrote:

> We have been in conference with our military advisers and have decided on the operations which are to be undertaken by the American and British forces in the first nine months of 1943. We wish to inform you of our intentions at once. We believe that these operations together with your powerful offensive, may well bring Germany to her knees in 1943.

In your next message, which I received on February 12, you wrote, specifying the date of the invasion of Western Europe, decided on by you and the President:

> We are also pushing preparations to the limit of our resources for a cross-Channel operation in August, in which British and United States units would participate. Here again, shipping and assault-landing craft will be the limiting factors. If the operation is delayed by the weather or other reasons, it will be prepared with stronger forces for September.

Last February, when you wrote to me about those plans and the date for invading Western Europe, the difficulties of that operation were greater than they are now. Since then the Germans have suffered more than one defeat: they were pushed back by our troops in the South, where they suffered appreciable loss; they were beaten in North Africa and expelled by the Anglo-American troops; in submarine warfare, too, the Germans found themselves in a bigger predicament than ever, while Anglo-American superiority increased substantially; it is also known that the Americans and British have won air superiority in Europe and that their navies and mercantile marines have grown in power.

It follows that the conditions for opening a second front in Western Europe during 1943, far from deteriorating, have, indeed, greatly improved.

That being so, the Soviet Government could not have imagined that the British and U.S. Governments would revise the decision to invade Western Europe, which they had adopted early this year. In fact, the Soviet Government was fully entitled to expect the Anglo-American decision would be carried out, that appropriate preparations were under way and that the second front in Western Europe would at last be opened in 1943.

That is why, when you now write that "it would be no help to Russia if we threw away a hundred thousand men in a disastrous cross-Channel attack," all I can do is remind you of the following:

First, your own Aide-Memoire of June 1942 in which you declared that preparations were under way for an invasion, not by a hundred thousand, but by an Anglo-American force exceeding one million men at the very start of the operation.

Second, your February message, which mentioned extensive measures preparatory to the invasion of Western Europe in August or September

1943, which, apparently, envisaged an operation, not by a hundred thousand men, but by an adequate force.

So when you now declare: "I cannot see how a great British defeat and slaughter would aid the Soviet armies," is it not clear that a statement of this kind in relation to the Soviet Union is utterly groundless and directly contradicts your previous and responsible decisions, listed above, about extensive and vigorous measures by the British and Americans to organise the invasion this year, measures on which the complete success of the operation should hinge.

I shall not enlarge on the fact that this responsible decision, revoking your previous decisions on the invasion of Western Europe, was reached by you and the President without Soviet participation and without inviting its representatives to the Washington conference, although you cannot but be aware that the Soviet Union's role in the war against Germany and its interest in the problems of the second front are great enough.

There is no need to say that the Soviet Government cannot become reconciled to this disregard of vital Soviet interests in the war against the common enemy.

You say that you "quite understand" my disappointment. I must tell you that the point here is not just the disappointment of the Soviet Government, but the preservation of its confidence in its Allies, a confidence which is being subjected to severe stress. One should not forget that it is a question of saving millions of lives in the occupied areas of Western Europe and Russia and of reducing the enormous sacrifices of the Soviet armies, compared with which the sacrifices of the Anglo-American armies are insignificant.

Roosevelt and Stalin on the "Four Policemen," at Teheran, 1943

The President then said the question of a post-war organization to preserve peace had not been fully explained and dealt with and he would like to discuss with the Marshal the prospect of some organization based on the United Nations.

The President then outlined the following general plan:

1. There would be a large organization composed of some 35 members of the United Nations which would meet periodically at different places, discuss and make recommendations to a smaller body.

Marshal Stalin inquired whether this organization was to be world-wide or European, to which the President replied, world-wide.

The President continued that there would be set up an executive committee composed of the Soviet Union, the United States, United Kingdom and China, together with two additional European states, one South American, one Near East, one Far Eastern country, and one British Dominion. He mentioned that Mr. Churchill did not like this proposal for the reason that the British Empire only had two votes. This Executive Committee would deal with all non-military questions such as agriculture, food, health, and economic questions, as well as the setting up of an International Committee. This Committee would likewise meet in various places.

Marshal Stalin inquired whether this body would have the right to make decisions binding on the nations of the world.

The President replied, yes and no. It could make recommendations for settling disputes with the hope that the nations concerned would be guided thereby, but that, for example, he did not believe the Congress of the United States would accept as binding a decision of such a body. The President then turned to the third organization which he termed "The Four Policemen," namely, the Soviet Union, United States, Great Britain, and China. This organization would have the power to deal immediately with any threat to the peace and any sudden emergency which requires this action. He went on to say that in 1935, when Italy attacked Ethiopia, the only machinery in existence was the League of Nations. He personally had begged France to close the Suez Canal, but they instead referred it to the League which disputed the question and in the end did nothing. The result was that the Italian Armies went through the Suez Canal and destroyed Ethiopia. The President pointed out that had the machinery of the Four Policemen, which he had in mind, been in existence, it would have been possible to close the Suez Canal. The President then summarized briefly the idea that he had in mind.

Marshal Stalin said that he did not think that the small nations of Europe would like the organization composed of the Four Policemen. He said, for example, that a European state would probably resent China having the right to apply certain machinery to it. And in any event, he did not think China would be very powerful at the end of the war. He suggested as a possible alternative, the creation of a European or a Far Eastern Committee and a European or a Worldwide organization. He said that in the European Commission there would be the United States, Great Britain, the Soviet Union and possibly one other European state.

The President said that the idea just expressed by Marshal Stalin was somewhat similar to Mr. Churchill's idea of a Regional Committee, one for Europe, one for the Far East, and one for the Americas. Mr. Churchill had also suggested that the United States be a member of the European Commission, but he doubted if the United States Congress would agree to the United States' participation in an exclusively European Committee which might be able to force the dispatch of American troops to Europe.

The President added that it would take a terrible crisis such as at present before Congress would ever agree to that step.

Marshal Stalin pointed out that the world organization suggested by the President, and in particular the Four Policemen, might also require the sending of American troops to Europe.

The President pointed out that he had only envisaged the sending of American planes and ships to Europe, and that England and the Soviet Union would have to handle the land armies in the event of any future threat to the peace. He went on to say that if the Japanese had not attacked the United States he doubted very much if it would have been possible to send any American forces to Europe. The President added that he saw two methods of dealing with possible threats to the peace. In one case if the threat arose from a revolution or developments in a small country, it might be possible to apply the quarantine method, closing the frontiers of the countries in question and imposing embargoes. In the second case, if the threat was more serious, the four powers, acting as policemen, would send an ultimatum to the nation in question and if refused, [it] would result in the immediate bombardment and possible invasion of that country. . . .

Marshal Stalin then stated he still was dubious about the question of Chinese participation.

The President replied that he had insisted on the participation of China in the 4 Power Declaration at Moscow not because he did not realize the weakness of China at present, but he was thinking further into the future and that after all China was a nation of 400 million people, and it was better to have them as friends rather than as a potential source of trouble.

The President, reverting to Marshal Stalin's statements as to the ease of converting factories, said that a strong and effective world organization of the 4 Powers could move swiftly when the first signs arose of the beginning of the conversion of such factories for warlike purposes.

Marshal Stalin replied that the Germans had shown great ability to conceal such beginnings.

The President accepted Marshal Stalin's remark. He again expressed his agreement with Marshal Stalin that strategic positions in the world should be at the disposal of some world organization to prevent a revival of German and Japanese aggression.

The Churchill-Stalin Percentage Deal, 1944

The moment was apt for business, so I said, "Let us settle about our affairs in the Balkans. Your armies are in Rumania and Bulgaria. We have interests, missions, and agents there. Don't let us get at cross-purposes in small ways. So far as Britain and Russia are concerned, how would it do for you to have ninety per cent predominance in Rumania, for us to have ninety per cent of the say in Greece, and go fifty-fifty about Yugoslavia?" While this was being translated I wrote out on a half-sheet of paper:

Rumania	
Russia	90%
The others	10%
Greece	

Great Britain	90%
(in accord with U.S.A.)	
Russia	10%
Yugoslavia	50–50%
Hungry	50–50%
Bulgaria	
Russia	75%
The others	25%

I pushed this across to Stalin, who had by then heard the translation. There was a slight pause. Then he took his blue pencil and made a large tick upon it, and passed it back to us. It was all settled in no more time than it takes to set down.

Of course we had long and anxiously considered our point, and were only dealing with immediate war-time arrangements. All larger questions were reserved on both sides for what we then hoped would be a peace table when the war was won.

After this there was a long silence. The pencilled paper lay in the centre of the table. At length I said, "Might it not be thought rather cynical if it seemed we had disposed of these issues, so fateful to millions of people, in such an offhand manner? Let us burn the paper." "No, you keep it," said Stalin.

The Yalta Protocol of Proceedings, 1945

The Crimea Conference of the Heads of the Governments of the United States of America, the United Kingdom, and the Union of Soviet Socialist Republics which took place from February 4th to 11th came to the following conclusions:

I. World Organization

It was decided:

1. that a United Nations Conference on the proposed world organization should be summoned for Wednesday, 25th April, 1945, and should be held in the United States of America.
2. the Nations to be invited to this Conference should be:
   a. the United Nations as they existed on the 8th February, 1945; and
   b. such of the Associated Nations as have declared war on the common enemy by 1st March, 1945. (For this purpose by the term "Associated Nations" was meant the eight Associated Nations and Turkey). When the Conference on World Organization is held, the delegates of the United Kingdom and United States of America will support a proposal to admit to original membership two Soviet Socialist Republics, i. e. the Ukraine and White Russia.

3. that the United States Government on behalf of the Three Powers should consult the Government of China and the French Provisional Government in regard to decisions taken at the present Conference concerning the proposed World Organization.
4. that the text of the invitation to be issued to all the nations which would take part in the United Nations Conference should be as follows:

Invitation

The Government of the United States of America, on behalf of itself and of the Governments of the United Kingdom, the Union of Soviet Socialist Republics, and the Republic of China and the Provisional Government of the French Republic, invite the Government of ———— to send representatives to a Conference of the United Nations to be held on 25th April, 1945, or soon thereafter, at San Francisco in the United States of America to prepare a Charter for a General International Organization for the maintenance of international peace and security.

The above named governments suggest that the Conference consider as affording a basis for such a Charter the Proposals for the Establishment of a General International Organization, which were made public last October as a result of the Dumbarton Oaks Conference, and which have now been supplemented by the following provisions for Section C of Chapter VI:

C. Voting

1. Each member of the Security Council should have one vote.
2. Decisions of the Security Council on procedural matters should be made by an affirmative vote of seven members.
3. Decisions of the Security Council on all other matters should be made by an affirmative vote of seven members including the concurring votes of the permanent members; provided that, in decisions under Chapter VIII, Section A, and under the second sentence of paragraph 1 of Chapter VIII, Section C, a party to a dispute should abstain from voting.

Further information as to arrangements will be transmitted subsequently.

In the event that the Government of ———— desires in advance of the Conference to present views or comments concerning the proposals, the Government of the United States of America will be pleased to transmit such views and comments to the other participating Governments.

Territorial Trusteeship. It was agreed that the five Nations which will have permanent seats on the Security Council should consult each other prior to the United Nations Conference on the question of territorial trusteeship.

The acceptance of this recommendation is subject to its being made clear that territorial trusteeship will only apply to (a) existing mandates of the League of Nations; (b) territories detached from the enemy as a result of the present war; (c) any other territory which might voluntarily be placed under trusteeship; and (d) no discussion of actual territories is contemplated at the forthcoming United Nations Conference or in the preliminary consultations, and it will be a matter for subsequent agreement which territories within the above categories will be placed under trusteeship.

II. Declaration on Liberated Europe

The following declaration has been approved:

The Premier of the Union of Soviet Socialist Republics, the Prime Minister of the United Kingdom and the President of the United States of America have consulted with each other in the common interests of the peoples of their countries and those of liberated Europe. They jointly declare their mutual agreement to concert during the temporary period of instability in liberated Europe the policies of their three governments in assisting the peoples of the former Axis satellite states of Europe to solve by democratic means their pressing political and economic problems.

The establishment of order in Europe and the rebuilding of national economic life must be achieved by processes which will enable the liberated peoples to destroy the last vestiges of Nazism and Fascism and to create democratic institutions of their own choice. This is a principle of the Atlantic Charter—the right of all peoples to choose the form of government under which they will live—the restoration of sovereign rights and self-government to those peoples who have been forcibly deprived of them by the aggressor nations.

To foster the conditions in which the liberated peoples may exercise these rights, the three governments will jointly assist the people in any European liberated state or former Axis satellite state in Europe where in their judgment conditions require (a) to establish conditions of internal peace; (b) to carry out emergency measures for the relief of distressed peoples; (c) to form interim governmental authorities broadly representative of all democratic elements in the population and pledged to the earliest possible establishment through free elections of governments responsible to the will of the people; and (d) to facilitate where necessary the holding of such elections.

The three governments will consult the other United Nations and provisional authorities or other governments in Europe when matters of direct interest to them are under consideration.

When, in the opinion of the three governments, conditions in any European liberated state or any former Axis satellite state in Europe make such action necessary, they will immediately consult together on the measures necessary to discharge the joint responsibilities set forth in this declaration.

By this declaration we reaffirm our faith in the principles of the Atlantic Charter, our pledges in the Declaration by the United Nations, and our determination to build in cooperation with other peace-loving nations world order under law, dedicated to peace, security, freedom and general well-being of all mankind.

In issuing this declaration, the Three Powers express the hope that the Provisional Government of the French Republic may be associated with them in the procedure suggested.

III. Dismemberment of Germany

It was agreed that Article 12 (a) of the Surrender Terms for Germany should be amended as follows:

The United Kingdom, the United States of America and the Union of Soviet Socialist Republics shall possess supreme authority with respect to Germany. In the exercise of such authority they will take such steps, including the complete disarmament, demilitarization and dismemberment of Germany as they deem requisite for future peace and security.

The study of the procedure for the dismemberment of Germany was referred to a Committee, consisting of Mr. Eden (Chairman), Mr. Winant and Mr. Gousev. This body would consider the desirability of associating with it a French representative.

IV. Zone of Occupation for the French and Control Council for Germany

It was agreed that a zone in Germany, to be occupied by the French Forces, should be allocated to France. This zone would be formed out of the British and American zones and its extent would be settled by the British and Americans in consultation with the French Provisional Government.

It was also agreed that the French Provisional Government should be invited to become a member of the Allied Control Council of Germany.

V. Reparation

The heads of the three governments agreed as follows:

1. Germany must pay in kind for the losses caused by her to the Allied nations in the course of the war. Reparations are to be received in the first instance by those countries which have borne the main burden of the war, have suffered the heaviest losses and have organized victory over the enemy.
2. Reparation in kind to be exacted from Germany in three following forms:
   a. Removals within 2 years from the surrender of Germany or the cessation of organized resistance from the national wealth of Germany located on the territory of Germany herself as well as outside her territory (equipment, machine-tools, ships, rolling stock, German investments abroad, shares of industrial, transport and other enterprises in Germany etc.), these removals to be carried out chiefly for purpose of destroying the war potential of Germany.
   b. Annual deliveries of goods from current production for a period to be fixed.
   c. Use of German labor.
3. For the working out on the above principles of a detailed plan for exaction of reparation from Germany, an Allied Reparation Commission will be set up in Moscow. It will consist of three representatives—one from the Union of Soviet Socialist Republics, one from the United Kingdom and one from the United States of America.
4. With regard to the fixing of the total sum of the reparation as well as

the distribution of it among the countries which suffered from the German aggression the Soviet and American delegations agreed as follows:

The Moscow Reparation Commission should take in its initial studies as a basis for discussion the suggestion of the Soviet Government that the total sum of the reparation in accordance with the points (a) and (b) of the paragraph 2 should be 20 billion dollars and that 50% of it should go to the Union of Soviet Socialist Republics.

The British delegation was of the opinion that pending consideration of the reparation question by the Moscow Reparation Commission no figures of reparation should be mentioned.

The above Soviet-American proposal has been passed to the Moscow Reparation Commission as one of the proposals to be considered by the Commission.

VI. Major War Criminals

The Conference agreed that the question of the major war criminals should be the subject of enquiry by the three Foreign Secretaries for report in due course after the close of the Conference.

VII. Poland

The following Declaration on Poland was agreed by the Conference:

A new situation has been created in Poland as a result of her complete liberation by the Red Army. This calls for the establishment of a Polish Provisional Government which can be more broadly based than was possible before the recent liberation of [the] Western part of Poland. The Provisional Government which is now functioning in Poland should therefore be recognized on a broader democratic basis with the inclusion of democratic leaders from Poland itself and from Poles abroad. This new Government should then be called the Polish Provisional Government of National Unity.

M. Molotov, Mr. Harriman and Sir A. Clark Kerr are authorized as a commission to consult in the first instance in Moscow with members of the present Provisional Government and with other Polish democratic leaders from within Poland and from abroad, with a view to the reorganization of the present Government along the above lines. This Polish Provisional Government of National Unity shall be pledged to the holding of free and unfettered elections as soon as possible on the basis of universal suffrage and secret ballot. In these elections all democratic and anti-Nazi parties shall have the right to take part and to put forward candidates.

When a Polish Provisional Government of National Unity has been properly formed in conformity with the above, the Government of the U. S. S. R., which now maintains diplomatic relations with the present Provisional Government of Poland, and the Government of the United Kingdom and the Government of the United States of America will establish diplomatic relations with the new Polish Provisional Government of National

Unity, and will exchange Ambassadors by whose reports the respective Governments will be kept informed about the situation in Poland.

The three Heads of Government consider that the Eastern frontier of Poland should follow the Curzon Line with digressions from it in some regions of five to eight kilometers in favor of Poland. They recognize that Poland must receive substantial accession of territory in the North and West. They feel that the opinion of the new Polish Provisional Government of National Unity should be sought in due course on the extent of these accessions and that the final delimitation of the Western frontier of Poland should therefore await the Peace Conference.

[Following this declaration, but omitted here, are brief statements on Yugoslavia, the Italo-Yugoslav frontier and Italo-Austrian frontier, Yugoslav-Bulgarian relations, Southeastern Europe, Iran, meetings of the three Foreign Secretaries, and the Montreux Convention and the Straits.]

Agreement on Soviet Entry into the War Against Japan, 1945

The leaders of the three Great Powers—the Soviet Union, the United States of America and Great Britain—have agreed that in two or three months after Germany has surrendered and the war in Europe has terminated the Soviet Union shall enter into the war against Japan on the side of the Allies on condition that:

1. The *status quo* in Outer-Mongolia (The Mongolian People's Republic) shall be preserved;
2. The former rights of Russia violated by the treacherous attack of Japan in 1904 shall be restored, viz:
   a. the southern part of Sakhalin as well as all the islands adjacent to it shall be returned to the Soviet Union,
   b. the commercial port of Dairen shall be internationalized, the preeminent interests of the Soviet Union in this port being safeguarded and the lease of Port Arthur as a naval base of the USSR restored,
   c. the Chinese-Eastern Railroad and the South-Manchurian Railroad which provides an outlet to Dairen shall be jointly operated by the establishment of a joint Soviet-Chinese Company; it being understood that the preeminent interests of the Soviet Union shall be safeguarded and that China shall retain full sovereignty in Manchuria;
3. The Kuril islands shall be handed over to the Soviet Union.

It is understood, that the agreement concerning Outer-Mongolia and the ports and railroads referred to above will require concurrence of Generalissimo Chiang Kai-shek. The President will take measures in order to obtain this concurrence on advice from Marshal Stalin.

The Heads of the three Great Powers have agreed that these claims of the Soviet Union shall be unquestionably fulfilled after Japan has been defeated.

For its part the Soviet Union expresses its readiness to conclude with the National Government of China a Pact of friendship and alliance between the USSR and China in order to render assistance to China with its armed forces for the purpose of liberating China from the Japanese yoke.

Roosevelt's Anger with Stalin, 1945

I have received with astonishment your message of April 3 containing an allegation that arrangements which were made between Field Marshals Alexander and Kesselring at Berne "permitted the Anglo-American troops to advance to the East and the Anglo-Americans promised in return to ease for the Germans the peace terms."

In my previous messages to you in regard to the attempts made in Berne to arrange a conference to discuss a surrender of the German army in Italy I have told you that: (1) No negotiations were held in Berne, (2) The meeting had no political implications whatever, (3) In any surrender of the enemy army in Italy there would be no violation of our agreed principle of unconditional surrender, (4) Soviet officers would be welcomed at any meeting that might be arranged to discuss surrender.

For the advantage of our common war effort against Germany, which today gives excellent promise of an early success in a disintegration of the German armies, I must continue to assume that you have the same high confidence in my truthfulness and reliability that I have always had in yours.

I have also a full appreciation of the effect your gallant army has had in making possible a crossing of the Rhine by the forces under General Eisenhower and the effect that your forces will have hereafter on the eventual collapse of the German resistance to our combined attacks.

I have complete confidence in General Eisenhower and know that he certainly would inform me before entering into any agreement with the Germans. He is instructed to demand and will demand unconditional surrender of enemy troops that may be defeated on his front. Our advances on the Western Front are due to military action. Their speed has been attributable mainly to the terrific impact of our air power resulting in destruction of German communications, and to the fact that Eisenhower was able to cripple the bulk of the German forces on the Western Front while they were still west of the Rhine.

I am certain that there were no negotiations in Berne at any time and I feel that your information to that effect must have come from German sources which have made persistent efforts to create dissension between us in order to escape in some measure responsibility for their war crimes. If that was Wolff's purpose in Berne, your message proves that he has had some success.

With a confidence in your belief in my personal reliability and in my determination to bring about, together with you, an unconditional surrender of the Nazis, it is astonishing that a belief seems to have reached the Soviet Government that I have entered into an agreement with the enemy without first obtaining your full agreement.

Finally I would say this, it would be one of the great tragedies of history if at the very moment of the victory, now within our grasp, such distrust, such lack of faith should prejudice the entire undertaking after the colossal losses of life, material and treasure involved.

Frankly I cannot avoid a feeling of bitter resentment toward your informers, whoever they are, for such vile misrepresentations of my actions or those of my trusted subordinates.

Roosevelt's Last Letter to Churchill, 1945

I would minimize the general Soviet problem as much as possible because these problems, in one form or another, seem to arise every day and most of them straighten out as in the case of the Berne meeting.

We must be firm, however, and our course thus far is correct.

✹ *E S S A Y S*

In his positive account of Roosevelt's wartime diplomacy, Gary R. Hess of Bowling Green University depicts the President as a "practical idealist" who understood the uses of American power, had clearly defined objectives consistent with American ideals, and provided successful leadership. Gaddis Smith of Yale University is far more critical in the second essay. Smith faults Roosevelt for delaying key decisions to protect himself politically, for giving the American people a false optimism about the state of Allied relations, and for failing to resolve Soviet-U.S. differences, in part because the President misjudged the Soviet Union.

Roosevelt as Practical Idealist

GARY R. HESS

"War," the German military theoretician, Karl von Clausewitz, wrote in the early nineteenth century, "is nothing but a continuation of politics by different means." As that quotation underscores, a nation engages in war not as an end in itself, but to achieve political objectives. Nations are usually driven to war by a belief that vital interests cannot be attained through peaceful means. Hence, during World War II the United States had objectives in Europe and Asia that it believed would be realized upon the defeat of the Axis powers.

The strength of the enemy, of course, necessitated the military alliance with Great Britain, the Soviet Union, China, and the other Allied nations: and each of the other powers brought their own long-term objectives into the alliance. In the Declaration of the United Nations that was signed on

Gary R. Hess, *The United States at War, 1941–1945* (Arlington Heights, Ill.: Harlan Davidson, 1986), 102–26.

January 1, 1942, the members of the Allied coalition agreed on their common purpose of defeating the Axis powers and creating a postwar world based on the principles of political freedom, economic cooperation, self-determination, and disarmament. Yet beyond that fundamental agreement, the Allied powers, especially in the relationship among the Big Three, constantly differed over military strategy and the postwar settlement. The United States, Great Britain, and the Soviet Union each brought into the alliance immediate and long-term objectives reflecting their histories, traditions, ideologies, and wartime experiences. The relationship among the major powers revealed constant points of difference, but in that respect, the World War II Allies were by no means unique. Writing in the late eighteenth century, the French diplomat, Comte de Segur, observed that alliances were "marriages followed promptly by divorce," for while a common enemy "momentarily unites, a constant jealousy separates."

Roosevelt set forth the American postwar objectives. In general, his vision looked to the preservation of the wartime alliance. The nations that fought together against the Axis were to cooperate in the preservation of international peace. To Roosevelt the "constant jealousy" or points of divergence among the Allies had to be minimized so this alliance would not be a "marriage followed promptly by divorce." Roosevelt's postwar objectives, broadly stated, can be summarized as envisioning (1) an expanded role for the United States in world affairs, (2) Soviet-American cooperation to help preserve peace, (3) China's emergence as a strong force for peace in Asia, and (4) the gradual demise of colonial empires leading eventually to independent states in Asia and Africa.

A "strong" president who had provided decisive leadership on domestic issues and foreign policy, Roosevelt, in the midst of a global war, became an even more dominant figure. Distrustful of the State Department and disdainful of Cordell Hull who served as secretary of state until late 1944, Roosevelt largely relied on his own instincts, a few close advisers, and a variety of special emissaries to help him define and implement the major elements of his foreign policy. (While Roosevelt frequently ignored the State Department, its leaders in Washington and its diplomatic personnel abroad generally shared Roosevelt's vision of the postwar world; the Department engaged extensively in postwar planning that provided the President with much useful information as he strove for the realization of his objectives.)

Roosevelt worked diligently to preserve the inherently fragile wartime coalition and to achieve his postwar goals. He corresponded frequently with Prime Minister Winston Churchill and Premier Josef Stalin. In addition, he met on several occasions with Churchill and twice undertook long trips to meet with both Churchill and Stalin. At the first Big Three Conference held at Teheran, Iran, in November 1943, an expectant and buoyant atmosphere prevailed because the Allies had gained military ascendancy in Europe and the Pacific. At the conference, the British and Americans finally promised to launch the cross-Channel invasion of German-occupied France the following spring, thus satisfying longstanding Russian demand for a "second front," in western Europe. For his part Stalin reaffirmed that following the defeat of Germany the Soviet Union would help the United States in the struggle against Japan. Beyond those military agreements, the Teheran Conference produced no important concrete results, but it did provide an opportunity for discussing postwar plans in a candid and forthright manner. Altogether, the conference led to much optimism that the Big Three would work together in the postwar world. Such expectations had been somewhat modified by the time of the second Big Three Conference, which was held at Yalta in the Soviet Union in February 1945. By that time Germany was on the verge of defeat and differences had developed between Russia and the Western Allies over the postwar status of eastern Europe (especially Poland) and the treatment of Germany. Circumstances required compromise which, Roosevelt believed, still provided the basis for a peaceful world.

Roosevelt's wartime diplomacy has been criticized from two perspectives. First, some contemporaries and scholars have argued that Roosevelt was too idealistic; that is, his objectives lacked a firm definition of American interests and reflected a misunderstanding of the behavior of other nations. Such criticisms of Roosevelt began during the late stages of the war and continued in the postwar period, especially when the United States encountered serious difficulties with the Soviet Union and China. In view of subsequent Cold War tensions with the Russians, some historians have maintained that Roosevelt's efforts to promote Soviet-American friendship were naive. He has been criticized for failing to understand the seriousness of Soviet-American differences and for relying too heavily on personal diplomacy to resolve problems. From this perspective Roosevelt's negotiations with Stalin are seen as futile; in particular, the agreements reached at the Yalta Conference of February 1945 are seen as evidence of a trusting Roosevelt being deceived by Stalin with the result that the United States tacitly sanctioned Russian control over eastern Europe. Likewise, Roosevelt's hope for promoting a strong China under the leadership of Chiang Kai-shek [Jiang Jieshi] has seemed in retrospect to be ill-considered in view of the deep divisions within China between Chiang's government and the communists led by Mao Tse-tung, and the ineffectiveness of Chiang's armies in fighting against the Japanese.

On the other hand, some contemporaries and scholars have criticized Roosevelt for failing to use American power and influence to achieve his ideals. From this perspective Roosevelt was not too idealistic; rather, his objectives would have been worthwhile and obtainable had he exercised American power effectively. Roosevelt is seen as impeding Soviet-American friendship by delaying the cross-Channel invasion. His plan for a strong China was undermined by the absence of military aid for the war in China caused by the priority given to the island campaign against Japan. And, finally, the Roosevelt commitment to ending colonialism was weakened by his failures to support nationalist movements, especially in India. According to his biographer, James MacGregor Burns, Roosevelt did not coordinate means and objectives:

So the more he preached his lofty ends and practiced his limited means, the more he . . . widened the gap between popular expectations and actual possibilities. Not only did this derangement of ends and means lead to crushed hopes, disillusion, and cynicism at home, but it helped sow the seeds of the Cold War during World War II, as the Kremlin contrasted Roosevelt's coalition rhetoric with his Atlantic First strategy and falsely suspected a bourgeois conspiracy to destroy Soviet Communism; and the Indians and Chinese contrasted Roosevelt's anticolonial words with his military concessions to colonial powers, and falsely inferred that he was an imperialist at heart and a hypocrite to boot.

But perhaps Roosevelt was neither naive nor indifferent to power. Roosevelt's leadership was realistic in the sense of its being firmly grounded on American interests and American capabilities. He recognized the forces that undermined his objectives and adjusted his plans accordingly. Roosevelt was aware of the inconsistency between rhetoric and practice, but his ability to translate plans into actions was limited by the diverse pressures of the wartime alliance and the vast demands on American resources. On close examination Roosevelt emerges as a thoughtful, calculating, well-informed leader whose efforts reflected American national interests and the potential, as well as the limits, of American power. Roosevelt himself summarized the character of his leadership when he wrote that, "I dream dreams, but am, at the same time, an intensely practical person." Roosevelt the practical idealist can be seen in the ways in which he endeavored to realize his four major objectives.

Roosevelt's commitment to an expanded role for the United States in international affairs resulted from his fear that the nation would retreat, as it had following World War I, from substantial responsibility for preserving world peace. To keep America vigilant, Roosevelt supported a new organization designed to replace the League of Nations. During the war various groups in the United States worked diligently to enlist popular and official backing for such an international organization, and the American public responded enthusiastically to this movement. American failure to join the League of Nations after World War I, many Americans believed, had led directly to World War II. The mistakes of the past should not be repeated. World War II offered Americans a second chance to prove their commitment to international peace. Support for a new international organization increased steadily, so that by early 1945 fully 90 percent of the American public favored inclusion in a world body. Eight out of ten Americans approved the use of force by the new organization in order to keep the peace. Recognizing the existence of widespread support among the public and in Congress for both a new international organization and unequivocal American participation in the forum, Roosevelt championed this movement and worked for the establishment of the desired organization. While the conference at San Francisco that formally established the United Nations met after his death, Roosevelt, especially in his negotiations with Stalin and Churchill at the Yalta Conference, had set forth clearly the American objectives for the new international body.

Roosevelt diverged from the public view of the United Nations on one important point. Most Americans assumed that the new organization would be based on the equality of nations, and that all members would participate in the preservation of international peace. They foresaw an organization which, like its predecessor the League of Nations, would rely on a system of collective security where all members would cooperate, economically and militarily, against aggressive nations. This idealistic vision had much appeal, for Americans tended to abhor suggestions of reliance on concepts such as the balance of power and spheres of influence, since those practices accepted the inequality of nations and seemed to have led to conflict in the past. Roosevelt appeared to share such views; indeed, when he addressed Congress after the Yalta Conference, he spoke of a postwar world free of power politics:

> It ought to spell the end of the system of unilateral action, the exclusive alliances, the spheres of influence, the balances of power, and all the other expedients that have been tried for centuries—and have always failed. We propose to substitute for all these, a universal organization in which all peace-loving nations will finally have a chance to join.

Roosevelt actually believed that international stability could only be achieved by strength and cooperation among the major powers; he considered collective security to be impractical. During the early part of the war, he spoke privately of the "four policemen"—the United States, the Soviet Union, Great Britain, and China—as principally responsible for the preservation of world peace. Each of the "policemen" was to be dominant in its area of the world (sphere of influence). As circumstances required, the four would cooperate to preserve international stability.

Roosevelt's concept of the postwar world assumed, not the end, but the continuation of power politics. As the plans for the United Nations progressed, Roosevelt's four-policemen concept took form in the Security Council; its permanent members (the four policemen plus France) were to be responsible for international peace. "Though the Four Policemen disappeared in substance," Robert Divine observes, "the grant of veto power to the permanent members of the Security Council continued Roosevelt's insistence on great-power control over the enforcement of peace."

How can Roosevelt's public promotion of a United Nations based on collective security and his personal commitment to big-power domination be reconciled? His support of the United Nations rested on the belief that it was necessary to involve the United States permanently in world affairs. Big-power control, Robert Dallek writes, was "obscure[d] . . . through a United Nations organization which would satisfy widespread demand in the United States for new idealistic or universalist arrangements for assuring the peace." Hence, membership in the United Nations capitalized on popular enthusiasm and was part of Roosevelt's strategy to ensure a permanent American involvement in world affairs.

The importance Roosevelt attached to big-power domination of the postwar world explains his determined efforts to cooperate with the Soviet Union and enhance China's status. Those two nations, in Roosevelt's thinking, were vital to a stable world order.

Among Roosevelt's most monumental challenges was to promote long-term Soviet-American cooperation. The mutual need to defeat Hitler created the "strange alliance" between the world's preeminent capitalist and communist nations. The Soviet and American governments had long distrusted one another; in Moscow, leaders recalled the Western hostility toward the communist revolution of 1917 and the prolonged period of American non-recognition of the Soviet government (until 1933 the United States did not extend diplomatic recognition). In Washington, officials could not ignore many aspects of Soviet rule: the efforts to promote communist revolutions internationally, the totalitarian character of the Soviet government which was vividly evident during the brutal purges of Stalin's political opponents in the late 1930s, Stalin's deal with the Germans (the Nazi-Soviet Non-Aggression Pact of August 1939) which facilitated Hitler's invasion of Poland, and the parallel Russian takeover of the Baltic states and its aggression against Finland.

Roosevelt shared the nation's disgust over much of what had occurred in Russia since 1917, but circumstances forced cooperation. "I can't take communism," he once wrote, "but to cross this bridge I would hold hands with the Devil." To build cooperation Roosevelt relied heavily on personal diplomacy, believing that through discussions and negotiations directly with Stalin, the Americans and Soviets could reach understandings. Following their first meeting at the Teheran Conference, Roosevelt reported that he had found in Stalin a man "something like me . . . a realist."

Roosevelt's aspirations for Soviet-American friendship found wide support among the American public. In a dramatic reversal of prewar sentiments, Americans came to look very favorably upon the Russian people and even the dictatorial government of Josef Stalin. Americans admired Russian resistance to the German invasion and appreciated in particular the rigors of the Battle of Stalingrad. When they were asked to characterize the Russian people by selecting from a list of twenty-five adjectives, Americans responded "hard-working" (61 percent) and "brave" (48 percent); few persons associated negative attributes with the Russians. On several occasions when public opinion polls asked which nation—Britain, China, the United States, or the Soviet Union—was contributing the most to winning the war, Americans always ranked either their own country or the Soviet Union first and the other second, and, in all cases, both were seen as contributing far more than China or Britain. Respect for the Soviet contribution was especially strong during the critical winter of 1942-1943 when Americans, despite their own offensives in north Africa and the Pacific, rallied around the Russians fighting the Battle of Stalingrad. Popular interest in that struggle has been described by [historian] Ralph Levering:

This, it was sensed even then, was the crucial battle of the war, and millions of attentive Americans followed the shifting tides in the streets of the city and on the Volga plain as they would follow a "crucial" televised football game. The hesitant American advances on small Pacific islands were as nothing compared with the epic quality of this struggle.

When the American public was asked in 1943 what *people*, not armies, were working hardest to win the war, they placed the Russians first (48 percent), themselves next (26 percent) and the British a distant third (13 percent).

The press, radio, and motion pictures reinforced these attitudes by consistently portraying the Soviet Union in positive terms. Several popular movies dramatized the fighting on the Eastern Front. The book *Mission to Moscow*, written by former Russian ambassador Joseph Davies, and the motion picture based on it presented Soviet leaders as men of honesty and integrity. Wendell Willkie, the Republican candidate for president in 1940, wrote the best-selling *One World* which spoke glowingly of Stalin and other Soviet leaders, and of the economic and social progress the Russian people had made under their communist government. *Life* and *Time* magazines— perhaps the most influential journals of the era—extolled Russian virtues. *Time* named Stalin its "Man of the Year" in 1943. A special issue of *Life*, featuring a smiling Stalin on the cover, was devoted entirely to the Soviet Union. From the several pro-Russian articles and pages of photographs, Americans learned that Lenin, the leader of the communist revolution of 1917, was "perhaps the greatest man of modern times" and that Stalin and his fellow leaders were "tough, loyal, capable administrators . . . 'Men of Good Will.' " *Life* concluded that the Russians were "one hell of a people" who "look like Americans, dress like Americans and think like Americans."

This identification with the Russians encouraged Americans to believe that the wartime alliance would lead to postwar cooperation. Repeatedly, public opinion polls revealed American confidence that the Russians could be trusted after the war. As a result Roosevelt enjoyed strong popular backing for his efforts to build Soviet-American cooperation. The public, however, was only dimly aware of the seriousness of points of Soviet-American disagreement.

Roosevelt assumed that he and his fellow realist, Stalin, could resolve their differences. And to a large extent they succeeded. Perhaps the most vexing issue was the future status of eastern Europe. The Soviets sought recognition of their dominance over that region which twice within the previous thirty years had been the path for a devastating German invasion of Russian territory. Soviet security, Stalin reiterated in messages to British and American officials, demanded friendly governments along Russia's western frontier. For the British and Americans, such claims posed great problems. The British had gone to war in 1939 to uphold Polish sovereignty; they were not prepared to see German control replaced by that of the Soviet Union. London was the headquarters of the Polish government-in-exile that had fled Warsaw at the time of the German invasion in 1939. Both British and American governments, as well as public opinion in those countries, held to the ideal of the self-determination of peoples. In the Atlantic Charter, Roosevelt and Churchill had pledged to oppose "territorial changes that do not accord with the freely expressed wishes of the peoples concerned" and to have "sovereign rights and self-government restored to those who have been forcibly deprived of them."

Yet Roosevelt recognized that increased Soviet influence in eastern Europe could not be denied; indeed, he assumed that the Russians would function as the "policemen" of that area. The question confronting the president was how to reconcile Russian influence with the concept of self-determination. Roosevelt delayed forthright negotiations on eastern Europe—especially the thorny subject of Poland-and permitted military developments to resolve the issues. Thus Roosevelt, in meetings with Stalin at the Teheran Conference, tacitly acknowledged Russian demands as reasonable, but urged that the eastern European question be handled by the Russians in ways that would not alienate world opinion. He pointedly observed that six to seven million American voters were of Polish descent and he could not risk losing their support by appearing to sanction the loss of their ancestral homeland's sovereignty.

By the time of the Big Three meeting at Yalta, the future of Poland had been substantially determined. In early 1944 Russian armies crossed into Polish territory and, as they pushed the Germans to the west, established a provisional government headed by Polish communists and headquartered at Lublin. This Committee of National Liberation became the vehicle for establishing Russian control over Poland. The British and the Polish government-in-exile protested bitterly but to no avail. Hence, when the Polish question was discussed at Yalta, Churchill and Roosevelt faced the fact of a functioning pro-Soviet government supported by the Russian army. Meeting with congressional leaders prior to his departure to Yalta, Roosevelt forthrightly acknowledged that spheres of influence were a reality the United States had to accept; he observed "that the Russians had the power in Eastern Europe, that it was obviously impossible to have a break with them and that, therefore, the only practical course was to use what influence we had to ameliorate the situation."

The Yalta Conference offered Roosevelt a compromise that under the circumstances provided the West with as much influence as it could possibly attain in Poland. Stalin agreed to the broadening of the Lublin government to include representatives of the government-in-exile and other important groups, and to the holding of timely free and democratic elections. Regarding the remainder of eastern Europe (where Russian armies by that time were well entrenched), the Big Three agreed to the Declaration on Liberated Europe. Like the Polish settlement, the declaration provided for participation of all political groups in provisional governments to be followed by free, democratic elections. While the agreements failed to provide any international guarantees for their implementation, they did, at least, place some moral obligation on the Soviet Union to act with restraint in their sphere. "For all intents and purposes," Dallek concludes, "[Roosevelt] conceded that Eastern Europe was a Soviet sphere of influence."

Clearly, Roosevelt regarded that concession as inevitable, given the Soviet military position and the need for continued Soviet cooperation. The settlements on eastern Europe were, simply, the best he could get. "Roosevelt's chief concern, John Gaddis maintains, "was cosmetic: to put the best possible face on a bad situation in order to make palatable to the American public the postwar expansion of Soviet influence."

Moreover, Roosevelt's acquiescence was made within the atmosphere of give-and-take on a number of questions, which included Soviet concessions to the interests of the United States. At Yalta Stalin promised to enter the war against Japan within three months of the end of the conflict in Europe; to Americans who anticipated that an invasion of the main Japanese islands would result in very substantial casualties, Russian support in the final campaign against the Japanese leader was considered a high priority. Also, the Soviet leader accepted the bases of American plans for a new international organization.

While Roosevelt worked throughout the war to reach understandings with the Soviet Union, his actions were not naive. A certain skepticism about the Russians was evident in his decision to withhold from them information about the development of the atomic bomb. Roosevelt did enter into secret confidences with Churchill about full postwar Anglo-American coordination in the development of atomic energy for military and commercial purposes. Excluding the Soviet Union from such understandings (while their agents in the United States were generally aware of the top-secret development of the bomb) was hardly reassuring to Stalin. This American policy led the Soviets to question the depth of the Roosevelt commitment to postwar alliance. From the perspective of Moscow, America's atomic monopoly appeared to be hostile to the Soviet Union. Whether Roosevelt meant to create that impression is unclear, but after the Yalta conference he became increasingly dubious about the prospects for Soviet-American cooperation. "We can't do business with Stalin," an exasperated Roosevelt exclaimed in late March, but in his last communique to Churchill, he wrote, "I would minimize the general Soviet problem as much as possible. . . . Most of [the problems] straighten out. . . . We must be firm, however, and our course thus far is correct."

Roosevelt was committed to aiding China so that it would be in a position to assume a prominent role in postwar Asia. The defeat of Japan would leave a power vacuum in Asia and the Pacific that a resurgent China, friendly with the United States, would help to fill. To raise China's international status during the war, the United States ended its longstanding, unequal treaty relationship with China and its policy of excluding Chinese immigrants. More important, Roosevelt insisted on treating China as a power equal to the Big Three. While he urged that Britain and the Soviet Union accord such recognition to the Chinese, neither Churchill nor Stalin shared American expectations for China. To make his point, Roosevelt, while en route to the first Big Three meeting at Teheran, arranged to confer with Chiang Kai-shek at Cairo. (A reluctant Churchill was also in attendance.) And China, again at American insistence, was given one of the permanent seats on the security council of the newly formed United Nations.

Although the United States treated China as a major power, the Chinese had not yet earned such status. Chinese armies had been unable to prevent Japanese conquest of most of northern and coastal China, which included the major centers of population in the country. The Chinese were badly divided politically, and the Kuomintang government, headed by Chiang Kai-shek, was steadily losing support. The Kuomintang faced much internal opposition, principally from the communist movement headed by Mao Tse-tung. During the war, the Communists increased their strength and appeal, especially among the rural peasantry. To Chiang the Communists were a danger far greater than the Japanese; the United States, he assumed, would eventually defeat Japan. Hence, at a time when the United States was directing its resources to the battle against Japan, its principal Asian ally was preoccupied with preparing for the final showdown in a prolonged internal struggle against the Communists.

American diplomatic and military personnel in wartime China recognized the significance of these developments. They came to deplore the massive corruption and inefficiency of the Kuomintang. That regime became increasingly repressive and appeared as brutal as the fascist nations against which the Allies were fighting. Conversely, the communist movement seemed to be progressive, as it introduced long-needed land reform programs in those rural areas under its control. Moreover, the communist forces were fighting against the Japanese. Few astute observers of the Chinese situation doubted that the future of the country rested with the Communists, not with the discredited Kuomintang.

These shortcomings of the Chinese war effort received scant attention in America, for the public generally identified closely with the Chinese and with the government of Chiang Kai-shek in the struggle against the hated Japanese. Under the influence of wartime propaganda, Americans rather uncritically expected that China was progressing toward democracy and major power status. When Americans were asked in 1942 which of twenty-five adjectives best described the Chinese, the predominant responses were "hard-working" (69 percent), "honest" (52 percent),and "brave" (48 percent). (Less than 5 percent attributed negative features—such as "cruel, warlike, treacherous"—to the Chinese; those were, however, the predominant characteristics given to the Japanese.)

Wartime news and information, motion pictures and propaganda glorified the heroic Chinese people. A series of popular films, including *The Battle of China*, *Inside Fighting China*, *Ravaged Earth*, *Burma Convoy*, *A Yank on the Burma Road*, *China Girl*, and *God Is My Co-Pilot*, dramatized the common American and Chinese cause against the Japanese. When Mrs. Chiang Kai-shek visited the United States in 1943, she was enthusiastically received. After her emotional plea to Congress for more American support, "tough-guys melted," according to according to *Time*, and one congressman said, " 'God-damnit, I never saw anything like it." Madame Chiang had me on the verge of bursting into tears.'' ' In this atmosphere, Harold Isaacs notes, ''a sympathetic image of the Chinese rose now to a unique pinnacle in a mass of American minds.'' The contrast between popular perceptions and realities could hardly have been sharper.

Despite the image of the Chinese struggle with the Japanese, the immediate challenge for the United States was to encourage Chinese political stability and military concentration on fighting against Japan. The Americans sent General Joseph Stilwell to serve as chief of staff of the Kuomintang Army. Stilwell's plans to improve Chinese military prowess failed completely when Stilwell and Chiang came to despise one another. To the American general, Chiang was a petty dictator (in the privacy of his diary, Stilwell contemptuously described Chiang as ''Peanut''). Stilwell's demands for reform threatened Chiang, who eventually demanded that Roosevelt recall Stilwell.

In addition to the Stilwell mission, the United States provided important air support for the Chinese, principally through the ''hump'' supply flights across the Himalayas from bases in India. Yet the Chinese always regarded American help as insufficient, and contrasted the low volume of supplies they were receiving with the flow of American supplies to the Soviet Union, Great Britain, and other Allies.

Why didn't the United States provide what Chiang demanded? Might that support have enabled him to fight more effectively against the Japanese? The failure to meet his demands resulted, in part, from the fact that the China theater always had had a low priority in the allocation of American resources. The Europe-first strategy dictated that the needs of European allies would receive primary consideration. And within the Pacific theater, China's needs were secondary to the island campaign. Moreover, the United States considered assistance as its most effective lever in forcing Chiang to fight more actively against the Japanese; increasing levels of support came to depend upon Chinese demonstration of willingness to fight the enemy. The Kuomintang, however, always insisted that American support had to come first—only then could its armies fight effectively. ''While the Americans refused to contribute more aid until the Chinese stepped up their war effort, Warren Cohen writes, ''the Chinese refused to step up their effort until they received more aid. At no time during the war was the circle broken.''

American efforts to encourage political change led to similar frustrations. Whenever American officials warned Chiang of his declining popularity or urged Kuomintang reforms to counter communist appeal, the Chinese leader refused to accept responsibility for his domestic problems. Rather, Chiang blamed the United States, charging that its policies were undermining his position.

For two and a half years after Pearl Harbor, Roosevelt and other officials promoted China's international status and encouraged military and political changes by the Kuomintang, but by late 1944, American patience was largely exhausted. By that time it had become evident that Chiang's followers would not undertake any major offensive against the Japanese. A special mission to China headed by Vice-President Henry Wallace in the spring of 1944 failed to change Chiang's attitudes toward his country's problems. And Roosevelt in the fall of 1944 reluctantly acquiesced to Chiang's demand for Stilwell's recall.

Roosevelt's enthusiasm for Chiang waned, but he still tried to ensure the emergence of a strong postwar China. Always the realist, Roosevelt adjusted his means as circumstances changed. In late 1944 and early 1945 he directed American policy toward fostering a coalition government for China in which the communists would join with the Kuomintang. Given the deep-seated antagonism between those two groups, forming a coalition was an unwieldy task that eventually proved impossible. But at the time a coalition seemed the only solution to China's internal divisions. (An important impetus for coalition was the number of Americans who had established a rapport with the communist movement through its leaders Mao Tse-tung and Chou En-lai; Mao and Chou in turn had considerable faith in the United States.)

Besides cultivating a Kuomintang-communist coalition, Roosevelt also worked to make certain that the Soviet Union would become a partner in America's plans for postwar Asia. At the Yalta Conference Roosevelt agreed to Stalin's demand for special concessions in China (particularly privileges in the province of Manchuria, an area of historic Russian interest). An allowance was considered necessary to help assure Soviet participation in the war against Japan. This concession was an affront to Chinese sovereignty. "To dispose of Chinese territory without China's prior consent," [historian Warren] Cohen observes, "was hardly calculated to make the Chinese rejoice." Yet Roosevelt also secured an important concession from Stalin which benefitted Chiang's government: the Russian leader agreed to enter into a treaty of friendship and alliance with the Kuomintang. The effects of this arrangement were to enhance Chiang's status and to commit, at least implicitly, the Soviets to the objective of working for a coalition government in China. As he endeavored to salvage American expectations of China, Roosevelt recognized the difficulties confronting the United States in that endeavor. At the Yalta Conference he remarked to Stalin that, "for some time we have been trying to keep China alive." And in the end the promotion of a coalition government and involvement of the Soviet Union seemed the most feasible means of stabilizing the Chinese situation.

Roosevelt's visions of China failed to appreciate the rapidity of political change there that led, shortly after World War II, to communist ascendancy in the renewed civil war. For as Chiang was discredited, defeated, and forced from the mainland, the United States—as his benefactor—suffered an immense loss of prestige. Roosevelt and later American leaders failed to recognize that the United States could not solve the internal problems of other lands. The China problem defied American solutions. The Chinese had to determine their own destiny.

Roosevelt's final objective—promotion of the self-determination of colonial peoples—dealt with the future of Asia and Africa. Western empires largely covered the area stretching from Southeast Asia to the Middle East and nearly all of the African continent. Parts of those empires had been disrupted by the war, in particular by the German-Italian encroachment in north Africa and the Japanese conquest of Southeast Asia.

The American government assumed that World War II would mark the beginning of the end of Western imperialism. Under Secretary of State Sumner Welles expressed American sentiments when he stated:

> If the war is in fact a war for the liberation of peoples, it must assure the sovereign equality of peoples throughout the world. . . . Our victory must bring in its train the liberation of all peoples. . . . The age of imperialism is ended. . . . The principles of the Atlantic Charter must be guaranteed to the world as a whole—in all oceans and in all continents.

This strong sense of anticolonialism led the State Department, in its extensive planning for the postwar world, to anticipate that the imperial powers would be called upon to train their colonial peoples in self-government leading eventually to independence. The American record in the Philippine Islands was advanced as the model for other imperial powers. After acquiring the Philippines, the United States had introduced substantial economic, social, and educational reforms; it also had provided for progressively greater self-government. Proud of its record in the Philippines, the United States expected that the British, French, Dutch, and Belgians would follow similar policies toward their colonial possessions.

This immodest American plan meant overhauling the imperial system. Henceforth, imperial powers would have to accept "international account-ability" for their actions; they would be expected to educate subject peoples in self-government. Such expectations were bitterly resented by the European imperial powers who were also America's wartime allies. The British, French, and Dutch had always looked upon their empires as possessions; the home government designed and implemented colonial policies in terms of their own national interests. American ideals of local self-determination were not shared by the European powers. Thus American anticolonialism triggered vigorous criticism, especially from the British who held the largest empire and who, throughout the war, were in the best position to speak on behalf of imperial interests. The question of the future of the imperial system exemplified the "constant jealousies" that can undermine wartime alliances.

The focus of the imperialism issue was Southeast Asia. Japan controlled this vast region that included the colonies of Britain (Malaya, Burma); France (French Indochina, that is, the present nations of Vietnam, Laos, Cambodia); the Netherlands (Netherlands East Indies, that is, the present nation of Indonesia); and, of course, the United States (the Philippines). The British, French, and Dutch assumed that, at the end of the war, they would re-establish the old imperial order. The critical question was: Would it be a return to "business as usual" or would there be a commitment to self-government?

Among the countries of Southeast Asia, Roosevelt took a strong personal interest in the future of French Indochina. In fact, he undertook to assure that the French would not re-establish control over their former colony. By promoting international administration in the form of a "trusteeship,"

Roosevelt attempted to provide for training in self-government leading to eventual independence. Why did Roosevelt champion the cause of Indochina? First, he had little regard for the French whom, he believed, had forfeited any claim to treatment as a major world power. France had been weak and ineffectual in the face of German aggression in 1940 and Japanese pressure on Indochina in 1940-1941. Moreover, in Roosevelt's opinion the French were the worst of the imperial powers; he repeatedly said they had shamelessly exploited the peoples of Indochina. Denial of French claims to Indochina was Roosevelt's way of punishing the French and of signalling their demise as a world power. Roosevelt's distaste for the French was intensified by his personal antagonism toward General Charles de Gaulle, the leader of the Free French. (This sentiment was not one-sided; de Gaulle also despised Roosevelt.)

Roosevelt also meant to make certain that the principle of anticolonialism would be achieved in at least one European-held colony. Unlikely to overcome British opposition to American anticolonial ideals, Roosevelt seized upon Indochina as an opportunity to prove that the war marked the "end of imperialism." An international trusteeship for Indochina would serve as a stimulus for the advancement of colonial peoples generally.

These American objectives for the colonial areas became the source of the most serious wartime tensions between the United States and Britain. In no other issue did the Americans and their closest ally find reconciliation of interest as intractable as in discussions of the future of Southeast Asia. "The differences between the two major Allies were indeed real and extensive enough," Christopher Thorne argues, "but they could at least have been clarified and faced more squarely. As it was, Southeast Asia remained an area where Anglo-American relations, so successful in many ways, were extremely poor."

As the war approached its end, America had to modify its plans for Southeast Asia. Since the region was not vital in the American plan to defeat Japan, the United States exercised little military influence in Southeast Asia (except, of course, for the Philippines). Accordingly, responsibility for military operations was given to a British command. As happened in other areas of the world, military occupation led to political domination. The British re-established their control in Burma and Malaya, assisted the French to retake Indochina, and helped the Dutch to regain the East Indies. As reality overcame idealism, the United States had to compromise with its western European allies to assure postwar cooperation. In the end the Americans agreed to a vague provision in the Charter of the United Nations which exhorted imperial powers to train subject peoples in self-government. Deferring to the British and other imperial powers, the United States rejected an alternative plan advanced by the Soviet Union which called for full national independence and self-determination in all colonial areas. Thus, by the end of the war the United States had retreated considerably from its earlier "end of imperialism" goal.

Yet in the long run Roosevelt's efforts against colonialism were prophetic. As the European imperial powers tried to resume "business as usual" in

Southeast Asia, they found that the war had brought fundamental changes heralding the true end of imperialism. Four years of Japanese administration had stimulated nationalist movements. The peoples of Southeast Asia sought their independence and rejected the imperial pretensions of the European powers; within a few more years most of Southeast Asia had gained that independence. Two decades after the end of World War II, virtually all of Asia and Africa was free from European domination.

The United States, as the nation that championed self-determination throughout the greater part of the war, contributed to this irrepressible nationalism. While the European imperial powers may have gained some short-term advantages at the end of the war, in overview, it was the American vision for colonial areas which was realized. For his role in bringing about self-determination, Roosevelt remains—decades after his death—a widely known and inspiring leader among peoples of Asia and Africa.

Franklin Delano Roosevelt died on April 12, 1945, just as the Allies were on the threshhold of victory. Throughout the last weeks of the war and into the immediate postwar era, Harry S Truman, who succeeded to the presidency, endeavored to follow Roosevelt's policies. While Roosevelt's objectives were not fully achieved, his diplomatic leadership during the war represented perhaps the most effective expression of American interests and ideals that the circumstances permitted. Those who criticize his actions must present feasible alternatives. Was it possible for the United States to "get tough" with the Soviet Union over eastern Europe at a time when Russian influence was firmly established there? Was it possible for the United States to alter the political situation in China? However much Americans disliked European colonialism, how could the United States force its allies to recognize the inevitability of independence in Asia? Politics is, after all, the art of the *possible*.

The Misleading Optimism and Misjudgments of Rooseveltian Diplomacy

GADDIS SMITH

Diplomatic historians are sometimes criticized for writing "palace history"—for concentrating too much on great figures at the expense of the thousands who shaped and implemented policies from below. But in the case of the American diplomatic experience during the Second World War, "palace history" is necessary and an understanding of President Roosevelt's attitudes and personality is essential. No president before or since has taken crucial diplomatic negotiations and decisions more completely into his own hands.

A good way to assess Roosevelt is to compare him with Woodrow Wilson. There was nothing cheerful about Wilson's solemn crusade of

From *American Diplomacy During the Second World War, 1941–1945*, Second Edition, 12–19, 177–81, 186–88, by Gaddis Smith. Copyright © 1985 by Newbery Award Records, Inc. Reprinted by permission of Alfred A. Knopf, Inc.

Christian good against the forces of evil. Roosevelt, in contrast, always gave the appearance of a happy man, sometimes to the point of inappropriate frivolity. Wilson found it hard to like many people with whom he was forced to deal; Roosevelt seemed to like almost everybody. Wilson was solitary; Roosevelt loved a crowd and the feeling of presiding over a numerous family. Wilson put millions of words on paper; Roosevelt thought by talking and listening and wrote comparatively little.

Associates found both Wilson and Roosevelt difficult to work with, for different reasons. Wilson would concentrate for long periods on a single issue and ignore others of equal importance. Roosevelt would dabble with a dozen issues simultaneously, acquiring a superficial acquaintance with thousands of details. He loved to ramble and he seldom studied deeply.

Wilson was stubborn and opinionated; his dislike for advice that did not conform to his own conclusions often became dislike for the adviser. Roosevelt, on the other hand, would feign agreement with an opinion rather than produce argument and disappointment. In domestic politics this habit of trying to please everyone caused confusion but no lasting harm. When Roosevelt's final views on an issue emerged, the person misled could resign. A few did.

But this Rooseveltian technique had doleful results when applied to international affairs, where all the favorable conditions that Roosevelt enjoyed at home were missing. Disagreements in affairs were over means, not basic objectives. All Americans desired a healthy economy, an end to unemployment, and a broadening of security among the whole population. There were no disagreements that could not be faced and thrashed out by men of goodwill. But how different the conduct of international affairs, especially in the emergency conditions of a world war. The nations in uneasy coalition against the Axis disagreed not only on the means of winning the war but also on fundamental objectives for the future. Differences were too profound to be dissolved by geniality. Disgruntled allies, unlike domestic subordinates, could not be ignored. Roosevelt either forgot these truths or else believed that his power to make friends was so irresistible that opposition could be charmed away. But in his defense, one must ask whether the American and Allied cause would have been better served had Roosevelt insisted on making every difference explicit and forcing every potential argument into the open and to a conclusion. His cavalier and casual ways may well have concealed a deeper realism.

As the most successful American politician of the century, Roosevelt had a superb sense of how much support he could command for domestic programs. But he had a timid grasp of what the people would accept in foreign affairs. This reinforced his tendency to shy away from problems lest publicity cause political damage at home. In general, he overestimated the strength of isolationism and underestimated the ability of the American people to absorb bad news and undertake new responsibility. As a result, Roosevelt sometimes gave the public a falsely optimistic picture, especially in regard to Russia and China. He also gave the Russians the impression that the United States would probably withdraw into partial isolation after victory and that Russia, therefore, need not worry about American opposition to its postwar ambitions.

Two further traits of Roosevelt's character should be noted. The president had a boy's delight in military and naval affairs. Under the Constitution he was commander in chief of the armed forces, and he gave practical as well as theoretical meaning to the title. He consulted closely with military and naval authorities. Usually he took the advice of the chiefs of staff, but on occasion he made important military decisions independently.

Finally, Roosevelt, unlike Wilson, was a practical man who knew that good and bad were always mixed together. He had no qualms about further blending the two or about settling by way of compromise for the best that seemed available. He was no metaphysician, losing sleep by wondering whether evil means could contaminate a worthy end. He was more inclined to act and let historians worry about the philosophical problems involved. Such practicality often served the nation and world well, but on occasion Roosevelt's means were questionable and the results worse.

Roosevelt's character produced the worst results in his diplomacy with Stalin; with Churchill, the best. Churchill and Roosevelt enjoyed the closest personal and official relationship that has ever existed between an American president and the head of another government. It was not, however, a relationship of equality. Churchill, acutely aware of the British Empire's dependence on the United States, kept Roosevelt informed with an almost daily stream of incomparably lucid and persuasive letters and telegrams. Frequently he traveled to meet Roosevelt in Washington, at Hyde Park, in Canada, and in the Mediterranean. Roosevelt never met with Churchill in Great Britain, although both Roosevelt and Churchill did meet Stalin on or near his home ground. No other man could have won Roosevelt's approval of such a large measure of British policy. But sometimes Roosevelt and his advisers did refuse Churchill's requests. On those occasions Churchill gave way with a grace both uncharacteristic and serviceable to the preservation of good Anglo-American relations.

Roosevelt's personal relations with Stalin were the least effective aspect of his diplomacy. The president met Stalin's displays of temper, suspicion, and churlish obstructionism with redoubled efforts at conciliation. Early in the war he tried to please Stalin by an implied promise of an immediate second front in Europe (a promise that was not and could not be kept), and later he remained almost silent in the face of barbarous Soviet conduct in Poland. Sometimes he tried to win Stalin's confidence by ridiculing Churchill and hinting at a Soviet-American alignment against British colonialism. In personal relations and in diplomacy it is unwise and dangerous to pretend to denounce a proven friend in order to ingratiate oneself with a third party. Churchill bore the humiliation manfully; Stalin was not fooled. He listened to Roosevelt's chatter, said little himself, and coolly pushed the Soviet advantage in Europe and Asia without regard to the idealistic principles of self-determination. Stalin acted on the assumption, which Roosevelt's words and behavior amply confirmed, that neither the United States nor Great Britain would or could raise any effective opposition to Russian expansion. Late in the war Churchill began to warn of ominous consequences and Roosevelt, too, had moments of uneasiness over Soviet behavior. But by that time, the Russian position had been consolidated. Short of an immediate and unthinkable transition from war with Germany to war with the Soviet Union, the outcome was inevitable.

The results of Roosevelt's contact with Chiang Kai-shek of China and Charles de Gaulle of France—the proud and haughty leaders who ranked just below the triumvirate—were poor. Chiang and de Gaulle each claimed to represent a great power suffering temporary eclipse; each was quick to resent the slightest reflection on his personal prestige or the prerogatives of his nation. Roosevelt treated them in opposite fashions—more in terms of his preconceived notions about France and China than on the basis of the actual situation. The president seemed an infatuated captive of the myth that China under Chiang was one of the world's four great powers and deserved to be treated as such. No amount of evidence concerning Chiang's maladministration, the disunity of the country, the strength of the opposition, or the inefficiency of his armies shook Roosevelt from his public maintenance of the illusion—although in private he had doubts. But again in Roosevelt's defense, one must ask whether public comment on Chiang Kai-shek's inadequacies would have served a useful purpose—except, perhaps, to have mitigated some of the subsequent American disillusionment.

For modern France, in contrast, Roosevelt had acquired an attitude of contempt as extreme as his admiration for China. He considered France a morally decadent nation which, by laying down before Hitler and giving way to Japan in Indochina, had forfeited the right to be respected. Roosevelt saw de Gaulle as a pompous adventurer who represented only a small clique and who aimed at dictatorial power. Ultimately, Roosevelt's attitudes led to severe friction with France and to bitter misunderstandings on the part of the American people when Chiang's regime collapsed so ignominiously in the civil war with the Communists.

Although wartime diplomacy dealt most frequently with military operations, one overriding question was always present: What kind of postwar world did the major allies desire? Each sought, first of all, a victory that would prevent yet another war while protecting its own interests. American leaders, in and out of government, gradually developed some broad ideas on how this might be done, but Roosevelt himself was loath to make commitments. Thus, despite a great deal of talk and writing during the war about the future, many decisions were postponed or left indefinite.

There were several ways the goal of American postwar security might be sought. Isolation had failed and was now discredited, more thoroughly than Roosevelt realized. A unilateral pax Americana in which every threat to security would be met by superior force was technically worth considering but not politically feasible. A pax Anglo-Americana in which the United States and Great Britain would run the world together had appeal for some Americans and briefly for President Roosevelt, but it, too, was not feasible. Roosevelt until 1944 favored a peace secured by the armed cooperation of the "four policemen": the United States, Great Britain, Russia, and China.

Little countries would be required to keep quiet and take orders. This concept had numerous flaws. A vacuum would appear in western Europe where, according to Roosevelt's conception, neither Germany nor France would be allowed power or influence. This would be dangerous if Roosevelt's assumption of cooperation between Russia and the West proved unfounded.

In Asia there was considerable doubt whether the Chiang Kai-shek regime in China could survive, much less serve as a policeman for others. In addition, the outcry of small nations at being herded about by the great powers would be too loud to ignore in the United States and Great Britain, countries that prided themselves on respecting the rights of others. There was also an incompatibility between the concept of four policemen preserving the status quo and the evolution of colonial regions to independent nationhood, an idea much favored by Roosevelt and many Americans.

Since the largest colonial regions in the world were British, Churchill feared that the United States was aiming at the dissolution of the British Empire. The prime minister's own program for securing the peace was equally objectionable to most Americans. Churchill's guiding star was the preservation of a traditional balance of power. He assumed that the fate of Europe would determine the fate of the world; that there was a fundamental conflict of interest between Russia and the West; that these differences should be faced openly and realistically; that western Europe had to be rehabilitated as quickly as possible, with France and eventually Germany forming a counterweight to Russia; and that the United States ought to join in checking Russian expansion. Churchill somewhat grudgingly accepted the inevitability of granting colonial peoples increased internal self-government, but he believed that imperial powers should continue to exercise responsibility for their colonies.

Roosevelt abandoned the concept of the four policemen not in favor of Churchill's balance-of-power program but in response to rising enthusiasm in the United States for a universal collective security organization, the United Nations. Secretary of State Cordell Hull, for example, argued that great-power cooperation must be embedded in a world organization which would, in effect, be a resurrection of the Wilsonian League of Nations. The alternative was a third world war. Hull's views were shared by thousands of opinion leaders: writers, teachers, clergy, labor leaders, senators, and congressmen. As Americans became fully committed to the idea of the United Nations, they became increasingly suspicious of Churchill's ideas. Some even believed that British colonialism and continued adherence to the idea of a balance of power were greater threats to security than anything the Soviet Union might do.

This does not mean that Americans were hostile to Great Britain; rather, they looked upon that nation as a misguided friend unfortunately wedded to dangerous and outmoded behavior. It was the duty of the United States to set the British right for their own good and the good of the world. The Americans who were most critical of Britain tended to be those most sympathetic to friendly but too scarred by unhappy memories to take the initiative. Russia's enormous loss of life—the final figure is generally estimated to be 20 million—strongly reinforced a sympathetic attitude. Those Americans who disputed this rosy picture were often denounced in internal debate as callous reactionaries.

While Roosevelt, Churchill, and their advisers privately wrestled with different theories for the maintenance of future security, the official public declaration of Anglo-American war aims remained the Atlantic Charter, a generalized statement drafted by the two leaders in August 1941 and subsequently accepted by all countries joining in war against the Axis. The Atlantic Charter denied that its adherents sought self-aggrandizement, condemned territorial changes against the will of the peoples concerned, favored the right of all people to choose their own form of government, advocated liberal international trading arrangements, called for the disarmament of aggressor nations, and glanced cautiously at a possible "permanent system of general security." The Soviet Union adhered to the charter—with the capacious qualification that "the practical application of these principles will necessarily adapt itself to the circumstances, needs, and historic peculiarities of particular countries." In other words, Russia would not be deflected in the slightest by the Atlantic Charter from the pursuit of its own aims in its own way. Churchill also had reservations concerning the applicability of self-determination to the parts of the British Empire.

Roosevelt thought that Russia wanted nothing but security from attack and that this could easily be granted. Personally uninterested in Communist or any other kind of theory, and president of a country where ideological passion was out of style, Roosevelt tended to assume that national security meant approximately the same thing in Moscow as it did in Washington. Russia's territorial objectives in Europe were clearly stated. They included restoration of the June 1941 boundary, which meant that Russia would enjoy the fruits of the 1939 Nazi-Soviet pact—specifically the annexation of the three Baltic states (Latvia, Lithuania, and Estonia), pieces of Finland and Rumania, and nearly half of prewar Poland. The Baltic states, it should be noted, had been Russian provinces from the eighteenth century until the end of the First World War. Germany was to be dismembered into a cluster of weak separate states, and hunks of territory were to be given to Poland and Russia. Russia insisted on "friendly" governments along its European borders. In practice this meant Communist regimes imposed by totalitarian means and the ruthless suppression of political liberty and democracy as it was understood in the United States. In Asia the Soviets sought the expulsion of Japan from the mainland and the restoration of Russia's position as it existed at the height of czarist imperial power in 1904. This would entail serious limitations on China's sovereignty in Manchuria.

Roosevelt shared these aims as far as they applied directly to Germany and Japan, but everything beyond that was in actual or potential conflict with the Atlantic Charter. By postponing decisions on these conflicts, Roosevelt convinced himself that he was preventing discord with Russia without making final concessions in violation of the Atlantic Charter. But postponement seemed to indicate a willingness to condone all Russian objectives on the assumption that once they were attained, Russia would feel secure and would cooperate without reservations in the new world organization.

In retrospect it seems clear that Roosevelt's assumptions were wrong. Russia could assign no limits to the requirements of security; expansion and security were sides of the same coin; ideology taught that communism and capitalism would forever be in conflict. Roosevelt misjudged the willingness of Americans to accept Soviet violations of democratic ideals and the ways in which disillusionment would inflame American domestic politics. . . .

The United States put first things first throughout the Second World War. No other considerations were ever permitted to interfere with or delay the victory over the Axis. In August 1945 the great achievement was complete. Hitler was dead and Germany lay powerless under Allied occupation. The emperor's wise decision to surrender meant that the landings on Japan were bloodless. Italy, ineffectual minor partner of the Axis, had withdrawn from the war two years before and, having repudiated fascism, was about to acquire a respected place among nations. Americans, virtually unaided, had beaten Japan back across the Pacific while providing the leadership and more than half the men for the attack on Hitler from the West. At the same time they had become the "arsenal of victory" and provided billions of dollars worth of arms for Britain, Russia, China, and dozens of smaller countries. American diplomacy had preserved the great coalition essential for victory, established the United Nations, and laid foundations for peace in Europe and Asia.

Victory had been achieved at an extraordinarily low cost in American lives—292,000 military dead from combat, 115,000 from other causes, virtually no civilians dead. This was a tribute to American industrial power, whereby the profligate use of weapons saved lives, and to Roosevelt's overall strategy. The Soviet Union, in contrast, lost 7 1/2 million soldiers and an estimated 12 1/2 million civilians—almost fifty times more people. Great Britain—with 30 percent of the population of the United States—lost 395,000, of whom 300,000 were in the armed services, 60,000 were civilians, and 35,000 were merchant seamen. China's losses are impossible to estimate because of the difficulty of separating death from starvation and social disintegration from combat losses, but they ran into millions. Enemy combat losses totaled about 6 million—more than half of which were inflicted by the Russians.

The public mood in the United States that August was one of exuberant celebration, even euphoria. But no informed American could be optimistic. There was far too much evidence that the legacy of victory was not automatic peace and prosperity for all humanity but, at best, a set of intractable problems that would require years of patient and arduous attention. At worst, the legacy could be continued suffering, unabated hatreds, and war.

The outcome appeared to depend overwhelmingly on the behavior of the two most powerful members of the wartime coalition: The United States and the Soviet Union. American leaders in 1945 were agreed that, a generation before, the United States had made a fateful mistake by repudiating the vision of Woodrow Wilson, refusing membership in the League of Nations, withdrawing from political involvement in European security affairs, following selfish economic policies that provoked retaliation and imitation from other nations, and permitting its armed forces to dwindle away. Now it appeared that the United States had a second chance to do the right things.

The second chance had three aspects. The first and most prominently discussed was the chance to create a workable world security organization in place of the League of Nations. The Charter of the United Nations had been signed at San Francisco on June 26, 1945, and would soon be approved overwhelmingly by the Senate. Perhaps American public enthusiasm for the United Nations was naive and perhaps it diverted attention from the complexity of the world's problems. Perhaps also an excessive faith in the United Nations may have contributed to subsequent disillusionment and denigration of the many useful but limited tasks that the world organization is capable of handling. Public statements by American leaders did contribute to "overselling" the UN, but in private President Truman and his advisers knew that the UN alone was no panacea.

The second aspect of the American opportunity to make amends for past mistakes was economic. The analysis went as follows: high tariff barriers and selfish economic restrictions had stultified world trade between the wars, caused massive unemployment, depressed standards of living, and prepared the way for dictators who promised to bring a better life with radical measures and an aggressive foreign policy. War was the result. Now the United States had a second chance to lead the world toward an open economy, a sophisticated version of the traditional American belief in the "open door" of equal economic opportunity for all nations. During the war, the United States had used the leverage of lend-lease aid as a means of winning commitment, especially from Great Britain, to open-door principles and abandonment of special trading blocks and preferential tariff arrangements. Correctly anticipating that aviation would soon replace shipping as the vehicle of international passenger transportation, the United States had also insisted (at the Chicago Aviation conference of 1944) on broad access by the American airlines to the routes and airports of the world—as against Britain's preference for tight restrictions that would protect its weak competitive position.

The United States had also convened the Bretton Woods conference, at an estate in New Hampshire in July 1944, where the International Monetary Fund (IMF) and the International Bank for Reconstruction and Development (World Bank) were established. The IMF was designed to stabilize national currencies and thus encourage trade. The International Bank was designed to aid economic growth. The United States, with the largest investment in both organizations, would be able to set policy. Some critics have argued that American economic policy was a form of imperialism whose purpose was American domination and preservation of capitalism. But the Americans who devised the new system sincerely believed they were acting for the welfare of all humanity and for the prevention of future war. They did not deny that they were also acting for the benefit of American economic interests, but they would have been astonished at the suggestion that there was any conflict between what was good for the world and what was good for the United States. Like their English forebears of the mid-nineteenth century, they elevated the concept of reducing trade barriers to something akin to religious dogma and were not moved by complaints from others that a nation with a lion's share of the world's industrial production could jolly well afford to be for free trade.

The final aspect of the perceived opportunity to avoid past mistakes was little discussed in public in 1945. It was the second chance to maintain a military establishment sufficient to deter and defeat aggression. President Truman and his closest advisers believed that the military weakness of the democracies, including the United States, had made possible the rise and early success of the Axis powers and had made the Second World War inevitable. They were determined that such a mistake would not be made again. But in the climate of 1945, when the public and Congress were calling for the boys to come home immediately, it was not politically feasible to call for big military budgets. Some advocates of military strength complained that the United States was in fact committing the mistake of 1919 over again, engaging (in the words of Secretary of the Navy James Forrestal) in the "swift evisceration of our armed strength." But the degree of demobilization never approached previous levels. The United States remained the world's greatest industrial base, biggest navy, largest air force, and the atomic bomb. In the days before intercontinental nuclear missiles, real military power was a question of what a nation could bring to bear in six months or a year after a war began. By that measure the United States was incomparably the military master of the world in 1945—notwithstanding the larger number of men the Soviet Union retained in uniform.

America's behavior was half the story. What of the Soviet Union? Here Americans divided into two points of view, two theories concerning the sources and nature of Soviet conduct. A few disciples of Roosevelt still believed at war's end that the Soviet Union wanted to cooperate in the interests of peace, but was inhibited by memories of past injuries inflicted by the West. But if the United States was generous and sympathetic, the Soviets would respond. The other viewpoint, soon prominently identified with the Soviet specialist and diplomat George F. Kennan, held that the Soviet Union was expansionist by history and ideology, immune to moral appeals, ruthless and realistic in pursuing its aims. According to this view, the United States and the West should not fear bruising Soviet sensibilities but should make its own opposition to Soviet expansion unequivocal, should demand quid pro quos for every concession, and should have the patience and toughness to contend with the Soviet Union over the very long haul.

The optimistic outline dominated American press and movie depictions of the Soviet Union during the war, but it was superficial and easily abandoned once the necessity of working together to defeat Germany had passed. Americans had long feared communism and their fears remained just below the surface, ready to reappear at the first sign of difficulty with the Soviet Union. Much of the internal bureaucratic history of wartime foreign policy involves a struggle by middle-echelon officials against what they saw as

Roosevelt's naiveté and lack of realism. Roosevelt, however, was a fox. It is probable that he had a less benign view of the Soviet Union than his public posture indicated. His style was to appear optimistic even when he had inner doubts. One should not confuse his public statements with what he really thought—or state confidently what that secretive man really did think.

Harry Truman, in contrast, was an open, contentious leader with a parochial distrust of foreign nations. He did not like the Russians or the pattern of their behavior as he witnessed it upon assuming the presidency. Also, he turned to those middle-echelon advisers who had never accepted Roosevelt's approach and who now felt a sense of liberation and recognition from a new president who would listen to and act on their advice. At war's end, optimism was fading fast, along with its advocates: Roosevelt was dead, Harry Hopkins was dying, Secretary of the Treasury Henry Morgenthau had been purged from Truman's cabinet. The last exponent, Secretary of Commerce Henry Wallace, would linger into 1946 before he too was fired. The hard-line view was in the saddle. . . .

One of the most somber aspects of the study of history is that it suggests no sure ways by which humanity could have avoided folly. Would the postwar world have been a happier and more secure place for the United States and for all people if Roosevelt had behaved differently during the war? Possibly. It might also have been worse. Russia treated as an adversary rather than a friend might, as people feared at the time, have reached a truce with Hitler. This seems unlikely, but the possibility was there. Or Stalin might have acted with less rather than more restraint in Europe and Asia. Might-have-beens can never be proved.

Critics of Roosevelt fall across a spectrum from political right to left. The right appeared first in print, during the early years of the Cold War. They argued that Roosevelt "lost" half of Europe and China to communism. The left were most active during the years of the Vietnam war, when all the established assumptions of American foreign policy were being scrutinized. Their charge was that the United States was insensitive to Russia's needs, opposed to radical movements of the left everywhere in the world, and bent on imposing an American-dominated capitalist order wherever it could. The far right and left share an implicit belief in American omnipotence. The right suggests that had the United States sought to exclude the Soviet Union from eastern Europe and to bring about a victory of Chiang Kai-shek in China, it would have succeeded. The left suggests that a cooperative, humane world would have emerged if the United States had been led by leftists less wedded to capitalism and the preservation of American economic power. Their case is not convincing. Both sets of critics imply that the United States between 1941 and 1945 ought not to have concentrated so hard on military victory but should have been maneuvering either to block the Soviet Union or in some vague way to facilitate the triumph of the forces of leftward movement around the world.

The first edition of [my] book, in 1965, condemned President Roosevelt for holding to stereotypes about other nations, for thinking that American approaches to political developments were applicable everywhere, for assuming that the Soviets used words like "democracy" in the same sense as Americans, and for doubting that the American people would be willing to support significant overseas commitments after the war. Scholarship and documentation appearing since 1965 indicate that Roosevelt was less naive than he once seemed and that he understood the complex nature of the world better than his simplistic comments to others would suggest. He was wrong about whether the United States would undertake postwar commitments, and his indomitable public optimism may have led to some disillusionment and have added to the pain of learning difficult lessons about the world after 1945. And yet those who expect the worst in international affairs often get it. Was not optimism a risk worth taking?

It was right that the first and overriding American priority was victory over the Axis. Other problems could not be solved until that was achieved. Roosevelt's leadership made possible the great result, and for that he and the United States government, armed services, and people deserve high acclaim. The difficulties the United States has encountered since 1945 cannot be blamed on Roosevelt—on the contrary, they should produce an enhanced appreciation of his achievement.

✖ *F U R T H E R   R E A D I N G*

Stephen E. Ambrose, *Eisenhower and Berlin, 1945* (1967)
———, *Rise to Globalism* (1985)
Robert Beitzell, *The Uneasy Alliance* (1972)
Richard Breitman and Alan M. Kraut, *American Refugee Policy and European Jewry, 1933–1945* (1987)
A. Russell Buchanan, *The United States and World War II* (1964)
Russell Buhite, *Decisions at Yalta* (1986)
James M. Burns, *Roosevelt: The Soldier of Freedom* (1970)
Thomas M. Campbell, *Masquerade Peace: America's UN Policy, 1944–1945* (1973)
Diane Shaver Clemens, *Yalta* (1970)
Wayne S. Cole, *Roosevelt and the Isolationists, 1932–1945* (1983)
R. D. Cuff and J. L. Granatstein, *Canadian-American Relations in Wartime* (1975)
Robert Dallek, *Franklin D. Roosevelt and American Foreign Policy, 1933–1945* (1979)
Richard E. Darilek, *A Loyal Opposition in Time of War* (1976)
Robert A. Divine, *Roosevelt and World War II* (1969)
———, *Second Chance* (1967)
John W. Dower, *War Without Mercy* (1986)
Herbert Feis, *Between War and Peace* (1960)
———, *Churchill, Roosevelt, Stalin* (1957)
Louis Fischer, *The Road to Yalta: Soviet Foreign Relations, 1941–1945* (1972)
Kent R. Greenfield, *American Strategy in World War II* (1963)
Stanley Hilton, *Hitler's Secret War in South America, 1939–1945* (1981)
Julian C. Hurstfield, *America and the French Nation, 1939–1945* (1986)
Akira Iriye, *Power and Culture* (1981)
Victor Israelian, *The Anti-Hitler Coalition* (1971)
Warren Kimball, "Churchill and Roosevelt: The Personal Equation," *Prologue*, 6 (1974), 169–82

Gabriel Kolko, *The Politics of War* (1968)

William Langer, *Our Vichy Gamble* (1947)

Eric Larrabee, *Commander in Chief* (1987)

Michael Leigh, *Mobilizing Consent: Public Opinion and American Foreign Policy, 1937–1947* (1976)

Ralph B. Levering, *American Opinion and the Russian Alliance* (1976)

William R. Louis, *Imperialism at Bay: The United States and the Decolonization of the British Empire* (1978)

Richard Lukas, *The Strange Alliance: The United States and Poland, 1941–1945* (1978)

William H. McNeill, *America, Britain, and Russia* (1953)

Vojtech Mastny, *Russia's Road to the Cold War* (1979)

Samuel Eliot Morison, *Strategy and Compromise* (1958)

William L. Neumann, *After Victory* (1967)

Raymond G. O'Connor, *Diplomacy for Victory: FDR and Unconditional Surrender* (1971)

Forrest C. Pogue, *George C. Marshall* (1963–1987)

Keith Sainsbury, *The Turning Point* (1985)

Michael S. Sherry, *Preparing for the Next Year* (1977)

Robert E. Sherwood, *Roosevelt and Hopkins* (1948)

John L. Snell, *Illusion or Necessity* (1963)

Ronald H. Spector, *Eagle Against the Sun* (1984)

Richard W. Steele, *The First Offensive, 1942* (1973)

Mark A. Stoler, *The Politics of the Second Front* (1977)

Kenneth W. Thompson, *Winston Churchill's World View* (1983)

Christopher Thorne, *Allies of a Kind* (1978)

——, *The Issue of War* (1985)

Adam Ulam, *Expansion and Coexistence: The History of Soviet Foreign Policy, 1917–1973* (1974)

Brian L. Villa, "The Atomic Bomb and the Normandy Invasion," *Perspectives in American History*, 2 (1977–1978), 461–502

Llewellyn Woodward, *British Foreign Policy in the Second World War* (1970–71)

David S. Wyman, *The Abandonment of the Jews: America and the Holocaust, 1941–1945* (1984)

The Origins of the Cold War

The Big Three alliance of World War II, often strained during the war itself, quickly splintered as the victors began to plan the peace. Questions of territorial boundaries, spheres of influence, atomic weaponry, trade, economic reconstruction, political principles, and international organizations divided Britain, the United States, and the Soviet Union. In Germany, Iran, Eastern Europe, China—indeed, on a global scale—the major powers, especially America and Russia, competed for postwar influence, using the economic, political, military, and ideological means available to them. The result was the Cold War.

Why the Cold War developed with such divisiveness is a topic of spirited debate among scholars and surviving participants of this postwar antagonism. Were the causes to be found in the flawed and broken international system itself? or in a totalitarian Soviet Union bent on aggression? or in a powerful, expansionist United States? or in the particular decisions of such strong personalities as Harry S Truman and Josef Stalin? Recent scholarship makes clear that there is no single explanation for the origins of the Cold War and that the historian's task is not to pin blame on one antagonist or the other but to probe for the complex national and international tensions and drives that pitted nation against nation.

✖ D O C U M E N T S

The first three documents speak to the American decision to use the atomic bomb against Japan and its impact on international relations. In early May 1945, Secretary of War Henry L. Stimson chaired the Interim Committee to advise on atomic energy and the uranium bombs the Manhattan Engineering District project was about to produce. The committee agreed on May 31, 1945 to keep the bomb project a secret from the Russians and to use the atomic bomb against the Japanese. On June 11, 1945, a group of atomic scientists in Chicago, headed by Jerome Franck, futilely petitioned Stimson for a noncombat demonstration of the bomb in order to improve chances for postwar international control. On September 11, 1945, Stimson himself sent President Harry S Truman a memorandum in which he argued that Russian-American relations were being "dominated by the problem of the atomic bomb." He now urged that the United States approach Russia to discuss controls, as the third document indicates.

In May 1945 Truman sent a special representative to Moscow to speak with Josef Stalin, but not about the atomic bomb. Harry Hopkins, who for years had advised Franklin D. Roosevelt, already knew the Soviet Premier. On May 27, as the fourth document reveals, they talked frankly about the abrupt American termination of Lend-Lease aid to Russia and the repressive Soviet presence in Poland. The next document, written by George F. Kennan, is his influential "long telegram" of February 22, 1946, which he, then attaché in the American Embassy in Moscow, sent to Washington to spell out what he thought were the underlying sources of Soviet behavior. Former British Prime Minister Winston S. Churchill's "iron curtain" speech of March 5, 1946, the sixth selection, delivered in Fulton, Missouri, stirred debate. The next document, a July 1946 memorandum given the President by Secretary of Commerce Henry A. Wallace, criticized Truman's "get tough" policies. Truman forced Wallace to resign in September. On March 12, 1947, the President addressed Congress to announce the "Truman Doctrine" or containment doctrine, reprinted here as the eighth document. The Marshall Plan soon followed. First suggested by Secretary of State George C. Marshall in June 1947, the American aid program for European reconstruction was launched by the Economic Cooperation Act of 1948, signed by the President on April 3. A portion of the act is reprinted as the ninth selection. The final document is a small part of National Security Council Paper No. 68 (NSC-68), dated April 7, 1950. This important report was alarmist in its depiction of a world beset by Soviet expansionism that only the United States could halt.

The Interim Committee on Military Use of the Atomic Bomb, 1945

Secretary Stimson explained that the Interim Committee had been appointed by him, with the approval of the President, to make recommendations on temporary war-time controls, public announcement, legislation and post-war organization. . . . He expressed the hope that the [four] scientists would feel completely free to express their views on any phase of the subject. . . .

The Secretary explained that General Marshall shared responsibility with him for making recommendations to the President on this project with particular reference to its military aspects; therefore, it was considered highly desirable that General Marshall be present at this meeting to secure at first hand the views of the scientists.

The Secretary expressed the view, a view shared by General Marshall, that this project not be considered simply in terms of military weapons, but as a new relationship of man to the universe. This discovery might be compared to the discoveries of the Copernican theory and of the laws of gravity, but far more important than these in its effect on the lives of men. While the advances in the field to date had been fostered by the needs of war, it was important to realize that the implications of the project went far beyond the needs of the present war. It must be controlled if possible to make it an assurance of future peace rather than a menace to civilization.

The Secretary suggested that he hoped to have the following questions discussed during the course of the meeting.

1. Future military weapons
2. Future international competition
3. Future research
4. Future controls
5. Future developments, particularly non-military.

At this point *General Marshall* discussed at some length the story of charges and counter-charges that have been typical of our relations with the Russians, pointing out that most of these allegations have proven unfounded. The seemingly uncooperative attitude of Russia in military matters stemmed from the necessity of maintaining security. He said that he had accepted this reason for their attitude in his dealings with the Russians and had acted accordingly. As to the post-war situation and in matters other than purely military, he felt that he was in no position to express a view. With regard to this field he was inclined to favor the building up of a combination among like-minded powers, thereby forcing Russia to fall in line by the very force of this coalition. General Marshall was certain that we need have no fear that the Russians, if they had knowledge of our project, would disclose this information to the Japanese. He raised the question whether it might be desirable to invite two prominent Russian scientists to witness the test.

Mr. Byrnes expressed a fear that if information were given to the Russians, even in general terms, Stalin would ask to be brought into the partnership. He felt this to be particularly likely in view of our commitments and pledges of cooperation with the British. In this connection *Dr. Bush* pointed out that even the British do not have any of our blue prints on plants. *Mr. Byrnes* expressed the view, *which was generally agreed to by all present*, that the most desirable program would be to push ahead as fast as possible in production and research to make certain that we stay ahead and at the same time make every effort to better our political relations with Russia.

It was pointed out that one atomic bomb on an arsenal would not be much different from the effect caused by any Air Corps strike of present dimensions. However, *Dr. Oppenheimer* stated that the visual effect of an atomic bombing would be tremendous. It would be accompanied by a brilliant luminescence which would rise to a height of 10,000 to 20,000 feet. The neutron effect of the explosion would be dangerous to life for a radius of at least two-thirds of a mile.

After much discussion concerning various types of targets and the effects to be produced, *the Secretary expressed the conclusion, on which there was general agreement, that we could not give the Japanese any warning; that we could not concentrate on a civilian area; but that we should seek to make a profound psychological impression on as many of the inhabitants as possible. At the suggestion of Dr. Conant the Secretary agreed that the most desirable target would be a vital war plant employing a large number of workers and closely surrounded by workers' houses.*

There was some discussion of the desirability of attempting several strikes at the same time. *Dr. Oppenheimer's* judgment was that several strikes would be feasible. *General Groves*, however, expressed doubt about this proposal and pointed out the following objections: (1) We would lose the advantage of gaining additional knowledge concerning the weapon at each successive bombing; (2) such a program would require a rush job on the part of those assembling the bombs and might, therefore, be ineffective; (3) the effect would not be sufficiently distinct from our regular Air Force bombing program.

The Franck Committee on a Noncombat Atomic Demonstration, 1945

The way in which the nuclear weapons, now secretly developed in this country, will first be revealed to the world appears of great, perhaps fateful importance.

One possible way—which may particularly appeal to those who consider the nuclear bombs primarily as a secret weapon developed to help win the present war—is to use it without warning on an appropriately selected object in Japan. It is doubtful whether the first available bombs, of comparatively low efficiency and small size, will be sufficient to break the will or ability of Japan to resist, especially given the fact that the major cities like Tokyo, Nagoya, Osaka and Kobe already will largely be reduced to ashes by the slower process of ordinary aerial bombing. Certain and perhaps important tactical results undoubtedly can be achieved, but we nevertheless think that the question of the use of the very first available atomic bombs in the Japanese war should be weighed very carefully, not only by military authority, but by the highest political leadership of this country. If we consider international agreement on total prevention of nuclear warfare as the paramount objective, and believe that it can be achieved, this kind of introduction of atomic weapons to the world may easily destroy all our chances of success. Russia, and even allied countries which bear less mistrust of our ways and intentions, as well as neutral countries, will be deeply shocked. It will be very difficult to persuade the world that a nation which was capable of secretly preparing and suddenly releasing a weapon, as indiscriminate as the rocket bomb and a thousand times more destructive, is to be trusted in its proclaimed desire of having such weapons abolished by international agreement. We have large accumulations of poison gas, but do not use them, and recent polls have shown that public opinion in this country would disapprove of such a use even if it would accelerate the winning of the Far Eastern war. It is true, that some irrational element in mass psychology makes gas poisoning more revolting than blasting by explosives, even though gas warfare is in no way more ''inhuman'' than the war of bombs and bullets. Nevertheless, it is not at all certain that the American public opinion, if it could be enlightened as to the effect of atomic explosives, would support the first introduction by our own country of such an indiscriminate method of wholesale destruction of civilian life.

Thus, from the ''optimistic'' point of view—looking forward to an international agreement on prevention of nuclear warfare—the military advantages and the saving of American lives, achieved by the sudden use of atomic bombs against Japan, may be outweighed by the ensuing loss of confidence and wave of horror and repulsion, sweeping over the rest of the world, and perhaps dividing even the public opinion at home.

From this point of view a demonstration of the new weapon may best be made before the eyes of representatives of all United Nations, on the desert or a barren island. The best possible atmosphere for the achievement of an international agreement could be achieved if America would be able to say to the world, "You see what weapon we had but did not use. We are ready to renounce its use in the future and to join other nations in working out adequate supervision of the use of this nuclear weapon."

This may sound fantastic, but then in nuclear weapons we have something entirely new in the order of magnitude of destructive power, and if we want to capitalize fully on the advantage which its possession gives us, we must use new and imaginative methods. After such a demonstration the weapon could be used against Japan if a sanction of the United Nations (and of the public opinion at home) could be obtained, perhaps after a preliminary ultimatum to Japan to surrender or at least to evacuate a certain region as an alternative to the total destruction of this target.

It must be stressed that if one takes a pessimistic point of view and discounts the possibilities of an effective international control of nuclear weapons, then the advisability of an early use of nuclear bombs against Japan becomes even more doubtful—quite independently of any humanitarian considerations. If no international agreement is concluded immediately after the first demonstration, this will mean a flying start of an unlimited armaments race. If this race is inevitable, we have all reason to delay its beginning as long as possible in order to increase our headstart still further. . . . The benefit to the nation, and the saving of American lives in the future, achieved by renouncing an early demonstration of nuclear bombs and letting the other nations come into the race only reluctantly, on the basis of guesswork and without definite knowledge that the "thing does work," may far outweigh the advantages to be gained by the immediate use of the first and comparatively inefficient bombs in the war against Japan. At the least, pros and cons of this use must be carefully weighed by the supreme political and military leadership of the country, and the decision should not be left to considerations, merely, of military tactics.

One may point out that scientists themselves have initiated the development of this "secret weapon" and it is therefore strange that they should be reluctant to try it out on the enemy as soon as it is available. The answer to this question was given above—the compelling reason for creating this weapon with such speed was our fear that Germany had the technical skill necessary to develop such a weapon without any moral restraints regarding its use.

Another argument which could be quoted in favor of using atomic bombs as soon as they are available is that so much taxpayers' money has been invested in those projects that the Congress and the American public will require a return for their money. The above-mentioned attitude of the American public opinion in the question of the use of poison gas against Japan shows that one can expect it to understand that a weapon can sometimes be made ready only for use in extreme emergency; and as soon as the potentialities of nuclear weapons will be revealed to the American people, one can be certain that it will support all attempts to make the use of such weapons impossible.

Henry L. Stimson's Appeal for Atomic Talks with Russia, 1945

The advent of the atomic bomb has stimulated great military and probably even greater political interest throughout the civilized world. In a world atmosphere already extremely sensitive to power, the introduction of this weapon has profoundly affected political considerations in all sections of the globe.

In many quarters it has been interpreted as a substantial offset to the growth of Russian influence on the continent. We can be certain that the Soviet Government has sensed this tendency and the temptation will be strong for the Soviet political and military leaders to acquire this weapon in the shortest possible time. Britain in effect already has the status of a partner with us in the development of this weapon. Accordingly, unless the Soviets are voluntarily invited into the partnership upon a basis of co-operation and trust, we are going to maintain the Anglo-Saxon bloc over against the Soviet in the possession of this weapon. Such a condition will almost certainly stimulate feverish activity on the part of the Soviet toward the development of this bomb in what will in effect be a secret armament race of a rather desperate character. There is evidence to indicate that such activity may have already commenced.

If we feel, as I assume we must, that civilization demands that some day we shall arrive at a satisfactory international arrangement respecting the control of this new force, the question then is how long we can afford to enjoy our momentary superiority in the hope of achieving our immediate peace council objectives.

Whether Russia gets control of the necessary secrets of production in a minimum of say four years or a maximum of twenty years is not nearly as important to the world and civilization as to make sure that when they do get it they are willing and co-operative partners among the peace-loving nations of the world. It is true if we approach them now, as I would propose, we may be gambling on their good faith and risk their getting into production of bombs a little sooner than they would otherwise.

To put the matter concisely, I consider the problem of our satisfactory relations with Russia as not merely connected with but as virtually dominated by the problem of the atomic bomb. Except for the problem of the control of that bomb, those relations, while vitally important, might not be immediately pressing. The establishment of relations of mutual confidence between her and us could afford to await the slow progress of time. But with the discovery of the bomb, they became immediately emergent. Those relations may be perhaps irretrievably embittered by the way in which we approach the solution of the bomb with Russia. For if we fail to approach them now and merely continue to negotiate with them, having this weapon rather ostentatiously on our hip, their suspicions and their distrust of our purposes and motives will increase. It will inspire them to greater efforts in an all-out effort to solve the problem. If the solution is achieved in that spirit, it is much less likely that we will ever get the kind of covenant we may desperately need in the future. This risk is, I believe, greater than the other, inasmuch as our objective must be to get the best kind of international bargain we can—one that has some chance of being kept and saving civilization not for five or for twenty years, but forever.

The chief lesson I have learned in a long life is that the only way you can make a man trustworthy is to trust him; and the surest way to make him untrustworthy is to distrust him and show your distrust.

If the atomic bomb were merely another though more devastating military weapon to be assimilated into our pattern of international relations, it would be one thing. We could then follow the old custom of secrecy and nationalistic military superiority relying on international caution to prescribe the future use of the weapon as we did with gas. But I think the bomb instead constitutes merely a first step in a new control by man over the forces of nature too revolutionary and dangerous to fit into the old concepts. It think it really caps the climax of the race between man's growing technical power for destructiveness and his psychological power of self-control and group control—his moral power. If so, our method of approach to the Russians is a question of the most vital importance in the evolution of human progress.

Since the crux of the problem is Russia, any contemplated action leading to the control of this weapon should be primarily directed *to* Russia. It is my judgment that the Soviet would be more apt to respond sincerely to a direct and forthright approach made by the United States on this subject than would be the case if the approach were made as a part of a general international scheme, or if the approach were made after a succession of express or implied threats or near threats in our peace negotiations.

My idea of an approach to the Soviets would be a direct proposal after discussion with the British that we would be prepared in effect to enter an arrangement with the Russians, the general purpose of which would be to control and limit the use of the atomic bomb as an instrument of war and so far as possible to direct and encourage the development of atomic power for peaceful and humanitarian purposes. Such an approach might more specifically lead to the proposal that we would stop work on the further improvement in, or manufacture of, the bomb as a military weapon, provided the Russians and the British would agree to do likewise. It might also provide that we would be willing to impound what bombs we now have in the United States provided the Russians and the British would agree with us that in no event will they or we use a bomb as an instrument of war unless all three Governments agree to that use. We might also consider including in the arrangement a covenant with the U.K. and the Soviets providing for the exchange of benefits of future developments whereby atomic energy may be applied on a mutually satisfactory basis for commercial or humanitarian purposes.

I would make such an approach just as soon as our immediate political considerations make it appropriate.

I emphasize perhaps beyond all other considerations the importance of taking this action with Russia as a proposal of the United States—backed by Great Britain but peculiarly the proposal of the United States. Action of any international group of nations, including many small nations who have not demonstrated their potential power or responsibility in this war would not, in my opinion, be taken seriously by the Soviets. The loose debates which would surround such proposal, if put before a conference of nations, would provoke but scant favor from the Soviet. As I say, I think this is the most important point in the program.

After the nations which have won this war have agreed to it, there will be ample time to introduce France and China into the covenants and finally to incorporate the agreement into the scheme of the United Nations. The use of this bomb has been accepted by the world as the result of the initiative and productive capacity of the United States, and I think this factor is a most potent lever toward having our proposals accepted by the Soviets, whereas I am most skeptical of obtaining any tangible results by way of any international debate. I urge this method as the most realistic means of accomplishing this vitally important step in the history of the world.

Harry Hopkins and Josef Stalin
Discuss Lend-Lease and Poland, 1945

Mr. Hopkins said that last night the Marshal had indicated that there were a number of questions concerning the United States which were worrying him. He asked Marshal Stalin if he would perhaps care to begin with these questions.

Marshal Stalin said he would not attempt to use Soviet public opinion as a screen but would speak of the feeling that had been created in Soviet governmental circles as a result of recent moves on the part of the United States Government. He said these circles felt a certain alarm in regard to the attitude of the United States Government. It was their impression that the American attitude towards the Soviet Union had perceptibly cooled once it became obvious that Germany was defeated, and that it was as though the Americans were saying that the Russians were no longer needed. He said he would give the following examples:. . .

[1] 3. The attitude of the United States Government towards the Polish question. He said that at Yalta it had been agreed that the existing government was to be reconstructed and that anyone with common sense could see that this meant that the present government was to form the basis of the new. He said no other understanding of the Yalta Agreement was possible. Despite the fact that they were simple

people the Russians should not be regarded as fools which was a mistake the West frequently made, nor were they blind and could quite well see what was going on before their eyes. It is true that the Russians are patient in the interests of a common cause but that their patience has its limits.

[2] 4. The manner in which Lend Lease had been curtailed. He said that if the United States was unable to supply the Soviet Union further under Lend Lease that was one thing but that the manner in which it had been done had been unfortunate and even brutal. For example, certain ships had been unloaded and while it was true that this order had been cancelled the whole manner in which it had been done had caused concern to the Soviet Government. If the refusal to continue Lend Lease was designed as pressure on the Russians in order to soften them up then it was a fundamental mistake. He said he must tell Mr. Hopkins frankly that [if] the Russians were approached frankly on a friendly basis much could be done but that reprisals in any form would bring about the exact opposite effect. . . .

Mr. Hopkins then said on the subject of Lend Lease he thought it had been clear to the Soviet Union that the end of the war with Germany would necessitate a reconsideration of the old program of Lend Lease to the Soviet Union.

Marshal Stalin said that was entirely understandable.

Mr. Hopkins continued that the history of Lend Lease showed that although in certain cases we had not always been able to meet every Soviet request we had nonetheless freely accepted commitments which we had done our best to carry out in spirit as well as in fact.

Marshal Stalin said that was undoubtedly true.

Mr. Hopkins stated that even prior to the end of the war in Europe we had made an agreement with the Soviet Union known as Annex 3 to Protocol 1 [IV], which involved delivery of supplies which might be of use in the Far East. He said that this grew out of recent conferences in which Far Eastern matters had been discussed. He emphasized that this commitment was accepted in full by the United States and we were in the process of carrying it out. In regard to the unloading of the ships he said that that was a technical misunderstanding and did not in any sense represent a decision of policy on the part of the United States. That it had been the action of one government agency involved in Lend Lease and that it had been countermanded promptly within twenty-four hours. He said that no one who was responsible for Lend Lease policy or American Government policy had had anything to do with that mistaken order. The only question which had to be reconsidered was the program of deliveries to the Soviet Union which had been based on the needs of the war against Germany and that it had been made clear that on the basis of this reconsideration we would be glad to reconsider any Soviet requests and that he thought some were now being considered. He said he wished to emphasize that he had seen no tendency on the part of those responsible for American policy to handle the question of future Lend Lease to the Soviet Union in an arbitrary fashion. It was in fact a question of law, since the basic Lend Lease Act made it clear that materials could only be delivered which would be useful in the process of the war. The United States Government, however, had interpreted this in its broadest sense and had included in addition to munitions of war foodstuffs and other non-military items.

Marshal Stalin said this was true.

Mr. Hopkins concluded by saying that there had naturally been considerable confusion in the United States Government as to the status of Lend Lease towards Russia at the end of the war and that there had been varying legal interpretations but that he wished to emphasize that the incident to which Marshal Stalin referred did not have any fundamental policy significance.

Marshal Stalin said he wished to make it clear that he fully understood the right of the United States to curtail Lend Lease shipments to the Soviet Union under present conditions since our commitments in this respect had been freely entered into. Even two months ago it would have been quite correct for the United States to have begun to curtail shipments but what he had in mind was the manner and form in which it was done. He felt that what was after all an agreement between two Governments had been ended in a scornful and abrupt manner. He said that if proper warning had been given to the Soviet Government there would have been no feeling of the kind he had spoken of; that this warning was important to them since their economy was based on plans. He added that they had intended to make a suitable expression of gratitude to the United States for the Lend Lease assistance during the war but the way in which this program had been halted now made that impossible to do.

Mr. Hopkins replied that what disturbed him most about the Marshal's statement was the revelation that he believed that the United States would use Lend Lease as a means of showing our displeasure with the Soviet Union. He wished to assure the Marshal that however unfortunate an impression this question had caused in the mind of the Soviet Government he must believe that there was no attempt or desire on the part of the United States to use it as a pressure weapon. He said the United States is a strong power and does not go in for those methods. Furthermore, we have no conflict of immediate interests with the Soviet Union and would have no reason to adopt such practices. . . .

Mr. Hopkins concluded the discussion of Lend Lease by stating that he thought it would be a great tragedy if the greatest achievement in co-operation which the Soviet Union and the United States had on the whole worked out together on the basis of Lend Lease were to end on an unsatisfactory note. He said he wished to add that we had never believed that our Lend Lease help had been the chief factor in the Soviet defeat of Hitler on the eastern front. That this had been done by the heroism and blood of the Russian army. . . .

Mr. Hopkins then said with the Marshal's permission he would like to review the position of the United States in regard to Poland. He said first of all he wished to assure the Marshal that he had no thought or indeed any right to attempt to settle the Polish problem during his visit here in Moscow, nor was he intending to hide behind American public opinion in presenting the position of the United States.

Marshal Stalin said he was afraid that his remark concerning Soviet public opinion has cut Mr. Hopkins to the quick and that he had not meant to imply that Mr. Hopkins was hiding behind the screen of American public opinion. In fact he knew Mr. Hopkins to be an honest and frank man.

Mr. Hopkins said that he wished to state this position as clearly and as forcibly as he knew how. He said the question of Poland per se was not so important as the fact that it had become a symbol of our ability to work out problems with the Soviet Union. He said that we had no special interests in Poland and no special desire to see any particular kind of government. That we would accept any government in Poland which was desired by the Polish people and was at the same time friendly to the Soviet Government. He said that the people and Government of the United States felt that this was a problem which should be worked out jointly between the United States, the Soviet Union and Great Britain and that we felt that the Polish people should be given the right to free elections to choose their own government and their own system and that Poland should genuinely be independent. The Government and people of the United States were disturbed because the preliminary steps towards the reestablishment of Poland appeared to have been taken unilaterally by the Soviet Union together with the present Warsaw Government and that in fact the United States was completely excluded. He said he hoped that Stalin would believe him when he said that this feeling was a fact. Mr. Hopkins said he urged that Marshal Stalin would judge American policy by the actions of the United States Government itself and not by the attitudes and public expressions of the Hearst newspapers and the *Chicago Tribune*. He hoped that the Marshal would put his mind to the task of thinking up what diplomatic methods could be used to settle this question keeping in mind the feeling of the American people. He said he himself was not prepared to say how it could be done but that he felt it must be done. Poland had become a symbol in the sense that it bore a direct relation to the willingness of the United States to participate in international affairs on a world-wide basis and that our people must believe that they are joining their power with that of the Soviet Union and Great Britain in the promotion of international peace and the well being of humanity. Mr. Hopkins went on to say that he felt the overwhelming majority of the people of the United States felt that the relations between the United States and the U.S.S.R. could be worked out in a spirit of cooperation despite the differences in ideology and that with all these factors in its favor he wished to appeal to the Marshal to help find a way to the solution of the Polish problem.

Marshal Stalin replied that he wished Mr. Hopkins would take into consideration the following factors: He said it may seem strange although it appeared to be recognized in United States circles and Churchill in his speeches also recognized it, that the Soviet Government should wish for a friendly Poland. In the course of twenty-five years the Germans had twice invaded Russia via Poland. Neither the British nor American people had experienced such German invasions which were a horrible thing to endure and the results of which were not easily forgotten. He said these German invasions were not warfare but were like the incursions of the Huns. He said that Germany had been able to do this because Poland had been regarded as a part of the cordon sanitaire around the Soviet Union and that previous European policy had been that Polish Governments must be hostile to Russia. In these circumstances either Poland had been too weak to oppose Germany or had let the Germans come through. Thus Poland had served as a corridor for the German attacks on Russia. He said Poland's weakness and hostility had been a great source of weakness to the Soviet Union and had permitted the Germans to do what they wished in the East and also in the West since the two were mixed together. It is therefore in Russia's vital interest that Poland should be both strong and friendly. He said there was no intention on the part of the Soviet Union to interfere in Poland's internal affairs, that Poland would live under the parliamentary system which is like Czechoslovakia, Belgium and Holland and that any talk of an intention to Sovietize Poland was stupid. He said even the Polish leaders, some of whom were communists, were against the Soviet system since the Polish people did not desire collective farms or other aspects of the Soviet system. In this the Polish leaders were right since the Soviet system was not exportable—it must develop from within on the basis of a set of conditions which were not present in Poland. He said all the Soviet Union wanted was that Poland should not be in a position to open the gates to Germany and in order to prevent this Poland must be strong and democratic. Stalin then said that before he came to his suggestion as to the practical solution of the question he would like to comment on Mr. Hopkins's remarks concerning future United States interests in the world. He said that whether the United States wished it or not it was a world power and would have to accept world-wide interests. Not only this war but the previous war had shown that without United States intervention Germany could not have been defeated and that all the events and developments of the last thirty years had confirmed this. In fact the United States had more reason to be a world power than any other state. For this reason he fully recognized the right of the United States as a world [power] to participate in the Polish question and that the Soviet interest in Poland does not in any way exclude those of England and the United States. Mr. Hopkins had spoken of Russian unilateral action in Poland and United States opinion concerning it. It was true that Russia had taken such unilateral action but they had been compelled to. He said the Soviet Government had recognized the Warsaw Government and concluded a treaty with it at a time when their Allies did not recognize this government. These were admittedly unilateral acts which would have been much better left undone but the fact was they had not met with any understanding on the part of their Allies. The need for these actions has arisen out of the presence of Soviet troops in Poland and it would have been impossible to have waited until such time as the Allies had come to an agreement on Poland. The logic of the war against Germany demanded that the Soviet rear be assured and the Lublin Committee had been of great assistance to the Red Army at all times and it was for this reason that these actions had been taken by the Soviet Government. He said it was contrary to the Soviet policy to set up [a] Soviet administration on foreign soil since this would look like occupation and be resented by the local inhabitants. It was for this reason that some Polish administration had to be established in Poland and this could be done only with those who had helped the Red Army. He said he wished to emphasize that these steps had not been taken with any desire to eliminate or exclude Russia's Allies. He must point out however that Soviet action in Poland had been more successful than British action in Greece and at no time had they been compelled to undertake the measures which they had done in Greece. Stalin then turned to his suggestion for the solution of the Polish problem.

Marshal Stalin said that he felt that we should examine the composition of the future Government of National Unity. He said there were eighteen or twenty ministries in the present Polish Government and that four or five of these portfolios could be given representatives of other Polish groups taken from the list submitted by Great Britain and the United States (Molotov whispered to Stalin who then said he meant four and not five posts in the government). He said he thought the Warsaw Poles would not accept more than four ministers from other democratic groups. He added that if this appears a suitable basis we could then proceed to consider what persons should be selected for these posts. He said of course that they would have to be friendly to the U.S.S.R. and to the Allies. He added that Mikolajczyk had been suggested and he thought he was acceptable and that the question was now who else. He inquired of Mr. Hopkins whether possibly Professor Lange might be willing to join the government.

Mr. Hopkins said he doubted whether Professor Lange, who was an American citizen, could be induced to give up his American citizenship for this purpose but that of course was only a private opinion.

Marshal Stalin then said it might be wise to ask some of the Warsaw leaders to come to Moscow now and to hear what they had to say and to learn more of what had been decided. He added that if we are able to settle the composition of the new government he felt that no differences remained since we were all agreed on the free and unfettered elections and that no one intended to interfere with the Polish people.

Mr. Hopkins said he would like to have some time to consider the Marshal's suggestion.

George F. Kennan's "Long Telegram," 1946

At bottom of Kremlin's neurotic view of world affairs is traditional and instinctive Russian sense of insecurity. Originally, this was insecurity of a peaceful agricultural people trying to live on vast exposed plain in neighborhood of fierce nomadic peoples. To this was added, as Russia came into contact with economically advanced West, fear of more competent, more powerful, more highly organized societies in that area. But this latter type of insecurity was one which afflicted rather Russian rulers than Russian people; for Russian rulers have invariably sensed that their rule was relatively archaic in form, fragile and artificial in its psychological foundation, unable to stand comparison or contact with political systems of Western countries. For this reason they have always feared foreign penetration, feared direct contact between Western world and their own, feared what would happen if Russians learned truth about world without or if foreigners learned truth about world within. And they had learned to seek security only in patient but deadly struggle for total destruction of rival power, never in compacts and compromises with it.

It was no coincidence that Marxism, which had smouldered ineffectively for half a century in Western Europe, caught hold and blazed for first time in Russia. Only in this land which had never known a friendly neighbor or indeed any tolerant equilibrium of separate powers, either internal or international, could a doctrine thrive which viewed economic conflicts of society as insoluble by peaceful means. After establishment of Bolshevist regime, Marxist dogma, rendered even more truculent and intolerant by Lenin's interpretation, became a perfect vehicle for sense of insecurity with which Bolsheviks, even more than previous Russian rulers, were afflicted. In this dogma, with its basic altruism of purpose, they found justification for their instinctive fear of outside world, for the dictatorship without which they did not know how to rule, for cruelties they did not dare not to inflict, for sacrifices they felt bound to demand. In the name of Marxism they sacrificed every single ethical value in their methods and tactics. Today they cannot dispense with it. It is fig leaf of their moral and intellectual respectability. Without it they would stand before history, at best, as only the last of that long succession of cruel and wasteful Russian rulers who have relentlessly forced country on to ever new heights of military power in order to guarantee external security of their internally weak regimes. This is why Soviet purposes must always be solemnly clothed in trappings of Marxism, and why no one should underrate importance of dogma in Soviet affairs. Thus Soviet leaders are driven [by?] necessities of their own past and present position to put forward a dogma which [apparent omission] outside world as evil, hostile and menacing, but as bearing within itself germs of creeping disease and destined to be wracked with growing internal convulsions until it is given final *coup de grace* by rising power of socialism and yields to new and better world. This thesis provides justification for that increase of military and police power of Russian state, for that isolation of Russian population from outside world, and for that fluid and constant pressure to extend limits of Russian police power which are together the natural and instinctive urges of Russian rulers. Basically this is only the steady advance of uneasy Russian nationalism, a centuries old movement in which conceptions of offense and defense are inextricably confused. But in new guise of international Marxism, with its honeyed promises to a desperate and war torn outside world, it is more dangerous and insidious than ever before.

It should not be thought from above that Soviet party line is necessarily disingenuous and insincere on part of all those who put it forward. Many of them are too ignorant of outside world and mentally too dependent to question [apparent omission] self-hypnotism, and who have no difficulty making themselves believe what they find it comforting and convenient to believe. Finally we have the unsolved mystery as to who, if anyone, in this great land actually receives accurate and unbiased information about outside world. In atmosphere of oriental secretiveness and conspiracy which pervades this Government, possibilities for distorting or poisoning sources and currents of information are infinite. The very disrespect of Russians for objective truth—indeed, their disbelief in its existence—leads them to view all stated facts as instruments for furtherance of one ulterior purpose or another. There is good reason to suspect that this Government is actually a conspiracy within a conspiracy; and I for one am reluctant to believe that Stalin himself receives anything like an objective picture of outside world. Here there is ample scope for the type of subtle intrigue at which Russians are past masters. Inability of foreign governments to place their case squarely before Russian policy makers—extent to which they are delivered up in their relations with Russia to good graces of obscure and unknown advisers who they never see and cannot influence—this to my mind is most disquieting feature of diplomacy in Moscow, and one which Western statesmen would do well to keep in mind if they would understand nature of difficulties encountered here. . . .

In summary, we have here a political force committed fanatically to the belief that with US there can be no permanent *modus vivendi*, that it is desirable and necessary that the internal harmony of our society be disrupted, our traditional way of life be destroyed, the international authority of our state be broken, if Soviet power is to be secure. This political force has complete power of disposition over energies of one of world's greatest peoples and resources of world's richest national territory, and is borne along by deep and powerful currents of Russian nationalism. In addition, it has an elaborate and far flung apparatus for exertion of its influence in other countries, an apparatus of amazing flexibility and versatility, managed by people whose experience and skill in underground methods are presumably without parallel in history. Finally, it is seemingly inaccessible to considerations of reality in its basic reactions. For it, the vast fund of objective fact about human society is not, as with us, the measure against which outlook is constantly being tested and re-formed, but a grab bag from which individual items are selected arbitrarily and tendenciously to bolster an outlook already preconceived. This is admittedly not a pleasant picture. Problem of how to cope with this force [is] undoubtedly greatest task our diplomacy has ever faced and probably greatest it will ever have to face. It should be point of departure from which our political general staff work at present juncture should proceed. It should be approached with same thoroughness and care as solution of major strategic problem in war, and if necessary, with no smaller outlay in planning effort. I cannot attempt to suggest all answers here. But I would like to record my conviction that problem is within our power to solve—and that without recourse to any general military conflict. And in support of this conviction there are certain observations of a more encouraging nature I should like to make:

1. Soviet power, unlike that of Hitlerite Germany, is neither schematic nor adventuristic. It does not work by fixed plans. It does not take unnecessary risks. Impervious to logic of reason, and it is highly sensitive to logic of force. For this reason it can easily withdraw—and usually does—when strong resistance is encountered at any point. Thus, if the adversary has sufficient force and makes clear his readiness to use it, he rarely has to do so. If situations are properly handled there need be no prestige-engaging showdowns.

2. Gauged against Western World as a whole, Soviets are still by far the weaker force. Thus, their success will really depend on degree of cohesion, firmness and vigor which Western World can muster. And this is factor which it is within our power to influence.

3. Success of Soviet system, as form of internal power, is not yet finally proven. It has yet to be demonstrated that it can survive supreme test of successive transfer of power from one individual or group to another. Lenin's death was first such transfer, and its effects wracked Soviet state for 15 years. After Stalin's death or retirement will be second. But even this will not be final test. Soviet internal system will now be subjected, by virtue of recent territorial expansions, to series of additional strains which once proved severe tax on Tsardom. We here are convinced that never since termination of civil war have mass of Russian people been emotionally farther removed from doctrines of Communist Party than they are today. In Russia, party has now become a great and—for the moment—highly successful apparatus of dictatorial administration, but it has ceased to be a source of emotional inspiration. Thus, internal soundness and permanence of movement need not yet be regarded as assured.

4. All Soviet propaganda beyond Soviet security sphere is basically negative and destructive. It should therefore be relatively easy to combat it by any intelligent and really constructive program.

For these reasons I think we may approach calmly and with good heart problem of how to deal with Russia. As to how this approach should be made, I only wish to advance, by way of conclusion, following comments:

1. Our first step must be to apprehend, and recognize for what it is, the nature of the movement with which we are dealing. We must study it with same courage, detachment, objectivity, and same determination not to be emotionally provoked or unseated by it, with which doctor studies unruly and unreasonable individual.

2. We must see that our public is educated to realities of Russian situation. I cannot over-emphasize importance of this. Press cannot do this alone. It must be done mainly by Government, which is necessarily more experienced and better informed on practical problems involved. In this we need not be deterred by [ugliness?] of picture. I am convinced that there would be far less hysterical anti-Sovietism in our country today if realities of this situation were better understood by our people. There is

nothing as dangerous or as terrifying as the unknown. It may also be argued that to reveal more information on our difficulties with Russia would reflect unfavorably on Russian-American relations. I feel that if there is any real risk here involved, it is one which we should have courage to face, and sooner the better. But I cannot see what we would be risking. Our stake in this country, even coming on heels of tremendous demonstrations of our friendship for Russian people, is remarkably small. We have here no investments to guard, no actual trade to lose, virtually no citizens to protect, few cultural contacts to preserve. Our only stake lies in what we hope rather than what we have; and I am convinced we have better chance of realizing those hopes if our public is enlightened and if our dealings with Russians are placed entirely on realistic and matter-of-fact basis.

3. Much depends on health and vigor of our own society. World communism is like malignant parasite which feeds only on diseased tissue. This is point at which domestic and foreign policies meet. Every courageous and incisive measure to solve internal problems of our own society, to improve self-confidence, discipline, morale and community spirit of our own people, is a diplomatic victory over Moscow worth a thousand diplomatic notes and joint communiques. If we cannot abandon fatalism and indifference in face of deficiencies of our own society, Moscow will profit—Moscow cannot help profiting by them in its foreign policies.

4. We must formulate and put forward for other nations a much more positive and constructive picture of sort of world we would like to see than we have put forward in past. It is not enough to urge people to develop political processes similar to our own. Many foreign peoples, in Europe at least, are tired and frightened by experiences of past, and are less interested in abstract freedom than in security. They are seeking guidance rather than responsibilities. We should be better able than Russians to give them this. And unless we do, Russians certainly will.

5. Finally we must have courage and self-confidence to cling to our own methods and conceptions of human society. After all, the greatest danger that can befall us in coping with this problem of Soviet communism, is that we shall allow ourselves to become like those with whom we are coping.

Winston S. Churchill's "Iron Curtain" Speech, 1946

The United States stands at this time at the pinnacle of world power. It is a solemn moment for the American democracy. With primacy in power is also joined an awe-inspiring accountability to the future. As you look around you, you feel not only the sense of duty done but also feel anxiety lest you fall below the level of achievement. Opportunity is here now, clear and shining, for both our countries. To reject it or ignore it or fritter it away will bring upon us all the long reproaches of the after-time. It is necessary that constancy of mind, persistency of purpose, and the grand simplicity of decision shall guide and rule the conduct of the English-speaking peoples in peace as they did in war. We must and I believe we shall prove ourselves equal to this severe requirement. . . .

Before we cast away the solid assurances of national armaments for self-preservation, we must be certain that our temple is built, not upon shifting sands or quagmires, but upon the rock. Anyone with his eyes open can see that our path will be difficult and also long, but if we persevere together as we did in the two World Wars—though not, alas, in the interval between them—I cannot doubt that we shall achieve our common purpose in the end.

I have, however, a definite and practical proposal to make for action. Courts and magistrates cannot function without sheriffs and constables. The United Nations Organization must immediately begin to be equipped with an international armed force. In such a matter we can only go step by step; but we must begin now. I propose that each of the powers and states should be invited to dedicate a certain number of air squadrons to the service of the world organization. These squadrons would be trained and prepared in their own countries but would move around in rotation from one country to another. They would wear the uniform of their own countries with different badges. They would not be required to act against their own nation but in other respects they would be directed by the world organization. This might be started on a modest scale and a grow [sic] as confidence grew. I wished to see this done after the First World War and trust it may be done forthwith.

It would nevertheless be wrong and imprudent to entrust the secret knowledge or experience of the atomic bomb, which the United States, Great Britain, and Canada now share, to the world organization, while it is still in its infancy. It would be criminal madness to cast it adrift in this still agitated and un-united world. No one in any country has slept less well in their beds because this knowledge and the method and the raw materials to apply it are at present largely retained in American hands. I do not believe we should all have slept so soundly had the positions been reversed and some Communist or neo-Fascist state monopolized, for the time being, these dread agencies. The fear of them alone might easily have been used to enforce totalitarian systems upon the free democratic world, with consequences appalling to human imagination. . . .

There is . . . an important question we must ask ourselves. Would a special relationship between the United States and the British Commonwealth be inconsistent with our overriding loyalties to the world organization? I reply that on the contrary, it is probably the only means by which that organization will achieve its full stature and strength. There are already the special United States relations with Canada and between the United States and the South American republics. We also have our twenty years' treaty of collaboration and mutual assistance with Soviet Russia. I agree with Mr. Bevin that it might well be a fifty-year treaty. We have an alliance with Portugal unbroken since 1384. None of these clash with the general interest of a world agreement. On the contrary they help it. "In my Father's house are many mansions.'' Special associations between members of the United Nations which have no aggressive point against any other country, which harbor no design incompatible with the charter of the United Nations, far from being harmful, are beneficial and, as I believe, indispensable. . . .

A shadow has fallen upon the scenes so lately lighted by the Allied victory. Nobody knows what Soviet Russia and its Communist international organization intends to do in the immediate future, or what are the limits, if any, to their expansive and proselytizing tendencies. I have a strong admiration and regard for the valiant Russian people and for my wartime comrade, Marshal Stalin. There is sympathy and good will in Britain—and I doubt not here also—toward the peoples of all the Russias and a resolve to persevere through many differences and rebuffs in establishing lasting friendships.

We understand the Russian need to be secure on her western frontiers from all renewal of German aggression. We welcome her to her rightful place among the leading nations of the world. Above all, we welcome constant, frequent, and growing contacts between Russian people and our own people on both sides of the Atlantic. It is my duty, however, to place before you certain facts about the present position in Europe.

From Stettin in the Baltic to Trieste in the Adriatic, an iron curtain has descended across the continent. Behind that line lie all the capitals of the ancient states of Central and Eastern Europe. Warsaw, Berlin, Prague, Vienna, Budapest, Belgrade, Bucharest, and Sofia, all these famous cities and the populations around them lie in the Soviet sphere and all are subject, in one form or another, not only to Soviet influence but to a very high and increasing measure of control from Moscow. Athens alone, with its immortal glories, is free to decide its future at an election under British, American, and French observation.

The Russian-dominated Polish government has been encouraged to make enormous and wrongful inroads upon Germany, and mass expulsions of millions of Germans on a scale grievous and undreamed of are now taking place. The Communist parties, which were very small in all these eastern states of Europe, have been raised to preeminence and power far beyond their numbers and are seeking everywhere to obtain totalitarian control. Police governments are prevailing in nearly every case, and so far, except in Czechoslovakia, there is no true democracy.

Turkey and Persia are both profoundly alarmed and disturbed at the claims which are made upon them and at the pressure being exerted by the Moscow government. An attempt is being made by the Russians in Berlin to build up a quasi-Communist party in their zone of occupied Germany by showing special favors to groups of left-wing German leaders. At the end of the fighting last June, the American and British Armies withdrew westward, in accordance with an earlier agreement, to a depth at some points of 150 miles on a front of nearly 400 miles, to allow the Russians to occupy this vast expanse of territory which the Western democracies had conquered.

If now the Soviet government tries, by separate action, to build up a pro-Communist Germany in their areas, this will cause new serious difficulties in the British and American zones, and will give the defeated Germans the power of putting themselves up to auction between the Soviets and the Western democracies. Whatever conclusions may be drawn from these facts—and facts they are—this is certainly not the liberated Europe we fought to build up. Nor is it one which contains the essentials of permanent peace.

In front of the iron curtain which lies across Europe are other causes for anxiety. In Italy the Communist party is seriously hampered by having to support the Communist-trained Marshall Tito's claims to former Italian territory at the head of the Adriatic. Nevertheless, the future of Italy hangs in the balance. Again, one cannot imagine a regenerated Europe without a strong France. . . .

However, in a great number of countries, far from the Russian frontiers and throughout the world, Communist fifth columns are established and work in complete unity and absolute obedience to the directions they receive from the Communist center. Except in the British Commonwealth, and in the United States, where communism is in its infancy, the Communist parties or fifth columns constitute a growing challenge and peril to Christian civilization. These are somber facts for anyone to have to recite on the morrow of a victory gained by so much splendid comradeship in arms and in the cause of freedom and democracy, and we should be most unwise not to face them squarely while time remains.

The outlook is also anxious in the Far East and especially in Manchuria. The agreement which was made at Yalta, to which I was a party, was extremely favorable to Soviet Russia, but it was made at a time when no one could say that the German war might not extend all through the summer and autumn of 1945 and when the Japanese war was expected to last for a further eighteen months from the end of the German war. In this country you are all so well informed about the Far East and such devoted friends of China that I do not need to expatiate on the situation there. . . .

Our difficulties and dangers will not be removed by closing our eyes to them; they will not be removed by mere waiting to see what happens; nor will they be relieved by a policy of appeasement. What is needed is a settlement, and the longer this is delayed, the more difficult it will be and the greater our dangers will become. From what I have seen of our Russian friends and allies during the war, I am convinced that there is nothing they admire so much as strength, and there is nothing for which they have less respect than for military weakness. For that reason the old doctrine of a balance of power is unsound. We cannot afford, if we can help it, to work on narrow margins, offering temptations to a trial of strength. If the Western democracies stand together in strict adherence to the principles of the United Nations Charter, their influence for furthering these principles will be immense and no one is likely to molest them. If, however, they become divided or falter in their duty, and if these all-important years are allowed to slip away, then indeed catastrophe may overwhelm us all.

Last time I saw it all coming, and cried aloud to my own fellow countrymen and to the world, but no one paid any attention. Up till the year 1933 or even 1935, Germany might have been saved from the awful fate which has overtaken her and we might all have been spared the miseries Hitler let loose upon mankind.

There never was a war in all history easier to prevent by timely action than the one which has just desolated such great areas of the globe. It could have been prevented without the firing of a single shot, and Germany might be powerful, prosperous, and honored today, but no one would listen and one by one we were all sucked into the awful whirlpool.

We surely must not let that happen again. This can only be achieved by reaching now, in 1946, a good understanding on all points with Russia under the general authority of the United Nations and by the maintenance of that good understanding through many peaceful years, by the world instrument, supported by the whole strength of the English-speaking world and all its connections.

Henry A. Wallace Questions the "Get Tough" Policy, 1946

How do American actions since V-J Day appear to other nations? I mean by actions the concrete things like $13 billion for the War and Navy Departments, the Bikini tests of the atomic bomb and continued production of bombs, the plan to arm Latin America with our weapons, production of B-29s and planned production of B-36s, and the effort to secure air bases spread over half the globe from which the other half of the globe can be bombed. I cannot but feel that these actions must make it look to the rest of the world as if we were only paying lip service to peace at the conference table. These facts rather make it appear either (1) that we are preparing ourselves to win the war which we regard as inevitable or (2) that we are trying to build up a predominance of force to intimidate the rest of mankind. How would it look to us if Russia had the atomic bomb and we did not, if Russia had ten thousand-mile bombers and air bases within a thousand miles of our coast lines and we did not?

Some of the military men and self-styled "realists" are saying: "What's wrong with trying to build up a predominance of force? The only way to preserve peace is for this country to be so well armed that no one will dare attack us. We know that America will never start a war."

The flaw in this policy is simply that it will not work. In a world of atomic bombs and other revolutionary new weapons, such as radioactive poison gases and biological warfare, a peace maintained by a predominance of force is no longer possible.

Why is this so? The reasons are clear:

First. Atomic warfare is cheap and easy compared with old-fashioned war. Within a very few years several countries can have atomic bombs and

---

Henry A. Wallace, "The Path to Peace with Russia," *New Republic*, 115 (1946), 401–406.

other atomic weapons. Compared with the cost of large armies and the manufacture of old-fashioned weapons, atomic bombs cost very little and require only a relatively small part of a nation's production plant and labor force.

Second. So far as winning a war is concerned, having more bombs— even many more bombs—than the other fellow is no longer a decisive advantage. If another nation had enough bombs to eliminate all of our principal cities and our heavy industry, it wouldn't help us very much if we had ten times as many bombs as we needed to do the same to them.

Third. The most important, the very fact that several nations have atomic bombs will inevitably result in a neurotic, fear-ridden, itching-trigger psychology in all the peoples of the world, and because of our wealth and vulnerability we would be among the most seriously affected. Atomic war will not require vast and time-consuming preparations, the mobilization of large armies, the conversion of a large proportion of a country's industrial plants to the manufacture of weapons. In a world armed with atomic weapons, some incident will lead to the use of those weapons.

There is a school of military thinking which recognizes these facts, recognizes that when several nations have atomic bombs, a war which will destroy modern civilization will result and that no nation or combination of nations can win such a war. This school of thought therefore advocates a "preventative war," an attack on Russia now, before Russia has atomic bombs. This scheme is not only immoral but stupid. If we should attempt to destroy all the principal Russian cities and her heavy industry, we might well succeed. But the immediate countermeasure which such an attack would call forth is the prompt occupation of all continental Europe by the Red Army. Would we be prepared to destroy the cities of all Europe in trying to finish what we had started? This idea is so contrary to all the basic instincts and principles of the American people that any such action would be possible only under a dictatorship at home.

Thus the "predominance of force" idea and the notion of a "defensive attack" are both unworkable. The only solution is the one which you have so wisely advanced and which forms the basis of the Moscow statement on atomic energy. That solution consists of mutual trust and confidence among nations, atomic disarmament and an effective system of enforcing that disarmament.

There is, however, a fatal defect in the Moscow statement, in the Acheson report, and in the American plan recently presented to the United Nations Atomic Energy Commission. That defect is the scheme, as it is generally understood, of arriving at international agreements by "easy stages," of requiring other nations to enter into binding commitments not to conduct research into the military uses of atomic energy and to disclose their uranium and thorium resources while the United States retains the right to withhold its technical knowledge of atomic energy until the international control and inspection system is working to our satisfaction. In other words, we are telling the Russians that if they are "good boys" we may eventually turn over our knowledge of atomic energy to them and to the other nations.

But there is no objective standard of what will qualify them as being "good" nor any specified time for sharing our knowledge.

Is it any wonder that the Russians did not show any great enthusiasm for our plan? Would we have been enthusiastic if the Russians had a monopoly of atomic energy, and offered to share the information with us at some indefinite time in the future at their discretion if we agreed now not to try to make a bomb and give them information on our secret resources of uranium and thorium? I think we should react as the Russians appear to have done. We would have put up counterproposal for the record, but our real effort would go into trying to make a bomb so that our bargaining position would be equalized. . . .

Insistence on our part that the game must be played our way will only lead to a deadlock. The Russians will redouble their efforts to manufacture bombs, and they may also decide to expand their "security zone" in a serious way. Up to now, despite all our outcries against it, their efforts to develop a security zone in Eastern Europe and in the Middle East are small change from the point of view of military power as compared with our air bases in Greenland, Okinawa and many other places thousands of miles from our shores. We may feel very self-righteous if we refuse to budge on our plan and the Russians refuse to accept it, but that means only one thing—the atomic armament race is on in deadly earnest.

I am convinced therefore that if we are to achieve our hopes of negotiating a treaty which will result in effective international atomic disarmament we must abandon the impractical form of the "step-by-step" idea which was presented to the United Nations Atomic Energy Commission. We must be prepared to reach an agreement which will commit us to disclosing information and destroying our bombs at a specific time or on terms of specified actions by other countries, rather than at our unfettered discretion. If we are willing to negotiate on this basis, I believe the Russians will also negotiate seriously with a view to reaching an agreement.

There can be, of course, no absolute assurance the Russians will finally agree to a workable plan if we adopt this view. They may prefer to stall until they also have bombs and can negotiate on a more equal basis, not realizing the danger to themselves as well as the rest of the world in a situation in which several nations have atomic bombs. But we must make the effort to head off the atomic bomb race. We have everything to gain by doing so, and do not give up anything by adopting this policy as the fundamental basis for our negotiation. During the transition period toward full-scale international control we retain our technical know-how, and the only existing production plants for fissionable materials and bombs remain within our borders. . . .

Our basic distrust of the Russians, which has been greatly intensified in recent months by the playing up of conflict in the press, stems from differences in political and economic organizations. For the first time in our history defeatists among us have raised the fear of another system as a successful rival to democracy and free enterprise in other countries and perhaps even our own. I am convinced that we can meet that challenge as we have in the past by demonstrating that economic abundance can be achieved without sacrificing personal, political and religious liberties. We cannot meet it, as Hitler tried to, by an anti-Comintern alliance.

It is perhaps too easy to forget that despite the deep-seated differences in our culture and intensive anti-Russian propaganda of some twenty-five years' standing, the American people reversed their attitudes during the crisis of war. Today, under the pressure of seemingly insoluble international problems and continuing deadlocks, the tide of American public opinion is again turning against Russia. In this reaction lies one of the dangers to which this letter is addressed.

I should list the factors which make for Russian distrust of the United States and of the Western world as follows: The first is Russian history, which we must take into account because it is the setting in which Russians see all actions and policies of the rest of the world. Russian history for over a thousand years has been a succession of attempts, often unsuccessful, to resist invasion and conquest—by the Mongols, the Turks, the Swedes, the Germans and the Poles. The scant thirty years of the existence of the Soviet government has in Russian eyes been a continuation of their historical struggle for national existence. The first four years of the new regime, from 1917 through 1921, were spent in resisting attempts at destruction by the Japanese, British and French, with some American assistance, and by the several White Russian armies encouraged and financed by the Western powers. Then, in 1941, the Soviet state was almost conquered by the Germans after a period during which the Western European powers had apparently acquiesced in the rearming of Germany in the belief that the Nazis would seek to expand eastward rather than westward. The Russians, therefore, obviously see themselves as fighting for their existence in a hostile world.

Second, it follows that to the Russians all of the defense and security measures of the Western powers seem to have an aggressive intent. Our actions to expand our military security system—such steps as extending the Monroe Doctrine to include the arming of the Western Hemisphere nations, our present monopoly of the atomic bomb, our interest in outlying bases and our general support of the British Empire—appear to them as going far beyond the requirements of defense. I think we might feel the same if the United States were the only capitalistic country in the world and the principal socialistic countries were creating a level of armed strength far exceeding anything in their previous history. From the Russian point of view, also, the granting of a loan to Britain and the lack of tangible results on their request to borrow for rehabilitation purposes may be regarded as another evidence of strengthening of an anti-Soviet bloc.

Finally, our resistance to her attempts to obtain warm water ports and her own security system in the form of "friendly" neighboring states seems, from the Russian point of view, to clinch the case. After twenty-five years of isolation and after having achieved the status of a major power, Russia believes that she is entitled to recognition of her new status. Our interest in establishing democracy in Eastern Europe, where democracy by and large has never existed, seems to her an attempt to reestablish the encirclement of unfriendly neighbors which was created after the last war and which might serve as a springboard of still another effort to destroy her.

If this analysis is correct, and there is ample evidence to support it, the action to improve the situation is clearly indicated. The fundamental objective of such action should be to allay any reasonable Russian grounds for fear, suspicions and distrust. We must recognize that the world has changed and that today there can be no "one world" unless the United States and Russia can find some way of living together. For example, most of us are firmly convinced of the soundness of our position when we suggest the internationalization and defortification of the Danube or of the Dardanelles, but we would be horrified and angered by any Russian counterproposal that would involve also the internationalizing and disarming of Suez or Panama. We must recognize that to the Russians these seem to be identical situations.

We should ascertain from a fresh point of view what Russia believes to be essential to her own security as a prerequisite to the writing of the peace and to cooperation in the construction of a world order. We should be prepared to judge her requirements against the background of what we ourselves and the British have insisted upon as essential to our respective security. We should be prepared, even at the expense of risking epithets of appeasement to agree to reasonable Russian guarantees of security. . . .

We should also be prepared to enter into economic discussions without demanding that the Russians agree in advance to discussion of a series of what are to them difficult and somewhat unrelated political and economic concessions. Although this is the field in which my department is most directly concerned, I must say that in my opinion this aspect of the problem is not as critical as some of the others, and certainly is far less important than the question of atomic energy control. But successful negotiation in this field might help considerably to bridge the chasm that separates us. The question of a loan should be approached on economic and commercial grounds and should be dissociated as much as possible from the current misunderstandings which flow from the basic differences between their system and ours. You have already clearly dissociated yourself and the American people from the expressions of anti-Soviet support for the British loan. If we could have followed up your statement on signing the British loan bill with a loan to the USSR on a commercial basis and on similar financial terms, I believe that it would have clearly demonstrated that this country is not attempting to use its economic resources in the game of power politics. In the light of the present Export-Import Bank situation it is now of the greatest importance that we undertake general economic discussions at an early date.

It is of the greatest importance that we should discuss with the Russians in a friendly way their long-range economic problems and the future of our cooperation in matters of trade. The reconstruction program of the USSR and the plans for the full development of the Soviet Union offers tremendous opportunities for American goods and American technicians.

American products, especially machines of all kinds, are well established in the Soviet Union. For example, American equipment, practices and methods are standard in coal mining, iron and steel, oil and nonferrous metals.

Nor would this trade be one-sided. Although the Soviet Union has been an excellent credit risk in the past, eventually the goods and services exported from this country must be paid for by the Russians by exports to us and to other countries. Russian products which are either definitely needed or which are noncompetitive in this country are various nonferrous metal ores, furs, linen products, lumber products, vegetable drugs, paper and pulp and native handicrafts. . . .

Many of the problems relating to the countries bordering on Russia could more readily be solved once an atmosphere of mutual trust and confidence is established and some form of economic arrangements is worked out with Russia. These problems also might be helped by discussions of an economic nature. Russian economic penetration of the Danube area, for example, might be countered by concrete proposals for economic collaboration in the development of the resources of this area, rather than by insisting that the Russians should cease their unilateral penetration and offering no solution to the present economic chaos there.

This proposal admittedly calls for a shift in some of our thinking about international matters. It is imperative that we make this shift. We have little time to lose. Our postwar actions have not yet been adjusted to the lessons to be gained from experience of Allied cooperation during the war and the facts of the atomic age.

It is certainly desirable that, as far as possible, we achieve unity on the home front with respect to our international relations; but unity on the basis of building up conflict abroad would prove to be not only unsound but disastrous. I think there is some reason to fear that in our earnest efforts to achieve bipartisan unity in this country we may have given away too much to isolationism masquerading as tough realism in international affairs.

The Truman Doctrine, 1947

The gravity of the situation which confronts the world today necessitates my appearance before a joint session of the Congress.

The foreign policy and the national security of this country are involved.

One aspect of the present situation, which I present to you at this time for your consideration and decision, concerns Greece and Turkey.

The United States has received from the Greek Government an urgent appeal for financial and economic assistance. Preliminary reports from the American Economic Mission now in Greece and reports from the American Ambassador in Greece corroborate the statement of the Greek Government that assistance is imperative if Greece is to survive as a free nation. . . .

The British Government has informed us that, owing to its own difficulties, it can no longer extend financial or economic aid to Turkey.

As in the case of Greece, if Turkey is to have the assistance it needs, the United States must supply it. We are the only country able to provide that help.

I am fully aware of the broad implications involved if the United States extends assistance to Greece and Turkey, and I shall discuss these implications with you at this time.

One of the primary objectives of the foreign policy of the United States is the creation of conditions in which we and other nations will be able to work out a way of life free from coercion. This was a fundamental issue in the war with Germany and Japan. Our victory was won over countries which sought to impose their will, and their way of life, upon other nations.

To ensure the peaceful development of nations, free from coercion, the United States has taken a leading part in establishing the United Nations. The United Nations is designed to make possible lasting freedom and independence for all its members. We shall not realize our objectives, however, unless we are willing to help free peoples to maintain their free institutions and their national integrity against aggressive movements that seek to impose upon them totalitarian regimes. This is no more than a frank recognition that totalitarian regimes imposed upon free peoples, by direct or indirect aggression, undermine the foundations of international peace and hence the security of the United States.

The peoples of a number of countries of the world have recently had totalitarian regimes forced upon them against their will. The Government of the United States has made frequent protests against coercion and intimidation, in violation of the Yalta agreement, in Poland, Rumania, and Bulgaria. I must also state that in a number of other countries there have been similar developments.

At the present moment in world history nearly every nation must choose between alternative ways of life. The choice is too often not a free one.

One way of life is based upon the will of the majority, and is distinguished by free institutions, representative government, free elections, guarantees of individual liberty, freedom of speech and religion, and freedom from political oppression.

The second way of life is based upon the will of a minority forcibly imposed upon the majority. It relies upon terror and oppression, a controlled press and radio, fixed elections, and the suppression of personal freedoms.

I believe that it must be the policy of the United States to support free peoples who are resisting attempted subjugation by armed minorities or by outside pressures.

I believe that we must assist free peoples to work out their own destinies in their own way.

I believe that our help should be primarily through economic and financial aid which is essential to economic stability and orderly political processes.

The world is not static, and the *status quo* is not sacred. But we cannot allow changes in the *status quo* in violation of the Charter of the United Nations by such methods as coercion, or by such subterfuges as political infiltration. In helping free and independent nations to maintain their freedom, the United States will be giving effect to the principles of the Charter of the United Nations.

It is necessary only to glance at a map to realize that the survival and integrity of the Greek nation are of grave importance in a much wider situation. If Greece should fall under the control of an armed minority, the effect upon its neighbor, Turkey, would be immediate and serious. Confusion and disorder might well spread throughout the entire Middle East.

Moreover, the disappearance of Greece as an independent state would have a profound effect upon those countries in Europe whose peoples are struggling against great difficulties to maintain their freedoms and their independence while they repair the damages of war.

It would be an unspeakable tragedy if these countries, which have struggled so long against overwhelming odds, should lose that victory for which they sacrificed so much. Collapse of free institutions and loss of independence would be disastrous not only for them but for the world. Discouragement and possibly failure would quickly be the lot of neighboring peoples striving to maintain their freedom and independence.

Should we fail to aid Greece and Turkey in this fateful hour, the effect will be far reaching to the West as well as to the East.

We must take immediate and resolute action.

I therefore ask the Congress to provide authority for assistance to Greece and Turkey in the amount of $400,000,000 for the period ending June 30, 1948. In requesting these funds, I have taken into consideration the maximum amount of relief assistance which would be furnished to Greece out of the $350,000,000 which I recently requested that the Congress authorize for the prevention of starvation and suffering in countries devastated by the war.

In addition to funds, I ask the Congress to authorize the detail of American civilian and military personnel to Greece and Turkey, at the request of those countries, to assist in the tasks of reconstruction, and for the purpose of supervising the use of such financial and material assistance as may be furnished. I recommend that authority also be provided for the instruction and training of selected Greek and Turkish personnel.

Finally, I ask that the Congress provide authority which will permit the speediest and most effective use, in terms of needed commodities, supplies, and equipment, of such funds as may be authorized.

If further funds, or further authority, should be needed for the purposes indicated in this message, I shall not hesitate to bring the situation before the Congress. On this subject the Executive and Legislative branches of the Government must work together.

This is a serious course upon which we embark.

I would not recommend it except that the alternative is much more serious. The United States contributed $341,000,000,000 toward winning World War II. This is an investment in world freedom and world peace.

The assistance that I am recommending for Greece and Turkey amounts to little more than 1/10 of 1 percent of this investment. It is only common sense that we should safeguard this investment and make sure that it was not in vain.

The seeds of totalitarian regimes are nurtured by misery and want. They spread and grow in the evil soil of poverty and strife. They reach their full growth when the hope of a people for a better life has died.

We must keep that hope alive.

The free peoples of the world look to us for support in maintaining their freedoms.

If we falter in our leadership, we may endanger the peace of the world— and we shall surely endanger the welfare of this Nation.

Great responsibilities have been placed upon us by the swift movement of events.

I am confident that the Congress will face these responsibilities squarely.

The Marshall Plan (Economic Cooperation Act of 1948)

Recognizing the intimate economic and other relationships between the United States and the nations of Europe, and recognizing that disruption following in the wake of war is not contained by national frontiers, the Congress finds that the existing situation in Europe endangers the establishment of a lasting peace, the general welfare and national interest of the United States, and the attainment of the objectives of the United Nations. The restoration or maintenance in European countries of principles of individual liberty, free institutions, and genuine independence rests largely upon the establishment of sound economic conditions, stable international economic relationships, and the achievement by the countries of Europe of a healthy economy independent of extraordinary outside assistance. The accomplishment of these objectives calls for a plan of European recovery, open to all such nations which cooperate in such plan, based upon a strong production effort, the expansion of foreign trade, the creation and maintenance of internal financial stability, and the development of economic cooperation, including all possible steps to establish and maintain equitable rates of exchange and to bring about the progressive elimination of trade barriers. Mindful of the advantages which the United States has enjoyed through the existence of a large domestic market with no internal trade barriers, and believing that similar advantages can accrue to the countries of Europe, it is declared to be the policy of the people of the United States to encourage these countries through a joint organization to exert sustained common efforts as set forth in the report of the Committee of European Economic Cooperation signed at Paris on September 22, 1947, which will speedily achieve that economic cooperation in Europe which is essential for lasting peace and prosperity. It is further declared to be the policy of the people of the United States to sustain and strengthen principles of individual liberty, free institutions, and genuine independence in Europe through assistance to those countries of Europe which participate in a joint recovery program based upon self-help and mutual cooperation: *Provided*, That no assistance to the participating countries herein contemplated shall seriously impair the economic stability of the United States. It is further declared to be the policy of the United States that continuity of assistance provided by the United States should, at all times, be dependent upon continuity of cooperation among countries participating in the program.

National Security Council
Paper No. 68 (NSC-68), 1950

Within the past thirty-five years the world has experienced two global wars of tremendous violence. It has witnessed two revolutions—the Russian and the Chinese—of extreme scope and intensity. It has also seen the collapse of five empires—the Ottoman, the Austro-Hungarian, German, Italian and Japanese—and the drastic decline of two major imperial systems, the British and the French. During the span of one generation, the international distribution of power has been fundamentally altered. For several centuries it had proved impossible for any one nation to gain such preponderant strength that a coalition of other nations could not in time face it with greater strength. The international scene was marked by recurring periods of violence and war, but a system of sovereign and independent states was maintained, over which no state was able to achieve hegemony.

Two complex sets of factors have now basically altered this historical distribution of power. First, the defeat of Germany and Japan and the decline of the British and French Empires have interacted with the development of the United States and the Soviet Union in such a way that power has increasingly gravitated to these two centers. Second, the Soviet Union, unlike previous aspirants to hegemony, is animated by a new fanatic faith, antithetical to our own, and seeks to impose its absolute authority over the rest of the world. Conflict has, therefore, become endemic and is waged, on the part of the Soviet Union, by violent or non-violent methods in accordance with the dictates of expediency. With the development of increasingly terrifying weapons of mass destruction, every individual faces the ever-present possibility of annihilation should the conflict enter the phase of total war.

On the one hand, the people of the world yearn for relief from the anxiety arising from the risk of atomic war. On the other hand, any substantial further extension of the area under the domination of the Kremlin would raise the possibility that no coalition adequate to confront the Kremlin with greater strength could be assembled. It is in this context that this Republic and its citizens in the ascendancy of their strength stand in their deepest peril.

The issues that face us are momentous, involving the fulfillment or destruction not only of this Republic but of civilization itself. They are issues which will not await our deliberations. With conscience and resolution this Government and the people it represents must now take new and fateful decisions. . . .

Our overall policy at the present time may be described as one designed to foster a world environment in which the American system can survive and flourish. It therefore rejects the concept of isolation and affirms the necessity of our positive participation in the world community.

This broad intention embraces two subsidiary policies. One is a policy which we would probably pursue even if there were no Soviet threat. It is a policy of attempting to develop a healthy international community. The other is the policy of "containing" the Soviet system. These two policies are closely interrelated and interact on one another. Nevertheless, the distinction between them is basically valid and contributes to a clearer understanding of what we are trying to do.

The policy of striving to develop a healthy international community is the long-term constructive effort which we are engaged in. It was this policy which gave rise to our vigorous sponsorship of the United Nations. It is of course the principal reason for our long continuing endeavors to create and now develop the Inter-American system. It, as much as containment, underlay our efforts to rehabilitate Western Europe. Most of our international economic activities can likewise be explained in terms of this policy.

In a world of polarized power, the policies designed to develop a healthy international community are more than ever necessary to our own strength.

As for the policy of "containment," it is one which seeks by all means short of war to (1) block further expansion of Soviet power, (2) expose the falsities of Soviet pretentions, (3) induce a retraction of the Kremlin's control and influence and (4) in general, so foster the seeds of destruction within the Soviet system that the Kremlin is brought at least to the point of modifying its behavior to conform to generally accepted international standards.

It was and continues to be cardinal in this policy that we possess superior overall power in ourselves or in dependable combination with other like-minded nations. One of the most important ingredients of power is military strength. In the concept of "containment," the maintenance of a strong military posture is deemed to be essential for two reasons: (1) as an ultimate guarantee of our national security and (2) as an indispensable backdrop to the conduct of the policy of "containment." Without superior aggregate military strength, in being and readily mobilizable, a policy of "containment"—which is in effect a policy of calculated and gradual coercion—is no more than a policy of bluff.

At the same time, it is essential to the successful conduct of a policy of "containment" that we always leave open the possibility of negotiation with the U.S.S.R. A diplomatic freeze—and we are in one now—tends to defeat the very purposes of "containment" because it raises tensions at the same time that it makes Soviet retractions and adjustments in the direction of moderated behavior more difficult. It also tends to inhibit our initiative and deprives us of opportunities for maintaining a moral ascendancy in our struggle with the Soviet system.

In "containment" it is desirable to exert pressure in a fashion which will avoid so far as possible directly challenging Soviet prestige, to keep open the possibility for the U.S.S.R. to retreat before pressure with a minimum loss of face and to secure political advantage from the failure of the Kremlin to yield or take advantage of the openings we leave it.

We have failed to implement adequately these two fundamental aspects of "containment." In the face of obviously mounting Soviet military strength ours has declined relatively. Partly as a byproduct of this, but also for other reasons, we now find ourselves at a diplomatic impasse with the Soviet Union, with the Kremlin growing bolder, with both of us holding on grimly to what we have and with ourselves facing difficult decisions. . . .

It is apparent from the preceding sections that the integrity and vitality of our system is in greater jeopardy than ever before in our history. Even if there were no Soviet Union we would face the great problem of the free society, accentuated many fold in this industrial age, of reconciling order, security, the need for participation, with the requirements of freedom. . . .

It is quite clear from Soviet theory and practice that the Kremlin seeks to bring the free world under its dominion by the methods of the cold war. The preferred technique is to subvert by infiltration and intimidation. Every institution of our society is an instrument which it is sought to stultify and turn against our purposes. Those that touch most closely our material and moral strength are obviously the prime targets, labor unions, civic enterprises, schools, churches, and all media for influencing opinion. The effort is not so much to make them serve obvious Soviet ends as to prevent them from serving our ends, and thus to make them sources of confusion in our economy, our culture and our body politic. The doubts and diversities that in terms of our values are part of the merit of a free system, the weaknesses and the problems that are peculiar to it, the rights and privileges that free men enjoy, and the disorganization and destruction left in the wake of the last attack on our freedoms, all are but opportunities for the Kremlin to do its evil work. Every advantage is taken of the fact that our means of prevention and retaliation are limited by those principles and scruples which are precisely the ones that give our freedom and democracy its meaning for us. None of our scruples deter those whose only code is, "morality is that which serves the revolution."

Since everything that gives us or others respect for our institutions is a suitable object for attack, it also fits the Kremlin's design that where, with impunity, we can be insulted and made to suffer indignity the opportunity shall not be missed, particularly in any context which can be used to cast dishonor on our country, our system, our motives, or our methods. Thus the means by which we sought to restore our own economic health in the '30's, and now seek to restore that of the free world, come equally under attack. The military aid by which we sought to help the free world was frantically denounced by the Communists in the early days of the last war, and of course our present efforts to develop adequate military strength for ourselves and our allies are equally denounced.

At the same time the Soviet Union is seeking to create overwhelming military force, in order to back up infiltration with intimidation. In the only terms in which it understands strength, it is seeking to demonstrate to the free world that force and the will to use it are on the side of the Kremlin, that those who lack it are decadent and doomed. In local incidents it threatens and encroaches both for the sake of local gains and to increase anxiety and defeatism in all the free world.

The possession of atomic weapons at each of the opposite poles of power, and the inability (for different reasons) of either side to place any trust in the other, puts a premium on a surprise attack against us. It equally puts a premium on a more violent and ruthless prosecution of its design by cold war, especially if the Kremlin is sufficiently objective to realize the improbability of our prosecuting a preventive war. It also puts a premium on piecemeal aggression against others, counting on our unwillingness to engage in atomic war unless we are directly attacked. We run all these risks and the added risk of being confused and immobilized by our inability to weigh and choose, and pursue a firm course based on a rational assessment of each.

The risk that we may thereby be prevented or too long delayed in taking all needful measures to maintain the integrity and vitality of our system is great. The risk that our allies will lose their determination is greater. And the risk that in this manner a descending spiral of too little and too late, of doubt and recrimination, may present us with ever narrower and more desperate alternatives, is the greatest risk of all. For example, it is clear that our present weakness would prevent us from offering effective resistance at any of several vital pressure points. The only deterrent we can present to the Kremlin is the evidence we give that we may make any of the critical points which we cannot hold the occasion for a global war of annihilation.

The risk of having no better choice than to capitulate or precipitate a global war at any of a number of pressure points is bad enough in itself, but it is multiplied by the weakness it imparts to our position in the cold war. Instead of appearing strong and resolute we are continually at the verge of appearing and being alternately irresolute and desperate; yet it is the cold war which we must win, because both the Kremlin design, and our fundamental purpose give it the first priority. . . .

A more rapid build-up of political, economic, and military strength and thereby of confidence in the free world than is now contemplated is the only course which is consistent with progress toward achieving our fundamental purpose. The frustration of the Kremlin design requires the free world to develop a successfully functioning political and economic system and a vigorous political offensive against the Soviet Union. These, in turn, require an adequate military shield under which they can develop. It is necessary to have the military power to deter, if possible, Soviet expansion, and to defeat, if necessary, aggressive Soviet or Soviet-directed actions of a limited or total character. The potential strength of the free world is great; its ability to develop these military capabilities and its will to resist Soviet expansion will be determined by the wisdom and will with which it undertakes to meet its political and economic problems. . . .

Our position as the center of power in the free world places a heavy responsibility upon the United States for leadership. We must organize and enlist the energies and resources of the free world in a positive program for peace which will frustrate the Kremlin design for world domination by creating a situation in the free world to which the Kremlin will be compelled to adjust. Without such a cooperative effort, led by the United States, we will have to make gradual withdrawals under pressure until we discover one day that we have sacrificed positions of vital interest.

It is imperative that this trend be reversed by a much more rapid and concerted build-up of the actual strength of both the United States and the other nations of the free world. The analysis shows that this will be costly and will involve significant domestic financial and economic adjustments. . . .

In summary, we must, by means of a rapid and sustained build-up of the political, economic, and military strength of the free world, and by means of an affirmative program intended to wrest the initiative from the Soviet Union, confront it with convincing evidence of the determination and ability of the free world to frustrate the Kremlin to the new situation. Failing that, the unwillingness of the determination and ability of the free world to frustrate the Kremlin design of a world dominated by its will. Such evidence is the only means short of war which eventually may force the Kremlin to abandon its present course of action and to negotiate acceptable agreements on issues of major importance.

The whole success of the proposed program hangs ultimately on recognition by this Government, the American people, and all free peoples, that the cold war is in fact a real war in which the survival of the free world is at stake. Essential prerequisites to success are consultations with Congressional leaders designed to make the program the object of non-partisan legislative support, and a presentation to the public of a full explanation of the facts and implications of the present international situation. The prosecution of the program will require of us all the ingenuity, sacrifice, and unity demanded by the vital importance of the issue and the tenacity to persevere until our national objectives have been attained.

✖ *E S S A Y S*

In the first essay, Barton J. Bernstein of Stanford University analyzes the thinking of officials in the Roosevelt and Truman administrations about the atomic bomb—its place as both a weapon in the war against the Axis and a diplomatic lever in the postwar peace. He agrees with most other historians that Truman ordered the use of the atomic bomb against civilians in Japan to end the war quickly and save American lives. But Bernstein also explores the bomb as a diplomatic "bonus" American leaders believed would give them advantages in bargaining with the Soviets in the future—in the Cold War. The second essay, by John Lewis Gaddis of Ohio University, points to Soviet unilateral behavior as the major cause of the Cold War. Gaddis depicts the United States as largely defensive and reactive, President Harry S Truman as a cautious leader, negative American views of Soviet intentions as reasonable, and the containment doctrine as realistic. Thomas G. Paterson of the University of Connecticut interprets the origins of the Cold War differently. He posits that the United States did not simply react to Soviet behavior, though he agrees that such behavior was often reprehensible. Rather, Truman was ill prepared and combative as a foreign policy leader in the early Cold War. Indeed, the President, moreover, understood the advantages of America's substantial postwar power in the unstable international system and pursued an activist, global foreign policy to expand American influence and interests. According to Paterson, Americans exaggerated the Soviet threat and then launched a simplistic containment doctrine.

The Atomic Bomb and Diplomacy

BARTON J. BERNSTEIN

Ever since the publication in 1965 of Gar Alperovitz's *Atomic Diplomacy*, scholars and laymen have developed a new interest in the relationship of the atomic bomb to wartime and postwar diplomacy and to the origins of the Cold War. This bold book revived and sometimes recast old themes and thereby sparked renewed interest in questions that once seemed settled: Why was the atomic bomb dropped on Japan? Why weren't other alternatives vigorously pursued? How did the bomb influence American policy before and after Hiroshima? Did the dropping of the bomb and postwar American atomic policies contribute to the cold war?

Unfortunately many studies of these questions have focused exclusively on the Truman period and thereby neglected the Roosevelt administration, which bequeathed to Truman a legacy of assumptions, options, and fears. Acting on the assumption that the bomb was a legitimate weapon, Roosevelt initially defined the relationship of American diplomacy and the atomic bomb. He decided to build the bomb, to establish a partnership on atomic energy with Britain, to bar the Soviet Union from knowledge of the project, and to block any effort at international control of atomic energy. These policies constituted Truman's inheritance—one he neither wished to abandon nor could easily escape. He was restricted politically, psychologically, and institutionally from critically reassessing this legacy.

Like Roosevelt, Truman assumed that the bomb was a legitimate weapon and also understood that it could serve as a bargaining lever, a military counterweight, a threat, or a combat weapon in dealing with the Soviet Union in the postwar world. In addition to speeding the end of the war, the combat use of the bomb, the Truman administration understood, offered the United States great advantages in the postwar world. Policy makers assumed that use of the bomb would help shape the world in a desirable mold: The bomb would impress the Soviets and make them more tractable. Contrary to some contentions, this consideration about the postwar world was not the controlling reason why the United States used the bomb. Rather, it was an additional reason reinforcing an earlier analysis. Ending the war speedily was the primary purpose; impressing the Soviet Union was secondary. This secondary aim did constitute a subtle deterrent to

From "Roosevelt, Truman and the Atomic Bomb, 1941–1945: A Reinterpretation." Reprinted with permission from the *Political Science Quarterly*, 90 (Spring 1975), 23–24, 30–32, 34–62.

reconsidering combat use of the bomb and to searching for alternative means of ending the war. Had the use of the bomb threatened to impair, rather than advance, American aims for the postwar peace, policy makers would have been likely to reassess their assumptions and perhaps to choose other alternatives. . . .

Running through the tangled skein of America's wartime policy on atomic energy is the persistent evidence of concern about the Soviet Union. Roosevelt knew that the Soviets were gathering information about the bomb project, and on September 9, 1943, Henry L. Stimson, the secretary of war, informed the president that spies "are already getting information about vital secrets and sending them to Russia." In late December 1944, at two sessions, they again discussed these issues. On December 31, Roosevelt told Stimson that he, too, was worried about how much the Soviets might know about the project, and they briefly discussed trading information for substantial Soviet concessions. As Stimson later summarized the conversation in his diary:

> I told him . . . that I knew they [Russia] were spying on our work but that they had not yet gotten any real knowledge of it and that, while I was troubled by the possible effect of keeping from them even now that work, I believed that it was essential not to take them into our confidence until we were sure to get a real quid pro quo from our frankness. I said I had no illusions as to the possibility of keeping permanently such a secret but that I did think that it was not yet time to share it with Russia. He said he thought he agreed with me.

They did not discuss the specific nature of the concessions, and perhaps Stimson and the president would not have agreed on how to use the bomb as a bargaining lever and what to demand from the Soviet Union. Whatever their unexplored differences on these issues, they did agree to continue for a period the same policy: exclusion of the Soviets. "It was quite clear," recorded General Leslie Groves, commanding general of the Manhattan Project, "that no one present was interested in bringing Russia into the picture, at least at this time." It is less clear why Roosevelt and Stimson, faced with the realization that the Soviet Union knew about the American research, still did not want formally to notify the Soviets about the bomb project. There is no direct evidence on this subject, but probably they feared that formal disclosure would lead to explicit Soviet inquiries and then to demands for participation that American leaders were not prepared to handle. As long as the United States technically kept the project secret, the Soviets could never raise issues about the bomb without admitting their espionage.

On March 15, 1945, at their last meeting together, Stimson and Roosevelt again discussed atomic energy. Roosevelt acknowledged that he would have to choose between (1) continuing the policy of secrecy and the Anglo-American partnership that barred the Soviets or (2) moving to international control with a sharing of information. Under Roosevelt, there was no further resolution of these issues. When he died in April, American policy had not advanced beyond the point where it had been in December.

Had Roosevelt lived, perhaps he would ultimately have reversed the policy of secrecy and decided to move toward international control in return for a *quid pro quo*—perhaps on Eastern Europe which he had "ceded" at Yalta to the Soviet Union. Any consideration of what 'might have happened" is, of course, a matter of speculation, since the evidence is skimpy and oblique on what Roosevelt might have done. What is clear is that he had maintained the strategy of excluding the Soviets from knowledge of the bomb and of reserving the options of using it in the future as a bargaining lever, threat, military counterweight, or even a weapon against the Soviets.

It was not that he lacked opportunities to reverse his policy. He did not want to change policy—at least not up to April. At Yalta, in February, for example, Roosevelt might have approached Stalin on the bomb, but the president neither discussed this subject nor the loan that the Soviets wanted, and thereby he simply kept open the options for the future of using economic leverage and the bomb to secure concessions. His position, then, made possible the future strategy of "atomic diplomacy"—of using the bomb as an implied or explicit threat to influence negotiations and to compel concessions from the Soviets. Would he have practiced "atomic diplomacy"? Probably. But that answer is speculative and rests principally upon the theory that he would not have wasted the options he was jealously guarding.

Roosevelt and his advisers had more clearly defined another issue: the combat use of the bomb. From the inception of the project, when it was directed primarily against Germany, they usually assumed, and most policy makers never questioned, that the bomb was a legitimate weapon to be used in combat. This assumption was phrased as policy on a number of occasions. In October 1942, for example, Stimson had directed Groves that the mission is "to produce [the bomb] at the earliest possible date so as to bring the war to a conclusion." Any time "that a single day could be saved," the general should save that day. In 1944, policy makers were also talking comfortably about "*after* S-1 [the bomb] is used." "At no time," Stimson later wrote,"did I ever hear it suggested by the President, or by any other responsible member of the government, that atomic energy should not be used in war.". . .

When Harry S Truman became president on April 12, 1945, he was only dimly aware of the existence of the Manhattan Project and unaware that it was an atomic-bomb project. Left uninformed of foreign affairs and generally ignored by Roosevelt in the three months since the inaugural, the new president inherited a set of policies and a group of advisers from his predecessor. While Truman was legally free to reverse Roosevelt's foreign policies and to choose new advisers on foreign policy, in fact he was quite restricted for personal and political reasons. Because Truman was following a very prestigious president whom he, like a great many Americans, loved and admired, the new president was not free psychologically or politically to strike out on a clearly new course. Only a bolder man, with more self-confidence, might have tried critically to assess the legacy and to act independently. But Truman lacked the confidence and the incentive. When, in fact, he did modify policy—for example, on Eastern Europe—he still believed sincerely, as some advisers told him, that he was adhering to his predecessor's agreements and wishes. When seeking counsel on foreign affairs, he usually did not choose new advisers but simply drew more heavily upon those members of Roosevelt's staff who were more anti-Soviet and relied less upon those who were more friendly to the Soviet Union. Even in this strategy, he believed that he was adhering to the policies of his predecessor, who, in his last weeks, Truman stressed, had become more suspicious of Stalin, more distressed by Soviet action in Eastern Europe, and more committed to resisting Soviet encroachments.

In the case of the international-diplomatic policy on the bomb, Truman was even more restricted by Roosevelt's decisions, for the new president inherited a set of reasonably clear wartime policies. Because Roosevelt had already decided to exclude the Soviets from a partnership on the bomb, his successor could not *comfortably* reverse this policy during the war— unless the late president's advisers pleaded for such a reversal or claimed that he had been about to change his policy. They did neither. Consider, then, the massive personal and political deterrents that blocked Truman from even reassessing this legacy. What price might he have paid at home if Americans learned later that he had reversed Roosevelt's policy and had launched a bold new departure of sharing with the Soviets a great weapon that cost the United States $2 billion? Truman, in fact, was careful to follow Roosevelt's strategy of concealing from Congress even the dimensions of the secret partnership on atomic energy with Britain.

Truman, depending as he did upon Roosevelt's advisers, could not easily reassess the prevailing assumption that the bomb was a legitimate weapon to be used in combat against Japan. Truman lacked the will and the incentive to reexamine this assumption, and his dependence upon Roosevelt's advisers and the momentum of the project confirmed this tendency. Only one close adviser, Admiral William Leahy, may have later challenged the use of the bomb, but he was an old "war horse," an expert on explosives of another era, who had often proclaimed that the bomb would not work, that the scientists were duping the administration, and that they were squandering $2 billion. His counsel could not outweigh the continuing legacy of assumptions and commitments, of advisers and advice, that Truman had inherited from Roosevelt. It was a subtle legacy, one that infiltrated decisions and shaped actions, so that Truman accepted it as part of his unquestioned inheritance. For Truman, the question would never be how openly to challenge this legacy, only how to fulfill it, how to remain true to it.

During his first weeks in office, Truman learned about the project from Stimson and from James F. Byrnes, Roosevelt's former director of the Office of War Mobilization and Reconversion who was to become Truman's secretary of state. Byrnes, despite his recent suspicions that the project might be a scientific boondoggle, told Truman, in the president's words, that "the bomb might well put us in a position to dictate our own terms at the end of the war." On April 25, Stimson discussed issues about the bomb more fully with Truman, especially the "political aspects of the S-1 [atomic bomb's] performance." The bomb, the secretary of war explained in a substantial memorandum, would probably be ready in four months and "would be the most terrible weapon ever known in human history [for it] . . . could destroy a whole city." In the future, he warned, other nations would be able to make atomic bombs, thereby endangering the peace and threatening the world. The bomb could be either a threat to or a guarantor of peace. "[I]n the light of our present position with reference to this weapon, the question of sharing it with other nations and, if so shared, upon what terms, becomes a primary question of our foreign relations," Stimson lectured the president. If "the problem of the proper use of this weapon can be solved, we would have the opportunity to bring the world into a pattern in which the peace of the world and our civilization can be saved."

The entire discussion, judging from Stimson's daily record and Groves's memorandum, assumed that the bomb was a legitimate weapon and that it would be used against Japan. The questions they discussed were not *whether* to use the bomb, but its relationship to the Soviet Union and the need to establish postwar atomic policies. Neither Stimson nor Truman sought then to resolve these outstanding issues, and Truman agreed to his secretary's proposal for the establishment of a high-level committee to recommend "action to the executive and legislative branches of our government when secrecy is no longer in full effect." At no time did they conclude that the committee would also consider the issue of whether to use the bomb as a combat weapon. For policy makers, that was not a question; it was an operating assumption.

Nor did Stimson, in his own charge to the Interim Committee, ever *raise* this issue. Throughout the committee's meetings, as various members later noted, all operated on the assumption that the bomb would be used against Japan. They talked, for example, about drafting public statements that would be issued after the bomb's use. They did not discuss *whether* but how to use it. Only one member ultimately endorsed an explicit advance warning to Japan, and none was prepared to suggest that the administration should take any serious risks to avoid using the bomb. At lunch between the two formal meetings on May 31, some members, perhaps only at one table, briefly discussed the possibility of a noncombat demonstration as a warning to Japan but rejected the tactic on the grounds that the bomb might not explode and the failure might stiffen Japanese resistance, or that Japan might move prisoners of war to the target area.

What impact would the bomb have on Japan? At the May 31 meeting, the Interim Committee, joined by its four-member scientific advisory panel discussed this question. Some felt, according to the minutes, that "an atomic bomb on an arsenal would not be much different in effect" from present bombing attacks. J. Robert Oppenheimer, the eminent physicist and member of the scientific panel, expecting that the bomb would have an explosive force of between 2,000 and 20,000 tons of TNT, stressed its visual effects ("a brilliant luminescence which would run to a height of

10,000 to 20,000 feet'') and its deadly power (''dangerous to life for a radius of at least two-thirds of a mile''). Oppenheimer's predictions did not answer the question. There were too many unknowns—about the bomb and Japan. According to the official minutes, Stimson concluded, with unanimous support: ''that we could not concentrate on a civilian area; but we should seek to make a profound psychological impression on as many of the inhabitants as possible.'' At Conant's suggestion, ''the Secretary agreed that the most desirable target would be a vital war plant employing a large number of workers and closely surrounded by workers' houses.'' (''I felt,'' Stimson later explained, ''that to extract a genuine surrender from the Emperor and his military advisers, they must be administered a tremendous shock . . . proof of our power to destroy the empire.'') The Interim Committee ruled out the strategy of several atomic strikes at one time, for, according to Groves, the United States would lose the benefit of additional knowledge from each successive bombing, would have to rush in assembling bombs and court error, and also would risk the possibility that multiple nuclear attacks ''would not be sufficiently distinct from our regular Air Force bombing program.''

Two weeks later, after the Franck Committee recommended a noncombat demonstration, Stimson's assistant submitted this proposal to the four-member scientific advisory panel for advice. The panel promptly rejected the Franck Committee proposal: ''we can propose no technical demonstration likely to bring an end to the war; we see no acceptable alternative to direct military use.'' Had the four scientists known that an invasion was not scheduled until November, or had they even offered their judgment after the unexpectedly impressive Alamogordo test on July 16, perhaps they would have given different counsel. But in June, they were not sure that the bomb explosion would be so dramatic, and, like many others in government, they were wary of pushing for a change in tactics if they might be held responsible for the failure of those tactics—especially if that failure could mean the loss of American lives.

A few days after the panel's report, the issue of giving Japan an advance warning about the bomb was raised at a White House meeting with the president, the military chiefs, and the civilian secretaries. On June 18, after they agreed upon a two-stage invasion of Japan, beginning on about November 1, Assistant Secretary of War John J. McCloy became clearly troubled by the omission of the bomb from the discussion and planning. When Truman invited him to speak, the assistant secretary argued that the bomb would make the invasion unnecessary. Why not warn the emperor that the United States had the bomb and would use it unless Japan surrendered? ''McCloy's suggestion had appeal,'' the official history of the AEC later recorded, ''but a strong objection developed'' to warning Japan in advance, ''which no one could refute—there was no assurance the bomb would work.'' Presumably, like the Interim Committee, they too feared that a warning, followed by a ''dud,'' might stiffen Japan's morale. There was no reason, policy makers concluded, to take this risk.

Though the Interim Committee and high administration officials found no reason not to use the bomb against Japan, many were concerned about the bomb's impact, and its later value, in Soviet-American relations. "[I]t was already apparent," Stimson later wrote, "that the critical questions in American policy toward atomic energy would be directly connected with Soviet Russia." At a few meetings of the Interim Committee, for example, members discussed informing the Soviets of the bomb before its use against Japan. When the issue first arose, Bush and Conant estimated that the Soviet Union could develop the bomb in about four years and argued for informing the Soviets before combat use as a preliminary to moving toward international control and thereby avoiding a postwar nuclear arms race. Conant and Bush had been promoting this strategy since the preceding September. Even though Roosevelt had cast them to the side in 1943, when he cemented the Anglo-American alliance, the two scientist-administrators had not abandoned hope for their notions. They even circulated to the Interim Committee one of their memoranda on the subject. But at the meetings of May 18 and 31 they again met defeat. General Groves, assuming that America was for more advanced technologically and scientifically and also that the Soviet Union lacked uranium, argued that the Soviets could not build a bomb for about twenty years. He contributed to the appealing "myth" of the atomic secret—that there was a secret and it would long remain America's monopoly. James Byrnes, with special authority as secretary of state-designate and Truman's representative on the committee, accepted Groves's analysis and argued for maintaining the policy of secrecy—which the committee endorsed. Byrnes was apparently very pleased, and Stimson agreed, as he told Truman on June 6, "There should be no revelation to Russia or anyone else of our work on S-1 [the atomic bomb] until the first bomb has been laid successfully on Japan."

At a later meeting on June 21, the Interim Committee, including Byrnes, reversed itself. Yielding to the pleas of Bush and Conant, who were strengthened by the scientific panel's recommendations, the Interim Committee advised Truman to inform the Soviets about the bomb before using it in combat. Like the Franck Committee, the Interim Committee concluded (as the minutes record):

> In the hope of securing effective future control and in view of the fact that general information concerning the project would be made public shortly after the [Potsdam] conference, the Committee *agreed* that there would be considerable advantage, if suitable opportunity arose, in having the President advise the Russians that we were working on this weapon with every prospect of success and that we expected to use it against Japan.
>
> The President might say further that he hoped this matter might be discussed some time in the future in terms of insuring that the weapon would become an aid to peace.

Because of this recommendation, and perhaps also because of the continuing prodding of Bush and Conant, Stimson reversed his own position. He concluded that if the United States dropped the bomb on Japan without first informing the Soviet Union, that act might gravely strain Soviet-American relations. Explaining the committee's position to Truman, Stimson proposed that if the President "thought that Stalin was on good terms with him" at the forthcoming Potsdam conference, he would inform Stalin that the United States had developed the bomb, planned to use it against Japan, knew the Soviets were working on the bomb, and looked forward to discussing international control later. This approach left open the option of "atomic diplomacy."

The issues of the bomb and the Soviet Union had already intruded in other ways upon policy and planning. Awaiting the bomb, Truman had postponed the Potsdam conference, delayed negotiations with Russia, and hoped that atomic energy would pry some concessions from Russia. Truman explained in late May to Joseph Davies, an advocate of Soviet-American friendship, and in early June to Stimson that he was delaying the forthcoming Potsdam conference until the Alamogordo test, when he would know whether the United States had a workable atomic bomb—what Stimson repeatedly called the "mastercard." Truman also told some associates that he was delaying because he wanted to work out budget matters, but it is unlikely that the budget was the controlling reason. Certainly, there was no reason that he should have told Davies, who, unlike Stimson, was not counseling delay of the conference, that he was waiting for the bomb. Stimson's counsel of caution, offered on May 15, had apparently triumphed: it would be "a terrible thing to gamble with such high stakes in diplomacy without having your master card in your hand. . . . Over [the] tangled wave of problems the S-1 secret would be dominant." This was not the counsel for a "delayed showdown," as some have wrongly argued, but for no showdown and for delaying some negotiations until the bomb test so that policy makers could determine whether they would have to make concessions to the Soviet Union.

For the administration, the atomic bomb, if it worked, had great potential value. It could reduce the importance of early Soviet entry into the war and make American concessions unnecessary. It could also be a lever for extracting concessions from the Soviet Union. On June 6, for example, Stimson discussed with Truman "quid pro quos which should be established for our taking them [Russia] into [a nuclear] partnership. He [Truman] said that he had been thinking of the same things that I was thinking of, namely the settlement of the Polish, Rumanian, Yugoslavian, and Manchurian problems." There is no evidence that they were planning explicitly to threaten the Soviets to gain these concessions, but, obviously, they realized that the Soviets would regard an American nuclear monopoly as threatening and would yield on some issues in order to terminate that monopoly and thereby reduce, or eliminate, the threat. Neither Stimson nor Truman discussed brandishing the bomb or using it explicitly as a threat to compel concessions. "Atomic diplomacy," as a conception, advanced no further than the notion of possibly trading in the future an atomic partnership, which was still undefined, for Soviet concessions.

For policy makers, the atomic weapons scheduled for combat use against Japan were intimately connected with the problem of Russia. In recent years some historians have focused on this relationship and raised troubling questions: Did the bomb, for policy makers, constitute an alternative to Soviet intervention in the Pacific war? Did they delay or even try to prevent Soviet entry because the bomb made it unnecessary? If so, did they do this in order to use the bomb? Was the bomb dropped on Japan primarily to influence Russia? Did the bomb influence American policy at Potsdam?

At Yalta, Roosevelt had granted the Soviet Union concessions in China in order to secure Soviet entry into the Pacific war, which Stalin promised, within two to three months after V-E Day (May 8). Stalin made it clear that Soviet entry would await a Sino-Soviet pact ratifying these concessions. At the time of Yalta, American military planners were counting on a Soviet attack in Manchuria to pin down the Kwantung army there and hence stop Japan from shifting these forces to her homeland to meet an American invasion.

But by April, war conditions changed and military planners revised their analysis: Japan no longer controlled the seas and therefore could not shift her army, so Soviet entry was not essential. In May, the State Department asked Stimson whether Soviet participation "at the earliest possible moment" was so necessary that the United States should abide by the Far East section of the Yalta agreement. Stimson concluded that the Soviets would enter the war for their own reasons, at their schedule, and with little regard to any American action, that the Yalta concessions would be largely within the grasp of Soviet military power, and that Soviet assistance would be useful, but not essential, if an American invasion was necessary. If there is an invasion, "Russian entry," he wrote, "will have a profound military effect in that almost certainly it will materially shorten the war and thus save American lives." But if the bomb worked, he implied in other discussions, then an invasion would probably not be necessary and Soviet help would be less important. As a result, he urged a delay in settling matters with Russia on the Far East until after the Alamogordo test, and the President apparently followed this counsel.

On June 18, when the joint chief of staffs, the civilian secretaries, and the president discussed plans for an American invasion of Kyushu on about November 1 and of Honshu during the following March, the issue of Soviet intervention again received attention. General George Marshall, the army chief of staff and the military leader Truman most admired, presented as his own views a JCS memorandum:

> It seems that if the Japanese are ever willing to capitulate short of complete military defeat in the field they will do it when faced by the completely hopeless prospect occasioned by (1) destruction already wrought by air bombardment and sea blockade, coupled with (2) a landing on Japan indicating the firmness of our resolution, and also perhaps coupled with (3) the entry or threat of Russian entry into the war.
>
> With reference to clean-up of the Asiatic mainland, our objective should be to get the Russians to deal with the Japs [sic] in Manchuria (and Korea). . . .
>
> An important point about Russian participation in the war is that the

impact of Russian entry on the already hopeless Japanese *may well be the decisive action* levering them into capitulation at that time or shortly thereafter *if* we land in Japan. [Emphasis added.]

Marshall's counsel was ambiguous and should have raised questions at this meeting. In one place, he said that Soviet entry, when combined with an invasion and other continued destruction, might lead to Japan's capitulation. In another place, he suggested that Soviet entry alone, or followed by an American invasion, might lead to Japan's capitulation. And he was unclear whether Russia's "clean-up of the Asiatic mainland" was necessary if Japan surrendered without an invasion.

None apparently noted the ambiguities or raised questions about Marshall's meaning. After the group approved plans for an invasion of Kyushu on about November 1, with possibly 30,000 casualties in the first thirty days, Truman indicated that one of his "objectives [at Potsdam] . . . would be to get from Russia all the assistance in the war that was possible." Admiral Ernest L. King, chief of Naval Operations, pointed out, according to the minutes, that the Soviets "were not indispensable and he did not think we should go as far as to beg them to come in. While the cost of defeating Japan would be greater, there was no question in his mind but that we should handle it alone. . . . [R]ealization of this fact should greatly strengthen the President's hand" at Potsdam. Admiral Leahy also expressed a "jaundiced view" of the need for Soviet participation.

Truman claimed that he went to Potsdam to secure Soviet entry and that he never changed his position. The first part of that claim is correct, but the second part is dubious, for Truman did nothing substantive at Potsdam to encourage Soviet intervention and much to delay or prevent it. The successful test at Alamogordo emphasized to policy makers that prompt Soviet entry was no longer necessary and that the United States might even be able to end the war without Soviet entry. After the unexpectedly glowing report of the test, Truman wanted to know whether Marshall considered Soviet entry necessary. "Marshall felt," Stimson recorded, "that now with our new weapon we would not need the assistance of the Russians to conquer Japan." "The bomb as a merely probable weapon had seemed a weak reed on which to rely, but the bomb as a colossal reality was very different," Stimson later explained. From Potsdam on July 23, Churchill cabled London: "It is quite clear that the United States do not at the present time desire Russian participation in the war against Japan." The bomb had eliminated the importance of Russia's prompt entry, since the planned American invasion no longer seemed necessary. Invasion and the bomb were the likely alternatives. As a result, Truman had no reason to offer concessions to secure early Soviet entry.

Could the United States keep the Soviet Union out of the war? Did policy makers try to do this? In mid-July Soviet troops were stationed on the Manchurian border and would soon be ready to intervene. Marshall concluded that even if Japan surrendered on American terms before Soviet entry, Russia could still march into Manchuria and take virtually whatever she wanted there in the surrender terms. Truman, if he believed Marshall's analysis, had nothing to gain politically from deterring Soviet entry, unless he feared, as did Stimson, that the Soviets might try to reach the Japanese homeland and put in a "claim to occupy and help rule it." Perhaps Truman followed the counsel of Stimson and Byrnes, who, for slightly different reasons, were eager to restrain the Soviets.

Byrnes, unlike Stimson, was sometimes naively optimistic. Part of the time he hoped to keep the Soviet Union out of the war, and not simply delay her entry, in order to protect China. On July 28, he explained to Secretary of the Navy James Forrestal (in Forrestal's words): "Byrnes said he was most anxious to get the Japanese affair over with before the Russians got in, with particular reference to Dairen and Port Arthur." These were the areas that both Stimson and Marshall acknowledged the Soviets could seize. Walter Brown, the friend who accompanied the secretary to Potsdam, recorded in his diary notes for July 20 Byrnes's strategy: "JFB determined to outmaneuver Stalin on China. Hopes Soong [the Chinese foreign minister] will stand firm and then Russians will not go in war. Then he feels Japan will surrender before Russia goes to war and this will save China." On July 24, four days later, Brown noted that Byrnes was linking the bomb and Japan's surrender but was less optimistic about excluding Russia: "JFB still hoping for time, believing after atomic bombing Japan will surrender and Russia will not get in so much on the kill, thereby [not] being in a position to press for claims against China."

Byrnes purposely impeded Sino-Soviet negotiations in order to *prevent* the Soviets from entering the war. Did Truman support Byrnes for the *same* reasons?—as Byrnes claimed later and as Truman obliquely denied. Perhaps. But, more likely, Truman supported his secretary's strategy for a different reason: the early entry of the Soviets was no longer important and, therefore, Truman did not want Chiang to make the required concessions, which would later weaken Chiang's government. In addition, Truman *may* have concluded that Russia's delayed entry would weaken her possible claims for a role in the postwar occupation government in Japan.

Why didn't Truman invite Stalin to sign the Potsdam Proclamation of July 26 calling for Japan's surrender? Some analysts argued later that this omission was part of a devious strategy: that Truman wanted to use the bomb and feared that Stalin's signature, tantamount to a declaration of war, might catapult Japan to surrender, thereby making a nuclear attack impossible. The major difficulty with this interpretation is that it exaggerates occasional, sometimes ambiguous, statements about the *possible* impact of Soviet entry and ignores the fact that this possible shock was not a persistent or important theme in American planning. Truman did not exclude the Soviets from the Proclamation in order to use the bomb. The skimpy, often oblique evidence *suggests* more plausible explanation and a less devious pattern: he wanted to avoid requesting favors from the Soviets. As a result, he did not try this one possible, but not very likely, way of ending the war without using atomic weapons.

At Potsdam, on July 24, Truman told Stalin casually that the United

States had developed "a new weapon of unusual destructive force" for use against Japan but did not specify an atomic weapon. Why didn't Truman explicitly inform Stalin about the atomic bomb? Was Truman, as some have suggested, afraid that the news would prompt Stalin to hasten Soviet intervention and therefore end the war and make combat use of the bomb impossible? Did Truman simply want to delay Soviet entry and did he, like Byrnes, fear that his news would have the opposite effect? Did Truman think that the destruction wrought by the bomb would not impress the Soviets as forcefully if they were informed in advance? Why did Truman reject the counsel of the Interim Committee, of Stimson, and even of Churchill, who, after the flowing news of the Alamogordo test, "was not worried about giving the Russians information on the matter but was rather inclined to use it as an argument in our favor in the negotiations"?

Many of these questions cannot be definitively answered on the basis of the presently available evidence, but there is enough evidence to refute one popular interpretation: that Truman's tactic was part of an elaborate strategy to prevent or retard Soviet entry *in order* to delay Japan's surrender and *thereby* make combat use of the bomb possible. That interpretation claims too much. Only the first part can be supported by some, albeit indirect, evidence: that he was probably seeking to delay or prevent Soviet entry. Byrnes later said that he feared that Stalin would order an immediate Soviet declaration of war if he realized the importance of this "new weapon"— advice Truman dubiously claimed he never received. Truman was not trying to postpone Japan's surrender *in order* to use the bomb. In addition to the reasonable theory that he was seeking to prevent or retard Soviet entry, there are two other plausible, complementary interpretations of Truman's behavior. First, he believed, as had some of his advisers earlier, that a combat demonstration would be more impressive to Russia without an advance warning and therefore he concealed the news. Second, he was also ill-prepared to discuss atomic energy with Stalin, for the president had not made a decision about postwar atomic policy and how to exploit the bomb, and probably did not want to be pressed by Stalin about sharing nuclear secrets. Perhaps all three theories collectively explain Truman's evasive tactics.

Even without explicit disclosure, the bomb strengthened American policy at Potsdam. The Alamogordo test stiffened Truman's resolve, as Churchill told Stimson after the meeting of the Big Three on July 22: "Truman was evidently much fortified . . . and . . . he stood up to the Russians in a most emphatic and decisive manner, telling them as to certain demands that they absolutely could not have." Probably, also, the bomb explains why Truman pushed more forcefully at Potsdam for the Soviets to open up Eastern Europe. It is less clear whether the bomb changed the substance of American policy at Potsdam. Probably Byrnes endorsed a reparations policy allowing the division of Germany because the bomb replaced Germany as a potential counterweight to possible Soviet expansion.

Not only did the bomb strengthen American resolve in dealing with the Soviets, but Stimson and Truman linked the bomb and the Soviet Union in another way: the selection of targets for atomic attacks. Kyoto, a city of religious shrines, was originally on the list, but Stimson removed it, with Truman's approval. Truman "was particularly emphatic in agreeing with my suggestion," Stimson wrote, because

> the bitterness . . . caused by such a wanton act might make it impossible during the long post war period to reconcile the Japanese to us in that area rather than to the Russians. It might thus, I pointed out, be the means of preventing what our policy demanded, namely, a sympathetic Japan to the United States in case there should be any aggression by Russia in Manchuria.

Scholars and laymen have criticized the combat use of the atomic bomb. They have contended, among other points, that the bombs were not necessary to end the war, that the administration knew or should have known this, that the administration knew that Japan was on the verge of defeat and *therefore* close to surrender, and that the administration was either short-sighted or had other controlling international-political motives (besides ending the war) for using the bomb. These varying contentions usually focus on the alleged failure of the United States to pursue five alternatives, individually or in combination, in order to achieve Japanese surrender before using the bomb: (1) awaiting Soviet entry, a declaration of war, or a public statement of intent (already discussed); (2) providing a warning and/or a noncombat demonstration (already discussed); (3) redefining unconditional surrender to guarantee the Imperial institution; (4) pursuing Japan's "peace feelers"; or (5) relying upon conventional warfare for a longer period. These contentions assume that policy makers were trying, or should have tried, to avoid using atomic bombs—precisely what they were not trying to do.

In examining these contentions, analysts must carefully distinguish between those writers (like Alperovitz) who maintain that there were ulterior motives for rejecting alternatives and those (like Hanson Baldwin) who regard policy makers as dangerously short sighted but without ulterior motives. It is logically possible to agree with Alperovitz and not Baldwin, or vice versa; but it is impossible logically to endorse both positions.

There were powerful reasons why the fifth alternative—the use of conventional weapons for a longer period *before* using atomic bombs—seemed undesirable to policy makers. The loss of American lives, while perhaps not great, would have been unconscionable and politically risky. How could policy makers have justified to themselves or to other Americans delaying the use of this great weapon and squandering American lives? Consider the potential political cost at home. In contrast, few Americans were then troubled by the mass killing of enemy citizens, especially if they were yellow. The firebombings of Tokyo, of other Japanese cities, and even of Dresden had produced few cries of outrage in the United States. There was no evidence that most citizens would care that the atomic bomb was as lethal as the raids on Dresden or Tokyo. It was unlikely that there would be popular support for relying upon conventional warfare and not using the atomic bomb. For citizens and policy makers, there were few, if any, moral restraints on what weapons were acceptable in war.

Nor were there any powerful advocates within the high councils of the administration who wanted to delay or not use the bomb and rely instead upon conventional warfare—a naval blockade, continued aerial bombings, or both. The advocates of conventional warfare were not powerful, and they did not directly oppose the use of the bomb. Admiral Ernest L. King, chief of Naval Operations, did believe that the invasion and the atomic bomb were not the only alternative tactics likely to achieve unconditional surrender. A naval blockade, he insisted, would be successful. The army, however, he complained, had little faith in sea power and, hence, Truman did not accept his proposal. Leahy had serious doubts about using the bomb, but as an old explosives expert who had long claimed that the bomb would never work, he carried little weight on this matter. Surprisingly, perhaps, he did not forcefully press his doubts on the president. Had Marshall plumped for the strategy of stepping up conventional warfare and delaying or not using the bomb, he might have been able to compel a reassessment. He had the respect and admiration of the president and could command attention for his views. But Marshall had no incentive to avoid the use of the bomb, prolong the war, and expend American lives. For him, nuclear weapons and invasion were likely alternatives, and he wanted to avoid invasion. If the bomb was used as quickly as possible, the invasion might be unnecessary and American lives would be saved.

For policy makers, the danger was not simply the loss of a few hundred American lives *prior* to the slightly delayed use of the bombs if the United States relied upon conventional warfare for a few more weeks. Rather the risk was that, if the nuclear attacks were even slightly delayed, the scheduled invasion of Kyushu, with perhaps 30,000 casualties in the first month, would be necessary. After the war, it became fashionable to assume that policy makers clearly foresaw and comfortably expected that an atomic bomb or two would shock Japan into a speedy surrender. But the evidence does not support this view. "The abrupt surrender of Japan came more or less as a surprise," Henry H. Arnold, commanding general of the air force, later explained. Policy makers were planning, if necessary, to drop at least three atomic bombs in August, with the last on about August 24, and more in September. Before Hiroshima, only occasionally did some policy makers imply (but never state explicitly) that one bomb or a few bombs might shock Japan into a prompt surrender: capitulation within a few days or weeks. Usually they were less optimistic, sometimes even pessimistic. They often assumed that the war might drag on after the nuclear attacks. Faced with this prospect, policy makers were unprepared to take risks and delay using the bombs. So unsure was Truman of the likelihood of a speedy surrender after the first atomic attack that he left domestic officials unprepared for the surrender and thereby seriously weakened his stabilization program and lost political support at home. Because policy makers feared that the attack on Hiroshima might not speedily end the war, they continued conventional bombing and also dropped the second bomb. Their aim was to end the war without a costly invasion of Kyushu. According to their analysis, atomic weapons, if employed promptly and combined with conventional attacks, were likely to achieve that goal. Delay was unconscionable, as Stimson later explained.

There have been criticisms of the administration for failing to pursue two other alleged opportunities: (1) redefining the unconditional surrender demands before Hiroshima to guarantee the Imperial institution; (2) responding to Japan's "peace feelers," which stressed the need for this guarantee. Byrnes and apparently Truman, however, were fearful at times that concessions might strengthen, not weaken, the Japanese military and thereby prolong, not shorten, the war. Some critics imply that Byrnes and Truman were not sincere in presenting this analysis and that they rejected concessions consciously in order to use the bomb. That is incorrect. Other critics believe that these policy makers were sincere but disagree with their assessment—especially since some intelligence studies implied the need for concessions on peace terms to shorten the war. Probably the administration was wrong, and these latter critics right, but either policy involved risks and some were very unattractive to Truman.

Truman, as a new president, was not comfortable in openly challenging Roosevelt's policy of unconditional surrender and modifying the terms. That was risky. It could fail and politically injure him at home. Demanding unconditional surrender meant fewer risks at home and, according to his most trusted advisers at times, fewer risks in ending the war speedily. Had his most powerful and trusted advisers pushed for a change in policy, perhaps he might have found reason and will to modify Roosevelt's policy well before Hiroshima. But most of Truman's closest advisers first counseled delay and then some moved into opposition. As a result, he too shifted from delay to opposition. At Potsdam, when Stimson pushed unsuccessfully for providing the guarantee in the proclamation, Truman refused but told Stimson that he would carefully watch Japan's reactions on this issue and implied that he would yield if it seemed to be the only impediment to surrender. After August 10, when Japan made the guarantee the only additional condition, Truman yielded on the issue. He deemed it a tactical problem, not a substantive one. But even then, Byrnes was wary of offering this concession, despite evidence that it would probably end the war promptly—precisely what he wanted in order to forestall Soviet gains in the Far East.

Within the administration, the issue of redefining the terms of surrender was a subject of discussion for some months before Hiroshima. Since at least April, Joseph Grew, undersecretary of state and at times acting secretary of state, urged the administration to redefine unconditional surrender to permit a guarantee of the Imperial institution. He argued that these moderate terms would speed Japan's surrender and perhaps make an invasion unnecessary. Within the Department of State, he met opposition from some high-ranking officials, including Dean Acheson and Archibald MacLeish, both assistant secretaries, who regarded the emperor as the bulwark of Japan's feudal-military tradition, which all wanted to destroy, and who feared that the American press and public opinion would be enraged by

Grew's proposed concession. Hirohito, Japan's emperor, like Hitler and Mussolini, had become a wartime symbol of a hated enemy, of depravity, of tyranny, and of inhumanity.

On May 28, President Truman, perhaps then sympathetic to Grew's proposal, told him to discuss it with Stimson, Forrestal, Marshall, and King. Unlike Acheson and MacLeish, these military leaders approved the principle but apparently agreed with Marshall that publication of softened terms at that time would be premature. Grew later explained, "for certain military reasons, not divulged, it was considered inadvisable for the President to make such a statement just now. The question of timing was the nub of the whole matter according to the views of those present." Though Grew knew about the atomic bomb, its connection with the delay never seemed to occur to him, and he thought that Marshall and others were concerned *only* about the impact of the announcement on the fighting on Okinawa. In his diary, Stimson explained the opposition more fully: "It was an awkward meeting because there were people present . . . [before] whom I could not discuss the real features which would govern the whole situation, namely S-1 [the atomic bomb]." Stimson never revealed this to Grew, who reported to Truman that they decided to postpone the statement—a position that the president endorsed.

Some analysts have argued, wrongly, that this evidence indicates that Stimson and the others blocked the statement *because* they wanted to use the bomb and did not want to risk a peace before the bomb could be used. That is incorrect. In view of Stimson's frequent judgments that the United States would issue a warning *after* the atomic bombing but before the scheduled attack on Kyushu, his objection was what Grew reported—an issue of timing. On July 2, for example, when Stimson proposed as part of the warning a guarantee of the Imperial institution, he was apparently assuming, as he stated explicitly a week earlier, that he hoped "to get Japan to surrender by giving her a warning after she had been sufficiently *pounded possibly with S-1*." Not until July 16, when Stimson learned of "the recent news of attempted approaches" by Japan for peace did he shift and call for a prompt warning *before* the atomic attacks.

"There was a pretty strong feeling" by mid-June, Stimson wrote in his diary, "that it would be deplorable if we have to go through [with] the military program with all its stubborn fighting to a finish." On June 18, Grew again went to Truman with his proposal, and the president told him, in Grew's words, that he "liked the idea [but] he had decided to hold this up until it could be discussed at the Big Three meeting" starting on July 16. Grew properly lamented that the government was missing an opportunity but did not speculate on whether the president had ulterior motives. Truman did not. A few hours later, he uneasily told associates that he, too, thought the requirement of unconditional surrender might drag out the war; that with "that thought in mind . . . [he] had left the door open for Congress to take appropriate action . . . [but] he did not feel that he could take any action at this time to change public opinion on the matter." Truman, apparently uneasy about departing from Roosevelt's policy, later explained that he delayed the guarantee until what he regarded as a more propitious time— the Potsdam conference, when the allies, by signing the proclamation, could forcefully demonstrate their "united purpose."

Had Cordell Hull, former secretary of state, Byrnes, and the JCS not intervened, Truman probably would have included in the Potsdam Proclamation a provision guaranteeing the Imperial institution. The provision was in early drafts. But Byrnes deleted it when Hull warned that it might stiffen Japan's resistance, and, if it failed, it could create serious political problems for the administration at home. The military chiefs, perhaps independently, also moved to delete the provision. Unlike Hull, they feared, among other problems, that the "guarantee would make it difficult or impossible to utilize the authority of the Emperor to direct a surrender of the Japanese forces in the outlying areas as well as in Japan proper." The guarantee, then, was not removed for ulterior purposes (because the administration wanted to use the bomb) but because advisers, with more power than Stimson and Grew, triumphed. Neither of these older men was close to Truman. Grew was headed for a quick retirement and was left behind in Washington when the president and top policy makers journeyed to Potsdam. Stimson, also headed for retirement, had so little influence by July that he was compelled to beg and scheme to attend the Potsdam conference and, while there, he was shunted to the side and seldom informed of negotiations.

Grew long maintained that America could have achieved peace without using atomic bombs if the United States had modified its demands and guaranteed the Imperial institution. In 1948, Stimson provided some support for this position: "It is possible, in the light of the final surrender, that a clearer and earlier exposition of American willingness to retain the Emperor would have produced an earlier ending to the war. Only on this question did [Stimson] . . . later believe," he wrote in his "autobiography," "that history might find that the United States, by its delay in stating its position, had prolonged the war." By implication, he was also criticizing the wartime fear—that he sometimes shared with Byrnes and most military advisers— that conciliatory offers would be interpreted in Japan "as an indication of [American] weakness" and thereby prolong the war. Probably policy makers were wrong in not acting earlier.

Let us look at the remaining, but connected, alternative—pursuing Japan's "peace feelers." Japan's so-called peace feelers were primarily a series of messages from the foreign minister to his nation's ambassador in Moscow, who was asked to investigate the possibility of having the Soviets serve as intermediaries in negotiating a peace. American intelligence intercepted and decoded all the messages. Most, if not all, were sent on to Potsdam, where Truman and Byrnes had access to them. Both men showed little interest in them, and may not even have read all of them, apparently because the proposed concessions were insufficient to meet American demands and because Truman and Byrnes had already decided that the peace party in Japan could not succeed until American attacks—including atomic bombs— crushed the military's hopes. The intercepted and decoded messages fell short of American expectations. Not only did Japan's foreign minister want to retain the Imperial institution, which was acceptable to some policy makers, but he also wanted a peace that would maintain his nation's "honor and existence," a phrase that remained vague. As late as July 27, the day after the Potsdam Proclamation, when Japan's foreign minister was planning a special peace mission to Russia, he was still unwilling or unable to present a "concrete proposal" for negotiations. What emerges from his decoded correspondence is a willingness by some elements in Japan's government to move toward peace, their fear of opposition from the military, and their inability to be specific about terms. Strangely, perhaps, though they feared that Stalin might be on the verge of entering the war, they never approached the United States directly to negotiate a peace settlement. For Truman and Byrnes, Japan was near defeat but not near surrender when the three powers issued the Potsdam Proclamation on July 26. When Japan's premier seemed to reject it, the president and secretary of state could find confirmation for their belief that the peace party could not triumph in Japan without more American "aid"—including nuclear attacks.

Given the later difficulties of Japan's peace party, even after the atomic bombings, after Soviet entry, and after more large-scale conventional bombings, top American policy makers could find evidence in the ambiguous record for their assessment that Japan's leaders were not ready to surrender before Hiroshima. More troubling were American policy makers' wartime convictions that any concessions or pursuit of unsure "peace feelers" might stiffen resistance. Most American leaders were fearful of softening demands. War had bred an attitude that any efforts at compromise might indicate to the enemy America's flaccidity of spirit and weakness of will. Toughness, for most policy makers, seemed to promise success.

Looking back upon these years, Americans may well lament the unwillingness of their leaders to make some concessions at this time and to rely upon negotiations before using the bombs. That lament, however, is logically separable from the unfounded charges that policy makers consciously avoided the "peace feelers" *because* they wanted to drop the bombs in order to intimidate the Soviets. It is true that American leaders did not cast policy in order to avoid using the atomic bombs. Given their analysis, they had no reason to avoid using these weapons. As a result, their analysis provokes ethical revulsion among many critics, who believe that policy makers should have been reluctant to use atomic weapons and should have sought, perhaps even at some cost in American lives, to avoid using them.

Truman inherited the assumption that the bomb was a legitimate weapon to use to end the war. No policy maker ever effectively challenged this conception. If the combat use of the bomb deeply troubled policy makers morally or politically, they might have been likely to reconsider their assumption and to search ardently for other alternatives. But they were generally inured to the mass killing of civilians and much preferred to sacrifice the lives of Japanese civilians to those of American soldiers. As a result, they were committed to using the bomb *as soon as possible* to end the war. "The dominant objective was victory," Stimson later explained. "If victory could be speeded by using the bomb, it should be used; if victory must be delayed in order to use the bomb, it should *not* be used. So far as . . . [I] knew, this general view was fully shared by the President and his associates." The morality of war confirmed the dictates of policy and reinforced the legacy that Truman had inherited. Bureaucratic momentum added weight to that legacy, and the relatively closed structure of decision making served also to inhibit dissent and to ratify the dominant assumption.

Had policy makers concluded that the use of the bomb would impair Soviet-American relations and make the Soviets intransigent, they might have reconsidered their assumption. But their analysis indicated that the use of the bomb would aid, not injure, their efforts to secure concessions from the Soviets. The bomb offered a bonus. The promise of these likely advantages probably constituted a subtle deterrent to any reconsideration of the use of the atomic bomb. Policy makers rejected the competing analysis advanced by the Franck Committee:

> Russia, and even allied countries which bear less mistrust of our ways and intentions, as well as neutral countries, will be deeply shocked. It will be very difficult to persuade the world that a nation which was capable of secretly preparing and suddenly releasing . . . [the bomb] is to be trusted in its proclaimed desire of having such weapons abolished by international agreement.

Instead, policy makers had come to assume that a combat demonstration would advance, not impair, the interests of peace—a position shared by Conant, Oppenheimer, Arthur H. Compton, Nobel laureate and director of the Chicago Metallurgical Laboratory, and Edward Teller, the Physicist and future father of the hydrogen bomb. In explaining the thinking of the scientific advisory panel in recommending combat use of the bomb, Oppenheimer later said that one of the two "overriding considerations . . . [was] the effect of our actions on the stability . . . of the postwar world." Stimson's assistant, Harvey H. Bundy, wrote in 1946, that some thought "that unless the bomb were used it would be impossible to persuade the world that the saving of civilization in the future would depend on a proper international control of atomic energy." The bomb, in short, would impress the Soviets.

In addition, there was another possible advantage to using the bomb: retribution against Japan. A few days after Nagasaki, Truman hinted at this theme in a private letter justifying the combat use of the bombs:

> Nobody is more disturbed over the use of Atomic bombs than I am but I was greatly disturbed over the unwarranted attack by the Japanese on Pearl Harbor. The only language they seem to understand is the one that we have been using to bombard them. When you have to deal with a beast you have to treat him as a beast. It is most regrettable but nevertheless true.

In this letter, one can detect strains of the quest for retribution (the reference to Pearl Harbor), and some might even find subtle strains of racism (Japan was "a beast"). The enemy was a beast and deserved to be destroyed. War, as some critics would stress, dehumanized victors and vanquished, and justified inhumanity in the name of nationalism, of justice, and even humanity.

In assessing the administration's failure to challenge the assumption that the bomb was a legitimate weapon to be used against Japan, we may conclude that Truman found no reason to reconsider, that it would have been difficult for him to challenge the assumption, and that there were also various likely benefits deterring a reassessment. For the administration, in short, there was no reason to avoid using the bomb and many reasons making it feasible and even attractive. The bomb was used primarily to end the war *promptly* and thereby to save American lives. There were other ways to end the war, but none of them seemed as effective. They would not produce victory as promptly and seemed to have greater risks. Even if Russia had not existed, the bombs would have been used in the same way. How could Truman, in the absence of overriding contrary reasons, justify not using the bombs, or even delaying their use, and thereby prolonging the war and sacrificing American lives?

Some who have searched for the causes of Truman's decision to use atomic weapons have made the error of assuming that the question was ever open, that the administration ever carefully faced the problem of *whether* to use the bombs. It was not a carefully weighed decision but the implementation of an assumption. The administration devoted thought to how, not whether, to use them. As Churchill later wrote, "the decision whether or not to use the atomic bomb to compel the surrender of Japan was never even an issue."

American Reactions to Soviet Unilateralism

JOHN LEWIS GADDIS

Wartime lack of concern over the powerful position the Soviet Union would occupy in the postwar world had been predicated upon the assumption that the Russians would continue to act in concert with their American and British allies. So long as the Grand Alliance remained intact, Western statesmen could assure each other, Moscow's emergence as the dominant Eurasian power would pose no threat. But during the final months of the war, there began to appear unsettling indications of a determination on Stalin's part to secure postwar interests without reference to the corresponding interests of his wartime associates. It was these manifestations of unilateralism that first set off alarm bells in the West about Russian intentions; the resulting uneasiness in turn stimulated deeper and more profound anxieties.

"I am becoming increasingly concerned," Secretary of State [Cordell] Hull warned Ambassador W. Averell Harriman early in 1944, "over the . . . successive moves of the Soviet Government in the field of foreign

From *The Long Peace*, 29–47, by John Lewis Gaddis. Copyright © 1987 by John Lewis Gaddis. Reprinted by permission of Oxford University Press.

relations.'' Hull went on to observe in this message, drafted by Soviet specialist Charles E. Bohlen, that whatever the legitimacy of Moscow's security interests in Eastern Europe—''and as you know we have carefully avoided and shall continue to avoid any disruption with the Soviet Government on the merits of such questions''—unilateral actions to secure those interests ''cannot fail to do irreparable harm to the whole cause of international collaboration.'' The American people would not be disposed to participate in any postwar scheme of world organization which would be seen ''as a cover for another great power to pursue a course of unilateral action in the international sphere based on superior force.'' It was ''of the utmost importance that the principle of consultation and cooperation with the Soviet Union be kept alive at all costs, but some measures of cooperation in relation to world public opinion must be forthcoming from the Soviet Government.''

This document reflects as well as any other the point from which American statesmen began to develop concerns about the postwar intentions of the Soviet Union. The United States had not challenged Moscow's determination to retain the boundaries it had secured as a result of Stalin's unsavory pact with Hitler in 1939, nor had it questioned the Russians' right to a postwar sphere of influence in what remained of Eastern Europe. It was prepared to grant similar concessions in East Asia in return for eventual U. S. S. R. participation in the war against Japan. But because the Roosevelt administration had justified American entry into the war as a defense of self-determination, and because it had committed the nation to participation in a postwar world collective security organization as a means of implementing that principle, it required from the Soviet Union a measure of discretion and restraint in consolidating these areas of control. Unilateral action seemed likely to endanger the balance of power, not by allowing the Russians to dominate areas beyond their borders—that domination was assumed—but rather by weakening the American capacity for countervailing action in the postwar world by provoking, first, public disillusionment and then, as a consequence, a revival of the isolationism the President and his advisers had fought so long and so hard to overcome.

The Russians, to put it mildly, were less than sensitive to these concerns. As their armies moved into Eastern Europe in 1944 they immediately set out to undermine potential sources of opposition, not just in the former enemy countries of Rumania, Bulgaria, and Hungry, but most conspicuously of all in Poland, which had been, after all, an ally. The callousness with which the Red Army allowed the Germans to decimate the anti-communist resistance in Warsaw late that summer shocked Western statesmen; meanwhile British and American representatives on Allied Control Commissions in the Balkans found themselves denied any significant influence in shaping occupation policies there as well. Moscow had interpreted Western restraint as a sign of weakness, Harrison reported in September: ''Unless we take issue with the present policy there is every indication that the Soviet Union will become a world bully wherever their interests are involved. . . . No written agreements can be of any value unless they are carried out in a spirit of give and take and recognition of the interests of other people.''

Franklin Roosevelt made valiant efforts at Yalta to make Stalin aware of the need to observe the proprieties in Eastern Europe, but these proved unsuccessful almost at once when the Soviet leader interpreted agreements made to hold free elections there as in fact license to impose still tighter control on Poland and Rumania. "Averell is right," Roosevelt complained three weeks before his death. "We can't do business with Stalin. He has broken every one of the promises he made at Yalta." F. D. R. had not been prepared, on the basis of these difficulties, to write off all possibilities of postwar cooperation with the Russians. But Soviet unilateralism does appear to have convinced him, by the time of his death, that efforts to win Stalin's trust had not worked; and that future policy toward the Soviet Union would have to be based on a strict *quid pro quo* basis.

Harry S Truman emphatically agreed. Although the new Chief Executive had had no direct experience in the conduct of foreign affairs, he could have hardly believed more firmly in the importance of keeping one's word. "When I say I'm going to do something, I do it," he once wrote, "or [I] bust my insides trying to do it." It was characteristic of him that he did not believe in divorce because "when you make a contract you should keep it." Convinced that the Yalta agreements on free elections in Eastern Europe were in fact contracts, determined to demonstrate decisiveness in an awesome and unexpected position of responsibility, Truman resolved— probably more categorically than Roosevelt would have done—to hold the Russians to what they had agreed to. It was this determination that occasioned the new President's sharp rejoinder to Soviet Foreign Minister V. M. Molotov after less than two weeks in office: "Carry out your agreements and you won't get talked to like that." A month later he complained again that the Russians were not honoring their agreements: they were, he told Henry Wallace, "like people from across the tracks whose manners were very bad."

The experience of meeting Stalin personally at Potsdam seems to have modified the President's attitude somewhat. The Soviet autocrat evoked memories of the Kansas City political boss Tom Pendergast, a man with whom deals could be made because he had always kept his word. "I can deal with Stalin," Truman noted in his diary at Potsdam. "He is honest— but smart as hell." Disturbed by rumors of the dictator's ill health, the President worried about what would happen "if Joe suddenly passed out" because his potential successors lacked sincerity. For several years afterward, there persisted in Truman's mind the notion that difficulties with the Russians reflected Stalin's internal political problems—interference from a recalcitrant Politburo was the most frequent explanation—rather than any personal desire on the Soviet leader's part to violate his word.

But deals had to be honored if they were to work, and with the return of peace instances of Soviet unilateralism began to proliferate. Reasonably free elections took place in Hungary and Czechoslovakia, but only in those countries: Moscow's grip on Poland, Rumania, and Bulgaria remained as tight as ever. The Russians joined the French in resisting central economic administration of occupied Germany; they also arbitrarily transferred a substantial portion of that country's eastern territory to Poland. Attempts to reunify another divided nation, Korea, came to naught as the Russians refused to tolerate anything other than a satellite government there. The Soviet Union rejected participation in the World Bank and the International Monetary Fund, institutions American planners regarded as critical for postwar economic recovery. And Stalin was showing strong signs, as 1945 ended, of exploiting the presence of Soviet troops in northern Iran to carve out yet another sphere of influence there. He was "trying to find a basis for an understanding which would give him confidence that an agreement reached with the Russians would be lived up to," Truman told his advisers in December, 1945. He had such confidence in dealing with the British, the Dutch, and the Chinese (though not the French), "but there is no evidence yet that the Russians intend to change their habits so far as honoring contracts is concerned."

The Chief Executive's initial inclination had been to regard these difficulties simply as failures of communication; with that explanation in mind, he had authorized Secretary of State [James F.] Byrnes to make one more effort to settle them at a hastily called meeting of foreign ministers in Moscow in December. By that time, though, public and Congressional impatience with Soviet unilateralism had considerably intensified. Sensitive to these pressures, irritated by Byrnes' eagerness to reach agreements without consulting him, Truman early in 1946 proclaimed to himself—if not directly to Byrnes, as he later claimed—his intention to stop "babying" the Soviets: "Unless Russia is faced with an iron fist and strong language another war is in the making. Only one language do they understand— 'how many divisions have you?' I do not think we should play at compromise any longer."

There was, in fact, no compromise when the Russians failed to meet their agreed-upon deadline for removing their troops from Iran: instead the administration confronted Moscow publicly in the United Nations Security Council and forced a humiliating withdrawal. Truman drew the appropriate conclusions: "Told him to tell Stalin I held him to be a man to keep his word," he noted in his appointment book after a meeting with the newly designated ambassador to the Soviet Union, Walter Bedell Smith, on March 23. "Troops in Iran after March 2 upset that theory." By June, he was writing to the author Pearl Buck that "the United States has performed no unfriendly act nor made a single unfriendly gesture toward the great Russian nation. . . . How has Russia met our friendly overtures?" The following month, after *New York Times* correspondent Brooks Atkinson had published a series of articles highly critical of the Russians, Truman pointedly invited him to the White House. That same day he told his advisers that he was "tired of our being pushed around," that "here a little, there a little, they are chiseling from us," and that "now is [the] time to take [a] stand on Russia."

It was in this spirit that the President authorized the first comprehensive study of Soviet-American relations to be carried out within the government. Compiled under the direction of his Special Counsel, Clark M. Clifford, and written after consultations with the Departments of State, War, Navy, the Joint Chiefs of Staff and the Director of Central Intelligence, the report acknowledged that agreements between nations were at times susceptible to differing interpretations. Nonetheless, it argued, there existed a persistent pattern on Moscow's part of either unilaterally implementing such agreements in such a way as to serve Soviet interest, or encouraging satellites to do so. "[T]here is no question," the report emphasized, "where the primary responsibility lies."

The implications could only be that the Soviet Union had no intention of cooperating with the West to maintain the existing balance of power; that it sought to expand its own influence as widely as possible without regard for the security requirements of its former allies; and that, when circumstances were right, it would be prepared to risk war to attain that objective. American policy could no longer be based upon the assumption of shared interests, therefore; priorities henceforth would have to be directed toward the accumulation of sufficient military strength to deter war if possible and to win it if necessary, while at the same time keeping open possibilities for dealing with the Russians should a change of heart in the Kremlin eventually occur. "[I]t is our hope," the report concluded, "that they will eventually change their minds and work out with us a fair and equitable settlement when they realize that we are too strong to be beaten and too determined to be frightened."

President Truman received the Clifford report on September 24, four days after he had fired Henry Wallace from the Cabinet for publicly advocating a more conciliatory policy toward the Soviet Union. There is no question that he agreed with its general conclusions: on the day before he dismissed Wallace he had complained in his diary about

> Reds, phonies, and . . . parlor pinks [who] can see no wrong in Russia's four and one half million armed forces, in Russia's loot of Poland, Austria, Hungary, Rumania, Manchuria. . . . But when we help our friends in China who fought on our side it is terrible. When Russia loots the industrial plant of those same friends it is all right. When Russia occupies Persia for oil that is heavenly.

But Truman chose not to use the Clifford report, as he might have, to justify increased military appropriations; instead he ordered all copies to be locked in the White House safe, where they remained for the duration of the administration. "There is too much loose talk about the Russian situation," he had written former Vice President John Nance Gerner on the day after Wallace's dismissal. "We are not going to have any shooting trouble with them but they are tough bargainers and always ask for the whole earth, expecting maybe to get an acre."

The President's cautious reaction to the manifestations of Soviet uni-lateralism catalogued in the Clifford report reflected a desire to avoid hasty and ill-considered action, but certainly no continuing assumption of common interest. Repeated demonstrations of Moscow's callousness to the priorities and sensibilities of its former allies had by this time virtually drained the reservoir of good will toward the Russians that had built up during the war. American leaders had been inclined, for many months, to give the Kremlin the benefit of the doubt: to assume, despite accumulating evidence to the contrary, that difficulties with Moscow had arisen out of misunderstandings rather than fundamental conflicts of interest. But such charitableness could not continue indefinitely, as Winston Churchill pointed out in the summer of 1946: "The American eagle sits on his perch, a large strong bird with formidable beak and claws. . . . Mr. Gromyko [Soviet ambassador] is sent every day to prod him with a sharp sickle, now on his beak, now under his wing, now in his tail feathers. All the time the eagle keeps quite still, but it would be a great mistake to suppose that nothing is going on inside the breast of the eagle."

In fact, a good deal was going on inside the breast of the eagle, all of it related in one way or another to attempting to explain the motivation for Moscow's puzzling behavior. Throughout the period of wartime co-operation there had lingered in the minds of most Americans latent but persistent suspicions about Russia, suspicions that extended back to, and even beyond, the Bolshevik Revolution. These grew out of the fact that the Soviet Union combined—as no other country in the world at that time did—two characteristics that Americans found particularly objectionable: arbitrary rule and ideological militancy. As long as the direct Axis threat remained, Americans had been willing to overlook these shortcomings, even to hope that in time they would disappear. But after 1945, with no common foe to compel unity, with ample evidence that the Russians intended to proceed on their own rather than in concert with their former allies to consolidate postwar interests, the predisposition to assume the worst about Moscow's intentions came out into the open once again.

Americans had not always found cooperation with authoritarian regimes to be impossible: the Russian-American relationship itself had been friendly throughout most of its early history, despite the vast cultural and political differences that separated the two countries. But toward the end of the 19th century a combination of circumstances—increasing repression within Russia, a keener American sensitivity to conditions inside other countries, growing rivalries between Washington and St. Petersburg over spheres of influence in East Asia—had produced in the United States the suspicion that a connection existed between autocratic rule at home and aggressiveness in foreign affairs. Parallel concerns had accompanied the deterioration of relations with imperial Germany prior to World War I; certainly participation in that conflict, which Woodrow Wilson justified by stressing the linkage between autocracy and aggression, served powerfully to reinforce this idea. Determination to remain aloof from European involvements caused Americans to worry less about such matters during the 1920's and early 1930's— indeed, the economic distress of the latter decade even produced in some circles a grudging respect for dictatorships—but the experience of fighting

Germany and Japan during World War II brought back repugnance for arbitrary rule with a vengeance. It would not take very many signs of aggressiveness on the part of totalitarian regimes in the postwar world—even totalitarian former allies—to convince Americans that the connection between domestic despotism and international expansionism still prevailed.

"If we fought Germany because of our belief that a police state and a democratic state could not exist in the same world," Rear Admiral Ellery W. Stone told Secretary of the Navy James Forrestal in July, 1946, then "it must necessarily follow that we could not afford to lie down before Russia." The simple fact that the Soviet Union was a totalitarian state raised suspicions that its foreign policy would proceed from priorities incompatible with those of the democracies—priorities now elaborately enshrined in the procedures the United Nations had established for settling international disputes. Totalitarian states, Americans assumed, relied upon force or the threat of force to secure their interests; such nations could hardly be expected to share Washington's aspiration to see the rule of law ultimately govern relations between nations. "[I]t is not Communism but Totalitarianism which is the potential threat," publisher Arthur Hays Sulzberger pointed out. ". . . [O]nly people who have a Bill of Rights are not the potential enemies of other people."

The point, for Truman, was fundamental. "Really there is no difference between the government which Mr. Molotov represents and the one the Czar represented—or the one Hitler spoke for," he privately wrote in November, 1946. And, again, informally, in May, 1947: "There isn't any difference in totalitarian states. . . . Nazi, Communist or Fascist, or Franco, or anything else—they are all alike. . . . The police state is a police state; I don't care what you call it." The President's public speeches during 1947 provided virtually a running commentary on the dangers of totalitarianism: "Freedom has flourished where power has been dispersed. It has languished where power has been too highly centralized." More than that, excessive concentrations of power produced temptations to use them. "The stronger the voice of a people in the formulation of national policies, the less the danger of aggression. When all governments derive their just powers from the consent of the governed, there will be enduring peace." There was no conflict between the requirements of justice and order: "The attainment of worldwide respect for essential human rights is synonymous with the attainment of world peace."

It was no accident, then, that when the President in the most famous speech of his career characterized the world as divided between two ways of life, one reflecting "the will of the majority," the other based "upon the will of a minority forcibly imposed upon the majority," it was the distinction between democracy and totalitarianism to which he referred. By so doing, he implicitly linked his own justification of American action to restore the balance of power in Europe to those advanced by Franklin Roosevelt in the Atlantic Charter and by Woodrow Wilson in the Fourteen Points: in each case the assumption was the ultimate incompatibility of autocratic and democratic institutions. The fact that this particular autocracy also embraced the ideology of communism was, for Truman, relatively insignificant.

That certainly was not the case for most Americans, though. Nothing—not even totalitarianism—did more to arouse suspicion about the Soviet Union's behavior than that country's long-standing and self-proclaimed intention to seek the overthrow of capitalist governments throughout the world. American hostility toward communism went back to the earliest days of the Bolshevik Revolution: to Russia's abandonment of the Allied cause in World War I; to the terror, expropriations, and executions that soon followed; to the postwar Red Scare, with its suggestion that even the United States might not be immune from the bacillus of revolution. The Soviet Union's commitment to communism had been the primary justification for Washington's refusal to recognize that country until 1933; and even after that date Moscow's claim to be the vanguard of world revolution had continued to plague relations with Washington. Stalin implicitly acknowledged the corrosive effects of ideology upon his dealings with the West in 1943 when, eager for an Anglo-American commitment to establish a Second Front, he abolished the Comintern, Lenin's designated instrument for bringing about the world proletarian revolution. But there could be no guarantee that such restraint would continue once Moscow's enemies had been defeated. As a Department of State memorandum put it in 1944, it was necessary to keep in mind the Soviet conviction that "there is an irreconcilable chasm between 'socialism' and 'capitalism' and that any temporary association in a common interest [is] an association of expediency for a specific purpose but with no underlying affinity of fundamental interest, civilization, or tradition."

"I expressed it as my view that it would not be difficult to work with Russia provided we were dealing with her only as a national entity," James Forrestal noted in his diary during the summer of 1945. "[T]he real problem was whether or not Russian policy called for a continuation of the Third International's objectives, namely, world revolution and the application of the political principles of the dialectical materialists for the entire world." Evidence that the Kremlin still harbored such ambitions arose from two sets of circumstances: the Russians' use of communist parties in Eastern Europe as instruments with which to create their sphere of influence there; and the increasing success of communist parties in Western Europe, the Eastern Mediterranean, and China. In retrospect, it is not at all clear that these phenomena were related: the popularity of communist parties outside the Soviet sphere grew primarily out of their effectiveness as resistance fighters against the Axis; in Eastern Europe the communists owed their prominence chiefly to Moscow's reliance on them to consolidate its control. Nor was it obvious that the Soviet Union's use of foreign communist parties to promote its interests necessarily proved an ideological motivation for its policies.

But these fine points were difficult to keep in mind as the end of the war brought increases in the militancy—and anti-American rhetoric—of all communist parties, not least that of the Soviet Union itself. When combined with the indisputable evidence of Moscow's unilateral expansionism, when considered against the record of how Nazi Germany had used "fifth columns" before the war, it is not surprising that concern about the ideological dimension of the Soviet challenge should have surfaced as well. "The tendency is increasingly marked," the British Embassy in Washington reported in August, 1946, "to detect the Soviet mind or hand behind every move which seems to threaten or embarrass the United States or its friends, and to link events in one part of the world with those in another." The editors of *Newsweek* put it more bluntly: "U. S. officials in the best position to judge fear they have confirmation that the Soviet Government has made up its mind that capitalism must be destroyed if Communism is to live."

Both the "totalitarian" and the "ideological" explanations of Soviet behavior had in common the assumption that one was dealing with a compulsive internally driven process, unresponsive to gestures of restraint or goodwill from the outside. There had been yet a third interpretation of Moscow's unilateralism, popular during the war, that had seen it as growing out of a quite understandable preoccupation with security capable of being alleviated by patient Western efforts to win the Russians' trust. President Roosevelt himself had made this "insecurity" theory the basis of his policy toward the Soviet Union, and it had remained very much alive—though under increasing challenge—during the first months of the Truman administration. But theories require validation if they are to be sustained: however persuasive the "insecurity" model of Soviet behavior may be in retrospect, what struck most observers at the time was the utter imperviousness of Stalin's regime to the gestures of restraint and goodwill that emanated from the West during and immediately after the war. Moscow's perceived failure to reciprocate these initiatives made it more and more difficult to sustain an interpretation of Soviet actions based on "insecurity," as Henry Wallace found out when he attempted during the spring and summer of 1946, to revive it within the inner councils of the government. The "totalitarian" and "ideological" models were the obvious alternatives.

It is ironic that the individual most influential in discrediting "insecurity" as an explanation of Soviet unilateralism shared many of its basic assumptions. George F. Kennan had never been inclined to interpret Soviet behavior in either strictly totalitarian or ideological terms. As a keen student of Russian history and culture, he was fully aware of the lack of self-confidence that plagued the Stalinist government, and of the extent to which its unilateralism was defensively motivated. But he emphatically did not share the view of Wallace and others that these attitudes could be modified from the outside. It was in an effort to bring official Washington to see that point that Kennan crafted the February, 1946, "long telegram," to this day the single most influential explanation of postwar Soviet behavior, and one which powerfully reinforced the growing tendency within the United States to interpret Moscow's actions in a sinister light.

The "long telegram" had the great influence that it did because it provided a way to fuse concerns about totalitarianism and communism in dealing with the Soviet Union. It portrayed that state as one in which an autocratic tradition had become incorporated within an ideological compulsion to treat the outside world as hostile. The conclusion was clear: no actions the United States or its Western allies could take would alleviate Stalin's suspicion; the best one could do was to look to one's own defenses—and to the strength and self-confidence of one's own society—and wait for the internal forces of change within the Soviet system to have their effect.

There is a definite psychological satisfaction, when confronted with a phenomenon one does not understand, in finding a simple but persuasive explanation. Whatever the actual intentions of its author, the "long telegram" performed that function within the government in 1946; a similar analysis would find a wider audience the following year in the form of the famous "X" article in *Foreign Affairs*. The "totalitarian-ideological" model of Soviet behavior provided a clear, plausible, and in many ways, gratifying explanation of the Russians' failure to cooperate with their former allies in building a lasting peace: it absolved the United States of responsibility for the breakdown of wartime cooperation; it made any future relaxation of tensions dependent upon changes of heart in Moscow, not Washington. Americans did not welcome the onset of the Cold War. But the rationale they worked out to account for its appearance at least had the advantage of allowing them to approach the coming contest with a reasonably clear conscience.

The Soviet Union's emergence as a potential adversary closed an obvious gap in Washington's thinking about the postwar world. A generalized sense of vulnerability, related both to historical experience and to technological change, had caused United States officials to regard preservation of a global balance of power as a vital interest even before specific challenges to that balance had manifested themselves. This situation of perceived vulnerability in the absence of apparent threat accounts for the failure of the United States to deploy forces and establish bases in the way one might have expected had the Russians been seen as the enemy from the beginning. But Soviet unilateralism, together with the conclusions about the roots of Soviet behavior that unilateralism provoked, had by 1947 created a credible source of danger, with the result that American strategy now took on a clearer and more purposeful aspect.

Central to it was the defense of Western Europe, a priority so basic that it was more often assumed than articulated. "[I]t is not a question of what men think now," the Joint Chiefs of Staff noted in the spring of 1947; "[it] is something that has been demonstrated by what we have had to do, though tardily, and therefore at greater risk and cost, in actual warfare in the past. . . . The entire area of Western Europe is in first place as an area of strategic importance to the United States." And yet, American planners had given remarkably little thought to the means by which that part of the world might be secured against Soviet expansionism. Their assumption— again mostly unstated—had been that Great Britain would provide the necessary counter presence, and that the United States could concern itself with other matters. It had done just that throughout 1946, concentrating on resisting Soviet pressures aimed at Iran and Turkey, consolidating its position in Japan and southern Korea, mediating the Chinese civil war, and attempting to resolve the diplomatic stalemate over Germany.

The British decision to withdraw military assistance from Greece and Turkey in February, 1947, forced a reconsideration of these priorities, not because two countries were of critical importance in and of themselves, but because of the way in which London's action dramatized the failure of Western Europe as a whole to recover from the war. A major consequence of that conflict had been, in [British geopolitician Sir Halford] Mackinder's terminology, a severe weakening of the "rimland" states surrounding the Soviet "heartland," leaving only the "world island"—effectively the United States—as a countervailing balance. But it was not until 1947 that Washington officials realized the full implications of that fact and set about taking corrective action.

At no point—despite references to the possibility of war in the 1946 Clifford report—did these officials seriously anticipate a Soviet military attack in Europe. Estimates of Moscow's intentions, whether from the Pentagon, the State Department, or the intelligence community, consistently discounted the possibility that the Russians might risk a direct military confrontation within the foreseeable future. Several considerations contributed to that judgment, not least of which was the damage the Soviet Union itself had suffered during the war and the still relatively primitive character of its air and naval forces. But these estimates also suggested that the Russians would not need to use force to gain their objectives, because of the ease with which war-weakened neighbors could be psychologically intimidated. "[I]f the countries of the world lose confidence in us," General George A. Lincoln of the War Department General Staff told the Senate Foreign Relations Committee early in April, 1947, "they may in effect pass under the Iron Curtain without any pressure other than the subversive pressure being put on them."

American planners assumed a direct correlation between economic health, psychological self-confidence, and the capacity for defense. As a State-War-Navy Coordinating Committee report noted that same month: "[E]conomic weaknesses may give rise to instability and subsequently to political shifts which adversely affect the security of the U. S." This could happen through "boring from within" tactics or the threat of overwhelming external force, but in either event the outcome from the standpoint of American interests would be grim. "Without further prompt and substantial aid from the United States," Under Secretary William Clayton argued, "economic, social and political disintegration will overwhelm Europe."

A Soviet-dominated Europe would pose obvious military dangers, even if military means were not used to secure it. In a clear echo of the wartime Mackinder-Spykman analysis [Professor Nicholas John Spykman, author of *America's Strategy in World Politics* (1942)], the Joint Chiefs of Staff pointed out that the Western hemisphere contained 40 percent of the earth's land surface but only 25 percent of its population. "The potential military strength of the Old World in terms of manpower . . . and war-making capacity is enormously greater than that of our area of defense commitments, in which the United States is the only arsenal nation." It was obvious, therefore, that in case of war "we must have the support of some of the countries of the Old World unless our military strength is to be overshadowed by that of our enemies." Western Europe was particularly important, not just because that region contained "almost all potentially strong nations who can reasonably be expected to ally themselves with the United States," but also because without access to the eastern shore of the Atlantic, "the shortest and most direct avenue of attack against our enemies will almost certainly be denied us."

The economic consequences of a European collapse were less clear. The Truman administration found it convenient to argue publicly that the effect on the American domestic economy, in terms of lost exports, would be little short of disastrous. What strikes one in retrospect, though, is how self-sufficient that economy actually was. Exports as a percentage of gross national product did not rise above 6.5 percent between 1945 and 1950, a figure lower than had normally been the case before the Great Depression, when the government had adamantly resisted any kind of official aid for European reconstruction. American investment in Western Europe in the early postwar years was actually less than European investment in the United States. It seems likely that administration officials stressed the economic implications of the crisis not because these stood out above others, but because Washington had chosen economic assistance as the quickest and most effective way to respond to it. It was easier to sell an unprecedented foreign-aid package as a program to ensure American prosperity than as a strategy for redressing the balance of power.

But it was the psychological implications of an extension of Soviet influence over Europe that probably most concerned American leaders. Although the term "domino theory" would not come into currency for another decade, administration officials worried deeply about the "bandwagon" effect that might ensue if the perception became widespread that the momentum in world affairs was on the Russians' side. And despite the United States' own history of isolationism, despite its relative self-sufficiency, there was a very real fear of what might happen if the nation were left without friends in the world. In one sense, this fear grew out of the tradition of American exceptionalism: the United States had always viewed itself as both apart from and a model for the rest of the world; it could hardly have regarded with equanimity evidence that its example was no longer relevant. But, in another sense, it was precisely the unexceptional character of Americans in relation to the rest of the world that was at issue here: who was to say that, buoyed by success in Europe, the totalitarian instinct might not take hold in the United States as well? "There is a little bit of the totalitarian buried somewhere, way down deep, in each and every one of us," George Kennan reminded students at the National War College in the spring of 1947. "It is only the cheerful light of confidence and security which keeps this evil genius down. . . . If confidence and security were to disappear, don't think that he would not be waiting to take their place."

The strategy of containment brought together the new American interest in maintaining a global balance of power with the perceived Muscovite challenge to that equilibrium in a part of the world that could hardly have been more pivotal—Western Europe. It sought to deal with that danger primarily by economic rather than military means; its goal was not so much the creation of an American hegemony as it was a re-creation of independent centers of power capable of balancing each other as well as the Russians. This is hardly the place to evaluate the success of that strategy or to trace its subsequent mutations and incarnations: these subjects have received excessively lengthy treatment elsewhere. Suffice it to say that the strategy could not have evolved without the perception of vulnerability brought about by the war, and the all-too-successful—if inadvertent—efforts of the Russians to give that abstraction an alarming reality.

Soviet historians have argued with unsurprising consistency through the years that the United States over-reacted to the "threat" posed by the U. S. S. R. in the wake of World War II. During the late 1960's and early 1970's, a number of American students of the early Cold War expressed agreement with that conclusion, though not with the methods that had been used to arrive at it. In an interesting inversion of Kennan's theory regarding Russian behavior, these accounts portrayed official Washington as having in one way or another fabricated the myth of a hostile Soviet Union in order to justify its own internally motivated drive for international hegemony. The difficulty with this argument was the impossibility of verifying it, for without access to Soviet sources there could be no definite conclusions regarding its accuracy: one cannot credibly assess responsibility when one can confirm the motives of only one side. The intervening years have brought us no nearer to a resolution of that problem, but they have witnessed the emergence of several new lines of historical interpretation that appear to call into question the thesis of American "over-reaction."

One of these involves a reconsideration of Stalin's policy by a new generation of scholars equally conversant, not only with the very limited number of Soviet and Eastern European sources that are available, but with the overwhelming array of recently declassified American and British documents as well. The effect of this work is to confirm neither the "totalitarian" nor the "ideological" explanations of Stalin's actions that were popular during the early Cold War years, but rather to see that dictator as having followed an "imperial" model of expansion: a pattern of behavior motivated by insecurity and characterized by caution, to be sure, but one that was also incapable of defining the limits of security requirements and that sought, as a result, to fill power vacuums where this could be done without encountering resistance. The effect of this policy was twofold: to incorporate within the Soviet sphere what Vojtech Mastny has called "a cluster of sullen dependencies" that probably contributed to more than they subtracted from Moscow's nervousness; and to alarm, and ultimately alienate, the United States and its Western European allies, who saw Stalin's inability to define the full extent of his security requirements as likely to undermine their own.

It may well be, as William Taubman has argued, that the West gave up on the possibility of cooperation with the West. But Taubman points out that any such cooperation would have been on the Kremlin leader's terms and for his purposes: it would have been designed "to foster Soviet control of Eastern Europe whether directly (in the case of Poland, Rumania, and Bulgaria) or indirectly (in Hungary and Czechoslovakia); to expand Soviet influence in Western Europe, the Near East and Asia; to position the USSR for even greater gains when the next Western economic crisis struck; and to achieve all this while subsidized to the tune of at least six billion dollars in American credits." Western statesmen may perhaps be pardoned for not having shared this particular vision of the postwar world.

Nor are they condemned, in the new historiography, for having resorted to a strategy of containment; indeed Mastny goes so far as to suggest that the West's responsibility for the coming of the Cold War lies more in the passive and dilatory character of its response than in its aggressiveness: "any Western policy likely to restrain [Stalin] would have had to follow a harder rather than a softer line; it would also have had a better chance to succeed if applied sooner rather than later." Containment no doubt reinforced Stalin's suspicion of the West, but it can hardly be said to have created it; without containment, according to this new line of interpretation, the fears Western statesmen held at the time regarding Soviet expansionism might well have become reality.

Historians are also beginning to study the involvement of third parties in the early Cold War; this work sheds new light on the question of who saw whom as a threat. What emerges from it so far is the extent to which states along the periphery of the U. S. S. R. tended to share Washington's concern about Soviet intentions, and indeed to welcome American intervention in their affairs as a counterweight. The Norwegian historian Geir Lundestad has pointed out that Washington's influence actually expanded more rapidly than did that of the Russians in the postwar world, but he argues that this happened because the United States was *encouraged* to assert its power in order to balance that of the Russians. Bruce Kuniholm has documented a similar pattern in the Near East: in 1946 the Iranian government was demanding not less but greater American interference in its internal affairs on the grounds, as the U. S. ambassador put it, that "[t]he only way they can think of to counteract one influence is to invite another." But the clearest case of all is the policy of Great Britain, which as Terry Anderson and Robert Hathaway have demonstrated, amounted almost to a conspiracy to involve the United States more actively in world affairs.

"If we cannot have a world community with the Russians as a constructive member," a British Foreign Office official minuted early in 1946, "it seems clear that the next best hope for peace and stability is that the rest of the world, including the vital North American arsenal, should be united in defense of whatever degree of stability we can attain." This is as good a summary of London's early Cold War policy, under both the Churchill and Attlee governments, as one is apt to find. The British had come earlier than their American allies to the conclusion that cooperation with the Russians was not going to be possible; certainly they welcomed—and, at times, sought to reinforce—the increasing indications from Washington throughout 1946 and early 1947 that the Truman administration had come to share that view. Their analysis of the reasons for Soviet unilateralism roughly paralleled that of the Americans; nor were they inclined to find fault—apart from some wincing at the rhetorical excesses involved—with the strategies Washington proposed to deal with that problem. Indeed, if anything, London's attitude was that the Americans were not doing enough: it was this conviction that led Foreign Secretary Ernest Bevin late in 1947 to propose to the United States a formal and permanent peacetime military alliance with Western Europe.

It is, of course, easy to see self-serving motivations at work in the invitations the British government and its counterparts in Western Europe and the Near East extended to the United States to expand its influence in their parts of the world. It could be argued that had that desire for an American presence not existed, these "third party" assessments of Russian intentions might have been considerably less alarmist than they were. But that is missing the point, for it is also the case that had a credible Soviet threat not presented itself, these countries would not have been seeking the expansion of American power in the first place. "It has really become a matter of the defence of western civilisation," the British Foreign Office concluded early in 1948:

> [N]ot only is the Soviet government not prepared at the present state to co-operate in any real sense with any non-Communist . . . Government, but it is actively preparing to extend its hold over the remaining portion of continental Europe and, subsequently, over the Middle East and no doubt the bulk of the Far East as well. . . . [P]hysical control of the Eurasian land mass and eventual control of the whole World Island is what the Politburo is aiming at—no less a thing than that. The immensity of the aim should not betray us into believing in its impracticality. Indeed, unless positive and vigorous steps are shortly taken by those other states who are in a position to take them . . . the Soviet Union will gain political and strategical advantages which will set the great Communist machine in action, leading either to the establishment of a World Dictatorship or (more probably) to the collapse of organised society over great stretches of the globe.

It is significant that this top-secret Foreign Office document, circulated only within the highest levels of the British government and declassified only after the passage of more than three decades, should have revealed an assessment of the Soviet threat more sweeping in character and apocalyptic in tone than anything in the record of private or public statements by major American officials at the time. The progression from Mackinder to [author of *The Decline of the West* Oswald] Spengler, it appears, was easier than one might think.

History, inescapably, involves viewing distant pasts through the prism of more recent ones. The incontestable fact that the United States over-reacted more than once during the subsequent history of the Cold War to the perceived threat of Soviet and/or "communist" expansionism has, to an extent, blinded us to the equally demonstrable fact that in the immediate postwar years the behavior of the Russians alarmed not just Americans but a good portion of the rest of the world as well. How well-founded that alarm was—how accurately it reflected the realities that shaped Soviet policy—are issues upon which there are legitimate grounds for disagreement. But to deny that the alarm itself was sincere, or that Americans were not alone in perceiving it, is to distort the view through the prism more than is necessary. Fear, after all, can be genuine without being rational. And, as Sigmund Freud once pointed out, even paranoids can have real enemies.

American Expansionism and Exaggerations of the Soviet Threat

THOMAS G. PATERSON

President Harry S Truman and his Secretary of State Dean Acheson, Henry A. Kissinger has remarked, "ushered in the most creative period in the history of American foreign policy." Presidents from Eisenhower to Reagan have exalted Truman for his decisiveness and success in launching the Truman Doctrine, the Marshall Plan, and NATO, and for staring the Soviets down in Berlin during those hair-trigger days of the blockade and airlift. John F. Kennedy and Lyndon B. Johnson invoked memories of Truman and the containment doctrine again and again to explain American intervention in Vietnam. Jimmy Carter has written in his memoirs that Truman had served as his model—that he studied Truman's career more than that of any other president and came to admire greatly his courage, honesty, and willingness "to be unpopular if he believed his actions were the best for the country." Some historians have gone so far as to claim that Truman saved humankind from World War III. On the other hand, he has drawn a diverse set of critics. The diplomat and analyst George F. Kennan, the journalist Walter Lippmann, the political scientist Hans Morgenthau, politicians of the left and right, like Henry A. Wallace and Robert A. Taft, and many historians have questioned Truman's penchant for his quick, simple answer, blunt, careless rhetoric, and facile analogies, his moralism that obscured the complexity of causation, his militarization of American foreign policy, his impatience with diplomacy itself, and his exaggeration of the Soviet threat.

Still, there is no denying the man and his contributions. He fashioned policies and doctrines that have guided leaders to this day. He helped initiate the nuclear age with his decisions to annihilate Hiroshima and Nagasaki with atomic bombs and to develop the hydrogen bomb. His reconstruction programs rehabilitated former enemies West Germany and Japan into thriving, industrial giants and close American allies. His administration's search for

From *Meeting the Communist Threat: Truman to Reagan*, by Thomas G. Paterson. Copyright © 1988 by Thomas G. Paterson. Reprinted by permission of Oxford University Press.

oil in Arab lands and endorsement of a new Jewish state in Palestine planted the United States in the Middle East as never before. Overall, Truman projected American power onto the world stage with unprecedented activity, expanding American interests worldwide, providing American solutions to problems afflicting countries far distant from the United States, establishing the United States as the pre-eminent nation in the postwar era.

Historians have given high marks to the President from Missouri with the memorable "give 'em hell Harry" style. In an elaborate polling of historians conducted in the early 1980s, Truman was judged "near great," just behind Andrew Jackson, Woodrow Wilson, and Theodore Roosevelt and just ahead of John Adams, Lyndon B. Johnson, and Dwight D. Eisenhower. He was also ranked seventh in a list of the most "controversial" Presidents—a list headed, of course, by Richard M. Nixon. When historians distinguished Truman's attributes, they usually mentioned his activism as a "doer," foreign policy accomplishments, expansion of executive power, decisiveness, shaping and using of public opinion, and personal integrity.

On April 12, 1945, Vice President Truman was presiding over the United States Senate. He was bored, his thoughts wandering to a poker game scheduled that evening with friends at the Statler Hotel. Shortly after gaveling the Senate to adjournment that afternoon, Truman dropped into the private office of Speaker of the House Sam Rayburn to discuss some legislation and to strike a few liquid blows for liberty. Soon Truman learned that the White House had called: he should come over immediately and quietly. He put down his bourbon and water, apologized to Rayburn for the hurried departure, and hailed his chauffeur. Once in the White House Truman was escorted to the second floor study of Eleanor Roosevelt. There sad faces signaled Truman for the first time that something momentous was about to happen. Mrs. Roosevelt placed her hand on Truman's shoulder and announced that President Franklin D. Roosevelt had died. "Is there anything I can do for you?" asked a stunned Truman. Eleanor Roosevelt shook her head and replied: "Is there anything we can do for you? For you are the one in trouble now."

Trouble indeed. As Truman confided to his diary that day, "the weight of the Government had fallen on my shoulders. . . . I knew the President had a great many meetings with Churchill and Stalin. I was not familiar with any of these things and it was really something to think about. . . ." In fact, Truman as Vice President had never been included in high-level foreign policy discussions; between the inauguration and the President's death, Truman had met only three times with Roosevelt. And foreign affairs had never been a primary interest of Truman's; he had not sat, for example, on the Foreign Relations Committee during his ten years as a senator. Shortly after becoming President, Truman admitted to the Secretary of State that he "was very hazy about the Yalta [Conference] matters," especially about Poland. Later he would lament that Roosevelt "never did talk to me confidentially about the war, or about foreign affairs or what he had in mind for the peace after the war." The weight of foreign policy had fallen on him, and he knew so little. "I was plenty scared." Apprehensive and insecure though he was, Truman was not content to sit in Roosevelt's shadow or brood about his inadequacies and new responsibilities. He would be "President in his own right," he told his first Cabinet meeting. And through trial and error he became so.

About three months after assuming office, a more self-assertive but still self-doubting Truman boarded a ship for Europe, there to meet at Potsdam, near Berlin, with two of recent history's most imposing figures, Winston Churchill and Josef Stalin. "I sure dread this trip, worse than anything I've had to face," he wrote his beloved wife Bess. On July 16, 1945, Truman visited Berlin, where he witnessed the heavy destruction of the city, like much of Europe, now reduced to rubble. "I was thankful," he wrote later, "that the United States had been spared the most unbelievable devastation of this war." At the Potsdam Conference Truman quickly took the measure of the eloquent Churchill and austere Stalin. "The boys say I gave them an earful," he boasted. He told his wife that "I reared up on my hind legs and told 'em where to get off and they got off."

Truman's assertiveness at Potsdam on such issues as Poland and Germany stemmed not only from his forthright personality, but also from his learning that America's scientists had just successfully exploded an atomic bomb which could be used against Japan to end World War II. And more, it might serve as a diplomatic weapon to persuade others to behave according to American precepts. The news of the atomic test's success gave Truman "an entirely new feeling of confidence . . . ," Secretary of War Henry L. Stimson recorded in his diary. "Now I know what happened to Truman yesterday," commented Churchill. "When he got to the meeting after having read this report he was a changed man. He told the Russians just where they got off and generally bossed the whole meeting."

Truman soon became known for what he himself called his "tough method." He crowed about giving Russia's Commissar for Foreign Affairs, V. M. Molotov, a "straight 'one-two to the jaw' " in their first meeting in the White House not long after Roosevelt's death. Yet Secretary Stimson worried about the negative effects of Truman's "brutal frankness," and Ambassador Harriman was skeptical that the President's slam-bang manner worked to America's advantage. Truman's brash, salty style suited his bent for the verbal brawl, but it ill-fit a world of diplomacy demanding quiet deliberation, thoughtful weighing of alternatives, patience, flexibility, and searching analysis of the motives and capabilities of others. If Truman "took 'em for a ride," as he bragged after Potsdam, the dangerous road upon which he raced led to the Cold War. "It isn't any use kicking a tough hound [like the Russians] around because a tough hound will kick back," retired Secretary Cordell Hull remarked after witnessing deteriorating Soviet-American relations.

The United States entered the postwar period, then, with a new, in-experienced, yet bold President who was aware of America's enviable power in a world hobbled by war-wrought devastation and who shared the popular notion of "Red Fascism." To study this man and the power at his command, the state of the world in which he acted, his reading of the

Soviet threat, and his declaration of the containment doctrine to meet the perceived threat further helps us to understand the origins of the Cold War. Truman's lasting legacy is his tremendous activism in extending American influence on a global scale—his building of an American "empire" or "hegemony." We can disagree over whether this postwar empire was created reluctantly, defensively, by invitation, or deliberately, by self-interested design. But few will deny that the drive to contain Communism fostered an exceptional, worldwide American expansion that produced empire and ultimately, and ironically, insecurity, for the more the United States expanded and drove in foreign stakes, the more vulnerable it seemed to become— the more exposed it became to a host of challenges from Communists and non-Communists alike.

In the aftermath of a war that bequeathed staggering human tragedy, rubble, and social and political chaos, "something new had to be created," recalled Dean Acheson. America's task "was one of fashioning, trying to help fashion what would come after the destruction of the old world." World order had to be reconstructed, societies, political systems, and economies had to be rebuilt. Europe lost more than 30 million dead in the Second World War. Of this total, the Russians suffered between 15 and 20 million dead, the Poles 5.8 million dead, and the Germans 4.5 million dead. Asian casualties were also staggering: Japan lost 2 million, and millions of Chinese also died. Everywhere, armies had trampled farms and bombs had crumbled cities. Everywhere, transportation and communications systems lay in ruins. Everywhere, water sources were contaminated and food supplies depleted. Everywhere, factories were gutted and lacked raw materials and labor. Everywhere, displaced persons searched for families and homes. One American journalist visited Warsaw, Poland, in 1945 and saw nothing but "rows of roofless, doorless, windowless walls. . . ." An American general described Berlin as a "city of the dead." In Greece one million people were homeless, agricultural production was down 50 percent, and 80 percent of railway rolling stock was inoperable. The bridges over the Danube River were demolished, and debris and bodies clogged the Rhine, Oder, and Elbe waterways. The Ukraine, once a center for coal, iron, steel, and farm goods, had been ravaged by the German scorched-earth policy. Much of the Soviet Union's national wealth had been destroyed. When the Secretary General of the United Nations visited Russia, he found "charred and twisted villages and cities . . . the most complete exhibit of destruction I have ever witnessed."

To recount this grisly story of disaster is to emphasize that economic, social, and hence political "disintegration" characterized the postwar international system. The question of how this disintegration could be reversed preoccupied Truman officials. Thinking in the peace and prosperity idiom, they believed that a failure to act would jeopardize American interests, drag the United States into depression and war, spawn totalitarianism and aggression, and permit the rise of Communists and other leftists who were eager to exploit the disorder. The prospects were grim, the precedents for action few, the necessities certain, the consequences of inaction grave. This formidable task of reconstruction drew the United States and the Soviet Union into conflict, for each had its own model for rebuilding states and each sought to align nations with its foreign policy.

Political turmoil within nations also drew America and Russia into conflict, for each saw gains to be made and losses to be suffered in the outcome of the political battles. Old regime leaders vied with leftists and other dissidents in state after state. In Poland, the Communist Lublin Poles dueled the conservative London Poles; in Greece the National Liberation Front contested the authority of the British-backed conservative Athens government; in China Mao Zedong's forces continued the civil war against Jiang Jieshi's (Chiang Kai-shek's) Nationalist regime. In occupied Germany, Austria, and Korea, the victors created competitive zones and backed different political groups. Much seemed at stake: economic ties, strategic bases, military allies, intelligence posts, and votes in international organizations. When the United States and the Soviet Union meddled in these politically unstable settings in their quest for influence, they collided— often fiercely.

The collapse of old empires also wrenched world affairs and invited confrontation between America and Russia. Weakened by the war and unable to sustain colonial armies in the field, the imperialists were forced to give way to nationalists who had long worked for independence. The British withdrew from India (and Pakistan) in 1947, from Ceylon and Burma the next year. The Dutch left Indonesia in 1949. The French clung to Indochina, engaged in bloody war, but departed in 1954. The European imperialists also pulled out of parts of Africa and the Middle East. The United States itself in 1946 granted independence to the Philippines. Decolonization produced a shifting of power within the international system and the emergence of new states whose allegiances both the Americans and Russians avidly sought.

With postwar economies, societies, politics, and empires shattered, President Truman confronted an awesome set of problems that would have bedeviled any leader. He also had impressive responsibilities and opportunities, because the United States had escaped from World War II not only intact but richer and stronger. America's abundant farmlands were spared from the tracks of marching armies, its cities were never leveled by bombs, and its factories remained in place. During the war, America's gross national product skyrocketed and every economic indicator, such as steel production, recorded significant growth. In the postwar years, Americans possessed the power, said Truman, "either to make the world economy work or, simply by failing to take the proper action, to allow it to collapse." To create the American-oriented world the Truman Administration desired, and to isolate adversaries, the United States issued or withheld loans (giving one to Britain but not to Russia), launched major reconstruction programs like the Marshall Plan, and offered technical assistance through the Point Four Program. American dollars and votes also dominated the World Bank and International Monetary Fund, transforming them into instruments of American diplomacy.

The United States not only possessed the resources for reconstruction, but also the implements of destruction. The United States had the world's largest Navy, floating in two oceans, the most powerful Air Force, a shrinking yet still formidable Army, and a monopoly of the most frightening weapon of all, the atomic bomb. Not until after the Korean War did the United States stockpile many atomic bombs, but Secretary of State James F. Byrnes, like other American leaders, was known to say that he liked to use the atomic bomb for diplomatic leverage at conferences. Once, during a social occasion at the London Conference in the fall of 1945, Byrnes and Molotov bantered. The Soviet Commissar asked Byrnes if he had an atomic bomb in his "side pocket." Byrnes shot back that the weapon was actually in his "hip pocket." And, "if you don't cut out all this stalling and let us get down to work, I am going to pull an atomic bomb out of my hip pocket and let you have it." Although Molotov apparently laughed, he could not have been amused, for he suspected that the Americans counted on the bomb as an implied threat to gain Soviet diplomatic concessions—and, as the supreme weapon, to blast the Soviet Union into smithereens in a war. Henry L. Stimson, for one, disapproved of "atomic diplomacy," because, he explained to the President, if Americans continued to have "this weapon rather ostentatiously on our hip, their [the Russians] suspicions and their distrust of our purposes and motives will increase."

Because of America's unusual postwar power, the Truman Administration could expand the United States sphere of influence beyond the Western Hemisphere and also intervene to protect American interests. But this begs a key question: Why did President Truman think it necessary to project American power abroad, to pursue an activist, global foreign policy unprecedented in United States history? The answer has several parts. First, Americans drew lessons from their experience in the 1930s. While indulging in their so-called "isolationism," they had watched economic depression spawn political extremism, which in turn, produced aggression and war. Never again, they vowed. No more appeasement with totalitarians, no more Munichs. "Red Fascism" became a popular phrase to express this American idea. The message seemed evident: To prevent a reincarnation of the 1930s, the United States would have to use its vast power to fight economic instability abroad. Americans felt compelled to project their power, second, because they feared, in the peace-and-prosperity thinking of the time, economic doom stemming from an economic sickness abroad that might spread to the United States, and from American dependency on overseas supplies of raw materials. To aid Europeans and other peoples would not only help them, but also sustain a high American standard of living and gain political friends, as in the case of Italy, where American foreign aid and advice influenced national elections and brought defeat to the left. The American fear of postwar shortages of petroleum also encouraged the Truman Administration to penetrate Middle Eastern oil in a major way. In Saudi Arabia, for example, Americans built and operated the strategically important Dhahran Airport and dominated that nation's oil resources.

Another reason why Truman projected American power so boldly derived from new strategic thinking. Because of the advent of the air age, travel across the world was shortened in time. Strategists spoke of the shrinkage of the globe. Places once deemed beyond American curiosity or interest now loomed important. Airplanes could travel great distances to deliver bombs. Powerful as it was, then, the United States also appeared vulnerable, especially to air attack. As General Carl A. Spaatz emphasized: "As top dog, America becomes target No. 1." He went on to argue that fast aircraft left no warning time for the United States. "The Pearl Harbor of a future war might well be Chicago, or Detroit, or even Washington." To prevent such an occurrence, American leaders worked to acquire overseas bases in both the Pacific and Atlantic, thereby denying a potential enemy an attack route to the Western Hemisphere. Forward bases would also permit the United States to conduct offensive operations more effectively. The American strategic frontier had to be pushed outward. Thus the United States took the former Japanese-controlled Pacific islands of the Carolines, Marshalls, and Marianas, maintained garrisons in Germany and Japan, and sent military missions to Iran, Turkey, Greece, Saudi Arabia, China, and to fourteen Latin American states. The Joint Chiefs of Staff and Department of State lists of desired foreign bases, and of sites where air transit rights were sought, included such far-flung spots as Algeria, India, French Indochina, New Zealand, Iceland, and the Azores. When asked where the American Navy would float, Navy Secretary James Forrestal replied: "Wherever there is a sea." Today we may take the presumption of a global American presence for granted, but in Truman's day it was new, even radical thinking, especially after the "isolationist" 1930s.

These several explanations for American globalism suggest that the United States would have been an expansionist power whether or not the obstructionist Soviets were lurking about. That is, America's own needs— ideological, political, economic, strategic—encouraged such a projection of power. As the influential National Security Council Paper No. 68 (NSC-68) noted in April 1950, the "overall policy" of the United States was "designed to foster a world environment in which the American system can survive and flourish." This policy "we would probably pursue even if there were no Soviet threat."

Americans, of course, did perceive a Soviet threat. Thus we turn to yet another explanation for the United States' dramatic extension of power early in the Cold War: to contain the Soviets. The Soviets unsettled Americans in so many ways. Their harsh Communist dogma and propagandistic slogans were not only monotonous; they also seemed threatening because of their call for world revolution and for the demise of capitalism. In the United Nations the Soviets cast vetoes and even on occasion walked out of the organization. At international conferences their "*nyets*" stung American ears. When they negotiated, the Soviets annoyed their interlocutors by repeating the same point over and over again, delaying meetings, or abruptly shifting positions. Truman labeled them "pigheaded," and Dean Acheson thought them so coarse and insulting that he once allowed that they were not "housebroken."

The Soviet Union, moreover, had territorial ambitions, grabbing parts of Poland, Rumania, and Finland, and demanding parts of Turkey. In Eastern

Europe, with their Red Army positioned to intimidate, the Soviets quickly manhandled the Poles and Rumanians. Communists in 1947 and 1948 seized power in Hungary and Czechoslovakia. Some Americans predicted that the Soviet military would roll across Western Europe. In general, Truman officials pictured the Soviet Union as an implacable foe to an open world, an opportunistic nation that would probe for weak spots, exploit economic misery, snuff out individual freedom, and thwart self-determination. Americans thought the worst, some claiming that a Soviet-inspired international conspiracy insured perennial hostility and a creeping aggression aimed at American interests. To Truman and his advisers, the Soviets stood as the world's bully, and the very existence of this menacing bear necessitated an activist American foreign policy and an exertion of American power as a "counterforce."

But Truman officials exaggerated the Soviet threat, imagining an adversary that never measured up to the galloping monster so often depicted by alarmist Americans. Even if the Soviets intended to dominate the world, or just Western Europe, they lacked the capabilities to do so. The Soviets had no foreign aid to dispense; outside Russia Communist parties were minorities; the Soviet economy was seriously crippled by the war; and the Soviet military suffered significant weaknesses. The Soviets lacked a modern navy, a strategic air force, the atomic bomb, and air defenses. Their wrecked economy could not support or supply an army in the field for very long, and their technology was antiquated. Their ground forces lacked motorized transportation, adequate equipment, and troop morale. A Soviet *blitzkrieg* invasion of Western Europe had little chance of success and would have proven suicidal for the Soviets, for even if they managed to gain temporary control of Western Europe by a military thrust, they could not strike the United States. So they would have to assume defensive positions and await crushing American attacks, probably including atomic bombings of Soviet Russia itself—plans for which existed.

Other evidence also suggests that a Soviet military threat to Western Europe was more myth than reality. The Soviet Union demobilized its forces after the war, dropping to about 2.9 million personnel in 1948. Many of its 175 divisions were under-strength, and large numbers of them were engaged in occupation duties, resisting challenges to Soviet authority in Eastern Europe. American intelligence sources reported as well that the Soviets could not count on troops of the occupied countries, which were quite unreliable, if not rebellious. At most, the Soviets had 700,000 to 800,000 troops available for an attack against the West. To resist such an attack, the West had about 800,000 troops, or approximate parity. For these reasons, top American leaders did not expect a Soviet onslaught against Western Europe. They and their intelligence sources emphasized Soviet military weaknesses, not strengths, Soviet hesitancy, not boldness.

Why then did Americans so fear the Soviets? Why did the Central Intelligence Agency, the Joint Chiefs of Staff, and the President exaggerate the Soviet threat? The first explanation is that their intelligence estimates were just that—estimates. The American intelligence community was still in a state of infancy, hardly the well-developed system it would become in the 1950s and 1960s. So Americans lacked complete assurance that their figures on Soviet force deployment or armaments were accurate or close to the mark. When leaders do not know, they tend to assume the worst of an adversary's intentions and capabilities, or to think that the Soviets might miscalculate, sparking a war they did not want. In a chaotic world, the conception of a single, inexorably aggressive adversary also brought a comforting sense of knowing and consistency.

Truman officials also exaggerated the Soviet threat in order "to extricate the United States from commitments and restraints that were no longer considered desirable." For example, they loudly chastised the Soviets for violating the Yalta agreements; yet Truman and his advisers knew the Yalta provisions were at best vague and open to differing interpretations. But, more, they purposefully misrepresented the Yalta agreement on the vital question of the composition of the Polish government. In so doing, they hoped to decrease the high degree of Communist participation that the Yalta conferees had insured when they stated that the new Polish regime would be formed by reorganizing the provisional Lublin (Communist) government. Through charges of Soviet malfeasance Washington sought to justify its own retreat from Yalta, such as its abandonment of the $20 billion reparations figure for Germany (half of which was supposed to go to the Soviet Union).

Another reason for the exaggeration: Truman liked things in black and white, as his aide Clark Clifford noted. Nuances, ambiguities, and counterevidence were often discounted to satisfy the President's preference for the simpler answer or his pre-conceived notions of Soviet aggressiveness. In mid-1946, for example, the Joint Chiefs of Staff deleted from a report to Truman a section that stressed Soviet weaknesses. American leaders also exaggerated the Soviet threat because it was useful in galvanizing and unifying American public opinion for an abandonment of recent and still lingering "isolationism" and support for an expansive foreign policy. Kennan quoted a colleague as saying that "if it [Soviet threat] had never existed, we would have had to invent it, to create a sense of urgency we need to bring us to the point of decisive action." The military particularly overplayed the Soviet threat in order to persuade Congress to endorse larger defense budgets. This happened in 1948–49 with the creation of the North Atlantic Treaty Organization. NATO was established not to halt a Soviet military attack, because none was anticipated, but to give Europeans a psychological boost—a "will to resist." American officials believed that the European Recovery Program would falter unless there was a "sense of security" to buttress it. They nurtured apprehension, too, that some European nations might lean toward neutralism unless they were brought together under a security umbrella. NATO also seemed essential to help members resist internal subversion. The exaggerated, popular view that NATO was formed to deter a Soviet invasion of Western Europe by conventional forces stems, in part, from Truman's faulty recollection in his published memoirs.

Still another explanation for why Americans exaggerated the Soviet threat is found in their attention since the Bolshevik Revolution of 1917 to the utopian Communist goal of world revolution, confusing goals with actual behavior. Thus Americans believed that the sinister Soviets and their Communist allies would exploit postwar economic, social, and political disorder, not through a direct military thrust, but rather through covert subversion. The recovery of Germany and Japan became necessary, then, to deny the Communists political opportunities to thwart American plans for the integration of these former enemies into an American system of trade and defense. And because economic instability troubled so much of Eurasia, Communist gains through subversion might deny the United States strategic raw materials.

Why dwell on this question of the American exaggeration of the Soviet threat? Because it over-simplified international realities by under-estimating local conditions that might thwart Soviet/Communist successes and by over-estimating the Soviet ability to act. Because it encouraged the Soviets to fear encirclement and to enlarge their military establishment, thereby contributing to a dangerous weapons race. Because it led to indiscriminate globalism. Because it put a damper on diplomacy; American officials were hesitant to negotiate with an opponent variously described as malevolent, deceitful, and inhuman. They especially did not warm to negotiations when some critics were ready to cry that diplomacy, which could produce compromises, was evidence in itself of softness toward Communism.

Exaggeration of the threat also led Americans to misinterpret events and in so doing to prompt the Soviets to make decisions contrary to American wishes. For example, the Soviet presence in Eastern Europe, once considered a simple question of the Soviets' building an iron curtain or bloc after the war, is now seen by historians in more complex terms. The Soviets did not seem to have a master plan for the region and followed different policies in different countries. Poland and Rumania were subjugated right away; Yugoslavia, on the other hand, was an independent Communist state led by Josip Tito, who broke dramatically with Stalin in 1948; Hungary conducted elections in the fall of 1945 (the Communists got only 17 percent of the vote) and did not suffer a Communist coup until 1947; in Czechoslovakia, free elections in May 1946 produced a non-Communist government that functioned until 1948; Finland, although under Soviet scrutiny, affirmed its independence. The Soviets did not have a firm grip on Eastern Europe before 1948—a prime reason why many American leaders believed the Soviets harbored weaknesses.

American policies were designed to roll the Soviets back. The United States reconstruction loan policy, encouragement of dissident groups, and appeal for free elections alarmed Moscow, contributing to a Soviet push to secure the area. The issue of free elections illustrates the point. Such a call was consistent with cherished American principle. But in the context of Eastern Europe and the Cold War, problems arose. First, Americans conspicuously followed a double standard which foreigners noted time and again; that is, if the principle of free elections really mattered, why not hold such elections in the United States' sphere of influence in Latin America, where an unsavory lot of dictators ruled? Second, free elections would have produced victories for anti-Soviet groups. Such results could only unsettle the Soviets and invite them to intervene to protect their interests in neighboring states—just as the United States had intervened in Cuba and Mexico in the twentieth century when hostile groups assumed power. In Hungary, for example, it was the non-Communist leader Ferenc Nagy who delayed elections in late 1946 because he knew the Communist Party would lose badly, thereby possibly triggering a repressive Soviet response. And, third, the United States had so little influence in Eastern Europe that it had no way of insuring free elections—no way of backing up its demands with power.

Walter Lippmann, among others, thought that the United States should tame its meddling in the region and make the best out of a bad arrangement of power. "I do believe," he said in 1947, "we shall have to recognize the principle of boundaries of spheres of influence which either side will not cross and have to proceed on the old principle that a good fence makes good neighbors." Kennan shared this view, as did one State Department official who argued that the United States was incapable of becoming a successful watchdog in Eastern Europe. American "barkings, growlings, snappings, and occasional bitings," Cloyce K. Huston prophesized, would only irritate the Soviets without reducing their power. Better still, argued some analysts, if the United States tempered its ventures into European affairs, then the Soviets, surely less alarmed, might tolerate more openness. But the United States did not stay out. Americans tried to project their power into a region where they had little chance of succeeding, but had substantial opportunity to irritate and alarm the always suspicious Soviets. In this way, it has been suggested, the United States itself helped pull down the iron curtain.

Another example of the exaggeration of the Soviet threat at work is found in the Truman Doctrine of 1947. Greece was beset by civil war, and the British could no longer fund a war against Communist-led insurgents who had a considerable non-Communist following. On March 12, Truman enunciated a universal doctrine: It "must be the policy of the United States to support free peoples who are resisting attempted subjugation by armed minorities or by outside pressures." Although he never mentioned the Soviet Union by name, his juxtaposition of words like "democratic" and "totalitarian" and his references to Eastern Europe made the menace to Greece appear to be the Soviets. But there was and is no evidence of Soviet involvement in the Greek civil war. In fact, the Soviets had urged both the Greek Communists and their allies the Yugoslavs to stop the fighting for fear that the conflict would draw the United States into the Mediterranean. And the Greek Communists were strong nationalists. The United States nonetheless intervened in a major way in Greek affairs, becoming responsible for right-wing repression and a military establishment that plagued Greek politics through much of its postwar history. As for Turkey, official Washington did not expect the Soviet Union to strike militarily against that bordering nation. The Soviets were too weak in 1947 to undertake such a major operation, and they were asking for joint control of the Dardanelles largely for defense, for security. Then why did the President, in the Truman Doctrine speech, suggest that Turkey was imminently threatened? American strategists worried that Russia's long-term objective was the subjugation of its neighbor. But they also wished to exploit an opportunity to enhance the American military position in the Mediterranean region and in a state bordering the Soviet Union. The Greek crisis and the Truman Doctrine speech provided an appropriate environment to build up an American military presence in the Eastern Mediterranean for use against the Soviets should the unwanted war ever come.

Truman's alarmist language further fixed the mistaken idea in the American mind that the Soviets were unrelenting aggressors intent upon undermining peace, and that the United States, almost alone, had to meet them everywhere. Truman's exaggerations and this commitment to the containment doctrine did not go unchallenged. Secretary Marshall himself was startled by the President's muscular anti-Communist rhetoric, and he questioned the wisdom of overstating the case. The Soviet specialist Llewellyn Thompson urged "caution" in swinging too far toward "outright opposition to Russia. . . ." Walter Lippmann, in reacting to both Truman's speech and George F. Kennan's now famous "Mr. 'X' "article in the July 1947 issue of the journal *Foreign Affairs*, labeled containment a "strategic monstrosity," because it made no distinctions between important or vital and not-so-important or peripheral areas. Because American power was not omnipresent, Lippmann further argued, the "policy can be implemented only by recruiting, subsidizing and supporting a heterogeneous array of satellites, clients, dependents and puppets." He also criticized the containment doctrine for placing more emphasis on confrontation than on diplomacy.

Truman himself came to see that there were dangers in stating imprecise, universal doctrines. He became boxed by his own rhetoric. When Mao Zedong's forces claimed victory in 1949 over Jiang's regime, conservative Republicans, angry Democrats, and various McCarthyites pilloried the President for letting China "fall." China lost itself, he retorted. But his critics pressed the point: if containment was to be applied everywhere, as the President had said in the Truman Doctrine, why not China? Truman appeared inconsistent, when, in fact, in the case of China, he was ultimately prudent in cutting American losses where the United States proved incapable of reaching its goals. Unable to disarm his detractors on this issue, Truman stood vulnerable in the early 1950s to political demagogues who fueled McCarthyism. The long-term consequences in this example have been grave. Democrats believed they could never lose "another China"—never permit Communists or Marxists, whether or not linked to Moscow, to assume power abroad. President John F. Kennedy later said, for example, that he could not withdraw from Vietnam because that might be perceived as "another China" and spark charges that he was soft on Communism. America, in fact, could not bring itself to open diplomatic relations with the People's Republic of China until 1979.

Jiang's collapse joined the Soviet explosion of an atomic bomb, the formation of the German Democratic Republic (East Germany) and the

Sino-Soviet Friendship Treaty to arouse American feeling in late 1949 and early 1950 that the Soviet threat had dramatically escalated. Although Kennan told his State Department colleagues that such feeling was "largely of our own making" rather than an accurate accounting of Soviet actions, the composers of NSC-68 preferred to dwell on a more dangerous Soviet menace in extreme rhetoric not usually found in a secret report. But because the April 1950 document was aimed at President Truman, we can certainly understand why its language was hyperbolic. The fanatical and militant Soviets, concluded NSC-68, were seeking to impose "absolute authority over the rest of the world." America had to frustrate the global "design" of the "evil men" of the Kremlin, who were unrelentingly bent on "piecemeal aggression" against the "free world" through military force, infiltration, and intimidation. The report called for a huge American and allied military build-up and nuclear arms development.

NSC-68, most scholars agree, was a flawed, even amateurish, document. It assumed a Communist monolith that did not exist, drew alarmist conclusions based upon vague and inaccurate information about Soviet capabilities, made grand, unsubstantiated claims about Soviet intentions, glossed over the presence of many non-democratic countries in the "free world," and recommended against negotiations with Moscow at the very time the Soviets were advancing toward a policy of "peaceful co-existence." One State Department expert on the Soviet Union, Charles E. Bohlen, although generally happy with the report's conclusions, faulted NSC-68 for assuming a Soviet plot for world conquest—for "oversimplifying the problem." No, he advised, the Soviets sought foremostly to maintain their regime and to extend it abroad "to the degree that is possible without serious risk to the internal regime." In short, there were limits to Soviet behavior. But few were listening to such cautionary voices. NSC-68 became American dogma, especially when the outbreak of the Korean War in June of 1950 sanctified it as a prophetic "we told you so."

The story of Truman's foreign policy is basically an accounting of how the United States, because of its own expansionism and exaggeration of the Soviet threat, became a global power. Truman projected American power after the Second World War to rehabilitate Western Europe, secure new allies, guarantee strategic and economic links, and block Communist or Soviet influence. He firmly implanted the image of the Soviets as relentless, worldwide transgressors with whom it is futile to negotiate. Through his exaggeration of the Soviet threat, Truman made it very likely that the United States would continue to practice global interventionism years after he left the White House.

FURTHER READING

Les K. Adler and Thomas G. Paterson, "Red Fascism," *American Historical Review*, 75 (1970), 1046–64

Gar Alperovitz, *Atomic Diplomacy* (1965 and 1985)

Stephen Ambrose, *Rise to Globalism* (1985)

Terry H. Anderson, *The United States, Great Britain, and the Cold War* (1981)

Barton J. Bernstein, ed., *The Atomic Bomb* (1975)

————, ed., *Politics and Policies of the Truman Administration* (1970)

Michael Boll, *Cold War in the Balkans* (1984)

Paul Boyer, *By the Bomb's Early Light* (1986)

Bulletin of the Atomic Scientists, 41 (1985), entire issue for August

Robert J. C. Butow, *Japan's Decision to Surrender* (1954)

Committee for the Compilation of Materials on Damage Caused by the Atomic Bombs in Hiroshima and Nagasaki, *Hiroshima and Nagasaki* (1981)

Hugh DeSantis, *The Diplomacy of Silence: The American Foreign Service, the Soviet Union, and the Cold War, 1933–147* (1980)

Robert J. Donovan, *Conflict and Crisis* (1977)

————, *Tumultuous Years* (1982)

Herbert Feis, *The Atomic Bomb and the End of World War II* (1966)

————, *From Trust to Terror* (1970)

Denna F. Fleming, *The Cold War and Its Origins* (1961)

Richard Freeland, *The Truman Doctrine and the Origins of McCarthyism* (1971)

John Lewis Gaddis, *Russia, the Soviet Union, and the United States* (1978)

————, *Strategies of Containment* (1982)

————, *The United States and the Origins of the Cold War* (1972)

Charles Gati, ed., *Caging the Bear: Containment and the Cold War* (1974)

Lloyd C. Gardner, *Architects of Illusion* (1970)

Richard Gardner, *Sterling-Dollar Diplomacy* (1969)

John Gimbel, *The American Occupation of Germany* (1968)

————, *The Origins of the Marshall Plan* (1976)

James L. Gormly, *The Collapse of the Grand Alliance, 1945–1948* (1987)

Louis Halle, *The Cold War as History* (1967)

Fraser J. Harbutt, *The Iron Curtain* (1986)

John L. Harper, *America and the Reconstruction of Italy* (1986)

Robert M. Hathaway, *Ambiguous Partnership: Britain and America, 1944–1947* (1981)

Gregg Herken, *The Winning Weapon* (1981)

George Herring, *Aid to Russia, 1941–1946* (1973)

Michael J. Hogan, *The Marshall Plan* (1987)

John O. Iatrides, *Revolt in Athens* (1972)

————, ed., *Greece in the 1940s* (1981)

Gabriel Kolko and Joyce Kolko, *The Limits of Power* (1972)

Bruce Kuklick, *American Reparations Policy and the Division of Germany* (1972)

Bruce Kuniholm, *The Origins of the Cold War in the Near East* (1980)

Walter LaFeber, *America, Russia, and the Cold War* (1985)

Deborah Larson, *Origins of Containment* (1985)

Melvyn P. Leffler, "The American Conception of National Security and the Beginnings of the Cold War, 1945–48," *American Historical Review*, 89 (1984), 346–81

Ralph Levering, *The Cold War, 1945–1987* (1988)

Walter Lippmann, *The Cold War* (1947)

Geir Lundestad, *The American Non-Policy Towards Eastern Europe, 1943–1947* (1975)

————, "Empire by Invitation," *Journal of Peace Research*, 23 (1986), 263–77

Mark H. Lyttle, *The Origins of the Iranian-American Alliance, 1941–1953* (1987)

Donald McCoy, *The Presidency of Harry S Truman* (1984)

David McLellan, *Dean Acheson* (1976)

Richard Mayne, *Recovery of Europe* (1973)

Robert L. Messer, *The End of an Alliance* (1982)

Aaron Miller, *Search for Security* (1980) (on Saudi Arabian oil)

James E. Miller, *The United States and Italy, 1940–1950* (1986)

Alan Milward, *The Reconstruction of Western Europe, 1945–51* (1984)
David S. Painter, *Oil and the American Century* (1986)
Thomas G. Paterson, ed., *Cold War Critics* (1971)
———, *On Every Front: The Making of the Cold War* (1979)
———, ed., *The Origins of the Cold War* (1974)
———, *Soviet-American Confrontation* (1973)
Michael Ruddy, *The Cautious Diplomat* (1986) (on Bohlen)
Arthur M. Schlesinger, Jr., "Origins of the Cold War," *Foreign Affairs*, 46 (1967), 22–52
Martin Sherwin, *A World Destroyed* (1975)
Nikolai V. Sivachev and Nikolai N. Yakovlev, *Russia and the United States* (1979)
Gaddis Smith, *Dean Acheson* (1972)
John Spanier, *American Foreign Policy Since World War II* (1983)
William Taubman, *Stalin's American Policy* (1982)
Athan G. Theoharis, *The Yalta Myths* (1970)
Hugh Thomas, *Armed Truce* (1987)
Kenneth W. Thompson, *Cold War Theories* (1981)
Robert W. Tucker, *The Radical Left and American Foreign Policy* (1971)
Adam Ulam, *The Rivals* (1971)
Walter Ullmann, *The United States in Prague, 1945–1948* (1978)
J. Samuel Walker, *Henry A. Wallace and American Foreign Policy* (1976)
Piotr S. Wandycz, *The United States and Poland* (1980)
Samuel F. Wells, Jr., "Sounding the Tocsin: NSC-68 and the Soviet Threat," *International Security*, 4 (1979), 116–58
Imanuel Wexler, *The Marshall Plan Revisited* (1983)
Lawrence S. Wittner, *American Intervention in Greece, 1943–1949* (1982)
Daniel Yergin, *Shattered Peace* (1977)

CHAPTER
8

Mao's China and the Chances for Sino-American Accommodation

From 1945 to the victory of Mao Zedong's (Mao Tse-tung's) Communists in 1949, the United States was deeply involved in the Chinese civil war. About three billion dollars flowed to the regime of Jiang Jieshi (Chiang Kai-shek), leader of the Guomindang (Kuomintang), or Nationalists. American officials also urged reforms upon Jiang, gave his army military advisers, and tried to mediate between the warring parties. Although Americans recognized the indigenous roots of the civil war, they feared the international consequences of a Communist triumph—especially a Sino-Soviet alliance. The failure to draw successfully the containment line in China aroused President Harry S Truman's critics, who believed he, Secretary of State Dean Acheson, and the China experts in the Foreign Service had "lost" China. The extreme anti-Communism of McCarthyism relentlessly pushed this charge, even accusing American leaders of Communist sympathies.

In this politically electric environment, the Truman administration considered whether to offer diplomatic recognition to the new People's Republic of China (PRC), or to back Jiang's exiled government on the island of Formosa, or Taiwan. Whether Truman and Acheson withheld recognition from Mao because of their fear of the domestic political consequences is a point of debate among historians. Some scholars suggest instead that the Truman administration was so inveterately anti-Communist that it interpreted the Communist victory as a Soviet thrust into Asia and hence passed up Chinese overtures for negotiations. Others have argued that the chances for Sino-American accommodation were minimal because of strong Chinese anti-Americanism. Historians agree, however, that the Korean War killed all chances. The origins of American nonrecognition policy, which lasted until 1979, is the subject of this chapter.

✹ *D O C U M E N T S*

In May and June 1949, the American Ambassador in China, John Leighton Stuart, was approached by Huang Hua, a Communist official. Stuart's two telegrams to Washington, the first document, reported the conversations and the tender of an "invitation from Mao and Chou to talk with them." In late May, Zhou Enlai (Chou En-lai), a high-ranking Chinese leader, made an indirect approach to the American Consulate General in Beijing. This demarche was reported to Washington by Consul General O. Edmund Clubb in a June 1 telegram, also reprinted here. The State Department's initial response to the Zhou overture is the next document, followed by President Truman's attitude toward the demarche.

On July 30, 1949, the Department of State issued a "White Paper"—a huge volume of documents and analysis that defended pre-1949 American policies toward China against charges that the United States had "lost" the nation. Secretary Dean Acheson's public letter transmitting the book to the President is included as the fifth selection. The next document is a speech of August 18 by Mao Zedong. Several weeks earlier he had announced that China was "leaning to one side"—the Soviet side in the Cold War. In his August speech he revealed strong anti-American views, accusing the United States of aggression. In the last document, Senator William Knowland of California, a McCarthyite and member of the "China lobby," argued against recognition of the People's Republic. His speech was delivered to the Senate on January 5, 1950.

John Leighton Stuart on Mao's Overture, 1949

Telegram of May 14, 1949

Huang [Hua] called my residence last evening remaining almost 2 hours. Our conversation was friendly and informal. I refrained from political remarks until he opened way which he did after few personal exchanges. I then spoke earnestly of great desire that peoples of all countries had for peace, including, emphatically, my own, of dangerous situation developing despite this universal popular will; of indescribable horrors of next war; of my conviction that much, but not all, present tension due to misunderstandings, fears, suspicions which could be cleared away by mutual frankness; of fears Americans and other non-Communists had of Marxist-Leninist doctrine, subscribed to by CCP [Chinese Communist Party], that world revolution and overthrow of capitalistic governments necessary, thus proclaiming subversive interference or armed invasion as fixed policy. Huang spoke of Chinese people's resentment at American aid to Kmt [Kuomintang, or Nationalist Party] and other "mistakes" of US Policy to which I briefly replied.

Huang asked about my plans and I told him of my instructions, adding that I was glad to stay long enough for symbolic purpose of demonstrating American people's interest in welfare of Chinese people as whole; that I wished to maintain friendly relations of past; that being near end of my active life I hoped to be able somewhat to help restore these relations as I knew my Government and people desired; that my aim was unity, peace, truly democratic government and international good will for which Huang knew I had worked all my life in China.

Huang expressed much interest in recognition of Communist China by USA on terms of equality and mutual benefit. I replied that such terms together with accepted international practice with respect to treaties would be only proper basis. He was greatly surprised at my explanation of status of armed forces in China particularly Marines in Shanghai. Our side of story, that is desire to protect American lives during civil disturbances and chaotic conditions brought on by war, appeared never to have occurred to him. He was obviously impressed. I explained question of national government was internal; that Communists themselves at present had none; that it was customary to recognize whatever government clearly had support of people of country and was able and willing to perform its international obligations; that therefore USA and other countries could do nothing but await developments in China. I hinted that most other nations would tend to follow our lead. I explained functions of foreign consulates in maintaining informal relations with *de facto* regional authorities.

Huang expounded upon needs of China for commercial and other relations with foreign countries. He said instructions had been issued to all military units to protect safety and interests of foreigners. Intrusion into my bedroom was discussed and he promised to do his best in constantly shifting military situation to trace offenders. He explained that first Communist troops in city had not been prepared or properly instructed on treatment of foreigners. . . .

Telegram of June 30, 1949

Huang Hua called on me by appointment June 28. He reported that he had received message from Mao Tse-tung and Chou En-lai assuring me that they would welcome me to Peiping if I wished to visit Yenching University. Background of this suggestion is as follows:

In early June Philip Fugh, in one of his conversations with Huang, asked casually, and not under instructions from me, if it would be possible for me to travel to Peiping to visit my old University as had been my habit in previous years on my birthday and Commencement. At that time Huang made no comment. However, 2 weeks later, June 18 to be precise, in discussing my return to Washington for consultation, Huang himself raised question with Fugh of whether time permitted my making trip to Peiping. Fugh made no commitment, commenting only that he himself had made this suggestion 2 weeks earlier. Neither Fugh nor I followed up this suggestion but apparently Huang did. Present message (almost an invitation) is reply.

Regardless whether initiation this suggestion is considered [by] Peiping to have come from me or from Communists, I can only regard Huang's message as veiled invitation from Mao and Chou to talk with them while ostensibly visiting Yenching. To accept would undoubtedly be gratifying to them, would give me chance to describe American policy; its anxieties regarding Communism and world revolution; its desires for China's future;

and would enable me to carry to Washington most authoritative information regarding CCP intentions. Such trip would be step toward better mutual understanding and should strengthen more liberal anti-Soviet element in CCP. It would provide unique opportunity for American official to talk to top Chinese Communists in informal manner which may not again present itself. It would be imaginative, adventurous indication of US open-minded attitude towards changing political trends in China and would probably have beneficial effect on future Sino-American relations.

On negative side, trip to Peiping before my return to US on consultation would undoubtedly start rumors and speculations in China and might conceivably embarrass Department because of American criticism. It would probably be misunderstood by my colleagues in Diplomatic Corps who might feel that US representative was first to break united front policy which we have sponsored toward Communist regime and might prove beginning of trek of chiefs of mission to Peiping on one pretext or another. Trip to Peiping at this time invariably suggests idea of making similar one to Canton before my return to US.

While visiting both capitals might effectively dramatize American interest in Chinese people as a whole, it might also appear as peace-making gesture, unwarranted interference in China's internal affairs, and would probably be misunderstood by Chinese Communists, thus undoing any beneficial effects of visit north. Finally, trip of US Ambassador to Peiping at this time would enhance greatly prestige, national and international, of Chinese Communists and Mao himself and in a sense would be second step on our part (first having been my remaining Nanking) toward recognition Communist regime.

I received clear impression that Mao, Chou and Huang are very much hoping that I make this trip, whatever their motives. I, of course, gave Huang no answer to Mao's message, replying that, while I enjoyed going back to Yenching, this year had assumed it would be out of question, that I had already delayed longer than intended my departure for Washington; that travel on as yet incompletely restored railway line to Peiping might be taxing for "feeble old man," et cetera. Question of using my airplane was raised. Huang objected on ground danger from Communists' anti-aircraft batteries; that it would take couple days at least to give proper instructions and that there would always be some risk. He continued Peiping trip can now be made in less than 3 days by train, adding that all facilities of railway would be put at my disposal. I could, if thought desirable, make airplane travel condition to visit Peiping and it is not to be excluded that permission would be granted. There is consideration that prestige of travel Peiping my own plane would somewhat offset negative features outlined above.

I have made this rather full statement of case for Department's consideration and decision. I am, of course, ready to make journey by either means should Department consider it desirable, and should be grateful for instructions earliest and nature of reply to Huang. . . .

Zhou Enlai's (Chou En-lai's) Demarche, 1949

Following message given Assistant Military Attaché [David D.] Barrett May 31 by reliable intermediary, origin being Chou En-lai. Chou desired message be transmitted highest American authorities on top secret level without his name being mentioned, said in fact that if it were attributed him he would positively disavow it. Essential there be no leak his name to outside channels. Chou approved transmittal via Barrett who gave message me to transmit, but wanted name unmentioned even to Barrett. Chou desired what he said be conveyed to British, expressed preference transmittal be through Department.

There were few disagreements in CCP Party [*sic*] during agrarian stage revolution but with arrival at urban stage there have now developed disagreements of serious nature primarily re industrial-commercial policies and questions international relations. There is still no actual split within party but definite separation into liberal and radical wings, with Chou being of liberal, and Liu Shao-chi of radical wing. Chou however said it would be as big mistake to base any policy toward China on idea there would develop major split in party as it was to attempt stop Communism in China by aiding Kmt [Kuomintang or Nationalist Party] para-liberal group; feels that country is in such bad shape that most pressing need is reconstruction without regard political theories and that Mao Tse-tung concepts regarding private capital should be effected. Group feels there should have been coalition with Kmt because of party lack necessary knowledge regarding reconstruction, did not favor coalition with elements Ho Ying-chin-Chen Li-fu type but felt that without coalition reconstruction might be so delayed that party would lose support people. Realistic coalition advocated by group failed after big dispute involving most of higher figures in party with exception Mao (Chou was most careful in references to Mao). Coalition having failed, party must make most of bad job and obtain aid from outside. USSR cannot give aid which, therefore, must come from USA or possibly Britain. Chou favors getting help from USA and does not accord Soviet attitude regarding USA. Chou professedly sincere Communist but feels there has developed in USA economy something which is outside Marxist theories and that present American economic situation is, therefore, not susceptible Marxian interpretation. Therefore, Soviet attitude this respect wrong, feels American economy will continue without internal collapse or revolution and that there is no real bar to relations between USA and other governments, different political type. Unequivocally opposed to American aid to Kmt but feels this was given from mistaken motives altruism rather than American viciousness. Feels USA has genuine interest in Chinese people which could become basis friendly relations between two countries.

Chou, speaking for liberal group, felt China should speedily establish *de facto* working relations with foreign governments.

This question will be prime issue in struggle between two wings. Radicals wish alliance with USSR, sort now existing between US and Britain, while liberals regard Soviet international policy as "crazy." Chou feels USSR is risking war which it is unable fight successfully and that good working relations between China and USA would have definite softening effect on party attitude toward Western countries. Chou desires these relations because he feels China desperately needs that outside aid which USSR unable give. Feels China on brink complete economic and physical collapse, by "physical" meaning breakdown physical well-being of people.

Chou feels USA should aid Chinese because: (1) China still not Communist and if Mao's policies are correctly implemented may not be so for long time; (2) democratic China would serve in international sphere as mediator between Western Powers and USSR; (3) China in chaos under any regime would be menace to peace Asia and world. Chou emphasized he spoke solely for certain people personally and not as member party, that he was not in position make formal or informal commitments or proposals. He hoped American authorities would recall wartime contacts with Communists and character and opinions of many whom they knew at that time. He hoped American authorities remembering this would believe there were genuine liberals in party who are concerned with everything connected with welfare Chinese people and "peace in our time" rather than doctrinaire theories. As spokesman for liberal wing he could say that when time came for Communist participation in international affairs his group would work within party for sensible solution impasse between USSR and west and would do its best make USSR discard policies leading to war. . . .

Chou emphasized that despite deficiencies, errors, disagreements, Communists had won military victory and in spite of same drawbacks would win future victory in reconstruction. Chou said Mao Tse-tung stands aside from party disputes using Chou, Liu Shao-chi and other liberals and radicals for specific purposes as he sees fit. Mao is genius in listening arguments various sides, then translating ideas into practical working policies.

Chou per source appeared very nervous and worried. . . .

The State Department's Response to the Demarche, 1949

US has traditionally maintained close and friendly relations with China and has thruout past 100 years Sino-US relations, particularly since end last century, taken lead in efforts obtain internatl respect for Chi territorial and administrative integrity to end that China might develop as stable, united and independent nation. Unique record US relations with China gives clear evidence US had no territorial designs on China and has sought no special privileges or rights which were not granted other fon nations; US has sought maintain relations on basis mutual benefit and respect. Basic US objectives and principles remain unchanged.

In present situation US hopes maintain friendly relations with China and continue social, economic and polit relations with that country insofar as these relations based upon principle mutual respect and understanding and principle equality and are to mutual benefit two nations. In absence these basic principles, it can hardly be expected that full benefit Sino-US relations can be attained.

In this connection, US Govt and people are naturally disturbed and seriously concerned over certain recent occurrences which represent significant departure from these principles and some of which, in fact, widely at variance with accepted internatl custom and practice: Repeated bitter propaganda misrepresenting US actions and motives in China and elsewhere in world; arbitrary restrictions on movement and denial communications ConGen Mukden and Commie failure reply to ConGen Peiping repeated representations this matter, including request withdraw ConGen and staff Mukden; and Commie failure take action release two US Marine flyers or reply ConGen Peiping representations this matter.

While we welcome expressions friendly sentiments, he must realize that they cannot be expected bear fruit until they have been translated into deeds capable of convincing American people that Sino-US relations can be placed upon solid basis mutual respect and understanding to benefit both nations. . . .

President Truman on the Demarche, 1949

I brought the President up to date with respect to the Chou En-lai *Demarche* and read to him the pertinent sections of our reply. He approved this course of action and directs us to be most careful not to indicate any softening toward the Communists but to insist on judging their intentions by their actions.

Dean Acheson in the "White Paper," 1949

When peace came the United States was confronted with three possible alternatives in China: (1) it could have pulled out lock, stock and barrel; (2) it could have intervened militarily on a major scale to assist the Nationalists to destroy the Communists; (3) it could, while assisting the Nationalists to assert their authority over as much of China as possible, endeavor to avoid a civil war by working for a compromise between the two sides.

The first alternative would, and I believe American public opinion at the time so felt, have represented an abandonment of our international responsibilities and of our traditional policy of friendship for China before we had made a determined effort to be of assistance. The second alternative policy, while it may look attractive theoretically and in retrospect, was wholly impracticable. The Nationalists had been unable to destroy the Communists during the 10 years before the war. Now after the war the Nationalists were, as indicated above, weakened, demoralized, and unpopular. They had quickly dissipated their popular support and prestige in the areas liberated from the Japanese by the conduct of their civil and military officials. The Communists on the other hand were much stronger than they had ever been and were in control of most of North China. Because of the ineffectiveness of the Nationalist forces which was later to be tragically demonstrated, the Communists probably could have been dislodged only by American arms. It is obvious that the American people would not have sanctioned such a colossal commitment of our armies in 1945 or later. We therefore came to the third alternative policy whereunder we faced the facts of the situation and attempted to assist in working out a *modus vivendi* which would avert civil war but nevertheless preserve and even increase the influence of the National Government. . . .

The reasons for the failures of the Chinese National Government appear in some detail in the attached record. They do not stem from any inadequacy of American aid. Our military observers on the spot have reported that the Nationalist armies did not lose a single battle during the crucial year of 1948 through lack of arms or ammunition. The fact was that the decay which our observers had detected in Chungking early in the war had fatally sapped the powers of resistance of the Kuomintang. Its leaders had proved incapable of meeting the crisis confronting them, its troops had lost the will to fight, and its Government had lost popular support. The Communists, on the other hand, through a ruthless discipline and fanatical zeal, attempted to sell themselves as guardians and liberators of the people. The Nationalist armies did not have to be defeated; they disintegrated. History has proved again and again that a regime without faith in itself and an army without morale cannot survive the test of battle. . . .

Fully recognizing that the heads of the Chinese Communist Party were ideologically affiliated with Moscow, our Government nevertheless took the view, in the light of the existing balance of forces in China, that peace could be established only if certain conditions were met. The Kuomintang would have to set its own house in order and both sides would have to make concessions so that the Government of China might become, in fact as well as in name, the Government of all China and so that all parties might function within the constitutional system of the Government. Both internal peace and constitutional development required that the progress should be rapid from one party government with a large opposition party in armed rebellion, to the participation of all parties, including the moderate non-communist elements, in a truly national system of government.

None of these conditions has been realized. The distrust of the leaders of both the Nationalist and Communist Parties for each other proved too deep-seated to permit final agreement, notwithstanding temporary truces and apparently promising negotiations. The Nationalists, furthermore, embarked in 1946 on an over-ambitious military campaign in the face of warnings by General Marshall that it not only would fail but would plunge China into economic chaos and eventually destroy the National Government. General Marshall pointed out that though Nationalist armies could, for a period, capture Communist-held cities, they could not destroy the Communist armies. Thus every Nationalist advance would expose their communications to attack by Communist guerrillas and compel them to retreat or to surrender their armies together with the munitions which the United States has furnished them. No estimate of a military situation has ever been more completely confirmed by the resulting facts.

The historic policy of the United States of friendship and aid toward the people of China was, however, maintained in both peace and war. Since V-J Day, the United States Government has authorized aid to Nationalist China in the form of grants and credits totaling approximately 2 billion dollars, an amount equivalent in value to more than 50 percent of the monetary expenditures of the Chinese Government and of proportionately greater magnitude in relation to the budget of that Government than the United States has provided to any nation of Western Europe since the end of the war. In addition to these grants and credits, the United States Government has sold the Chinese Government large quantities of military and civilian war surplus property with a total procurement cost of over 1 billion dollars, for which the agreed realization to the United States was 232 million dollars. A large proportion of the military supplies furnished the Chinese armies by the United States since V-J Day has, however, fallen into the hands of the Chinese Communists through the military ineptitude of the Nationalist leaders, their defections and surrenders, and the absence among their forces of the will to fight.

It has been urged that relatively small amounts of additional aid—military and economic—to the National Government would have enabled it to destroy communism in China. The most trustworthy military, economic, and political information available to our Government does not bear out this view.

A realistic appraisal of conditions in China, past and present, leads to the conclusion that the only alternative open to the United States was full-scale intervention in behalf of a Government which had lost the confidence of its own troops and its own people. Such intervention would have required the expenditure of even greater sums than have been fruitlessly spent thus far, the command of Nationalist armies by American officers, and the probable participation of American armed forces—land, sea, and air—in the resulting war. Intervention of such a scope and magnitude would have been resented by the mass of the Chinese people, would have diametrically reversed our historic policy, and would have been condemned by the American people.

It must be admitted frankly that the American policy of assisting the Chinese people in resisting domination by any foreign power or powers is now confronted with the gravest difficulties. The heart of China is in Communist hands. The Communist leaders have foresworn their Chinese heritage and have publicly announced their subservience to a foreign power, Russia, which during the last 50 years, under czars and Communists alike, has been most assiduous in its efforts to extend its control in the Far East. In the recent past, attempts at foreign domination have appeared quite clearly to the Chinese people as external aggression and as such have been bitterly and in the long run successfully resisted. Our aid and encouragement have helped them to resist. In this case, however, the foreign domination has been masked behind the facade of a vast crusading movement which apparently has seemed to many Chinese to be wholly indigenous and national. Under these circumstances, our aid has been unavailing.

The unfortunate but inescapable fact is that the ominous result of the civil war in China was beyond the control of the government of the United

States. Nothing that this country did or could have done within the reasonable limits of its capabilities could have changed that result; nothing that was left undone by this country has contributed to it. It was the product of internal Chinese forces, forces which this country tried to influence but could not. A decision was arrived at within China, if only a decision by default.

And now it is abundantly clear that we must face the situation as it exists in fact. We will not help the Chinese or ourselves by basing our policy on wishful thinking. We continue to believe that, however tragic may be the immediate future of China and however ruthlessly a major portion of this great people may be exploited by a party in the interest of a foreign imperialism, ultimately the profound civilization and the democratic individualism of China will reassert themselves and she will throw off the foreign yoke. I consider that we should encourage all developments in China which now and in the future work toward this end.

In the immediate future, however, the implementation of our historic policy of friendship for China must be profoundly affected by current developments. It will necessarily be influenced by the degree to which the Chinese people come to recognize that the Communist regime serves not their interests but those of Soviet Russia and the manner in which, having become aware of the facts, they react to this foreign domination. One point, however, is clear. Should the Communist regime lend itself to the aims of Soviet Russian imperialism and attempt to engage in aggression against China's neighbors, we and the other members of the United Nations would be confronted by a situation violative of the principles of the United Nations Charter and threatening international peace and security.

Meanwhile our policy will continue to be based upon our own respect for the Charter, our friendship for China, and our traditional support for the Open Door and for China's independence and administrative and territorial integrity.

Mao Zedong (Mao Tse-tung) on United States "Imperialism," 1949

The war to turn China into a U. S. colony, a war in which the United States of America supplies the money and guns and Chiang Kai-shek the men to fight for the United States and slaughter the Chinese people, has been an important component of the U. S. imperialist policy of world-wide aggression since World War II. The U.S. policy of aggression has several targets. The three main targets are Europe, Asia and the Americas. China, the centre of gravity in Asia, is a large country with a population of 475 million; by seizing China, the United States would possess all of Asia. With its Asian front consolidated, U. S. imperialism could concentrate its forces on attacking Europe. U. S. imperialism considers its front in the Americas relatively secure. These are the smug over-all calculations of the U. S. aggressors.

But in the first place, the American people and the peoples of the world do not want war. Secondly, the attention of the United States has largely been absorbed by the awakening of the peoples of Europe, by the rise of the People's Democracies in Eastern Europe, and particularly by the towering presence of the Soviet Union, this unprecedentedly powerful bulwark of peace bestriding Europe and Asia, and by its strong resistance to the U. S. policy of aggression. Thirdly, and this is most important, the Chinese people have awakened, and the armed forces and the organized strength of the people under the leadership of the Communist Party of China have become more powerful than ever before. Consequently, the ruling clique of U. S. imperialism has been prevented from adopting a policy of direct, large-scale armed attacks on China and instead has adopted a policy of helping Chiang Kai-shek fight the civil war.

U.S. naval, ground and air forces did participate in the war in China. There were U. S. naval bases in Tsingtao, Shanghai and Taiwan. U. S. troops were stationed in Peiping, Tientsin, Tangshan, Chinwangtao, Tsingtao, Shanghai and Nanking. The U. S. air force controlled all of China's air space and took aerial photographs of all China's strategic areas for military maps. At the town of Anping near Peiping, at Chiutai near Changchun, at Tangshan and in the Eastern Shantung Peninsula, U. S. troops and other military personnel clashed with the People's Liberation Army and on several occasions were captured. Chennault's air fleet took an extensive part in the civil war. Besides transporting troops for Chiang Kai-shek, the U. S. air force bombed and sank the cruiser *Chungking*, which had mutinied against the Kuomintang. All these were acts of direct participation in the war, although they fell short of an open declaration of war and were not large in scale, and although the principal method of U. S. aggression was the large-scale supply of money, munitions and advisers to help Chiang Kai-shek fight the civil war.

The use of this method by the United States was determined by the objective situation in China and the rest of the world, and not by any lack of desire on the part of the Truman-Marshall group, the ruling clique of U. S. imperialism, to launch direct aggression against China. Moreover, at the outset of its help to Chiang Kai-shek in fighting the civil war, a crude farce was staged in which the United States appeared as mediator in the conflict between the Kuomintang and the Communist Party; this was an attempt to soften up the Communist Party of China, deceive the Chinese people and thus gain control of all China without fighting. The peace negotiations failed, the deception fell through and the curtain rose on the war.

Liberals or "democratic individualists" who cherish illusions about the United States and have short memories! Please look at Acheson's own words:

> When peace came the United States was confronted with three possible alternatives in China: (1) it could have pulled out lock, stock and barrel; (2) it could have intervened militarily on a major scale to assist the Nationalists to destroy the Communists; (3) it could, while assisting the Nationalists to assert their authority over as much of China as possible, endeavor to avoid a civil war by working for a compromise between the two sides.

Why didn't the United States adopt the first of these policies? Acheson says:

> The first alternative would, and I believe American public opinion at the time felt, have represented an abandonment of our international responsibilities and of our traditional policy of friendship for China before we had made a determined effort to be of assistance.

So that's how things stand: the "international responsibilities" of the United States and its "traditional policy of friendship for China" are nothing but intervention against China. Intervention is called assuming international responsibilities and showing friendship for China; as to non-intervention, it simply won't do. Here Acheson defiles U. S. public opinion; his is the "public opinion" of Wall Street, not the public opinion of the American people.

Why didn't the United States adopt the second of these policies? Acheson says:

> The second alternative policy, while it may look attractive theoretically and in retrospect, was wholly impracticable. The Nationalists had been unable to destroy the Communists during the 10 years before the war. Now after the war the Nationalists were, as indicated above, weakened, demoralized and unpopular. They had quickly dissipated their popular support and prestige in the areas liberated from the Japanese by the conduct of their civil and military officials. The Communists on the other hand were much stronger than they had ever been and were in control of most of North China. Because of the ineffectiveness of the Nationalist forces which was later to be tragically demonstrated, the Communists probably could have been dislodged only by American arms. It is obvious that the American people would not have sanctioned such a colossal commitment of our armies in 1945 or later. We therefore came to the third alternative policy. . . .

What a splendid idea! The United States supplies the money and guns and Chiang Kai-shek the men to fight for the United States and slaughter the Chinese people, to "destroy the Communists" and turn China into a U. S. colony, so that the United States may fulfill its "international responsibilities" and carry out its "traditional policy of friendship for China." . . .

What matter if we have to face some difficulties? Let them blockade us! Let them blockade us for eight or ten years! By that time all of China's problems will have been solved. Will the Chinese cower before difficulties when they are not afraid even of death? Lao Tzu said, "The people fear not death, why threaten them with it?" U. S. imperialism and its running dogs, the Chiang Kai-shek reactionaries, have not only "threatened" us with death but actually put many of us to death. Besides people like Wen Yi-to, they have killed millions of Chinese in the last three years with U. S. carbines, machine-guns, mortars, bazookas, howitzers, tanks and bombs dropped from aeroplanes. This situation is now coming to an end. They have been defeated. It is we who are going in to attack them, not they who are coming out to attack us. They will soon be finished. True, the few problems left to us, such as blockade, unemployment, famine, inflation and rising prices, are difficulties, but we have already begun to breathe more easily than in the past three years. We have come triumphantly through the ordeal of the last three years; why can't we overcome these few difficulties of today? Why can't we live without the United States?

When the People's Liberation Army crossed the Yangtse River, the U. S. colonial government at Nanking fled helter-skelter. Yet His Excellency Ambassador Stuart sat tight, watching wide-eyed, hoping to set up shop under a new signboard and to reap some profit. But what did he see? Apart from the People's Liberation Army marching past, column after column, and the workers, peasants and students rising in hosts, he saw something else—the Chinese liberals or democratic individualists turning out in force, shouting slogans and talking revolution together with the workers, peasants, soldiers and students. In short, he was left out in the cold, "standing all alone, body and shadow comforting each other." There was nothing more for him to do, and he had to take to the road, his briefcase under his arm.

There are still some intellectuals and other people in China who have muddled ideas and illusions about the United States. Therefore we should explain things to them, win them over, educate them and unite with them, so they will come over to the side of the people and not fall into the snares set by imperialism. But the prestige of U. S. imperialism among the Chinese people is completely bankrupt, and the White Paper is a record of its bankruptcy. Progressives should make good use of the White Paper to educate the Chinese people.

Leighton Stuart has departed and the White Paper has arrived. Very good. Very good. Both events are worth celebrating.

William Knowland Argues Against Recognition, 1950

Mr. President and Members of the Senate, within the last 90 days two catastrophic events have taken place. These are the Soviet success in atomic development, as announced by the President of the United States on September 23, 1949, and the establishment of a Soviet-recognized Communist regime in China. Only in retrospect will we be able to finally determine which event will have the most far-reaching influence. Both have set off chain reactions that have not yet run their full course.

Fifty years of friendly interest on the part of our people and our Government in a free and independent China and the overwhelming contribution made by our Army, Navy, and Air Force in the Pacific during World War II gave us the power, the prestige, and the opportunity for constructive action no western nation had ever before possessed. We could have pioneered in exporting the ideals that inspired men who loved freedom everywhere following our own breakaway from colonial status.

All this opportunity has been frittered away by a small group of willful men in the Far Eastern Division of the State Department who had the backing of their superiors.

In Europe where the record of Soviet aims was clearly outlined in Poland, Czechoslovakia, Bulgaria, Hungary, Rumania, Latvia, Lithuania, and Estonia we finally stood up to communism in Greece, Turkey, Iran, Berlin, and western Germany.

Knowing that communism thrives on economic and political chaos we gave economic aid through the ECA [Economic Cooperation Administration, or Marshall Plan] and with the North Atlantic Pact and the arms-implementation legislation, we have given moral and material support for the protection of western Europe and the Middle East from overt aggression. In that area we have given hope and support to those advancing the cause of a free world of freemen.

Munich certainly should have taught us that appeasement of aggression, then as now, is but surrender on the installment plan. Mr. Chamberlain, Prime Minister of Great Britain 10 years ago, may have sincerely thought that he was gaining "peace in our time" by consenting to the destruction of a free and independent Czechoslovakia by Nazi Germany. We know now that paying such international blackmail only increased later demands that made World War II inevitable.

The men in the Kremlin are as power hungry as the Nazis, and their system is as destructive of human liberty as was Hitlerism with which they were bedfellows while Poland was being dismembered in 1939. They have, however, learned some new techniques.

Communism is destructive of human liberty everywhere in the world. It is no less destructive in China or Korea than it is in Poland, Czechoslovakia, Latvia, Estonia, Lithuania, Hungary, Rumania, or Bulgaria. The pattern may differ slightly. In Poland the opposition leader, Mikolajczyk, was forced to flee; in Bulgaria Petkov was hanged; in Rumania the King was given a 2-hour ultimatum to change the government regardless of the constitution; in Czechoslovakia Masaryk's life was forfeited when it became apparent that coalition with communism would not work.

A Chinese official put it clearly by saying to me recently that there can be no real coalition with a tiger unless you are inside the tiger.

The President's State of the Union message of January 4 was notable for its silence on the question of China. In what we hope will be a free world of freemen does the administration have less concern with human liberty in Asia than it does in Europe? On what basis does the administration write off freemen in China? . . .

In Europe we have had a foreign policy in which the Republicans and the Democrats have contributed to the initiation and formulation of doctrines that are understandable. In the Far East there has been no bipartisan foreign policy. The Republicans in Congress have not been consulted in the moves leading up to the bankrupt policy which now stands revealed in all its sorry detail. . . .

Our long-standing far eastern policy was first compromised at Yalta. We gave to the Soviet Union vital rights in Manchuria which were not ours to give. It was done without the consent or approval of the American

Congress or the American people. It was done in violation of the open-door policy of John Hay and of Woodrow Wilson's concept of "open covenants, openly arrived at." The Yalta agreement made Soviet domination of Manchuria and other border provinces inevitable. It made possible Chinese Communist domination of the balance of continental China and has opened the door to bringing the entire continent of Asia, with more than a billion people and vast resources, into the orbit of international communism. Sitting with our American delegation at Yalta was Alger Hiss.

Following VJ-day the representatives of our Department of State persistently tried to get the Government of the Republic of China to form a coalition with the Communists. When they refused we placed an embargo against the shipments of any arms or ammunition to the legal government of the country while during those same months the Soviet army of occupation in Manchuria, as the result of the Yalta agreement, was turning over to the Communist forces large amounts of captured Japanese war stocks.

Like a person with a bad conscience, the State Department on August 6 released the China white paper. All the blame was placed on the National Government, then with its back to the wall. It was apparently issued with the hope that our own sorry part and share of responsibility might be overlooked. . . .

The basic objective the United States should have kept constantly in mind was to preserve a free, independent, united non-Communist China. In the postwar illness of that nation we prescribed that the strychnine of communism be taken. The State Department having contributed greatly to the Chinese disaster, still proclaims that we must follow a hands off policy, or that we must wait for the dust to settle, or we must investigate some more. Are they preparing for a post mortem rather than a consultation? . . .

In a very well-written article in the January 7 issue of the *Saturday Evening Post*, Joseph Alsop has this to say about State Department excuses as contained in the China white paper:

> But there is also one carefully concealed defect in the State Department argument. If you have kicked a drowning friend briskly in the face as he sank for the second and third times, you cannot later explain that he was doomed anyway because he was such a bad swimmer. The question that must be answered is not whether the Chinese did their best to save themselves, which they most certainly did not. The question is whether we did our best to save China.
>
> The answer to this question is contained in the strange, still secret inner history of our China policy. And this is true history for which the State Department could find no room in all the 1,054 pages of the white paper may be simply, if grimly, summarized:
>
> Throughout the fatal years in China, the American representatives there actively favored the Chinese Communists. They also contributed to the weakness, both political and military, of the National Government. And in the end they came close to offering China up to the Communists,

like a trussed bird on a platter, over 4 years before the eventual Communist triumph. . . .

It is a sad commentary that Britain, which itself was in such a desperate plight after Dunkerque, which joined us in complaining of Mussolini's stab in the back when France was down but not quite out, should now be contemplating abandoning the Republic of China and giving recognition, aid, and comfort to the Communists who are so closely allied with the same international Communist conspiracy that threatens human freedom in Europe.

Like Mr. Chamberlain at Munich, there are some in this country and in Great Britain who believe that by appeasing the Communists they may change their way of life. This is naive, and such a viewpoint is dangerous to the peace of the world and the security of this country. . . .

It is my judgment that history will record the recognition of Communist China as being as great a betrayal of human freedom as was the Pact of Munich. . . .

The question is asked "Can anything be done at this late date?" I believe that it can. While desperate, the situation is not more desperate than it was at the time of Dunkerque or Valley Forge.

First, of course, we need a foreign policy in the Far East. We have none there today. As a basis for such a foreign policy, I suggest the following:

First. That we make clear that we have no intention of recognizing the Communist regime in China at this time nor in the immediate future and that we make known to the powers associated with us that we do not look with favor upon such recognition by others.

It is of course not sufficient merely to delay our own recognition if, with a wink of the eye or tongue in cheek the State Department leaves doubt in the minds of others as to the course of action we may pursue.

Second. That we have a major shakeup in the Far Eastern Division of the State Department. We cannot expect to get inspired leadership for a new policy in the Far East from those who have been receivers of the bankrupt policy we have been following.

Third. Our policy itself, of course, will have to be set by our constitutional officers, the President, his advisers, and the Congress. Once we have a foreign policy there is great need for it to be coordinated in both its economic and defense phases. As coordinator, either Gen. Douglas MacArthur or some other comparable figure should be selected so that in that area of the world the right hand will know what the left is doing.

Fourth. We should give supervised aid to the legal Government of China in the same way we gave it to the legal Governments of Greece and Korea when they were threatened by communism. I have never favored giving unsupervised assistance. A mission headed by a man of the caliber of General Wedemeyer could supervise the requests for aid, be sure that the Chinese Government was properly training the troops in the use of equipment, and make certain from a logistical point of view that the supplies were received at the points where they were needed.

✸ *E S S A Y S*

Warren I. Cohen of Michigan State University argues in the first essay that Dean Acheson hoped to drive a wedge between the Soviet Union and the People's Republic of China, with recognition of the PRC as one means. But President Truman, McCarthyism, and the outbreak of the Korean War wrecked his plans. William W. Stueck, Jr., of the University of Georgia does not agree that Acheson was willing to deal with the Chinese Communists. He notes the consequences of the United States's failure to talk and speculates about what might have come from such discussions. The last essay, by Steven M. Goldstein of Smith College, doubts the chances for accommodation, given Chinese Communist hostility toward the United States.

Acheson's Search for Accommodation

WARREN I. COHEN

Acheson was a commanding presence as secretary of state. Nothing seems clearer than the fact that the opinion neither of his subordinates, of Congress, nor of the public, could sway him once he had made up his mind. The president, however, open to such influences, could and did on occasion reject, modify, or otherwise impose his wishes on Acheson's recommendations.

Acheson had little interest in Chinese affairs. In 1946, however, he had worked in support of [presidential envoy George C.] Marshall's effort to avert the civil war and had shared the frustration Marshall suffered in his dealings with Chiang. He had no intention of enduring any such nonsense in 1949. He was aware that the Communists were on the verge of victory, regretted the situation, but was quite content to follow the course upon which Marshall had settled. As new questions arose, he relied for information and analysis on [Walton] Butterworth, who became his assistant secretary for Far Eastern affairs; Dean Rusk, his deputy undersecretary and later Butterworth's successor; and his close friend and alter ego Philip C. Jessup, appointed ambassador-at-large. Although he looked less to Policy Planning than had Marshall, Acheson often received ideas from [George F.] Kennan and from John P. Davies, the PPS [Policy Planning Staff] specialist on China. In 1950 John Foster Dulles was brought into the department, at Rusk's suggestion, to attempt to salvage bipartisan support for policy toward Asia. Despised by Acheson, Dulles nonetheless served him loyally, working primarily with Rusk and, to a lesser extent, with Jessup.

Eager to contain Soviet influence everywhere, Acheson was, however, an Atlanticist for whom Western Europe was the highest priority. His principal concerns in 1949 were European recovery and creation of the North Atlantic Treaty Organization. Stopping communism across the Pacific

From "Acheson, His Advisors, and China, 1949–1950" in *Uncertain Years: Chinese-American Relations, 1947–1950,* edited by Dorothy Borg and Waldo Heinrichs (New York: Columbia University Press, 1980). Reprinted by permission of the publisher.

was also highly desirable, but a task of lesser importance. He had little interest in Asia beyond a determination to link Japan, like Germany, to the West. Jessup, Rusk, Kennan, and Davies were troubled by his neglect of East Asia, but they had little effect on his policy recommendations prior to the Korean War. He allowed them only symbolic acts, shows of concern—nothing that required a major commitment of American resources or power. . . .

Between the time Acheson took office and the onset of the Korean War, the department's concerns regarding China fell into three general areas. First, there was a need to determine policy toward the retreating Kuomintang and whatever factions emerged. Second, a decision had to be made about Formosa. Third, policy toward the emerging Communist regime had to be defined. In each area Acheson's intent was thwarted, in several instances by the perceived need for temporary delays in order to win a national consensus, and in every instance by the Korean War and the Sino-American conflict that developed from it.

Ten days before Acheson was sworn in, the National Security Council (NSC) agreed to continue efforts to prevent China from becoming "an adjunct of Soviet power." Council members also agreed that efforts toward China would be "of lower priority" than efforts where the benefits to American security were "more immediately commensurate" with the expenditure of resources.

By the end of January [1949] all of China north of the Yangtze was in Communist hands and Mao's legions were massing at the river. Chiang went home to Fenghua and left the government in the hands of Li Tsung-jen, who began peace overtures to the Communists. To Acheson and others in Washington it seemed clear that the time had come to stop aid. On February 3 the NSC recommended that the United States suspend shipments to China. Several days later, however, Congressional leaders urged the president not to take any formal action. That their concern was not for the fortunes of the Kuomintang but rather to soothe their colleagues and constituents was manifest in their willingness to have shipments delayed by informal action. Truman accepted the advice. Aid would not be suspended, but ways would be found to slow shipments. American political leaders feared that a public announcement of the cessation of aid would lead to the immediate collapse of the Kuomintang regime, and that they would be held responsible. Acheson had his orders.

By the end of February General Albert C. Wedemeyer, more sympathetic to Chiang than most American leaders, had concluded that it would be worse than useless to send aid to Chiang's forces: it would be seized almost immediately by the Communists. In mid-March Acheson wrote to Senator Tom Connally, chairman of the Senate Foreign Relations Committee, to oppose a bill calling for $1.5 billion in aid for China, insisting that even massive military assistance would not reverse the tide. But he agreed that it would be undesirable to cut off aid to Kuomintang-controlled areas "precipitously." Several days later, addressing the committee in executive session, Acheson was franker. He reported that he was persuaded by his advisers "that at the present time to continue aid to anybody in China is going to have the opposite result from what we want to achieve."

A few weeks later Acheson indicated confidence that he had won the support necessary to end aid to the Kuomintang and to seek an accommodation with the Chinese Communists. He told Ernest Bevin, the British foreign secretary, that Chiang's regime was "washed up," that the Communists now had a free hand in China. The Chinese people were tired and further aid to the Kuomintang would anger them. "We had," he explained to Bevin, "abandoned the idea of supporting the regime and were only extending to June 2 a further 58 million dollars under the China Aid Act." It was difficult to withdraw support publicly, but he thought "the extreme supporters of Chiang Kai-shek in Congress were gaining a better appreciation of realities." Most significantly, Acheson promised Bevin, "The U. S. henceforth will pursue a more realistic policy respecting China."

In mid-April Wellington Koo, near despair over his failure to win adequate American support for his government, met with Dulles. He reported finding Acheson preoccupied with Europe and blamed Marshall's influence for the State Department's indifference to China's plight. Dulles agreed and added that Senator Arthur H. Vandenberg, the key Republican foreign policy spokesman in the Senate, would no longer press for aid. The State Department had persuaded Vandenberg that the Kuomintang could not win, no matter how much aid the United States sent.

By the spring of 1949 Acheson was persuaded that the consensus necessary to withdraw support from the Kuomintang had been obtained. On June 2, when the China Aid Act expired, the United States would cease wasting its resources. Kuomintang China was dead. There remained only the need for last rites, to persuade the American people. Acheson turned to an earlier recommendation by Kennan that the public be informed of the reasons for American policy before it was misled by partisan criticism. Marshall had read the suggestion to the cabinet in November 1948, but Truman had rejected it. The people needed the facts, but to reveal Chiang's ineptness and the corruption of his regime would be tantamount to the United States' delivering the final blow. Nine months later, however, Truman agreed that the time had come. He supported Acheson over the objections of the secretary of defense and the Joint Chiefs, and "The China White Paper" was published. Awareness of the ties between Chiang's lobbyists and Republican critics may have facilitated the decision.

Acheson's determination to publish the White Paper, despite concern over Mao's "leaning to one side" speech, strong opposition from the Pentagon, reservations within the department and on Capitol Hill, and while the Kuomintang still held Canton, is explicable only as a decision to drive in the last nail. He was determined to end American involvement in the Chinese civil war, to quash in advance any new onslaught by Chiang's American friends, and to prepare for an accommodation with the Communist regime. Acheson failed, but not for want of trying. His *bete noire*, Chiang Kai-shek, escaped to Formosa and reopened the issue on a basis less susceptible to Acheson's arguments. . . .

The principal reason for Acheson's determination to cut off aid to Chiang and to acquiesce in the fall of Formosa was the desire to establish the best possible relationship with Mao's regime. The Communist victory posed dangers for the United States because of evident Soviet influence among Mao's colleagues. Acheson and his advisers were eager to lessen that influence and to develop among the Chinese Communist leaders a sense of a need for ties to the West.

The State Department considered trade, recognition, and Chinese representation on the UN Security Council as means of achieving tolerable relations with the Communists. Trade would be used as a weapon, to demonstrate the extent of Chinese dependence on the West. Eventual recognition was assumed, but it would not be automatic. Recognition, too, might be useful as a lever with which to gain advantage for the United States. Policy on the Security Council representation question would have to be more flexible. The People's Republic might well be seated without American approval. There would be no attempt to use the veto.

A variety of domestic restraints and Chinese Communist actions delayed recognition, but these were diminishing in importance. There were indications that the United States would grant recognition to the People's Republic after the elections of November 1950. "Formal, regularized relations . . . not intimate but proper" were anticipated. The department assumed that Peking's representatives would represent China in the UN as early as February or March 1950. But Acheson's preparations for overcoming public and Congressional opposition to an accommodation with the Communists were halted by the coming of war in Korea and abandoned after Chinese intervention in that war.

Kennan and his staff set the tone for dealing with the Chinese Communists in November 1948. The Kuomintang government would soon disappear, and the United States should determine its policy on recognition when that happened. Aid to Chiang was useless, but American ends in China might be achieved by using economic bargaining power to exact concessions, presumably from the successor Communist regime.

Butterworth reflected the same position in talks with British officials in January and February 1949. They agreed that trade and recognition provided opportunities for bargaining. Butterworth was also prepared to cut off all Economic Cooperation Administration (ECA) operations in Communist-controlled areas to make it "just as difficult for the Communists as possible, in order to force orientation to the West." On the other hand, he favored restoration of trade relations with Communist China as "the most feasible means of maintaining contact" and thought it desirable to allow the Communists to import petroleum products "in order that they might develop a sense of dependence on the West."

The department's premises were detailed in NSC 41, drafted by the State Department in late February 1949. The goal was to prevent "Soviet domination of China for strategic ends." The alternatives posed were political and economic warfare to isolate and intimidate the Chinese, or restoration of economic relations and efforts to divide the Chinese and Russian Communists. The department insisted that the first course would force Mao into complete subservience to the Soviet Union, was obviously undesirable, and should not be risked except in extremis. The second alternative might produce an independent regime and was the policy to be pursued.

Reports from the field, from Moscow as well as from offices in China, reinforced hope of an independent Communist regime. There was evidence of tension between Russian and Chinese leaders. There was suspicion that Russian-controlled Chinese Communists were worried by Mao's apparent interest in mutually beneficial relations with the United States. John M. Cabot, consul-general at Shanghai after a tour in Yugoslavia, sent a number of thoughtful letters and cables indicating his belief that a Sino-Soviet split was inevitable. The critical question of *when* might be affected by American policy. In March Acheson authorized Ambassador J. Leighton Stuart to approach Communist leaders. He was cautioned to avoid any ultimatums and any publicity. Acheson was eager to explore issues with Mao and Chou En-lai, but reports of talks were to be sent "eyes only for the secretary." The American public and the president were not quite ready to acknowledge the conquerors.

In April, as the People's Liberation Army poised to cross the Yangtze, Acheson advised diplomats in China not to demand recognition of their official consular status from the Communists. Such action would convey a sense of "de jure relations in which we [are] unable [to] reciprocate," presumably because the Kuomintang still controlled China south of the Yangtze. After the Yangtze defenses were breached, Acheson raised with Stuart the question of de facto recognition. He was concerned about Communist attitudes toward American officials and property. Was de facto recognition the best hope for protecting American interests, or would the Communists become more demanding? Would they immediately want de jure recognition "which the United States might be unprepared to grant in absence [of] some sense of international responsibility?" Stuart conceded that de facto recognition would probably lead to a more correct attitude on the part of the Communists, but only if it were treated as tantamount to de jure recognition. Stuart clearly preferred sharper bargaining before dispensing what he saw as a reward for good behavior. Increasingly, discussions in the department on how to handle the Chinese Communists seemed liked a seminar on adolescent psychology.

On June 1, O. Edmund Clubb, the consul-general at Peking, reported an unusual initiative attributed to Chou En-lai. Chou indicated, as Mao had on previous occasions, that he was interested in American trade and investment on terms of mutual advantage. But he also noted that there were party leaders opposed to friendly relations with the United States. A more forthcoming attitude would be welcome, timely, and mutually advantageous.

Acheson was in Paris when the department received and formulated a response to Chou's message. Clubb and Stuart advised the acting secretary to be wary. Clubb suspected the Communists wanted the best of both worlds, to obtain American aid while supporting the Soviet Union. Stuart wanted the Chinese to demonstrate their desire for good relations by their actions. The president agreed emphatically: there was to be no indication of any softening toward the Communists. Nothing came of Chou's demarche.

In May and June Stuart met several times with Huang Hua, his former student who was serving as chief of the Communists' Office of Alien Affairs. These meetings culminated in an invitation for Stuart to visit Yenching University in Peking, where he could expect to be welcomed by Mao and Chou. Word of the invitation generated excitement within the Department of State, but Butterworth and Davies feared an adverse public reaction. Davies thought Stuart should accept the opportunity to berate Mao and Chou about proper behavior and believed the public would approve a trip for that purpose. Butterworth devised an elaborate scheme for disguising the trip as a mission to rescue the staff of the Mukden consulate-general. The president would have none of it; "under no circumstances" was Stuart to visit Peking. An extraordinary opportunity to explore terms of accommodation was brushed aside, apparently because the president did not wish to be held responsible for applying the *coup de grace* to the Kuomintang. But this was only one of several times Truman resisted department recommendations designed to improve relations with the Communists. Indeed it was only with great difficulty that Acheson was able to dissuade Truman from ordering Stuart to visit Kuomintang headquarters at Canton instead of Peking.

In an unrelated action on the day Acheson informed Stuart of the president's decision, Mao contributed to the difficulty of reaching an accommodation. He denounced the United States and declared that China would lean to the side of the Soviet Union; it would not allow itself to become dependent on the West. Acheson expected such rhetoric and had tried to prepare Congress and the President for it. In mid-March he had predicted to the Senate Foreign Relations Committee that Chinese Communist leaders, as they gained control of China, would "go out of their way to show their sympathetic attitude of cooperation with the Russians. I think they are going to show a considerable amount of hostility to us and to the West." As Sino-Soviet tensions developed, he expected the Chinese to become even more insistent on their kinship with the Russians. He would be patient. But if Acheson was unperturbed by Mao's speech, it nevertheless increased his problems in persuading the president, Congress, and the public of the wisdom of his course.

The equanimity with which Acheson approached policy toward China was not shared by most of his advisers. Kennan, Davies, Rusk, and Jessup feared that the apparent inaction of the United States in East Asia was upsetting to Americans and Asians. In July Kennan called for a "change of climate" in policy toward East and South Asia. Rusk converted Kennan's idea into a forty-seven-point "action program" that included a "declaration of nonrecognition" of Communist China, continued support for Kuomintang China in the UN, and assistance to "non-Communist China." In August Kennan, Davies, and Jessup devised a twenty-one-point program containing a call for a policy of "frank hostility to the Chinese Communists." They wanted to demonstrate American willingness to use force, to react with strength, "with majesty and greatness." A week later Davies suggested bombing a few installations in Manchuria to demonstrate that the United States would not tolerate the Chinese behaving like "bandits and blackmailers."

Acheson refused to encourage Truman to play Teddy Roosevelt and continued preparing the country for the accommodation with the People's Republic that he assumed was inevitable. Nonetheless his aides persisted in efforts to manipulate trade and recognition policies in order to reform Chinese Communist behavior and appease public, Congressional, and presidential opinion. In September a high-level department meeting concluded that the British were eager to normalize relations with China. Rusk and Butterworth urged delay, and Acheson agreed to ask Bevin to exact satisfactory performance on China's international obligations. He indicated to Bevin that it was of great importance to the United States to let the dust settle, to let events rather than an act of the West proclaim a Communist victory. Clearly, Acheson was prepared to wait until after the annihilation of Chiang Kai-shek and his forces, another inevitability he did not wish to delay.

A number of remarks attributed to the president in the summer and fall of 1949 indicated his preference for more active opposition to the Chinese Communists than Acheson was advocating. At least once there was a suggestion in his remarks of doubt that the department was following his wishes. Several weeks after denying permission for Stuart to go to Peking, Truman began pressing for revision of NSC 41, which had precluded economic warfare against the new regime. On October 1 he "indicated strongly" his desire that the department do nothing to subvert the Kuomintang blockade of mainland ports. Acting Secretary James E. Webb reported that "the President stressed again the fact that his policy was to permit the blockade to work effectively, to which policy he expected strict adherence." Two days later he remarked that the United States should be in no hurry to recognize the People's Republic, noting that the country had waited many years to recognize the Russian regime. Not long afterward, when Consul-General Angus Ward was imprisoned in Manchuria, Truman contemplated using force to liberate the consular staff.

In these circumstances, Acheson's failure to respond to the Chinese interest in recognition was less remarkable than his success in restraining his colleagues and the president from more aggressive action. He delayed two months before responding to the president's call for revision of NSC 41, and then argued against a change of policy. No recommendation for a show of force against the People's Republic went forward from the department. Instead, Acheson had a study prepared on recognition policy, lectured congressmen on the meaning of recognition, and used Jessup as choreographer for a series of elaborate dances that consumed approximately six months, their only significant result. He was confident that time was on the side of sensible policy and that his opponents understood precisely what he was doing. Wellington Koo complained bitterly as Jessup and outside consultants studied policy and as Jessup embarked on a sea voyage to examine conditions in East Asia. Koo realized that the department was stalling until everyone agreed it was too late to help Kuomintang China.

Keeping the door open for recognition of the People's Republic was a more difficult, and ultimately impossible, task. Nonetheless, the record of Acheson's efforts is clear. Throughout 1949 and the first half of 1950 he persisted in his attempt to persuade Truman that efforts to detach the Peking regime from Moscow did not constitute appeasement, that harassment would be a mistake. No doubt reluctantly, apprehensively, Truman stayed with him. When confronted with outrageous Chinese behavior, Acheson argued that vital American interests had not been affected, that policies likely to drive Mao closer to Stalin were not warranted. In May 1949, before the Ward case came to a head, he argued that it be viewed as a special situation. In November, as Ward was brought to trial and public outrage verged toward explosion, Acheson stressed the fact that no Americans had been killed in Communist-controlled areas. He argued that, considering the circumstances of revolution and civil war and the refusal of the United States to recognize the regime, American consular posts had "on the whole not fared badly." The public explosion came, but the torrents of abuse did not move him and he held the president's support.

In January 1950 both the department and the Communist regime misplayed a minor problem in Peking to the benefit of opponents of Sino-American accommodation. Acheson thought he had given the Communists a clear signal of American intent to establish formal relations as soon as practicable. But the Chinese were impatient and pressed the United States and other regimes that still withheld recognition, threatening to requisition their property in Peking, including the consular premises of the governments involved. Acheson devised a compromise that seemed sensible. The Communists were informed that they could take a large part of the area, but not the building the United States planned to use for its chancellery. Such an arrangement might give the Communists face without creating an uproar in the United States. The Peking regime was warned, however, that seizure of the building in question would be unacceptable and result in the withdrawal of all American diplomatic personnel in China. The Chinese seized the building and American officials were ordered out of China. Each side apparently thought the other was bluffing. The results were unfortunate, but neither Edmund Clubb in Peking nor Acheson perceived the action as a final break. Indeed, withdrawal had long been advocated by Jessup and others in the department as a means of avoiding incidents that would inflame public opinion against the Chinese.

A few weeks after the incident Trygve Lie, secretary general of the UN, met with Acheson to express his fear about the consequences. Acheson's "let the dust settle" speech of January 12 had reassured him about American intentions, but he feared Peking's action might complicate and delay a settlement. He feared the United States might try to keep the People's Republic out of the UN, resulting in a permanent Russian withdrawal. Rusk, who was present, indicated his expectation that "in a matter of several weeks seven members of the Security Council will have recognized the communist regime and when that happens a communist representative will be seated on a procedural vote.'' Rusk left no doubt that the United States regarded the issue as procedural and that ''we would neither ourselves exercise the veto nor acquiesce in a veto by anyone else.''

Rather than being distraught about the prospects for normalization of relations with the People's Republic, Acheson was anticipating better opportunities when Mao returned from his protracted negotiations with Stalin. He planted rumors of Stalin's attempts at extortion with Cyrus Sulzberger, Paris-based correspondent for the *New York Times*. But the alliance Mao and Stalin signed in February was clearly a setback. In April Clubb's informants gave him little hope for an early open break between Peking and Moscow. There appeared to be but a slight chance for a more conciliatory attitude toward the United States for several years. Still Acheson was in no hurry. Kuomintang resistance on the mainland had been virtually eliminated. Chiang's flight to Formosa was another complication, but the CIA estimated that the problem would disappear before the end of the year. Perhaps the president would be ready to act after the November elections. In the interim, nonrecognition might please the French, who were worried about Chinese support for Ho Chi Minh in Indochina. So long as Chiang was destroyed, so long as there was no chance of further involving the United States in the Chinese civil war, Acheson could wait. There was no compelling reason for more immediate action.

The war in Korea brought an end to Acheson's complacency about East Asia. His position on Formosa was immediately undermined and his efforts to hold course on recognition, UN representation, and aid to the Kuomintang ended in failure after the Chinese intervened. . . .

Acheson's goal was to reach an accommodation with the People's Republic under the most advantageous terms for the United States. He hoped to encourage the Peking regime to distance itself from the Soviet Union and to recognize the importance of its historic ties to the West. The quest for advantage doubtless contributed to delay, and ultimately to failure. But Acheson saw no reason to be eager about the normalization of relations with the new regime. His determination to proceed deliberately was strengthened when Mao and Chou indicated a desire for American aid and voiced the doctrinaire assumption that American capitalism required trade with China to avoid depression. He assumed that the Russians could not provide the economic and technical assistance China needed and that it would be useful for the People's Republic to perceive that it needed the United States more than the United States needed it. Such an awareness might prompt good behavior.

He opposed overt involvement with Formosa because the aim of American policy was to separate the People's Republic from Moscow's control, in part by focusing on Soviet imperialism. It was essential not to provide the Communists with a concrete anti-American issue. His interest in even covert operations to save Formosa vanished when he realized that Chiang would soon be ensconced there, that the native independence movement lacked the power to throw out the Kuomintang.

Acheson's confidence in his passive policy toward Asia was founded on his indifference to the region. He was not persuaded that much of consequence to the United States could happen on the Asian mainland. He was much more interested in British and French opinion, in pacifying major allies, than in the fate of Chiang Kai-shek or Southeast Asia. When his advisers became frantic in their concern over his disinterest, he agreed to exercises in political theater—invitations to Asian leaders, statements of the importance of Asia, and Jessup's extended tour. When Jessup reported that no major expenditure of American power or resources was required, only a little aid and a little psychological warfare, he was telling the secretary precisely what he wanted to hear.

Acheson was also certain of his ability to cope with Congressional and public opinion. Indeed, public opinion polls showed a low regard for Chiang and little inclination to aid him—before the Korean War. The polls did indicate opposition to recognition of the Communist regime or a place for it in the UN, but it was reasonable to assume these reservations would disappear when Chiang did. Republican opposition to his policies and attacks by McCarthyites irritated Acheson, but he was not apprehensive. He had worked with Vandenberg and Dulles to surmount such problems in the past, and he assumed "the primitives" were still manageable.

The second important ingredient in American policy toward China appears to have been Truman's greater responsiveness to domestic pressures. Congressional leaders feared the disruptive influence of the China bloc, and Democrats concerned about reelection in 1950 were uneasy. Truman delayed the termination of aid to the Kuomintang and prevented steps that might have led to an early normalization of relations with the Communists. Acheson and Truman thought they had time, that foreign policy goals would not be jeopardized by obeisance to temporary domestic political needs.

In the spring of 1950 there seemed to be a race between Rusk's efforts to change policy and the tolling of the bells that would sound Chiang's doom. Delays caused by the inability to get the desired responses from Mao, by Truman, perhaps also by French apprehension about Peking's intentions in Southeast Asia allowed a third ingredient—war in Korea— to win a reprieve for Chiang. But even the coming of war in Asia did not preclude accommodation with the People's Republic. Acheson worked desperately to keep that option retrievable, and he might well have succeeded had it not been for the decision to send UN forces across the 38th parallel [in Korea]. Even then Acheson tried to stave off an association with Chiang that would prevent a settlement with the Chinese Communists.

Acheson's performance was not perfect, but it was perfectly creditable until the decision to cross the 38th parallel. Conceivably Rusk understated the danger of Chinese intervention. Perhaps Acheson deferred to a Pentagon led by Marshall and Deputy Defense Secretary Robert A. Lovett, two of the few men he respected. Or, most obviously, the temptation to disarm domestic critics by "liberating" Korea proved irresistible. But Acheson's response to Chinese intervention was senseless. He knew full well that the United States, thanks to MacArthur, was sending confusing signals to Peking. In the heat of battle and bearing a burden of guilt as Americans died at Chinese hands, he blamed the Chinese for their anger at the United States. He assumed it would take too long for the Sino-Soviet split to manifest itself. Mao might be independent, but he was intensely anti-American and his hostility had to be reciprocated, had to be the basis of policy. Nonetheless, Acheson refused alliance with Kuomintang China, leaving that mistake for the succeeding administration.

In 1951 Acheson and the Truman administration squared off against the plague of McCarthyism, a kind of public constraint he could never have imagined and could not ignore. By its disastrous decision to cross the 38th parallel the administration had rearmed the "primitives"—and it spent its last years staggering under McCarthy's attack.

The American Failure to Negotiate

WILLIAM W. STUECK, JR.

The issue of political relations with a Chinese Communist regime was closely tied to commercial matters. The Communists might survive a Western economic boycott, but State Department officials believed that the new masters of China would at least temporarily want trade with the capitalist powers. Yet, during late 1948 and early 1949, as the Communists moved into cities of Manchuria and North China in which American consular personnel resided, they refused to acknowledge the official standing of the representatives of foreign governments. Communist leaders also announced their intention to abrogate U. S. treaties with Nationalist China.

American officials deeply resented this attitude. Not only were representatives of the United States accustomed to favored treatment in China, they, as well as top policymakers in Washington, regarded the upholding of treaty obligations as "basic to relations among modern States." This view, together with the belief that, for commercial reasons, the Communists would soon adopt a less extreme course, produced a tough position regarding the formal recognition of Peking. As Ambassador Stuart put it, "the Communists, rather than nations with well-established tradition[s] and accepted international standards," should be placed "on trial." In early May 1949, Acheson decided that the United States should not initiate moves toward recognition, and he instructed American officials to impress upon Western European governments the desirability of developing a "common front" on the issue. Weeks before the secretary, responding to political pressures at home, outlined publicly the criteria for establishing political relations, he privately had adopted the Jeffersonian model. A Communist regime would be judged in three areas: its capacity to control the territory it purported to govern, its "ability and willingness . . . to discharge its international obligations," and the "general acquiescence" of the people of the country under its rule.

This attitude led to rejection of an apparent opportunity for an American official to talk directly to Mao and other top men in Peking. Ironically, just

From *The Road to Confrontation: American Policy Toward China and Korea, 1947–1950* by William W. Stueck, Jr. Copyright 1981 The University of North Carolina Press. By permission of the publisher.

after the United States moved to create a united front among the Western powers on the recognition question, Huang Hua, head of the Communist Alien Affairs Bureau in Nanking, approached Ambassador Stuart. On 13 May, the two men talked for nearly two hours. Raising the matter of recognition, Huang expressed much interest in Communist relations with the United States on a basis of "equality and mutual benefit." Stuart outlined the criteria recently established in Washington. The Chinese official then apologized for a recent incident in which Communist soldiers had trespassed on Stuart's living quarters.

Then, at the end of the month, Chou En-lai, a powerful figure in the Chinese Communist Party, made an indirect approach to the American consulate general at Peking through Michael Keon, an Australian journalist employed by the United Press. Chou talked of a division within the Communist camp between a liberal group, of which he was a leader, and a radical faction, headed by Liu Shao-chi. The liberals desired friendly relations with the Western democracies, especially the United States and Great Britain, as a means of obtaining the assistance necessary for economic reconstruction at home. The radicals demurred, desiring a close alliance with the Soviet Union. The State Department authorized O. Edmund Clubb, the consul general at Peking, to respond that Washington hoped for amicable relations with the new China on the basis of "mutual respect" and "equality," but was deeply disturbed by Communist treatment of American representatives in the country and propaganda attacks on the United States. President Truman approved this reply, though he emphasized that Clubb must avoid any indication of a "softening" American attitude toward the Communists. When Clubb sought to transmit the message directly to Chou or his secretary, however, the Communist leader abruptly broke off contact.

In the meantime, Stuart's talks with Huang in Nanking had continued. On 28 June, only days after Chou had squelched his own initiative in Peking, Huang told the ambassador that Mao would welcome him in the northern city if he wished to visit Yenching University. This proposal was a response to a query from Philip Fugh, Stuart's secretary and confidant, regarding the feasibility under present circumstances of the ambassador's annual July pilgrimage to his former school. Stuart immediately cabled Washington for instructions. In the State Department, both Butterworth and John Paton Davies considered the invitation to be significant, but they feared the domestic reaction if Stuart accepted. They proposed to skirt this problem. The ambassador could stop in Peking after traveling to Mukden to pick up Angus Ward, the American consul general there, who, along with his staff, was being held under house arrest; or Washington could announce that Stuart had gone to Peking to read Communist leaders "the riot act" regarding mistreatment of American diplomats.

On 1 July, however, Acheson wired Stuart and stated that a decision had been reached at the "highest level" against a journey to Peking. Communist attitudes toward American officials in China, of which the Ward case was only the most extreme expression, and toward treaties concluded by the National government, were foremost in reaching this verdict. On 16 June 1949, President Truman had instructed Webb to be "most careful not to indicate any softening toward the Communists but to insist on judging their intentions by their actions." A trip by Stuart to Peking also might have disrupted American efforts to unite Western governments on a cautious policy regarding recognition, and, to Acheson, a united front was a prerequisite to applying effective pressure on the Communists. Moreover, the Communists had not yet officially proclaimed themselves the government of China. The United States continued to recognize the National government. A trip to Peking by the American ambassador could not be kept secret, and Stuart was known to be inclined to deviate from instructions. His journey would detract from the already diminished prestige of the Nationalists and bolster the Communists at a time when their capacity to rule China remained uncertain. In a narrow legal sense, talks between the United States and a Chinese party, against the wishes of the recognized government, were inappropriate.

From the standpoint of politics in the United States, the trip would add fuel to the already intense attacks from Capitol Hill on Truman administration China policy. On 24 June, twenty-two Senators, including six Democrats, sent a letter to the President urging him to withhold recognition of the Communists. A week later, on the very day that the proposed Stuart trip to Peking was rejected, Acheson wrote to Senator Connally outlining the previously established criteria for recognition; the secretary assured him he would consult the Foreign Relations Committee before acting on the matter. The North Atlantic Treaty was then before the Senate, and the military assistance program, considered essential to give teeth to the pact, had not yet been sent to Congress. The specter, which had been so pervasive in late 1947 and early 1948, of a China bloc on Capitol Hill withholding support for critical enterprises in Europe, reappeared.

Yet domestic political concerns probably only reinforced Truman's and Acheson's inclination against the Huang overture. Had they believed that a major opportunity was at hand to advance American interests in China, they surely would have moved with less dispatch to stifle it. Certainly they would have explored the possibility of using Clubb at Peking to initiate talks with Communist leaders, a procedure that stood an excellent chance of remaining secret. If revealed to the public, it could be explained away, both to international lawyers and hostile politicians, far more easily than the Stuart trip. In all likelihood, Acheson advised Truman to reject the Huang initiative, and the president, already inclined in that direction, agreed. To them, a more positive response might encourage the Communists to persist in their aggressive behavior toward American officials in China, and undermine administration efforts to maintain a united Western front on recognition.

Both temperamentally and intellectually, Acheson was poorly suited to deal in an astute manner with the Communists. For one thing, he was preoccupied with the European theater. It was there, he felt, that the great issues of international politics would be played out. Furthermore, as Dean Rusk noted many years later, Acheson never had much respect for Asian peoples. He was a Europeanist not only in American foreign policy, but in culture as well. Finally, he had a passion for order. "In fact, I was always a conservative," he was to declare in 1969: "I sought to meet the Soviet menace and help create some order out of the world. I was seeking stability and never had much use for revolution. As a friend once said, we had plenty of chaos, but not enough to make a world." From this perspective, it was up to Communist China to demonstrate its worthiness to enter into the family of nations. Although the secretary of state was far from inflexible on China policy, neither was he anxious to explore every possible opportunity for constructive relations with the Communists. . . .

Few American decisions toward China in the postwar period were as unfortunate as the outright rejection of the Huang overture. To be sure, much of Communist behavior in preceding months evinced strong hostility toward the United States. Then, on 1 July—and probably unknown to Truman and Acheson at the time of their decision—Mao published an essay, "On People's Democratic Dictatorship," in which he asserted that the United States was the "one great imperialist power" remaining on earth. Because America sought "to enslave the world," he claimed, China must ally itself "with the Soviet Union, with every New Democratic country, and with the proletariat and broad masses in all other countries."

Such statements, however, do not eliminate the possibility that a careful probing of Peking's position in the summer of 1949 could have been useful to the United States. As John M. Cabot, the outspoken American consul general in Shanghai, observed, "Virulent anti-American propaganda is natural in view of our aid to the Nationalists." That aid was ineffectual in sustaining the Nationalists in China, but it added significantly to the anti-Communist resistance there. Even so, Communist leaders expressed interest in relations with the United States. On 15 June, Mao stated in a speech that his regime was

> willing to discuss with any foreign government the establishment of diplomatic relations on the basis of the principles of equality, mutual benefit and mutual respect for territorial integrity and sovereignty, provided it is willing to sever relations with the Chinese reactionaries, stops conspiring with them or helping them and adopts an attitude of genuine, and not hypocritical, friendship toward People's China.

Other evidence existed that the Communists were, as Stuart put it, "far from a Soviet Punch and Judy show." Clearly they were not anxious to eliminate the American presence in China. Throughout 1949, the Communist attitude toward American missionaries encouraged them to remain in China. Some American-owned businesses had similar experiences. Relations between the Peking regime and the Shanghai Power Company, for instance, remained smooth for months after the May 1949 Communist takeover of Shanghai.

Talks with Communist leaders could have served a variety of purposes. They could have been used to protest the treatment of American representatives in China. To avoid conveying a sense of American weakness or desperation, the United States could have held to a firm position on this issue. Top officials in Peking might well have demonstrated flexibility on the matter. It was by no means certain, after all, either then or later, that the harassment of American officials represented a centrally coordinated policy of the Communists or merely the independent acts of local forces.

Acheson could have minimized confusion and resentment among Western European nations by keeping their leaders informed of the proceedings. The mere fact of discussions in Peking need not have detracted from caution and unity on the recognition question. In fact, Peking talks might actually have strengthened Western harmony. If they went poorly, tendencies, already apparent in Great Britain and France, to open relations with the Communists once they formed a government, might have been weakened.

On the other hand, conversations in Peking might have been a basic step toward mutual toleration between Communist China and the West. Washington's failure to pursue discussions diminished such prospects. As Cabot noted, the out-and-out rejection of the Huang overture may "have placed those Communists favoring better relations with the West in an impossible situation." The American response was especially damaging because the ambassador's secretary had initiated the idea of a Stuart visit to Peking. The Communists probably viewed the suggestion as a concrete overture by the United States. When Washington squelched it, therefore, Peking was understandably embarrassed and displeased. Indeed, between July and September 1949 there emerged little new evidence that Communist leaders desired a "working relationship with the United States." Even Chou En-lai made strong anti-American speeches. And Communist officials in Mukden, who on 21 June had notified Ward that transportation facilities would be made available for him and his staff to leave the city, hardened their position toward the American diplomat. Although a variety of considerations may have dictated against Stuart traveling to Peking, Acheson should at least have communicated to the Communists that the United States desired talks but wanted, for the present, to pursue them through Clubb.

Direct contacts between the United States and the Communist Chinese were especially desirable in view of continued American aid to Chiang. In the absence of diplomatic exchanges between Peking and Washington, Communist leaders inevitably saw an American plot behind every Nationalist move. In late June, for example, in an effort to impede Communist efforts to rule China, the Nationalists blockaded Shanghai. The action consisted of both air and naval maneuvers to prevent foreign ships from unloading cargoes there. Although the United States did not approve the move, the Communists soon labeled it as American-inspired. This characterization may have been part of a Communist strategy of exploiting popular resentments against foreigners for the purpose of building unity at home. But past American support for the Nationalists—which continued, albeit at a low level—coupled with Washington's rejection of Peking's overtures, made it just as likely that the Communists truly believed that the United States was responsible for the blockade.

In addition to the possibility that talks would have increased Communist understanding of the American position, they also might have added to the Truman administration's grasp of events in China. Washington's perceptions of the Communists already had suffered from insufficient contact. Although the State Department had tentatively concluded—perhaps in part because of the recent example of Yugoslavia—that, in a positive sense, there was little the United States could or need do to influence Communist relations with the Soviet Union, more extensive knowledge might have led to a different judgment. As *New York Times* correspondent Seymour Topping has noted, even if the Truman administration could not have influenced Mao "to adopt a neutral position in the East-West struggle," conversations with the Communist leader might have "led at least to the establishment of a channel of communication between Peking and Washington." "If Americans had continued to talk to the Chinese Communists," Topping maintains, "many of the misunderstandings and much of the agony in Asia over the next two decades might have been averted." . . .

The administration's top priority was to maintain a united front against early recognition. The American effort faced serious difficulties, for the Labor government in Great Britain, in the face of pressures from commercial interests at home, leaned toward the establishment of relations with the Mao government. India's Prime Minister Jawaharlal Nehru also favored quick action. A succession of other Western European and Asian governments undoubtedly would follow the British and Indian lead. Rather than planning to move with the tide, Acheson summoned his persuasive powers in an attempt to reverse it. He failed in the endeavor; India recognized the People's Republic in December, and Great Britain took the same course a week later. By 18 January 1950, nine more non-Communist regimes had taken similar action.

Acheson's stand enjoyed widespread congressional and public support. Gallup polls of the summer and fall of 1949 indicated that Americans with opinions on the matter—only about 60 percent of those questioned—opposed recognition by more than a two to one margin. In late November, the Committee to Defend America by Aiding Anti-Communist China launched a "nationwide drive" against recognition with a rally at Carnegie Hall in New York. Several members of Congress attended the event. On 29 December, Senator Connally, following the overwhelming opinion expressed in letters to him from private citizens, announced his opposition to recognition.

James Reston, Washington correspondent for the *New York Times*, reported that State Department officials conceded in private that the domestic climate alone was delaying American recognition. As earlier, however, this consideration merely reinforced Acheson's inclinations, for Communist China's comportment in international matters genuinely disturbed him. On 24 October 1949, Angus Ward was jailed in Mukden for an alleged assault on a former Chinese servant at the American consulate. The State Department managed to obtain his release a month later, but Communist aggressiveness toward American officials and property in China did not end. On 14 January 1950, the Chinese government seized American consular compounds in Peking. In response to this action, and to the termination two months later of American radio communications with its representatives on the mainland, the United States withdrew completely from China. To the secretary of state, these were only the most overt manifestations of a generally intolerable state of mind that prevailed within the new government. Although he did not desire to slam the door permanently on American recognition, a halt to the "active abuse of us" in Peking was a prerequisite to a reevaluation of his position.

In early 1950, there was little movement on the question. Acheson toyed with the idea of using continued Nationalist air attacks on Shanghai—which often damaged American property—as a pretext for a total break with the Nationalist government, but such a break never occurred. In March, on the eve of Clubb's final departure from Peking, the secretary of state suggested that the consul general seek "an informal discussion with high Commie authorities of outstanding points of friction" between the United States and the new regime. Acheson emphasized, however, that Clubb must avoid "any inference [that] such [a] discussion constituted [a] move toward recognition or is a preliminary to such a move," or that the overture resulted from Communist "pressure" or American "weakness." Concern for American credibility abroad remained a barrier to flexible diplomacy.

In early April, Communist Chinese officials made it clear that termination of United States support for Chiang was a quid pro quo for talks on other issues. For all practical purposes, this exchange closed the matter. Clubb left China before the end of the month. Intent on avoiding any implication that Communist pressure could soften American policy, Acheson held firmly to the view that the Mao regime must submit to generally accepted standards of international conduct before the United States would talk about halting aid to the Nationalists and recognizing Peking. If the domestic political factor was critical, it was so only in an indirect sense: the American failure during 1949 to abandon the Nationalists completely—which was partially a result of pressures at home—influenced the Communist attitude toward the United States which, in turn, shaped the State Department position on relations with the Mao regime.

Another factor early in the fall of 1949 concerned pockets of armed resistance to the Communists in China. Although American officials recognized the probable futility of such activity, they did not want to openly discourage it. The desire remained strong to make the road to power of the Communists as rocky as possible. By mid-November, however, this consideration was no longer a significant impediment to recognition.

Concern for resistance to Communism on China's borders continued to influence Acheson's deliberations. On 16 December, he sent telegrams to his representatives in Southeast Asia requesting their views on the impact of American recognition. In the next two weeks, the secretary received replies from the consul general in Saigon, the chargé in Burma, and the ambassadors to Thailand and the Philippines. All of them emphasized the negative impact early recognition might have on efforts to bolster anti-Communist forces south and east of China's borders. This negative consideration took on decisive weight when combined with the prevailing State Department view that little could be done, in a positive vein, to alter the essentially hostile attitude of the Communists toward the United States.

From a domestic political standpoint, the Truman administration's best opportunity to talk to Peking was in the last months of 1949. The Communist government had been officially established, and the Atlantic Pact and the Military Assistance Plan had passed Congress. Public and congressional opinion did not necessitate a negative policy on recognition. In October, for instance, the State Department's Office of Public Opinion Studies reported that "most observers" in the press, while seeing "little need for haste, . . . expected eventual *de facto* recognition as the most 'realistic' course." Even after the Ward case made headlines in late October, most commentators "did not discount the possibility or desirability of recognition at some time in the future." Most Asian experts in the academic community, most Protestant church organizations, and many businessmen with interests in China favored early recognition. Admittedly, Catholic organizations and much of organized labor disagreed, as did large pluralities of those Americans queried by pollsters. The firmness of much of this opposition, however, especially in the general citizenry, may be doubted. Recognizing Peking would not take money or jobs away from many Americans, nor would it lead directly to physical setbacks to the security of the United States. Surely a public-relations offensive by the administration in favor of recognition would have had some impact.

Furthermore, if the hostility of the Chinese Communists toward the United States was related to American hostility toward them, and if the antagonism of many Americans toward recognition derived in part from Peking's antagonism to the United States, then American overtures to Mao might have led ultimately to a decline of public opposition to relations with the new government. In the absence of American initiatives toward Peking, on the other hand, Communist hostility was virtually certain to continue, as was the tendency of the American public to oppose recognition. In fact, much can be said for the argument that the Truman administration's best chance of overcoming the charge that it had "lost" China rested in the cautious but active pursuit of rapprochement with the Communists.

What were the prospects for rapprochement? Although the hostile acts in Mukden in late October 1949 and in Peking in the following January indicated to many the total hostility of the Communists, it remains uncertain that the incidents reflected decisions by a unified national leadership. One plausible explanation of the Ward affair is that Kao Kang, the pro-Russian head of the Northeastern People's Government, which was seated in Mukden—a government that had been established in late August and that temporarily maintained a degree of autonomy—took the action without prior approval from Peking. Clubb believed that the Soviet Union had instigated Ward's arrest in retaliation for the prosecution in the United States of Valentin Gubichev, a Russian citizen who the Kremlin asserted had diplomatic immunity. The State's Department's Office of European Affairs suspected a direct connection between the Ward case and the October 1949 arrest in the United States of officials in the Soviet-owned Amtorg Trading Corporation for failing to register as foreign agents. Whatever the reasons for Ward's arrest, its occurrence so soon after Clubb had seen evidence that the Communists genuinely desired to establish relations with the United States suggests that powerful forces were pulling in opposite directions within China. Whether or not the United States could have influenced the situation remains a mystery. It is certain, however, that in October 1949 the State Department rejected an opportunity to explore the possibility.

Initially, Clubb, based on information from a "reliable source," interpreted events in Peking during January 1950 as representing a Communist effort to pressure the United States into recognizing the new regime. British consular property had not been confiscated, he observed, and this fact appeared to be related to London's recognition of the Communists. Years later, Clubb suggested that confiscation of American consular property was the brainstorm of a faction within the Chinese Communist party, rather than the act of a monolithic leadership. The move, after all, came while Mao was in Moscow attempting to negotiate a treaty of alliance with the Russians. The time it took to achieve this purpose—nearly two months— and the meager assistance received by China as a result of the Treaty of Friendship, Alliance, and Mutual Assistance that was signed on 14 February, indicates that all was not smooth in the Sino-Soviet relationship. Prior to the emergence of the pact, the State Department had reliable reports that Mao was seriously dissatisfied with the Soviet position on several points. During the previous fall, Clubb's contacts in Peking had indicated that the Chinese leader was a "moderate" on the question of relations with the United States. It is unlikely that such a man would choose the middle of tough discussions with the Kremlin to intentionally burn all bridges to Washington.

Sino-American talks in Peking in October 1949 would have run into difficulties in two areas: continued American assistance to the Nationalists and the status of treaties between the United States and the Chiang regime. Agreement could have come only through concessions on both sides. The United States undoubtedly would have been expected to end economic and military aid to Taiwan. Past Sino-American agreements would have needed to be renegotiated. Pressures from the pro-Soviet faction in China and the China bloc in the United States made flexibility difficult for either government.

Nevertheless, an exchange of views might have shown compromise to be possible. For instance, the United States might have offered to end all assistance to the Nationalists after 15 February 1950, the termination date for the commitment of funds through the China Aid Act. The United States might also have agreed to revise old pacts between the two countries, provided that changes were more of form than of substance. In a Sino-American agreement of 1943, the United States had renounced the most blatant privileges in the "unequal treaties" of the nineteenth and early twentieth centuries, but dissatisfaction remained among the Communists in certain areas, including the status of part of the United States consular compound in Peking, which had been seized in 1900 as a barracks for

American troops in the foreign intervention against the Boxer Rebellion. A protocol of 1901 had given the United States title to this land, and the agreement of 1943, though calling for an end to all rights received in the earlier pact, provided for the continued American use of property allocated for its diplomatic quarters. It may be wondered here if relatively minor concessions by Washington would have satisfied Communist determination to remove all vestiges of "imperialist" domination. A demonstrated willingness on the part of the United States to discuss the matter might at least have prevented precipitous action such as occurred on 14 January 1950.

Perhaps the Communists, fearing the Kremlin's reaction, would have shied away from serious talks with the United States. The Soviets maintained a strong, possibly even dominant, presence in Manchuria, and—in the aftermath of Yugoslavia's revolt against Stalin's direction—were particularly sensitive to any Peking flirtations with the West. Walter McConaughy, who during the previous summer had replaced Cabot as consul general at Shanghai, had information that Mao's trip to Moscow was the result of a "strong and rather sudden . . . pressure" from the Kremlin in response to "moves" by Great Britain and other non-Communist nations toward recognition and an impending visit by Philip Jessup to the western Pacific. On the other hand, McConaughy also reported a "rapidly swelling tide [of] Chinese charges and bitterness re[garding] Soviet greed [and] encroachments" in Manchuria. Had Washington demonstrated greater flexibility toward the new regime, it might have evaluated its options somewhat differently.

But the cold war had so come to dominate Acheson's mentality that common bargaining was unthinkable with a Communist government that repudiated widely accepted standards of international conduct—standards, by the way, that China had had no role in constructing—and showed open allegiance to Moscow. To Acheson, there was little to discuss and nothing to concede. If "keeping a foot in the door" and avoiding the diversion of potential Chinese irredentist sentiments against Russia in the north were of sufficient worth to merit a degree of restraint on the part of the United States, they warranted little in the way of positive effort. And Acheson received little pressure within the administration, from either above or below, to loosen his stance.

No Lost Chance: Chinese Anti-Americanism

STEVEN M. GOLDSTEIN

The Communist armies that crossed the Yangtze in April 1949 were well disciplined, battle-hardened troops. They were euphoric as they finally entered China's great cities to garner the fruits of their victory. They were

From "Chinese Communist Policy Toward the United States: Opportunities and Constraints, 1944–1950" in *Uncertain Years: Chinese-American Relations, 1947–1950*, edited by Dorothy Borg and Waldo Heinrichs (New York: Columbia University Press, 1980). Reprinted by permission of the publisher.

also highly politicized armies. For nearly three years the troops had been lectured on the indignities visited upon the Chinese nation by the imperialist United States. Awaiting them in the cities were workers who shared their intense anti-Americanism.

Anti-Americanism had been strong at the grass-roots level among the Chinese Communists ever since 1945–46. In August 1946, Chou En-lai candidly stated to Ambassador Stuart that resentment against the presence of American troops in China was "hotter among the lower classes than the higher classes of Communists." By the beginning of 1949 hostility to the United States was rampant among the masses, especially in the major Chinese cities that contained large foreign communities. Missionaries, according to their own accounts, had to bear the brunt of much popular ill will despite the restraining efforts of Communist leaders. In Nanking members of the United States Embassy were targets of anti-American outbursts from middle-and low-ranking Communist officials. In Shanghai the pent-up animosity of the workers toward the United States erupted in spontaneous demonstrations after the Communists took over the city. Leftist tendencies pervaded the workers' movement, anxious to settle scores with foreign and domestic entrepreneurs.

Prominent among the foreigners who had expected to stay in China after the Communists came to power were American businessmen in the main urban centers. Many were eager to do business with the new China. In their own eyes, they had been compassionate observers of the Chinese scene and were now prepared to make concessions to the Chinese Communists' sensitivities. Still, like most foreign residents in China they had, consciously or unconsciously, become accustomed to occupying a highly privileged position and were unprepared to cope with the broad-based antiforeign feeling that developed in 1949 and quickly led to the elimination of their special status. By the end of the year most of the American businessmen who originally intended to remain in China had returned to the United States.

Much of the anti-American and antiforeign outburst that occurred in 1949 was clearly contrary to the wishes of the CCP leadership. In the early months of 1949 the CCP had hoped to differentiate between the imperialist governments and their people. While warning the Communist troops before they entered the cities against hostile acts likely to be instigated by foreign governments they also instructed them "to protect the lives and property" of all foreign nationals in China. In the spring of 1949 Mao himself wrote: "The Chinese people wish to have friendly cooperation with the people of all countries and to resume and expand international trade in order to promote economic prosperity."

The distinction between imperialist governments and their nationals proved, however, difficult to make in practice, especially in relation to the United States. Given the intensity of their feeling against the United States, the Chinese people were in no mood to draw fine lines between official and unofficial America. American nationals in China were beneficiaries of the unjust, imperialist system. If the CCP had been conciliatory toward individual

American businessmen, many Chinese would have felt that the Party was violating one of its most vital tenets: the eradication of imperialism in China. To recognize or even merely to reform the old commercial system in China— a system which many Americans and other Westerners regarded as essential for the conduct of business—was patently a political impossibility. As a member of the Democratic league, one of the Chinese political parties then outlawed by the Kuomintang, reported to a U. S. official:

> General intransigence of labor whether under foreign or Chinese employment is exploiting opportunity to extent which Communists disapprove but cannot afford suppress, irrespective rights and wrongs, for fear seeming to champion capitalists, imperialists, and losing urgently needed mass support.

The Party leaders not only recognized the political dangers of modifying their anti-imperialist position but also realized the benefits that might be obtained from capitalizing on it. The civil war had entered a crucial phase. The Communists were now in the cities, the very places where they had the most to gain from demonstrating their loyalty to the anti-imperialist cause. Throughout the summer of 1949 the Chinese Communist press prominently published accounts of incidents in which Westerners, who had allegedly mistreated Chinese, were forced to pay compensation, indicating that the day of Western supremacy in China was over. Accounts of this nature merely intensified the public's hostility toward foreigners and thus committed the Party even more deeply to opposing the imperialists.

Domestic political considerations, therefore, left the CCP little room for making any adjustments in its relations with Americans. Moreover the actions of the United States Government, as interpreted by the CCP, most certainly did not justify any moderation of its anti-American policy. America's global policy continued to be bellicose, as evinced by the founding of NATO. Its China policy was seen as no different. As noted above, from the end of 1948 the Party leaders had predicted that the hostility of the United States government to the CCP would increase as the defeat of the Kuomintang drew nearer. By mid-summer of 1949 they felt their predictions had been substantiated to an alarming degree. The Truman administration was apparently acquiescing in the naval blockade imposed by the Kuomintang in June against the ports under Chinese Communist control and in August the State Department issued the famous White Paper.

From the Chinese Communists' point of view it would be difficult to imagine a more inflammatory document than the White Paper. The CCP immediately launched a massive "anti–White Paper" campaign. A large body of documentation was produced to substantiate the oft-made charge that the United States must bear a major share of the responsibility for the civil war in China. The campaign was above all an attack on the hope expressed in the White Paper that "democratic individualism" would emerge in China and that the Chinese Communists would follow the road of Titoism. This American approach intensified a long-held CCP concern, and the Chinese Communists asserted that in attempting to foster "democratic individualism" (which they translated as "democratic individualists") the United States was trying to construct a fifth column in China. They moreover took the occasion of a renewal of the anti-Tito campaign by the Soviet bloc to reemphasize their earlier position that to advocate Titoism was to be ensnared by an imperialist trick to win China over to the American side. In the international world, they were convinced, there was no middle ground between the reactionary and democratic camps. Any Chinese who favored neutrality was at best unpatriotic, at worse treasonous.

As 1949 developed there seemed to be little incentive for the CCP to change its anti-American posture. Domestic restraints existed and American actions—in China and the world—conformed to the adversary relationship the CCP anticipated would develop as their victory grew nearer. China would have to confront the forces of imperialism. . . .

The American side of the story is told elsewhere in this volume. As the civil war developed and the Communists gained the upper hand, the United States government was forced to keep its distance from the CCP. While public opinion was generally permissive, the pro-KMT lobby in Congress was strong—or at least appeared so to the policymakers in Washington. The president and the State Department were still reluctant to give a wartime ally the coup de grace by dealing with its enemy. In addition the administration's options were limited by foreign policy commitments elsewhere. It was difficult to maintain simultaneously an anti-Communist posture in Europe and an accommodating position toward a major Communist movement in Asia. In short it was impossible, in 1949, for American policymakers to deal with the emerging Chinese regime as it was—a pro-Soviet, anti-imperialist movement, humiliating one of America's wartime allies and driving uncompromisingly against United States interests in China.

But what of the CCP? If Washington had not had these inhibitions, would the Chinese Communists have established friendly relations at this time? Could they have dealt with the United States as it was—a capitalist nation with significant economic and political stakes in China moving toward a global confrontation with the Soviet Union? I do not think so.

Unlike the pre-1947 period, in 1949 CCP statements about the United States were almost uniformly hostile. The animosity they reflected was strong and clear and any suggestions of possible ties with the United States were vague. There are, however, a few reports of Chinese Communists approaching American officials with a view to establishing friendly relations between the CCP and the Truman Administration. Of these, two have received considerable attention.

The first involves an alleged demarche by Chou En-lai through Michael Keon, an Australian journalist, in Peking in June 1949. Chou purportedly sent a "top secret" message through Keon to the American consul general in Peking for transmittal to the State Department. The message suggested inter alia that Chou was part of a "liberal" faction that was seeking ties with the United States and was eager to act as a mediating agency between America and the Soviet Union. In response the Acting Secretary of State,

James E. Webb, drafted a statement of conditions for discussions with the CCP. Nothing materialized as Chou En-lai suddenly became elusive.

This story has evoked much skepticism. American specialists on China, who were in Peking at the time, strongly question its validity. A few months earlier Keon had been denounced by the Chinese Communists for reportorial distortions and would therefore seem an unlikely choice to serve as messenger on a mission of this nature. Moreover it is improbable that, in the period of Cominform opposition to Tito, Chou En-lai would have maintained that China's place was between the United States and the Soviet Union.

A second account of a demarche has somewhat more substance. On June 28, 1949, Huang Hua, then director of the Communist Alien Affairs Office in Nanking, suggested that Ambassador Stuart, who had been president of Yenching University for almost three decades, might consider returning to Peking for his annual birthday visit. Huang strongly implied that, while in Peking, Stuart could hold a meeting with Mao Tse-tung and Chou En-lai. Two days later, while Huang's suggestion was under consideration in Washington, Mao delivered his "lean to one side" speech. On July 1 the proposed trip was vetoed by the State Department, to all appearances under instructions from President Truman, bringing the episode to an end.

Some scholars have suggested that, if a meeting between Ambassador Stuart and the Chinese leaders had been held, it would have changed the course of history materially. There is little to substantiate such a thesis. Indeed if the constant exchanges in Nanking between American and Chinese officials in the period before late June 1949 are a guide, Ambassador Stuart, Mao Tse-tung, and Chou En-lai might well have found that neither side was willing to yield on matters perceived as essential. In the Nanking meetings the responses of the Chinese officials to American initiatives were tentative and evasive. Despite the greater stature of the leaders in Peking there is no ground for supposing their reaction would have been any different. The CCP simply did not believe existing domestic or international conditions permitted the establishment of positive relations with the United States.

The domestic conditions that in the CCP's judgment ruled out an understanding with the administration in Washington are apparent. As indicated earlier, when the Chinese Communists entered the cities and began to confront imperialism in its economic, social, and political reality, they were greatly impressed by the strength of the popular reaction to the anti-imperialist issue. In the summer of 1949 the Party leaders apparently feared that to relent on the strident anti-Americanism that had characterized the CCP's foreign policy for years would incur grave political costs in the urban areas. It might also create serious organizational problems, as there was considerable hostility to the United States throughout the Party and the army. Moreover the CCP leadership was deeply concerned with the effect that any lessening of tension between the Chinese Communists and the Truman Administration might have upon the Chinese intellectuals. Although the Chinese intellectuals were firmly opposed to American imperialism, they generally still admired the United States, especially in comparison with the Soviet Union. The CCP had long feared that, under certain circumstances, many Chinese intellectuals would consciously or unconsciously promote the interests of the American imperialists. A detente between the Chinese Communists and Washington could provide just such an opportunity.

While the domestic situation, in the CCP's view, therefore suggested that there was more to lose than to gain from reaching an understanding with the United States, the international situation in 1949 seemed to point to the same conclusion. The events after 1946 had only confirmed the Party's earlier judgment that revolutionary China's struggle with imperialism was inextricably bound to the global confrontation between the forces of reaction and of progress. As the Cold War quickened, the CCP became increasingly impressed with the benefits to be derived from a policy of leaning to the side of the Soviet Union.

Admittedly there had been developments following the war—especially Stalin's advice to the CCP to negotiate with the Nationalists and the Soviets' self-serving actions in Manchuria—that might have increased the CCP's misgivings regarding the Soviet Union. Yet it would be a serious mistake to conclude that Mao's relations with Stalin in 1949 contained more areas of discord than of agreement. The spirit of Communist interdependence remained strong. From 1947 to 1949, the CCP consistently supported the Soviets on matters of global policy. Such support was more than a mere gesture. The CCP adhered to its often unpopular alignment with Moscow at considerable domestic political cost. But it was obviously willing to pay the price. Whatever second thoughts the Party may have had concerning Soviet actions were more than offset by the increased American threat and the consequent importance of relying on the USSR.

It has often been stated that even if the Communists were committed to a lean-to-one-side policy they may still have been prepared to establish some limited economic or other ties with the United States. But there are a number of considerations that argue against such a thesis. In addition to the existing domestic situation and the CCP's assessment of the United States as a threat, the ideological trend within the international Communist movement in the late 1940s was against any association with the imperialist camp. The expulsion of Tito from the Cominform and the subsequent purges of other East European Communist leaders clearly conveyed the message that Stalin would not look with favor upon any dalliance with the bourgeois world. Under such circumstances the CCP was not likely to enter into any arrangements with the enemy which at best would achieve only marginal gains and might result in the alienation of the USSR, China's only real friend among the great powers. While the lean-to-one-side policy need not have precluded ties with the West, the CCP had long recognized that under certain circumstances it might do so. Such was the case in 1949–50.

It is common to view the crisis-ridden beginnings of Sino-American relations as the result of a "failure" of American diplomacy. While some impugn the motives of the Truman administration, more sympathetic proponents of this view depict the administration as severely constrained by political considerations of a domestic and international nature. Discussions of the Chinese side rarely mention comparable constraints. Mao and the

CCP leadership often seem to be making policy in splendid isolation from such factors.

This paper asserts, to the contrary, that an appreciation of similar constraints on the CCP leaders is indispensable to an understanding of United States-China relations in the years from 1944 to 1950. Peking, too, was constrained in what it could do by the weight of past policies and perceptions and, more immediately, the pressures of domestic public opinion and international commitments. There was no "lost chance" for the simple reason that neither side was in a position to take a chance.

✖ F U R T H E R   R E A D I N G

Robert M. Blum, *Drawing the Line* (1982)
Russell Buhite, *Patrick J. Hurley and American Foreign Policy* (1973)
——, *Soviet-American Relations in Asia, 1945–1954* (1982)
Warren I. Cohen, *America's Response to China* (1980)
——, "The United States and China Since 1945," in Warren I. Cohen, ed., *New Frontiers in American East Asian Relations* (1983)
John P. Davies, *Dragon by the Tail* (1972)
John K. Fairbank, *The United States and China* (1979)
Herbert Feis, *The China Tangle* (1953)
John Gittings, *The World and China, 1922–1972* (1974)
Akira Iriye, *The Cold War in Asia* (1974)
Arnold Xiangze Jiang, *The United States and China* (1988)
E. J. Kahn, *The China Hands* (1972)
Ross Koen, *The China Lobby in American Politics* (1974)
David McLean, "American Nationalism, the China Myth, and the Truman Doctrine: The Question of Accommodation with Peking, 1949–50," *Diplomatic History*, 10 (1986), 25–42
Edwin Martin, *Divided Counsel: The Anglo-American Response to Communist Victory in China* (1986)
Ernest R. May, ed., *The Truman Administration and China, 1945–1949* (1975)
Gary May, *China Scapegoat: The Diplomatic Ordeal of John Carter Vincent* (1979)
David Mayers, *Cracking the Monolith: U. S. Policy Against the Sino-Soviet Alliance* (1986)
Thomas G. Paterson, *Meeting the Communist Threat* (1988)
James Reardon-Anderson, *Yenan and the Great Powers* (1980)
Michael Schaller, *The U. S. Crusade in China, 1938–1945* (1978)
——, *The United States and China in the Twentieth Century* (1979)
William W. Stueck, Jr., *The Wedemeyer Mission* (1984)
Tang Tsou, *America's Failure in China, 1941–1950* (1963)
Barbara Tuchman, "If Mao Had Come to Washington," *Foreign Affairs*, 51 (1972), 44–64
——, *Stilwell and the American Experience in China, 1911–1945* (1971)
Nancy Tucker, *Patterns in the Dust: Chinese-American Relations and the Recognition Controversy, 1949–1950* (1983)
Paul Varg, *The Closing of the Door: Sino-American Relations, 1936–1947* (1973)
H. Bradford Westerfield, *Foreign Policy and Party Politics* (1955)
Donald Zagoria, "Choices in the Postwar World: Containment and China," in Charles Gati, ed., *Caging the Bear* (1974)

CHAPTER
9

The Korean War

Before the outbreak of the Korean War in June 1950, the United States had launched a number of Cold War programs—the Truman Doctrine, the Marshall Plan, and NATO—and had weathered several crises: in Iran, Greece, and Berlin, for example. Yet in Asia, the American policy of containment faltered in China, where Mao Zedong's (Mao Tse-tung's) Communists unseated Jiang Jieshi's (Chiang Kai-shek's) Nationalists in late 1949 and created the People's Republic of China. Americans considered the new Chinese government a Soviet puppet.

Another shock wave hit the United States in August 1949, when the Soviet Union successfully exploded a nuclear device, thereby ending the American atomic monopoly. Many Americans jumped to the conclusion that the United States was losing the Cold War. The phenomenon of McCarthyism began in early 1950. Then the Korean War erupted. The Truman administration quickly decided to intervene—to draw the containment line.

Since then, questions have challenged contemporaries and scholars alike: Why did the Truman administration intervene? Should the United States have intervened? Was the Korean War an example of global, Soviet-engineered Communist aggression? Or was it essentially a Korean civil war? Did Soviets plan and order the North Korean invasion? Why did Truman decide to order American troops across the 38th parallel? What exactly was China's role, and why did it intervene? Why was General Douglas MacArthur fired? Should Americans have conducted the "limited" war that they did?

✖ *D O C U M E N T S*

On January 12, 1950, Secretary of State Dean Acheson delivered a major speech, reprinted here. He defined the American defense perimeter in Asia, which excluded Korea. Critics later charged that this omission gave the Soviet Union the incentive to use its North Korean allies to attack South Korea. The second document is the first North Korean statement on the outbreak of war in June 1950, blaming South Korea for provoking hostilities. During the opening days of the crisis, President Truman met with key advisers at Blair House, a building near the White House. The third document is a record of the June 26,

1950, meeting, in which Acheson recommended several important policies, not only for Korea but also for the Philippines, Formosa, and Indochina. The fourth document, dated August 7, 1950, is a top secret Defense Department memorandum that made the case for sending American troops across the 38th parallel. Truman accepted this advice, and on September 15 American Marines landed at Inchon and began the penetration of North Korea.

At a meeting with Truman on Wake Island on October 15, 1950, General Douglas MacArthur assured the President that the Chinese would not enter the war even in the face of an American advance through North Korea toward the Chinese border. This conversation is printed here as the fifth selection. In the sixth document, a November 28, 1950, speech to the United Nations, People's Republic of China official Wu Xinchnan (Wu Hsiu-ch'uan) explained why China felt compelled to join the Korean War. Truman summarized American war policy in a speech on April 11, 1951, shortly after he relieved MacArthur of his command (the seventh selection). The last document is MacArthur's rebuttal of April 19, delivered as a speech to Congress.

Dean Acheson on the Defense Perimeter in Asia, 1950

What is the situation in regard to the military security of the Pacific area, and what is our policy in regard to it?

In the first place, the defeat and the disarmament of Japan has placed upon the United States the necessity of assuming the military defense of Japan so long as that is required, both in the interest of our security and in the interests of the security of the entire Pacific area and, in all honor, in the interest of Japanese security. We have American—and there are Australian—troops in Japan. I am not in a position to speak for the Australians, but I can assure you that there is no intention of any sort of abandoning or weakening the defenses of Japan and that whatever arrangements are to be made either through permanent settlement or otherwise, that defense must and shall be maintained.

This defensive perimeter runs along the Aleutians to Japan and then goes to the Ryukyus. We hold important defense positions in the Ryukyu Islands, and those we will continue to hold. In the interest of the population of the Ryukyu Islands, we will at an appropriate time offer to hold these islands under trusteeship of the United Nations. But they are essential parts of the defensive perimeter of the Pacific, and they must and will be held.

The defensive perimeter runs from the Ryukyus to the Philippine Islands. Our relations, our defensive relations with the Philippines are contained in agreements between us. Those agreements are being loyally carried out and will be loyally carried out. Both peoples have learned by bitter experience the vital connections between our mutual defense requirements. We are in no doubt about that, and it is hardly necessary for me to say an attack on the Philippines could not and would not be tolerated by the United States. But I hasten to add that no one perceives the imminence of any such attack.

So far as the military security of other areas in the Pacific is concerned, it must be clear that no person can guarantee these areas against military attack. But it must also be clear that such a guarantee is hardly sensible or necessary within the realm of practical relationship.

Should such an attack occur—one hesitates to say where such an armed attack could come from—the initial reliance must be on the people attacked to resist it and then upon the commitments of the entire civilized world under the Charter of the United Nations which so far has not proved a weak reed to lean on by any people who are determined to protect their independence against outside aggression. But it is a mistake, I think, in considering Pacific and Far Eastern problems to become obsessed with military considerations. Important as they are, there are other problems that press, and these other problems are not capable of solution through military means. These other problems arise out of the susceptibility of many areas, and many countries in the Pacific area, to subversion and penetration. That cannot be stopped by military means. . . .

That leads me to the other thing that I wanted to point out, and that is the limitation of effective American assistance. American assistance can be effective when it is the missing component in a situation which might otherwise be solved. The United States cannot furnish all these components to solve the question. It can not furnish determination, it can not furnish will, and it can not furnish the loyalty of a people to its government. But if the will and if the determination exists and if the people are behind their government, then, and not always then, is there a very good chance. In that situation, American help can be effective and it can lead to an accomplishment which could not otherwise be achieved. . . .

Korea

In Korea, we have taken great steps which have ended our military occupation, and in cooperation with the United Nations, have established an independent and sovereign country recognized by nearly all the rest of the world. We have given that nation great help in getting itself established. We are asking the Congress to continue that help until it is firmly established, and that legislation is now pending before the Congress. The idea that we should scrap all of that, that we should stop half way through the achievement of the establishment of this country, seems to me to be the most utter defeatism and utter madness in our interests in Asia. . . .

So after this survey, what we conclude, I believe, is that there is a new day which has dawned in Asia. It is a day in which the Asian peoples are on their own, and know it, and intend to continue on their own. It is a day in which the old relationships between east and west are gone, relationships which at their worst were exploitation, and which at their best were paternalism. That relationship is over, and the relationship of east and west must now be in the Far East one of mutual respect and mutual helpfulness. We are their friends. Others are their friends. We and those others are willing to help, but we can help only where we are wanted and only where the conditions of help are really sensible and possible. So what we can see is that this new day in Asia, this new day which is dawning, may go on to a glorious noon or it may darken and it may drizzle out. But that decision lies within the countries of Asia and within the power of the Asian people. It is not a decision which a friend or even an enemy from the outside can decide for them.

North Korea Blames South Korea
for Starting the War, 1950

Official announcement made by the Home Affairs Bureau of the People's Republic of Korea. The so-called "defense army" of the South Korea puppet regime started a surprise invasion of the north along the whole front of the 38th parallel line at dawn on the 25th. The enemy, who started the surprise operation, invaded the territory north of the 38th parallel line one to two kilometers at three points west of Haeju, Kumchon, and Chorwon. The Home Affairs Bureau of the People's Republic of Korea has issued an order to the security army of the People's Republic to repulse the enemy. At this moment, our security army is putting up stiff counter-operations against the enemy. The People's Republic army succeeded in repulsing the enemy force which penetrated into the north at Yangyang. In this connection, the People's Republic of Korea wishes to remind the South Korea puppet regime of the fact that, unless the puppets immediately suspend their adventurous military actions, the People's Republic will be obliged to resort to decisive countermeasures. At the same time the People's Republic entrusted the Home Affairs Bureau to call the attention of the South Korea puppet regime to the fact that the whole responsibility for the grave consequences arising from their reckless venture would squarely rest on the shoulders of the South Korea puppet regime.

Truman and His Advisers at the
"Blair House Meeting," June 26, 1950

GENERAL [HOYT S.] VANDENBERG reported that the First Yak plane had been shot down.

THE PRESIDENT remarked that he hoped that it was not the last.

GENERAL VANDENBERG read the text of the orders which had been issued to our Air Forces calling on them to take "aggressive action" against any planes interfering with their mission or operating in a manner unfriendly to the South Korean forces. He indicated, however, that they had been avoiding combat where the direct carrying-out of their mission was not involved.

MR. [DEAN] ACHESON suggested that an all-out order be issued to the Navy and Air Force to waive all restrictions on their operations in Korea and to offer the fullest possible support to the South Korean forces, attacking tanks, guns, columns, etc., of the North Korean forces in order to give a chance to the South Koreans to reform.

THE PRESIDENT said he approved this.

MR. [FRANK] PACE inquired whether this meant action only south of the 38th parallel.

MR. ACHESON said this was correct. He was making no suggestion for any action across the line.

GENERAL VANDENBURG asked whether this meant also that they should not fly over the line.

MR. ACHESON said they should not.

THE PRESIDENT said this was correct; that no action should be taken north of the 38th parallel. He added "not yet."

MR. PACE said that care should be used to avoid hitting friendly forces.

GENERAL [J. LAWTON] COLLINS agreed but suggested that the orders themselves should not put restrictions on the operation.

MR. ACHESON said that if it was considered useful the orders could add that the purpose which the orders would implement is to support South Korean forces in conformity with the resolution of the Security Council.

MR. ACHESON said that the second point he wished to bring up was that orders should be issued to the Seventh Fleet to prevent an attack on Formosa.

THE PRESIDENT said he agreed.

MR. ACHESON continued that at the same time the National Government of China should be told to desist from operations against the mainland and that the Seventh Fleet should be ordered to see that those operations would cease.

MR. ACHESON said his third point was an increase in the United States military forces in the Philippines and an acceleration of aid to the Philippines in order that we might have a firm base there.

THE PRESIDENT said he agreed.

MR. ACHESON said his fourth point was that aid to Indochina should be stepped up and that a strong military mission should be sent.

He suggested that on all these matters if orders were issued tonight it would be desirable for the President to make a statement tomorrow. He handed the President a rough draft of the type of statement which might be issued.

THE PRESIDENT said he would work on the statement tonight. The President continued that he wished consideration given to taking Formosa back as part of Japan and putting it under MacArthur's Command.

MR. ACHESON said that he had considered this move but had felt that it should be reserved for later and should not be announced at this time. It required further study.

THE PRESIDENT said that he had a letter from the Generalissimo about one month (?) ago to the effect that the Generalissimo might step out of the situation if that would help. He said this was a private letter and he had kept it secret. He said that we might want to proceed along those lines in order to get Chinese forces helping us. He thought that the Generalissimo might step out if MacArthur were put in.

MR. ACHESON said that the Generalissimo was unpredictable and that it was possible that he might resist and "throw the ball game." He said that it might be well to do this later.

THE PRESIDENT said that was alright. He himself thought that it was the next step.

MR. [LOUIS A.] JOHNSON said that the proposals made by the Secretary of State pleased him very much. He thought that if we hold the line as indicated that that was alright.

MR. ACHESON added in regard to the Formosan situation that he thought it undesirable that we should get mixed up in the question of the Chinese administration of the Island.

THE PRESIDENT said that we were not going to give the Chinese "a nickel" for any purpose whatever. He said that all the money we had given them is now invested in United States real estate.

MR. JOHNSON added or in banks in the Philippine Islands.

ADMIRAL [FORREST P.] SHERMAN said that the Command of the Seventh Fleet could be either under Admiral Radford at Pearl Harbor or under General MacArthur. He said that under the orders issued yesterday the Seventh Fleet had been ordered to proceed to Japan and placed under General MacArthur's Command. He said that the orders in regard to Formosa would be issued from the Joint Chiefs of Staff to General MacArthur so to employ the forces allocated by Admiral Radford to General MacArthur.

No objection was raised to this statement.

MR. ACHESON said that the Security Council would meet tomorrow afternoon and that the Department had prepared a further resolution for adoption. Our reports were that we would get full support. He noted that even the Swedes were now supporting us.

MR. [JOHN D.] HICKERSON read the draft of the Security Council resolution recommending that UN members render such assistance as was needed to Korea to repel the attack.

THE PRESIDENT said that was right. He said we wanted everyone in on this, including Hong Kong.

GENERAL [OMAR] BRADLEY reported that British Air Marshall Tedder had come to see him, was generally in accord with our taking the firm position, and gave General Bradley a full report of the forces which the British have in that area.

MR. [DEAN] RUSK pointed out that it was possible the Russians would come to the Security Council meeting and cast a veto. In that case we would still take the position that we could act in support of the Charter.

THE PRESIDENT said that was right. He rather wished they would veto. He said we needed to lay a base for our action in Formosa. He said that he would work on the draft of his statement tonight and would talk to the Defense and State Departments in the morning regarding the final text.

MR. RUSK pointed out that it was Mr. Kennan's estimate that Formosa would be the next likely spot for a Communist move.

SECRETARY JOHNSON reported that SCAP's guess was that the next move would be on Iran. He thought there should be a check on this.

GENERAL COLLINS said that SCAP did not have as much global information as they have in Washington. He and Mr. Pace stated that they have asked for full reports all over the world in regard to any developments, particularly of Soviet preparations.

SECRETARY JOHNSON suggested to Mr. Acheson that it would be advisable to have some talks with the UK regarding possible action in Iran.

MR. ACHESON said he would talk with both the British and French.

MR. ACHESON asked Admiral Sherman whether he desired that any action should be taken regarding the utilization of the Sakishimas, south of Okinawa.

ADMIRAL SHERMAN said he would leave this to General MacArthur. . . .

MR. ACHESON suggested that the President might wish to get in Senator Connolly and other members of the Senate and House and tell them what had been decided.

THE PRESIDENT said that he had a meeting scheduled for 10:00 tomorrow morning with the Big Four and that he would get in any others that the Secretary thought should be added. He suggested that Secretaries Acheson and Johnson should also be there. . . .

GENERAL COLLINS stated that the military situation in Korea was bad. It was impossible to say how much our air can do. The Korean Chief of Staff has no fight left in him.

MR. ACHESON stated that it was important for us to do something even if the effort were not successful.

MR. JOHNSON said that even if we lose Korea this action would save the situation. He said this action "suits me". He then asked whether any of the military representatives had any objection to the course of action which had been outlined. There was no objection.

GENERAL VANDENBERG, in response to a question from Mr. Finletter, said that he bet a tank would be knocked out before dark.

THE PRESIDENT said he had done everything he could for five years to prevent this kind of situation. Now the situation is here and we must do what we can to meet it. He had been wondering about the mobilization of the National Guard and asked General Bradley if that was necessary now. If it was he must go to Congress and ask for funds. He was merely putting the subject on the table for discussion. He repeated we must do everything we can for the Korean situation—"for the United Nations".

GENERAL BRADLEY said that if we commit our ground forces in Korea we cannot at the same time carry out our other commitments without mobilization. He wondered if it was better to wait now on the question of mobilization of the National Guard. He thought it would be preferable to wait a few days.

THE PRESIDENT said he wished the Joint Chiefs to think about this and to let him know in a few days time. He said "I don't want to go to war."

GENERAL COLLINS stated that if we were going to commit ground forces in Korea we must mobilize.

MR. ACHESON suggested that we should hold mobilization in reserve.

MR. JOHNSON said he hoped these steps already authorized will settle the Korean question.

THE PRESIDENT said the next question would be the mobilization of the Fleet Reserve.

ADMIRAL SHERMAN said there must be a degree of balance.

THE PRESIDENT noted that there is some pretty good air in the National Guard. He had never been in favor of this and thought it should be like the Naval Reserve.

GENERAL VANDENBERG said he was very glad to hear the President say this.

ADMIRAL SHERMAN asked whether MacArthur could anchor the fleet in Formosan ports if necessary.

THE PRESIDENT asked Mr. Acheson what he thought about this.

MR. ACHESON said that they should go ahead and do it.

ADMIRAL SHERMAN said this would be the best procedure.

GENERAL COLLINS remarked that if we had had standing orders we could have stopped this. We must consider this problem for the future.

THE PRESIDENT said he agreed.

MR. JOHNSON said that if there was danger of a Russian veto in the Security Council the President's statement should be put out before the Security Council meets tomorrow.

MR. ACHESON agreed.

The Defense Department's Case for Crossing the 38th Parallel to Reunite the Two Koreas, 1950

The following principles form the basis for consideration of U. S. actions:

a. The unification of Korea conforms with Korean aspirations, U.S. policies, and the objectives of the United Nations.

b. The establishment of a free and united Korea and the elimination of the North Korea Communist regime, following unprovoked military aggression, would be a step in reversing the dangerous strategic trend in the Far East of the past twelve months.

c. The 38th parallel, in and of itself, has no military significance other than such an artificial barrier as would limit if not prevent a military victory.

d. The chief potential limitation on the objective of unifying Korea will be Soviet military countermeasures including the use of Chinese Communist troops, or Soviet diplomatic and political actions in the UN.

e. Consequently, the timing and speed of U. S. politico-military operations are crucial, and call for especially close working relationships.

f. In the long run, a maximum UN effort will be needed in securing peace in Korea and in meeting the acute problems of political and economic reconstruction.

g. The continued functioning of the Republic of Korea, as the only sovereign government in Korea, is indispensable to the re-establishment of the rule of law in Korea and is necessary to the fulfillment of U.S. objectives.

h. Long-range policies in support of independence for Korea conform to the general objectives of the United States in Asia.

In consonance with the above principles and in pursuit of its basic long-range objectives with respect to Korea, the U.S. should take measures to effect:

a. The establishment of a free, independent and stable Korea oriented toward the U. S.
b. The security of Korea against foreign aggression and internal subversion.
c. The reconstruction of Korea in political, economic, and social fields to develop a stable, self-sustaining, and advancing state.

As the basis for realizing these objectives, the United States should take the following series of actions:

a. Statements of Aims:

1. At an appropriate time, the President should proclaim that our peace aim is a united, free, and independent Korea, as envisaged by the UN. Such a statement should be supported by a Joint Resolution of Congress.
2. Again at an appropriate time, the U.S. should seek to translate this aim into UN objectives. In view of the possibility that uncoordinated measures would provoke Soviet counter-action, either in the military or diplomatic field or both, the United States should seek UN action in two stages: first, at the 1950 meeting of the General Assembly, the United Nations should immediately endorse the resolutions of 25 and 27 June and 7 July, of the Security Council and seek maximum support for the unified command; second, at a later date, at the moment when the unified command has taken the offensive, the United Nations should re-affirm the basic UN aims in Korea along the lines of the General Assembly Resolution of 14 November 1947.
3. No statement of U.S. general objectives should be made until the unified command has launched offensive military measures to carry out the military objectives listed below. Until such time, great caution and discretion should be taken in public discussion of the 38th parallel.
4. In the meantime, the U.S. should use all its diplomatic means to forestall any Soviet effort to mediate the conflict on any terms short of the unification of all Korea on a free and representative basis under UN auspices.

b. Military Objectives:

1. The unified command should seek to occupy Korea and to defeat North Korean armed forces wherever located north or south of the 38th parallel.
2. To achieve this objective, the Commanding General of the unified com-

mand should pursue military operations in Korea without regard to the 38th parallel.

Douglas MacArthur on the Likelihood of Chinese Intervention, 1950

THE PRESIDENT: What are the chances for Chinese or Soviet interference?
GENERAL MAC ARTHUR: Very little. Had they interfered in the first or second months it would have been decisive. We are no longer fearful of their intervention. We no longer stand hat in hand. The Chinese have 300,000 men in Manchuria. Of these probably not more than 100/125,000 are distributed along the Yalu River. Only 50/60,000 could be gotten across the Yalu River. They have no Air Force. Now that we have bases for our Air Force in Korea, if the Chinese tried to get down to Pyongyang there would be the greatest slaughter.

With the Russians it is a little different. They have an Air Force in Siberia and a fairly good one, with excellent pilots equipped with some jets and B-25 and B-29 planes. They can put 1,000 planes in the air with some 2/300 more from the Fifth and Seventh Soviet Fleets. They are probably no match for our Air Force. The Russians have no ground troops available for North Korea. They would have difficulty in putting troops into the field. It would take six weeks to get a division across and six weeks brings the winter. The only other combination would be Russian air support of Chinese ground troops. Russian air is deployed in a semicircle through Mukden and Harbin, but the coordination between the Russian air and the Chinese ground would be so flimsy that I believe Russian air would bomb the Chinese as often as they would bomb us. Ground support is a very difficult thing to do. Our Marines do it perfectly. They have been trained for it. Our own Air and Ground Forces are not as good as the Marines but they are effective. Between untrained Air and Ground Forces an air umbrella is impossible without a lot of joint training. I believe it just wouldn't work with Chinese Communist ground and Russian air. We are the best.

The Chinese Case for Intervention, 1950

Under the pretext of the Korean civil war, which was of its own making, the United States Government launched armed aggression simultaneously against Korea and Taiwan. From the very outset the United States armed aggression against Korea gravely threatened China's security. Korea is about 5,000 miles away from the boundaries of the United States. To say that the civil war in Korea would affect the security of the United States is a flagrant, deceitful absurdity. But there is only a narrow river between Korea and China. The United States armed aggression in Korea inevitably threatens China's security. That the United States aggression forces in

Korea have directly threatened China's security is fully borne out by the facts.

From 27 August to 10 November 1950, the military aircraft of the United States aggression forces in Korea have violated the territorial air of North-East China ninety times; they have conducted reconnaissance activities, strafed and bombed Chinese cities, towns and villages, killed and wounded Chinese peaceful inhabitants and damaged Chinese properties. . . .

Now the United States forces of aggression in Korea are approaching our north-eastern frontiers. The flames of the war of aggression waged by the United States against Korea are swiftly sweeping towards China. Under such circumstances the United States armed aggression against Korea cannot be regarded as a matter which concerns the Korean people alone. No, decidedly not. The United States aggression against Korea gravely endangers the security of the People's Republic of China. The Korean People's Democratic Republic is a country bound by close ties of friendship to the People's Republic of China. Only a river separates the two countries geographically. The Chinese people cannot afford to stand idly by in the face of this serious situation brought about by the United States Government's aggression against Korea and the dangerous tendency towards the extension of the war. . . .

One of the master-planners of Japanese aggression, Tanaka, once said: to conquer the world, one must first conquer Asia; to conquer Asia, one must first conquer China; to conquer China, one must first conquer Manchuria and Mongolia; to conquer Manchuria and Mongolia, one must first conquer Korea and Taiwan.

Ever since 1895, the course of aggression taken by imperialist Japan has exactly corresponded to the Tanaka plan. In 1895, imperialist Japan invaded Korea and Taiwan. In 1931, imperialist Japan occupied the whole of NorthEast China. In 1937, imperialist Japan launched the war of aggression against the whole of China. In 1941, it started the war aimed at the conquest of the whole of Asia. Naturally, as everyone knows, before it had realized this design, Japanese imperialism collapsed. American imperialism, by its aggression against Taiwan and Korea, in practice plagiarizes Tanaka's memorandum and follows the beaten path of the Japanese imperialist aggressors. The Chinese people are maintaining a sharp vigilance over the progress of American imperialist aggression. They have already acquired the experience and learned the lesson from history as to how to defend themselves from aggression.

American imperialism has taken the place of Japanese imperialism. It is now following the old track of aggression against China and Asia on which Japanese imperialism set forth in 1894–95, only hoping to proceed with greater speed. But after all, 1950 is not 1895; the times have changed, and so have the circumstances. The Chinese people have arisen. The Chinese people who have victoriously overthrown the rule of Japanese imperialism and of American imperialism and its lackey, Chiang Kai-shek on China's mainland, will certainly succeed in driving out the United States aggressors and recover Taiwan and all other territories that belong to China. . . .

Truman Defends American Policy, 1951

In the simplest terms, what we are doing in Korea is this: We are trying to prevent a third world war.

I think most people in this country recognized that fact last June. And they warmly supported the decision of the Government to help the Republic of Korea against the Communist aggressors. Now, many persons, even some who applauded our decision to defend Korea, have forgotten the basic reason for our action.

It is right for us to be in Korea. It was right last June. It is right today.

I want to remind you why this is true.

The Communists in the Kremlin are engaged in a monstrous conspiracy to stamp out freedom all over the world. If they were to succeed, the United States would be numbered among their principal victims. It must be clear to everyone that the United States cannot—and will not—sit idly by and await foreign conquest. The only question is: When is the best time to meet the threat and how?

The best time to meet the threat is in the beginning. It is easier to put out a fire in the beginning when it is small than after it has become a roaring blaze.

And the best way to meet the threat of aggression is for the peace-loving nations to act together. If they don't act together, they are likely to be picked off, one by one.

If they had followed the right policies in the 1930's—if the free countries had acted together, to crush the aggression of the dictators, and if they had acted in the beginning, when the aggression was small—there probably would have been no World War II.

If history has taught us anything, it is that aggression anywhere in the world is a threat to peace everywhere in the world. When that aggression is supported by the cruel and selfish rulers of a powerful nation who are bent on conquest, it becomes a clear and present danger to the security and independence of every free nation.

This is a lesson that most people in this country have learned thoroughly. This is the basic reason why we joined in creating the United Nations. And since the end of World War II we have been putting that lesson into practice—we have been working with other free nations to check the aggressive designs of the Soviet Union before they can result in a third world war.

That is what we did in Greece, when that nation was threatened by the aggression of international communism.

The attack against Greece could have led to general war. But this country came to the aid of Greece. The United Nations supported Greek resistance. With our help, the determination and efforts of the Greek people defeated the attack on the spot.

Another big Communist threat to peace was the Berlin blockade. That too could have led to war. But again it was settled because free men would not back down in an emergency.

The aggression against Korea is the boldest and most dangerous move the Communists have yet made.

The attack on Korea was part of a greater plan for conquering all of Asia. . . .

They want to control all Asia from the Kremlin. . . .

The whole Communist imperialism is back of the attack on peace in the Far East. It was the Soviet Union that trained and equipped the North Koreans for aggression. The Chinese Communists massed 44 well-trained and well-equipped divisions on the Korean frontier. These were the troops they threw into battle when the North Korean Communists were beaten. . . .

So far, by fighting a limited war in Korea, we have prevented aggression from succeeding and bringing on a general war. And the ability of the whole free world to resist Communist aggression has been greatly improved.

We have taught the enemy a lesson. He has found out that aggression is not cheap or easy. Moreover, men all over the world who want to remain free have been given new courage and new hope. They know now that the champions of freedom can stand up and fight and that they will stand up and fight.

Our resolute stand in Korea is helping the forces of freedom now fighting in Indochina and other countries in that part of the world. It has already slowed down the timetable of conquest. . . .

But you may ask: Why can't we take other steps to punish the aggressor? Why don't we bomb Manchuria and China itself? Why don't we assist Chinese Nationalist troops to land on the mainland of China?

If we were to do these things, we would be running a very grave risk of starting a general war. If that were to happen, we would have brought about the exact situation we are trying to prevent.

If we were to do these things, we would become entangled in a vast conflict on the continent of Asia and our task would become immeasurably more difficult all over the world.

What would suit the ambitions of the Kremlin better than for our military forces to be committed to a full-scale war with Red China?

It may well be that, in spite of our best efforts, the Communists may spread the war. But it would be wrong—tragically wrong—for us to take the initiative in extending the war.

The dangers are great. Make no mistake about it. Behind the North Koreans and Chinese Communists in the front lines stand additional millions of Chinese soldiers. And behind the Chinese stand the tanks, the planes, the submarines, the soldiers, and the scheming rulers of the Soviet Union.

Our aim is to avoid the spread of the conflict.

The course we have been following is the one best calculated to avoid an all-out war. It is the course consistent with our obligation to do all we can to maintain international peace and security. Our experience in Greece and Berlin shows that it is the most effective course of action we can follow.

First of all, it is clear that our efforts in Korea can blunt the will of the Chinese Communists to continue the struggle. The United Nations forces have put up a tremendous fight in Korea and have inflicted very heavy casualties on the enemy. Our forces are stronger now than they have been before. These are plain facts which may discourage the Chinese Communists from continuing their attack.

Second, the free world as a whole is growing in military strength every day. In the United States, in Western Europe, and throughout the world, free men are alert to the Soviet threat and are building their defenses. This may discourage the Communist rulers from continuing the war in Korea— and from undertaking new acts of aggression elsewhere.

If the Communist authorities realize that they cannot defeat us in Korea, if they realize it would be foolhardy to widen the hostilities beyond Korea, then they may recognize the folly of continuing their aggression. A peaceful settlement may then be possible. The door is always open. . . .

I believe that we must try to limit the war to Korea for these vital reasons: to make sure that the precious lives of our fighting men are not wasted; to see that the security of our country and the free world is not needlessly jeopardized; and to prevent a third world war.

A number of events have made it evident that General MacArthur did not agree with that policy. I have therefore considered it essential to relieve General MacArthur so that there would be no doubt or confusion as to the real purpose and aim of our policy.

It was with the deepest personal regret that I found myself compelled to take this action. General MacArthur is one of our greatest military commanders. But the cause of world peace is more important than any individual.

MacArthur's "No Substitute for Victory" Speech, 1951

While I was not consulted prior to the President's decision to intervene in the support of the Republic of Korea, that decision from a military standpoint proved a sound one. As I say, a brief and sound one as we hurled back the invaders and decimated his forces. Our victory was complete and our objectives within reach when Red China intervened with numerically superior ground forces. This created a new war and an entirely new situation, a situation not contemplated when our forces were committed against the North Korean invaders, a situation which called for new decisions in the diplomatic sphere to permit the realistic adjustment of military strategy. Such decisions have not been forthcoming.

While no man in his right mind would advocate sending our ground forces into continental China—and such was never given a thought—the new situation did urgently demand a drastic revision of strategic planning if our political aim was to defeat this new enemy as we had defeated the old.

Apart from the military need as I saw it to neutralize sanctuary, protection given to the enemy north of the Yalu, I felt that military necessity in the conduct of the war made necessary:

First, the intensification of our economic blockade against China.

Second, the imposition of a naval blockade against the China coast.

Third, removal of restrictions on air reconnaissance of China's coastal areas and of Manchuria.

Fourth, removal of restrictions on the forces of the Republic of China on Formosa with logistical support to contribute to their effective operation against the Chinese mainland.

For entertaining these views all professionally designed to support our forces committed to Korea and bring hostilities to an end with the least possible delay and at a saving of countless American and Allied lives, I have been severely criticized in lay circles, principally abroad, despite my understanding that from a military standpoint the above views have been fully shared in the past by practically every military leader concerned with the Korean campaign, including our own Joint Chiefs of Staff.

I called for reinforcements, but was informed that reinforcements were not available. I made clear that if not permitted to utilize the friendly Chinese force of some 600,000 men on Formosa; if not permitted to blockade the China coast to prevent the Chinese Reds from getting succor from without; and if there were to be no hope of major reinforcements, the position of the command from the military standpoint forbade victory. We could hold in Korea by constant maneuver and at an approximate area where our supply advantages were in balance with the supply line disadvantages of the enemy, but we could hope at best for only an indecisive campaign, with its terrible and constant attrition upon our forces if the enemy utilized his full military potential. I have constantly called for the new political decisions essential to a solution. Efforts have been made to distort my position. It has been said in effect that I was a warmonger. Nothing could be further from the truth. I know war as few other men now living know it, and nothing to me is more revolting. . . .

But once war is forced upon us, there is no other alternative than to apply every available means to bring it to a swift end. War's very object is victory-not prolonged indecision. In war, indeed, there can be no substitute for victory.

There are some who for varying reasons would appease Red China. They are blind to history's clear lesson. For history teaches with unmistakable emphasis that appeasement but begets new and bloodier war. It points to no single instance where the end has justified that means—where appeasement has led to more than a sham peace. Like blackmail, it lays the basis for new and successively greater demands, until, as in blackmail, violence becomes the only other alternative. Why, my soldiers asked of me, surrender military advantages to an enemy in the field? I could not answer. Some may say to avoid spread of the conflict into an all-out war with China; others, to avoid Soviet intervention. Neither explanation seems valid. For China is already engaging with the maximum power it can commit and the Soviet will not necessarily mesh its actions with our moves. Like a cobra, any new enemy will more likely strike whenever it feels that the relativity in military or other potential is in its favor on a world-wide basis.

The tragedy of Korea is further heightened by the fact that as military action is confined to its territorial limits, it condemns that nation, which it is our purpose to save, to suffer the devastating impact of full naval and air bombardment, while the enemy's sanctuaries are fully protected from such attack and devastation. Of the nations of the world, Korea alone, up to now, is the sole one which has risked its all against communism. . . .

I am closing my 52 years of military service. When I joined the Army even before the turn of the century, it was the fulfillment of all my boyish hopes and dreams. The world has turned over many times since I took the oath on the plain at West Point, and the hopes and dreams have long since vanished. But I since remember the refrain of one of the most popular barrack ballads of that day which proclaimed most proudly that—

"Old soldiers never die; they just fade away." And like the old soldier of that ballad, I now close my military career and just fade away—an old soldier who tried to do his duty as God gave him the light to see that duty.

Good-by.

❇ *E S S A Y S*

Peter Lowe, a historian at Manchester University in Great Britain, has determined that the Korean War started as a civil war between rival Korean governments and leaders, north and south, both of whom sought to unite their divided nation after 1945. Although the United States and the Soviet Union had different interests and goals in Korea, it was the turmoil in Korean society and politics, not meddling by foreign powers, that sparked war. Noting that we still do not know for sure what role the Soviets played in the outbreak of the war, Lowe agrees, in the first essay, with historian Bruce Cumings that North Korea, not the Soviet Union, initiated the war in June 1950. In the second essay, James I. Matray of New Mexico State University studies the controversial United States decision to unite the two Koreas by advancing across the 38th parallel. That decision changed the American war objective from saving South Korea to "liberating" North Korea, and the military advance toward the Chinese border ultimately brought China into the war. Matray discounts the view that Truman acted because he sought to improve his faltering political standing at home or because Americans suffered from exaggerated optimism after their success at Inchon. Matray stresses instead Truman's commitment to the principle of self-determination and his hope that, after the war, Koreans would be free to choose their own—preferably non-Communist—government.

The Origins of the Korean War: Civil War

PETER LOWE

In August to September 1945 Korea was in a ferment of revolutionary upheaval. The pent-up tensions and emotions of colonial servitude had been cast off, even though many Japanese were still in posts in south Korea at

---

the request of the incoming American military administration. Political and social revolution was in the air and Koreans of all political persuasions longed for unity. To a combustible internal situation in August 1945 was added the beginnings of great power rivalry and animosity, which would ensure that the deadly hatreds within Korean society would be resolved amid a framework of hostility between superpowers that would have profound repercussions for Korea.

In August 1945 Korea, as with the other parts of the Japanese colonial empire, faced turmoil and uncertainty on a massive scale. The vacuum created by the sudden termination of the Pacific War raised enormous questions on the combustible internal situation in the territories affected, on allied policies, and on the relationship that would exist between local representatives of the allied powers and their home governments. American officials had shown greater interest in Korea from 1943 onwards as part of the State Department's preparations for handling the consequences of Japan's defeat. The assumption was that Korea would require a period of trusteeship in which the United States and the Soviet Union would play the principal roles, before Korea became independent as a unitary state. Concern was felt over ambitions that might be stimulated in Moscow with the result that Korea could become a focal point of tension. The Soviet Union entered the Pacific War in its dying moments in August 1945 to fulfil Stalin's wish that the Russian voice should be raised to influence postwar developments in East Asia. Decisions on the administration of Korea had to be reached swiftly and the United States would be dependent on Soviet goodwill at first, since American forces were not immediately available to occupy south Korea. American-Soviet agreement on respective zones in Korea was attained through acceptance of the 38th parallel as the dividing line between the Soviet-controlled area to the north and the American-controlled area to the south.

There was nothing magical about the choice. The 38th parallel was an obvious line to adopt and had the merit from the American viewpoint of placing the border north of Seoul; this maximised the territory under American direction. Korea south of the 38th parallel included the bulk of the population and was predominantly rural; north Korea contained most of the industry, previously linked with the Japanese economic interests in Manchuria. Soviet troops advanced into Korea to accept the surrender of Japanese forces; Stalin kept his word and when American troops arrived on 8 September, they assumed responsibility to the 38th parallel. Stalin adhered to the agreement because he wished to maintain satisfactory relations with the United States if possible and perhaps because he felt that sooner or later Korea would fall into the Soviet sphere in any case.

Within Korea in 1945–46 a revolutionary situation and spirit existed. This has been thoroughly assessed by Bruce Cumings in the first volume of his study of the antecedents of the Korean War. Fundamental to everything was the bitter experience of Japanese colonialism and the determination to eliminate the legacy of that experience together with those who had collaborated with the Japanese. Much of the old Korean élite had worked with the Japanese for the material rewards and defence of their interests; the police force was the most hated feature of the colonial era and the vengeance taken on police guilty of torture, extortion and corruption was savage. The collapse of Japanese authority was followed by the emergence throughout Korea of "people's committees"; they appeared at various levels—province, city, county and village. The committees functioned effectively in north Korea in the initial stage of communist rule before their independent characteristics were curbed as the northern regime consolidated itself. In the south the people's committees operated in over half the counties. Cumings has remarked, "These people's committees are examples of that rarest of Korean political forms, locally rooted and responsive organization." The emergence of the people's committees was promoted by the significant improvement in the communications network in Korea during the Japanese era and through the population growth and mobility of the population under colonialism. The people's committees connoted a manifestation of profound discontent against deprivation and oppression: high rents, interest rates, large grain collections, the exactions and interventions of landowners and police contributed to a spontaneous revolutionary environment. The people's committees were of radical outlook in the main, representing the aspirations of the "have-nots" of Korean rural society. However, the most vital feature in eligibility for participation in the committees was the attitude or relationship previously adopted to the Japanese: if village elders had shunned the colonial regime, they could be chosen to play a leading part in the work of the committees. The American occupation misunderstood the nature of the unrest in south Korea and attributed it to the machinations of the communists. In fact the people's committees were a genuinely spontaneous growth in which communist agitation was involved only to a minor extent. The existence of the committees posed problems for both the American and the Soviet occupations in the sense that any vigorous, independent organization represents a latent challenge to outside authority. However, the challenge was bound to be more difficult for the Americans to handle, since they opposed drastic change while the Russians desired it.

The most important individual for deciding the direction of United States policy in Korea was the head of the military occupation, from 1945 to 1948, General John Reed Hodge. Hodge was frequently criticised by contemporaries for his inability to grasp the finer points of the problems confronting him and for reacting in too blunt a manner. Much of the criticism was justified but to be fair to Hodge, he had been placed in an invidious position and, blinkered as he was, in some respects, he was correct in appreciating that a rebuilding of the Korean right offered the only means of preventing communist success in south Korea. . . . One of Hodge's advisers was George Z. Williams, born in Korea and the son of a missionary; Williams was strongly anti-communist and well connected with the rightists in Korea. From the moment he arrived in Korea, Hodge was concerned with the maintenance of order and of developing quickly a viable framework of control. Circumstances in Korea, as in China and South-East Asia, pressured the Americans into relying on Japanese administrators and police in the early months of the occupation. Whilst to begin with inevitable, Hodge and his colleagues need not have relied so heavily or for so long on Japanese personnel. Many Koreans were affronted at the liberation of August 1945 being followed by the continued presence of Japanese and of the odious methods they had employed to suppress dissent. The Korean police, as reorganised under the occupation, included numerous former collaborators, operating as in the past but serving different masters. Ordinary Koreans wishing to see their country independent, unified and tackling its social and economic problems radically felt betrayed at the deep conservatism that distinguished the occupation.

The political situation in south Korea in August–September 1945 was largely dominated by the Committee for the Preparation of Korean Independence (CPKI), founded by Yo Un-hyong and his supporters. Yo was left of centre but not militant; in the dying moments of the Japanese administration he was invited to form a transitional administration and agreed to do so, on the basis of the release of political prisoners and of no interference with the organisation of workers, peasants, students and youths. Yo regarded the CPKI as a temporary, transitional, administration pending the arrival of the allies and the formulation of more permanent plans. Political debate soon raged at different levels throughout Korean society; an intoxicating sense of freedom prevailed. Workers and peasants meetings developed spontaneously in August and September; later from November to December 1945, the new mass organisations came to be more tightly controlled from above. The CPKI was a typical umbrella nationalist movement characteristic of the struggle for independence before divergent ideological approaches had shattered the organisation. The CPKI was broadly divided into a faction supporting Yo Un-hyong, which was leftist but not communist, and a faction that consisted chiefly of communists. The CPKI issued a statement on 28 August advocating radical reform and "mass struggle against the anti-democratic and reactionary forces" which had collaborated with Japan "and committed crimes against the nation." The leading personality in the growth of communism in south Korea was Pak Hon-yong, who established the reconstructed Korean Communist Party on 8 September. Two days earlier a CPKI meeting in Seoul proclaimed the establishment of the Korean People's Republic (KPR). The action demonstrated the belief that Korea was ready for independence and was intended to forestall a lengthy American occupation or the Americans advancing Koreans of their own choice. The danger of internal dispute was recognised and the KPR strove to achieve coalescence of all elements whether right or left, that had been opposed to the Japanese. This was illustrated in the list of cabinet members, which included Syngman Rhee, Kim Ru, Ho Hon and Kim Kyu-sik. The statement of KPR policy objectives included the elimination of feudalism, imperialism, the implementation of radical land policies, the nationalisation of major industries, and the encouragement of industrialisation. Civil liberties were guaranteed, the franchise was extended to all over the age of eighteen, and an enlightened approach was urged for the industrial and education spheres. The KPR was unduly idealistic in aspirations and it proclaimed a programme that was too grandiose. The communists within the CPKI moved to take over as much power as they could for themselves in August–September and this, too, weakened the KPR.

The Korean right was weak, despondent and lacking in effective leadership. Many rightists had worked closely with the Japanese and had so discredited themselves. The two most prominent rightists were Kim Ku and Syngman Rhee. Both had been associated with the exiled "government" based at Chungking from 1938 to 1945. This was a shadowy body with few supporters but at least it represented definite opposition to the Japanese presence. . . . Rhee never doubted that he was destined to lead Korea and acted with a strange mixture of arrogance, duplicity, cunning and tenacity to establish his power. It took him a considerable time to do so but he succeeded and left a deep mark on Korea only equalled or exceeded by his arch-rival, Kim Il Sung in north Korea. . . . Hodge and those around him believed Syngman Rhee should be encouraged and believed he could be controlled; they were later to regret having aided Rhee's ambitions to the extent that they had done when they found themselves exposed to Rhee's mordant censure. . . .

The Moscow conference of American, British and Russian foreign ministers met in December 1945 against a sombre background of anxiety at the deterioration of relations between the powers since the end of the European War. The conference was misleadingly regarded as a success and as reversing the trend in relations. Korea was fully discussed at the conference and agreement was secured, which later ran into the sands. The United States advocated trusteeship. The Soviet Union submitted a scheme envisaging the establishment of a joint commission by the Soviet and American military commands in Korea, which would advise on the formation of a provisional Korean government. The powers approved the Soviet scheme with slight amendments. The outcome was that the concept of trusteeship was played down: the agreement concentrated on the creation of a provisional government. Trusteeship would not be considered until after a government had been established and after the Joint Commission had been approached. As Cumings observes, this was open to the interpretation that trusteeship might not be proceeded with at the end of the day. The Moscow agreement could have offered the basis for a settlement had the United States and the Soviet Union cooperated and had the bulk of opinion in Korea accepted it. Instead the United States was soon to swing against it with General Hodge undermining it, and most opinion in south Korea was hostile to it. . . .

The United States moved steadily away from the Moscow agreement in the first half of 1946. The worsening of relations with the Soviet Union in Europe meant that Hodge's policy of constructing a viable right-centre opposition to left communism won growing support in Washington. The next significant development occurred with the formation of the Representative Democratic Council (RDC) as the nucleus of a south Korean administration. The body emerged in February 1946 and resulted from the actions of Hodge, Rhee and the mysterious M. Preston Goodfellow. Goodfellow had worked in American intelligence during the Pacific War and became deputy director of the OSS. Rhee met Goodfellow during the war and they assisted each other's interests from then onwards. Goodfellow went to Korea in November 1945 and remained there until the following summer. He worked to achieve a coalition of right-centre political groups under Rhee's leadership. Hodge worked to advance the RDC as the coalition of rightist elements that would strengthen the American hand in the impending negotiations with the Soviet Union in the Joint Commission. The RDC comprised twenty-eight political leaders, almost all rightists. Rhee stated that the RDC would "represent the Korean people in its dealings with General Hodge and the Military Government." The deliberations of the RDC revealed that it was intended to pave the way for the establishment of a provisional government. Hodge supported and utilised the RDC until November 1946 when the Interim Legislature came into existence. The polarisation in south Korea was underlined with the formation of the Democratic National Front (DNF) as a coalition of left-centre groups embracing moderate leftists and communists. It included Yo Un-hyong, who had refused to attend the RDC, and Pak Hon-yong. Bruce Cumings has shown that the DNF was not run by communists trained by the Soviet Union, as Hodge alleged, but was designed as an authentic voice of independent leftist opinion. While most obviously a reaction to the coalescence of the right, it was also a reaction against the establishment in north Korea on 14 February of the Interim People's Committee under the leadership of Kim Il Sung. . . .

At the end of 1946 and beginning of 1947 speculation centred on the prospects of a south Korea split by bitter political and social tensions. The suppression of the autumn harvest uprisings dealt a fatal blow to the "people's committees" in many areas; the right was strengthened further. Rhee became more vocal and extreme in advancing his ambition. The Americans endeavoured to persuade the Russians to reconvene the Joint Commission but without success. Inflation had become a particularly serious and contentious subject. . . .

The atmosphere in Seoul was extremely tense. The rightists, whipped up by Syngman Rhee and Kim Ku, organised demonstrations attacking the Soviet Union and the American military government. The Joint Commission reconvened in a final attempt to make some progress. In a speech in Seoul on 27 April Rhee cleverly sought to reconcile his own vigorous hostility to communism with the American approach to world problems. He welcomed the Truman Doctrine and claimed he had frequently predicted tne development to Hodge:

> With the change of the international trends, not only have the gloomy prospects of the Korean people become bright, but also General Hodge's policy to South Korea will be changed in accordance with the policy of his country.
>
> The American authorities told me that I should make a general election law and arrange that the Korean people rule themselves. In view of this we must enact election laws as soon as possible. After this we must participate in the UNO and try to unify North and South Korea by negotiating with Russia from the standpoint of freedom. On the other hand I have

considered the problem of supporting the Great Korean Provisional Government, but we must cooperate with the MG [military government] as much as possible and then talk about the provisional government. . . .

We must fulfil our task by ourselves and we must not create any cause for an American and Russian war. If a new war should occur no country will suffer as much as Korea would. . . .

The Joint Commission reconvened in late May. At first it appeared that some progress was being made. A joint bulletin issued on 7 June stated that agreement had been reached over methods of consulting Korean democratic parties and other relevant organisations on developments leading to the creation of a unified government and that the text of agreement would be issued shortly. General Hodge reported that the reopening of the Joint Commission was a disappointment for Rhee and the extreme right in that they had campaigned vociferously for the past year against further American-Soviet discussion. The Joint Commission soon became bogged down in renewed argument over the eligibility of various groups for consultation, with the Russians reiterating refusal to consult rightists currently denouncing the Soviet Union vehemently and demonstrating noisily in Seoul. On 23 June rightist demonstrations took place in Seoul and in other parts of south Korea; Hodge ordered American tanks on to the streets to disperse the crowds. The exchanges in the Joint Commission again ended in deadlock and this marked the termination of the discussions set in train at the Moscow conference. . . .

Political unrest in south Korea increased appreciably in June and July 1947, stimulated by Rhee's intrigues. Hodge reported on 7 July that Rhee had issued a statement criticising the Americans for not supporting him; this was in keeping with Rhee's denunciation of the State Department and of an alleged plot to assassinate General Brown. Rhee was encouraged by certain people in Washington and Hodge named Oliver, Staggers and Jerome Williams; Staggers and Williams were respectively president and vice-president of the American World Trade Export-Import Company Inc. Shortly afterwards Hodge described the political unrest as worsening with the anti-trusteeship campaign having become a campaign against the Joint Commission, the Soviet Union and the United States. The possibility existed of Rhee forming a government unilaterally. Hodge lamented the rift between the military government and the rightists after their earlier cooperation. It was, he sadly reflected, impossible to keep the Koreans away from factionalism and skulduggery. . . .

Clearly the point had arrived in September 1947 where fundamental decisions had to be taken on the American commitment to Korea. The vital questions were aptly summarised by Jacobs on 19 September. Was Korea of sufficient importance for the United States to accept a substantial financial and political involvement? If the answer was that American global strategy required an allocation of priorities in geographical terms could south Korea be abandoned in favour of a stand being made in Japan or elsewhere? These would be central to the arguments over defence policy that resounded or echoed through the State Department and Pentagon until the beginning of

July 1950. If Korea was deemed vital, Jacobs recommended liquidation of the Moscow agreement as rapidly as possible and the full implications in cost and personnel worked out. If the United States decided to get out of south Korea, it should not be difficult to transfer the burden to the UN where an agreement could be reached; this would incorporate simultaneous withdrawal of American and Russian forces. Bloodshed would ensue as the rival sides fought each other, as had happened in India after British withdrawal and as was happening in China. However, American involvement would be at an end. The Joint Chiefs of Staff assessed Korea in September and concluded that "from the standpoint of military security, the United States has little strategic interest in maintaining the present troops and bases in Korea . . . ." If war broke out in the Far East "our present forces in Korea would be a military liability and could not be maintained there without substantial reinforcement prior to the initiation of hostilities." Any offensive operations which the United States might have to conduct on the Asiatic continent would probably avoid the Korean peninsula. If an enemy developed powerful air and naval bases in Korea, American communications and operations in east China, Manchuria, the Yellow Sea, the Sea of Japan and contiguous areas could be adversely affected. Such enemy forces based in Korea could be neutralised through air action. The latter would be more feasible and less expensive than large-scale ground operations. Since the American army was under pressure with the impact of economy measures, the two divisions of approximately 45,000 men in south Korea could be deployed more profitably elsewhere. Withdrawal would not undermine the military position of the Far Eastern Command unless the Soviet Union built up military strength in south Korea sufficient to implement an attack on Japan. As George Kennan has remarked, the heavy emphasis upon American air power was a characteristic error of the period; the extent of the misjudgment became abundantly clear in early July 1950.

Opinion in Washington therefore moved to the conclusion that on balance it would be best to reduce American involvement in Korea and to request the UN to assist in achieving an acceptable solution. In the Joint Commission, which had reached the end of its futile labours, General Shtikov proposed in early October the withdrawal of foreign troops from Korea as a prelude to the various Korean factions agreeing on a provisional government to lead the peninsula to unified independence. Shtikov's proposal was warmly welcomed by the Korean left and viewed with alarm by the right. Although the right had advocated foreign withdrawal they were well aware that the retention of some American troops was needed to prevent communist domination—"Under Shtikov's proposal, [a] strong Korean Communist Army in [the] North of Korea would be free to sweep down on the virtually unarmed south and quickly over-run it." Rhee reacted by toning down his recent criticisms of the Americans and he urged that a small force be left in south Korea until the south could defend itself effectively. The United States wished to secure a transitional period in which limited American military and economic aid would be extended to south Korea in the hope that the communists would be kept at bay, at least for a decent interval.

The role of the UN would be to supervise elections, if possible throughout Korea but if not in south Korea alone, and to afford some measure of protection to the infant state as it moved to independence. . . .

The UN was a relatively small body in 1947 and effectively dominated by the United States. The Soviet Union possessed a veto in the Security Council but there was little doubt that the United States could convince the UN General Assembly to accept a proposal of reasonable character. The motion providing for the establishment of the UN Temporary Commission on Korea (UNTCOK) was carried easily against Soviet opposition on 14 November 1947. The members were India, Canada, Australia, France, China, El Salvador, the Philippines and Syria; the Ukrainian Soviet Socialist Republic declined to serve. The chairman was the Indian representative Kumara P. S. Menon. The successor body, UNCOK, had the same membership with the exception of Canada. It was established by a motion carried on 12 December 1948.

[I have] so far focused mainly upon south Korea and on the American-Soviet deliberations upon producing a unified administration. This . . . section will look concisely at the construction of north Korea between 1945 and the beginning of 1948. It was widely believed in the western world that north Korea was simply created by the Soviet Union in a manner similar to that used by the Soviet Union in eastern Europe. There were some similarities but it would be wrong to consider north Korea as analogous to Bulgaria or Hungary. Stalin was less interested in Korea and the type of state that developed was of idiosyncratic character, in some respects resembling the Soviet Union and in others the kind of communist party devised by Mao Tse-tung during the Yenan era. Before 1945 Korean Marxists had cooperated with the Soviet Union from bases in Soviet far eastern territories and had worked with the Chinese communists at Yenan. Of Korean communists associated with Russia, the best known was Kim Il Sung but he had also been involved with the CCP [Chinese Communist party]. . . . Kim was frequently regarded in the West as a Soviet stooge but this was erroneous. Kim was a passionate nationalist imbued with determination to restore self-respect to Korea and to unify the peninsula, to liquidate feudalism and to remove foreign dominance—American or Russian—from Korea. Admittedly these characteristics became more obvious later on; Kim Il Sung was dependent on the Soviet Union for assistance in the early years in north Korea and had to tread warily. . . .

The Soviet Union had made few preparations for occupation of north Korea in August 1945. Improvisation was necessary in the haste of the Soviet attack on Japan. People's committees operated extensively, comprising progressive non-communists and communists; the Soviet task was helped by the will for reform and change. The initial behaviour of the Soviet forces was bad, including rape and plunder; this was explicable through the rawness of troops and inadequate provision for the occupation—some soldiers lacked proper uniform or shoes. They were permitted by their superiors to take personal booty back with them. From the beginning of 1946 Soviet troops were efficient and well disciplined; they were not liked but were respected.

In 1945–46 Soviet policy was to encourage cooperation between the moderate leftists and the communists until an administrative framework had been created. The independence of the people's committees was not ultimately compatible with communist rule in north Korea and problems occurred in the first few months of communist dominance. The Russians were helped through the fleeing southwards of many of those who might have obstructed them. The coalition between moderate leftists and communists was shattered by the trusteeship crisis of January 1946. The beginning of the north Korean state dates from this period. Kim Il Sung soon established his authority. He became leader of the northern branch of the Communist Party in December 1945; there was always latent rivalry between Kim and Pak Hon-yong, the leader of the southern branch. It is likely that Pak would have been more amenable to the Russians than Kim but Kim was the tougher of the two and had the opportunities, which he fully exploited. Kim put forward a blend of Russian and Chinese approaches, which marked the beginning of the independent and sometimes eccentric path subsequently trodden by Kim. In a speech on 17 December 1945 Kim stressed the necessity for creating a wide range of party organisations in factories, enterprises and villages with the formulation of suitable criteria for party membership so as to eliminate some of the dubious elements which had recently joined the party. He emphasised the importance of a tightly organised centralised party on Leninist lines but also injected Mao Tse-tung's views with stress on working with the masses.

The North Korean Interim People's Committee (NKIPC) developed in February 1946 as a reaction to the trend of events in the south; it was meant to assist in the process that would lead to a government for the whole of Korea. Kim Il Sung headed the NKIPC; the membership was disparate and it took some time for Kim to establish his control. Gradually autonomous organisations in north Korea were curbed by Kim and the Soviet forces. The north Korean army originated in a coalescence of Kim's guerrilla supporters and the Yenan Koreans; it was only lightly armed prior to the departure of Soviet forces in 1948. Thereafter it evolved rapidly into a formidable force. Land reform policies were swiftly implemented on lines similar to China with the poor peasants and landless labourers constituting the spearhead. Landlords and rich peasants were identified as the enemy and their power broken. The changes were carried through with relatively little bloodshed.

 . . . . As it was, Kim Il Sung worked successfully to establish his authority. By the beginning of 1948 his position was strong but could still be challenged. The emerging north Korean state was solidly based and possessed much more cohesion than its counterpart in the south. The two leaders of Korea, Syngman Rhee and Kim Il Sung, confronted one another, both intensely nationalistic, ruthless, driven on by a sense of destiny and confidence that he—whether Rhee or Kim—would unite Korea and lead the nation to a glorious future. . . .

The leading members of the government of the DPRK were Kim Il Sung and Pak Han-yong; Pak was simultaneously Foreign Minister and leader of the South Korean Labour Party (SKLP). Pak's presence strengthened the argument for regarding the government as representing the whole of Korea and underlined the hopes that Korean unification could be achieved through a major rebellion in the south. The turbulent history of much of South Korea since 1945 suggested the likelihood of this eventuality and was further strengthened by the bloody fighting in Cheju island in October 1948, which will be discussed below. Much obscurity surrounds the views within the North Korean leadership and what exactly were the perceptions of the probable evolution of politics in the south. Pak Hon-yong needed to bolster his own role in the North Korean government and the maintenance of a revolutionary spirit in the south would assist that objective. The revolutionary impetus was declining, however, in 1949–50 amid the harsh repression by the South Korean government. North Korea was forced more upon itself as a result of American success in manipulating UN recognition of the ROK. Kim and Pak visited Moscow in March 1949 for discussions with Stalin and it was evidently on this occasion—if Nikita Khrushchev's recollections are reliable—that Stalin gave somewhat grudging approval to a future North Korean attack, on the assumption that there would be a significant rebellion in the south.

Between 1948 and 1950 the Soviet Union helped in building the armed strength of North Korea to a powerful level. Regular intelligence assessments of North Korean strength were prepared by different American agencies with varying results. John J. Muccio informed Washington in November 1948 that military intelligence pointed to North Korea defeating South Korea in the event of war occurring. There were frequent rumours of North Korean invasion plans down to June 1950. . . .

Syngman Rhee had established a strong but not invincible position in 1948. He was the most tenacious politician in South Korea and an adroit manipulator but lacking in popularity. John J. Muccio, the first ambassador to the ROK, knew Rhee well and appreciated the President's strengths and weaknesses. In retirement, Muccio recalled that Rhee was very intelligent, determined and assertive; he had reached the top at a late age and was too set in his ways, his attitude having been determined by his lengthy period in exile, amid the seemingly forlorn struggle to save Korea from Japanese colonialism. When Rhee was in a logical frame of mind, he showed an excellent historical perspective but when he became emotional, he became particularly awkward to deal with. Rhee was highly autocratic yet claimed to represent the desire for genuine democracy in Korea. Rhee was concerned with consolidating his own power base, building up the strength of his regime, securing American economic and military assistance, and with achieving the unification of Korea under his leadership; this would be the crowning attainment of his long struggle. The omens for the new state were not encouraging in the first months of its existence. Muccio reported in November 1948 that economic developments were disturbing, with inflation reaching worrying proportions. Politically the situation was contentious and Rhee had not shown the correct touch in tackling domestic problems. It was possible that this ineptitude revealed incipient senility. Corruption was a serious problem and the success of the Chinese communists had made people feel jittery.

There was much anxiety as to how South Korea would cope when American troops were withdrawn. Internal disaffection was significant in certain areas, accentuated by communist infiltration. Fear of a North Korean invasion was real and military intelligence indicated the probability of North Korean success if they attacked. During 1948 unrest in South Korea reached its most serious level since the autumn harvest uprisings of 1946. A major rebellion started on Cheju Island on 3 April 1948 with guerrillas advancing into coastal towns from their bases on the higher volcanic summit of the island. The timing was explicable because of the vigorous SKLP campaign against separate elections. The conflict was peculiarly bloody with both sides responsible for committing atrocities. Extra police and groups of rightists went to Cheju-do to assist in restoring order. American naval and air units acted to deter the rebels. The fighting diminished after the elections but developed again in October 1948 and January 1949. It has been estimated that the Cheju rebellion involved 30,000 deaths, approximately 10 per cent of the population. The guerrillas fought fiercely and effectively. The nature of the rebellion is explained by the social character of the island with a cohesive clan structure and social solidarity; the leaders included radicals who had returned from Japan and schoolteachers. The SKLP had a number of loyal supporters including some among the local police. John Merrill has concluded that the rebellion was probably not the result of conspiracy but rather of the geographical remoteness of the island, the tenuous nature of government authority, and ancient grievances against Seoul. On 19 October 1948 the Yosu rebellion occurred when police about to be sent to Cheju-do rebelled. Communist infiltration of the police was clearly shown in the mutiny. It is likely that about 3,000 people, divided roughly equally between supporters and opponents of the rebellion, perished.

Thereafter guerrilla activity gradually subsided and the most dangerous period faced by South Korea from the viewpoint of internal unrest had been surmounted. Rhee combated dissension with a mixture of harsh suppression, new security provisions and drastic purges of dubious elements in the police force. . . .

The policy of the United States regarding the defence of South Korea was to continue in 1949 with the withdrawal of American troops so that the process was completed by 30 June 1949. Economic and military aid would be furnished to render the ROK government capable of defending itself but without being very explicit as to what this meant. The NSC [National Security Council] reviewed Korean policy in March 1949 in very similar terms to NSC 8, approved in April 1948. Once again the dilemma of maintaining the independence of South Korea without involving the United States in an open-ended commitment was examined. Once more the conclusion was that a middle policy was appropriate. All American forces would be withdrawn by 30 June 1949. An American military advisory group should be established formally, taking over from the provisional group already in existence. Congress should be asked to continue economic and military aid with the objective of achieving a well-trained, efficient army of 65,000 men, including air detachments adequate for maintaining political order inside South Korea, a coastguard of 4,000 men, and a police force of 35,000 possessing small arms and ammunition. "In publicly announcing the withdrawal of its remaining occupation forces from Korea, the US should make it unmistakably clear that this step in no way constitutes a lessening of US support of the Government of the Republic of Korea, but constitutes rather another step towards the regularisation by the US of its relations with that Government and a fulfilment on the part of the US of the relevant provision of the GA Resolution [UN General Assembly] of December 12, 1948." This sentence admirably encapsulates the ambiguities in American policy. The ROK armed forces were to be developed so as to be capable of handling internal dissent but the issue as to its capacity for reacting effectively to North Korea was side-stepped. The ambiguity was the product of two factors: unwillingness to pay for larger armed forces and doubts as to the policy of South Korea itself. With reference to the former, Congress was unlikely to pour out vast sums of money for Korea. As regards the latter, Rhee had stated on many occasions that Korea must be reunited; given his advanced age, the President might well be tempted to accomplish this sooner rather than later.It would be dangerous to supply too much to South Korea since Rhee could not be trusted to behave responsibly if he possessed powerful forces. . . .

American apprehension at the danger of the ROK provoking North Korea from across the 38th parallel was reinforced by serious incidents in early May 1949. General Roberts stated that on 6 May a unit of the ROK army had advanced north of the 38th parallel to a depth of 2.5 miles (4 km) and had attacked several settlements. Muccio discussed the incidents at Kaesong and Chunchon with Rhee on 10 May; he reminded the President that UNCOK was observing developments and it would hardly benefit the cause of South Korea if the impression was conveyed to the UN that South Korea was indulging in aggression. Rhee reiterated the strategic importance of Kaesong and the necessity of standing firm against communist aggression. He gave an understanding that his government would not adopt aggressive measures in future. Muccio's considered opinion in June 1949 was that the departure of Russian and American troops left the two sides in Korea evenly balanced and that neither side was likely to risk "an all-out invasion" in the foreseeable future. The 38th parallel offered frequent opportunities for incidents, and reports indicated strengthening of the North Korean forces. The morale of the South Korean army had improved recently. Muccio blamed North Korea for provoking two serious incidents at Kaesong and Ongjin within the past six weeks. Minor incidents would doubtless continue to arise in future. The Army Department reviewed commitments in Korea and wrote to the State Department that Korea possessed "little strategic value" in the view of the Joint Chiefs of Staff—"To apply the Truman Doctrine to Korea would require prodigious effort and vast expenditure far out of proportion to the benefits to be expected."

Rhee therefore failed to secure the definite promises of American support that he deemed to be essential. Indeed the tone of reports emanating from Washington between August 1949 and May 1950 gave cause for increasing alarm in Seoul over ultimate American intentions. The publication of the China White Paper in August 1949 worried Rhee, since it connoted a virtual collapse of American support for Chiang Kai-shek and the possibility of the United States preparing to recognise Communist China. The statement by President Truman on 5 January 1950, to be followed a week later by Dean Acheson's address to the National Press Club, deeply concerned Rhee, for they seemed to show that South Korea was expendible or, at any rate, that American intentions towards South Korea were ambiguous. Equally disturbing was the fact that the House of Representatives noted narrowly on 19 January 1950, by 193 votes to 191, to reject the administration's Korean Aid Bill. The defeat was attributable to resentment at the Truman administration's bankrupt policy in China, to complacency regarding the Korean bill, and to the grave ill health of Senator [Arthur] Vandenberg. It did not reflect particular animus over Korea but more a feeling of frustration at the setbacks encountered by American policy in the Far East in the previous two years. There was, however, growing concern over the effects of inflation in the ROK. Acheson visited Vandenberg in the hospital on 21 January and the senator emphasised his support for Acheson's policy. Vandenberg was shocked at the House vote and the stupidity of many of his fellow Republicans. "He thought that as good a case could be made for our efforts in Korea—and probably a better one—as almost anything we had done in the foreign field." In his memoirs Acheson lays much stress on the impact of the House vote and sought to play down criticisms of his own speech of 12 January; the latter criticisms had focused on Acheson having given encouragement to a North Korean attack by not making clear what the American reaction would be in these circumstances. The criticisms were to be renewed after 25 June 1950. The House vote was soon reversed and Economic Cooperation Administration (ECA) aid for Korea approved. The House carried a bill on 9 February authorising sixty million US dollars for the second part of the fiscal year 1950. . . .

In domestic politics in South Korea Rhee's growing authoritarianism and the accelerating acrimony between Rhee and his political opponents did not augur well for stability. Rhee had long displayed intolerance of dissent and his obsession with his mission to unite Korea under his leadership led him to equate criticism with treachery. Jessup reported in January 1950 that the dominance of Rhee was unquestioned and few people stood up to him. The national security law was responsible for the fears of a police state. Anyone could be arrested and accused of communist sympathies; such a person would be tried by a special court consisting of four judges from which no appeal was allowed. The South Korean justification to Jessup was that no one would be convicted, unless he or she was taking orders from a foreign power. Supposedly no danger existed of an individual being prosecuted for happening to disagree with the government but Jessup was understandably sceptical. It was obvious that Rhee had intimidated the national assembly with threats of arrest. The growth of criticism of Rhee led to speculation that he might seek to postpone the elections scheduled for May 1950. Muccio recommended on 1 April 1950 that Rhee be warned that autocratic actions could adversely affect relations with Washington. Dean Acheson sent an *aide-memoire* to the ROK ambassador on 3 April protesting at the state of the economy and firmly warning against any idea of postponing the general election. Despite the American criticism of Rhee, the British ambassador in Washington, Sir Oliver Franks, believed that the Truman administration was identifying itself more closely with South Korea. Feeling in Congress was less critical than it had been and Senator William F. Knowland (Republican, California), a lively critic of the administration, supported it over Korean aid while castigating the administration for the serious economic plight in which the Koreans found themselves. The elections were duly held in May 1950 with more than 2,000 candidates standing for 200 positions. Numerous independents stood and did well in the elections. The outcome was widely regarded as a considerable rebuff for Rhee and a weakening of his position, underlined by the number of successful independents. However, John Merrill has qualified this assessment by pointing out that Rhee himself encouraged many independents to stand because of the weakness of his own political organisation; while a reverse for Rhee, his position after the election was rather stronger than it appeared to be. . . .

Therefore in May 1950 the balance sheet of strengths and weaknesses between the two Korean states could be summarised as follows. North Korea was tightly organised and directed by a tough, ruthless élite. The armed forces were efficient with good equipment. There were significant factional divisions, particularly between the followers of Kim Il Sung and Pak Hon-yong. There was probably a tendency in the north to exaggerate the potential for a guerrilla-led insurrection in South Korea. As for the ROK, it was divided politically but dominated by the intransigent Syngman Rhee. Grave economic and political problems existed and the army was clearly inferior to its opponents. However, South Korea had overcome the armed challenge from within. Tension along the 38th parallel had been serious since 1948 but was worse on some occasions than on others. There was always the possibility of an obscure clash escalating into full-scale conflict. The situation in the Korean peninsula was in essence one of civil war. As in other civil wars the big question mark was the approaches to be adopted by the great powers. The responses of the United States, the Soviet Union and China would soon become clear. . . .

To turn now to the tortuous events in the Korean peninsula in June 1950. What exactly happened? Did North Korea launch a sudden, well-coordinated onslaught against South Korea as was generally believed? Or did South Korea attack first and thus provoke the conflict? It is impossible to determine with absolute accuracy precisely what occurred on 25 June 1950, since wildly divergent accounts were given by the two sides and their respective supporters. It is appropriate to begin with the report of UNCOK, since the task of this body was to observe the situation, particularly along the 38th parallel. The key report on behalf of UNCOK was submitted by two Australian military observers appointed in May, as a response to a request by UNCOK. The observers were Major F. S. B. Peach and Squadron Leader R.J. Rankin. They devoted the period from 9 June to 23 June to inspecting ROK troops stationed along the parallel. Peach and Rankin stated that the ROK forces were organised "entirely for defence" and were "in no condition to carry out an attack on a large scale against the forces of the north." South Korean troops were not concentrated and there was no massing at any point. In certain places the North Korean forces were effectively in possession of salients on the south side of the parallel and there was no indication that South Korean troops were about to act against them. Some South Korean troops were engaged in anti-guerrilla operations when guerrillas had infiltrated. The inadequate resources of the ROK army, in particular the absence of armour, air support and heavy artillery, rendered a South Korean invasion impossible in military terms. There were no signs that the ROK army was preparing an attack: their commanders demonstrated an attitude of "vigilant defence." As regards the position north of the parallel, civilians had recently been transferred from areas adjacent to the parallel northwards. A report that there was military activity near Chwiyari just north of the parallel, had been received. "No report, however, had been received of any unusual activity on the part of the North Korean forces that would indicate any imminent change in the general situation of the parallel." Peach and Rankin submitted their report on 24 June and it was fundamental to the conclusion of UNCOK that North Korea was responsible for the military action that marked the beginning of the war. At 5 p.m. on 25 June the field observers had reported that North Korean forces had that morning mounted a surprise attack all along the 38th parallel. Kim Il Sung had claimed in a broadcast made on 26 June at 9.20 a.m. that South Korea had attacked the north in the section of Haeju, thus provoking counter-attacks. In the light of the report by Peach and Rankin, UNCOK unanimously rejected the North Korean contention and stated categorically that no offensive could possibly have been launched by South Korea; UNCOK continued:

> The invasion launched by the North Korean forces on 25 June cannot have been the result of a decision taken suddenly in order to repel a mere border attack or in retaliation for such an attack. Such an invasion involving amphibious landings and the use of considerable numbers of troops carefully trained for aggressive action and in relation to the area of great quantities of weapons and other war material, presupposes a long-premeditated, well prepared and well-timed plan of aggression. The subsequent steady advance of the North Korean forces supplies further evidence if further evidence is needed of the extensive nature of the planning and preparation for the aggression.
>
> It is the considered opinion of the commission that this planning and preparation were deliberate and an essential part of the policy of the North Korean authorities. The objective of this policy was to secure by force what could not be gained by any other means. In furtherance of this policy the North Korean authorities on 25 June initiated a war of aggression without provocation and without warning.

The phraseology was emphatic but the fact remained that UNCOK was not clear exactly what had happened at the moment when fighting commenced. In addition, they side-stepped the question of the inflammatory rhetoric emanating from Rhee, revealing his ardent desire to unite the country, and ignored the provocation for which South Korea had been responsible on occasions in 1949–50 and which had worried KMAG.

What were the views of North Korea, the Soviet Union and China in June 1950? Who took the initiative in the chain of events? There is considerable obscurity over the decision-making process and the responsibilities of each. It was widely held in June-July 1950 that the Soviet Union had masterminded the North Korean attack and that Kim Il Sung was a puppet of Stalin's. Few believed that Kim was sufficiently independent to seize the initiative himself. Some, subscribing to a monolithic, conspiratorial view of world communism, believed that China was supporting the Soviet Union in inspiring the North Korean attack; others maintained that China was not involved. Khruschev's reminiscences, if a reliable source, indicate that Kim Il Sung first proposed the attack and that Stalin acquiesced, as did Mao Tse-tung. Bruce Cumings has investigated the evidence and maintains that North Korea was most probably the vital agent. Kim Il Sung was intensely nationalistic, proud, possessed of a mission to unify his country and contemptuous of opposition. The North Korean army had been strengthened through the entry of battle-hardened veterans who had fought with the Chinese communists and who constituted 80 per cent of the officers. Cumings adduces a small but significant piece of information pointing to the likelihood of North Korea having launched the attack on 25 June: notebooks belonging to North Korean mechanics and technicians reveal that planes were being prepared for action in mid-June instead of undergoing the usual routine maintenance. Cuming's thesis is convincing: Kim Il Sung wished to attack South Korea in fulfilment of his policy and that Stalin either acquiesced grudgingly or was not consulted at all. Kim Il Sung was motivated not simply by determination to unite Korea but by the aim of ending political dependence upon the Soviet Union or China.

As for the Soviet Union, Stalin preferred to see the Korean peninsula ruled by a communist regime but it was not something he felt passionately about. Korea was important in that she bordered Soviet far eastern territories but it was almost certainly not a priority in Stalin's mind that Korea should be unified. Stalin was normally highly cautious in his international policy and was disinclined to gamble. Admittedly he could have reasoned that a Korean crisis might be worth the risk in terms of embarrassing the United States and that a North Korean attack might succeed at little cost. Stalin did not desire a major crisis in Korea and had no intention of involving the Soviet Union deeply in the peninsula's problems. This is borne out by his decision, evidently taken about a week after the Korean War began, to pull out Russian pilots and other advisers from North Korea so as to minimise the dangers of Soviet commitment. It might be argued that Stalin would have gained from a diversionary war in the Far East, which could have hindered American efforts to rebuild western Europe. However, such a diversionary conflict could also unite Americans and lead to much increased defence expenditure; the latter indeed resulted. It is important to keep in mind the activities of Guy Burgess, Donald Maclean and Kim Philby. Stalin received invaluable information from the highly placed spies and he must have been reasonably clear—or as clear as anyone was—on the likely trend of American policy-making. Policy document NSC 68, formally adopted in April 1950, and its strategy for American global containment of communism would surely have pointed to the probability of the United States reacting firmly to any crisis connoting a challenge to an American-supported regime. On balance it is unlikely that the Soviet Union manipulated North Korea in June 1950 but it is still a possibility.

China had no motive for unleashing war in Korea. Chinese leaders had more than enough challenges with having to eliminate the last vestiges of opposition on the mainland, erect a viable political system and above all cope with the horrendous problems of the Chinese economy. Taiwan remained to be conquered, presumably in 1950 or 1951. Sino-American relations were bad but there was no reason for Mao Tse-tung to foster a Korean clash. Kim Il Sung was identified with a pro-Russian stance rather than one sympathetic to China and Mao would hardly benefit from strengthening Kim's authority. Naturally China was bound to be deeply concerned at war in Korea but there was little chance of China intervening while the purpose of the UN was to restore the status quo ante. Advancing beyond the 38th parallel would be another matter, however, and an approach towards the Yalu would be viewed by China as a direct threat and treated appropriately.

Now to consider the political situation in South Korea in June and developments in American policy-making. Syngman Rhee's support had waned in 1949–50 following the President's increasingly autocratic behaviour, the effects of inflation, and the revelations of corruption and incompetence in the administration. Rhee experienced a setback in the general election held on 30 May with those supporting him suffering appreciable losses. The most striking feature was the large increase in the number of independents. There were various minor groups but the independents clearly constituted the key element. The British minister in Seoul summarized by predicting that some independents would subsequently join Rhee but that the defeat of men prominent in public life could only be interpreted "as a demonstration of public feeling against the President and his associates and the Police". North Korea launched a propaganda campaign on 7 June with Pyongyang radio broadcasting an appeal from the Democratic Front for all Koreans— except Rhee's clique—to coalesce in support of unification: this would be achieved through holding a general election for the whole of Korea on 5 August with a new national legislature meeting in Seoul on 15 August; political leaders of north and south, again excluding Rhee and his close associates, would assemble to decide on arrangements for holding the election and UNCOK would be excluded from advising on the unification process. Rhee was still confident of retaining control and the tone of his pronouncements on the future of Korea under his leadership did not change significantly. The nature of the assembly elected on 30 May pointed to Rhee encountering more problems with the body in future but the President revealed few signs of doubting his ability to surmount any problems.

Rhee's most significant engagement in mid-June was to receive an important American visitor, John Foster Dulles. Mystery surrounds the precise motives for Dulles's visit to Seoul. Dulles had accepted appointment in April 1950 as special consultant to the State Department with particular responsibility for handling the negotiations over the Japanese peace treaty. He was a firm advocate of resisting communism and his statements in Seoul were generally but not entirely encouraging to Rhee. The principal reason for Dulles's trip was to visit Tokyo for talks on the peace treaty and it was agreed after deliberations in the State Department that Dulles should go to Seoul. John J. Muccio had drawn attention to the feeling of isolation in South Korea and the absence of distinguished American visitors seemed to underline lack of interest in the fate of Korea. Given the tougher approach being adopted behind the scenes in Washington over Taiwan, a visit to Seoul was opportune. Dulles was accompanied by John M. Allison, a leading State Department official and a hardliner where encounters against communism were concerned. The South Korean assembly met on 19 June and was addressed by Dulles. He compared the Korean struggle for independence after colonial oppression to the American experience in escaping from British imperialism. The generosity of the United States in assisting peoples to secure and maintain their freedom was emphasised. He concluded, in the words of the British minister, "with an eloquent assurance that the American people welcomed the Koreans as an equal partner in the great company of those who comprised the Free World, a world which commanded vast moral and material power and in which any despotism which waged aggressive war doomed itself to unalterable disaster."

Dulles met Rhee for private talks on 19 June at the President's request. Rhee wanted greater American commitment in Korea and East Asia in total. Dulles regarded subversion as a more likely danger for South Korea than a direct North Korean attack; to combat subversion it was essential that governments took "active steps to create conditions within their countries which would prohibit growth of communism." This required "true allegiance to the principles of representative government and a real effort to self-control and hard work to create a stable economy and a government which deserved the support of its people. . . ." Dulles's public rhetoric conveyed the image of a more assertive American role which when taken in conjunction with his activity in working for a Japanese peace treaty, must have alarmed North Korea. In a famous photograph, afterwards produced in North Korean literature, Dulles was shown wearing his characteristic Homburg hat, peering intently across the 38th parallel at the communist hordes to the north. This was regarded in Pyongyang as demonstrating Dulles's aggressive intentions. Dulles's purpose certainly was to put more backbone into South Korea but he did not anticipate the developments that were shortly to take place. Alvary Gascoigne, head of the British liaison mission in Japan, reported to London on Dulles's return to Tokyo. Dulles described Syngman Rhee's mood as ebullient and said that far from passively awaiting an attack from

North Korea, Rhee might instead take an initiative against the north. A British official in London commented with some embarrassment:

> It is quite clear that Mr. Dulles had not the faintest inklings of what was impending. Read in the light of subsequent events, Mr. Dulles's words seem unfortunate. It is true that Syngman Rhee who, although very reactionary is no realist, has talked in terms of solving the problem of Korean disunity by force. It is clear, however, that Mr. Dulles merely meant to indicate that the South Koreans were in a buoyant frame of mind.

The CIA produced a lengthy assessment of the capabilities of North Korea on 19 June, based on information made available on 15 May. It examined political, economic and strategic aspects. The chief points brought out were the degree of Soviet control, the disciplined character of the state with efficient armed forces; and that while factionalism existed, it did not represent a serious problem. The morale of North Korean troops was good. The ultimate objective of the Soviet Union was to unify the Korean peninsula under a communist government. The vulnerability of South Korea to a determined onslaught from the north was underlined, although it was felt that Soviet or Chinese participation would be necessary to ensure total military victory over the south. To observers in Seoul on the eve of the war, all appeared relatively calm and there was no suggestion of imminent crisis. Holt, the British minister, wrote to the Foreign Office on 22 June that the most impressive occurrence had been the arrival of rain, which averted the threatened drought. At 10 A.M. on 25 June, John J. Muccio reported urgently to Washington that North Korean forces had invaded the south at several places that morning. Action had started at about 4 A.M. when Ongjin was attacked by North Korean artillery fire. Two hours later North Korean infantry began crossing the parallel in the vicinity of Ongjin and in the areas of Kaesong and Chunchon; an amphibious landing on the east coast south of Kangnung was also reported. Kaesong had apparently been captured at 9 A.M. and fighting was proceeding at the places indicated. It should be pointed out that there was thirteen hours' difference in local time between Seoul and Washington; between the hours of 12 midnight and 1 P.M. Korea was one day ahead of Washington. Muccio's message sparked off hectic activity in Washington, New York and in world capitals. The United States faced the first real challenge of the Cold War, in terms of contemplating the use of appreciable numbers of American forces in a "hot" war and one that could escalate into a far greater conflict involving the Soviet Union and (or) China. . . .

Finally why did the Korean War occur? Most wars take place because of a mixture of aggression or perceived aggression and of miscalculation. Usually muddle is more conspicuous than malevolence but the latter should not be discounted. Korea was in a chronically unstable position from 1945 to 1950. There were deep social divisions within the country, accelerated and brought to a climax by the Japanese colonial occupation from 1910 to 1945. Left to her own devices Korea would probably have become a radical and very possibly communist state but one that would not have been sub-

servient to the Soviet Union or China. The intervention of the United States
and the Soviet Union ensured that a unified Korea finding her own salvation
would not be the outcome. The United States did not wish to see South
Korea incorporated within the communist sphere but would not make the
defence of the ROK a priority before June 1950. The Soviet Union believed
that sooner or later South Korea would fall into the communist camp and
perhaps felt the risk of North Korean action could be accepted in June
1950, although it is impossible to say with certainty what the Russian
attitude was. China was not deeply involved before June or even October
1950 and then acted because of the American threat to Manchuria. Historians
have emphasised that the events of June 1950 must be seen in the context
of the endemic civil war in the Korean peninsula since August 1945. We
do not know precisely what happened before the outbreak of the open,
large-scale conflict in June 1950. It is likely that North Korea took the
initiative in advancing but Bruce Cumings is surely right in stressing that
this action has to be understood in terms of the bitter hostility between the
two Korean states and that South Korea had done much to provoke the
north. Kim Il Sung certainly erred in his gamble and Syngman Rhee had
erred equally in his shrill boasts between 1948 and 1950. Responsibility for
the outbreak and escalation of the war has to be shared widely. North and
South Korea had inflamed matters, as had the United States and the Soviet
Union. China could have acted with more consistency and effect in the
nature of the warnings forwarded in September and October 1950. Korea
was a victim of her own murderous internal animosities and of the mutual
suspicion and hatred of the superpowers in the Cold War.

Ensuring Korea's Freedom: The Decision to Cross the Thirty-Eighth Parallel

JAMES I. MATRAY

Although historians have devoted considerable attention in recent years to
Harry S Truman's foreign policy, one incident has escaped significant controversy. Few writers challenge the conclusion that Truman's decision to
cross the thirty-eighth parallel and seek forcible reunification of the Korean
peninsula was ill-considered and disastrous. American military operations
north of the parallel constituted a clear escalation of hostilities and prompted
Chinese intervention in the Korean conflict. Subsequently, American involvement in the prolonged and costly military stalemate undermined Truman's
leadership both at home and abroad.

Some scholars have argued that Truman's primary motive for ordering
American combat forces across the thirty-eighth parallel was political gain.

From James I. Matray, "Truman's Plan for Victory: National Self-Determination and the
Thirty-Eighth Parallel Decision in Korea," *Journal of American History*, 66 (September 1979),
314–333. Copyright Organization of American Historians, 1979.

Popular happiness over Korean reunification would increase sharply the popularity of the Democratic party and lead to a sweep of the 1950 midterm congressional elections. Domestic politics may have been an important consideration, but Truman ultimately decided to cross the thirty-eighth parallel because he believed that the reunification of Korea would inflict a momentous defeat on the strategy of Soviet expansion. Once the United States destroyed the North Korean army, the administration was confident that a united Korea would reject the communist model for national development. In crossing the parallel, Truman sought to guarantee for all Koreans the right of national self-determination.

Truman's decision to cross the thirty-eighth parallel was in large part the outgrowth of past policy. Ever since the Cairo Conference in December 1943, Washington's objective in Korea had been the creation of an independent, united, western-oriented nation that would possess a progressive and democratic government. Following the death of Franklin D. Roosevelt, Truman devised a strategy that appeared to ensure the realization of this goal. If American forces liberated Korea unilaterally, Truman reasoned, then the United States could reconstruct this Asian nation without Soviet interference. Josef Stalin's decision to send the Red Army into Korea before the United States had an opportunity to land troops on the peninsula forced Truman to settle for a line dividing Korea at the thirty-eighth parallel into zones of occupation. The Soviet-American partition of Korea meant that only a diplomatic agreement among the great powers could produce peaceful reunification.

After World War II Truman sought to reunify Korea under a government that reflected the American rather than the Soviet model of political and economic development. At the Moscow Conference in December 1945, the United States and the Soviet Union appeared to agree on an international trusteeship as the best method for resolving the Korean problem. When Stalin refused to accept the American interpretation of the Moscow decision, Truman rejected further negotiations and ultimately turned to the policy of containment in an effort to break the deadlock. Truman's strategy for containing Soviet expansion in Korea, in contrast to western Europe, was limited and required only that the United States provide economic aid, technical advice, and small amounts of military assistance. If successful, containment in Korea would foster the emergence of a strong and stable government south of the thirty-eighth parallel closely allied with the United States and capable of self-defense.

American objectives in Korea were, however, far more grandiose, since Truman and his advisors believed that containment would act as a liberating force. Arthur C. Bunce, the American economic advisor in Korea, indicated the nature of Washington's expectations in a revealing letter that expressed his hope that the South Korean leaders "will institute a whole series of necessary reforms which will so appeal to the North Koreans that their army will revolt, kill all the nasty Communists, and create a lovely liberal democracy to the everlasting credit of the U.S.A.!" Once containment registered its first victory for national self-determination in Korea, many

American leaders hoped that other Asian nations would reject communism as well and thereby frustrate Stalin's strategy for expansion.

Unfortunately, the administration submitted its aid bill for Korea to Congress at the height of the acrimonious debate over Truman's China policy. Republican critics of the administration voiced immediate opposition to the proposal arguing that unless Truman increased the American commitment to prevent a communist victory in China, further assistance to South Korea would be pointless. Many of Truman's major advisors testified before the House Committee on Foreign Affairs in an effort to overcome Republican opposition, but by the end of 1949 Congress still had not approved the Korean aid bill. Secretary of State Dean G. Acheson's now famous National Press Club speech of January 12, 1950, was designed in part to convince Congress that passage of Truman's aid program was vital to South Korea's survival.

In analyzing the Press Club speech, scholars have pointed to Acheson's exclusion of Korea from America's "defensive perimeter" as evidence of the absence of an American commitment to defend South Korea. This argument has tended, however, to divert attention from Acheson's statement of the actual nature of Truman's Korea policy. Washington believed that it could achieve peace and stability, not only in Korea but elsewhere in Asia, without a positive guarantee of military protection. If Asian nations developed strong democratic institutions and stable economies, Acheson argued, they could withstand communist "subversion and penetration." The United States could best contribute to the growth of stability in Asia through providing economic aid, technical knowledge, and administrative advice. Such a strategy, Acheson stressed, would be particularly successful in Korea, because, in contrast to China, the Republic of Korea not only wanted American aid but would use it effectively. Acheson indicated the importance of Korea to America's strategy when he concluded that "we have a greater opportunity to be effective" in South Korea than anywhere else on the Asian mainland.

In May 1950 the administration decided to request approval from Congress for a substantial increase in military assistance to South Korea. The following month, Truman dispatched John Foster Dulles on a fact-finding mission to the Republic of Korea. In an address before the Korean legislature, Dulles proclaimed that South Korea was "in the front line of freedom." The Republic of Korea's "great strides" toward political liberty and economic prosperity proved that the task of opposing Soviet expansionism was not hopeless. Dulles then made specific reference to the power of containment as a liberating force, when he predicted that South Korea's "wholesome society of steadily expanding well-being . . . will set up a peaceful influence which will disintegrate the hold of Soviet communism on your fellows in the north and irresistibly draw them into unity with you." To American leaders containment represented a particularly attractive policy alternative, since it promised to achieve a great deal at a relatively limited cost in terms of men and material. While avoiding the necessity of resorting to military means, the United States could progressively reduce the Soviet sphere of influence and ultimately obtain victory in the Cold War. At least that was the hope.

Truman and his advisors were totally unprepared for the North Korean invasion of South Korea in June 1950. The logic of containment precluded the possibility that Moscow would revert to open military aggression to further its expansionist aims. During the senate hearings regarding the subsequent dismissal of General Douglas MacArthur, Acheson indicated the nature of the administration's assumptions: "The view was generally held that since the Communists had far from exhausted the potentialities for obtaining their objectives through guerilla and psychological warfare, political pressure and intimidation, such means would probably continue to be used rather than overt military aggression." Acheson explained that the administration recognized that the situation was serious, "but it was not believed that the attack would take place at that time." North Korea's decision to pursue forcible reunification had a decisive impact on Truman's strategy for ending the Korean partition. American economic assistance and military advice alone would not provide sufficient means for resolving the Korean problem on terms advantageous to the United States. Since the Soviet challenge was now essentially military and for more aggressive, Truman concluded that he had to alter his Korea policy accordingly.

American leaders relied heavily on a global interpretation of the Korean conflict in the formulation of subsequent policy alternatives. Dulles spoke for the administration when he exclaimed that "one thing is certain, they [the North Koreans] did not do this purely on their own but as part of the world strategy of international communism." He stressed that South Korea was making tremendous progress toward political freedom and economic stability just prior to the attack. For the Soviet Union, this "promising experiment in democracy" in Asia was a source of embarrassment. Stalin and his cohorts had "found that they could not destroy it by indirect aggression, because the political, economic, and social life of the Republic was so sound that subversive efforts, which had been tried, had failed." The Truman administration reasoned that the very success of containment in Korea forced Moscow to alter its tactics. Since Asians would reject communism if given a free choice, Stalin turned to open military conquest to expand the area of Soviet control.

Stalin's decision to use armed force for the destruction of "wholesome" nations appeared to justify, if not demand, an American willingness to employ its military power to counter the new Soviet strategy. As Dulles explained at the time, "The Korean affair shows that communism cannot be checked merely by building up sound domestic economies." Such an approach had only encouraged military aggression. Washington now feared that Moscow would initiate similar thrusts into such areas as Yugoslavia and Indochina. Perhaps more alarming, if Stalin had attacked South Korea because of its political and economic progress, there was a strong possibility of "Soviet application [of] similar reasoning to Western Europe. . . ." "Since international communism may not be deterred by moral principles backed by *potential* might," Dulles concluded, "we must back those principles with military strength-in-being, and do so quickly."

North Korea's invasion of South Korea also destroyed all basis for continued faith in the power of containment as a liberating force. Soon after the attack, the administration recognized that the United States could achieve reunification of Korea under a desirable government only if American forces crossed the thirty-eighth parallel and eliminated the communist regime by military means. Initially, however, American leaders stated that the objective in Korea was merely to restore the status quo ante bellum. During a meeting on June 27, 1950, George F. Kennan assured the North Atlantic Treaty Organization (NATO) ambassadors that the United States had no intention of pursuing forcible reunification. Two days later, Acheson declared publicly that American efforts in Korea were aimed only at upholding the rule of law in international affairs and preserving the credibility of the United Nations. He stated categorically that military action "is solely for the purpose of restoring the Republic of Korea to its status prior to the invasion from the north and of reestablishing the peace broken by that aggression."

Once the United States had intervened in the Korean conflict with combat troops, certain individuals in the administration began to press for an American commitment to cross the thirty-eighth parallel in pursuit of reunification. Perhaps the most vocal member of this group was John M. Allison, the director of the Office of Northeast Asian Affairs. In a statement dated July 1, 1950, he wrote:

> I understand that there has been some suggestion that in the speech which is being prepared for President Truman to make on the Korean situation should be included a statement to the effect that United States forces and presumably South Korean forces will only attempt to drive the North Koreans back to the 38th parallel and will not go any further. I most strongly urge that no such statement be included in the speech. In my opinion it would be fatal to what may be left of South Korean morale if such a statement were made. It would also appear to me to be most unrealistic in the present situation. I believe there is ample justification in the last part of the second Resolution of the Security Council for any action which may be deemed appropriate at the time which will contribute to the permanent restoration of peace and stability in that area. I am convinced that there will be no permanent peace and stability in Korea as long as the artificial division at the 38th parallel continues. I believe the time has come when we must be bold and willing to take even more risks than we have already and, while I certainly would not advocate saying in the speech that we would proceed beyond the 38th parallel, nevertheless we should not commit ourselves at this time not to do so.

Allison strongly recommended that the United States establish military control over the entire peninsula and then sponsor the free election of a government to rule a reunited Korea.

MacArthur clearly shared Allison's point of view with respect to the thirty-eighth parallel. During the first week of July, American forces were unable to halt the North Korean advance, yet MacArthur was already considering offensive action. On July 4, American military leaders in Tokyo began to discuss the feasibility of an amphibious landing behind enemy lines. MacArthur speculated that the operation could begin as early as July 22. Three days later, he informed Washington of his intention to halt the North Korean advance as soon as possible and then launch a counteroffensive in coordination with an amphibious landing behind enemy lines that would permit the United States to "compose and unite" Korea. . . .

Paul Nitze, head of the Policy Planning Staff, voiced strong opposition to forcible reunification and counseled against crossing the thirty-eighth parallel under any circumstances. The United Nations would never sanction the military conquest of North Korea, while the Soviet Union would perceive such an operation as a clear threat to its national security. Nitze's Policy Planning Staff favored instead an attempt to restrict the conflict to south of the parallel and thereby avoid the dangers involved in pursuing reunification by force: "The risks of bringing on a major conflict with the U.S.S.R. or Communist China, if U.N. military action north of the 38th parallel is employed in an effort to reach a 'final' settlement in Korea, appear to outweigh the political advantages that might be gained from such further military action." If Washington sought only to repel aggression and restore the status quo, the United States could gain a settlement more quickly and implement it with a smaller number of combat troops. The Policy Planning Staff recognized that a permanent peace would require positive guarantees for the security of South Korea. Such an approach would also entail certain political hazards, since "public and Congressional opinion in the United States might be dissatisfied with any conclusion falling short of what it would consider a 'final' settlement of the problem."

Allison found these recommendations unpalatable and registered his "emphatic dissent." If the United States fought only for the status quo ante bellum, the United Nations would be starting at the same point as in 1947. "The aggressor would be informed," Allison explained, "that all he had to fear from aggression was being compelled to start over again." Not only were the present actions of North Korea in clear violation of the will of the United Nations, but the very existence of the communist regime was a moral and factual illegality. Allison insisted that if "a correct solution of the immediate problem is not reached, a correct long term solution will be impossible." The United States possessed a moral obligation to destroy the North Korean army and implement the United Nations resolutions providing for Korea's reunification, even at the risk of global war. For Allison the issue was clear—the United States could either stand up to and defeat "raw aggression" or admit that the Soviet strategy for expansion had won.

Allison's objections forced the Policy Planning Staff to alter its position paper. The new draft stated plainly that the ultimate objective in Korea was reunification, but stressed that "we have no commitment to use armed force in the effort to bring about Korean independence and unity." Since no clear consensus existed on immediate war aims, the paper offered the following conclusions and recommendations:

The Korean problem must be dealt with in the wider framework of the conflict between the communist and non-communist countries. The necessity to maintain a realistic balance between our military strength on the one hand and commitments and risks on the other hand, together with the need for additional information . . . , make it impossible to make decisions now regarding our future course of action in Korea. It seems clear that our national security and interest will be best served at present by maintaining the greatest possible degree of flexibility and freedom of action.

Allison reluctantly approved the revised draft but continued to express dissatisfaction. Acheson, on the other hand, apparently supported the paper. At that point in the conflict, he would agree only that "no arbitrary prohibition against crossing the parallel should be imposed."

American military leaders initially voiced support for the Kennan-Nitze position. They were quite fearful of widening the war and opposed consideration of offensive action north of the thirty-eighth parallel. On July 21 the Joint Chiefs of Staff (JCS) submitted a policy paper that warned against any "excessive commitment of United States military forces and resources in those areas of operations which would not be decisive." Truman's military advisors were apprehensive that Moscow would exploit American involvement in Korea and stage new acts of aggression in areas of greater strategic importance to the United States. Even if the Soviet Union intervened militarily in support of North Korea, the JCS believed that "the U.S. should prepare to minimize its commitment in Korea and prepare to execute war plans." Events on the Korean battlefield appeared to warrant the adoption of a cautious approach. By July 18 the North Korean army had advanced one hundred miles south of Seoul and seemed to be on the verge of total victory.

Despite the desperate nature of the situation, MacArthur was urging the administration to grant early approval of his plan for an amphibious landing behind enemy lines at Inchon. On July 23 he supplied Washington with the details and expressed confidence that the operation would sever North Korea's "main line of communication and enable us to deliver a decisive and crushing blow." If the United States refused to implement such a plan, MacArthur warned, a costly and prolonged frontal assault would be the only other feasible alternative. It was obvious, however, that the JCS would not grant approval as long as the North Korean offensive continued. As a result, MacArthur traveled to Korea on July 26 and informed the Eighth Army commander Walton H. Walker that he would not tolerate further retreat. This "stand or die" order was evidently effective; battlelines stabilized during the first week of August. MacArthur's army rapidly consolidated its position and on August 7 launched its first counterattack. That same day, MacArthur wrote to former Secretary of War Robert P. Patterson that "in spite of great odds, I am sure that before too long a time has passed we will again be on the winning end."

MacArthur's successful halting of the North Korean military advance had a decisive impact on the administration's attitude toward crossing the thirty-eighth parallel. American leaders who had been reluctant to support forcible reunification now began to reconsider their position. Significantly, the JCS advised Truman on July 31 that the occupation of North Korea was desirable if the Soviet Union did not intervene and "the United States would mobilize sufficient resources to attain the objective and strengthen its military position in all other areas of strategic importance." Improved conditions on the Korean battlefield undoubtedly produced a new sense of optimism among Truman's civilian advisors as well. In all probability, Truman and his advisors decided during the second week of August to cross the thirty-eighth parallel in pursuit of a final settlement to the Korean problem. American actions at the United Nations provide strong support for such a conclusion.

On August 17 Ambassador Warren Austin delivered a pivotal speech to the General Assembly in response to an Indian request for an American statement of peace terms. At the outset Austin reminded his listeners that the United States supported Korea's freedom and independence and would not have intervened in the absence of North Korea's aggression. "The Security Council," he declared, "has set as its first objective the end of the breach of the peace. This objective must be pursued in such a manner that no opportunity is provided for another attempt at invasion." The United Nations had to establish complete individual and political freedom in Korea. The ambassador then proclaimed, "Shall only a part of the country be assured this freedom? I think not." The United Nations had a moral obligation to assist all Koreans in creating a reunited and democratic nation eligible for admission as a member of the international organization.

Having decided to pursue forcible reunification of the Korean peninsula, the Truman administration now turned its attention to formulating plans for the achievement of this objective. Despite its support for military ground operations north of the parallel, the JCS continued to emphasize the need for caution, particularly in regard to MacArthur's Inchon landing project. On August 19 [Army Chief of Staff J. Lawton] Collins and Navy Chief of Staff Forrest Sherman traveled to Tokyo and reminded MacArthur of the serious risks involved in his plan. All those present during the subsequent discussions agreed that Inchon would be an extremely dangerous operation, but MacArthur delivered an extemporaneous speech that by all accounts was a masterful job of persuasion. He convinced his audience that the element of surprise alone guaranteed success. "We shall land at Inchon," MacArthur perorated, "and I shall crush them."

Perhaps the most significant aspect of the conference, however, was that a consensus existed on the need to cross the thirty-eighth parallel. Collins, Sherman, and MacArthur agreed that the United States had to destroy the North Korean army completely or the threat of invasion would remain. Since the Soviet Union had not as yet intervened militarily in Korea, MacArthur expressed confidence that Moscow would not become involved in the future. MacArthur adopted the global perspective and focused attention on the wider importance of total victory in Korea when he argued: "The Oriental follows a winner. If we win, the Chinese will not follow the USSR." Upon their return to Washington, Collins and Sherman informed Truman of MacArthur's plans. The president now instructed his advisors to formulate a detailed course of action for the occupation of North Korea and the reunification of the peninsula.

On August 28 the JCS tentatively approved the Inchon landing project and set September 15 as the target date. The administration simultaneously completed work on its plans for an offensive across the thirty-eighth parallel. On September 1 the JCS submitted a memorandum predicting that the Soviet Union would probably attempt to retain possession of North Korea. Once the United Nations reached the thirty-eighth parallel, Moscow would either call for a ceasefire or intervene militarily "under the guise of . . . maintaining law and order." The JCS then outlined a course of action designed to forestall such an eventuality:

> Our objective of unifying Korea, however, can be accomplished if we forestall Soviet action by early entry of United Nations forces into North Korea. Such a maneuver would deny to the Soviets the initiative, deal them a major political rebuff, and, if properly timed, may not necessarily increase the risk of collision with Soviet troops.

For American military leaders, time was of the essence if the United States hoped to reunify Korea without at the same time starting a global war.

American leaders were also concerned that the Soviet Union would apply pressure on the United Nations to accept a compromise settlement in Korea. India had already demonstrated that it would ignore American opposition and respond favorably to such a Soviet proposal. To avoid a possible stalemate at the United Nations, the National Security Council (NSC) recommended that the State Department inaugurate immediate and "vigorous action on the psychological and diplomatic front." The United States had to prevail upon its allies to support postponement at the United Nations of consideration of a compromise settlement. Once MacArthur had launched a successful offensive for reunification, the entire issue would become academic.

American leaders summarized plans for Korean reunification in a NSC report. The document proceeded from the basic assumption that the United Nations, in three previous resolutions, had established as its "political objective" in Korea the achievement of a completely independent and united nation. "If the present United Nations action in Korea can accomplish this political objective without substantial risk of general war with the Soviet Union or Communist China," the paper continued, "it would be in our interest to advocate the pressing of the United Nations action to this conclusion." It would be ill-advised to pursue forcible reunification, however, if it led to global war or sacrificed American support at the United Nations. To reduce the possibility of either occurrence, the report recommended certain precautions. First, MacArthur would offer peace terms to the North Koreans prior to crossing the thirty-eighth parallel. Second, the JCS would instruct MacArthur to permit only Korean forces in the most northern provinces. Finally, the United States should obtain the explicit support of the United Nations for reunification.

The report emphasized that "a clear legal basis" existed for such American "military actions north of the thirty-eighth parallel as are necessary" to compel the North Korean army to withdraw from South Korea. The United Nations resolutions did not, however, authorize the pursuit of the political aim of establishing Rhee's control over the entire peninsula. To counter opposition in the United Nations to offensive action north of the parallel, the paper urged the administration to concentrate on the military disadvantages of merely restoring the status quo ante bellum. If the United Nations permitted North Korea to survive, it would also have to provide sufficient military power on the peninsula to enforce the ceasefire.

The report also advised the administration to expect the outbreak of global war and prepare for such an eventuality. Since American military capabilities remained relatively limited, the JCS should instruct MacArthur to cross the thirty-eighth parallel only if there were no apparent threat or indication of Soviet or Chinese intervention. If Moscow intervened, MacArthur should withdraw to the parallel and notify the United Nations. The international organization would then either increase its military commitment to achieve reunification or condemn the Soviet Union for aggression. If, however, the Chinese intervened, the JCS should instruct MacArthur to continue military operations "as long as action by UN military forces offers a reasonable chance of successful resistance."

Finally, the report discussed the reconstruction of a reunited Korea. It stressed that the American military force had to act as an army of "liberation" in order to maximize support for Rhee's government in North Korea. The United States had to withdraw its troops from the peninsula as soon as practicable after the conclusion of hostilities. The United Nations would supervise free elections throughout Korea and consult with the South Korean government regarding any problems hampering reunification. Washington would then press for the neutralization of Korea and the adoption of guarantees for the future sovereignty of the nation. The report also expressed hope that the United Nations would foster "the reorientation of the North Korean people toward the outlook of free peoples who accept the standards of international behavior set forth in the United Nations Charter." Korea would retain its independence and unity, the report concluded, only if the United Nations remained involved in the peninsula until its stability was secure.

On September 7, 1950, the JCS informed Truman of its strong support for the NSC recommendations. Thus American leaders abandoned their earlier opposition to crossing the thirty-eighth parallel and now advocated the pursuit of forcible reunification. Although Kennan and probably Nitze continued to warn against military action north of the parallel, Allison's views now appeared to represent the attitude of most of Truman's diplomatic advisors. During a radio interview on August 27, Ambassador-at-Large Philip C. Jessup emphasized that both the United States and the United Nations were committed to the creation of a free and united Korea. Although it was an entirely United Nations decision, Washington intended to impress upon the international organization that only strong action would deter further aggression and build confidence in the effectiveness of collective security.

Assistant Secretary of State Dean Rusk was perhaps the most influential advocate of crossing the thirty-eighth parallel. In a speech delivered on September 9, he pointed out that the United States was attempting to foster the triumph of national self-determination throughout Asia. Rusk then declared that American leaders "believe that the United Nations must have the opportunity to give effect to its long-standing policy in favor of a free and united Korea. . . . We have tried every other method to build peace—we must now make it clear to any aggressor that aggression carries with it their certain destruction." International security demanded that all nations rely upon peaceful and legal means to settle disputes. Rusk viewed it as imperative that the United Nations punish those governments refusing to follow established rules for proper conduct.

Truman approved the NSC report on September 11 after only minor alterations. MacArthur did not receive a complete copy of the paper until September 22, largely because Truman had just replaced Louis Johnson with George C. Marshall as secretary of defense. The United States was now committed to the pursuit of forcible reunification in Korea as long as military action north of the parallel did not ignite a major war. For Truman and his advisors, success in Korea was a matter of global importance. As State Department official H. Freeman Matthews revealed in a memorandum to the JCS, if the United States reunified Korea militarily, "the resultant defeat to the Soviet Union and to the Communist world will be of momentous significance." It was Washington, then, and not MacArthur, that made the decision to seek the destruction of North Korea. When the general crossed the thirty-eighth parallel, he "was not violating policy but putting it into effect."

Truman was careful not to admit publicly that he had instructed MacArthur to cross the thirty-eighth parallel. At a press conference on September 21, a newsman asked the president if he had reached a decision with respect to military action in North Korea. Truman stated flatly: "No, I have not. That is a matter for the United Nations to decide. That is a United Nations force, and we are one of the many who are interested in that situation. It will be worked out by the United Nations and I will abide by the decision that the United Nations makes." Truman remained fearful that the Soviet Union would be able to mobilize sufficient support at the United Nations for a compromise settlement to block offensive action north of the parallel. It was vital for the United States to avoid any appearance of unilateralism that might undermine its position at the United Nations. Washington could forestall a prolonged debate at the General Assembly if crossing the thirty-eighth parallel appeared to be a matter of military necessity.

American efforts to minimize the possibility of United Nations interference in the military advance north of the thirty-eighth parallel are important in understanding the administration's instructions to MacArthur during the final week of September. Truman and his advisors demonstrated an acute sensitivity to any public reference to the parallel. In a cable to MacArthur on September 29, for example, Secretary Marshall expressed alarm over rumors that the Eighth Army commander had announced his intention to halt at the parallel and await authorization from the United Nations to cross into northern Korea. The secretary of defense then explained the reason for Washington's displeasure: "We want you to feel unhampered tactically and strategically to proceed north of 38th parallel. Announcement above referred to may precipitate embarrassment in the UN where evident desire is not to be confronted with necessity of a vote on passage, rather to find you have found it militarily necessary to do so." In response, MacArthur assured Marshall that the report was erroneous and the parallel was "not a factor in the mil[itary] employment of our forces." "Unless and until the enemy capitulates," the general emphasized, "I regard all of Korea open for our mil[itary] operations."

MacArthur apparently failed to comprehend the basis for Washington's concern. On October 1 he informed the JCS of his desire to issue a "dramatic" statement announcing his intention to pursue and destroy North Korean forces throughout the peninsula. The proclamation would warn the enemy that "the field of our military operations is limited only by military exigencies and the international boundaries of Korea." The JCS cabled MacArthur immediately that Washington considered "it unwise to issue your statement. In accordance with General Marshall's message . . . We desire that you proceed with your operations without any further explanation or announcement and let action determine the matter." The JCS continued: "Our Government desires to avoid having to make an issue of the 38th parallel until we have accomplished our mission of defeating the North Korean forces." The Truman administration was probably following the advice of its allies in adopting such an approach. The strategy was successful; on October 7 the United Nations passed a resolution instructing MacArthur to "ensure conditions of stability throughout Korea."

Acheson later insisted that the administration never advocated as a war aim the achievement of an independent and united Korea. Washington's sole objective was to destroy the North Korean army and restore peaceful conditions in the area, which required the crossing of the thirty-eighth parallel. Only the Korean people themselves could realize the "political objective" of a united and democratic government through participation in free elections under the sponsorship of the United Nations. Critics subsequently maintained that Acheson was engaged in a feeble attempt to counter charges that Truman had abandoned reunification as a war aim after Chinese intervention. In reality, the secretary of state's explanation illustrates well the administration's perception of what would soon transpire.

Since 1945 Truman and his advisors had believed that the vast majority of the Korean populace favored reunification under a western-oriented, democratic government. The illegitimate North Korean regime had managed to deny its people freedom of choice until the application of containment in South Korea began to erode the foundations of communist control. North Korea's invasion of South Korea demonstrated that only the military destruction of the Soviet puppet would permit all Koreans to exercise the right of national self-determination. Most American leaders certainly recognized that elections, even in a united Korea, would not be truly free or democratic. Yet Truman was determined to impress upon the international community that, in crossing the thirty-eighth parallel, the United States sought not to compel, but to allow, the Korean people to choose the American model for political and economic development.

Truman's decision to pursue the complete destruction of North Korea was an extremely dangerous policy in both military and political terms. When the administration reverted to the restoration of the status quo ante bellum as its military objective early in 1951, the Republicans began to denounce Truman for engaging in appeasement. MacArthur also exploited popular dissatisfaction with Truman's apparent retreat. During the MacArthur hearings he stressed that his "mission was to clear out all North Korea, to unify it and to liberalize it." According to MacArthur, Truman placed unwarranted restrictions on his command and thereby prevented the fulfillment of his assignment. The administration found it difficult to counter these charges. General Omar N. Bradley insisted that Washington had never issued orders of a political nature and that MacArthur's sole mission was to destroy the North Korean army. Chinese intervention had forced the United States to abandon this "military objective," but the administration never wavered in its commitment to the creation of a united Korea through free elections. Bradley stressed that the United States had not altered its "political objective" in Korea.

Public criticism of the administration probably would have been even more severe had Truman refused to authorize military action across the parallel. Few Americans raised any words of opposition to MacArthur's offensive into North Korea. In fact, most commentators demanded a "final" settlement in Korea. In one senate speech the Democratic chairman of the Senate Foreign Relations Committee, Tom Connally, called upon the United Nations to reaffirm its commitment to the creation of a united Korea. Republicans were even more enthusiastic about the prospects for victory in Korea. Dulles explained in one private letter that "if we have the power to do otherwise, it would be folly to go back to the division of Korea at the 38th Parallel." Dulles conveyed his opinion to the administration in a memorandum to Nitze. "If we have the opportunity to obliterate the line as a political division," he reasoned, "certainly we should do so in the interest of 'peace and security in the area. ''Even liberals voiced support for crossing the thirty-eighth parallel and anticipated the establishment of a united, democratic, and reform-minded government in Korea.

In the final analysis, Truman's decision to order American forces across the thirty-eighth parallel was the culmination of America's persistent efforts to resolve the Korean predicament. MacArthur's offensive into North Korea sought to guarantee for all Koreans the right of national self-determination, which had been the primary aim of America's Korea policy since World War II. Truman's decision to cross the parallel was not the product of "military momentum" or "a surge of optimism" following the Inchon landing, since the President had adopted this course of action early in August. The

Truman administration turned to military means as a last resort and only after concluding that force alone would ensure Korea's freedom to determine its own destiny.

If the United States had halted at the thirty-eighth parallel, it would have registered a significant victory. The successful defense of South Korea would have secured the interests of the United States by maintaining American international credibility and prestige. Unfortunately, the assumptions underlying American foreign policy prevented the administration from being satisfied with a mere restoration of the status quo. American leaders interpreted the Korean conflict in the larger context of the global Soviet-American competition and believed a decisive victory was within easy grasp.

Yet Truman and his advisors never perceived the American offensive north of the parallel as aggressive and struggled to avoid any indication that the United States intended to force its will on the Korean people. American leaders sought instead to portray the operation as essentially negative and designed only to create conditions in which all Koreans would enjoy, or at least appear to possess, freedom of choice. The election of a united Korean government, rather than the destruction of the North Korean army, would inflict a momentous defeat on the Soviet strategy of expansion. When a united Korea produced economic prosperity, social stability, and the appearance of democracy, Truman believed that the popularity of communism throughout the world would begin to wane. The international community would soon realize that only national self-determination could produce "final" settlements. Crossing the thirty-eighth parallel was then only the prelude to the fulfillment of Truman's plan for victory in Korea and around the globe.

✹ FURTHER READING

Frank Baldwin, ed., *Without Parallel* (1975)

Clay Blair, *The Forgotten War* (1988)

Ronald J. Caridi, *The Korean War and American Politics* (1969)

Bruce Cumings, ed., *Child of Conflict* (1983)

———, "Korean-American Relations," in Warren I. Cohen, ed., *New Frontiers in American-East Asian Relations* (1983)

———, *The Origins of the Korean War* (1981)

Charles Dobbs, *The Unwanted Symbol* (1981)

Rosemary Foot, *The Wrong War* (1985)

Alexander L. George and Richard Smoke, *Deterrence in American Foreign Policy* (1974)

Joseph Goulden, *Korea* (1982)

Karunaker Gupta, "How Did the Korean War Begin?" *China Quarterly*, no. 52 (1972), 699–716. Critics' comments in no. 54 (1973), 354–68

Allen Guttmann, ed., *Korea: Cold War and Limited War* (1972)

Francis H. Heller, ed., *The Korean War* (1977)

D. Clayton James, *The Years of MacArthur* (1985)

Burton I. Kaufman, *The Korean War* (1986)

Gabriel Kolko and Joyce Kolko, *The Limits of Power* (1972)

Callum A. MacDonald, *Korea* (1987)

David McLellan, *Dean Acheson* (1976)

James I. Matray, *The Reluctant Crusade* (1985)

Ernest R. May, *"Lessons" of the Past* (1973)

Yonosuke Nagai and Akira Iriye, eds., *The Origins of the Cold War in Asia* (1977)

Glenn D. Paige, *The Korean Decision* (1968)

——, ed., *1950: Truman's Decision* (1970)

David Rees, *Korea, The Limited War* (1964)

Robert R. Simmons, *The Strained Alliance* (1975)

Gaddis Smith, *Dean Acheson* (1972)

John W. Spanier, *The Truman-MacArthur Controversy* (1959)

Russell Spurr, *Enter the Dragon: China's Involvement in the Korean War* (1988)

I. F. Stone, *The Hidden History of the Korean War* (1952)

William Stueck, "The Korean War as International History," *Diplomatic History*, 10 (1986), 291–309

——, *The Road to Confrontation* (1981)

John E. Wiltz, "Truman and MacArthur, The Wake Island Meeting," *Military Affairs*, 42 (1978), 169–76

Allen Whiting, *China Crosses the Yalu* (1960)

The Eisenhower-Dulles
Foreign Policy of the 1950s

In 1953 the leadership of the two major antagonists of the Cold War changed hands. In Soviet Russia, Josef Stalin died and Nikita Khrushchev eventually took command. In the United States, Dwight D. Eisenhower won the 1952 election, entered the White House, and named John Foster Dulles his Secretary of State. The problems they faced were familiar: Korea, Indochina, Berlin, China, Eastern Europe, and the nuclear arms race. But new problems arose in the Third World, as emerging nations asserted their independence. The Middle East and Latin America became more unsettled and hence more dangerous to international stability.

The Eisenhower-Dulles team had to respond to both the Cold War issues and the new realities. Their response has prompted questions about the foreign policy of the 1950s: Was there continuity or discontinuity between Truman diplomacy and Eisenhower-Dulles diplomacy? Who was most responsible for shaping foreign policy—Eisenhower or Dulles? What kind of President was Eisenhower? Was he an effective leader? Did the Eisenhower administration restrain or exacerbate the Cold War and the nuclear arms race? How skillful did American leaders handle revolutionary nationalism and crises in the Third World? Why were alternative policies rejected, such as the acceptance of neutralism? And, finally, why has Eisenhower's reputation improved in recent years?

✖ D O C U M E N T S

Before taking office, Secretary of State John Foster Dulles told the Senate Foreign Relations Committee that he favored the "liberation" of China and Eastern Europe from Communist domination. Neither in his statement of January 15, 1953—the first document—nor in others did he explain how he would accomplish this.

In 1954, when a leftist Guatemalan government under Jacobo Arbenz Guzman expropriated lands owned by the mammoth United Fruit Company, President Eisenhower ordered the Central Intelligence Agency to topple Arbenz. One of the tactics was to use propaganda to depict him as a Communist. Guatemalan Guillermo Toriello Garido defended the integrity of his nation in a speech on March 5, 1954, reprinted here as the second document. On June 30 of the same year, after Arbenz had been forced from office by CIA-backed forces, Dulles cheered the change as a victory over "international communism" (the third selection).

The fourth document is a portion of Eisenhower's press conference of April 7, 1954, in which he spelled out what he meant by the "domino theory" and its relationship to Indochina. The President announced the "Eisenhower Doctrine" in a speech on January 5, 1957 (the fifth selection); it sought to draw the containment line in the Middle East. The last document is Eisenhower's farewell address of January 17, 1961, which aroused interest by including a warning against a "military-industrial complex."

John Foster Dulles on Liberation, 1953

THE CHAIRMAN: I am particularly interested in something I read recently, to the effect that you stated you were not in favor of the policy of containment. I think you advocated a more dynamic or positive policy. Can you tell us more specifically what you have in mind? . . .

MR. DULLES: There are a number of policy matters which I would prefer to discuss with the committee in executive session, but I have no objection to saying in open session what I have said before: namely, that we shall never have a secure peace or a happy world so long as Soviet communism dominates one-third of all of the peoples that there are, and is in the process of trying at least to extend its rule to many others.

These people who are enslaved are people who deserve to be free, and who, from our own selfish standpoint, ought to be free because if they are the servile instruments of aggressive despotism, they will eventually be welded into a force which will be highly dangerous to ourselves and to all of the free world.

Therefore, we must always have in mind the liberation of these captive peoples. Now, liberation does not mean a war of liberation. Liberation can be accomplished by processes short of war. We have, as one example, not an ideal example, but it illustrates my point, the defection of Yugoslavia, under Tito from the domination of Soviet communism. Well, that rule of Tito is not one which we admire, and it has many aspects of despotism, itself; but at least it illustrates that it is possible to disintegrate this present monolithic structure which, as I say, represents approximately one-third of all the people that there are in the world.

The present tie between China and Moscow is an unholy arrangement which is contrary to the traditions, the hopes, the aspirations of the Chinese people. Certainly we cannot tolerate a continuance of that, or a welding of the 450 million people of China into the servile instruments of Soviet aggression.

Therefore, a policy which only aims at containing Russia where it now is, in itself, an unsound policy; but it is a policy which is bound to fail because a purely defensive policy never wins against an aggressive policy. If our only policy is to stay where we are, we will be driven back. It is only by keeping alive the hope of liberation, by taking advantage of that wherever opportunity arises, that we will end this terrible peril which dominates the world, which imposes upon us such terrible sacrifices and so great fears for the future. But all of this can be done and must be done in ways which will not provoke a general war, or in ways which will not provoke an insurrection which would be crushed with bloody violence, such as was the case, for example, when the Russians instigated the Polish revolt, under General Bor, and merely sat by and watched them when the Germans exterminated those who were revolting.

It must be and can be a peaceful process, but those who do not believe that results can be accomplished by moral pressures, by the weight of propaganda, just do not know what they are talking about.

I ask you to recall the fact that Soviet communism itself has spread from controlling 200 million people some 7 years ago to controlling 800 million people today, and it has done that by methods of political warfare, psychological warfare and propaganda, and it has not actually used the Red Army as an open aggressive force in accomplishing that.

Surely what they can accomplish, we can accomplish. Surely if they can use moral and psychological force, we can use it; and, to take a negative defeatest attitude is not an approach which is conducive to our own welfare, or in conformity with our own historical ideas.

Guatemala Defends Its Reforms, 1954

The people of Guatemala are enormously disturbed to find that a respected people, freed of brutal tyrannies, eager to progress and to put in practice the most noble postulates of democracy; determined to put an end to the abuses of the past, trying to wipe out feudalism and colonial procedures and the iniquitous exploitation of its most humble citizens, finds itself faced with the dismaying reality that those who boast of encouraging other peoples to travel the road to economic and political liberty decide to bring them to a halt, only because the decisions and the efforts of these peoples injure unjust interests and because the highest interest of these peoples is incompatible with the maintenance of privileges granted by tyrants in evil times as a means of achieving impunity and a guarantee that they not be moved from the throne of their despotism. And these privileges are so important for the satisfaction of intemperate ambitions and the privileged ones are so powerful that, despite the noble postulates of Pan Americanism, they have unleashed against Guatemala the most iniquitous campaign, and have been unashamed to have recourse to the most cowardly weapons to defame, to deceive, to discredit one of the purest movements that this hemisphere has ever witnessed. . . .

What is the reason for this campaign of defamation? What is the real and effective reason for describing our Government as communist? From what source comes the accusation that we threaten continental solidarity and security? Why do they wish to intervene in Guatemala?

The answers are simple and evident. The plan of national liberation being carried out with firmness by my Government has necessarily affected the privileges of the foreign enterprises that are impeding the progress and the economic development of the country. The highway to the Atlantic, besides connecting the important productive zones it traverses, is destroying the monopoly of internal transportation to the ports now held by the Ferrocarriles Internacionales de Centro América (an enterprise controlled by the United Fruit Company), in order to increase foreign trade free of grievous and discriminatory charges. With construction of national ports and docks, we are putting an end to the monopoly of the United Fruit Company, and we will thus make it possible for the nation to increase and to diversify its foreign trade through the use of maritime transport other than the White Fleet, also belonging to the United Fruit Company, which now controls this essential instrument of our international commercial relations.

With the realization of the plan of national electrification, we shall put and [sic] end to foreign monopoly of electric power, indispensable to our industrial development, which has been delayed by the lack, the scarcity, or the distribution failures of that important means of production.

With our Agrarian Reform, we are abolishing the latifundia, including those of the United Fruit Company itself. Following a dignified policy, we have refused to broaden the concessions of that company. We have insisted that foreign investment be in accordance with our laws, and we have recovered and maintained absolute independence in our foreign policy. . . .

These bases and purposes of the Guatemalan revolution cannot be catalogued within a Communist ideology or policy: a political-economic platform like that put forward by the government of Guatemala, which is settling in rural areas thousands of individual landowners, individual farmers, can never be conceived of as a Communist plan. Far from that, we believe that raising the standard of living and the income of rural and urban workers alone stimulates the capitalistic economic development of the country and the sociological bases of a genuinely Guatemalan functional democracy. . . .

International reaction, at the same time it is pointing out Guatemala as a "threat to continental solidarity," is preparing vast interventionist plans, such as the one recently denounced by the Guatemalan government. The published documents—which the Department of State at Washington hastened to call Moscow propaganda—unquestionably show that the foreign conspirators and monopolistic interests that inspired and financed them sought to permit armed intervention against our country, as "a noble undertaking against communism." Let us emphasize before this Conference the gravity of these events. Non-intervention is one of the most priceless triumphs of Pan Americanism and the essential basis of inter-American unity, solidarity, and cooperation. It has been fully supported in various inter-American instruments, and specifically in Article 15 of the Charter of the Organization of American States. The Secretary General of the Organization, Dr. Alberto Lleras Camargo, in his report on the Ninth International Conference of American States, in commenting on this article, states categorically that with it "the doubt that seemed to arise recently, as to whether intervention carried out collectively would be so considered, has thus been dispelled."

Dulles on "International Communism" in Guatemala, 1954

For several years international communism has been probing here and there for nesting places in the Americas. It finally chose Guatemala as a spot which it could turn into an official base from which to breed subversion which would extend to other American Republics.

This intrusion of Soviet despotism was, of course, a direct challenge to our Monroe Doctrine, the first and most fundamental of our foreign policies. . . .

In Guatemala, international communism had an initial success. It began 10 years ago, when a revolution occurred in Guatemala. The revolution was not without justification. But the Communists seized on it, not as an opportunity for real reforms, but as a chance to gain political power.

Communist agitators devoted themselves to infiltrating the public and private organizations of Guatemala. They sent recruits to Russia and other Communist countries for revolutionary training and indoctrination in such institutions as the Lenin School at Moscow. Operating in the guise of "reformers" they organized the workers and peasants under Communist leadership. Having gained control of what they call "mass organizations," they moved on to take over the official press and radio of the Guatemalan Government. They dominated the social security organization and ran the agrarian reform program. Through the technique of the "popular front" they dictated to the Congress and the President.

The judiciary made one valiant attempt to protect its integrity and independence. But the Communists, using their control of the legislative body, caused the Supreme Court to be dissolved when it refused to give approval to a Communist-contrived law. Arbenz, who until this week was President of Guatemala, was openly manipulated by the leaders of communism.

Guatemala is a small country. But its power, standing alone, is not a measure of the threat. The master plan of international communism is to gain a solid political base in this hemisphere, a base that can be used to extend Communist penetration to the other peoples of the other American Governments. It was not the power of the Arbenz government that concerned us but the power behind it.

If world communism captures any American State, however small, a new and perilous front is established which will increase the danger to the entire free world and require even greater sacrifices from the American people.

This situation in Guatemala had become so dangerous that the American States could not ignore it. At Caracas last March the American States held their Tenth Inter-American Conference. They then adopted a momentous statement. They declared that "the domination or control of the political institutions of any American State by the international Communist movement . . . would constitute a threat to the sovereignty and political independence of the American States, endangering the peace of America."

There was only one American State that voted against this declaration. That State was Guatemala.

This Caracas declaration precipitated a dramatic chain of events. From their European base the Communist leaders moved rapidly to build up the military power of their agents in Guatemala. In May a large shipment of arms moved from behind the Iron Curtain into Guatemala. The shipment was sought to be secreted by false manifests and false clearances. Its ostensible destination was changed three times while en route.

At the same time, the agents of international communism in Guatemala intensified efforts to penetrate and subvert the neighboring Central American States. They attempted political assassinations and political strikes. They used consular agents for political warfare.

Many Guatemalan people protested against their being used by Communist dictatorship to serve the Communists' lust for power. The response was mass arrests, the suppression of constitutional guaranties, the killing of opposition leaders, and other brutal tactics normally employed by communism to secure the consolidation of its power.

In the face of these events and in accordance with the spirit of the Caracas declaration, the nations of this hemisphere laid further plans to grapple with the danger. The Arbenz government responded with an effort to disrupt the inter-American system. Because it enjoyed the full support of Soviet Russia, which is on the Security Council, it tried to bring the matter before the Security Council. It did so without first referring the matter to the American regional organization as is called for both by the United Nations Charter itself and by the treaty creating the American organization.

The Foreign Minister of Guatemala openly connived in this matter with the Foreign Minister of the Soviet Union. The two were in open correspondence and ill-concealed privity. The Security Council at first voted overwhelmingly to refer the Guatemala matter to the Organization of American States. The vote was 10 to 1. But that one negative vote was a Soviet veto. . . .

Throughout the period I have outlined, the Guatemalan Government and Communist agents throughout the world have persistently attempted to obscure the real issue—that of Communist imperialism—by claiming that the United States is only interested in protecting American business. We regret that there have been disputes between the Guatemalan Government and the United Fruit Company. We have urged repeatedly that these disputes be submitted for settlement to an international tribunal or to international arbitration. That is the way to dispose of problems of this sort. But this issue is relatively unimportant. All who know the temper of the U.S. people and Government must realize that our overriding concern is that which, with others, we recorded at Caracas, namely, the endangering by international communism of the peace and security of this hemisphere.

The people of Guatemala have now been heard from. Despite the armaments piled up by the Arbenz government, it was unable to enlist the spiritual cooperation of the people.

Led by Colonel Castillo Armas, patriots arose in Guatemala to challenge the Communist leadership—and to change it. Thus, the situation is being cured by the Guatemalans themselves.

Dwight D. Eisenhower Explains the "Domino Theory," 1954

QUESTION. Robert Richards, *Copley Press*: Mr. President, would you mind commenting on the strategic importance of Indochina to the free world? I think there has been, across the country, some lack of understanding on just what it means to us.

THE PRESIDENT: You have, of course, both the specific and the general when you talk about such things.

First of all, you have the specific value of a locality in its production of materials that the world needs.

Then you have the possibility that many human beings pass under a dictatorship that is inimical to the free world.

Finally, you have broader considerations that might follow what you would call the "falling domino" principle. You have a row of dominoes set up, you knock over the first one, and what will happen to the last one is the certainty that it will go over very quickly. So you could have a beginning of a disintegration that would have the most profound influences.

Now, with respect to the first one, two of the items from this particular area that the world uses are tin and tungsten. They are very important. There are others, of course, the rubber plantations and so on.

Then with respect to more people passing under this domination, Asia, after all, has already lost some 450 million of its peoples to the Communist dictatorship, and we simply can't afford greater losses.

But when we come to the possible sequence of events, the loss of Indochina, of Burma, of Thailand, of the Peninsula, and Indochina following, now you begin to talk about areas that not only multiply the disadvantages that you would suffer through loss of materials, sources of materials, but now you are talking really about millions and millions and millions of people.

Finally, the geographical position achieved thereby does many things. It turns the so-called island defensive chain of Japan, Formosa, of the Philippines and to the southward; it moves in to threaten Australia and New Zealand.

It takes away, in its economic aspects, that region that Japan must have as a trading area or Japan, in turn, will have only one place in the world to go—that, toward the Communist areas in order to live.

So, the possible consequences of the loss are just incalculable to the free world.

The Eisenhower Doctrine, 1957

The action which I propose would have the following features.

It would, first of all, authorize the United States to cooperate with and assist any nation or group of nations in the general area of the Middle East in the development of economic strength dedicated to the maintenance of national independence.

It would, in the second place, authorize the Executive to undertake in the same region programs of military assistance and cooperation with any nation or group of nations which desires such aid.

It would, in the third place, authorize such assistance and cooperation to include the employment of the armed forces of the United States to secure and protect the territorial integrity and political independence of such nations, requesting such aid, against overt armed aggression from any nation controlled by International Communism.

Eisenhower on the "Military-Industrial Complex," 1961

A vital element in keeping the peace is our military establishment. Our arms must be mighty, ready for instant action, so that no potential aggressor may be tempted to risk his own destruction.

Our military organization today bears little relation to that known by any of my predecessors in peacetime, or indeed by the fighting men of World War II or Korea.

Until the latest of our world conflicts, the United States had no armaments industry. American makers of plowshares could, with time and as required, make swords as well. But now we can no longer risk emergency improvisation of national defense; we have been compelled to create a permanent armaments industry of vast proportions. Added to this, three and a half million men and women are directly engaged in the defense establishment. We annually spend on military security more than the net income of all United States corporations.

This conjunction of an immense military establishment and a large arms industry is new in the American experience. The total influence—economic, political, even spiritual—is felt in every city, every State house, every office of the Federal government. We recognize the imperative need for this development. Yet we must not fail to comprehend its grave implications. Our toil, resources and livelihood are all involved; so is the very structure of our society.

In the councils of government, we must guard against the acquisition of unwarranted influence, whether sought or unsought, by the military-industrial complex. The potential for the disastrous rise of misplaced power exists and will persist.

We must never let the weight of this combination endanger our liberties or democratic processes. We should take nothing for granted. Only an alert and knowledgeable citizenry can compel the proper meshing of the huge industrial and military machinery of defense with our peaceful methods and goals, so that security and liberty may prosper together.

Akin to, and largely responsible for the sweeping changes in our industrial-military posture, has been the technological revolution during recent decades.

In this revolution, research has become central; it also becomes more formalized, complex, and costly. A steadily increasing share is conducted for, by, or at the direction of, the Federal government.

Today, the solitary inventor, tinkering in his shop, has been overshadowed by task forces of scientists in laboratories and testing fields. In the same fashion, the free university, historically the fountainhead of free ideas and scientific discovery, has experienced a revolution in the conduct of research. Partly because of the huge costs involved, a government contract becomes virtually a substitute for intellectual curiosity. For every old blackboard there are now hundreds of new electronic computers.

The prospect of domination of the nation's scholars by Federal employment, project allocations, and the power of money is ever present—and is gravely to be regarded.

Yet, in holding scientific research and discovery in respect, as we should, we must also be alert to the equal and opposite danger that public policy could itself become the captive of a scientific-technological elite.

It is the task of statesmanship to mold, to balance, and to integrate these and other forces, new and old, within the principles of our democratic system—ever aiming toward the supreme goals of our free society. . . .

Down the long lane of the history yet to be written America knows that this world of ours, ever growing smaller, must avoid becoming a community of dreadful fear and hate, and be, instead, a proud confederation of mutual trust and respect.

Such a confederation must be one of equals. The weakest must come to the conference table with the same confidence as do we, protected as we are by our moral, economic, and military strength. That table, though scarred by many past frustrations, cannot be abandoned for the certain agony of the battlefield.

Disarmament, with mutual honor and confidence, is a continuing imperative. Together we must learn how to compose differences, not with arms, but with intellect and decent purpose. Because this need is so sharp and apparent I confess that I lay down my official responsibilities in this field with a definite sense of disappointment. As one who has witnessed the horror and the lingering sadness of war—as one who knows that another war could utterly destroy this civilization which has been so slowly and painfully built over thousands of years—I wish I could say tonight that a lasting peace is in sight.

Happily, I can say that war has been avoided. Steady progress toward our ultimate goal has been made. But, so much remains to be done. As a private citizen, I shall never cease to do what little I can to help the world advance along that road.

✸ E S S A Y S

In a reassessment of the Eisenhower presidency in the first essay, Fred I. Greenstein of Princeton University challenges the once-popular view that Secretary Dulles dominated the making of foreign policy. He also questions the related view that President Eisenhower was a passive, noninvolved leader. According to Greenstein, Eisenhower was an energetic, skilled, and activist president in command of decision making; he practiced a "hidden-hand leadership."

Arthur M. Schlesinger, Jr., a historian at the City University of New York and a former assistant to President John F. Kennedy, agrees in the second essay that new scholarly research has corrected the distorted picture of Eisenhower as a bumbling, purposeless, politically inept leader. But Schlesinger doubts the effectiveness of the "hidden-hand" style and faults Eisenhower for evading difficult issues. Schlesinger also critically examines his record on matters of war and peace, especially the gap between his rhetoric and his decisions. In the end, Schlesinger argues, Eisenhower was a hawk who threatened nuclear war and advanced the arms race.

In the final essay, Robert J. McMahon of the University of Florida also disputes Eisenhower "revisionism" by scrutinizing the President's diplomacy toward the Third World, where nationalism and revolution stirred and new nations were emerging from colonialism. Summarizing recent scholarship on the subject and drawing upon his own research in documents of the period, McMahon concludes that the Eisenhower administration profoundly misunderstood Third World developments. The United States clung to the status quo, suffered major setbacks, and ensured long-term instability in the Third World.

Eisenhower Revised: The Activist President

FRED I. GREENSTEIN

The administration of Dwight D. Eisenhower is commonly thought to be devoid of interest to those who seek insight into the range of feasible ways to conduct the presidency in the era since the responsibilities and demands of that office mushroomed under Franklin D. Roosevelt. Most of the scholarly and serious journalistic commentators on Eisenhower as president have characterized him as an aging hero who reigned more than he ruled and who lacked the energy, motivation, and political skill to have a significant impact on events. If Eisenhower was an exemplar, to their minds, it was in the negative sense of showing how one ought *not* to be president.

From "Eisenhower as an Activist President: A Look at New Evidence." Reprinted with permission from the *Political Science Quarterly,* 94 (Winter 1979–80), 575–583.

In recent years, however, there has been a slowly but steadily rising tide of Eisenhower revisionism. Some of the new interest in Eisenhower stems from nostalgia for the alleged placid, uncomplicated nature of the 1950s. Other interest derives from "postliberal" attraction to the kinds of policies he espoused—for example, curbs on defense spending, mildly incremental approaches to expanding welfare policies, and efforts to hold down inflation. A third category of revisionism, which might be called "instrumental revisionism," arises from reassessments of Eisenhower's performance as a political practitioner. In view of the debacles of his successors, the conduct in office of the only post-Twenty-second Amendment president to be elected to and complete two terms (and with continuingly high levels of public support at that) seems worthy of reconsideration on that ground alone.

Instrumental revisionist reexamination of Eisenhower's performance has to date been largely deductive. The two writers who have argued most forcefully that Eisenhower was not inept but instead a skilled politician who practiced the art of ruling in a deceptively veiled fashion are journalists who have relied heavily on close readings of the published record. Both have ingeniously reconstructed what seems to them the logic of Eisenhower's actions in various widely publicized events. They also have drawn on passages from writings of his contemporaries, such as the following by Richard Nixon in his 1962 memoir:

> [Eisenhower] was a far more complex and devious man than most people realized, and in the best sense of these words. Not shackled to a one-track mind, he always applied two, three or four lines of reasoning to a single problem and he usually preferred the indirect approach where it would serve him better than the direct attack on a problem.

The observations on Eisenhower's presidential style adduced in this article differ from those of previous instrumental revisionists in that they are inductive rather than deductive. They are based mainly on one of the many newly available primary sources on his presidency, namely the collection of several thousand documents in the Whitman File at the Eisenhower Library. This archival trove, which is named after Eisenhower's personal secretary, Ann Whitman, was opened for scholarly perusal in the mid-1970s. The Whitman File provides far more thorough documentation of Eisenhower's day-to-day activities than has been preserved for other presidencies, including: daily lists of the president's appointments; detailed minutes of formal meetings such as those of the cabinet, National Security Council (NSC), and legislative leaders; extensive notes and numerous transcripts of informal meetings between the president and other political figures; transcripts or summaries of his face-to-face and telephone conversations; texts of pre-press conference briefings; and many observations by Mrs. Whitman of comings and goings in the White House, of offhand remarks by the president, and even of fluctuations in his mood and temper.

The Whitman File also contains Eisenhower's copious comments on and interpolations in the numerous drafts of his speeches; his memoranda and notes to colleagues; an extraordinary number of "personal and confidential" letters he dictated to correspondents; and his private diary, which reaches back to Eisenhower's service in the 1930s as aide to General Douglas MacArthur in the Philippines and extends forward into his late retirement years. The Eisenhower presidency is further illuminated by the unpublished diaries and oral histories of his personal associates, many of whom are now more disposed to be interviewed than would have been the case shortly after the end of his administration.

The conclusions I draw from an extensive reading of the archival materials are more consistent with the inferences of the instrumental revisionists than with the traditional lore deprecating Eisenhower's leadership skills and efforts. Eisenhower was politically astute and informed, actively engaged in putting his personal stamp on public policy, and applied a carefully thought-out conception of leadership to the conduct of his presidency.

The term activism is commonly used to refer to three presidential attributes that in fact may vary independently of one another: sheer extent of activity; commitment to use the office so as to have an impact on public policy; and actual success in affecting policy. Despite the widespread belief that Eisenhower was not an activist president in any of these respects, he worked hard and both intended to and did have an impact on policy. Moreover, as will be illustrated throughout this essay, his activism has not been evident to many observers of his presidency due to the "low-profile" nature of his leadership style. I shall begin by considering the extent of activity of this president who often was portrayed as being more attentive to golf than to government.

The extent of Eisenhower's activity can be assessed by examining the lists of his appointments and meetings for each official day. The lists for some days can be supplemented by taking account of the prodigious amount of correspondence he dictated and other paper work he engaged in along with his numerous telephone conversations. Furthermore, oral histories and interviews with people who worked with him provide information on Eisenhower's activities during the time not covered by the appointment lists— between appointments and before and after his official day.

The appointment list for October 13, 1960, which falls at about the median in number of appointments, is quite instructive, because in addition to demonstrating the sheer extent of his activity, it suggests the distinctive nature and style of certain aspects of Eisenhower's activism. The conventional view of him as an inactive president is manifestly inaccurate. He arrived at his office at 8:12 A.M., but his work had begun much earlier. Before leaving the White House residential quarters, Eisenhower often held 7:30 meetings over breakfast. On many days, moreover, he chatted with his closest confidant, his brother Milton, who regularly spent three-day weekends living in Washington and using an office in the Executive Office Building. And by the time Milton Eisenhower, Press Secretary James Hagerty, and the staff members who each morning briefed President Eisenhower on intelligence matters saw him, he had closely read several newspapers—

papers to which he paid particular attention were the *New York Times*, *New York Herald Tribune*, and the *Christian Science Monitor*.

The October 13 log lists seventeen meetings during the morning and afternoon, ranging from brief exchanges with his appointments secretary to the weekly meeting of the National Security Council. The first part of the log continues from 8:12 A.M.to 5:13 P.M., with a forty-five minute preluncheon break for the rest and exercise prescribed by Eisenhower's doctors. Ordinarily, his work day would have continued for perhaps another hour, and there probably would have been a predinner hour session of informal business conducted over cocktails in the official residence. This last hour was when Eisenhower met with his major friendly adversaries, House Speaker Sam Rayburn and Senate Majority Leader Lyndon Johnson, and it often was an occasion for reflective discussion with John Foster Dulles or Milton Eisenhower.

But on this evening, Head of State ceremonies were scheduled. President and Mrs. Eisenhower attended a dinner given for them by King Frederick and Queen Ingrid of Denmark at the Danish embassy, along with a performance of the Danish Royal Ballet (with reception of guests during the intermission). The Eisenhowers dropped off the king and queen at Blair House at 11:32 P.M. and arrived at the Executive Mansion at 11:37 P.M.

If Eisenhower typically was as busy as the log of activities on October 13, 1960, suggests, how did the misimpression of his lassitude arise? For one thing, the administration did not release to the press full lists of Eisenhower's meetings. For another, it was not deemed appropriate that some of the meetings be announced—indeed this was the case with three of those held on the day under consideration, which were listed as officially "off-the-record." The nature of these meetings helps to alter the impression of Eisenhower as a passive, apolitical president who "delegated away" authority to make decisions on major issues. . . .

Whether Eisenhower "delegated away" powers he himself should have exercised is a question that meetings like the third off-the-record meeting of October 13, 1960, shed light on. This was a fifty-five-minute session with a variety of high national security and foreign-policy officials (for example, the secretaries of state and defense and the director of the Central Intelligence Agency) which immediately preceded the official meeting of the National Security Council. It falls into a class of decision-making conferences that have been described by Douglas Kinnard, who drew on the minutes of the regular pre-NSC meeting conference. The NSC meetings and administrative machinery were at that time being criticized by Washington insiders such as Senators Henry Jackson and John F. Kennedy for being an unimaginative bureaucratic setting in which routine presentation of turgid position papers occurred. [Professor Douglas] Kinnard has shown, however, that the preliminary sessions were occasions for genuine policy debate and policymaking. Indeed these sessions had a give-and-take quality quite like that recommended by scholars who call for the avoidance of "groupthink" in policy deliberations. (The official NSC meetings also were occasions for discussion, but their main function was that of "spreading the word," that is, promulgating administration policy to those who were to execute it.) Not only in pre-NSC conferences and cabinet meetings but also in general, Eisenhower favored discussions that were preceded by careful staff work, but in which contending advocates were brought together and asked to argue vigorously for their policy options. Eisenhower usually reserved comment until the other participants had spoken. Then he—not his subordinates—made the final choices, which were followed by systematic attention by staff aides to insure implementation.

Decision making by the president after vigorous debate among advisers was not a product of the so-called new Eisenhower of 1959–60; rather, this procedure was followed throughout his first six years in office as well. During those years, Eisenhower still had in his employ Sherman Adams and John Foster Dulles, to each of whom he is commonly believed to have abdicated fundamental policy-making powers. Eisenhower did strongly hold that the ability to delegate power and to utilize staff support was a necessary condition for effective leadership of large, complex organizations. As far back as 1942, immediately on assuming command of Allied forces in the European theater of World War II, he stressed in a briefing to his aides that they were "free to solve their own problems wherever possible and not to get in the habit of passing the buck up." But his delegation practices were informed by a well-developed sense of whom he could entrust with what amount of decision-making power and of the need to be vigilant about possible failures by line and staff officials to adhere to their chief's policies.

Eisenhower did entrust important responsibilities to Adams and Dulles. He prized the service of both men, but he was not awed by them. In his view, both were overly gruff and insensitive to their abrasive effect on others, but these shortcomings were more than compensated for by the high quality and prodigious quantity of their work. In numerous private diary entries Eisenhower made from time to time (much like the performance evaluations of military associates he made in World War II and immediately thereafter as chief of staff of the army), he registered judgments on their deficiencies as well as on their strengths. For example, in a note Eisenhower dictated to himself summing up accomplishments and disappointments in his first year as president, he said of Adams: "Honesty, directness, and efficiency have begun to win friends among people who initially were prone to curse him because he had no time for flattery or cajolery, or even pleasantries over the telephone." With respect to Dulles, Eisenhower wrote this assessment: "He is well informed and [on matters of foreign affairs] at least is deserving, I think, of his reputation as a 'wise' man. . . . But he is not particularly persuasive in presentation and, at times, seems to have a curious lack of understanding as to how his words and manner may affect another personality."

The evidence required for close, if not definitive, analysis of the Eisenhower-Dulles and Eisenhower-Adams relationships is now accessible. It includes not only the Eisenhower Library sources enumerated above, but also the several hundred oral histories in the Columbia University Eisenhower Administration collection, the papers and oral histories in the Princeton University John Foster Dulles collection, and Adams's papers in the library of Dartmouth College.

Richard Immerman has reported preliminary findings of a study of how Eisenhower and Dulles worked together. The evidence overwhelmingly indicates that their relationship was collaborative. The two men agreed in their basic policy goals as well as their assessments of the political realities of the time and the strategies appropriate to deal with them, although they differed from time to time on matters of tactics. Their common beliefs and perceptions were reinforced by daily contact—direct meetings when Dulles was in Washington, electronic communication when he was traveling. Eisenhower, it should be noted, conferred with and issued policy instructions to members of the foreign-policy community besides Dulles. He used Dulles partly as roving emissary, partly as official foreign-policy spokesman, and partly in his "wise man" capacity as a participant in a continuing dialogue on general and specific facets of foreign policy.

Eisenhower and Dulles practiced a division of labor resembling that of a client with his attorney—a client who has firm overall purposes and an attorney who is expected to help him devise ways to accomplish those purposes and to argue his case. The public impression that emanated from the quite different personal styles of these men—Dulles the austere cold warrior, Eisenhower the warm champion of peace—contributed to a further division of labor. Dulles was assigned the "get tough" side of foreign-policy enunciation, thus placating the fervently anti-Communist wing of the Republican party. Meanwhile, amiable Ike made gestures toward peace and international humanitarianism—for example, Atoms for Peace, Open Skies, and summitry at Geneva. . . .

In addition to the regular meetings with the cabinet and legislative leaders, the newspaper reading, conversations with his brother Milton, and intelligence briefings, Eisenhower had many other ways of seeking and receiving information. He read an extraordinary volume of official documents and maintained a voluminous "personal and confidential" correspondence with his extensive network of friends in the business and military communities and in other walks of life. His periodic stag dinners with carefully selected national figures were still another source of knowledge. Finally, it is instructive to note that although Adams had the impression that Eisenhower rarely used the telephone, the telephone logs for some days contain as many as a dozen calls in which Eisenhower sought information, gave instructions, rallied support, and made policy decisions.

Adams, in short, was an expediter of the president's policies and a like-minded agent, not a prime policy mover—this notwithstanding the not uncommon view that "O.K., S.A." was tantamount to adoption of a given course of action by "D.D.E." In this connection, the matter of "O.K., S.A." sheds light on a way that Adams's services had some of the same effect for Eisenhower as did Dulles's. The major policy papers and correspondence that went to the president did *not* bear this inscription. Rather, it was largely to be found on recommendations for minor patronage positions. Apart from being time consuming, such decisions are a notorious source of recrimination. It was much to Eisenhower's advantage that Adams take the blame for the bulk of them. (Eisenhower was able to benefit from those he informally arranged and then instructed Adams to implement.) More broadly, Adams's reputation as "abominable no man," like Dulles's as grim cold warrior, preserved Eisenhower's ability to appear as a benevolent national and international leader.

Stephen Hess has described Eisenhower's general approach to delegation of authority as one that "artfully constructed . . . an elaborate maze of buffer zones." Hess adds that "Eisenhower gave himself considerable freedom of action by giving his subordinates considerable latitude to act." It should be emphasized that Eisenhower's buffering practices did not consist exclusively of allowing subordinates to carry out the more controversial components of administration policy. But the division of labor in which the subordinate protected the president's ability to be perceived as being above the fray was in some instances a conscious strategy. For example, Press Secretary James Hagerty (one of the staff members who had regular, direct access to the president) once reminisced:

> President Eisenhower would say, "Do it this way." I would say, "If I go to that press conference and say what you want me to say, I would get hell." With that, he would smile, get up and walk around the desk, pat me on the back and say, "My boy, better you than me."

The uses by Eisenhower and subordinates of this type of strategy are better described as acts of "pseudo-delegation" than of true delegation. In these cases the policy was Eisenhower's, but in its promulgation Eisenhower's hand was hidden. There is much further evidence of a variety of ways in which Eisenhower practiced what I shall designate as "hidden hand leadership."

Covert or hidden hand leadership is an alternative political tactic to seeking to enhance one's professional reputation. [Richard] Neustadt, it will be recalled, argues that the principal sources of presidential influence are the president's "professional reputation" among other politicians as a skilled leader, his prestige with the general public, and his use of formal powers. Eisenhower was prepared to sacrifice the first for the second. Further, he preferred informal to formal means of influence.

One type of hidden hand leadership Eisenhower practiced involved working through intermediaries. An example is provided by the following rough notes summarizing a telephone conversation in which Eisenhower charged Treasury Secretary Humphrey with the task of urging Eisenhower's friend, the Texas oil millionaire, Sid Richardson, to persuade Lyndon Johnson to be more cooperative.

> Called Secy. Humphrey—asking him to speak to Sid Richardson (who was really the angel for Johnson when he came in). Ask him what it is that Tex wants. We help out in drought, take tidelands matter on their side, & tax bill. But question is, how much influence has Sid got with

Johnson? He tells Sid he's supporting us, then comes up here & disapproves it (yesterday for instance). Perhaps Sid could get him into right channel, or threaten to get Shivers into primary & beat him for Senate. Humphrey says this is exactly the time to do it, too; & if he talks to Sid, it can't be said that DDE is taking advantage of long-time friendship. DDE admits Sid himself has helped us; but can't let Johnson do as he pleases. He nagged George on Bricker, now on this one. If Sid is friend of fine conservative govt., he'd better pull away from Johnson. Humphrey and Johnson's alibi to Sid this time was, "They wait until we are committed; then they come after us." But we just can't tell them things in advance—they always give it to the press. Sid understands rough language; Humphrey can use it, & will!

Another element of Eisenhower's deliberately unpublicized kind of activism consisted of exploitation of his putative lack of political skill. This is illustrated by an episode described in his private diary in which he took the blame for a diplomatic error on the part of Secretary of State Dulles. The diary entry was stimulated by a meeting with the retiring ambassador to the Court of St. James, "my good friend, Walter Gifford."

While Eisenhower was still at Supreme Headquarters Allied Powers Europe (SHAPE), he had learned of Gifford's plan to retire as soon as the next administration was in office. "With this knowledge, I of course was interested in the task of selecting a completely acceptable and useful successor. We started this job shortly after election in early November and it was not long before we determined that all things considered Winthrop Aldrich would be our best bet. This selection was made on the most confidential basis, but to our consternation it was soon public knowledge." Because Dulles felt the situation embarrassing and in need of public announcement, Eisenhower authorized this, but "put in my word of caution that Walter Gifford would have to be protected in every possible way."

In the haste to act quickly, Gifford's planned resignation and Aldrich's intended appointment were announced promptly, without clearing the matter with the British. Eisenhower continues:

> This upset the British government very badly—and I must say most understandably. As Anthony Eden pointed out in his informal protest to Walter Gifford, this meant that Britain was being subjected to pretty rough treatment when there was no effort made to get the usual "agreement." He said that with this precedent, any small nation could pursue the same tactics and if Britain should protest, they could argue that since the United States had done this and Britain had accepted it, no real objection could be made. To guard against any such development as this, I am going to advise Anthony, when I see him next month, to lay the blame for this whole unfortunate occurrence squarely on me. He will have the logical explanation that my lack of formal experience in the political world was the reason for the blunder. Actually, I was the one who cautioned against anything like this happening, but manifestly I can take the blame without hurting anything or anybody, whereas if the Secretary of State would have to shoulder it his position would be badly damaged.

Perhaps the most striking example of hidden hand leadership, at least in domestic politics, was Eisenhower's extensive behind-the-scenes partic-ipation in the sequence of events that culminated in the Senate's censure of Joseph McCarthy in December 1954. Working most closely with Press Secretary Hagerty, Eisenhower conducted a virtual day-to-day campaign via the media and congressional allies to end McCarthy's political effec-tiveness. The overall strategy was to avoid *direct mention* of McCarthy in the president's public statements, lest McCarthy win sympathy as a spunky David battling against the presidential Goliath. Instead Eisenhower system-atically condemned the *types* of actions in which McCarthy engaged.

Hagerty arranged with sympathetic newspaper reporters, publishers, and broadcasters for coverage that underscored the president's implicit condemnation of McCarthy. In addition, an arrangement was made whereby an administration spokesman rather than McCarthy received network air-time on an occasion when Adlai Stevenson castigated the Republican party for McCarthyism. Finally, much attention was given to persuading congres-sional leaders to conduct the hearings evaluating McCarthy's conduct in a fashion that would vitiate McCarthy's usual means of defending himself against counterattack. Eisenhower's orchestration of the covert aspects of the events that led to McCarthy's censure even now have not been documented in the published literature on the period.

Eisenhower's published discourse was a principal source of the many deprecations of his fitness for presidential leadership. His unpublished dis-course—both writings and transcripts of discussions—leads to an impression quite different from that conveyed by the published record. Eisenhower's critics derided his apparent inability to think and express himself clearly along with his seeming lack of knowledge. The evidence that gave rise to their view was the fuzzy and tangled prose in his answers at press conferences; his frequent professions of ignorance in response to reporters' questions about issues one would expect any self-respecting president to discuss knowledgeably; and the middle-brow, middle-America rhetoric of a large portion of his speeches.

Three kinds of evidence in the Whitman File make necessary a reeval-uation of Eisenhower's level of knowledge and his rhetorical and cognitive styles: the transcripts of Eisenhower's conversations and conferences; his markups and insertions in the numerous drafts through which all of his major speeches went; and his personal correspondence. These sources reveal a skilled, sophisticated use of language on Eisenhower's part and extend my description of the nature and style of his activism.

A large number of the papers preserved in the Whitman File are transcripts or paraphrases of Eisenhower's conversations and conferences dealing with specifics of policy, in numerous instances matters that many people believed Eisenhower was neither interested in nor attentive to. An example is a transcribed paraphrase of a meeting with the chairman of the Council of Economic Advisers, in which the president requested a shift of emphasis in a passage of a draft of the 1959 Annual Economic Report. This document reveals the man who allegedly read only simplified one-page memos both reading and commenting upon a good many pages of complex subject matter.

The President called Dr. Saulnier in and said that he had read the first two chapters of the proposed economic report. He liked them, but felt there was one very definite omission. He felt that in these two chapters there would be some account of the history of the weakness of the automobile market. He thinks it very important to say what caused this weakness—and he listed the causes as (1) lack of statesmanship in the search for market and (2) overextension in the use of credit terms. This latter had the effect of encouraging buying and unusual wage demands.

The transcripts of conversations and conferences also include minutes of pre-press conference briefings. Some of these explain one verbal regularity that led president-watchers to take it for granted that Eisenhower was poorly informed—his frequent statements in press conferences that he was unfamiliar with an issue. Eisenhower made such claims when he preferred not to discuss a matter. For example, in the July 31, 1957, briefing, Eisenhower was reminded that Egyptian President Nasser had made a series of speeches criticizing the United States and that the "Egyptians are trying to say [these speeches] have disturbed us." Eisenhower replied that if asked about Nasser's speeches he would state that he had not read them, whereas in fact hypothetical questions and answers on the topic were present in that session's briefing papers. It turned out, as was often the case with topics discussed in the preliminary conferences, that no journalist asked a question about Nasser's speeches.

Numerous similar assertions of Eisenhower's intention to deny knowledge of a sticky issue about which he was informed, or to say that he had not kept up with the technicalities of a matter, can be found in the pre-press conference transcripts. These assertions are borne out by abundant examples of followthrough. Virtually all of Eisenhower's press conferences include remarks such as "Well, this is the first I have heard about that," "You cannot expect me to know the legal complexities of that issue," and so on. No doubt all presidents have feigned ignorance or "stonewalled" occasionally, but out-and-out denials of knowledge are far more common in Eisenhower's press conferences than in those of the other modern presidents.

Insight into Eisenhower's confusing prose in press conferences is provided by the report, in his memoirs, of the following incident. In March 1955, two months after the passage of the Formosa Straits Resolution, reporters were still seeking unequivocal answers to such questions as whether, under what circumstances, and with what kinds of weapons the United States would defend the Nationalist Chinese-held islands of Quemoy and Matsu, if they were attacked from the mainland. In the March 16 conference, Eisenhower warned that in the event of a "general war" in Asia, the United States was prepared to use tactical nuclear weapons "on strictly military targets and for strictly military purposes." Just before the next week's conference, the State Department urgently requested, through Press Secretary James Hagerty, that the president refuse to discuss this delicate matter further.

> "Don't worry Jim," I told him as we went out the door of my office, "if that question comes up, I'll just confuse them."

One question on this subject came that morning from Joseph C. Harsch, of the *Christian Science Monitor*: "If we got into an issue with the Chinese, say, over Matsu and Quemoy, that we wanted to keep limited, do you conceive of using [atomic weapons] in that situation or not?"

I said that I could not answer that question in advance. The only thing I knew about war was two things: the most unpredictable factor in war was human nature, but the only unchanging factor in war was human nature.

"And the next thing," I said in answer to Mr. Harsch, "is that every war is going to astonish you in the way it occurred, and in the way it is carried out.

"So that for a man to predict, particularly if he has the responsibility for making the decision, to predict what he is going to use, how he is going to do it, would I think exhibit his ignorance of war; that is what I believe.

"So I think you just have to wait; and that this is the kind of prayerful decision that may some day face a President."

The July 17, 1957, pre-press conference briefing is illuminating on both the vagueness of his press conference statements and the nature of the Eisenhower-Dulles relationship. Eisenhower expressed to his staff annoyance that on the previous day the secretary of state, in his own press conference, had "wandered" into a discussion of a national security matter that Eisenhower felt should not have been commented upon at all, namely the disposition of American missiles in Europe. After checking by telephone with Dulles about precisely what had been said, Eisenhower informed his associates that if this matter were to arise in that day's press conference, "I will be evasive," as he in fact was.

Not only Eisenhower's claims of ignorance and ambiguous language, but also his fractured syntax led 1950s observers to deprecate his professional skills and, for that matter, his intelligence. Prudential calculation and personal style conspired to produce the garbled phrases quoted in so many writings drawing on Eisenhower's press conference utterances. The element of calculation is portrayed by Eisenhower in his memoirs, where he discusses the intra-administration objection to his decisions to release transcripts and later tapes on the ground that "an inadvertent misstatement in public would be a calamity." He explains that, "by consistently focusing on ideas rather than on phrasing, I was able to avoid causing the nation a serious setback through anything I said in many hours, over eight years, of intensive questioning."

The element of style involved a personal trait Eisenhower was well aware of, namely his tendency in spontaneous discourse to ramble and to stop and start. This trait derived from his tendency to have more ideas than he could readily convert into orderly sentences. Interestingly, in the absence of an audience waiting to seize upon controversial misstatements, he could dictate lengthy letters of noteworthy clarity. In press conferences, wary of misstatement and prone to a conversational mode of sputtering, he continually edited his discourse while talking. Overall, both the calculated and unintentional aspects of Eisenhower's press conference style had the same effect as his approach to delegation of authority: they damaged his reputation among the political cognoscenti, but protected his options as a decision maker and insulated him from blame by the wider public for controversial or potentially controversial utterances and actions.

Speech writing and editing were hardly novel experiences to Eisenhower when he entered partisan politics. For a number of the interwar years he had been speech writer for none other than Douglas MacArthur. His Post-V-E Day Guild Hall speech in London had received wide acclaim for its eloquence. In view of this background, it should come as no surprise that as president, Eisenhower devoted great attention to his speeches. Mrs. Whitman estimates that twenty to thirty hours of the president's time, with much intervening response by speech writers, was spent on any speech of consequence.

The president's comments on the first draft of his 1954 State of the Union Message, of which thirty-eight were specific and four overarching, will serve to demonstrate his markups and insertions. The specific comments included two kinds of word changes and instructions to insert new paragraphs (which he dictated). The major purpose of one kind of Eisenhower's changes was to simplify language, striving to make the speeches more persuasive to the segment of the population to which he thought the Republican party ought to extend its appeal—members of normally Democratic population groups, such as white-collar workers and people who had completed high school but had not gone to college. To this end, Eisenhower eliminated phrases such as "substantial reductions in size and cost of Federal government" and "attacks on deficit financing," on the ground that the "man we are trying to reach" understands usages such as "purchasing power of the dollar" and stability "in the size of his market basket." Hence it was neither an accident nor an indicator of Eisenhower's own verbal limitations that when contrasted with the high-culture rhetoric of the principal Democratic spokesman of the time, Adlai Stevenson, Eisenhower's utterances seemed banal.

The second kind of change, editing with a view to perfecting diction and step-by-step progression of the exposition, probably was not necessary for rhetorical effectiveness with the general public. It was consistent with an enduring aspect of Eisenhower's cognitive style, namely intellectual precision. His demand for logical, carefully organized presentations is exemplified in the overarching recommendations concerning his 1954 message that he made to speech writer Bryce Harlow. They are the sort of recommendations one expects from experienced teachers of English composition: "Use blue pencil"; reexamine the structure of presentation by thinking through the sequence in which the paragraphs are put; "sections need to be more distinctly marked. Do not be afraid to say 'I come now to so-and-so'. . . . you cannot take the human mind from subject to subject . . . as quickly [as the present draft of this speech has attempted to do]." An illustration of the many suggestions for more precise diction is the instruction, accompanied by its rationale, to change a statement from "confidence has developed" to "constantly increasing confidence" in order to make clear that a "continuing action" is being described. (Eisenhower ranked tenth in his West Point class in English composition.)

Eisenhower's correspondence ranges from "personal and confidential" letters, many of which are quite long, to brief memoranda to aides and administration officials. In the long, confidential communications, the prose is crisp, the phrasing elaborate, and the reasoning logical and clear. It is remarkable that these highly focused letters were usually dictated in one draft that required little editing.

One such communication is a four-page, single-spaced, "eyes only" memorandum dated September 21, 1953, to Walter Bedell Smith (then under secretary of state), concerning the defection of and subsequent award of bounty to a North Korean pilot who supplied the United Nations forces with a MIG aircraft. The gist of the episode is that defectors were no longer wanted, for as a result of recent defections of pilots in Europe there was nothing more to learn technically from a MIG plane. Eisenhower's concern was with the impact of the response by the United States on world propaganda. He had gone along with his advisers' proposal and the government had paid the bounty, kept the plane (in order to justify paying the bounty), and canceled the offer.

Eisenhower agreed that the bounty had to be paid and that the offer should be canceled. But he believed that the United States also should propose to return the plane, since a propaganda victory would attend that course of action—for the United States would be able "to stand before the world as a very honorable people, maintaining that while we had not been guilty of a real violation of the Armistice, we were anxious to avoid any implication of violating the spirit." The style and approach taken in the letter is more relevant in the present context than is the episode itself (a trivial way-station in the cold war).

In the memorandum, Eisenhower musters an orderly series of arguments that weigh the pros, cons, and probabilities of international propaganda gains against those of possible difficulties in justifying the action to the American people and of failing to take advantage of an opportunity to weaken the North Korean Air Force. In systematic progression, he considers fall-back positions the policymakers might take, depending upon anticipated responses to their initial actions. For example, if there is domestic criticism, he suggests that it be asserted that since the plane was inspected before it was returned, the United States was able to learn whether any recent changes in MIG design have been made. (Incidentally, several days after his memorandum was dispatched, the United States did offer to return the plane.)

Unlike the fairly long memoranda such as the one to Bedell Smith, much of Eisenhower's correspondence to aides and administration officials is quite brief, conveying suggestions or information rather than elaborate arguments. For instance, Eisenhower's comments on and proposed changes in drafts of his aides' letters and speeches were often phrased as polite suggestions or ideas he wanted his colleagues to consider, rather than as commands. Nonetheless, they appear to have been understood as directions, not suggestions. The passage that follows, an attempt to soften the dour tone of a Dulles speech draft, exemplifies the correspondence under consideration here.

> I have read the draft of your talk to the CIO and I must say that, in general, I enthusiastically approve. The suggestions that follow may have sufficient validity that you will want to consider them briefly:
>
> I. On page 6, at the point marked, I suggest that it might be well to expand your idea a little bit, somewhat as follows: "Based upon this clear understanding, the present Administration believes that the formulation and execution of a clear, positive, and effective American foreign policy are impossible except as it is presented against a background of American prosperity, well-being, and opportunity that extends from the most to the least fortunate among us. Specifically and concretely, this Administration is committed to the development of policies that will bring the greatest good to the greatest number. This means that appropriate governmental connection with our entire economy must be so adjusted as to develop and sustain a prosperous agriculture, manufacturing, and services, and above all such an equitable distribution of the resulting products that 60 million people will constitute always the finest advertisement for freedom." [Eisenhower makes four other suggestions and concludes], if any of the above suggestions prove helpful, I shall be pleased. If not, throw them away with a clear conscience.

Dulles revised the speech, incorporating Eisenhower's five proposed changes.

Eisenhower the Hawk

ARTHUR M. SCHLESINGER, JR.

Eisenhower never sank so low as [Herbert] Hoover in the esteem of historians, but his comeback has been still more impressive. The fashion in the 1980s is to regard Hoover rather as Hoover himself regarded Prohibition—"a great social and economic experiment, noble in motive and far-reaching in purpose." He is seen as a deep social thinker but as a failed statesman. Eisenhower, on the other hand, has come with time to be seen as above all a successful statesman. The year after he left office, historians and political scientists in my father's poll of 1962 rated him twenty-second among American Presidents. In a poll taken by Steve Neal of the *Chicago Tribune* twenty years later, Eisenhower rose to ninth place. In Professor Robert K. Murray's poll the next year he finished eleventh. (Hoover meanwhile, despite revisionist ardor, dropped from nineteenth in 1962 to twenty-first in 1982 and 1983 polls.)

There are obvious reasons for Eisenhower's upward mobility. At the

From *The Cycles of American History*, 387–90, 392–395, 398–405, by Arthur M. Schlesinger, Jr. Copyright © 1986 by Arthur M. Schlesinger, Jr. Reprinted by permission of Houghton Mifflin Company.

time the 1950s seemed an era of slumber and stagnation, the bland leading the bland. After intervening years of schism and hysteria, the Eisenhower age appears in nostalgic retrospect a blessed decade of peace and harmony. Moreover, the successive faults of Eisenhower's successors—Kennedy's activism, Johnson's obsessions, Nixon's crookedness, Ford's mediocrity, Carter's blah, Reagan's ideology—have given his virtues new value. Historians should not overlook the capacity of Presidents to do more for the reputations of their predecessors than for their own. The final impetus was provided by the swing of the political cycle back to the private-interest mood of Eisenhower's own Presidency.

The opening of the papers in the Eisenhower Library in Abilene, Kansas, has speeded the revaluation by placing his character in striking new light. When he was President, most Americans cherished him as the national hero reigning benignly in the White House, a wise, warm, avuncular man who grinned a lot and kept the country calm and safe. His critics, whom he routed in two presidential elections, saw him as an old duffer who neglected his job, tripped up in his syntax, read Westerns, played golf and bridge with millionaires and let strong associates run the country in his name, a "captive hero." Both views assumed his kindness of heart and benevolence of spirit.

The Eisenhower papers powerfully suggest that the pose of guileless affability was a deliberate put-on and that behind the masquerade an astute leader moved purposefully to achieve his objectives. Far from being an openhearted lover of mankind, Eisenhower now appears a wily fellow, calculating, crafty and unerringly self-protective. Far from being a political innocent, he was a politician of the first water, brilliantly exploiting the popular illusion that he was above politics. Far from being an amiable bumbler, he feigned his incoherence to conceal his purposes. Far from being passive and uninterested, he had large and vigorous concerns about public policy.

The man who emerges, for example, from *The Eisenhower Diaries* is shrewd, confident and masterful. He is hard and cold in his judgment of his associates. Some entries reveal the famous Eisenhower temper. ("One thing that might help win this war is to get someone to shoot King," he wrote in 1942 about the imperious Chief of Naval Operations.) Others betray, while denying, his ambition. Occasional passages of ponderous philosophizing read as if they had been carefully indited for posterity.

We thought at the time that he lacked political experience. How wrong we were! Politics has few tougher training schools than the United States Army. Eisenhower, who began as a protégé of General MacArthur and then rose to eminence as a protégé of MacArthur's detested rival, General Marshall, was obviously endowed with consummate political talent. His later skill as President in distancing himself from his unpopular party infuriated Republican professionals but testified to his dazzling instinct for survival.

We must assume now that, however muddled he often appeared, Eisenhower knew perfectly what he was up to most of the time—not least when he encouraged his fellow citizens to think of him as (Good Old) Ike.

Once, when the State Department pleaded with him to say nothing in a press conference about the then explosive question of Quemoy and Matsu, the besieged islands off the coast of China, he told James Hagerty, his press secretary "Don't worry Jim, if that question comes up, I'll just confuse them." He confused us all. As Richard Nixon put it, Eisenhower was "a far more complex and devious man than most people realized, and in the best sense of those words."

Martin Van Buren, John Randolph of Roanoke once said, "rowed to his object with muffled oars." Phrased less elegantly, this is Fred I. Greenstein's thesis in his influential study of Eisenhower's administrative techniques. Greenstein ascribes six "political strategies" to Eisenhower—"hidden-hand" leadership; "instrumental"—i.e., manipulative—use of language; refusal to engage in personalities; taking action nevertheless on the basis of private personality analysis; selective delegation; and building public support. While the author concedes that these strategies were hardly exclusive to Eisenhower, the loving care with which they are described gives the impression of attributing uniquely to Eisenhower practices that are the stock in trade of political leaders. Thus: "Eisenhower ran organizations by deliberately making simultaneous use of both formal and informal organizations." What President does not?

I do not think that Greenstein fully considers the implications of a "hidden-hand Presidency." For in a democracy, politics must be in the end an educational process, resting above all on persuasion and consent. The Presidency in Franklin D. Roosevelt's words, is "preeminently a place of moral leadership." The hidden-hand Presidency represents an abdication of the preeminent presidential role. The concept is even a little unjust to Eisenhower, who was not entirely averse to using the Presidency as a pulpit.

On the whole, however, as his political confidant Arthur Larson later wrote, "He simply did not believe that the President should exploit his influence as a dominant national figure to promote good causes that were not within his constitutional function as Chief Executive." In consequence, Larson regretfully continued, Eisenhower denied the country the "desperately needed . . . educational guidance and moral inspiration that a President with a deep personal commitment to the promotion of human rights could supply." Larson was talking about civil rights. His point applies equally to civil liberties.

Racial justice and McCarthyism were the great moral issues of the Eisenhower years. Eisenhower evaded them both. This may be in part because of his severely constricted theory of the Presidency. But it was partly too because Eisenhower did not see them as compelling issues. He did not like to use law to enforce racial integration, and, while he disliked McCarthy's manners and methods, he basically agreed with his objectives. His failure, as his biographer Stephen E. Ambrose has said, "to speak out directly on McCarthy encouraged the witch-hunters, just as his failure to speak out directly on the *Brown v. Topeka* [school integration] decision encouraged the segregationists." It can be added that Eisenhower's failure to speak out directly on the Pentagon, at least before his Farewell Address, encouraged the advocates of the arms race.

Yet, whatever his defects as a public leader, we may stipulate that behind the scene Eisenhower showed more energy, interest, purpose, cunning and command than many of us understood in the 1950s; that he was the dominant figure in his administration whenever he wanted to be (and he wanted to be more often than it seemed at the time); and that the very talent for self-protection that led him to hide behind his reputation for muddle and to shove associates into the line of fire obscured his considerable capacity for decision and control. . . .

It is on his handling of the problems of peace and war that Eisenhower's enhanced reputation rests. Robert A. Divine conveniently sums up the case for "a badly underrated President" in his *Eisenhower and the Cold War* (1981):

> For eight years he kept the United States at peace, adroitly avoiding military involvement in the crises of the 1950s. Six months after taking office, he brought the fighting in Korea to an end; in Indochina, he resisted intense pressure to avoid direct American military intervention; in Suez, he courageously aligned the United States against European imperialism while maintaining a staunch posture toward the Soviet Union. He earnestly sought a reduction in Cold War tensions.

Professor Divine draws a particular contrast with his predecessor, claiming that the demands of foreign policy outran Truman's ability and that the result was "overreaction and tragedy for the nation and the world."

In fact, Eisenhower thought that Truman underreacted to the Soviet menace. "In the fiscal years, 1947, 1948, 1949, and 1950," Eisenhower wrote in his diary the day after his inauguration, "the defense fabric continued to shrink at an alarming extent—and this in spite of frequent . . . warnings that people like Jim Forrestal had been expressing time and time again." Forrestal had been Eisenhower's mentor regarding the "threat by the monolithic mass of communistic imperialism." When Forrestal killed himself in 1949, Eisenhower recalled their talks in 1945 about the Russians: "He insisted they hated us, which I had good reason to believe myself. I still do." In May 1953 Eisenhower complained to the legislative leaders that Truman "had let our armed forces dwindle after World War II and had thus invited the attack on Korea."

Revisionists exalt Eisenhower not only over his predecessor but over his successor as well, contrasting Eisenhower's conciliatoriness with Kennedy's alleged bellicosity. N. S. Khrushchev, who was perhaps in a better position to judge, offers a different assessment. "If I had to compare the two American presidents with whom I dealt—Eisenhower and Kennedy—" Khrushchev tells us in his memoirs, "the comparison would not be in favor of Eisenhower. . . . I had no cause for regret once Kennedy became President. It quickly became clear he understood better than Eisenhower that an improvement in relations was the only rational course. . . . He impressed me as a better statesman than Eisenhower."

Winston Churchill stands high on the revisionist hit list of Cold War villains. But Churchill knew Eisenhower well and when he heard that Eisenhower had defeated Adlai Stevenson in 1952 told his wartime private secretary John Colville: "For your private ear, I am greatly disturbed. I think this makes war much more probable." After Stalin's death in March 1953, the new Soviet regime signaled in various ways, as in the Austrian treaty negotiations, interest in the relaxation of tensions. Churchill, now Prime Minister again, rightly or wrongly perceived a major change in Soviet policy. "A new hope," he wrote Eisenhower, "has been created in the unhappy, bewildered world." "If we fail to strive to seize this moment's precious chances," he wrote in a Top Secret minute, "the judgement of future ages would be harsh and just." Churchill was now an old man (seventy-nine), but he had been around, and his thoughts deserved at least as much respect as those of John Foster Dulles. Eisenhower, who had decided that Churchill was gaga, took the Dulles line. Churchill, Colville noted in his diary, was "very disappointed in Eisenhower whom he thinks both weak and stupid."

When Eisenhower and Churchill met in Bermuda in December 1953, Churchill argued that the policy of strength toward the Soviet Union should be combined with the hand of friendship. "Ike followed," Colville recorded, "with a short, very violent statement in the coarsest terms." As regards the Prime Minister's belief that there was a new look in Soviet policy, Eisenhower said, "Russia was a woman of the streets and whether her dress was new, or just the old one patched, it was certainly the same whore underneath. America intended to drive her off her present 'beat' into the back streets." Colville wrote: "I doubt if such language has ever before been heard at an international conference. Pained looks all round."

Eisenhower fully accepted the premises of the Cold War. He appointed the high priest of the Cold War as his Secretary of State. He allowed Dulles to appease Joe McCarthy, to purge the Foreign Service, to construct a network of military pacts around the globe and to preach interminably about godless communism and going to the brink and massive retaliation. Lord Salisbury, the quintessential British Tory and a leading figure in the Churchill cabinet, found Eisenhower in 1953 "violently Russophobe, greatly more so than Dulles," and believed him "personally responsible for the policy of useless pinpricks and harassing tactics the U.S. is following against Russia in Europe and the Far East."

Eisenhower's superiority to the other Cold War Presidents, revisionists argue, lay not in the premises of policy but in the "prudence" with which he conducted the struggle. It is true that, as a former general, Eisenhower was uniquely equipped among recent Presidents to override the national security establishment. Convinced that excessive government spending and deficits would wreck the economy, he kept the defense budget under control. He knew too much about war to send regular troops into combat lightly, especially on unpromising Third World terrain. Perhaps for this as well as for budgetary reasons—nuclear weapons cost less than large conventional forces—he contrived a military posture that made it almost impossible for the United States to fight anything short of nuclear war.

The doctrine of massive retaliation left the United States the choice, when confronted by local aggression in a distant land, of dropping the bomb or doing nothing. Eisenhower's critics feared he would drop the bomb. Most of the time his preference was for doing nothing—not always a bad attitude in foreign affairs. When the Democrats took over in 1961, they briskly increased conventional forces. Their theory was that enlarging the capability to fight limited wars would reduce the risk of nuclear war. The result was the creation of forces that enabled and emboldened us to Americanize the war in Vietnam. Had the Eisenhower all-or-nothing strategy survived, we might have escaped that unmitigated disaster. Or we might have had something far worse.

Eisenhower's budgetary concerns—"a bigger bang for a buck"—and his skepticism about the regular Army and Navy also had their disadvantages. They led him to rely exceptionally, and dangerously, on unconventional forms of coercive power: upon the covert operations of the Central Intelligence Agency, and upon nuclear weapons. . . .

We are sensitive these days about the limitless horror of nuclear war. Revisionist historians condemn Truman for his allegedly unrepentant decision to drop the bomb in 1945. In fact, Truman behaved like a man much shaken by the decision. He had directed that the bomb be used "so that military objectives . . . are the target and not women and children," and he was considerably disturbed when he learned that most of those killed at Hiroshima were civilians.

The day after Nagasaki he ordered that further atomic bombing be stopped. He told his cabinet, as Henry Wallace recorded in his diary that "the thought of wiping out another 100,000 people was too horrible. He didn't like the idea of killing, as he said, 'all those kids.' " 'After the cabinet meeting he remarked to Wallace that he had had bad headaches every day. Four months later, when the question came up at cabinet as to how many atomic bombs there were, Truman said that he didn't really want to know.

Nor did he press the production of bombs in the next years. The best estimates of the number of bombs stockpiled in early 1948 range from less than six to two dozen. When the Secretary of the Army proposed using the bomb to break the Soviet blockade of Berlin, Truman told him, "You have got to understand that this isn't a military weapon. It is used to wipe out women and children and unarmed people, and not for military use. So we have to treat this differently from rifles and cannon and ordinary things like that." At the worst moment of the Korean War, when the Red Chinese were storming down the Korean peninsula, Truman remarked in casual answer to a press conference question that the United States would employ "every weapon" to end the war. But in fact the Joint Chiefs of Staff (though, as always, it had contingency plans) never recommended the use of the bomb, and Truman, as Gregg Herken writes, "consistently refused to be stampeded by the bad news from Korea into a precipitous decision on its use in the Far East. Reflecting about Korea in 1954, Truman wrote in a private memorandum that, to be effective, the bomb would have had to be used against China. Distinguishing the Korean case from ending the war against Japan, he wrote, "I could not bring myself to order the slaughter of 25,000,000 noncombatants. . . . I know I was *right*."

Revisionist historians are similarly severe in condemning Kennedy for running the risk of nuclear war to get the Soviet missiles out of Cuba in 1962. They seem strangely unconcerned, however, that Eisenhower used the threat of nuclear war far more often than any other American President has done, before or since. Nuclear blackmail was indeed the almost inevitable consequence of the military posture dictated by "massive retaliation." It is said in his defense that Eisenhower used the threat in a context of American nuclear superiority that minimized the risk. But the same condition of nuclear superiority prevailed for, and must equally absolve, Truman and Kennedy.

Eisenhower began by invoking the nuclear threat to end the fighting in Korea. He let the Chinese know, he later told Lyndon Johnson, that "he would not feel constrained about crossing the Yalu, or using nuclear weapons." Probably the effectiveness of this threat has been exaggerated. The Chinese had compelling reasons of their own to get out of the war. The decisive shift in their position away from the forced repatriation of prisoners of war took place, as McGeorge Bundy has pointed out, after the death of Stalin in March 1953—and before Eisenhower sent his signals to Peking. In May 1953 General J. Lawton Collins, the Army Chief of Staff, declared himself "very skeptical about the value of using atomic weapons tactically in Korea." Eisenhower replied that "it might be cheaper, dollar-wise, to use atomic weapons in Korea than to continue to use conventional weapons." If the Chinese persisted, "it would be necessary to expand the war outside of Korea and . . . to use the atomic bomb." In December Eisenhower said that, if the Chinese attacked again, "we should certainly respond by hitting them hard and wherever it would hurt most, including Peiping itself. This . . . would mean all-out war." A joint memorandum from the State Department and the Joint Chiefs of Staff called for the use of atomic weapons against military targets in Korea, Manchuria and China.

The next crisis came in 1954 in Vietnam. In March, according to Divine, Eisenhower was "briefly tempted" by the idea of American intervention, refusing, as he put it, to "exclude the possibility of a single [air] strike, if it were almost certain this would produce decisive results. . . . Of course, if we did, we'd have to deny it forever." As envisaged by General Twining of the Air Force and Admiral Radford, the strike would involve three atomic bombs. Opposition by Congress and by the British killed the idea. Whether this was Eisenhower's hope when he permitted Dulles to carry the air strike proposal to London remains obscure. It was at this time that he propounded what he called "the 'falling domino' principle . . . a beginning of a disintegration that would have the most profound influences," a disintegration that, he said, could lead to the loss of Indochina, then Burma, then Thailand,

Malaya, Indonesia, then Japan, Formosa and the Philippines. This theory of the future entrapped Eisenhower's successors in the quicksands of Vietnam. The dominos did indeed fall in Indochina, as we all know now. But, with communist China invading communist Vietnam because communist Vietnam had invaded communist Cambodia, the dominos fell against each other, not against the United States.

Whatever Eisenhower's intentions regarding Vietnam, he definitely endorsed in May 1954 the recommendation by the Joint Chiefs to use atomic bombs in case of Chinese intervention if Congress and allies agreed. "The concept" in the event of a large-scale Vietminh attack, Dulles said in October, "envisions a fight with nuclear weapons rather than the commitment of ground forces."

Eisenhower tried nuclear blackmail again during the Quemoy-Matsu crisis of 1955. In March of that year Dulles publicly threatened the use of atomic weapons. Eisenhower added the next day in his press conference, "I see no reason why they shouldn't be used just exactly as you would use a bullet or anything else." In the 1958 replay of the Quemoy-Matsu drama, Dulles said that American intervention would probably not be effective if limited to conventional weapons; "the risk of a more extensive use of nuclear weapons, and even of general war, would have to be accepted." "There [is] no use of having stuff," Dulles remarked over the phone to General Twining, "and never being able to use it."

"The beauty of Eisenhower's policy," Divine writes with regard to Quemoy and Matsu, "is that to this day no one can be sure whether or not . . . he would have used nuclear weapons." Nuclear blackmail may strike some as the beauty part, though we did not use to think so when Khrushchev tried it. In Eisenhower's case it was associated with an extraordinary effort to establish the legitimacy of nuclear war. One restraint on the use of the bomb was the opposition of American allies and of world opinion. This resistance Eisenhower was determined to overcome. As Dulles told the National Security Council on 31 March 1953, while "in the present state of world opinion we could not use an A-bomb, we should make every effort now to dissipate this feeling." The minutes of the meeting add: "The President and Secretary Dulles were in complete agreement that somehow or other the tabu which surrounds the use of atomic weapons would have to be destroyed."

Eisenhower's campaign to legitimate the bomb appalled America's British ally. In their Bermuda meeting Eisenhower sought Winston Churchill's support for nuclear war if the Korean truce broke down. Churchill sent Jock Colville to Eisenhower with a message of concern. According to Colville's notes on the meeting, Eisenhower said "that whereas Winston looked on the atomic bomb as something entirely new and terrible, he looked upon it as just the latest improvement in military weapons. He implied that there was no distinction between 'conventional weapons' and atomic weapons: all weapons in due course become conventional." Colville wrote later, "I could hardly believe my ears." In his diaries Eisenhower portrays the Churchill of the 1950s as on the verge of senility. The old man made a good deal of sense at Bermuda.

The British were no happier the next year when Eisenhower asked their support for intervention in Vietnam. Churchill, who had received a long letter from Eisenhower lecturing him about Munich and the dangers of appeasement, was unmoved. "What we were being asked to do," he said to his Foreign Secretary, "was to assist in misleading Congress into approving a military operation, which would in itself be ineffective, and might well bring the world to the verge of a major war." He told Admiral Radford that the British, having let India go, were not about to give their lives to keep Indochina for France. "I have known many reverses myself," he said. "I have not given in. I have suffered Singapore, Hong Kong, Tobruk; the French will have Dien Bien Phu." The Indochina War, he said, could only be won by using "that horrible thing," the atomic bomb. Eisenhower was enraged.

In December 1954 Eisenhower ordered the Atomic Energy Commission to relinquish control of nuclear weapons to the Department of Defense. At the same time, he ordered Defense to deploy overseas a large share of the nuclear arsenal—36 percent of the hydrogen bombs, 42 percent of the atomic bombs—many on the periphery of the Soviet Union. The movement of American policy continued to disturb our British allies.

According to the official minutes, Lord Salisbury told the cabinet in this period, "Some believed that the greatest threat to world peace came from Russians. He [Salisbury] himself believed that the greater risk was that the United States might decide to bring the East-West issue to a head while they still had overwhelming superiority in atomic weapons."

Nor were the British happier when Eisenhower argued in 1955 for nuclear weapons in defense of Quemoy and Matsu. The British Chiefs of Staff, according to Harold Macmillan, saw "no purpose in it" and rejected Eisenhower's contention "that the smaller explosions produced no fallout. . . . [British Foreign Minister Anthony] Eden and I proposed a firm line in opposition to the American argument." (Why one must ask parenthetically do Eisenhower revisionists write about his foreign policy almost exclusively from American sources?)

Eisenhower's persevering effort was to abolish the "firebreak" between conventional and nuclear weapons. Fortunately for the world, this effort failed. By 1964 nearly everyone agreed with Lyndon Johnson when he said, "Make no mistake. There is no such thing as a conventional nuclear weapon."

In his first years in the White House, Eisenhower regarded nuclear attack as a usable military option. He hoped to destroy the taboo preventing the use of nuclear weapons. But in fact he never used them. As Ambrose points out, "Five times in one year [1954] the experts advised the President to launch an atomic strike against China. Five times he said no." His campaign to legitimate the bomb was happily only a passing phase.

As the Soviet Union increased its nuclear arsenal, Eisenhower came to believe more and more strongly in the horror of nuclear war. The outlook was ever closer, he said in 1956, "to destruction of the enemy and suicide for ourselves." When both sides recognized that "destruction will be reciprocal and complete, possibly we will have sense enough to meet at the conference table with the understanding that the era of armaments has ended and the human race must conform its actions to this truth or die."

For all his early talk about the "same old whore," Eisenhower now sought better relations with the Soviet Union. As Sherman Adams, Eisenhower's chief of staff on domestic matters, later observed, "The hard and uncompromising line that the United States government took toward Soviet Russia and Red China between 1953 and the early months of 1959 was more a Dulles line than an Eisenhower line." But Dulles retained his uses for Eisenhower, both in frightening the Russians and in enabling the President to reserve for himself the role of man of peace.

In his later mood, Eisenhower strove, less anxiously than Churchill and later Macmillan but a good deal more anxiously than Dulles, to meet the Russians at the conference table. In 1953 at the United Nations he set forth his Atoms for Peace plan, by which the nuclear powers would contribute fissionable materials to an International Atomic Energy Agency to promote peaceful uses of atomic energy. This well-intentioned but feckless proposal assumed that atoms for peace could be segregated from atoms for war— an assumption abundantly refuted in later years and the cause of dangerous nuclear proliferation in our own time. In 1955 at the Geneva summit he came up with a better idea, the creative Open Skies plan. A system of continuous reciprocal monitoring, Eisenhower argued, would reduce fears of surprise attack. The Russians turned Open Skies down as an American espionage scheme. Open Skies was a good idea; it deserves revival. In his second term, against the opposition of many in his own administration, Eisenhower fitfully pursued the project of a nuclear test ban.

He resented the mounting pressure from the Democrats and from the Pentagon to accelerate the American nuclear build-up. The Pentagon did not impress him. He knew all the tricks, having employed them himself. He used to say that he "knew too much about the military to be fooled." He refused to be panicked by perennial Pentagon alarms about how we were falling behind the Russians and dismissed the 'missile gap' of the late 1950s with richly justified skepticism.

Yet he weakly allowed the build-up to proceed. In 1959 he complained that the Pentagon, after agreeing a few years earlier that hitting seventy key targets would knock out the Soviet system, now insisted on hitting thousands of targets. The military, he said, were getting "themselves into an incredible position—of having enough to destroy every conceivable target all over the world, plus a threefold reserve." The radioactivity from atomic blasts at this level, he said, would destroy the United States too. The United States already had a stockpile of "five thousand or seven thousand weapons or whatnot." Why did the Atomic Energy Commission and the Department of Defense want more? "But then," writes Ambrose, "he reluctantly gave way to the AEC and DOD demands."

In 1960, when informed at a National Security Council meeting that the United States could produce almost 400 Minuteman missiles a year, Eisenhower with "obvious disgust" (according to his science adviser George Kistiakowsky) burst out, "Why don't we go completely crazy and plan on a force of 10,000?" The nuclear arsenal had now grown to a level that the Eisenhower of 1954 had considered "fantastic," "crazy" and "unconscionable." There were approximately 1000 nuclear warheads when Eisenhower entered the White House, 18,000 when he left.

For all his concern about nuclear war, for all his skepticism about the Pentagon, for all the unique advantage he enjoyed as General of the Armies in commanding confidence on defense issues, he never seized control of the military-industrial complex. "Being only one person," he lamely explained, he had not felt he could oppose the "combined opinion of all his associates." In the measured judgment of the Regius Professor of History at Oxford, the military historian Michael Howard, "The combination of his constant professions of devotion to disarmament and peace with his reluctance to take any of the harsh decisions required to achieve those professed objectives leaves an impression, if not of hypocrisy, then certainly of an ultimate lack of will which, again, denies him a place in the first rank of world statesmen."

Though Eisenhower carefully avoided war himself, he was surprisingly bellicose in his advice to his successors. He told Kennedy before the inauguration not only to go full speed ahead on the exile invasion of Cuba but, if necessary, "to intervene unilaterally" in Laos. So bent was Eisenhower on American intervention in Laos that Kennedy persuaded Macmillan to explain to him in detail the folly of such an adventure. When Vietnam became the issue in the mid-1960s, Eisenhower advised Lyndon Johnson to avoid gradualism, "go all out," declare war, seek victory, not negotiations, warn China and the Soviet Union, as Eisenhower himself had done over Korea, that the United States might feel compelled to use nuclear weapons to break the deadlock, and, if the Chinese actually came in, "to use at least tactical atomic weapons." The antiwar protest, Eisenhower declared, "verges on treason." When Johnson announced in 1968 that he was stopping most of the bombing of North Vietnam, Eisenhower, Ambrose writes, "was livid with anger, his remarks [to Ambrose] about Johnson's cutting and running unprintable." Eisenhower was more a hawk than a prince of peace.

"It would perhaps have been better for him, as in the last century for Wellington and Grant," Sir John Colville concludes, "if he had rested on his military laurels." Walter Lippmann remarked in 1964 that Eisenhower's was "one of the most falsely inflated reputations of my experience"—and he was speaking before the inflation was underway. In later years the Eisenhower boom has gathered momentum in cyclical response to a need and a time.

In due course the pendulum will doubtless swing back toward the view of Eisenhower presented in the illuminating early memoirs by men close to him—Sherman Adams's *Firsthand Report* (1961), Emmet Hughes's *The Ordeal of Power* (1963), Arthur Larson's *Eisenhower: The President Nobody Knew* (1968). In these works of direct observation, Eisenhower emerges as a man of intelligence, force and restraint who did not always understand and control what was going on, was buffeted by events and was capable of misjudgment and error. I lunched with Emmet Hughes in 1981. "Eisenhower was much more of a President than you liberals thought at the time," he said. "But Eisenhower revisionism has gone too far. Take Fred Greenstein of Princeton, for example. He is a nice fellow. But his thesis these days— Eisenhower the activist President—is a lot of bullshit."

Yet we were wrong to have underestimated Eisenhower's genius for self-presentation and self-preservation—the best evidence of which lies in his capacity to take in a generation of scholars.

Eisenhower's Failure in the Third World

ROBERT J. MCMAHON

Within the past decade, revisionism about Dwight D. Eisenhower's presidency has become a veritable cottage industry. A torrent of books and articles has already appeared—with many more undoubtedly on the way—that have forced a major reassessment of the Eisenhower presidency, and especially of its foreign policy. According to the new literature, the former image of the popular general as an amiable but bumbling leader who presided over the "great postponement" of critical national and international issues during the 1950s can no longer be sustained by the evidence. On the contrary, writes one historian, he was "intelligent, decisive, and perceptive, a strong leader who guided his administration with a deft hand and a president who led his nation peacefully through eight tortuous years of Cold War." In the words of another scholar: "He now appears to be a more astute and more sophisticated politician, a stronger and more concerned chief executive, a more successful president both in domestic and foreign affairs, a more prescient and imaginative leader and a more energetic, perceptive, and compassionate person." Certainly the new scholarship on Eisenhower is not uncritical, nor is it unanimous in its judgments on the various facets of the administration's record. Nonetheless, there does appear to be a consensus developing on the part of the majority of the new Eisenhower scholars that, at least within the realm of foreign affairs, Eisenhower must rank as one of the most skilled and probably the most successful of all the postwar presidents.

Fueled by a combination of new sources and fresh perspectives, revisionist accounts of the Eisenhower presidency have challenged earlier studies on two broad grounds: first, the Eisenhower revisionists have portrayed the general, in the words of one scholar, as a "skilled tactician and a master of his administration"; and, second, they have argued that his foreign policy was astute, restrained, and largely successful. The two contentions, of

Robert J. McMahon, "Eisenhower and Third World Nationalism: A Critique of the Revisionists." Reprinted with permission from *Political Science Quarterly* 101, no. 3 (1986), 453–73.

course, deal with separate issues and are often advanced by scholars with different sets of interests.

Given the weight of evidence presented by the Eisenhower revisionists, the first contention now appears virtually unassailable. Robert Ferrell's wry remark in his introduction to the *Eisenhower Diaries* [1981] that "the general-president knew what he was doing" aptly captures the new consensus. As Richard H. Immerman has persuasively argued, contrary to the conventional wisdom Eisenhower exercised strong executive control in foreign affairs, often reining in his bombastic secretary of state. Even Arthur M. Schlesinger, Jr., hardly a sympathetic observer, concedes that "the Eisenhower papers . . . unquestionably alter the old picture. . . . Eisenhower showed much more energy, interest, self-confidence, purpose, cunning, and command than many of us supposed in the 1950s."

These new revelations about Eisenhower's leadership capabilities and uses of presidential power have added an important dimension to our understanding of the man and his presidency. Despite the intrinsic value of such work, however, it has serious limitations for the student of American foreign relations. For those interested in examining the goals and results of American diplomacy during the 1950s, the preoccupation with the decision-making process appears at best peripheral. This debate focuses on the means of presidential leadership, not the ends. As Fred I. Greenstein concedes in his acclaimed book, *The Hidden-Hand Presidency* [1982], his interest is exclusively in Ike's style of leadership—which he admires—and not with the president's aims and accomplishments.

The second contention, involving longer-term perspectives and more intricate standards of evaluation, has inevitably sparked more controversy. Do Eisenhower's accomplishments in foreign affairs place him in the first rank among postwar presidents? Despite inevitable differences on particulars, the revisionists are virtually unanimous in applauding Ike's consistent exercise of mature judgment, prudence, and restraint and in celebrating his signal accomplishment of maintaining peace during an unusually perilous period in international relations.

Robert Divine has ably summarized the revisionist perspective in his recent book, *Eisenhower and the Cold War* [1981]. "The essence of Eisenhower's strength," Divine writes, "and the basis for any claim to presidential greatness, lies in his admirable self-restraint. . . . Nearly all of Eisenhower's foreign policy achievements were negative in nature. He ended the Korean War, he refused to intervene militarily in Indochina, he refrained from involving the United States in the Suez crisis, he avoided war with China over Quemoy and Matsu, he resisted the temptation to force a showdown over Berlin, he stopped exploding nuclear weapons in the atmosphere. . . . His moderation and prudence served as an enduring model of presidential restraint—one that his successors ignored to their eventual regret. Tested by a world as dangerous as any that an American leader has ever faced, Eisenhower used his sound judgment and instinctive common sense to guide the nation safely through the first decade of the thermonuclear age."

Despite the general consensus among Eisenhower revisionists on the success of his diplomacy, these scholars have been curiously ambivalent on one major topic: the efficacy of Eisenhower's approach to the emerging nations of the Third World. As Robert Divine's examples—Korea, Indochina, Suez, the Taiwan Straits—would suggest, the wisdom of the President's policies toward the Third World constitutes an important element in the favorable assessment of at least some historians. To the litany of achievements cited by Divine, moreover, other scholars have added the limited but effective use of force to help overthrow unfriendly governments in Iran and Guatemala and to help prop up a friendly one in Lebanon. Other Eisenhower scholars, however, including Peter Lyon, Charles C. Alexander, and Stephen E. Ambrose, have criticized the President's handling of certain Third World problems. They have nonetheless concluded their evaluations by praising the President's overall diplomatic legacy. Thus Lyon, whose critique of the administration's record in the Third World is both sustained and sharp, closes his largely sympathetic "portrait of the hero" with the observation that Eisenhower must be praised for the pacific nature of his two terms in office.

This seeming contradiction is actually quite easily explained. Regardless of whether they see success, failure, or a mixed record in the Third World, the Eisenhower revisionists do not consider that aspect of Ike's diplomacy crucial to their overall evaluation. It is such issues as maintaining the peace, managing relations with the Soviet Union, gaining control over the nuclear arms race, and understanding the limits of American power that these scholars typically emphasize when calculating the balance sheet on the Eisenhower years. Given that perspective, Third World issues fade in importance; only the President's refusal to commit American troops to any open-ended Third World conflict appears critical to the new consensus on Eisenhower.

That perspective, however, is certainly open to question. Undoubtedly the concerns mentioned above were critical ones during the Eisenhower years. With the ever-present threat of nuclear confrontation—a threat compounded by the advent of the H-Bomb and intercontinental ballistic missiles—U.S.-Soviet relations certainly had to top Ike's diplomatic agenda. Still, the single most dynamic new element in international affairs during the 1950s was the emergence of a vigorous, broad-based, and assertive nationalism throughout the developing world. Those nationalist stirrings, moreover, constituted not only a major challenge to the world order that Eisenhower and his advisers sought to preserve, but promised as well to exacerbate tensions between Washington and Moscow as the two superpowers competed for the loyalty and resources of the newly emerging areas. The nature of the administration's response to Third World nationalism, in its varying manifestations, must therefore rank as a fundamental consideration in any overall assessment of Eisenhower's diplomatic record. This article will argue that the failure of the Eisenhower revisionists to appreciate the centrality of Third World nationalism has led them to present a distorted and over-simplified view of American foreign relations during a critical eight-year period.

The publication in recent years of a series of detailed studies on U.S. relations with different parts of the developing world, either focusing specifically on the Eisenhower years or spanning a broader time frame, has considerably enhanced our understanding of this important subject. Considered as a whole, this work offers an assessment of Eisenhower's foreign policy sharply at odds with that drawn by the revisionists. Indeed, a brief review of some of the more important recent work on U.S. relations with Asia, the Middle East, Latin America, and Africa reveals that Eisenhower scholarship actually is moving in two very different directions. Instead of applauding restraint, the authors of these studies often criticize intervention; instead of seeing a prudent administration aware of the limitations of American power, they often see an administration self-consciously expanding American involvement in all corners of the globe and trying to manage the internal affairs of other nations to an unprecedented degree.

Although recent literature on U.S.-Third World relations during the Eisenhower years varies considerably in scope, quality, depth of research, and interpretive thrust, it does suggest the plausibility of an alternative interpretation of Eisenhower's foreign policy. That view might be summarized as follows. The Eisenhower administration grievously misunderstood and underestimated the most significant historical development of the mid-twentieth century—the force of Third World nationalism. This failure of perception, furthermore, constituted a major setback for American diplomacy. The Eisenhower administration insisted on viewing the Third World through the invariably distorting lens of a Cold War geopolitical strategy that saw the Kremlin as the principal instigator of global unrest. As a result, it often wound up simplifying complicated local and regional developments, confusing nationalism with communism, aligning the United States with inherently unstable and unrepresentative regimes, and wedding American interests to the status quo in areas undergoing fundamental social, political, and economic upheaval. Rather than promoting long-term stability in the Third World, the foreign policy of the Eisenhower administration contributed to its instability, thus undermining a basic American policy goal. In this critical area, then, the Eisenhower record appears one of persistent failure. The new Eisenhower revisionism, which largely overlooks, downplays, or misinterprets this record, may consequently be a castle built upon sand.

Eisenhower's response to Asian developments well illustrates this larger theme. Nearly all of the new revisionist writers applaud the President's decisions to extricate the United States from the Korean quagmire and to avoid the considerable pressures for American intervention at Dienbienphu in Indochina. In addition, most of these scholars similarly praise Ike's astute avoidance of conflict with China over the Quemoy and Matsu imbroglio. The President, Herbert Parmet contends, was ''cautious and fully cognizant of the hazards involved in military commitment, held the controls during the Indochinese crisis of 1954 and, together with John Foster Dulles, maneuvered with care and skillfully avoided enticements to involvement during two crises over the islands of Quemoy and Matsu.''

The revisionist reasoning in this regard is as logical as it is compelling: the former general, who well understood the limits of military force, carefully steered the nation clear of open-ended military commitments, a policy of restraint that stands in sharp relief when compared to that pursued by both his predecessor and successors in the Oval Office. At least in the case of Indochina, this judgment appears sound. John Prados's *"The Sky Would Fall"* [1983], a book based on newly-declassified records, concludes that the pressures for intervention were even stronger than previously suspected. Accordingly, Ike's firm stand against U.S. military involvement in the face of strong contrary advice from many of his leading military and civilian advisers appears both bold and farsighted. Despite the considerable evidence that Prados amasses to demonstrate how close the United States did come to intervention, the salient fact remains that the President ultimately exercised sound judgment. In a new study of "the day we didn't go to war," George C. Herring and Richard H. Immerman conclude that "there seems little reason to quarrel with the view that the administration acted wisely in staying out of war in 1954."

The Korean case is somewhat more problematic. Our understanding of how the President negotiated an end to that conflict has until very recently been hindered by the unavailability of essential documentary sources. Critics of his policy, however, suggest that he may have relied far too heavily on the threat of nuclear weapons to break the negotiating logjam, thus initiating a "brinksmanship" policy that gravely endangered world peace.

Scholars have advanced similar arguments with regard to the Taiwan Straits crises of 1955 and 1958. Divine approves of the President's brinksmanship in those twin showdowns with China, arguing that "the beauty of Eisenhower's policy is that to this day no one can be sure whether or not . . . he would have used nuclear weapons." That brandishing nuclear weapons could be a thing of beauty under any circumstances is a value judgment that some historians have been unwilling to make. Lyon faults the President for placing the United States in "an untenable position" during the 1958 crisis, "which, by maladroit diplomacy, was transformed into an intolerable dilemma, one that could apparently be resolved only by nuclear catastrophe or Chinese restraint." Likewise, John Gaddis's brief account of these episodes in his suggestive book, *Strategies of Containment* [1982], also raises serious doubts about the efficacy of Ike's brinksmanship. "Far from validating the administration's strategy," he writes, "these incidents—particularly the one of 1958—in fact thoroughly discredited it in the eyes of the American public and allies overseas by revealing how little it would take to push the administration into a war with China involving the probable use of nuclear weapons." Decrying the riskiness of brinksmanship in the Taiwan Straits and elsewhere, Gaddis argues that "in retrospect the most startling deficiency of the administration's strategy was its bland self-confidence that it could use nuclear weapons without setting off an all-out nuclear war."

The real problem with the interpretation of the President's Asian policy advanced by the Eisenhower revisionists is not just that their assessments of his remarkable restraint in the incidents noted above are open to question. Rather, it is that they build a case based on a narrow, highly selective and episodic approach that largely ignores the crucial question of nationalism. How well did the President accommodate American foreign policy to the transforming dynamic of Asian nationalism? Given the framework sketched above, that question should be critical to any rigorous analysis of Eisenhower's diplomatic record in Asia. Yet it is missing from most of the revisionist accounts. Most importantly, posing that question necessitates a very different evaluation of the administration's policy toward Asia since, according to much of the recent literature, its response to Asian nationalism was often inadequate and at times even disastrous.

Indochina is a case in point. While the revisionists routinely cite Ike's nonintervention at Dienbienphu to bolster their overall interpretative thrust, they rarely evaluate the more general issue of American policy toward Indochina during the post-Geneva period. Those revisionists who do discuss this aspect of the administration's record invariably temper their judgments. Lyon, for example, praises the President for his staunch refusal to aid the French in 1954, but adds that "the decisions to make massive commitments of military and financial aid to the puppet government in Saigon were Eisenhower's, as were the decisions to authorize hostile acts, 'dirty tricks,' acts of war against the Viet Minh undertaken by Americans under the direction of Americans." George C. Herring's important study of U.S. involvement in Vietnam, *America's Longest War* [2d ed., 1986], renders a harsh verdict on Eisenhower's Vietnam policy. "Certain that the fall of Vietnam to Communism would lead to the loss of all of Southeast Asia," he writes, "the Eisenhower administration after Geneva firmly committed itself to creating in the southern part of the country a nation that would stand as a bulwark against Communist expansion and serve as a proving ground for democracy in Asia." But this experiment in nation building, Herring argues, was a "high-risk gamble" that by the close of Eisenhower's second term was on the verge of collapse. Despite massive military and economic assistance—aid that by 1961 had catapulted South Vietnam to fifth place among recipients of U.S. support worldwide—the Americans never succeeded in laying the foundation for a genuinely independent nation; on the contrary, the American financial stake tended to foster dependence. As renewed guerrilla warfare erupted in the south in 1957, the inefficacy of the U.S. effort became painfully apparent. Only "the quirks of the electoral calendar," Herring contends, "spared Eisenhower from the ultimate failure of his policies in Vietnam."

The administration's record in Laos, conveniently ignored by most of the Eisenhower revisionists, constituted another effort at nation building whose outcome was less than a triumph for U.S. policy objectives. Charles Stevenson, whose book *The End of Nowhere* [1972] remains the most detailed and informed account of American relations with that struggling young country, offers a scathing indictment of the Eisenhower policy. He charges that the administration was animated exclusively by that nation's supposed significance to the Free World in its struggle against international communism. But by reducing complex Lao developments to broad Cold War categories, the United States almost completely misread and distorted the internal dynamics of Lao society. Stevenson demonstrates the futility of the U.S. effort to create an anticommunist bastion in Laos by pumping enormous sums of money into the Lao army. As Ike's second term came to a close, the deepening U.S. involvement in Laos had elevated a limited, local struggle against a communist-led guerrilla movement to global significance. Yet, as in Vietnam, U.S. objectives were further from realization than ever before.

U.S.-Indonesian relations, another subject largely ignored by the Eisenhower revisionists, provide even more dramatic evidence of the administration's failure to understand the depth and appeal of Asian nationalism. Specialists in this area have argued that the Eisenhower administration's virtual obsession with the prospects for a communist takeover of Southeast Asia's largest and most important nation blinded it to the complex internal developments that were shaking Indonesian society to its very core. The result was a policy that proved almost entirely counter productive in terms of long-range U.S. objectives in that country. By providing clandestine support to Indonesian dissidents, whose long-simmering regional rebellion erupted into full-scale civil war in 1958, Eisenhower apparently hoped that he could help topple President Sukarno's left-leaning regime and replace it with a more pliant, moderate, and pro-American government. But the administration's bold gamble backfired when Sukarno quickly suppressed the rebels; not only did the United States support the losing side, but its covert support for that side was embarrassingly exposed when Sukarno's troops shot down a CIA pilot flying bomber missions for the rebels. The heavy-handed U.S. intervention wound up strengthening Sukarno's hand while simultaneously offending nationalists of nearly all political hues with what was universally denounced as imperialist intervention. As a former Indonesian Foreign Minister later recalled, "the general opinion in Indonesia was unanimous that the CIA had a hand in the rebellion" and this suspicion "was to linger on for a long time and was the main cause of further deterioration in Indonesia-U.S. relations. . . ."

In comparison to the continuing crises in Indochina and Indonesia, U.S.-Philippine relations during the Eisenhower years appear remarkably placid. Indeed, as a recent study by Stephen Shalom makes clear, by the mid-1950s U.S. policy makers looked upon the Philippines as a real American success story: the Huk rebellion had been suppressed; economic collapse had been averted; a staunch U.S. ally, Ramon Magsaysay—with timely help from the CIA—had been installed in the presidency; U.S. economic and strategic interests had been secured; and nationalist sentiment appeared largely neutralized. Beneath this surface tranquility, however, lay festering problems, and Shalom shows how pent-up Filipino frustrations with their nation's neocolonial status—symbolized by the mammoth U.S. military bases and the unequal trade relationship between the two nations—led to an explosion of nationalist sentiment in the mid-1950s. As a result, the negotiations over a revised military bases agreement became harshly acrimonious and were broken off in 1956 as the United States could not satisfy Filipino demands for even limited sovereignty. It was U.S. recalcitrance in the face of enhanced Filipino nationalism, Shalom argues, that led both to the collapse of the talks and to a searching reexamination by Manila of its relationship with Washington. The significance of the Philippine case is that it demonstrates how, even in the most moderate, American-oriented Asian nation, nationalism posed a formidable threat to American objectives; the American response to that nationalist challenge proved at best halting and inadequate.

Another important topic rarely examined by the Eisenhower revisionists, U.S. policy toward South Asia, can best be understood as part of this general pattern. Recent work in this area by scholars such as Selig S. Harrison, M. S. Venkataramani, and Stanley Wolpert has suggested that the Eisenhower administration proved incapable of appreciating the deeply-felt neutralist stance of the region's most important power, India. Instead of cultivating India's friendship as the key to regional stability, the Eisenhower administration made a major strategic blunder by aligning itself with Pakistan, first through a military assistance agreement in 1954, and subsequently through Pakistani membership in the Southeast Asia Treaty Organization (SEATO) and the Baghdad Pact. This decision, based on a global geopolitical approach that viewed Pakistan as a valuable strategic asset and thus an important anchor in America's worldwide containment network, proved counterproductive, however; it helped foster an arms race between India and Pakistan, rendered an amicable resolution of the tangled Kashmir dispute increasingly unlikely, alienated Afghanistan, and opened the door for greater Russian involvement in both India and Afghanistan. In short, the Eisenhower administration's decision to provide Pakistan with arms and to align it with the West increased regional instability and, as Indian Prime Minister Jawaharlal Nehru charged at the time, brought the Cold War to South Asia.

Turning to another important region of the developing world, it can be argued with equal force that the major stumbling block to the accomplishment of American objectives in the Middle East during the Eisenhower years was, as in Asia, the rising tide of indigenous nationalism. Here too the President's record provides little comfort for the revisionists. Judging from recent scholarly accounts, Ike's policy toward the region was characterized by missed opportunities, strategic miscalculations, and counterproductive actions. It foundered, in short, on the rock of Arab nationalism. "The Eisenhower Administration," asserts Robert W. Stookey in his book *America and the Arab States* [1975], "never arrived at a clear distinction between communism and revolutionary Arab nationalism." He contends that the administration's inability to come to terms with this nationalism quickly erased the momentarily favorable impression created by its opposition to the Suez invasion of 1956. By foolishly intervening in a series of domestic Arab crises in the post-Suez period, the United States wound up "reinforcing its own neocolonialist image and facilitating the infiltration of Soviet influence." Similarly, in her study of U.S.-Egyptian relations Gail E. Meyer states that the administration "usually failed to make any practical distinction between communists and Arab nationalists." The Eisenhower policy was counterproductive, she argues, since "American support for unpopular regimes that tried to repress [nationalists] drove the wedge between the United States and these same nationalists ever deeper and actually forced the nationalists to turn to the Soviet Union for help." Consequently, "American policy unified and strengthened Arab nationalist resistance while ignoring its tremendous popular appeal."

The revisionists, of course, use a different standard of evaluation. Wedded to the thesis that the President well understood the uses as well as the limits of military power, they typically cite Ike's restraint during the Suez crisis and his limited but effective use of force during the Lebanon operation of 1958 to illustrate the point. "When the Suez war of 1956 threatened either American intervention or estrangement from the Western allies," writes Herbert Parmet, "Eisenhower avoided either hazard. When he sent the Marines into Lebanon, he did so after choosing a time, place, and display of power that minimized the risks and ensured success." "Nothing exemplifies better than the Lebanon intervention," adds William Bragg Ewald, "the American people's reasons for wanting Eisenhower as Commander in Chief." Ike's guiding principle, he notes approvingly, was that when resorting to force one does so overwhelmingly, thus ensuring success. Although the revisionists are divided on the appropriateness of covert operations, many also add the Iranian coup of 1953 to the list of Ike's Middle East triumphs; not only was CIA intervention in Iran successful, in their view, but it well served American interests in that strategic country and was accomplished at a remarkably minimal cost.

The foregoing interpretation of Eisenhower's Middle East policy, while compelling, is also open to serious question, since it largely ignores the crucial nationalist equation. Barry Rubin's study of American-Iranian relations suggests some of the complexities involved in any effort to evaluate the coup of 1953. Although the operation was without doubt a success in the short run, he points out that "in the long run the CIA's support for the shah's return would breed Iranian anti-Americanism and play a central role in shaping the attitudes of the post-shah regime." The myth propagated by Eisenhower and Director of the CIA Allen Dulles, moreover, that Prime Minister Mohammed Mossadegh's government had been a communist-dominated regime, in Rubin's view, "encouraged a tragic confusion between militant nationalism and Marxism-Leninism that plagued United States policy elsewhere in the Third World." Divine as well, despite his general approval of Eisenhower's Middle East policy, questions the efficacy of the Iranian operation, concluding that "in this case, a short-term triumph led to a long-term defeat for the United States."

A broad evaluation of the Suez invasion also casts some doubt on the validity of the revisionist framework. Donald Neff, who bases his recent book *Warriors at Suez* [1981] on much newly declassified material, partially supports the revisionists' case by concluding that Ike's "firm insistence that the rule of law be obeyed was one of the high points of his presidency."

He quickly adds, however, that in the aftermath of the invasion the administration squandered a unique opportunity to improve relations with Egypt and other emerging nations. The problem, Neff suggests, was that Eisenhower and his advisers had a deep aversion to Gamal Abdel Nasser and the radical Arab nationalism that he represented. "Such blind prejudice," Neff asserts, "allowed a unique opportunity to slip by." Steven L. Spiegel adds in his new study, *The Other Arab-Israeli Conflict* [1985]: while on one level Eisenhower's Suez policy was a success, he failed to understand the two underlying causes of the crisis, Arab nationalism and Israeli isolation. Instead of trying to come to grips with the true sources of regional instability— Arab-Israeli tensions and intra-Arab rivalries—the administration concentrated on a phony communist menace "and any instability in the area was perceived as originating behind the Kremlin walls."

Gail E. Meyer, who analyzes the Eisenhower administration's Middle East policy through the lens of Egyptian-American relations, offers a similar perspective. She argues that a chronic American "aversion to Arab nationalism" proved to be an implacable impediment to the establishment of a constructive relationship with Nasser's Egypt, the key to the region. By sponsoring a Baghdad Pact grouping that encouraged Iraq's ambitions for Middle Eastern leadership, the United States undercut Egypt and exacerbated regional tensions. With Iraq challenging Egypt's cherished role as leader of the Arab world and the Eisenhower administration unwilling to meet its demands for arms, Egypt believed it had no choice but to embrace neutralism and to move in an increasingly antiwestern direction. Meyer insists that the Suez crisis must be placed within the context of American opposition to Nasser's ambitions, its support for Egypt's rivals, especially Iraq, its refusal to sell arms to Cairo, and, most important, its humiliating withdrawal of the promised Aswan Dam financing in the wake of Egypt's arms deal with Czechoslovakia. Like Neff, she suggests that the United States managed to preserve a modicum of prestige and influence by its Suez policy, but she also sees this as a transitory phenomenon since Washington remained unwilling to appraise its attitude toward Egypt and Arab nationalism. The Syrian and Jordanian crises of 1957 demonstrated the bankruptcy of Eisenhower's Middle East policy. By refusing to come to terms with Arab nationalism and treating local and regional problems within a global anticommunist framework, the United States ironically fostered the regional instability that its policy was presumably designed to quell.

It is equally hazardous to view the 1958 Lebanon invasion as an unambiguous triumph for U.S. interests in the Middle East. Divine praises the landing of American troops, which he says "was designed to impress Arab leaders with American strength and determination." Eisenhower, he observes, had "a clear sense of the strategic value of Persian Gulf oil and acted boldly to protect that vital national interest." But even Divine concedes that the danger of communist subversion in Lebanon, which served as a pretext for the invasion, was in fact nonexistent. "Arab nationalism," he says, "not Soviet communism, was the source of danger to American hopes for a stable Middle East." His own evidence suggests the plausibility of an alternative evaluation: that by viewing local developments within a global perspective Eisenhower wound up responding with an excessive and wholly inappropriate use of force that in the long run harmed America's position in the region. Lyon emphasizes that the intervention alienated rather than impressed the Arab states, and only managed to stoke the flames of radical Arab nationalism. He speculates that the real reason for the invasion was the misplaced hope that Lebanon could serve as a base of operations against the new revolutionary regime in Iraq.

Viewing Eisenhower's Middle East policy from a broad perspective, Robert W. Stookey offers the following assessment of the President's record: "Lacking a sufficient appreciation of the difference (in fact, the incompatibility) of communism with Arab nationalism and neutralism, the United States was led into unilateral actions that, far from shielding the Near East from the cold war, actually tended to draw it into the confrontation and lent substance to communist assertions, eagerly adopted by Arab nationalists, that the United States had become the leader of a Western imperialism opposed to Arab freedom and progress."

Steven L. Spiegel's evaluation is equally scathing. "In evaluating the record, policies, and decision-making style of the administration," he writes, "the contrast is dramatic between its high hopes and great attention and limited results. For every Middle East policy problem, the policy had failed by the time Eisenhower left office. . . . By attempting to maneuver between the conflicting interests of Egypt, Israel, Britain, and France, the administration has alienated all of them."

As in other regions, so too in Latin America an explosive nationalism posed the principal challenge to American interests during the Eisenhower years. Recent literature on inter-American relations during this period, much of which draws heavily on documentation from the Eisenhower Library, suggests that the administration adapted poorly to the problems—and opportunities—presented by this renewed nationalism. Only the threat of communist penetration could arouse high-level interest in Latin American issues during Ike's presidency; otherwise, the administration pursued a policy of benign neglect, calculating that in comparison to more pressing international hot spots Latin America could safely be placed on the proverbial back burner. The result of this policy, according to most recent accounts, was nothing short of disastrous. Throughout the 1950s inter-American relations steadily deteriorated, a fact dramatically illustrated by the angry mobs that greeted Vice President Richard Nixon in Venezuela and elsewhere during his goodwill tour in 1958, the establishment of a revolutionary regime in Cuba in 1959, and Eisenhower's belated efforts to repair relations within the hemisphere during the waning months of his presidency. In his new study of U.S. relations with Central America, *Inevitable Revolutions* [1983], Walter LaFeber states flatly that the Eisenhower administration simply could not "come to terms with history." Even the episode that some Eisenhower revisionists point to as a successful and limited defense of American interests—the CIA-led overthrow of the leftist Jacobo Arbenz regime in Guatemala in 1954—has been severely criticized in recent works.

The studies of Blanche Weisen Cook, Stephen Schlesinger and Stephen Kinzer, and Richard Immerman offer the fullest account yet of the Guatemalan coup, an operation still shrouded in secrecy. They agree that the intervention in Guatemala was not only unjustified by nearly any standard, but set a dangerous precedent for the expanded use of covert operations as an instrument of American policy. Cook insists that the Guatemalan model has been used time and again, with only minor modifications. There are important differences in emphasis in these works. In *Bitter Fruit* [1982], Schlesinger and Kinzer argue that the American intervention was motivated by concern with the confiscation of the properties of the powerful United Fruit Company. In *The CIA in Guatemala* [1982], Immerman takes a broader and more convincing view, suggesting that an all-embracing Cold War ethos led the United States to fear radical social experimentation in Guatemala and equate it, despite the lack of hard evidence, with communism. They do agree wholeheartedly, however, on the baleful impact of the operation. Of course, it was a resounding short-term success; Arbenz was ousted and replaced by a leader beholden to the United States. In the long-run, though, Immerman and Schlesinger and Kinzer see the intervention as detrimental not only to the evolution of democratic institutions in Guatemala, but also to the achievement of long-term U.S. interests in the country and in the region. Arbenz sought to end centuries of social and economic injustice, Immerman asserts, but "the CIA's 1954 coup made moderation impossible." He sees the guerrilla struggle currently raging in Guatemala as "the final irony— and legacy" of the Eisenhower administration's intervention in that tragic land. Schlesinger and Kinzer are equally biting in their indictment of the CIA's meddling in Guatemala. "Over the longer term," they contend, "the coup gravely damaged American interests in Latin America. The gusto with which the United States had ended the Guatemalan revolution embittered many Latins, and strengthened deep-seated anti-Americanism throughout the continent." Partly as a result of the coup, they conclude, "movements toward peaceful reform in the region were set back, dictators were strengthened and encouraged, and activists of today look to guerrilla warfare rather than elections as the only way to produce change."

U.S. insensitivity toward the rising tide of Latin American nationalism took a less dramatic form in Brazil, but the results were just as detrimental to the accomplishment of long-term American objectives in the hemisphere. In his essay, "The United States, Brazil, and the Cold War, 1945–1960" [*Journal of American History*, 1981], Stanley E. Hilton contends that the Eisenhower administration's neglect of the region's largest and most important nation brought about an eclipse in the special relationship between the two countries that had long served U.S. and Brazilian interests. As a result, by the late-1950s the Brazilian leadership began to replace dependence on and cooperation with the United States with a more independent policy, one that would eventually lead Brazil to proclaim solidarity with the neutralist nations of the Third World and to seek common cause with fellow Latin states. The Truman and Eisenhower administrations "bear responsibility for that shift," according to Hilton. By foolishly ignoring its leaders' incessant pleas for the maintenance of a privileged relationship, he writes, "Washington alienated Brazil, formerly an eager ally in hemisphere matters. It also contributed powerfully to the long-range decline of American influence in the region by propelling Brazil along the path of solidarity with its historical antagonists, the Spanish Americans."

Stephen G. Rabe's important new book on U.S.-Venezuelan relations presents another chronicle of insensitivity and missed opportunities during the Eisenhower era. "Perhaps what distinguished its policies from the previous administration," Rabe notes, "was the Eisenhower administration's unabashed embrace of military dictatorships and its failure to criticize, however mutely, the rampant political and civil repression in Latin America." This failure was particularly evident in Venezuela, where the U.S. heaped medals and accolades on the brutal dictator, Marcos Pérez Jiménez, for his staunch anticommunism and his favorable treatment of U.S. oil companies. When Perez Jimenez was toppled in January 1958, the unqualified support for a leader who had managed to alienate nearly all segments of Venezuelan society produced a vicious backlash against the United States. The angry mob that nearly killed Nixon in Caracas in May 1958, "shocked the United States," Rabe writes; "relations with the model Latin American country were in a shambles." In the aftermath of the assault on the Vice President, the Eisenhower administration scrambled to repair relations with some limited success. Support for the liberal democrat Romulo Betancourt certainly represented a welcome reversal of previous policy. Nonetheless, Rabe contends that the Eisenhower administration's failure to adapt to the stirrings of economic nationalism in Venezuela laid the seeds of future problems. The Eisenhower administration continually blocked any Venezuelan efforts to gain more control over their only important resource: oil. And when the President announced price cuts and import quotas on Venezuelan petroleum in 1959, Venezuelan leaders responded by founding the Organization of Petroleum Exporting Countries (OPEC), a cartel that would raise fundamental problems for the United States in succeeding years.

Without doubt, Fidel Castro's revolution in Cuba presented the most serious immediate threat to the accomplishment of the administration's objectives in the region. It is the verdict of much recent scholarship on Cuban-American relations that the Eisenhower administration's response to that challenge was rash, poorly planned, and ultimately counterproductive. As former Ambassador Philip W. Bonsal recalled in a 1972 memoir: "The Russian presence in Cuba is largely the consequence of the American reaction to Castro's provocations. . . . Russia came to Castro's rescue only after the United States had taken steps designed to overthrow him." Richard E. Welch's *Response to Revolution* [1985], the most recent and balanced account of these events, concludes that "the Cuban policy of the Eisenhower years can only be judged a failure. Its legacy was one of defeat and animosity." Eisenhower, moreover, must be charged with the primary responsibility for the Bay of Pigs fiasco. "It was Eisenhower," writes Peter Lyon, "who had ordered that the attack be prepared, just as the operation was carried out under the purview of officials . . . who were completing what they had begun at Eisenhower's instigation." Peter Wyden, whose *Bay of Pigs: The Untold Story* [1979] is the fullest account to date of that failed operation, offers a savage indictment of an ill-conceived and poorly-planned "wild gamble" that he calls "Eisenhower's baby." Even Cole Blasier, who accepts the still hotly-debated theory that Eisenhower was correct in believing that Castro, from the very inception of his rule, sought to radicalize Cuban society and establish close relations with the Soviet Union, insists that the President's decisions "to arm a counterrevolutionary force and cut the sugar quota were counterproductive. . . . U.S. policies seem to have removed whatever slight chances may have existed for Castro's demise and facilitated his alignment with the USSR."

For the Eisenhower revisionists—indeed, for nearly all specialists in postwar American diplomacy—Africa remains virtually uncharted territory. This neglect of Africa is, of course, understandable since most scholars agree that it posed relatively few problems for the United States during Eisenhower's two terms. Yet, at the same time, the emergence of vigorous nationalist movements in Africa and the creation of numerous new states out of former colonial areas—eighteen in 1960 alone—parallels developments elsewhere in the Third World. Ike's response to the shifting currents of African nationalism, moreover, well conforms to the pattern sketched above of an administration largely insensitive to this new force and prone to view radical nationalism through the distorting prism of U.S.-Soviet relations. As Thomas J. Noer notes in his impressively researched account of the U.S. response to white minority regimes: "By continuing a 'Europe first' approach at the expense of alienating the newly independent countries, Eisenhower may have insured immediate support for America's Cold War efforts, but he identified Washington with the dwindling pockets of white rule." Cold War blinders joined with deference to the former European colonial powers, writes Richard D. Mahoney in a provocative new study, to frustrate the development of constructive relations between Washington and the new African states.

The Congo crisis provides a case in point. When an independent government emerged out of the former Belgian Congo in 1960, under the leadership of the charismatic if erratic and left-leaning Patrice Lumumba, the United States quickly interpreted developments there as a new Cold War battleground. In her recent study of that crisis, Madeleine G. Kalb states that the Eisenhower administration saw Lumumba as "a Castro or worse" and determined that he must be eliminated lest his calls for Soviet intervention upset U.S interests in Africa. She offers a chilling account of various U.S. assassination plots, prominently featuring a CIA agent known only as "Joe from Paris," whose assignment was to provide lethal injections for the would-be assassins. But was Lumumba a protocommunist and a direct threat to U.S. interests? The Eisenhower administration, argues Stephen R. Weissman, simply failed to understand the political force of nationalism represented by Lumumba and instead mistakenly based its policy on international communist conspiracies that were completely illusory. Nationalism was the issue in the Congo, not communism. Lumumba's policies "were rationally related to the militant nationalism which was his basic formula," writes Weissman. "But the Eisenhower Administration regarded Lumumba's acceptance of Soviet military aid as a last of a series of actions tending to prove 'Communist influence.'"

The foregoing review raises some troubling questions about the new Eisenhower revisionism. Certainly the revisionists are to be congratulated for combining new evidence with fresh perspectives to give us a challenging reinterpretation of the Eisenhower presidency. Many of their findings, moreover, appear basically sound; that the general was a strong leader who often exercised prudence and restraint in the conduct of international relations seems veritably unassailable now. In their zeal to revise, however, some revisionists have badly overstated their case. This paper has tried to demonstrate that they often ignore, downplay, or misinterpret major elements of the President's policies toward the Third World, and thus seriously distort the Eisenhower record. It is particularly revealing that the revisionists offer judgments about American diplomacy that are widely at variance from those drawn by scholars who have focused more narrowly on U.S. relations with particular developing nations or regions. If one accepts the premise that Eisenhower's response to the Third World, and especially its nationalist stirrings, must be at least one critical ingredient in any overall evaluation of his foreign policy, then the revisionist case for Ike appears far weaker than many recent accounts would have us believe.

There are several possible explanations for the contrasting perspectives offered in the two sets of literature. Since the nature and availability of documentary evidence inevitably shapes the judgments rendered by scholars, it is tempting to see interpretive differences as a function of the reliance on different sources. Such an explanation, however, would risk gross oversimplification. To be sure, many of the studies of U.S.-Third World relations discussed above are painstakingly researched, while some of the revisionist works—Robert Divine's *Eisenhower and the Cold War* is a prime example—are general accounts based solely on secondary literature. Yet other revisionist works certainly do mine important primary sources. Herbert Parmet, Peter Lyon, Fred I. Greenstein, and Stephen E. Ambrose all rely heavily on newly released documentation from the Eisenhower Library. Ambrose's magisterial biography, *Eisenhower, the President* [1984], reflects its author's exceptional grasp of the available primary sources.

Depth and breadth of research alone simply cannot explain such sharp differences in interpretation. All studies of the Eisenhower presidency to date, after all, despite the boasts of some specialists, are based on a woefully incomplete documentary record. Many of the most important sources on the Eisenhower years—including most of the critically significant minutes of the National Security Council's weekly meetings—remain classified. Not even the most diligent researcher can compensate for the tightening web of governmental security regulations. The Department of State, moreover, has yet to publish more than a handful of volumes in its indispensable documentary series, *Foreign Relations of the United States*. In comparison, studies of the Truman presidency have been based on a far broader empirical base; scholarly reconstructions of Truman's foreign policy have consequently been more numerous, more comprehensive, and more sophisticated.

Varying perspectives and conflicting methods of evaluation more accurately explain these contradictory trends in Eisenhower scholarship. What criteria does one use to evaluate the relative success or failure of any administration in international affairs? On this crucial question the revisionists and their critics differ profoundly. As noted above, the revisionists emphasize several key considerations in analyzing Eisenhower's foreign policy: maintaining the peace, managing relations with the Soviet Union, and understanding the limits of American power. On every point they award Ike high marks, contrasting his accomplishments, either implicitly or explicitly, with those of other postwar occupants of the White House.

Rather than reject these sweeping claims directly, many specialists in the field of U.S. relations with the developing nations simply investigate areas and topics outside the standard purview of the revisionists. Thus many of the nations discussed above—Laos, Indonesia, India, Pakistan, Egypt, Iraq, Brazil, Venezuela—are virtually ignored in revisionist accounts of Eisenhower's presidency. Yet the issues raised by these case studies speak directly to the conclusions reached by revisionist scholars. Using different standards of measurement—such as the *impact* of American actions on developing nations and the gap between goals and results—they reach strikingly different conclusions. If these authors are correct about the meager results of American initiatives, the detrimental long-term effects of many U.S. actions, and the chasm between expectations and accomplishments in so many parts of the world, then it becomes nearly impossible to view Ike's foreign policy in such a favorable light. Nor do the occasionally rash and often counterproductive actions detailed in these studies bolster the image of Ike's administration as consistently wise, prudent, and restrained.

Most important, this work on U.S.-Third World relations provides the basis for a fuller and more sophisticated understanding of Eisenhower's foreign policy. It promises to move the traditionalist/revisionist debate to a new plane. If any one theme emerges clearly from the recent literature on postwar American diplomacy it is the global nature of American interests. To understand a global foreign policy requires a systematic explanation of *all* the areas of the world in which the United States tried to exert influence or affect developments. The studies discussed above certainly move us closer to that ultimate goal.

As the authors of those studies typically emphasize the continuity in American policy toward the developing nations, another question must be addressed: Is it fair to single out the Eisenhower administration for criticism in this area? Or, to rephrase the question: Is the Eisenhower administration any more to blame for American policy failures in the Third World than those of Harry S Truman, John F. Kennedy, Lyndon B. Johnson, or other recent presidents? Although that question cannot be answered with precision until far more detailed work on U.S.-Third World relations during those administrations has been published, it is certainly germane to this discussion. If Eisenhower's policies toward the Third World are in fact just part of a continuum in postwar American foreign relations, as some of the studies discussed above suggest, then this article's emphasis on the failures of one particular administration may be misplaced. At the same time, the revisionist's emphasis on discontinuity—the heart of their argument for Ike's diplomatic success—might be equally misplaced.

Many additional questions remain unanswered. The most basic of these is *why* did the Eisenhower administration fail to develop constructive relations with the emerging nations of the Third World? Were there truly prospects for an accommodation with Third World nationalism that were missed, as some authors assert? Or was militant nationalism itself, whether influenced by the Kremlin or not, simply perceived as a significant threat to American interests that demanded a vigorous response? If so, how then did Eisenhower administration officials define those interests? Were they primarily economic in nature, or strategic and political? Can the administration fairly be accused of a failure of vision in its approach to the developing nations? Or is it more properly a failure of strategy? Is it the administration's preoccupation with the Soviet Union that best explains its failures in the Third World? Or is Eisenhower's relative neglect of Third-World nationalism simply characteristic of the Europe-first orientation of a whole generation of American leaders? Did indifference or aversion to Third-World issues by key congressional leaders or by the American public as a whole set limits on the Eisenhower administration's freedom of action? And what of the President's personal views toward the newly emerging areas? Did he truly appreciate the dynamism of Third-World nationalism, as some of his defenders insist? If so, then why was he so unsuccessful in translating those insights into workable policies? These questions should rank high on the future research agenda of Eisenhower scholars.

✖ *F U R T H E R   R E A D I N G*

Stephen Ambrose, *Eisenhower: The President* (1984)
———, *Ike's Spies* (1981)
———, *Nixon* (1987)
Howard Ball, *Justice Downwind: America's Atomic Testing Program in the 1950s* (1986)
Michael Beschloss, *MAYDAY* (1986) (U-2 affair)
H. W. Brands, Jr., *Cold Warriors: Eisenhower's Generation and American Foreign Policy* (1988)
Cole Blasier, *The Hovering Giant* (1976)
William J. Burns, *Economic Aid and American Policy Toward Egypt, 1955–1981* (1985)
Blanche W. Cook, *The Declassified Eisenhower* (1981)
Robert A. Divine, *Blowing on the Wind: The Nuclear Test Ban Debate, 1954–1960* (1978)
———, *Eisenhower and the Cold War* (1981)

Alexander L. George and Richard Smoke, *Deterrence in American Foreign Policy* (1974)

Louis Gerson, *John Foster Dulles* (1968)

Richard Gould-Adams, *Time of Power* (1962)

Norman Graebner, ed., *The National Security: Its Theory and Practice, 1945–1960* (1987)

Fred I. Greenstein, *The Hidden-Hand Presidency* (1982)

Michael Guhin, *John Foster Dulles* (1972)

Gregg Herken, *Counsels of War* (1985)

George Herring, *America's Longest War* (1986)

Townsend Hoopes, *The Devil and John Foster Dulles* (1973)

Emmet J. Hughes, *The Ordeal of Power* (1963)

Richard H. Immerman, *The CIA in Guatemala* (1982)

———, "Eisenhower and Dulles: Who Made the Decisions?" *Political Psychology*, I (1979), 3–20

Burton I. Kaufman, *Trade and Aid: Eisenhower's Foreign Economic Policy, 1953–1961* (1982)

Gabriel Kolko and Joyce Kolko, *The Limits of Power* (1972)

Walter LaFeber, *America, Russia, and the Cold War* (1985)

———, *Inevitable Revolutions* (1983) (on Central America)

Peter Lyon, *Eisenhower* (1974)

Richard A. Melanson and David Mayers, eds., *Reevaluating Eisenhower* (1987)

Gail Meyer, *Egypt and the United States* (1980)

Donald Neff, *Warriors at Suez* (1981)

Thomas Noer, *Cold War and Black Liberation* (1985)

Herbert S. Parmet, *Eisenhower and the Great Crusades* (1972)

Thomas G. Paterson, *Meeting the Communist Threat* (1988)

Ronald W. Pruessen, *John Foster Dulles: The Road to Power* (1982)

George H. Quester, "Was Eisenhower a Genius?" *International Security*, 4 (1979), 159–79

Stephen G. Rabe, *Eisenhower and Latin America* (1988)

———, *The Road to OPEC* (1982) (on Venezuela)

Barry Rubin, "America and the Egyptian Revolution, 1950–1957," *Political Science Quarterly*, 97 (1982), 73–90

Bennett C. Rushkoff, "Eisenhower, Dulles and the Quemoy-Matsu Crisis, 1954–1955," *Political Science Quarterly*, 96 (1981), 465–80

Stephen Schlesinger and Stephen Kinzer, *Bitter Fruit: The Untold Story of the American Coup in Guatemala* (1982)

Thomas F. Soapes, "A Cold Warrior Seeks Peace: Eisenhower's Strategy for Nuclear Disarmament," *Diplomatic History*, 4 (1980), 55–71

I. F. Stone, *The Haunted Fifties* (1963)

Stephen R. Weissman, *American Foreign Policy in the Congo, 1960–1964* (1974)

Richard E. Welch, Jr., *Response to Revolution* (1985) (on Cuba)

CHAPTER
11

Cuba and the Missile Crisis

*In October 1962, American U-2 reconnaissance planes photographed Soviet mis-
sile sites in Cuba. After meeting for days with his advisers, President John F.
Kennedy gave a dramatic television address in which he announced a blockade
of the island and demanded withdrawal of the missiles. A chilling war scare
gripped Moscow, Havana, and Washington, and the rest of the world waited
anxiously, for this was the closest the superpowers had ever come to nuclear
war. Premier Nikita Khrushchev and President Kennedy (Cuban Premier Fidel
Castro was not consulted) finally settled the crisis: the Soviet Union pledged to
withdraw its missiles from Cuba, and the United States promised not to invade
Cuba (as it had done with Cuban exiles in April 1961 at the Bay of Pigs).
Behind the missile crisis, as the no-invasion promise suggests, lay years of Cuban-American antagonism over the course of the island's revolution and Castro's
defiance of United States authority in the hemisphere. Before and after the missile crisis, the United States tried but failed, through a variety of economic, political, and covert programs, to oust Castro and cripple the Cuban Revolution.*

*Although the answers must remain tentative until the documentary archives
of the United States, Soviet Union, and Cuba are opened wide to scholars, the
questions for this topic are well defined: Why were Cuba and the United States
at such odds? Why did the Soviets place the missiles in Cuba? And why did the
Cubans welcome Soviet military assistance? Did American assassination plots
against Fidel Castro and other covert operations influence Cuban and Soviet decisions? Did the missiles seriously affect the strategic balance of power? How well
did the American decision-making process work? Why did Kennedy initially
shun private negotiations in favor of a public confrontation? Why was the blockade or quarantine selected, and what were the alternatives? Was the crisis necessary? Who won? Were opportunities for a more comprehensive settlement possible? What lessons have Americans drawn from the experience, and what impact
did the crisis have thereafter on international relations?*

✳ D O C U M E N T S

The first document is part of a November 1975 report by the Senate Select Committee to Study Governmental Operations with Respect to Intelligence Activities.
Some of the assassination plots against Fidel Castro are recounted here. The

second document is a portion of a hard-hitting April 20, 1961, speech President John F. Kennedy gave after the failure at the Bay of Pigs, where Cubans defeated a Central Intelligence Agency-run exile invasion. In the third document, exerpted from his memoirs, published in 1970, Soviet Premier Nikita Khrushchev explains that the missiles were sent to Cuba to thwart American intervention. The fourth document is a speech by Cuban President Osvaldo Dorticos. Delivered to the United Nations on October 8, 1962, before the missile crisis, it defended a Cuban military buildup as necessary to counter United States "aggression."

The fifth document includes parts of the transcribed record of Kennedy's first two meetings with his high-level advisers on October 16, 1962, the day he was informed that Soviet missile sites were being built in Cuba. The next document is Kennedy's October 22 television address to the nation, in which he announced an American naval "quarantine" of Cuba. The seventh selection, Khrushchev's October 27 letter, offered proposals to defuse the crisis. The President ignored this letter, which asked that American missiles be removed from Turkey, and answered an earlier, more moderate letter that had not mentioned such a swap.

The last document was written for *Time* magazine on the twentieth anniversary of the missile crisis by several men who had served with Kennedy in 1962: Dean Rusk, Robert McNamara, George W. Ball, Roswell L. Gilpatric, Theodore Sorensen, and McGeorge Bundy. They summarize the lessons they have drawn from the confrontation.

Assassination Plots Against Fidel Castro (1960–1965), 1975

We have found concrete evidence of at least eight plots involving the CIA to assassinate Fidel Castro from 1960 to 1965. Although some of the assassination plots did not advance beyond the stage of planning and preparation, one plot, involving the use of underworld figures, reportedly twice progressed to the point of sending poison pills to Cuba and dispatching teams to commit the deed. Another plot involved furnishing weapons and other assassination devices to a Cuban dissident. The proposed assassination devices ran the gamut from high-powered rifles to poison pills, poison pens, deadly bacterial powders, and other devices which strain the imagination. . . .

Efforts against Castro did not begin with assassination attempts.

From March through August 1960, during the last year of the Eisenhower Administration, the CIA considered plans to undermine Castro's charismatic appeal by sabotaging his speeches. According to the 1967 Report of the CIA's Inspector General, an official in the Technical Services Division (TSD) recalled discussing a scheme to spray Castro's broadcasting studio with a chemical which produced effects similar to LSD, but the scheme was rejected because the chemical was unreliable. During this period, TSD impregnated a box of cigars with a chemical which produced temporary disorientation, hoping to induce Castro to smoke one of the cigars before delivering a speech. The Inspector General also reported a plan to destroy Castro's image as "The Beard" by dusting his shoes with thallium salts, a strong depilatory that would cause his beard to fall out. The depilatory was to be administered during a trip outside Cuba, when it was anticipated

Castro would leave his shoes outside the door of his hotel room to be shined. TSD procured the chemical and tested it on animals, but apparently abandoned the scheme because Castro cancelled his trip. . . .

A notation in the records of the Operations Division, CIA's Office of Medical Services, indicates that on August 16, 1960, an official was given a box of Castro's favorite cigars with instructions to treat them with lethal poison. The cigars were contaminated with a botulinum toxin so potent that a person would die after putting one in his mouth. The official reported that the cigars were ready on October 7, 1960; TSD notes indicate that they were delivered to an unidentified person on February 13, 1961. The record does not disclose whether an attempt was made to pass the cigars to Castro.

In August 1960, the CIA took steps to enlist members of the criminal underworld with gambling syndicate contacts to aid in assassinating Castro. The origin of the plot is uncertain. According to the 1967 Inspector General's Report,

> [Richard] Bissell recalls that the idea originated with J. C. King, then Chief of W. H. Division, although King now recalls having only had limited knowledge of such a plan and at a much later date—about mid-1962.

Bissell testified that:

> I remember a conversation which I would have put in early autumn or late summer between myself and Colonel Edwards [Director of the Office of Security], and I have some dim recollection of some earlier conversations I had had with Colonel J. C. King, Chief of the Western Hemisphere Division, and the subject matter of both of those conversations was a capability to eliminate Castro if such action should be decided upon.

The earliest concrete evidence of the operation is a conversation between DDP Bissell and Colonel Sheffield Edwards, Director of the Office of Security. Edwards recalled that Bissell asked him to locate someone who could assassinate Castro. Bissell confirmed that he requested Edwards to find someone to assassinate Castro and believed that Edwards raised the idea of contacting members of a gambling syndicate operating in Cuba.

Edwards assigned the mission to the Chief of the Operational Support Division of the Office of Security. The Support Chief recalled that Edwards had said that he and Bissell were looking for someone to "eliminate" or "assassinate" Castro.

Edwards and the Support Chief decided to rely on Robert A. Maheu to recruit someone "tough enough" to handle the job. Maheu was an ex-FBI agent who had entered into a career as a private investigator in 1954. A former FBI associate of Maheu's was employed in the CIA's Office of Security and had arranged for the CIA to use Maheu in several sensitive covert operations in which "he didn't want to have an Agency person or a government person get caught." Maheu was initially paid a monthly retainer by the CIA of $500, but it was terminated after his detective agency became more lucrative. The Operational Support Chief had served as Maheu's case officer since the Agency first began using Maheu's services, and by 1960 they had become close personal friends.

Sometime in late August or early September 1960, the Support Chief approached Maheu about the proposed operation. As Maheu recalls the conversation, the Support Chief asked him to contact John Rosselli, an underworld figure with possible gambling contacts in Las Vegas, to determine if he would participate in a plan to "dispose" of Castro. The Support Chief testified, on the other hand, that it was Maheu who raised the idea of using Rosselli.

Maheu had known Rosselli since the late 1950's. Although Maheu claims not to have been aware of the extent of Rosselli's underworld connections and activities, he recalled that "it was certainly evident to me that he was able to accomplish things in Las Vegas when nobody else seemed to get the same kind of attention."

The Support Chief had previously met Rosselli at Maheu's home. The Support Chief and Maheu each claimed that the other had raised the idea of using Rosselli, and Maheu said the Chief was aware that Rosselli had contacts with the gambling syndicate.

At first Maheu was reluctant to become involved in the operation because it might interfere with his relationship with his new client, Howard Hughes. He finally agreed to participate because he felt that he owed the Agency a commitment. The Inspector General's Report states that:

> Edwards and Maheu agreed that Maheu would approach Rosselli as the representative of businessmen with interests in Cuba who saw the elimination of Castro as the first essential step to the recovery of their investments.

The Support Chief also recalled that Maheu was to use this cover story when he presented the plan to Rosselli, but Rosselli said that the story was developed after he had been contacted, and was used as a mutual "cover" by him, the Chief, and Maheu in dealing with Cubans who were subsequently recruited for the project. The Support Chief testified that Maheu was told to offer money, probably $150,000, for Castro's assassination.

According to Rosselli, he and Maheu met at the Brown Derby Restaurant in Beverly Hills in early September 1960. Rosselli testified that Maheu told him that "high government officials" needed his cooperation in getting rid of Castro, and that he asked him to help recruit Cubans to do the job. Maheu's recollection of that meeting was that "I informed him that I had been asked by my Government to solicit his cooperation in this particular venture."

Maheu stated that Rosselli "was very hesitant about participating in the project, and he finally said that he felt that he had an obligation to his government, and he finally agreed to participate." Maheu and Rosselli both testified that Rosselli insisted on meeting with a representative of the Government.

A meeting was arranged for Maheu and Rosselli with the Support Chief at the Plaza Hotel in New York. The Inspector General's Report placed the meeting on September 14, 1960. Rosselli testified that he could not recall the precise date of the meeting, but that it had occurred during Castro's visit to the United Nations, which the New York Times Index places from September 18 through September 28, 1960.

The Support Chief testified that he was introduced to Rosselli as a business associate of Maheu. He said that Maheu told Rosselli that Maheu represented international business interests which were pooling money to pay for the assassination of Castro. Rosselli claimed that Maheu told him at that time that the Support Chief was with the CIA.

It was arranged that Rosselli would go to Florida and recruit Cubans for the operation. Edwards informed Bissell that contact had been made with the gambling syndicate.

During the week of September 24, 1960 the Support Chief, Maheu, and Rosselli met in Miami to work out the details of the operation. Rosselli used the cover name "John Rawlston" and represented himself to the Cuban contacts as an agent of ". . . some business interests of Wall Street that had . . . nickel interests and properties around in Cuba, and I was getting financial assistance from them."

Maheu handled the details of setting up the operation and keeping the Support Chief informed of developments. After Rosselli and Maheu had been in Miami for a short time, and certainly prior to October 18, Rosselli introduced Maheu to two individuals on whom Rosselli intended to rely: "Sam Gold," who would serve as a "back-up man," or "key" man and "Joe," whom "Gold" said would serve as a courier to Cuba and make arrangements there. The Support Chief, who was using the name "Jim Olds," said he had met "Sam" and "Joe" once, and then only briefly.

The Support Chief testified that he learned the true identities of his associates one morning when Maheu called and asked him to examine the "Parade" supplement to the *Miami Times*. An article on the Attorney General's ten-most-wanted criminals list revealed that "Sam Gold" was Momo Salvatore Giancana, a Chicago-based gangster, and "Joe" was Santos Trafficante, the Cosa Nostra chieftain in Cuba. The Support Chief reported his discovery to Edwards, but did not know whether Edwards reported this fact to his superiors. The Support Chief testified that this incident occurred after "we were up to our ears in it," a month or so after Giancana had been brought into the operation, but prior to giving the poison pills to Rosselli.

Maheu recalled that it was Giancana's job to locate someone in Castro's entourage who could accomplish the assassination, and that he met almost daily with Giancana over a substantial period of time. Although Maheu described Giancana as playing a "key role," Rosselli claimed that none of the Cubans eventually used in the operation were acquired through Giancana's contacts. . . .

The Inspector General's Report described conversations among Bissell, Edwards, and the Chief of the Technical Services Division (TSD), concerning the most effective method of poisoning Castro. There is some evidence that Giancana or Rosselli originated the idea of depositing a poison pill in Castro's drink to give the "asset" a chance to escape. The Support Chief recalled Rosselli's request for something "nice and clean, without getting into any kind of out and out ambushing," preferably a poison that would disappear without a trace. The Inspector General's Report cited the Support Chief as stating that the Agency had first considered a "gangland-style killing" in which Castro would be gunned down. Giancana reportedly opposed the idea because it would be difficult to recruit someone for such a dangerous operation, and suggested instead the use of poison.

Edwards rejected the first batch of pills prepared by TSD because they would not dissolve in water. A second batch, containing botulinum toxin, "did the job expected of them" when tested on monkeys. The Support Chief received the pills from TSD, probably in February 1961, with assurances that they were lethal, and then gave them to Rosselli.

The record clearly establishes that the pills were given to a Cuban for delivery to the island some time prior to the Bay of Pigs invasion in mid-April 1961. There are discrepancies in the record, however, concerning whether one or two attempts were made during that period, and the precise date on which the passage[s] occurred. The Inspector General's Report states that in late February or March 1961, Rosselli reported to the Support Chief that the pills had been delivered to an official close to Castro who may have received kickbacks from the gambling interests. The Report states that the official returned the pills after a few weeks, perhaps because he had lost his position in the Cuban Government, and thus access to Castro, before he received the pills. The Report concludes that yet another attempt was made in April 1961, with the aid of a leading figure in the Cuban exile movement. . . .

In early April 1962, Harvey, who testified that he was acting on "explicit orders" from [Richard] Helms, requested Edwards to put him in touch with Rosselli. The Support Chief first introduced Harvey to Rosselli in Miami, where Harvey told Rosselli to maintain his Cuban contacts, but not to deal with Maheu or Giancana, whom he had decided were "untrustworthy" and "surplus." The Support Chief recalled that initially Rosselli did not trust Harvey although they subsequently developed a close friendship.

Harvey, the Support Chief and Rosselli met for a second time in New York on April 8–9, 1962. A notation made during this time in the files of the Technical Services Division indicates that four poison pills were given to the Support Chief on April 18, 1962. The pills were passed to Harvey, who arrived in Miami on April 21, and found Rosselli already in touch with the same Cuban who had been involved in the pre–Bay of Pigs pill passage. He gave the pills to Rosselli, explaining that "these would work anywhere and at any time with anything." Rosselli testified that he told Harvey that the Cubans intended to use the pills to assassinate Che Guevara as well as Fidel and Raul Castro. According to Rosselli's testimony, Harvey approved of the targets, stating "everything is all right, what they want to do."

The Cuban requested arms and equipment as a *quid pro quo* for carrying out the assassination operation. With the help of the CIA's Miami station which ran covert operations against Cuba (JM/WAVE), Harvey procured explosives, detonators, rifles, handguns, radios, and boat radar costing about $5,000. Harvey and the chief of the JM/WAVE station rented a U-Haul Truck under an assumed name and delivered the equipment to a parking lot. The keys were given to Rosselli, who watched the delivery with the Support Chief from across the street. The truckload of equipment was finally picked up by either the Cuban or Rosselli's agent. Harvey testified that the arms "could" have been for use in the assassination attempt, but that they were not given to the Cuban solely for that purpose.

Rosselli kept Harvey informed of the operation's progress. Sometime in May 1962, he reported that the pills and guns had arrived in Cuba. On June 21, he told Harvey that the Cuban had dispatched a three-man team to Cuba. The Inspector General's report described the team's mission as "vague" and conjectured that the team would kill Castro or recruit others to do the job, using the poison pills if the opportunity arose.

Harvey met Rosselli in Miami on September 7 and 11, 1962. The Cuban was reported to be preparing to send in another three-man team to penetrate Castro's bodyguard. Harvey was told that the pills, referred to as "the medicine," were still "safe" in Cuba.

Harvey testified that by this time he had grave doubts about whether the operation would ever take place, and told Rosselli that "there's not much likelihood that this is going anyplace, or that it should be continued." The second team never left for Cuba, claiming that "conditions" in Cuba were not right. During early January 1963, Harvey paid Rosselli $2,700 to defray the Cuban's expenses. Harvey terminated the operation in mid-February 1963. At a meeting with Rosselli in Los Angeles, it was agreed that Rosselli would taper off his communications with the Cubans. Rosselli testified that he simply broke off contact with the Cubans. However, he never informed them that the offer of $150,000 for Castro's assassination had been withdrawn.

The agency personnel who dealt with Rosselli attributed his motivation to patriotism and testified that he was not paid for his services. According to the Support Chief, Rosselli "paid his way, he paid his own hotel fees, he paid his own travel. . . . And he never took a nickel, he said, no, as long as it is for the Government of the United States, this is the least I can do, because I owe it a lot."

Edwards agreed that Rosselli was "never paid a cent," and Maheu testified that "Giancana was paid nothing at all, not even for expenses, and that Mr. Rosselli was given a pittance that did not even begin to cover his expenses." It is clear, however, that the CIA did pay Rosselli's hotel bill during his stay in Miami in October 1960. The CIA's involvement with Rosselli caused the Agency some difficulty during Rosselli's subsequent prosecutions for fraudulent gambling activities and living in the country under an assumed name.

As [for the question of authorization], both Helms and the high Kennedy Administration officials who testified agreed that no direct order was ever given for Castro's assassination and that no senior Administration officials, including McCone, were informed about the assassination activity. Helms testified, however, that he believed the assassination activity was permissible and that it was within the scope of authority given to the Agency. McCone and other Kennedy Administration officials disagreed, testifying that assassination was impermissible without a direct order and that Castro's assassination was not within the bounds of the MONGOOSE operation.

As DDP, Helms was in charge of covert operations when the poison pills were given to Rosselli in Miami in April 1962. Helms had succeeded to this post following Bissell's retirement in February 1962. He testified that after the Bay of Pigs:

> Those of us who were still [in the Agency] were enormously anxious to try and be successful at what we were being asked to do by what was then a relatively new Administration. We wanted to earn our spurs with the President and with other officers of the Kennedy Administration.

John F. Kennedy After the Bay of Pigs: The "Struggle" Against Communism, 1961

Any unilateral American intervention, in the absence of an external attack upon ourselves or an ally, would have been contrary to our traditions and to our international obligations. But let the record show that our restraint is not inexhaustible. Should it ever appear that the inter-American doctrine of non-interference merely conceals or excuses a policy of nonaction—if the nations of this Hemisphere should fail to meet their commitments against outside Communist penetration—then I want it clearly understood that this Government will not hesitate in meeting its primary obligations which are to the security of our Nation!

Should that time ever come, we do not intend to be lectured on "intervention" by those whose character was stamped for all time on the bloody streets of Budapest! Nor would we expect or accept the same outcome which this small band of gallant Cuban refugees must have known that they were chancing, determined as they were against heavy odds to pursue their courageous attempts to regain their Island's freedom.

But Cuba is not an island unto itself; and our concern is not ended by mere expressions of nonintervention or regret. This is not the first time in either ancient or recent history that a small band of freedom fighters has engaged the armor of totalitarianism.

It is not the first time that Communist tanks have rolled over gallant men and women fighting to redeem the independence of their homeland. Nor is it by any means the final episode in the eternal struggle of liberty against tyranny, anywhere on the face of the globe, including Cuba itself. . . .

Meanwhile we will not accept Mr. Castro's attempts to blame this nation for the hatred [with] which his onetime supporters now regard his repression. But there are from this sobering episode useful lessons for us all to learn. Some may be still obscure, and await further information. Some are clear today.

First, it is clear that the forces of communism are not to be underestimated, in Cuba or anywhere else in the world. The advantages of a police state— its use of mass terror and arrests to prevent the spread of free dissent— cannot be overlooked by those who expect the fall of every fanatic tyrant. If the self-discipline of the free cannot match the iron discipline of the maileu fist—in economic, political, scientific and all the other kinds of struggles as well as the military—then the peril to freedom will continue to rise.

Secondly, it is clear that this Nation, in concert with all the free nations of this hemisphere, must take an ever closer and more realistic look at the menace of external Communist intervention and domination in Cuba. The American people are not complacent about Iron Curtain tanks and planes less than 90 miles from their shore. But a nation of Cuba's size is less a threat to our survival than it is a base for subverting the survival of other free nations throughout the hemisphere. It is not primarily our interest or our security but theirs which is now, today, in the greater peril. It is for their sake as well as our own that we must show our will.

The evidence is clear—and the hour is late. We and our Latin friends will have to face the fact that we cannot postpone any longer the real issue of survival of freedom in this hemisphere itself. On that issue, unlike perhaps some others, there can be no middle ground. Together we must build a hemisphere where freedom can flourish; and where any free nation under outside attack of any kind can be assured that all of our resources stand ready to respond to any request for assistance.

Third, and finally, it is clearer than ever that we face a relentless struggle in every corner of the globe that goes far beyond the clash or armies or even nuclear armaments. The armies are there, and in large numbers. The nuclear armaments are there. But they serve primarily as the shield behind which subversion, infiltration, and a host of other tactics steadily advance, picking off vulnerable areas one by one in situations which do not permit our own armed intervention. . . .

We dare not fail to see the insidious nature of this new and deeper struggle. We dare not fail to grasp the new concepts, the new tools, the new sense of urgency we will need to combat it—whether in Cuba or South Viet-Nam. And we dare not fail to realize that this struggle is taking place every day, without fanfare, in thousands of villages and markets—day and night—and in classrooms all over the globe.

The message of Cuba, of Laos, of the rising din of Communist voices in Asia and Latin America—these messages are all the same. The complacent, the self-indulgent, the soft societies are about to be swept away with the debris of history. Only the strong, only the industrious, only the determined, only the courageous, only the visionary who determine the real nature of our struggle can possibly survive.

Nikita Khrushchev Recalls His Decision to Deploy the Missiles (1962), 1970

Cuba's geographical position has always made it very vulnerable to its enemies. The Cuban coast is only a few miles from the American shore, and it is stretched out like a sausage, a shape that makes it easy for attackers and incredibly difficult for the island's defenders. There are infinite opportunities for invasion, especially if the invader has naval artillery and air support.

We were sure that the Americans would never reconcile themselves to the existence of Castro's Cuba. They feared, as much as we hoped, that a Socialist Cuba might become a magnet that would attract other Latin American countries to Socialism. Given the continual threat of American interference in the Caribbean, what should our own policy be? This question was constantly on my mind, and I frequently discussed it with the other members of the Presidium. Everyone agreed that America would not leave Cuba alone unless we did something. We had an obligation to do everything in our power to protect Cuba's existence as a Socialist country and as a working example to the other countries of Latin America. It was clear to me that we might very well lose Cuba if we didn't take some decisive steps in her defense.

The fate of Cuba and the maintenance of Soviet prestige in that part of the world preoccupied me even when I was busy conducting the affairs of state in Moscow and traveling to the other fraternal countries. While I was on an official visit to Bulgaria, for instance, one thought kept hammering away at my brain: what will happen if we lose Cuba? I knew it would have been a terrible blow to Marxism-Leninism. It would gravely diminish our stature throughout the world, but especially in Latin America. If Cuba fell, other Latin American countries would reject us, claiming that for all our might the Soviet Union hadn't been able to do anything for Cuba except to make empty protests to the United Nations. We had to think up some way of confronting America with more than words. We had to establish a tangible and effective deterrent to American interference in the Caribbean. But what exactly? The logical answer was missiles. The United States had already surrounded the Soviet Union with its own bomber bases and missiles. We knew that American missiles were aimed against us in Turkey and Italy, to say nothing of West Germany. Our vital industrial centers were directly threatened by planes armed with atomic bombs and guided missiles tipped with nuclear warheads. As Chairman of the Council of Ministers, I found myself in the difficult position of having to decide on a course of action which would answer the American threat but which would also avoid war. Any fool can start a war, and once he's done so, even the wisest of men are helpless to stop it—especially if it's a nuclear war.

It was during my visit to Bulgaria that I had the idea of installing missiles with nuclear warheads in Cuba without letting the United States find out they were there until it was too late to do anything about them. I knew that first we'd have to talk to Castro and explain our strategy to him in order to get the agreement of the Cuban government. My thinking went like this: if we installed the missiles secretly and then if the United States discovered the missiles were there after they were already poised and ready

---

to strike, the Americans would think twice before trying to liquidate our installations by military means. I knew that the United States could knock out some of our installations, but not all of them. If a quarter or even a tenth of our missiles survived—even if only one or two big ones were left—we could still hit New York, and there wouldn't be much of New York left. I don't mean to say that everyone in New York would be killed— not everyone, of course, but an awful lot of people would be wiped out. I don't know how many: that's a matter for our scientists and military personnel to work out. They specialize in nuclear warfare and know how to calculate the consequences of a missile strike against a city the size of New York. But that's all beside the point. The main thing was that the installation of our missiles in Cuba would, I thought, restrain the United States from precipitous military action against Castro's government. In addition to protecting Cuba, our missiles would have equalized what the West likes to call "the balance of power." The Americans had surrounded our country with military bases and threatened us with nuclear weapons, and now they would learn just what it feels like to have enemy missiles pointing at you; we'd be doing nothing more than giving them a little of their own medicine. And it was high time America learned what it feels like to have her own land and her own people threatened. . . .

All these thoughts kept churning in my head the whole time I was in Bulgaria. I paced back and forth, brooding over what to do. I didn't tell anyone what I was thinking. I kept my mental agony to myself. But all the while the idea of putting missiles in Cuba was ripening inside my mind. After I returned to Moscow from Bulgaria I continued to think about the possibility. Finally we convened a meeting and I said I had some thoughts to air on the subject of Cuba. I laid out all the considerations which I've just outlined. I presented my idea in the context of the counterrevolutionary invasion [Bay of Pigs] which Castro had just resisted. I said that it would be foolish to expect the inevitable second invasion to be as badly planned and as badly executed as the first. I warned that Fidel would be crushed if another invasion were launched against Cuba and said that we were the only ones who could prevent such a disaster from occurring.

In the course of discussions inside the Government, we decided to install intermediate-range missiles, launching equipment, and Il-28 bombers in Cuba. Even though these bombers were obsolete, they would be useful against an enemy landing force. The Il-28 was too slow to fly over enemy territory because it could easily be shot down, but was well suited for coastal defense. The Il-28 was our first jet bomber. In its time it had been god of the air, but by the time we gave military assistance to Cuba, the IL-28 had already been taken out of production. . . .

I want to make one thing absolutely clear: when we put our ballistic missiles in Cuba, we had no desire to start a war. On the contrary, our principal aim was only to deter America from starting a war. We were well aware that a war which started over Cuba would quickly expand into a world war. Any idiot could have started a war between America and Cuba. Cuba was eleven thousand kilometers away from us. Only a fool would think that we wanted to invade the American continent from Cuba. Our goal was precisely the opposite: we wanted to keep the Americans from invading Cuba, and, to that end, we wanted to make them think twice by confronting them with our missiles. This goal we achieved—but not without undergoing a period of perilous tension.

The Cuban Case Against the United States, 1962

It was enough for us to promulgate laws which affected the United States monopolistic interests in our country, it was enough to promulgate the land reform act at a period when our revolutionary development was not yet shaped by socialist principles, for aggressive action against our homeland to be undertaken by the United States Government.

That was the start of the insolent diplomatic notes and piratical flights over our territory. Then the Cuban sugar quota was eliminated from the United States market, supplies of petroleum to our country were stopped, and diplomatic measures were taken aimed at isolating Cuba from the continent. Finally there was a whole series of eminently aggressive activities which generated this tension, long before—I repeat—long before we proclaimed that our revolution was a socialist one.

And what has happened since?

It would be unduly tedious, I think, to recapitulate all the acts of aggression committed by the United States against Cuba. Suffice it to mention all the efforts designed to subvert our country from within, the acts of sabotage, the attacks on persons and the espionage activities on our soil. In brief, suffice it to recall the armed invasion of our country by mercenary forces financed, trained in warfare, militarily protected and commanded by the Government of the United States: the invasion of Playa Girón [Bay of Pigs]. And what happened after Playa Girón, that ridiculous fiasco? Did they perchance learn a great lesson of history from it? Did they perchance have sufficient perception and knowledge to realize what immense forces can be marshalled by a nation firmly resolved to preserve its freedom and independence? That is not what happened. We immediately became the victims of further acts of aggression with the infiltration of agents landed on our coasts and trained by the Central Intelligence Agency, new attempts at sabotage, the military training of groups to carry out the hitherto unsuccessful internal subversion of our country and the increase of economic pressure on our homeland—tenaciously and doggedly applied in the hope that it would undermine our revolution and that, as a result, their sole objective would be attained: the downfall of the Revolutionary Government of Cuba. . . .

These aggressive acts continue, like the United States warships that lie near the coast off our harbours. Every day those of us who live in Havana must see with our own eyes these warships lurking around our island, making a show of war or of preparation for war.

This is the situation today but we can also say that it is qualitatively different from the situation which existed before the invasion of our country at Playa Girón, for the following reasons. Before Playa Girón, the Government of the United States had on more than one occasion stated that it had no aggressive intentions towards our country. It is obvious that after Playa Girón even the President of the United States publicly and officially acknowledged his responsibility and his sympathy and support for that invasion.

Today the situation is different, for while it is true that once again it is being asserted—as the Head of the United States delegation has stated here—that there are no aggressive designs on our country, on the other hand there are records, and there have been statements and official resolutions which authorize armed aggression against Cuba and seek to justify it in advance. The fact is that the object—as acknowledged recently in a statement by the State Department of the United States—of the foreign policy of the United States Government in regard to Cuba is clearly and obviously the overthrow of the revolutionary Government and the destruction of our glorious revolution. . . .

Cuba does not stand alone; it has friends, it can count on the solidarity of other nations and relies on friendly countries which must enable it to carry on its international trade.

But there is something more, something to which I emphatically wish to draw the attention of the Assembly. At the beginning of my address I said that the situation as regards Cuban-United States relations before the invasion at Playa Girón was qualitatively different from the present situation. And I said so because in the United States there have been statements and official resolutions designed to build up a case in advance for direct armed aggression against our country. By way of proof it is sufficient to take a brief look at the operative part of the joint resolution of the United States Congress.

"*Resolved by the Senate and House of Representatives of the United States of America in Congress assembled,*

"That the United States is determined

"(*a*) To prevent by whatever means may be necessary, including the use of arms"—I repeat, including the use of arms—"the Marxist-Leninist regime in Cuba from extending, by force or the threat of force, its aggressive or subversive activities to any part of this hemisphere." . . .

Of course we should have preferred to devote all those human and material resources, all the energies we have had to employ in strengthening our military defences, to the development of our economy and culture. We have armed ourselves against our wishes and contrary to our aspirations, because we were driven to strengthen our military defences lest we should jeopardize the sovereignty of our nation and the independence of our homeland. We have armed ourselves because the people of Cuba have a legitimate right, sanctioned by history, to defend their sovereign decisions and to steer their country on the historic course which, in the exercise of their sovereignty, they have chosen.

I ask you, so that you may answer in all sincerity to your own consciences: what would have happened if we had not strengthened our military defences when a division armed and trained by the United States Government invaded our country at Playa Girón? Our revolution would not, of course, have been defeated nor the tide of our history turned back; but no doubt the struggle would have been long and bloody, and many more lives and more wealth than our country actually lost would have been destroyed. We wiped out this invasion, this unjustified act of aggression and arrogance towards our country, in seventy-two hours, because we had exercised in time the right to strengthen our defensive military capability in order to safeguard our sovereignty, our independence and our revolution.

If the United States could give assurances, by word and by deed, that it would not commit acts of aggression against our country, we solemnly declare that there would be no need for our weapons and our armies, because we want peace and we want to carry on our work in peace. . . .

Cuba does not, as has been stated here, represent a problem between the East and the West. Cuba poses a problem of sovereignty and independence. The Cuban problem is a problem involving the sovereign decision of a people and the right of that people to self-determination. Cuba has not wanted to be drawn into the cold war. Cuba merely wants to pursue its economic and cultural development and to shape its own future in peace, and it is ready to demonstrate these intentions at any time. And if it is not true that there is an intention to attack our country—although we consider that such an intention certainly exists—we urge the head of the United States delegation specifically to guarantee before this Assembly that his Government does not intend to attack Cuba. We urge him, however, to back up these guarantees not merely by words, but more especially by deeds. Verbal guarantees were given before Playa Girón, and when the invasion took place, many Members of the Assembly heard the representative of the United States Government state that there was no such invasion and that his Government had not planned one; yet only a few days later, the President of the United States himself publicly and officially assumed the responsibility for that invasion.

Missiles Photographed in Cuba: Kennedy's First Meetings with His Advisers, October 16, 1962

Meeting of 11:50 A.M.–12:57 P.M.

LUNDAHL*: This is a result of the photography taken Sunday, sir.

JFK: Yeah.

LUNDAHL: There's a medium-range ballistic missile launch site and two new military encampments on the southern edge of Sierra del Rosario in west central Cuba.

---

*Art Lundahl, National Photographic Interpretation Center

JFK: Where would that be?

LUNDAHL: Uh, west central, sir. That. . . .

JFK: Yeah. . . .

LUNDAHL: Well, on site on one of the encampments contains a total of at least fourteen canvas-covered missile trailers measuring 67 feet in length, 9 feet in width. The overall length of the trailers plus the tow-bars is approximately 80 feet. The other encampment contains vehicles and tents but with no missile trailers. . . .

JFK: How far advanced is this? . . . How do you know this is a medium-range ballistic missile?

LUNDAHL: The length, sir.

JFK: The what? The length?

LUNDAHL: The length of it. Yes.

JFK: The length of the missile? Which part? I mean which . . .

LUNDAHL: . . . the missile [word unintelligible] indicates which one is [words unintelligible]. . . .

JFK: Is this ready to be fired?

GRAYBEAL*: No, sir.

JFK: How long have we got. . . . We can't tell, I take it . . .

GRAYBEAL: No, sir.

JFK: . . . how long before it can be fired?   .

GRAYBEAL: That depends on how ready the . . .

JFK: But, what does it have to be fired from?

GRAYBEAL: It would have to be fired from a stable hard surface. This could be packed dirt; it could be concrete or, or asphalt. The surface has to be hard, then you put a flame deflect-, a deflector plate on there to direct the missile.

McNAMARA**: Would you care to comment on the position of nuclear warheads—this is in relation to the question from the president—explain when these can be fired?

GRAYBEAL: Sir, we've looked very hard. We can find nothing that would spell nuclear warhead in term of any isolated area or unique security in this particular area. The mating of the nuclear warhead to the missile from some of the other short range missiles there would take about, uh, a couple of hours to do this.

McNAMARA: This is not defensed, I believe, at the moment?

LUNDAHL: Not yet, sir. . . .

RUSK***: Don't you have to assume these are nuclear? . . .

McNAMARA: There's no question about that. The question is one of readiness of the, to fire and—and this is highly critical in forming our plans—that the time between today and the time when the readiness to fire capability

---

*Sidney Graybeal.
**Robert McNamara, secretary of defense
***Dean Rusk, secretary of state

develops is a very important thing. To estimate that we need to know where these warheads are, and we have not yet found any probable storage of warheads and hence it seems extremely unlikely that they are now ready to fire or may be ready to fire within a matter of hours or even a day or two. . . .

JFK: Secretary Rusk?

RUSK: Yes. [Well?], Mr. President, this is a, of course, a [widely?] serious development. It's one that we, all of us, had not really believed the Soviets could, uh, carry this far. Uh, they, uh, seemed to be denying that they were going to establish bases of their own [in the same?] [words unintelligible] with a Soviet base, thus making it [essential to or essentially?] Cuban point of view. The Cubans couldn't [word unintelligible] with it anyhow, so. . . . Now, uhm, I do think we have to set in motion a chain of events that will eliminate this base. I don't think we [can?] sit still. The questioning becomes whether we do it by sudden, unannounced strike of some sort, or we, uh, build up the crisis to the point where the other side has to consider very seriously about giving in, or, or even the Cubans themselves, uh, take some, take some action on this. The thing that I'm, of course, very conscious of is that there is no such thing, I think, as unilateral action by the United States. It's so [eminently or heavily?] involved with 2 allies and confrontation in many places, that any action that we take, uh, will greatly increase the risks of direct action involving, uh, our other alliances and our other forces in other parts of the world. Uhm, so I think we, we have to think very hard about two major, uh, courses of action as alternatives. One is the quick strike. The point where we [make or think?], that is the, uh, overwhelming, overriding necessity to take all the risks that are involved doing that. I don't think this in itself would require an invasion of Cuba. I think that with or without such an invasion, in other words if we make it clear that, uh, what we're doing is eliminating this particular base or any other such base that is established. We ourselves are not moved to general war, we're simply doing what we said we would do if they took certain action. Uh, or we're going to decide that this is the time to eliminate the Cuban problem by actual eliminate the island.

The other would be, if we have a few days—from the military point of view, if we have the whole time—uh, then I would think that, uh, there would be another course of action, a combination of things that, uh, we might wish to consider. Uhm, first, uh, that we, uh, stimulate the OAS procedure immediately for prompt action to make it quite clear that the entire hemisphere considers that the Rio Pact has been violated [and actually?] what acts should [we take or be taken?] in, under the terms of the Rio Pact. . . .

I think also that we ought to consider getting some word to Castro, perhaps through the Canadian ambassador in Havana or through, uh, his representative at the U.N. Uh, I think perhaps the Canadian ambassador would be best, the better channel to get to Castro [apart?] privately and tell him that, uh, this is no longer support for Cuba, that Cuba is being victimized here, and that, uh, the Soviets are preparing Cuba for destruction or betrayal.

You saw the [*New York*] *Times* story yesterday morning that high Soviet officials were saying, "We'll trade Cuba for Berlin." This ought to be brought to Castro's attention. It ought to be said to Castro that, uh, uh, this kind of a base is intolerable and not acceptable. The time has now come when he must take the interests of the Cuban people, must now break clearly with the Soviet Union, prevent this missile base from becoming operational.

And I think there are certain military, uhm, uh, actions that we could, we might well want to take straight away. First, to, uh, to call up, uh, highly selective units [no more than?] 150,000. Unless we feel that it's better, more desirable to go to a general national emergency so that we have complete freedom of action. If we announce, at the time that we announce this development—and I think we do have to announce this development some time this week—uh, we announce that, uh, we are conducting a surveillance of Cuba, over Cuba, and we will enforce our right to do so. We reject the mission of secrecy in this hemisphere in any matters of this sort. We, we reinforce our forces in Guantanamo. We reinforce our forces in the southeastern part of the United States— whatever is necessary from the military point of view to be able to give, to deliver an overwhelming strike at any of these installations, including the SAM sites. And, uh, also, to take care of any, uh, MIGs or bombers that might make a pass at Miami or at the United States. Build up heavy forces, uh, if those are not already in position. . . .

I think also that we need a few days, uhm, to alert our other allies, for consultation with NATO. I'll assume that we can move on this line at the same time to interrupt all air traffic from free world countries going into Cuba, insist to the Mexicans, the Dutch, that they stop their planes from coming in. Tell the British, who, and anyone else who's involved at this point, that, uh, if they're interested in peace, that they've got to stop their ships from Cuban trade at this point. Uh, in other words, isolate Cuba completely without at this particular moment a, uh, a forceful blockade. . . .

But I think that, by large, there are, there are these two broad alternatives: one, the quick strike; the other, to alert our allies and Mr. Khrushchev that there is utterly serious crisis in the making here, and that, uh. . . . Mr. Khrushchev may not himself really understand that or believe that at this point. I think we'll be facing a situation that could well lead to general war. . . .

McNAMARA: Mr. President, there are a number of unknowns in this situation I want to comment upon, and, in relation to them, I would like to outline very briefly some possible military alternatives and ask General Taylor to expand upon them.

But before commenting on either the unknowns or outlining some military alternatives, there are two propositions I would suggest that we ought to accept as, uh, foundations for our further thinking. My first is that if we are to conduct an air strike against these installations, or against any part of Cuba, we must agree now that we will schedule that prior to the time these missile sites become operational. I'm not prepared to say when that will be, but I think it is extremely important that our talk and our discussion be founded on this premise: that any air strike will be planned to take place prior to the time they become operational. Because, if they become operational before the air strike, I do not believe we can state we can knock them out before they can be launched; and if they're launched there is almost certain to be, uh, chaos in part of the east coast or the area, uh, in a radius of six hundred to a thousand miles from Cuba.

Uh, secondly, I, I would submit the proposition that any air strike must be directed not solely against the missile sites, but against the missile sites plus the airfields plus the aircraft which may not be on the airfields but hidden by that time plus all potential nuclear storage sites. Now, this is a fairly extensive air strike. It is not just a strike against the missile sites; and there would be associated with it potential casualties of Cubans, not of U.S. citizens, but potential casualties of Cubans in, at least in the hundreds, more likely in the low thousands, say two or three thousand. It seems to me these two propositions, uh, should underlie our, our discussion.

Now, what kinds of military action are we capable of carrying out and what may be some of the consequences? Uh, we could carry out an air strike within a matter of days. We would be ready for the start of such an air strike within, within a matter of days. If it were absolutely essential, it could be done almost literally within a matter of hours. I believe the chiefs would prefer that it be deferred for a matter of days, but we are prepared for that quickly. The air strike could continue for a matter of days following the initial day, if necessary. Uh, presumably there would be some political discussions taking place either just before the air strike or both before and during. In any event, we would be prepared, following the air strike, for an air, invasion, both by air and by sea. . . . Associated with this air strike undoubtedly should be some degree of mobilization. Uh, I would think of the mobilization coming not before the air strike but either concurrently with or somewhat following, say possibly five days afterwards, depending upon the possible invasion requirements. The character of the mobilization would be such that it could be carried out in its first phase at least within the limits of the authority granted by Congress. There might have to be a second phase, and then it would require a declaration of a national emergency.

Now, this is very sketchily the military, uh, capabilities, and I think you may wish to hear General Taylor, uh, outline his choice. . . .

TAYLOR*: Uh, we're impressed, Mr. President, with the great importance

---

*General Maxwell Taylor, chairman of the Joint Chiefs of Staff

of getting a, a strike with all the benefits of surprise, uh, which would mean *ideally* that we would have all the missiles that are in Cuba above ground where we can take them out. Uh, that, that desire runs counter to the strong point the secretary made if the other optimum would be to get every missile before it could, becomes operational. Uh, practically, I think the, our knowledge of the timing of the readiness is going to be so, so, uh, difficult that we'll never have the, the exact permanent, uh, the perfect timing. . . .It's a little hard to say in terms of time how much I'm discussing. But we must do a good job the first time we go in there, uh, pushing a 100 percent just as far, as closely as we can with our, with our strike. . . .

I would also mention among the, the military actions we should take that once we have destroyed as many of these offensive weapons as possible, we should, should prevent any more coming in, which means a naval blockade. . . .

JFK: What is the, uh, advant-. . . . Must be some major reason for the Russians to, uh, set this up as a. . . . Must be that they're not satisfied with their ICBMs. What'd be the reason that they would, uh. . . .

TAYLOR: What it'd give 'em is primary, it makes the launching base, uh, for short range missiles against the United States to supplement their rather [deceptive?] ICBM system, for example. There's one reason. . . .

RUSK: Still, about why the Soviets are doing this, uhm, Mr. McCone* suggested some weeks ago that one thing Mr. Khrushchev may have in mind is that, uh, uh, he knows that we have a substantial nuclear superiority, but he also knows that we don't really live under fear of his nuclear weapons to the extent that, uh, he has to live under fear of ours. Also we have nuclear weapons nearby, in Turkey and places like that.

JFK: How many weapons do we have in Turkey?

TAYLOR?: We have Jupiter missiles. . . .

McNAMARA?: About fifteen, I believe it is. . . .

RUSK: Uhm, and that Mr. McCone expresses the view that Khrushchev may feel that it's important for us to learn about living under medium-range missiles, and he's doing that to sort of balance that, uh, that political, psychological [plank?]. I think also that, uh, Berlin is, uh, very much involved in this. Uhm, for the first time, I'm beginning really to wonder whether maybe Mr. Khrushchev is entirely rational about Berlin. We've [hardly?] talked about his obsession with it. And I think we have to, uh, keep our eye on that element. But, uh, they may be thinking that they can either bargain Berlin and Cuba against each other, or that they could provoke us into a kind of action in Cuba which would give an umbrella for them to take action with respect to Berlin. In other words like the Suez-Hungary combination. If they could provoke us into taking the first overt action, then the world would be confused and they would have, uh, what they would consider to be justification for making a move

---

*John A. McCone, director of the Central Intelligence Agency

somewhere else. But, uh, I must say I don't really see the rationality of, uh, the Soviets' pushing it this far unless they grossly misunderstand the importance of Cuba to this country. . . .

JFK: Uh, eh, well, this, which . . . What you're really talking about are two or three different, uh, [tense?] operations. One is the strike just on this, these three bases. One, the second is the broader one that Secretary McNamara was talking about, which is on the airfields and on the SAM sites and on anything else connected with, uh, missiles. Third is doing both of those things and also at the same time launching a blockade, which requires really the, uh, the, uh, third and which is a larger step. And then, as I take it, the fourth question is the, uh, degree of consultation.

RFK*: Mr. President.

JFK: Yes.

RFK: We have the fifth one, really, which is the invasion. I would say that, uh, you're dropping bombs all over Cuba if you do the second, uh, air, the airports, knocking out their planes, dropping it on all their missiles. You're covering most of Cuba. You're going to kill an awful lot of people, and, uh, we're going to take an awful lot of heat on it . . .

JFK: I don't believe it takes us, at least, uh. . . . How long did it take to get in a position where we can invade Cuba? Almost a month? Two months?

McNAMARA: No, sir. . . .

JFK: I think we ought to, what we ought to do is, is, uh, after this meeting this afternoon, we ought to meet tonight again at six, consider these various, uh, proposals. In the meanwhile, we'll go ahead with this maximum, whatever is needed from the flights, and, in addition, we will. . . . I don't think we got much time on these missiles. They may be. . . . So it may be that we just have to, we can't wait two weeks while we're getting ready to, to roll. Maybe just have to just take *them out*, and continue our other preparations if we decide to do that. That may be where we end up. I think we ought to, beginning right now, be preparing to. . . . Because that's what we're going to do *anyway*. We're certainly going to do number one; we're going to take out these, uh, missiles. Uh, the questions will be whether, which, what I would describe as number two, which would be a general air strike. That we're not ready to say, but we should be in preparation for it. The third is the, is the, uh, the general invasion. At least we're going to do number one, so it seems to me that we don't have to wait very long. We, we ought to be making *those* preparations.

BUNDY**: You want to be clear, Mr. President, whether we have *definitely* decided *against* a political track. I, myself, think we ought . . .

TAYLOR:? Well, we'll have . . .

BUNDY: . . . to work out a contingency on that.

TAYLOR?: We, we'll develop both tracks.

---

*Robert F. Kennedy
**McGeorge Bundy, assistant for national security affairs

Meeting of 6:30–7:55 P.M.

McNamara: Mr. President, could I outline three courses of action we have considered and speak very briefly on each one? The first is what I would call the political course of action, in which we, uh, follow some of the possibilities that Secretary Rusk mentioned this morning by approaching Castro, by approaching Khrushchev, by discussing with our allies. An overt and open approach politically to the problem [attempting, or in order?] to solve it. This seemed to me likely to lead to no satisfactory result, and it almost stops subsequent military action. . . .

A second course of action we haven't discussed but lies in between the military course we began discussing a moment ago and the political course of action is a course of action that would involve declaration of open surveillance; a statement that we would immediately impose an, uh, a blockade against *offensive* weapons entering Cuba in the future; and an indication that with our open-surveillance reconnaissance which we would plan to maintain indefinitely for the future. . . .

But the third course of action is any one of these variants of military action directed against Cuba, starting with an air attack against the missiles. The Chiefs are strongly opposed to so limited an air attack. But even so limited an air attack is a very extensive air attack. It's not twenty sorties or fifty sorties or a hundred sorties, but probably several hundred sorties. Uh, we haven't worked out the details. It's very difficult to do so when we lack certain intelligence that we hope to have tomorrow or the next day. But it's a substantial air attack. . . . I don't believe we have considered the consequences of any of these actions satisfactorily, and because we haven't considered the consequences, I'm not sure we're taking all the action we ought to take now to minimize those. I, I don't know quite what kind of a world we live in after we've struck Cuba, and we, we've started it. . . .

Taylor: And you'll miss some [missiles].

McNamara: And you'll miss some. That's right. Now after we've launched sorties, what kind of a world do we live in? How, how do we stop at that point? I don't know the answer to this. I think tonight State and we ought to work on the consequences of any one of these courses of actions, consequences which I don't believe are entirely clear. . . .

JFK: If the, uh, it doesn't increase very much their strategic, uh, strength, why is it, uh, can any Russian expert tell us why they. . . . After all Khrushchev demonstrated a sense of caution [thousands?]. . .

Speaker?: Well, there are several, several possible . . .

JFK: . . . Berlin, he's been cautious, I mean, he hasn't been, uh . . .

Ball*: Several possibilities, Mr. President. One of them is that he has given us word now that he's coming over in November to, to the UN.

---

*George W. Ball, under secretary of state

If, he may be proceeding on the assumption, and this lack of a sense of *apparent* urgency would seem to, to support this, that this *isn't* going to be discovered at the moment and that, uh, when he comes over this is something he can do, a ploy. That here is Cuba armed against the United States, or possibly use it to try to trade something in Berlin, saying he'll disarm Cuba, if, uh, if we'll yield some of our interests in Berlin and some arrangement for it. I mean, that this is a, it's a trading ploy.

BUNDY: I would think one thing that I would still cling to is that he's not likely to give Fidel Castro nuclear warheads. I don't believe that has happened or is likely to happen.

JFK: Why does he put these in there though?

BUNDY: Soviet-controlled nuclear warheads [of the kind?] . . .

JFK: That's right, but what is the advantage of that? It's just as if we suddenly began to put a major number of MRBMs [Medium-Range Ballistic Missiles] in Turkey. Now that'd be goddam dangerous, I would think.

BUNDY: Well, we *did*, Mr. President. . . .

JFK: Yeah, but that was five years ago. . . .

BALL: Yes, I think, I think you, you look at this possibility that this is an attempt to, to add to his strategic capabilities. A second consideration is that it is simply a trading ploy, that he, he wants this in so that he could, he could [words unintelligible]. . . .

SPEAKER?: Isn't it puzzling, also, there are no evidence of any troops protecting the sites?

TAYLOR: Well, there're troops there. At least there're tents. . . .

McNAMARA: But they look like [words unintelligible]. It's as if you could walk over the fields into those vans.

JFK: Well, it's a goddam mystery to me. I don't know enough about the Soviet Union, but if anybody can tell me any other time since the Berlin blockade where the Russians have given us so clear provocation, I don't know when it's been, because they've been awfully cautious really. The Russians, I never. . . . Now, maybe our mistake was in not saying some time *before* this summer that if they do this we're [word unintelligible] to act. . . .

John F. Kennedy's Television Address, October 22, 1962

This Government, as promised, has maintained the closest surveillance of the Soviet military buildup on the island of Cuba. Within the past week unmistakable evidence has established the fact that a series of offensive missile sites is now in preparation on that imprisoned island. The purpose of these bases can be none other than to provide a nuclear strike capability against the Western Hemisphere.

Upon receiving the first preliminary hard information of this nature last Tuesday morning [October 16] at 9:00 a.m., I directed that our surveillance be stepped up. And having now confirmed and completed our evaluation of the evidence and our decision on a course of action, this Government feels obliged to report this new crisis to you in fullest detail.

The characteristics of these new missile sites indicate two distinct types of installations. Several of them include medium-range ballistic missiles capable of carrying a nuclear warhead for a distance of more than 1,000 nautical miles. Each of these missiles, in short, is capable of striking Washington, D.C., the Panama Canal, Cape Canaveral, Mexico City, or any other city in the southeastern part of the United States, in Central America, or in the Caribbean area.

Additional sites not yet completed appear to be designed for intermediate-range ballistic missiles capable of traveling more than twice as far—and thus capable of striking most of the major cities in the Western Hemisphere, ranging as far north as Hudson Bay, Canada, and as far south as Lima, Peru. In addition, jet bombers, capable of carrying nuclear weapons, are now being uncrated and assembled in Cuba, while the necessary air bases are being prepared.

This urgent transformation of Cuba into an important strategic base— by the presence of these large, long-range, and clearly offensive weapons of sudden mass destruction—constitutes an explicit threat to the peace and security of all the Americas, in flagrant and deliberate defiance of the Rio Pact of 1947, the traditions of this nation and hemisphere, the Joint Resolution of the 87th Congress, the Charter of the United Nations, and my own public warnings to the Soviets on September 4 and 13.

This action also contradicts the repeated assurances of Soviet spokesmen, both publicly and privately delivered, that the arms buildup in Cuba would retain its original defensive character and that the Soviet Union had no need or desire to station strategic missiles on the territory of any other nation.

The size of this undertaking makes clear that it has been planned for some months. Yet only last month, after I had made clear the distinction between any introduction of ground-to-ground missiles and the existence of defensive antiaircraft missiles, the Soviet Government publicly stated on September 11 that, and I quote, "The armaments and military equipment sent to Cuba are designed exclusively for defensive purposes," and, and I quote the Soviet Government, "There is no need for the Soviet Government to shift its weapons for a retaliatory blow to any other country, for instance Cuba," and that, and I quote the Government, "The Soviet Union has so powerful rockets to carry these nuclear warheads that there is no need to search for sites for them beyond the boundaries of the Soviet Union." That statement was false.

Only last Thursday, as evidence of this rapid offensive buildup was already in my hand, Soviet Foreign Minister Gromyko told me in my office that he was instructed to make it clear once again, as he said his Government had already done, that Soviet assistance to Cuba, and I quote,"pursued solely the purpose of contributing to the defense capabilities of Cuba," that, and I quote him, "training by Soviet specialists of Cuban nationals in handling defensive armaments was by no means offensive," and that "if it were otherwise," Mr. Gromyko went on, "the Soviet Government would never become involved in rendering such assistance." That statement also was false.

Neither the United States of America nor the world community of nations can tolerate deliberate deception and offensive threats on the part of any nation, large or small. We no longer live in a world where only the actual firing of weapons represents a sufficient challenge to a nation's security to constitute maximum peril. Nuclear weapons are so destructive and ballistic missiles are so swift that any substantially increased possibility of their use or any sudden change in their deployment may well be regarded as a definite threat to peace.

For many years both the Soviet Union and the United States, recognizing this fact, have deployed strategic nuclear weapons with great care, never upsetting the precarious *status quo* which insured that these weapons would not be used in the absence of some vital challenge. Our own strategic missiles have never been transferred to the territory of any other nation under a cloak of secrecy and deception; and our history, unlike that of the Soviets since the end of World War II, demonstrates that we have no desire to dominate or conquer any other nation or impose our system upon its people. Nevertheless, American citizens have become adjusted to living daily on the bull's eye of Soviet missiles located inside the U.S.S.R. or in submarines.

In that sense missiles in Cuba add to an already clear and present danger—although it should be noted the nations of Latin America have never previously been subjected to a potential nuclear threat.

But this secret, swift, and extraordinary buildup of Communist missiles— in an area well known to have a special and historical relationship to the United States and the nations of the Western Hemisphere, in violation of Soviet assurances, and in defiance of American and hemispheric policy— this sudden, clandestine decision to station strategic weapons for the first time outside of Soviet soil—is a deliberately provocative and unjustified change in the *status quo* which cannot be accepted by this country if our courage and our commitments are ever to be trusted again by either friend or foe.

The 1930's taught us a clear lesson: Aggressive conduct, if allowed to grow unchecked and unchallenged, ultimately leads to war. This nation is opposed to war. We are also true to our word. Our unswerving objective, therefore, must be to prevent the use of these missiles against this or any other country and to secure their withdrawal or elimination from the Western Hemisphere.

Our policy has been one of patience and restraint, as befits a peaceful and powerful nation, which leads a worldwide alliance. We have been determined not to be diverted from our central concerns by mere irritants and fanatics. But now further action is required—and it is underway; and these actions may only be the beginning. We will not prematurely or un- necessarily risk the costs of worldwide nuclear war in which even the fruits of victory would be ashes in our mouth—but neither will we shrink from that risk at any time it must be faced.

Acting, therefore, in the defense of our own security and of the entire Western Hemisphere, and under the authority entrusted to me by the Constitution as endorsed by the resolution of the Congress, I have directed that the following *initial* steps be taken immediately:

First: To halt this offensive buildup, a strict quarantine on all offensive military equipment under shipment to Cuba is being initiated. All ships of any kind bound for Cuba from whatever nation or port will, if found to contain cargoes of offensive weapons, be turned back. This quarantine will be extended, if needed, to other types of cargo and carriers. We are not at this time, however, denying the necessities of life as the Soviets attempted to do in their Berlin blockade of 1948.

Second: I have directed the continued and increased close surveillance of Cuba and its military buildup. The Foreign Ministers of the OAS in their communique of October 3 rejected secrecy on such matters in this hemisphere. Should these offensive military preparations continue, thus increasing the threat to the hemisphere, further action will be justified. I have directed the Armed Forces to prepare for any eventualities; and I trust that, in the interest of both the Cuban people and the Soviet technicians at the sites, the hazards to all concerned of continuing this threat will be recognized.

Third: It shall be the policy of this nation to regard any nuclear missile launched from Cuba against any nation in the Western Hemisphere as an attack by the Soviet Union on the United States, requiring a full retaliatory response upon the Soviet Union.

Fourth: As a necessary military precaution I have reinforced our base at Guantanamo, evacuated today the dependents of our personnel there, and ordered additional military units to be on a standby alert basis.

Fifth: We are calling tonight for an immediate meeting of the Organ of Consultation, under the Organization of American States, to consider this threat to hemispheric security and to invoke articles 6 and 8 of the Rio Treaty in support of all necessary action. The United Nations Charter allows for regional security arrangements—and the nations of this hemisphere decided long ago against the military presence of outside powers. Our other allies around the world have also been alerted.

Sixth: Under the Charter of the United Nations, we are asking tonight that an emergency meeting of the Security Council be convoked without delay to take action against this latest Soviet threat to world peace. Our resolution will call for the prompt dismantling and withdrawal of all offensive weapons in Cuba, under the supervision of U.N. observers, before the quarantine can be lifted.

Seventh and finally: I call upon Chairman Khrushchev to halt and eliminate this clandestine, reckless, and provocative threat to world peace and to stable relations between our two nations. I call upon him further to abandon this course of world domination and to join in an historic effort to end the perilous arms race and transform the history of man. He has an opportunity now to move the world back from the abyss of destruction— by returning to his Government's own words that it had no need to station missiles outside its own territory, and withdrawing these weapons from Cuba—by refraining from any action which will widen or deepen the present crisis—and then by participating in a search for peaceful and permanent solutions.

This nation is prepared to present its case against the Soviet threat to peace, and our own proposals for a peaceful world, at any time and in any forum—in the OAS, in the United Nations, or in any other meeting that could be useful—without limiting our freedom of action.

We have in the past made strenuous efforts to limit the spread of nuclear weapons. We have proposed the elimination of all arms and military bases in a fair and effective disarmament treaty. We are prepared to discuss new proposals for the removal of tensions on both sides—including the possibilities of a genuinely independent Cuba, free to determine its own destiny. We have no wish to war with the Soviet Union, for we are a peaceful people who desire to live in peace with all other peoples.

But it is difficult to settle or even discuss these problems in an atmosphere of intimidation. That is why this latest Soviet threat—or any other threat which is made either independently or in response to our actions this week—must and will be met with determination. Any hostile move anywhere in the world against the safety and freedom of peoples to whom we are committed—including in particular the brave people of West Berlin—will be met by whatever action is needed.

Finally, I want to say a few words to the captive people of Cuba, to whom this speech is being directly carried by special radio facilities. I speak to you as a friend, as one who knows of your deep attachment to your fatherland, as one who shares your aspirations for liberty and justice for all. And I have watched and the American people have watched with deep sorrow how your nationalist revolution was betrayed and how your fatherland fell under the reign domination. Now your leaders are no longer Cuban leaders inspired by Cuban ideals. They are puppets and agents of an international conspiracy which has turned Cuba against your friends and neighbors in the Americas—and turned it into the first Latin American country to become a target for nuclear war, the first Latin American country to have these weapons on its soil.

These new weapons are not in your interest. They contribute nothing to your peace and well-being. They can only undermine it. But this country has no wish to cause you to suffer or to impose any system upon you. We know that your lives and land are being used as pawns by those who deny you freedom.

Many times in the past the Cuban people have risen to throw out tyrants who destroyed their liberty. And I have no doubt that most Cubans today look forward to the time when they will be truly free—free from foreign domination, free to choose their own leaders, free to select their own system, free to own their own land, free to speak and write and worship without fear or degradation. And then shall Cuba be welcomed back to the society of free nations and to the associations of this hemisphere.

My fellow citizens, let no one doubt that this is a difficult and dangerous effort on which we have set out. No one can foresee precisely what course it will take or what costs or casualties will be incurred. Many months of sacrifice and self-discipline lie ahead—months in which both our patience and our will will be tested, months in which many threats and denunciations will keep us aware of our dangers. But the greatest danger of all would be to do nothing.

The path we have chosen for the present is full of hazards, as all paths are; but it is the one most consistent with our character and courage as a nation and our commitments around the world. The cost of freedom is always high—but Americans have always paid it. And one path we shall never choose, and that is the path of surrender or submission.

Our goal is not the victory of might but the vindication of right—not peace at the expense of freedom, but both peace *and* freedom, here in this hemisphere and, we hope, around the world. God willing, that goal will be achieved.

Khrushchev's Second Letter to the President, October 27, 1962

I understand your concern for the security of the United States, Mr. President, because this is the first duty of the president. However, these questions are also uppermost in our minds. The same duties rest with me as chairman of the USSR Council of Ministers. You have been worried over our assisting Cuba with arms designed to strengthen its defensive potential—precisely defensive potential—because Cuba, no matter what weapons it had, could not compare with you since these are different dimensions, the more so given up-to-date means of extermination.

Our purpose has been and is to help Cuba, and no one can challenge the humanity of our motives aimed at allowing Cuba to live peacefully and develop as its people desire. You want to relieve your country from danger and this is understandable. However, Cuba also wants this. All countries want to relieve themselves from danger. But how can we, the Soviet Union and our government, assess your actions which, in effect, mean that you have surrounded the Soviet Union with military bases, surrounded our allies with military bases, set up military bases literally around our country, and stationed your rocket weapons at them? This is no secret. High-placed American officials demonstratively declare this. Your rockets are stationed in Britain and in Italy and pointed at us. Your rockets are stationed in Turkey.

You are worried over Cuba. You say that it worries you because it lies at a distance of 90 miles across the sea from the shores of the United States. However, Turkey lies next to us. Our sentinels are pacing up and down and watching each other. Do you believe that you have the right to demand security for your country and the removal of such weapons that you qualify as offensive, while not recognizing this right for us?

You have stationed devastating rocket weapons, which you call offensive, in Turkey literally right next to us. How then does recognition of our equal military possibilities tally with such unequal relations between our great states? This does not tally at all.

It is good, Mr. President, that you agreed for our representatives to meet and begin talks, apparently with the participation of U.N. Acting Secretary General U Thant. Consequently, to some extent, he assumes the role of intermediary, and we believe that he can cope with the responsible mission if, of course, every side that is drawn into this conflict shows good will.

I think that one could rapidly eliminate the conflict and normalize the situation. Then people would heave a sigh of relief, considering that the statesmen who bear the responsibility have sober minds, an awareness of their responsibility, and an ability to solve complicated problems and not allow matters to slide to the disaster of war.

This is why I make this proposal: We agree to remove those weapons from Cuba which you regard as offensive weapons. We agree to do this and to state this commitment in the United Nations. Your representatives will make a statement to the effect that the United States, on its part, bearing in mind the anxiety and concern of the Soviet state, will evacuate its analogous weapons from Turkey. Let us reach an understanding on what time you and we need to put this into effect.

After this, representatives of the U.N. Security Council could control on-the-spot the fulfillment of these commitments. Of course, it is necessary that the Governments of Cuba and Turkey would allow these representatives to come to their countries and check fulfillment of this commitment, which each side undertakes. Apparently, it would be better if these representatives enjoyed the trust of the Security Council and ours—the United States and the Soviet Union—as well as of Turkey and Cuba. I think that it will not be difficult to find such people who enjoy the trust and respect of all interested sides.

We, having assumed this commitment in order to give satisfaction and hope to the peoples of Cuba and Turkey and to increase their confidence in their security, will make a statement in the Security Council to the effect that the Soviet Government gives a solemn pledge to respect the integrity of the frontiers and the sovereignty of Turkey, not to intervene in its domestic affairs, not to invade Turkey, not to make available its territory as a place d'armes for such invasion, and also will restrain those who would think of launching an aggression against Turkey either from Soviet territory or from the territory of other states bordering on Turkey.

The U.S. Government will make the same statement in the Security Council with regard to Cuba. It will declare that the United States will respect the integrity of the frontiers of Cuba, its sovereignty, undertakes not to intervene in its domestic affairs, not to invade and not to make its territory available as place d'armes for the invasion of Cuba, and also will restrain those who would think of launching an aggression against Cuba either from U.S. territory or from the territory of other states bordering on Cuba.

Of course, for this we would have to reach agreement with you and to arrange for some deadline. Let us agree to give some time, but not to delay, two or three weeks, not more than a month.

The weapons on Cuba, that you have mentioned and which, as you say, alarm you, are in the hands of Soviet officers. Therefore any accidental use of them whatsoever to the detriment of the United States of America is excluded. These means are stationed in Cuba at the request of the Cuban Government and only in defensive aims. Therefore, if there is no invasion of Cuba, or an attack on the Soviet Union, or other of our allies then, of course, these means do not threaten anyone and will not threaten. For they do not pursue offensive aims.

If you accept my proposal, Mr. President, we would send our representatives to New York, to the United Nations, and would give them exhaustive instructions to order to come to terms sooner. If you would also appoint your men and give them appropriate instructions, this problem could be solved soon.

Why would I like to achieve this? Because the entire world is now agitated and expects reasonable actions from us. The greatest pleasure for all the peoples would be an announcement on our agreement, on nipping in the bud the conflict that has arisen. I attach a great importance to such understanding because it might be a good beginning and, specifically, facilitate a nuclear test ban agreement. The problem of tests could be solved simultaneously, not linking one with the other, because they are different problems. However, it is important to reach an understanding to both these problems in order to make a good gift to the people, to let them rejoice in the news that a nuclear test ban agreement has also been reached and thus there will be no further contamination of the atmosphere. Your and our positions on this issue are very close.

All this, possibly, would serve as a good impetus to searching for mutually acceptable agreements on other disputed issues, too, on which there is an exchange of opinion between us. These problems have not yet been solved but they wait for an urgent solution which would clear the international atmosphere. We are ready for this.

These are my proposals, Mr. President.

Dean Rusk and Other Leaders on the Lessons of the Missile Crisis, 1982

In the years since the Cuban missile crisis, many commentators have examined the affair and offered a wide variety of conclusions. It seems fitting now that some of us who worked particularly closely with President Kennedy during that crisis should offer a few comments, with the advantages both of participation and of hindsight.

Dean Rusk et al., "The Lessons of the Cuban Missile Crisis," *Time Magazine,* 52 (September 27, 1982), 85–86. Reprinted by permission of Dean Rusk and McGeorge Bundy.

First: The crisis could and should have been avoided. If we had done an earlier, stronger and clearer job of explaining our position on Soviet nuclear weapons in the Western Hemisphere, or if the Soviet government had more carefully assessed the evidence that did exist on this point, it is likely that the missiles would never have been sent to Cuba. *The importance of accurate mutual assessment of interests between the two superpowers is evident and continuous.*

Second: Reliable intelligence permitting an effective choice of response was obtained only just in time. It was primarily a mistake by policymakers, not by professionals, that made such intelligence unavailable sooner. But it was also a timely recognition of the need for thorough overflight, not without its hazards, that produced the decisive photographs. The usefulness and scope of inspection from above, also employed in monitoring the Soviet missile withdrawal, should never be underestimated. *When the importance of accurate information for a crucial policy decision is high enough, risks not otherwise acceptable in collecting intelligence can become profoundly prudent.*

Third: The President wisely took his time in choosing a course of action. A quick decision would certainly have been less carefully designed and could well have produced a much higher risk of catastrophe. The fact that the crisis did not become public in its first week obviously made it easier for President Kennedy to consider his options with a maximum of care and a minimum of outside pressure. Not every future crisis will be so quiet in its phase, but *Americans should always respect the need for a period of confidential and careful deliberation in dealing with a major international crisis.*

Fourth: The decisive military element in the resolution of the crisis was our clearly available and applicable superiority in conventional weapons within the area of the crisis. U.S. naval forces, quickly deployable for the blockade of offensive weapons that was sensibly termed a quarantine, and the availability of U.S. ground and air forces sufficient to execute an invasion if necessary, made the difference. American nuclear superiority was not in our view a critical factor, for the fundamental and controlling reason that nuclear war, already in 1962, would have been an unexampled catastrophe for both sides: the balance of terror so eloquently described by Winston Churchill seven years earlier was in full operation. No one of us ever reviewed the nuclear balance for comfort in those hard weeks. *The Cuban missile crisis illustrates not the significance but the insignificance of nuclear superiority in the face of survivable thermonuclear retaliatory forces. It also shows the crucial role of rapidly available conventional strength.*

Fifth: The political and military pressure created by the quarantine was matched by a diplomatic effort that ignored no relevant means of communication with both our friends and our adversary. Communication to and from our allies in Europe was intense, and their support sturdy. The Organization of American States gave the moral and legal authority of its regional backing to the quarantine, making it plain that Soviet nuclear weapons were profoundly unwelcome in the Americas. In the U.N., Ambassador Adlai Stevenson drove home with angry eloquence and unanswerable photographic evidence the facts of the Soviet deployment and deception.

Still more important, communication was established and maintained, once our basic course was set, with the government of the Soviet Union. If the crisis itself showed the cost of mutual incomprehension, its resolution showed the value of serious and sustained communication, and in particular of direct exchanges between the two heads of government.

When great states come anywhere near the brink in the nuclear age, there is no room for games of blindman's bluff. Nor can friends be led by silence. They must know what we are doing and why. *Effective communication is never more important than when there is a military confrontation.*

Sixth: This diplomatic effort and indeed our whole course of action were greatly reinforced by the fact that our position was squarely based on irrefutable evidence that the Soviet government was doing exactly what it had repeatedly denied that it would do. The support of our allies and the readiness of the Soviet government to draw back were heavily affected by the public demonstration of a Soviet course of conduct that simply could not be defended. In this demonstration no evidence less explicit and authoritative than that of photography would have been sufficient, and it was one of President Kennedy's best decisions that the ordinary requirements of secrecy in such matters should be brushed aside in the interest of persuasive exposition. *There are times when a display of hard evidence is more valuable than protection of intelligence techniques.*

Seventh: In the successful resolution of the crisis, restraint was as important as strength. In particular, we avoided any early initiation of battle by American forces, and indeed we took no action of any kind that would have forced an instant and possibly ill-considered response. Moreover, we limited our demands to the restoration of the *status quo ante,* that is, the removal of any Soviet nuclear capability from Cuba. There was no demand for "total victory" or "unconditional surrender." These choices gave the Soviet government both time and opportunity to respond with equal restraint. *It is wrong, in relations between the superpowers, for either side to leave the other with no way out but war or humiliation.*

Eighth: On two points of particular interest to the Soviet government, we made sure that it had the benefit of knowing the independently reached positions of President Kennedy. One assurance was public and the other private.

Publicly we made it clear that the U.S. would not invade Cuba if the

Soviet missiles were withdrawn. The President never shared the view that the missile crisis should be "used" to pick a fight to the finish with Castro; he correctly insisted that the real issue in the crisis was with the Soviet government, and that the one vital bone of contention was the secret and deceit-covered movement of Soviet missiles into Cuba. He recognized that an invasion by U.S. forces would be bitter and bloody, and that it would leave festering wounds in the body politic of the Western Hemisphere. The no-invasion assurance was not a concession, but a statement of our own clear preference—once the missiles were withdrawn.

The second and private assurance—communicated on the President's instructions by Robert Kennedy to Soviet Ambassador Anatoli Dobrynin on the evening of Oct. 27—was that the President had determined that once the crisis was resolved, the American missiles then in Turkey would be removed. (The essence of this secret assurance was revealed by Robert Kennedy in his 1969 book *Thirteen Days*, and a more detailed account, drawn from many sources but not from discussion with any of us, was published by Arthur M. Schlesinger Jr. in *Robert Kennedy and His Times* in 1978. In these circumstances, we think it is now proper for those of us privy to that decision to discuss the matter.) This could not be a "deal"— our missiles in Turkey for theirs in Cuba—as the Soviet government had just proposed. The matter involved the concerns of our allies, and we could not put ourselves in the position of appearing to trade their protection for our own. But in fact President Kennedy had long since reached the conclusion that the outmoded and vulnerable missiles in Turkey should be withdrawn. In the spring of 1961 Secretary Rusk had begun the necessary discussions with high Turkish officials. These officials asked for delay, at least until Polaris submarines could be deployed in the Mediterranean. While the matter was not pressed to a conclusion in the following year and a half, the missile crisis itself reinforced the President's convictions. It was entirely right that the Soviet government should understand this reality.

This second assurance was kept secret because the few who knew about it at the time were in unanimous agreement that any other course would have had explosive and destructive effects on the security of the U.S. and its allies. If made public in the context of the Soviet proposal to make a "deal," the unilateral decision reached by the President would have been misread as an unwilling concession granted in fear at the expense of an ally. It seemed better to tell the Soviets the real position in private, and in a way that would prevent any such misunderstanding. Robert Kennedy made it plain to Ambassador Dobrynin that any attempt to treat the President's unilateral assurance as part of a deal would simply make that assurance inoperative.

Although for separate reasons neither the public nor the private assurance ever became a formal commitment of the U S. Government, the validity of both was demonstrated by our later actions; there was no invasion of Cuba, and the vulnerable missiles in Turkey (and Italy) were withdrawn, with allied concurrence, to be replaced by invulnerable Polaris submarines.

Both results were in our own clear interest, and both assurances were helpful in making it easier for the Soviet government to decide to withdraw its missiles.

In part this was secret diplomacy, including a secret assurance. Any failure to make good on that assurance would obviously have had damaging effects on Soviet-American relations. But it is of critical importance here that the President gave no assurance that went beyond his own presidential powers; in particular he made no commitment that required congressional approval or even support. The decision that the missiles in Turkey should be removed was one that the President had full and unquestioned authority to make and execute.

When it will help your own country for your adversary to know your settled intentions, you should find effective ways of making sure that he does, and a secret assurance is justified when a) you can keep your word, and b) no other course can avoid grave damage to your country's legitimate interests.

Ninth: The gravest risk in this crisis was not that either head of government desired to initiate a major escalation but that events would produce actions, reactions or miscalculations carrying the conflict beyond the control of one or the other or both. In retrospect we are inclined to think that both men would have taken every possible step to prevent such a result, but at the time no one near the top of either government could have that certainty about the other side. *In any crisis involving the superpowers, firm control by the heads of both governments is essential to the avoidance of an unpredictably escalating conflict.*

Tenth: The successful resolution of the Cuban missile crisis was fundamentally the achievement of two men, John F. Kennedy and Nikita S. Khrushchev. We know that in this anniversary year John Kennedy would wish us to emphasize the contribution of Khrushchev; the fact that an earlier and less prudent decision by the Soviet leader made the crisis inevitable does not detract from the statesmanship of his change of course. We may be forgiven, however, if we give the last and highest word of honor to our own President, whose cautious determination, steady composure, deep-seated compassion and, above all, continuously attentive control of our options and actions brilliantly served his country and all mankind.

✖ *E S S A Y S*

Arthur M. Schlesinger, Jr., has chronicled the Kennedy years in two books: *A Thousand Days* (1965) and *Robert Kennedy and His Times* (1978). The one-time Kennedy aide now teaches at the City University of New York. In the first essay, he presents the Cuban-American story after the Bay of Pigs. In attempting to exonerate the Kennedy brothers from wrongdoing toward Cuba before the missile crisis, Schlesinger studies Operation Mongoose and the assassination plots. For Schlesinger, the Central Intelligence Agency made mistakes, but the Kennedys demonstrated masterful statesmanship in their handling of the missile crisis.

In the second essay, Thomas G. Paterson of the University of Connecticut places the missile crisis in the context of the tense Cuban-American relationship and Kennedy's Cold War anti-Communism. He suggests that the Soviet military presence in Cuba derived from Castro's fears of an American invasion; hence, the sources of the missile crisis can be found in large part in the Kennedy administration's unrelenting multitrack effort to overthrow the Cuban government. Paterson also questions the view that President Kennedy and his advisers engaged in a superb example of crisis management. The Kennedys' fixation with Cuba ignited crises—and the myriad programs to destroy the Cuban Revolution failed.

The Kennedys and Cuba:
The Ultimate Triumph of Diplomacy

ARTHUR M. SCHLESINGER, JR.

"The Cuba matter is being allowed to slide," Robert Kennedy said on June 1 [1961]. "Mostly because nobody really has the answer to Castro. Not many are really prepared to send American troops in there at the present time but maybe that is the answer. Only time will tell." The Attorney General was unquestionably right on one point: nobody had the answer to Castro.

John Kennedy politely asked Richard Nixon, "What would you do now in Cuba?" "I would find a proper legal cover," Nixon replied (by his own account), "and I would go in." In mid-June the Cuba Study Group chimed in. "There can be no long-term living with Castro as a neighbor," Maxwell Taylor, Robert Kennedy and their associates solemnly concluded. The group saw two possible policies: either to hope that time and internal discontent would eventually end the threat, "or to take active measures to force its removal. . . . Neither alternative is attractive. . . . While inclining personally to a positive course of action against Castro without delay, we recognize the danger of dealing with the Cuban problem outside of the world Cold War situation."

Senator Mike Mansfield, who was regularly wiser on questions of foreign policy than most members of the National Security Council, offered the best answer. "If we yield to the temptation to give vent to our anger at our own failure," he wrote the President, "we will, ironically, strengthen Castro's position." Mansfield sensibly recommended "gradual disengagement of the U.S. government from anti-Castro revolutionary groups, . . . a taciturn resistance to the political blandishments or provocations from those at home who would urge that we act directly in Cuba, . . . a cessation of violent verbal attacks on Castro by officials of the government" and full steam ahead on the Alliance for Progress because without economic progress *"Castroism is likely to spread elsewhere in Latin America whether or not Castro remains in power in Cuba."* Robert Kennedy agreed over the long run. "If the Alliance for Progress goes into operation fully," he said in 1963, "if reforms, social, economic and political, are put into effect, then Communism and Castroism will collapse in Latin America." . . .

But neither the Alliance for Progress nor the diplomatic and economic isolation of Cuba promised immediate results. With his brother under Communist harassment in Berlin and Southeast Asia and under Republican harassment in the United States, with Castro's operatives plotting against democratic regimes in Latin America, Robert Kennedy was determined to find quicker ways of striking back. . . .

With sure bureaucratic instinct, the Agency [CIA] seized on the Cuban problem as the way of making its comeback from the Bay of Pigs. "We wanted to earn our spurs with the President," as Richard Helms said. But as usual it thought it alone knew how to do the job. The CIA wished to organize Castro's overthrow itself from *outside* Cuba, as against those in the White House, the Attorney General's office and State who wished to support an anti-Castro movement *inside* Cuba. The CIA's idea was to fight a war; the others hoped to promote a revolution. Any successful anti-Castro movement inside Cuba would have to draw on disenchanted Castroites and aim to rescue the revolution from the Communists. This approach, stigmatized as *Fidelismo sin Fidel*, was opposed by businessmen, both Cuban and American, who dreamed of the restoration of nationalized properties. But the CIA alternative was probably dictated less by business interests than by the Agency's preference for operations it could completely control— especially strong in this case because of the Cuban reputation for total inability to keep anything secret.

As I wrote in July 1961 to Richard Goodwin, the White House liaison for Cuba, the CIA's Cuban Covert Plan contemplated "a CIA underground formed on criteria of operational convenience rather than a *Cuban* underground formed on criteria of building political strength sufficient to overthrow Castro." The CIA specifications favored those Cubans "most willing to accept CIA identification and control" and discriminated against Cubans who insisted on running their own show. I had in mind the anti-Castro radical Manuel Ray, who was believed to have the most effective network on the island. "The practical effect," I concluded, "is to invest our resources in the people least capable of generating broad support within Cuba."

These disagreements were temporarily papered over at the end of August 1961 when the Cuba Task Force—which included George Ball and some Latin Americanists from State, Goodwin from the White House and a CIA delegation led by Richard Bissell—came up with a formula. They all agreed, as Goodwin reported to the President, on a campaign directed "toward the destruction of targets important to the economy, e.g., refineries, plants using U.S. equipment, etc." This was the CIA plank; but Goodwin also won nominal CIA acceptance of "the principle that para-military activities ought to be carried out through Cuban revolutionary groups which have a potential for establishing an effective political opposition to Castro within Cuba."

But the Goodwin plank was against the CIA's operational code. The Agency could not bring itself to trust those it could not control. In the early fall Bissell was told, perhaps in a meeting with the President and the Attorney General, to "get off your ass about Cuba." After a meeting with Bissell, Esterline and other Agency people on October 23, I noted: "At bottom, there is a conflict between operational interests and diplomatic interests. CIA wants to subordinate everything else to tidy and manageable operations; hence it prefers compliant people, like [Joaquin] Sanjenis [head of Operation 40, a right-wing clandestine group funded by the CIA] to proud and independent people, like Miro [Cardona, the head of the Cuban Revolutionary Council and Castro's first prime minister]." Hoping to bring the CIA into line, Goodwin proposed to the President in early November that Robert Kennedy "would be the most effective commander of the anti-Castro campaign." At just this point, the famed General Lansdale returned from a trip to Saigon. Robert Kennedy, remembering Lansdale's doctrine of pre-empting the revolution and aware that the Army did not want him in Vietnam, thought that the savior of Magsaysay might have the answer to Castro.

On November 4, 1961, Cuba was the subject of a White House meeting. Present, according to Robert Kennedy's handwritten notes, were

> McNamara, Dick Bissell, Alexis Johnson [the deputy under secretary of state for political affairs], Paul Nitze, Ed Lansdale (the Ugly American). McN said he would make latter available for me—I assigned him to make survey of situation in Cuba—the problems & our assets.
>
> My idea is to stir things up on island with espionage, sabotage, general disorder, run & operated by Cubans themselves with every group but Batistaites & Communists. Do not know if we will be successful in overthrowing Castro but we have nothing to lose in my estimate.

Lansdale made his survey. He recommended "a very different course" from the CIA "harassment" operations of the summer, conceived and led as they were by Americans. Instead, the United States, Lansdale argued, should seek out Cubans who had opposed Batista and then had become disillusioned with Castro. His theory was to work within Cuba, taking care not to "arouse premature actions, not to bring great reprisals on the people there." The objective was to depose Castro in the same way Castro had deposed Batista—to have "the people themselves overthrow the Castro regime rather than U.S. engineered efforts from outside Cuba."

The President decided in favor of the Goodwin-Lansdale thesis and against the CIA. At the end of November he put out a top secret instruction "to use our available assets . . . to help Cuba overthrow the Communist regime." Lansdale was appointed chief of operations, reporting to a new review committee known as the Special Group (Augmented). Operation Mongoose was born. . . .

Mongoose, like the baby in the old story, was attended at the cradle by good fairies with divergent wishes. The President's wish was that, as Taylor described it, "all actions should be kept in a low key." Since "anything big was going to be charged to the United States," Mongoose had to be kept small, functioning at what was known in intelligence circles as a low noise level. The American hand was to be concealed. Nor did the President wish undue activity to jeopardize the lives of the Bay of Pigs prisoners.

The Attorney General had a separate wish, as rendered in CIA notes of a meeting at Justice with Mongoose planners in January 1962: that "no time, money, effort—or manpower . . . be spared." Mongoose was "top priority." But he was never clear how the time, money, etc., were to be used.

Lansdale's wish was activity—a lot of it—leading to internal revolution. He had a multitude of ideas: nonlethal chemicals to incapacitate sugar workers; "gangster elements" to attack police officials; defections "from the top echelon of the Communist gang"; even (at least according to one witness before the Church committee; Lansdale later disclaimed the project) spreading word that Castro was anti-Christ and that the Second Coming was imminent—an event to be verified by star shells sent up from an American submarine off the Cuban coast ("elimination by illumination," a waspish critic called it). In February, Lansdale presented a six-phase plan designed to culminate the next October in an "open revolt and overthrow of the Communist regime." All this was a little rich for the Special Group (Augmented), which directed him instead to make the collection of intelligence the "immediate priority objective of U.S. efforts in the coming months." While the group was willing to condone a little concurrent sabotage, the acts "must be inconspicuous," it told Lansdale, and on a scale "short of those reasonably calculated to inspire a revolt." It further insisted that all "sensitive" operations, "sabotage, for example, will have to be presented in more detail on a case by case basis."

The Augmented Group could prescribe policy to Lansdale. It was harder for Lansdale to prescribe operations, which remained in the hands of CIA. Task Force W, the CIA unit for Mongoose, soon had four hundred American employees in Washington and Miami, over fifty proprietary fronts, its own navy of fast boats, a rudimentary air force and two thousand Cuban agents. The Miami headquarters became for a season the largest CIA station in the world. All this cost over $50 million a year. The CIA had its special wish for Mongoose too. Whereas the Special Group (Augmented) had accepted the presidential decision that "the one thing that was off limits was military invasion," the Agency persisted in seeing the objective as the creation of "internal dissension and resistance leading to eventual U.S. intervention" (October 1962). The Agency, in short, was more bent than ever on fighting a war. It proved this by the men to whom it offered command of Task Force W.

Bissell's first choice, if Howard Hunt can be believed, was Hunt himself, an operative notorious in the Cuban community for his division of the exiles into (as one anti-Castro exile put it) the "good guys," who did his bidding, and the "bad guys," who "refused to be coerced into accepting his standard operating procedures." Hunt, however, declined the job on the ground that "it was obvious there was no serious interest in overthrowing Castro, and I was reluctant to conduct operations for their own sake, to give the appearance of activity."

The next CIA candidate was no more amenable to the Lansdale-Goodwin political strategy. William King Harvey had begun as an FBI counterespionage agent, renowned for having turned the Nazi spy William Sebold into a double agent during the Second World War. Fired by Hoover for drunkenness in 1947, he caught on with the CIA and became one of its celebrated operators. His great coup, the "Berlin tunnel," had enabled the CIA for many months in 1955–56 to intercept communications between East Berlin and Moscow. He was a histrionic fellow who always packed a gun, even in CIA headquarters in Langley. "If you ever know as many secrets as I do," he would say mysteriously, "then you'll know why I carry a gun." Far from wanting the independent Cuban movement envisaged by Lansdale, Harvey was determined to reduce his Cuban operatives to abject dependence. "Your CO [case officer] was like your priest," one of Harvey's Cubans said later. ". . . You learned to tell him everything, your complete life."

Lansdale found Harvey intensely secretive, almost paranoid. Lansdale finally said to him, "I'm not the enemy. You can talk to me." But the momentum of the overblown Miami establishment generated its own excesses. "Mostly the things we needed were not the things they wanted to do," Lansdale said later. "Still, if the equipment exists, the temptation to use it becomes irresistible." Lansdale would ask what they expected random hit-and-run raids to accomplish. They had no good answer. A bridge would be blown up. "Why did you do it?" Lansdale would say. "What communications were you trying to destroy?" Harvey would reply, "You never told us not to blow up the bridge." Lansdale made his directives increasingly precise in the hope of stopping aimless sabotage and saving courageous Cubans from pointless death.

Harvey protested to McCone about the "tight controls exercised by the Special Group" and the "excruciating detail" he was expected to provide. The controls must have had some effect. "They never let us fight as much as we wanted to," lamented Ramón Orozco, a Cuban commando, "and most of the operations were infiltrations and weapons drops." In October 1962 Robert Kennedy pointed out that, after almost a year of Mongoose, "there had been no acts of sabotage and that even the one which had been attempted [against the Matahambre copper mines] had failed twice." CIA itself complained that same month, "Policymakers not only shied away from the military intervention aspect but were generally apprehensive of sabotage proposals."

Still Harvey's Cubans evidently did more than Washington imagined. "The difficulties of control were so great," Taylor Branch and George Crile have written, "that the Agency [itself] often didn't know which missions were leaving in which directions." Harvey's people included soldiers of fortune like William (Rip) Robertson, a flamboyant figure who, in defiance of presidential orders, had landed on the beach at the Bay of Pigs. "When we didn't go [on missions]," said Orozco, "Rip would feel sick and get very mad." Once Robertson told Orozco "I'll give you $50 if you bring me back an ear." Orozco brought him two, and "he laughed and said, 'You're crazy,' but he paid me $100, and he took us to his house for a turkey dinner." They all sounded crazy. It was the 'dirty dozen' spirit, action for action's sake, without concern for the safety of the Cubans involved or for the reprisal effect or for political follow-up.

Lansdale, Robert Kennedy said in 1964, "came to cross purposes with CIA and they didn't like his interferences." "Revolutions have to be indigenous," Lansdale said in retrospect. ". . . We have a tendency as a people to want to see things done right—and, if they aren't, we step in and try to do them ourselves. That is fatal to a revolution." Harvey, however, had the decisive advantage of operational control. The political strategy fell by the wayside. As for Robert Kennedy, he found Harvey and his meaningless melodrama destestable. "Too much 'Gunsmoke stance' for the Attorney General," said Howard Hunt. "Why lose lives," Kennedy used to say to Taylor and to Lansdale, "if the return isn't clearly, clearly worth it?" As for Harvey, he "hated Bobby Kennedy's guts," said a CIA colleague, "with a purple passion."

The Attorney General was always dissatisfied with Mongoose. He wanted it to do more, the terrors of the earth, but what they were he knew not. He was wildly busy in 1962—a trip around the world in February, the steel fight in April, civil rights always, Ole Miss in September, organized crime, Hoffa, apportionment, fighting with Lyndon Johnson about minority employment, fighting with Edgar Hoover about everything. Castro was high on his list of emotions, much lower on his list of informed concerns. When he was able to come to meetings of Special Group (Augmented), as he did his best to do, he made up in pressure for what he lacked in knowledge. His style there, as everywhere, was to needle the bureaucracy. If there was a problem, there had to be a solution. He conveyed acute impatience and urgency. With the intelligence-collection phase ending in August 1962, the Mongoose group meditated a "stepped up Course B Plus" intended to inspire open revolt. Kennedy, who was away on the west coast, endorsed B Plus in a message to Taylor. "I do not feel," he said, "that we know yet what reaction would be created in Cuba for an intensified program. Therefore, I am in favor of pushing ahead rather than taking any step backward."

In October he urged the Augmented Group, in the name of the President, to give more priority to sabotage. The group responded by calling for "new and imaginative approaches with the possibility of getting rid of the Castro regime." The State Department recommended the use of Manuel Ray, the anti-Castro radical. "I do believe," Lansdale wrote Robert Kennedy on October 15, "we should make a real hard try at this—since helping Cubans to help themselves was the original concept of Mongoose and still has validity." But CIA had always rejected Ray as too independent. Lansdale added: "I believe you will have to hit CIA over the head personally. I can then follow through, to get the action desired." . . . On the same day, CIA experts were poring over photographs just taken by a U-2 plane over western Cuba. . . .

The CIA had yet another program against Castro, the one initiated in 1960 and dedicated to his death. The Agency had considered assassination within its purview since the early Eisenhower years when it gave a special unit responsibility for, among other things, kidnapping and murder. The Church committee found no evidence that this special unit tried to kill any foreign leaders. There are indications, however, that CIA operatives abroad tried, or at least wished, to kill Chou En-lai in 1955. But the fever seems not to have struck in full force until the last Eisenhower year. In August 1960 the CIA decided to kill Patrice Lumumba, the pro-Soviet Premier of the newly independent Congo, and delivered a bag of poison to Leopoldville for that purpose. (Lumumba's actual murder the following January was, however, the work of his fellow countrymen and not of the CIA.) In August also, the CIA set in motion the plot to kill Castro.

The early planning was evidently confided to a team of humorists. One idea was to dust Castro's shoes, if he chanced to leave them outside his hotel room, with thallium salts in the expectation that this would cause his beard to fall out and destroy his charisma. Another was to lace a box of cigars with a chemical that produced temporary disorientation and get Castro to smoke one before delivering a speech. Since Castro's speeches often gave an impression of disorientation anyway, it is not clear how much difference the toxic cigar would have made. By August 1960 the Agency had progressed to the project of impregnating cigars with botulinum, a poison so deadly that a man would die after putting one in his mouth. The cigars were ready in October and were delivered to an unidentified person the following February.

The Agency also may have recruited Marie Lorenz, a pretty German girl whom Castro had taken as a mistress in 1959 and later cast off. She fell in with Frank Fiorini, an adventurer who had fought beside Castro, but turned against him and went to work for CIA; under the name of Frank Sturgis, Fiorini figured in the Bay of Pigs and later in Watergate. The CIA, Lorenz claimed in 1976, appealed to her patriotism, promised her money for her old age and asked her to kill Castro. Sturgis gave her two poison capsules, which she secreted in a jar of cold cream. When she arrived in Havana, Castro greeted her warmly, took his phone off the hook, ordered food and coffee and then fell asleep on the bed with a cigar, evidently not a CIA model, in his mouth. Lorenz went to the bathroom and opened the cold cream. "I couldn't find the capsules," she said in 1976. "They had melted. It was like an omen. . . . I thought, 'To hell with it. Let history take its course.'"

The Agency decided to turn to experts. When Castro's revolution swept into Havana at the end of 1958, it swept out not only Batista but the dictator's partners in the North American mob. Batista and the criminal entrepreneur Meyer Lansky fled on the same day. The closing of the casinos, the bordellos and the drug traffic cost the mob perhaps $100 million a year. Back in God's country, Lansky was reputed to have persuaded his associates to join in a pledge of a million dollars for Castro's head. Frank Sturgis claimed in 1975 that the mob had offered him $100,000 in 1959 to kill Castro. The masterminds of CIA now decided the syndicate possessed uniquely both the motives and skills required to rid the world of the Cuban revolutionary. Since the mob had its own grudge against Castro, a gangland hit would be less likely to lead back to the American government.

The CIA commissioned Robert Maheu—a former FBI agent, later a private eye involved for a time with Hoffa's friend Eddie Cheyfitz and now working for Howard Hughes—to put out the contract. Maheu subsequently said that assassination was presented to him as "a necessary ingredient . . . of the overall invasion plan." Maheu brought in John Rosselli, a minor crook-about-town he had known in Las Vegas. Rosselli, who had no illusions about his middling rank in the underworld, brought in the Chicago big shot Sam Giancana, who was a don and could make the right connections. Giancana's vital connection for this purpose was Santos Trafficante, Jr., the boss of organized crime in Florida; not so long before, in Havana.

CIA case officers made their contact with the underworld notables before they informed their own chief, Allen Dulles. One would have supposed that an alliance between the CIA and the mob might have required prior approval at least by the CIA director, if not by the Special Group. That this was not the case suggests the liberties casually taken even by lesser CIA officials in the Agency's golden age.

In the fall of 1960, CIA installed Giancana and Rosselli in a Miami Beach hotel. The Agency stuck staunchly by Giancana even after J. Edgar Hoover sent Bissell in October a report that, "during recent conversations with several friends, Giancana stated that Fidel Castro was to be done away with shortly." For his part Giancana, plotting away in Miami and jealously apprehensive that his girl, the singer Phyllis McGuire, might have her own plots in Las Vegas, asked the CIA to arrange an illegal wiretap in the room of his putative rival, the comedian Dan Rowan. The Agency obliged: anything to keep Giancana happy. When the tap was discovered, the Agency did its best to stop prosecution.

As for Trafficante, he was a leader in his field. He had been a prime suspect in the barbershop murder of Albert Anastasia in 1957. Later that year he had been picked up at the Appalachin seminar. Havana was his base, and he was the only syndicate boss to stay on after the revolution.

Castro imprisoned him in 1959. For an enemy of the people, Trafficante lived behind bars in surprising comfort. Chums from the mainland visited him, among them the Dallas hood Jack Ruby. On release in September 1959, Trafficante went to Tampa. With his Cuban business presumably destroyed, but with part of the gang still in Havana, Trafficante had both motives and men for the CIA job.

It may have been more complicated than that. Why, after all, had Castro let Trafficante go? A Federal Narcotics Bureau document in July 1961 reported rumors in the exile community that Castro had "kept Santo [sic] Trafficante, Jr., in jail to make it appear that he had a personal dislike for Trafficante, when in fact Trafficante is an agent of Castro. Trafficante is allegedly Castro's outlet for illegal contraband in the country. While banning drugs at home, Castro might have wished to earn foreign exchange by permitting them to flow through Cuba to the United States, as they had done so lucratively under Batista. He might also have hoped to promote drug addiction in the United States—even as Chou En-lai organized the export of Chinese opium in order to demoralize American troops in Vietnam. If Trafficante was indeed a double agent, one can see why Castro survived so comfortably the ministrations of the CIA. . . .

Their first idea was to slip some pills into Castro's drink shortly before the Bay of Pigs. After one batch of CIA pills failed to dissolve, a more soluble batch killed some innocent monkeys and was deemed suitable. The obliging Trafficante produced a Cuban who, he said, had access to one of Castro's favorite restaurants. Maheu gave the Cuban the pills and $10,000. Castro survived. A second attempt was made in April immediately before the Bay of Pigs. Castro survived.

After the Bay of Pigs, the Castro project was, in the CIA patois, "stood down"—i.e., suspended. In the meantime William K. Harvey had entered the picture. In January 1961, before Kennedy's inauguration, Bissell discussed with Harvey, and soon directed him to establish, an "executive action capability," for the disabling of foreign leaders, including assassination as a "last resort." No one has been able to discover that the executive-action crowd did much apart from Cuba. In April 1962, Richard Helms, who had now succeeded Bissell, ordered Harvey to reactivate the Castro Project. Whatever else, Harvey was, he was a professional, and he found the six-link operation—CIA to Maheu to Rosselli to Giancana to a Cuban exile to a Cuban assassin—intolerably loose. He thereupon instructed Rosselli to cut out Maheu and Giancana. Now it all started again: poison pills in April 1962; a three-man assassination team in June; talk of a new team in September; Castro always in perfect health. Harvey began to doubt whether the operation was going anyplace. He finally terminated it in February 1963. The mob's conning of CIA came to an end.

CIA's stalking of Castro did not. Some genius proposed that James Donovan, during his negotiations for the Bay of Pigs prisoners, give Castro a scuba diving suit contaminated by a tubercle bacillus and dusted inside with a fungus designed to produce skin disease. Donovan, who knew nothing of this, innocently foiled the Agency by giving Castro a clean diving suit on his own. Then Desmond FitzGerald, who replaced Harvey as head of Task Force W in January 1963, suggested depositing a rare seashell, rigged to explode, in a place where Castro might skin-dive and pick it up. This inspiration proved beyond the Agency's technical capacity. . . .

Though the assassination plan was confided to Robert Maheu, though it became a staple of Sam Giancana's table talk and a joke among the mob, there is *no* evidence that any Agency official ever mentioned it to any President—Eisenhower in 1960, Kennedy after 1960, Johnson after 1963—except (in Johnson's case) for operations already terminated. The practice of "plausible denial" had, as Colonel William R. Corson, a veteran intelligence officer, put it, "degenerated to the point where the cover stories of presidential ignorance really are fact, not fiction."

Nor was the Castro murder plan submitted to the Special Group, the supposed control mechanism for covert action, either in 1960 or thereafter; nor to the Special Group (Augmented), sitting on top of Mongoose. Nor was it disclosed after the Bay of Pigs to Maxwell Taylor and his review board. Rusk, McNamara, Bundy, Taylor, Gilpatric, Goodwin, Rostow, all testified under oath that they had never heard of it (nor had Kenneth O'Donnell, nor, for that matter, had I). On every occasion in the Kennedy years when CIA officials might naturally have brought it up—Bissell's briefings of his old Yale friend Mac Bundy after the inauguration, the Bay of Pigs meeting, the Taylor board, the missile crisis—they studiously refrained from saying a word.

The argument that the Kennedys knew and approved of the assassination plan comes down, in the end, to the argument that they *must* have known—an argument that, of course, applies with equal force to Eisenhower and Johnson. The CIA, it is said, would never have undertaken so fearful a task without presidential authorization.

In John Kennedy's case, Bissell and Helms offered contradictory theories about the nature of that authorization. Bissell assumed the project had been cleared with Kennedy, as with Eisenhower, in ways that were tacit, "circumlocutious," camouflaged, leaving no record. Helms thought CIA's authority was derived, not from supposed "circumlocutious" talks, but from the "intense" pressure the Kennedys radiated against Castro. The CIA operators were undoubtedly misled by the urgency with which the Kennedys, especially Robert, pursued Mongoose. "We cannot overemphasize the extent," the CIA inspector general said in 1967, "to which responsible Agency officers felt themselves subject to the Kennedy Administration's severe pressure to do something about Castro and his regime." "It was the policy at the time to get rid of Castro," said Helms, "and if killing him was one of the things that was to be done in this connection, that was within what was expected." Having been asked "to get rid of Castro," Helms added, ". . . there were no limitations put on the means, and we felt we were acting well within the guidelines." No member of the administration told Helms to kill Castro, but no one had ever specifically ruled it out, so the Agency, he believed, could work for Castro's overthrow as it deemed best.

Moreover, as Helms said, "Nobody wants to embarrass a President . . . by discussing the assassination of foreign leaders in his presence."

Still it seems singular that, even if the CIA people believed they had an original authorization of some yet undiscovered sort from Eisenhower, they never inquired of Kennedy whether he wished these risky and disagreeable adventures to continue. The project after all had begun as part of the Cuban invasion plan. In this context the murder of Castro had an arguably rational, if wholly repellent, function. After the Bay of Pigs and the abandonment of invasion fantasies, the radical change in context ought surely to have compelled reconsideration both of the project itself and of the alleged authorization. The Mongoose committee was demanding at this time that all "sensitive" operations be presented in "excruciating" detail, case by case. But the Agency, without consulting superior authority, resuscitated the assassination project on its own, the murder of Castro now becoming, without the invasion, an end in itself—a quite pointless end, too, in the unconsulted judgment of the CIA's Intelligence Branch. In October 1961 the Special Group asked for a contingency plan in the event Castro died from whatever cause. The CIA Board of Estimates responded that Castro's death "by assassination or by natural causes . . . would almost certainly not prove fatal to the regime." Its main effect would probably be to strengthen the Communist position in Cuba. Unfortunately the Intelligence Branch and the Clandestine Services were hardly on speaking terms.

It appears that the CIA regarded whatever authorization it thought it had acquired in 1960 as permanent, not requiring review and reconfirmation by new Presidents or, even more astonishingly, by new CIA directors. For neither Bissell nor Helms even told John McCone what his own Agency was up to. Harvey, after supplying Rosselli with a new batch of poison pills in 1962, briefed Helms and, according to the 1967 report by the CIA inspector general, "obtained Helms' approval not to brief the Director." "For a variety of reasons which were tossed back and forth," Harvey said later, "we agreed that it was not necessary or advisable to brief him."

The available evidence clearly leads to the conclusion that the Kennedys did not know about the Castro assassination plots before the Bay of Pigs or about the pursuit of those plots by the CIA after the Bay of Pigs. There is a final consideration. No one who knew John and Robert Kennedy well believed they would conceivably countenance a program of assassination. Like McCone, they were Catholics. Robert, at least, was quite as devout as McCone. Theodore Sorensen's statement about John Kennedy applied to them both: assassination "was totally foreign to his character and conscience, foreign to his fundamental reverence for human life and his respect for his adversaries, foreign to his insistence upon a moral dimension in U.S. foreign policy and his concern for this country's reputation abroad and foreign to his pragmatic recognition that so horrendous but inevitably counterproductive a precedent committed by a country whose own chief of state was inevitably vulnerable could only provoke reprisals." "I find," said McGeorge Bundy, "the notion that they separately, privately encouraged, ordered, or arranged efforts at assassination totally inconsistent with what I knew of both of them, . . . their character, their purposes, and their nature and the way they confronted international affairs." McNamara said it would have been "totally inconsistent with everything I knew about the two men." I too find the idea incredible that these two men, so filled with love of life and so conscious of the ironies of history, could thus deny all the values and purposes that animated their existence. . . .

But had the American secret war against Castro left the Russians no alternative but to send nuclear missiles secretly to Cuba? Certainly Castro had the best grounds for feeling under siege. Even if double agents had not told him the CIA was trying to kill him, the Mongoose campaign left little doubt that the American government was trying to overthrow him. It would hardly have been unreasonable for him to request Soviet protection. But did he request nuclear missiles?

The best evidence is that he did not. Castro's aim was to deter American aggression by convincing Washington that an attack on Cuba would be the same as an attack on the Soviet Union. This did not require nuclear missiles. "We thought," he told Jean Daniel of *L'Express* in November 1963, "of a proclamation, an alliance, conventional military aid." It was Khrushchev who thought of nuclear missiles. "The initial idea," Castro said, "originated with the Russians and with them alone." Khrushchev's proposal, Castro said to Daniel with emphasis, *"surprised us at first and gave us great pause."* No doubt he worried (rightly) that the Soviet missile bases in Cuba would be an intolerable provocation to Washington. So he resisted the missiles. "When Castro and I talked about the problem," Khrushchev recalled, "we argued and argued. Our argument was very heated. But, in the end, Fidel agreed with me." "We felt that we could not get out of it," Castro told Claude Julien of *Le Monde* the next March. "This is why we accepted them. It was not in order to ensure our own defense, but primarily to strengthen socialism on the international plane." "We finally went along," Castro told Daniel, "because on the one hand the Russians convinced us that the United States would not let itself be intimidated by conventional weapons and secondly because it was impossible for us not to share the risks which the Soviet Union was taking to save us. . . . It was, in the final analysis, a question of honor."

Why did Khrushchev wish to force nuclear weapons on Castro? In his memoirs he alleged the protection of Cuba as his primary motive. The thought, he wrote, was "hammering away at my brain; what will happen if we lose Cuba?"—much as in American brains the thought was starting to hammer away about the dire consequences if Washington 'lost' Vietnam. Losing Cuba, Khrushchev believed, would be a "terrible" blow, gravely diminishing Soviet influence throughout the Third World, especially in Latin America—the domino theory, I expect. It would also, though Khrushchev did not say this, expose the Soviet Union to devastating ideological attack by Peking.

Still, if the protection of Cuba had been the only point, this could have been done far more simply, as Castro had proposed, through a proclamation or an alliance or the stationing of Soviet troops on the island. If nuclear weapons were to be used, tactical weapons would have been easier to install, harder to detect and less likely to provoke. As Graham Allison later wrote in his careful study of the crisis: "It is difficult to conceive of a Soviet deployment of weapons less suited to the purpose of Cuban defense than the one the Soviets made." Long-range nuclear missiles, in short, served Russian, not Cuban, purposes. Khrushchev, as Castro told Herbert Matthews in 1967, "was acting solely in Russian interests and not in Cuban interests." The secret war against Castro was therefore *not* the cause of the Soviet attempt to make Cuba a nuclear missile base.

By 1962 Khrushchev was in a state of acute frustration—blocked in Berlin, at odds with Peking, stalled in the Third World, left badly behind by the inordinate American missile build-up. Inside the Soviet Union industrial growth was slowing down; agriculture was in its usual trouble; generals were demanding a larger share of limited resources for the military budget; old-line Stalinists were grumbling against internal liberalization. Khrushchev was desperate for a change of fortune.

The emplacement of nuclear missiles in Cuba would prove the Soviet ability to act with impunity in the very heart of the American zone of vital interest—a victory of high significance for the Kremlin, which saw the world in terms of spheres of influence and always inflexibly guarded its own. It would go far to close the Soviet Union's own missile gap, increasing by half again Soviet first-strike capacity against American targets. It would do so without the long wait and awful budgetary strain attendant on an intensified missile production program. Secrecy would conceal the missiles until they were deployed. Once they were operational, Kennedy, as a rational man, would not go to nuclear war in order to expel them. If they were discovered prematurely, the congressional elections, not to speak of Kennedy's past irresolution on Cuban matters, would delay the American response. With one roll of the nuclear dice, Khrushchev might redress the strategic imbalance, humiliate the Americans, rescue the Cubans, silence the Stalinists and the generals, confound the Chinese and acquire a potent bargaining counter when he chose to replay Berlin. The risks seemed medium; the rewards colossal.

A plunger, he plunged. He sent 42 medium-range (1100-mile) nuclear missiles, 24 intermediate-range (2200-mile) missiles (which never arrived), 42 IL-28 nuclear bombers, 24 antiaircraft missile sites (SAMs) and 22,000 Soviet troops and technicians. This was something, he bragged to Castro, Stalin would never have done. He explained his objective in his memoirs: "Our missiles would have equalized . . . 'the balance of power. '' 'As Mikoyan put it in a secret meeting with Communist diplomats in Washington on November 30, 1962, the purpose of the deployment was to achieve "a definite shift in the power relationship between the socialist and the capitalist worlds." . . .

Critics have called it a needless crisis. Kennedy's conduct, according to R. J. Walton, was "irresponsible and reckless to a supreme degree." Driven by "the *machismo* quality" in his character, by rage over deception, by egotistical concern over personal prestige, by fear of setbacks in the elections, by a spurious notion of international credibility, Kennedy exaggerated the danger, rejected a diplomatic resolution and instead insisted on a public showdown. His purpose was the conspicuous humiliation of Khrushchev—eyeball to eyeball. Pursuing so insensate a course, he risked the incineration of the world in order to satisfy his own psychic and political needs. . . .

R. J. Walton was an exception among the revisionists in conceding that, "given the political realities, Kennedy had to get the missiles removed." But he and others have asserted that, instead of negotiating them out, Kennedy manufactured a public crisis. Even if he had not sought a showdown in August, he definitely sought one in October: both for personal reasons— obsession with his image, Irish temper, machismo, etc.—and for political reasons—the November election. He should, say, have discussed the missiles when Andrei Gromyko, the Soviet foreign minister, called on him at the White House three days after their discovery. If the Executive Committee had not yet figured out what to do, why did he not call Gromyko back as soon as the decision was made and before instituting the quarantine? Why did he not yield to Khrushchev at once the things that would enable the Soviet leader to remove the missiles with dignity: a no-invasion guarantee for Cuba and the removal of American Jupiter missiles from Turkey?

Charles Bohlen, that brilliant aficionado of Soviet policy, attended the meetings on the first two days. Departing on the third day, to take up new duties as ambassador to France, he left Kennedy a valedictory memorandum. The missiles, Bohlen agreed, had to be eliminated; and "no one can guarantee that this can be achieved by diplomatic action—but it seems to me essential that this channel should be tested out before military action is employed." On the same day, Sorensen, summing up the discussion thus far, defined a choice between what he called "the Rusk or the Bohlen approaches." Rusk, he said, favored a limited strike without prior warning. Bohlen and "all blockade advocates" favored a "prompt letter to Khrushchev, deciding after the response whether we use air strike or blockade. . . . If you accept the Bohlen plan, we can then consider the nature of the letter to K[hrushchev]."

Critics claim that Kennedy rejected the "Bohlen plan." In fact Kennedy did his best to pursue the plan. For two days, at his direction, Sorensen and others worked on letters to the Kremlin. On October 20, Sorensen reported to the President: "No one has been able to devise a satisfactory message to Khrushchev to which his reply could not outmaneuver us"— by, for example, demanding submission of the dispute to the UN or to a summit meeting, thereby plunging the whole affair into a protracted diplomatic wrangle and making other forms of American reaction difficult while the missile bases were rushed to completion. The not unreasonable decision was therefore to announce the quarantine *before* beginning talks with the Russians. . . .

Why had Khrushchev given up? "This is a mystery," Castro said bitterly the next March. "Maybe historians will be able to clarify this twenty or thirty years hence. I don't know." The assurances about the Cuban guarantee [no future U.S. invasion] and the Turkish missiles [Robert Kennedy promised their withdrawal] undoubtedly helped sweeten his retreat. But the political concessions were face savers. The real reason Khrushchev pulled out was his hopeless military situation. In his explanation to the Supreme Soviet in December 1962, he emphasized that Cuba was to be attacked in two or three days. An American invasion of Cuba would have been a disaster for Khrushchev personally and for the Soviet claim to world revolutionary leadership—especially when Khrushchev's own recklessness had handed America the pretext. What Communist state would trust Soviet promises thereafter? And, if Kennedy were serious about invasion, Khrushchev could do nothing about it, short of nuclear war against a stronger nuclear power. He was not suicidal. "It would have been preposterous," Khrushchev said later, "for us to unleash a war against the United States from Cuba. Cuba was 11,000 kilometers from the Soviet Union. Our sea and air communications were so precarious that an attack against the U.S. was unthinkable." Lacking conventional superiority in the Caribbean, he could neither break the blockade nor protect Cuba against invasion. Lacking strategic superiority, Khrushchev could not safely retaliate elsewhere in the world. . . .

The record demands the revision of the conventional portraits of Kennedy during the crisis: both the popular view, at the time, of the unflinching leader fearlessly staring down the Russians until they blinked; and the later left-wing view of a man driven by psychic and political compulsions to demand unconditional surrender at whatever risk to mankind. Far from rejecting diplomacy in favor of confrontation, Kennedy in fact took the diplomatic path after arranging the military setting that would make diplomacy effective.

The hard-liners thought him fatally soft. Dean Acheson in another year: "So long as we had the thumbscrew on Khrushchev, we should have given it another turn every day. We were too eager to make an agreement with the Russians." Richard Nixon inevitably thought that Kennedy's doves had "enabled the United States to pull defeat out of the jaws of victory." Or Daniel Patrick Moynihan in 1977: "The Cuban Missile Crisis was actually a *defeat*. . . . When anybody puts missiles into a situation like that, he should expect to have a lot of trouble with the United States, and real trouble—and all that happened was the agreement: 'O.K., you can have your man down there permanently.'"

The revisionists, on the other hand, portrayed Kennedy as reckless and irresponsible. This was not the view of those in the best position to judge— neither of Khrushchev nor, in the end, of Castro himself. In a time of "serious confrontation," Khrushchev said, ". . . one must have an intelligent, sober-minded counterpart with whom to deal. . . . I believe [Kennedy] was a man who understood the situation correctly and who genuinely did not want war. . . . Kennedy was also someone we could trust. . . . He showed great flexibility and, together, we avoided disaster. . . . He didn't let himself become frightened, nor did he become reckless. . . . He showed real wisdom and statesmanship." In 1967 Castro told Herbert Matthews that he thought Kennedy had "acted as he did partly to save Khrushchev, out of fear that any successor would be tougher." And in 1975 Castro told George McGovern: "I would have taken a harder line than Khrushchev. I was furious when he compromised. But Khrushchev was older and wiser. I realize in retrospect that he reached the proper settlement with Kennedy. If my position had prevailed, there might have been a terrible war. I was wrong."

In all this, Robert Kennedy was the indispensable partner. Without him, John Kennedy would have found it far more difficult to overcome the demand for military action. Even Senator Fulbright, in Kennedy's meeting with congressional leaders before his television speech, had advocated the invasion of Cuba as a "wiser course" than the quarantine. It was Robert Kennedy who oversaw the Executive Committee, stopped the air-strike madness in its tracks, wrote the reply to the Khrushchev letter, conducted the secret negotiations with Dobrynin. "Throughout the entire period of the crisis," McNamara said in 1968, "a period of the most intense strain I have ever operated under, he remained calm and cool, firm but restrained, never nettled and never rattled." "For this happy outcome to such long and agonizing negotiations," Adlai Stevenson wrote him, "I think you are entitled to our gratitude." Khrushchev, recalling the discussions during the crisis, said the Americans "had, on the whole, been open and candid with us, especially Robert Kennedy." "Looking back on it," said Harold Macmillan, "the way that Bobby and his brother played this hand was absolutely masterly. . . . What they did that week convinced me that they were both great men."

The Kennedys' Fixation: The War Against Cuba

THOMAS G. PATERSON

"My God," muttered Richard Helms of the Central Intelligence Agency, "these Kennedys keep the pressure on about Castro." Another CIA officer heard it straight from the Kennedy brothers: "Get off your ass about Cuba." Defense Secretary Robert McNamara remembered that "we were hysterical about Castro at the time of the Bay of Pigs and thereafter." As someone said, Cuba was one of the four-letter words of the 1960s.

President John F. Kennedy spent as much or more time on Cuba as on any other foreign policy issue. Cuba stood at the center of his administration's admitted greatest failure, the Bay of Pigs, and its alleged greatest success, the missile crisis. Contrary to some Kennedy memoirists and

Adapted from Thomas G. Paterson, "Fixation with Cuba: The Bay of Pigs, Missile Crisis, and Covert War Against Castro," in Thomas G. Paterson, ed., *Kennedy's Quest for Victory: American Foreign Policy, 1961–1963* (New York: Oxford University Press, 1989) Reprinted by permission of the author.

scholars who have claimed that Kennedy was often trapped by a bureaucracy he could not control and distracted by other time-consuming issues, the President was knowledgeable, engaged, and influential on matters Cuban.

Why did President Kennedy and his chief advisers indulge such a fixation with Cuba and direct so many United States resources to an unrelenting campaign to monitor, harass, isolate, and ultimately destroy Havana's radical regime? One answer springs from a candid remark by Robert F. Kennedy. Looking back at the early 1960s, he wondered "if we did not pay a very great price for being more energetic than wise about a lot of things, especially Cuba." The Kennedys' famed eagerness for action became exaggerated in the case of Cuba. They always wanted to get moving on Cuba, and Castro dared them to try. The popular, intelligent, but erratic Cuban leader, who came down from the Sierra Maestra Mountains in January 1959 to overthrow the United States ally Fulgencio Batista, hurled harsh words at Washington and defiantly challenged the Kennedy model of evolutionary, capitalist development so evident in the Alliance for Progress. As charismatic figures charting new frontiers, the President and *Jefe Máximo* often personalized the Cuban-American contest. Kennedy harbored a "deep feeling against Castro," as one White House aide noted, and the Cuban thought the American "an intelligent and able leader of American imperialism." After the Bay of Pigs invasion, Castro branded Kennedy a new Hitler. To Kennedy's great annoyance, Castro could not be wheedled or beaten.

Kennedy's ardent war against *Fidelismo* may also have stemmed from his feeling that Castro had double-crossed him. As a senator, Kennedy had initially joined many Americans in welcoming the Cuban Revolution as a decided advancement over the "oppressive" Batista dictatorship. Linking Castro to the legacy of Bolívar, Kennedy urged a "patient attitude" toward the new government, which he did not see as Communist. Denying repeatedly that he was a Communist, Castro had in fact proclaimed his allegiance to democracy and private property. But in the process of legitimizing his revolution and resisting United States pressure, Castro became increasingly radical. Americans grew impatient with the regime's highly charged anti-Yankeeism, postponement of elections, jailing of critics, and nationalization of property. The President rejected the idea that intense United States hostility to the Cuban Revolution may have contributed to Castro's tightening political grip and flirtation with the Soviet Union. Nor did Kennedy and other Americans wish to acknowledge the measurable benefits of the revolution—improvements in education, medical care, and housing and the elimination of the island's infamous corruption that once had been the American mafia's domain. Instead, Kennedy officials concluded that Cuba's was a "betrayed revolution."

Richard N. Goodwin, the young White House and State Department official with responsibilities for Latin America, provided another explanation for the Kennedy fixation with Cuba. He remarked that "the entire history of the Cold War, its positions and assumption, converged upon the 'problem of Cuba.' " Indeed, the Cold War dominated international politics, and in the zero-sum accounting of the time, a loss for "us" meant a gain for "them." As Cuban-American relations steadily deteriorated, Cuban-Soviet relations gradually improved. Not only did Americans come to believe that a once-loyal ally had jilted them for the tawdry embrace of the Soviets; they also grew alarmed that Castro sneered at the Monroe Doctrine by inviting the Soviet military to the island. When Castro in late 1961 declared himself a Marxist-Leninist, Americans who had long denounced him as a Communist then felt vindicated. American leaders began to speak of Cuban membership in the "Sino-Soviet bloc," thus providing Communists with a "spearhead" to penetrate the Western Hemisphere. From the moment of victory, Castro had called for Cuban-style revolutions throughout Latin America, and Havana had sent agents and arms to other nations to kindle radical fires. Castro's revolutionary mission happened to coincide with Nikita Khrushchev's alarming statement that the Soviet Union supported wars of national liberation worldwide. It mattered little to Americans that the two appeals appeared independently or that Havana and Moscow differed markedly over the best method for promoting revolutionary change—the Soviets insisted on utilizing Communist parties within political systems, whereas the Cubans espoused peoples' rebellions. Cuba came to represent the Cold War in the United States' backyard.

Besides the Kennedy style and the Cold War, American politics influenced the administration's Cuba policy. In the 1960 presidential campaign, Kennedy had seized the Cuban issue to counter Richard Nixon's charge that the inexperienced Democratic candidate would abandon Quemoy and Matsu to Communism and prove no match for the hard-nosed Khrushchev. "In 1952 the Republicans ran on a program of rolling back the Iron Curtain in Eastern Europe," Kennedy jabbed. "Today the Iron Curtain is 90 miles off the coast of the United States." Privately he asked, "How would *we* have saved Cuba if we had [had] the power?" but he nonetheless valued the political payback from his attack. "What the hell," he informed his aides, "they never told us how they would have saved China [in 1949]." He did recommend a controversial method to reclaim Cuba for the American system. Apparently unaware that President Dwight D. Eisenhower had initiated a clandestine CIA program to train Cuban exiles for an invasion of the island, candidate Kennedy bluntly called for just such a project. After exploiting the Cuban issue, Kennedy, upon becoming President, could not easily have retreated. Partisan politics kept his gaze fixed on the defiant Caribbean leader. Everyone seemed eager to know when Kennedy would knock Castro off his perch, and many expected the President to act before the next election.

Overarching all explanations for Kennedy's obsession with Cuba is a major phenomenon of twentieth-century world history: the steady erosion of the authority of imperial powers, which had built systems of dependent, client, and colonial governments. The strong currents of decolonization, anti-imperialism, revolutionary nationalism, and social revolution, sometimes in combination, undermined the instruments the imperial nations had used to maintain control and order.

The Cuban revolution constituted an example of this process of breaking up and breaking away. American leaders reacted so hostilely to this revolution not simply because Castro and his 26th of July Movement taunted them or because domestic politics and the Cold War swayed them, but because Cuba, as symbol and reality, challenged United States hegemony in Latin America. The specter of "another Cuba" haunted President Kennedy, not just because it would hurt him politically but because, as George W. Ball put it, "the game would be up through a good deal of Latin America." Americans refused to accept a revolution that not only targeted Batista and their island assets but also the Monroe Doctrine and the United States' claim to political, economic, and military leadership in the hemisphere. Given this fundamental conflict, a breakdown in Cuban-American relations seemed inevitable: Cuba sought independence and radical social change, which would necessarily come at the expense of the United States, and the latter, not unexpectedly, defended its interests against revolutionary nationalism. As Castro once remarked, "The United States *had* to fight his revolution." Khrushchev, in pondering the American campaign against Cuba, once asked: "Why should an elephant be afraid of a mouse?" The Soviet leader, who certainly knew his own nation's imperial record in suppressing its neighbors when they became too independent-minded, surely knew that the answer to his question could be found in the intense American fear that the Cuban Revolution would become contagious and further diminish United States hegemony in the Western Hemisphere.

After the United States helped expel Spain from Cuba in 1898 and imposed the Platt Amendment on the island in 1903, Americans gained influence through military interventions, occupations, threats, economic penetration, and political manipulation. By 1959 Americans dominated Cuba's oil, telephone, mining, and electric industries and produced more than a third of its sugar. That year, too, the United States bought 74 percent of Cuba's exports and supplied 65 percent of the island's imports. Because the United States had such tremendous economic favors to dispense (especially a quota system that guaranteed Cuba sugar sales in the American market), Washington wielded political influence in Havana. The United States also stationed a military mission in Cuba and sent arms to Batista's forces. The CIA infiltrated political groups and helped Batista organize an anti-Communist police unit.

After having underestimated Castro's 26th of July Movement and the depth of unrest on the island, the Eisenhower Administration tried to manipulate Cuba on the very eve of Castro's victory. With the President's blessing and CIA instructions, William D. Pawley, owner of Cuban lands and former Ambassador to Brazil, traveled to Havana to press Batista to resign in favor of a military junta in order to prevent the 26th of July Movement's imminent triumph. The Cuban President balked, and Pawley's mission aborted. Even after this setback, the United States' continued sense of its strength in Cuba appeared in a CIA report: it concluded that "no sane man undertaking to govern and reform Cuba would have chosen to pick a fight with the US." Because Castro did not honor traditional United States power in his nation, he must have possessed a "psychotic personality," argued CIA officers. Americans, unable or unwilling to acknowledge that the Cuban Revolution tapped deep nationalistic feelings and that their own repeated interventionism and island interests made the United States a primary target, preferred to depict Fidel Castro as a crazed *guerrillero* whose temporarily frenzied people would toss him out when their rationality returned.

The Eisenhower Administration bequeathed to its successor an unproductive tit-for-tat process of confrontation with Cuba and a legacy of failure. In 1959–1960, with Ambassador Philip Bonsal thinking that Castro suffered "mental unbalance at times" and Eisenhower concluding that the Cuban leader "begins to look like a madman," Havana and Washington traded punch for punch. In November 1959 the President decided to encourage anti-Castro groups within Cuba to "check" or "replace" the revolutionary regime, and thus end an anti-Americanism that was "having serious adverse effects on the United States position in Latin America and corresponding advantages for international Communism." In March of the next year Eisenhower ordered the CIA to train Cuban exiles for an invasion of their homeland—this shortly after Cuba signed a trade treaty with the Soviet Union. The CIA, as well, hatched assassination plots against Castro and staged hit-and-run attacks along the Cuban coast. As Cuba undertook land reform that struck at American interests and nationalized American-owned industries, the United States in 1960 suspended Cuba's sugar quota and forbade American exports to the island, drastically cutting a once-flourishing commerce. On January 3, 1961, fearing an invasion and certain that the American embassy was a "nest of spies" aligned with counterrevolutionaries who were burning cane fields and sabotaging buildings, Castro heatedly demanded that the embassy staff be reduced to the small size of the Cuban delegation in Washington. The United States promptly broke diplomatic relations with Cuba.

Eisenhower failed to topple Castro, but American pressure accelerated the radicalization of the revolution and helped open the door to the Soviets. Moscow bought sugar, supplied technicians, armed the militia, and offered generous trade terms. Although the revolution's radicalization was probably inevitable, it was not inexorable that Cuba would end up in the Soviet camp. Hostile United States policies ensured that outcome. Revolutionary Cuba needed outside assistance to survive. "Russia came to Castro's rescue," as Bonsal himself has concluded, "only after the United States had taken steps designed to overthrow him."

Kennedy's foreign policy troubles have sometimes been explained as inheritances from Eisenhower that shackled the new president with problems not of his own making. To be sure, Kennedy inherited the Cuban problem from Eisenhower. But he did not simply continue his predecessor's anti-Castro policies. Kennedy greatly exaggerated the Cuban threat, attributing to Castro a capability to export revolution that the Cuban leader never had and lavishing on him an attention he did not deserve. Castro was "an affront to our pride" and a "mischief maker," Walter Lippmann wisely wrote, but he was not a "mortal threat" to the United States. Because of his obsession with Cuba, Kennedy significantly increased the pressures against the upstart island. He thus helped generate major crises, including the October 1962 missile crisis. Kennedy inherited the Cuban problem—and he made it worse.

The questions of whether and under what conditions to approve an exile expedition dominated the President's discussion of Cuba in his first few months in office. Although Kennedy always reserved the authority to cancel the operation right up to the moment of departure, his choices, made after much deliberation, pointed in one direction: Go. National security adviser McGeorge Bundy later said that the president "really was looking for ways to make it work . . . and allowed himself to be persuaded it would work and the risks were acceptable." Not simply a prisoner of events or of the Eisenhower legacy, Kennedy associated so closely with the covert operation that it became identified as *his*. He listened to but rejected the counsel of doubting advisers, and he never revealed moral or legal qualms about violently overthrowing a sovereign government. He never requested a contingency plan to disband the exile brigade. In questioning aides, the President worried most about which methods would deliver success and whether the guiding hand of the United States could be concealed. Kennedy sought deniability of an American role but never the demise of the project.

The Bay of Pigs plan began to unravel from the start. As the brigade's old, slow freighters plowed their way to Cuba, B-26 airplanes took to the skies from Nicaragua. On April 15, D-Day-minus-2, the brigade pilots destroyed several parked planes of Castro's meager air force. That same day, as part of a preinvasion ploy, a lone, artificially damaged B-26 flew directly to Miami, where its pilot claimed that he had defected from the Cuban military and had just bombed his country's airfields. But the cover story soon cracked. Snooping journalists noticed that the nose cone of the B-26 was metal; Cuban planes had plastic noses. They observed too that the aircraft's guns had not been fired. The American hand was being exposed. The President, still insistent upon hiding American complicity, decided to cancel a D-Day (or second) air strike against the remnants of the Cuban air force. CIA officials protested, because they believed the invasion force could not succeed unless Castro's few planes were knocked out. After conferring with Secretary Dean Rusk, Kennedy stuck with his decision.

Shortly after midnight on April 17, more than 1,400 commandos motored in small boats to the beaches at Bahía de Cochinos. The invaders immediately tangled with Castro's militia. Some commandos never made it because their boats broke apart on razor-sharp coral reefs. Castro's marauding airplanes shot down two brigade B-26s and sank ships carrying essential communications equipment and ammunition. The brigade fought ferociously but nonetheless failed to establish a beachhead. Would Washington try to salvage the mission? Kennedy turned down CIA appeals to dispatch planes from the nearby USS *Essex*, but he did permit some jets to provide air cover for a new B-26 attack from Nicaragua. Manned this time by American CIA pilots, the B-26s arrived an hour after the jets had come and gone. Cuban aircraft downed the B-26s, killing four Americans. With Castro's boasting that the *mercenarios* had been foiled, the final toll was grim: 114 of the exile brigade dead and 1,189 captured. A pall settled over the White House.

"How could I have been so stupid, to let them go ahead?" Kennedy asked an assistant. Stupid or not, Kennedy knew the answers to his own question. First, he dearly sought to oust Castro and score a victory in the Cold War. Second, his personality and style encouraged action. Always driven to win, Kennedy believed, as one aide said, "that his disapproval of the plan would be a show of weakness inconsistent with his general stance." One foreign policy observer explained "how the President got such bad advice from such good advisers":

> The decision on which they were asked to advise was presented as a choice between action and inaction. . . . None of the President's advisers wants it said of him by his colleagues . . . that he . . . loses his nerve when the going gets hot. The Harvard intellectuals are especially vulnerable, the more so from being new on the scene. They are conscious of the fact that the tough-minded military suspect them of being soft-headed. They have to show that they are he-men too, that they can act as well as lecture.

Third, fear of nasty political repercussions influenced the President. Told to disband, brigade members might have refused to give up their arms or even have mutineed. In any case, Republicans would have scorned a weak-kneed administration. Kennedy approved the operation, finally, because he felt a sense of urgency. CIA analysts advised that time was on Castro's side. Delay would permit the Soviets to strengthen the Cuban military, perhaps with MiG fighters, and the rainy season was about to begin, making military maneuver difficult. As well, the Guatemalan president, facing awkward questions about Cuban trainees in his country, beseeched Washington to move the exiles out by late April.

Failures in intelligence, operations, decision-making, and judgment doomed the Bay of Pigs undertaking. The most controversial operational question remains the cancelled second D-Day air strike. Postcrisis critics have complained that the President lost his nerve and made a decision that condemned the expedition to disaster. Castro and Bissell have agreed that Cuban air supremacy was important to Cuba's triumph. But was it decisive? A preemptive strike on D-Day against the Cuban air force would not have delivered victory to the invaders. After the first air attack, Castro had dispersed his planes; the brigade's B-26s would have encountered considerable difficulty in locating and destroying them. And even if a D-Day assault had disabled all of Castro's planes, then what? *La brigada*'s 1,400 men would have had to face Castro's army of 25,000 and the nation's 200,000 militia. The commandos most likely would not have survived the overwhelming power of the Cuban military.

Kennedy and his advisers believed that the invasion would ignite a popular revolt against an unpopular government. No rebellion erupted. Kennedy also assumed that should the brigade prove incapable of taking territory, it could melt into the mountains and become a guerrilla army. But the mountains lay 80 miles away, with impassable swamps between.

The guerrilla option, which like the belief in a rebellion, probably led Kennedy to suppress doubts about the operation, was actually impossible. As well, Kennedy officials nurtured the fiction that American participation could be hidden and plausibly denied. "Trying to mount an operation of this magnitude from the United States," a CIA official later wrote, "is about as covert as walking nude across Times Square without attracting attention." Nonetheless, until his decision to cancel the second strike, Kennedy clung to his wishful thinking about deniability.

"Mr. President, it could have been worse," remarked an assistant to Ambassador to the United Nations Adlai Stevenson. How? asked Kennedy. "It might have succeeded." Had all gone well with the chain reaction of beachhead, rebellion, and Castro's death (the CIA planned to kill him before the invasion) or departure, the victory, observed one diplomat, would have "exchanged a Castro pesthouse for a post-Castro asylum." Tainted as an American stooge, the head of the new government would have struggled to win public favor. Castro and his many well-armed followers would probably have initiated a protracted guerrilla war against the American-created regime. The Soviets might have helped Castro's forces, and volunteers from around the world might have swelled the resistance—like the Spanish Civil War of the 1930s, as historian-turned-presidential-adviser Arthur M. Schlesinger, Jr., had warned at the time. The United States would have had to save its puppet government through military aid, advisers, and maybe even troops. To have sustained a successful Bay of Pigs invasion, then, the Kennedy Administration probably would have had to undertake a prolonged and expensive occupation of the island.

As it was, defeat did not chasten the administration. While a secret presidential panel investigated the disaster, Kennedy and his advisers huddled. At the April 20 Cabinet meeting, Under Secretary of State Chester Bowles, who had opposed the operation, found his colleagues "almost savage." Robert Kennedy became especially agitated, Bowles told his diary, and "there was an almost frantic reaction for an action program which people would grab onto." Under Secretary Bowles was "yellowed-bellied," press secretary Pierre Salinger snorted, and "we're going to get him." White House aide Harris Wofford shot back: "Why don't you get those who got us into this mess?" Kennedy pushed Bowles out of the State Department later in the year.

On April 20 the beleaguered President spoke out. "Let the record show," he boomed, "that our restraint is not inexhaustible." Indeed, the United States intended to carry on a "relentless" struggle with Communism in "every corner of the globe." In familiar words, Kennedy declared that "the complacent, the self-indulgent, the soft societies are about to be swept away with the debris of history. Only the strong . . . can possibly survive." That day, too, Kennedy ordered American military advisers in Laos to put on their uniforms to show United States resolution in the face of defeat. "A new urgency" was injected into "Kennedy's concern for counterinsurgency," recalled General Maxwell Taylor.

Robert Kennedy told counterinsurgency specialist Colonel Edward

Lansdale that the Bay of Pigs "insult needed to be redressed rather quickly." But that redressing faced some heady obstacles. The anti-Castro underground lay shattered. Cuban security forces, before and after the landing, rounded up, jailed, killed, or converted thousands of anti-regime subversives, most of whom were surprised because the CIA had not forewarned them about D-Day. In the United States the Cuban Revolutionary Council splintered as the demoralized and angry Cuban community descended once again into fierce factionalism. Castro triumphantly exploited patriotic nationalism to strengthen his regime. Instead of driving the Soviets out of Cuba, the botched Bay of Pigs operation drew Havana and Moscow closer together. Understandably fearing another invasion, perhaps with American troops, Castro sought Soviet military assistance. The Soviets shipped small arms, machine guns, howitzers, armored personnel carriers, patrol boats, tanks, surface-to-air missiles, and, ultimately, nuclear missiles that could reach into the United States itself.

Persuaded that "there can be no long-term living with Castro as a neighbor," Kennedy officials launched a multitrack program of covert, economic, diplomatic, and propagandistic elements. Encouraged by the White House, the CIA created a huge operations station in Miami called JMWAVE to recruit and organize Cuban exiles. In Washington, Robert Kennedy became a ramrod for action. At a November 4 White House meeting, the Attorney General made his pitch: "stir things up on the island with espionage, sabotage, general disorder." The President himself asked Colonel Lansdale to direct Operation Mongoose—"to use our available assets . . . to help Cuba overthrow the Communist regime."

Operation Mongoose and JMWAVE, although failing to unseat Castro, punished Cubans. CIA-handled saboteurs burned cane fields and blew up factories and oil storage tanks. In a December 1961 raid, for example, a seven-man team blasted a railroad bridge, derailed an approaching train, and torched a sugar warehouse. Myriad exile groups, from Alpha 66 to the Revolutionary Student Directorate, left the Florida Keys to stage hit-and-run attacks along Cuba's coast. CIA agents contaminated goods leaving European ports for Cuba, and they bribed European manufacturers to produce faulty equipment for Cuba—as when a German industrialist shipped off-center ball bearings. British-made Leland buses were sabotaged too. These spoiling operations compelled the Castro government to divert scarce resources from economic and social programs to coastal defense and internal surveillance. They also pushed Cuba toward greater dependence upon the Soviet Union.

The CIA devised new plots to kill Castro. Poisonous cigars, pills, and needles were directed Castro's way, but to no avail. Did the Kennedys know about these death schemes? Robert Kennedy learned about them in mid-1962, and his biographer Arthur M. Schlesinger, Jr., claims that the Attorney General ordered an end to assassination projects—but they did not end. John Kennedy said at the time that in general he disapproved the killing of foreign leaders. The President apparently never directly ordered the assassination of Castro; at least no trail of documents leads to the

Kennedy White House. But, of course, the word *assassination* was never uttered in the presence of the President or committed to paper so that he could be protected by the principle of plausible deniability. What was always mentioned was the need to remove Castro. "And if killing him was one of the things that was to be done in this connection," assassination was attempted because "we felt we were acting within the guidelines." So bespoke Bissell's replacement, Richard Helms. President Kennedy may or may not have known about the assassination plots, but he did set the general guidelines.

Intensified economic coercion joined assassination and sabotage as methods to undermine the Castro government. American officials did not expect the economic denial program alone to force Castro's fall. But they did seek to inhibit the island's economic development, thereby decelerating socialization, spurring Cuban discontent, and diminishing Cuba's appeal as a model for Latin America. In February 1962 Kennedy further tightened the economic screws by banning most imports of Cuban products (especially tobacco). *El bloqueo*, as the Cubans called the embargo, hurt. Cuba was forced to pay higher freight costs, enlarge its foreign debt, and suffer innumerable factory shutdowns due to the lack of spare parts once bought in the United States. Cuba's economic woes also stemmed from the flight of technicians and managers, a decline in tourism, high workers' absenteeism rates, the drying up of foreign capital investment, hastily conceived policies to diversify the economy, and suffocating government controls. The overall effect on Cuba of American economic measures was not what Washington intended: greater political centralization, more state management, closer ties to the Soviet Union. By 1962, 82 percent of Cuba's exports flowed to Communist countries, and 85 percent of its imports came from them. As with military defense, so with the economy: the Soviet Union became Cuba's lifeline.

The Kennedy Administration also lobbied the OAS (Organization of American States) to isolate Cuba. Eisenhower had grown frustrated with the regional organization's refusal to "do something about Castro." But after Castro declared himself a Marxist-Leninist in late 1961, the United States managed to obtain the votes to oust Cuba from the OAS, even though Mexico voted "nay" and Argentina, Brazil, Chile, Bolivia, and Ecuador abstained. The expulsion registered loudly in Havana, which interpreted it as "political preparation for an invasion." By early 1962, moreover, fifteen Latin American states had answered Washington's call to break relations with Cuba.

By the spring of 1962, then, Cuba was losing on several fronts in its contest with the United States: diplomatic isolation in the hemisphere, ouster from the OAS, economic embargo, CIA assistance to anti-Castro rebels in Cuba, exile raids and sabotage, assassination plots, Operation Mongoose, and the successful launching of the anti-Cuban Alliance for Progress. After the American failure at the Bay of Pigs and in the face of the studied American effort to cripple the Cuban Revolution, "Were we right or wrong to fear direct invasion [next]?" Fidel Castro later asked.

Although Kennedy had actually ruled out invasion as a method to overthrow Castro, in large part because Latin American opinion would have been so negative and American casualties would have been so staggering, Castro could think only the worst in 1962. After all, some Washington politicians were shouting for invasion, and Kennedy officials spoke frankly about getting rid of Castro.

It may be plausibly argued, then, that had there been no exile expedition, no destructive covert activities, and no economic and diplomatic boycott—had there been no concerted United States vendetta to quash the Cuban Revolution—there would not have been an October missile crisis. The principal source for that frightening crisis lay in Kennedy's unvarnished hostility toward Cuba and in Castro's understandable apprehension that an invasion by the United States was inevitable.

The origins of the missile crisis, in other words, derived largely from United States–Cuban tensions. To stress only the global dimension of Soviet-American competition, as is commonly done, is like saying that a basketball game can be played without a court. Cuba was the court. To slight the local or regional sources of the conflict is to miss a central point: Nikita Khrushchev would never have had the opportunity to begin his dangerous missile game if Kennedy had not been attempting to expunge Castro and his revolution from the hemisphere. This interpretation does not dismiss but incorporates the view, predominant in the scholarly literature, that the emplacement of nuclear missiles in Cuba served the Soviet strategic goal of catching up in the nuclear arms race. Rather, this interpretation emphasizes that both Cuba and the Soviet Union calculated that their interests would be served by putting medium- and intermediate-range rockets on the island. Havana hoped to gain deterrent power to thwart an expected American invasion and Moscow hoped to enhance its deterrent power in the Cold War and save a new ally. From Castro's perspective, the United States would not start a local, conventional war out of fear that it would then have to risk a nuclear war. "We'd carried out the Bay of Pigs operation, never intending to use American military force—but the Kremlin didn't know that," Defense Secretary Robert McNamara recalled. "We were running covert operations against Castro [and] people in the Pentagon were even talking about a first strike [nuclear policy]. . . . So the Soviets may well have believed we were seeking Castro's overthrow *plus* a first strike capability. This may have led them to do what they did in Cuba."

Cuba's eagerness for Soviet military assistance is well documented in the contemporary record. Castro and other Cuban officials made repeated, consistent, and compelling statements that their nation faced an American onslaught. "Cuba took measures to defend its security against a systematic policy of hostility and aggression," Castro privately explained to United Nations Secretary General U Thant during the October crisis. Contemporary, secret, now declassified United States documents also reveal that American decision-makers knew that the Cuban-Soviet military linkage, which included the June 1962 agreement on nuclear missiles, grew from Cuba's fear of invasion. They did not say so publicly, of course, for such would have acknowledged their own responsibility for generating what the CIA called "invasion scares." In early October, for example, the Department of State cabled its diplomatic posts that Castro feared an American invasion and that "the available evidence suggests strongly that this crash build-up of military and economic assistance did not represent a Soviet initiative but rather a response to insistent demands from Castro for help."

On October 14 an American U-2 plane photographed missile sites in Cuba, providing the first "hard" evidence, as distinct from the "soft" reports of exiles, that the island was becoming a nuclear base. "He can't do that to me!" snapped Kennedy when he saw the pictures on October 16. He had warned the Soviets that the United States would not suffer "offensive" weapons in Cuba, although the warnings had come after the Cuban-Soviet decision of early summer. The President convened his top advisers on October 16. His first questions focused on the firing readiness of the missiles and the probability that they carried nuclear warheads. The tentative answers were negative, although he was advised that the missiles could become operational in a brief time. Discussion of military options (invasion? air strike?) dominated this first meeting. Kennedy's immediate preference became clear: "We're certainly going . . . to take out these . . . missiles." McGeorge Bundy urged consideration not only of military plans but of a "political track" or diplomacy. But Kennedy showed little interest in negotiations. When McNamara mentioned that diplomacy might precede military action, the President immediately switched the discussion to another question: How long would it take to get air strikes organized?

At a second meeting on October 16, Rusk argued against the surprise air strike that General Maxwell Taylor had bluntly advocated. The Secretary of State recommended instead "a direct message to Castro." At the close of Rusk's remarks, Kennedy immediately asked: "Can we get a little idea about what the military thing *is*?" Bundy then posed a question now central to the history of the missile crisis: "How gravely does this change the strategic balance?" McNamara thought "not at all," but Taylor disputed him. Kennedy himself was uncertain, but he did complain that the missile emplacement in Cuba "makes them look like they're co-equal with us." And, added Treasury Secretary C. Douglas Dillon, who obviously knew the President's competitive personality, the presence of the missiles made it appear that "we're scared of the Cubans."

Then the rambling discussion turned to Khrushchev's motivation. The Russian leader had been cautious on Berlin, Kennedy said. "It's just as if we suddenly began to put a major number of MRBMs in Turkey," the President went on. "Now that'd be goddam dangerous." Bundy jumped in: "Well, we *did*, Mr. President." Not liking the sound of a double standard, Kennedy lamely answered, "Yeah, but that was five years ago." Actually, the American Jupiter missiles in Turkey, under a 1959 agreement with Ankara, were put into launch position in mid-1961—during the Kennedy Administration—and not turned over to Turkish forces until October 22, 1962, the very day Kennedy informed Moscow that it must withdraw its SS-4 or medium-range (1,020 miles) missiles from Cuba.

For the next several days, Kennedy's group of advisers, named the Executive Committee or Ex Comm, met frequently in tight secrecy. Taylor later summarized policy options: "talk them out," "squeeze them out," or "shoot them out." In exhausting sessions marked by frank disagreement and changing minds, Ex Comm members weighed the advantages and disadvantages of invasion, bombing, quarantine, and diplomacy. The President gradually moved with a majority of Ex Comm advisers toward a quarantine or blockade of Cuba: incoming ships would be stopped and inspected for military cargo. McNamara persistently argued this alternative against the generals, Dillon, CIA Director John McCone, and Dean Acheson, all of whom urged an air strike. When queried if an air strike would knock out all of the known missiles, Taylor replied: "The best we can offer you is to destroy 90 percent. . . ." In other words, some missiles in Cuba would remain in place for firing against the United States. Robert Kennedy also worried that the Soviets might react unpredictably with military force, "which could be so serious as to lead to general nuclear war." In any case, the Attorney General insisted, there would be no "Pearl Harbor type of attack" on *his* brother's record.

By October 22 the President had made two decisions. The chief decision was to quarantine Cuba to prevent further military shipments and to impress the Soviets with American resolve to force the missiles out. If the Soviets balked, more drastic measures would be undertaken. The second decision was to inform the Soviets of United States policy through a television address rather than through diplomatic channels. Ex Comm advisers have dubiously argued that a surprise public speech was necessary to rally world opinion behind United States policy and to prevent Khrushchev from issuing a "blustering ultimatum." At least two Ex Comm participants recommended that negotiations be tried first. Former Ambassador to the Soviet Union Charles Bohlen advised that Moscow would have to retaliate against the United States if its technicians were killed by American bombs. As an alternative, a stern letter to Khrushchev should be "tested" as a method to gain withdrawal of the missiles. "I don't see the urgency of military action," Bohlen told the President. And a grim Ambassador to the United Nations Adlai Stevenson appealed to an unreceptive Kennedy: "The existence of nuclear missile bases anywhere is negotiable before we start anything." Going into the crisis, Kennedy refused to negotiate with either Khrushchev or Castro.

In his evening television speech on October 22, Kennedy recalled the special United States relationship with the Western Hemisphere, and he reminded Americans that the lessons of the 1930s taught them to resist aggression and surrender. The President lectured the Soviets to reverse their "deliberately provocative" decision by dismantling their "strategic" missiles in Cuba, and he announced the Caribbean quarantine as an "initial" step. The missile crisis soon became an international war of nerves. More than sixty American ships went on patrol to enforce the blockade. The Strategic Air Command went on nuclear alert, moving upward to Defense Condition (DEFCON) 2 for the first time ever (the next level is deployment for combat). B-52 bombers, loaded with nuclear weapons, stood ready, and men and equipment moved to the southeastern United States to prepare for an invasion (thousands of road maps of Cuba were distributed). American diplomats hastened to inform NATO allies; the OAS voted to endorse United States policy. Strangely, the Soviets did not mobilize or redeploy their huge military, nor did they take measures to make their strategic forces less vulnerable. The Soviets also refrained from testing the quarantine: their ships turned around and went home. But what next? On October 26, Kennedy and some Ex Comm members, thinking that the Soviets were stalling, soured on the quarantine. Sentiment for military action strengthened.

The "first real blink" in the crisis came in the afternoon of the twenty-sixth. A Soviet embassy officer, Aleksander Fomin, called ABC correspondent John Scali and asked for a meeting. They talked in a Washington restaurant, where Scali was surprised to hear Fomin urge him to carry a message to the television journalist's high-level friends in the State Department: the Soviet Union would withdraw the missiles if the United States would promise not to invade Cuba. Scali scurried to Rusk, who sent the unusual emissary back to Fomin with the reply that American leaders were interested in discussing the proposal. In the meantime, a private Khrushchev letter arrived with the same offer, as well as with a pointed reminder for Kennedy: the missiles were in Cuba only because the United States had been threatening the island.

The next morning, another letter came. Khrushchev now upped the stakes: he would trade the missiles in Cuba for the American missiles in Turkey. An angry Kennedy felt boxed because "we are now in the position of risking war in Cuba and in Berlin over missiles in Turkey which are of little military value." Indeed, the President in early 1961 had expressed doubts about the military efficacy of the Jupiters in Turkey and had later directed the Defense Department to prepare a study for phasing them out. But he had not ordered their removal. Now they seemed to stand in the way of settling the October crisis, for Kennedy hesitated to accept a swap—first, because he did not want to appear to be giving up anything in the face of Soviet provocation; second, because he knew the proud Turks would be upset with the appearance of being "traded off in order to appease an enemy"; and third, because acceptance of a missile trade would lend credence to charges that the United States all along had been applying a double standard. Kennedy told his Ex Comm advisers that Khrushchev's offer caused "embarrassment," for most people would think it "a very fair trade." Indeed, Moscow had played "a very good card." Some of Kennedy's advisers had explored the issue days before Khrushchev's second letter. Stevenson had recommended a horse trade, and Ambassador W. Averell Harriman counseled that America's "ring of bases" around the Soviet Union had proved "counter-productive." The way out of the crisis, Harriman said, was to let Khrushchev save face through an agreement to withdraw the Jupiters. Such a bargain would also permit Khrushchev to gain politically on his tough-minded military and "swing" toward improved relations with the United States.

This discussion raises another question: What if the Soviets and Cubans had *announced* in the summer of 1962 that they were deploying a limited number of missiles—the same number as Americans had stationed in Turkey (and Italy)? Would the United States have been able to compel reversal of a publicly announced decision and prevent emplacement without having to abandon the Jupiters in Turkey in a negotiated deal? Some Ex Comm advisers later suggested that, in such a case, Washington might not even have sought to force withdrawal of the SS-4s from Cuba. Many people abroad, including some European allies, would have asked if the USSR had any less right than the United States to practice deterrence. Moscow no doubt calculated differently—that Washington would attempt to halt shipments of missiles—and thus tried to sneak them in.

In the afternoon of October 27, more bad news rocked the White House: an American U-2 plane had overflown the eastern part of the Soviet Union, probably because its equipment malfunctioned. Soviet fighters scrambled to intercept it, and American jets from Alaska took flight to rescue the errant aircraft. Although the spy plane flew home without having sparked a dog fight, Moscow might have read the incident as provocative. Worse still, a U-2 was shot down over Cuba by a surface-to-air missile (SAM). *Cubans*, after having fought Soviet soldiers for control of the SAM sites, may have brought down the U-2. American decision-makers assumed at the time that the Soviets manned the SAM batteries; thus the shoot-down seemed to constitute a dangerous escalation. A distressed McNamara now thought "invasion had become almost inevitable." But Kennedy hesitated to retaliate, surely scared about taking a step in the direction of nuclear war. Upon brother Robert's advice, the President decided to ignore Khrushchev's second letter and answer the first. And he dispatched the Attorney General to deliver an ultimatum to Soviet Ambassador Anatoly Dobrynin: start pulling out the missiles within forty-eight hours or "we would remove them." After Dobrynin asked about the Jupiters in Turkey, Robert Kennedy presented an important American concession: they would be dismantled if the problem in Cuba were resolved. As the President had said in an Ex Comm meeting, "We can't very well invade Cuba with all its toil . . . when we could have gotten them out by making a deal on the same missiles in Turkey." But should the Soviets leak word of a "deal," Robert Kennedy told the Soviet ambassador, the United States would disavow the offer. Just in case this unusual style of diplomacy failed, the President ordered the calling up of Air Force reservists. In the last Ex Comm meeting on October 27, McNamara reminded his colleagues that the United States had to have two contingencies ready if a diplomatic settlement could not be reached: a response to expected Soviet action in Europe and a government to take power in Cuba after an American invasion. Someone remarked: "Suppose we make Bobby mayor of Havana."

On October 28, faced with an ultimatum, a concession, and the possibility that the Cubans would shoot down another U-2 and precipitate a Soviet-American conflagration, Khrushchev retreated. An agreement, although not written, was struck: the Soviet Union agreed to dismantle the MRBMs under United Nations supervision, and the United States pledged not to invade Cuba. In April 1963 the Jupiter missiles came down in Turkey. Castro remained skeptical of the no-invasion pledge. As he once remarked to U Thant, it was difficult for Cubans to believe a simple American "promise not to commit a crime."

John F. Kennedy's handling of the Cuban missile crisis has received high grades as a success story and model for crisis management. But it was a near miss. "We were in luck," Ambassador John Kenneth Galbraith ruminated, "but success in a lottery is no argument for lotteries." Many close calls threatened to send the crisis to greater levels of danger. Besides the two U-2 incidents, there was the serious possibility that a "crackpot" exile group would attempt to assassinate Castro or raid the island during the crisis. As well, Operation Mongoose sabotage teams were inside Cuba during the crisis and could not be reached by their CIA handlers. What if this "half-assed operation," Robert Kennedy worried, ignited trouble? One of these teams actually did blow up a Cuban factory on November 8. To cite another mishap: not until October 27 did the administration think to inform the Soviets that the quarantine line was an arc measured at 500 nautical miles from Cape Maisi, Cuba. What if a Soviet captain inadvertently piloted his ship into the blockade zone? When the commander of the Strategic Air Command issued DEFCON 2 alert instructions, he did so in the clear instead of in code because he wanted to impress the Soviets. Alerts serve to prepare American forces for war, but they also carry the danger of escalation, because movement to a higher category might be read by an adversary as American planning for a first strike. Under such circumstances, the adversary might be tempted to strike first. Finally, the Navy's anti-submarine warfare activities carried the potential of escalating the crisis. Soviet submarines prowled near the quarantine line, and, following standing orders, Navy ships forced several of them to surface. In one case, a Navy commander exercised the high-risk option of dropping a depth charge on a Soviet submarine. As in so many of these examples, decision-makers in Washington actually lost some control of the crisis to personnel at the operational level.

Ex Comm members represented considerable intellectual talent and experience, and the policy they urged upon the President ultimately forced the Soviets to back down. But a mythology of grandeur, illusion of control, and embellishment of performance have obscured the history of the committee. The group never functioned independently of the President. In an example of what scholar Richard Ned Lebow has called "promotional leadership," Kennedy picked his advisers, directed them to drive the missiles out, and used his brother as a "policeman" at meetings. Ex Comm debated alternatives under "intense strain," often in a "state of anxiety and emotional exhaustion." Apparently two advisers suffered such stress that they became passive and unable to perform their responsibilities. An assistant to Adlai Stevenson recalled that he had had to become an Ex Comm "back-up" for the ambassador because, "while he could speak clearly, his memory wasn't very clear." Asked if failing health produced this condition, Vice-Admiral Charles

Wellborn answered that the "emotional state and nervous tension that was involved in it [missile crisis] had this effect." Stevenson was feeling "pretty frightened." So apparently was Dean Rusk. Robert Kennedy remembered that the Secretary of State "frequently could not attend our meetings" because "he had a virtually complete breakdown mentally and physically." We cannot determine how stress affected the advice Ex Comm gave Kennedy, but we know that the crisis managers struggled against time, sleep, exhaustion, and themselves, and they did not always think clearheadedly at a time when the stakes were very high. Had Stevenson and Rusk, both of whom recommended diplomacy and compromise, been steadier, the option of negotiations *at the start* might have received a better hearing and the world might have been spared the grueling confrontation.

Contemporaries and scholars have debated Kennedy's shunning of formal, private negotiations and traditional, diplomatic channels and his opting instead for a public showdown through a surprise television speech. It does not appear that he acted this way because he thought the Soviets would protract talks until the missiles had become fully operational. Even before his television address, he knew that many of the missiles were ready to fire, and Ex Comm worked under the assumption that the SS-4s were armed with nuclear warheads. Nor did Kennedy initially stiff-arm negotiations in order to score a foreign policy victory just before the November congressional elections. Politics does not explain his decisions; indeed, the most popular political position most likely would have been an air strike and invasion to rid the island of both the missiles and Castro. Did Kennedy initially reject diplomacy because the Soviet missiles intolerably altered the strategic balance? Kennedy seems to have leaned toward McNamara's argument that the missiles in Cuba did not make a difference, given the fact that the Soviets already possessed enough capability to inflict unacceptable damage on some American cities.

President Kennedy eschewed diplomatic talks before October 22 because his strong Cold War views, drawing of lessons from the past, and personal hostility toward Castro's Cuba recommended confrontation. His conspicuous style of boldness, toughness, and craving for victory also influenced him, and he resented that Khrushchev had tried to trick him by stating that no offensive weapons would be placed in Cuba and then clandestinely sending them. Kennedy had warned Moscow not to station such weapons on the island; if he did not force the Soviets to back down, he worried, his personal credibility would have been undermined. And even if the missiles did not markedly change the strategic balance, the new missiles in Cuba gave the appearance of doing so. One Ex Comm member remarked that the question is "psychological," and Kennedy agreed that the matter was as much "political" as "military." Kennedy acted so boldly, too, because the Soviet missile deployment challenged the Monroe Doctrine and United States hegemony in Latin America. Finally, with other tests in Berlin and Southeast Asia looming, the United States believed it had to make emphatic its determination to stand firm in the Cold War. Remember, Rusk has said, "aggression feeds upon success."

President Kennedy helped precipitate the missile crisis by harassing Cuba through his multitrack program. Then he reacted to the crisis by suspending diplomacy in favor of public confrontation. In the end, he frightened himself. In order to postpone doomsday, or at least to prevent a high-casualty invasion of Cuba, he moderated the American response and compromised. Khrushchev withdrew his mistake while gaining what Ambassador Llewellyn Thompson thought was the "important thing" for the Soviet leader: being able to say, "I saved Cuba. I stopped an invasion."

Kennedy may have missed an opportunity to negotiate a more comprehensive settlement: he did not give serious attention to a Brazilian proposal, offered in the United Nations on October 25, to denuclearize Latin America. This proposal also sought to guarantee the territorial integrity of each nation in the region. Harriman recommended a day later that the United States accept the Brazilian plan but enlarge it: the United States and the Soviet Union would agree not to place nuclear weapons in any nation in the world other than in nuclear powers. Thus Great Britain could hold American missiles, but Turkey and Italy could not. Nor could Soviet missiles be deployed in Cuba or Eastern Europe. Looking beyond the crisis, Harriman presented his scheme "as a first and important step towards disarmament." Perhaps there could have been another aspect of a far-reaching agreement: the United States would turn Guantánamo over to Cuba in exchange for a Cuban pledge to end the Soviets' military presence on the island. In short, under these provisions, both American and Soviet militaries would leave Cuba, Latin America would become off-limits to nuclear weapons, Cuba's territorial integrity would be guaranteed, and Moscow and Washington would make a modest nod toward arms control. Would the Cubans have accepted such a deal? Given his extreme anger with Moscow after the Soviets disengaged the missiles, Castro may well have grasped an opportunity to begin a process toward improved relations with Washington. Such a bargain, of course, would have required *Cuban-American* discussions. Yet Kennedy never seemed open to such talks. Why? Because they would have legitimized the Castro-Communist government and signified a Cold War defeat.

In the end, Castro remained in power, the Soviets continued to garrison troops on the island and subsidize the Cuban economy, the United States persisted in its campaign of harassment, and new Soviet-American contests over Cuba erupted (1970 and 1979). The Soviets, exposed as nuclear inferiors, vowed to catch up in the arms race. At the same time, perhaps the "jagged edges" of Kennedy's Cold Warriorism were smoothed. In the aftermath of the missile crisis, Moscow and Washington installed a teletype "hot line" to facilitate communication. The nuclear war scare during the missile crisis also nudged the superpowers to conclude the long-standing talks on a test ban treaty. Negotiated by Harriman in Moscow, the treaty, signed on July 25, 1963, was limited, not comprehensive (banning only tests in the atmosphere, outer space, and beneath the surface of the oceans). Although some analysts have trumpeted the treaty as a major accomplishment because it started the superpowers on a path toward arms control, the agreement did not prevent a plethora of underground nuclear detonations or slow the cascading arms race. It nonetheless stands as one of just a few successes in the diplomatic record of the Kennedy Administration.

After the missile crisis, Cubans complained, Kennedy played a "double game." The President showed some interest in accommodation at the same time that he reinvigorated anti-Cuban programs. Washington intended by early 1963 to "tighten the noose" around Cuba. Operation Mongoose had been put on hold during the October crisis, but raids by exiles, some of them no doubt perpetrated with CIA collaboration, and most of them monitored but not stopped by American authorities, remained a menace. In March 1963, after an exile "action group" attacked a Soviet ship in Cuban waters, Kennedy speculated that such freelance raids no longer served a "useful purpose." Did they not strengthen the "Russian position in Cuba and the Communist control of Cuba and justify repressive measures within Cuba. . . ?" The President ordered restrictions on unauthorized exile activities because they had failed to deliver "any real blow at Castro." Raiding parties still managed to slip out of the Florida Keys to sabotage and kill in Cuba, and the administration itself, to mollify the more than 500 anti-Castro groups, may have "backed away" from enforcing its own restrictions.

After the missile crisis, Castro sought better relations with Washington, and he made gestures toward détente. He sent home thousands of Soviet military personnel and released some political prisoners, including a few Americans. He remarked in April 1963 that the prisoner release could mark a beginning toward rapprochement. But then the mercurial leader departed for a four-week trip to the Soviet Union, where he patched up relations with Khrushchev and won promises of more foreign aid. Washington stirred against Moscow's "grandiose" reception of Castro, his "tone of defiance rather than conciliation," and the refurbished Soviet-Cuban alliance. Soon Robert Kennedy asked the CIA to "develop a list of possible actions which might be undertaken against Cuba." In mid-June the National Security Council approved a new sabotage program. The CIA quickly cranked up new dirty tricks and revitalized its assassination option by making contact with a traitorous Cuban official, Rolando Cubela Secades. Code-named AM/LASH, he plotted with the CIA to kill Fidel Castro. In Florida, American officials intercepted and arrested saboteurs heading for Cuba, but they usually released them and seldom prosecuted. Alpha 66 and Commando L raiders hit oil facilities, sugar mills, and industrial plants.

In the fall of 1963 Cuba continued to seek an accommodation. Through contact with a member of Stevenson's United Nations staff, William Attwood, the Cuban government signaled once again its interest in improving relations. The President authorized an eager Attwood to work up an agenda with the Cubans. Yet on November 18, Kennedy sounded less the conciliator and more the warrior. In a tough-minded speech, he reiterated the familiar charges against Castro's "small band of conspirators." The President, Bundy privately reported, sought to "encourage anti-Castro elements within Cuba to revolt" and to "indicate that we would not permit another Cuba in the hemisphere."

On November 22, while Castro was discussing chances for Cuban-American détente with French journalist Jean Daniel, the news of the assassination in Dallas arrived. "This is bad news," the stunned Cuban mumbled repeatedly. What would become of his overture? Castro wondered. In Washington, the new Lyndon B. Johnson Administration decided to put the "tenuous" and "marginal" contacts "on ice." Castro also worried that he would be held personally responsible for Kennedy's death because assassin Lee Harvey Oswald had professed to be pro-Castro (he may actually have been leading a covert life as an anti-Castro agitator). Some Americans did blame the Cuban regime. And although several official investigations have concluded that Cuban officials played no part in the assassination, conspiracy theories persist. One theory actually points an accusing finger at disgruntled anti-Castro Cuban exiles in the United States.

At the time of his death, Kennedy's Cuba policy was moving in opposite directions—probing for talks but sustaining multitrack pressures. "How can you figure him out?" Castro had asked in late October 1963. On the day that Kennedy died, AM/LASH rendezvoused with CIA agents in Paris, where the Cuban spy received a ballpoint pen rigged with a poisonous hypodermic needle intended to produce Castro's death instantly. But AM/LASH was but one obstacle to improved Cuban-American relations. For Kennedy and Castro to have reached détente, each would have had to suppress strong views and national interests as they defined them at the time. Would Castro have risked a cooling of his close relationship with the Soviet Union and Cuban Communists at a time when Washington still worked for his ouster, some Americans yelped constantly for a United States invasion, and the next presidential election might send a conservative Republican to the White House or keep the hawkish Johnson there? Would Castro have been willing to sever his lifeline? Would Castro have abandoned his bonds with Latin American revolutionaries in order to win a lifting of American economic sanctions?

From the Kennedy 1960s to the Reagan 1980s, United States policy has consistently demanded two Cuban concessions: an end to support for revolutions in the hemisphere and an end to the Soviet military presence on the island. Havana has just as consistently refused to budge on either point before seeing United States concessions: abolition of the economic embargo and American respect for Cuban sovereignty. As for Kennedy, could he have quieted the Cuban exile community, disciplined the CIA, and persuaded hard-line State Department officials? Would he have been willing to withstand the political backlash from his dealing with "Communist Cuba"? More important, did he want to improve relations with Cuba? Would he have shelved his intense, sometimes personal, three-year war against Cuba and disbanded the myriad spoiling operations? Would he ever have accepted the legitimacy of a radical revolution in the United States sphere of influence? It does not seem likely that either Kennedy, had he lived, or Castro could have overcome the roadblocks that they and their national interests had erected.

The Cuban-American confrontation was and is a question of the Cold

War, domestic American politics, and personalities. Above all else, it has been primarily a question of faltering United States hegemony in the hemisphere. Kennedy struggled to preserve that hegemony. In the end, he failed because he could not achieve his well-defined and ardently pursued goals for Cuba. His administration bequeathed to successors an impressive fixation both resistant to diplomatic opportunity and attractive to political demagoguery.

✖ *F U R T H E R   R E A D I N G*

Graham Allison, *Essence of Decision* (1971)

Barton J. Bernstein, "The Cuban Missile Crisis: Trading the Jupiters in Turkey?" *Political Science Quarterly*, 95 (1980), 97–125

——, "The Week We Almost Went to War," *Bulletin of the Atomic Scientists*, 30 (1976), 13–21

Cole Blasier, *The Hovering Giant* (1976)

Dan Caldwell, "A Research Note on the Quarantine of Cuba, October 1962," *International Studies Quarterly*, 22 (1978), 625–33

Fidel Castro, *Atlas Armas* (1963)

Abram Chayes, *The Cuban Missile Crisis: International Crisis and the Role of Law* (1974)

David Detzer, *The Brink* (1979)

Herbert Dinerstein, *The Making of a Missile Crisis: October 1962* (1976)

Jorge I. Domínguez, *Cuba: Order and Revolution* (1978)

Theodore Draper, *Castroism* (1965)

A. A. Gromyko, "The Caribbean Crisis," *Soviet Law and Government*, 11 (1972), 3–53

Donald L. Hafner, "Bureaucratic Politics and 'Those Frigging Missiles': JFK, Cuba, and U.S. Missiles in Turkey," *Orbis*, 21 (1977), 307–33

Maurice Halperin, *The Rise and Decline of Fidel Castro* (1972)

——, *The Taming of Fidel Castro* (1981)

Jim Heath, *Decade of Disillusionment* (1975)

Trumbull Higgins, *The Perfect Failure* (1987) (on the Bay of Pigs invasion)

Irving L. Janis, *Groupthink* (1982)

Haynes B. Johnson, et al., *The Bay of Pigs* (1964)

Montague Kern, Patricia W. Levering, and Ralph B. Levering, *The Kennedy Crises: The Press, the Presidency, and Foreign Policy* (1983)

Richard Ned Lebow, *Between Peace and War* (1981)

Lee Lockwood, *Castro's Cuba, Cuba's Fidel* (1967)

Frank Mankiewicz and Kirby Jones, *With Fidel* (1975)

Morris Morley, *Imperial State and Revolution: The United States and Cuba, 1952–1987* (1987)

James Nathan, "The Missile Crisis," *World Politics*, 27 (1975), 256–81

Lewis J. Paper, *The Promise and the Performance* (1975)

Henry M. Pachter, *Collision Course* (1963)

Herbert S. Parmet, *JFK* (1983)

Thomas G. Paterson, "Bearing the Burden: A Critical Look at JFK's Foreign Policy," *Virginia Quarterly Review*, 54 (1978), 193–212

Arthur M. Schlesinger, Jr., *A Thousand Days* (1965)

Glenn T. Seaborg and Benjamin J. Loeb, *Kennedy, Khrushchev, and the Test Ban* (1981)

Thomas J. Schoenbaum, *Waging Peace and War* (1988) (on Rusk)

Ronald Steel, "Endgame," *New York Review of Books*, March 13, 1969, pp. 15–22.

Tad Szulc, *Fidel* (1986)

————, and K.E. Meyer, *The Cuban Invasion* (1962)

Lucien S. Vandenbroucke, "Anatomy of a Failure: The Decision to Land at the Bay of Pigs," *Political Science Quarterly*, 99 (1984), 471–91

Richard Walton, *Cold War and Counterrevolution* (1972)

Richard E. Welch, Jr., *Response to Revolution* (1985)

Peter Wyden, *Bay of Pigs* (1979)

CHAPTER

12

The Vietnam War

For thirty years after World War II, the United States was involved in the Indo-chinese country of Vietnam. In 1945 America tolerated the reimposition of French colonialism; in 1950 the United States began giving massive aid to the French to quell the Vietnamese insurgency; from 1954 to 1961 America helped to organize and maintain a non-Communist regime in the South; in 1961 American military personnel began to fight in Vietnamese jungles; in 1964 American bombers began a tremendous campaign of raids against North Vietnam; in 1968 peace talks began; in 1973 a peace settlement was reached and the United States continued to support the South Vietnamese regime; but in 1975 the remaining Americans were driven pell-mell from Vietnam when the Vietcong and North Vietnamese seized the southern capital of Saigon, renaming it Ho Chi Minh City. Over 58,000 American servicemen died in Vietnam, and the United States spent more than $150 billion in Southeast Asia between 1950 and 1975. Millions of Asians died, and the countries of Indochina lay in ruins.

In the 1960s, when the American military intervention escalated, peace demonstrations and debates swept the United States, putting pressure on politicians to rethink American policy. The question posed in the 1960s is the same as that asked by recent scholars: Why did the United States become so deeply involved in Vietnam and stay for so long? The answers have varied greatly: security, containment of Communism, economic needs, hegemony, lessons of the past, maintenance of international stature as the "number one" power, rampant globalism, imperialism, arrogance of power, immorality, inadvertence (the "quagmire" thesis), an imperial presidency, and bureaucratic imperatives.

It is not surprising that the longest war in American history should produce so many explanations, for the causes of the Vietnamese conflict seemed less clear-cut than those of previous wars in which the United States had fought, and the tragedy and ultimate defeat were so wrenching.

※ D O C U M E N T S

Resistance to foreigners is an enduring theme in Vietnamese history. During World War II, the Vietnamese battled the Japanese. On September 2, 1945, Ho Chi Minh and other nationalists wrote a Declaration of Independence for the Democratic Republic of Vietnam. The document, reprinted here, resembled the

568

1776 American declaration. But the French denied independence and reclaimed their colony. From 1945 to 1954 Vietnam was rocked by anti-colonial rebellion. The beleaguered French ultimately decided to withdraw, and at the Geneva Conference of May 8–July 21, 1954, the warring parties and their allies, including the United States, prepared peace terms and long-range plans for Indochina. The Geneva accords, which the United States refused to sign, were summarized in the Final Declaration, reprinted here as the second selection. Thereafter, Ho's communists governed North Vietnam, and the United States backed a regime in the south.

The Tonkin Gulf Resolution, the third document, which passed the Senate on August 10, 1964, with only two dissenting votes, authorized the President to use the force he deemed necessary in Vietnam. American war managers interpreted this important document as the equivalent of a declaration of war. The fourth selection, President Lyndon B. Johnson's vigorous speech at The Johns Hopkins University on April 7, 1965, explains the reasons why the United States was fighting in Vietnam. The fifth document presents notes of a discussion between President Johnson and Under Secretary of State George W. Ball on July 21, 1965, when Johnson questioned his advisers about a Joint Chiefs of Staff request for a major increase in American troops in Vietnam. Ball dissented, and his answers to Johnson's incisive questions illuminate some of the troubles Americans faced in the Vietnam War. The next document is a portion of Chinese General Lin Biao's (Lin Piao's) 1965 statement that "people's war" would overcome American imperialism in the "testing ground" of Vietnam. Such views alarmed American leaders and led some to argue that the United States was drawing the line against "Red Chinese" aggression in Southeast Asia.

J. William Fulbright, chairman of the Senate Foreign Relations Committee, became a vocal critic of the Vietnam War. In the seventh selection, a speech on May 5, 1966, he protested an American "arrogance of power." The eighth document is an excerpt from an article by Clark M. Clifford, secretary of defense, 1968–1969, recalling his disconcerting conferences with military leaders in the shattering aftermath of the early-1968 Tet Offensive. The last selection is a transcript of a November 24, 1969, interview between Mike Wallace of the Columbia Broadcasting System and Vietnam veteran Private Paul Meadlo, who had participated in the 1968 massacre of Vietnamese civilians at My Lai.

The Vietnamese Declaration of Independence, 1945

All men are created equal. They are endowed by their Creator with certain inalienable rights, among these are Life, Liberty and the pursuit of Happiness.

This immortal statement was made in the Declaration of Independence of the United States of America in 1776. In a broader sense, this means: All the peoples on the earth are equal from birth, all the peoples have a right to live, to be happy and free.

The Declaration of the French Revolution made in 1791 on the Rights of Man and the Citizen also states: "All men are born free and with equal rights, and must always remain free and have equal rights."

Those are undeniable truths.

Nevertheless, for more than eighty years, the French imperialists, abusing the standard of Liberty, Equality and Fraternity, have violated our Fatherland

and oppressed our fellow-citizens. They have acted contrary to the ideals of humanity and justice.

In the field of politics, they have deprived our people of every democratic liberty.

They have enforced inhuman laws; they have set up three distinct political regimes in the North, the Centre and the South of Viet Nam in order to wreck our national unity and prevent our people from being united.

They have built more prisons than schools. They have mercilessly slain our patriots; they have drowned our uprisings in rivers of blood.

They have fettered public opinion; they have practised obscurantism against our people.

To weaken our race they have forced us to use opium and alcohol.

In the field of economics, they have fleeced us to the backbone, impoverished our people and devastated our land.

They have robbed us of our ricefields, our mines, our forests and our raw materials. They have monopolized the issuing of banknotes and the export trade.

They have invented numerous unjustifiable taxes and reduced our people, especially our peasantry, to a state of extreme poverty.

They have hampered the prospering of our national bourgeoisie; they have mercilessly exploited our workers. . . .

For these reasons, we, members of the Provisional Government, representing the whole Vietnamese people, declare that from now on we break off all relations of a colonial character with France; we repeal all the international obligation[s] that France has so far subscribed to on behalf of Viet Nam and we abolish all the special rights the French have unlawfully acquired in our Fatherland.

The whole Vietnamese people, animated by a common purpose, are determined to fight to the bitter end against any attempt by the French colonialists to reconquer their country.

We are convinced that the Allied nations which at Teheran and San Francisco have acknowledged the principles of self-determination and equality of nations, will not refuse to acknowledge the independence of Viet Nam.

A people who have courageously opposed French domination for more than eighty years, a people who have fought side by side with the Allies against the fascists during these last years, such a people must be free and independent.

For these reasons, we, members of the Provisional Government of the Democratic Republic of Viet Nam, solemnly declare to the world that Viet Nam has the right to be a free and independent country—and in fact it is so already. The entire Vietnamese people are determined to mobilize all their physical and mental strength, to sacrifice their lives and property in order to safeguard their independence and liberty.

Final Declaration of the Geneva Conference on Indochina, 1954

1. The Conference takes note of the agreements ending hostilities in Cambodia, Laos and Viet Nam and organising international control and the supervision of the execution of the provisions of these agreements. . . .

4. The Conference takes note of the clauses in the agreement on the cessation of hostilities in Viet Nam prohibiting the introduction into Viet Nam of foreign troops and military personnel as well as of all kinds of arms and munitions. . . .

5. The Conference takes note of the clauses in the agreement on the cessation of hostilities in Viet Nam to the effect that no military base under the control of a foreign State may be established in the regrouping zones of the two parties [above and below the 17th parallel], the latter having the obligation to see that the zones allotted to them shall not constitute part of any military alliance and shall not be utilised for the resumption of hostilities or in the service of an aggressive policy. . . .

6. The Conference recognises that the essential purpose of the agreement relating to Viet Nam is to settle military questions with a view to ending hostilities and that the military demarcation line [at the 17th parallel] is provisional and should not in any way be interpreted as constituting a political or territorial boundary. The Conference expresses its conviction that the execution of the provisions set out in the present declaration and in the agreement on the cessation of hostilities creates the necessary basis for the achievement in the near future of a political settlement in Viet Nam.

7. The Conference declares that, so far as Viet Nam is concerned, the settlement of political problems, effected on the basis of respect for the principles of independence, unity and territorial integrity, shall permit the Vietnamese people to enjoy the fundamental freedoms, guaranteed by democratic institutions established as a result of free general elections by secret ballot. In order to ensure that sufficient progress in the restoration of peace has been made, and that all the necessary conditions obtain for free expression of the national will, general elections shall be held in July 1956, under the supervision of an international commission composed of representatives of the Member States of the International Supervisory Commission, referred to in the agreement on the cessation of hostilities. Consultations will be held on this subject between the competent representative authorities of the two zones from July 20, 1955, onwards. . . .

12. In their relations with Cambodia, Laos and Viet Nam, each member of the Geneva Conference undertakes to respect the sovereignty, the independence, the unity and the territorial integrity of the above-mentioned States, and to refrain from any interference in their internal affairs. . . .

The Tonkin Gulf Resolution, 1964

To promote the maintenance of international peace and security in southeast Asia.

Whereas naval units of the Communist regime in Vietnam, in violation of the principles of the Charter of the United Nations and of international law, have deliberately and repeatedly attacked United States naval vessels lawfully present in international waters, and have thereby created a serious threat to international peace; and

Whereas these attacks are part of a deliberate and systematic campaign of aggression that the Communist regime in North Vienam has been waging against its neighbors and the nations joined with them in the collective defense of their freedom; and

Whereas the United States is assisting the peoples of southeast Asia to protect their freedom and has no territorial, military or political ambitions in that area, but desires only that these peoples should be left in peace to work out their own destinies in their own way: Now, therefore, be it *Resolved by the Senate and House of Representatives of the United States of America in Congress assembled*, That the Congress approves and supports the determination of the President, as Commander in Chief, to take all necessary measures to repel any armed attack against the forces of the United States and to prevent further aggression.

Sec. 2. The United States regards as vital to its national interest and to world peace the maintenance of international peace and security in southeast Asia. Consonant with the Constitution of the United States and the Charter of the United Nations and in accordance with its obligations under the Southeast Asia Collective Defense Treaty, the United States is, therefore, prepared, as the President determines, to take all necessary steps, including the use of armed force, to assist any member or protocol state of the Southeast Asia Collective Defense Treaty requesting assistance in defense of its freedom.

Sec. 3. This resolution shall expire when the President shall determine that the peace and security of the area is reasonably assured by international conditions created by action of the United Nations or otherwise, except that it may be terminated earlier by concurrent resolution of the Congress.

Lyndon B. Johnson Explains
Why Americans Fight in Vietnam, 1965

Why must this nation hazard its ease, its interest, and its power for the sake of a people so far away?

We fight because we must fight if we are to live in a world where every country can shape its own destiny, and only in such a world will our own freedom be finally secure.

This kind of world will never be built by bombs or bullets. Yet the infirmities of man are such that force must often precede reason and the waste of war, the works of peace.

We wish that this were not so. But we must deal with the world as it is, if it is ever to be as we wish.

The world as it is in Asia is not a serene or peaceful place.

The first reality is that North Viet-Nam has attacked the independent nation of South Viet-Nam. Its object is total conquest.

Of course, some of the people of South Viet-Nam are participating in attack on their own government. But trained men and supplies, orders and arms, flow in a constant stream from North to South.

This support is the heartbeat of the war.

And it is a war of unparalleled brutality. Simple farmers are the targets of assassination and kidnaping. Women and children are strangled in the night because their men are loyal to their government. And helpless villages are ravaged by sneak attacks. Large-scale raids are conducted on towns, and terror strikes in the heart of cities.

The confused nature of this conflict cannot mask the fact that it is the new face of an old enemy.

Over this war—and all Asia—is another reality: the deepening shadow of Communist China. The rulers in Hanoi are urged on by Peking. This is a regime which has destroyed freedom in Tibet, which has attacked India and has been condemned by the United Nations for aggression in Korea. It is a nation which is helping the forces of violence in almost every continent. The contest in Viet-Nam is part of a wider pattern of aggressive purposes.

Why are these realities our concern? Why are we in South Viet-Nam?

We are there because we have a promise to keep. Since 1954 every American President has offered support to the people of South Viet-Nam. We have helped to build, and we have helped to defend. Thus, over many years, we have made a national pledge to help South Viet-Nam defend its independence.

And I intend to keep that promise.

To dishonor that pledge, to abandon this small and brave nation to its enemies, and to the terror that must follow, would be an unforgivable wrong.

We are also there to strengthen world order. Around the globe from Berlin to Thailand are people whose well being rests in part on the belief that they can count on us if they are attacked. To leave Viet-Nam to its fate would shake the confidence of all these people in the value of an American commitment and in the value of America's word. The result would be increased unrest and instability, and even wider war.

We are also there because there are great stakes in the balance. Let no one think for a moment that retreat from Viet-Nam would bring an end to conflict. The battle would be renewed in one country and then another. The central lesson of our time is that the appetite of aggression is never satisfied. To withdraw from one battlefield means only to prepare for the next. We must say in Southeast Asia—as we did in Europe—in the words of the Bible: "Hitherto shalt thou come, but no further."

There are those who say that all our effort there will be futile—that China's power is such that it is bound to dominate all Southeast Asia. But there is no end to that argument until all of the nations of Asia are swallowed up.

There are those who wonder why we have a responsibility there. Well, we have it there for the same reason that we have a responsibility for the defense of Europe. World War II was fought in both Europe and Asia and when it ended we found ourselves with continued responsibility for the defense of freedom.

Our objective is the independence of South Viet-Nam and its freedom from attack. We want nothing for ourselves—only that the people of South Viet-Nam be allowed to guide their own country in their own way.

We will do everything necessary to reach that objective and we will do only what is absolutely necessary.

In recent months attacks on South Viet-Nam were stepped up. Thus, it became necessary for us to increase our response and to make attacks by air. This is not a change of purpose. It is a change in what we believe that purpose requires.

We do this in order to slow down aggression.

We do this to increase the confidence of the brave people of South Viet-Nam who have bravely borne this brutal battle for so many years with so many casualties.

And we do this to convince the leaders of North Viet-Nam—and all who seek to share their conquest—of a simple fact:

We will not be defeated.

We will not grow tired.

We will not withdraw, either openly or under the cloak of a meaningless agreement.

We know that air attacks alone will not accomplish all of these purposes. But it is our best and prayerful judgment that they are a necessary part of the surest road to peace.

We hope that peace will come swiftly. But that is in the hands of others besides ourselves. And we must be prepared for a long continued conflict. It will require patience as well as bravery—the will to endure as well as the will to resist. . . .

These countries of Southeast Asia are homes for millions of impoverished people. Each day these people rise at dawn and struggle through until the night to wrestle existence from the soil. They are often wracked by diseases, plagued by hunger, and death comes at the early age of forty.

Stability and peace do not come easily in such a land. Neither independence nor human dignity will ever be won though by arms alone. It also requires the works of peace. The American people have helped generously in times past in these works, and now there must be a much more massive effort to improve the life of man in that conflict-torn corner of our world.

The first step is for the countries of Southeast Asia to associate themselves in a greatly expanded co-operative effort for development. We would hope that North Viet-Nam would take its place in the common effort just as soon as peaceful co-operation is possible.

The United Nations is already actively engaged in development in this area, and as far back as 1961 I conferred with our authorities in Viet-Nam in connection with their work there. And I would hope tonight that the Secretary General of the United Nations could use the prestige of his great office and his deep knowledge of Asia to initiate, as soon as possible, with the countries of that area, a plan for co-operation in increased development.

For our part I will ask the Congress to join in a billion dollar American investment in this effort as soon as it is underway.

And I would hope that all other industrialized countries, including the Soviet Union, will join in this effort to replace despair with hope and terror with progress.

The task is nothing less than to enrich the hopes and existence of more than a hundred million people. And there is much to be done.

The vast Mekong River can provide food and water and power on a scale to dwarf even our own T.V.A.

The wonders of modern medicine can be spread through villages where thousands die every year from lack of care.

Schools can be established to train people in the skills needed to manage the process of development.

And these objectives, and more, are within the reach of a cooperative and determined effort.

I also intend to expand and speed up a program to make available our farm surpluses to assist in feeding and clothing the needy in Asia. We should not allow people to go hungry and wear rags while our own warehouses overflow with an abundance of wheat and corn and rice and cotton.

So I will very shortly name a special team of outstanding, patriotic, and distinguished Americans to inaugurate our participation in these programs. This team will be headed by Mr. Eugene Black, the very able former president of the World Bank.

This will be a disorderly planet for a long time. In Asia, and elsewhere, the forces of the modern world are shaking old ways and uprooting ancient civilizations. There will be turbulence and struggle and even violence. Great social change—as we see in our own country—does not always come without conflict.

We must also expect that nations will on occasion be in dispute with us. It may be because we are rich, or powerful, or because we have made some mistakes, or because they honestly fear our intentions. However, no nation need ever fear that we desire their land, or to impose our will, or to dictate their institutions.

But we will always oppose the effort of one nation to conquer another nation.

We will do this because our own security is at stake.

But there is more to it than that. For our generation has a dream. It is a very old dream. But we have the power, and now we have the opportunity to make that dream come true.

For centuries nations have struggled among each other. But we dream of a world where disputes are settled by law and reason. And we will try to make it so.

For most of history men have hated and killed one another in battle. But we dream of an end to war. And we will try to make it so.

For all existence most men have lived in poverty, threatened by hunger. But we dream of a world where all are fed and charged with hope. And we will help to make it so.

Johnson Questions the Dissenting George Ball, 1965

Morning Meeting of July 21

THE PRESIDENT: Is there anyone here of the opinion we should not do what the [Joint Chiefs of Staff] memorandum says [increase U.S. troops in Vietnam by 100,000]? If so, I want to hear from him now, in detail.

BALL: Mr. President, I can foresee a perilous voyage, very dangerous. I have great and grave apprehensions that we can win under these conditions. But let me be clear. If the decision is to go ahead, I am committed.

THE PRESIDENT: But, George, is there another course in the national interest, some course that is better than the one McNamara proposes? We know it is dangerous and perilous, but the big question is, can it be avoided?

BALL: There is no course that will allow us to cut our losses. If we get bogged down, our cost might be substantially greater. The pressures to create a larger war would be inevitable. The qualifications I have are not due to the fact that I think we are in a bad moral position.

THE PRESIDENT: Tell me then, what other road can I go?

BALL: Take what precautions we can, Mr. President. Take our losses, let their government fall apart, negotiate, discuss, knowing full well there will be a probable take-over by the Communists. This is disagreeable, I know.

THE PRESIDENT: I can take disagreeable decisions. But I want to know can we make a case for your thoughts? Can you discuss it fully?

BALL: We have discussed it. I have had my day in court.

THE PRESIDENT: I don't think we can have made any full commitment, George. You have pointed out the danger, but you haven't really proposed an alternative course. We haven't always been right. We have no mortgage on victory. Right now, I am concerned that we have very little alternatives to what we are doing. I want another meeting, more meetings, before we take any definitive action. We must look at all other courses of possibility carefully. Right now I feel it would be more dangerous to lose this now, than endanger a great number of troops. But I want this fully discussed.

Reprinted from *Planning a Tragedy: The Americanization of the War in Vietnam*, 107–10, by Larry Berman, by permission of W.W. Norton & Company, Inc. Copyright © 1982 by Larry Berman.

Afternoon Meeting of July 21

BALL: We cannot win, Mr. President. The war will be long and protracted. The most we can hope for is a messy conclusion. There remains a great danger of intrusion by the Chinese. But the biggest problem is the problem of the long war. The Korean experience was a galling one. The correlation between Korean casualties and public opinion showed support stabilized at 50 percent. As casualties increase, the pressure to strike at the very jugular of North Vietnam will become very great. I am concerned about world opinion. If we could win in a year's time, and win decisively, world opinion would be alright. However, if the war is long and protracted, as I believe it will be, then we will suffer because the world's greatest power cannot defeat guerrillas. Then there is the problem of national politics. Every great captain in history was not afraid to make a tactical withdrawal if conditions were unfavorable to him. The enemy cannot even be seen in Vietnam. He is indigenous to the country. I truly have serious doubts that an army of Westerners can successfully fight Orientals in an Asian jungle.

THE PRESIDENT: This is important. Can Westerners, in the absence of accurate intelligence, successfully fight Asians in jungle rice paddies? I want McNamara and General Wheeler to seriously ponder this question.

BALL: I think we all have underestimated the seriousness of this situation. It is like giving cobalt treatment to a terminal cancer case. I think a long, protracted war will disclose our weakness, not our strength. The least harmful way to cut losses in SVN [South Vietnam] is to let the government decide it doesn't want us to stay there. Therefore, we should put proposals to the GVN [Government of Vietnam] that they can't accept. Then, it would move to a neutralist position. I have no illusions that after we were asked to leave South Vietnam, that country would soon come under Hanoi control. . . .

THE PRESIDENT: But George, wouldn't all these countries say that Uncle Sam was a paper tiger, wouldn't we lose credibility breaking the word of three presidents, if we did as you have proposed? It would seem to be an irresponsible blow. But I gather you don't think so?

BALL: No sir. The worse blow would be that the mightiest power on earth is unable to defeat a handful of guerrillas.

Lin Biao (Lin Piao) on People's War, 1965

Ours is the epoch in which world capitalism and imperialism are heading for their doom and socialism and communism are marching to victory. Comrade Mao Tse-tung's theory of people's war is not only a product of the Chinese revolution, but has also the characteristics of our epoch. The new experience gained in the people's revolutionary struggles in various countries since World War II has provided continuous evidence that Mao Tse-tung's thought is a common asset of the revolutionary people of the whole world. This is the great international significance of the thought of Mao Tse-tung.

Since World War II, U.S. imperialism has stepped into the shoes of German, Japanese, and Italian fascism and has been trying to build a great American empire by dominating and enslaving the whole world. It is actively fostering Japanese and West German militarism as its chief accomplices in unleashing a world war. Like a vicious wolf, it is bullying and enslaving various peoples, plundering their wealth, encroaching upon their countries' sovereignty and interfering in their internal affairs. It is the most rabid aggressor in human history and the most ferocious common enemy of the people of the world. Every people or country in the world that wants revolution, independence and peace cannot but direct the spearhead of its struggle against U.S. imperialism.

Just as the Japanese imperialists' policy of subjugating China made it possible for the Chinese people to form the broadest possible united front against them, so the U.S. imperialists' policy of seeking world domination makes it possible for the people throughout the world to unite all the forces that can be united and form the broadest possible united front for a converging attack on U.S. imperialism.

At present, the main battlefield of the fierce struggle between the people of the world on the one side and U.S. imperialism and its lackeys on the other is the vast area of Asia, Africa, and Latin America. In the world as a whole, this is the area where the people suffer worst from imperialist oppression and where imperialist rule is most vulnerable. Since World War II, revolutionary storms have been rising in this area, and today they have become the most important force directly pounding U.S. imperialism. The contradiction between the revolutionary peoples of Asia, Africa, and Latin America and the imperialists headed by the United States is the principal contradiction in the contemporary world. The development of this contradiction is promoting the struggle of the people of the whole world against U.S imperialism and its lackeys.

Since World War II, people's war has increasingly demonstrated its power in Asia, Africa, and Latin America. The peoples of China, Korea, Vietnam, Laos, Cuba, Indonesia, Algeria and other countries have waged people's wars against the imperialists and their lackeys and won great victories. The classes leading these people's wars may vary, and so may the breadth and depth of mass mobilization and the extent of victory, but the victories in these people's wars have very much weakened and pinned down the forces of imperialism, upset the U.S. imperialist plan to launch a world war, and become mighty factors defending world peace.

Today, the conditions are more favorable than ever before for the waging of people's wars by the revolutionary peoples of Asia, Africa, and Latin America against U.S. imperialism and its lackeys.

Since World War II and the succeeding years of revolutionary upsurge, there has been a great rise in the level of political consciousness and the degree of organization of the people in all countries, and the resources available to them for mutual support and aid have greatly increased. The whole capitalist-imperialist system has become drastically weaker and is in the process of increasing convulsion and disintegration. After World War I, the imperialists lacked the power to destroy the new-born socialist Soviet state, but they were still able to suppress the people's revolutionary movements in some countries in the parts of the world under their own rule and so maintain a short period of comparative stability. Since World War II, however, not only have they been unable to stop a number of countries from taking the socialist road, but they are no longer capable of holding back the surging tide of the people's revolutionary movements in the areas under their own rule.

U.S. imperialism is stronger, but also more vulnerable, than any imperialism of the past. It sets itself against the people of the whole world, including the people of the United States. Its human, military, material and financial resources are far from sufficient for the realization of its ambition of dominating the whole world. U.S. imperialism has further weakened itself by occupying so many places in the world, overreaching itself, stretching its fingers out wide and dispersing its strength, with its rear so far away and its supply lines so long. As Comrade Mao Tse-tung has said, "Wherever it commits aggression, it puts a new noose around its neck. It is besieged ring upon ring by the people of the whole world."

When committing aggression in a foreign country, U.S. imperialism can only employ part of its forces, which are sent to fight an unjust war far from their native land and therefore have a low morale, and so U.S. imperialism is beset with great difficulties. The people subjected to its aggression are having a trial of strength with U.S. imperialism neither in Washington nor New York, neither in Honolulu nor Florida, but are fighting for independence and freedom on their own soil. Once they are mobilized on a broad scale, they will have inexhaustible strength. Thus superiority will belong not to the United States but to the people subjected to its aggression. The latter, though apparently weak and small, are really more powerful than U.S. imperialism.

The struggles waged by the different peoples against U.S. imperialism reinforce each other and merge into a torrential world-wide tide of opposition to U.S. imperialism. The more successful the development of people's war in a given region, the larger the number of U.S. imperialist forces that can be pinned down and depleted there. When the U.S. aggressors are hard pressed in one place, they have no alternative but to loosen their grip on others. Therefore, the conditions become more favorable for the people elsewhere to wage struggles against U.S. imperialism and its lackeys.

Everything is divisible. And so is this colossus of U.S. imperialism. It can be split up and defeated. The peoples of Asia, Africa, Latin America and other regions can destroy it piece by piece, some striking at its head and others at its feet. That is why the greatest fear of U.S. imperialism is that people's wars will be launched in different parts of the world, and particularly in Asia, Africa and Latin America, and why it regards people's war as a mortal danger.

U.S. imperialism relies solely on its nuclear weapons to intimidate people. But these weapons cannot save U.S. imperialism from its doom. Nuclear weapons cannot be used lightly. U.S. imperialism has been condemned by the people of the whole world for its towering crime of dropping two atom bombs on Japan. If it uses nuclear weapons again, it will become isolated in the extreme. Moreover, the U.S. monopoly of nuclear weapons has long been broken; U.S. imperialism has these weapons, but others have them too. If it threatens other countries with nuclear weapons, U.S. imperialism will expose its own country to the same threat. For this reason, it will meet with strong opposition not only from the people elsewhere but also inevitably from the people in its own country. Even if U.S.imperialism brazenly uses nuclear weapons, it cannot conquer the people, who are indomitable.

However highly developed modern weapons and technical equipment may be and however complicated the methods of modern warfare, in the final analysis the outcome of a war will be decided by the sustained fighting of the ground forces, by the fighting at close quarters on battlefields, by the political consciousness of the men, by their courage and spirit of sacrifice. Here the weak points of U.S. imperialism will be completely laid bare, while the superiority of the revolutionary people will be brought into full play. The reactionary troops of U.S. imperialism cannot possibly be endowed with the courage and the spirit of sacrifice possessed by the revolutionary people. The spiritual atom bomb which the revolutionary people possess is a far more powerful and useful weapon than the physical atom bomb.

Vietnam is the most convincing current example of a victim of aggression defeating U.S. imperialism by a people's war. The United States has made South Vietnam a testing ground for the suppression of people's war. It has carried on this experiment for many years, and everybody can now see that the U.S. aggressors are unable to find a way of coping with people's war. On the other hand, the Vietnamese people have brought the power of people's war into full play in their struggle against the U.S. aggressors. The U.S. aggressors are in danger of being swamped in the people's war in Vietnam. They are deeply worried that their defeat in Vietnam will lead to a chain reaction. They are expanding the war in an attempt to save themselves from defeat. But the more they expand the war, the greater will be the chain reaction. The more they escalate the war, the heavier will be their fall and the more disastrous their defeat. The people in other parts of the world will see still more clearly that U.S. imperialism can be defeated, and that what the Vietnamese people can do, they can do too.

History has proved and will go on proving that people's war is the most effective weapon against U.S. imperialism and its lackeys. All revolutionary people will learn to wage people's war against U.S. imperialism and its lackeys. They will take up arms, learn to fight battles and become skilled in waging people's war, though they have not done so before. U.S imperialism, like a mad bull dashing from place to place, will finally be burned to ashes in the blazing fires of the people's wars it has provoked by its own actions.

J. William Fulbright on the "Arrogance of Power," 1966

The attitude above all others which I feel sure is no longer valid is the arrogance of power, the tendency of great nations to equate power with virtue and major responsibilities with a universal mission. The dilemmas involved are preeminently American dilemmas, not because America has weaknesses that others do not have but because America is powerful as no nation has ever been before and the discrepancy between its power and the power of others appears to be increasing. . . .

We are now engaged in a war to "defend freedom" in South Vietnam. Unlike the Republic of Korea, South Vietnam has an army which [is] without notable success and a weak, dictatorial government which does not command the loyalty of the South Vietnamese people. The official war aims of the United States Government, as I understand them, are to defeat what is regarded as North Vietnamese aggression, to demonstrate the futility of what the communists call "wars of national liberation," and to create conditions under which the South Vietnamese people will be able freely to determine their own future. I have not the slightest doubt of the sincerity of the President and the Vice President and the Secretaries of State and Defense in propounding these aims. What I do doubt—and doubt very much—is the ability of the United States to achieve these aims by the means being used. I do not question the power of our weapons and the efficiency of our logistics; I cannot say these things delight me as they seem to delight some of our officials, but they are certainly impressive. What I do question is the ability of the United States, or France or any other Western nation, to go into a small, alien, undeveloped Asian nation and create stability where there is chaos, the will to fight where there is defeatism, democracy where there is no tradition of it and honest government where corruption is almost a way of life. Our handicap is well expressed in the pungent Chinese proverb: "In shallow waters dragons become the sport of shrimps."

Early last month demonstrators in Saigon burned American jeeps, tried to assault American soldiers, and marched through the streets shouting "Down with the American imperialists," while one of the Buddhist leaders made a speech equating the United States with the communists as a threat to South Vietnamese independence. Most Americans are understandably shocked and angered to encounter such hostility from people who by now would be under the rule of the Viet Cong but for the sacrifice of American lives and money. Why, we may ask, are they so shockingly ungrateful? Surely they must know that their very right to parade and protest and demonstrate depends on the Americans who are defending them.

The answer, I think, is that "fatal impact" of the rich and strong on the poor and weak. Dependent on it though the Vietnamese are, our very strength is a reproach to their weakness, our wealth a mockery of their poverty, our success a reminder of their failures. What they resent is the disruptive effect of our strong culture upon their fragile one, an effect which we can no more avoid than a man can help being bigger than a child. What they fear, I think rightly, is that traditional Vietnamese society cannot survive the American economic and cultural impact. . . .

The cause of our difficulties in southeast Asia is not a deficiency of power but an excess of the wrong kind of power which results in a feeling of impotence when it fails to achieve its desired ends. We are still acting like boy scouts dragging reluctant old ladies across the streets they do not want to cross. We are trying to remake Vietnamese society, a task which certainly cannot be accomplished by force and which probably cannot be accomplished by any means available to outsiders. The objective may be desirable, but it is not feasible. . . .

If America has a service to perform in the world—and I believe it has—it is in large part the service of its own example. In our excessive involvement in the affairs of other countries, we are not only living off our assets and denying our own people the proper enjoyment of their resources; we are also denying the world the example of a free society enjoying its freedom to the fullest. This is regrettable indeed for a nation that aspires to teach democracy to other nations, because, as Burke said, "Example is the school of mankind, and they will learn at no other." . . .

There are many respects in which America, if it can bring itself to act with the magnanimity and the empathy appropriate to its size and power, can be an intelligent example to the world. We have the opportunity to set an example of generous understanding in our relations with China, of practical cooperation for peace in our relations with Russia, of reliable and respectful partnership in our relations with Western Europe, of material helpfulness without moral presumption in our relations with the developing nations, of abstention from the temptations of hegemony in our relations with Latin America, and of the all-around advantages of minding one's own business in our relations with everybody. Most of all, we have the opportunity to serve as an example of democracy to the world by the way in which we run our own society; America, in the words of John Quincy Adams, should be "the well-wisher to the freedom and independence of all" but "the champion and vindicator only of her own." . . .

If we can bring ourselves so to act, we will have overcome the dangers of the arrogance of power. It will involve, no doubt, the loss of certain glories, but that seems a price worth paying for the probable rewards, which are the happiness of America and the peace of the world.

Clark M. Clifford Recalls
His Post-Tet Questions (1968), 1969

I took office on March 1, 1968. The enemy's Tet offensive of late January and early February had been beaten back at great cost. The confidence of

From "A Viet Nam Reappraisal: The Personal History of One Man's View and How It Evolved." Excerpted by permission of *Foreign Affairs*, July 1969. Copyright 1969 by the Council on Foreign Relations, Inc.

the American people had been badly shaken. The ability of the South Vietnamese government to restore order and morale in the populace, and discipline and esprit in the armed forces, was being questioned. At the President's direction, General Earle G. Wheeler, Chairman of the Joint Chiefs of Staff, had flown to Viet Nam in late February for an on-the-spot conference with General Westmoreland. He had just returned and presented the military's request that over 200,000 troops be prepared for deployment to Viet Nam. These troops would be in addition to the 525,000 previously authorized. I was directed, as my first assignment, to chair a task force named by the President to determine how this new requirement could be met. We were not instructed to assess the need for substantial increases in men and materiel; we were to devise the means by which they could be provided.

My work was cut out. The task force included Secretary Rusk, Secretary Henry Fowler, Under Secretary of State Nicholas Katzenbach, Deputy Secretary of Defense Paul Nitze, General Wheeler, CIA Director Richard Helms, the President's Special Assistant, Walt Rostow, General Maxwell Taylor and other skilled and highly capable officials. All of them had had long and direct experience with Vietnamese problems. I had not. I had attended various meetings in the past several years and I had been to Viet Nam three times, but it was quickly apparent to me how little one knows if he has been on the periphery of a problem and not truly in it. Until the day-long sessions of early March, I had never had the opportunity of intensive analysis and fact-finding. Now I was thrust into a vigorous, ruthlessly frank assessment of our situation by the men who knew the most about it. Try though we would to stay with the assignment of devising means to meet the military's requests, fundamental questions began to recur over and over.

It is, of course, not possible to recall all the questions that were asked nor all of the answers that were given. Had a transcript of our discussions been made—one was not—it would have run to hundreds of closely printed pages. The documents brought to the table by participants would have totalled, if collected in one place—which they were not—many hundreds more. All that is pertinent to this essay are the impressions I formed, and the conclusions I ultimately reached in those days of exhausting scrutiny. In the colloquial style of those meetings, here are some of the principal issues raised and some of the answers as I understood them:

"Will 200,000 more men do the job?" I found no assurance that they would.

"If not, how many more might be needed—and when?" There was no way of knowing.

"What would be involved in committing 200,000 more men to Viet Nam?" A reserve call-up of approximately 280,000, an increased draft call and an extension of tours of duty of most men then in service.

"Can the enemy respond with a build-up of his own?" He could and he probably would.

"What are the estimated costs of the latest requests?" First calculations were on the order of $2 billion for the remaining four months of that fiscal year, and an increase of $10 to $12 billion for the year beginning July 1, 1968.

"What will be the impact on the economy?" So great that we would face the possibility of credit restrictions, a tax increase and even wage and price controls. The balance of payments would be worsened by at least half a billion dollars a year.

"Can bombing stop the war?" Never by itself. It was inflicting heavy personnel and materiel losses, but bombing by itself would not stop the war.

"Will stepping up the bombing decrease American casualties?" Very little, if at all. Our casualties were due to the intensity of the ground fighting in the South. We had already dropped a heavier tonnage of bombs than in all the theaters of World War II. During 1967, an estimated 90,000 North Vietnamese had infiltrated into South Viet Nam. In the opening weeks of 1968, infiltrators were coming in at three to four times the rate of a year earlier, despite the ferocity and intensity of our campaign of aerial interdiction.

"How long must we keep on sending our men and carrying the main burden of combat?" The South Vietnamese were doing better, but they were not ready yet to replace our troops and we did not know when they would be.

When I asked for a presentation of the military plan for attaining victory in Viet Nam, I was told that there was no plan for victory in the historic American sense. Why not? Because our forces were operating under three major political restrictions: The President had forbidden the invasion of North Viet Nam because this could trigger the mutual assistance pact between North Viet Nam and China; the President had forbidden the mining of the harbor at Haiphong, the principal port through which the North received military supplies, because a Soviet vessel might be sunk; the President had forbidden our forces to pursue the enemy into Laos and Cambodia, for to do so would spread the war, politically and geographically, with no discernible advantage. These and other restrictions which precluded an all-out, no-holds-barred military effort were wisely designed to prevent our being drawn into a larger war. We had no inclination to recommend to the President their cancellation.

"Given these circumstances, how can we win?" We would, I was told, continue to evidence our superiority over the enemy; we would continue to attack in the belief that he would reach the stage where he would find it inadvisable to go on with the war. He could not afford the attrition we were inflicting on him. And we were improving our posture all the time.

I then asked, "What is the best estimate as to how long this course of action will take? Six months? One year? Two years?" There was no agreement on an answer. Not only was there no agreement, I could find no one willing to express any confidence in his guesses. Certainly, none of us was willing to assert that he could see "light at the end of the tunnel" or that American troops would becoming home by the end of the year.

After days of this type of analysis, my concern had greatly deepened.

I could not find out when the war was going to end; I could not find out the manner in which it was going to end; I could not find out whether the new requests for men and equipment were going to be enough, or whether it would take more and, if more, when and how much; I could not find out how soon the South Vietnamese forces would be ready to take over. All I had was the statement, given with too little self-assurance to be comforting, that if we persisted for an indeterminate length of time, the enemy would choose not to go on.

And so I asked, "Does anyone see any diminution in the will of the enemy after four years of our having been there, after enormous casualties and after massive destruction from our bombing?"

The answer was that there appeared to be no diminution in the will of the enemy. . . .

And so, after these exhausting days, I was convinced that the military course we were pursuing was not only endless, but hopeless. A further substantial increase in American forces could only increase the devastation and the Americanization of the war, and thus leave us even further from our goal of a peace that would permit the people of South Viet Nam to fashion their own political and economic institutions. Henceforth, I was also convinced, our primary goal should be to level off our involvement, and to work toward gradual disengagement.

Paul Meadlo Explains
the My Lai Massacre, 1969

MEADLO: Captain Medina had us all in a group, and oh, he briefed us, and I can't remember all the briefing.

WALLACE: How many of them were you? A. Well, with the mortar platoon, I'd say there'd be about 60–65 people, but the mortar platoon wasn't with us, and I'd say the mortar platoon had about 20–25—about 25 people in the mortar platoon. So we didn't have the whole company in the Pinkville [My Lai], no we didn't.

Q. There weren't about 40–45—A. . . . right. . . .

Q. —that took part in all of this? A. Right.

Q. Now you took off from your base camp. A. . . . yes—Dolly.

Q. . . . Dolly. At what time? A. I wouldn't know what time it was. . . .

Q. . . . in the early morning. . . . A. . . . In the early morning. It was—it would have been a long time ago.

Q. And what had you been briefed to do when you got to Pinkville?

A. To search and to make sure that there weren't no N.V.A. in the village and expecting to fight—when we got there. . . .

Q. To expect to fight? A. To expect to fight.

Q. Un-huh. So you took off and—in how many choppers?

New York Times, November 25, 1969. © 1969 by The New York Times Company. Reprinted by permission.

A. Well, I'd say the first wave was about four of us—I mean four choppers, and. . . .

Q. How many men aboard each chopper?

A. Five of us. And we landed next to the village, and we all got in line and we started walking toward the village. And there was one man, one gook in the shelter, and he was all huddled up down in there, and the man called out and said there's a gook over here.

Q. How old a man was this? I mean was this a fighting man or an older man?

A. An older man. And the man hauled out and said that there's a gook over here, and then Sergeant Mitchell hollered back and said shoot him.

Q. Sergeant Mitchell was in charge of the 20 of you? A. He was in charge of the whole squad. And so then the man shot him. So we moved on into the village, and we started searching up the village and gathering people and running through the center of the village.

Q. How many people did you round up? A. Well, there was about 40–45 people that we gathered in the center of the village. And we placed them in there, and it was like a little island, right there in the center of the village, I'd say. And—

Q. What kind of people—men, women, children?

A. Men, women, children.

Q. Babies?

A. Babies. And we all huddled them up. We made them squat down, and Lieutenant Calley came over and said you know what to do with them, don't you? And I said yes so I took it for granted that he just wanted us to watch them. And he left, and came back about 10 to 15 minutes later, and said, how come you ain't killed them yet? And I told him that I didn't think you wanted us to kill them, that you just wanted us to guard them. He said, no, I want them dead. So—

Q. He told this to all of you, or to you particularly?

A. Well, I was facing him. So, but, the other three, four guys heard it and so he stepped back about 10, 15 feet, and he started shooting them. And he told me to start shooting. So I started shooting, I poured about four clips into the group.

Q. You fired four clips from your . . . . A. M-16.

Q. And that's about—how many clips—I mean how many—

A. I carried seventeen rounds to each clip.

Q. So you fired something like 67 shots—A. Right.

Q. And you killed how many? At that time?

A. Well, I fired them on automatic, so you can't—you just spray the area on them and so you can't know how many you killed 'cause they were going fast. So I might have killed ten or fifteen of them.

Q. Men, women and children? A. Men, women and children.

Q. And babies?

A. And babies.

Q. Okay, then what? A. So we started to gather them up, more people, and we had about seven or eight people, that we was gonna put into the hootch, and we dropped a hand grenade in there with them.

Q. Now you're rounding up more?

A. We're rounding up more, and we had about seven or eight people. And we was going to throw them in the hootch, and well, we put them in the hootch and then we dropped a hand grenade down there with them. And somebody holed up in the ravine, and told us to bring them over to the ravine, so we took them back out, and led them over to—and by that time, we already had them over there, and they had about 70–75 people all gathered up. So we threw ours in with them and Lieutenant Calley told me, he said, Meadlo, we got another job to do. And so he walked over to the people, and he started pushing them off and started shooting. . . .

Q. Started pushing them off into the ravine?

A. Off into the ravine. It was a ditch. And so we started pushing them off and we started shooting them, so altogether we just pushed them all off, and just started using automatics on them. And then—

Q. Again—men, women, children? A. Men, women and children.

Q. And babies?

A. And babies. And so we started shooting them and somebody told us to switch off to single shot so that we could save ammo. So we switched off to single shot and shot a few more rounds. And after that, I just— we just—the company started gathering up again. We started moving out, and we had a few gooks that was in—as we started moving out, we had gooks in front of us that was taking point, you know. . . .

Q. Why did you do it? A. Why did I do it? Because I felt like I was ordered to do it, and it seemed like that, at the time I felt like I was doing the right thing, because like I said I lost buddies. I lost a damn good buddy, Bobby Wilson, and it was on my conscience. So after I done it, I felt good, but later on that day, it was getting to me.

Q. You're married? A. Right.

Q. Children? A. Two.

Q. How old? A. The boy is two and a half, and the little girl is a year and a half.

Q. Obviously, the question comes to my mind . . . the father of two little kids like that . . . how can he shoot babies? A. I didn't have the little girl. I just had a little boy at the time.

Q. Uh-huh. How do you shoot babies? A. I don't know. It's just one of them things.

Q. How many people would you imagine were killed that day? A. I'd say about 370.

Q. How do you arrive at that figure? A. Just looking.

Q. You say, you think, that many people, and you yourself were responsible for how many of them? A. I couldn't say.

Q. Twenty-five? Fifty? A. I couldn't say . . . just too many.

Q. And how many men did the actual shooting? A. Well, I really couldn't say that, either. There was other . . . there was another platoon in there and . . . but I just couldn't say how many.

Q. But these civilians were lined up and shot? They weren't killed by cross-fire? A. They weren't lined up . . . they [were] just pushed in a ravine or just sitting, squatting . . . and shot.

Q. What did these civilians—particularly the women and children, the old men—what did they do? What did they say to you? A. They weren't much saying to them. They [were] just being pushed and they were doing what they was told to do.

Q. They weren't begging or saying, "No . . . no," or—A. Right, they were begging and saying, "No, no." And the mothers was hugging their children and, but they kept right on firing. Well, we kept right on firing. They was waving their arms and begging. . . .

Q. Was that your most vivid memory of what you saw? A. Right.

Q. And nothing went through your mind or heart? A. Many a times . . . many a times. . . .

Q. While you were doing it? A. Not while I was doing it. It just seemed like it was the natural thing to do at the time. I don't know . . . I was getting relieved from what I'd seen earlier over there.

Q. What do you mean? A. Well, I was getting . . . like the . . . my buddies getting killed or wounded or—we weren't getting no satisfaction from it, so what it really was, it was just mostly revenge.

Q. You call the Vietnamese "gooks?" A. Gooks.

Q. Are they people to you? Were they people to you?

A. Well, they were people. But it was just one of them words that we just picked up over there, you know. Just any word you pick up. That's what you call people, and that's what you been called.

Q. Obviously, the thought that goes through my mind—I spent some time over there, and I killed in the second war, and so forth. But the thought that goes through your mind is, we've raised such a dickens about what the Nazis did, or what the Japanese did, but particularly what the Nazis did in the second world war, the brutalization and so forth, you know. It's hard for a good many Americans to understand that young, capable, American boys could line up old men, women and children and babies and shoot them down in cold blood. How do you explain that?

A. I wouldn't know.

Q. Did you ever dream about all of this that went on in Pinkville?

A. Yes, I did . . . and I still dream about it.

Q. What kind of dreams? A. About the women and children in my sleep. Some days . . . some nights, I can't even sleep. I just lay there thinking about it.

✵ *E S S A Y S*

James C. Thomson, Jr., now of Harvard University, was a policymaker in the State Department and White House from 1961 to 1966. He became a dissenter from American policy. In his essay on why the United States committed itself to war in Vietnam, he stresses a number of factors, including the influence of lessons from the past, bureaucratic inertia, lack of expertise, and miscalculation.

Thomson's autopsy of the subject differs from the radical perspective of Gabriel Kolko of York University, Canada. Kolko does not believe that the war was an American mistake or that Washington was simply acting according to the containment doctrine—to check the advance of Communism. Rather, he argues in the second essay that the United States deliberately intervened in Southeast Asia in order to maintain its economic hegemony in the Third World. Vietnam, Kolko concludes, became a symbolic test case of America's ability to continue its economic supremacy in the face of leftist opposition.

George C. Herring of the University of Kentucky, whose book *America's Longest War* (1986) is one of the best studies of the Vietnam War, asks in the last essay why the United States failed to win. He questions those scholars, politicians, and publicists who came to argue that the United States could have won. He discusses the powerful current of Vietnamese nationalism, the deficiencies of American-backed governments, the destructive American conduct of the war, and the shortcomings of the containment doctrine. America, he suggests, was caught in a "no-win situation."

Historical Legacies and Bureaucratic Procedures

JAMES C. THOMSON, JR.

As a case study in the making of foreign policy, the Vietnam War will fascinate historians and social scientists for many decades to come. One question that will certainly be asked: How did men of superior ability, sound training, and high ideals—American policy-makers of the 1960s— create such costly and divisive policy?

As one who watched the decision-making process in Washington from 1961 to 1966 under Presidents Kennedy and Johnson, I can suggest a preliminary answer. I can do so by briefly listing some of the factors that seemed to me to shape our Vietnam policy during my years as an East Asia specialist at the State Department and the White House. I shall deal largely with Washington as I saw or sensed it, and not with Saigon, where I have spent but a scant three days, in the entourage of the Vice President, or with other decision centers, the capitals of interested parties. Nor will I deal with other important parts of the record: Vietnam's history prior to 1961, for instance, or the overall course of America's relations with Vietnam.

Yet a first and central ingredient in these years of Vietnam decisions does involve history. The ingredient was *the legacy of the 1950s*—by which I mean the so-called "loss of China," the Korean War, and the Far East policy of Secretary of State Dulles.

This legacy had an institutional by-product for the Kennedy Administration: in 1961 the U.S. government's East Asian establishment was undoubtedly the most rigid and doctrinaire of Washington's regional divisions

James C. Thomson, Jr., "How Could Vietnam Happen? An Autopsy," *Atlantic Monthly*, 221 (1968), 47–53. © 1968 James C. Thomson, Jr. Reprinted by permission.

in foreign affairs. This was especially true at the Department of State, where the incoming Administration found the Bureau of Far Eastern Affairs the hardest nut to crack. It was a bureau that had been purged of its best China expertise, and of far-sighted, dispassionate men, as a result of McCarthyism. Its members were generally committed to one policy line: the close containment and isolation of mainland China, the harassment of "neutralist" nations which sought to avoid alignment with either Washington or Peking, and the maintenance of a network of alliances with anti-Communist client states on China's periphery.

Another aspect of the legacy was the special vulnerability and sensitivity of the new Democratic Administration on Far East Policy issues. The memory of the McCarthy era was still very sharp, and Kennedy's margin of victory was too thin. The 1960 Offshore Islands TV debate between Kennedy and Nixon had shown the President-elect the perils of "fresh thinking." The Administration was inherently leery of moving too fast on Asia. As a result, the Far East Bureau (now the Bureau of East Asian and Pacific Affairs) was the last one to be overhauled. Not until Averell Harriman was brought in as Assistant Secretary in December, 1961, were significant personnel changes attempted, and it took Harriman several months to make a deep imprint on the bureau because of his necessary preoccupation with the Laos settlement. Once he did so, there was virtually no effort to bring back the purged or exiled East Asia experts.

There were other important by-products of this "legacy of the fifties":

The new Administration inherited and somewhat shared *a general perception of China-on-the-march*—a sense of China's vastness, its numbers, its belligerence; a revived sense, perhaps, of the Golden Horde. This was a perception led by Chinese intervention in the Korean War (an intervention actually based on appallingly bad communications and mutual miscalculation on the part of Washington and Peking; but the careful unraveling of that tragedy, which scholars have accomplished, had not yet become part of the conventional wisdom).

The new Administration inherited and briefly accepted a *monolithic conception of the Communist bloc*. Despite much earlier predictions and reports by outside analysts, policy-makers did not begin to accept the reality and possible finality of the Sino-Soviet split until the first weeks of 1962. The inevitably corrosive impact of competing nationalisms on Communism was largely ignored.

The new Administration inherited and to some extent shared *the "domino theory" about Asia*. This theory resulted from profound ignorance of Asian history and hence ignorance of the radical differences among Asian nations and societies. It resulted from a blindness to the power and resilience of Asian nationalisms. (It may also have resulted from a subconscious sense that, since "all Asians look alike," all Asian nations will act alike.) As a theory, the domino fallacy was not merely inaccurate but also insulting to Asian nations; yet it has continued to this day to beguile men who should know better.

Finally, the legacy of the fifties was apparently compounded by an uneasy sense of a worldwide Communist challenge to the new Administration after the Bay of Pigs fiasco. A first manifestation was the President's traumatic Vienna meeting with Khrushchev in June, 1961; then came the Berlin crisis of the summer. All this created an atmosphere in which President Kennedy undoubtedly felt under special pressure to show his nation's mettle in Vietnam—if the Vietnamese, unlike the people of Laos, were willing to fight.

In general, the legacy of the fifties shaped such early moves of the new Administration as the decisions to maintain a high-visibility SEATO (by sending the Secretary of State himself instead of some underling to its first meeting in 1961), to back away from diplomatic recognition of Mongolia in the summer of 1961, and most important, to expand U.S. military assistance to South Vietnam that winter on the basis of the much more tentative Eisenhower commitment. It should be added that the increased commitment to Vietnam was also fueled by a new breed of military strategists and academic social scientists (some of whom had entered the new Administration) who had developed theories of counterguerrilla warfare and were eager to see them put to the test. To some, "counter-insurgency" seemed a new panacea for coping with the world's instability.

So much for the legacy and the history. Any new Administration inherits both complicated problems and simplistic views of the world. But surely among the policy-makers of the Kennedy and Johnson Administrations there were men who would warn of the dangers of an open-ended commitment to the Vietnam quagmire?

This raises a central question, at the heart of the policy process: Where were the experts, the doubters, and the dissenters? Were they there at all, and if so, what happened to them?

The answer is complex but instructive.

In the first place, the American government was sorely *lacking in real Vietnam or Indochina expertise.* Originally treated as an adjunct of Embassy Paris, our Saigon embassy and the Vietnam Desk at State were largely staffed from 1954 onward by French-speaking Foreign Service Personnel of narrowly European experience. Such diplomats were even more closely restricted than the normal embassy officer—by cast of mind as well as language—to contacts with Vietnam's French-speaking urban elites. For instance, Foreign Service linguists in Portugal are able to speak with the peasantry if they get out of Lisbon and choose to do so; not so the French speakers of Embassy Saigon.

In addition, the *shadow of the "loss of China"* distorted Vietnam reporting. Career officers in the Department, and especially those in the field, had not forgotten the fate of their World War II colleagues who wrote in frankness from China and were later pilloried by Senate committees for critical comments on the Chinese Nationalists. Candid reporting on the strengths of the Viet Cong and the weaknesses of the Diem government was inhibited by the memory. It was also inhibited by some higher officials, notably Ambassador Nolting in Saigon, who refused to sign off on such cables.

In due course, to be sure, some Vietnam talent was discovered or developed. But a recurrent and increasingly important factor in the decision-making process was *the banishment of real expertise*. Here the underlying cause was the "closed politics" of policy-making as issues become hot: the more sensitive the issue, and the higher it rises in the bureaucracy, the more completely the experts are excluded while the harassed senior generalists take over (that is, the Secretaries, Undersecretaries, and Presidential Assistants). The frantic skimming of briefing papers in the back seats of limousines is no substitute for the presence of specialists; furthermore, in times of crisis such papers are deemed "too sensitive" even for review by the specialists. Another underlying cause of this banishment, as Vietnam became more critical, was the replacement of the experts, who were generally and increasingly pessimistic, by men described as "can-do guys," loyal and energetic fixers unsoured by expertise. In early 1965, when I confided my growing policy doubts to an older colleague on the NSC staff, he assured me that the smartest thing both of us could do was to "steer clear of the whole Vietnam mess"; the gentleman in question had the misfortune to be a "can-do guy," however, and is now highly placed in Vietnam, under orders to solve the mess.

Despite the banishment of the experts, internal doubters and dissenters did indeed appear and persist. Yet as I watched the process, such men were effectively neutralized by a subtle dynamic: *the domestication of dissenters*. Such "domestication" arose out of a twofold clubbish need: on the one hand, the dissenter's desire to stay aboard; and on the other hand, the nondissenter's conscience. Simply stated, dissent, when recognized, was made to feel at home. On the lowest possible scale of importance, I must confess my own considerable sense of dignity and acceptance (both vital) when my senior White House employer would refer to me as his "favorite dove." Far more significant was the case of the former Undersecretary of State, George Ball. Once Mr. Ball began to express doubts, he was warmly institutionalized: he was encouraged to become the inhouse devil's advocate on Vietnam. The upshot was inevitable: the process of escalation allowed for periodic requests to Mr. Ball to speak his piece; Ball felt good, I assume (he had fought for righteousness); the others felt good (they had given a full hearing to the dovish option); and there was minimal unpleasantness. The club remained intact; and it is of course possible that matters would have gotten worse faster if Mr. Ball had kept silent, or left before his final departure in the fall of 1966. There was also, of course, the case of the last institutionalized doubter, Bill Moyers. The President is said to have greeted his arrival at meetings with an affectionate, "Well, here comes Mr. Stop-the-Bombing . . ." Here again the dynamics of domesticated dissent sustained the relationship for a while.

A related point—and crucial, I suppose, to government at all times— was *the "effectiveness" trap*, the trap that keeps men from speaking out, as clearly or often as they might, within the government. And it is the trap that keeps men from resigning in protest and airing their dissent outside the government. The most important asset that a man brings to bureaucratic life is his "effectiveness," a mysterious combination of training, style, and connections. The most ominous complaint that can be whispered of a bureaucrat is: "I'm afraid Charlie's beginning to lose his effectiveness." To preserve your effectiveness, you must decide where and when to fight the mainstream of policy; the opportunities range from pillow talk with your wife, to private drinks with your friends, to meetings with the Secretary of State or the President. The inclination to remain silent or to acquiesce in the presence of the great men—to live to fight another day, to give on this issue so that you can be "effective" on later issues—is overwhelming. Nor is it the tendency of youth alone; some of our most senior officials, men of wealth and fame, whose place in history is secure, have remained silent lest their connection with power be terminated. As for the disinclination to resign in protest: while not necessarily a Washington or even American specialty, it seems more true of a government in which ministers have no parliamentary back-bench to which to retreat. In the absence of such a refuge, it is easy to rationalize the decision to stay aboard. By doing so, one may be able to prevent a few bad things from happening and perhaps even make a few good things happen. To exit is to lose even those marginal chances for "effectiveness."

Another factor must be noted: as the Vietnam controversy escalated at home, there developed *a preoccupation with Vietnam public relations as opposed to Vietnam policy-making.* And here, ironically, internal doubters and dissenters were heavily employed. For such men, by virtue of their own doubts, were often deemed best able to "massage" the doubting intelligentsia. My senior East Asia colleague at the White House, a brilliant and humane doubter who had dealt with Indochina since 1954, spent three quarters of his working days on Vietnam public relations: drafting presidential responses to letters from important critics, writing conciliatory language for presidential speeches, and meeting quite interminably with delegations of outraged Quakers, clergymen, academics, and housewives. His regular callers were the late A. J. Muste and Norman Thomas; mine were members of the Women's Strike for Peace. Our orders from above: keep them off the backs of busy policy-makers (who usually happened to be nondoubters). Incidentally, my most discouraging assignment in the realm of public relations was the preparation of a White House pamphlet entitled *Why Vietnam*, in September, 1965; a gesture toward my conscience, I fought—and lost—a battle to have the title followed by a question mark.

Through a variety of procedures, both institutional and personal, doubt, dissent, and expertise were effectively neutralized in the making of policy. But what can be said of the men "in charge"? It is patently absurd to suggest that they produced such tragedy by intention and calculation. But it is neither absurd nor difficult to discern certain forces at work that caused decent and honorable men to do great harm.

Here I would stress the paramount role of *executive fatigue*. No factor seems to me more crucial and underrated in the making of foreign policy. The physical and emotional toll of executive responsibility in State, the Pentagon, the White House, and other executive agencies is enormous; that toll is of course compounded by extended service. Many of today's Vietnam policy-makers have been on the job for from four to seven years. Complaints may be few, and physical health may remain unimpaired, though emotional health is far harder to gauge. But what is most seriously eroded in the deadening process of fatigue is freshness of thought, imagination, a sense of possibility, a sense of priorities and perspective—those rare assets of a new Administration in its first year or two of office. The tired policy-maker becomes a prisoner of his own narrowed view of the world and his own cliched rhetoric. He becomes irritable and defensive—short on sleep, short on family ties, short on patience. Such men make bad policy and then compound it. They have neither the time nor the temperament for new ideas or preventive diplomacy.

Below the level of the fatigued executives in the making of Vietnam policy was a widespread phenomenon: *the curator mentality* in the Department of State. By this I mean the collective inertia produced by the bureaucrat's view of his job. At State, the average "desk officer" inherits from his predecessor our policy toward Country X; he regards it as his function to keep that policy intact—under glass, untampered with, and dusted—so that he may pass it on in two to four years to his successor. And such curatorial service generally merits promotion within the system. (Maintain the status quo, and you will stay out of trouble.) In some circumstances, the inertia bred by such an outlook can act as a brake against rash innovation. But on many issues, this inertia sustains the momentum of bad policy and unwise commitments—momentum that might otherwise have been resisted within the ranks. Clearly, Vietnam is such an issue.

To fatigue and inertia must be added the factor of internal confusion. Even among the "architects" of our Vietnam commitment, there has been persistent *confusion as to what type of war we were fighting* and, as a direct consequence, *confusion as to how to end that war.* (The "credibility gap" is, in part, a reflection of such internal confusion.) Was it, for instance, a civil war, in which case counterinsurgency might suffice? Or was it a war of international aggression? (This might invoke SEATO [Southeast Asia Treaty Organization] or UN commitment.) Who was the aggressor—and the "real enemy"? The Viet Cong? Hanoi? Peking? Moscow? International Communism? Or maybe "Asian Communism"? Differing enemies dictated differing strategies and tactics. And confused throughout, in like fashion, was the question of American objectives; your objectives depended on whom you were fighting and why. I shall not forget my assignment from an Assistant Secretary of State in March, 1964: to draft a speech for Secretary McNamara which would, *inter alia*, once and for all dispose of the canard that the Vietnam conflict was a civil war. "But in some ways, of course," I mused, "it *is* a civil war." "Don't play word games with me!" snapped the Assistant Secretary.

Similar confusion beset the concept of "negotiations"—anathema to much of official Washington from 1961 to 1965. Not until April, 1965, did "unconditional discussions" become respectable, via a presidential speech; even then the Secretary of State stressed privately to newsmen that nothing had changed, since "discussions" were by no means the same as "negotiations." Months later that issue was resolved. But it took even longer to obtain a fragile internal agreement that negotiations might include the Viet Cong as something other than an appendage to Hanoi's delegation. Given such confusion as to the whos and whys of our Vietnam commitment, it is not surprising, as Theodore Draper has written, that policy-makers find it so difficult to agree on how to end the war.

Of course, one force—a constant in the vortex of commitment—was that of *wishful thinking*. I partook of it myself at many times. I did so especially during Washington's struggle with Diem in the autumn of 1963 when some of us at State believed that for once, in dealing with a difficult client state, the U.S. government could use the leverage of our economic and military assistance to make good things happen, instead of being led around by the nose by men like Chiang Kai-shek and Syngman Rhee (and, in that particular instance, by Diem). If we could prove that point, I thought, and move into a new day, with or without Diem, then Vietnam was well worth the effort. Later came the wishful thinking of the air-strike planners in the late autumn of 1964; there were those who actually thought that after six weeks of air strikes, the North Vietnamese would come crawling to us to ask for peace talks. And what, someone asked in one of the meetings of the time, if they don't? The answer was that we would bomb for another four weeks, and that would do the trick. And a few weeks later came one instance of wishful thinking that was symptomatic of good men misled: in January, 1965, I encountered one of the very highest figures in the Administration at a dinner, drew him aside, and told him of my worries about the air-strike option. He told me that I really shouldn't worry; it was his conviction that before any such plans could be put into effect, a neutralist government would come to power in Saigon that would politely invite us out. And finally, there was the recurrent wishful thinking that sustained many of us through the trying months of 1965–1966 after the air strikes had begun: that surely, somehow, one way or another, we would "be in a conference in six months," and the escalatory spiral would be suspended. The basis of our hope: "It simply can't go on."

As a further influence on policy-makers I would cite the factor of *bureaucratic detachment*. By this I mean what at best might be termed the professional callousness of the surgeon (and indeed, medical lingo—the "surgical strike" for instance—seemed to crop up in the euphemisms of the times). In Washington the semantics of the military muted the reality of war for the civilian policy-makers. In quiet, air-conditioned, thick-carpeted rooms, such terms as "systematic pressure," "armed reconnaissance," "targets of opportunity," and even "body count" seemed to breed a sort of games-theory detachment. Most memorable to me was a moment in the late 1964 target planning when the question under discussion was how heavy our bombing should be, and how extensive our strafing, at some midpoint in the projected pattern of systematic pressure. An Assistant Secretary of State resolved the point in the following words: "It seems to me that our orchestration should be mainly violins, but with periodic touches of brass." Perhaps the biggest shock of my return to Cambridge, Massachusetts, was the realization that the young men, the flesh and blood I taught and saw on these university streets, were potentially some of the numbers on the charts of those faraway planners. In a curious sense, Cambridge is closer to this war than Washington.

There is an unprovable factor that relates to bureaucratic detachment: the ingredient of *crypto-racism*. I do not mean to imply any conscious contempt for Asian loss of life on the part of Washington officials. But I do mean to imply that bureaucratic detachment may well be compounded by a traditional Western sense that there are so many Asians, after all; that Asians have a fatalism about life and a disregard for its loss; that they are cruel and barbaric to their own people; and that they are very different from us (and all look alike?). And I *do* mean to imply that the upshot of such subliminal views is a subliminal question whether Asians, and particularly Asian peasants, and most particularly Asian Communists, are really people— like you and me. To put the matter another way: would we have pursued quite such policies—and quite such military tactics—if the Vietnamese were white?

It is impossible to write of Vietnam decision-making without writing about language. Throughout the conflict, words have been of paramount importance. I refer here to the impact of *rhetorical escalation* and to the *problem of oversell*. In an important sense, Vietnam has become of crucial significance to us *because we have said that it is of crucial significance.* (The issue obviously relates to the public relations preoccupation described earlier.)

The key here is domestic politics: the need to sell the American people, press, and Congress on support for an unpopular and costly war in which the objectives themselves have been in flux. To sell means to persuade, and to persuade means rhetoric. As the difficulties and costs have mounted, so has the definition of the stakes. This is not to say that rhetorical escalation is an orderly process; executive prose is the product of many writers, and some concepts—North Vietnamese infiltration, America's "national honor," Red China as the chief enemy—have entered the rhetoric only gradually and even sporadically. But there is an upward spiral nonetheless. And once you have *said* that the American Experiment itself stands or falls on the Vietnam outcome, you have thereby created a national stake far beyond any earlier stakes.

Crucial throughout the process of Vietnam decision-making was a conviction among many policy-makers: that Vietnam posed a *fundamental test of America's national will*. Time and again I was told by men reared in the tradition of Henry L. Stimson that all we needed was the will, and we would then prevail. Implicit in such a view, it seemed to me, was a curious assumption that Asians lacked will, or at least that in a contest between Asian and Anglo-Saxon wills, the non-Asians must prevail. A corollary to the persistent belief in will was a *fascination with power* and an awe in the face of the power America possessed as no nation or civilization ever before. Those who doubted our role in Vietnam were said to shrink from the burdens of power, the obligations of power, the uses of power, the responsibility of power. By implication, such men were soft-headed and effete.

Finally, no discussion of the factors and forces at work on Vietnam policy-makers can ignore the central fact of *human ego investment*. Men who have participated in a decision develop a stake in that decision. As they participate in further, related decisions, their stake increases. It might have been possible to dissuade a man of strong self-confidence at an early stage of the ladder of decision; but it is infinitely harder at later stages since a change of mind there usually involves implicit or explicit repudiation of a chain of previous decisions.

To put it bluntly: at the heart of the Vietnam calamity is a group of able, dedicated men who have been regularly and repeatedly wrong—and whose standing with their contemporaries, and more important, with history, depends, as they see it, on being proven right. These are not men who can be asked to extricate themselves from error.

The various ingredients I have cited in the making of Vietnam policy have created a variety of results, most of them fairly obvious. Here are some that seem to me most central:

Throughout the conflict, there has been *persistent and repeated miscalculation* by virtually all the actors, in high echelons and low, whether dove, hawk, or something else. To cite one simple example among many: in late 1964 and early 1965, some peace-seeking planners at State who strongly opposed the projected bombing of the North urged that, instead, American ground forces be sent to South Vietnam; this would, they said, increase our bargaining leverage against the North—our "chips"—and would give us something to negotiate about (the withdrawal of our forces) at an early peace conference. Simultaneously, the air-strike option was urged by many in the military who were dead set against American participation in "another land war in Asia"; they were joined by other civilian peace-seekers who wanted to bomb Hanoi into early negotiations. By late 1965, we had ended up with the worst of all worlds: ineffective and costly air strikes against the North, spiraling ground forces in the South, and no negotiations in sight.

Throughout the conflict as well, there has been *a steady give-in to pressures for a military solution* and only minimal and sporadic efforts at a diplomatic and political solution. In part this resulted from the confusion (earlier cited) among the civilians—confusion regarding objectives and strategy. And in part this resulted from the self-enlarging nature of military investment. Once air strikes and particularly ground forces were introduced, our investment itself had transformed the original stakes. More air power was needed to protect the ground forces; and then more ground forces to protect the ground forces. And needless to say, the military mind develops its own momentum in the absence of clear guidelines from the civilians. Once asked to save South Vietnam, rather than to "advise" it, the American military could not but press for escalation. In addition, sad to report, assorted military constituencies, once involved in Vietnam, have had a series of cases to prove: for instance, the utility not only of air power (the Air Force) but of supercarrier-based air power (the Navy). Also, Vietnam policy has suffered from one ironic byproduct of Secretary McNamara's establishment of civilian control at the Pentagon: in the face of such control, interservice rivalry has given way to a united front among the military—reflected in the new but recurrent phenomenon of JCS unanimity. In conjunction with traditional congressional allies (mostly Southern senators and representatives) such a united front would pose a formidable problem for any President.

Throughout the conflict, there have been *missed opportunities, large and small, to disengage ourselves from Vietnam on increasingly unpleasant but still acceptable terms.* Of the many moments from 1961 onward, I shall cite only one, the last and most important opportunity that was lost: in the summer of 1964 the President instructed his chief advisers to prepare for him as wide a range of Vietnam options as possible for postelection consideration and decision. He explicitly asked that all options be laid out. What happened next was, in effect, Lyndon Johnson's slow-motion Bay of Pigs. For the advisers so effectively converged on one single option—juxtaposed against two other, phony options (in effect, blowing up the world, or scuttle-and-run)—that the President was confronted with unanimity for bombing the North from all his trusted counselors. Had he been more confident in foreign affairs, had he been deeply informed on Vietnam and Southeast Asia, and had he raised some hard questions that unanimity had submerged, this President could have used the largest electoral mandate in history to de-escalate in Vietnam, in the clear expectation that at the worst a neutralist government would come to power in Saigon and politely invite us out. Today, many lives and dollars later, such an alternative has become an elusive and infinitely more expensive possibility.

In the course of these years, another result of Vietnam decision-making has been *the abuse and distortion of history.* Vietnamese, Southeast Asian, and Far Eastern history has been rewritten by our policy-makers, and their spokesmen, to conform with the alleged necessity of our presence in Vietnam. Highly dubious analogies from our experience elsewhere—the "Munich" sellout and "containment" from Europe, the Malayan insurgency and the Korean War from Asia—have been imported in order to justify our actions. And more recent events have been fitted to the Procrustean bed of Vietnam. Most notably, the change of power in Indonesia in 1965–1966 has been ascribed to our Vietnam presence; and virtually all progress in the Pacific region—the rise of regionalism, new forms of cooperation, and mounting growth rates—has been similarly explained. The Indonesian allegation is undoubtedly false (I tried to prove it, during six months of careful investigation at the White House, and had to confess failure); the regional allegation is patently unprovable in either direction (except, of course, for the clear fact that the economies of both Japan and Korea have profited enormously from our Vietnam-related procurement in these countries; but that is a costly and highly dubious form of foreign aid).

There is a final result of Vietnam policy I would cite that holds potential danger for the future of American foreign policy: *the rise of a new breed of American ideologues who see Vietnam as the ultimate test of their doctrine.* I have in mind those men in Washington who have given a new life to the missionary impulse in American foreign relations; who believe that this nation, in this era, has received a threefold endowment that can transform the world. As they see it, that endowment is composed of, first, our unsurpassed military might; second, our clear technological supremacy; and third, our allegedly invincible benevolence (our "altruism," our affluence, our lack of territorial aspirations). Together, it is argued, this threefold endowment provides us with the opportunity and the obligation to ease the nations of the earth toward modernization and stability: toward a full-fledged *Pax Americana Technocratica.* In reaching toward this goal, Vietnam is viewed as the last and crucial test. Once we have succeeded there, the road ahead is clear. In a sense, these men are our counterpart to the visionaries of Communism's radical left: they are technocracy's own Maoists. They do not govern Washington today. But their doctrine rides high.

Long before I went into government, I was told a story about Henry L. Stimson that seemed to me pertinent during the years that I watched the Vietnam tragedy unfold—and participated in that tragedy. It seems to me more pertinent than ever as we move toward the election of 1968.

In his waning years Stimson was asked by an anxious questioner, "Mr. Secretary, how on earth can we ever bring peace to the world?" Stimson is said to have answered: "You begin by bringing to Washington a small handful of able men who believe that the achievement of peace is possible.

"You work them to the bone until they no longer believe that it is possible.

"And then you throw them out—and bring in a new bunch who believe that it is possible."

To Master the Third World

GABRIEL KOLKO

There is no comprehensive theory of the contemporary world crisis. That both conventional academic or Left scholars have failed or been unable to assess the causes and meaning of the most significant events of our time

From *Roots of American Foreign Policy: An Analysis of Power and Purpose,* 48–55, 83–86, 88–90, by Gabriel Kolko, Copyright © 1969 by Gabriel Kolko. Reprinted by permission of Beacon Press.

in large part reflects their willingness to confront directly the nature of American interest and power. Theories of imperialism are now the dry-as-dust topics of academic tomes, and all too few have been made a serious effort to scratch beneath the ideology of American expansion to define its larger needs, imperatives, and functions as a system.

Earlier studies of imperialism left no doubt as to what one had to examine in order to comprehend the role of a state in the world. Whether it was imperialist rivalries for economic and strategic power, the atavism of feudal ideologies, reaction and counterrevolution, or the desire to integrate and stabilize a world economy, the study of foreign policy was specific, real, and discounted the notion of error, myth, and exuberance as the sources of conduct as explanations sufficient only for national patriots. American scholars have not translated their ability to perceive correctly the roots of diplomacy in the past into a description of contemporary American policy, even though the same categories and analogies may be equally relevant today.

To understand the unique economic interests and aspirations of the United States in the world, and the degree to which it benefits or loses within the existing distribution and structure of power and the world economy, is to define a crucial basis for comprehending as well as predicting its role overseas. The nature of the international crisis, and the limited American responses to it, tell us why the United States is in Vietnam and why in fact American intervention inevitably colors the direction of the vast changes in the world political and social system which are the hallmarks of modern history. In brief, the manner in which the United States has expanded its problems and objectives overseas, transforming the American crisis into a global one, also explains its consistent interventionism.

It is critical, as part of a comprehensive theory of the world crisis, to study the control and organization of the international economy, who gains and who loses in it, and how we have arrived at the present impasse. We should neither dismiss nor make too much of the issue of ideology or the less systematic belief, as former Secretary of Defense James Forrestal once put it, that ". . . our security is not merely the capacity or ability to repeal invasion, it is our ability to contribute to the reconstruction of the world. . . ." For American ideology is a vague synthesis that embodies, once its surface is scratched, economic and strategic objectives and priorities that a thin rhetoric rationalizes into doctrines more interesting for what they imply than for what they state. . . . I shall deal only with the structure and the material components of the world economy that set the context for the repeated local interventions and crises that are the major characteristics of the modern world scene.

The role of raw materials is qualitative rather than merely quantitative, and neither volume nor price can measure their ultimate significance and consequences. The economies and technologies of the advanced industrial nations, the United States in particular, are so intricate that the removal of even a small part, as in a watch, can stop the mechanism. The steel industry must add approximately thirteen pounds of manganese to each ton of steel, and though the weight and value of the increase is a tiny fraction of the total, a modern diversified steel industry *must* have manganese. The same analogy is true of the entire relationship between the industrial and so-called developing nations: The nations of the Third World may be poor, but in the last analysis the industrial world needs their resources more than these nations need the West, for poverty is nothing new to peasantry cut off from export sectors, and trading with industrial states has not ended their subsistence living standards. In case of a total rupture between the industrial and supplier nations, it is the population of the industrial world that proportionately will suffer the most.

Since the Second World War the leaders of the United States have been acutely aware of their vital reliance on raw materials, and the fact, to quote Paul G. Hoffman, former Marshall Plan administrator, that ". . . our own dynamic economy has made us dependent on the outside world for many critical raw materials." Successive Administrations have been incessantly concerned over the ability and necessity of the United States to develop these resources everywhere, given the paucity of local capital and technology, and their interest extends for beyond short-term profits of investment. In areas such as Africa this obsession has defined American policy on every major issue.

At the beginning of this century the United States was a net earner in the export of minerals and commodities, but by 1926–30 it had a vast annual deficit of crude materials, and in 1930 imported 5 percent of its iron ore, 64 percent of its bauxite (aluminum), 65 percent of its copper, 9 percent of its lead, and 4 percent of its zinc. Imports of these five critical metals by 1960 had increased to 32 percent for iron ore, 98 percent of bauxite, 35 percent for lead, and 60 percent for zinc, and only in the case of copper declined to 46 percent. As a percentage of the new supply, the United States in 1956 imported at least 80 percent of thirty-nine necessary commodities, 50 to 79 percent of fifteen commodities, 10 to 49 percent of twenty commodities, and less than 10 percent of another twenty-three—all with a total import value of $6.6 billion. There was no doubt, as one Senate report concluded in 1954, that Washington knew that should the mineral-rich nations cut off these sources, "To a very dangerous extent, the vital security of this Nation is in serious jeopardy."

By 1956–60 the United States was importing over half of all its required metals and almost 60 percent of its wool. It imported all tropical foodstuffs, such as cocoa, coffee, and bananas, as well as over half the sugar supply. When, in 1963, Resources for the Future completed its monumental survey of raw materials and projected American needs for the next forty years, it predicted a vast multiplication of American demands that made imperative, in its estimate, ". . . that in the future even larger amounts of certain items will have to be drawn from foreign sources if demand is to be satisfied without marked increases in cost." Its medium projections suggested immensely increased needs for nearly all metals, ranging as high as nine times for molybdenum to about two and one-half times for lead. Within three years, however, all of the critical output, consumption, and population assumptions upon which the Resources for the Future experts based their speculations proved to be far too conservative, the omnivorous demands of the economy were far greater than they had expected.

A critical shift in the location of the world's most vital mineral output and reserves has accompanied the imperative need for raw materials in the United States. In 1913 the developing nations accounted for 3 percent of the world's total iron ore output and 15 percent of its petroleum, as opposed to 37 percent and 65 percent, respectively, in 1965. Its share of bauxite output increased from 21 percent in 1928 to 69 percent in 1965. The United States share of world oil output fell from 61 percent in 1938 to 29 percent in 1964, as the known world reserves shifted toward the Middle East.

Despite the introduction of synthetics between 1938 and 1954, which reduced by about one-fifth the quantity of natural raw materials needed for the average constant quantity of goods produced in the industrial nations, the vast increase in world industrial output has more than compensated for the shift and greatly increased pressures on raw materials supplies from the industrial nations. In effect, the United States has become more dependent on imported raw materials as its share of the consumption of the world's total has declined sharply in the face of European and Japanese competition for supplies. The United States, which consumed slightly less than half of the world's total output of copper, lead, zinc, aluminum, and steel in 1948–50, consumed slightly over one-quarter in 1960, save for aluminum, where the percentage decline was still great. This essentially European demand, which has grown far more rapidly than in the United States, has challenged the American predominance in the world raw materials trade in a manner which makes the maintenance and expansion of existing sources in the ex-colonial regions doubly imperative to it.

American and European industry can find most of these future sources of supply, so vital to their economic growth, only in the continents in upheaval and revolution. Over half of the United States iron ore imports in 1960 came from Venezuela and three equally precarious Latin American countries. Over half the known world reserves of manganese are in Russia and China, and most of the remainder is in Brazil, India, Gabon, and South Africa. South Africa and Rhodesia account for nearly all the world's chromium reserves, Cuba and New Caledonia for half the nickel, China for over two-thirds the tungsten, and Chile, Northern Rhodesia, Congo, and Peru for well over two-thirds of the foreign copper reserves. Guyana has about six times the American reserves of bauxite, and China has three times, while Malaya, Indonesia, and Thailand alone have two-thirds of the world tin reserves, with Bolivia and the Congo possessing most of the balance. Only zinc and lead, among the major metals, are in politically stable regions, from the American viewpoint.

It is extraordinarily difficult to estimate the potential role and value of these scarce minerals to the United States, but certain approximate definitions are quite sufficient to make the point that the future of American economic power is too deeply involved for this nation to permit the rest of the world to take its own political and revolutionary course in a manner that imperils the American freedom to use them. Suffice it to say, the ultimate significance of the importation of certain critical raw materials is not their cost to American business but rather the end value of the industries that *must* employ these materials, even in small quantities, or pass out of existence. And in the larger sense, confident access to raw materials is a necessary precondition for industrial expansion into new or existing fields of technology, without the fear of limiting shortages which the United States' sole reliance on its national resources would entail. Intangibly, it is really the political and psychological assurance of total freedom of development of national economic power that is vital to American economic growth. Beyond this, United States profits abroad are made on overseas investments in local export industries, giving the Americans the profits of the suppliers as well as the consumer. An isolated America would lose all this, and much more.

It is not enough, therefore, to state that nonfood raw materials imports doubled in value between 1953 and 1966, and that $16.6 billion in imports for the food and industrial users in 1966 was virtually necessary to American prosperity. More relevant is the fact that in 1963 the Census valued the iron and steel industry's shipments at $22.3 billion, the aluminum's at $3.9 billion, metal cans at $2.1 billion, copper at $3.1 billion, asbestos at a half billion, zinc at a half billion, coffee at $1.9 billion, sugar and chocolate at $1.7 billion—and that all of these industries and many others to some critical extent, depended on their access to the world's supply of raw materials. Without the availability of such goods for decades, at prices favorable to the United States, the American economy would have been far different—and much poorer.

To suggest that the United States could solve its natural shortages by attempting to live within its raw materials limits would also require a drastic reduction in its exports of finished goods, and this the leaders of the American system would never voluntarily permit, for it would bring profound economic repercussions for a capitalist economy in the form of vast unemployment and lower profits. While only four or five percent of American steel mill products went to exports in 1955–60, this proportion reached nearly one-quarter in the aluminum and one-fifth in the copper industries. In this context the United States had become a processor of the world's raw materials in a number of fields not simply to satisfy domestic needs but also its global export trade and military ambitions. At home, a policy of self-sufficiency would, in the case of aluminum, seriously affect the building construction industry, consumer and producer durables, and transport industries. The same is true for copper, which is critical for producer durables, building construction, communications, and electric power. Minor metals, of which the United States is largely deficient, are essential to any technologically advanced nation, especially to the chemical, electrical, and electronics industries.

America's ability to procure at will such materials as it needs, and at a price it can afford, is one of the keystones of its economic power in this century. The stakes are vast, and its capacity to keep intact something like the existing integrated but unequal relations between the poor, weak nations and the United States is vital to the future of its mastery of the international economy.

The dominant interest of the United States is in world economic stability, and anything that undermines that condition presents a danger to its present hegemony. Countering, neutralizing and containing the disturbing political and social trends thus becomes the most imperative objective of its foreign policy. . . .

In their brilliant essay on the political economy of nineteenth century British imperialism, John Gallagher and Ronald Robinson have described a process that parallels the nature of the United States expansion after 1945:

> Imperialism, perhaps may be defined as a sufficient political function of this process of integrating new regions into the expanding economy; its character is largely decided by the various and changing relationships between the political and economic elements of expansion in any particular region and time. Two qualifications must be made. First, imperialism may be only indirectly connected with economic integration in that it sometimes extends beyond areas of economic development, but acts for their strategic protection. Secondly, although imperialism is a function of economic expansion, it is not a necessary function. Whether imperialist phenomena show themselves or not, is determined not only by the factors of economic expansion, but equally by the political and social organization of the regions brought into the orbit of the expansive society, and also by the world situation in general.
>
> It is only when the politics of these new regions fail to provide satisfactory conditions for commercial or strategic integration and when their relative weakness allows, that power is used imperialistically to adjust those conditions. Economic expansion, it is true, will tend to flow into the regions of maximum opportunity, but maximum opportunity depends as much upon political considerations of security as upon questions of profit. Consequently, in any particular region, if economic opportunity seems large but political security small, then full absorption into the extending economy tends to be frustrated until power is exerted upon the state in question. Conversely, in proportion as satisfactory political frameworks are brought into being this way, the frequency of imperialist intervention lessens and imperialist control is correspondingly relaxed. It may be suggested that this willingness to limit the use of paramount power to establishing security for trade is the distinctive feature of the British imperialism of free trade in the nineteenth century, in contrast to the mercantilist use of power to obtain commercial supremacy and monopoly through political possession.

In today's context, we should regard United States political and strategic intervention as a rational overhead charge for its present and future freedom to act and expand. One must also point out that however high that cost may appear today, in the history of United States diplomacy specific American economic interests in a country or region have often defined the national interest on the assumption that the nation can identify its welfare with the profits of some of its citizens—whether in oil, cotton, or bananas. The cost to the state as a whole are less consequential than the desire and profits of specific class strata and their need to operate everywhere in a manner that, collectively, brings vast prosperity to the United States and its rulers.

Today it is a fact that capitalism in one country is a long-term physical and economic impossibility without drastic shift in the distribution of the world's income. Isolated, the United States would face those domestic back-logged economic and social problems and weaknesses it has deferred confronting for over two decades, and its disappearing strength in a global context would soon open the door to the internal dynamics which might jeopardize the very existence of liberal corporate capitalism at home. It is logical to regard Vietnam, therefore, as the inevitable cost of maintaining United States imperial power, a step toward saving the future in something akin to its present form by revealing to others in the Third World what they too may encounter should they also seek to control their own development. That Vietnam itself has relatively little of value to the United States is all the more significant as an example of America's determination to hold the line as a matter of principle against revolutionary movements. What is at stake, according to the "domino" theory with which Washington accurately perceives the world, is the control of Vietnam's neighbors, Southeast Asia and, ultimately, Latin America.

The contemporary world crisis, in brief, is a by-product of United States response to Third World change and its own definitions of what it must do to preserve and expand its vital national interests. At the present moment, the larger relationships in the Third World economy benefit the United States, and it is this type of structure America is struggling to preserve. Moreover, the United States requires the option to expand to regions it has not yet penetrated, a fact which not only brings it into conflict with Third World revolutions but also with an increasingly powerful European capitalism. Where neo-colonial economic penetration via loans, aid, or attacks on balanced economic development or diversification in the Third World are not sufficient to maintain stability, direct interventions to save local *compradors* and oligarchies often follow. Frequently such encroachments succeed, as in Greece and the Dominican Republic, but at times, such as Vietnam, it is the very process of intervention itself that creates its own defeat by deranging an already moribund society, polarizing options, and compelling men to choose—and to resist. Even the returns to the United States on partial successes have warranted the entire undertaking in the form not just of high profit ratios and exports, but in the existence of a vast world economic sector which supplies the disproportionately important materials without which American prosperity within its present social framework would eventually dry up.

The existing global political and economic structure, with all its stagnation and misery, has not only brought the United States billions but has made possible, above all, a vast power that requires total world economic integration not on the basis of equality but of domination. And to preserve this form of world is vital to the men who run the American economy and politics at the highest levels. If some of them now reluctantly believe that Vietnam was not the place to make the final defense against tides of unpredictable revolutionary change, they all concede that they must do it somewhere, and the logic of their larger view makes their shift on Vietnam a matter of expediency or tactics rather than of principle. All the various American leaders believe in global stability which they are committed to defend against revolution that may threaten the existing distribution of economic power in the world. . . .

The intervention of the United States in Vietnam is the most important single embodiment of the power and purposes of American foreign policy since the Second World War, and no other crisis reveals so much of the basic motivating forces and objectives—and weaknesses—of American global politics. A theory of the origins and meaning of the war also discloses the origins of an American malaise that is global in its reaches, impinging on this nation's conduct everywhere. To understand Vietnam is also to comprehend not just the present purposes of American action but also to anticipate its thrust and direction in the future.

Vietnam illustrates, as well, the nature of the American internal political process and decision-making structure when it exceeds the view of a major sector of the people, for no other event of our generation has turned such a large proportion of the nation against its government's policy or so profoundly alienated its youth. And at no time has the government conceded so little to democratic sentiment, pursuing as it has a policy of escalation that reveals that its policy is formulated not with an eye to democratic sanctions and compromises but rather the attainment of specific interests and goals scarcely shared by the vast majority of the nation.

The inability of the United States to apply its vast material and economic power to compensate for the ideological and human superiority of revolutionary and guerrilla movements throughout the world has been the core of its frustration in Vietnam. From a purely economic viewpoint, the United States cannot maintain its existing vital dominating relationship to much of the Third World unless it can keep the poor nations from moving too far toward the Left and the Cuban or Vietnamese path. A widespread leftward movement would critically affect its supply of raw materials and have profound long-term repercussions. It is the American view of the need for relative internal stability within the poorer nations that has resulted in a long list of United States interventions since 1946 into the affairs of numerous nations, from Greece to Guatemala, of which Vietnam is only the consummate example—but in principle no different than numerous others. The accuracy of the "domino" theory, with its projection of the eventual loss of whole regions to American direction and access, explains the direct continuity between the larger United States global strategy and Vietnam.

Yet, ironically, while the United States struggles in Vietnam and the Third World to retain its own mastery, or to continue that once held by the former colonial powers, it simultaneously weakens itself in its deepening economic conflict with Europe, revealing the limits of America's power to attain its ambition to define the preconditions and direction of global economic and political developments. Vietnam is essentially an American intervention against a nationalist, revolutionary agrarian movement which embodies social elements in incipient and similar forms of development in numerous other Third World nations. It is in no sense a civil war, with the United States supporting one local faction against another, but an effort to preserve a mode of traditional colonialism via a minute, historically opportunistic *comprador* class in Saigon. For the United States to fail in Vietnam would be to make the point that even the massive intervention of the most powerful nation in the history of the world was insufficient to stem profoundly popular social and national revolutions throughout the world. Such a revelation of American weaknesses would be tantamount to a demotion of the United States from its present role as the world's dominant superpower.

Why the United States Failed in Vietnam

GEORGE C. HERRING

During the past few months [of 1981], a new phrase has entered the American political vocabulary. It is called the "Vietnam syndrome." It was apparently coined by Richard Nixon. As employed by the Reagan administration, it presumably means that America's failure in Vietnam and the backlash from it have been primarily responsible for the malaise that has allegedly reduced the United States to a state of impotence in a menacing world. Doctor Reagan and his associates seem determined to cure the disease. Some of the administration's defenders have even justified intervention in El Salvador as essential to that end; and although the White House and State Department may not go that far, their public statements leave no doubt to their determination to exorcise the Vietnam syndrome.

The notion of a Vietnam syndrome presupposes a view of the war which, although rarely articulated in full, nevertheless clearly influences the administration's foreign policy. Reagan himself has stated—contrary to a long-prevailing view—that Vietnam was "in truth a noble war," an altruistic attempt on the part of the United States to help a "small country newly free from colonial rule" defend itself against a "totalitarian neighbor bent on conquest." He and Secretary of State Alexander M. Haig, Jr. have also insisted that it was a necessary war, necessary to check the expansionist designs of the Soviet Union and its client states and to uphold the global position of the United States. They have left no doubt that they regard it as a war that we should have won. America failed, Reagan recently stated, not because it was defeated but because the military was *"denied permission to win."* Haig has argued that the war could have been won at any of several junctures if American leaders had been willing to "apply the full range of American power to bring about a successful outcome." The defeat was thus self-inflicted, and the consequences have been enormous. "America

From "The 'Vietnam Syndrome' and American Foreign Policy," © *Virginia Quarterly Review*, LVII (Fall, 1981). Reprinted by permission of the author and publisher.

is no longer the America it was," Haig has stated, and "that is largely attributable to the mistakes of Vietnam."

These views are not, of course, new, nor is it surprising that they have gained credence in recent years. The aggressiveness of the Soviets and the Hanoi regime have made it easier for us to justify our own actions morally and in terms of national security. An explanation of failure which places blame on ourselves rather than elsewhere is probably easier for us to live with. Scholars had begun to revise conventional dovish views of the war well before Reagan took office, and films such as *The Deerhunter*, whatever their artistic merit, promoted to a form of redemption. What *is* significant is that this now [1981] seems to be the official view and is also a partial basis for major policy decisions. Equally important, it is getting little challenge from Congress and the media, the centers of respectable dissent in the late 1960's and early 1970's. From all appearances, to apply an Oriental usage, 1981 is the year of the hawk.

It seems particularly urgent, therefore, that we examine this view critically in terms of the following very difficult questions: was Vietnam a just and necessary war as is now being proclaimed? Was it a winnable war, our failure primarily the result of our own mistakes? . . .

Let me begin with a caveat. The questions I have just raised cannot now be answered definitively. We are still very close to Vietnam, and it is difficult to appraise the war with the sort of detachment and perspective we would like. The evidence is far from complete. We have no more than roughly 15 percent of the documentation on the American side, and Hanoi has given no indication that it plans to initiate a freedom of information act. More important, some of the major questions concerning the war can never be answered with finality. We cannot know, for example, what would have happpened if we had not intervened in Vietnam or if we had fought the war differently. We can do no more than speculate, an inexact science at best.

With these qualifications in mind, we can turn to the essential questions that have been raised about the war and its consequences. For many of those who experienced the Vietnam era, Reagan's "noble war" statement seemed so far off the wall that it could not be taken seriously. But it touched a responsive chord, and this is not surprising. The charges of American atrocities and war guilt that echoed across the land just a few years ago ran across the grain of our traditional sense of our own righteousness. Every war has its elements of nobility, moreover, and it is perhaps proper and even necessary for us to recognize the acts of heroism, sacrifice, and compassion that were as much a part of Vietnam as the atrocities. Certainly it was wrong for us to lay on the veterans the guilt which all of us share in one way or another, and Reagan's statement may have been addressing this point, at least obliquely.

His argument was based on the specific premise that we intervened in defense of a "free government" against "outside aggression," however, and this interpretation badly distorts the origins and nature of the war. In fact, we tried to contain an indigenous revolution that, although Communist led, expressed the deepest and most powerful currents of Vietnamese nationalism. The Vietnam conflict cannot be understood by looking at the situation in 1965, when the major U.S. commitments were made. It is necessary to go back to 1945 or even earlier. The revolution that erupted in Vietnam at the end of World War II sought to eliminate French colonialism and to unify a country that had been divided for several centuries. During the ensuing war against France, the revolution generated widespread popular support, and its leader, Ho Chi Minh, came to symbolize for many Vietnamese the spirit of national independence just as George Washington did for the revolutionary generation of Americans. Ho's Vietminh defeated the French in 1954, despite the massive aid given France by the United States. It would probably have unified Vietnam after 1954, had the United States not stepped in and helped to make permanent a division at the 17th parallel the Geneva Conference had intended to be temporary. The Vietcong revolution, which erupted spontaneously in the south in the late 1950's, and subsequent North Vietnamese support of it, were extensions of the revolution of 1945, a fact which explains their unusual staying power in the face of tremendous adversity. This is not to endow the revolution with a higher morality, as the rhetoric of the antiwar movement frequently did. Its leaders were ruthless in pursuit of their goals and were capable of great brutality toward their own people and others. The point rather is that throughout much of the 30-year war, Ho's revolution represented the most powerful political force in Vietnam, and we can talk of outside aggression only in the most narrow, ahistorical sense.

Moreover, the governments we supported—by and large our own creations—were free primarily in the sense that they were non-Communist. It should be recalled in this connection that our first crucial commitment in Vietnam came in 1950 in support of French colonialism. When the French departed after Geneva, we inherited what was left of the puppet government they had created in 1949. We grafted onto it the trappings of Western-style democracy and gave it a measure of international respectability. But in fact, the government of Ngo Dinh Diem and his successors were narrowly based oligarchies, held up mainly by American power, at times quite repressive, and generally unresponsive to the needs and concerns of the predominantly rural population of southern Vietnam. It can be argued, of course, that they were better than their counterpart in the north and provided an alternative to the many Vietnamese who did not want Communism. This may well be true, but it blurs the issue, and we should be wary in the aftermath of the war of endowing the governments we supported with qualities they did not have.

A third point that must be stressed is this: whatever our intent, the way we conducted the war had a devastating impact on the land and people we professed to be serving. In trying to ennoble our cause, we must not forget the consequences of our actions. We prolonged for as much as 20 years a war that might have ended much earlier, with losses of human lives that ran into the millions. The heavy bombing and artillery fire of the high-technology war we fought permanently scarred the landscape of southern

Vietnam, obliterating an area roughly the size of Massachusetts and leaving an estimated 21 million craters. Along with Vietcong terrorism, our military operations made refugees of nearly one-third of the population of South Vietnam. We destroyed the economic and social fabric of the nation for which we had assumed responsibility. Despite the moral pretensions on both sides, it seems evident, as Henry Kissinger once observed, that in Vietnam, no one had a "monopoly of anguish and no one . . . had a monopoly of moral insight."

Finally, I would argue that the major American decisions in Vietnam were made primarily on the basis of self-interest, not altruism. This is a sticky wicket, to be sure. It is difficult to separate the two, and American policy makers certainly felt they were acting on the basis of principle as well as self-interest. To put it another way, however, had it been merely a matter of saving a free people from outside aggression, they would not have acted as they did. At every step along the way, they were convinced that the national interests of the United States required them to escalate the commitment.

What were these interests and why were they felt to be so compelling? From 1950 at least into the late 1960's, we viewed Vietnam primarily in terms of the Cold War and the doctrine of containment, the overarching principle of our Cold War foreign policies. The basic assumption of that policy was that we faced a monolithic, tightly unified world Communist movement, orchestrated by Moscow, and committed to world revolution. We viewed the world as split into two hostile blocs, irreconcilably divided by ideology and existing in a precarious equilibrium. Particularly after the fall of China to communism in 1949, we saw the Cold War as a zero sum game in which any gain for communism was automatically a loss for what we called the "free world." To contain the global Communist menace, we constructed a world-wide network of alliances, intervened freely in the affairs of other nations, and went to war in Korea.

From the beginning to near the end, we viewed the conflict in Vietnam primarily from this perspective. Because the revolution was led by Moscow-trained Communists, we assumed it was but an instrument of the Kremlin's drive for world domination. In the early stages, we felt it necessary to block Communist conquest of Vietnam lest it set off a domino effect which could cause the loss of all of Southeast Asia, with presumably incalculable strategic, political, and economic consequences for the United States. Later, we escalated the commitment because of a felt need to uphold our credibility. We had to prove that we would stand by our commitments to dissuade the Communists from further aggressions that could drastically undermine our global position or perhaps plunge us into a global war.

This leads directly to question number two: were these assumptions valid? Was the war necessary, as many now allege, to stop the advance of communism and uphold our world position? It is impossible to answer these questions with absolute certainty because we can never know precisely what would have happened if we had not intervened. It seems probable that there would have been war of some kind and that Vietnam would have been unified by force. What then? Would the dominoes have fallen in Southeast Asia? Would there have been a new wave of aggression elsewhere? Obviously, we can never know. I would argue, however, that we badly misperceived the nature of the struggle in Vietnam and that we may have exaggerated the possible consequences of a Communist victory.

The containment policy was misguided both generally and in its specific application to Vietnam. The simplistic, black and white assumptions from which it derived never bore much resemblance to reality. Soviet goals were (and remain) as much the product of traditional Russian nationalism as ideology, and they fell considerably short of world domination. The so-called Communist bloc was never a monolith—it was torn by divisions from the start, and the fragmentation has become more pronounced. In the Third World, nationalism and resistance to any form of outside influence have been the driving force. And there has never been a zero sum game. What appeared to be a major victory for the Soviet Union in China in 1949, for example, has turned out to be a catastrophic loss. In most parts of the world, neither the Soviet Union nor the United States has prevailed, and pluralism and fragmentation have been the norm.

In applying the containment policy to Vietnam, we drastically misjudged the internal dynamics of the conflict. We attributed the war to an expansionist communism bent on world domination. In fact, as I have suggested, it began as a revolution against French colonialism. Ho Chi Minh and his cohorts were Communists, to be sure, rigid and doctrinaire in their views and committed to structure their society along Marxist-Leninist lines. But they were never mere instruments of Moscow. The Soviet Union did not instigate the revolution and in fact exerted very little influence on it until after the United States initiated the bombing in 1965. The Chinese Communists exerted some influence in the early stages, but traditional Vietnamese suspicions of China, the product of a long history of Chinese imperialism, restricted the closeness of these ties. "I would rather sniff French dung for a few more years than eat Chinese for a lifetime," Ho Chi Minh once said, expressing Vietnam's deep-seated fear of its larger northern neighbor. Throughout the 30-year war, the Soviet Union and China supported Vietnam when it was expedient to do so, but they also abandoned it at several critical junctures. North Vietnam played the two off against each other for essentially Vietnamese ends—to rid the country of foreign influence and unify it under one government.

Our rigid application of the containment doctrine in Vietnam had fateful consequences. By placing ourselves against the strongest force in an otherwise politically fragmented country, first in the war against France, later on our own, we may have ensured our ultimate failure. By ascribing the war to international rather than local forces, we underestimated the enemy's commitment, a vital point to which I will return later. Our intervention probably gave the war an international significance it did not have at the outset. Indeed, we may have driven the Vietnamese closer into the arms of their Communist allies than they would have preferred to go.

I also believe that we exaggerated the possible consequences of nonintervention. We will never know whether the domino theory would have operated if Vietnam had fallen earlier, but there is reason to doubt that it would have. Nationalism has proven the most potent and enduring force in recent history, and the nations of Southeast Asia, with their long tradition of opposition to China and Vietnam, would have resisted mightily. By making the war a test case of our credibility, we may have made its consequences greater than they would otherwise have been. By rigidly adhering to a narrow, one-dimensional world view, without adequately taking into account the nature and importance of local forces, we may have placed ourselves in an untenable position.

Question number three: was Vietnam a winnable war, our failure there primarily the result of our mistakes, our lack of will, the disunity within our society? Because it has such profound implications for future policy decisions, this is the most important of our questions and deserves the most extended commentary. Those who argue that our defeat was self-inflicted focus on the misuse of our admittedly vast military power. Instead of using air power to strike a knockout blow against the enemy, they contend, Lyndon Johnson foolishly hedged it about with restrictions, applied it gradually, and held back from the sort of massive, decisive bombing attacks that could have assured victory. Similarly, they argue, had Johnson permitted U.S. ground forces to invade North Vietnamese sanctuaries in Laos, Cambodia, and across the 17th parallel, General Westmoreland's strategy of attrition could have worked and the war could have been won.

These criticisms are not without merit. Johnson's gradual expansion of the bombing did give North Vietnam time to disperse its resources and develop a highly effective air defense system, and the bombing may have encouraged the will to resist rather than crippled it as Johnson had intended. A strategy of attrition could not work as long as the enemy enjoyed sanctuary. If losses reached unacceptable proportions, the enemy could simply retreat to safety, regroup and renew the battle at times and places of his own choosing. He retained the strategic initiative.

To jump from here to the conclusion that the unrestricted use of American power could have produced victory at acceptable costs raises some troubling questions, however. Could an unrestricted bombing campaign have forced North Vietnam to accept a settlement on our terms? Obviously, there is no way we can ever know, but there is reason to doubt that it would have. The surveys conducted after World War II raised some serious doubts about the effect of bombing on the morale of the civilian population of Germany and Japan, and the capacity of air power to cripple a pre-industrial society such as North Vietnam may have been even more limited. There is evidence to suggest that the North Vietnamese were prepared to resist no matter what the level of the bombing, even if they had to go underground. The United States could probably have destroyed the cities and industries of North Vietnam, but what then? Invasion of the sanctuaries and ground operations in North Vietnam might have made the strategy of attrition more workable, but they would also have enlarged the war at a time when the United States was already stretched thin. Each of these approaches would have greatly increased the costs of the war without resolving the central problem—the political viability of South Vietnam.

We must also consider the reasons why Johnson refused to expand the war. He feared that if the United States pushed North Vietnam to the brink of defeat, the Soviet Union and/or China would intervene, broadening the war to dangerous proportions, perhaps to a nuclear confrontation. Johnson may, of course, have overestimated the risks of outside intervention, but the pressures would certainly have been large and he would have been irresponsible to ignore the dangers. And even if the United States had been able militarily to subdue North Vietnam without provoking outside intervention, it would still have faced the onerous, expensive, and dangerous prospect of occupying a hostile nation along China's southern border.

Those who argue that the war was winnable also emphasize the importance of American public opinion in sealing our defeat. They shift blame from those who waged the war to those who opposed it, contending that an irresponsible media and a treacherous antiwar movement turned the nation against the war, forcing Johnson and later Nixon to curtail U.S. involvement just when victory was in grasp. As much mythology has developed around this issue as any other raised by the war, and we probably know as little about it as any. Studies of public opinion do indicate that despite an increasingly skeptical media and noisy protest in the streets, the war enjoyed broad, if unenthusiastic support until that point early in 1968 when it became apparent that the costs might exceed any possible gains—and, even then, Nixon was able to prolong it for four more years. Until the early 1970's, moreover, the antiwar movement was probably counterproductive in terms of its own goals, the majority of Americans finding the protestors more obnoxious than the war. Indeed, it seems likely that the antiwar protest in a perverse way may have strengthened support for the government. After 1969, public opinion and Congress did impose some constraints on the government, and the media probably contributed to this. But to pin the defeat on the media or the antiwar movement strikes me as a gross oversimplification.

The problem with all these explanations is that they are too ethnocentric. They reflect the persistence of what a British scholar has called the illusion of American omnipotence, the traditional American belief that the difficult we do tomorrow, the impossible may take awhile. When failure occurs, it must be *our* fault, and we find scapegoats in our own midst: the poor judgment of our leaders, the media, or the antiwar movement. The flaw in this approach is that it ignores the other side of the equation, in this case, the Vietnamese dimension. I would contend that the sources of our frustration and ultimate failure rest primarily, although certainly not exclusively, in the local circumstances of the war: the nature of the conflict itself, the weakness of our ally, the relative strength of our adversary.

The Vietnam War posed extremely difficult challenges for Americans. It was fought in a climate and on a terrain that were singularly inhospitable. Thick jungles, foreboding swamps and paddies, rugged mountains. Heat that could "kill a man, bake his brains, or wring the sweat from him until he died of exhaustion," Philip Caputo tells us in [A] *Rumor of War.* "It was as if the sun and the land itself were in league with the Vietcong," Caputo adds, "wearing us down, driving us mad, killing us." Needless to say, those who had endured the land for centuries had a distinct advantage over outsiders, particularly when the latter came from a highly industrialized and urbanized environment.

It was a people's war, where the people rather than territory were the primary objective. But Americans as individuals and as a nation could never really bridge the vast cultural gap that separated them from all Vietnamese. Not knowing the language or the culture, they did not know what the people felt or even how to tell friend from foe. "Maybe the dinks got things mixed up," one of the novelist Tim O'Brien's bewildered G.I.'s comments in *Going After Cacciato* after a seemingly friendly farmer bowed and smiled and pointed the Americans into a minefield. "Maybe the gooks cry when they're happy and smile when they're sad." Recalling the emotionless response of a group of peasants when their homes were destroyed by an American company, Caputo notes that they did nothing "and I hated them for it. Their apparent indifference made me feel indifferent." The cultural gap produced cynicism and even hatred toward the people Americans were trying to help. It led to questioning of our goals and produced a great deal of moral confusion among those fighting the war and those at home.

Most important, perhaps, was the formless, yet lethal, nature of guerrilla warfare in Vietnam. It was a war without distinct battlelines or fixed objectives, where traditional concepts of victory and defeat were blurred. It was, Caputo writes, "a formless war against a formless enemy who evaporated into the morning jungle mists only to materialize in some unexpected place." This type of war was particularly difficult for Americans schooled in the conventional warfare of World War II and Korea to fight. And there was always the gnawing question, first raised by John Kennedy himself—how can we tell if we're winning? The only answer that could be devised was the notorious body count, as grim and corrupting as it was unreliable as an index of success. In time, the strategy of attrition and the body count came to represent for sensitive G.I.'s and for those at home killing for the sake of killing. And the light at the end of the tunnel never glimmered. "Aimless, that's what it is," one of O'Brien's G.I.'s laments, "a bunch of kids trying to pin the tail on the Asian donkey. But no . . . tail. No . . . donkey."

Far more important in explaining our failure is the uneven balance of forces we aligned ourselves with in Vietnam. With the passage of time, it becomes more and more apparent that in South Vietnam we attempted a truly formidable undertaking on the basis of a very weak foundation. The "country" to which we committed ourselves in 1954 lacked most of the essential ingredients for nationhood. Had we looked all over the world, in fact, we could hardly have found a less promising place for an experiment in nation-building. Southern Vietnam lacked a viable economy. The French had destroyed the traditional political order, and their departure left a gaping vacuum, no firmly established political institutions, no native elite capable of exercising effective political leadership. Southern Vietnam was rent by a multitude of conflicting ethnic and religious forces. It was, in the words of one scholar, a "political jungle of war lords, bandits, partisan troops, and secret societies." When viewed from this perspective, there were probably built-in limits to what the United States or any outside nation could have accomplished there.

For nearly 20 years, we struggled to establish a viable nation in the face of internal insurgency and external invasion, but the rapid collapse of South Vietnam after our withdrawal in 1973 suggests how little was really accomplished. We could never find leaders capable of mobilizing the disparate population of southern Vietnam. We launched a vast array of ambitious and expensive programs to promote sound and effective government, win the support of the people, and wage war against the Vietcong. When our client state was on the verge of collapse in 1965, we filled the vacuum by putting in our own military forces. But the more we did, the more we induced a state of dependency among those we were trying to help. Tragically, right up to the fall of Saigon in 1975, the South Vietnamese elite expected us to return and save them from defeat. This is not to denigrate the leaders or people who sided with us or to make them scapegoats for our failure. The point rather is that given the history of southern Vietnam and the conditions that prevailed there in 1954, the creation of a viable nation by an outside power may have been an impossible task.

The second point central to understanding our failure is that we drastically underestimated the strength and determination of our adversary. I do not wish to imply here that the North Vietnamese and Vietcong were supermen. They made blunders. They paid an enormous price for their success. They have shown a far greater capacity for making war than for building a nation. In terms of the balance of forces in Vietnam, however, they had distinct advantages. They were tightly mobilized and regimented and fanatically committed to their goals. They were fighting on familiar soil, and they employed methods already perfected in the ten years' war against France. The Vietcong were close to the rural population of South Vietnam, adapted its ideology and tactics to traditional Vietnamese political culture, and used the American presence to exploit popular distrust of outsiders. North Vietnam skillfully employed the strategy of protracted war, perceiving that the Americans, like the French, could become impatient, and if they bled long enough they might tire of the war. "You will kill ten of our men, but we will kill one of yours," Ho once remarked, "and in the end it is you who will tire." The comment was made to a French general in 1946, but it could easily have been said of the Second Indochina War.

Our fatal error, therefore, was to underestimate our adversary. We rather casually assumed that the Vietnamese, rational beings like ourselves, would know better than to stand up against the most powerful nation in the world. It would be like a filibuster in Congress, Lyndon Johnson speculated, enormous resistance at first, then a steady whittling away, then Ho Chi Minh hurrying to get it over with. Years later, Henry Kissinger confessed great surprise with the discovery that his North Vietnamese counterparts were "fanatics." Since our own goals were limited and from our standpoint more than reasonable, we found it hard to understand the total, unyielding commitment of the enemy, his willingness to risk everything to achieve his objective.

The circumstances of the war in Vietnam thus posed a dilemma that we never resolved. To have achieved our goal of an independent non-Communist South Vietnam required means that were either morally repugnant to us, posed unacceptable risks, or were unlikely to work. Success would have required the physical annihilation of North Vietnam, but given our limited goals, this would have been distasteful and excessively costly, and it held out a serious threat of Soviet or Chinese intervention. The only other way was to establish a viable South Vietnam, but given the weak foundation we worked from and the cultural gap, not to mention the strength of the internal revolution, this was probably beyond our capability. To put it charitably, we may very well have placed ourselves in a classic, no-win situation.

✸ F U R T H E R   R E A D I N G

Loren Baritz, *Backfire* (1985)
Richard J. Barnet, *Intervention and Revolution* (1972)
Lawrence Bassett and Stephen Pelz, "The Failed Search for Victory," in Thomas
     G. Paterson, ed., *Kennedy's Quest for Victory* (1989)
Larry Berman, *Planning a Tragedy* (1982)
William C. Berman, *William Fulbright and the Vietnam War* (1988)
Melanie Billings-Yun, *Decision Against War: Eisenhower and Dien Bien Phu, 1954*
     (1988)
Peter Braestrup, *Big Story* (1977)
——, ed., *Vietnam as History* (1984)
Bernard Brodie, *War and Politics* (1973)
Joseph Buttinger, *Vietnam: A Political History* (1970)
Michael Charlton and Anthony Moncrieff, eds., *Many Reasons Why* (1978)
Warren I. Cohen, *Dean Rusk* (1980)
Chester Cooper, *The Lost Crusade* (1970)
Bernard Fall, *The Two Vietnams* (1967)
——, *Vietnam Witness, 1953–1966* (1966)
Frances FitzGerald, *Fire in the Lake* (1972)
Robert L. Gallucci, *Neither Peace nor Honor* (1975)
Lloyd C. Gardner, *Approaching Vietnam* (1988)
Leslie H. Gelb and Richard K. Betts, *The Irony of Vietnam* (1979)
Philip Geyelin, *Lyndon B. Johnson and the World* (1966)
William C. Gibbons, *The U.S. Government and the Vietnam War* (1986–1987)
Allen E. Goodman, *The Lost Peace* (1978)
David Halberstam, *The Best and the Brightest* (1972)
Daniel C. Hallin, *The "Uncensored War"* (1986)
James P. Harrison, *The Endless War* (1982)
John Hellman, *American Myth and the Legacy of Vietnam* (1986)
Herbert Hendin and Ann P. Haas, *Wounds of War: The Psychological Aftermath
     of Combat in Vietnam* (1985)
George C. Herring, *America's Longest War* (1986)
Gary Hess, *The United States Emergence as a Southeast Asian Power* (1987)

Stanley Hoffmann et al., "Vietnam Reappraised," *International Security*, 6 (1981), 3–26

Townsend Hoopes, *The Limits of Intervention* (1969)

George McT. Kahin, *Intervention* (1986)

————, and John W. Lewis, *The United States in Vietnam* (1969)

David E. Kaiser, "Vietnam, Was the System the Solution?" *International Security*, 4 (1980), 199–218

Stanley Karnow, *Vietnam* (1983)

Paul M. Kattenburg, *The Vietnam Trauma in American Foreign Policy, 1945–1975* (1980)

Douglas Kinnard, *The War Managers* (1977)

Gabriel Kolko, *Anatomy of a War* (1986)

Andrew F. Krepinevich, Jr., *The Army and Vietnam* (1986)

Walter LaFeber, "The Last War, the Next War, and the New Revisionists," *democracy*, 1 (1981), 93–103

Anthony Lake, ed., *The Vietnam Legacy* (1976)

Guenter Lewy, *America in Vietnam* (1978)

William L. Lunch and Peter W. Sperlich, "American Public Opinion and the War in Vietnam," *Western Political Quarterly*, 32 (1979), 21–44

Terry Nardin and Jerome Slater, "Vietnam Revised," *World Politics*, 33 (1981), 436–48

Robert E. Osgood, *Limited War Revisited* (1979)

Bruce Palmer, Jr., *The 25-Year War* (1984)

Archimedes L. A. Patti, *Why Viet Nam?* (1980)

Douglas Pike, *History of Vietnamese Communism* (1978)

————, *PAVN: People's Army of Vietnam* (1986)

————, *Viet Cong* (1972)

————, *Vietnam and the Soviet Union* (1987)

Norman Podhoretz, *Why We Were in Vietnam* (1982)

Gareth Porter, *A Peace Denied* (1975)

Earl C. Ravenal, *Never Again* (1978)

Andrew J. Rotter, *The Path to Vietnam* (1987)

William J. Rust, *Kennedy in Vietnam* (1985)

Herbert Y. Schandler, *The Unmaking of a President* (1977) (on Johnson)

Thomas J. Schoenbaum, *Waging Peace and War* (1988) (on Rusk)

Robert Shaplen, *A Turning Wheel* (1979)

————, *Time Out of Hand* (1970)

William Shawcross, *Sideshow: Kissinger, Nixon, and the Destruction of Cambodia* (1979)

Melvin Small, *Johnson, Nixon, and the Doves* (1988)

Ronald H. Spector, *The United States Army in Vietnam* (1983)

Shelby L. Stanton, *The Rise and Fall of an American Army* (1985)

Harry G. Summers, *On Strategy* (1981)

James C. Thompson, *Rolling Thunder* (1980)

W. Scott Thompson and Donaldson D. Frizzill, eds., *The Lessons of Vietnam* (1977)

Kathleen J. Turner, *Lyndon Johnson's Dual War* (1985) (on the press)

Marilyn B. Young, "Revisionists Revised: The Case of Vietnam," *The Society for Historians of American Foreign Relations Newsletter*, 10 (1979), 1–10

Nancy Zaroulis and Gerald Sullivan, *Who Spoke Up?* (1984)

Nixon, Kissinger, and Détente

President Richard M. Nixon and Henry A. Kissinger had a grand design for achieving international stability based upon superpower arrangements. As an influential Assistant for National Security Affairs (1969–1973) and Secretary of State (1973–1977), Kissinger became a major architect of détente with both the People's Republic of China and the Soviet Union. His management of the Strategic Arms Limitation Talks (SALT) led to major agreements. His secret negotiations helped extricate the United States from Vietnam. And his "shuttle diplomacy" cooled crisis in the Middle East. Admirers and critics alike applauded the Nixon administration's diplomatic achievements in the 1970s.

But the Nixon-Kissinger record was mixed, as scholars have shown. Interventions and crises in Indochina, Chile, Cyprus, Bangladesh, Angola, and elsewhere undermined détente and stability, and they raised doubts about the judgment and morality of the Nixon Administration. The international economy deteriorated. Despite SALT, the nuclear arms race persisted. Too much was claimed for détente, and people felt disappointed whenever the Cold War seemed to heat up. Kissinger and Nixon conducted their diplomacy in high secrecy and resented the congressional role in foreign policy. Eventually the President resigned and the administration fell because of the array of corruptions revealed in the "Watergate crisis." Scholarship on the Nixon-Kissinger diplomacy remains at an early stage. Nonetheless, the objectives and consequences of the Nixon administration's foreign policy can be delineated from the documents available. And if the answers are not yet clear, the questions, as the selections in this chapter demonstrate, are legion.

✻ D O C U M E N T S

Richard M. Nixon, elected President in 1968, came to office with a reputation as a hard-line Cold Warrior. But the first document, from his memoirs, shows that he saw new opportunities through negotiations to contain the Soviet Union and end the war in Vietnam. One method for doing so was the exploitation of the Sino-Soviet split, sometimes called the "China card." The second selection, a Nixon statement on Asian self-help given during an interview on July 25, 1969, became known as the Nixon Doctrine. The third document, from Kissinger's memoirs, recounts the American movement toward détente with the People's Republic of China. In 1972 the Soviet Union and the United States signed the Strategic Arms Limitation Talks agreements, or SALT-I. The next document is the United States Arms Control and Disarmament Agency's explanation of the two SALT pacts: the Anti-Ballistic Missile (ABM) Treaty and the Interim Agreement on offensive ballistic missile systems. In a September 19, 1974, appearance before the Senate Foreign Relations Committee, Kissinger defined détente and its accomplishments. His statement is reprinted here as the fifth selection.

Chile became a trouble spot from the Nixon-Kissinger perspective in 1970 when a Marxist, Salvador Allende, was elected president of that South American nation. The United States had attempted to prevent his election. When those covert operations failed, the Nixon administration worked to destabilize his government. The sixth document is a 1975 report from the United States Senate Select Committee on Intelligence Activities—the "Church Committee"—on covert activities in Chile, 1963–1973. The last document is a January 13, 1977, editorial by Anthony Lewis of the *New York Times*, a writer who sharply indicted Kissinger's diplomatic record.

Richard Nixon Recalls His Initial Goals (1968), 1978

For twenty-five years, I had watched the changing face of communism. I had seen prewar communism, luring workers and intellectuals with its siren call of equality and justice, reveal itself as an aggressive imperialistic ideology during the postwar period of the Marshall Plan. Despite the most nobly ringing rhetoric, the pattern was tragically the same: as soon as the Communists came to power, they destroyed all opposition. I had watched the Soviets' phenomenal recovery from the devastation of war and their costly but successful struggle to achieve for communism the selling point of potential prosperity. At home I had seen the face of underground subversive communism when it surfaced in the Hiss case, reminding people not only that it existed, but that its purpose was deadly serious.

In the late 1940s and during the 1950s I had seen communism spread to China and other parts of Asia, and to Africa and South America, under the camouflage of parties of socialist revolution, or under the guise of wars of national liberation. And, finally, during the 1960s I had watched as Peking and Moscow became rivals for the role of leadership in the Communist world.

Never once in my career have I doubted the Communists mean it when they say that their goal is to bring the world under Communist control. Nor have I ever forgotten Whittaker Chamber's chilling comment that when he left communism, he had the feeling he was leaving the winning side. But unlike some anticommunists who think we should refuse to recognize or deal with the Communists lest in doing so we imply or extend an ideological respectability to their philosophy and their system, I have always believed

---

Excerpts from *RN: The Memoirs of Richard Nixon*, © 1978 by Richard Nixon. Reprinted by permission of Grosset & Dunlap, Inc.

that we can and must communicate and, when possible, negotiate with Communist nations. They are too powerful to ignore. We must always remember that they will never act out of altruism, but only out of self-interest. Once this is understood, it is more sensible—and also safer—to communicate with the Communists than it is to live in icy cold-war isolation or confrontation. In fact, in January 1969 I felt that the relationship between the United States and the Soviet Union would probably be the single most important factor in determining whether the world would live at peace during and after my administration.

I felt that we had allowed ourselves to get in a disadvantageous position vis-à-vis the Soviets. They had a major presence in the Arab states of the Middle East, while we had none; they had Castro in Cuba; since the mid-1960s they had supplanted the Chinese as the principal military suppliers of North Vietnam; and except for Tito's Yugoslavia they still totally controlled Eastern Europe and threatened the stability and security of Western Europe.

There were, however, a few things in our favor. The most important and interesting was the Soviet split with China. There was also some evidence of growing, albeit limited, independence in some of the satellite nations. There were indications that the Soviet leaders were becoming interested in reaching an agreement on strategic arms limitation. They also appeared to be ready to hold serious talks on the anomalous situation in Berlin, which, almost a quarter century after the war had ended, was still a divided city and a constant source of tension, not just between the Soviets and the United States, but also between the Soviets and Western Europe. We sensed that they were looking for a face-saving formula that would lessen the risk of confrontation in the Mideast. And we had some solid evidence that they were anxious for an expansion of trade.

It was often said that the key to a Vietnam settlement lay in Moscow and Peking rather than in Hanoi. Without continuous and massive aid from either or both of the Communist giants, the leaders of North Vietnam would not have been able to carry on the war for more than a few months. Thanks to the Sino-Soviet split, however, the North Vietnamese had been extremely successful in playing off the Soviets and the Chinese against each other by turning support for their war effort into a touchstone of Communist orthodoxy and a requisite for keeping North Vietnam from settling into the opposing camp in the struggle for domination within the Communist world. This situation became a strain, particularly for the Soviets. Aside from wanting to keep Hanoi from going over to Peking, Moscow had little stake in the outcome of the North Vietnamese cause, especially as it increasingly worked against Moscow's own major interests vis-à-vis the United States. While I understood that the Soviets were not entirely free agents where their support for North Vietnam was concerned, I nonetheless planned to bring maximum pressure to bear on them in this area. . . .

During the transition period Kissinger and I developed a new policy for dealing with the Soviets. Since U.S.-Soviet interests as the world's two competing nuclear superpowers were so widespread and overlapping, it was unrealistic to separate or compartmentalize areas of concern. Therefore we decided to link progress in such areas of Soviet concern as strategic arms limitation and increased trade with progress in areas that were important to us—Vietnam, the Mideast and Berlin. This concept became known as linkage.

Lest there be any doubt of my seriousness in pursuing this policy, I purposely announced it at my first press conference when asked a question about starting SALT talks. I said, "What I want to do is to see to it that we have strategic arms talks in a way and at a time that will promote, if possible, progress on outstanding political problems at the same time—for example, on the problem of the Mideast and on other outstanding problems in which the United States and the Soviet Union acting together can serve the cause of peace."

Linkage was something uncomfortably new and different for the Soviets, and I was not surprised when they bridled at the restraints it imposed on our relationship. It would take almost two years of patient and hard-nosed determination on our part before they would accept that linkage with what we wanted from them was the price they would have to pay for getting any of the things they wanted from us. . . .

The most pressing foreign problem I would have to deal with as soon as I became President was the war in Vietnam. During the transition Kissinger began a review of all possible policies toward Vietnam, distilling them into specific options that ran the gamut from massive military escalation to immediate unilateral withdrawal. A strong case could be made for each option.

For example, it could be argued that military victory was still possible if I would remove the restrictions Johnson had placed on our commanders in the field and allow them to use our massive power to defeat the enemy. The most serious of these constraints was the bombing halt; because of it the Communists had been able to regroup their forces and amass supplies for a new offensive. Those who favored the escalation option argued that just the threat of an invasion of North Vietnam would tie down North Vietnamese troops along the DMZ; that mining Haiphong Harbor would cripple the enemy's supply lines; and that free pursuit of the Communist forces into Laos and Cambodia would blunt their ability to continue making hit-and-run attacks against our forces in South Vietnam. Renewed bombing would reinforce these other moves. That, in essence, was the escalation option. It was an option we ruled out very early.

The opinion polls showed a significant percentage of the public favored a military victory in Vietnam. But most people thought of a "military victory" in terms of gearing up to administer a knockout blow that would both end the war and win it. The problem was that there were only two such knockout blows available to me. One would have been to bomb the elaborate systems of irrigation dikes in North Vietnam. The resulting floods would have killed hundreds of thousands of civilians. The other possible knockout blow would have involved the use of tactical nuclear weapons. Short of one of these methods, escalation would probably have required up to six months of highly intensified fighting and significantly increased casualties before the Communists would finally be forced to give up and accept a peace settlement. The domestic and international uproar that would have accompanied the use of either of these knockout blows would have got my administration off to the worse possible start. And as far as escalating the conventional fighting was concerned, there was no way that I could hold the country together for that period of time in view of the numbers of casualties we would be sustaining. Resorting to the escalation option would also delay or even destroy any chance we might have to develop a new relationship with the Soviet Union and Communist China.

At the other end of the spectrum from escalation was the case for ending the war simply by announcing a quick and orderly withdrawal of all American forces. If that were done, the argument went, the Communists would probably respond by returning our POWs after the last American had departed. . . .

I began my presidency with three fundamental premises regarding Vietnam. First, I would have to prepare public opinion for the fact that total military victory was no longer possible. Second, I would have to act on what my conscience, my experience, and my analysis told me was true about the need to keep our commitment. To abandon South Vietnam to the Communists now would cost us inestimably in our search for a stable, structured, and lasting peace. Third, I would have to end the war as quickly as was honorably possible. . . .

The Vietnam war was complicated by factors that had never occurred before in America's conduct of a war. Many of the most prominent liberals of both parties in Congress, having supported our involvement in Vietnam under Kennedy and Johnson, were now trying to back off from their commitment. Senators and congressmen, Cabinet members and columnists who had formerly supported the war were now swelling the ranks of the antiwar forces. In 1969 I still had a congressional majority on war-related votes and questions, but it was a bare one at best, and I could not be sure how long it would hold. Another unusual aspect of this war was that the American news media had come to dominate domestic opinion about its purpose and conduct and also about the nature of the enemy. The North Vietnamese were a particularly ruthless and cruel enemy, but the American media concentrated primarily on the failings and frailties of the South Vietnamese or of our own forces. In each night's TV news and in each morning's paper the war was reported battle by battle, but little or no sense of the underlying purpose of the fighting was conveyed. Eventually this contributed to the impression that we were fighting in military and moral quicksand, rather than toward an important and worthwhile objective.

More than ever before, television showed the terrible human suffering and sacrifice of war. Whatever the intention behind such relentless and literal reporting of the war, the result was a serious demoralization of the home front, raising the question whether America would ever again be able to fight an enemy abroad with unity and strength of purpose at home. As *Newsweek* columnist Kenneth Crawford wrote, this was the first war in our history when the media was more friendly to our enemies than to our allies. I felt that by the time I had become President the way the Vietnam war had been conducted and reported had worn down America's spirit and sense of confidence.

As I prepared to enter the presidency, I regarded the antiwar protesters and demonstrators with alternating feelings of appreciation for their concerns, anger at their excesses, and, primarily, frustration at their apparent un-willingness to credit me even with a genuine desire for peace. But whatever my estimation of the demonstrators' motives—and whatever their estimate of mine—I considered that the practical effect of their activity was to give encouragement to the enemy and thus prolong the war. They wanted to end the war in Vietnam. So did I. But they wanted to end it immediately, and in order to do so they were prepared to abandon South Vietnam. That was something I would not permit.

The Nixon Doctrine, 1969

I believe that the time has come when the United States, in our relations with all of our Asian friends, [must] be quite emphatic on two points: One, that we will keep our treaty commitments, our treaty commitments, for example, with Thailand under SEATO; but, two, that as far as the problems of internal security are concerned, as far as the problems of military defense, except for the threat of a major power involving nuclear weapons, that the United States is going to encourage and has a right to expect that this problem will be increasingly handled by, and the responsibility for it taken by, the Asian nations themselves.

I believe, incidentally, from my preliminary conversations with several Asian leaders over the past few months that they are going to be willing to undertake this responsibility. It will not be easy, but if the United States just continues down the road of responding to requests for assistance, of assuming the primary responsibility for defending these countries when they have internal problems or external problems, they are never going to take care of themselves.

Henry Kissinger on Rapprochement with China (1972), 1979

When we completed drafting the communiqué announcing my secret visit to China in July 1971, Chou En-lai remarked that the announcement would shake the world. He was right. Not only was it a sensation for the media; overnight it transformed the structure of international politics. After twenty bitter years of isolation an American emissary had stepped onto the mysterious soil of Peking; and his President would shortly follow. It was abrupt and astonishing, but behind the climax were thirty months of patient and deliberate preparation as each side feft its way, gingerly, always testing the ground so that a rebuff would not appear humiliating, graduating its steps so that exposure would not demoralize nervous allies or give a new strategic opportunity to those who did not wish them well.

We took even ourselves by surprise. Originally we had not thought reconciliation possible. We were convinced that the Chinese were fanatic and hostile. But even though we could not initially see a way to achieve it, both Nixon and I believed in the importance of an opening to the People's Republic of China.

Events came to our assistance, but I doubt whether the rapprochement could have occurred with the same decisiveness in any other Presidency. Nixon had an extraordinary instinct for the jugular. He was less interested in tactics or the meticulous accumulation of nuance; too much discussion of details of implementation, indeed, made him nervous. Once he had set a policy direction, he almost invariably left it to me to implement the strategy and manage the bureaucracy. But though I had independently come to the same judgment as Nixon, and though I designed many of the moves, I did not have the political strength or bureaucratic clout to pursue such a fundamental shift of policy on my own. Nixon viscerally understood the essence of the opportunity and pushed for it consistently. He had the political base on the right, which protected him from the charge of being "soft on Communism." And his administrative style lent itself to the secretive, solitary tactics the policy required. If the NSC system of elaborating options interested him for anything, it was for the intelligence it supplied him about the views of a bureaucracy he distrusted and for the opportunity it provided to camouflage his own aims.

There was a marginal difference in our perspectives. Nixon saw in the opening to China a somewhat greater opportunity than I to squeeze the Soviet Union into short-term help on Vietnam; I was more concerned with the policy's impact on the structure of international relations. Nixon tended to believe that ending the isolation of 800 million Chinese itself removed a great threat to peace. To me a China active in foreign policy would call for very skillful diplomacy to calibrate our policies in the more complicated context that would evolve and that would alter all international relationships. But these differences rested on the same fundamental judgment: that if relations could be developed with both the Soviet Union and China the triangular relationship would give us a great strategic opportunity for peace. . . .

Thus by the end of 1969, America's relationship with the Communist world was slowly becoming triangular. We did not consider our opening to China as inherently anti-Soviet. Our objective was to purge our foreign policy of all sentimentality. There was no reason for us to confine our contacts with major Communist countries to the Soviet Union. We moved toward China not to expiate liberal guilt over our China policy of the late 1940s but to shape a global equilibrium. It was not to collude against the Soviet Union but to give us a balancing position to use for constructive ends—to give each Communist power a stake in better relations with us.

Such an equilibrium could assure stability among the major powers, and even eventual cooperation, in the Seventies and Eighties. . . .

. . . Nixon was exposed for the first time to the Chinese style of diplomacy. The Soviets tend to be blunt, the Chinese insinuating. The Soviets insist on their prerogatives as a great power. The Chinese establish a claim on the basis of universal principles and a demonstration of self-confidence that attempts to make the issue of power seem irrelevant. The Soviets offer their goodwill as a prize for success in negotiations. The Chinese use friendship as a halter in advance of negotiation; by admitting the interlocutor to at least the appearance of personal intimacy, a subtle restraint is placed on the claims he can put forward. The Soviets, inhabiting a country frequently invaded and more recently expanding its influence largely by force of arms, are too unsure of their moral claims to admit the possibility of error. They move from infallible dogma to unchangeable positions (however often they may modify them). The Chinese, having been culturally preeminent in their part of the world for millennia, can even use self-criticism as a tool. The visitor is asked for advice—a gesture of humility eliciting sympathy and support. This pattern also serves to bring out the visitor's values and aims; he is thereby committed, for the Chinese later can (and often do) refer to his own recommendations. The Soviets, with all of their stormy and occasionally duplicitous behavior, leave an impression of extraordinary psychological insecurity. The Chinese stress, because they believe in it, the uniqueness of Chinese values. Hence they convey an aura of imperviousness to pressure; indeed, they preempt pressure by implying that issues of principle are beyond discussion.

In creating this relationship Chinese diplomats, at least in their encounters with us, proved meticulously reliable. They never stooped to petty maneuvers; they did not haggle; they reached their bottom line quickly, explained it reasonably, and defended it tenaciously. They stuck to the meaning as well as the spirit of their undertakings. As Chou was fond of saying: "*Our* word counts." . . .

The trip [by Richard Nixon to China, February 1972] was increasingly perceived as a great success. As the American public gained hope from the China visit, Vietnam became less an obsession and more a challenge to be mastered. The Administration that had revolutionized international relations could not so easily be accused of neglecting the deepest concern of the American people.

Once more, though, we encountered the curious phenomenon that success seemed to unsettle Nixon more than failure. He seemed obsessed by the fear that he was not receiving adequate credit. He constantly badgered his associates to press a public relations campaign that would call more attention to the China visit. He followed the press carefully, so that any criticism could be immediately countered. He read some commentator's criticism that the Chinese statements of their position in the Shanghai Communiqué were more aggressive than the statements of our position. On March 9, therefore, he sent me a memorandum asking me to make clear to the press the deep thought and analysis that lay behind this "decision" to state our position moderately. His preference for this approach dated back, he said, to a speech he gave in the Soviet Union in 1959, which he urged me to read in his book *Six Crises*. Though Chou En-lai had originally proposed the idea of separate and conflicting statements, though Chou and I had drafted almost all of that part of the text in October 1971 without reference to Washington, and though Nixon had learned of both the approach and the content only after I returned, he wanted me to explain to the press—and I believe had convinced himself—that he had conceived it:

> You could begin by pointing out that I made the decision with regard to the tone of the statement of our position for two basic reasons. First, the more aggressive we stated our position the more aggressive the Chinese would have to be in stating their position. As a result of our presenting our position in a very firm, but non-belligerent manner, their position, while it was also uncompromising on principle, was not nearly as rough in its rhetoric as has been the case in previous statements they have issued over the years. . . .
>
> I was determined that in this document, which would be the first time Chinese leaders, and cadres, and to a certain extent even Chinese masses, would ever hear the American position expressed, I had to make the strongest possible effort to set it in a tone which would not make it totally incredible when they heard it. It would not have been credible, of course, had we set forth our position in more aggressive terms because 22 years of propaganda at the other extreme would have made it impossible for the reader of the communiqué, or those who heard it read on radio, to believe it at all if the tone was too harsh.

Nixon, of course, deserves full credit for the Shanghai Communiqué. A President is always responsible for the policy, no matter who does the technical labors. A less courageous President could have pulled back from the separate statements, when I presented them to him upon my return in October, in favor of a more orthodox presentation. This trivial incident does not derogate from Nixon's boldness in his historic opening to China. What it illustrates, however, is the tendency for illusion to become reality, a brooding and involuted streak that, together with starker character traits, at first flawed, and later destroyed, a Presidency so rich in foreign policy achievements. . . .

The SALT-I Agreements, 1972

The ABM [Anti-Ballistic Missile] Treaty is a definitive long-term agreement which contributes in a fundamental way to our security. The possibility of nuclear war has been dramatically reduced by this Treaty. It sets forth at the outset the joint commitment not to build a nationwide ABM defense nor provide a base for such defense. In this undertaking both countries have, in effect, agreed not to challenge the credibility of each other's deterrent missile forces by deploying a widespread defense against them. This is the central consequence of this Treaty, and its importance to avoidance of nuclear war cannot be overestimated. Both major nuclear powers have agreed that they will not attempt to build a shield against penetration by the other's missile forces which serve to deter nuclear attack.

The ABM Treaty limits the United States and the Soviet Union to two ABM sites each—one for the protection of the national capital, and the other for the defense of an ICBM complex. At each site, there can be no more than 100 ABM launchers and 100 associated interceptor missiles. In addition to numerical limitations on ABM launchers and missiles at each complex, the areas permitted for ABM deployment are limited geographically and in size.

To assure that these two complexes do not form a basis for a nationwide ABM system, the two sides agreed that they must be separated by a distance of at least 1300 kilometers (800 miles). In addition, each ABM system deployment area is restricted to a radius of 150 kilometers (94 miles).

ABM radars are an essential element of an ABM system and are its long-lead-time component. Defining appropriate limits on ABM radars—a highly complex subject—occupied a great deal of time in the negotiations. In addition to the technical restrictions on ABM radars specified in the Treaty, there are limitations on the deployment of certain types of non-ABM radars in order to reduce the possibility of their use as elements of an ABM system.

In order to assure further that there would be adequate restraints on ABM capabilities, the Treaty provides for significant qualitative limitations on ABM systems. The two sides agreed not to develop, test, or deploy ABM launchers for launching more than one interceptor missile at a time, not to modify launchers to provide them with such a capability, nor to develop, test, or deploy automatic or semiautomatic or other similar systems for rapid reload of ABM launchers. It was also agreed that these prohibitions included a ban on more than one independently guided warhead for an ABM missile.

An additional important qualitative limitation is the prohibition on development and testing, as well as deployment, of sea, air, space-based and land-mobile ABM systems and components.

Another important element is the agreement that if future types of ABM systems or components based on physical principles different from present technology become feasible, specific limitations thereon will be a subject of discussion and agreement in accordance with treaty provisions regarding amendments. An example of such a future system would be one depending on the use of laser beams for destruction of missile reentry vehicles.

To avoid possible circumvention of the ban on a nationwide ABM defense through developments in non-ABM systems, e.g., antiaircraft surface-to-air missiles, the Parties agreed to prohibit conversion or testing of such other systems, or components thereof, to perform an ABM role. For much the same reasons, they also agreed to restrict certain categories of large phased-array radars. These provisions deal with what had come to be known in this country as the "SAM-upgrade problem" (upgrading surface-to-air defense missiles for an ABM role).

It has been the position of the United States that a limitation on ABMs alone would not make as great a contribution to stability and security as would limitations on both offensive and defensive strategic systems. However, problems over definition of strategic systems made clear that it would be extremely difficult to negotiate a single comprehensive agreement.

The Interim Agreement is essentially a holding action which freezes existing levels of land and sea-based offensive ballistic missile systems until a more complete agreement, taking into account the complex asymmetries and implications involved, can be reached. Both nations have expressed the belief that a permanent agreement limiting strategic offensive systems can be reached before the 5-year duration of the Interim Agreement has expired.

The May 20, 1971, understanding focused discussions of strategic offensive systems on ICBMs and SLBMs, setting aside consideration of bombers and forward based systems.

The inclusion of ICBMs was never at issue. However, SLBMs became the subject of intense discussions. The Soviet Union was engaged in a very rapid buildup of its nuclear-missile submarine fleet, deploying additional sea-based ballistic missiles at the rate of about 100 per year. In the U.S. view, it was inconsistent with the purpose of the interim offensive freeze to leave the Soviet buildup unconstrained. It was only in late April, 1972, however, that the Soviets agreed in principle to limit SLBMs in some way. The final details were worked out during the 4 weeks leading up to the Moscow Summit Meeting.

The Interim Agreement is limited in duration and scope. The first two Articles deal with ICBM launchers. The Parties commit themselves not to construct additional fixed land-based ICBM launchers or to relocate existing ICBM launchers. In addition, they commit themselves not to convert launchers for light or older ICBMs into launchers for modern heavy ICBMs. This constitutes an important qualitative constraint which prevents the Soviets from replacing older missiles with SS-9s, the largest and most powerful missile in the Soviet inventory. Unrestrained growth in the number of SS-9s has been a concern of U.S. strategic planners.

Under the terms of the agreement, both sides are allowed to continue to modernize their existing ICBM forces. However, an understanding was reached that the dimensions of land-based ICBM silos will not be significantly increased.

The negotiators were unable to reach full agreement on the definition of a "heavy" missile to supplement the prohibition on conversion of existing light missiles to heavy missiles. The United States therefore made a formal unilateral interpretation of this matter, stating that we "would consider any ICBM having a volume significantly greater than that of the largest light ICBM now operational on either side to be a heavy ICBM."

The agreement does not cover land-mobile ICBMs. The Soviet Union did not want them included in the temporary freeze, arguing that neither side presently had such a system. Although no agreement was reached on mobile systems, the United States served notice to the Soviets in a formal statement that deployment of operational land-mobile ICBMs during the interim period would be considered inconsistent with the objectives of the agreement.

SLBM launchers and modern ballistic submarines are dealt with in Article III of the Interim Agreement and in the Protocol which accompanies the Agreement.

Taking into account current levels of strategic submarine fleets on the two sides, together with other factors in the U.S.-Soviet strategic equation, SLBM limitations were arrived at as follows: For the U.S.S.R., a ceiling of 62 was set on the number of modern, nuclear-powered submarines, and a limit of 950 established for the total number of modern SLBM launchers on either nuclear or diesel-powered submarines. However, for every modern Soviet SLBM launcher over 740 and up to the agreed ceiling of 950, the Soviet Union must, under agreed procedures, retire older land-based launchers (SS-7s and SS-8s) or launchers on older nuclear submarines. In other words, the 741st SLBM launcher on a modern nuclear-powered submarine must be a replacement for a currently deployed launcher. The rapid buildup which, in recent times, had been taking place in the Soviet strategic submarine fleet was thus constrained.

The United States has, under these arrangements, the existing level of 656 SLBM launchers, and the right to have, through replacement of 54 Titan II ICBMs, up to 710 SLBM launchers on 44 modern submarines.

The conversion of U.S. ICBM launchers to handle Minuteman III missiles and the conversion of current Polaris submarines to handle Poseidon missiles are not affected by the freeze.

The undertakings in the ABM Treaty and in the Interim Agreement are to be verified by national technical means of verification. For the types of obligations contained in these agreements, national technical means of verification are practical and effective. Both Parties have made the commitment not to interfere with the national technical means of verification of the other. This would, for example, prohibit interference with a satellite in orbit used for verification purposes. In addition, the Parties have committed themselves not to use deliberate concealment measures to impede the effectiveness of national means of verification. These commitments are landmarks in the joint effort to bring the strategic confrontation under manageable control.

Related to the question of compliance is the provision for a Standing Consultative Commission. This Commission will meet on a regular basis to consider questions of compliance and other aspects of implementation of both the ABM Treaty and the Interim Agreement.

Kissinger on Détente, 1974

Since the dawn of the nuclear age the world's fears of holocaust and its hopes for peace have turned on the relationship between the United States and the Soviet Union.

Throughout history men have sought peace but suffered war; all too often deliberate decisions or miscalculations have brought violence and destruction to a world yearning for tranquility. Tragic as the consequences of violence may have been in the past, the issue of peace and war takes on unprecedented urgency when, for the first time in history, two nations have the capacity to destroy mankind.

The destructiveness of modern weapons defines the necessity of the task; deep differences in philosophy and interests between the United States and the Soviet Union point up its difficulty.

Paradox confuses our perception of the problem of peaceful coexistence: If peace is pursued to the exclusion of any other goal, other values will be compromised and perhaps lost; but if unconstrained rivalry leads to nuclear conflict, these values, along with everything else, will be destroyed in the resulting holocaust.

There can be no peaceful international order without a constructive relationship between the United States and the Soviet Union. There will be no international stability unless both the Soviet Union and the United States conduct themselves with restraint and unless they use their enormous power for the benefit of mankind.

Thus, we must be clear at the outset on what the term ''détente'' entails. It is the search for a more constructive relationship with the Soviet Union. It is a continuing process, not a final condition. And it has been pursued by successive American leaders though the means have varied as have world conditions.

Some fundamental principles guide this policy:

The United States does not base its policy solely on Moscow's good intentions. We seek, regardless of Soviet intentions, to serve peace through a systematic resistance to pressure and conciliatory responses to moderate behavior.

We must oppose aggressive actions, but we must not seek confrontations lightly.

We must maintain a strong national defense while recognizing that in the nuclear age the relationship between military strength and politically usable power is the most complex in all history.

Where the age-old antagonism between freedom and tyranny is concerned, we are not neutral. But other imperatives impose limits on our ability to produce internal changes in foreign countries. Consciousness of our limits is a recognition of the necessity of peace—not moral callousness. The preservation of human life and human society are moral values, too.

We must be mature enough to recognize that to be stable a relationship must provide advantages to both sides and that the most constructive international relationships are those in which both parties perceive an element of gain.

America's aspiration for the kind of political environment we now call détente is not new.

The effort to achieve a more constructive relationship with the Soviet Union is not made in the name of any one administration, or one party, or for any one period of time. It expresses the continuing desire of the vast majority of the American people for an easing of international tensions, and their expectation that any responsible government will strive for peace. No aspect of our policies, domestic or foreign, enjoys more consistent bipartisan support. No aspect is more in the interest of mankind.

In the postwar period repeated efforts were made to improve our relationship with Moscow. The spirits of Geneva, Camp David, and Glassboro were evanescent moments in a quarter century otherwise marked by tensions and by sporadic confrontation. What is new in the current period of relaxation of tensions is its duration, the scope of the relationship which has evolved and the continuity and intensity of contact and consultation which it has produced.

We sought to explore every avenue toward an honorable and just accommodation while remaining determined not to settle for mere atmospherics. We relied on a balance of mutual interests rather than Soviet intentions.

Our approach proceeds from the conviction that in moving forward across a wide spectrum of negotiations, progress in one area adds momentum to progress in other areas. We did not invent the interrelationship; it was a reality because of the range of problems and areas in which the interests of the United States and the Soviet Union impinge on each other. By acquiring a stake in this network of relationships with the West the Soviet Union may become more conscious of what it would lose by a return to confrontation. Indeed, it is our expectation that it will develop a self-interest in fostering the entire process of relaxation of tensions.

Cooperative relations, in our view, must be more than a series of isolated agreements. They must reflect an acceptance of mutual obligations and of the need for accommodation and restraints.

To set forth principles of behavior in formal documents is hardly to guarantee their observance. But they are reference points against which to judge actions and set goals.

The first of the series of documents is the Statement of Principles signed in Moscow in 1972. It affirms: (1) the necessity of avoiding confrontation; (2) the imperative of mutual restraint; (3) the rejection of attempts to exploit tensions to gain unilateral advantages; (4) the renunciation of claims of special influence in the world; and (5) the willingness, on this new basis, to coexist peacefully and build a firm long-term relationship.

An Agreement on the Prevention of Nuclear War based on these Principles was signed in 1973. But it emphasizes that this objective presuppose the renunciation of any war or threat of war not only by the two nuclear superpowers against each other, but also against allies or third countries. In other words, the principle of restraint is not confined to relations between the United States and the U.S.S.R. It is explicitly extended to include all countries.

These statements of principles are not an American concession; indeed, we have been affirming them unilaterally for two decades. Nor are they a legal contract; rather, they are an aspiration and a yardstick by which we assess Soviet behavior. We have never intended to rely on Soviet compliance with every principle; we do seek to elaborate standards of conduct which the Soviet Union would violate only to its cost. And if over the long term the more durable relationship takes hold, the basic principles will give it definition, structure, and hope.

One of the features of the current phase of United States-Soviet relations is the unprecedented consultation between leaders either face to face or through diplomatic channels.

It was difficult in the past to speak of a United States-Soviet bilateral relationship in any normal sense of the phrase. Trade was negligible. Contacts between various institutions and between the peoples of the two countries were at best sporadic. Today, by joining our efforts even in such seemingly apolitical fields as medical research or environmental protection, we and the Soviets can benefit not only our two peoples, but all mankind.

Since 1972 we have concluded agreements on a common effort against cancer, on research to protect the environment, on studying the use of the ocean's resources, on the use of atomic energy for peaceful purposes, on studying methods for conserving energy, on examining construction techniques for regions subject to earthquakes, and on devising new transportation methods.

Each project must be judged by the concrete benefits it brings. But in their sum—in their exchange of information and people as well as in their establishment of joint mechanisms—they also constitute a commitment in both countries to work together across a broad spectrum.

During the period of the cold war economic contact between ourselves and the U.S.S.R. was virtually nonexistent.

The period of confrontation should have left little doubt, however, that economic boycott would not transform the Soviet system or impose upon it a conciliatory foreign policy. Throughout this period the U.S.S.R. was quite prepared to maintain heavy military outlays and to concentrate on capital growth by using the resources of the Communist world alone.

The question then became how trade and economic contact—in which the Soviet Union is obviously interested—could serve the purposes of peace.

We have approached the question of economic relations with deliberation and circumspection and as an act of policy not primarily of commercial opportunity. As political relations have improved on a broad basis, economic issues have been dealt with on a comparably broad front. A series of interlocking economic agreements with the U.S.S.R. has been negotiated, side by side with the political progress already noted. The 25-year-old lend-lease debt was settled; the reciprocal extension of the most-favored-nation treatment was negotiated, together with safeguards against the possible disruption of our markets and a series of practical arrangements to facilitate the conduct of business; our Government credit facilities were made available for trade with the U.S.S.R.; and a maritime agreement regulating the carriage of goods has been signed.

This approach commanded widespread domestic approval. It was considered a natural outgrowth of political progress. At no time were issues regarding Soviet domestic political practices raised. Indeed, not until after the 1972 agreements was the Soviet domestic order invoked as a reason for arresting or reversing the progress so painstakingly achieved.

This sudden, ex post facto form of linkage raises serious questions.

The significance of trade, originally envisaged as only one ingredient of a complex and evolving relationship, is inflated out of all proportion;

The hoped-for results of policy become transformed into preconditions for any policy at all.

We recognize the depth and validity of the moral concerns expressed by those who oppose—or put conditions on—expanded trade with the U.S.S.R. But a sense of proportion must be maintained about the leverage our economic relations give us.

Denial of economic relations cannot by itself achieve what it failed to do when it was part of a determined policy of political and military confrontation.

The economic bargaining ability of most-favored-nation status is marginal. MFN grants no special privilege; it is a misnomer, since we have such agreements with over 100 countries. To continue to deny it is more a political than an economic act.

The actual and potential flow of credits from the United States represents a tiny fraction of the capital available to the U.S.S.R. domestically and elsewhere, including Western Europe and Japan.

Over time, trade, and investment may leaven the autarkic tendencies of the Soviet system, invite gradual association of the Soviet economy with the world economy, and foster a degree of interdependence that adds an element of stability to the political relationship.

We cannot expect to relax international tensions or achieve a more stable international system should the two strongest nuclear powers conduct an unrestrained strategic arms race. Thus, perhaps the single most important component of our policy toward the Soviet Union is the effort to limit strategic weapons competition.

The competition in which we now find ourselves is historically unique: Each side has the capacity to destroy civilization as we know it.

Failure to maintain equivalence could jeopardize not only our freedom but our very survival.

The lead time for technological innovations is so long, yet the pace of change so relentless that the arms race and strategic policy itself are in danger of being driven by technological necessity.

When nuclear arsenals reach levels involving thousands of launchers and over 10,000 warheads, and when the characteristics of the weapons of the two sides are so incommensurable, it becomes difficult to determine what combination of numbers of strategic weapons and performance capabilities would give one side a military and political superiority. At a minimum clear changes in the strategic balance can be achieved only by efforts so enormous and by increments so large that the very attempt is highly destabilizing.

The prospect of a decisive military advantage, even if theoretically possible, is politically intolerable; neither side will passively permit a massive shift in the nuclear balance. Therefore, the probable outcome of each succeeding round of competition is the restoration of a strategic equilibrium, but at increasingly higher and more complex levels of forces.

The arms race is driven by political as well as military factors. While a decisive advantage is hard to calculate, the appearance of inferiority—whatever its actual significance—can have serious political consequences. Thus, each side has a high incentive to achieve not only the reality but the appearance of equality. In a very real sense each side shapes the military establishment of the other.

If we are driven to it, the United States will sustain an arms race. But the political or military benefit which would flow from such a situation would remain elusive. Indeed, after such an evolution it might well be that both sides would be worse off than before the race began.

The Soviet Union must realize that the overall relationship with the United States will be less stable if strategic balance is sought through unrestrained competitive programs. Sustaining the buildup requires exhortations by both sides that in time may prove incompatible with restrained international conduct. The very fact of a strategic arms race has a high potential for feeding attitudes of hostility and suspicion on both sides, transforming the fears of those who demand more weapons into self-fulfilling prophecies.

The American people can be asked to bear the cost and political instability of a race which is doomed to stalemate only if it is clear that every effort has been made to prevent it. That is why every President since Eisenhower has pursued negotiations for the limitation of strategic arms while maintaining the military programs essential to strategic balance.

SALT has become one means by which we and the Soviet Union could enhance stability by setting mutual constraints on our respective forces and by gradually reaching an understanding of the doctrinal considerations that underlie the deployment of nuclear weapons. SALT, in the American conception, is a means to achieve strategic stability by methods other than the arms race. . . .

To be sure, the process of détente raises serious issues for many people. We will be guided by these principles.

First, if détente is to endure, both sides must benefit.

Second, building a new relationship with the Soviet Union does not entail any devaluation of traditional alliance relations.

Third, the emergence of more normal relations with the Soviet Union must not undermine our resolve to maintain our national defense.

Fourth, we must know what can and cannot be achieved in changing human conditions in the East.

We shall insist on responsible international behavior by the Soviet Union. Beyond this, we will use our influence to the maximum to alleviate suffering and to respond to humane appeals. We know what we stand for, and we shall leave no doubt about it.

United States Covert Action
in Chile (1963–1973), 1975

The pattern of United States covert action in Chile is striking but not unique. It arose in the context not only of American foreign policy, but also of covert U.S. involvement in other countries within and outside Latin America. The scale of CIA involvement in Chile was unusual but by no means unprecedented. . . .

The most extensive covert action activity in Chile was propaganda. It was relatively cheap. In Chile, it continued at a low level during "normal" times, then was cranked up to meet particular threats or to counter particular dangers.

The most common form of a propaganda project is simply the development of "assets" in media organizations who can place articles or be asked to write them. The Agency provided to its field Stations several kinds of guidance about what sorts of propaganda were desired. For example, one CIA project in Chile supported from one to five media assets during the seven years it operated (1965–1971). Most of those assets worked for a major Santiago daily which was the key to CIA propaganda efforts. Those assets wrote articles or editorials favorable to U.S. interests in the world (for example, criticizing the Soviet Union in the wake of the Czechoslovakian invasion); suppressed news items harmful to the United States (for instance about Vietnam); and authored articles critical of Chilean leftists.

The covert propaganda efforts in Chile also included "black" propaganda—material falsely purporting to be the product of a particular individual or group. In the 1970 election, for instance, the CIA used "black" propaganda to sow discord between the Communists and the Socialists and between the national labor confederation and the Chilean Communist Party.

Table 1   Techniques of Covert Action: Expenditures in Chile, 1963–73*

TECHNIQUES	AMOUNT
Propaganda for elections and other support for political parties	$8,000,000
Producing and disseminating propaganda and supporting mass media	4,300,000
Influencing Chilean institutions (labor, students, peasants, women) and supporting private sector organizations	900,000
Promoting military coup d'etat	<200,000

---

* Figures rounded to nearest $100,000.

In some cases, the form of propaganda was still more direct. The Station financed Chilean groups who erected wall posters, passed out political leaflets (at times prepared by the Station) and engaged in other street activities. Most often these activities formed part of larger projects intended to influence the outcomes of Chilean elections (see below), but in at least one instance the activities took place in the absence of an election campaign.

Of thirty-odd covert action projects undertaken [in] Chile by the CIA between 1961 and 1974, approximately a half dozen had propaganda as their principal activity. Propaganda was an important subsidiary element of many others, particularly election projects. (See Table I.) Press placements were attractive because each placement might produce a multiplier effect, being picked up and replayed by media outlets other than the one in which it originally came out.

In addition to buying propaganda piecemeal, the Station often purchased it wholesale by subsidizing Chilean media organizations friendly to the United States. Doing so was propaganda writ large. Instead of placing individual items, the CIA supported—or even founded—friendly media outlets which might not have existed in the absence of Agency support.

From 1953 through 1970 in Chile, the Station subsidized wire services, magazines written for intellectual circles, and a right-wing weekly newspaper. According to the testimony of former officials, support for the newspaper was terminated because it became so inflexibly rightist as to alienate responsible conservatives.

By far, the largest—and probably the most significant—instance of support for a media organization was the money provided to *El Mercurio*, the major Santiago daily, under pressure during the Allende regime. That support grew out of an existing propaganda project. In 1971 the Station judged that *El Mercurio*, the most important opposition publication, could not survive pressure from the Allende government, including intervention in the newsprint market and the withdrawal of government advertising. The 40 Committee [a Sub-Cabinet level body of the executive branch which reviewed covert plans] authorized $700,000 for *El Mercurio* on September 9, 1971, and added another $965,000 to that authorization on April 11, 1972. A CIA project renewal memorandum concluded that *El Mercurio* and other media outlets supported by the Agency had played an important role in setting the stage for the September 11, 1973, military coup which overthrew Allende.

Through its covert activities in Chile, the U.S. government sought to influence the actions of a wide variety of institutions and groups in Chilean society. The specific intent of those activities ran the gamut from attempting to influence directly the making of government policy to trying to counter communist or leftist influence among organized groups in the society. That most of these projects included a propaganda component is obvious.

From 1964 through 1968, the CIA developed contacts within the Chilean Socialist Party and at the Cabinet level of the Chilean government.

Projects aimed at organized groups in Chilean society had more diffuse purposes than efforts aimed at government institutions. But the aim was similar: influencing the direction of political events in Chile.

Projects were directed, for example, toward:
- Wresting control of Chilean university student organizations from the communists;
- Supporting a women's group active in Chilean political and intellectual life;

- Combating the communist-dominated *Central Unica de Trabajadores Chilenos* (CUTCh) and supporting democratic labor groups; and
- Exploiting a civic action front group to combat communist influence within cultural and intellectual circles.

Covert American activity was a factor in almost every major election in Chile in the decade between 1963 and 1973. In several instances the United States intervention was massive.

The 1964 presidential election was the most prominent example of a large-scale election project. The Central Intelligence Agency spent more than $2.6 million in support of the election of the Christian Democratic candidate, in part to prevent the accession to the presidency of Marxist Salvador Allende. More than half of the Christian Democratic candidate's campaign was financed by the United States, although he was not informed of this assistance. In addition, the Station furnished support to an array of pro-Christian Democratic student, women's, professional and peasant groups. Two other political parties were funded as well in an attempt to spread the vote.

In Washington, an inter-agency election committee was established, composed of State Department, White House and CIA officials. That committee was paralleled by a group in the embassy in Santiago. No special task force was established within the CIA, but the Station in Santiago was reinforced. The Station assisted the Christian Democrats in running an American-style campaign, which included polling, voter registration and get-out-the-vote drives, in addition to covert propaganda.

The United States was also involved in the 1970 presidential campaign. That effort, however, was smaller and did not include support for any specific candidate. It was directed more at preventing Allende's election than at insuring another candidate's victory. . . .

Most covert American support to Chilean political parties was furnished as part of specific efforts to influence election outcomes. However, in several instances the CIA provided subsidies to parties for more general purposes, when elections were not imminent. Most such support was furnished during the Allende years, 1970–1973, when the U.S. government judged that without its support parties of the center and right might not survive either as opposition elements or as contestants in elections several years away.

In a sequence of decisions in 1971 through 1973, the 40 Committee authorized nearly $4 million for opposition political parties in Chile. Most of this money went to the Christian Democratic Party (PDC), but a substantial portion was earmarked for the National Party (PN), a conservative grouping more stridently opposed to the Allende government than was the PDC. An effort was also made to split the ruling Popular Unity coalition by inducing elements to break away. . . .

As part of its program of support for opposition elements during the Allende government, the CIA provided money to several trade organizations of the Chilean private sector. In September 1972, for instance, the 40 Committee authorized $24,000 in emergency support for an anti-Allende businessmen's organization. At that time, supporting other private sector organizations was considered but rejected because of the fear that those organizations might be involved in anti-government strikes.

The 40 Committee authorized $100,000 for private sector organizations in October 1972, as part of the March 1973 election project. According to the CIA, that money was spent only on election activities, such as voter registration drives and get-out-the-vote drives. In August 1973, the Committee authorized support for private sector groups, but with disbursement contingent on the agreement of the Ambassador and State Department. That agreement was not forthcoming. . . .

United States covert efforts to affect the course of Chilean politics reached a peak in 1970: the CIA was directed to undertake an effort to promote a military coup in Chile to prevent the accession to power of Salvador Allende [a project known as "Track II"]. . . . A brief summary here will demonstrate the extreme in American covert intervention in Chilean politics.

On September 15, 1970—after Allende finished first in the election but before the Chilean Congress had chosen between him and the runner-up, Alessandri,—President Nixon met with Richard Helms, the Director of Central Intelligence, Assistant to the President for National Security Affairs Henry Kissinger and Attorney General John Mitchell. Helms was directed to prevent Allende from taking power. This effort was to be conducted without the knowledge of the Department of State and Defense or the Ambassador. Track II was never discussed at a 40 Committee meeting.

It quickly became apparent to both White House and CIA officials that a military coup was the only way to prevent Allende's accession to power. To achieve that end, the CIA established contact with several groups of military plotters and eventually passed three weapons and tear gas to one group. The weapons were subsequently returned, apparently unused. The CIA knew that the plans of all groups of plotters began with the abduction of the constitutionalist Chief of Staff of the Chilean Army, General René Schneider. The Committee has received conflicting testimony about the extent of CIA/White House communication and of White House officials' awareness of specific coup plans, but there is no doubt that the U.S. government sought a military coup in Chile.

On October 22, one group of plotters attempted to kidnap Schneider. Schneider resisted, was shot, and subsequently died. The CIA had been in touch with that group of plotters but a week earlier had withdrawn its support for the group's specific plans.

The coup plotting collapsed and Allende was inaugurated President. After his election, the CIA and U.S. military attachés maintained contacts with the Chilean military for the purpose of collecting intelligence. Whether those contacts strayed into encouraging the Chilean military to move against Allende; or whether the Chilean military—having been goaded toward a coup during Track II—took encouragement to act against the President from those contacts even though U.S. officials did not intend to provide it: these are major questions which are inherent in U.S. covert activities in the period of the Allende government. . . .

In addition to providing information and cover to the CIA, multinational corporations also participated in covert attempts to influence Chilean politics. . . .

In 1970, the U.S. government and several multinational corporations were linked in opposition to the candidacy and later the presidency of Salvador Allende. This CIA-multinational corporation connection can be divided into two phases. Phase I comprised actions taken by either the CIA or U.S.-based multinational companies at a time when it was official U.S. policy not to support, even covertly, any candidate or party in Chile. During this phase the Agency was, however, authorized to engage in a covert "spoiling" operation designed to defeat Salvador Allende. Phase II encompassed the relationship between intelligence agencies and multinational corporations after the September 1970 general election. During Phase II, the U.S. government opposed Allende and supported opposition elements. The government sought the cooperation of multinational corporations in this effort.

A number of multinational corporations were apprehensive about the possibility that Allende would be elected President of Chile. Allende's public announcements indicated his intention, if elected, to nationalize basic industries and to bring under Chilean ownership service industries such as the national telephone company, which was at that time a subsidiary of ITT.

In 1964 Allende had been defeated, and it was widely known both in Chile and among American multinational corporations with significant interests in Chile that his opponents had been supported by the United States government. John McCone, a former CIA Director and a member of ITT's Board of Directors in 1970, knew of the significant American government involvement in 1964 and of the offer of assistance made at that time by American companies. Agency documents indicate that McCone informed Harold Geneen, ITT's Board Chairman, of these facts.

In 1970 leaders of American multinational corporations with substantial interests in Chile, together with other American citizens concerned about what might happen to Chile in the event of an Allende victory, contacted U.S. government officials in order to make their views known.

In July 1970, a CIA representative in Santiago met with representatives of ITT and, in a discussion of the upcoming election, indicated that Alessandri could use financial assistance. The Station suggested the name of an individual who could be used as a secure channel for getting these funds to the Alessandri campaign.

Shortly thereafter John McCone telephoned CIA Director Richard Helms. As a result of this call, a meeting was arranged between the Chairman of the Board of ITT and Chief of the Western Hemisphere Division of the CIA. Geneen offered to make available to the CIA a substantial amount of money to be used in support of the Alessandri campaign. In subsequent meetings ITT offered to make $1 million available to the CIA. The CIA rejected the offer. The memorandum indicated further that CIA's advice was sought with respect to an individual who might serve as a conduit of ITT funds to the Alessandri campaign.

The CIA confirmed that the individual in question was a reliable channel which could be used for getting funds to Alessandri. A second channel of funds from ITT to a political party opposing Allende, the National Party, was developed following CIA advice as to a secure funding mechanism utilizing two CIA assets in Chile. These assets were also receiving Agency funds in connection with the "spoiling" operation.

During the period prior to the September election, ITT representatives met frequently with CIA representatives both in Chile and in the United States and CIA advised ITT as to ways in which it might safely channel funds both to the Alessandri campaign and to the National Party. CIA was kept informed of the extent and the mechanism of the funding. Eventually at least $350,000 was passed by ITT to this campaign. A roughly equal amount was passed by other U.S. companies; the CIA learned of this funding but did not assist in it. . . .

Anthony Lewis on Kissinger, 1977

Henry Kissinger is leaving office in a blaze of adulation. The National Press Club produces a belly dancer for him and gives standing applause to his views on world peace. The Harlem Globetrotters make him an honorary member. Senators pay tribute to his wisdom.

Historians of the next generation will find it all very puzzling. Because they will not have seen Mr. Kissinger perform, they will have to rely on the record. And the record of his eight years in Washington is likely to seem thin in diplomatic achievement and shameful in human terms.

The one outstanding accomplishment is Mr. Kissinger's Middle East diplomacy. He restored United States relations with the Arab world, and he set in motion the beginnings of an Arab-Israeli dialogue. Of course, the work is incomplete. But to start something after so many years of total failure was a great breakthrough and it was essentially the work of one man: Henry Kissinger.

The other undoubtedly positive entry on the record is the opening to China, but that was in good part Richard Nixon's doing. Also, the beginnings of a relationship with the People's Republic were not followed up as they might have been, and the failure may prove damaging.

With the Soviet Union, Mr. Kissinger took the familiar idea of easing tensions and glamorized it as détente. The glamor was dangerous. It fostered the illusion that détente could prevent conflict all over the world, and many Americans turned sour on the whole idea when it did not. At times Mr.

Anthony Lewis, "This Way to the Egress," *New York Times*, January 13, 1977, p. 37, © 1977 by the New York Times Company. Reprinted by permission.

Kissinger himself seemed to believe the illusion—and became apoplectic when it failed as in Angola. Détente's real achievements are scant; not much more than a halting step toward nuclear arms control.

Ignorance and ineptitude marked his policy in much of the rest of the world. In Cyprus, his blundering led to human tragedy and left America's reputation damaged in both Greece and Turkey. His insensitivity to Japanese feelings had traumatic effects on a most important ally.

In dealing with Portugal and its African territories Mr. Kissinger decided in succession that (1) the Portuguese were in Africa to stay, (2) the U.S. should help Portugal's dictatorship, (3) after the dictatorship's fall the Communists were bound to prevail in Portugal and (4) the U.S. could decide the outcome in Angola by covert aid. That parade of folly was matched in his African policy generally: years of malign neglect, then last-minute intervention for majority rule in Rhodesia.

He often talked about freedom, but his acts show a pre-eminent interest in order. Millions lost their freedom during the Kissinger years, many to dictatorships that had crucial support from his policies, as in Chile and the Philippines. He expressed little open concern for the victims of Soviet tyranny, and he did little to enforce the human rights clauses of the Helsinki Agreement.

The American constitutional system of checks and balances he treated as an irritating obstacle to power. In his valedictory to the Press Club his only reference to Watergate was an expression of regret at "the disintegration of Executive authority that resulted."

Secrecy and deceit were levers of his power; he had no patience for the democratic virtues of openness and consultation. By keeping all the facts to himself and a few intimates, he centralized control. He practiced deceit with a kind of gusto, from petty personal matters to "peace is at hand."

His conduct in the wiretapping of his own staff gave ugly insight into his character. He provided names for investigation—and then, when the story came out, wriggled and deceived in order to minimize his role. He never expressed regret, even to those who had been closest to him, for the fact that their family conversations had been overheard for months. But when someone ransacked his garbage, he said his wife had suffered "grave anguish."

History will remember him most of all for his policy in Indochina. In the teeth of evidence well known by 1969, this supposed realist pressed obsessively for indefinite maintenance of the status quo. To that end, in his time, 20,492 more Americans died in Vietnam and hundreds of thousands of Vietnamese. The war was expanded into Cambodia, destroying that peaceable land. And all for nothing.

With such a record, how is it that people vie to place laurels on the head of the departing Secretary of State? The answer became clear the other night during an extraordinarily thoughtful Public Broadcasting television program on Mr. Kissinger's career: He has discovered that in our age publicity is power, and he has played the press as Dr. Miracle played his violin. He is intelligent and hard-working and ruthless, but those qualities are common enough. His secret is showmanship.

Henry Kissinger is our P. T. Barnum—a Barnum who plays in a vastly larger tent and whose jokes have about them the air of the grave. That we honor a person who has done such things in our name is a comment on us.

✳ E S S A Y S

The author of the first essay, John G. Stoessinger, a political scientist and friend of Henry Kissinger, has written a sympathetic study of the Secretary of State. He commends Kissinger's search for and partial success in achieving a stable world order. In the second essay, Stanley Hoffmann of Harvard University reviews the first volume of Kissinger's memoirs, delineating the diplomat's style, world view, and goals. Critical of Kissinger's anti-Soviet "grand design," Hoffmann also questions his behavior within the American political system. Finally, Hoffmann thinks Kissinger's global view of a Soviet threat influenced him toward "universal intervention" and a tragic misreading of the internal problems of other countries.

A Safer World

JOHN G. STOESSINGER

"I know I have a first-rate mind," Henry Kissinger once told me many years ago, "but that's no source of pride to me. Intelligent people are a dime a dozen. But I am proud of having character."

Henry Kissinger never had much patience with mediocrities or fools. But when, in the rolling cadences of his Bavarian accent, he would describe some luckless academic as a "characterless bastard," he meant to convey a bottomless contempt. Kissinger reserved this ultimate epithet for those unfortunates who did not have the courage to *act* on their convictions. A man who said one thing but did another was even more certain to incur his wrath than someone who had no convictions whatsoever. The move to Washington did little to change Kissinger's opinion. "The worst kinds of bastards in this town," he declared three years after he had come to power, "are those who hold high positions and then go out and say they really didn't believe in Administration policies. If anyone would ever say I didn't believe in what Nixon is doing, I would publicly dispute him. I like the President. I agree with him. We've gone through all this for three years, like two men in a foxhole. . . ."

"Character" to Kissinger, had little to do with intelligence. What he admired was a man's capacity to stand up for his convictions in the world of action, alone if necessary. When, in a rare unguarded moment, Kissinger

Reprinted from *Henry Kissinger: The Anguish of Power*, by John G. Stoessinger, by permission of W.W. Norton & Company, Inc. Copyright © 1976 by W.W. Norton & Company, Inc.

had said, "I have always acted alone," he had revealed a deep emotional conviction. Even though his intellect reminded him that "a policy that was conceived in the mind of one, but resided in the hearts of none," was doomed to failure, this *emotional* preference for solitude remained. It is for this reason that Kissinger preferred Castlereagh to Metternich. Castlereagh had a grand design and, even though it had "outdistanced the experience of his people," he had found the moral courage to remain loyal to his vision. Metternich, on the other hand, despite his brilliance and his cunning, had never found the courage to "contemplate an abyss as a challenge to overcome or to perish in the process." Thus, he had ultimately doomed himself to sterility, and with him, Imperial Austria.

Among contemporary statesmen, Kissinger most admired those who had not only conceived a vision, but had found the courage to translate it into action, even in the face of anguish and adversity. The fact that most of the men who shared these qualities happened to be adversaries, did not deter him in the least. When as a scholar at Harvard, he was preoccupied with Europe, he had often expressed considerable admiration for the strength and steadfastness of Charles de Gaulle, the *bête noire* of the North Atlantic Treaty. After he had come to power, he spoke with genuine respect of Mao Tse-tung and Chou En-lai and of their courage in adversity. Among his fellow intellectuals, he was most drawn to Hans Morgenthau, even though the older scholar had often attacked his policies on Indochina and the Middle East. But he admired Morgenthau's vision in having been the first to oppose Indochina policy under Kennedy and Johnson and his courage in making that early opposition known despite official ridicule and even harassment.

In Kissinger's hierarchy of values, courage and decisiveness came first. Loyalty, too, was prized by him. Intelligence, even brilliance, he considered fairly commonplace. If they were coupled with indecisiveness and weakness in a man, that combination was sure to arouse Kissinger's contempt. Whether one chose to describe Kissinger's ideal in the romantic terms of Hegel's *Zeitgeist*, or in the more rustic image of an embattled cowboy in a Western town, its essence was the same: a man must know how to think and act *alone*.

A great deal has been written about Henry Kissinger's personal diplomacy. His insistence on conducting important negotiations personally and his habit of establishing close relationships with adversary leaders are well known characteristics of his statecraft. His low opinion of the bureaucracy has also been widely commented upon. This penchant for the solo performance has been variously attributed to Kissinger's "enormous ego," his "obsessive secrecy" or to his "elemental need for power and for glory."

I should like to submit another interpretation. I believe that, in order for Kissinger to succeed in his most historic diplomatic initiatives, he *had to* establish personal dominance over the bureaucracy. To establish such control moreover, he had to act decisively, often secretly, and, at times, alone.

Kissinger had never had much patience with bureaucracy. When a professor at Harvard, he had reserved his most acid comments for university administrators. His tolerance for bureaucracy in government was not much greater. After having studied the American "foreign policy-making apparatus" he had come to the conclusion that it was a kind of feudal network of competing agencies and interests, in which there was a "powerful tendency to think that a compromise among administrative proposals (was) the same thing as a policy." The bureaucratic model for making a decision, in Kissinger's opinion, was a policy proposal with three choices: the present policy bracketed by two absurd alternatives.

Kissinger had been a consultant to both the Kennedy and Johnson administrations. While he never said so publicly, he had been deeply disappointed. So much had been promised; so much less had been attempted and, in his judgment, so little had been done. He had had the opportunity to observe government decision-making from a fairly close perspective. What impressed him most was that the foreign policy bureaucracy had a way of smothering initiative by advocating a path of least resistance. The lawyers, businessmen, and former academics who ran the hierarchy generally seemed to place a premium on safety and acceptance rather than on creativity and vision. The result was that any innovative statesmanship tended to expire in the feudal fiefs of the bureaucracy or come to grief on the rocks of organizational inertia.

There was ample basis for Kissinger's impatience. SALT might have been initiated at the Glassboro summit in 1967, between Lyndon Johnson and the Soviet leaders, but there had been no decisive leadership. Nor had there been a clear-cut stand on the possible limitation of strategic arms. Instead, there were endless arguments among the Joint Chiefs of Staff, the Pentagon, the State Department, and academic experts in the field of arms control. Similarly, the Arab-Israeli war of 1967 had presented opportunities for American diplomacy and mediation, but there had been no one with a plan, let alone the courage to place himself between competing claims. Instead, there emerged from the bowels of the bureaucracy countless position papers by learned academic experts. There was no agreement on an overall strategy for mediation in the Middle East, only an almost fatalistic sense of hopelessness and drift.

This was the reason why Kissinger decided, immediately after January 20, 1969, to establish personal control over the bureaucracy. Those whom he could not dominate, he would manipulate. And those whom he could not manipulate, he would try to bypass. He embarked on this course of action as a result of a rational decision. He simply feared that *unless* he dominated, bypassed, or manipulated, nothing would get done. He, too, would ultimately be submerged in a long twilight struggle of modern feudal baronies. This he was simply not prepared to accept.

In his position as Assistant for National Security Affairs, Kissinger came to dominate the bureaucracy as no other figure before him had done, and as no other is likely to do for a very long time to come. He promptly established his control through the establishment of a few small committees each of which he personally chaired. These were a number of interdepartmental groups: a Review Group, a Verification Panel for SALT, a Vietnam Special Studies Group, the Washington Special Actions Group for Crisis Control, and the Forty Committee which dealt with covert intelligence operations.

It was out of these committees that Kissinger forged the great initiatives that have assured his place in history: SALT I in 1969, the opening to China after his secret trip to Peking in 1971, and the diplomatic mediation in the Middle East after the October war in 1973. It is true, of course, that some of the more dubious decisions also had their genesis in this small elitist structure, particularly in the Forty Committee. The "destabilization" of the Allende government in Chile in 1971, alleged payments to Italian neo-fascists in 1972, and the denouement in Indochina are some of the more disturbing examples. Only history can provide the necessary distance for a balanced assessment of these various initiatives. But what can already be asserted with a fair amount of certainty is that Kissinger was right in his assumption that, in order to put into effect a coherent global policy, he would have to concentrate as much power in his hands as possible.

Kissinger's pursuit of power had a very clear-cut purpose. During two decades of reflection he had evolved a theory of global order which, in his judgment, would bring the world a few steps closer to stability and peace. Nothing was more important to him in 1969 than the chance to test that theory. He believed with the most absolute conviction that he was the one best qualified. On one occasion, in 1968, when Rockefeller's speech writers had made some changes in a Kissinger position paper, the author exclaimed furiously: "If Rockefeller buys a Picasso, he doesn't hire four housepainters to improve on it." In Kissinger's own view, this was not an arrogant statement. It was merely the reflection of an enormous, though quite genuine, intellectual self-confidence. He believed, quite matter-of-factly, that he was the Picasso of modern American foreign policy.

Henry Kissinger believed that, in creating a design for world order, realism was more compassionate than romanticism. The great American moralists, in his judgment, had been failures. In the end, Woodrow Wilson had proved ineffectual and John Foster Dulles had turned foreign policy into a crusade that had led straight into the Indochina quagmire. Kissinger did not make peace or justice the objective of his policy nor was he particularly interested in "making the world safe for democracy." He merely wished to make the world safer and more stable. This was a lesser goal, one that offered no illusions, but also brought fewer disappointments. It was also not quite in the mainstream of American history. But then, Kissinger was a European in America, his thought rooted firmly in the European philosophical tradition.

There has been a great deal of confusion about Kissinger's intellectual debt to Metternich for his vision of stability. Kissinger himself has made it abundantly clear that he never looked to Metternich for guidance on *substantive problems* of statecraft: "Most people associate me with Metternich. And that is childish . . . there can be nothing in common between me and Metternich. He was chancellor and foreign minister at a time when it took three weeks to travel from Central Europe to the ends of the Continent, when wars were conducted by professional soldiers and diplomacy was in the hands of the aristocracy. . . ." What Kissinger admired in Metternich was the Austrian diplomat's *conceptual insight* in having recognized the revolutionary character of the Napoleonic challenge, the need to neutralize that challenge without humiliating retribution, and, having achieved that end, his commitment to stability and balance which ushered in a century without a global war.

If Castlereagh taught Kissinger that a statesman must create a vision and remain faithful to it even in adversity, Metternich taught him how to adjust that vision to reality. If Castlereagh taught him about courage and a grand design, Metternich taught him about cunning and manipulation. But when all was said and done, the lessons Kissinger could learn from these two nineteenth century aristocrats were limited. In the end, Kissinger, too, had to stand alone.

Henry Kissinger once told me that a statesman, to be successful, had to have some luck. He knew well that he was no exception to this rule. His appearance on the world stage coincided most fortuitously with a new nadir in the relations between China and the Soviet Union. By 1969, Mao Tse-tung and Brezhnev feared each other more than they feared America, and thus had become more concerned with moderating their relations with the United States than with the pursuit of revolutionary goals of conquest vis-à-vis the West. Thus, the timing of Kissinger's arrival as a world statesman could not have been more fortunate for the particular objective that he had in mind: a new stability in the relations among the world's three great powers.

The drawing up of any balance sheet on the centerpiece of Kissinger's foreign policy—détente with the Soviet Union—must remain a highly personal business on which thoughtful people may have widely differing opinions. Any such analysis must enter in the realm of competing values, since in creating that centerpiece, choices had to be made and a price had to be paid. Hence, it is only fair that, as we enter this discussion, I reveal the basis of my judgment and share my values and prejudices with the reader.

I believe that Henry Kissinger was right when he declared that the overriding reason for détente with Russia was the avoidance of a nuclear catastrophe. I believe that if such a world cataclysm has become less likely, this is in no small measure to be credited to Kissinger. I am fully aware that the American relationship with Russia leaves a great deal to be desired. But there is no question in my mind that the danger of nuclear war has substantially receded. It no longer intrudes into our daily lives the way it did when Kissinger and I were students. Mothers worried about radioactive waste and strontium-90 in their children's milk; and a decade later, John F. Kennedy almost went to nuclear war with Khrushchev over missiles in Cuba. Today, we argue with the Soviet Union about strategic arms control, trade, and human rights, but we no longer live in daily terror of a nuclear exchange. The fearful scenarios that were conjured up in Herman Kahn's *Thinking the Unthinkable* today read almost like horrible anachronisms. In addition to the elements of luck and timing, it was also Kissinger's design and courage that made détente possible at all.

I know the price that Kissinger has paid on behalf of the United States has been enormous. But, to be fair, we must ask ourselves in each case whether the alternatives would have yielded better results. In strategic arms control, Kissinger's accusers have blamed him for his acceptance in SALT I of Soviet superiority in missile numbers. They have also been suspicious of his lack of interest in alleged evidence that the Soviet Union had violated the spirit and perhaps even the letter of SALT I. Critics have also taken umbrage at his reported willingness—during the SALT II negotiations—to exclude the Soviet Backfire bomber from an overall ceiling while including the American cruise missile.

But the critics, in my judgment, have never given a convincing answer to Kissinger's own question: "What in God's name," he asked in 1974, "is strategic superiority? What is the significance of it, politically, militarily, operationally, at these levels of numbers? What do you do with it?" Kissinger simply did not believe that a marginal "overkill" capacity on either side could be translated into a meaningful strategic or political advantage. To my mind, there is no conclusive evidence that such a translation can in fact be made.

The "great grain robbery" of 1972 was not one of Kissinger's proudest moments. The Russian harvest was so poor that the Soviet leadership probably would have paid a better price. As it turned out, however, the American taxpayer helped to underwrite the Soviet purchases and got in return only a few ephemeral benefits: a little Soviet help in Hanoi and Brezhnev's decision to meet with Nixon at the Moscow summit despite the President's decision to place mines in Haiphong harbor.

Kissinger was right, however, in my judgment, in his dispute with Senator Henry Jackson over the linking of most-favored-nations status for the Soviet Union with emigration of Soviet Jews to Israel. It was unreasonable for Jackson to couple an international agreement with Russia to a demand for internal changes within the Soviet state. How would Jackson have responded if the Soviet leadership had linked the conclusion of SALT I to a demand for a lifting of all American immigration quotas? The point I am making is not that the demand was ethically unjustified, but that it was asymmetrical. A *quid pro quo* of Soviet cooperation in the Middle East would have been more sensible and would not have brought up the delicate issue of Soviet internal politics. To those who argued that he was insensitive to the human rights of Jews wishing to emigrate to Israel, Kissinger could point to his record with not inconsiderable pride. Before the Soviets cancelled the 1972 trade agreement in their anger over the Jackson amendment, the annual figure of Jewish emigrants from Russia reached 35,000. After Jackson made his public demands, this figure was cut by more than half. In this instance, without a doubt, private diplomacy tactfully conducted had yielded better results than open covenants stridently demanded.

The great paradox of Kissinger's conception of détente is in his relative tolerance vis-à-vis the Soviet Union, still the fountainhead of communism, and his combativeness toward local Communist movements in peripheral areas. How can Kissinger proclaim détente with the Soviet Union, the supporter of Communist causes everywhere, and yet fight communism to the death in Indochina, warn Western European heads of state against coalition governments with Communists, and demand action against the Communists in Angola?

The key to this riddle is to be found in Kissinger's primary commitment to stability. In the central relationship between the superpowers, there can be no decisive change in the power balance, short of nuclear war. The balance could be changed dramatically, however, if a minor nation shifted its allegiance from one side to the other and thus added appreciably to the strength of one of the two main contenders. The direct jockeying for mutual advantage between Russia and the United States was not likely to affect the global balance. But Communist advances elsewhere could, at least cumulatively, affect the balance of power in the world. Hence, Kissinger's concern with stemming Communist advances in peripheral areas.

This logic, however, runs into serious difficulties. It may stand up in an area such as Angola where thousands of Cuban troops were imported to do battle for the Communist cause. In such a case, there was at least good circumstantial evidence for direct Soviet-sponsored intervention. But there was little, if any evidence that the Soviet Union was very active in helping the Communists in Portugal, Italy, or France. The growth of the Italian Communist movement in Italy under Enrico Berlinguer might be attributable more to that Italian's "historic compromise" with democratic socialism than to subversion by the Soviet Union. Yet, Kissinger accused the Portuguese Foreign Minister of being a "Kerensky," quarantined Portugal from NATO, and had secret payments made to a neo-fascist Italian general. In such cases, a good argument can be made that, by his indiscriminate opposition to all local forms of communism, Kissinger might force breakaway groups back into Moscow's arms and thus bring about the very developments he was so eager to prevent.

On a deeper level, Hans Morgenthau has made the most telling criticism:

> Since the causes and effects of instability persist, a policy committed to stability and identifying instability with communism is compelled by the logic of its interpretation of reality to suppress in the name of anticommunism all manifestations of popular discontent and stifle the aspirations for reform. Thus, in an essentially unstable world, tyranny becomes the last resort of a policy committed to stability as its ultimate standard.

This is how, in Morgenthau's opinion, Kissinger, despite his extraordinary brilliance, often failed. He tended to place his great gifts at the service of lost causes, and thus, in the name of preserving stability and order, aligned the United States on the wrong side of the great historic issues.

Morgenthau may be a little harsh in such a judgment. What if the Italian Communists renounced their "historic compromise," made common cause with Moscow, and other European countries followed suit? The result could well be a catastrophe for the United States. Morgenthau, as critic, does not have to make that awesome choice. But can a statesman dare to take such risks at a moment when he must base his decisions on conjecture rather than on facts? Here the scholar, in my judgment, owes the statesman a measure of empathy and tolerance.

In this entire realm of argument, Kissinger is most vulnerable, in my view, on his Indochina policy. No one, of course, can blame him for the escalation which he regarded as a national disaster. But I have always differed with his judgment that the presence of 500,000 Americans had settled the importance of Vietnam since credibility was now at stake. Rather, it was my impression that American credibility rose rather than fell when that suicidal commitment finally came to an end. I have also never understood Kissinger's answer to the argument that a negotiated settlement could have been attained in 1969 on terms at least as favorable as those that he finally negotiated in 1973. His explanation that for three years the North Vietnamese had refused to accept his "double track" plan of separating military from political matters always struck me as rather unconvincing. Finally, the Cambodian invasion that dragged a neutral nation into a war that it might have been able to avoid, struck me as the greatest, and possibly most tragic, blunder. And, in the end, when Saigon fell in April 1975, Kissinger looked like all the other Americans who had come to Indochina to lose their reputation to Ho Chi Minh and the Vietcong.

There may be a psychological interpretation of Kissinger's paradoxical approach to Communism. It may be found in his profound suspicion of the revolutionary as the greatest threat to a stable world order. In theory, as Kissinger had made clear in an essay on Bismarck, it made little difference to him whether a revolutionary was "red" or "white." But in practice, he always feared the "red" revolutionary infinitely more. It is not that he approved of a Greek or Chilean junta, but he simply did not believe that it posed the kind of threat to international stability as that presented by a Cunhal, an Allende, a Castro, or a Ho Chi Minh. These were the types of leaders, rather than a Brezhnev or a Mao Tse-tung, who were most likely to upset the global balance. They still retained that messianic revolutionary quality that had a vast potential for dislocation and contagion. In relation to the Soviet Union and China, one could afford to take some chances without risk to equilibrium. But when it came to the smaller revolutionaries, Kissinger believed that the war-maker still made the most effective peacemaker.

The opening to China was probably Kissinger's most uncontaminated triumph in his tenure as a statesman. It was also his greatest diplomatic adventure. Once he perceived the depth of the rift between China and the Soviet Union, he became convinced that rapprochement with China might make the Soviet Union more receptive to a genuine détente. In short, China, in his view, had become the key to Russia. In addition to establishing this triangular linkage, Kissinger's secret trip to Peking in 1971 had made him the first messenger of reconciliation. Furthermore to discover that beyond the Himalayas, there were men who elicited his admiration and respect only added to his elation. One of the few times that I heard Kissinger happily admit that he had been wrong was an occasion when he discussed his change of heart about Mao Tse-tung and Chou En-lai. In 1966, during the "Cultural Revolution," he had perceived the Chinese leaders as the two most dangerous men on earth. Five years later, he had come to regard them as rational statesmen who pursued China's national interest in a manner not altogether inconsistent with the rules of international stability. But then it was Henry Kissinger who had once said about himself that while he had a first-rate mind, he had a third-rate intuition about people. In the case of China, fortunately, the reality turned out to be more pleasant than the fantasy.

As for the charge that Kissinger's relationships with adversaries were often better than his relationships with friends, I would hardly cloak this statement in a mantle of universal application. There is, however, ample evidence for it if one contemplates Kissinger's policies toward the continent where he was born. Europe brought out the darker side of his personal diplomacy and his reluctance to delegate responsibility. His declaration of a "Year of Europe" in 1973 had come almost as an afterthought in response to complaints by Western European statesmen that their capitals had become little more than refueling stops for Kissinger on his way to or back from Moscow. It reminded one European diplomat of an unfaithful husband's decision to declare a "year of the wife." Kissinger's outbursts of exasperation in moments of frustration did little to improve relations. When he exclaimed in a moment of anger that he "didn't care what happened to NATO," this momentary lapse was taken seriously by his NATO partners. And his lectures to the Portuguese aroused their anger and resentment. In many of these instances, Kissinger followed his own judgment and generally ignored the advice of experienced foreign service officers.

The case that combined all the weaknesses of personal diplomacy, of course, was Cyprus. Kissinger made policy decisions with regard to Cyprus almost absentmindedly. Distracted by the final act of Watergate, he paid only the most cursory attention to events on that tormented island. His dislike for Archbishop Makarios prompted him to lean toward the Greek extremist, Nikos Sampson, of whose reputation he knew little. When the Turks, predictably enough, responded by mounting an invasion, Kissinger did little to deter them even though a democratic government in the meantime had assumed control in Athens. Thus, Kissinger managed to alienate *both* Greece and Turkey in an amazingly short period of time. Perhaps even more serious, the failure of his Cyprus policy led directly to the first of many strictures to be imposed upon him by an increasingly suspicious and hostile Congress.

Since Kissinger's main objective has always been the pursuit of international stability, his attention had been focussed on the world's major power wielders. The pawns on the global chessboard seemed quite expendable to him, until quite suddenly and without warning, some of them decided to improve their lowly status. The Arab oil embargo and the demands for a "new international economic order" that swept through the Third World like a hurricane, convinced Kissinger that he finally would have to pay attention to the smaller nations of Africa, Latin America, and Asia. He quickly realized that his vision of stability would have to become bifocal. Unless he did so, his policies might prevent World War III, but they were certain to prepare the ground for World War IV.

When, in the spring of 1976, Kissinger declared his clear support for black majority rule in southern Africa, he reversed a long tradition of American equivocation. While this reversal was triggered primarily by the Soviet victory in Angola, it was also motivated by Kissinger's desire to build détente between the races and the rich and poor. And when he pledged a dedicated effort to "roll back the desert" in famine-stricken African lands, his promise had the ring of truth. This compassion for the world's dispossessed came late, but when it came, it was sincere.

For almost thirty years, the United Nations had existed in the suburbs of Henry Kissinger's consciousness. Its lack of authority and power had convinced him that he could ignore it with impunity. The increase of Third World bloc voting, however, and a rise of a "tyranny of the majority," made him pay attention. When this majority, having driven the United States into the role of opposition, finally passed an Orwellian resolution that equated Zionism with racism, Kissinger's antennae, always sensitive to power, registered an ominous alert.

Somber warnings that the United Nations might become an empty shell, coupled with Ambassador Moynihan's blunt rhetoric, placed the Third World nations on guard that they were not immune to Kissinger's favorite mixture of diplomacy and force. When Moynihan, however, engaged in so much bluntness that it began to resemble "overkill," Kissinger became alarmed. The differences between the two men finally led to the ambassador's resignation. Even a Kissinger weakened by mounting criticism and congressional opposition was still a formidable adversary.

We cannot say with certitude whether the critics of the step-by-step approach to peace in the Middle East were justified in their assertions that Kissinger avoided the heart of the conflict by refusing to address himself to the Palestinian problem. What the record does indicate, however, is that Kissinger has managed to narrow the differences between Israel and the Arabs more successfully than any other mediator in the long history of that tragic conflict.

The essence of Kissinger's Middle East diplomacy has been the avoidance of the appearance of victory. Convinced that only a stalemate could contain the seeds of peace, he steered the October war to an inconclusive end. In doing so, he resisted enormous pressure from each side hungering for military victory. It was in the aftermath of this military stalemate that he succeeded in negotiating the two disengagement accords, first between Israel and Egypt and then, between Israel and Syria. The two agreements were achieved in no small measure because of Kissinger's personal tenacity. The Sinai agreement which followed in September 1975, was the first accord reached by Israel and an Arab state that was not an armistice to end a war. It was a voluntary agreement reached in times of peace. Even when shortly afterward Syria temporarily linked its future to the PLO, Kissinger's approach of "peace by pieces" had already achieved remarkable results.

It is in the Middle East that Kissinger's intellectual courage had to undergo its acid test. It was not easy always to negotiate between a hammer and an anvil. His striving for balance and equilibrium was never popular with either side. As a Jew, he did not find it easy to deny victory to the state of Israel. Personally, he endured considerable suffering. Yet, he remained faithful to his intellectual conviction that a victor's peace would plant the seeds of yet another war. He might be mistaken in this belief though history provides considerable evidence to back him up. But while his judgment may be open to debate, his sincerity is not. Nowhere in his statesmanship has Henry Kissinger shown greater courage than in his quest for a Middle Eastern peace.

If there is any iron law of history, Kissinger once said, it is that no longing is ever completely fulfilled. His own pursuit of a stable world order is no exception to this general rule.

After Nixon's resignation Kissinger remained the only major figure in the government who had been closely associated with the former president. He now had to pay the price exacted by a resurgent Congress in the post-imperial presidency.

Kissinger's autocratic temperament, highly personal style, and persistent secrecy, now made him a natural target. What had been admired in him earlier now was questioned and condemned. Within one year, between 1974 and 1975, the Congress placed severe restrictions on his freedom to maneuver in virtually every single area of foreign policy, Turkey to Angola. The man who could do nothing wrong now suddenly could do nothing right. As Kissinger himself observed, "I have been praised excessively, so now I am being blamed excessively." Seldom has a man been more exposed to the fickleness of popular acclaim.

While Kissinger was still widely perceived as an asset to the United States as a *nation* in its relationships abroad, many Americans, by 1976, were deeply ambivalent about his impact on America as a *people* at home. Kissinger himself has been consistent. He has never wavered in his striving for a stable world order. But he was fated to experience in practice what he had learned in theory a quarter of a century before: that a statesman who removes himself too much from the experience of his people may doom himself to disappointment and despair. In February 1976, he stated that America was more endangered by her "domestic divisions than by her overseas adversaries." "A great nation that does not shape history," he continued, "eventually becomes its victim." In his frustration with a Congress that had persistently disavowed his policies and had simply refused to heed his counsel on Angola, he sounded a bleak and somber warning:

> Unless the country ends its divisions, our only option is to retreat—to become an isolated fortress in a hostile and turbulent global sea, awaiting the ultimate confrontation with the only response we will not have denied ourselves—massive retaliation.

Once again, Kissinger walked as a loner, with the ghost of Oswald Spengler by his side. His career showed clearly that vision and courage may not be enough to ensure success. As he himself had written, popular support was essential as well. Luck and timing also played a crucial role. Thucydides had realized this long ago in ancient Athens when he had elevated fortune to the rank of goddess.

Perhaps the most haunting questions about Henry Kissinger's foreign policy are of a philosophical nature. What is the role of ethics in Kissinger's world of stability and power? What is the relationship between personal and political morality? What room does Kissinger's pursuit of a stable world order leave for justice? What should be our criterion for success—his intentions or the consequences of his actions? In short, what must concern us, in conclusion, is the problem of statesmanship and moral choice.

There is little doubt that Kissinger, when facing Goethe's dilemma— the choice "between justice and disorder, on the one hand, and injustice and order, on the other," has tended to prefer the latter. In Kantian terms Kissinger made the pursuit of a stable world order the categorical imperative of his foreign policy. If, in the process, the human element had to be sacrificed at times on the altar of stability or of a larger strategic vision, so be it, because without stability, peace could not be born at all and justice, too, would be extinguished. He felt that, in a tragic world, a statesman was not able to choose between good and evil, but only among different forms of evil. Indeed, whatever decision he would make, *some* evil consequences were bound to flow from it. All that a realistic statesman could do in such a world was to choose the lesser evil.

The competing claims of stability and justice permeate the world of Henry Kissinger. A few examples from the record will suffice to demonstrate the pervasiveness of this terrible dilemma.

In the Indochina war, the problem presented itself in its starkest form in the Nixon decision to mine the ports of North Vietnam and to order all-out bombing attacks on Hanoi and Haiphong in 1972. These actions, which were publicly supported by Kissinger, tested the determination of the Soviet Union and China to stand by their North Vietnamese ally. When no action was forthcoming either from Moscow or Peking, Nixon and Kissinger realized that they had managed to isolate North Vietnam. The war was therefore brought to an end for American combat soldiers, but at a price that aroused the moral indignation of many nations and that of many Americans as well. The question that remains is whether this brutal means was justified to attain the desired objective of a "peace with honor," a peace which, in the end, proved to be ephemeral. Could not another, less dreadful, way have been found?

In his relations with the Soviet Union, Kissinger has also been accused of indifference to the human element. As Richard Falk has observed in a thoughtful essay, "Kissinger's effectiveness in dealing with foreign governments arose from his capacity to avoid unpleasant criticisms about their domestic indecencies." Since most powerful states have skeletons hidden in their closets, most statesmen, Falk observed, "found Kissinger's Machiavellian posture a welcome relief." If, in short, a choice had to be made between détente and human rights within the borders of the Soviet Union, there was little doubt how Kissinger would choose.

When India went to war with Pakistan in 1971, Kissinger "tilted" toward Yahya Khan. Not only had the Pakistani president helped in the preparations for the secret trip to China, but an Indian alliance with the Soviet Union threatened to dismember a weakened Pakistan. When Yahya Khan turned on his Bengali fellow-Moslems in a ferocious civil war, and drove ten million of them into exile, Kissinger remained silent. The imperatives of the strategic balance, once again, had overshadowed the human tragedy.

Until the nations of the Third World gained a measure of power through the oil embargo and bloc alignments in the United Nations, Kissinger had little time for the problems of the small and poor. Until famines in the Third World reached catastrophic dimensions, they remained on the periphery of his political awareness. Falk observed of Kissinger's early attitude that "it was inconceivable that afflictions of this magnitude in the Northern Hemisphere would not have been perceived as a catastrophe of historic significance." "Kissinger's outlook," Falk continued, "presupposed that it (was) possible to manage international relations mainly by moderating conflictual relations among governments in the Northern Hemisphere." Once more, Kissinger stood accused of ignoring humanity in the name of order.

It would not be fair to Kissinger to let these judgments stand without giving him a hearing. On Indochina, the question he might ask is this: What is more merciful and more compassionate, an end with horror or a horror without end? On the problem of ignoring human rights in Russia, he might well respond by asking whether the avoidance of an atomic holocaust was not itself the highest moral imperative of our age. On India and Pakistan, he might query his accuser as to whether Soviet domination of the Indian sub-continent might not have been the greater evil. And on the matter of the world's poor and dispossessed, Kissinger could now respond that his numerous proposals to build bridges between the world's rich and poor more than compensated for his earlier indifference.

When Henry Kissinger entered Harvard as an undergraduate in 1946, another Jewish refugee, almost a generation older, had just published his first book in the United States. Hans Morgenthau's *Scientific Man versus Power Politics* contained a paragraph that foreshadowed Kissinger's dilemma in all its awesome starkness:

> We have no choice between power and the common good. To act successfully, that is, according to the rules of the political art, is political wisdom. To know with despair that the political act is inevitably evil, and to act nevertheless, is moral courage. To choose among several expedient actions the least evil one is moral judgment. In the combination of political wisdom, moral courage and moral judgment, man reconciles his political nature with his moral destiny. That this condition is nothing more than a *modus vivendi*, uneasy, precarious, and even paradoxical, can disappoint only those who prefer to gloss over and to distort the tragic contradictions of human existence with the soothing logic of a specious concord.

In such a world, is it not easier to abstain from any decision altogether? Kissinger has never thought so. He knew that abstention from evil did not affect the existence of evil in the world, but only destroyed the faculty of choice. As Albert Camus had said, not to choose, too, was a choice.

When history would make its judgment on the foreign policy of Henry Kissinger, the chronicle would not pay much attention to his personal anguish when forced to choose between competing claims. Its iron pen would merely register the objective consequences of his acts. Nor would history reveal its alternatives had he acted otherwise. He would never know where the road *not* taken might have led. The unending quest for meaningful choices in a tragic world in which the only certainty was risk simply was a statesman's lot. It was, therefore, in action in the present that courage and humanity were born.

When a quarter of a century ago, on that October day in 1950, I first met Henry Kissinger, I had a premonition that one day he might enter history. I think the world is a safer place today because of his courage and his vision. It might even be a little better. No mortal man could ask for more.

Flawed Design and Diplomatic Disaster

STANLEY HOFFMANN

Some people owe their psychological or sociological insight exclusively to their resentments and their fears. This is not Kissinger's case. These may sharpen his wits, and dip his brush in acid. But he has three great gifts which serve him equally well in his writings and his statecraft.

One is an almost devilish psychological intuition, an instinct for grasping the hidden springs of character, of knowing what drives or what dooms another person. He was at his best as a face-to-face negotiator precisely because of this rare talent. Had he been less tempted by action and more capable of that "fantasy life" of "romantic imaginings" in which, he says, Nixon indulged, he might have been a good novelist. The gallery of portraits is the best part of the book. Each reader will have his own favorites (and all will notice that some statesmen with whom Kissinger had many dealings hardly appear, Willy Brandt being the most conspicuous). My favorites are the vivid portraits of Chou, Heath, Brezhnev, and Mao—who is described with a power and subtlety that seem worthy of him. As in his account of Nixon, for example, Kissinger backs up his incisive analysis of character with incisive anecdotes. We see Chou, late at night, taking Kissinger on a walk where they cross two bridges, without a word referring to a conversation months before when Kissinger had told Chou that he felt like a character in Kafka's *Castle*—the plumber who is summoned and denied entrance—because of the presence of soldiers guarding the bridges connecting the various guest cottages, and Brezhnev trying to make a toy cannon work during a conference and strutting "like a prizefighter who has knocked out his opponent" when the cannon finally went off.

All of the portraits convey the relation between a personality and the culture that has shaped it. And Kissinger's second gift is that of a man particularly attuned to the nuances of cultural difference (the word "nuance" is one of his favorites, along with "intangible," "comparison," "exalted," "insecure," "petty," and "unsentimental"). People who have been transplanted from one country into another, who have a certain distance both from the history and mores of the society from which they were uprooted and from the memories and rituals of their adopted country, often develop this sense. They lose it only if they are too eager to assimilate into the mainstream of their new culture—something that was never Kissinger's case.

Kissinger is very good at evoking atmospheres, and their relation to the business of power: Washington dinner parties and receptions, where "the relationships are created without which the machinery of government would soon stalemate itself," the president's lonely hideaway room, the villa filled with Fernand Léger paintings where Kissinger met the North Vietnamese, the peculiarities of protocol in each country he visited. One of the most fascinating sides of this book is the analysis of different political styles, molded by distinctive historical experiences and geographical imperatives. Kissinger thus compares brilliantly the Chinese and the Soviet styles of negotiation (not to mention cuisines). "The Soviets insist on their prerogatives as a great power. The Chinese establish a claim on the basis of universal principles and a demonstration of self-confidence that attempts to make the issue of power irrelevant." Mao and Chou represented a nation that "had absorbed conquerors and had proved its inward strength by imposing its social and intellectual style on them. Its leaders were aloof, self-assured, composed. Brezhnev represented a nation that had survived not by civilizing its conquerors but by outlasting them . . . he sought to obscure his lack of assurance by boisterousness."

The Vietnamese, he notes, have outlasted their conquerors by driving them insane. A Japanese leader "does not announce a decision, he evokes it." Japanese decision-making by consensus is endless, but execution is disciplined; in the US, it is the other way around. In the Middle East, "formal positions are like the shadows in Plato's cave—reflections of a transcendent reality almost impossible to encompass in the dry legalisms of a negotiating process."

Nobody has analyzed more pithily Western European ambivalence toward the US—the fear of American rigidity compounded by the fear either of American retreat or of superpower condominium. French foreign policy under the Fifth Republic was prickly but "serious and consistent," at times "steadier and more perceptive than our own," whereas British statesmen "were content to act as honored consultants to our deliberations." And "one sometimes could not avoid the impression that to discuss international affairs with [Italy's] foreign minister was to risk boring him." One could cull a bestiary of negotiating styles from this book.

One could also draw from it a vast monograph on the workings of American bureaucracy in foreign affairs, and a short Little Red (or rather White) Book, an appendix to *The Prince*, on the art of diplomatic bargaining. For Kissinger's third gift is one that puts into practice his insights into personalities and cultures: it is the gift for the manipulation of power— exploiting the weaknesses and strengths of character of his counterparts, either by neutralizing them (if they were adversaries) or turning them into allies or accomplices by addressing their needs and playing on their fears of other countries. This did not always work: his attempt at negotiating a textile agreement with the Japanese began as "an intricate Kabuki play" which "turned out to be more like a Kafka story."

Kissinger's prerequisite for the exercise of this gift, as he suggests throughout the book, is a firm control of the US bureaucracy—which is precisely what Nixon also wanted. The president "was determined to run foreign policy from the White House," and Kissinger devised the machinery that was supposed to make it possible. But it never worked well enough, and those who believe that confusion and cacophony began with the Carter administration are in for a surprise.

If there is one constant theme that runs through every chapter of this complex book, it is that of the battle for control between, on the one hand, Nixon and Kissinger and, on the other, the bureaucracy—the State Department, Defense, the CIA, the Treasury during Connally's "frontal assault on the White House staff system." It was a vicious circle: Nixon and Kissinger, exasperated by the bureaucrats' lack of imagination, frequent resistance, and propensity to leaks, reserved more and more control over the key issues to themselves, but this only compounded the problem, since the execution of policies had to be largely entrusted to departments that had not been consulted or even informed. More and more Kissinger carried on the real business of foreign policy through secretive "back channels"— with Dobrynin over SALT and all other Soviet-American relations, with Chou, with Ambassador Rabin and Golda Meir (at the expense of Foreign Minister Abba Eban), later with Sadat. But the same issues were being treated simultaneously by the State Department, or in the formal SALT negotiation at Helsinki.

This created frequent confusion when America's negotiators did not know the agreements in the making through the back channels; it also gave the Soviets opportunities to try to play one team against the other. It created deep resentments among American diplomats ignored or undercut by the White House. It even created suspicion in Moscow and Peking, for Soviet and Chinese diplomats wondered why the Americans wanted so much secrecy. It meant that vital decisions (for instance, those concerning Cambodia in April 1970) were taken behind the backs or against the opposition of Secretaries Rogers and Laird. It meant that at the summits in Peking and Moscow, set up without Roger's participation, Kissinger had to enlist the cooperation of Chou and of Gromyko in handling our own resentful State Department. (In China, this did not work: when the State Department, which had been kept in the dark, was informed of the text of what became the Shanghai communiqué, it demanded a host of changes—and obtained some, behaving exactly as Thieu was going to do, a few months later, when he was finally informed of the text of the peace agreement Kissinger had negotiated alone with Le Duc Tho.)

When Kissinger was charged with executing a policy, the sluggishness and opposition of the bureaucracy could complicate and delay, but no more. When responsibilities were shared, or supposedly belonged to the State Department but were subject to White House review, policy could become incoherent: for instance in the Middle East in 1969–1970, when Rogers launched peace plans which Nixon and Kissinger did not endorse, or during the Bangladesh crisis when Rogers opposed the "tilt" toward Pakistan. The bureaucracy, in what it deemed "its" domain, often failed to consult the White House! Nixon's startling announcement of August 15, 1971— the monetary and economic measures that provoked a crisis with Western Europe and Japan—was made without either Rogers or Kissinger being consulted.

> The Nixon method of government worked well when the military problem was relatively straightforward and could be carried out in one daring move. . . . It was effective also for purposeful solitary diplomacy conducted by a trusted associate working with a small staff. . . . Difficulties arose when a sustained military effort was needed . . . or when the diplomacy was too complex to be handled by the security adviser's office. . . . Then the absence of consensus or even understanding inhibited coherence and commitment.

Nixon's reluctance to impose his will perpetuated the lack of discipline, and drove him increasingly into secrecy and distrust. Thus his methods made possible some remarkable initiatives, but also led straight to the crisis which destroyed him in 1974, and weakened the presidency.

Kissinger was more than willing to overlook those risks, both when in office and in writing most of his memoir. For the brand of diplomacy he wanted to perform cannot tolerate pluralism in the various institutions concerned with foreign policy, or the long delays that building a consensus among them would entail. He concentrated on the games to be played with foreign interlocutors, not domestic bureaucrats. For him the job of the US bureaucracies was to give him the data for the decisions he and Nixon would make, and to carry out these decisions.

Bureaucratic maneuver annoys him. What fascinates him is diplomatic maneuver, as he makes clear in countless maxims and comments on the art of relating force to goals, on the advantages and perils of crises. These confer "an unusual capacity for creative action," but they must be "overpowered early." "One's actions must be sustained; they must appear relentless, inexorable." In the final phase one must resist "the natural temptation to relax and perhaps to ease the process by a gesture of goodwill. . . . The time for conciliation is after the crisis is surmounted."

He tells us the requirements of secret diplomacy, the way of linking issues in a bargain so as to extract advantages, and the way of delaying agreement on the issues which one's opponent is in a hurry to settle until he has given in on the others. One must never appear too eager, yet one should not (as the Soviets tend to do) compromise one's gains by being too greedy or by asking for something unattainable; one should not make any unilateral concessions, yet one ought to avoid excessive haggling.

Kissinger also instructs us on triangular diplomacy (which "must rely on the natural incentives and propensities of the players" and "avoid the impression that one is 'using' either of the contenders against the other"), on giving an opponent "a formal reassurance intended to unnerve as much as to calm; and which would defeat its purpose if it were actually believed," on the error of raising too soon an issue on which "readiness to compromise does not exist," on the occasional need to substitute boldness if one lacks power, on the uses of insolence, "the armor of the weak."

If there seems considerable self-satisfaction in such advice, it is true that during the period covered by this book he was rarely caught at his own game: pathetically, his only personal diplomatic defeat was inflicted by Thieu, in October 1972, when the South Vietnamese leader turned the deadline agreed upon by Kissinger and the North Vietnamese into a weapon against the whole agreement as brilliantly as Kissinger had used the deadline of the US election in order to extract a "cascade" of concessions from Hanoi. (Both Thieu and Le Duc Tho used insolence to "stonewall" when in positions of weakness. Kissinger in this book does the same in reply to criticism from the left and from liberals.) Like an athlete reminiscing about a game he won because he was in top form, Kissinger relives his tactical calculations and manipulations with relish, and thus reveals what sustains a master politician in the daily drudgery of dealing with "the contingent." But what was the design which all the ingenuity he so fondly recalls was supposed to serve? What strategy required these tactics?

Kissinger's tactical maxims leave no doubt: the professed disciple of Kant, he is a follower of Hobbes in his assessment of human nature and of the behavior of states in the international state of nature. (Twice he mentions, with some awe, that Pompidou, who helped him conduct his secret negotiations with the North Vietnamese, "never used these kindnesses to extract anything in return.") As he sees them, nations are driven by diffidence, greed, and glory; they are often propelled by the murderous certainties of ideology, compelled to use their power for their preservation or their expansion. What order can nations achieve in this "state of war" which Hobbes deemed bearable in his day, but which has become a threat to the common survival in the age (foreseen by Kant) when total destruction is possible and nations are so intimately interdependent?

Americans, Kissinger tells us, have had three traditions: "an idealistic tradition that sees foreign policy as a contest between evil and good," a pragmatic tradition of problem-solving, and a legalistic tradition. They had all failed. "Emotional slogans" had kept America oscillating from over-involvement to isolationism. The time had come when "moral exuberance" could no longer be condoned: "we were becoming like other nations in the need to recognize that our power, while vast, had limits." "It was my conviction that a concept of our fundamental national interests would provide a ballast of restraint and an assurance of continuity." What America needed, and Kissinger wanted to establish, was a geopolitical tradition. ("By 'geopolitical' I mean an approach that pays attention to the requirements of equilibrium.")

Kissinger the realist sounds here like Hans Morgenthau writing on the balance of power. But Morgenthau has often been severely critical of Kissinger. The drama of this doctrine of realism is that, while it conceives of world order as the product of a careful balancing of power, as a set of restraints on excessive ambitions, and as a compromise between conflicting interests, it allows for many different versions of nirvana, and different evaluations of threats and opportunities. Containment too—as described by George Kennan, and as executed (not to Kennan's satisfaction) by Acheson and (not to Acheson's satisfaction) by Dulles—had been an attempt to teach realism to Americans. But Kissinger is critical of containment: it "treated power and diplomacy as distinct elements or phases of policy"; by concentrating on building "situations of strength" at a time when we were strong and the Soviets weak, we allowed them to catch up, and thus to be in a much more favorable position on the distant day of negotiation. "Treating force and diplomacy as discrete phenomena caused our power to lack purpose and our negotiations to lack force." We had to learn a better integration of power and policy in an age of nuclear weapons, competing ideologies, and diffusion of political power.

The question remains: for what purpose? What was the "geopolitical design"? It is here that surprises begin. In the first place, Kissinger's repeated assertions about the need for a policy purged of emotional excesses and reconciled "to imperfect choices, partial fulfillment, the unsatisfying tasks of balance and maneuver" are nowhere accompanied by a description of the kind of world Kissinger was trying to bring about. If there was a vision beyond the geopolitical game, if the complex manipulation of rewards and punishments needed to create equilibrium and to restrain the troublemakers was aimed at a certain ideal of world order, we are left free to guess what it might have been. Maybe it is Kissinger's horror of grand designs mass-produced by "the wayward representatives of American liberalism" which explains this reticence. At any rate, he is much more mysterious about his purposes than about his method, about his destination than about his approach.

Secondly, the approach itself reminds one that geopolitics was a German school of thought based on the notion of constant and inevitable struggle. And Kissinger now reminds one of Karl Schmitt's fundamental distinction—in which he saw the key to politics—between friends and foes. Kissinger recognizes that the nuclear stalemate between the superpowers results in a kind of fragmentation of world politics: there is both a global balance of nuclear power, and a series of regional balances (or imbalances). But at the heart of his conception there are two propositions.

The first is that the decisive and dominant issue is the conflict between the US and the Soviet Union. This extends to every part of the world and, given the nature of Soviet ideology, includes "the internal policies and social structures of countries" as well. Soviet policy, whatever its "ultimate aims'' or the Soviet leaders' "real intentions" (wrong questions, says Kissinger), wants "to promote the attrition of adversaries by gradual increments." Soviet strategy is "one of ruthless opportunism." There is no "terminal point to international tension" that could be achieved by "sentimental conciliation" or "liturgical belligerence," for we are "dealing with a system too ideologically hostile for instant conciliation and militarily too powerful to destroy."

The second fundamental proposition is that "to foreclose Soviet opportunities is thus the essence of the West's responsibility." It is a permanent task, not (as containment was thought to be) "an exertion that has a foreseeable end." The nature of that task is the management of the balance of power, which requires "perseverance, subtlety, not a little courage, and above all understanding of its requirements."

What are these requirements? Above all, we must create in our adversary a perception of "an equality of power": if it is perceived, "it will not be tested." "Calculation must include potential as well as actual power, not only the possession of power but the will to bring it to bear." We must understand that our performance in any part of the world has an effect on this balance of real and perceived power; therefore, the way in which we respond to any local crisis ought to be related to, and determined by its relation to, the central contest.

Kissinger rigorously applied this maxim in cases such as Chile, where he saw in Allende's election "a challenge to our national interest" not only because of Allende's revolutionary and anti-American program but because it happened "against the backdrop of the Syrian invasion of Jordon" (Syria being a Soviet ally) "and our effort to force the Soviet Union to dismantle its installation for servicing nuclear submarines in the Caribbean." He acted in the same way in the Middle East, where in 1969 "delay was on the whole in our interest because it enabled us to demonstrate even to radical Arabs that we were indispensable to *any* progress and that it cannot be extorted from us by Soviet pressure." The division of the world into radicals and moderates is as important to Kissinger as the division between Moscow and Washington, Moscow being seen as the ally of the radicals, and Washington the protector of the moderates.

Vietnam was of course part of the same chain: he tells us many times that his "initiatives with Peking and Moscow would have been impossible had we simply collapsed in Vietnam." He supported Pakistan against India because Pakistan was our ally, and China's friend, whereas India had signed a treaty with Moscow, and India's war threatened "our geopolitical design." Our friends must be supported whatever they may do within their own countries: hence Kissinger's determination to stick by Yahya Khan, Thieu, Lon Nol, the Shah, etc. . . . Still, when their acts could adversely affect the central conflict, we must check their course: thus as Nixon "frostily" reminded Willy Brandt, we did not support his *Ostpolitik*, we merely "did not object"; but we gave "the inevitable a constructive direction" by linking it to America's own policy toward the Soviet Union, and thus we "became responsible for the ultimate success of Brandt's policy." Our enemies, defined as whoever aligns himself with the Soviets, must be resisted and frustrated; our friends must be guided.

Kissinger's notion of linkage applies not only to power relations among nations and entire regions but also to political issues arising with the Soviets. Not only are "the actions of a major power inevitably related," and not only do they have "consequences beyond the issue or region immediately concerned," but we must try to link "deliberately" separate objectives in a negotiation, "using one as a leverage on the other." Hence the efforts of the Nixon administration to make "progress in settling the Vietnam war something of a condition for advance in areas of interest to the Soviets, such as the Middle East, trade or arms limitation"; and we linked SALT to the Berlin negotiation, on whose success, in turn, the Soviet–West German treaty depended. "We saw linkage, in short, as synonymous with an overall strategic and geopolitical view. To ignore the interconnection of events was to undermine the coherence of all policy."

Linkage was part of the attempt to restrain the Soviets with a careful mixture of penalties and incentives. Trade, for instance, was treated as "a political instrument," to be favored "in measured doses" when the Soviets behaved cooperatively, and withheld otherwise. "Penalties for adventurism" include "military assistance to friends resisting Soviet or Cuban or radical pressures." They also include the use of force.

On this point, Kissinger is prolix: on the one hand, the "basic choice is to act or not to act": "there are no rewards for exhibiting one's doubts in vacillation: statesmen get no praise for failing with restraint. Once committed they must prevail." "Gradual escalation tempts the opponent to match every move"; a leader, once committed, has the "obligation to end the confrontation rapidly. For this he must convey implacability."

On the other hand, the purpose of force is to restore a balance of power, without which negotiations are bound to be counterproductive for one's own side. And it is best to resort to force quickly, when a major crisis can still be avoided and the adversary is not yet fully committed. The objective of this strategy is "an end of the constant Soviet pressure against the global balance of power," to which "in our minds efforts to reduce the danger of nuclear war by the control of arms had to be linked." Reacting strongly, violently if necessary, in the early stages of Soviet expansion would save us from having to choose between either "the collapse of the balance of power or a colossal confrontation."

It must be clear that Kissinger's geopolitical design is not at all adequately described by the word détente. It was a scheme for universal, permanent, and successful containment, marshaling all our instruments of power more effectively than before, and aiming at "an end to the constant probing for openings and the testing of every equilibrium." Kissinger, indeed, appears as the Compleat Cold Warrior. To be sure, he would allow for some co-operation with Moscow, but as a reward for good behavior, as an incentive to moderation, and because of the risks in the nuclear age.

Détente was a name for the forced Soviet acceptance of the status quo, obtained by "a firm application of psychological and physical restraints and determined resistance to challenge." It was also "a device to maximize Soviet dilemmas," a tactic aimed at demonstrating "to our public and to our allies that we were not the cause of conflict." "We could not permit the Soviets to monopolize the world's yearning for peace." SALT I made us give up one weapon—the ABM—Congress was going to destroy anyhow, but it froze the Soviet offensive build-up (a debatable point) while allowing us to catch up. Triangular diplomacy has to serve the aim of containing the Soviets without provoking them into greater aggressiveness, and

> it was a three-dimensional game, but any simplification had the makings of catastrophe. If we appeared irresolute or leaning toward Moscow, Peking would be driven to accommodations with the Soviet Union. If we adopted the Chinese attitude, however, we might not even help Peking: we might, in fact, tempt a Soviet preemptive attack on China and thus be faced with decisions of enormous danger.

Kissinger asks whether the Soviet's shift to détente was a tactical maneuver— a question that could be put to him.

This was, as I have written elsewhere, a design of Bismarckian proportions. "Our relations to possible opponents should be such, I considered, that our options toward both of them were always greater than their options toward each other." The US was to be the supreme manipulator of the triangle, and of course the supreme beneficiary of détente: the Soviets would be contained all over the world, and rewarded with measured deliveries of grain. Their proxies would be either punished, or induced to turn to us, as in the Middle East, from where, Kissinger announced in 1969, we wanted to expell the Soviets. "Three years later," he now claims, "we made this prediction come true"—another debatable point. Balance of power and American hegemony become synonymous. Just as "it is up to *us* to define the limits of Soviet aims," it is up to us to teach everyone else the boundaries of the permissible, to trace the borders of their diplomatic and social experiments.

The problems with this ambitious strategy were legion, and Kissinger is singularly unwilling to confront them. In the first place, it assumed a far greater ability to force the Soviets to play "our" game than it was wise to expect. During the period in question Soviet military might and their capacity to project it grew, in no small part because the US was bogged down in Vietnam. Not only the weaknesses but the strengths of our own friends and allies created openings for Soviet influence—in the Middle East and in southern Africa, for example. Were we really in a position to deny them "all opportunities for expansion"? Since we wanted to keep them out of our *chasses gardées*, and since they wanted to preserve the autonomy of their political and economic system, how many chances "for genuine cooperation" could we dangle before their eyes so as to "inculcate habits of moderation and bring about a more constructive future?"

Kissinger had criticized the containment doctrine for its suggestion that creating situations of strength would ultimately lead to harmony. But his own strategy left room for only two options: a constant manning of barricades, permanent crisis management, an endless vista of confrontations and tests, or else Soviet acceptance of the inevitable US dominance. The latter was unlikely, for it presumed total success by the US, for which the conditions existed neither at home nor in the world. The former was bleak.

Let us assume that the design made sense. Was it compatible with the American system of government? First, it required an extraordinary capacity for acting swiftly and flexibly all over the globe. Centralization of command allows for speed and suppleness. But it also entails concentration on a few fronts: a small staff can't cope with everything. The beast in Kafka's fable can't run to all the corners of the burrow at once. Kissinger tells us that his plan for the Middle East, in 1969–1972, was, through intransigence— i.e., by our refusing to put pressure on Israel to make any accommodation whatever with Moscow and its allies—to get to the point where "some Arab state showed a willingness to separate from the Soviets, or the Soviets were prepared to dissociate from the maximum Arab program." By the early spring of 1972, *both* of these developments had occurred: the Soviets were hinting strongly at their desire to deviate from that program (although they could not initiate this deviation themselves). At the summit they agreed on a weak statement of principles (Kissinger says he "never understood" why they did so) which Sadat indeed interpreted as a Soviet breach of solidarity with the Arabs. And Sadat himself, disillusioned with the Soviets, had opened a secret channel to Kissinger and suggested an American initiative.

Even after Sadat's expulsion of the Soviets in July, 1972, however, the U.S. took no such initiative. Kissinger—in the only chapter that sounds faintly embarrassed—pleads unconvincingly that Soviet proposals were unacceptable because they assumed a permanent Soviet presence in the Middle East. And yet—knowing what was happening to their position in Egypt—the Russians had offered to withdraw in the event of a comprehensive settlement. As for Sadat, Kissinger recognizes that he thought for too long that Nasser's successor was still playing Nasser's game: "great men are so rare that they take some getting used to!" In other words, opportunities were missed (and the October war made more likely), partly by Kissinger's fixation on the Soviet angle of the Middle Eastern problem, partly by the simple fact that the summits and Vietnam left him little time, partly by the fact that 1972 was an election year: "I was too immersed in Vietnam and Nixon in the campaign to do any serious negotiating." This is far from the only case where Kissinger's conception and manipulation of grand strategy are shown as defective by his own evidence.

In the second place, Kissinger's strategy required that domestic politics allow American leaders to pursue their delicate game abroad without constraints or pressures. He denounces, from chapter to chapter, those who wanted to cut the military budget at a time when the Soviets were building large missiles, or who sympathized with India over Bangladesh, or who tried to limit the Executive's freedom of military action in Cambodia, Laos, and Vietnam. But there can be no guarantee that a policy whose success depends largely on secrecy and speed will be automatically supported by a public and a Congress that are simply told to wait for the results. Surely the secrecy of the 1969 bombing of the sanctuaries in Cambodia was due at least as much to the desire not to sharpen domestic opposition as to the desire to protect Sihanouk. The tools of Kissinger's strategy—linkage, the unrestrained use of force for specific objectives—could be effective only in the hands of one person. Yet their very nature tempted others, in Congress or in the public, to try to impose different ways (more crude or more moderate) of using them.

The style of Kissinger's strategy was itself an invitation to damaging leaks, which in turn would provoke more or less legal retaliation, such as the wiretaps or the onslaught on Daniel Ellsberg; and these measures in turn would make Congress and the public more restive. In this sense, Kissinger cannot escape all responsibility for Watergate, if we mean by Watergate a pattern of Executive abuses. Watergate became a personal tragedy for Kissinger not only because it was the price of having served Nixon but also because it symbolized the revolt of the very democracy on whose behalf the geopolitical battle was being waged.

We have assumed so far that the design at least made sense abroad. But this too is open to challenge. The problem is not *whether* Soviet designs ought to be thwarted; the debate is over *how* to do it, and about the conception of the world that underlies Kissinger's strategy. To Kissinger, the struggle between Moscow and Washington is not just global in scope, it absorbs, so to speak, every other conflict or issue. Peace, or containment, is therefore indivisible. Every crisis anywhere tests our ability to stand up to the Soviets. And the credibility of the US depends on our capacity to meet every test. Thus, in case after case, Kissinger's policy was to make the Soviets squarely responsible for what was happening, and to act in such a way that they would either put pressure on their clients to cease and desist, or dissociate themselves from their clients.

Is this the real world? Or does it not substitute for the real world an artificially simple and tidy one, in which friends and foes, radicals and moderates are neatly lined up, and in which nationalism—surely as important a force as communism—gets thoroughly discounted? If one sees the world as more complex and fluid than in Kissinger's scheme, if one realizes that most states are not simply the superpowers' proxies—India and Syria are described as waging "proxy wars" for the Soviets—but pursue their own interests, the notion of indivisible credibility and of a strategy geared exclusively to the Soviet Union becomes eminently questionable. A Soviet presence or privileged position is not necessarily permanent. We may have a good reason for being occasionally on the same side as the Soviets in order to prevent them from capturing a cause or movement. And we may have many incentives to deal with Soviet clients while they still are beholden to the Soviets, precisely because they may not want to mortgage their independence, or because their radicalism is rhetorical, or compatible with our concerns. Looking to Moscow for a key (as Kissinger did, in early 1969, when he wanted to send Cyrus Vance there were with a peace plan for Vietnam) can be a mistake. On the other hand, as we discovered in Vietnam, some "proxies" are of such a hostile will of their own that neither Soviet pressure nor Soviet political disengagement helps us much.

Kissinger's conception can thus be criticized in the first place because—

strange as it seems—it limits America's flexibility and may turn into a set of self-fulfilling prophecies. It obliges us to treat practically all unfavorable events as confrontations, and yet it may be very wise to avoid confrontations one can't win—and some situations (as in the Horn of Africa) offer little or no scope for American success. Kissinger wanted us to establish priorities. Yet in his design every incident must be treated seriously, since even if it has no great intrinsic significance, losing the test would encourage our adversary to test us again. But if the Soviets are indeed intent on seizing every good opportunity, why would they fail to exploit one just because we blocked them elsewhere earlier?

To treat countries allied to Moscow (for their own national reasons) merely as Soviet proxies risks tightening their bonds to Moscow (it was Chou En-lai who wisely advised Kissinger to end the Vietnam war rapidly so as to reduce Soviet influence in Indochina), or putting oneself on the losing side (as in the Bangladesh crisis), or missing opportunities (as with Sadat). Indeed, to treat one's own allies as proxies may bring rude awakenings: Thieu, in the last part of 1972, derailed our negotiations by asserting his own interests. And Kissinger has some trouble defending, in a footnote, our friend the Shah's decision to press for high oil prices through OPEC.

Kissinger's conception is one which, in its obsession with Moscow, discounts the internal problems of other countries, and dismisses local circumstances. This is a recipe for disaster. Thus he reduces the Chilean domestic situation of 1969 to a simple choice between revolutionary communism and democracy, either ignoring or misreading the complexities of the Allende coalition and the opposition to it. In 1972, Kissinger refused to support Brandt—who was having trouble getting his *Ostpolitik* treaties through the Bundestag—because the Soviets weren't helpful in Vietnam: had Brandt lost, there would have been a major crisis in US-West German relations (Schmidt has been more generous in trying to help Carter with SALT II).

In the case of Bangladesh, Kissinger blames "the majority of informed opinion" for having "sought to judge the confrontation on the subcontinent on the merits of the issue that had produced the crisis." We had to stay associated with Pakistan because dissociation would have been tantamount "to the US-Soviet condominium so dreaded by Peking." There would therefore have been no Peking summit, and without it there could be no Moscow summit. But the one thing, it seems, we could not do was to ask Yahya Khan to release Mujib, without whom Kissinger's dream of a "peaceful" solution of the Bangladesh problem (after so much bloodshed) was bound to remain a mirage, at Indira Gandhi's mercy. "The merits of the issue" not only produce a crisis: they are also the key to a solution.

The signing by Sadat of a treaty with Moscow was wrongly seen by Kissinger as evidence of Soviet domination and confirmation of the conviction he expressed to Rabin (see the latter's *Memoirs*, p. 201) that no settlement could be concluded without a Soviet-American understanding—on our terms. The geopolitical vision Kissinger advocates looks above all at military balances. Yet in the Middle East, where the US provided huge military assistance to Israel, William Quandt rightly notes that "the military balance proved not to be the key to regional stability and the prevention of war."

Kissinger's conception can be criticized for another reason as well. Like Metternich, he is caught in a contradiction. He seeks an order of restraint, yet his global view obliges him to universal intervention. He wants the Soviets to separate their domestic ideology and practices from their external conduct, yet his very recognition of the fact that "a domestic upheaval in any country can cause a major shift in international alignments" leads him to justify as blatant an intervention in another nation's affairs as the attempt to prevent Allende from becoming president. Indeed, he regrets that the US did not use arms and economic assistance as political weapons earlier and better in Chile. Our failure to do so "transformed us by 1970 from the dominant element of 1964 into a sort of mother hen clucking nervous irrelevancies from the sidelines." Kissinger wants to "shape events in the light of our own purposes"—those events may be another nation's own political life. But of course, in Kissinger's view, nobody's affairs are exclusively his own.

The third criticism arises from the human cost of such a strategy—admittedly a "sentimental" concern. Kissinger's conception turns people into pawns, countries into tools. Kissinger and the CIA encouraged the Kurds to agitate in Iraq so as to divert Iraqi forces from the Arab-Israeli conflict. When, in 1975, the Shah decided to "settle the Kurdish problem with Iraq" (a nice unsentimental euphemism), we approved. Chile's General Schneider was killed as result of a half-comic, half-serious confusion produced by the famous Forty Committee's orders (Frei, the former Chilean president, whom we had financed in the past, refused to play the part Kissinger had assigned to him). And the classic case of a people sacrificed is of course Cambodia. Had we not intervened, Kissinger writes, "Vietnamization and American withdrawal would then come unstuck." "Cambodia was not a moral issue. . . . What we faced was essentially a tactical choice." "Strategically, Cambodia could not be considered a country separate from Vietnam."

This does not mean that Kissinger presents his strategy as amoral: morality is defined as the defense of our values and the resistance to totalitarianism. But this is an ethics of intentions, or purposes, which neglects consequences, and makes of "credibility," in effect, the highest value. Whether a nation ensures its credibility by fighting unwinnable wars, by intervening blatantly in the affairs of others, by turning secondary issues into tests of strength, and by sacrificing others to its design is, at least, an open question. De Gaulle asked Kissinger in 1969 why the U.S. did not leave Vietnam; he answered that "a sudden withdrawal might give us a credibility problem." De Gaulle asked where; Kissinger mentioned the Middle East. "How very odd," de Gaulle replied. "It is precisely in the Middle East that I thought your enemies had the credibility problem."

Indivisible credibility is a recipe for political hubris, military overextension, and moral callousness. "Those without strong values cannot withstand the ambiguities, pressures, and anguish that are inseparable from great responsibility." But "strong values" can apparently carry you anywhere. In Kissinger's conception, the ends justify the means, and the end (in both meanings of the word)—the stable, balanced world where the radicals and the Soviets will have been tamed—is attractive enough to vindicate a great deal of misery on the way. Kissinger wanted to put an end to America's oscillations from one form of idealism—isolation—to another—crusades. But he fails to see both how his division of the world into friends and foes resembles the crusaders' itch to divide it into good and evil, and how the way in which he proposed "to teach our people to face their permanent responsibility" was bound to produce a new swing toward the sentimental liberalism he despises.

If Kissinger's book is, at times, oppressive, it is because the "historian's perspective" he says he brought with him to power is both so grim and so thin. This is a world in which power is all: equilibrium is not just the prerequisite to order, the precondition for justice, it *is* order, it amounts to justice. Inspiration is provided not by an ideal, not by the attractiveness of the outcome—unless one makes a fetish out of a condition (balance)—but by the magnitude of the stakes. Ultimately, it is not surprising if no substantial conception of world order emerges. Religions are poor at describing paradise: it is with this world that they deal. And geopolitics is Kissinger's religion—its god is the balance of power, its dogma is linkage, faith is credibility, the high priest is a United States acting on Henry Kissinger's maxims.

All the flaws in Kissinger's conception come together in his discussion of Vietnam and Cambodia. It fills one-third of the volume. Just as Kissinger's ultimate vision of world order is elusive, he does not begin by telling us what his and Nixon's policy in Vietnam was trying to achieve. He tells us what was to be avoided—we had "the duty" to prove that the North Vietnamese ambition of imposing communist rule (or a fake coalition government) in Saigon was wrong—and what was at stake: "the future of other people depended on their confidence in America." Thus we had to fight on "until Hanoi's perceptions of its possibilities changed." What did this mean?

There were never more than two possible outcomes when Kissinger was in office. One was a victory of Hanoi—either on the battlefield or at the conference table. The other was a defeat of Hanoi—the North Vietnamese accepting in effect the survival of the regime of Saigon, under American protection, just as South Korea has survived since 1953. The fundamental ambiguity in Kissinger's account is revealed when he talks of the agreement negotiated in 1972 as a compromise—which is why, he says, up to the "breakthrough" of October 1972, both sides had rejected his strategy: each one "still yearned for a decisive victory." But a compromise was ultimately impossible, because it was not acceptable in the long run to either side and it could be no more than a lull. Ultimately either Saigon or Hanoi had to be in control.

Consider what Kissinger calls a satisfactory compromise, one with which he was so happy in October 1972 that he pleaded with Nixon to let him sign it almost at once, and did not communicate the text to Thieu until the last moment in the belief that Thieu would be impressed by the magnitude of Hanoi's concessions. What he saw as a compromise provided Saigon not merely with a "decent interval" but with "a decent settlement." Saigon, "generously armed and supported by the United States," could cope with "moderate violations," the US "would stand by to enforce the agreement and punish major violations," Hanoi would be deterred by the prospect of such punishment and the incentives of economic aid. In other words, this was victory—not complete, since Hanoi did not have to withdraw its forces in the South, but it could not reinforce them and they occupied little ground.

The reason for Thieu's fury was not just that "the South Vietnamese after eight years of American participation, simply did not feel ready to confront Hanoi without our direct involvement"—although the reluctance of much of the South Vietnamese population to fight on behalf of the ruling regime had long been a fundamental problem for the US. It is also that Thieu doubted that indirect American involvement would be forthcoming. Kissinger hoped that "joint exertions" between American and South Vietnamese would preserve the peace; he writes that "if doubts as to compliance were to be allowed to block a satisfactory agreement, then the war would never come to a negotiated end." But doubts were justified, both about compliance (by either Saigon or Hanoi), and about American's willingness permanently to act as policeman to exact compliance from Hanoi. Here again Watergate—and the decline in support for Nixon's Vietnam policy that accompanied it—serves Kissinger as a convenient excuse for failure.

But even without Watergate, there was no justification for believing that an agreement that "depended on the vigor with which it was enforced" could rely on the only effective deterrent: the certainty of US forces reintervening. Nixon promised this to Thieu, but it was not credible even before Watergate. For years Congress had been trying to accelerate America's withdrawal; the two escalations of 1972, which involved no ground forces, provoked storms at home; Vietnamization had been an attempt to meet such criticisms (in vain).

Kissinger condemns those domestic upheavals throughout his book. Either he knew that the internal balance of forces in US politics would not allow the US to restore the external one in South Vietnam if there were a violation by Hanoi, in which case Thieu's suspicions would be justified, and the agreement was no more than a time- and face-saving charade. Or else (and this is undoubtedly the case) he once again underestimated domestic battle fatigue, misjudged his ability to make Americans believe that their standing in the world depended on their persistence in a hopeless undertaking, and absurdly overestimated Nixon's capacity to repeat in the future the temporary rescue of Saigon in 1972.

When, after Thieu's request for sixty-three changes in the agreement, Hanoi in turn reopened many issues (with the rather obvious aim of forcing the US to return to the October text), Kissinger concluded that "they have not in any way abandoned their objectives or ambitions with respect to South Vietnam" (report to Nixon). How could he have believed they had, and if they hadn't, could he believe that "reestablishing a better balance of risks" (another euphemism for bombing) would be available forever?

The Christmas bombing may not have been the horror some critics denounced at the time; nevertheless it killed at least hundreds of people simply because Thieu needed time and a psychological lift that would enable him to sign at last. Returning to the October test after Thieu had so violently rejected it would have been "tantamount to wrecking the South Vietnamese government." Kissinger writes that "though I considered the agreement a good one" in October, "intervening events would turn acceptance of it into a debacle." This was a bloody charade—we got Hanoi to accept trivial changes that made no difference at all in the end.

Is one more "credible" for recognizing the inevitable early, and cutting one's losses, or for pursuing a futile course, escalating not only the means but the stakes, and adding to the sufferings which the winner was going to impose at the end, those inflicted by the attempt to delay his inevitable victory? When Kissinger finally obtained the separation of Peking and Moscow from Hanoi, what the China initiative had started was completed: he had "reduced Indo-China to its proper scale—a small peninsula on a major continent." Yet even then he acted as if American credibility demanded the vindication of the policies we had pursued from Eisenhower to LBJ, just as his geopolitical design was meant to be an apotheosis of containment.

There are bad places for a fight. In Vietnam, we (and the hapless South Vietnamese) never had a good alternative. We could "bug out," either unilaterally or by negotiating a "coalition" formula to save some face. Or we could dig in and stick to our protégé in order to reassure our other allies—but our enemy would still be there, unless we destroyed him completely, something our values, as well as our calculation of risks, prevented us from doing. And in the meantime the futility of the effort would ensure that we'd look for a way out. At the end, the "honor" we had saved in 1973 was "lost" in 1975. Although Kissinger proclaims that "the security of free peoples everywhere would [have been] jeopardized by an essentially narcissistic act of abdication," our allies were less than delighted to see what we were doing for them. They doubted its worth, and they feared that our exertions in this dubious cause might drain us of energy for better ones. In Vietnam, geopolitics were against us, and neither linkage nor dissociation could help.

Having however declared our policy moral, and all alternatives immoral as well as geopolitically dangerous, Kissinger can indeed affirm that he had little choice when the Cambodian crisis of 1970 broke out. There is a mad logic at work here. The new Nixon-Kissinger strategy, aimed at the same old objective of saving Saigon, entailed a greater willingness to use force outside South Vietnam (remember Kissinger's strictures against gradualism). And it also entailed Vietnamization: the combination of American withdrawals and South Vietnamese build-up. Cambodia, whose neutrality had been dented by Hanoi (as had that of Laos)—no one denies it—was the natural victim of these changes. As early as January 8, Nixon ordered a report on "what, if anything, we are doing to destroy the buildup there": the secret bombing was at least as much caused by this desire to loosen old constraints as by the North Vietnamese offensive at the end of February 1969.

The bombing did, as William Shawcross has shown [in *Sideshow*, 1979], begin to undermine Sihanouk. Kissinger denies what General Abrams has acknowledged to a Senate Committee: the bombing and other operations started pushing the North Vietnamese deeper into Cambodia. When Lon Nol's coup occurred, the North Vietnamese, and Peking, tried to get an agreement from Lon Nol about the sanctuaries. Even though no direct aid was provided to him for several weeks, according to Kissinger, Lon Nol's ultimate intransigence must have had something to do with an expectation of American support.

On the other hand, Nixon authorized (contrary to Kissinger's wishes, he tells us) South Vietnamese attacks across the border; and several Khmer units trained in Vietnam were "launched on a grand scale into Cambodia." The North Vietnamese started moving westward. They must have known that the American command in Saigon was preparing an attack against one of the sanctuaries. Kissinger minimizes the importance of the South Vietnamese raids. When he says that "there had been no consideration of attacking the sanctuaries before April 21," he surely does not mean in Saigon, as is shown in the memo to Nixon which he quoted in an earlier version of his book and then removed. He claims that the North Vietnamese were threatening Phnom Penh, and that Sihanouk, by "effectively declaring war on the new government," had ceased to be a possible alternative: his "return would have meant not a restoration of neutrality but the victory of his new communist patrons, whom he had lost all capacity to control." But it was not to the North Vietnamese advantage to take charge of a vast and unfriendly country (in which Lon Nol was fostering massacres of Vietnamese); it was in their interest to have in power someone who would let them maintain their line of communication and their sanctuaries.

What made it impossible for us to deal with Sihanouk was neither Le Duc Tho's rhetoric (which supported Sihanouk) nor Sihanouk's alliance with his communist ex-foes but our "geopolitical" notion that whoever sides with the communists must be opposed, and above all the requirements of Vietnamization. The North Vietnamese in Cambodia were threatening a vital part of South Vietnam; we had to withdraw without endangering Saigon's survival; Nixon had expressed anger at the existence of the sanctuaries from the beginning. The fall of Sihanouk and the westward moves of the North Vietnamese provided the opportunity to embroil them in Cambodia—by our helping Lon Nol, as Nixon wanted to do almost at once—as well as the opportunity to hit them from South Vietnam.

For America's strategy, a restoration of Sihanouk under North Vietnamese "protection" would have been a major setback. But for the Cambodian people, it would have provided a far better alternative than the war that ravaged the country and allowed, at the end, the Khmer Rouge—not the North Vietnamese—to take over. In 1970, the Khmer Rouge were a handful, with no prospects of power. Kissinger several times attributes the devastation of Cambodia to the U.S. opponents of the war, who crippled the scope of US military assistance legally available for Lon Nol, and thus obliged the Cambodian forces "to rely on our planes as their only strategic reserve."

But he does not include in his account what Shawcross stressed: that it was Kissinger who chose the most ambitious strategic option for the war in Cambodia, and got it approved by the National Security Council in October 1970. This strategy, designed to help Vietnamization, became a liability, both because of Lon Nol's incompetence and because the South Vietnamese, to whom the departing Americans were entrusting ever bigger missions, had to overstretch their resources to keep the North Vietnamese from taking over Cambodia. Our way of helping "free Cambodia" by relentlessly destructive bombing for several years prolonged the agony and did much to prepare for Pol Pot's rule. Kissinger may be right in saying that the Nixon administration had inherited the war in Vietnam. But not only did it accept the legacy, it extended the war to Cambodia.

The same geopolitical needs, global and local, kept Kissinger from trying to deal with Sihanouk before the peace agreement in Vietnam (and, as Shawcross shows, not much more actively later): "negotiations with him could not succeed so long as he was titular head of the communist force, insisting on total victory." He "could not resume his pre-1970 balancing role unless there were two parties left to balance." But by 1973, Sihanouk could not have returned except as head of the anti-Lon Nol forces (which would have been far better for the Cambodians than Pol Pot). We remained inhibited both by the belief that the North Vietnamese could somehow "deliver" the Khmer Rouge—it took Kissinger a long time to recognize that their relation to Hanoi was rather like that of Hanoi to Peking—and by the fear that a negotiation with Sihanouk while the war in Cambodia persisted could undermine the shaky regime in Phnom Penh, and perhaps by the belief that a continuing war in Cambodia might provide relief for our ally in Saigon. Thus, as in Saigon, we stuck to our client, and encouraged him to persist; but in Cambodia we could not even obtain a cease-fire.

External triumphs destroyed by domestic tragedy: a president's weird character, an irresponsible Congress. This is one of the main themes of this volume, and it will undoubtedly be the thread of its successor. But the questions Kissinger's relentless and impressive work leaves in the reader's mind are quite different. To what extent were the successes proof of the validity of Kissinger's "geopolitical" design? Was the détente of 1972 a vindication of his approach, or a passing episode? Was it only an attempt by Brezhnev "to calm the threat from Russia's Western past so that he could deal with its Chinese future," rather than an assent to Kissinger's theory of linkages, networks, rewards, and penalties?

Was the China summit a triumph of triangular diplomacy, or a delicate marriage of convenience, in which one of the partners wants a far closer embrace than the other deems in his interest, although he may have to submit to it lest the more ardent partner should feel jilted and resume a flirtation with their mutual enemy? How wise was American policy in the Middle East and in Iran during those years? Was the colossal effort to find an "honorable" way out of Vietnam proportional to the result? Also, was the pursuit of so single-minded and intense a policy compatible with America's institutions, and if not, what were the alternatives open to us? Kissinger, immersed in tactics, recounting the bureaucratic battles, and imperturbable in his reading of history, does not raise these questions.

✠ FURTHER READING

Robert J. Alexander, *The Tragedy of Chile* (1978)
Stephen Ambrose, *Nixon* (1987)
Richard J. Barnet, *The Giants* (1977)
———, *The Lean Years* (1980)
Coral Bell, *The Diplomacy of Détente* (1977)
Henry Brandon, *The Retreat of American Power* (1973)
Seyom Brown, *The Faces of Power* (1983)
Dan Caldwell, ed., *Henry Kissinger* (1983)
David Calleo, *The Imperious Economy* (1982)
Thomas M. Franck and Edward Weisband, *Foreign Policy by Congress* (1979)
Edward Friedland et al., *The Great Détente Disaster* (1975)
John L. Gaddis, *Strategies of Containment* (1982)
Lloyd C. Gardner, ed., *The Great Nixon Turnaround* (1973)
Raymond Garthoff, *Détente and Confrontation* (1985)
Charles Gati and Toby Trister Gati, *The Debate over Détente* (1977)
Matti Golan, *The Secret Conversations of Henry Kissinger* (1976)
Stephen Graubard, *Kissinger: Portrait of a Mind* (1973)
Seymour M. Hersh, *The Price of Power: Kissinger in the White House* (1983)
Stanley Hoffmann, *Primacy or World Order* (1978)
———, "The Return of Henry Kissinger," *New York Review of Books*, 29 (April 29, 1982), 14ff
William G. Hyland, *Mortal Rivals* (1987)
Robert C. Johansen, *The National Interest and the Human Interest* (1980)
Loch K. Johnson, *A Season of Inquiry: The Senate Intelligence Investigation* (1985)
Bernard Kalb and Marvin Kalb, *Kissinger* (1974)
David Landau, *Kissinger: Uses of Power* (1972)
Thomas B. Larson, *Soviet-American Rivalry* (1978)
Robert S. Litwak, *Détente and the Nixon Doctrine* (1984)
Michael Mandelbaum, *The Nuclear Question* (1979)
Roger Morris, *Uncertain Greatness: Henry Kissinger and American Foreign Policy* (1977)
Fred Warner Neal, ed., *Détente or Debacle* (1979)
John Newhouse, *Cold Dawn: The Story of SALT* (1973)
James Petras and Morris Morley, *The United States and Chile* (1975)
Richard Pipes, *U.S.-Soviet Relations in the Era of Détente* (1981)
Robert D. Schulzinger, "The Naive and Sentimental Diplomat: Henry Kissinger's Memoirs," *Diplomatic History*, 4 (1980), 303–15
Edward R. F. Sheehan, *The Arabs, Israelis, and Kissinger* (1976)
Paul E. Sigmund, *The Overthrow of Allende and the Politics of Chile, 1964–1976* (1977)
Lewis Sorley, *Arms Transfers Under Nixon* (1983)
Harvey Starr, *Henry Kissinger* (1984)
Richard Stevenson, *The Rise and Fall of Détente* (1985)
Tad Szulc, "How Kissinger Did It: Behind the Vietnam Cease-Fire Agreement," *Foreign Policy*, No. 15 (1974), 21–61
———, *The Illusion of Peace* (1978)
Adam B. Ulam, *Dangerous Relations: The Soviet Union in World Politics, 1970–1982* (1983)
Garry Wills, *Nixon Agonistes* (1970)

Carter, Reagan, Cold War, and Global Crisis

After the Vietnam tragedy, the waning of détente, and Watergate, Presidents Jimmy Carter and Ronald Reagan pledged to revive American prestige and power. Carter initially emphasized human rights, attention to long-range, global questions like the environment and the law of the sea, negotiations rather than military interventions, and the importance of seeing Third World issues as North-South, rather than East-West, problems. He continued the process toward stronger nuclear arms controls and a negotiated peace in the Middle East. The Carter administration, often utilizing the President's personalized diplomacy, achieved an Egyptian-Israeli accord, the Panama Canal treaties, normalization of relations with the People's Republic of China, improved relations with the Third World, and the SALT-II agreement, although the Senate did not approve the last. But by the time Carter left office in early 1981, the Cold War had come once again to dominate American foreign policy. Soviet-American relations deteriorated badly, and, after the Soviet invasion of Afghanistan, the containment doctrine was refurbished as the Carter Doctrine. The Carter administration negotiated the placement of American Pershing II and cruise missiles in NATO nations. Overall, Carter failed to satisfy many of his goals, and, handicapped by the Iranian hostage crisis and bureaucratic infighting that made his administration look immobilized and confused, he lost the 1980 election to Ronald Reagan.

In the 1980 campaign, Reagan charged that Carter had let American power, especially its military power, slip. Beginning with denunciations of Soviet imperialism in raw anti-Communist rhetoric, huge increases in military expenditures, and super-patriotic declarations about America's "reawakening," the Reagan administration revitalized the Cold War even more. Blaming most of the world's troubles on the Soviet Union, Reagan discouraged arms control talks, stepped up American support for anti-Communist groups abroad under the Reagan Doctrine, and tied foreign aid to other nations' willingness to embrace private-enterprise capitalism. The expansion and use of the military and a preference for military solutions—sending the Marines to Lebanon, bombing raids on Libya, the contra *war against Nicaragua, the invasion of Grenada, the Strategic Defense Initiative, and the largest military budget in peacetime history, to name a few examples—meant that the Reagan Administration enjoyed very few diplomatic successes (the treaty on eliminating intermediate nuclear forces in Europe being the major exception). United States relations with the Third World plummeted, America's domestic budget and foreign trade deficits climbed dangerously, and a global economic crisis marked by Third World debt, famine, and trade wars threatened world order. Near the end of his second term, Reagan was rocked by the Iran-contra scandal. All the while, he claimed that America had restored its stature, that Americans were once again "standing tall." Critics complained that the administration had ignored seething global issues that portended a dark future not only for international stability but also for American well-being at home and influence abroad.*

This chapter studies the Carter and Reagan records, but it also explores fundamental questions of Cold War, global crisis, world order, and the decline of American power in the complex international system of the 1970s and 1980s. Was bipolarity the best insurance for international stability? Did nuclear deterrence actually serve rather than undermine world peace? Or was the escalating nuclear arms race destabilizing? Was the Soviet-American relationship the central feature of world politics? Or had North-South—Third World—questions become the most compelling? That is, were the superpowers capable of managing world conflict? And if, as most observers agree, the United States declined in the Carter and Reagan years, losing the hegemonic power it once held, how do we explain this change? inexorable international factors beyond the nation's control? domestic economic stagnation? Soviet malevolence? an abandonment of basic American principles that has robbed the United States of support abroad? defeatism, timidity, or subversion on the part of some Americans? a penchant for interventionism and military power that has overreached American capabilities and resources? or some other reason? The debate among scholars is lively and revealing; it seems, however, that American leaders pay more attention to immediate, day-to-day matters and crises than to the systemic, structural, or long-term sources of the United States's troubled place in the world community.

�֎ D O C U M E N T S

During the 1976 presidential campaign between Democrat Jimmy Carter and Republican President Gerald Ford, Henry Kissinger's foreign policy and America's post-Vietnam international standing became subjects of heated political controversy. In the first document, a portion of the October 7, 1976, televised presidential debate between the two candidates, Carter lambasted the Nixon-Kissinger-Ford record and forecast some of the themes that would characterize his own administration. The second document, a speech to the nation on July 15, 1979, represented Carter's rather agonized reading of what ailed America—a "crisis of confidence." The next selection is the Carter Doctrine, announced in the President's State of the Union Address of January 23, 1980. The fourth document, a portion of Ronald Reagan's speech to the Republican National Convention on July 17, 1980, after he won his party's nomination, scorned the Carter administration for "weakness" and "vacillation." He explained the Reagan Doctrine, the next document, in the State of the Union Address of February 6, 1985, among other places. The last document, from a Reagan speech of February 26, 1986, reveals the President's emphasis on restoration and military power as the best means to meet the Soviet threat.

Jimmy Carter's Critique of the
Nixon-Ford-Kissinger Foreign Policy, 1976

Our country is not strong anymore; we're not respected anymore. We can only be strong overseas if we're strong at home, and when I become President we will not only be strong in those areas but also in defense—a defense capability second to none.

We've lost in our foreign policy the character of the American people. We've ignored or excluded the American people and the Congress from participation in the shaping of our foreign policy. It's been one of secrecy and exclusion. In addition to that we've had a chance to become now—contrary to our longstanding beliefs and principles—the arms merchant of the whole world. We've tried to buy success from our enemies, and at the same time we've excluded from the process the normal friendship of our allies.

In addition to that we've become fearful to compete with the Soviet Union on an equal basis. We talk about détente. The Soviet Union knows what they want in détente, and they've been getting it. We have not known what we wanted, and we've been outtraded in almost every instance. . . .

What we were formerly so proud of—the strength of our country, its moral integrity, the representation in foreign affairs of what our people or what our Constitution stands for—has been gone. And in the secrecy that has surrounded our foreign policy in the last few years, the American [people] and the Congress have been excluded. . . .

We've seen in the past the destruction of elected Governments, like in Chile, and the strong support of military dictatorship there. These kinds of things have hurt us very much. . . .

I notice that Mr. Ford didn't comment on the prisons in Chile. This is a typical example, maybe of many others, that this Administration overthrew an elected government and helped to establish a military dictatorship.

This has not been an ancient history story. Last year under Mr. Ford, of all the Food for Peace that went to South America, 85 percent went to the military dictatorship in Chile.

Another point I want to make is this. He said we have to move from one area of the world to another. That's one of the problems with this Administration's so-called shuttle diplomacy. While the Secretary of State's in one country, there are almost 150 others that are wondering what we're going to do next, what will be the next secret agreement. We don't have a comprehensive understandable foreign policy that deals with world problems or even regional problems. . . .

This election will also determine what kind of world we leave our children. Will it be a nightmare world threatened with the proliferation of atomic bombs, not just in five major countries but dozens of smaller countries that have been permitted to develop atomic weapons because of a failure of our top leadership to stop proliferation?

Will we have a world of hunger and hatred and will we be living in an arms camp stripped of our friendship and allies, hiding behind a tight defense that's been drawn around us because we are fearful of the outside world?

Will we have a government of secrecy that excludes the American people from participation in making basic decisions and therefore covers up mistakes and makes it possible for our government—our government—to depart from the principles of our Constitution and Bill of Rights?

Or will we have a world of peace with the threat of atomic weapons eliminated, with full trade, with our people at work, inflation controlled, openness in government, our people proud once again, Congress, citizens, President, Secretary of State working in harmony and unity toward a common future? Or will our people have enough to eat and a world where we care about those who don't? Can be become breadbasket of the world instead of the arms merchant of the world? . . .

I want to see our nation return to a posture and an image and a standard to make us proud once again. I remember the world of NATO and the world of Point Four and the world of the Marshall Plan and the world of the Peace Corps. Why can't we have that once again? We ought to be a beacon for nations who search for peace and who search for freedom, who search for individual liberty, who search for basic human rights. We haven't been lately. We can be once again.

We'll never have that world leadership until we are strong at home, and we can have that strength if we return to the basic principles.

It ought not to be a strength of bombast and threats. It ought to be a quiet strength based on the integrity of our people, the vision of the Constitution and in a strong will and purpose that God's given us in the greatest nation on earth—the United States.

Carter on the "Crisis of Confidence," 1979

Ten days ago I had planned to speak to you again about a very important subject—energy. For the fifth time I would have described the urgency of the problem and laid out a series of legislative recommendations to the Congress. But as I was preparing to speak, I began to ask myself the same question that I now know has been troubling many of you. Why have we not been able to get together as a nation to resolve our serious energy problem?

It's clear that the true problems of our Nation are much deeper—deeper than gasoline lines or energy shortages, deeper even than inflation or recession. And I realize more than ever that as President I need your help. So, I decided to reach out and listen to the voices of America.

I invited to Camp David people from almost every segment of our society—business and labor, teachers and preachers, Governors, mayors, and private citizens. And then I left Camp David to listen to other Americans, men and women like you. . . .

These 10 days confirmed my belief in the decency and the strength and the wisdom of the American people, but it also bore out some of my longstanding concerns about our Nation's underlying problems.

I know, of course, being President, that government actions and legislation can be very important. That's why I've worked hard to put my campaign promises into law—and I have to admit, with just mixed success. But after listening to the American people I have been reminded again that all the legislation in the world can't fix what's wrong with America. So, I want to speak to you first tonight about a subject even more serious than energy or inflation. I want to talk to you right now about a fundamental threat to American democracy.

I do not mean our political and civil liberties. They will endure. And I do not refer to the outward strength of America, a nation that is at peace tonight everywhere in the world, with unmatched economic power and military might.

The threat is nearly invisible in ordinary ways. It is a crisis of confidence. It is a crisis that strikes at the very heart and soul and spirit of our national will. We can see this crisis in the growing doubt about the meaning of our own lives and in the loss of a unity of purpose of our Nation.

The erosion of our confidence in the future is threatening to destroy the social and the political fabric of America.

The confidence that we have always had as a people is not simply some romantic dream or a proverb in a dusty book that we read just on the Fourth of July. It is the idea which founded our Nation and has guided our development as a people. Confidence in the future has supported everything else—public institutions and private enterprise, our own families, and the very Constitution of the United States. Confidence has defined our course and has served as a link between generations. We've always believed in something called progress. We've always had a faith that the days of our children would be better than our own.

Our people are losing that faith, not only in government itself but in the ability as citizens to serve as the ultimate rulers and shapers of our democracy. As a people we know our past and we are proud of it. Our progress has been part of the living history of America, even the world. We always believed that we were part of a great movement of humanity itself called democracy, involved in the search for freedom, and that belief has always strengthened us in our purpose. But just as we are losing our confidence in the future, we are also beginning to close the door on our past.

In a nation that was proud of hard work, strong families, close-knit communities, and our faith in God, too many of us now tend to worship self-indulgence and consumption. Human identity is no longer defined by what one does, but by what one owns. But we've discovered that owning things and consuming things does not satisfy our longing for meaning. We've learned that piling up material goods cannot fill the emptiness of lives which have no confidence or purpose.

The symptoms of this crisis of the American spirit are all around us. For the first time in the history of our country a majority of our people believe that the next 5 years will be worse than the past 5 years. Two-thirds of our people do not even vote. The productivity of American workers is actually dropping, and the willingness of Americans to save for the future has fallen below that of all other people in the Western world.

As you know, there is a growing disrespect for government and for churches and for schools, the news media, and other institutions. This is not a message of happiness or reassurance, but it is the truth and it is a warning.

These changes did not happen overnight. They've come upon us gradually over the last generation, years that were filled with shocks and tragedy.

We were sure that ours was a nation of the ballot, not the bullet, until the murders of John Kennedy and Robert Kennedy and Martin Luther King, Jr. We were taught that our armies were always invincible and our causes were always just, only to suffer the agony of Vietnam. We respected the Presidency as a place of honor until the shock of Watergate.

We remember when the phrase "sound as a dollar" was an expression of absolute dependability, until 10 years of inflation began to shrink our dollar and our savings. We believed that our Nation's resources were limitless until 1973, when we had to face a growing dependence on foreign oil.

These wounds are still very deep. They have never been healed.

Looking for a way out of this crisis, our people have turned to the Federal Government and found it isolated from the mainstream of our Nation's life. Washington, D.C., has become an island. The gap between our citizens and our Government has never been so wide. The people are looking for honest answers, not easy answers; clear leadership, not false claims and evasiveness and politics as usual.

What you see too often in Washington and elsewhere around the country is a system of government that seems incapable of action. You see a Congress twisted and pulled in every direction by hundreds of well-financed and powerful special interests. You see every extreme position defended to the last vote, almost to the last breath by one unyielding group or another. You often see a balanced and a fair approach that demands sacrifice, a little sacrifice from everyone, abandoned like an orphan without support and without friends.

Often you see paralysis and stagnation and drift. You don't like it, and neither do I. What can we do?

First of all, we must face the truth, and than we can change our course. We simply must have faith in each other, faith in our ability to govern ourselves, and faith in the future of this Nation. Restoring that faith and that confidence to America is now the most important task we face. It is a true challenge of this generation of Americans.

One of the visitors to Camp David last week put it this way: "We've got to stop crying and start sweating, stop talking and start walking, stop cursing and start praying. The strength we need will not come from the White House, but from every house in America."

We know the strength of America. We are strong. We can regain our unity. We can regain our confidence. We are the heirs of generations who survived threats much more powerful and awesome than those that challenge us now. Our fathers and mothers were strong men and women who shaped a new society during the Great Depression, who fought world wars, and who carved out a new charter of peace for the world.

We ourselves are the same Americans who just 10 years ago put a man on the Moon. We are the generation that dedicated our society to the pursuit of human rights and equality. And we are the generation that will win the war on the energy problem and in that process rebuild the unity and confidence of America.

We are at a turning point in our history. There are two paths to choose. One is a path I've warned about tonight, the path that leads to fragmentation and self-interest. Down that road lies a mistaken idea of freedom, the right to grasp for ourselves some advantage over others. That path would be one of constant conflict between narrow interests ending in chaos and immobility. It is a certain route to failure.

All the traditions of our past, all the lessons of our heritage, all the promises of our future point to another path, the path of common purpose and the restoration of American values. That path leads to true freedom for our Nation and ourselves. We can take the first steps down that path as we begin to solve our energy problem.

Energy will be the immediate test of our ability to unite this Nation, and it can also be the standard around which we rally. On the battlefield of energy we can win for our Nation a new confidence, and we can seize control again of our common destiny.

In little more than two decades we've gone from a position of energy independence to one in which almost half the oil we use comes from foreign countries, at prices that are going through the roof. Our excessive dependence on OPEC has already taken a tremendous toll on our economy and our people. This is the direct cause of the long lines which have made millions of you spend aggravating hours waiting for gasoline. It's a cause of the increased inflation and unemployment that we now face. This intolerable dependence on foreign oil threatens our economic independence and the very security of our Nation.

The energy crisis is real. It is worldwide. It is a clear and present danger to our Nation. These are facts and we simply must face them. . . .

In closing, let me say this: I will do my best, but I will not do it alone. Let your voice be heard. Whenever you have a chance, say something good about our country. With God's help and for the sake of our Nation, it is time for us to join hands in America. Let us commit ourselves together to a rebirth of the American spirit. Working together with our common faith we cannot fail.

The Carter Doctrine, 1980

An attempt by any outside force to gain control of the Persian Gulf region will be regarded as an assault on the vital interests of the United States of America, and such an assault will be repelled by any means necessary, including military force.

Ronald Reagan's Critique
of Carter's Foreign Policy, 1980

A Soviet combat brigade trains in Cuba, just 90 miles from our shores.

A Soviet army of invasion occupies Afghanistan, further threatening our vital interests in the Middle East.

America's defense strength is at its lowest ebb in a generation, while the Soviet Union is vastly outspending us in both strategic and conventional arms.

Our European allies, looking nervously at the growing menace from the East, turn to us for leadership and fail to find it.

And incredibly, more than 50, as you've been told from this platform so eloquently already, more than 50 of our fellow Americans have been held captive for over eight years—eight months—by a dictatorial foreign power that holds us up to ridicule before the world.

Adversaries large and small test our will and seek to confound our resolve, but we are given weakness when we need strength, vacillation when the times demand firmness. . . .

You know, there may be a sailor at the helm of the ship of state, but the ship has no rudder. Critical decisions are made at times almost in comic fashion, but who can laugh?

Who was not embarrassed when the Administration handed a major propaganda victory in the United Nations to the enemies of Israel, our staunch Middle East ally for three decades, and then claimed that the American vote was a "mistake," the result of a "failure of communication" between the President, his Secretary of State and his U.N. Ambassador?

Who does not feel a growing sense of unease as our allies, facing repeated instances of an amateurish and confused Administration, reluctantly conclude that America is unwilling or unable to fulfill its obligations as leader of the free world?

Who does not feel rising alarm when the question in any discussion of foreign policy is no longer, "Should we do something?" but "Do we have the capacity to do anything?"

The Administration which has brought us to this state is seeking your endorsement for four more years of weakness, indecision, mediocrity and incompetence. No. No. No American should vote until he or she has asked: Is the United States stronger and more respected now than it was three-and-a-half years ago? Is the world safer, a safer place in which to live?

It is the responsibility of the President of the United States, in working for peace, to insure that the safety of our people cannot successfully be threatened by a hostile foreign power. As President, fulfilling that responsibility will be my No. 1 priority.

We're not a warlike people. Quite the opposite. We always seek to live in peace. We resort to force infrequently and with great reluctance— and only after we've determined that is is absolutely necessary. We are awed—and rightly so—by the forces of destruction at loose in the world in this nuclear era.

But neither can we be naive or foolish. Four times in my lifetime

America has gone to war, bleeding the lives of its young men into the sands of island beachheads, the fields of Europe and the jungles and rice paddies of Asia. We know only too well that war comes not when the forces of freedom are strong. It is when they are weak that tyrants are tempted.

We simply cannot learn these lessons the hard way again without risking our destruction.

Of all the objectives we seek, first and foremost is the establishment of lasting world peace. We must always stand ready to negotiate in good faith, ready to pursue any reasonable avenue that holds forth the promise of lessening tensions and furthering the prospects of peace. But let our friends and those who may wish us ill take note: the United States has an obligation to its citizens and to the people of the world never to let those who would destroy freedom dictate the future course of life on this planet. I would regard my election as proof that we have renewed our resolve to preserve world peace and freedom. That this nation will once again be strong enough to do that. . . .

Everywhere we've met thousands of Democrats, Independents and Republicans from all economic conditions, walks of life bound together in that community of shared values of family, work, neighborhood, peace and freedom. They are concerned, yes, they're not frightened. They're disturbed, but not dismayed. They are the kind of men and women Tom Paine had in mind when he wrote, during the darkest days of the American Revolution. "We have it in our power to begin the world over again."

Nearly 150 years after Tom Paine wrote those words, an American President told the generation of the Great Depression that it had a "rendezvous with destiny." I believe this generation of Americans today also has a rendezvous with destiny. . . .

I have thought of something that's not a part of my speech and worried over whether I should do it. Can we doubt that only a Divine Providence placed this land, this island of freedom, here as a refuge for all those people in the world who yearn to breathe free? Jews and Christians enduring persecution behind the Iron Curtain; the boat people of Southeast Asia, Cuba and of Haiti; the victims of drought and famine in Africa, the freedom fighters in Afghanistan, and our own countrymen held in savage captivity.

I'll confess that I've been a little afraid to suggest what I'm going to suggest. I'm more afraid not to. Can we begin our crusade joined together in a moment of silent prayer?

God Bless America.

The Reagan Doctrine, 1985

We must stand by all our democratic allies. And we must not break faith with those who are risking their lives—on every continent, from Afghanistan to Nicaragua—to defy Soviet-supported aggression and secure rights which have been ours from birth.

The Sandinista dictatorship of Nicaragua, with full Cuban-Soviet bloc support, not only persecutes its people, the church, and denies a free press but arms and provides bases for communist terrorists attacking neighboring states. Support for freedom fighters is self-defense and totally consistent with the OAS and UN Charters. It is essential that the Congress continue all facets of our assistance to Central America. I want to work with you to support the democratic forces whose struggle is tied to our own security.

Reagan on the Rebuilding of American Military Power, 1986

We know that peace is the condition under which mankind was meant to flourish. Yet, peace does not exist of its own will. It depends on us—on our courage to build it and guard it and pass it on to future generations. George Washington's words may seem hard and cold today, but history has proven him right again and again: "To be prepared for war," he said, "is one of the most effective means of preserving peace." Well, to those who think strength provokes conflict, Will Rogers had his own answer. He said of the world heavyweight champion of his day: "I've never seen anyone insult Jack Dempsey."

The past 5 years have shown that American strength is once again a sheltering arm for freedom in a dangerous world. Strength is the most persuasive argument we have to convince our adversaries to negotiate seriously and to cease bullying other nations. . . .

We need to remember where America was 5 years ago. We need to recall the atmosphere of that time—the anxiety that events were out of control, that the West was in decline, that our enemies were on the march. It was not just the Iranian hostage crisis or the Soviet invasion of Afghanistan, but the fear, felt by many of our friends, that America could not, or would not, keep her commitments. Pakistan, the country most threatened by the Afghan invasion, ridiculed the first offer of American aid as "peanuts." Other nations were saying that it was dangerous—deadly dangerous—to be a friend of the United States.

It was not just years of declining defense spending but a crisis in recruitment and retention and the outright cancellation of programs vital to our security. The Pentagon horror stories at the time were about ships that couldn't sail, planes that couldn't fly for lack of spare parts, and army divisions unprepared to fight.

And it was not just a one-sided arms agreement that made it easy for one side to cheat, but a treaty that actually permitted increases in nuclear arsenals. Even supporters of SALT II [strategic arms limitation talks] were demoralized, saying, well, the Soviets just won't agree to anything better. . . .

We set out to narrow the growing gaps in our strategic deterrent. And we're beginning to do that. Our modernization program—the MX, the Trident submarine, the B-1 and Stealth bombers—represents the first significant improvement in America's strategic deterrent in 20 years.

Those who speak so often about the so-called arms race ignore a central fact: in the decade before 1981, the Soviets were the only ones racing. . . .

Finally, we've set out to reduce the danger of nuclear war. Here, too, we're achieving what some said couldn't be done. We've put forth a plan for deep reductions in nuclear systems; we're pushing forward our highly promising Strategic Defense Initiative (SDI)—a security shield that may one day protect us and our allies from nuclear attack, whether launched by deliberate calculation, freak accident, or the isolated impulse of a madman. Isn't it better to use our talents and technology to build systems that destroy missiles, not people?

Our message has gotten through. The Soviets used to contend that real reductions in nuclear missiles were out of the question. Now, they say they accept the idea. Well, we shall see. Just this week, our negotiators presented a new plan for the elimination of intermediate-range nuclear missiles, and we're pressing the Soviets for cuts in other offensive forces as well. One thing is certain: if the Soviets truly want fair and verifiable agreements that reduce nuclear forces, we will have those agreements.

✖ *E S S A Y S*

In the first essay, John Lewis Gaddis of Ohio University points to the absence of a world war since 1945. He attributes this Cold War "long peace" to several characteristics of the postwar international system, including bipolarity and the nuclear deterrent. In the second selection, a critique of Carter's foreign policy, Stanley Hoffmann of Harvard University believes that the "simplicities of Cold War containment and bipolarity" to which Carter succumbed rest at the very heart of America's struggle to devise a new strategy for a world of diffused power. In the third essay, George W. Ball, a high-ranking policymaker in the Kennedy and Johnson administrations, searches for why, by the mid-1980s, United States influence and prestige had waned and Soviet-American relations had turned so sour. He scrutinizes, in particular, Reagan's policy toward the Middle East and nuclear arms. The last selection, by Paul Kennedy of Yale University, takes a broad look at America's relative decline by comparing the U.S. experience to that of hegemonic powers of the past. Domestic and foreign problems generated by "imperial overstretch," he argues, have sorely burdened the nation. Still, as all of the authors agree, the United States remains a superpower with impressive resources. The question of how that power will be used and protected to ensure American prosperity and security became—and remains— the major problem for the nation's leaders as they look toward the twenty-first century.

The Long Peace: Stability in the International System

JOHN LEWIS GADDIS

The fortieth anniversary of the end of World War II, and, simultaneously, of the beginning of the Cold War as well, was greeted in some circles with an odd sense of surprise that we were still around to celebrate it. Recognition

Originally published as "The Long Peace: Elements of Stability and Instability in the Postwar International System," in *The Future of U.S.-U.S.S.R. Relations: Lessons from Forty Years without World War*, ed. Robert K. German (Austin: Lyndon B. Johnson School of Public Affairs, University of Texas at Austin, 1986), pp. 39–45.

had begun to dawn that four decades of superpower rivalry without superpower war is an impressive, if unanticipated, development; that the international system set in place so haphazardly and arbitrarily in 1945 has evolved into one stable enough to bear comparison, in longevity at least, to the great and now wistfully recalled nineteenth-century systems of Bismarck and Metternich. Without realizing it, without having set out in any conscious way to achieve it, the great powers have managed somehow to construct an international order that, even if it should come apart tomorrow, would be considered by whatever historians survive the collapse to have been one of remarkable durability.

The essay that follows is one historian's attempt to account for that durability, drawing not only on what his fellow historians have concluded about the Cold War, but also on such insights as he has been able to comprehend from that not always comprehensible discipline known as political science. It tries to take a systemic perspective: that is, to look at international relations since 1945, not as the product of a narrow bilateral relationship existing between the Soviet Union and the United States, but rather as a discrete and describable international system, the characteristics of which add up to something more than the sum of its parts.

Systems theorists point out that there are two kinds of systems: those that are self-regulating and those that are not. The cruise control in an automobile, if it works right, is a self-regulating system; the O-ring seal on the space shuttle obviously wasn't. By definition, self-regulating systems tend to last longer than those that fly apart; hence, it seems logical to assume that there have been certain self-regulating mechanisms at work in the international system since 1945. This essay is an attempt to identify some of them.

In doing such an analysis, it is important to distinguish between those self-regulating mechanisms that were put in place as the result of conscious decisions by statesmen and the governments within which they function, and those that evolved quite unconsciously from the workings of the international system itself. Political success grows out of a combination of both skill and luck; both factors need to be taken into account in the kinds of things that we are going to be talking about here.

Let us first consider those self-regulating mechanisms that lie beyond the ability of either superpower to shape, as a matter of conscious policy.

The first of these that has helped to preserve the stability of the postwar international system has been the largely bipolar character of the international system since 1945, at least in comparison to those that immediately preceded it. The assertion that bipolar systems have a greater capacity for self-regulation than do multipolar systems does not seem convincing at first glance. This is because people tend to equate world politics with furniture, and to assume therefore that because tables and chairs require three or more points of support to achieve stability, international systems must also.

But geopolitics is not geometry. In fact, the bipolar configuration of power that we have had since 1945 has been remarkably stable, at least insofar as the positions of the major actors within it are concerned. This has been the case in part because bipolarity accurately reflected the postwar distribution of power in the world; one need only compare it with the multipolar settlement of 1919—which effectively left out Germany and Soviet Russia—to see the difference. Bipolarity also had the advantages of simplicity, which meant that sophisticated leadership was not required to maintain it. That, too, has been fortunate, since neither the Soviet nor the American political system has been geared toward producing statesmen of the caliber of Metternich or Bismarck, or toward entrusting those few who approach that standard with political responsibility for very long. Bipolarity also simplifies the business of maintaining coalitions: it encourages stability and durability—NATO and the Warsaw Pact have been partners in competition for more than three decades now—but paradoxically it also seems more tolerant of defections than earlier multipolar coalitions have been. The fact that a nation the size of China could switch sides twice within the past four decades with so little impact on the overall bipolar system says something about the stability that is inherent within it.

The second self-regulating mechanism that has proceeded at more or less an unconscious level has to do with the obvious—but little discussed—fact that the two most powerful nations in the world are also its most self-sufficient. Now self-sufficiency, in the past, has had a bad press. The argument has been around since at least the eighteenth century that if only nations could become more interdependent, the likelihood of wars being fought between them would correspondingly decrease. Unfortunately, there is hardly a shred of historical evidence to confirm this pleasant theory: even a cursory glance at the record will show that the nations that have most often fought one another have generally been the nations that were economically involved with one another, rather than the other way around.

There has never been a war between Russia and the United States, despite the fact that both of us, at one time or another, have managed to fight the British, the French, the Germans, the Italians, the Austro-Hungarians, and the Japanese. This is, as the Russians like to say, "no accident." It stems, in part, from our good fortune in occupying substantial portions of the earth, at opposite sides of the earth. That means that we have had no perpetual boundary disputes to quarrel about—no Alsace-Lorraines, no West Banks, no Shatt el Arab waterways. But this absence of war, I suspect, also grows out of the fact that neither country is or has been critically dependent upon the other for vital commodities that might be withheld in an effort to coerce one or the other to act against its will.

I would not want this argument to be misunderstood: I am not trying to suggest that trade, cultural exchange, and people-to-people contacts are therefore bad things, and that we ought to stop them lest they lead to war. What I am saying is that they won't automatically prevent war, either. Considering the number of nations who have had intimate people-to-people contacts and who, as a result, have taken an intense dislike to each other—French and Germans, Russians and Poles, Chinese and Japanese, Greeks and Turks, English and Irish, Arabs and Israelis—it becomes apparent that maintaining a certain distance, and independence in preference to interdependence, is perhaps no bad thing.

The third self-regulating mechanism and again one that proceeds more or less independently of the deliberate decisions of statesmen—has to do with domestic structures in each country: is there anything in the domestic cultural or institutional makeup of the Soviet Union or the United States that would predispose either nation to glorify war as an instrument of national policy? The question is not an insignificant one, given the fact that there have been cultures and institutions, in other countries at other times, that have in fact had this attitude toward war, and have generally had war as a result.

Once again, we—the Russians and the Americans—have been fortunate. With all the accusations we hurl at each other about our respective military-industrial complexes, with all the rhetorical sabre-rattling our respective political leaders have indulged in over the years, there really is no evidence on either side of a culturally or institutionally based predisposition to war: we both have had painful experience with it; we both have a pretty good idea of what it means; and we do not, either of us, take it lightly. That, again, has been a very lucky thing.

But what about those aspects of the Soviet-American relationship that do not fall within the realm of luck? What self-regulating mechanisms have statesmen, through their conscious actions, succeeded in creating?

The first and most important of these, I am convinced, has been the existence of nuclear weapons. Students of the causes of wars assert that war is almost never something that develops exclusively from the workings of impersonal social and economic forces, or from the effects of arms races, or even by accident. It requires conscious decisions on the part of national leaders; more than that, it requires calculations on their part that the gains to be derived from war will outweigh the probable costs. "Recurring optimism," Geoffrey Blainey has written, "is a vital prelude to war. Anything which dampens that optimism is a cause of peace."

It would be hard to quarrel with the proposition that nuclear weapons have had a dampening effect on the optimism of anyone in either Moscow or Washington who might have contemplated going to war during the past forty years. The existence of these devices—and, more to the point, the fact that we have direct evidence of what they can do when used against human beings—has given this generation of statesmen a painfully vivid awareness of the realities of war that no previous generation has had. Pessimism, in a nuclear era, is a permanent accompaniment of our thinking about war, and that, as Blainey reminds us, is a cause of peace.

But it is important to recognize that nuclear weapons have not been the only consciously imposed self-regulating mechanism that has held the postwar international system together. There have been others, and one that has been almost as important as the "nuclear revolution" has been the "reconnaissance revolution," the ability of the United States and the Soviet Union now to assess each other's *capabilities,* if not *intentions,* to a degree unparalleled in the history of international relations, and thereby to reduce the danger of surprise attack.

The philosopher Michael Walzer has suggested that espionage, if it facilitated the exchange of information between two antagonistic states, might actually serve the cause of peace; and indeed this has been largely the effect of the reconnaissance programs that began with the U-2 and have since evolved—chiefly by means of satellites—into what is really quite a remarkable system of mutually tolerated and for the most part quite polite spying. There was nothing inevitable about this: the fate of one particular U-2—the one piloted by Francis Gary Powers—shows how easily things might have gone the other way. The fact that that episode became the exception rather than the rule, that by 1963 both we and the Russians had made the conscious decision not to try to shoot down each other's spy satellites, provides quite a remarkable demonstration of the extent to which we have come to place our common interest in systemic stability above even our very natural instinct to keep secrets from one another.

A third consciously determined self-regulating mechanism has been the tendency, present in both the United States and the Soviet Union, to modify ideology when it inconveniently gets in the way. We are, it has often been said, two of the most ideological nations on the face of the earth, and if we had both interpreted our respective ideologies literally, it is difficult to see how coexistence would have been possible.

The fact is, of course, that we haven't interpreted ideology literally: both we and the Russians have shown ourselves capable, over the years, of moderating ideological positions that might have required challenging the other's internal system. In the case of the Soviet Union, the doctrine of "inevitable conflict" between communism and capitalism has evolved into that of "peaceful coexistence"; the Russians even assure us now that this is what Lenin meant all along. In the case of the United States, the Wilsonian notion that a state that was autocratic at home would necessarily behave aggressively beyond its borders—an attitude very much enshrined in the World War II doctrine of "unconditional surrender"—gave way after the war to the strategy of containment, which implied coexistence with, but never destruction of, the Soviet Union.

Both of us, therefore, even though we don't much like to admit it, have compromised ideological positions in the interests of preserving the existing international system. The moderation of ideologies must be considered, then, along with nuclear deterrence and mutually tolerated reconnaissance, as one of the major conscious self-regulating mechanisms of postwar international relations.

Still another conscious self-regulating mechanism has been the development of certain tacitly agreed-upon "rules of the game": rules of superpower competition. It is through mutual agreement on such rules that vigorous competition is possible in international relations, even in the absence of an umpire or a referee. Several of the most important of these "rules" are as follows:

1. Respect each other's spheres of influence. Challenges to such spheres have tended to come only where the resolve or the ability of a superpower to maintain its sphere had, for whatever reason, been left unclear.

2. Avoid direct military confrontations between the two states. When

we and the Russians have sought to expand our influence in the world, or when we felt called upon to use military force, we have tended more often than not to do it through proxies; in those few instances where direct confrontations between Soviet and American forces occurred—Berlin and Cuba, for example—they were handled with great caution.

3. Use nuclear weapons only as a last resort. The tradition of not using nuclear weapons in limited war situations is one of the most important "rules of the game," and it is one that could very easily have gone the other way, given the fact that the United States possessed an effective monopoly over these devices for roughly the first decade of the Cold War and could have used them during that period with relative impunity. That it did not is, among other things, one of the few clear demonstrations of the importance of moral considerations in international politics.

4. Prefer predictable anomaly over unpredictable rationality. Both we and the Russians have fallen into the habit of tolerating a whole series of awkward and illogical regional arrangements. Who in their right mind would ever have sat down consciously to design such things as the division of Germany, or the position of Berlin inside a divided Germany, or the Korean demilitarized zone, or the existence of Cuba as a Soviet satellite ninety miles off the coast of Florida, or, even more paradoxically, the existence of a major American military base in the middle of the same Soviet satellite that is ninety miles off the coast of Florida? None of this makes very much sense; and yet, we have lived with it all of these years because we prefer even irrational familiarity to the uncertainty that attempts to rationalize these illogical arrangements might bring.

5. Refrain from attempts to undermine the position of each other's leadership. Leadership crises have occurred in both countries over the years; but, quite interestingly, neither of us has made any sustained or significant effort to try to take advantage of them.

By all of these mechanisms—those that have evolved as a result of conscious design as well as those that were largely a matter of unconscious good fortune—a certain stability has been brought to the superpower relationship that functions quite apart from formal agreements or from the levels of angry rhetoric that may exist on each side.

Now, I would not want to make any attempts to predict how long this system will hold together. Historians quite properly are cautious about making predictions in this matter. If we think ahead to the kinds of things that might possibly endanger the stability of this system in the future, the one that seems most plausible would be a sustained decline in the power of one of the superpowers at a time when the power of the other one is either increasing or remaining roughly stable. And that in turn raises an interesting question.

It would be helpful if in international politics it could be arranged for great powers to decline and approach senility at roughly the same rate, because a certain symmetry and balance would be provided in that way, and disparities of power would not develop. History, however, is rarely so accommodating. One of the major questions we must ponder, if we consider long-term prospects for this forty-year system of international stability, is how that system might in fact accommodate what will inevitably happen sooner or later: that is, the decline as a world power of one or the other of the major actors that make it up.

But even if that breakup of the system should occur tomorrow, sufficient time has now passed without World War III for historians to begin to regard the post–World War II era, quite properly, not as a "Cold War" at all, but as a wholly unanticipated—though no less thankfully received—"Long Peace."

The Tragic Return to Cold War Bipolarity

STANLEY HOFFMANN

Rarely has an administration had as few defenders as Jimmy Carter's. The election of Ronald Reagan has been generally interpreted as a repudiation both of Carter's economic policies and of his foreign policy. Thus, it may be useful to ask three questions: What was done well, what went wrong, and what should be learned from the Carter presidency?

At a time when realpolitik is regaining prestige, it may not be very popular to state that the almost aggressive reassertion of American idealism by the Carter administration in its first year was one of its greatest achievements. There have been too many disappointments and difficulties since then for most Americans to appreciate today how welcome the tone set by Carter and his team was at that time. At home, he appealed to the national reservoir of moral enthusiasm and the urge to behave in world affairs not merely as a great power but also as the champion of certain values. He was determined to redefine the national interest to make it coincide with the moral impulse. These efforts did much to help Americans overcome the bitter divisions, and the sense of shame and guilt, engendered by the war in Vietnam and by the Watergate scandal.

Abroad, many governments were as suspicious of American flings of idealism—easily translated into, or perceived as, alarming mixes of naiveté and benevolent arrogance—as they usually are of brutal or cynical power plays by big states. But it soon became apparent that Carter's human rights emphasis was not merely rhetorical, that steps were actually taken to turn it into a policy, and that even mere sermons or lofty pronouncements by an American president cannot fail to have some effect when they clearly reflect his wishes and his will. As this policy began to liberate political prisoners, put repressive governments on the defensive, and encourage dissidents everywhere, the prestige of the United States—tarnished by American behavior in Vietnam, Chile, Cyprus, and Bangladesh—soared again in many parts of the world.

Good Machiavellians will discount the sympathy for America felt by opponents of Filipino President Ferdinand Marcos or by Indonesians released

Stanley Hoffmann, "Requiem," reprinted with permission from *Foreign Policy*, No. 42 (Spring 1981), 3–26. Copyright 1981 by the Carnegie Endowment for International Peace.

from camps or by many black Africans or by citizens of Panama. But just as it is not enough to be loved in the global contest for influence, it is certainly not sufficient to be feared. The Soviet quandary in Poland testifies both to the subversive potential of human rights and to the unenviable choices facing a power that relies almost entirely on fear.

The second merit of the Carter administration was its attempt to come to terms with the world as it is. The administration may have harbored far too many illusions about the ease with which this world, or even the United States, could be managed. But in important respects, the original analysis was right. The Carter administration understood that, in an era marked by the diffusion of power to new actors insistent on asserting themselves and on rejecting the dependencies fashioned by colonialism or by long economic subordination to more advanced nations, the conditions for U.S. influence had changed. In a world characterized both by the contagion of independence and by the complex bonds, restraints, and manipulations of interdependence, Marina v.N. Whitman's formula of "leadership without hegemony" was the only possible one.

That this was later denounced as a quasi-retreat from leadership, as an abdication from power, says more about the critics than about the administration. Those who tend to equate power with displays of military might, or with periodic military outbursts, have failed to understand that power is neither a mystical gift nor a stock of goods, but a relationship. If the purpose of the exercise of power is to influence the behavior of others, the first requirement is to understand the concerns, interests, and fears of those one tries to affect and the costs and limits of control.

There was often too much glibness in the proclaimed intention to be on the side of change: Not all changes are desirable, and there was always a tension between the drive for human rights and the accommodation of the developing nations' desires. But those very Americans who were disturbed by U.S. defeats in the United Nations in the early 1970s and unresigned to the spectacle of the United States as a mere, albeit vocal, opposition in the General Assembly, should have been the first to note that under Carter the United States ceased being on the defensive and achieved some remarkable successes in the U.N. General Assembly and Security Council. The negotiation of the Panama Canal treaties symbolized the new U.S. willingness to accept, even in its own domain, the reality of a post-colonial era.

The Carter administration's original analysis was correct again in stressing that this ever more complex world could be neither managed by the superpowers nor reduced to the relationship between them. Until his last years as secretary of state, Henry Kissinger had maintained an intensely bipolar view of the world. In 1973 it became clear that superpower control of regional conflicts and internal developments in Third World countries was limited and imperfect. Opportunities for superpower influence arose from local politics and could not be easily eliminated or offset unless the local circumstances were propitious.

The best way of coping with Soviet advances and maneuvers in the Third World is through preventive diplomacy. Not every Soviet success can be avoided at a reasonable cost or constitutes a threat to a major U.S. interest. Not every loss is a defeat. And the division of the world into two camps—moderates versus radicals—is an artificial and ultimately self-defeating procrustean formula. It gives up as lost and treats as foes countries or forces whose extremism, or whose ties to the Soviets, may well be temporary and counts as allies regimes or groups whose internal weaknesses or external ambitions may turn them into liabilities for the United States and opportunities for the Soviet Union. Carter's steadfast refusal to apply this mischievous Manichaean division to Rhodesia was entirely justified.

A third merit of the Carter administration was its determination to cope with major, long-term problems, rather than to concentrate only on the most urgent ones. The emphasis on global issues, many of which had been dealt with only timidly before, was far sighted, whatever one may say about the way in which policies were carried out. Human rights, non-proliferation, arms sales, arms control beyond the confines of SALT or of Europe, the law of the seas, international trade, and the Arab-Israeli conflict were all subjects of enormous long-range importance.

In some instances, little more was achieved than consciousness raising. In others, partial victories were won: The rate of nuclear proliferation has slowed, and the range of consensus among suppliers of nuclear fuels and technology has increased; the Tokyo round of the General Agreement on Tariffs and Trade has been a success; an agreement on the law of the seas is in sight.

Fourth, those who now speak of the Carter legacy as one of disaster and peril will soon realize that the great improvements of which they will undoubtedly boast in a few months were all carefully prepared by the Carter administration. Thus, Carter and Harold Brown, the secretary of defense, initiated a variety of programs designed to neutralize the Soviet strategic nuclear build-up by increasing America's counterforce capabilities; obtained West European consent to a modernization of North Atlantic Treaty Organization (NATO) forces and to the establishment of long-range theater nuclear weapons in Western Europe; pressured Japan, with some success, for an increase in its defense effort; and created the Rapid Deployment Force and negotiated access to various bases and facilities for it. Also, the Carter administration normalized relations with the Soviet Union's most uncompromising enemy—China—and began to fashion a strategic relationship with the new Chinese leadership.

Critics of the Carter administration ritualistically deplore what they view as its major defeats—Moscow's grip on Ethiopia, Vietnamese control of Kampuchea, the Soviet invasion of Afghanistan, the collapse of America's position in Iran, and turmoil in Central America. But there were also major victories—the solidity of America's main alliances, the progress in relations with China, the breakthrough at Camp David, the decline of Soviet influence in the Arab world, the trend of elections in the Caribbean, the end of the Rhodesian civil war, and the support of Angola and Mozambique for major Western objectives in Southern Africa. This is not a picture of decline and retreat. Yet it has been so perceived by many, at home and abroad.

The general impression of failure is not caused by the fact that Carter pursued policies at the end of his term that were far different—indeed almost the opposite—from those he had announced when he first took office. A team that had wanted to conduct a diplomacy freed from the "inordinate fear" of communism and to play down the relationship between the superpowers ended up so preoccupied with the bipolar conflict that it had little time and energy left for anything else, except the Iran hostage crisis. But other administrations had shown the same contradiction between their original course and their later trajectory: The Harry Truman of the Cold War was far different from the Truman of 1945–1946; Kissinger's global diplomacy of 1975–1976 was vastly different from his détente policy of 1971–1973.

Nor is the impression of failure caused largely by the hostage crisis. Most Americans agreed that the return of the hostages was the primary national objective. A declaration of war followed by military operations would have been fatal to the hostages, dangerous for America's relations with its allies, and rich in opportunities for Soviet gain. A blockade with or without a declaration of war would have embroiled the United States in confrontations with third powers and jeopardized the world's oil supply without necessarily helping the hostages. Waiting until the dust settled in Iran and until other events—such as the Iran-Iraq war—changed Iranian priorities proved to be frustrating; but few outside the United States believe that America practiced appeasement or was humiliated because of its show of restraint.

Indeed, the contrast between American patience toward Iran and Soviet brutality in Afghanistan has not been unnoticed. Those who believe that the United States should have put national honor or pride ahead of the lives of the hostages ought to ask themselves what the spectacle of a great power bombing or otherwise assaulting a weaker country with which it had been previously involved—to put it mildly—in an unhappy and unfortunate relationship would have done for America's prestige.

The main failures of the Carter administration can be found in four different but interrelated areas: style, strategy, economics, and politics. Style is almost as important as substance. A policy based on a faulty design can impress friends and skeptics abroad and generate enthusiasm at home, if it is carried out with a sense of mastery and a dash of drama. Style can convey the illusion of coherence and continuity at a time when a policy is floundering, the original design is in pieces, and diplomacy is reduced to improvisation.

Any student of the late French President Charles de Gaulle or of Kissinger's diplomacy knows that skill in manipulating the perceptions of the public and of leaders can go a long way toward offsetting miscalculations or even a deficiency of power. But the Carter administration from the very beginning developed a style of clumsiness that amplified misgivings and specific grievances abroad into a general conviction of incompetence.

The administration suffered from an almost total addiction to erratic tactics. The complaint of friends and foes alike—that Carter was unpredictable—was based in large part on the bumpiness of the administration's style. There were policy zigzags on the status of U.S. troops in South Korea, the neutron bomb, high technology transfers to the Soviet Union, relations with Somalia, the Soviet role in a Middle East settlement, the March 1980 U.N. resolution on Israeli settlements, and other issues.

There was plain incoherence, such as when the president authorized the hostage rescue mission in Iran immediately after he had obtained allied support for economic sanctions by promising military restraint. Moments of complacency—the absence of reaction to the April 1978 communist coup in Afghanistan and Carter's failure at and immediately after Camp David to press Israeli Prime Minister Menachem Begin on the issue of Israeli West Bank settlements—alternated with brusque, screeching fortissimos— the initial confrontation with Bonn over the West German-Brazilian nuclear deal, the "discovery" of a Soviet brigade in Cuba, and the post-Afghanistan avalanche of sanctions against the Soviet Union. There was, above all, what might be called tactical fission: some officials sounding the alarm about African or Caribbean developments while others were shrugging it off, the U.S. embassy in Tehran pursuing one course at the time of the fall of Shah Mohammad Reza Pahlavi while Washington seemed to be pursuing at least two others—one non-interventionist, one pro-shah.

This tactical infelicity had three causes. One was institutional. A president may want to receive diverse kinds of advice. He may even want to institutionalize diversity. But then he must be able to impose his own views, achieve his own synthesis, and be the master of the administration's tactics. Otherwise, diversity enshrined in different administrative sanctuaries becomes cacophony. At no point, except at Camp David, did the president give the impression of being in command of the daily course.

There was not only the well-publicized conflict of views and of styles between the national security adviser and the secretary of state, and between either of these and Andrew Young, the U.S. ambassador to the United Nations. There were also tensions between the domestic advisers, with their eyes on the polls—and on the Jewish vote—and the foreign policy experts; between the regional bureaus and the champions of global or functional issues; between the arms controllers and the military or its supporters. Such divergencies are inevitable. But when each group or clan is allowed, or feels free, to launch its own initiatives, and the others then try to cancel these moves or to neutralize them with moves of their own, the style that emerges is deplorable.

The second cause was personal. Each of the main players had his own flaws. Carter has often been blamed for his addiction to detail; but detail and tactics turned out not to be synonymous. The attempt to master detail— always a dubious goal for a president—becomes particularly futile when specific knowledge is not translated into a steady course of action. In domestic as well as in foreign affairs, Carter often behaved as if his minute understanding of a problem and his definition of goals were all a policy needed for success.

Former Secretary of State Cyrus Vance was a believer in case-by-case negotiation. Tactically, this was a fine bent, but one that failed to address two problems: the need or itch for occasional spectaculars—a need neglected at great peril not only in democracies but also in multilateral diplomacy, which tends toward paralysis if there are not some crescendos from time to time—and the opportunity a lack of style gives to flashier, if clumsier, players, who then provide the crescendos on their own, at the wrong moment or far too loud. National Security Adviser Zbigniew Brzezinski's fascination with tactics was not wedded to talent for negotiation or regard for steadiness. In his case, institutional and personal characteristics merged to handicap the administration: No national security adviser should be a principal negotiator, an enforcer of policy, and a public spokesman; but this is especially true when the adviser likes quick moves, grand gestures, and tough tactics.

The third cause of the clumsy style was the most important and resulted in part from the other two: the Carter administration's strategic incoherence. This factor is of such importance that it must be treated as an independent one. Never did the administration succeed in integrating its excellent intuitions and assumptions into a strategy. Contradictions remained unmanaged until the end.

From the beginning, the core of the failure was in the area of Soviet-U.S. relations. It was impossible both to improve these relations and to pursue—in the Middle East, the Far East, and with respect to human rights—a policy the Soviets would view as one of exclusion or confrontation. It was impossible simultaneously to demote the Soviet-U.S. relationship from its perch as the top American concern and to expect the Soviets—keen on competition and unhappy with the U.S. interpretation of the "Basic Principles of U.S.-Soviet Relations" agreed to in 1972—to let themselves be relegated to the periphery of American concerns. It was wrong to believe that world affairs could somehow be packaged into two separate categories: the Soviet-U.S. contest, to be dealt with by the alliances and by a mix of military and arms control measures; and all the rest.

Indeed, the more one wanted to be able to concentrate on that remainder, to cope with global issues, to make progress on regional ones, to examine them on their own merits, the more important it was to manage the Soviet-American contest intelligently. Otherwise, the duel between the superpowers would again spill over into all areas and dominate U.S. attention, either totally obscuring or distorting the other issues. Third World conflicts and global problems do have roots autonomous of the superpowers. But when superpower competition moves toward confrontation, worldwide strategic considerations—the fear of the cumulative effect of discrete, and perhaps separately insignificant, Soviet advances; the worry about U.S. credibility and reliability—begin to overwhelm the concern for local realities. U.S. ability to deal with these, and with global issues, is at the mercy of the superpower contest: The latter is not the only or even the determining force in world affairs, but it remains the central one.

The biggest charge that can be made against the Carter administration is that it failed to define what it wanted out of Soviet-U.S. relations. It failed to decide and to communicate, through deeds as well as words, which Soviet activities were intolerable, and which were compatible with Washington's concept of the bipolar contest. The Carter administration thus compromised its own innovative insights and intentions.

Those who believe that the superpower contest is the one overriding issue and that foreign policy and security policy are synonymous have of course been critical of Carter's initial belief that the competition could lose its saliency and of his persistent, discombobulated groping for a mix of cooperation and confrontation. But those who think that the administration was right in trying to remove the blinders of bipolarity from American eyes have a very different reason for being critical of Carter. At the time of his victory, the American people had already gone through one rich experience. The détente policy of Richard Nixon and Kissinger aimed at moderating Soviet behavior through incentives, punishments, and barricades had already run into formidable obstacles: Many Americans were suspicious of providing the Soviets with economic rewards, the Soviets were unwilling to forgo political gains in the Third World, Washington was unwilling to interpret the 1972 statement of principles in the way Moscow read it—as a promise of condominium and an assertion that the arms race would continue, especially on the Soviet side.

Three lessons seemed clear. First was the difficulty of waging a long-range, mixed policy toward Moscow, which could lead to Soviet restraint in the long run even if there were, on the way, occasional setbacks and confrontations. For every such setback tends to be seen as a reason to remove rewards, and every resort to a sanction is treated not as a normal application of the theory of incentives, but as evidence of failure of the whole policy. The second lesson was the difficulty of waging such a policy when the climate is poisoned by a quickening arms race. The third was the formidable reservoir of antagonism in the United States to any policy other than one of hostility and traditional containment toward the Soviet Union— a state rightly felt to be a threat both to U.S. power and to America's most fundamental values, and much more questionably, held to have few genuinely common interests with America.

The Carter administration did not draw the consequences from these lessons. Kissinger's failed attempt at an integrated strategy was replaced not with a different integrated policy, but with a declaratory policy of juxtapositions. The United States would, in Brzezinski's words, both ''recognize the continuing relevance of power'' and be ''responsive to the new political realities of the world.'' It would have both competition and co-operation in Soviet-American relations. Amen! Yet how would the search for either half not drown out the other?

The administration never made up its mind on linkage. Kissinger's attempt had apparently not worked after 1972. But rather than determining why it had failed—because it had not really been tried, thanks to the Jackson-Vanik amendment; or because it had attempted to achieve the impossible by demanding Soviet acceptance of the U.S. concept of stability; or even because it could never work once the Soviets had reached the original objectives of their switch to détente—the members of the Carter administration oscillated from moments when the very notion of linkage seemed abandoned, to others when linkage-as-punishment was discussed, to the final orgy of linkage after the invasion of Afghanistan.

But linkage is above all a means to an end; and the end—defining acceptable Soviet behavior—was never clarified. If a modicum of cooperation with the Soviet Union was deemed essential, both as a way to curtail the growth of the Soviet war machine and as a way to make the new Carter global strategy possible, then a very clear priority ought to have been given to arms control. The longer it took to negotiate SALT II, the more the United States exposed itself to dangerous schizophrenia in the realm of security—to a situation in which there would appear to be a contradiction between U.S. arms control policy and a renewed U.S. military effort, required by the failure to curb the Soviet build-up by mutual agreements and intended to prevent a further deterioration of the balance.

The administration appeared divided between a security policy increasingly driven by mounting fears of Soviet capabilities and intentions and an arms control policy based on moderate assumptions about the two sides' strategic plans. And such schizophrenia could not fail to lead to the defeat of the arms control component, if global political and military events appeared to vindicate what might be called the Committee on the Present Danger's analysis of Soviet behavior. The imperatives were therefore either a quick arms control agreement as a major component of the cooperative dimension or, if no such rapid success seemed possible, a major attempt at joint U.S.-Soviet crisis management in the meantime to accompany America's military efforts. Neither was achieved, and the latter was not even undertaken.

In the absence of either, decisions about redressing the military balance seemed to be a vindication of the committee's warnings and a frantic effort to buy votes for SALT II, rather than a part of a balanced strategy. With a deteriorating diplomatic climate at the end of the SALT II negotiations, attention increasingly was concentrated not on the future of Washington's political relationship with Moscow but on the nightmare scenarios of Minuteman missile vulnerability. The shrinking of the cooperative dimension with Moscow tended to make of a most improbable worst-case hypothesis— a disarming Soviet first strike—not only the tail that wagged the dog of strategic decisions and doctrines, but also, absurdly enough, an additional reason for rejecting SALT II, since the treaty did nothing to remove that particular threat.

Indeed, U.S. military policy is increasingly driven by an apparent belief that the United States needs capabilities that mirror theoretical Soviet ones, either those required to win a nuclear war or those in the Persian Gulf area. The questions that ought to be asked are: What are American objectives, and what is entailed by them? Instead, Americans seem to ask: What are, or rather what might be, Soviet goals and what does the United States need to match Soviet capabilities?

Another unfortunate effect of this U.S. failure was the gap between Washington's Soviet policy and that of its European allies. The West Europeans have clearly chosen a mixed strategy, one that does not entail linkages and aims above all at stability in Europe. Given their economic and diplomatic links with Moscow, they see little contradiction between those links and an arms effort. France began to increase its defense budget several years before NATO and West German Chancellor Helmut Schmidt raised the issue of the Euro-strategic balance. As long as the United States has no network of relations with Moscow of comparable density, Washington will be quick to resort to sanctions—suspending grain sales or shelving SALT II when Moscow misbehaves. As long as Western Europe, in its bundle of bonds with Moscow, does not have any arms agreement of its own, it will insist on arms control—at both the central and the theater level. Moreover, arms control is a necessary companion of any rearmament effort, if for no other reason than domestic opinion. This trans-Atlantic contrast is a perfect recipe for mutual recrimination.

A third consequence was the administration's inability to choose between a policy of balance toward Moscow and Beijing, and a quasi-alliance with China. Each has had its champions. A fourth consequence has been felt in those very areas that the administration wanted to rescue, so to speak, from bipolarity. The prerequisite for such a rescue was a better and more stable, but not necessarily uncompetitive, Soviet-U.S. relationship. In the absence of that kind of relationship, the Carter administration did not feel free to pursue its own instincts and postulates in sensitive areas; but by continuing to act as if the Soviet-American contest had to be the determining factor, the administration often made mistakes, or worse. In other words, the weakness of its political strategy both compromised what was right and new, and reinforced what was old and wrong.

Carter inherited the policy of regional influentials in the Middle East. He continued to see in the shah of Iran a bulwark for stability and so, American policy in Iran continued to depend on the shah. Once the revolution began, there was—short of military intervention nobody advocated—no way of avoiding that the shah's fall would also be a U.S. debacle. The fear of Soviet influence in the Middle East and the habit of looking at Israel as a bastion of security there partly explain Carter's failure to try to extract bigger concessions on the Palestinian issue from Begin. The fear of Cuban influence, or of the charge of being blind to Cuban expansionism, largely explains the administration's protracted unwillingness to acknowledge a revolutionary situation, first in Nicaragua, later in El Salvador. The same zero-sum-game view has thwarted efforts to recognize Angola or Vietnam in order to diminish the strength of their ties to Moscow.

Asserting that nothing was thought through does not mean that devising a strategy radically different from the two varieties of containment—the Cold War and the détente versions—would have been easy. Establishing a mixed relationship with Moscow will remain a most difficult undertaking. It must be acceptable to the U.S. public and deemed satisfactory in Moscow. It must provide for enough cooperation with the Soviets to restrain the means and intensify the contest in gray areas, without amounting to the superpower condominium Moscow seeks but nobody else wants. It must not lead to a division of the world into exclusive spheres of domination that would risk self-destruction whenever turbulence attributable to one side's efforts hits a zone of influence of the other.

Nor is it easy, when the Soviets behave in an unacceptable way, to choose between a response "in the area and in kind" only (for this may be deemed too weak, both within the United States and in Moscow) and linkage across the board (for every incident then threatens to unravel the whole policy). Nor is it easy to integrate arms control and security concerns: What is best for the former may not always be the best solution for the latter. But the tragedy of the Carter failure is that, far from furthering an intelligent discussion of the issues, it has thrown us back to the simplicities of cold war containment and bipolarity. . . .

A third major failure was the inability to understand quickly enough that the soundness of the U.S. economy was as important a pre-condition for an effective foreign policy as a strong military establishment. In the realm of energy, the responsibility for failure lies largely with Congress. However, it remains true that U.S. policy in the late 1970s was designed to convince the Persian Gulf states to produce more and to moderate the Organization of Petroleum Exporting Countries prices; this increased U.S. dependence on Persian Gulf oil. Neither conservation nor strategic reserves were pushed hard enough.

The vast U.S. balance of payments deficits caused by increasing imports of oil and by the domestic expansion policies promoted by Carter in 1977–1978 led to further deterioration of the dollar. With the Iranian revolution, this resulted in additional massive increases in the price of oil. These proved far more difficult for Bonn and Tokyo to absorb than the earlier price shock of 1973. This had the triple effect of weakening West Germany's ability to provide for aid abroad and to pay for arms increases at home, of inciting Japan to an export drive that threatens the U.S. automobile industry and revives the danger of U.S. protectionism, and of worsening the prospects of bankruptcy for many oil-importing developing nations. As political scientist Robert Keohane has shown, the American loss of monetary and economic power since the late 1960s is largely the result of U.S. policies; this was as true under Carter as before. The turnaround of late 1978, when inflation became Carter's top priority, entailed a willingness to provoke a recession. The resulting combination of inflation and recession made the administration and the Congress highly reluctant to provide resources for developing countries, thus emptying of substance one of the major global policies announced earlier by Carter. . . .

The last failure was Carter's inability to master the politics of foreign policy. One political task was to obtain the cooperation of Congress. Carter did achieve two major successes: a painful one, the Senate's consent to the Panama treaties, and a triumphant one, the management of the multilateral trade negotiations. Probably no administration could have prevented Congress from legislating its own frequently contradictory and fragmentary preferences and dislikes in areas such as nuclear proliferation and human rights. But the distant relations between Carter and congressional leaders, when their authority was weaker than in the days of the seniority system and of stabler coalitions, did not help provide the administration with enough support to save it from the obligation to fight and to rally a different mix of friends or clients on each issue.

Above all, the absence of a coherent strategy got the administration into trouble with Congress over the crucial question of Soviet-U.S. relations. The Senate's skepticism over SALT II did not receive sufficient attention in time. When a concerted administration counteroffensive developed at last, Carter's officials far too often seemed to fight on their adversaries' terrain and to defend the treaty as harmless rather than as beneficial, except insofar as it allowed the United States to undertake every needed and planned arms build-up. But more damaging was Carter's inept handling of the issue of the Soviet brigade in Cuba, which was allowed to delay consideration of the SALT treaty once more, this time fatally.

The decisive battleground was the public. If Congress, in 1979, seemed to listen more attentively to the champions of the new orthodoxy that finally prevailed on November 4, 1980, than to Carter, it was because a divided administration had allowed the opposition to gain control of the agenda and of the minds of the American people. The president and his top aides did not, as Brzezinski recognized, "adequately emphasize the importance of formal speeches, broadly conceptual-type statements which would convey to the American public on a continuing basis the sense of direction."

There were such speeches, but they conveyed no such sense. Either they were no more than lofty sermons, or they juxtaposed but did not reconcile or integrate policies pointing in opposite directions, or they provided shopping lists rather than clear priorities. To Carter, politics seemed to mean the strategy and tactics of coming to power; government meant the management of issues. But the successful management of issues requires politics in the double sense of coalition building and educating. This is particularly indispensable when there is no clear consensus on a policy at the onset. When Carter took over, there was consensus on two points only: Idealism had to be revived, and new Vietnams avoided. The shocks of recent years have destroyed both, and the Carter administration failed to move the public and Congress beyond these points.

When the original cold war consensus was dissolved by the Vietnam war, Nixon and Kissinger did not attempt to fashion one by coalition building and by public education. They tried to obtain public assent through success and spectacle. It worked for a while, but not after 1974. The Carter administration chose to be resolutely unspectacular. Except for Camp David, its biggest successes were negative—troubles avoided—or atmospheric. Its fiascoes, real or apparent, were sensational—the Soviet airlift to Ethiopia, the convulsions of Iran, the invasion of Afghanistan. . . .

Without a strategy and without skill in political maneuver and persuasion, the Carter administration left the domestic battlefield to its adversaries. They would not have prevailed if Soviet behavior had not appeared to vindicate the cold warriors. Even though Soviet behavior is objectively expansionist, it matters whether one interprets Moscow's moves as a necessary result of the essence of an imperial or of a revolutionary system or as the complex outcome of external ambitions, external frustrations, miscalculations, internal weaknesses, bureaucratic drives, and atavisms. Policy responses ought to be widely different, depending on the interpretation. But the new orthodoxy would not have prevailed either, if it had not had so many secret, or not-so-secret, sympathizers within the administration and if the president had not given the impression first that he did not always see the difference between his advisers' views, and later, that Afghanistan had forced him, belatedly and somewhat abjectly, to recognize the error of his earlier ways.

There were several lessons for the future. First, U.S. leaders must insure the unity of domestic and foreign policy. Reagan asserts he wants to do just that by reviving the U.S. economy as well as American military strength, and by restoring American productivity and self-confidence as well as U.S. leadership. But in an era of finite resources and protracted economic difficulties, tough decisions will have to be made. Some of the domestic transformations required for a sound foreign policy—a shift in industrial structures that would save the United States from the choice between protectionism and industrial disasters, an energy policy that would drastically reduce domestic consumption and dependence on imports— might require the kind of *dirigisme* that the Reagan ideology deems intolerable, indeed un-American. And an obsession with America's military might could lead to further inflation, or, if it is combined with drastic cuts in social services or results in dubious military interventions abroad, it could crack the very superficial consensus that swept Carter out of office and bring new convulsions to the body politic.

The second imperative for any U.S. administration is to erase from the minds of its leaders and from its public vocabulary any hyperbole and any illusion about the quick coming of that great American dream: the elimination or the moderation of conflict in international affairs, the advent of harmony. Three different visions of postwar U.S. diplomacy all nurtured such hopes, and even though such statesmen as Dean Acheson or Kissinger were too skeptical and realistic to harbor these hopes themselves, they were not above letting them slip into their rhetoric. The Cold War vision looked forward to the mellowing of a Soviet Union persuaded by external barriers and situations of strength that reasonable, responsible behavior would be in its interest. The détente vision promised a Soviet Union playing the game of stability in exchange for symbolic status rewards and material incentives, to the point of cooperating with the United States in the management and resolution of third party conflicts. The Carter vision added to this the dream of convergence between U.S. deeds and Third World aspirations, of the acceptance of American political ideals by foreign regimes, and the miracle (or mirage) of a world in which nuclear weapons would be on their way out. . . .

The third lesson, however, is about the difficulty of curing Americans of their seemingly congenital fondness for simplicity. Two of the three visions entailed complex policies. Kissinger moved from bipolar competition to a triangular game and tried to turn Soviet-U.S. relations into a mix of containment and cooperation. Carter tried to apply the notion of mixed relationships even to friends and allies. He attempted to move from a strategy centered on great power geopolitics to a policy that gave precedence both to regional realities and to global issues.

Both Kissinger and Carter found themselves attacked for reasons that had little to do with their conceptions—Kissinger for the secrecy of his methods and the amorality of his inspiration; Carter for his incoherence and clumsiness. Yet both men were also savaged by those who could not accept any vision more subtle than that of a cold war crusade. Kissinger was criticized either for consorting with communist regimes or for not playing the China card against the Soviets hard enough, and for making deals with Moscow that—since the Kremlin wanted them—could be only in the enemy's interest. . . .

It is as if two archetypes only were competing for American approval: the Popeye archetype of the United States as the guardian of law and order, insuring stability and general happiness through strength and toughness; and the archetype of the missionary United States helping the poor abroad and bringing its values to those who suffer in the dark. Today's world fits neither scheme. But the reactions of much of the American political class, of some in the intellectual establishment, and of a majority of the public reminds one of the behavior of a patient who, disliking what he reads on his thermometer, breaks it.

Instead of examining the reasons for the divorce between those archetypes and the real world, many Americans prefer to blame other Americans. The purists tend to indict a corrupt, militaristic, or capitalist establishment for the failure of America's missionary vocation to rid the world of political and economic diseases. Those in the grip of a High Noon vision of America's role abroad blame the naive idealists, the tiresome exponents of complexity, the liberals who do not understand power, the writers who may be soft on communism, or that famous McGovern wing of the Democratic party that supposedly captured the Carter administration. They have gone dangerously far in convincing not only themselves, and the American public, but even America's friends and perhaps its foes that America has been dragged into decline by their domestic enemies. Internal settlements of accounts substitute for an appraisal of the state of the world.

It is this craving for simplicity rather than, as sociologist Michel Crozier says in his book *Le mal américain*, an inability to recognize and cope with evil, that is distinctively American; and it may well be one of America's major forms of parochialism, even in an age of inevitable involvement. Isolationism is dead, but the insular spirit that bred both of these activist archetypes lives on. Indeed, the last lesson is that the most distinctive American belief, generated by America's origins and confirmed by so much of American's history, remains the most resilient: faith in American exceptionalism.

Kissinger, toward the end of his tenure in office, said that America had to learn to behave as an ordinary nation. Carter, by his understated manner and his reluctance toward grand imperial moves, his apparent meekness toward the challenges of pygmies, his willingness to accept not only military equality but also certain kinds of inequality with the Soviet Union, made people believe that he too accepted decline as inevitable. In the process, he allowed them to forget how much of the missionary archetype could be found in his original approach to world affairs. The Reagan victory was a revenge of exceptionalist faith.

The idea of a world in which the United States would be merely one actor like any other, or even a great power like so many others in history, remains intolerable. But if the denial of complexity and the dogma of exceptionalism, of the "city on the hill," are so deep and tenacious, yet incompatible with external realities, can one be confident that the new administration will be capable of offering more than an atavistic display of axiomatic assertiveness? Will the new administration be able to devise anything more than a mere series of ad hoc responses once it becomes obvious that nostalgia provides no road map, and military strength no panacea?

The Abandonment of Principles and the Erosion of America's Global Standing

GEORGE W. BALL

The nature of the rivalry between the two superpowers was progressively defined after 1945 as Americans became increasingly aware that the conclusion of World War II had meant not the end of conflict but merely the substitution of one adversary for another. Not only did the Soviet Union command greater military resources than the Axis, but it also offered an ideology seductively attractive to some of the nations emerging from colonialism. For a time many Americans persisted in thinking of the Soviets merely as prickly allies—as they had been during the war. But when Stalin's aggressiveness and persistent bellicosity revealed the dimensions of Soviet ambitions, the United States reacted with ugly excesses such as McCarthyism.

Then, beginning in 1956, when Khrushchev's speech at the Twentieth Party Congress started a progressive destalinization, relations with the United States acquired a more civil tone. In the wake of the Cuban missile crisis— a climactic test of will—the Kennedy Administration negotiated the Partial Test Ban Treaty. Ten years later, in 1972, by laying the foundation of a new relationship with China, President Nixon exorcised the specter of a monolithic Communist bloc. All this led to the brief Indian summer of détente.

As they appeared in 1972, relations between the two superpowers seemed destined for further improvement, and there was reason to hope that we might achieve a safer world. SALT I put a cap on the buildup of offensive

George W. Ball, "Erosion of U.S. Foreign Relations," *Bulletin of the Atomic Scientists*, 41 (August 1985), 110–13. Reprinted by permission of the *Bulletin of the Atomic Scientists*, a magazine of science and world affairs. Copyright © 1985 by the Educational Foundation for Nuclear Science, 6042 S. Kimbark Ave., Chicago, IL 60637.

weapons and restricted the deployment of anti-ballistic-missile (ABM) systems. Meanwhile, the United States began to develop a network of ties and contacts with the Soviet Union at various levels in a variety of cultural, technical, professional, and commercial areas.

If U.S.-Soviet relations showed improvement during the first 20 years, U.S. relations with the noncommunist nations also developed and matured. Since the United States was the only major power to emerge strengthened rather than weakened by World War II, it was compelled abruptly to revise long-established parochial attitudes and to adjust to a new leadership role. And before long the United States began to enjoy the yeasty experience of world power and responsibility. Since all the world seemed to depend on the United States, it is not hard to see why, in the exuberance of new-felt importance, Americans failed to comprehend the limits of their nation's power or to appraise the priority of its interests.

In the exercise of leadership the United States drew strength not only from its physical, financial, and military resources but also from its moral authority as a democratic power guided by a body of principles and practices that reflect a respect for human rights and the rule of law. To be sure, the country sometimes compromised those principles, as when it launched the Bay of Pigs fiasco. But, during those first 20 years, successive administrations usually practiced what they preached, behaving with a magnanimity and a spacious vision which commanded world respect. The United States devised the Marshall Plan to rebuild Europe, and later the Point Four programs that led to some sharing of its wealth with Third World countries. It organized Western defenses through NATO, encouraged Europe to unite, undertook negotiations to untangle the obstructions to the free flow of goods and capital that arose from the war and the interwar period, and established international institutions to stabilize commercial and financial relations. Finally—and by no means the least important—the United States took the lead in creating the United Nations, which provided the essential mechanism for helping a billion people move from colonial dependence to some kind of juridical independence. It is no wonder that many now look back on those two decades as golden years.

Détente unfortunately survived only for a brief period, and, since it had been oversold, the disillusionment as it faded was stronger than events justified. As a result of the Carter Administration's clumsy approach to arms control and its overreaction to the 1979 Soviet invasion of Afghanistan, U.S. relations with the Soviet Union began to deteriorate. With the advent of the Reagan Administration relations between the superpowers were systemically chilled by a reversion to incivility and the injection of a Manichean antipathy. Today those relations are at a dangerously low point.

Paradoxically, just when much of the gas has escaped from the Soviets' ideological balloon, the U.S. government is pursuing a more ideological line than at any time since John Foster Dulles was the secretary of state, 30 years ago. President Reagan, in his actions and attitude, has denied the hope of achieving a more stable and pacific relationship with the Soviet Union. Indeed he has frequently asserted that the United States cannot bargain with a godless country. "How," he has asked, "do you compromise between good and evil? . . . How do you compromise with men who say . . . there is no God?"

In basing security solely on physical means while rejecting diplomatic efforts to exploit a common interest in survival, President Reagan has insisted on an enormous buildup of offensive military power. Consistent with his reliance on mechanistic means for security, he put forward his "Star Wars" program. Regardless of the ultimate findings of the intensive research program he proposes, the president's decision will almost certainly mean acceleration in the massive buildup of weapons on both sides, since it will force the Soviet Union to concentrate on countering or overwhelming U.S. defenses with a greater number of ICBMs and cruise missiles, and on developing its own Star Wars program.

The Star Wars decision will also inevitably weaken U.S. credibility in an already skeptical international environment. Once other nations fully comprehend the president's expressed—if unrealistic—hope to create a world resembling one in which nuclear weapons never existed, they will feel betrayed. Rightly or wrongly, Europeans count on the U.S. nuclear umbrella as the one hope for halting the continuous cycle of wars they have known for generations. And Third World countries will look with dismay at what appears to be an effective abandonment by the nuclear powers of any serious intention to achieve arms control through agreement. That, it should never be forgotten, was the explicit condition on which many of them signed the Nuclear Non-Proliferation Treaty.

Here arises another paradox: while Americans are preoccupied as never before with the nuclear menace, the President is urging a project that— while purporting to gratify the antinuclear movement by promising an end to nuclear weapons—will result in an enormous escalation of both offensive and defensive nuclear arms and may well halt serious efforts to contain the arms spiral.

But if U.S. relations with the Soviet Union are now worse than they were a decade or so ago, so also is U.S. influence with the noncommunist nations. Until disenchanted by the Vietnam War most Americans uncritically accepted the worldwide scope of U.S. responsibilities. The Truman Doctrine had declared that "it must be the policy of the United States to support free peoples who are resisting attempted subjugation by armed minorities or by outside pressure." And John F. Kennedy had announced in his inaugural address that the United States would "pay any price, bear any burden, meet any handicap, support any friend, oppose any foe to assure the survival and the success of liberty."

In the light of the present U.S. mood, it may be difficult to understand why few Americans initially challenged the need to try to prevent the National Liberation Front and North Vietnamese from overrunning South Vietnam. But the United States' leaders at that time tended to believe that the country's interests were affected by almost any major development in almost any part of the world—particularly when that development might even remotely advance communist influence. The United States had fought for three years in Korea to throw back first the North Koreans and then the Chinese, and the progressive involvement in Vietnam seemed merely another chapter in the continuous effort to prevent the spread of communist power. Any suggestion that Hanoi and the NLF might be more than instruments of Moscow and Peking was dismissed as reflecting a soft-headed attitude toward the communist menace. The defense of the ersatz government of South Vietnam was declared to be "vital" to U.S. interests—and that ended the argument.

The Vietnam ordeal was an exorbitant way to learn the limitations of U.S. capabilities, and the country is still paying heavily for that long, agonizing aberration and its demoralizing effect on national life. Perhaps an even larger cost of the war has been its effect in weakening the moral and psychological authority of U.S. leadership, for it raised questions in the minds of many otherwise friendly nations as to the United States' continued fidelity to democratic principles and reputation for international decency and good sense.

Nor was the Vietnamese imbroglio the only reason for U.S. loss of standing. In two additional geographical areas—the Middle East and Central American—the United States for the past two decades has also pursued policies not supported by most other nations. Indeed, the U.S. government's persistent practice of giving uncritical support to almost any Israeli actions— even when they violated the principles of international law and the U.N. Charter—and the insistence on blocking the efforts of the other Security Council members to uphold those principles have done more than anything else to impair the U.S. reputation for justice and fair-mindedness and have seriously damaged the effectiveness of the United Nations itself.

Prior to the Six-Day Arab-Israeli War in 1967, the United States had sought to maintain a relatively impartial policy toward the Middle East. In pursuance of the Tripartite Agreement [the 1950 agreement among the United States, the United Kingdom, and France guaranteeing the territorial integrity of all Middle Eastern states], it refused to supply arms to nations in the area, including Israel, in order to forestall an arms buildup on both sides. In 1956 President Eisenhower effectively demonstrated his support for the United Nations and the principles it represented by compelling Israel to withdraw its forces from the Sinai, just as the United States had forced the French and British to do.

But after the 1967 war, President Lyndon Johnson reversed the established policy. Instead of seeking to maintain an arms balance, he concentrated on making Israel militarily stronger than any potential combination of its Arab neighbors. The practical consequence was, of course, to accelerate the arms race, leading the Arab nations to augment their military expenditures so that today the Arab states lying to the east of Suez have more soldiers, guns, tanks, and planes than NATO. At the same time, bowing to pressure from pro-Israeli interests, the United States has refused to sell arms to friendly Arab nations.

Meanwhile, the United States has increased its annual subsidy to Israel to unprecedented levels for a country with roughly the population of Detroit. And that assistance is not limited to the economic and military spheres.

Equally important, the United States has faithfully run political interference to defend even Israel's most extreme actions from U.N. censure or sanctions. In 1967, the United States sat by while Israel annexed East Jerusalem and opposed any U.N. action that might force it to reverse that seizure. And it protested only weakly when, in December 1981, Israel annexed the Golan Heights and then went on to invade Lebanon. The United States continued to increase its subsidy to Israel even after that country had commenced systematically preempting the land and water supply of the West Bank through its settlement program in order, as Israeli leaders frankly admitted, to create "new facts" that would preclude the return of territory as called for under Security Council Resolution 242.

Nor did the United States merely avert its eyes from violations of established international legal principles and the Geneva conventions, but during the 1982 Israeli invasion of Lebanon, it meekly accepted Israel's violations of contractual obligations restricting use of U.S.-provided military equipment strictly to self-defense purposes. That was unconscionable discrimination since we had earlier applied heavy sanctions against Turkey for a similar violation.

The price the United States has paid for its uncritical support of Israel cannot be measured only in terms of the $30 billion of assistance provided so far; even more costly has been the destruction of the U.S. reputation as a nation that stands for and supports established principles of international decency and conduct. That loss of authority is dramatically revealed by the deteriorating U.S. position in U.N. councils. For 25 years, from the establishment of the United Nations in 1945 until 1970, the United States was able to defend and advance its policies through persuasion, friendship, and moral authority. During that period the United States not only refrained from exercising the veto it possessed as a permanent member of the Security Council, but regarded the use of the veto as, in effect, a rejection of the central concept of the United Nations. Indeed, during my days in the State Department, we took pride in pointing out that the Soviets had cast 103 vetoes while the U.S. had cast none—a sure sign of which side held the allegiance and respect of other members of the world community.

But in shifting its Middle East policies after the 1967 War, the United States became so out of step with the opinions of other nations that it could no longer prevail by persuasion. Having once cast a veto in 1970, the United States became hooked on the habit. Thus, since 1970, the United States has cast 40 vetoes, of which 16 have been to prevent censure of, or sanction against, Israel; five to prevent the expulsion of or sanctions against South Africa; five on the issue of Namibian independence; and five to defend positions regarding Vietnam. During that same period, the Soviet Union has cast only nine vetoes—fewer than one-fourth as many.

The United States' improvident use of its veto powers has not only disclosed the degree to which its prestige and influence have diminished, but the fact that the most powerful nation constantly thwarts the will of other Security Council nations has greatly diminished that body's authority, while infusing many Americans with a childish sense of outrage because their nation can no longer command the support of others for its policies.

That frustration has led many—even some diplomats accredited to the United Nations—to mount an unseemly and irrational attack on that world institution; thus, instead of supporting the body it helped to create, the United States is mindlessly tearing it down.

The list of international principles the United States has abandoned is distressingly long. By use of its veto the United States has sanctioned the retention of territory taken by force. It has opposed extending even the basic right of self-determination to the Palestinians, despite the fact that it insisted on writing that principle into the U.N. Charter and the president regularly espouses it in political speeches. To be sure, the president has offered to support a "Jordanian solution." But since he specifically rejects an independent Palestinian state, that solution recalls Henry Ford's assurance that the American people could buy a Ford car of any color, provided it was black. President Reagan has gone even further than his predecessors in refusing to acknowledge the illegality of Israel's settlement program on the West Bank even though those settlements plainly violate Articles 47,49, and 53 of the Geneva Convention of 1949, and have been declared illegal by the State Department's own legal adviser.

Principles have integrity only if they are uniformly and impartially applied, and it is likely that the United States' progressive transgression of principle with respect to Vietnam and Israel has contributed to the general disdain for the rule of law expressed in the reversion to gunboat diplomacy in Central American and the Caribbean. Applying what is, in effect, an American Brezhnev doctrine, the United States has already committed such outrages as mining Nicaraguan harbors, assisting in the bombing of Nicaraguan targets, and instructing the insurgents in the odious arts of assassination. These are acts of war, taken with the approval of Congress; and no plausible justification has been forthcoming. Finally, the United States—out of guilt and desperation—has demonstrated a total disrespect for the rule of law by refusing to submit to the arbitrament of the World Court.

Thus, as a result of this creeping attrition of its principles, the United States finds itself today more and more tempted to lower its standards and to pursue the same sordid practices as the Soviets. Indeed, the process of moral deterioration the United States is suffering seems to prove the old French adage that one tends to acquire the visage of his adversary.

Economic Decline and Imperial Overstretch

PAUL KENNEDY

In February of 1941, when Henry Luce's *Life* magazine announced that this was the "American century," the claim accorded well with the economic realities of power. Even before the United States entered the Second World War, it produced about a third of the world's manufactures, which was

Adapted from *The Rise and Fall of the Great Powers* by Paul Kennedy. Copyright © 1987 by Paul Kennedy. Reprinted by permission of Random House, Inc. and Unwin Hyman Limited. This essay originally appeared as "The (Relative) Decline of America," *Atlantic*, CCLX (August 1987), 29–38.

more than twice the production of Nazi Germany and almost ten times that of Japan. By 1945, with the Fascist states defeated and America's wartime allies economically exhausted, the U.S. share of world manufacturing output was closer to half—a proportion never before or since attained by a single nation. More than any of the great world empires—Rome, Imperial Spain, or Victorian Britain the United States appeared destined to dominate international politics for decades, if not centuries, to come.

In such circumstances it seemed to American decision-makers natural (if occasionally awkward) to extend U.S. military protection to those countries pleading for help in the turbulent years after 1945. First came involvement in Greece and Turkey; and then, from 1949 onward, the extraordinarily wide-ranging commitment to NATO; the special relationship with Israel and, often contrarily, with Saudi Arabia, Jordan, Egypt, and lesser Arab states; and obligations to the partners in such regional defense organizations as SEATO, CENTO, (Central Treaty Organization in the Middle East) and ANZUS, (Australia, New Zealand, United States pact). Closer to home, there was the Rip Pact and the special hemispheric defense arrangements with Canada. By early 1970, as Ronald Steel has pointed out, the United States "had more than 1,000,000 soldiers in 30 countries, was a member of 4 regional defense alliances and an active participant in a fifth, had mutual defense treaties with 42 nations, was a member of 53 international organizations, and was furnishing military or economic aid to nearly 100 nations across the face of the globe." Although the end of the Vietnam War significantly reduced the number of American troops overseas, the global array of U.S. obligations that remained would have astonished the Founding Fathers.

Yet while America's commitments steadily increased after 1945, its share of world manufacturing and of world gross national product began to decline, at first rather slowly, and then with increasing speed. In one sense, it could be argued, such a decline is irrelevant: this country is nowadays far richer, absolutely, than it was in 1945 or 1950, and most of its citizens are much better off in absolute terms. In another sense, however, the shrinking of America's share of world production is alarming because of the implications for American grand strategy—which is measured not by military forces alone but by their integration with all those other elements (economic, social, political, and diplomatic) that contribute toward a successful long-term national policy.

The gradual erosion of the economic foundations of America's power has been of several kinds. In the first place, there is the country's industrial decline relative to overall world production, not only in older manufactures, such as textiles, iron and steel, shipbuilding, and basic chemicals, but also— though it is harder to judge the final outcome at this stage of industrial-technological combat—in robotics, aerospace technology, automobiles, machine tools, and computers. Both areas pose immense problems: in traditional and basic manufacturing the gap in wage scales between the United States and newly industrializing countries is probably such that no efficiency measures will close it; but to lose out in the competition in future technologies, if that indeed should occur, would be even more disastrous.

The second, and in many ways less expected, sector of decline is agriculture. Only a decade ago experts were predicting a frightening global imbalance between food requirements and farming output. But the scenarios of famine and disaster stimulated two powerful responses: the first was a tremendous investment in American farming from the 1970s onward, fueled by the prospect of ever larger overseas food sales; the second was a large-scale investigation, funded by the West, into scientific means of increasing Third World crop outputs. These have been so successful as to turn growing numbers of Third World countries into food exporters, and thus competitors of the United States. At the same time, the European Economic Community has become a major producer of agricultural surpluses, owing to its price-support system. In consequence, experts now refer to a "world awash in food," and this state of affairs in turn has led to sharp declines in agricultural prices and in American food exports—and has driven many farmers out of business.

Like mid-Victorian Britons, Americans after 1945 favored free trade and open competition, not just because they held that global commerce and prosperity would be advanced in the process but also because they knew that they were most likely to benefit from a lack of protectionism. Forty years later, with that confidence ebbing, there is a predictable shift of opinion in favor of protecting the domestic market and the domestic producer. And, just as in Edwardian Britain, defenders of the existing system point out that higher tariffs not only might make domestic products *less* competitive internationally but also might have other undesirable repercussions—a global tariff war, blows against American exports, the undermining of the currencies of certain newly industrializing countries, and an economic crisis like that of the 1930s.

Along with these difficulties affecting American manufacturing and agriculture has come great turbulence in the nation's finances. The uncompetitiveness of U.S. industrial products abroad and the declining sales of agricultural exports have together produced staggering deficits in visible trade—$160 billion in the twelve months ending with April of 1986—but what is more alarming is that such a gap can no longer be covered by American earnings on "invisibles," which are the traditional recourse of a mature economy. On the contrary, the United States has been able to pay its way in the world only by importing ever larger amounts of capital. This has, of course, transformed it from the world's largest creditor to the world's largest debtor nation in the space of a few years.

Compounding this problem—in the view of many critics, causing this

Federal Deficit, Debt, and Interest (in billions)

	DEFICIT	DEBT	INTEREST ON DEBT
1980	$59.6	$914.3	$52.5
1983	$195.4	$1,381.9	$87.8
1985	$202.8	$1,823.1	$129.0

problem—have been the budgetary policies of the U.S. government itself.

A continuation of this trend, alarmed voices have pointed out, would push the U.S. national debt to around $13 *trillion* by the year 2000 (fourteen times the debt in 1980) and the interest payments on the debt to $1.5 *trillion* (twenty-nine times the 1980 payments). In fact a lowering of interest rates could make those estimates too high, but the overall trend is still very unhealthy. Even if federal deficits could be reduced to a "mere" $100 billion annually, the compounding of national debt and interest payments by the early twenty-first century would still cause unprecedented sums of money to be diverted in that direction. The only historical examples that come to mind of Great Powers so increasing their indebtedness *in peacetime* are France in the 1780s, where the fiscal crisis finally led to revolution, and Russia early in this century.

Indeed, it is difficult to imagine how the American economy could have got by without the inflow of foreign funds in the early 1980s, even if that had the awkward consequence of inflating the dollar and thereby further hurting U.S. agricultural and manufacturing exports. But, one wonders, what might happen if those funds are pulled out of the dollar, causing its value to drop precipitously?

Some say that alarmist voices are exaggerating the gravity of what is happening to the U.S. economy and failing to note the "naturalness" of most of these developments. For example, the midwestern farm belt would be much less badly off if so many farmers had not bought land at inflated prices and excessive interest rates in the late 1970s. The move from manufacturing into services is understandable, and is occurring in all advanced countries. And U.S. manufacturing *output* has been rising in absolute terms, even if employment (especially blue-collar employment) in manufacturing has been falling—but that too is a "natural" trend, as the world increasingly moves from material-based to knowledge-based production. Similarly, there is nothing wrong in the metamorphosis of American financial institutions into world financial institutions, with bases in Tokyo and London as well as New York, to handle (and profit from) the heavy flow of capital; that can only increase the nation's earnings from services. Even the large annual federal deficits and the mounting national debt are sometimes described as being not very serious, after allowance is made for inflation; and there exists in some quarters a belief that the economy will "grow its way out" of these deficits, or that government measures will close the gap, whether by increasing taxes or cutting spending or both. A too hasty attempt to slash the deficit, it is pointed out, could well trigger a major recession.

The positive signs of growth in the American economy are said to be even more reassuring. Because of the boom in the service sector, the United States has been creating jobs over the past decade faster than it has done at any time in its peacetime history—and certainly a lot faster than Western Europe has been. America's far greater degree of labor mobility eases such transformations in the job market. Furthermore, the enormous American commitment to high technology—not just in California and New England but also in Virginia, Arizona, and many other places—promises ever greater production, and thus national wealth (as well as ensuring a strategic edge over the Soviet Union). Indeed, it is precisely because of the opportunities existing in the American economy that the nation continues to attract millions of immigrants and to generate thousands of new entrepreneurs, and the capital that pours into the country can be tapped for further investment, especially in research and development. Finally, if long-term shifts in the global terms of trade are, as economists suspect, leading to steadily lower prices for foodstuffs and raw materials, that ought to benefit an economy that still imports enormous amounts of oil, metal ores, and so on (even if it hurts particular American interests, such as farmers and oilmen).

Many of these points may be valid. Since the American economy is so large and diverse, some sectors and regions are likely to be growing while others are in decline—and to characterize the whole with generalizations about "crisis" or "boom" is therefore inappropriate. Given the decline in the price of raw materials, the ebbing of the dollar's unsustainable high exchange value since early 1985, the reduction that has occurred in interest rates, and the impact of all three trends on inflation and on business confidence, it is not surprising that some professional economists are optimistic about the future.

Nevertheless, from the viewpoint of American grand strategy, and of the economic foundation necessary to an effective long-term strategy, the picture is much less rosy. In the first place, American's capacity to carry the burden of military liabilities that it has assumed since 1945 is obviously less than it was several decades ago, when its shares of global manufacturing and GNP were much larger, its agriculture was secure, its balance of payments was far healthier, the government budget was in balance, and it was not in debt to the rest of the world. From that larger viewpoint there is something in the analogy that is made by certain political scientists between America's position today and that of previous "declining hegemons." . . .

In particular, there could be serious implications for American grand strategy if the U.S. industrial base continues to shrink. If there were ever in the future to be a large-scale war that remained conventional (because of the belligerents' fear of triggering a nuclear holocaust), one must wonder, would America's productive capacities be adequate after years of decline in certain key industries, the erosion of blue-collar employment, and so on? One is reminded of the warning cry of the British nationalist economist Professor W.A.S. Hewins in 1904 about the impact of British industrial decay upon that country's power:

> Suppose an industry which is threatened [by foreign competition] is one which lies at the very root of your system of National defense, where are you then? You could not get on without an iron industry, a great Engineering trade, because in modern warfare you would not have the means of producing, and maintaining in a state of efficiency, your fleets and armies.

It is hard to imagine that the decline in American industrial capacity could be so severe: America's manufacturing base is simply much broader than Edwardian Britain's was, and—an important point—the so-called defense-related industries not only have been sustained by Pentagon procurement but also have taken part in the shift from materials-intensive to knowledge-intensive (high-tech) manufacturing, which over the long term will also reduce the West's reliance on critical raw materials. Even so, the expatriation from the United States of, say, semiconductor assembly, the erosion of the American shipping and shipbuilding industry, and the closing down of so many American mines and oil fields represent trends that cannot but be damaging in the event of another long, Great Power, coalition war. If, moreover, historical precedents have any validity at all, the most critical constraint upon any surge in wartime production will be the number of skilled craftsmen—which causes one to wonder about the huge long-term decline in American blue-collar employment, including the employment of skilled craftsmen.

A problem quite different but equally important for sustaining a proper grand strategy concerns the impact of slow economic growth on the American social-political consensus. To a degree that amazes most Europeans, the United States in the twentieth century has managed to avoid overt "class" politics. This, one imagines, is a result of America's unique history. Many of its immigrants had fled from socially rigid circumstances elsewhere; the sheer size of the country had long allowed those who were disillusioned with their economic position to escape to the West, and also made the organization of labor much more difficult than in, say, France or Britain; and those same geographic dimensions, and the entrepreneurial opportunities within them, encouraged the development of a largely unreconstructed form of laissez-faire capitalism that has dominated the political culture of the nation (despite occasional counterattacks from the left). In consequence, the earnings gap between rich and poor is significantly larger in the United States than in any other advanced industrial society, and state expenditures on social services claim a lower share of GNP than in comparable countries except Japan, whose family-based support system for the poor and the aged appears much stronger.

This lack of class politics despite obvious socio-economic disparities has been possible because the nation's overall growth since the 1930s has offered the prospect of individual betterment to a majority of the population, and, disturbingly, because the poorest third of American society has not been mobilized to vote regularly. But given the different birthrates of whites on the one hand and blacks and Hispanics on the other, given the changing composition of the flow of immigrants into the United States, given also the economic metamorphosis that is leading to the loss of millions of relatively high-paying jobs in manufacturing, and the creation of millions of poorly paid jobs in services, it may be unwise to assume that the prevailing norms of the American political economy (such as low government social expenditures and low taxes on the rich) would be maintained if the nation entered a period of sustained economic difficulty caused by a plunging dollar and slow growth. An American polity that responds to external challenges by increasing defense expenditures, and reacts to the budgetary crisis by cutting existing social expenditures, runs the risk of provoking an eventual political backlash. There are no easy answers in dealing with the constant three-way tension between defense, consumption, and investment as national priorities.

This brings us, inevitably, to the delicate relationship between slow economic growth and high defense spending. The debate over the economics of defense spending is a heated one and—bearing in mind the size and variety of the American economy, the stimulus that can come from large government contracts, and the technological spin-offs from weapons research—the evidence does not point simply in one direction. But what is significant for our purposes is the comparative dimension. Although (as is often pointed out) defense expenditures amounted to ten percent of GNP under President Eisenhower and nine percent under President Kennedy, America's shares of global production and wealth were at that time around twice what they are today, and, more particularly, the American economy was not then facing challenges to either its traditional or its high-technology manufactures. The United States now devotes about seven percent of its GNP to defense spending, while its major economic rivals, especially Japan, allocate a far smaller proportion. If this situation continues, then America's rivals will have more funds free for civilian investment. If the United States continues to direct a huge proportion of its research and development activities toward military-related production while the Japanese and West Germans concentrate on commercial research and development, and if the Pentagon drains off the ablest of the country's scientists and engineers from the design and production of goods for the world market, while similar personnel in other countries are bringing out better consumer products, then it seems inevitable that the American share of world manufacturing will decline steadily, and likely that American economic growth rates will be slower than those of countries dedicated to the marketplace and less eager to channel resources into defense.

It is almost superfluous to say that these tendencies place the United States on the horns of a most acute, if long-term, dilemma. Simply because it is *the* global superpower, with military commitments far more extensive than those of a regional power like Japan or West Germany, it requires much larger defense forces. Furthermore, since the USSR is seen to be the major military threat to American interests around the globe, and is clearly devoting a far greater proportion of its GNP to defense, American decision-makers are inevitably worried about "losing" the arms race with Russia. Yet the more sensible among the decision-makers can also perceive that the burden of armaments is debilitating the Soviet economy, and that if the two superpowers continue to allocate ever larger shares of their national wealth to the unproductive field of armaments, the critical question might soon be, Whose economy will decline *fastest*, relative to the economics of such expanding states as Japan, China, and so forth? A small investment in armaments may leave a globally overstretched power like the United States feeling vulnerable everywhere, but a very heavy investment in them, while bringing greater security in the short term, may so erode the commercial competitiveness of the American economy that the nation will be less secure in the long term.

Here, too, the historical precedents are not encouraging. Past experience shows that even as the relative economic strength of number-one countries has ebbed, the growing foreign challenges to their position have compelled them to allocate more and more of their resources to the military sector, which in turn has squeezed out productive investment and, over time, led to a downward spiral of slower growth, heavier taxes, deepening domestic splits over spending priorities, and a weakening capacity to beat the burdens of defense. If this, indeed, is the pattern of history, one is tempted to paraphrase Shaw's deadly serious quip and say: "Rome fell. Babylon fell. Scarsdale's turn will come."

How is one to interpret what is going on? And what, if anything, can be done about these problems? Far too many of the remarks made in political speeches suggest that while politicians worry more than they did about the nation's economic future, they tend to believe that the problems have quick and simple-minded solutions. For example, some call for tariffs—but they fail to address the charge that whenever industry and agriculture are protected, they become less productive. Others urge "competitiveness"—but they fail to explain how, say, American textile workers are to compete with textile workers earning only a twentieth of American wages. Still others put the blame for the decline of American efficiency on the government, which they say takes too much of the national income—but they fail to explain how the Swiss and the Germans, with their far higher tax rates, remain competitive on the world market. There are those who want to increase defense spending to meet perceived threats overseas—but they rarely concede that such a policy would further unbalance the economy. And there are those who want to reduce defense spending—but they rarely suggest which commitments (Israel? Korea? Egypt? Europe?) should go, in order to balance means and ends.

Above all, there is rarely any sense of the long-term context in which this American dilemma must be seen, or of the blindingly obvious point that the problem is not new. The study of world history might be the most useful endeavor for today's decision-makers. Such study would free politicians from the ethnocentric and temporal blinkers that so often restrict vision, allowing them to perceive some of the larger facts about international affairs.

The first of these is that the relative strengths of the leading nations have never remained constant, because the uneven rates of growth of different societies and technological and organizational breakthroughs bring greater advantage to one society than to another. For example, the coming of the long-range-gunned sailing ship and the rise of Atlantic trade after 1500 were not uniformly beneficial to the states of Europe—they benefited some much more than others. In the same way, the later development of steam power, and of the coal and metal resources upon which it relied, drastically increased the relative power of certain nations. Once their productive capacity was enhanced, countries would normally find it easier to sustain the burdens of spending heavily on armaments in peacetime, and of maintaining and supplying large armies and fleets in wartime. It sounds crudely mercantilistic to express it this way, but wealth is usually needed to underpin military power, and military power is usually needed to acquire and protect wealth. If, however, too large a proportion of a state's resources is diverted from the creation of wealth and allocated instead to military purposes, that is likely to lead to a weakening of national power over the long term. And if a state overextends itself strategically, by, say, conquering extensive territories or waging costly wars, it runs the risk that the benefits ultimately gained from external expansion may be outweighed by the great expense—a problem that becomes acute if the nation concerned has entered a period of relative economic decline. The history of the rise and fall of the leading countries since the advance of Western Europe in the sixteenth century—that is, of nations such as Spain, the Netherlands, France, Great Britain, and, currently, the United States—shows a significant correlation over the long term between productive and revenue-raising capacity on the one hand and military strength on the other.

Of course, both wealth *and* power are always relative. Three hundred years ago the German mercantilistic writer Philip von Hornigk observed that "whether a nation be today mighty and rich or not depends not on the abundance or security of its power or riches, but principally on whether its neighbors possess more or less of it."

The Netherlands in the mid-eighteenth century was richer in absolute terms than it had been a hundred years earlier, but by that stage it was much less of a Great Power, because neighbors like France and Britain had more power and riches. The France of 1914 was, absolutely, more powerful than the one of 1850—but that was little consolation when France was being eclipsed by a much stronger Germany. Britain has far greater wealth today than it had in its mid-Victorian prime, and its armed forces possess far more powerful weapons, but its share of world product has shrunk from about 25 percent to about three percent. If a nation has "more of it" than its contemporaries, things are fine; if not, there are problems.

This does not mean, however, that a nations's relative economic and military power will rise and fall in parallel. Most of the historical examples suggest that the trajectory of a state's military-territorial influence lags noticeably behind the trajectory of its relative economic strength. The reason for this is not difficult to grasp. An economically expanding power—Britain in the 1860s, the United States in the 1890s, Japan today—may well choose to become rich rather than to spend heavily on armaments. A half century later priorities may well have altered. The earlier economic expansion has brought with it overseas obligation; dependence on foreign markets and raw materials, military alliances, perhaps bases and colonies. Other, rival powers are now expanding economically at a faster rate, and wish in their turn to extend their influence abroad. The world has become a more competitive place, and the country's market shares are being eroded. Pessimistic observers talk of decline; patriotic statesmen call for "renewal."

In these more troubled circumstances the Great Power is likely to spend much more on defense than it did two generations earlier and yet still find the world to be less secure—simply because other powers have grown faster, and are becoming stronger. Imperial Spain spent much more money on its army in the troubled 1630s and 1640s than it had in the 1580s, when the Castilian economy was healthier. Britain's defense expenditures were far greater in 1910 than they were, say, at the time of Palmerston's death, in 1865, when the British economy was at its relative peak; but did any Britons at the later date feel more secure? The same problem appears to confront both the United States and the Soviet Union today. Great Powers in relative decline instinctively respond by spending more on security, thereby diverting potential resources from investment and compounding their long-term dilemma.

After the Second World War the position of the United States and the USSR as powers in a class by themselves appeared to be reinforced by the advent of nuclear weapons and delivery systems. The strategic and diplomatic landscape was now entirely different from that of 1900, let alone 1800. And yet the process of rise and fall among Great Powers had not ceased. Militarily, the United States and the USSR stayed in the forefront as the 1960s gave way to the 1970s and 1980s. Indeed, because they both interpret international problems in bipolar, and often Manichean, terms, their rivalry has driven them into an ever-escalating arms race that no other powers feel capable of joining. Over the same few decades, however, the global productive balances have been changing faster than ever before. The Third World's share of total manufacturing output and GNP, which was depressed to an all-time low in the decade after 1945, has steadily expanded. Europe has recovered from its wartime batterings and, in the form of the EEC, become the world's largest trading unit. The People's Republic of China is leaping forward at an impressive rate. Japan's postwar economic growth has been so phenomenal that, according to some measures, Japan recently overtook the Soviet Union in total GNP. Meanwhile, growth rates in both the United States and the USSR have become more sluggish, and those countries' shares of global production and wealth have shrunk dramatically since the 1960s. . . .

Although the United States is at present still pre-eminent economically and perhaps even militarily, it cannot avoid the two great tests that challenge the longevity of every major power that occupies the number-one position in world affairs. First, in the military-strategic realm, can it preserve a reasonable balance between the nation's perceived defense commitments and the means it possesses to maintain those commitments? And second, as an intimately related question, can it preserve the technological and economic bases of its power from relative erosion in the face of the ever-shifting patterns of global production? This test of American abilities will be the greater because America, like Imperial Spain around 1600 or the British Empire around 1900, bears a heavy burden of strategic commitments, made decades earlier, when the nation's political, economic, and military capacity to influence world affairs seemed so much more assured. The United States now runs the risk, so familiar to historians of the rise and fall of Great Powers, of what might be called "imperial overstretch": that is to say, decision-makers in Washington must face the awkward and enduring fact that the total of the United States's global interests and obligations is nowadays far too large for the country to be able to defend them all simultaneously.

To be sure, it is hardly likely that the United States would be called upon to defend all of its overseas interests simultaneously and unilaterally, unaided by the NATO members in Western Europe, Israel in the Middle East, or Japan, Australia, and possibly China in the Pacific. Nor are all the regional trends unfavorable to the United States with respect to defense. For example, while aggression by the unpredictable North Korean regime is always possible, it would hardly be welcomed by Beijing—furthermore, South Korea has grown to have more than twice the population and four times the GNP of the North. Also, while the expansion of Soviet forces in the Far East is alarming to Washington, it is balanced by the growing threat that China poses to the USSR's land and sea lines of communication in that area. The recent sober admission by Secretary of Defense Caspar Weinberger that "we can never afford to buy the capabilities sufficient to meet all of our commitments with one hundred percent confidence" is surely true; but it is also true that the potential anti-Soviet resources in the world (the United States, Western Europe, Japan, China, Australasia) are far greater than the resources lined up on the USSR's side.

Despite such consolations, the fundamental grand-strategic problem remains: the United States today has roughly the same enormous array of military obligations across the globe that it had a quarter century ago, when its shares of world GNP, manufacturing production, military spending, and armed-forces personnel were much larger than they are now. In 1985, forty years after America's triumph in the Second World War and more than a decade after its pull-out from Vietnam, 526,000 members of the U.S. armed forces were abroad (including 64,000 afloat). That total is substantially more than the overseas deployments in peacetime of the military and naval forces of the British Empire at the height of its power. Nevertheless, in the opinion of the Joint Chiefs of Staff, and of many civilian experts, it is simply not enough. Despite a near-trebling of the American defense budget since the late 1970s, the numerical size of the armed forces on active duty has increased by just five percent. As the British and the French military found in their time, a nation with extensive overseas obligations will always have a more difficult manpower problem than a state that keeps its armed forces solely for home defense, and a politically liberal and economically laissez-faire society sensitive to the unpopularity of conscription will have a greater problem than most.

Ultimately, the only answer to whether the United States can preserve its position is *no*—for it simply has not been given to any one society to remain permanently ahead of all the others, freezing the patterns of different growth rates, technological advance, and military development that have existed since time immemorial. But historical precedents do not simply imply that the United States is destined to shrink to the relative obscurity of former leading powers like Spain and the Netherlands, or to disintegrate like the Roman and Austro-Hungarian empires; it is too large to do the former, and probably too homogeneous to do the latter. Even the British analogy, much favored in the current political-science literature, is not a good one if it ignores the differences in scale. The geographic size, population, and natural resources of Great Britain suggest that it ought to possess roughly three or four percent of the world's wealth and power, all other things being equal. But precisely because all other things are never equal, a peculiar set of historical and technological circumstances permitted Great Britain to possess, say, 25 percent of the world's wealth and power in its prime. Since those favorable circumstances have disappeared, all that it has been doing is returning to its more "natural" size. In the same way, it may be argued, the geographic extent, population, and natural resources of the United States suggest wealth and power. But because of historical and technological circumstances favorable to it, that share rose to 40 percent or more by 1945, and what we are witnessing today is the ebbing away from that extraordinary high figure to a more natural share. That decline is being masked by the country's enormous military capability at present, and also by its success in internationalizing American capitalism and culture. Yet even when it has declined to the position of occupying no more than its natural share of the world's wealth and power, a long time into the future, the United States will still be a very significant power in a multipolar world, simply because of its size.

The task facing American statesmen over the next decades, therefore, is to recognize that broad trends are under way, and that there is a need to manage affairs so that the relative erosion of America's position takes place slowly and smoothly, unaided by policies that bring short-term advantage but long-term disadvantage. Among the realities that statesmen, from the President down, must be alert to are these: that technological and therefore socioeconomic change is occurring in the world faster than it has ever before; that the international community is much more politically and culturally diverse than has been assumed, and is defiant of simplistic remedies offered by either Washington or Moscow for its problems; that the economic and productive power balances are no longer tilted as favorably in America's direction as they were in 1945. Even in the military realm there are signs of a certain redistribution of the balances, away from a bipolar and toward a multipolar system, in which American economic and military strength is likely to remain greater than that of any other individual country but will cease to be as disproportionate as it was in the decades immediately after the Second World War. In all the discussions about erosion of American leadership it needs to be repeated again and again that the decline is relative, not absolute, and is therefore perfectly natural, and that a serious threat to the real interests of the United States can come only from a failure to adjust sensibly to the new world order.

Just how well can the American system adjust to a state of relative decline? Already, a growing awareness of the gap between U.S. obligations and U.S. power has led to questions by gloomier critics about the overall political culture in which Washington decision-makers have to operate. It has been suggested to reformulate its grand strategy in the light of the larger, uncontrollable changes taking place in world affairs may be ill served by an electoral system that seems to paralyze foreign-policy decision-making every two years. Foreign policy may be undercut by the extraordinary pressures applied by lobbyists, political-action committees, and other interest groups, all of whom, by definition, are prejudiced in favor of this or that policy change, and by the simplification of vital but complex international and strategic issues, inherent to mass media whose time and space for such things are limited and whose raison d'être is chiefly to make money and only secondarily to inform. It may also be undercut by the still powerful escapist urges in the American social culture, which are perhaps understandable in terms of the nation's frontier past but hinder its coming to terms with today's complex, integrated world and with other cultures and ideologies. Finally, the country may not always be helped by the division of decision-making powers that was deliberately created when it was geographically and strategically isolated from the rest of the world, two centuries ago, and had time to find a consensus on the few issues that actually concerned foreign policy. This division may be less serviceable now that the United States is a global superpower often called upon to make swift decisions vis-à-vis countries that enjoy far fewer constraints. No one of these obstacles prevents the execution of a coherent, long-term American grand strategy. However, their cumulative effect is to make it difficult to carry out policy changes that seem to hurt special interests and occur in an election year. It may therefore be here, in the cultural and political realms, that the evolution of an overall American policy to meet the twenty-first century will be subjected to the greatest test.

Nevertheless, given the considerable array of strengths still possessed by the United States, it ought not in theory to be beyond the talents of successive Administrations to orchestrate this readjustment so as, in Walter Lippmann's classic phrase, to bring "into balance . . . the nation's commitments and the nation's power." Although there is no single state obviously preparing to take over America's global burdens, in the way that the United States assumed Britain's role in the 1940s, the country has fewer problems than had Imperial Spain, besieged by enemies on all fronts, or the Netherlands, squeezed between France and England, or the British Empire, facing numerous challengers. The tests before the United States as it heads toward the twenty-first century are certainly daunting, perhaps especially in the economic sphere; but the nation's resources remain considerable, *if* they can be properly utilized and *if* there is a judicious recognition of both the limitations and the opportunities of American power.

FURTHER READING

George W. Ball, *Error and Betrayal in Lebanon* (1984)
Richard J. Barnet, *The Alliance* (1983)
———, *Real Security* (1981)
Seweryn Bialer and Michael Mandelbaum, eds., *Gorbachev's Russia and American Foreign Policy* (1988)
Terry Boswell and Albert Bergesen, eds., *America's Changing Role in the World System* (1987)
David P. Calleo, *Beyond American Hegemony* (1987)

Kenneth M. Coleman and George C. Herring, eds., *The Central American Crises* (1985)

Robert Dallek, *Ronald Reagan* (1984)

Alexander Dallin, *Black Box: KAL 007 and the Superpowers* (1985)

Tami R. Davis and Sean M. Lynn-Jones, "City Upon a Hill," *Foreign Policy*, No. 66 (1987), 20–38

I. M. Destler et al., *Our Own Worst Enemy* (1984)

Tom J. Farer, *The Lost Consensus* (1987)

Richard E. Feinberg, *The Intemperate Zone* (1983)

John Lewis Gaddis, *The Long Peace* (1988)

Raymond L. Garthoff, *Détente and Confrontation* (1985)

Alexander George et al., eds., *U.S.-Soviet Security Cooperation* (1988)

Robert Gilpin, *The Political Economy of International Relations* (1987)

Betty Glad, *Jimmy Carter* (1980)

Norman A. Graebner, "The Decline of America: A Countering Appraisal," *Virginia Quarterly Review*, 58 (1982), 369–91

Roy Gutman, *Banana Diplomacy* (1988)

Seymour M. Hersh, *The Target is Destroyed* (1986) (on KAL 007)

Ole Holsti and James Rosenau, *American Leadership in World Affairs* (1984)

Jerry F. Hough, *Russia and the West* (1988)

William Hyland, ed., *The Reagan Foreign Policy* (1987)

Charles O. Jones, *The Trusteeship Presidency: Jimmy Carter and the United States Congress* (1988)

Michael Klare and Cynthia Arnson, *Supplying Repression* (1981)

Jonathan Kwitny, *Endless Enemies* (1986)

Walter LaFeber, *Inevitable Revolutions* (1983) (on Central America)

——, *The Panama Canal* (1978)

——, "The Reagan Administration and Revolutions in Central America," *Political Science Quarterly*, 99 (1984), 1–25

Thomas McCormick, " 'Every System Needs a Center Sometimes': An Essay on Hegemony and Modern American Foreign Policy," in Lloyd C. Gardner, ed., *Redefining the Past* (1986)

David McLellan, *Cyrus Vance* (1985)

Walter R. Mead, *Mortal Splendor: The American Empire in Transition* (1987)

Morris H. Morley, ed., *Crisis and Confrontation: Ronald Reagan's Foreign Policy* (1988)

James Nathan and James Oliver, *Foreign Policy Making and the American Political System* (1987)

Robert Nisbet, *The Present Age* (1987)

Kenneth Oye et al., eds., *Eagle Defiant* (1983)

——, *Eagle Entangled* (1979)

——, *Eagle Resurgent?* (1987)

Robert A. Pastor, *Condemned to Repetition* (1987) (on Nicaragua)

William B. Quandt, *Camp David: Peacemaking and Politics* (1986)

Cheryl Rudenberg, *Israel and the American National Interest* (1986)

Barry Rubin, *Paved with Good Intentions* (1980) (on Iran)

Lars Schoultz, *National Security and the United States Policy toward Latin America* (1987)

Simon Serfaty, "Lost Illusions," *Foreign Policy*, No. 66 (1987), 3–19

Gaddis Smith, *Morality, Reason and Power* (1986) (on Carter)

Strobe Talbott, *Deadly Gambits* (1984)

——, *Endgame: The Inside Story of SALT-II* (1979)

——, *The Russians and Reagan* (1984)

Sanford J. Ungar, ed., *Estrangement: America and the World* (1985)

Thomas W. Walker, ed., *Reagan and the Sandinistas* (1987)

Marina v. N. Whitman, "Leadership without Hegemony," *Foreign Policy*, No. 20 (1975), 138–160

Thomas W. Wolfe, *The SALT Experience* (1979)